Wicklow
HISTORY & SOCIETY

Interdisciplinary Essays on the History of an Irish County

Editors:
KEN HANNIGAN
WILLIAM NOLAN

GEOGRAPHY PUBLICATIONS

The editors and publisher are very grateful to
AVONDALE CHEMICAL COMPANY, RATHDRUM
and
WICKLOW COUNTY COUNCIL
for their generous subventions to this publication.

Published in Ireland by
Geography Publications,
Kennington Road,
Templeogue, Dublin 6W

ISBN 0 906602 30 O

Design and typesetting by Phototype-Set, Lee Road, Dublin Industrial Estate
Printed by Colour Books.
Bound by Museum Bookbindings, Dublin

Contents

Preface and Acknowledgments

This book on Wicklow is the seventh volume in the Irish County History series. It follows the volumes on Tipperary (1985), Wexford (1987), Kilkenny (1990), Dublin (1992) and Cork (1993).

Wicklow, more than most others, is a county of contrasts. Its wild and rugged mountainous core lies only a few miles from the metropolis of Dublin: both mountain and city have shaped its political and social development. Mountain locked glens provided an ideal setting for the monastic settlement of Glendalough in the early christian period and were later a refuge for the last of the O'Byrne chieftains in the early modern period. Wicklow's proximity to Dublin prioritised its subjugation in Elizabethan times but also attracted a large, resident landed gentry in the eighteenth and nineteenth centuries. The mountain barrier divides the west of the county from the coast. Districts west of the mountains, such as Blessington and Baltinglass, have more in common with those in the neighbouring counties of Carlow, Dublin and Kildare than with the coastal towns of Bray, Wicklow and Arklow in the east.

Wicklow is the youngest county in Ireland, having being formed in 1606. By the early nineteenth century, however, it had changed from being thoroughly gaelic to being, linguistically, the most completely anglicised of Irish counties. Once subdued in the early seventeenth century, gaelic culture and society all but vanished as the area became the focus for an acculturation process as intensive as any in Ireland. In the sixteenth century the writ of the crown did not prevail in Wicklow, but nineteenth century Wicklow became the most law abiding and tranquil of Irish counties.

Wicklow has several times experienced the ebb and flow of industrial development. Its rich woodlands became the focus for intensive exploitation in the seventeenth century, both for iron smelting and for the export of timber. In the early nineteenth century its mineral wealth, particularly in the Avoca valley, spawned the phenomenon of a gold rush and to more sober minds its rich seams of iron, lead and copper seemed to offer the base on which large scale industrialisation could be built. Later still the valleys, which had echoed to the sounds of industry fell silent and, having regained the wilderness, became the raw material of modern tourism.

The essays in this volume give some measure of these contrasts. It does not claim to be a comprehensive account of Wicklow's history but represents the most recent research on Wicklow's development in a wide range of disciplines. Conscious that the current state of research does not allow for a seamless garment, we are confident, nevertheless, that this book provides the most thorough analysis yet attempted of vital periods in the county's development.

In compiling this volume we have drawn on the resources and the generosity of many people. Chief among them have been the contributors who responded so positively when we issued our initial invitations to join us. Within county Wicklow we are greatly indebted to the many friends who gave of their time and their expertise to teach us something of the county. We are deeply grateful to John Anderson of Mount Usher, Edward Bayly of Ballyarthur, Aisling Broderick of Wicklow, Jim Burke of Templelyon, Charles Byrne of Clara Vale, Emmet Byrne of Newrath, Owen and Maureen Byrne of Castletimon, Val Cosgrave of Ballinaclogh, Harry and Molly Delahunt of Furzeditch, Donatienne and Philippe de Patoul of Kilbride, Bill Dolan of Wicklow, Rob and Kathleen Douglas of Kilnamanagh, Michael Doyle of Cranagh, Maeve Flannery of Wicklow, Michael Fogarty of Carrigmore, Michael Owen Fogarty of Aughrim, Bill Lott of Cullen, Syl Lott of Furzeditch, Martha McDonald and Ann McDonald-Hill of Dunganstown, Darren MacEiteagain of Knockrobin, Fr James Murphy of Barndarrig, Nigel Pratt of Coolacork, Jim Rees of Arklow and Tommy Sheehan and Hester Storm of Ballynagran, all of whom shared their knowledge of the topography, history and antiquities of county Wicklow with us.

Many of the chapters in this volume were presented as papers at the monthly meetings of Wicklow Historical Society, or to the annual symposium of the Roundwood and District History and Folklore Society, and we are grateful to the members of these societies who responded with many stimulating comments and helpful suggestions. We are particularly grateful to Jimmy Cleary and John Finlay of the Wicklow Historical Society, Ian Cantwell, Sean Kavanagh and Frank McGillick of the Roundwood society, and also to the officers and members of the historical societies in Arklow, Ashford, Bray and West Wicklow who have shared their knowledge with us over the years.

We are also deeply grateful to the staff of the many archives, libraries and museums who have facilitated research for this book, especially to Brid Dolan of the Royal Irish Academy, Paul Ferguson of the Map Library, Trinity College Dublin, Gerry Lyne, Catherine Fahy and Eugene Hogan, of the National Library of Ireland, Fergus Mac Giolla Easpaig of the Genealogical Office, Máire Kennedy of the Gilbert Library, Dublin, Gerry Maher, Wicklow County Librarian, Joe Hayes, the former Wicklow County Librarian and to their ever-helpful and courteous staff, George McClafferty of the Glendalough Interpretative Centre, Joan Kavanagh, the supervisors and trainees of the County Wicklow

Heritage Project who never failed to help when called upon. We must record our thanks also to Charles Acton, Declan Doyle, Paul Gorry, Christine Kinealy, Ernie Shepherd, Matthew Stout and Sarah Ward-Perkins. We owe special thanks to our colleagues in the National Archives and University College Dublin, particularly the Director of the National Archives, Dr. David V. Craig, and the Dean of the Faculty of Arts, University College Dublin, Dr. Fergus A. D'Arcy, and also to Dr. Mary Daly, Lorcan Farrell, Stephen Hannon, Dr Arnold Horner, Aideen Ireland, Rena Lohan, Sile MacMurrough, Eamonn Mullally, Gregory O'Connor, Professor Cormac Ó Grada, Dr. Jean Michel Picard, Ken Robinson and Tony Roach. We also wish to thank the Audio-visual Centre in University College Dublin, An Bord Fáilte, the Curator, Cambridge University Collection of Air Photographs, the Irish Architectural Archive and Mr. Aidan Heavey for photographs. The Faculty of Arts Revenue Committee, University College Dublin provided financial assistance for fieldwork associated with chapter sixteen.

We wish to express our gratitude to the members of Wicklow County Council and especially to the Chairman, Michael Lawlor, the County Manager, Blaise Treacy, and the County Development Officer, Tom Broderick.

Our typesetters, Phototype-Set, Glasnevin, especially Michael Lynam, Rory O'Neill, Noel Murphy and Christy Nolan were assiduous in their attention to detail, and Colour Books were unsparing in their efforts to ensure that this volume matched the same high quality as its predecessors. We also wish to thank Deasún FitzGerald for indexing and editorial help.

We owe a very special debt to Dr. Phil Connolly of the National Archives and to Dr. Kevin Whelan of the Royal Irish Academy.

Finally we wish to thank our families. Teresa, John, Sadbh, Brianán and Róisin Nolan; Carolyn, Justin, William and Alex Hannigan have endured much in the course of this volume's preparation and have contributed in many ways to its completion. We and the volume have benefited greatly by their patience, support, help and encouragement.

List of Figures

List of Plates

Plates Insert

List of Abbreviations

A.F.M.	*Annála ríoghachta Éireann:* Annals of the kingdom of Ireland by the Four Masters from the earliest period to the year 1616, ed. John O'Donovan, 5 vols (Dublin, 1848-51). This earliest edition appeared in two divisions. The early medieval material was printed in vol 1 of the first division published in 1851.
AGWU	Agricultural and General Workers' Union.
Alen's reg.	*Calendar of Archbishop Alen's register, c.1172-1534; prepared and edited from the original in the united dioceses of Dublin and Glendalough and Kildare,* ed. Charles MacNeill; index by Liam Price (Dublin, 1950).
Anal. Boll.	*Analecta Bollandiana* (Paris and Brussels, 1882).
Anal. Hib.	*Analecta Hibernica,* including the reports of the Irish Manuscripts Commission.
Ann. Clon.	*The Annals of Clonmacnoise, being annals of Ireland from the earliest period to AD 1408, translated into English , AD 1627, by Conell Mageoghagan,* ed. Denis Murphy (Royal Society of Antiquaries of Ireland, Dublin, 1896).
Ann. Conn.	*Annála Connacht ... (AD 1224-1544),* ed. A. Martin Freeman (Dublin Institute for Advanced Studies, 1944).
Ann. Inisf.	The Annals of Inisfallen (MS Rawlinson B 503), ed. and trans. Sen Mac Airt (Dublin Institute for Advanced Studies, 1951).
Ann. Tig.	'The Annals of Tigernach' ed. W. Stokes in Revue Celtique, xvi-xviii (1895-7).
Annals of Clyn	*The Annals of Ireland by Friar John Clyn,* ed. Richard Butler.
Archiv. Hib.	*Archivium Hibernicum: or Irish historical records.*
Arklow His. Soc. Jn.	Journal of the Arklow Historical Society.
A.P.C.	Arklow Property Company.
A.P.C. O.S. volume	Arklow Property Company, Ordnance Survey volume.

A.U.	Annla Uladh, *The Annals of Ulster (to AD 1131)*, Part 1, ed. S. Mac Airt and G. Mac Niocaill (Dublin, 1983).
Bicknor's Account	James Lydon (ed.), 'The enrolled account of Alexander Bicknor, treasurer of Ireland, 1308-14' in *Anal. Hib.*, no. 30 (1982).
Bk. Leinster	*The Book of Leinster, formerly Lebar na Núachongbála* ed. R.I. Best, Osborn Bergin and M.A. O'Brien (5 vols, Dublin Institute for Advanced Studies, 1954-67).
Bk. Rights	*Lebor na Cert; The Book of Rights*, ed. Myles Dillon (Irish Texts Society, Dublin, 1962).
Bks survey & dist.	*Books of survey and distribution: being abstracts of various surveys and instruments of title*, Public Record Office, Dublin.
B.L.	British Library.
B.M.	British Museum.
Brit. Acad. Proc.	*Proceedings of the British Academy* (London, 1903–).
Cal. Carew Mss	*Calendar of Carew manuscripts preserved in the archiepiscopal library at Lambeth.* 1515-74 (etc.) 6 vols (London, 1867-73).
Cal. doc. Ire./C.D.I.	*Calendar of documents relating to Ireland*, ed. H.S. Sweetman and G.F. Handcock, 5 vols (London, 1875-86).
Cal. justic. rolls Ire.	*Calendar of the justiciar rolls of Ireland*, ed. James Mills, *et al*, 3 vols (Dublin, 1905–).
Cal. papal letters	*Calendar of entries in the papal registers relating to Great Britain and Ireland: papal letters, 1198-1304 (etc)* (London, 1893–).
Cal. pat. rolls Ire.	*Calendar of patent and close rolls of chancery in Ireland, Charles I, years 1 to 8*, ed. James Morrin (Dublin, 1864).
Cal. pat. rolls Ire. Hen. VII-Eliz.	*Calendar of patent and close rolls of chancery in Ireland, Henry VII to 18th Elizabeth*, ed. James Morrin (Dublin, 1861).
Cal. pat. rolls Ire. Jas 1	*Irish patent rolls of James 1: facsimile of the Irish record commissioners' calendar prepared prior to 1830*, with foreword by M.C. Griffith (Dublin, 1966).
Ca. S.P. Ire.	*Calendar of the state papers relating to Ireland 1509-73* (etc.) 24 vols London, 1860-1911).

Cal. S.P. Dom.	*Calendar of state papers, domestic series, 1547-80* (etc.) (London, 1856-).
Chartul. St Mary's	*Dublin Chartularies of St Mary's Abbey, Dublin ... and annals of Ireland, 1162-1370*, ed. J.T. Gilbert (2 vols, 1884-6).
Chron. Scot.	*Chronicum Scotorum: a chronicle of Irish affairs ... to 1135, and supplement ... 1141-1150*, ed. W.M. Hennessy (London, 1866).
Cork Arch. Hist. Soc. Jn.	*Journal of the Cork Archaeological and Historical Society.*
Corpus Gen. Hib.	*Corpus Genealogiarum Hiberniae*, 1, ed. M.A. O'Brien (Dublin, 1962).
Crede Mihi	J. T. Gilbert (ed.), *"CREDE MIHI" The most ancient register book of the archbishops of Dublin before the reformation* (Dublin, 1897).
D.E.P.	*Dublin Evening Post.*
D.K.R.	*Deputy Keeper's Report.*
Dublin Hist. Rec.	*Dublin Historical Record.*
Econ. Hist. Rev.	*Economic History Review.*
E.H.R.	*English Historical Review.*
Etudes Celt	*Etudes Celtiques.*
Expug.Hib.	*The conquest of Ireland by Geraldus Cambriensus*, A.B. Scott and F.X. Martin ed. (Dublin, 1978)
Facs. nat. MSS Ire.	*Facsimiles of the national manuscripts of Ireland*, ed. J.T. Gilbert (4 vols, Dublin, 1874-84).
F.J.	*Freeman's Journal.*
G.O.	Genealogical Office , Dublin
Gormanston reg.	*Calendar for the Gormanston register*, ed. James Mills and M.J. McEnery (Royal Society of Antiquaries of Ireland, Dublin, 1916).
G.P.O.	General Post Office.
Hand, Eng. law in Ire.	Geoffrey J. Hand, *English law in Ireland, 1290-1324* (Cambridge, 1697).
H.C.	House of Commons.
Hist & mun. doc. Ire.	*Historic and municipal documents of Ireland, 1172-1320*, ed. J.T. Gilbert (London, 1870).
H.M.C.	Historical Manuscripts Commission.
H.M.S.O.	Her Majesty's Stationary Office.
Holt Mss	Holt's manuscript memoirs.
I.F.C.	Irish Folklore Commission.
I.H.S.	*Irish Historical Studies.*

I.M.C.	Irish Manuscripts Commission.
Inq. cancell. Hib. repert.	*Inquisitionum in officio cancellariae hiberniae ... repertorium* (2 vols, Dublin, 1826-9).
Ir. Cartul. Llanthony	*The Irish Chartularies of Llanthony Prima & Secunda*, ed. St John Brooks (Irish Manuscripts Commission, Dublin, 1953).
Ir. Econ. Soc. Hist. Jn.	*Journal of Irish Economic and Social History.*
Ir. Geog.	*Irish Geography (bulletin of the Geographical society of Ireland)* (vols i-iv, Dublin, 1944-63); continued as *The Geographical Society of Ireland*, Irish Geography (vol v –, Dublin, 1964–).
Ir. Kings	F.J. Byrne, *Irish kings and high kings* (London, 1973).
Irish Naturists Jn.	*The Irish Naturalists' Journal.*
I.T.G.W.U.	Irish Transport and General Worker's Union.
I.T.U.C.	Irish Trade Union Congress.
I.W.W.U.	Irish Women Workers' Union.
Jn. Ir. Arch.	*Journal of Irish Archaeology.*
Kildare Arch. Soc. Jn.	*Journal of the Kildare Archaeological Society.*
M.P.	Member of Parliament.
Ms; Mss	manuscript; manuscripts.
M.J.	*Mining Journal.*
NAI	National Archives Ireland.
NAI 620	Rebellion papers
NAI CBS	Chief Secretary's Office, Crime Branch Special files
NAI D/JUS	Department of Justice
NAI D/LG	Department of Local Government
NAI D/T	Department of the Taoiseach
NAI OP	Official papers [1st series]
NAI OR	Chief Secretary's Office, Outrage Reports
NAI QRO	Quit Rent Office
NAI RLF COM	Relief Commission
NAI SOC	State of the Country Papers [1st and 2nd series – consecutive numbering , 2nd series begins at 3000]
N.H.I.	*A New History of Ireland* (Oxford, 1976–).
N.L.I; L.N.	National Library of Ireland, Leabharlann Náisiúnta na hEireann.
N.M.I.	National Museum of Ireland.
no.; nos	number; numbers.

N.P.	not published.
O.P.W.	Office of Public Works.
O.S.	Ordnance Survey of Ireland.
O.S. letters Wicklow	Letters containing information relative to the antiquities of the county of Wicklow collected during the progress of the Ordnance Survey in 1835, reproduced under the direction of Rev. Michael O'Flanagan [from the originals in the Royal Irish Academy] (typescript, 42 vols in 35 bindings, Bray, 1926-8).
O.S. name-books Wicklow	Books containing information relative to the placenames of the county of Wicklow collected during the progress of the Ordnance Survey in 1834, ed. Rev Michael O'Flanagan, from the originals in the Ordnance Survey, Phoenix Park (typescript, 76 vols, Bray)]
Orpen, Normans	G.H. Orpen, *Ireland under the Normans, 1169-1333* (4 vols, Oxford 1911-20; reprint, 4 vols, Oxford, 1968).
Otway-Ruthven *Med. Ire.*	A.J. Otway-Ruthven, *A history of medieval Ireland* (London, 1968).
pers. comm.	personal communication.
Pipe roll Ire. 1211-12	'The Irish pipe roll of 14 John, 1211-1212,' ed. Oliver Davies and David B. Quinn in *Ulster Journal of Archaeology,* 3rd series, iv, supp. (July, 1941).
Plummer, *Vitae SS Hib. C.*	C. Plummer (ed.), *Vitae sanctorum Hiberniae, partim hactenus ineditre* ... (2 vols, Oxford, 1910).
Price, *Placenames*	Liam Price, *The placenames of county Wicklow,* 7 vols (Dublin, 1945-1967).
Private coll.	private collection.
P.R.O.	Public Record office of England.
Proc. Belfast Nat. Hist. and Phil. Soc.	*Proceedings of the Belfast Natural History and Philosophical Society.*
Proc. 7th Viking Cong.	*Proceedings of Seventh Viking Congress.*
Proc. Soc. Antiquities Scotland	*Proceedings of the Society of Antiquities of Scotland.*
P.R.O., H.O.	Public Record Office, Home Office.
P.R.O.N.I.	Public Record Office of Northern Ireland.
Rawl. B.502	*Rawlinson B 502: a collection of pieces in*

	prose and verse in the Irish language ... from the original manuscript in the Bodleian, with introduction by Kuno Meyer (facsimile, Oxford, 1909).
R.D.	Registry of Deeds, Dublin.
R.D.S. Scient. Proc.	*Royal Dublin Society Scientific Proceedings.*
revd. edition	revised edition.
R.I.A.; A.R.E.	Royal Irish Academy; Acadámh Ríoga na hÉireann.
R.I.A. Proc.	*Proceedings of the Royal Irish Academy.*
R.I.A. Trans.	*Transactions of the Royal Irish Academy,* 33 vols (Dublin 1876-1907).
R.S.A.I. Jn.	*Journal of the Royal Society of Antiquaries of Ireland.*
Red Bk. Ormond	*The Red Book of Ormond,* ed. N.B. White (Dublin, 1932).
Reg. St John Baptist, Dublin	*Register of St John Baptist, Dublin,* ed. E. St J. Brooks (Dublin, 1936).
Reg. St Thomas Dublin	*Register of the Abbey of St Thomas the Martyr,* Dublin ed. J.T. Gilbert (London, 1889).
Reportorium Novum	*Reportorium Novum: Dublin Diocesan Historical Record.*
Richardson & Sayles *Admin. Ire.*	H.G. Richardson and G.O. Sayles, *The administration of Ireland 1172-1377* (Dublin, 1963).
Rot. pat. Hib.	*Rotulorum patentium et clausorum cancellariae Hiberniae calendarium* (Dublin, 1828).
Roundwood His. & Folklore Jn.	*Journal of the Roundwood and District History and Folklore Society.*
Royal Hist. Soc. Trans.	*Transactions of the Royal Historical Society.*
Sayles, Affairs	*Documents on the affairs of Ireland before the King's Council* (Dublin 1979).
Sheehy, Pontifica Hib.	M.P. Sheehy (ed.), *Pontificia Hibernica: medieval papal chancery documents concerning Ireland, 640-1261* (2 vols, Dublin, 1962, 1965).
S.I.P.T.U.	Services, Industrial, Professional Trade Union.
S.M.R. Wicklow	Sites and Monuments Record survey of county Wicklow
S.N.L.	*Saunder's Newsletter.*
S.P. Henry viii	*State Papers, Henry viii* (11 vols, London, 1830-52).

Stat. Ire.	*John-Hen.v Statutes and ordinances, and acts of the parliament of Ireland, King John to Henry v*, ed. H.F. Barry (Dublin, 1907).
T.C.D.	Library of Trinity College Dublin.
Technology Ir.	*Technology Ireland.*
Topog. dict. Ire.	*Topographical Dictionary of Ireland.*
Trip. Life	*The tripartite life of Patrick, with other documents*, ed. W. Stokes (London, 1887).
U.J.A.	*Ulster Journal of Archaeology.*
Wakefield, *Account of Ire.*	Edward Wakefield, *An account of Ireland statistical and political* (2 vols, Dublin, 1812).
vol.; vols	volume; volumes.
West Wicklow Hist Soc. Jn.	*Journal of the West Wicklow Historical Society.*
Wexford Hist. Soc. Jn.	*Journal of the Wexford Historical Society.*
Wicklow Hist. Soc. Jn.	*Journal of the Wicklow Historical Society.*
W.N.L.	*Wicklow Newsletter.*
Z.C.P.	*Zeitschrift für celtische Philologie* (Halle, 1896-1943, 23 vols; Tübingen, 1953–).

ERRATA

For Russborough in Table of Contents, page xii, read Powerscourt.

For Russborough in plates insert, between pages 490 and 491, read Powerscourt.

Editors and Contributors

F. H. A. Aalen
Senior Lecturer, Department of Geography, Trinity College Dublin.

Thomas Bartlett
Associate Professor, Department of History, University College Galway.

Ross M. Connolly
Trade union official
Blacklion, Greystones, County Wicklow.

Des Cowman
Teacher, Knockane, Annestown, County Waterford.

Louis M. Cullen
Professor of Modern Irish History, Trinity College Dublin.

Brian Donnelly
Archivist, National Archives of Ireland.

Colmán Etchingham
Lecturer, Department of History, St. Patrick's College, Maynooth.

R. F. Foster
Carroll Professor of Irish History, Hertford College, Oxford.

Nicholas Grene
Associate Professor, Department of English, Trinity College Dublin.

Ken Hannigan
Senior Archivist, National Archives of Ireland.

Joan Kavanagh
Director, County Wicklow Heritage Project, Wicklow.

Mary Kelly Quinn
Newman Scholar, Department of Botany, University College Dublin.

Rolf Loeber
Pittsburg.

Harry Long
Post-graduate student, Department of Medieval History, Trinity College Dublin.

J. F. Lydon
Professor Emeritus, Department of Medieval History, Trinity College Dublin.

Geraldine Lynch
Teacher, Wicklow.

Fiachra MacGabhann
Department of Celtic Studies, The Queen's University, Belfast.

Ailbhe Mac Shamhráin
Teacher, post-graduate researcher, Department of Medieval History, Trinity College Dublin

William Nolan
Lecturer in Geography, University College Dublin.

Conor O'Brien
Annacurra., County Wicklow

Eva Ó Cathaoir
Local Historian, Bray, County Wicklow.

Ruan O' Donnell
Post-graduate scholar, Australian National University, Canberra, Australia.

Patrick J. Power
Local historian, Arklow.

Linzi Simpson
Archaeologist, Dublin.

Alfred Smyth
Master of Keynes College, University of Kent, Canterbury, England

Geraldine Stout
Archaeologist, Office of Public Works, Dublin.

Chapter 1

WICKLOW'S PRESHISTORIC LANDSCAPE

GERALDINE STOUT

Introduction

In 1934 Liam Price published a study of early communities in Wicklow entitled 'The Ages of Stone and Bronze in county Wicklow'.[1] The culmination of many years of tireless fieldwork and research, it marked a watershed in research on Wicklow prehistory and it is a tribute to Price's scholarship that many of his observations have been substantiated in subsequent work. Among his enduring conclusions must firstly be the primacy of north-west Wicklow as a core area of early settlement before and into the pre-Christian period and secondly the necessary caution with which he approached the much quoted association of Wicklow with the technological revolution of the Irish Bronze Age, an issue which still remains controversial. Almost sixty years on, it is time to re-appraise growing evidence for prehistoric communities in Wicklow drawn from excavation and fieldwork. In the latter regard, Wicklow has benefited from the efforts of archaeologist and fieldworker Paddy Healy and the results of a 'Preliminary Report' on the monuments of archaeological interest in county Wicklow published by An Foras Forbartha.[2] More recently the Sites and Monuments Record, Office of Public Works have identified over fourteen hundred areas of archaeological interest in the county,[3] and this work has been further advanced by a field-based survey undertaken by the Archaeological Survey of Ireland.

Within contemporary Wicklow there is a gradual shift from traditional farming practices to the promotion of forestry and tourism which threaten its Stone and Bronze Age landscapes. This Brussels-driven land-use policy is causing a revolution in land-use and landscape which has been compared in degree to the transition from the Mesolithic to the Neolithic, or to the Enclosure movement of the eighteenth century.[4] In addition to presenting a picture of prehistoric settlement in the county, this essay concludes with an assessment of the risks inherent in such a strategy for some of Wicklow's finest archaeological monuments.

As Price observed,[5] the physical characteristics of the county explain many of its early settlement patterns. Wicklow is a maritime county

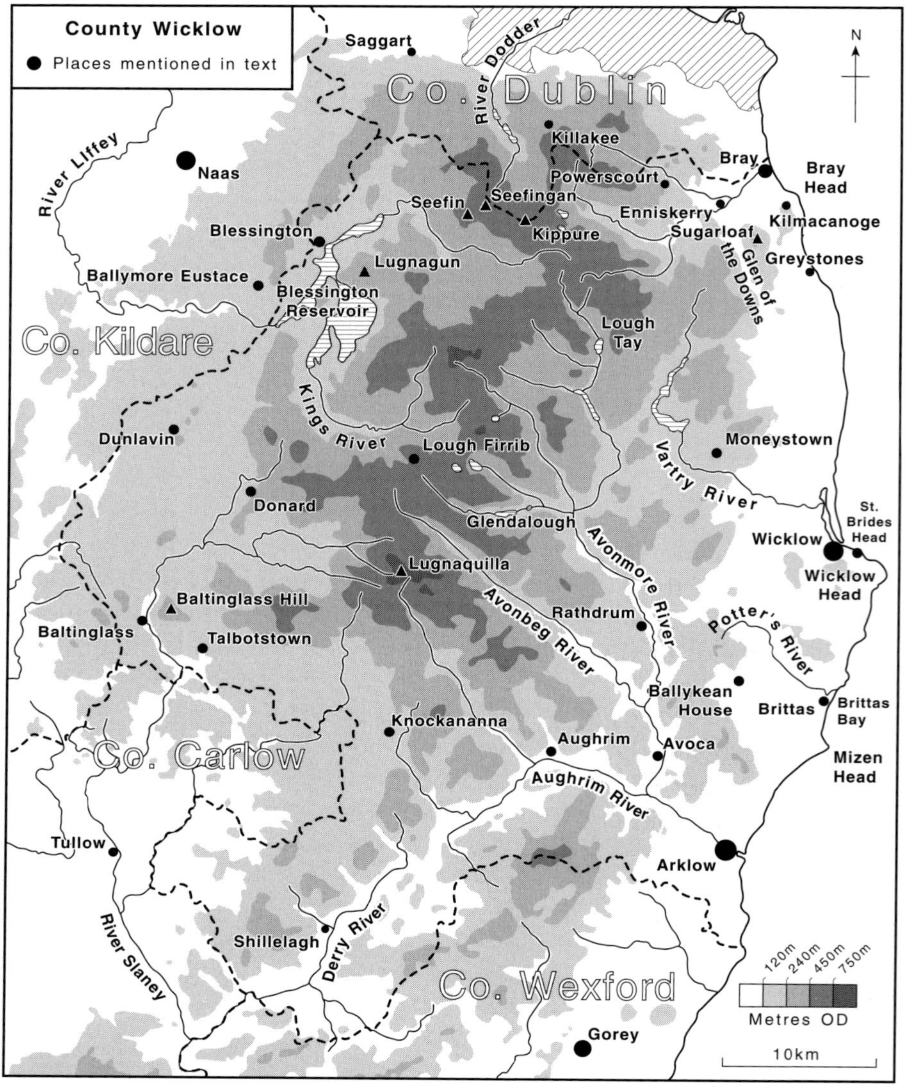

Figure 1.1 County Wicklow: Location map.

situated on the east coast of Ireland (fig. 1.1) with a great sweep of granite running through the heart of the county, extending south-westwards from the southern shores of Dublin Bay for a distance of some seventy miles to Mount Brandon in Kilkenny.[6] This elevated mountain tract naturally divides the coastal district of east Wicklow from the upland communities of north-west Wicklow whilst at the same time uniting communities on the Dublin/Wicklow mountain border. These granitic rocks form rounded hills about Lugnaquillia (926m), the highest peak in central Wicklow, and many of the other peaks which rise above 610m. South-west of Lugnaquilla, the mountain chain narrows to become a ridge of hills dissected by a number of rivers, the largest being the Slaney and its tributaries. In the north and west this mountain range overlooks the lowland plain developed on carboniferous limestone of Dublin and Kildare. To the south-west lie the Tullow lowlands formed on granite, and to the east is a narrow plain based on Palaeozoic rocks. In the foothills to the north-east a series of glacial drainage channels have created valleys such the Glen of the Downs and the Scalp. On the western edge of the mountains, the valleys are broad and well developed; in contrast, they are deeper in the east owing to the difference in the length of their courses.[7]

The soils of the county have developed on glacial material deposited by successive glaciations during the Pleistocene (fig. 1.2a). Evidence for four glacial episodes has been identified in the county.[8] Two of these were marked by ice-sheets that originated outside Wicklow and banked up against the mountains from the north-west and north-east. The deposits of these two encircling ice-sheets are characterised by a high limestone content with chert and other rocks foreign to the Wicklow mountain district which is composed of granite, schist and slate. These limestone gravels reach a maximum elevation of 366m at the extreme northern end of the mountains in Wicklow which experienced the full force of the ice-sheets advancing southwards. The deposits of other mountain glaciations are formed of local rocks and the most recent episode in the mountain glaciation laid down a granitic drift. Generally the soils in Wicklow are fertile with a wide use range (fig. 1.2b), except for the peaty podsols which formed in the central Wicklow upland where there is no drift cover, and the sticky gleys – called the maccamores – which run in a coastal strip south of Mizen Head into county Wexford.

Hunter-gatherers

The earliest evidence for a human presence in Ireland dates to around 7000BC and is associated with a community of hunter-gatherers who lived in timber-framed huts on the banks of the River Bann at Mount Sandel, county Derry, the most famous early Mesolithic (Middle Stone Age) site in north-east Ireland.[9] Base camps such as these were probably occupied for a substantial part of the year. Available resources rotated on a seasonal basis and included salmon, eel, wild boar, fruit and nuts. The most diagnostic of their stone tools is the microlith, a small flint blade worked and hafted for use in hunting and fishing. It is still a matter of some conjecture as to the origin of these first colonists; did they come from across the Irish Sea or from the Isle of Man, or were they part of an

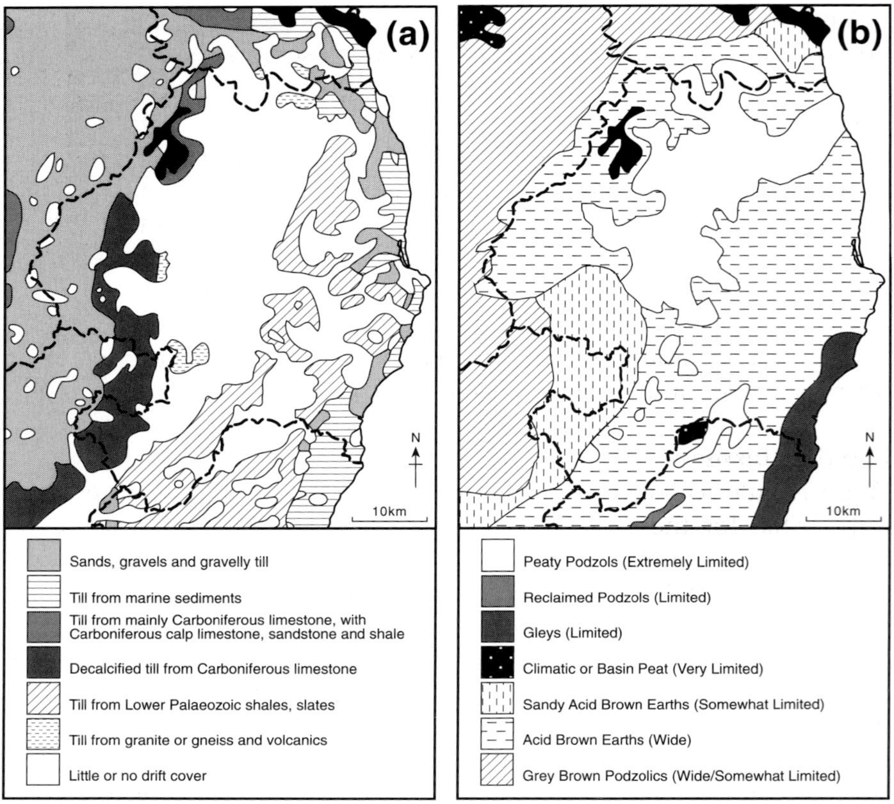

Figure 1.2 (a) Glacial drift in county Wicklow (after F.M. Synge in *Atlas of Ireland* (1979), pp 18-19); (b) Soils of county Wicklow with land use range in brackets (after M.J. Gardiner in *Atlas of Ireland* (1979), pp 24-5).

early movement of peoples from south-western France, through Britain, to Ireland?[10] There is, however, considerable evidence that the south of Ireland was colonised as early as north-east Ireland, on the basis of stone tool finds from the Blackwater valley in Cork, and assemblages from Rathjordan, county Limerick and Lough Boora in county Offaly.[11] No early Mesolithic sites have been identified in county Wicklow; the nearest ones are in north county Dublin.[12] This absence in Wicklow is possibly a result of natural erosion. Early occupation could have taken place on a lowland plain along the Wicklow coast which has been subsequently inundated by the sea. An examination of the contouring of the Irish Sea Basin has suggested that around 7000BC a considerable area of the existing sea floor would have been exposed.[13] However, remnants of *later* Mesolithic culture have been identified in Wicklow. In 1932, Charles Martin fortuitously discovered a cave on St Bride's Head one mile east of Wicklow town. The entrance to the cave was about

1.20m high and its floor was littered with broken flints and flint pebbles. He observed that this material bore a distinct resemblance to flints found on raised beaches in other parts of the country.[14] These were remains of tools used by hunter-gatherers who lived along the east coast between 5500 and 3500BC. Many years later, G. F. Mitchell, following in Martin's footsteps, discovered similar later Mesolithic implements on an exposed cliff edge at a golf links just south of Wicklow town.[15] Impressed by these finds he investigated further south along the Wicklow coast, finding quite a number of small flint working sites buried in the sands. His most productive site lay at the southern end of Brittas Bay, where he found a large scatter of flint debris near a small stream including scrapers, blades and rough-outs for other implements.

The first farmers

There is little to suggest that these hunter-gatherer communities were responsible for the technological and ritual revolution which was to take place in county Wicklow over the next millennia. There are a number of coastal settlement sites in Leinster, such as that in Bannow Bay in county Wexford and Sutton in county Dublin,[16] which show some evidence for cross fertilisation between Mesolithic and farming communities. But one still retains the distinct impression that this remained a separate form of settlement tied to the coast and its resources. If this is the case, then at what stage was the interior of Wicklow first settled? In general, the beginning of farming in Ireland is associated with the first appearance of the megalithic tomb builders. Within county Wicklow the distribution of these tombs represents a dramatic shift from a coastal to an upland economy. These tombs are concentrated in north-west Wicklow with smaller clusters south of Rathdrum and east along the coast at Brittas (fig. 1.3, appendix I). Our earliest evidence for activity in the interior has come from a burial in Ballintruer More in west Wicklow, excavated by the National Museum in 1970. It comprised a polygonal-shaped cist (stone box) containing the burial of an adult male accompanied by a highly decorated pot. This site has been favourably compared with a growing number of similar 'Linkardstown type' burials discovered in the south of Ireland which were believed to date from the end of the Neolithic. However, the C14 date for this site, which is now calibrated to 4300+ –70BC, indicates that these burials can be placed at the earlier rather than the later end of the Neolithic.[17] Dates from similar burials further substantiate the view that single inhumations in a cist under a round mound is a burial custom which started very early in the south of Ireland. These isolated tombs may indicate an incipient stage of colonisation in the south-east. However, it is the passage tomb builders

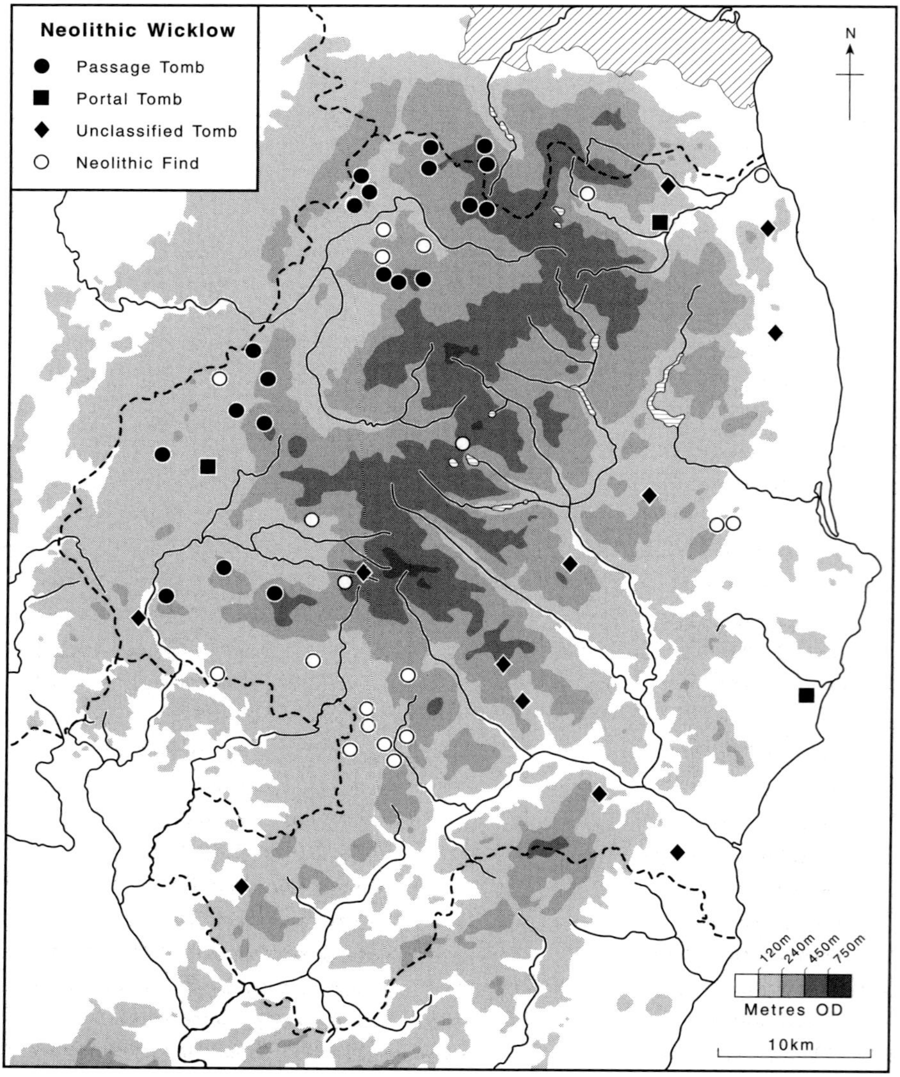

Figure 1.3 Distribution of Neolithic tombs and finds in county Wicklow.

who formed the most coherent and distinctive group (fig. 1.4). Their tombs are a prominent feature of the west Wicklow/south Dublin uplands, crowning its western and northern summits between Saggart in Dublin and Baltinglass in county Wicklow.[18] In general they lie above the 240m contour and beyond the present limits of agriculture. Below these tombs lie the plains of Dublin and Kildare. The area is drained by the Dodder in the north, the north-westerly flowing Liffey and King's rivers and, in the south, by the upper reaches of the Slaney.

Neolithic environment

The exposed and now partially peat-covered landscape chosen by the passage-tomb builders is currently classified as marginal. However, the physical presence of these tombs testifies to more favourable climatic conditions during the Neolithic and this is borne out by evidence from excavations on Baltinglass Hill and palaeobotanical research on four sites in the county. With the help of pollen analysis it is possible to reconstruct the prehistoric environment of these stone-age communities and the large-scale changes to vegetation brought about by them with the introduction of farming. In 1967, Doherty sampled a blanket bog site within the boundary of the Wicklow granite area on a saddle of land between Seefin and Seefingan.[19] Both of these peaks are crowned by impressive passage tombs. He was also able to compare his results with pollen diagrams from Kippure (fig. 1.4), Lough Firrib, and Moneystown which lies to the east of the Wicklow granite (fig. 1.1). The basal sample from Seefin was from a rich-limestone drift horizon showing evidence for a forest cover of pine and elm (fig. 1.5). Above this drift horizon Doherty identified typical landnam features, i.e. a decline in elm and pine associated with the occurrence of plantain, thought to be an agricultural indicator. This dramatic elm decline has usually been interpreted as indicating widespread clearance of elm-dominated woodland but many scientists now believe that a disease similar to Dutch elm disease caused these changes about 4000BC.[20] However, there were also quite considerable peaks in grass pollen in the Seefin profile indicating large areas of upland used for grazing. A decline in forest cover was also apparent in the other Wicklow pollen diagrams, though the elm decline was not as marked at the Moneystown site in east Wicklow. There, the soil was sandy and a marked hazel peak in the profile indicates an oak forest, since hazel apparently acts as a pioneer invader following the clearance of oak forest.[21] The time scale for these pollen diagrams is difficult to determine without C14 dating, but it would seem that the early 'landnam' phase was followed by the spread of blanket bog. At Seefin this began as a heath type community and there is some evidence to suggest the burning of this heath by these communities. However, this would have resulted in further podsolisation of the subsoil. Moore has suggested that the granite bedrock of west Wicklow would have podsolised quicker than the mineral-rich schist in east Wicklow.[22] Scientists are now ascribing this spread of blanket bogs to the major impact of early farming on this vegetation and soil over a long period.[23]

Excavations of a passage tomb on Baltinglass Hill showed evidence for pre-tomb habitation floors on the old ground surface below the cairn.[24] The finds from these floors include a polished stone axehead,

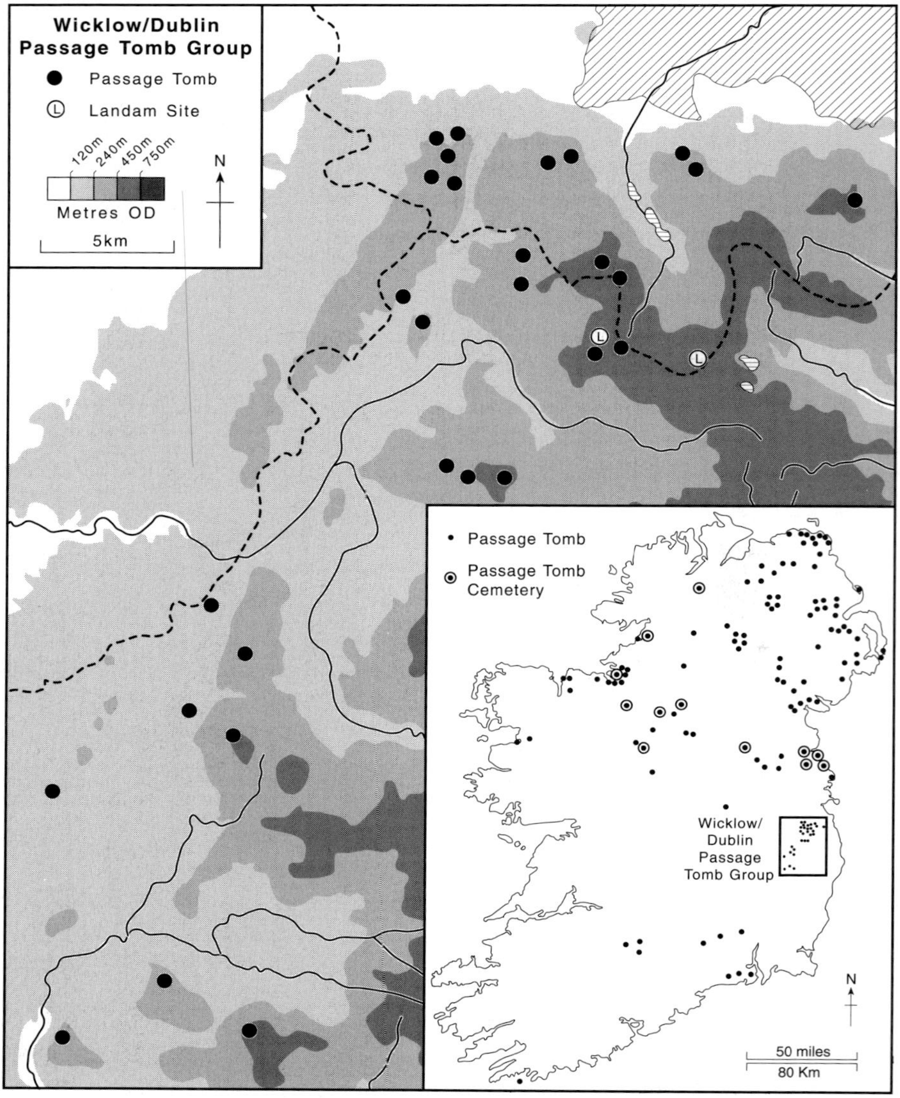

Figure 1.4 The Wicklow/Dublin passage tomb group; Inset: The distribution of passage tombs and passage tomb cemeteries in Ireland (after Eogan (1986), p. 91, fig. 45).

flint scrapers and a quantity of wheat grains. In 1980, Cooney discovered a saddle quern in part of the cairn on Baltinglass Hill. This, he argued, could have been used by the pre-tomb settlers and further substantiates evidence for cereal cultivation in the vicinity of the hilltop during the Neolithic.[25] Cooney has further argued that the presence of cereal crops at these prehistoric sites suggest that boundaries surrounding tillage plots would have been a feature of the early farmed

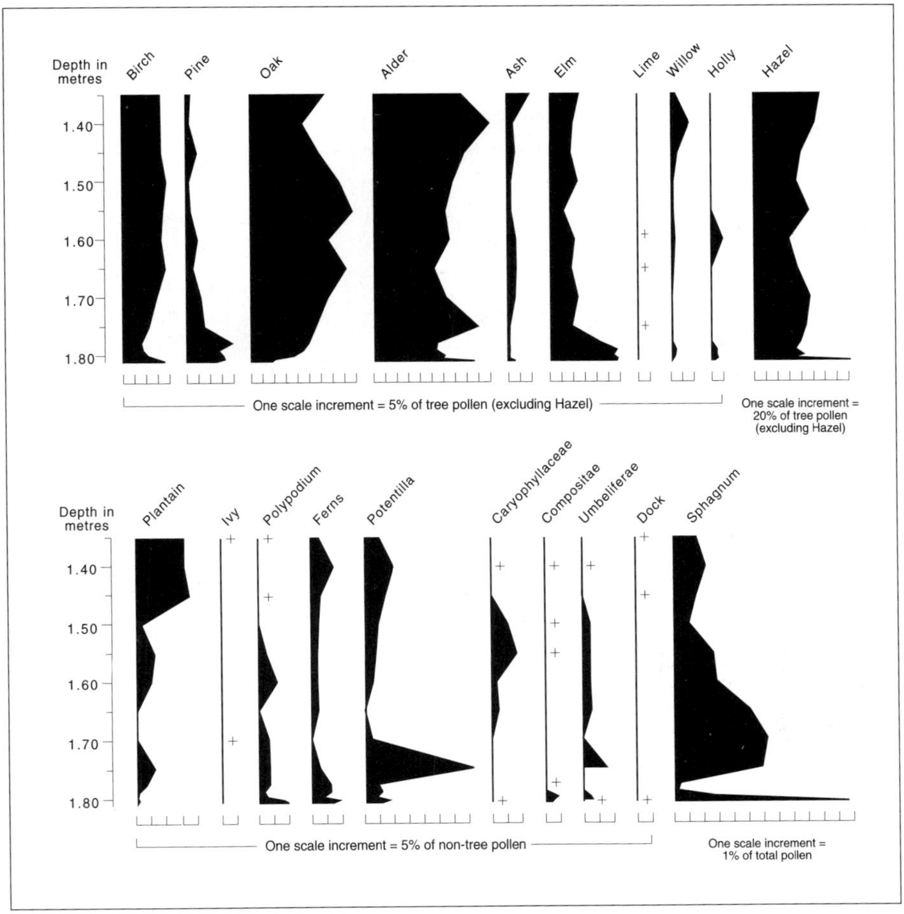

Figure 1.5 Pollen diagram from Seefin, county Wicklow (after Doherty [1967]).

landscape.[26] The making of fields would have been an integral part of this agricultural activity particularly in this key 'core' area of settlement in north-west Wicklow. This highlights the landscape context of these tombs and the need to preserve a large area around them from development. These very sites appear to be now under threat by intensive afforestation.

From a broader perspective, the passage tombs of north-west Wicklow and south Dublin demarcate a sacred and political territory (fig. 1.4). Their builders were the first to clear large tracts of the forest and impose a structure on the Wicklow landscape. This was achieved by a major communal enterprise in a community integrated by religious unity and shared burial customs, expressed in tomb architecture and symbolism. The tombs are positioned on strategic commanding positions along the western and northern summits of the Dublin/ Wicklow border land. It is not clear whether this was for ritual purposes or stemmed from the desire to demarcate a discrete territory. Cooney has recently examined the relationship of tombs within cemeteries and has outlined common characteristics within the more notable passage tomb groupings. These include a focal tomb in a key position upon which other tombs are oriented, intervisibility between two tombs and distinct patterning around the main tomb.[27] The Dublin/ Wicklow mountain group shares some of these characteristics, i.e. intervisibility and a well-defined territory. There is however little evidence for a focal tomb within the group and definite orientations are difficult to pinpoint because entrances are known only at Lackan (NSW), Baltinglass (SW, NW and N) and Seefin (NE). There are variations in scale indicating some hierarchy within the tombs larger ones at Seefin and Baltinglass contrast in scale with smaller examples at Ballyfolan, Lackan and Kilbride. The high visibility of this group, as expressed in its hilltop positioning, is more indicative of territorial demarcation than ritual placement in the landscape in a cemetery arrangement.

The art of these tomb builders has been recorded on three of the Wicklow passage tombs, namely Seefin, Baltinglass Hill and on a kerbstone from a now destroyed tomb in Tornant Upper near Dunlavin.[28] The art which covers the upper portion of the stone has been described in terms of 'tall boxed U's'.[29] The two decorated stones at Seefin are in the passage which leads to the chamber and were exposed during excavations in the 1930s. Incised on these stones are large-scale chevrons and lozenges which cover the stone and the art has been compared in style with that occurring on the Breton tombs, the best parallels for it coming from the site at Gavrinis in Morbihan.[30] Additional art was recently identified by Richard Dowling.[31] The megalithic art at Baltinglass occurs on five stones, in the chamber and on the kerbstones. Geometrical motifs are employed in the form of circles, spirals and triangles. Particular designs were preferred for individual features of the tomb; spirals in chamber 11 and circles on the kerbstones. Recent research on passage grave art has shown that positioning was an important consideration and that there was a conscious effort to place particular designs in specific parts of the tomb, suggesting that certain meanings were associated with the various symbols.[32] A stylistic development has been observed in this passage grave art with an earlier depictive style based on geometric elements and a later plastic style which has a greater visual impact.[33] At Knowth in the Boyne Valley, for instance, the depictive style was used in the building of the structure and the plastic style was used afterwards. Some stones were actually re-ornamented with bold carvings superimposed on the earlier geometric designs. The art on the Wicklow tombs appears to represent the earlier depictive style of decoration.

In contrast to the concentrated distribution of passage tombs in north-west Wicklow, the three portal tombs in the county display a more disparate pattern. However, the site in Onagh is part of a group which spreads across the county boundary into Dublin and includes the tombs at Kiltiernan, Ballybrack and Brenanstown. In 1934 Price commented on the likely relationship between these tombs.[34] There is an impressive isolated example along the coast at Brittas standing near the mouth of the Potter's river in an area rich in antiquities.[35] All that remains of the dolmen in Broomfield are the uprights which are incorporated into a field fence.[36] The low-lying setting of these simpler tombs may indicate a greater penetration into the more heavily wooded countryside by their builders than that attempted by the passage tomb folk and possibly a more mixed farming economy. That both communities existed side by side in well demarcated territories is suggested by the mutually exclusive nature of their distribution in south Dublin.[37] Ó Nualláin has established the significance of coasts and rivers in the distribution and diffusion of these tombs which represent a seaborne movement of communities into Wicklow during the third millennium BC.[38]

The most durable artifacts to have survived from the Neolithic period of Wicklow's past are the stone tools used in early land clearance. There have been at least sixteen isolated discoveries of stone axes in the county (fig. 1.3). The frequency of finds is relatively low when compared with other parts of the country such as counties Meath and Limerick, for instance.[39] However, the actual find spots of these axes can be very significant in that they indicate early settlement in areas where there is no tomb presence, thereby expanding our picture of where people were living at this time in county Wicklow. There is, for example, a cluster of stone axe finds in the Knockanna area in south-west Wicklow, quite a distance from the nearest known Neolithic tombs. Some axes found along the foothills of the mountains in north-west Wicklow further substantiate the settlement evidence of the tombs. Others have been discovered during turf cutting operations – such as that from Rathcot, Moyne and Kyle[40] – and alert us to the real possibilities of finding early settlement in large tracts of Wicklow which are now bog covered. Stone axe finds can also be an indicator of the extent of communications between communities in Wicklow and other parts of the country. Of particular interest from the point of view of possible trading links is a pair of porcelainite axeheads found at a farmhouse in Killamoat. The source for these axes is thought to have been Rathlin Island and Tievebulliagh in north-east Ireland, which were areas of large-scale axe production from 3800BC to 2500BC.[41] The Killamoat finds are part of a scatter of axes identified along the eastern seaboard. They may have been transported to Wicklow from the source as rough-outs and finished locally. Another possible imported item brought in from north-east Ireland to Wicklow is finely produced flint javelinheads.[42] They have been found at Camaderry, Knockanna and on the pre-tomb occupation floors at Baltinglass.[43]

The Bronze Age in Wicklow: Technology

Wicklow has long been associated with the technological revolution that was underway in Ireland from about 2000BC. There is an old tradition that it was Tighearnmas who first caused gold to be smelted in Ireland and that it was Uchadan, an artificer of the men of Cuala in Wicklow, who smelted it.[44] Indeed, until the 1960s it was assumed that county Wicklow was the main source of alluvial gold in the Irish Early Bronze Age. However, the results of a detailed metallurgical survey of all the gold objects in National Museums of Europe indicated otherwise.[45] Hartmann, who undertook this metallurgical analysis, concluded that virtually all the objects showed no connection with the gold nuggets from Wicklow except for some of the earliest ones which comprise discs, earrings and a solid bronze bracelet. However, Hartmann admitted that he was unable to trace most of the remaining gold content from a source outside Ireland so it is still possible that other types of gold from Wicklow were used.[46] Jackson has identified early ore workings in Avoca which were rich in gold. The natural action of ice passing over these surfaces would have scoured out large quantities of this ore, thereby concentrating the native gold in alluvial gravels.[47] Certainly, the presence of standing stones, burials and rock art in the Avoca area suggests an expansion of settlement in the area in the Early Bronze Age (fig. 1.6). The primacy of Wicklow as a source for raw materials in the Bronze Age remains questionable, and the archaeological record does not provide much evidence for the importance of Wicklow as a manufacturing centre at this time. There is one gold lunula in the British Museum from Blessington.[48] Besides this luxurious item there is a limited range of metal objects which were being produced at the early stages of the Bronze Age such as the copper or bronze axehead, of which over one thousand examples are known from Ireland.[49] A relatively small proportion of these were found in county Wicklow. The first metal workers in Ireland were journeymen, and a hoard of one of these travelling craftsmen was found in a gravel pit at Monastery north-east of the bridge outside Enniskerry.[50] This hoard contained three flat axes, all broken, and two fragments of copper cake. These are the earliest type of axes made in Ireland. A similar axe, in the Ulster Museum, is from 'county Wicklow'

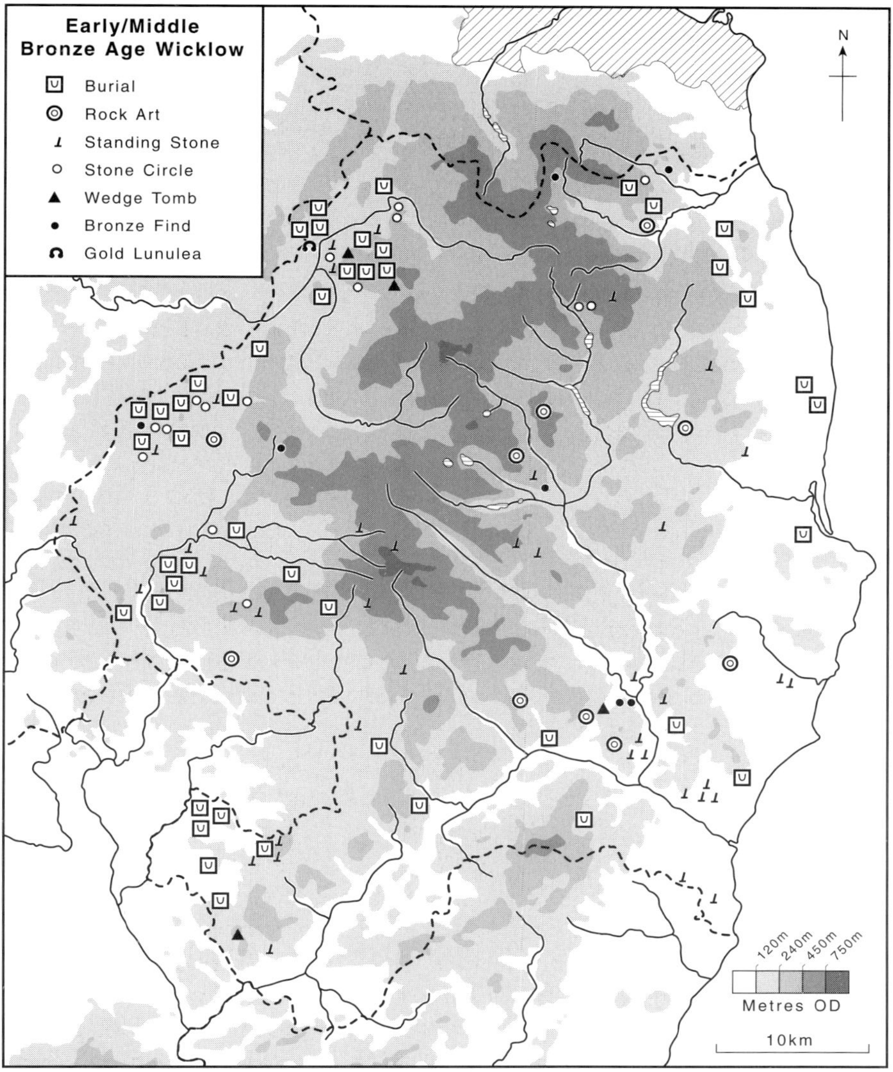

Figure 1.6 Distribution of Early to Middle Bronze Age finds and monuments in county Wicklow.

and there are four early axes from the county in the National Museum (fig. 1.6, appendix II). Another five Early Bronze Age axes have been found in various parts of Wicklow. Taken as a whole, these finds do not indicate that this area was a major hub of manufacturing in the Early Bronze Age. Not until the Later Bronze Age, when we have evidence for the production of weapons and socketed implements on an industrial scale inside the hillfort at Rathgall, does any site in Wicklow feature as a manufacturing centre.

Bronze Age ritual practices

A better indicator of the wealth and significance of Wicklow in the Bronze Age is the presence in the county of some of the finest ritual monuments to be found in Leinster (fig. 1.6, appendix III). Stone circles and standing stones were erected, rock art was inscribed on isolated boulders as a focus for communal ceremonial activity, and the building of communal tombs continued in north-west and south Wicklow. The Donard/Dunlavin area has a group of stone circles remarkable for their distinctive regional characteristics which include embankments, ceremonial avenues and stone outliers (fig. 1.7).[51] Amongst the better known examples are Athgreany near Hollywood, the 'griddle stones' at Boleycarrigeen and the 'Davidstown ring' at Castleruddery near Donard.[52] The Castleruddery circle has impressive entrance stones of white quartz and standing stones to the east of the site suggest a ceremonial avenue into the circle. An outer ditch and possible pit circle around the embanked circle, visible on a Cambridge University photograph (CUCAP BDR 39) of the site, indicates its complex nature. This regional group of circles lies south of the Liffey valley and the upper reaches of the Slaney on limestone till. Similar circles are found in contiguous county Kildare with multiple stone circles at Broadleas Commons and Whiteleas, just south of Ballymore-Eustace on the fringes of the Curragh.[53] On Brewel Hill the remains of a circle is enclosed by two earthen banks.[54] Features such as the stone lined entrances and enclosing embankments are characteristic of henge monuments – the ceremonial enclosures of the Late Neolithic/Early Bronze Age period in Britain and Ireland. The closest analogy to the Castleruddery sites is the circle in Grange, near Lough Gur, county Limerick, excavated by Ó Ríordáin in 1947.[55] Grange produced Beaker and Coarse Ware pottery together with a wide ranging flint assemblage. Both of these stone embanked enclosures appear to be local variants of the 'Boyne Type' embanked enclosure identified in the Boyne region and presumed to have succeeded passage tombs as a focus for ritual practice around 2000BC.[56]

Nineteenth-century reports indicate an even greater number of stone circles in north-west Wicklow. Many were being robbed for building purposes when John O'Donovan was compiling information for the Ordnance Survey in the 1830s.[57] An impressive circle had been removed during road building at Blessington Demesne, its location fortunately recorded by the Ordnance Survey as the 'Piper Stones (site of)'.[58] Another site at Athgreany, west of the better known stone circle, had been partially cleared.[59] The less well known stone circles at Ballyfoyle, Carrig and Sroughan in the Blessington area have been identified by Healy.[60] These are a type of site which presents problems

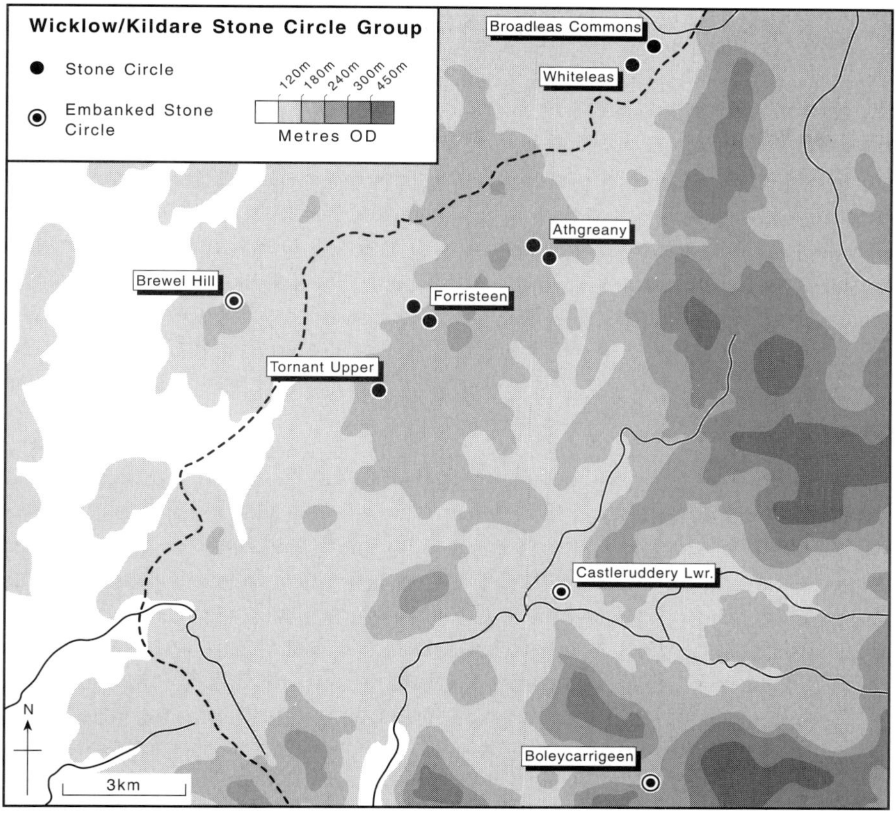

Figure 1.7 The Wicklow/Kildare stone circle group.

in interpretation without excavation evidence and have been confused in the past with foundations for house sites. A case in point is a 'circle' at Rath East/Knockeen just beside the hillfort at Rathgall.[61] This was formed of tightly spaced, relatively small standing stones (0.60m to 1.20m in height) when surveyed by Raftery in 1972.[62] A portion of a saddle quern and a rim sherd of coarse pottery were retrieved indicating a domestic rather than a ritual function. In general, finds from stone circles are a rarity. The only other occurrence in Wicklow of a stone circle is at Forristeen 2.4km east of Dunlavin which was disturbed during land reclamation projects in the 1940s. This site produced 'crocks' containing ashes.[63]

A simpler version of these ritual stone monuments, the standing stone, has a more widespread distribution in the county extending into central and south-east Wicklow, overlapping with the distribution of funerary sites (fig. 1.6, appendix VI). There are thirty-seven standing stones including a stone pair at Laragh East and multiple stones at

Slievemaan/Farbreaga and Carrycole Hill.[64] The best known example is the 'Longstone' at Ballintruer More which is situated near the bed of a stream at the junction of the main Dublin/Baltinglass road with that leading to Talbotstown.[65] The function of these standing stones has been the subject of much debate. Some may have acted as demarcators of property or territorial boundaries, others may have been grave markers. In a recent study of sixty-five excavated and disturbed standing stones from Ireland, fifty (89 per cent) were associated with burial predominantly Beaker or Early Bronze Age in date. This indicates that their primary function was as grave markers.[66] At Carrig, near Blessington, a burial contained in a crude inverted urn was found in a pit beside the socket for a standing stone close to a cemetery cairn of Early Bronze Age date.[67] Across the county boundary into Kildare, cist graves have been found at the base of some standing stones. At Longstone Rath, Furness, county Kildare cremated remains of five adults together with pottery sherds, stone beads, a flint scraper and fragments of a stone wrist guard were recovered. There was a short cist at the base of a stone without accompanying grave goods at the 'Longstone', Punchestown.[68]

There are ten areas where rock art dating from this period has been identified (fig. 1.6, appendix V), only two of which are in west Wicklow. One is at Merginstown Demesne, a 'cupped stone' found near a cist cemetery[69] and the other at Humewood Castle, undoubtedly the finest example of rock art in the county. This stone was found sometime before 1870 during the construction of an artificial lake in the neighbouring townland of Barraderry East.[70] These are part of the lands attached to Humewood Castle south-east of Baltinglass. It is incised with the classic cup and circle markings, one of which has a groove running through it. The stone was re-erected as a curiosity in front of Humewood Castle where it stands today. The remaining rock art in the county is much more simplistic in style. As early as the 1830s Kinahan commented on the particularly simple version of rock art to be seen in the Wicklow/Wexford area.[71] This comprises multiple cups and grooves which could not be interpreted as a natural phenomenon. The most remarkable cluster of decorated stones he recorded lies in the fields north and south of Ballykean House, 5km south-east of Rathdrum.[72] This form of rock art has been, in general, dated to the Early Bronze Age and is associated with a Food Vessel culture. It is a form used to decorate cist-graves in northern England and Scotland.[73] Evidence from Wicklow certainly substantiates this cultural connection. For instance, the inscribed stone at Merginstown Demesne was found near a cist cemetery which contained a Food Vessel. However, the rock art in Wicklow has a much more restricted distribution than that of the cist graves (fig. 1.6). The only other associations with rock art in Wicklow is the stone with cup markings found 400 yards south of the Glaskenny dolmen'[74] and at least two decorated stones found within a few hundred yards of the wedge tomb at Mongnacool.[75] MacWhite has proposed influences from as far afield as north-west Iberia or Galicia for some of the Wicklow rock art such as the stones at Barraderry East and Baltynamina,[76] but other parallels lie much closer to hand.

Bronze Age burial practices

The main body of archaeological evidence for Bronze Age activity in the county is the funerary record which provides the best indication of the extent of settlement in Wicklow from *circa* 2000BC to 1500BC. Most of these sites have been discovered during gravel extraction which may account for their riverine distribution focused on the Liffey, Slaney and to a lesser extent, the Avoca valley and its tributaries (fig. 1.6, appendix VI). The one exception to this pattern is a concentration around Dunlavin in the midst of the stone circles previously described. The timing of some of the findings coincides with the active phase of demesne development in the late eighteenth century. For instance, in 1764 six urns were discovered 'in one of the moats near Powerscourt, county Wicklow... and each urn was covered by a small flat stone and filled with black dirt, which possibly might have been ashes reduced to that condition by time...'.[77] In 1785 William Hamilton described the discovery of a 'small stone enclosure of eight stones' (a cist?) and cremated bones, found when the estate of Greenville House in Kilranelagh was being laid out.[78]

There are records of forty-six Bronze Age burials in the county. The main burial mode is a short cist or stone box containing a cremation or inhumation accompanied by a Bowl or Vase Food Vessel. Both of these pottery types occur equally in the county. There are only six reports of unprotected burials. These are all large cinerary urn burials with the exception of a cremation with an accompanying incense cup found near Dunlavin.[79] On at least seven occasions the cist burials were accompanied by flint artifacts (Fassaroe, Newcastle Upper, Kelshamore, Rathmoon, Carrig, Ballybrew), and there was a bronze razor with the burials at Newcastle Upper and Carrig.[80] In general, we are dealing with a single burial tradition but multiple remains have been identified enclosed in one cist. At Rathmoon, for instance, a short cist under a circular mound contained three adults and two children. These were discovered when the site was bulldozed in 1958.[81] Multiple cists are frequently found either in unmarked flat cemeteries as at Clonshannon and Saundersgrove or under a mound such as that at Merginstown Demesne which contained at least two cists with three accompanying

Food Vessels.[82] The cemetery mounds are particularly significant in that they incorporate a variety of burial modes, indicating a range of burial options available simultaneously. At Crehelp, for instance, there were two cist-like structures and a slab covered pit containing two Vase Food Vessels and a pygmy cup.[83] Excavations at these sites have shed some light on the ritual practices involved in the placement of the human remains and the probable status of those individuals interned. One of the cists exposed in a gravel pit at Ballybrew contained the skeleton of a woman.[84] She had been laid on her right side with her head towards the east facing a Food Vessel which stood in the north-east corner of the cist. Her right hand was placed under her head and the left arm bent at right angles, the hand having been placed near the knee. She lay on rush matting over a paved floor in the cist with a lignite bracelet and flint scraper placed in the burial with her. A low cairn at Carrig on the west slopes of Lugnagun, recently excavated by Eoin Grogan, contained four cists enclosing ten separate burials; all were cremations.[85] These bodies had been burned in a funeral pyre near the cairn. Although approximately twenty individuals ranging in age from newborn to over fifty had been burned in this pyre, only ten of the individuals had been placed in the actual cists. The small number of individuals in the grave suggested that only the most important members of society were entitled to more formal burial. Mount, in his recent study of Bronze Age burials in south Leinster, develops this point further: he believes that women and children were discriminated against because predominantly more adult males than females were in these burials and few children are represented.[86]

Wedge tombs in Ireland show a marked regional distribution; the majority are located in the south and west of the country.[87] Therefore, the Dublin/Wicklow tombs and the Wexford group form an outlier in the south-east. There are two tombs in the north-west of the county at Carrig and Blackrock on Lugnagun Spur near Blessington, and two others in the south of the county at Mongnacool Lower and Moylisha[88] (fig. 1.6, appendix I). Both of the south Wicklow wedge tombs were excavated in the last century and produced rather unsatisfactory results. The 'fairy house' at Mongnacool Lower situated between Ballynaclash and Aughrim was excavated *circa* 1880.[89] Kinahan, the excavator, found some evidence for burning in the chamber but there were no finds. Canon Ffrench spent a day digging the tomb of 'Labbansigh' at Moylisha, near Clonegal in 1877 with little result.[90] However, a re-excavation of the site in the 1930s proved more successful. Ffrench's spoil heaps were found to contain some handmade coarse ware pottery. More of this pottery and flint was discovered in the east end of the main chamber as well as two stone discs in the end chamber. A sandstone mould for a bronze socketed spearhead was found under cairn material and thought to be primary.[91] The discovery of this mould, which dated from the Late Bronze Age, raises the question of dating for wedge tombs in county Wicklow. Factors such as the proximity of the north Wicklow wedge tombs at Carrick and Blackrock to Early Bronze Age cemeteries, the association of rock art with the Mongnacool Lower example, and the presence of this spearhead mould under the cairn at Moylisha strongly suggest that they come late in the tomb building tradition.

In broader terms, the Early to Middle Bronze Age in Wicklow was a period of considerable expansion in settlement with a movement into east Wicklow and along the river valleys onto the heavier lowland soils. This was assisted by technological advances at the time and driven to some extent by a deterioration in the upland soils which led to the spread of blanket bog. It is likely that the unique mineral wealth of the county was recognised and exploited during this period, particularly the gold ores in the Avoca area, which shows extensive evidence for human activity from this period. The earlier tradition of building communal tombs was to continue in north-west Wicklow and in isolated pockets in the south of the county, but in general, burial became less formalised and much more diverse in practice. A social hierarchy is still prevalent in this funerary record with only a small percentage of the dead receiving formalised burial. Ritual and communal worship continued to play an important role in the lives of the communities and large scale enclosures were erected to facilitate these ceremonies, the most impressive group of these being the stone-embanked enclosures in the Donard/Dunlavin area.

Late Bronze Age/Early Iron Age Wicklow

The Later Bronze Age period constitutes a more turbulent phase of the county's prehistory. Centres of power were being re-defined and territories consolidated. On the high ground north of Rathgall and east of Baltinglass lie a major group of hilltop fortifications, seven in number (fig. 1.8, appendix VII). These represent the greatest concentration of multivallate hillforts in the country. From their great heights they dominate the Leinster plains and the Slaney valley below. The only other area in Wicklow where we find hillforts is in the Glen of the Downs. These are near the coast where there are single banked (univallate) hillforts at Downshill and Coolagad/Kindlestown Upper.[92] The core group in west Wicklow combines univallate, bivallate and multivallate types. The ramparts are constructed mainly of earth and stone facings or a single stone rampart such as that which encloses the hilltop at Brusselstown.[93] A possible lower line of defence around the

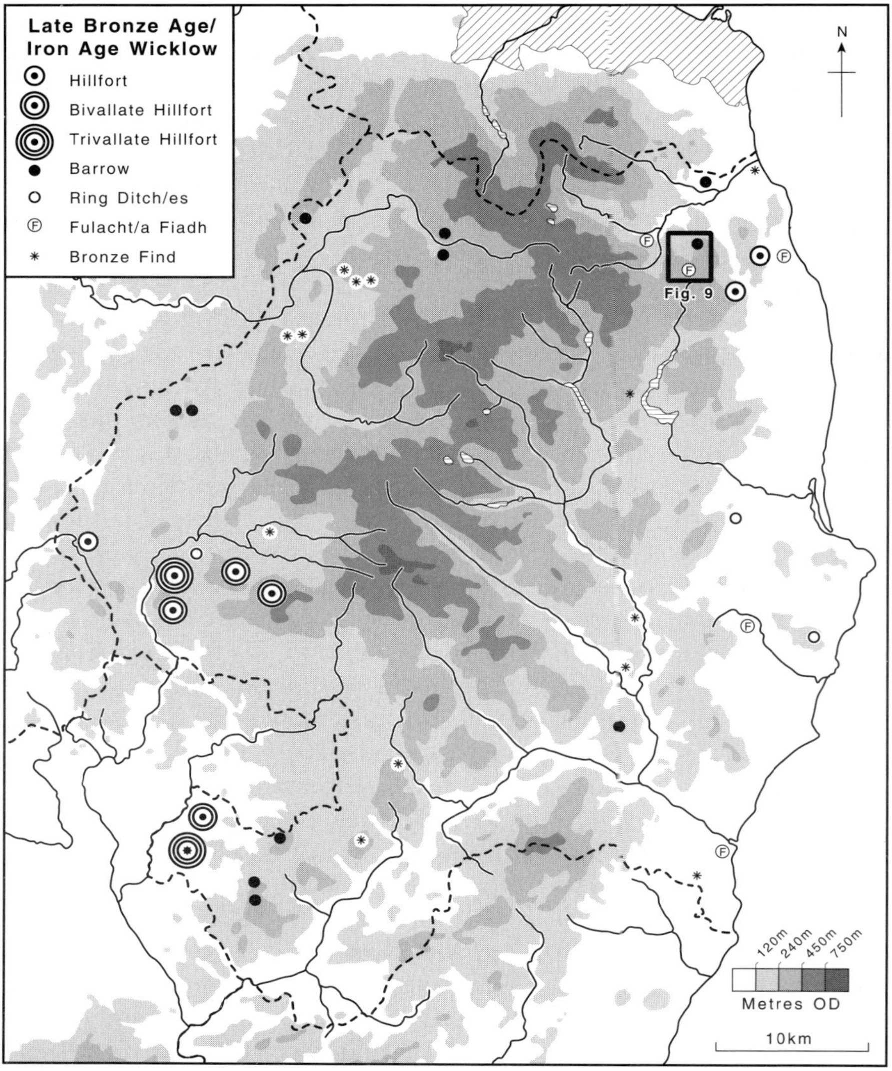

Figure 1.8 Distribution of Late Bronze Age/Iron Age finds and monuments in county Wicklow.

upper slopes of Brusselstown and encompassing Spinans Hill has recently been identified from aerial photography.[94] In some cases these defences follow the contour, as at Tinoranhill, Coolagad/Kindlestown Upper, are located off the hillslope, as at 'Rathnagree' on Tuckmill Hill, or are on the summit as is 'Rathgall' in Rath East.[95] These hillforts are all over 300m in diameter, the largest example being the site on Tinoranhill (500m). Within some of these fortifications are stone enclosures or 'citadels' such as that called the 'round O' on Tinoranhill and in

'Rathnagree' on Tuckmill Hill.[96] There is a probable burial mound within the site at Knockeen[97] and a passage grave on the summit of Baltinglass Hill was excavated in the 1930s.[98] Raftery has commented on the repeated occurrences of passage graves within hillforts and interprets it as the attraction of particular hills with some pre-existing sanctity.[99] Rathgall is the only site within this core area which has been scientifically excavated. It comprises four lines of rampart which enclose over eighteen acres. The excavations have revealed that the impressive ramparts around this low hill at Rath East were constructed during the Late Bronze Age, and that settlement took place on the hill from this period into the Iron Age, the early centuries AD and again during the thirteenth and fourteenth centuries.[100] In the centre of the site, excavations exposed a workshop structure which produced hundreds of clay mould fragments used in the production of sword, spears and other socketed implements. These testify to the manufacture of weaponry on an industrial scale within the hillfort at Rathgall during the seventh and sixth centuries BC. No other manufacturing centre from the Later Bronze Age is at present known in the county but isolated finds of weapons and tools have been discovered (fig. 1.8, appendix VIII). The most impressive assemblage of material is that contained in the hoard from Kish, south of Arklow, which was found in the last century during the removal of a field fence. This contained a socketed spearhead, two axeheads and a knife.[101]

Undoubtedly, Rathgall was a high status site and Orpen has argued on the basis of rather tenuous documentary evidence that 'Rathgall' is synonymous with the 'Dún na nGalian' of the Book of Leinster, the fortress associated in early Irish literature with Labraid Loingsech, the ancestor-deity of the Laigin or Leinstermen, and the city called 'Dunum' identified by Ptolemy in the second century AD.[102] This hypothesis has been rejected by O'Rahilly who would prefer to equate these places with the more ambiguous site 'Dind Ríg' supposedly on the Barrow near Leighlinbridge.[103] Beyond dispute, however, is the strong archaeological evidence which testifies to the presence of a major group of hillforts which, in turn, demonstrate that the district around Rathgall and Baltinglass was a major hub of power in south Leinster, indeed within Ireland, at the beginning of the historic period in Wicklow.

Settlement evidence, other than that identified in the hillfort at Rathgall, is difficult to pinpoint for the Later Bronze Age period in the county. However, the recent recognition and dating of the ancient cooking places known as fulachta fiadh may reveal the nature of lowland settlement during this period in Wicklow. Scientific dating of a randomly excavated sample of these sites from Ireland places them firmly in the Bronze Age with a predominance of second millennium

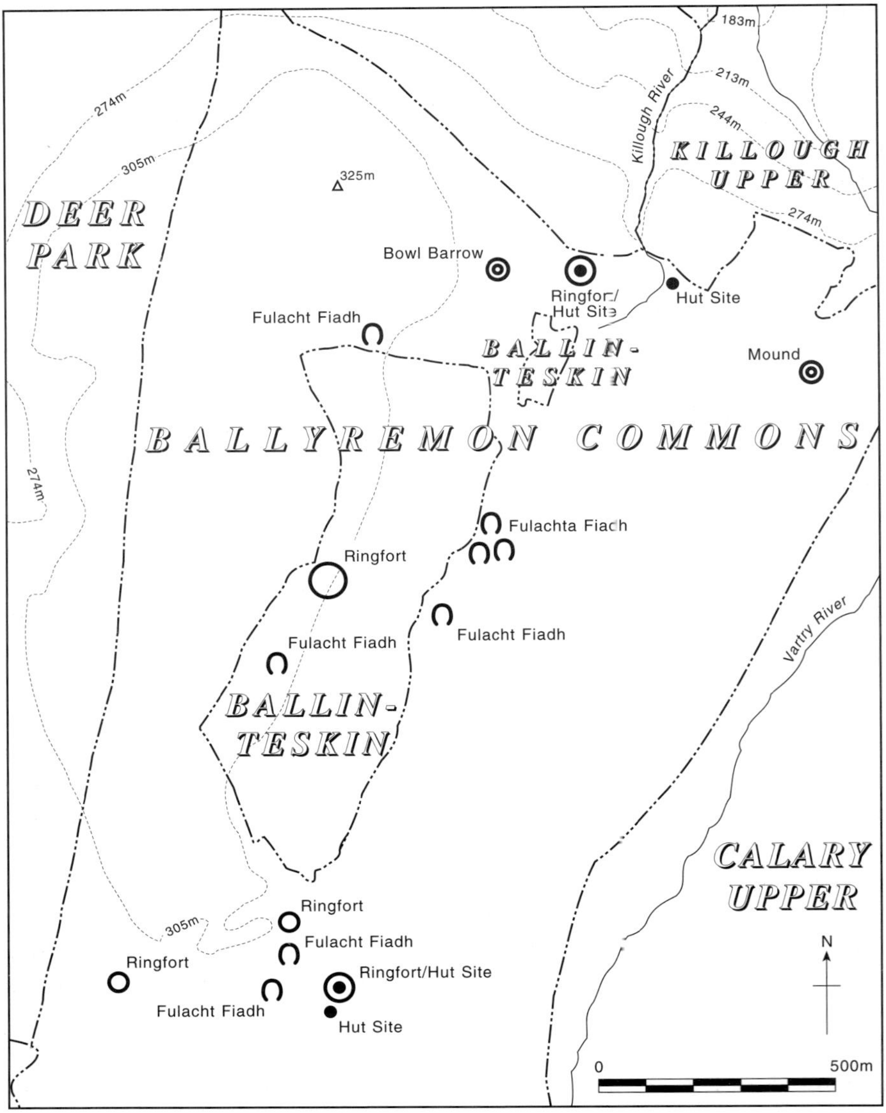

Figure 1.9 The Ballyremon Common fulachta fiadh/barrow group.

BC dates for their use.[104] This dating is further substantiated by the finds evidence associated with the monument.[105] Known fulachta fiadh have a limited distribution in Wicklow, confined to the eastern half of the county (fig. 1.8, appendix VIII). The monument survives usually as a crescent-shaped mound made up of small pieces of shattered stone, near a stream or in marshy ground. A wooden trough or dry-lined pit is often found in the area surrounded by the mound. Stones were heated from a fire close-by and placed in the water-filled trough which resulted in a steady rise in temperature and the food was then placed in the hot water to cook. The hot stones often shattered on contact with the water and were discarded, which resulted in their build-up to a mound over a long period of use. The most extensive group of these sites had been identified in Ballyremon Commons on the western foothills of the Sugarloaf Mountain near the village of Kilmacanogue (fig. 1.9). A total of eight sites has been identified in association with a bowl barrow, a possible burial mound, hut-sites and enclosures. In 1983 one of the fulachta fiadh on the commons was excavated by Victor Buckley and Paddy Healy. The investigations exposed a clay-lined pit; axe sharpened stakes had been placed at an angle into the side of this pit indicating that a wooden tripod was erected above the pit. The stone used to heat the water was the local granite, apparently an effective, re-usable stone type for this particular purpose. A C14 date from the site of 3410+40 B.P. (uncalibrated) places the site in the middle of the second millennium BC.[106] Another fulacht fiadh was recently discovered at Killincarrig, near Greystones. Sherds of Late Bronze Age coarse ware and evidence for flint knapping were found close to this site.[107]

The burial record is inconclusive for the Later Bronze Age. From present evidence the indigenous burial rite appears to have been cremation, deposited either in an upright clay vessel or directly into a small pit within or associated with a circular enclosure. A burial complex at Rathgall uncovered during excavations by Raftery provided important evidence for this practice.[108] The burial consisted or a shallow V-sectioned ditch enclosing a circular area 16m in diameter within which there were three cremation burials. Beside these burial pits were other pits, one of these containing a fragment of the blade of a bronze leaf-shaped sword, an incomplete socketed bronze spearhead and a chisel(?). Two amber beads and coarse pottery were found in the enclosing ditch. This burial complex was associated with an extensive settlement dating to the first millennium BC. Ring ditches identified from aerial photography at Ballintruer More, Monduff and Kilpoole Upper may prove to be further examples of this form of burial.[109]

The rite of cremation continued into the Iron Age in Wicklow under simple mounds, sometimes ditched, and within ring barrows with low central mounds.[110] Beads, bracelets and brooches are the types of items laid with the cremations. Ring barrows with a central mound have a longer history; the site at Lemonstown which produced Bronze Age burials illustrates their antiquity;[111] at the opposite end of the spectrum, ditched mounds excavated at Blessington Demesne proved to be landscape features on which trees were planted in the nineteenth century.[112] Dating these features remains a significant barrier to interpreting their distribution. Barrows have been identified in eight different locations in the county (fig. 1.8). The most significant association is that between the barrows at Ballyremon Commons and the large group of fulachta fiadh and house sites, already referred to (fig. 1.9, appendix IX). The gradual replacement of the cremation rite by inhumation in the early centuries AD has been associated with stronger contacts between the Roman world and Ireland:[113] the practice of extended inhumation burial in slab lined cists in the early centuries AD has been seen as an adoption of Roman forms of burial, although the Irish long cists did not contain grave goods. The seven slab-lined graves discovered between 1943 and 1964 at Tinnapark Demesne illustrate this practice.[114] A fine example of the intrusive burial type is seen in the group of partially protected extended inhumations, heads to the west, discovered by workmen in 1835 beside the beach at Bray, between Victoria and Convent avenues.[115] These were accompanied by coins of Trajan (97-117AD) and Hadrian (117-138AD).[116]

The future of Wicklow's prehistoric landscapes in the Age of Brussels

Many of the monuments described above survive in a landscape which is undergoing major changes in land-use.[117] This Brussels-driven land-use policy in Ireland will lead to a massive increase in the area under forestry in the coming years; the government's National Development Plan (1989-1993) is aimed at a doubling of the area planted in Ireland to 30,000ha per year by 1993.[118] This increase presents a potential threat to the survival of our upland archaeological heritage. For instance, the Bray division of Coillte Teoranta, The Irish Forestry Board, which administers Wicklow, Wexford and parts of Kildare and Dublin, holds 44,000ha and this does not include the private sector holdings.[119] Forestry operations have damaged and continue to damage archaeological remains and their wider setting. Damage can occur in all stages of the forestry process from initial ploughing through to clear felling. Ploughing can churn up site stratigraphy and diminish the potential of future excavations, making it impossible to reconstruct the history of a monument. Where planting has taken place at the edge of a monument, the whole landscape setting has been eliminated.[120] A recent report on forestry damage to Wicklow's archaeology lists fifty-six instances of disturbance and highlights the wide range of monuments involved.[121] The hillforts at Downshill and Coolagad/Kindlestown Upper have had their interiors ploughed and planted; cairns at Lugnagroagh, Cloghleagh and Castleman have been damaged; at Cloghleagh, trees were planted on the cairn itself. Twenty years ago Ireland's rich lowland archaeology was adversely affected by new agricultural technology. It is estimated that as much as one third of existing field monuments was destroyed in some areas during the 1970s.[122]

The EU's awareness of the potential for damage in this policy led to an EU Directive which requires an Environmental Impact Assessment (EIA) for forestry developments over 200ha.[123] However, most Irish tree planting projects cover only 30ha to 70ha thus falling below the EIA threshold. As a result, all grant aided afforestation projects are not subject to pre-planting field based assessments. Little monitoring procedure exists to deal with archaeological monuments in forestry plantations. No Archaeological Forestry Unit has been established within the Forest Service – where all applications are approved – to facilitate these requirements. A prototype for such a unit exists in Scotland where the Royal Commission on the Ancient and Historical Monuments of Scotland (RCAHMS) has set up a survey unit to work in areas threatened by afforestation: the Historic Buildings and Monuments Branch have also made funds available for rapid assessments related to specific grant applications.[124]

A significant step in ensuring a future for some of Wicklow's early monuments has been the establishment of a national park in the county. In April 1990 the government announced the creation of a Wicklow Mountains National Park with a commitment to an eventual target area of 29,000ha, stretching from Killakee in the north to south of Lugnaquilla[125] (fig. 1.10). Its main objective will be nature conservation but it will also contribute enormously to preserving places of cultural heritage. At least thirty-four archaeological monuments have been identified in the target area. These include many of the finest prehistoric monuments discussed in this paper: passage tombs at Seefin and Seefingan, stone circles at Ballinastoe and barrows at Athdown and Ballynabrockey. The presence of this designated conservation zone should help authorities resist proposals from developers. An indication of the positive impact a national park can have on an area has been the increased input of the Office of Public Works into the County Development Plan and in county planning in Donegal since the establishment of the Glenveagh National Park. One of the more immediate advantages in Wicklow has been prohibition of commercial afforestation by Coillte in the park area. The freeze has yet to be extended to the private sector planting which currently accounts for an estimated 50 per cent of afforestation in Ireland.

The archaeology of county Wicklow provides a physical reminder that the Irish landscape is continually changing. The ages of stone and bronze altered the landscape in dramatic ways, and now the age of Brussels has the same effect. While this chapter has attempted to chart

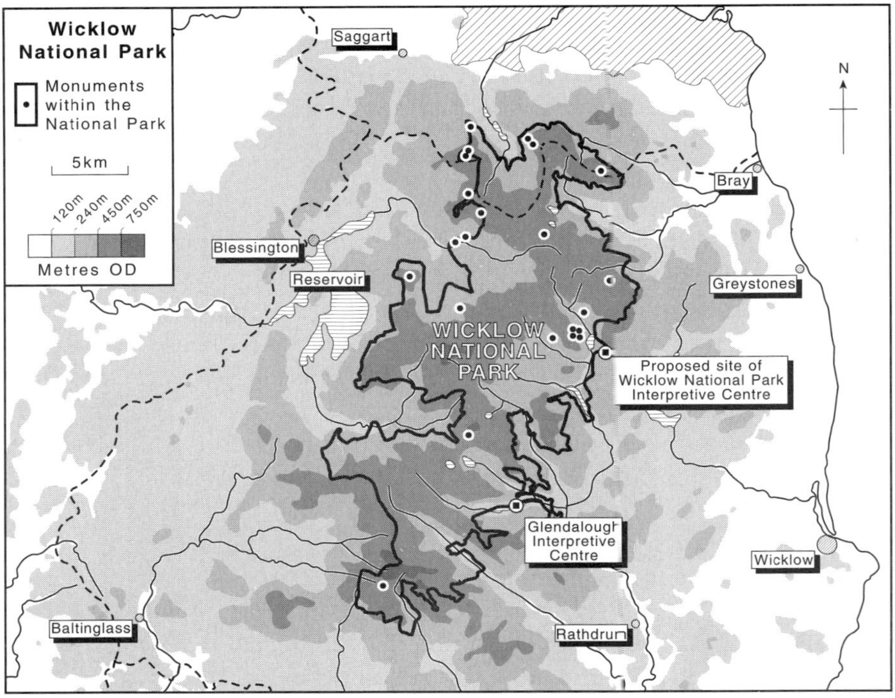

Figure 1.10 The Wicklow National Park.

developments in prehistory, it cannot change the past, but I draw attention to the present impact of EU policy on the landscape because it is in our power to shape the future.

Acknowledgements

I wish to thank the following for their contributions to this paper; the Commissioners of Public Works for permission to use the Sites and Monuments database; Ms. Katherine Daly, Ms. Patricia Dunford and Mr. Gerry Walsh (Sites and Monuments Record Office, Office of Public Works) who prepared the S.M.R. for county Wicklow; Dr. Michael Ryan and the staff of the National Museum of Ireland for providing information from their museum registers; Mr. Paddy Healy; Mr. Matthew Stout who typed the final draft and drew figures 1-10.

References

1. L. Price, 'The ages of stone and bronze in county Wicklow' in *R.I.A. Proc.*, xlii (1934), C, pp 31-64.
2. M. Reynolds and R. Haworth, *A preliminary report on the monuments of archaeological interest in county Wicklow* (Dublin, 1973).

3. G. Stout, G. Walsh, P. Dunford and K. Daly, *Sites and monuments record for county Wicklow* (Dublin, 1986).
4. C. Moriarty, 'Introduction' in *The right trees in the right places* (Dublin, 1991), p. 11.
5. Price, 'Ages of stone and bronze', p. 31.
6. G. L. Davies, 'The age and origin of the Leinster Mountain chain; a study of the evolution of south-eastern Ireland from the upper Palaeozoic to the Later Tertiary' in *R.I.A. Proc.*, lxi (1960-61), B, p. 79.
7. A. Farrington, 'The glaciation of the Wicklow Mountains' in *R.I.A. Proc.*, xlii (1934), B, p. 175.
8. A. Farrington, 'The granite drift near Brittas on the border between county Dublin and county Wicklow' in *R.I.A. Proc.*, xlvii (1942), B, p. 285.
9. P. Woodman, *Excavations at Mount Sandel, 1973-77* (Belfast, 1985).
10. P. Woodman, 'Problems in the colonisation of Ireland' in *Ulster Jn. Arch.*, il (1986), pp 7-17.
11. Ibid., p. 10.
12. G. Stout and M. Stout, 'Patterns in the past: county Dublin 50000 BC – 1000AD' in F. Aalen and K. Whelan (ed.), *Dublin city and county: from prehistory to present* (Dublin, 1992), pp 5-42.
13. P. Woodman, 'The post-glacial colonisation of Ireland: the human factor' in D. Ó Corráin (ed.), *Irish Antiquity: Essays and studies presented to Professor M.J. O'Kelly* (Cork, 1981), p. 96.
14. C.P. Martin, 'Human flints in east county Wicklow' in *Irish Naturalists Jn.*, iv (1932-33), p. 58.
15. F. Mitchell, *The way that I followed* (Dublin, 1990), pp 46-7.
16. T. Butler, *A parish and its people: history of the parish of Carrig-on-Bannow* (Wellingtonbridge, 1985), pp 8-9; G.F. Mitchell, 'An early kitchen midden at Sutton, county Dublin' in *R.S.A.I. Jn.*, lxxxvi (1956), pp 1-26; ibid., 'Further excavations of the early kitchen middens at Sutton, county Dublin' in *R.S.A.I. Jn.*, cii (1972), pp 151-9.
17. J. Raftery, 'A Neolithic burial mound at Ballintruer More, county Wicklow' in *R.S.A.I. Jn.*, ciii (1973), pp 214-19; A.L. Brindley, J.N. Lanting and W.G. Mook, 'Radiocarbon dates from Neolithic burials at Ballintruer More, county Wicklow and Ardcroney, county Tipperary' in *Jn. Ir. Arch.* (1988), pp 1-9.
18. M. Herity, *Irish passage graves* (Dublin, 1974); S. Ó Nualláin, *Survey of the megalithic tombs of Ireland, Vol. v, county Sligo* (Dublin, 1989).
19. C. Doherty, Palaeoecological investigations of a peat profile adjoining a Bronze Age passage grave at Seefin, county Wicklow, unpublished B.Sc. thesis, Botany Department, University College Dublin (1967).
20. M. O'Connell, 'The Neolithic environment' in M. Ryan (ed.), *The illustrated archaeology of Ireland* (Dublin, 1991), p. 46.
21. Doherty, 'Palaeoecological investigations', p. 9.
22. Ibid., p. 10.
23. M. O'Connell, 'The environment and human activity in Bronze Age Ireland' in M. Ryan, *Illustrated Archaeology*, p. 66.
24. P.J. Walsh, 'The excavation of a burial cairn on Baltinglass Hill, county Wicklow' in *R.I.A. Proc.* xlvi (1941), C, pp 221-36.
25. G. Cooney, 'A saddle quern from Baltinglass Hill, county Wicklow' in *R.S.A.I. Jn.*, cxi (1981), pp 102-6. In this context, note also some recent findings from pollen analysis in Ulster which indicate that it may have been in upland areas that

cereals were cultivated during the Neolithic. See A.G. Smith, 'The Neolithic' in I. Simmons and M. Tooley (ed.), *The environment in British prehistory* (London, 1981), pp 125-209.

26. G. Cooney, 'Irish Neolithic landscapes and land use systems: the implications of field systems' in *Rural History*, xi (1991), pp 123-39.
27. G. Cooney, 'The place of Megalithic tomb cemeteries in Ireland' in *Antiquity*, lvi (1990), pp 741-53.
28. E. Shee-Twohig, *The megalithic art of Western Europe* (Oxford, 1981), pp 222-3, 225; P.J. Walsh, 'The antiquities of the Dunlavin-Donard district' in *R.S.A.I. Jn.*, lxi (1931), p. 120, pl. 1b.
29. Shee-Twohig, *Megalithic art*, p. 225.
30. R.A.S. MacAlister, 'A burial cairn on Seefin Mountain' in *R.S.A.I. Jn.*, lvii, (1932), pp 153-7; E. Rynne, 'The decorated stone at Seefin' in *R.S.A.I. Jn.*, xciii (1963), pp 85-6; Shee-Twohig, *Megalithic art*, pp 222-3, fig. 269.
31. Dowling (pers. comm.).
32. G. Eogan, *Knowth and the passage tombs of Ireland* (London, 1986), pp 177-95.
33. M. O'Sullivan, 'A stylistic revolution in the megalithic art of the Boyne valley' in *Arch. Ir.*, iii (1989), pp 138-142.
34. Price, 'Ages of stone and bronze', p. 32; S. Ó Nualláin, 'Irish portal tombs: topography, siting and distribution' in *R.S.A.I. Jn.*, cxiii (1983), pp 81-2.
35. Price, 'Ages of stone and bronze', pp 32-3, 37.
36. Walsh, 'Antiquities of Dunlavin-Donard', pp 125-6.
37. Stout and Stout, 'Patterns in the past', pp 7-8.
38. Ó Nualláin, 'Irish portal tombs', p. 75.
39. E. Grogan and G. Cooney, 'A preliminary distribution map of stone axes in Ireland' in *Antiquity*, lxiv (1990), pp 559-61.
40. Price, 'Ages of stone and bronze', pp 61-2.
41. E. Rynne, 'Two stone axeheads from Killamoat Upper, county Wicklow' in *Kildare Arch. Soc. Jn.,* xiv (1964-70), pp 50-3; J. A. Sheridan, 'Porcelainite artifacts: a new survey' in *Ulster Jn. Arch*., il (1986), pp 19-32.
42. A. Collins, 'The flint javelin heads of Ireland' in Ó Corráin (ed.), *Irish Antiquity*, pp 111-33.
43. Price, 'Ages of stone and bronze', pp 60-1; Walsh, 'A burial cairn on Baltinglass Hill', pp 227-8.
44. Price, 'Ages of stone and bronze', p. 43.
45. J. Raftery, 'Irish prehistoric gold objects: new light on the source of the metal' in *R.S.A.I. Jn.*, ci (1971), pp 101-5.
46. P. Harbison, 'Hartmann's gold analysis: a comment' in *R.S.A.I. Jn.*, ci (1971), pp 159-60.
47. J.S. Jackson, 'Mining in Ireland: some guidelines from the past' in *Technology Ir.* (Oct. 1971), p. 32.
48. Price, 'Ages of stone and bronze', p. 56.
49. L. Flanagan, 'The Irish earlier Bronze Age in perspective' in *R.S.A.I. Jn.*, cxii (1982), pp 93-101.
50. P. Harbison, 'Catalogue of Irish Early Bronze Age: associated finds containing copper and bronze' in *R.I.A. Proc*., lxxvii (1968-9), C, p. 55; L. Price, 'Miscellanea: finds of copper axes at Monastery, county Wicklow' in *R.S.A.I. Jn.*, lxviii (1938), pp 305-6.
51. S. Ó Nualláin, 'The stone circle complex of Cork and Kerry' in *R.S.A.I. Jn.*, cv (1975), p. 111; A. Burl, *The stone circles of the British Isles* (Yale, 1975), pp 232-4.

52. Walsh, 'Antiquities of Dunlavin-Donard', pp 128-30; Price, 'Ages of stone and bronze', pp 39-40; Walsh, 'Antiquities of Dunlavin-Donard', pp 131-4; H.G. Leask, 'Miscellanea: a stone circle, Castleruddery, county Wicklow' in *R.S.A.I. Jn.*, lxxv (1945), pp 266-7.
53. Ó Nualláin, 'Stone circle complex of Cork and Kerry', p. 112 ; Burl, *Stone circles*, p. 234.
54. G.M. Thornton [Stout], A survey of earthen enclosures of the Boyne Valley and related sites, unpublished M.A. thesis, University College Dublin (1980), p. 142, Fig. 42.
55. S.P. Ó Ríordáin, 'Lough Gur excavations; the great stone circle (B) in Grange townland' in *R.I.A. Proc.*, lvi (1951), C, pp 37-74.
56. G. Stout, 'The embanked enclosures of the Boyne region' in *R.I.A. Proc.*, xci (1991), C, pp 281, 284.
57. M. O'Flanagan (ed.), *Letters containing information relative to the antiquities of Wicklow collected during the progress of the Ordnance Survey* (1927), pp 136-7, 81.
58. L. Price and P. Walsh, 'Stone and Bronze Age antiquities in the barony of Lower Talbotstown, county Wicklow, with a description of the excavation of Haylands Mote near Blessington' in *R.S.A.I. Jn.*, lxiii (1933), p. 47.
59. O'Flanagan (ed.), *Letters*, pp 135-6.
60. P. Healy, pers. comm.
61. G.H. Orpen, 'Rathgall, county Wicklow' in *R.S.A.I. Jn.*, xli (1911), pp 142-3.
62. I. Churcher, A survey of stone circles in southern Leinster, unpublished B.A. dissertation, Department of Archaeology, University of Durham (1985).
63. Walsh, 'Antiquities of Dunlavin-Donard', p. 128.
64. M. Medlycott, Standing stones in central Leinster, unpublished M.A. thesis, University College Dublin (1989), vol. ii, p. 159 (Laragh East), p. 189 (Farbregga); OS 6 inch sheet (1910) (Slievemaan).
65. Walsh, 'Antiquities of Dunlavin-Donard', p. 139.
66. M. Medlycott, 'Letters to the editor', in *Arch. Ir.*, v (1991), p. 30.
67. E. Grogan, 'Bronze Age cemetery at Carrig, county Wicklow', in *Arch. Ir.*, iv (1990), pp 12-14.
68. S.P. Ó Ríordáin, *Antiquities of the Irish countryside*, R. de Valera (ed.), fifth ed. (London, 1979), p. 143.
69. T.J. Westropp, 'On Irish motes and early Norman castles' in *R.S.A.I. Jn.*, xxxiv (1904), pp 319-20.
70. Price, 'Ages of stone and bronze', p. 42.
71. G.H. Kinahan, 'Proceedings' in *R.S.A.I. Jn.*, xvi (1883-4), pp 224-32.
72. Ibid., pp 224-8.
73. E.G. Amati, 'New petroglyphs at Derrynablaha, county Kerry' in *Cork Hist. Arch. Soc. Jn.*, lxviii (1963), pp 1-15.
74. Price, 'Ages of stone and bronze', p. 42.
75. Kinahan, 'Proceedings', pp 229-32.
76. E. MacWhite, 'A new view on Irish Bronze Age rock scribings' in *R.S.A.I. Jn.*, lxxvi (1946), pp 59-80.
77. Price, 'Ages of stone and bronze', p. 55.
78. W. Hamilton, 'Account of an ancient urn found in the parish of Kilranelagh in the county of Wicklow from a letter written by Thomas Green, Esq.' in *R.I.A. Trans.*, i (1785-87), pp 161-2.
79. R. Kavanagh, 'Pygmy cups in Ireland' in *R.S.A.I. Jn.*, cvii (1977), pp 61-95.

80. L. Price, 'Miscellanea: cremated burial found near Enniskerry, county Wicklow' in *R.S.A.I. Jn.*, lxv (1935), pp 325-9 (Fassaroe); J. MacEniry, 'On the opening of a sepulchral mound near Newcastle, county Wicklow' in *R.S.A.I. Jn.*, xviii (1887-8), pp 163-4; NMI 1872:33 (Newcastle Upper); P.J. Hartnett, 'Bronze Age Burials in county Wicklow' in *R.S.A.I. Jn.*, lxxxii (1982), pp 153-62; NMI 1951:125-6 (Kelshamore); A.T. Lucas 'Miscellanea: burial mound at Rathmoon, county Wicklow' in *R.S.A.I. Jn.*, xc (1960), pp 84-8 (Rathmoon); E. Grogan, 'Bronze Age cemetery', pp 12-4 (Carrig); C.P. Martin, L. Price and G.F. Mitchell, 'On two short cist internments found at Ballybrew in county Wicklow' in *R.I.A. Proc.*, xliii (1936), pp 255-70 (Ballybrew).
81. Lucas, 'Burial mound at Rathmoon', pp 84-8.
82. A. Mahr and L. Price, 'Excavation of urn burials at Clonshannon, Imaal, county Wicklow' in *R.S.A.I. Jn.*, lxiii (1932), pp 75-90 (Clonshannon); J. Waddell, *Bronze Age burials* (Galway, 1990), p. 166 (Saundersgrove); Price and Walsh, 'Stone and Bronze Age antiquities', pp 59-61 (Merginstown Demesne).
83. Walsh, 'Antiquities of Dunlavin-Donard', p. 121.
84. Martin, Price and Mitchell, 'Two short cist internments', pp 255-70.
85. Grogan, 'Bronze Age cemetery', pp 12-14.
86. C. Mount, 'Early Bronze Age burials: the social implications', in *Arch. Ir.*, xi (1991), pp 21-3.
87. Ó Ríordáin, *Antiquities,* pp 123-6.
88. Price, *Placenames,* iii, p. 239 (Carrig); Ó Nualláin, *Megalithic tombs,* v, p. 140; Reynolds and Haworth, *Preliminary report,* p. 23 (Blackrock); Ó Nualláin, *Megalithic tombs,* v, p. 140 (Mongnacool Lower); G. Ó hIceadha, 'The Moylisha megalith, county Wicklow' in *R.S.A.I. Jn.*, lxxvi (1946), pp 120-8 (Moylisha).
89. G.H. Kinahan, 'Megalithic structure, Mongnacool Lower, county Wicklow' in *R.S.A.I. Jn.*, xv (1879-80), pp 253-7.
90. Committee, 'Proceedings' in *R.S.A.I. Jn.*, xiv (1877), pp 183-4.
91. Ó hIceadha, 'Moylisha megalith', pp 120-8.
92. O'Flanagan (ed.), *Letters,* pp 77-8; P. Healy, pers. comm.; Reynolds and Haworth, *Preliminary report,* p. 34 (Downshill); Geological Survey of Ireland aerial photograph (GSIAP) O62/63 (1973); SMR 8:15 (Coolagad/Kindlestown Upper).
93. Price, *Placenames,* iii, pp 162-5.
94. T. Condit, 'Ireland's hillfort capital' in *Arch. Ir.*, vi (1992), pp 16-20.
95. OS 1:10560 sheet (1910) (Tinoranhill); Irish Tourist Authority (ITA) survey (1943) (Tuckmill Hill); G.H. Orpen, 'Rathgall, county Wicklow' in *R.S.A.I. Jn.*, xli (1911), pp 138-50; G.H. Orpen, 'Rathgall: the Rath of the foreigners' in *Kildare Arch. Soc. Jn.,* xi (1930), pp 31-5; B. Raftery, 'Irish hillforts' in C. Thomas (ed.) *The Iron Age in the Irish Sea Province* (London, 1972), p. 46 (Rathgall).
96. Ibid., p. 46.
97. Price, *Placenames,* iii, p. 150 (Tinoranhill); Ibid., p. 143 (Tuckmill Hill)
98. Orpen, 'Rathgall', p. 142 (Knockeen); Walsh, 'Burial cairn on Baltinglass Hill, pp 221-36 (Baltinglass).
99. Raftery, 'Irish hillforts', p. 44.
100. B. Raftery, 'The Rathgall Hillfort, county Wicklow' in *Antiquity,* xliv (1970), pp 51-4.
101. G. Eogan, *Hoards of the Irish Later Bronze Age* (Dublin, 1983), pp 173, 312.
102. Orpen, 'Rath of the foreigners', pp 31-5.
103. T.F. O'Rahilly, *Early Irish history and mythology* (Dublin, 1946), pp 13, 115.
104. A.L. Brindley and J.N. Lanting, 'The dating of fulachta fiadh' in V. Buckley

(comp.), *Burnt Offerings: International contributions to burnt mound archaeology* (Dublin, 1990), pp 55-6.

105. S. Cleary, 'The finds from fulachta fiadh' in Buckley (comp.), *Burnt Offerings,* pp 49-54.
106. V. Buckley. 'Experiments using a reconstructed fulacht fiadh' in Buckley (comp.), *Burnt Offerings,* p. 171.
107. M. Gowen, pers. comm.
108. B. Raftery, 'Rathgall, a late Bronze Age burial in Ireland' in *Antiquity,* xlvii (1973), pp 293-5.
109. Cambridge University Committee for Archaeology, photograph (CUCAP) ASH 41, ASH 44, BDR 40 (Ballintruer More); CUCAP BDP 15 (Monduff); CUCAP BDJ 180 (Kilpoole Upper).
110. B. Raftery, 'Iron Age burials in Ireland' in Ó Corráin (ed.), *Irish Antiquity,* pp 175-204.
111. Price and Walsh, 'Stone and Bronze Age antiquities', pp 48-9.
112. H.M. Roe and E. Prendergast, 'Excavation of a mound at Blessington, county Wicklow' in *R.S.A.I. Jn.*, lxxvi (1946), pp 1-12.
113. E. O'Brien, 'Iron Age burial practices in Leinster: continuity and change' in *Emania,* vii (1990), pp 37-42.
114. J. Raftery, 'A long stone cist in county Wicklow', in *R.S.A.I. Jn.*, lxxiv (1944), pp 166-9; A.T. Lucas, 'National Museum of Ireland archaeological acquisitions in the year 1963' in *R.S.A.I. Jn.*, xcvi (1966), pp 12-13; A.T. Lucas, 'National Museum of Ireland archaeological acquisitions in the year 1964' in *R.S.A.I. Jn.*, xcvii (1967), p. 11.
115. K.M. Davies, 'A note on the location of a Roman burial site at Bray, county Wicklow' in *Arch. Ir.*, iii (1989), pp 108-9.
116. R. Warner, 'Some observations on the context and importation of exotic material in Ireland from the first century B.C. to the second century A.D.' in *R.I.A. Proc.*, lxxvi (1976), C, pp 275, 279, 288.
117. C. Moriarty, 'Introduction' in C. Mollan and M. Mahoney (ed.), *The right trees in the right places* (Dublin, 1991), p. 11
118. D. Hickie, *Forestry in Ireland: policy and practice* (Dublin, 1990), p. 1.
119. Coillte Teoranta, *Coillte: annual report and accounts* (Dublin, 1989), p. 37.
120. G. Stout, M. Gibbons, and C. Foley, 'Forestry and archaeology', unpublished discussion document compiled for the Irish Association of Professional Archaeologists (1991).
121. E. Grogan, pers. comm.
122. T.B. Barry, 'The destruction of Irish archaeological monuments' in *Ir. Geog.*, xii (1979), pp 111-3; G. Stout, *Archaeological survey of the barony of Ikerrin* (Roscrea, 1984), p. 5.
123. Hickie, *Forestry in Ireland,* p. 23.
124. J.N.G. Ritchie, *Pre-Afforestation Survey* (Edinburgh, 1988)
125. Parks Section, Office of Public Works, 'The Wicklow Mountains National Park', unpublished internal report (1990).

Appendix I: Megalithic tombs in county Wicklow

SMR No	OS Sheet	Townland	Site	Reference
1:11	1	Ballyfolan	Passage tomb/ Ringcairn	Price and Walsh (1933), pp 47-48
1:13	1	Ballyfolan	Tumulus	Reynolds and Haworth (1973), p. 23
1:18	1	Goldenhill	Passage tomb (possible)	Herity (1974), p. 257
1:19	1	Kilbride	Passage tomb (possible)	Reynolds and Haworth (1973), p. 20
5:57	5	Knockieran	Passage tomb (possible)	Ó Nualláin (1989), p. 140
5:58	5	Blackrock	Wedge Tomb	Reynolds and Haworth (1973), p. 23
5:79	5	Carrig	Wedge Tomb	Price (1953), p. 239; Ó Nualláin (1989), p. 140
5:92	5	Lackan	Passage tomb	Price (1929), p. 239; Ó Nualláin (1989), p. 132
5:100	5	Lugnagun Great/ Kilbeg	Passage tomb (possible)	Herity (1974), p. 257
6:3	6	Scurlocksleap	Passage tomb	Ó Nualláin (1989), p. 132
6:4	6	Athdown/Shankill	Passage tomb	Price and Walsh (1933), p. 47; Price (1953), p. 278; Ó Nualláin (1989), p. 132
7:21	7	Parknasilloge	Megalithic tomb	W.C. Borlase (London, 1897), *The dolmens* (possible) *of Ireland* ii, p. 412; Price (1934), pp 32, 54
7:33	7	Onagh	Portal tomb	Borlase (1897), ii, pp 412-3; Powell (1941), pp 9-22; Ó Nualláin (1989), p. 127
8:24	8	Ballynamuddagh	Megalithic tomb	O'Flanagan (1927), p. 36 (destroyed)
9:8	9	Lugnagroagh	Passage tomb (possible)	Herity (1974), p. 258
12:2	12	Powerscourt Paddock/ Glasnamullen	Cairn	O'Flanagan (1927), p. 29
13:33	13	Woodstock Demesne	Megalithic tomb (possible)	Reynolds and Haworth (1973), p. 21
15:25	15	Mullycagh Upper	Passage tomb (possible)	Price (1953), p. 226; Herity (1974), p. 258
15:29	15	Ballymooney	Passage tombs (2) (possible)	Price and Walsh (1933), p. 47; Price (1934), p. 34; Ó Nualláin (1968), p 29; Herity (1974), p. 258
15:36	15	Tornant Upper	Passage tomb	Price (1934), p. 38; Price (1953), p. 200; Ó Nualláin (1989), p. 132
15:61	15	Broomfields	Portal tomb	Walsh (1931), pp 125-6; Ó Nualláin (1983), p. 103
22:28	22	Lugnaquillia	Megalithic tomb	O'Flanagan (1927), p. 60
24:7	24	Parkmore	Megalithic tomb (possible)	Price (1967), vii, p. 510

27:17	27	Spinans Hill	Passage tomb (possible)	Herity (1974), p. 259
27:26	27	Tuckmill Hill/ Coolinarrig Upper	Passage tomb	Walsh (1941), pp 221-36; Price (1949), pp 129, 135
27:45	27	Muckduff Upper	Passage tomb (possible)	Herity (1974), p. 260
27:47	27	Lathaleere	Megalithic tomb (destroyed)	Borlase (1897), ii, p. 413; Price (1934), pp 35-6; Powell (1941), p. 22
29:1	29	Ballintonbay Upper	Megalithic tomb (possible)	Borlase (1897), ii, p. 413
34:31	34	Three Wells	Megalithic tomb (possible)	Price (1946), p. 72
35:23	35	Mongnacool Lower	Wedge tomb	Kinahan (1879-80), pp 253-7; Borlase (1897), ii, pp 413-4; Price (1934), pp 34-5; Ó Nualláin (1989), p. 140
35:51	35	Cronebeg	Megalithic tomb (possible)	NMI correspondence file (6/9/1930)
36:8	36	Brittas	Portal tomb	Price (1934), pp 32-3, 37
39:42	39	Kilpipe	Megalithic tomb (possible)	NMI correspondence 9/4/35
40:40	40	Knocknamohill	Megalithic tomb (destroyed)	Price (1934), p. 37; Powell (1941), pp 13, 21
42:20	42	Barnacashel	Megalithic tomb (possible)	NMI correspondence file (20/2/1967)
42:36	42	Moylisha	Wedge tomb	Ó hIceadha (1946), pp 120-8

Appendix II: Bronze Age artifacts from county Wicklow

OS Sheet	Location	Find	Reference
2	Glencree	Flat bronze axe	P. Harbison (Munich, 1969), *The axes of the Early Bronze Age*, p. 11, pl. 15; NMI 1945:151
3/7	Monastery	Flat bronze axes (3), copper cake fragments (2)	Harbison (1968-9), p. 55
4	Bray	Bronze axe with flanges and stop ridge	Price (1934), p. 57
5	Ballynasculloge Lower	Flat axe	Harbison (1969), no. 842, pl. 38, 8
5	Blessington	Gold lunulae	Price (1934), p. 56
5	Sroughan	Socketed bronze spearhead	NMI 1980:2
5	Valleymount	Bronze ingot	NMI 1975:237
5	Valleymount	Socketed bronze axehead	E92:388
13/19	Newcastle	Dagger (MBA)	Price (1934), p. 59
15	Dunlavin	Flat bronze axe	Price and Walsh (1933), p. 66; Harbison (1969), p. 56, no. 1696
15-6/21	Kilcoagh	Flat bronze axe	NMI 1872: 3

17	Brockagh and Camaderry	Flat bronze axe	Harbison (1969), p. 59, no. 1672
30/34-5	'Ballinaclash'	Flat bronze axe, bronze axe with flanges and stop ridge, bronze socketed axe, bronze dagger	Price (1934), pp 57-8; Harbison (1969), p. 65, no. 1991
33	Rathcot	Bronze axe with flanges and stop ridge	Price (1934), p. 57
38/43	Muskeagh	Bronze axe with flanges and stop ridge	Price (1934), p. 57
45	Kish	Spearhead with basal loops, looped socketed axeheads (2), socketed knife	Eogan (1983), p. 173, fig. 96
	Glen of Imaal	Socketed spearhead	Price (1934), p. 59
	'Knockatemple'	Leaf-shaped sword	G. Eogan, *Catalogue of Irish bronze swords* (Dublin, 1965), p. xiv; NMI 1915:11
	Roundwood		
	Lackan	Flanged and decorated bronze axehead	NMI 1971:1049
	Lackan	Bronze palstave	NMI 1967:186
	Rathdrum	Bronze axe with flanges	Price (1934) p. 57
	Co. Wicklow	Bronze axe with flanges and stop ridge	Price (1934) p. 57
	Co. Wicklow	Flat bronze axe	NMI 1931:201; Harbison (1969), ix, pp 39
	Co. Wicklow	Flat bronze axe	NMI 1959:68; A. Lucas, 'Archaeological aquisitions in 1959' in *R.S.A.I. Jn.* (1961), xci, pp 72-5; Harbison (1969), ix, p. 14;
	Co. Wicklow	Flat bronze axe	NMI 1959:70 Lucas (1961), p. 73; Harbison (1969), ix, p. 48
	Co. Wicklow	Flat bronze axe (unfinished)	NMI 1959:69; Lucas (1961), p. 73 Harbison (1969), ix, p. 53
	Co. Wicklow	Flat bronze axe (unfinished)	NMI 1959:71; Lucas (1961), p. 73 Harbison (1969), ix, p. 53
	Co. Wicklow	Ogival dagger	Harbison (1969), ix, p.13
	Co. Wicklow	Flat copper axe	Harbison (1969), ix, p. 14
	Co. Wicklow	Looped socketed axehead, pennanular bracelet	Eogan (1983), p. 174, fig. 95

Appendix III: Stone circles in county Wicklow

SMR No	OS Sheet	Townland	Site	Reference
3:33	3	Ballybrew	Stone circle (possible)	O'Flanagan (1927), i, p. 17
5:5	5	Ballyfoyle	Stone circle	P. Healy (pers. comm.)
5:14	5	Blessington	Stone circle	Price and Walsh (1933), p. 47;

		Demesne	(destroyed)	Price (1953), p. 263
5:39	5	Ballyward	Multiple stone circle	Reynolds and Haworth (1973), p. 22; P. Healy (pers. comm.)
5:81	5	Carrig	Stone circle	P. Healy (pers. comm.)
5:86	5	Sroughan	Stone circle (possible)	P. Healy (pers. comm.)
12:41	12	Ballinastoe	Stone circle	O'Flanagan (1927), i, p. 81
12:42	12	Ballinastoe	Stone circle	Ibid., i, p. 81
15:8	15	Athgreany	Stone circles (2)	Ibid., i, pp 135-6;Walsh (1931), pp 128-30; Ó Nuallaín (1975), p. 111
15:10	15	Athgreany	Embanked stone circle	Walshe (1931), pp 128-30; Ó Nuallaín (1975), pp 111-2
15:17	15	Forristeen	Stone circle	Walsh (1931), p. 128
15:18	15	Forristeen	Stone circle (destroyed)	ITA survey (1943)
15:37	15	Tornant Upper	Stone circle	Price (1934), pp 38-9; Churcher (1985), pp 14, 23, 27, fig. 3, pl. iii
21:32	21	Castleruddery Lower	Embanked stone circle	Walsh (1931) pp 131-4; Leask (1945), pp 266-7; Ó Nuallaín (1975), pp 111-2
27:39	27	Boleycarrigeen	Embanked stone circle	Price (1934), pp 39-40; Ó Nuallaín (1975), pp 111-2

Appendix IV: Standing stones in county Wicklow

SMR No	OS Sheet	Townland	Site	Reference
5:51	5	Knockieran Lower	Standing stone	P. Healy, (pers. comm.)
5:82	5	Sroughan	Standing stone	Ibid.
5:102	5	Oldcourt	Standing stone	O'Flanagan (1927), i, pp 34-5
	12	Kilmurry	Standing stone	Medlycott (1989), p. 157
12:1	12	Ballinastoe/ Powerscourt Mountain/ Powerscourt Paddock	Standing stone	Ordnance Survey field name books for county Wicklow (1838-40), p. 254
15:6	15	Crehelp	Standing stone (holed)	Walsh (1931), pp 134-5; Price (1933), p. 48
15:39	15	Tornant Upper	Standing stone	Price (1934), pp 38-39
	17	Laragh East	Standing stones (pair)	Medlycott (1989), p. 159
19:30	19	Moorstown	Standing stone	Price (1934), p. 41
20:1	20	Knockdoo	Standing stone	Price (1949), p. 149
	20	White Hills	Standing stone	Medlycott (1989), p. 167
21:27	21	Ballintruer More	Standing stone	Walsh (1931), p. 139
	21	Coolamaddra	Standing stone	Medlycott (1989), p. 175
22:14	22	Cannow	Standing stone	Stout, *et. al.* (1986)
22:15	22	Leoh	Standing stone	Price (1949), p. 176
23:33	23	Cullentragh Big	Standing stone	OS 6 inch (1911)

23:35	23	Cullentragh Little	Standing stone	OS 6 inch (1911)
24:7	24	Parkmore	Standing stone	OS 6 inch (1908)
27:9	27	Tuckmill Upper	Standing stone	Price (1934), pp 41, 46-7
	27	Boley	Standing stone	Medlycott (1989), p. 181
	27	Castlequarter/ Cloughnagaune	Standing stone	Medlycott (1989), pp 183, 185
28:2	28	Slievemaan	Multiple standing stones	OS 6 inch (1910)
28:23	28	Farbreaga	Multiple standing stones	Medlycott (1989), p. 189
31:33-4	31	Dunganstown West	Multiple standing stones	O'Flanagan (1927), p. 123
33:22	33	Ardnaboy	Standing stone	Price (1946), p. 97
	35	Cherrymount	Standing stone	Medlycott (1989), p. 193
	35	Knockanree Lower	Standing stone	NMI report (12-3-32)
35:4	35	Kingston	Standing stone	Price (1934), p. 40
35:17	35	Cronebane	Standing stone	Lord Killanin and M. Duignan *The Shell guide to Ireland* (London, 1967), pp 405-6
37:23	37	Gowle	Standing stone	OS 6 inch (1909)
37:26	37	Killabeg	Standing stone	Price (1934), p. 41
	40	Carrycole Hill	Standing stones (5)	Medlycott (1989), pp 201-10
40:16	40	Sheepwalk	Standing stone	Price (1967), p. 474
42:8	42	Killabeg	Standing stone	Price (1934), p. 41
42:46	42	Newry	Standing stone	Price (1934), p. 41
45:13	45	Ballintombay	Standing stone	Medlycott (1989), p. 215
46:6	46	Newry	Standing stone	Price (1934), p. 41; Medlycott (1989), p. 213

Appendix V: Rock art in county Wicklow

SMR No	**OS Sheet**	**Townland**	**Site**	**Reference**
7:34	7	Onagh	Rock art	Price (1934), p. 42
15:41	15	Merginstown Demesne	Rock art	Westropp (1904), pp 319-20
17:2	17	Carrigeenshinagh	Rock art	Price (1934), p. 42
18:5	18	Baltynanima	Rock art (4)	Price (1934), p. 42; MacWhite (1946), p. 78
23:9	23	Sevenchurches or Camderry	Rock art	Kinahan (1883-4), p. 229
27:64	27	Barraderry East (original position) Humewood (present)	Rock art	Price (1934), p. 42
30:23-5/ 35:11-3	30/35	Ballykean (Penrose)	Rock art (14)	Kinahan (1883-4), pp 224-8
34:26/ 35:52	34-5	Crone beg	Rock art (possible)	OPW topographical files; NMI correspondence (6/12/50)
35:22	35	Mongnacool Lower	Rock art (6)	Kinahan (1883-4), pp 229-32
35:49/ 40:30	35/40	Ballinapark	Rock art	Kinahan (1883-4), pp 232-3

Appendix VI: Bronze age burials in county Wicklow

SMR No	OS Sheet	Townland	Site	Reference
1:36/ 5:105	1/5	Kilbride	Pit burial	Walsh and Price (1933), p. 62; NMI 1959:18;
3:35	3	Fassaroe	Cist burial	Price (1935), pp 325-9; Waddell (1990), p. 160
	3	Ballybrew	Cist burials (3)	Martin, Price and Mitchell (1936), pp 255-70
	3/7	Near Powercourt	Cemetery mound	Ibid., p. 166
5:1	5	Dillonsdown	Cist burial	NMI 1934:11, 118-9
5:25	5	Haylands	Cemetery mound	Price (1934), p. 45
5:52	5	Butterhill	Cist burial (possible)	Walsh and Price (1933), p. 48
5:76	5	Burgage More	Cist burial	NMI report 1933-4; Price (1953), p. 251; Waddell (1970), p. 138
5:83	5	Carrig	Cemetery mound	E. Grogan (pers. comm.)
5:84	5	Carrig	Cemetery mound	NMI 1984: 224; Grogan (1990), pp 12-4
5:95-6	5	Lackan	Cist burials (2)	SMR office
5:105	5	Kilbride	Pit burial (possible)	Walsh and Price (1933), p. 62
7:50	7	Calary Lower	Cist burial	Price (1939), pp 157-9; Waddell (1990), p. 138
7:65	7	Kilmacanoge North Kilmacanoge South	Cist burial	Waddell (1970), p. 139; Kavanagh (1977), p. 91; Waddell (1990), p. 163
9:10	9	Lemonstown	Burial mound	NMI 1818:3; NMI 1883:378, AB 311
9:22/ 10:36	9/10	Lugnagroagh	Cist burial	Kavanagh (1973), p. 91; NMI R849A, WK 83, W 21, AB 402; Waddell (1990) p. 165
13:58	13	Newcastle	Cist bural	Anon (1897), pp 189-90; Price (1980), pp 50-1
15:19 15:21	15	Friarhill	Cemetery mound	Walsh (1931), p. 121; Price (1953), 203; Waddell (1990), p. 162
15:22	15	Crehelp	Cemetery mound	Walsh (1931), p. 122; Kavanagh (1977), p. 90
15:41	15	Merginstown Demesne	Cemetery mound (with rock art)	NMI 1931:14, 16; Price and Walsh (1933), pp 59-61
15:80	15	Tornant Upper	Cist burial	NMI 1885:155, WK 104, AB 318; Price (1933), p. 63;
19:3	19	Newcastle Upper	Cist burial	NMI 1872:33; MacEniry (1887-8), pp 163-4
19:8	19	Blackditch	Cist burial	Coffey, Browne and Westropp, 'Report on a prehistoric burial near Newcastle, county Wicklow' in *R.I.A. Proc.*, xx (1897), pp 559-62; Waddell (1990), p. 138
21:36	21	Kelshamore	Cist burials (?)	NMI 1951: 125-6; Hartnett (1952), pp 153-61

21:74	21	Saundersgrove	Flat cemetery	Waddell (1990), p. 166
22:17	22	Clonshannon	Flat cemetery	NMI 1931:434, 434A, 434B, 446, 446A; 1932:5628A, 5628B, 5629; Mahr and Price (1932), pp 75-90; Waddell (1970), p. 138
25:14	25	Ballynerrin	Cist burial	NMI register P1932:3; Hartnett (1952), pp 161-2
26:6	26	Rathmoon	Cist burial	NMI 1959:749; Lucas (1960), pp 84-8
27:8	27	Tuckmill Upper	Cist burial	Hamilton (1785-7), pp 161-2; NMI correspondence 1930; Price (1934), pp 41, 46-7
27:69	27	Kilranelagh	Cist burial	Waddell (1990), p. 163
27:74	27	Tuckmill Upper	Cist burial (destroyed)	NMI 1969:735-7
28:20	28	Ballyknockan	Cist burial	P.T. Walsh, 'Miscellanea: cist burial at Ballyknockan, parish of Kiltegan, county Wicklow' in *R.S.A.I. Jn.*, lxiv (1934), pp 259-60; Waddell (1970), p. 138
33:19	33	Rathcot	Pit burial	NMI 1932:6163, 6163A; Price (1934), pp 47-8
	33	Deerpark	Urn burial	Waddell (1990), p. 159
34:32	34	Near Aughrim	Pit burial	NMI 19[illegible]4:7; Waddell (1990), p. 159
35:41	35	Knockanree Lower	Cist burial	W.F. Dargan, , 'Cist burial in Co. Wicklow' in *R.S.A.I. Jn.*, xlvi (1916), pp 77-8; NMI 1933:1242
37:1	37	Liscolman	Cemetery mound	Ó Ríordáin (1955), p. 303
37:10	37	Ballyconnell	Cist burial	Ó Ríordáin (1955), pp 300-3
39:37	39	Ballinglen	Cist burial	Waddell (1990), p. 159
40:29F	40	Ferrybank	Urn burials (?)	Price (1934), p. 51
40:36-7	40	Glenteige (?)	Cist burial Kilbride parish	Price (1967), vii, p. 471; Waddell (1990), p. 138
40:41	40	Mooreshill	Burial mound	Price (1934), p. 51; NMI 1944:246, 247
42:4	42	Rath	Cist burial	NMI 1944, pp 246-7; Raftery (1969), pp 95-6
42:7	42	Killabeg	Pit burial	F.T. Riley, 'Urn with cremation found at Killabeg, near Shillelagh, Co. Wicklow' in *R.S.A.I. Jn.*, lvii (1937), pp 308-9
42:44	42	Money Upper	Cist burial	NMI 1985:14-14A

Appendix VII: Hillforts in county Wicklow

SMR No	**OS Sheet**	**Townland**	**Site**	**Reference**
8:15	8	Coolagad/ Kindlestown Upper	Univallate hillfort	GS AP O62/63 (1973)
13:1	13	Downshill	Univallate hillfort	O'Flanagan (1927), i, pp 77-8; P. Healy (pers. comm.)

26:4	26	Tinoran Hill	Bivallate hillfort	OS 6 inch sheet (1910)
27:10	27	Tuckmill Hill Tuckmill Upper	Trivallate hillfort	ITA survey (1943); Price (1949), iii, p. 143
27:18	27	Brusselstown	Bivallate hillfort	Ordnance Survey field name books for Donagmore parish, county Wicklow (1838-40), p. 91 (103); ITA survey (1945); Price (1949), iii, pp 162-5; Condit (1992), pp 16-20
27:43	27	Keadeen	Hillslope enclosure	GS AP S127/128 (1973)
27:26	27	Coolinarrig Upper/ Pinnacle/ Tuckmill Hill	Bivallate hillfort	Ordnance Survey field name books for Baltinglass parish, countyWicklow (1838-40), pp 155 (5), 158 (26), 265 (3), 280 (44); O'Flanagan (1927), i, p. 36 (94)
37:16	37	Rath East	Multivallate hillfort	Orpen (1911), pp 138-50; Ibid., (1930), pp 31-5; Price (1958), p. 366; Raftery (1970), pp 51-4; Ibid., (1972), pp 45-6, 55
37:18	37	Knockeen	Bivallate hillfort	OS 6 inch sheet (1839); Orpen (1911), p. 142; CUCAP AHK 73; AHK 78

Appendix VIII: Fulachta Fiadh in county Wicklow

SMR No	OS Sheet	Townland	Site	Reference
7:42 7:47-8	7	Ballyremon Commons	Fulachta Fiadh (5)	Stout *et. al.* (1986); Buckley (1990), p. 171; P. Healy (pers. comm.); G. Bird (pers. comm.)
	7	Bahana	Fulacht Fiadh	G. Bird (pers. comm.)
	7	Ballinteskin	Fulacht Fiadh (possible)	G. Bird (pers. comm.)
	9	Killincarrig	Fulacht Fiadh	M. Gowen (pers. comm.)
12:5-6	12	Ballyremon	Fulachta Fiadh (2) Commons	Stout *et. al.* (1986); P. Healy (pers. comm.)
	31	Balllinameesda Lower	Fulacht Fiadh	OPW files
41:4	41	Johnstown North	Fulacht Fiadh	Stout *et. al.* (1986)

Appendix IX: Late Bronze Age/Iron Age burials in county Wicklow

SMR No	OS Sheet	Townland	Site	Reference
5:13	5	Blessington Demesne	Ring barrows (?)	Roe and Prendergast (1946), pp 1-12
7:23	7	Monastery	Bowl barrow	Stout *et. al.* (1986)

7:43	7	Ballyremon Commons	Bowl barrow	O'Flanagan (1927), i, pp 18-9; P. Healy (pers. comm.)
15:78	15	Tornant Upper	Barrow	Price (1953), p. 200
15:79	15	Tornant Upper	Barrow	Killanin and Duignan (1962), p. 266
21:54	21	Ballintruer More	Ring ditches (?)	CUCAP ASH 41; ASH 44; BDR 40
25:6	25	Monduff	Ring ditch	CUCAP BDP 15
31:12	31	Kilpoole Upper	Ring ditches (?)	CUCAP BDJ 80
35:40	35	Ballygahan Upper	Ring barrow	Stout *et. al.* (1986)
37:25	37	Gowle/Seskin/ Kilquiggin	Ring barrow	Haworth and Reynolds (1973), p. 24; P. Healy (pers. comm.)
42:21	42	Boley	Ring barrow	Haworth and Reynolds (1973), p. 23; P. Healy (pers. comm.)
42:29	42	Aghowle Lower	Ring barrow	Haworth and Reynolds (1973), p. 23; P. Healy (pers. comm.)

Rathcoran, Baltinglass.

Chapter 2

KINGS, SAINTS AND SAGAS

ALFRED P. SMYTH

The coming of Christianity and the dawn of history

The great massif of the Wicklow Hills – with its labyrinth of secluded glens, fenced off from each other by impassible and inhospitable bare granite peaks – provided a refuge in all centuries for people who were in political decline and in retreat from aggressive neighbours. Wicklow is best known as a survival area for later medieval Gaelic peoples, who held on grimly to a vanishing way of native Irish life into the reign of Elizabeth I. The O'Byrnes and O'Tooles survived as Gaelic lords ruling over their embattled territories until the end of the sixteenth century. Wicklow – so near to the centre of English power at Dublin Castle – was not marked off as a shire in its own right until as late as 1605, and for two centuries afterwards continued to be a dangerous and lawless territory for the English administration. But the role of this mountainous region of east Leinster as a survival area goes back much further than the sixteenth and early seventeenth centuries. Wicklow, because of its inaccessible terrain, no doubt provided a refuge to peoples set on the path to political extinction back in prehistory, and we can trace its role as a region of survival from the time when Ireland's earliest historical records begin. The O'Byrnes (Ua Bhroin) of Críoch Bhranach and Gabhal Raghnaill in Wicklow, and the O'Tooles (Ua Thuathail) of Imaal and Fercullen, were, by Irish standards, newcomers to the Wicklow Hills in the later Middle Ages. The O'Byrne ancestors had once ruled from their fort at Naas over the Liffey plain in the richest lands of north Kildare, under the dynastic name of Uí Fáeláin. The O'Tooles – very distant cousins of the O'Byrnes – had earlier ruled over south Kildare as the Uí Muiredaig (table 2.6). These cousinly dynasties were known collectively as Uí Dúnlainge when they established themselves as kings of North Leinster (Laigin Tuathgabair) in the second quarter of the seventh century. They went on to rule as kings of all the Leinstermen from the early eighth century until the eleventh, when they began to lose out to their rivals the Uí Cheinnselaig who controlled the kingship of South Leinster (Laigin Desgabair). With the Anglo-Norman conquest of the Barrow and Liffey basins in the years immediately following 1170, the O'Tooles and O'Byrnes were forced to retreat into those very

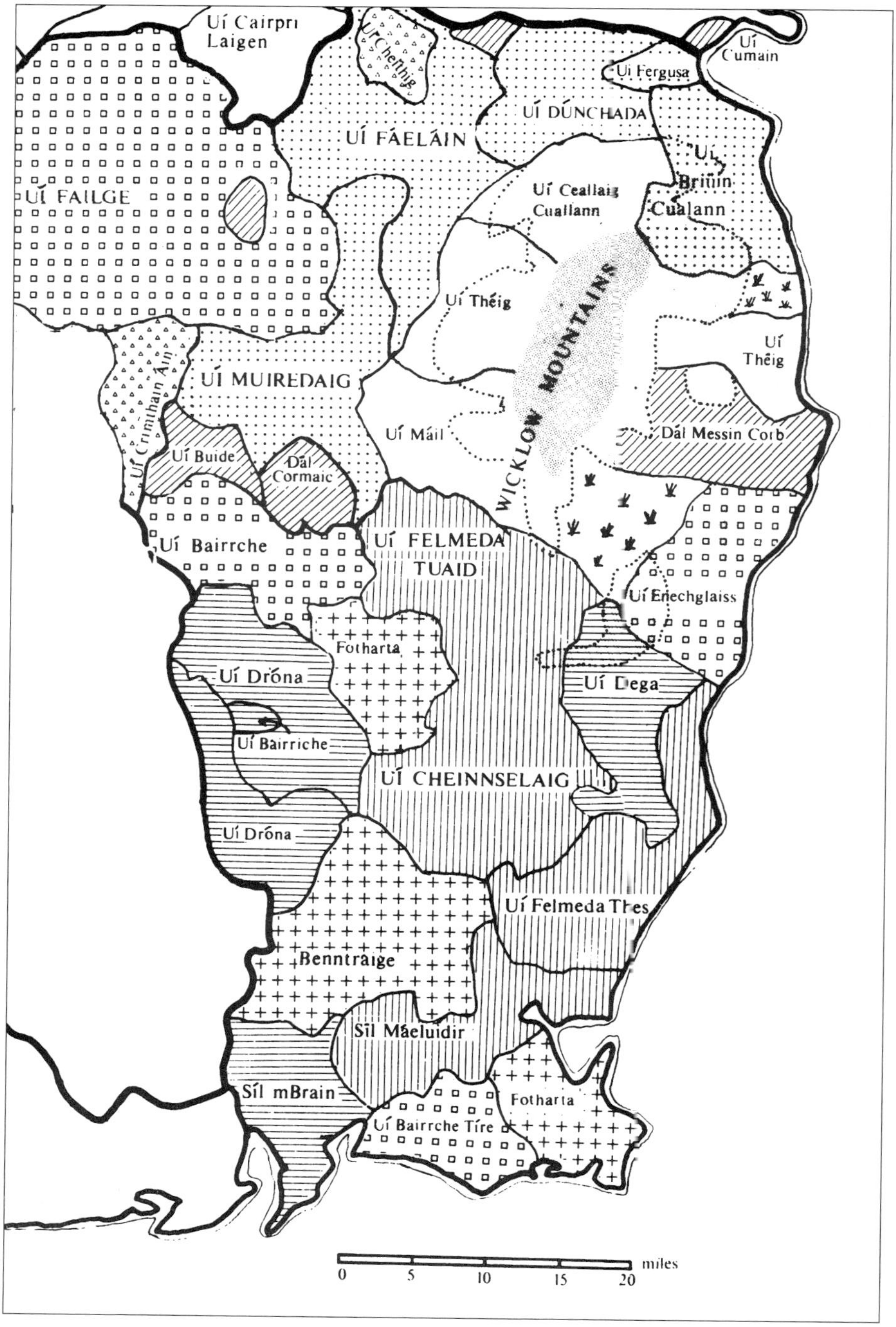

Figure 2.1 Leinster Tribes *c.*A.D. 750.

mountains of Wicklow where their own ancestors had driven their defeated enemies back in the seventh and eighth centuries.

The historical geography of Wicklow presents the student of this region with a paradox. On the one hand, Wicklow, with its enduring mountains, presents the strongest environmental personality, and one which has changed least from interference by man. So, compared with the boglands of Offaly, for instance, which have been transformed by human action and by modern technology in the past three centuries, Wicklow – apart from the loss of its great forests – has remained relatively unchanged. But Wicklow as a county is an early seventeenth-century creation, and it is impossible to discuss the early history of that region without taking into account the history of those lands in south Dublin, east Kildare, north Wexford and Carlow which formed a continuum with the Wicklow massif. So, the Uí Máil, one of the most powerful of the Wicklow tribes, ruled not only in central and west Wicklow, but they also extended over greater and lesser parts of east Kildare as their power waxed and waned in the seventh and eighth centuries. The Uí Chellaig Cualann, a branch of the Uí Máil, ruled over Cualu – a territory which spanned the foothills of the western and north-western area of the Wicklow massif and covered parts of modern east Kildare, south-west Dublin, and of course, north-west Wicklow. Similarly the Uí Felmeda of north-east Carlow, who were a branch of the powerful Uí Cheinnselaig of south Leinster, at one period in the sixth century were pushing north into the Glen of Imaal, a region which as its name (Glenn Ua Máil) implies, was otherwise associated with the heartland of the Wicklow Uí Máil. The most southern region of modern Wicklow, now represented by the barony of Shillelagh, must have formed a unity with southern Leinster Uí Cheinnselaig lands of Carlow and north Wexford in Celtic times, while the Uí Enechglais (table 2.12), a tribe settled along the eastern coast, straddled the modern boundary between Wicklow and Wexford extending from the Avoca to the Inch rivers. The Uí Garrchon (table 2.11), that Wicklow people *par excellence*, were associated with the central coastal region to the west and south of Arklow. Yet even this people, whose main tribal territory seemed completely contained within the modern county of Wicklow, had as we shall see, extensive contacts with scattered territories to the west, in Kildare and elsewhere. Finally, the Uí Briúin Chualann were a people who ruled the mountain foothills from Rathmichael in south Dublin, past Bray to Delgany in Wicklow. In spite of this seeming territorial chaos, the mountains in Celtic times, as today, provided the dominant unifying factor to all this region. And just as today, farmers in Glencullen in south Dublin have more in common with their Wicklow and even with their north Wexford colleagues, than

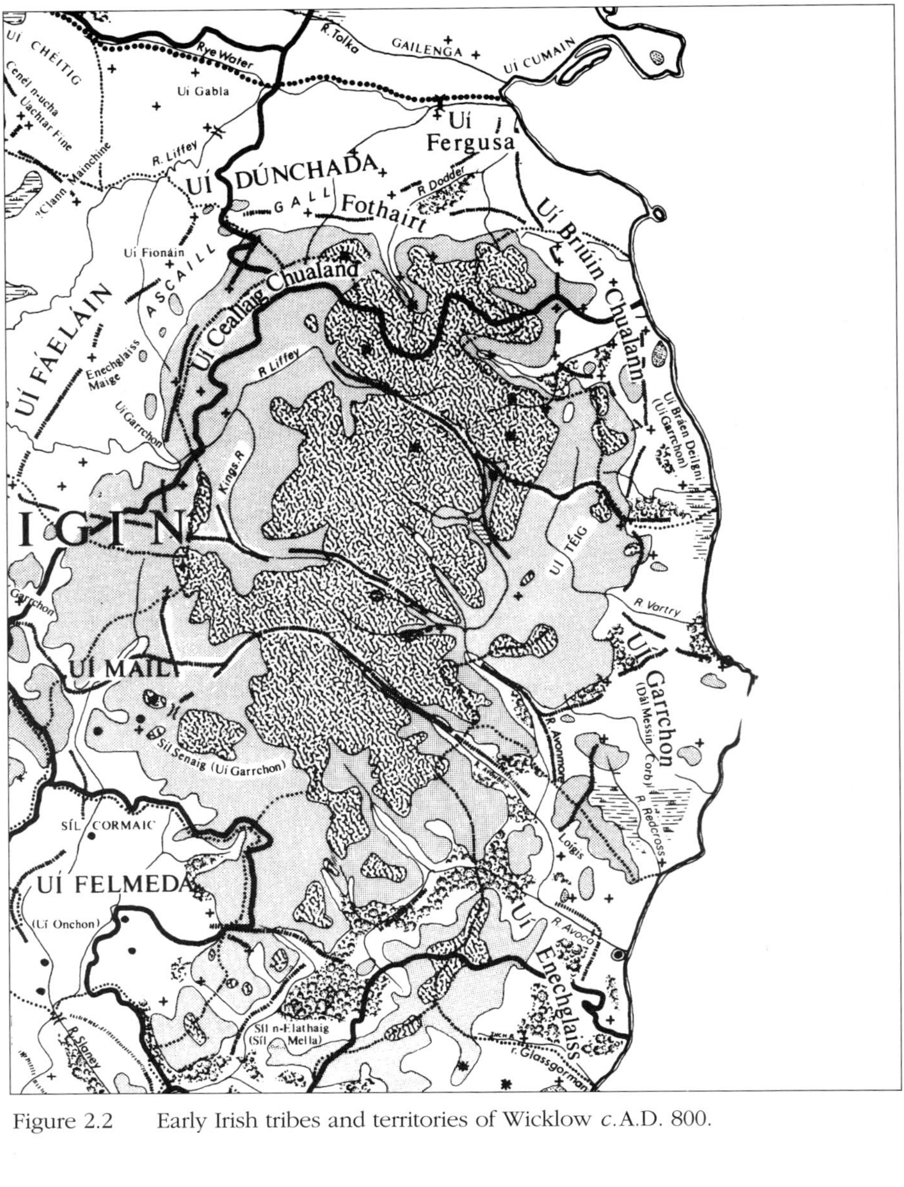

Figure 2.2 Early Irish tribes and territories of Wicklow *c.*A.D. 800.

they have with the rich graziers of Fingal in north Dublin, so too, in Celtic times, the otherwise very diverse tribes of the *Fortuatha Laigen* ('Alien people among the Leinstermen') in the Wicklow massif, were grouped collectively under that name in recognition of their special political and geographical status among the Wicklow Hills.

The Wicklow mountains, and especially the coastal strip stretching from Bray down to Arklow and further south, was unquestionably a political backwater in early Ireland. The coastal area was not only cut off from the richer Irish interior by a formidable mountain chain, but it was also poorly drained and very heavily forested, and its rivers ran west to east from the mountains to the sea, obstructing the path of travellers striving to move up or down the coastal hinterland from Dublin to Wexford.[1] Liam Price remarked as long ago as 1940 on the scarcity of Neolithic and Bronze Age remains in the area from Delgany to the north of Arklow, and on the scarcity of Iron Age ring forts in the Delgany/Brittas region compared with numerous examples of those Celtic habitation sites to the west of the mountains.[2] Price was in a stronger position to comment on the placename evidence, observing that with the exception of Rathnew there were few early placenames in the east of the county and that the incidence of *cell* placenames in the east only highlighted the deserted character of a forested region which attracted only hermits.[3] As for the name of Rathnew or *Raith Nuí* in Uí Garrchon, the Book of Leinster *Dindshenchas* or 'Lore of Places' claims that it was founded by Nuí who came from Mag Rechet (Heath of Maryborough) in Loígis. While Nuí and his brother, Másc, the supposed founder of Dún Másc (Dunamase, county Leix) have no claim to historicity, the orientation of the story is cast from the point of view of a people settled in the Leinster interior and who believed they had expanded eastwards across the Wicklow mountains to the coast.[4] The first Germanic settlers in Ireland – seaborne Vikings of the ninth century – found this ideal coastal territory for the establishing of bases at Wicklow and Arklow with easy access to Britain and with natural protection from the more powerful Leinster kingdoms in the Irish interior. For the Irish tribes of this region, however, their own presence here signified their eclipsed political status, far removed from the centres of Leinster power at Rathvilly, Mullaghmast, Knockaulin (Dún Ailinne) and Naas.

But the study of early Irish population groups of Wicklow does not necessarily lead us into a backwater of early Irish History. On the contrary, the story of the tribes of this region takes us far beyond the confines of Wicklow and helps us to understand some of the major developments in early Ireland as a whole. In spite of the mountainous summits, dense forest and blanket bog, which made this a region of 'deserted places' so vividly described in the *Life* of St. Kevin of Glendalough, a study of the people who lived here frequently helps us towards a greater understanding of the earliest strata in Irish historical records, taking us back even into realms of prehistory. For just as the O'Byrnes and O'Tooles of the sixteenth century were survivors and representatives of peoples who once claimed the kingship of all Leinster several centuries before, so too, in the seventh and eighth centuries, the tribal kings of the Wicklow Hills – the *Fortuatha Laigen* – were themselves descendants of once powerful warlords who controlled the Kildare plains. Nor can life in the mountains have been wholly grim. While the unavailability of good farmland must have placed severe limits on population growth, nevertheless, reasonable farmland was to be found, not only in valleys but also (and perhaps more so) on the well-drained foothills of the massif. Even the high plateau, for instance, between Sugar Loaf Mountain and past Calary to Roundwood, continues to support mixed farming communities to this day. The forests and high summits offered a protection to ordinary men and women which must have been the envy of their counterparts who lived at the mercy of feuding warlords out on the exposed plain of Liffey. And the mountain massif, while offering protection, was not entirely land-locked. Major passes leading from Wicklow (Inber dá Glas) and from Arklow (Inber Dee) via Sally Gap, Glendalough and Wicklow Gap, and through Glenmalure (Glenn Maoil 'oraidh), saw a lucrative trade in goods exported and imported to and from Britain, and carried over the mountains to richer centres of royal power inland at Naas, Rathangan and elsewhere. Such trade must have offered an income by way of tolls to the remote tribes who inhabited the Wicklow seaboard and who controlled key passes which joined the inner heartlands of Leinster with the east coast.

Too often this trade is thought of in terms of hunting dogs and raw materials such as furs and wool, exported to Britain in exchange for luxury goods for the warlords of Leinster and beyond. No doubt such trade was significant, and it was this, supplemented by slave-trading, which eventually fell into the hands of the Vikings on the Wicklow coast in the ninth century. A Viking presence at Arklow is first vouched for in the Annals of Ulster in 836, but Arklow was clearly a port of some significance in pre-Viking times. Muirchú moccu Machthéni in his late seventh-century *Life* of Patrick refers to Arklow as 'a harbour of some repute among us called Inber Dee (*portum apud nos clarum, qui vocatur Hostium Dee*).'[5] By the middle of the seventh century, it must surely have been the rich and well organised monastic centres such as Kildare which were dominating trade. Early Irish monastic houses quickly developed a decadent taste for exotic manuscript illumination and craftsmanship in precious metals, which in turn must have generated a need for luxuries such as glass, silver and gold, gemstones, ivory, and exotic liturgical fabrics, as well as the necessary altar wine. Monasteries such as Kildare and Kilcullen in north Leinster, as well as other houses such as Killeigh in Uí Failge and Clonenagh in Lóigis further west, together with Moone, Killabban, Aghowle, and Clonmore in the centre and south of the province, must all have generated trading

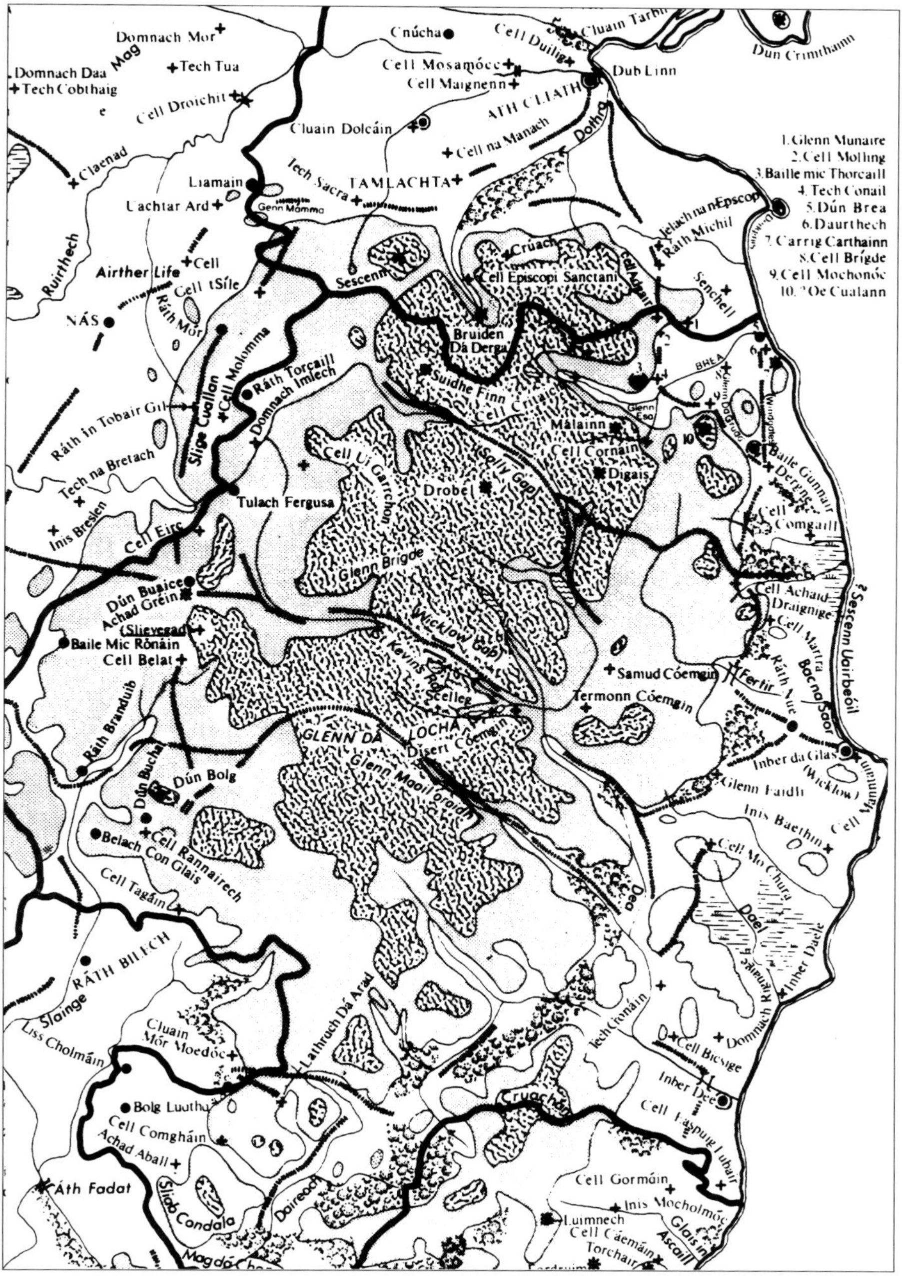

Figure 2.3 Topography of the Wicklow region *c.*A.D. 800.

activity across the Wicklow mountains. It is likely that Glendalough, because of its key position *vis-à-vis* the Wicklow Gap, grew rich in handling that trade with the Leinster interior. And it was that monastic trade of his own time which led Muirchú, writing in the late seventh century, to fantasise that Patrick's ship, taking him to convert the Irish, landed at Arklow laden 'with wonderful religious treasures from across the sea (*cum transmarinis mirabilibus spiritalibusque tessauris*)'.[6]

The story of Glendalough, its founding by the saintly Kevin, and its development into a monastic *civitas* or 'city', is in many ways representative of the history of all early medieval Wicklow. For Glendalough, in spite of its isolation in the heart of the Wicklow mountains, grew rich on its contacts with the wider world to the west, and its connection with royal patrons takes us to the heart of early Leinster history. Its founder, Kevin or *Coemgen* ('Beautifully born one'), died in 622. His various *Lives* credit him with the great age of 120, but assuming he lived to a less remarkable ripe old age of 75 or 80, we may surmise that he was born *c.*540-50. There is an early genealogical tradition, backed by the Latin *vita* of Kevin, which claims he belonged to the tribe of Dál Messin Corb. This ancient people controlled the kingship of the Leinstermen in the fifth century and, indeed, the earliest historical king of Leinster was Fróech mac Finchada (table 2.11) of this tribe who was slain by Eochu son of Coirpre, the grandson of Niall Noígiallach in 495. At that time, the Dál Messin Corb ruled the Kildare plains, and Fróech lost his life trying to retain northern Kildare territory later covered by the barony of Carbery. The Leinstermen lost out in that struggle, and Carbery took its name from Coirpre son of Niall who annexed it to Uí Néill lands of Brega (in county Meath) to the north of Leinster. The outcome of that struggle weakened the Dál Messin Corb hold on the Leinster confederacy, and the over-kingship of Leinster was then seized by the Uí Failge who led the defence of the province against Uí Néill aggression in the Midlands in what was Fir Chell and what is now central and southern county Offaly. The Dál Messin Corb on the other hand, declined and were overtaken by their neighbours the Uí Máil who became the dominant tribe in north-east Leinster in the sixth and seventh centuries. When historical sources become fuller and more diversified from the eighth century onwards, we find the main descendants of the Dál Messin Corb – the Uí Garrchon – settled east of the Wicklow mountains in the hinterland of Arklow. But there is an accumulation of evidence of an early and reliable sort which suggests that the original home of this people lay to the west of the massif on the Kildare-Wicklow border, in a region known as Cualu in the historical period. Price suggested that Kevin's birthplace at *Ráith an Tobair Gil* ('Fort of the bright well') was Tipperkevin in county Kildare.[7]

The names of Kevin's earliest monastic tutors – Eógan, Lochán and Énna – identify their base as being at Cell na Manach or Cell Manach Escrach in Uí Dúnchada (Kilnamanagh, near Tallaght, county Dublin), rather than at Kilnamanagh near Glenealy in Wicklow. Significantly, we find from the earliest Rawlinson genealogies, that Kevin's tutors, like their pupil, were all from the Uí Náir, a sept of the Dál Messin Corb.[8] A strong feature in the *Lives* of Kevin is the tale of the young saint's migration in search of a desert place. The account of Kevin's crossing of the mountains to seek out his retreat in Glendalough, although devoid of specific directional details, suggests an origin for this saint in the fertile lands of Kildare or south Dublin which he abandoned when 'he crossed the summits' and travelled alone 'through deserted regions' until he reached that remote 'Glen of the Two Lakes' (*Glenn dá Locha*).[9]

If Kevin and the monastic founders associated with him in his early life all belonged to the Dál Messin Corb and were associated with northern Cualu in south Dublin and east Kildare, evidence for the tribal origins of other early saints and their churches point in the same direction. The Dál Messin Corb saint, Berchán, and the obscure Dál Messin Corb sept of Uí Amsáin were located about Shankill (Senchell) north of Bray in south Dublin. Finán Cam, a saintly founder at Kinneigh (Cenn Eich) close to the Wicklow border in Kildare, was a Dál Messin Corb saint, as was Mo-Ṡenóc of Dunmanogue (Dún mo Ṡenóc Mugna) who settled a few miles west of Castledermot in county Kildare. The Uí Lopéni – yet another branch of the Dál Messin Corb – were located at Kilranelagh (Cell Rannairech), a place otherwise associated with the centre of Uí Máil power in the Glen of Imaal.[10] This evidence, taken together, suggests that prior to the downfall of the Dál Messin Corb kings at the beginning of the sixth century, their tribe controlled the Leinster confederacy from the western foothills of the Wicklow massif, and their main strength was most likely concentrated in eastern Kildare and in the Glen of Imaal. As the Dál Messin Corb yielded their dominant position to the Uí Máil, they withdrew across the mountains to the Arklow region, leaving the Uí Máil to dominate Cualu or all the fertile lowlands of west Wicklow.

Hagiographical tales relating to St Patrick also highlight the importance of the Dál Messin Corb (or their sub-group of Uí Garrchon) in late fifth-century Leinster and suggest that they once controlled the Kildare plains. The late seventh-century *Life* of Patrick by Muirchú and the later *Tripartite Life* (*Vita Tripartita*) of Patrick, compiled *c.*900, both claim that Patrick began his Irish mission by landing at Arklow or Inber Dee. The information seems pointless since Patrick did not stay there or accomplish anything at the spot. Indeed he is said, rather, to have proceeded immediately to seek out his former master, Miliucc, in Ulster. Since Patrick proceeded northwards along the Irish coast by ship, the mention of his landfall at Arklow seems even more pointless.[11] But the Dál Messin Corb tribe of Uí Garrchon and their king, Driccriu, who were based near Arklow, reappear in the Patrick story as told in the *Tripartite Life*, and the prominence which this otherwise obscure people are given there demands an explanation. The Tripartite *Life* takes Patrick on an apocryphal circuit of Ireland by way of Ulster to Brega (in Meath) and on to Naas in north Leinster, where he was alleged to have baptised the sons of Dúnlang and the daughters of Ailill mac Dúnlainge. The whole notion of Patrick ever having evangelised in north Leinster is open to serious doubt, and as for Dúnlang and his sons, there is no good evidence to show that they ever held the kingship of Leinster, or indeed ruled in any capacity in the Naas area, as early as the fifth century.

It was the Dál Messin Corb who were dominant at that time, and it is for that reason that the abrupt change of focus in the Tripartite *Life* at this point in the Kildare itinerary assumes significance. While still concerned with Patrick's visit to the Liffey plain, the writer of the Tripartite *Life* tells us that when Patrick arrived in Leinster, Driccriu, the king of Uí Garrchon refused to invite the saint to his feast at Ráith Inbir, which was probably near Arklow, and as the *inber* element in the name implies, was most certainly on the east coast of Leinster.[12] Patrick then proceeded to travel across the plain of Liffey (Mag Liphi) to Killashee and Kilcullen, south of Naas. Earlier in the *Tripartite Life*, when Patrick was supposed to have landed in Ireland for the first time while on his mission, we are told that Nath-Í, son of Garrchú (see table 2.11) repulsed him.[13] All this is hagiographical shorthand for showing how St Patrick was alleged to have influenced the destinies of Irish tribes and dynasties for centuries after his time. It states, in effect, that kings of Uí Garrchon, by slighting Patrick, were to condemn their descendants to permanent political eclipse, while Patrick's Uí Dúnlainge friends were to inherit the kingship of the Leinstermen. The Uí Dúnlainge did indeed become kings of all Leinster, though not in the fifth century, but rather in the eighth. The message also carried political threats and propaganda for the time of the writer of the *Tripartite Life* – 'Befriend Armagh, the church of Patrick, and you will prosper. Oppose Armagh and you will suffer dire political consequences.'

Several important points emerge in relation to the Leinster episode in the Tripartite *Life*. Firstly, the refusal of Driccriu, the king of Uí Garrchon, to invite Patrick to his feast at Ráith Inbir makes no sense in the context of a journey through the plain of Liffey. Clearly, the original tradition, for what it was worth, understood that the Uí Garrchon king was in close proximity to Naas, rather than on the Wicklow coast. Secondly, the statement that he was married to a daughter of Niall Noígiallach ('of the Nine Hostages') the progenitor of the Uí Néill highkings of Tara, is suggestive of a powerful king – a king of all the Leinstermen – who was worthy of such a prestigious marriage alliance.[14] Just as Patrick's initial landfall on the Wicklow coast makes little sense in the Ulster or Miliucc episode of Muirchú and the *Tripartite Life*, so too, Patrick's communication with the Uí Garrchon of east Wicklow is also meaningless when narrated in the context of his visit to the Liffey plain. Clearly, we are dealing with a tradition already established in Muirchú's time in the late seventh century, which somehow associated the Dál Messin Corb with early Christian happenings in the Liffey basin in the Patrician era. By the time these traditions came to be written down, the Dál Messin Corb kings who once featured at the centre of the story had long since fallen from power and had retreated from Kildare across the Wicklow Hills to the coast. And yet the tradition of the involvement of the Dál Messin Corb (and their major sept of Uí Garrchon) in the initial christianisation of Leinster proved so strong, that a role for this defeated tribe had to be found in the Patrick saga. The original tradition involving the Dál Messin Corb is unlikely to have contained any reference to Patrick at all. It probably dealt with the early missionary labours of men such as Mac Táil of Old Kilcullen, Iserninus of northern Carlow, and perhaps also it included Palladius – missionaries who arrived in Leinster with the message of Christianity when the Dál Messin Corb ruled that province. The fact that the Uí Garrchon descendants of the Dál Messin Corb were shown to be hostile to Patrick was nothing more than an attempt to explain and exploit their later weak political position and geographical isolation on the periphery of Leinster. Those who lost out politically, it could be argued, were those who had opposed Patrick and his church of Armagh.

Muirchú, although aware that Palladius had reached Ireland as a bishop charged with the care of the early Irish church before Patrick, does not tell us where Palladius landed. But the Tripartite *Life* of Patrick is not silent on this subject. It boldly claims that the elusive Palladius (who was dispatched to Ireland by Pope Celestine in 431), also first came into contact with the Uí Garrchon. Landing at Arklow (Inber Dee), Palladius like Patrick after him, was expelled by Nath-Í mac Garrchon.[15] Price needlessly accepted that this showed the Uí Garrchon were already in position around Arklow in the fifth century. The tradition – like others relating to Patrick at Arklow – if it has any value at all, merely associates the earliest missionary activity in Leinster with a time when the Dál Messin Corb were supreme in that province, and at a time, when they most likely had not even begun their trek eastwards over the Wicklow Hills. As for *Cell Fine* – that place in Uí Garrchon where, according to the *Tripartite Life*, Palladius left relics of Peter and Paul, his books, and a writing tablet – we ought not to seek for it in the hinterland of Arklow. *Cell Fine* is surely Kileen Cormac (Cell Fhine Chormaic) in Kildare, which lies north of Moone and Mullaghmast, and within a few miles of the Wicklow border. This place, with its ogham inscriptions and other remarkable remains, was within Dál Messin Corb territory in the fifth and sixth centuries. Similarly, the obsolete placename *Cellugarrconn* (Cell Uí Garrchon, 'The church of the Ua Garrchon') near Lackan in Wicklow, and by the side of Blessington reservoir, testifies to the presence of this people further north in Cualu in early Christian times.[16] The Dál Messin Corb, then, were kings of the Leinstermen at a time when the first Christian evangelists were arriving in Leinster. Those wandering holy men had probably nothing to do with Patrick and may never even have heard of him. It is in the context of this evidence for the patronage of early Christian evangelists by Dál Messin Corb rulers that we must view the emergence of the Dál Messin Corb's own indigenous saints such as Kevin who was born near the Kildare-Wicklow border *c.* 540-550.

Glendalough: Monastic oasis in a mountainous desert

Kevin's earliest association with Glendalough was in the ascetic tradition of the Desert Fathers. His *Lives*, both Latin and Irish, show him as a recluse living on herbs supplemented by a fish diet on the inaccessible southern shore of the Upper Lake at Glendalough. His ascetic exercises, sleeping in his cave – the prehistoric rock-cut tomb of Kevin's Bed – and praying waist-deep in the waters of the Upper Lake, are classic examples of early Celtic asceticism, and remind us of Bede's account of Dryhthelm praying in the icy waters of the Northumbrian Tweed.[17] The hagiographical lore relating to Kevin living in the tree-tops and praying in the trees owes something to the motif of the wild man in early Irish literature, as well as to the stylite movement among ascetics in Syria and elsewhere in the Near East. Kevin's earliest settlement at Dísert Cóemgin by the Upper Lake, probably dates to *c.* 575. The earliest mention of a successor to Kevin in the Annals of Ulster is the record of the death of Colmán of Glendalough in 660.[18] Colmán is very unlikely to have been Kevin's immediate successor, given that the average rule of abbots in the late eighth and early ninth centuries (when documentation is available) did not extend beyond ten years. Early annalistic documentation on Glendalough is patchy and very similar to that of Ferns in Wexford. The records of neither monastery can compare with the detailed notices offered on Kildare

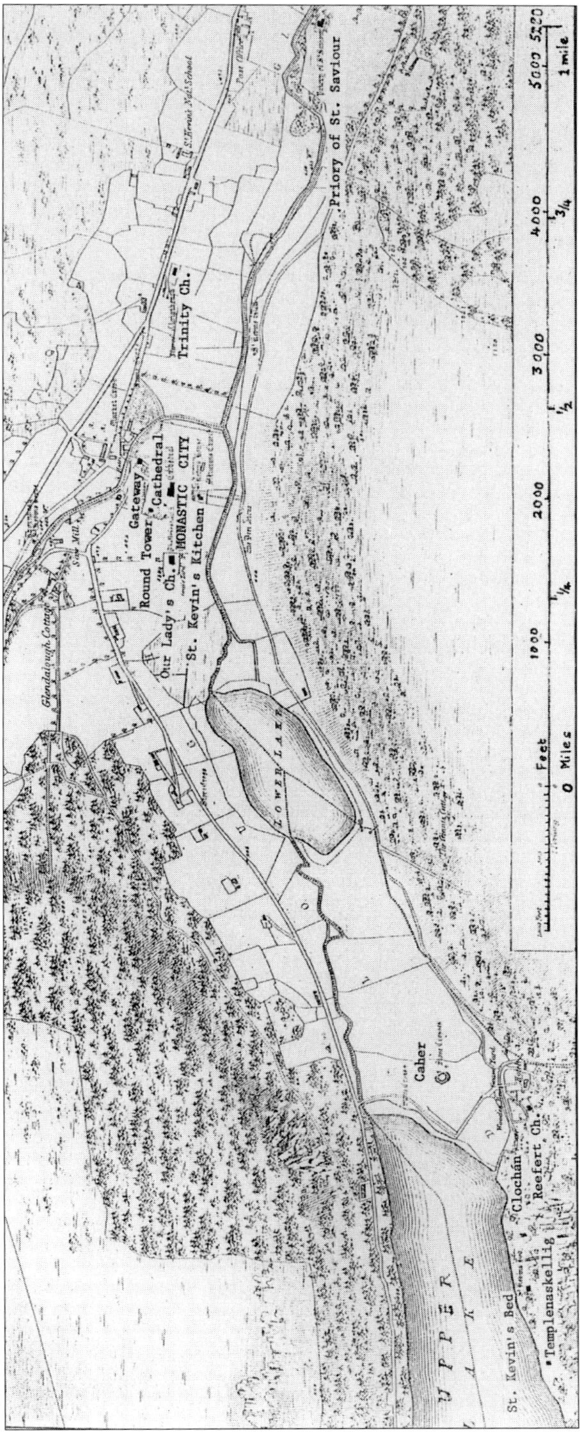

Figure 2.4 Glendalough.

and Clonard in the late seventh and throughout the eighth centuries. Nor are the existing records sufficiently detailed to indicate to which tribes the earliest abbots and bishops of Glendalough belonged. The precise nature, for instance, of Colmán's office at Glendalough is not specified in the Annals of Ulster. We are justified, on the basis of our knowledge of abbatial succession on Iona and elsewhere, in assuming that Kevin's earliest nameless successors belonged to his own tribe of Dál Messin Corb which may have exercised a proprietorial right over Glendalough. But the tribal origins of Colmán (+ 660), or of abbots Do-Chuma Conoc (+ 687), and Dub Guala (+ 712) are unknown. With the decline of the founder's dynasty, Glendalough became a rich resource for powerful local warlords to exploit, and some of those early abbots may have been imposed on the monastery by Uí Máil or Uí Dúnlainge kings of Leinster. There is some evidence, however, to the contrary. Dairchell, the bishop of Glendalough who died in 678 is described in the Annals of Ulster as *m. Curetai* which ought to be read as *moccu Retai* 'of the [tribe of Dál] Riata' in north-east Ireland and Argyll in Scotland. If Bishop Dairchell did come from the distant Ulaid – and *moccu Retai* can scarcely refer to any other people – we have evidence that the bishop of a great *paruchia* such as Glendalough was an outsider who was free of local tribal politics and loyalties. Dairchell was remembered as a holy man, whose festival, according to the Martyrology of Tallaght, was kept on 3 May.[19]

There is a hiatus in the record for Glendalough in the Annals of Ulster between the death of Abbot Dub Guala in 712 and that of Abbot Encorach Ua Doadán in 769, and thereafter the meagre evidence suggests that Glendalough, if it had not become decadent, had at any rate become rich. The burning of the monastery in 775, in a year when Armagh and Kildare suffered the same fate, may have been accidental, but it is likely that the *combustio* was caused by a violent attack on the community by local tribes hostile to the established ecclesiastical rulers of the place. The *comotatio* of the relics of St Kevin is recorded for 790.[20] This event may have consisted of the formal *translatio* of the remains of the saint, which were taken from the founder's tomb and solemnly installed in a splendid shrine in the monastic church, or alternatively it could refer to the taking of that shrine on a circuit of dependent houses within the *paruchia* of Glendalough. Whatever its precise meaning, the *comotatio* had, at the centre of its ritual, a magnificent shrine displaying the goldsmiths' and enamel workers' high art-forms of the late eighth century. Finian's relics had been so honoured in Clonard in 776 and Conláed's bones were housed in a gold and silver shrine in Kildare in 800. Architectural improvements went hand in hand with shrine production during this period of new-found opulence. Killeigh in north-west Leinster was provided with a new oratory in 805. Glendalough by 790, then, had come to share in the increasing wealth of Irish monastic culture, and there can be little doubt that its later abbots – Máel Combair (+ 790), Ceithernach (+ 799), Mimtenacha (+ 800), Guaire (+ 810), Bishop Eiterscél son of Cellach (+ 814), Suibne son of Joseph (+ 836), Daniél (+ 868) and Fechtnach (+ 875) – were all princely abbots, who in other monasteries were described as *principes* at this time. From what we know of the office of monastic *princeps* in eighth-century Ireland, it was synonymous with that of abbot, and with the notable exception of Iona, these princely churchmen constituted dynasties of married men who controlled rich monastic communities and represented the interests of the local warrior aristocracy. On the other hand, it may be that the absence of the term *princeps* for the ruler of Glendalough in the early annals does suggest something more positive. It may be that Kevin's isolated community preserved something of the sanctity of Iona's monks during the eighth century and later. The very trace of Kevin's powerful association with this hauntingly beautiful valley may have kept the spark of ascetic idealism alive here. And Glendalough's extreme geographical isolation from powerful warlords may have helped even more. For unlike most other major monastic houses, Glendalough, like Iona, was not so close to a centre of political power as to become a royal chapel for any one tribal king. Certainly there is no record of unedifying fracas in the monastic precincts such as the battles fought at Ferns in 783 between the abbot and the steward, or the slaughter involving the communities of Clonmacnoise and Birr in 760, or the battle between Clonmacnoise and Durrow in 764.[21] We even read of a battle actually *in* the monastery of Kildare (*inna cill*) on 29 August 833.[22] But the very expansion and great physical extent of the surviving early medieval monastic remains at Glendalough testify to the growing wealth and power of the place.

There are essentially three monastic complexes at Glendalough – the earliest on the shores of the Upper Lake under Kevin's Bed, the next oldest at the Reefert Church between the Upper and Lower Lakes, and finally the monastic 'city' or *civitas* built to house an ever-expanding community at the eastern end of the Lower Lake and at the mouth of the Vale of Glendalough. The Latin *Life* of Kevin and some of the Irish *Lives* preserve memories of the debate within the community regarding the migration of the settlement to the eastern end of the valley. The controversy generated by that move – which took place perhaps in the eighth century – is resolved in the *Lives* by making an angel appear to Kevin, commanding him to remove his community further down the valley to a more roomy location. The reluctant saint only agreed to this move having won from the angel the privilege that no monk would be lost to Heaven who was buried there.[23] A community of monks which began life fleeing from the world to a remote mountain glen *c*.A.D. 600 eventually found that Kevin's reputation for sanctity conspired to bring Glendalough into the limelight. Its location, furthermore, on a key passway leading from the Irish Sea over the Wicklow Gap to Naas, combined with the very fame of its founder to make it increasingly rich. The compiler of the Latin *Life* striving to reconcile these contradictory aspects of Glendalough makes the angel predict to St Kevin just how rich his humble community will become:[24]

> Kings and powerful ones of Ireland will honour it with a religious veneration on thine account. It will be enriched with lands, gold and silver, precious gems and silken garments, with gifts from beyond the sea, as with royal treasure and abundance.

The *muneribus transmarinis* reminds us of Muirchú's *transmarinis mirabilibus ... tessauris* which Patrick was supposed to have brought in his ship to Arklow. The place where the angel pointed out to Kevin for his expanding community was the Reefert foundation between the two lakes of Glendalough. The word *Reefert* comes from *Ríg Ferta*, 'The Cemetery of the Kings', with the obvious implication that this part of Glendalough provided a mausoleum for neighbouring kings who ruled over the Wicklow Hills. One of the fragmentary sagas relating to the Leinster champion, Máelodrán, claims that he was buried in Glendalough, whence it was said:

> Máelodrán's grave is conspicuous
> In the Glen against the whirling wind.

Máelodrán: champion in a heroic tradition

It is significant that the Leinster warrior Máelodrán, who was supposed to have lived in the middle of the seventh century, was understood in the *senchus* to have been a member of the Dál Messin Corb and to have been a formidable enemy of the Uí Néill kings of Brega and the neigbouring kings of Uí Máil in Leinster. In those very general terms, the sagas of Máelodrán, which are inserted at the end of the *Scélshenchus Laigen* ('Historical Sagas of the Leinstermen'), reflect a genuine historical reality. Scholars who seek to wrest more exact historical data from saga material such as this, fail to understand the nature of the Old Irish *scél*. Such a saga was never intended to fulfil the needs of modern historical scholarship, and although it might deal with historical incidents which had made a deep impression on tribal memories, those incidents were handled by professional storytellers with the primary aim of entertaining and flattering their audiences. So, historical accuracy in relation to minutiae, could be, and was, sacrificed in the service of narration, and when this is not appreciated by modern scholars, distortions in our evaluation of this genre are the inevitable result. When Price consulted the two sagas of Máelodrán, he found there an unwarranted historical accuracy that supported his own hypotheses, while Paul Walsh despaired of reconciling these sagas' details with those of conventional sources. David Greene compounded the problem by heaping up a catalogue of seemingly irreconcilable material and leaving questions unresolved to the confusion of his readers and to the great disservice of the subject.[25] Máelodrán's sagas may be summarised as follows:

The Death of the Three Sons of Diarmait Mac Cerbaill[26]

Diarmait mac Cerbaill was the son of Fergus Cerrbél, and he was the ancestor of the two Southern Uí Néill dynasties of the Síl nÁedo Sláine of Brega in county Meath – called after Diarmait's son, Áed Sláine (+ 604) – and the Clann Cholmáin of Mide in Westmeath – called after Diarmait's son Colmán Mór (+ 555). According to the saga of Máelodrán, three sons of Diarmait son of Fergus Cerrbél were slain by Máelodrán who had them crushed to death in a mill where they had taken refuge, having slain Máelodrán's personal servant, Déoraid, on a raid into Leinster. The names of these Uí Néill princes are given as Dúnchad, Conall and Máelodor, – styled collectively as *Uí Cerbaill* (Grandsons of Cerball). The genealogical details from the saga are summarised in table 2.1.

The Annals of Ulster record the 'killing of two sons of Bláthmac son of Áed Sláine in 651. The compiler clearly equated this killing with the tale of Máelodrán's revenge on the sons of Diarmait, for two verses from Máelodrán's saga are entered in the margin by the main or first hand of the manuscript.

The genealogical details of the record in the Annals of Ulster are set out in table 2.2.

The descendants of Diarmait mac Cerbaill

We see that two of the names of the slain Uí Néill princes are the same as in the saga, while a third – that of Máelodor – has been added in the saga. Price suggested that the saga compiler had confused the slain sons of Bláthmac with sons of his brother Diarmait, but it is perhaps easier to conclude that the saga tradition has omitted the two generations of Áed Sláine and his son Bláthmac, and by this telescoping of genealogy, the slain Uí Néill princes are made out to be

Table 2.1 Genealogy from the Saga of the Three Sons of Diarmait

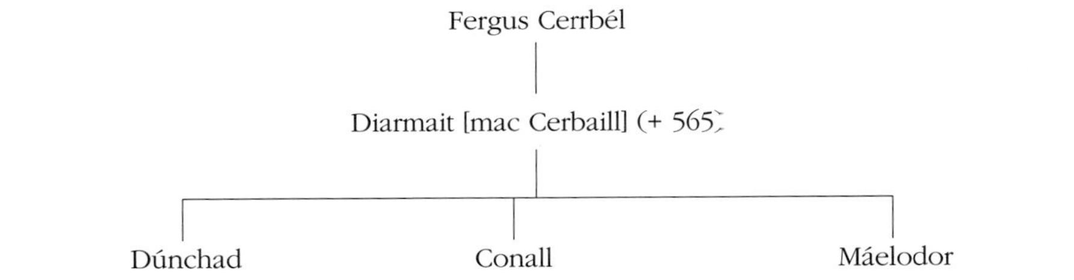

Table 2.2 The descendants of Diarmait mac Cerbaill

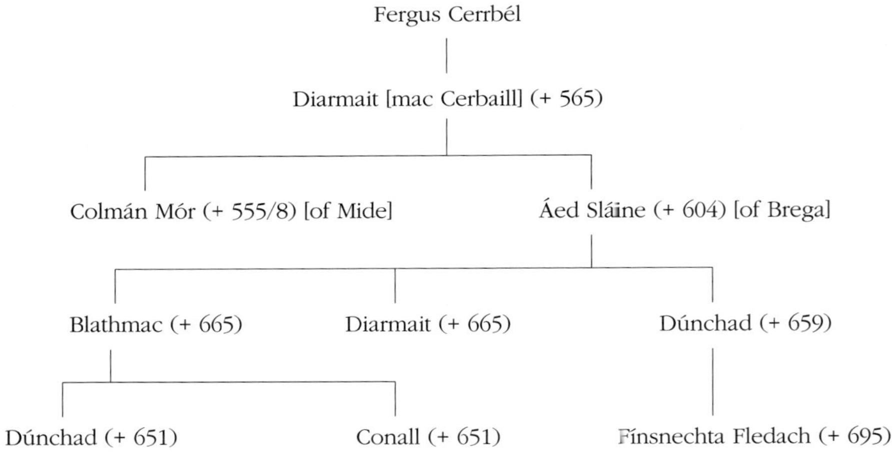

the sons of Diarmait mac Cerbaill, one of the best-known early Uí Néill kings, who was himself the subject of saga traditions. Such re-arranging of historical and genealogical data was normal for early Irish storytellers as it was for later compilers of Icelandic sagas. To a Leinster audience, it meant more to be told that their hero, Máelodrán, had inflicted a devastating blow on Diarmait mac Cerbaill than on his more obscure relative, Bláthmac son of Áed Sláine. The notes to the *Félire Óengusso* (*Calendar of Óengus*) claim that the Uí Néill victims were sons of Bláthmac as stated in the Annals of Ulster, and confirms the name of one as Dúnchad, but gives the other as Cathal instead of Conall.[27] The saga alone knows of the third son, Máelodor. Finally, the *Félire Óengusso* names the slayer of these princes as Marcán, another Leinster champion mentioned elsewhere in the Máelodrán sagas. But it is the Annals of Ulster that must remain our guide, and all that we can safely conclude is that the slaying of the sons of Bláthmac (an Uí Néill high-king, and also a king of Brega), in 651, was associated in later centuries with the exploits of the Leinster champion, Máelodrán. Máelodran's saga concludes with Diarmait mac Cerbaill demanding that the Leinstermen yield up Máelodrán to him as a hostage. The Leinstermen refuse, but Máelodrán goes voluntarily and alone to confront Diarmait at his crannóg or lake-fortress at Lagore near Dunshaughlin in county Meath. Máelodrán takes a boat to the fortress after dark and gains the advantage over the Uí Néill king who happened to emerge alone from his hall to defecate in the darkness. Peace was eventually established between Diarmait and Máelodrán and with Mugain, Diarmait's queen.

This Lagore episode has caused needless controversy as to whether Diarmait mac Cerbaill actually resided on that crannóg, which has yielded such a wealth of archaeological finds from the Harvard Archaeological Expedition of the 1930s. If the saga relates to any particular king, it must be to Bláthmac son of Áed Sláine who died in 665, and who as king of Brega may well have ruled from Lagore. We shall see that in 677 – only some 26 years after the slaying of Bláthmac's sons – the Leinstermen did indeed launch an attack on the Uí Néill 'in a place near Lagore' which was repulsed by Fínsnechta Fledach, the Uí Néill high-king, who was the nephew of Bláthmac. So, in so far as it reflects tales of Leinster heroism against Uí Néill enemies belonging to the House of Bláthmac and Áed Sláine, involving the slaying of Uí Néill princes and confrontations at Lagore crannóg, *The tragic death of the three sons of Diarmait mac Cerbaill* (*Orgguin Trí Mac Diarmata mic Cerbaill*) when used with caution, is a useful source for the historian. This does not mean that we accept all its details – many of which are patently distortions of historical realities – but such sagas can shed valuable light on the general historical background for the time at least in which they were composed, and their greatest value is what they tell us about the attitudes of the audience for whom they were composed.

The sagas relating to Máelodrán were composed among the Dál Messin Corb soon after that tribe had been ousted from power by the Uí Máil. Máelodrán's tribal and family origins are stressed. He is described as *mac Dima Croin* ('son of Dímmae Crón'), or *ua Díma Chróin di Scorbraige Lagen* ('grandson or descendant of Dímmae Crón of the Scorbrige of the Leinstermen'), and we are also told that Máelodrán was of 'Dál Messin Corb of Leinster' (*do Dáil Moss Corb Laigen*). Máelodrán and his ancestor Dímmae Crón do indeed feature in the Rawlinson genealogies of the Dál Messin Corb and it was unquestionably to this tribe that the hero of the Leinster tales involving the death of Uí Néill princes belonged. Dímmae Crón is given in the genealogies as the son of Fintán and grandson of Branán, and Máelodrán son of Dícuill (*mac Dícolla*) is given as fourth in descent from Dímmae Crón (see table 2.11).

The death of Máelodrán (*Aided Máelodráin*)[28]

Máelodrán's inveterate enemies, in the saga relating how the champion died, were the Uí Máil and their king, Aithechda or Athechda, whose daughter was Máelodrán's wife. We are told that the Uí Máil were *comaithig* or 'neighbours' to the Dál Messin Corb, which in the mid-seventh century was indeed the case, with the Uí Máil holding the western approaches to the Wicklow mountains (including the Glen of Imaal, Glenn Ua Máil) and with the main body of Dál Messin Corb pushed eastwards towards Arklow. Máelodrán's wife agreed with her father to betray her husband into the hands of her Uí Máil kindred. The trap which she set for Máelodrán – an ambush in some isolated cabin went badly wrong. Máelodrán escaped after slaughtering his attackers and a temporary peace was patched up with his Uí Máil father-in-law. Eventually, Máelodrán was cruelly slain while bathing as a guest in Aithechda's house, being pierced by Aithechda with his own magic spear – the Carr of Belach Duirgen. Aithechda then took yet another wife of the slain Máelodrán to his own bed. A full year after this killing, the ghost of the dead Máelodrán re-appeared to Aithechda and slew him with that same wondrous spear of Máelodrán which Aithechda had kept as a trophy on a rack in his hall. We are told that Máelodrán, while in life, had reduced the Uí Máil from thirty hundred – the nominal tribal muster or *trícha chét* – to twenty seven (thrice nine), and he slaughtered them as a quern might crush corn.[29] In his prime he had raced around Imlech Ech, a place somewhere in Uí Bairrche in northern Carlow – a short distance across the Barrow valley from Uí Máil where warriors from the Wicklow Hills might be expected to visit on bravado raiding parties against their Leinster neighbours. And, finally, we are told Máelodrán's grave was in Glendalough, perhaps in the Reefert cemetery between the two lakes.

In these two sagas dealing with the exploits of Máelodrán, we discern echoes of a vanishing world of warlords of the Dál Messin Corb, as told to an audience in the Wicklow Hills in the eighth and ninth centuries.

The kingship of the Leinstermen

Leinster court historians of the later Uí Dúnlainge have tampered so drastically with the king-list for the kings of all Leinster covering the sixth century that it may never be possible to recover a full and accurate succession for that time. This does not mean that the Leinster king-list is flawed throughout, but it does mean that a desire on the part of the Uí Dúnlainge to show their ancestors were in control of sixth-century Leinster has seriously distorted the original record for that period. A glance at the Uí Dúnlainge genealogy (table 2.3) which supposedly covers this time, highlights the forging which is evident at this point in the Leinster king-list.

If we were to believe the king-list, then Ailill, his brother (Illann), his son (Cormac), grandson (Coirpre) and great-grandson (Colmán Mór) all inherited the kingship of the Leinstermen in unbroken succession. Such a tightly ordered succession was never true for the Uí Dúnlainge even when they eventually managed to monopolise the Leinster kingship from the eighth century onwards. For even in that later period, three cousinly septs shared royal power. Not even the Uí Néill, who had developed the most regular and tightly organised succession within narrow degrees of kindred, could ever have matched this forged order of succession for sixth-century Leinster. Back in the sixth century, we know that royal power oscillated not only between cousins, but between rival tribes in the confederacy. The succession, therefore, from Illann (no. 5 in the king-list) to Cólmán Mór (no. 9) must be rejected out of hand. Significantly, these names have been inserted in the Leinster list between the rule of the Dál Messin Corb king, Fróech mac

Table 2.3 The early Uí Dúnlainge. Cf. table 2.6.

- Dúnlang
  - (5) Illann + 527
  - (6) Ailill + 548 *Ann. Tig.*
    - (7) Cormac + 552 *Ann. Tig.*
      - (8) Coirpre + 563 *Ann. Tig.*
        - (9) Colmán Mór + 576 A.F.M.
          - Áed Find
            - Óengus (abbot of Kildare)
          - (14) Fáelán fl. 628
            - Conall
              - (16) Bran Mut (+ 693)
          - Áed Dub (+ 639)
          - Rónán

Numbers in round brackets indicate numerical order as found in the Leinster king-list in the Book of Leinster.

Findchada (no. 4 and see table 2.11) and Áed Cerr (no. 10). Áed Cerr, in spite of attempts by a forger to show otherwise, was not of the Uí Dúnlainge, but of the Uí Máil (table 2.7). The intrusion of these names of bogus Uí Dúnlainge kings into the Leinster king-list is matched, as we have seen, by later assertions in the *Vita Tripartita* that Patrick baptised Illann and Ailill, the sons of Dúnlang, at the fort of Naas.

The name of Áed Cerr is inserted tenth in the Leinster king-list after that of Colmán Mór. Áed's name is entered as *Áed Cerr mac Cólmáin.* Above the line of this record in the *Book of Leinster* and repeated in the margin, the alternative reading *Senaig* is given for the name of Áed Cerr's father.[30] Paul Walsh correctly identified this Áed Cerr as Áed Díbchíne son of Senach Díbech of the Uí Máil (see table 2.10), whose territory occupied the present Wicklow-Kildare border district.[31] The assertion that this Áed was a son of Colmán was an attempt by a later editor to identify Áed with a son of Colmán Mór of the Uí Dúnlainge (no. 9) of the Liffey plain, and thus enlarge on the fiction that the later dominance of the Uí Dúnlainge in eighth- and ninth-century Leinster enjoyed a much earlier history than in fact it ever had. Genuine genealogical records facilitated the forger in his search for possible Uí Dúnlainge kings. We find that in the Uí Dunlainge pedigree (see table 2.3), Colmán Mór had not one, but two sons called Áed – distinguished by the epithets Áed *Find* ('Fair' Áed) and Áed *Dub* ('Dark' Áed). But any later confusion of the Leinster king, Áed son of Senach, with an Áed son of Cólmán must be dismissed as being quite false. There is no reliable historical evidence to show that Colmán Mór of the Uí Dúnlainge ever held the kingship of Leinster and there is no record even of his death in the Annals of Ulster. We may conclude that on the collapse of the Uí Failge and Dál Messin Corb in the face of southern Uí Néill expansion, the Uí Máil presented themselves as serious challengers for the kingship of Leinster. This is the struggle which is reflected in the sagas relating to Máelodrán, where that Dál Messin Corb hero is confronted with Uí Néill enemies from outside, and with Uí Máil rivals from within his own Leinster borders. At this time, too, clearly the ancestors of the Uí Dúnlainge were fighting their way to power – a power which they eventually attained when Fáelán (no. 14, table 2.3), the son of Colmán Mór of the Uí Dúnlainge, seized the kingship of the Leinstermen in 633. According to the saga of *The death of Máelodrán*, the inveterate enemy and slayer of that Dál Messin Corb champion is named as Aithechda. In the saga, Aithechda is described as king of Uí Máil (*rí hua Máil*). *Aithechdae* was never common as a name in early Irish records and it may be significant that a great-grandson of Colmán Mór of the Uí Dúnlainge was called Aithechda (son of Máel-Ochtraig son of Rónán, see table 2.8). The Uí Dúnlainge

Aithechda ought to have been active in the 690s since he had one great-uncle, Fáelán, who became king of Leinster in 633 and another, Áed Dub, who died in 639. The chronology does not quite fit for making this Aithechda the slayer of Máelodrán, for Máelodrán is assumed to have been responsible for the slaying of the sons of Bláthmac of the Uí Néill back in 651. But it was no business of saga makers to present their audience with a coherent chronological and historical framework. What our historical records do tell us is that the Uí Dúnlainge rise to power in Leinster was slow, and that during the sixth century they can have made little progress in asserting their claim to the Leinster kingship. That kingship was contested by the Uí Failge, the Dál Messin Corb and the Uí Máil. Áed Díbchíne mac Senaig Díbig of the Uí Máil began to rule as king of the Leinstermen sometime around 580-5. We know from the Annals of Ulster that his successor, Brandub, of the Uí Cheinnselaig held the Leinster kingship by 590 at the latest. In spite of Uí Cheinnselaig opposition, Áed Díbchíne of the Uí Máil established his successors in that Wicklow tribe as the dominant dynasty throughout the seventh century. Áed's son, Crimthann, his grandson, Fiannamail, and his great-great-grandson, Cellach Cualann, all ruled as Uí Máil kings of Leinster over the period 630-715 (see tables 2.7 and 2.10).

Brandub: defender of a province

Brandub mac Echach was king of the Leinstermen at the opening of the seventh century. He has been viewed as an exotic king by many historians partly because of his prominent place in the saga of the *Bóruma Laigen* ('The Cattle-tribute of the Leinstermen') – a tale of Leinster's resistance to the levying of tribute by the Uí Néill kings of Tara – and partly because of his supposedly unique position as an Uí Cheinnselaig over-king of the Leinstermen who came from the far south of the province. At the time when Brandub seized the kingship of the Leinstermen, there was no tribal group strong enough to enforce a monopoly on that kingship, which was competed for by a number of tribal groups, including the Uí Cheinnselaig and the Uí Máil of west Wicklow. Brandub was not the first Uí Cheinnselaig king of the Leinstermen. At least one of his Uí Cheinnselaig predecessors, Crimthann, son of Énna Cennselach (table 2.4), ruled as king of all Leinster before his death at *c.* 483. And Brandub, contrary to once received opinion, did not usurp the kingship of Leinster from the Uí Dúnlainge, that dominant dynastic group who controlled the provincial kingship throughout the ninth and tenth centuries. The Uí Dúnlainge at this early period were only beginning to aspire to their claim over Leinster – as were the Uí Cheinnselaig themselves, to whom Brandub belonged. Brandub's immediate predecessor in the kingship of Leinster was Áed mac Senaig, a king of the Uí Máil who ruled from the western foothills of the Wicklow mountains. It is also incorrect to maintain that Brandub was the last king of Uí Cheinnselaig to hold the kingship of the Leinstermen until his dynasty again asserted its claim in the eleventh century. Brandub's successors, Rónán mac Colmáin (+ 624), together with Crundmáel Erbuilg mac Rónáin (+ 656) and Áed mac Colggen (+ 738) were all kings of Leinster who came from the Uí Cheinnselaig (see table 2.4). Historians have further exaggerated the unique quality of Brandub's reign by pointing out that when his dynasty returned to power many centuries after his time, the Síl Fáelchon branch were then the dominant group who did not count Brandub in their pedigree at all – since he belonged to the Uí Felmeda. This observation is based more on selective editing of the extensive Uí Cheinnselaig genealogies by modern historians and by the failure to collate those pedigrees with the Uí Cheinnselaig king-list rather than to any unique qualities of Brandub himself, or of his immediate kindred. A glance at the complex Uí Cheinnselaig genealogy in table 2.4 will show that the tribal kingship of Uí Cheinnselaig was shared between not one or two dynastic segments but between at least six competing groups into the eighth and ninth centuries. So, if Brandub's sept of Síl Felmeda eventually lost out in the struggle to monopolise the kingship of Uí Cheinnselaig, so also did the septs of Síl Chormaic and Síl Máeluidir (from which the Barony of Shelmalier gets its name), for instance, which had provided far more kings for the tribe of Uí Cheinnselaig than that of Brandub's Uí Felmeda.

The on-going strife between the Brega and Uí Failge alliance on the one hand, against the Uí Néill enemies of Mide on the other, provides us with a background against which we may view the rise of new and powerful dynasties in Leinster at the opening of the seventh century.[32] Brandub mac Echach, king of the Uí Cheinnselaig, was one of those new leaders who forced himself upon the attention of the annalists during the period 590 to 605. To understand the reason for Brandub's success we must turn to the king-list of the Uí Cheinnselaig dynasty to which he belonged. This king-list[33] provides a reliable historical source even for this early period, in contrast to the confused record for the kings of Uí Failge and the partially-forged list of the kings of all Leinster. On collating the names of the kings in the Uí Cheinnselaig list with the genealogies of the Uí Cheinnselaig, it is possible to follow the royal succession of this tribal confederacy through the sixth and seventh centuries. The complexities of the Uí Cheinnselaig genealogies make it highly unlikely that the king-list has been invented from the genealogies or *vice versa*. The genealogical record contains a maze of inter-connecting pedigrees from which the modern researcher can reconstruct an over-view not given to early medieval scribes. The kingship of the Uí Cheinnselaig for this early period was not confined exclusively to any one branch of the dynasty – much less to the line which was to monopolise it in later centuries, so that it is safe to assume that re-editing, although present in the king-list, is minimal. Furthermore, there are rulers named in the king-list who are not found in the genealogies – always a healthy sign – and it is sometimes possible to tie such individuals into their proper place in the genealogies on the evidence of the patronymics which are usually provided in the king-lists.

The succession to the kingship of Uí Cheinnselaig may be followed by means of the numbered sequence set out on the genealogical chart in table 2.4. It will be seen that Brandub mac Echach is marked no. 12 on the Uí Cheinnselaig king-list. Brandub belonged to the Uí Felmeda branch of the dynasty. His father, Eochu (no. 10), his grandfather, Muiredach (no. 8), and his great-grandfather, Óengus (no. 5), had all held the kingship of Uí Cheinnselaig before him. The succession from Óengus to his great-grandson, Brandub, was not continuous, unlike that spurious succession-list we have already encountered for the north Leinster Uí Dúnlainge. In this genuine Uí Cheinnselaig document, we see that competing dynastic segments also participated in the succession, in typical early Irish fashion. Between Óengus (no. 5) and Muiredach (no. 8), Fáelán Senchustal (no. 6) and Éogan Cáech (no. 7), two sons of Nath-Í, intervened. Between Muiredach (no. 8) and Eochu (no. 10), we note the intervention of Fáelán (no. 9) of the Síl Mella, who was the grandson of Éogan Cáech (no. 7). Nevertheless, the continuity of succession within Brandub's Uí Felmeda branch is not parallelled in any other segment of the Uí Cheinnselaig at this early period – not even in the Síl Coluim (Chormaic) line – and emphasises that when Brandub came to power as king of all the Leinstermen *c.*600, his Uí Felmeda dynasty at that time constituted the dominant Uí Cheinnselaig group which had held power in the south-west Wicklow and Carlow region for over four generations. The name of Brandub's immediate predecessor in the Uí Cheinnselaig king-list, *Forannán mac Máel Udir*, is not found in the genealogies. Forannán was very probably a son of Máeloder son of Guaire, the founder of the Síl Máeluidor dynasty (see table 2.4) who have given their name to the Barony of Shelmalier in Wexford. If that is correct, then Brandub's predecessor was a descendant of Crimthann son of Énna Cennselach rather than of Fedelmid, the ancestor of Brandub.

Brandub first appears in the historical record in 590, and since his career was later to become a focus for sagas and eulogistic poetry, it is best to begin with the record of the Annals of Ulster.

590: Brandub defeated the Uí Néill at the battle of Mag Ochtair.
597: Cummascach son of Áed mac Ainmerech was slain by Brandub at Dún Buchat.
598: The slaughter of Dún Bolg where Áed mac Ainmerech was slain by Brandub. Bécc mac Cuanach, king of the Uí Maicc Uais of Airgialla (county Tyrone), was also slain on the side of Áed.
605: The battle of *Slaebhre* in which Brandub was defeated by the Uí Néill.

[A later hand in the TCD MS H.1.7 claims that Áed Uaredach, then overlord of the Uí Néill, led the Uí Néill army. The main entry continues by claiming that Brandub was assassinated by one of his own people through treachery (*per dolum*). This is followed by a genealogy of Brandub together with a mixed entry in Latin and Irish – all in a later hand, which claims Brandub reigned for 30 years in Leinster, and was slain in the battle of Dam Chluain or by Sárán Saobhderg, the *oirchinnech* (hereditary warden) of Senboth Sine. This statement is backed by a stanza of verse repeating that Sárán was Brandub's slayer.]

Brandub's first appearance in 590 concerns his victory over the Uí Néill at Mag Ochtair. The exact location of this place is specified in the Annals of Tigernach (followed by the Four Masters) as being 'by the hill over Cluain Conaire Tomain to the south (*isin telaigh os Cluain Conaire Tomain andes*)'.[34] Mag Ochtair was in the vicinity of Cloncurry in north Kildare on the border of Leinster with the Southern Uí Néill and at one of the few crossing points between the two provincial kingdoms, on a pass leading to Rathcore (Dún Cuair) in county Meath. We see here, then, for the first time, a south Leinster king taking upon himself the defence of the whole province against Uí Néill attack. We may reasonably assume that it was the Northern Uí Néill (rather than their southern cousins in Brega and Mide) who were defeated by Brandub in this battle, since it was only the northern branch who subsequently opposed Brandub in what became a classic blood-feud ending in the slaying of the leading protagonists on both sides. The Southern Uí Néill, for their part, were too preoccupied with damaging feuds within their own dynastic territories to have been capable of mounting a major offensive against the Leinstermen at the turn of the sixth century.

The next reference to Brandub in the Annals of Ulster occurs seven years later, in 597, when we are told he slew Cummascach son of Áed mac Ainmerech of the Cenél Conaill – that Northern Uí Néill sept based in north-western territory later known as Tír Conaill or Donegal. Áed mac Ainmerech was at this time overlord of the Uí Néill north and south, and the claim that Brandub slew his son in 597 and that he slew Áed himself in the following year, appears in the laconic Latin record of the original hand in the TCD manuscript. There is no reason to doubt this record of Brandub's triumph over the most powerful royal house in late sixth-century Ireland – a triumph which forms the basis of his high profile in later Leinster saga and hagiography. Áed mac Ainmerech met his death at Dún Bolg in 598 in an abortive attempt to avenge the death of his son in the previous year at Dún Buchat. The precise locations of Dún Bolg and Dún Buchat are not known for certain, but Dún Bolg was in the immediate vicinity of Baltinglass (Belach Con Glais), in south-west Wicklow, while it is clear from the *Bóruma* saga that Dún Buchat was also located in west Wicklow. Price identified Dún Bolg with the Iron Age hillfort at Brusselstown Ring, and he placed Dún Buchat in the immediate vicinity at Kilranelagh (Cell Rannairech).[35] Brandub in the *Bóruma* tradition was also said to have had a fortress or *dún* on the Slaney near Baltinglass, variously named as *Tech mBranduib*, *Ráith Branduib*, or *Ráith Brainn*. Price identified this ráth with a ring-fort in Gibralter townland on the Slaney, two miles from Baltinglass, which up until the eighteenth century was included in the nearby townland of Rathbran.[36]

Bóruma Laighen: 'the cattle tribute of the Leinstermen'

Brandub is the central hero of the saga of the *Bóruma Laigen* ('Cattle-tribute of the Leinstermen') and the tale of how he resisted Uí Néill aggression and slew first Cummascach son of Áed Mac Ainmerech and then Áed himself, forms the centrepiece to that saga. The *Bóruma* in its developed form relates the history of the levying of an exorbitant tribute of cows, swine, wethers, mantles, silver chains and copper cauldrons on the Leinstermen by the Uí Néill from the time of the legendary Tuathal Techtmar in prehistory down to the time of the Leinster king, Bran [Mut] son of Conall, who died *c.*693 (table 2.3). It is clear, however, that the longer pseudo-history of the cattle-tribute was written up later to provide a background to the saga of Brandub's resistance to Uí Néill aggression in the late sixth century, and more immediately to provide an historical context for the supposed achievement of St Moling (died 697) in tricking the Uí Néill into remitting the tribute forever. For while the central action in the *Bóruma* is located in west Wicklow and focusses on Brandub, it is clear that the saga in its most developed form was put together at St Mullins in the Barrow Valley in county Carlow. The mark of a St Mullins compiler on the *Bóruma* is unmistakeable. The army of the legendary Finn mac Cumaill is said to have encamped at Ros mBroc (the site of the future St Mullins) on their way to join the Leinstermen in battle against Cairpre Lifechair of the Uí Néill. While at Ros mBroc, one of Finn's warriors had a vision of Moling and his attendant clerics who would adorn that place in a future time. In the resulting battle, the Leinstermen supported by Finn and his fianna – and by implication, supported also by St. Moling – utterly destroyed the Uí Néill at Cnamros.[37] The *Bóruma* ends with Moling entering the conflict like a Homeric god, to negotiate between the beleaguered Leinster king, Bran son of Conall, and the invading Uí Néill ruler, Fínshnechta Fledach (died 695). Moling emerges as the ultimate hero of the tale, having tricked Fínsnechta into remitting the cattle-tribute till the Day of Doom.

If the finishing touches were put to the *Bóruma* at St Mullins – where it was transformed into a 'history' saga by tagging together disjointed anecdotes and listings of battles relating to age-old conflicts between the Uí Néill and the Leinstermen – the main body of material which the St Mullins compiler went to work on related to events in west Wicklow and in the Glen of Imaal in particular. We are told that Cummascach son of Áed mac Ainmerech invaded Leinster on a stripling's circuit of Ireland, claiming the right to sleep with the wives of his father's subject kings *en route*. Brandub pretended to comply with this Uí Néill *droit de seigneur* but was careful to withdraw from his house (*tech*) at Belach nDubthaire or Baltinglass, before Cummascach arrived there. Brandub's queen managed to slip away to Dún Buchat (at Kilranelagh) while Brandub with the help of the Uí Failge kings, Airnelach and Óengus, the sons of Airmedach, set fire to the hall at Baltinglass, where Cummascach was feasting with his entourage of 300 kings' sons. Cummascach escaped the inferno only to be slain near the green (*faithche*) of Kilranelagh by Loíchín Lonn, the grandson of Lonán, erenach or warden of Kilranelagh.[38] The slaying of Cummascach provided the saga-writer with a classic revenge motif, whereby Cummascach's father, Áed mac Ainmerech, invaded Leinster across the King's River, seeking vengeance against Brandub and the Leinstermen for the loss of his son. Once again the action is firmly centred on Wicklow, for while we are told that Brandub was then at Scadharc in Uí Cheinnselaig, he marched north to prepare against the invasion, over [Mag] Fea in Carlow, and across the Slaney to his own *dún* at Baltinglass. Bishop Áedán of Glendalough then informed Brandub that his Uí Néill enemies were encamped at Baeth Abha by Dún Buaice (Dunboyke, south of Hollywood) further north in west Wicklow. Brandub retired to Ráth Branduib on the Slaney, while the Uí Néill host pushed south along the west Wicklow foothills of Cualu into Belach Dúin Bolg, through Berna na Sciath to Cell Belat (Kilbaylet) north of Donard. The Ulaid forces were now persuaded by the Leinstermen to withdraw from the Uí Néill camp at Sliabh in Chotaig (Slievegad or Church Mountain, to the north of Kilbaylet). The Leinstermen, through a ruse which recalls the Trojan Horse motif, gained access to the Uí Néill camp concealed in hampers, supposedly delivered to provision the invading army. In the mayhem that followed, Rón Cerr, son of Dubhánach, king of Uí Máil, slew the northern kings of Airgialla and of Tulach Óg, and he finally beheaded Áed mac Ainmerech himself. Rón presented Brandub with the severed head of his fallen enemy on the morrow, and to underline the self-contained nature of this centrepiece to the *Bóruma*, this section of the narrative is rounded off with the statement 'There, then, you have the battle of Dún Bolg, an episode in the history of the *Bóruma*.'[39]

The *Bóruma* saga in its developed form cannot be earlier than *c.*700, or the era of Fínsnechta Fledach, Bran son of Conall, and the saints, Moling and Adomnán – all of whom feature in its closing episode. Its folk-motifs involving kings disguised as servants spying out the camps of their enemies, together with the Trojan Horse motif, and the grotesque caricaturing of the holy men, Moling and Adomnán, all suggest a time of writing some centuries later than the events described. So, too, does the ambiguous presence of Máedóc grandson of Dúnlang who presented Brandub with gifts of a flesh-hook, cauldron and weapons, and we are introduced to an Áedán, bishop of Glendalough, who acted as Brandub's ambassador and who is stated to have been the half-brother of Áed mac Ainmerech. Máedóc Ua Dunlainge was the saint associated with Clonmore in Uí Felmeda, just over the Wicklow border in north-east Carlow.[40] Although his monastery was located within Brandub's own territory, this Máedóc seems to have been a saint of the rival Uí Dunlainge. Other episodes such as the defection of the Ulstermen to the Leinster side contain glaring anachronisms which show that the *Bóruma* in its present form cannot have been compiled prior to *c.*825. The confused reference to the Ulsterman, Diarmait the founder of Castledermot (Dísert Diarmata), in south Kildare, who died in 825, can scarcely have found its way into the *Bóruma* until at least a century of time had elapsed to allow for the confused association of Diarmait with events of *c.*600. It is possible that the notion of an alliance between the Leinstermen and the men of Ulster was inspired by just such an alliance in the time of the Leinster king, Diarmait mac Maíl na mBó (1042-72).[41] But earlier evidence for traditional friendship between the Laigin and the Ulaid does exist. In the tenth-century *March Roll of the Leinstermen* the Ulaid are accorded special status as traditional allies of the Leinstermen. This work consists of a series of stanzas constructed on the formula *If the tribe of X attack* *the Leinstermen, then the Leinster tribe of Y will defend the Province.* So for instance, we are told that if the Clann Conaill and [Cenél] nEógain of the Northern Uí Néill attack Leinster, then the Fortuatha of the Leinstermen (the Wicklow tribes) or the Men of Cualu 'will raise a red weaponed fight against them'. But the author goes on to say of the Ulstermen: 'I must not caution the great province of the blessed Brandub against the men of Ulster. So long as the Lord rules over Heaven, they shall not come to fight against my communities.'

The reference to Leinster as the province of Brandub may suggest that the compiler was thinking here of the treaty concluded between the Ulaid and the Laigin during the invasion of Áed Mac Ainmerech in 598 as narrated in the *Bóruma* saga. It does appear that the eleventh century is far too late a time for the *Bóruma* to have taken shape.

There is a case to be made for the antiquity of some of the traditions at the core of that section of the *Bóruma* which centres on Brandub and the battle of Dún Bolg, in spite of obvious saga elements. The chief players on the Leinster side in Brandub's camp are identified as the kings of Uí Failge and the Uí Máil. These rulers are clearly presented as Brandub's principal satellite kings – and by implication, suitable candidates for the kingship of all the Leinstermen. It was the Uí Failge who brought about the death of Cummascach, while Rón Cerr of the Uí Máil is named as the slayer of Áed mac Ainmerech. Indeed, Brandub is seen to have had little or no part in the slaughter of the Uí Néill army and he clearly was not responsible (in the saga at least) for the slaying of Áed mac Ainmerech – all of which was engineered by Rón Cerr of Uí Máil. This is not what we should expect from a saga concocted by Uí Cheinselaig warlords from say the late tenth century onwards, when the Uí Failge and Uí Máil would scarcely have provided kings of suitable rank as chief sub-kings for the king of all the Leinstermen.

Whatever the precise historical status of Áedán, bishop of Glendalough, it is remarkable that Glendalough and Clonmore (in north-east Carlow) play leading roles along with Kilranelagh as the holy places in the tale of Brandub's victory. Ferns, on the other hand, – that later centre of Uí Cheinnselaig power – finds no mention. In the Latin *Life* of Kevin of Glendalough, the hounds of Brandub are said to have pursued a boar which took refuge in Kevin's oratory.[42] Later in the *Life* we are introduced to 'a certain king of the Leinstermen' who sought out Kevin at Glendalough to obtain the holy man's advice on how to deal with an invading Uí Néill army. Kevin did not allow the ruler to enter the valley, but delivered his advice to the king, admonishing him to defend his people if all else failed.[43] The ruler is nowhere named, but Brandub was most likely intended, since Fáelán of the Uí Dúnlainge – that other Leinster ruler taken into contact with Kevin while yet a boy – cannot have been meant. This *Life* of Kevin is remarkable for the high profile which it affords to Brandub and elsewhere to the Uí Cheinnselaig generally, who do not appear as a distant people to the south, but as neighbouring warlords. There is mention, for instance, of brigands of Uí Dega of the Uí Cheinnselaig who had lodged themselves in the mountains of Glendalough and were preying off the Uí Máil inhabitants of that region.[44] So Brandub's friendly contact in the *Bóruma* saga, with Áedán, bishop of Glendalough, as well as the west Wicklow location there, of his military operations, all supports a case for some early traditions being enshrined in the *Bóruma*.

Byrne was correct in identifying the Brandub section of the *Bóruma* as essentially a king-saga in the *Scél Senchus* of the Leinstermen.[45] That in itself does not prove its antiquity, but it does suggest it may have originated, at least, in the same early historical tradition as *The tales of Máelodrán* or the *Fingal Rónáin*, and may well be much earlier in its original composition than the apochryphal anecdotes attached to it, relating to Adomnán and Moling, or to Diarmait son (*recte* grandson) of Áed Rón of Ulster. Whether or not we agree with all the details of Price's topographical discussion on the *Bóruma*, we must accept that the places mentioned in the annals and the *Boruma* saga, associating Brandub with his two consecutive victories at Dún Buchat and Dún Bolg, all relate to the west Wicklow region and to the territory of the Uí Máil in particular. The question presents itself as to why Brandub, a supposedly south Leinster king, was campaigning over a sustained period so far north within Leinster. While his presence at Mag Ochtair in north Kildare can be explained as a response to the threat of an invasion of Leinster from her northern enemies, the later Uí Néill attacks on Brandub in 597 and 598 in the Glen of Imaal region cannot be so easily explained topographically. The *Bóruma* saga's heavy emphasis on the upper Slaney and Imaal region in Wicklow is also surprising, as it is suggestive of an early tradition. Had the *Bóruma* been a later medieval work, we should have expected it to have associated Brandub with the later tenth- and eleventh-century Uí Cheinnselaig homeland in Wexford and south Carlow, but instead it follows the topographical tradition laid down in the early annals.

The settlement of the Uí Cheinnselaig in Wexford may have been a comparatively late phenomenon. The genealogies show that the centre of dispersal of the Uí Cheinnselaig in the sixth and seventh centuries was located in northern Carlow and south-west Wicklow, and that from there, various branches moved south through Carlow and eventually into Wexford. The main branch of Síl Fáelchon moved into northern

Wexford, where Ferns was to become the chief centre of the dynasty up to the time of Diarmait mac Murchada and the Anglo-Norman invasion. At the opening of the seventh century, this migration can only have been in its initial stages. Tullow (Tulach mic Fheilmeda) in northern Carlow was probably one of the earliest centres of Uí Cheinnselaig power. Ambitious Uí Cheinnselaig kings who coveted the kingship of all the Leinstermen would have been tempted to expand north from there in order to obtain a central foothold in Leinster politics – geographically as well as politically. The region to the south was inevitably peripheral to the life of the rich heartland of Leinster in the upper Barrow valley and in the Liffey plain. Any expansion from the Tullow region could best have been achieved by pushing north along the western foothills of the Wicklow mountains. In view of the weakness of the Uí Failge and Dál Messin Corb – those older tribes who once supplied kings for the whole province – it is not surprising to find Brandub trying to push north and establish himself in west Wicklow.

The *Life* of Finian of Clonard shows that saint receiving land for his monastery at Aghowle (Achad Aball), in the extreme south-west of Wicklow, from the Uí Cheinnselaig king, Muiredach [Máel-Brugach] mac Óengusa. Finian is also said to have blessed Muiredach's queen and through her, their child, Eochu, and their grandson, Brandub mac Eachach. All of these men, as we have seen (table 2.4), had ruled in their turn as kings of Uí Cheinnselaig. Since Brandub died in 605, we should expect that his grandfather, Muiredach, was active *c.*520-40, an estimate which tallies well with the fact that his contemporary, Finian, died of the Great Plague in 549. Aghowle was founded early on in Finian's Irish monastic career, perhaps *c.*530, for that saint eventually founded Clonard (Cluain Iraird) in the extreme south of county Meath near the later Leinster border with Brega. Aghowle is about five miles east and south-east of Tullow, and this episode in the *Life* of Finian confirms the concentration of Uí Cheinnselaig power in south and south-west Wicklow in the first half of the sixth century. The region about Baltinglass is but a short distance from Tullow, and the numerous forts which command a view of the fertile lowlands of the Barrow and Slaney valleys, testify to the strategic importance of this region. Whoever held the Glen of Imaal not only controlled the lowlands to the west, but also held a key pass along which goods, traded from Britain through the estuaries at Arklow and Wicklow, were carried over the mountains and into the interior of Leinster and beyond. But to achieve his objective in west Wicklow, Brandub had to overcome the Uí Máil who remained the single most powerful dynasty in Leinster at this time and who dominated the kingship of all the

Leinstermen throughout the late sixth and the seventh centuries. Brandub of the Uí Cheinnselaig, for all his prowess, real and fictitious, was but one of a number of successful challengers who won fame for their dynasties by temporarily wresting the Leinster kingship from the Uí Máil, who continued to act as the holders of that office long after Brandub's time.

Brandub must have reached the height of his power when he defeated and slew the Uí Néill overking, Áed mac Ainmerech, at Dún Bolg in Wicklow in 598. His victory was all the greater since Áed had clearly embarked on an expedition to avenge the death of his son, Cummascach, at the hands of Brandub in the previous year. The Annals of Ulster show that Áed had come with allies, since the king of Uí Maicc Uais was slain in his army, while the *Bóruma* includes other, more unlikely, allies of Áed, such as the Ulaid who were said to have betrayed the Uí Néill on this expedition.[46] The Leinster victories at Dún Buchat and Dún Bolg in 597-8 may be viewed as part of a wider struggle between the Leinstermen and the Uí Néill in the sixth century. While the Leinstermen successfully repulsed Uí Néill invaders and thwarted their attempts at vengeance in 598, the outcome of that wider struggle for dominance over the Central Plain of Ireland was clearly to lie with the Uí Néill in the longer term. It was the Uí Néill who controlled the greatest resources in terms of land and of tributary allies, stretching from Malin Head to Birr. And while the Uí Néill could not have hoped to conquer Leinster, they seemed determined to bring that province into a tributary position. The Southern Uí Néill must have considered the Leinstermen as a threat to their hold over the Plain of Brega (county Meath) and to their domination of the southern midlands in Mide and central county Offaly. So, Brandub's last battles in 605 ended in his downfall at the hands of Uí Néill aggressors. He was defeated in the battle of *Slaebre* and like many a weakened Irish warlord, before and after him, he was subsequently slain by his own kinsmen. A later hand in the Annals of Ulster attributes his death to Sarán Saebderg, *oirichinneach* or hereditary warden of Templeshanbo (Senboth Sine, to the east of Mount Leinster, county Wexford). An alternative later tradition (also in the Annals of Ulster) located his end in a battle at Dam Chluain. The Annals of Tigernach claim that Sarán, the slayer of Brandub, was the *cliamuin* or son-in-law of the Leinster king.[47]

A later hand (H2) in the Annals of Ulster (supported by the Annals of Tigernach) attributes Brandub's defeat to Áed Uairidnach, who was a successor of Áed mac Ainmerech in the overkingship of the Uí Néill. Áed Uairidnach was of the Cenél nÉogain (in the Tyrone area) and it would have been to his advantage to avenge the slaying of his Cenél

Conaill predecessor and uphold the honour of the northern holders of the Uí Néill kingship. It is noticeable that Áed Sláine of Brega, who ruled immediately after Áed mac Ainmerech and before Áed Uairidnach, does not seem to have attacked Leinster, and held aloof from this feud. I have shown elsewhere that Áed Sláine was in fact allied with the Leinster Uí Failge.[48] The Annals of Ulster is the only source to claim that Brandub had a reign of thirty years over the Leinstermen. He is credited with a reign of ten years in his own Uí Cheinnselaig king-list and in the king-lists of the kings of all Leinster. While the figure in the king-lists cannot be accepted without question, it provides a more plausible estimate than the later account of a thirty-year reign in the entry of Brandub's death in the Annals of Ulster.

Early Uí Cheinnselaig Kings: A case study in early Irish royal succession

The fall of Brandub seems to have brought about the eclipse of his Uí Felmeda sept among the Uí Cheinnselaig. One other member of the Uí Felmeda held the Uí Cheinnselaig kingship after Brandub's time, namely his first cousin, Crimthann son of Ailill (no. 14, table 2.4). The kingship did not, however, become the sole property of the rival descendants of Nath-Í, the Síl Chormaic, Síl Fáelchon and Síl Máeluidir. From the Síl Felmeda it passed for a time into the hands of the Síl nÁeda meic Óengusa who were very distant relatives of the descendants of Nath-Í. Conall (no. 13) and Dúnchad (no. 15) belonged to this line, whose genealogy was not recorded in the major collections after that of Dúnchad's son, Óengus. Rónán son of Colman appears as sixteenth king in the Uí Cheinnselaig king-list, and from his time onwards the tribal kingship remained with the septs descended from Nath-Í son of Crimthann. It is almost certainly this Rónán son of Colmán of the Uí Cheinnselaig whose death is entered in the Annals of Ulster in 624. This entry was taken by Paul Walsh and by John Ryan to refer to Rónán of the Uí Dúnlainge,[49] but there is good evidence to suggest that the Uí Dúnlainge had not yet established a successful candidate in the kingship of all Leinster by this time. The evidence, on the contrary, points to Rónán son of Colmán who died in 624 as an Uí Cheinnselaig king. The Annals of Ulster note the death of Crundmáel Erbuilg son of Rónán in 656 and Crundmáel was certainly the son of Rónán of the Uí Cheinnselaig. Crundmáel's name appears as no.18 in the Uí Cheinnselaig king-list (table 2.4) while he is styled 'king of the Leinstermen' (*regis Lagenensium*) at his death in 656 in the Annals of Ulster. It is more likely that the Rónán son of Colmán who died in 624 was indeed the father of Crundmáel Erbuilg of Uí Cheinnselaig who died in 656 rather than being of the Uí Dúnlainge of north Leinster.

Brandub died in 605 and we may conclude that several kings ruled over the Leinstermen between that time and the death of Crundmáel of Uí Cheinnselaig in 656. We find this, indeed, to have been the case. The king-list of the overlords of the Leinstermen (as opposed to tribal kingships) shows that the first of these rulers was Rónán son of Colmán, followed by Crimthann Cualann of the Uí Máil of Wicklow, Fáelán of the Uí Dúnlainge, and finally by Crundmáel [Erbuilg] of the Uí Cheinnselaig (see table 2.7). The reference to Crundmáel Erbuilg in the Leinster king-list is ambiguous. After listing Brandub in the kingship, the king-list of the Leinstermen continues:

> Ronan son of Colman [reigned] nine years. He died of a haemorrhage. Others say that Crundmáel son of Rónán took the kingship.

Crundmáel's name was most likely excised from the earliest version of this list by later Uí Dúnlainge historians, and at some later time still, an editor with access to an earlier tradition inserted the present note as found in the Book of Leinster. Whatever the reason for the confusion, we need to bear in mind that the Annals of Ulster vouch for Crundmáel's status as king of the Leinstermen in 656. The Annals of Ulster do not specify that Rónán son of Colmán who died in 624 was king of the Leinstermen, but the very mention of the death of a Leinster ruler at this early time, clearly implies that he was either king of the province or at least aspiring to that office. Walsh overcame the difficulty of Crundmáel son of Rónán being referred to as king of the Leinstermen in the Annals of Ulster in 656, by preferring the reading of the Four Masters at 650 who describe Crundmáel as *toísech* or 'leader' of South Leinster (*Laigen Desgabhair*). The use of *toísech* is foreign to the earliest strata of the annals and the Four Masters provide merely a garbled version of the Annals of Tigernach who describe Crundmáel as 'king of south Leinster (*Ríg Laigen Desgabair*)'. This title does not in any way contradict the testimony of the Annals of Ulster. Crundmáel's name appears in both the king-list of all the Leinstermen and in the king-list of his own tribe of Uí Cheinnselaig. This is what we should expect, for the king of the province would also have been king of one of the leading tribes of the Leinster confederacy.

The genealogists name the sons of Rónán son of Colmán of the Uí Dúnlainge as Máelochtraig, Máelcháich and Máeltuile (table 2.8), and they make no mention of a Crundmáel. One of the two recorded sons of Rónán mac Colmáin of the Uí Cheinnselaig, however, is Crundmáel (table 2.4) whose numerous descendants played an important role in the kingship of Uí Cheinnselaig. Uí Néill hostility continued against the

Table 2.4 Kings of Uí Cheinnselaig A.D. 500-1072

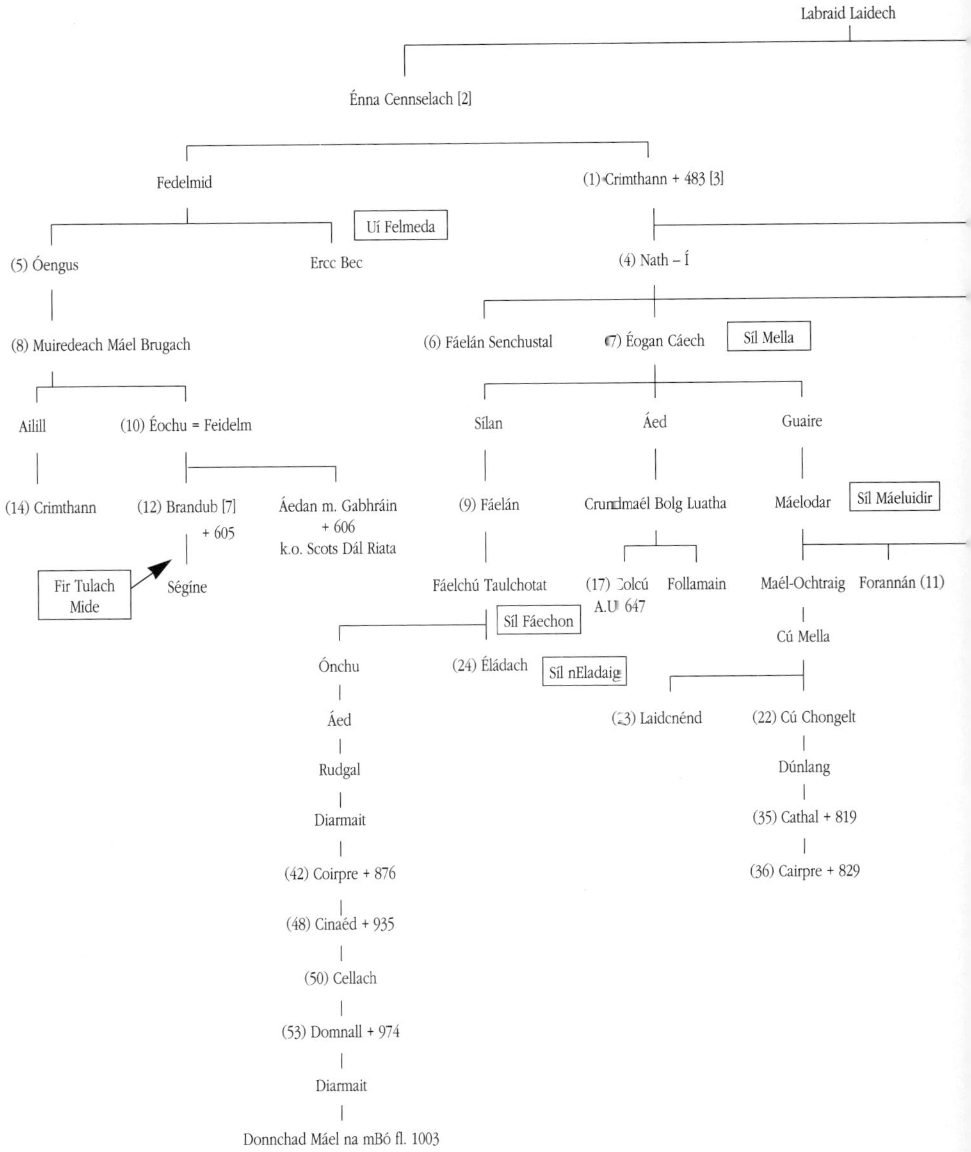

(6) Numbers in round brackets indicate order of succession to Uí Cheinnselaig kingship.
[6] Numbers in square brackets indicate order of succession to Leinster kingship.
A.U. = Annals of Ulster
k.o. = king of
* Fróech and Findchad were probably kings of Dál Messin Corb.

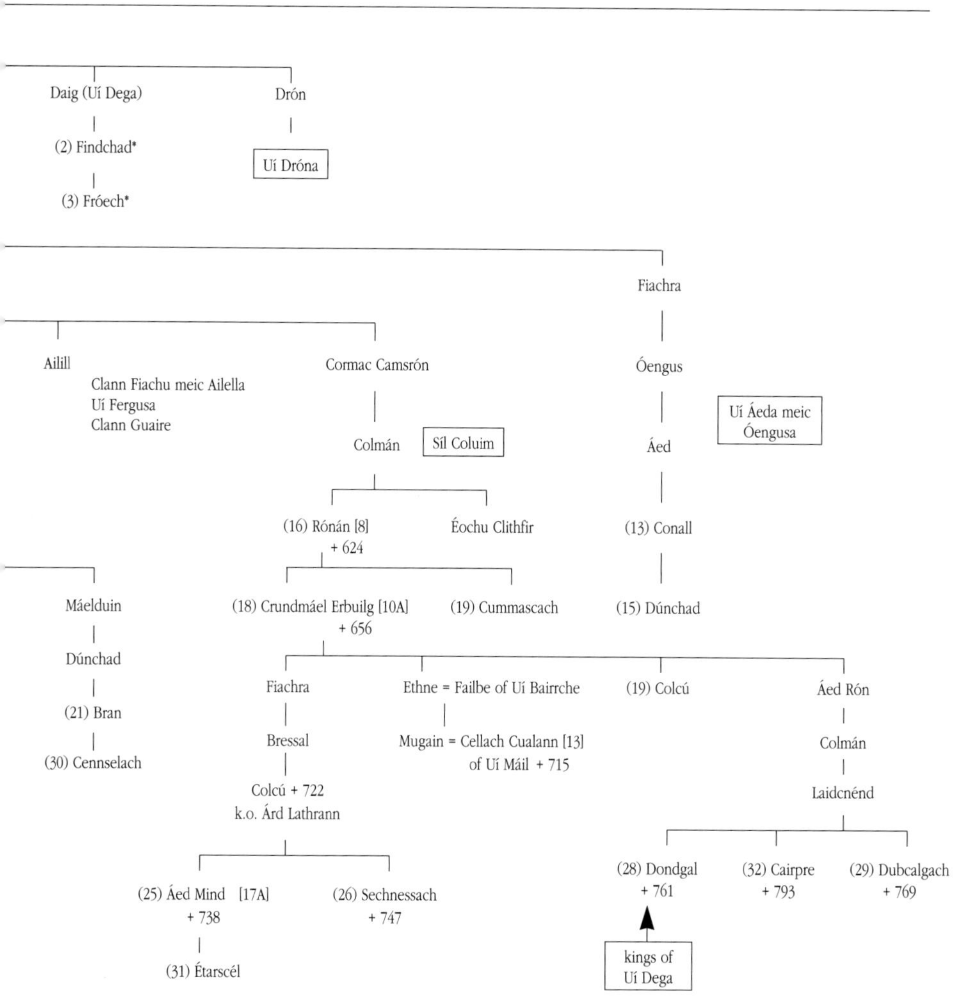

Notes:
Uí Cheinnselaig kings not accounted for in genealogy:

(20) Colum mac in espuic

(27) Cathal hua Cinaid

The full order of Uí Cheinnselaig succession is provided from nos. 1 to 32 only.

Uí Cheinnselaig in the period between 625 and 650. This was also a time when the Uí Cheinnselaig struggled with their Uí Máil and other rivals, to hold on to their share in the circulating kingship of the province of Leinster. We can only dimly perceive these events in the south-east corner of Ireland, from a series of very obscure entries in the Annals of Ulster. These entries refer not to one, but to two quite distinct Uí Cheinnselaig rulers called Crundmáel.

A.D. 626 *Obsessio Boilg Luatha a nepotis Néill.*

628 *Bellum Boilgg Luatho, in quo Fáelán filius Colmáin, rex Laegen uictor erat.*

647 *Bellum Colgan mic Crunnmáel Builg Luatho righ Haue Ceinnselaigh.*

656 *Mors Crunnmael Erbuilc mac Ronain regis Lagenensium.*

Translation:

626 The besieging of Bolg Lúatha by the Uí Néill.

628 The battle of Bolg Lúatha in which Fáelán son of Colmán, king of Leinster, was victor.

647 The battle of Colgu son of Crundmáel Bolg Lúatha, king of Uí Cheinnselaig.

656 The death of Crundmáel Erbuilg son of Rónán, king of the Leinstermen.

The first question centres on the identity of Bolg Lúatha ('Sack of Ashes'). The name could refer to a place – in which case we would read *Crunnmael Builg Lúatho* as 'Crundmáel of Bolg Luatha'. If it were a nickname personal to Crundmáel, we should read *Crunnmáel Bolg Lúatho* ('Crundmáel, the Bag of Ashes'). It may be that Bolg Lúatha was a place – a hillfort or ring-fort associated with the kings of Uí Cheinnselaig in the first half of the seventh century. The association of this place with Crundmáel was such that the place became synonymous with that of the warlord (Crundmáel) who held it. It is probable that Bolg Lúatha which is first mentioned as besieged by the Uí Néill in 626 was none other than Dún Bolg or Brusselstown Ring near Baltinglass in Wicklow, the scene of the slaying of the Uí Néill overlord, Áed mac Ainmerech in 598. The third of these three difficult entries in the Annals of Ulster – the battle involving Colgu in 647 – provides the key to the other two entries relating to Bolg Luatha, 626 and 628. The 647 entry reveals that Crundmáel Bolg Luatha had a son, Colgu, who was king of the Uí Cheinnselaig. This Crundmáel Bolg Luatha is shown from the genealogies to have been quite distinct from his contemporary Crundmáel Erbuilg son of Rónán, who was also an Uí Cheinnselaig king and who died in 656. According to the Book of

Lecan, which alone enables us to tie in his line, Crundmáel Bolg Luatha was the son of Áed son of Éogan Cáech, son of Nath-Í (table 2.4). It will be seen from that genealogical chart that Crundmáel Bolg Lúatha's posterity did not share in the kingship of Uí Cheinnselaig. This cannot, of course, be used in our assessment of Crundmáel himself. We see that his grandfather, Éogan (no. 7), had been king of Uí Cheinnselaig and we should expect that either he or his sons would seek to revive their claim, before the kingship passed out of the ambit of their immediate family or *derbfine*. It will be seen, too, that Crundmáel Bolg Luatha's first cousin, Fáelán son of Sílan (no. 9), eventually established the kingship in his branch of the family (Síl Fáelchon) to the exclusion of many other lines. Crundmáel Bolg Luatha's only recorded son in the genealogies is Follamain, but we have seen from the annals that in 647, another son, Colgu, is accorded the title 'king of Uí Cheinnselaig'. In this, the Annals of Ulster are supported by the king-list of the Uí Cheinnselaig. At this point in the Uí Cheinnselaig king-list, the names of two kings are duplicated, but fortunately a marginal direction enables us to reject the first couple in favour of the second. The correct sequence of the king-list reads as follows:

[16] Rónán mac Coluim .xx	[*A.U.* A.D. 624]
[17] Colgu mac Crundmáel .xi.	[*A.U.* A.D. 647]
[18] Crundmáel Erbuilg mac Rónáin .iiii.	[*A.U.* A.D. 656]
[19] Cummascach mac Rónáin xui.	

The order of names in the king-list is crucial. If Colgu (no. 17) were the son of Crundmáel Erbuilc (no. 18) we would have the highly unusual situation of a father succeeding his son in the kingship. But the order as it stands is in complete harmony with the chronological sequence offered by the Annals of Ulster, where the name of Colgu appears under 647 and the notice of the death of his successor, Crundmáel Erbuilc, at 656.[50] We are not told Colgu died in the battle of 647. He may have done, but if the reign length of the king-list can be trusted, Colgu may not have died until 651. The Uí Cheinnselaig king-list, therefore, is not only in harmony with the evidence of the Annals of Ulster, but also confirms the evidence of the genealogies that Crundmáel Bolg Lúatha and Crundmáel Erbuilc were two quite distinct Uí Cheinnselaig leaders.

We return then, to the record of the Annals of Ulster concerning Crundmáel Bolg Luatha, in the knowledge that although he himself was not king of Uí Cheinnselaig, he was close to it by kin, and his son, Colgu, succeeded Rónán son of Colmán in that kingship. It was this Rónán, rather than his namesake of the Uí Dúnlainge, who also aspired to the kingship of all the Leinstermen on the death of Brandub. We see, therefore, that Crundmáel Bolg Lúatha and his son, Colgu, as heirs to the victories of Brandub, must have inherited, too, his feud with the Northern Uí Néill, and they may well have inherited his ambitions to establish a foothold in west Wicklow. The record, therefore, of the besieging of Bolg Luatha by the Uí Néill in 626, falls into place as a continuation of Uí Néill hostility against the Uí Cheinnselaig, and the tentative identification of Bolg Luatha with Dún Bolg near Baltinglass is also in accord with earlier confrontations between the Uí Cheinnselaig and Uí Néill in this very region in the time of Brandub. Two years later, in 628, Domnall, the new Northern Uí Néill overlord, ravaged Leinster in an inaugural raid. Domnall was the son of Áed mac Ainmerech, and his father and brother had been slain by Brandub. Such a king had every incentive to seek vengeance from the Leinstermen. Crundmáel Bolg Luatha had been defeated in battle (probably earlier) in that year at the hands of Fáelán son of Colmán who was then a challenger for the kingship of all the Leinstermen. The Annals of Tigernach suggest that Crundmáel lost his life in that battle. The victor Fáelán is the earliest attested member of the Uí Dúnlainge who can be shown to have ruled as king of Leinster. His dynasty at this time was establishing its hold over the Liffey plain in northern Kildare. The Annals of Tigernach locate Crundmáel Bolg Luatha's last battle at *Duma Aichir*. There were several places of this name, but Duma Aichir 'in Uí Felmeda in Leinster (*i nUíb Felmeda i Laighnib*)' in north-west county Carlow (Uí Felmeda Tuaid), seems the most appropriate location for a conflict involving the Uí Cheinnselaig at this time.

The front line in the Uí Cheinnselaig wars of expansion from *c.*500 to 650 was located in northern Carlow and south-west Wicklow. Uí Cheinnselaig successes on this front must have been at the expense of the Uí Máil in west Wicklow and the Uí Bairrche in north Carlow. There is ample evidence from the annals and elsewhere for an on-going feud between the Uí Máil and the Uí Cheinnselaig. The Latin *Life* of Fintán of Cluain Édnech (Clonenagh, county Leix) reveals a similar state of hostility between the Uí Cheinnselaig and Uí Bairrche in the period *c.*590. Fintán died in 603, and although he settled in north-west Leinster at Clonenagh, he is shown in his *Life* to have been active further south in Leinster in Uí Dróna (Idrone) in northern Carlow, and not far from Old Leighlin – in that area of conflict between the Uí Bairrche and the expanding Uí Cheinnselaig. We have already encountered Muiredach, the grandfather of Brandub, welcoming St Finian of Clonard to Aghowle *c.* 530. In the *Life* of Fintán, however, we encounter another Uí Cheinnselaig king, Colum or Colmán mac Cormaic, the father of that Rónán, king of all Leinster who died in 624, and grandfather of

Table 2.5 Inter-Tribal Genealogy of the Leinstermen

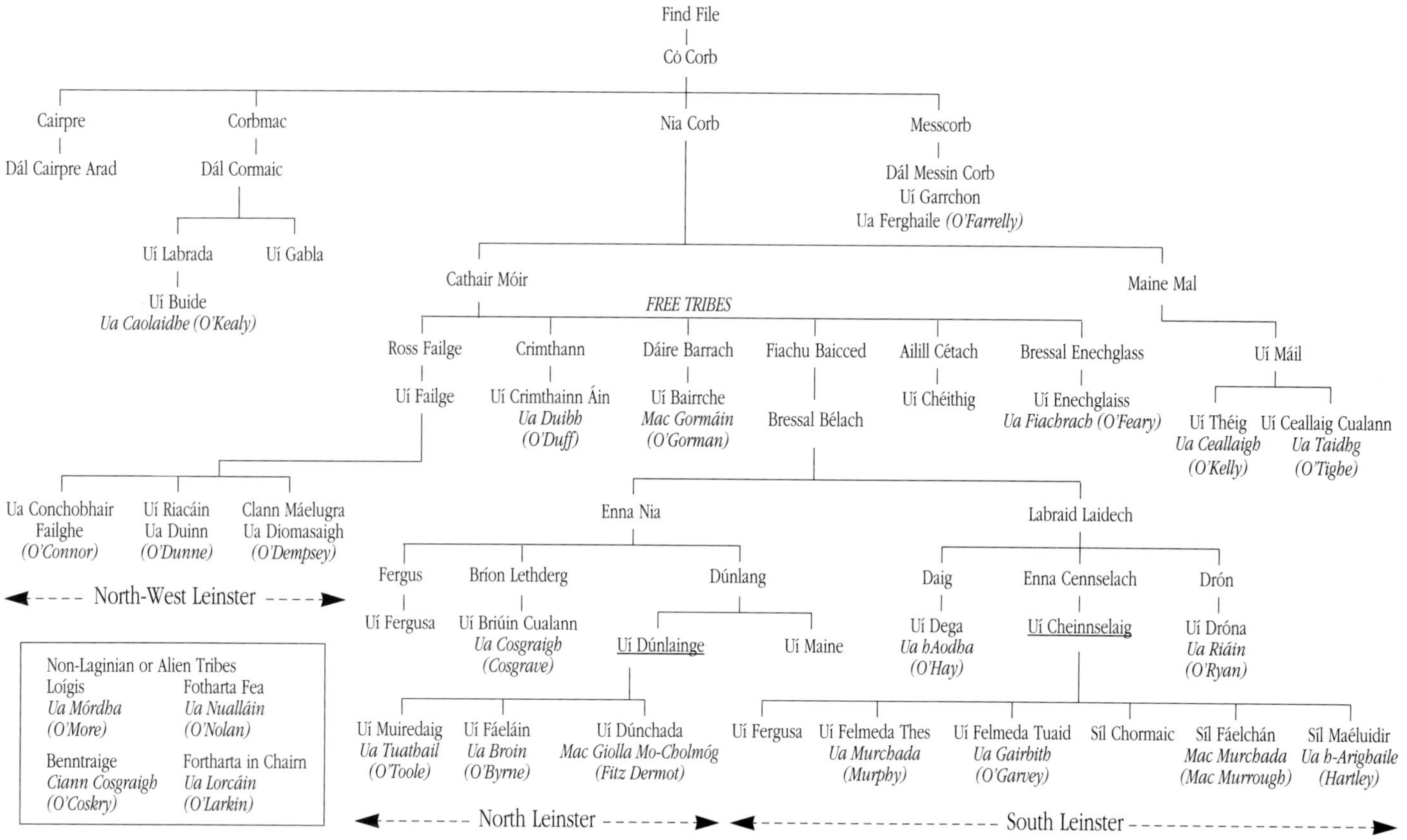

Crundmáel Erbuilg who died in 656. This Colmán, who was the progenitor of the powerful Uí Cheinnselaig sept of Síl Coluim, is given a bad press by the writer of Fintán's *Life*.[51] He is portrayed there as a cruel king who had imprisoned Cormac mac Diarmata, the king of Uí Bairrche, with the intention of putting him to death. Cormac of the Uí Bairrche, on the other hand, was remembered with affection by hagiographers who recorded his piety as a king, and who noted his friendship with St Comgall in distant Bangor in Ulster, where the Uí Bairrche king ended his days in retirement as a monk. Both the *Life* of Comgall and that of Fintán describe Cormac mac Diarmata of Uí Bairrche as king of Uí Cheinnselaig, a term which betrays the late time of compilation of these *lives* when the word *Uí Cheinnselaig* had become synonomous with 'South Leinster'.[52] The *Life* of Fintán describes Colum son of Cormac, who was indeed an Uí Cheinnselaig king as 'king of the Northern Leinstermen (*rex aquilcnalium Laginensium*)'.[53] This may be little more than a hagiographical distortion of an earlier and more reliable tradition. On the other hand, the presence of this anecdote relating to Uí Bairrche and Uí Cheinnselaig hostilities, and dealing as it does with a most obscure period of local Leinster history, underlines the very early nature of the traditions which are embodied in some later Leinster hagiographical collections. What looks at first sight like a passing and garbled reference to an obscure tribal leader whose identity eluded scholars from the time of John Colgan down to our own time, turns out to be a reference to a powerful Uí Cheinnselaig king. Colum mac Cormaic was active in the last quarter of the sixth century. His son probably died in 624, and his grandson certainly died in 656. Colum was indeed a contemporary of Fintán of Cluain Édnech, but the two men were geographically far removed from each other, and they were certainly not candidates for a later forger to invent stories about. Colum's immediate descendants were remarkably successful in their efforts to control the kingship of Uí Cheinnselaig. No less than eleven of his direct descendants had become kings of Uí Cheinnselaig within two centuries of his death. Even more remarkable for an Uí Cheinnselaig king, Colum's son, Rónán, and his grandson, Crundmáel, ruled as kings of all the Leinstermen. The Latin *Life* of Fintán, in describing Colum as 'king of the Northern Leinstermen' may well be accurately reflecting Uí Cheinnselaig domination of North Leinster (Laigen Tuath Gabair) by Colum's house at this time, or shortly afterwards, in the seventh century.

The rise of the Uí Dúnlainge

The early Uí Dúnlainge kings of Leinster are credited by later medieval Irish historians, hagiographers and genealogists with ruling the province and controlling the Liffey plain from the time of St Patrick. These spurious claims to kingship and political dominance of the Uí Dúnlainge were invented by later medieval compilers and synthesisers writing in the tenth century and later, when Uí Dúnlainge descendants had indeed established a monopoly over the kingship of the province. The earlier historical reality, however, was very different from that which later historians strove so hard to invent. The battle between Fáelán and Crundmáel Bolg Lúatha in 628 is the earliest incontrovertible historical reference to the Uí Dúnlainge in early Irish records. And here also, for the first time, we have evidence for the Uí Dúnlainge entering the field as challengers for the kingship of all the Leinstermen. The only Uí Dúnlainge prince who has any claim to a place in the Leinster king-list prior to Fáelán son of Colman, is Rónán mac Colmáin, and we have seen that Rónán of the Uí Cheinnselaig is much more likely to have held the kingship than Rónán of the Uí Dúnlainge. That Rónán, who died in 624, was succeeded in the kingship of the Leinstermen by the Uí Máil king, Crimthann Cualann. Crimthann was slain in the battle of Áth Goan 'in western Liffey plain' in 633. He is identified very fully in the Annals of Ulster as 'Crimthann son of Áed son of Senach, king of the Leinstermen'. His father, Áed Cerr, had been king of the Leinstermen in the late sixth century. Crimthann was an Uí Máil king from west Wicklow (see table 2.10), and his nickname *Cualann* ('of Cualu') associates him with the north-western and western foothills of the Wicklow massif. Since Crimthann Cualann's reign as documented by the Annals of Ulster ran from 624 to 633, the twenty-eight-year reign ascribed to him in the Leinster king-list cannot be correct. But equally, since Fáelán of the Uí Dúnlainge succeeded Crimthann (according to the king-list), and since Crimthann did not die until 633, then the reference to Fáelán in the Annals as king of the Leinstermen as early as 628 cannot be correct.

Fáelán son of Colmán of the Uí Dúnlainge ought not to be confused with his namesake, Fáelán son of Murchad, of that same dynasty, who died in 738 and who founded the Uí Fáeláin branch of Uí Dúnlainge in the eighth century (table 2.6). Ryan accepted the Four Masters' date of 665 for the death of Fáelán mac Colmáin, but a significant point in connection with this king is that his death is ignored by the Annals of Ulster. Dobbs computed a lifespan of 92 years for Fáelán, by accepting the Four Masters' date of 576 for the death of his father, Colmán, and since Fáelán had to be born before that time, his life would have spanned from at least as early as 576 to 665.[54] These dates cannot be taken seriously. The Four Masters date for Fáelán's death (in 665) was borrowed from the Annals of Tigernach. While that compilation may provide an accurate version of a core text for the early annals, its earlier sections also contain computed dates and incorporate whole entries from other later sources such as the Leinster king-lists.

We learn more of Fáelán's place in the Leinster kingship from a study of the genealogies than we can hope to recover from fictitious dates offered by some of the annals. The family connections of Fáelán, as recovered from the genealogies, not only add to our knowledge of the political scene in seventh-century Leinster, but their broad agreement with evidence arrived at independently from the Annals of Ulster and king-lists underlines the accuracy and integrity of much of early Leinster source material. Fáelán's mother, Fedelm, was of the Uí Théig, and of the Uí Maine branch of that sept in particular (table 2.5). Dobbs, who studied the female Leinster genealogies with great care, was not aware that the Uí Théig were a branch of the Uí Máil, to which tribe, Lassi, the grandmother of Fedelm also belonged.[55] Fáelán's succession – perhaps as the first of his line – to the kingship of all the Leinstermen, must have been helped by the fact that his mother and grandmother belonged to the Uí Máil which was at this time the dominant dynasty within Leinster. Fáelán's family alliances were widely spread. His own queen was Sarnat, daughter of Eochu of the Leinster Fothairt, the tribe from whom St Brigit was sprung, and who up to this time controlled the monastery of Kildare. This house, as we learn from Cogitosus, had already become one of the most renowned and wealthy monasteries in Ireland by the seventh century.[56] That Fáelán's marriage alliance with the Fothairt had somehow helped to annex the prestige of Kildare to his Uí Dúnlainge dynasty, is confirmed by our knowledge that Áed Dub, the brother of Fáelán, is described in the genealogies as 'a royal bishop of Kildare'. Kildare may never have been entirely free from powerful outside political influences. Even in the days of its founder, St Brigit, her first bishop Conláed (died 520), was a member of the Dál Messin Corb who at that time were overlords of the Liffey plain. But in the 630s Kildare was taken over by new patrons.

The significance of the new-found Uí Dúnlainge influence at Kildare was not lost on the early compiler of the Annals of Ulster who only included those people in his record whom he considered to be the leading players on the political and ecclesiastical scene in his time. The first contemporary reference to the monastery of Kildare occurs as late as 639 and indeed, it is the first mention of any sort of this place – apart from the record of the death of its founder, Brigit, in 524. The record in 639 refers to the death of Áed Dub, abbot of Kildare.[57] Áed is also described as a bishop in that entry, and he no doubt fulfilled the episcopal functions necessary for the ordination of clergy and other liturgical duties throughout the great *paruchia* of the abbess of Kildare. The entry of Kildare into the annalistic record, therefore, was prompted by the political implications of Áed Dub's position in that monastery. So, too, that same bishop is described in the genealogies as 'royal bishop of Kildare and of all Leinster' – a bold claim, emphasising not only sweeping claims for the ecclesiastical jurisdiction of Kildare, but also emphasising the new political dominance of the Uí Dúnlainge.[58] This Uí Dúnlainge presence at Kildare did not end with the death of Bishop Áed Dub. His nephew, Óengus (table 2.3), was also an abbot of that monastery,[59] and Uí Dúnlainge control here, which began *c.*630, persisted for several centuries. We find that in the ninth and tenth centuries, the Uí Dúnchada branch of Uí Fáeláin (later Mac Giolla Mocholmóc) were running Kildare as if it were part of their royal demesne. The Uí Dúnchada king, Fínsnechta Cetharderc died in Kildare in 808 (table 2.6). His sister Muirenn died as abbess there in 831, and his two brothers, Fáelán (died 804) and Áed (died 829) ruled as royal abbots (*principes*) of that same house. Fínsnechta's great-grandson, Muiredach (died 885) combined the royal abbacy of Kildare with that of the kingship of all the Leinstermen, and his grandson in turn (yet another Muiredach), is described by the Four Masters as abbot of Kildare and 'royal heir of the Leinstermen (*ríoghdhamhna Laighean*)'. This last Muiredach was slain by Olaf Cuarán, the Norse king of Dublin in 967.[60] Nor was the Kildare connection confined to the Uí Dúnchada descendants of the Uí Dúnlainge. An O'Toole ancestor, Tuathal of Uí Muiredaig who died in 854 and who was no. 27 in succession to the kingship of the Leinstermen (table 2.6) is described as 'son of Máel Brigte' (*mac Máele Brigti*) in the Annals of Ulster. Tuathal's father was Muiredach, son of the Leinster king, Bran Ardchenn (table 2.6), and the fact that he was also known by the name *Máel Brigte* or 'Servant of St Brigit' is yet another indication of the close ties between the ruling Leinster house and Kildare in the mid-ninth century. It may be, too, that Glendalough's isolation did not, in the end, save it from the greed of the Uí Fáeláin. We read of an Eiterscél son of Cellach, bishop of Glendalough who died in 814.[61] The designation 'son of Cellach' is ominous, for in spite of the frequency of this name in the annals, Fínshnechta, that ruthless king of the Leinstermen and his two abbot-brothers of Kildare, were all sons of Cellach, the Uí Dúnchada king of Leinster who died in 776. If Glendalough had fallen a prey to Uí Dúnlainge control, that would explain the significance of the invasion of Leinster by the Uí Néill high-king, Áed Oirdnide in 819, when we are told by the annalist that he laid waste 'the land of Cualu as far as Glendalough'.[62] When kings attacked monasteries, they were not attacking the church *per se*, but rather their political rivals who controlled its lucrative resources.

The Latin *Life* of St Kevin of Glendalough brings Fáelán of the

Table 2.6 Descendants of the Uí Dúnlainge A.D. 650-1000

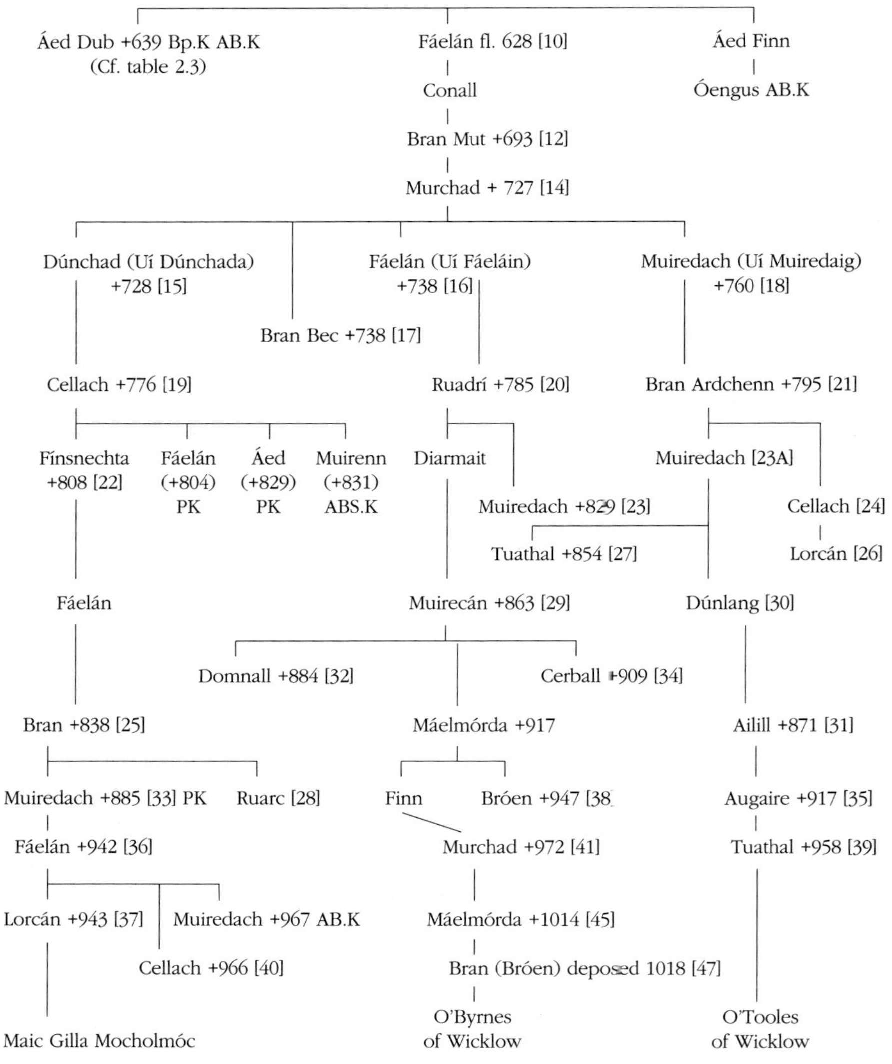

AB.K = Abbot of Kildare ABS.K = Abbess of Kildare
Bp.K = Bishop of Kildare PK = *Princeps* (Royal Abbot) of Kildare.
Numbers in square brackets indicate order of succession to kingship of Leinster. Cf. tables 2.3, 2.7 and 2.8.

Uí Dúnlainge into close association with that monastery. Glendalough, although founded, as we have seen, by a Dál Messin Corb saint, was one of the chief monastic houses located within Uí Máil territory, and became one of Uí Máil's chief monasteries and cult centres on a par with other leading Leinster houses such as Kildare, St Mullins or Ferns. We are told in the Latin *Life* of Kevin that Colmán son of Coirpre, who was a *dux* over a fourth part of northern Leinster, had divorced a certain noblewoman whom he had married in his youth. This woman slew all Colmán's children which he had by a second wife, through magic arts, and when a son, Fáelán, was born to Colmán, he sent him to Kevin for protection and eventually to be educated in Glendalough. Kevin had the boy brought up, not as an oblate, but in the habit of a layman. Eventually the wicked step-mother arrived at Glendalough practising her lethal sorcery against Fáelán from on top of the mountain called *Eanach*, 'which rises over the southern side of the *civitas* or monastic city'. Kevin ordered Fáelán to be hidden from the gaze of the sorceress and he prayed against her as she roved about the mountain-top. She fell from the top of *Eanach* over a steep precipice and headlong into the valley of *Cassain* below.[63] When Fáelán had become a youth, Kevin sent him to Mochonne, a holy man who prophesied Fáelán's greatness and the greatness of his descendants.[64] None of this material is in any way suggestive of a genuine historical tradition. The wicked step-mother motif is universal to folklore, and forecasts of Uí Dúnlainge greatness reflect a situation appropriate to the eighth century and later. Mention of the burial of Fáelán's posterity in Glendalough may even look ahead to much later times.[65] In the seventh and eighth centuries, Uí Dúnlainge warlords were most likely buried at Cell, or Kill, near Naas.

Other anecdotes relating to the infant Fáelán are even less reassuring – such as Kevin's blessing of a willow tree in Glendalough which produced apples to satisfy the young Fáelán, or the tale of Fáelán's escape from his enemies in the form of a deer.[66] On the other hand, it is possible chronologically for Fáelán of the Uí Dúnlainge who first came to prominence in 628 to have been a boy under the tutelage of Kevin, who died in 622. Notable, too, is the gloss on Fáelán's name in the Rawlinson genealogies to the effect that he was the foster-child or *dalta* of Kevin,[67] and we have seen how Fáelán's mother and grand-mother belonged to the Uí Máil, in whose territory Glendalough lay. It is more likely, however, that these traditions about Fáelán and St Kevin tell us that from the eighth century onwards, the Uí Dúnlainge of Kildare were anxious to invent an association between their ancestors and the founder of Glendalough, which in turn helped to legitimise their control over that monastery. The tale of Kevin's struggle with the royal sorceress is perhaps the longest surviving anecdote in the popular folk memory of county Wicklow. In the later medieval Irish *Lives* of Kevin, the jealous queen of Colmán was replaced by a fairy witch called Caineog, accompanied by her attendant fairy women, who were eventually turned into stones by St Kevin 'on the brink of the Lough which is in the Glen.'[68] The tale survived the Middle Ages and after much distortion re-appeared in modern times in the form of a popular ballad recounting how Kevin cast a woman over the rocks to her death in the waters of the Upper Lake. Unlike the medieval tale, in the modern version the woman followed Kevin to his monastic retreat at St Kevin's Bed, in order to seduce him.

Although Fáelán was preceded and followed in the Leinster kingship by Uí Máil kings,[69] and although he was married to a daughter of that house, it would be rash to conclude that he remained on friendly terms with what was essentially a rival dynasty. It would appear that Crimthann Cualann who fell in the battle of Áth Goan in Western Liffey in 633 was in fact slain by Fáelán who then seized the kingship of Leinster for himself. The Annals of Tigernach name Fáelán as one of the victors over the slain Crimthann in that battle. Tigernach also names Conall son of Suibne, the Southern Uí Néill king of Mide (Westmeath) and Failbe Flann, king of Munster, as the allies of Fáelán in the battle.[70] The presence of the Munster king is also vouched for in the Annals of Inisfallen.[71] There is further evidence to support the notion of an alliance between Fáelán and the Uí Néill of Mide. Various annals note the death of Uasal, daughter of Suibne, and sister of Conall of Mide, in 643. While the Annals of Ulster give a garbled version of the obit, Tigernach and *Chronicum Scotorum* claim that Uasal was the queen (*rígan*) of Fáelán, king of Leinster.[72] Fáelán, as we have seen, was also married to Sarnat of the Fothairt, but it was usual for early Irish kings to enter into several marriage alliances with neighbouring dynasties. Fáelán's father, the elusive Colmán, was believed to have been married first to Fedelm of the Wicklow Uí Théig and secondly to Cummine of the Déisi, and Cummine outlived her Uí Dúnlainge husband and went on to marry Brandub of the Uí Cheinnselaig. It might seem tempting to identify Fedelm of the Uí Théig as the wicked step-mother of hagiography who pursued Fáelán to Glendalough – a place which lay within her people's territory. But according to the *Bansenchus*, Fedelm was the mother of Fáelán, and so the spectre of the wicked step-mother recedes once more into the realms of folktale. The study of royal marriages, which is better documented for women in seventh-century Ireland than for most other contemporary societies in Europe, has been much neglected by historians and anthropologists. Royal women 'rotated' among rival Leinster warlords (table 2.5) somewhat as the kingship of the province rotated among those same warlords (table 2.7), who constantly fought each other for that prize in every generation. And just as securing the kingship for any one contender assured the status of his sept (as candidates for kingship in the future) for at least three generations, so too, marriage to a rotating queen – even from an enemy tribe – consolidated a king's standing among leading contenders for kingship within the province. There can be no question that women, because of their royal blood, and because of their ability to move outside their fathers' tribal kingdoms, provided a crucial ingredient in the complex political manoeuvres associated with the sharing out of royal power in early Ireland.[73]

In 604, twenty-nine years before Conall, king of Mide, invaded the plain of Western Liffey, that same Uí Néill king brought about the destruction of a king of Uí Failge. Now in 633 we find Conall assisting his brother-in-law, Fáelán, in gaining the kingship of Leinster at the expense of the Uí Máil. The battle of Áth Goan heralded the success of the Uí Dúnlainge dynasty in Leinster, and the presence of the king of Mide in that conflict on the side of the Uí Dúnlainge may well explain a great deal of Uí Dúnlainge success. It may help to explain, too, something of the paradox that was afterwards inherent in the Uí Dúnlainge dynasty. While they went on eventually to monopolise the kingship of the Leinstermen from the eighth to the eleventh century, and while they controlled that kingship through a tightly organised dynastic succession, they seem to have remained something of a puppet dynasty at the mercy of the Uí Néill. The essentially satellite nature of Uí Dúnlainge kingship is shown by subsequent events involving Leinster relations with the Uí Néill. Inter-marriage with Uí Néill overlords was to continue, and helped to consolidate Leinster alliances to the advantage of the Uí Néill. Bran Ardchenn, the Leinster king of Uí Muiredaig (later O'Tooles) was married to Eithne the daughter of Domnall Mide. Eithne was the daughter of one Uí Néill high-king (Domnall, died 763) and the sister of another (Donnchad Mide, died 797). She and her husband were burned to death by Fínsnechta Cetharderc, a rival Uí Dúnlainge king of Uí Dúnchada (table 2.6), in Cell Cúile Dumai in 795. John Ryan, following O'Donovan, located the scene of this outrage at Kilcoole, south of Greystones, in Wicklow.[74] Such a remote coastal location – far removed from the centre of political power in Leinster – seems most unlikely. Hogan was correct in identifying Cell Cúile Dumai with Coole near Abbeyleix.[75] Fínsnechta succeeded in seizing the kingship of the Leinstermen, having brutally removed the opposition, but his triumph did not go unnoticed by the Uí Néill. Áed Oirdnide, the Uí Néill high-king, entered Leinster in 804 and compelled Fínsnechta to submit to his overlordship. He returned in the following year to depose Fínsnechta and divided the kingship of Leinster between Muiredach son of Ruadrí of Uí Fáeláin (later O'Byrnes) and Muiredach son of the unfortunate Bran Ardchenn who had been slain in 795. In

818, Áed Oirdnide was back meddling in Leinster affairs again, this time dividing the kingship of the Leinstermen between two grandsons of Bran, and in the following year he laid waste the lands of Cualu in West Wicklow as far south as Glendalough. The heady days of the *Bóruma* appear to have been at an end by the ninth century. Leinster, instead of defiantly refusing tribute to the Uí Néill, was by then reduced to what amounted to satellite status.

The hegemony of Uí Máil

Although the Annals of Ulster do not record the date of Fáelán's death, we may arrive at a reasonable approximation of it from the obits of his brother and of his immediate descendants. Counting back thirty-three years to the generation from the death of Murchad, great-grandson of Fáelán who died in 727, we arrive at a date of *c*.628 for Fáelán himself. Similarly counting back over two generations from the death of Bran, a grandson of Fáelán who died in 693, we arrive at a date of 627 for the death of Fáelán. Fáelán was, of course alive and active in 628 when he defeated Crundmáel Bolg Lúatha of Uí Cheinnselaig, and again in 633 when he wrested the kingship of Leinster from the Uí Máil. His brother, Áed Dub, died in 639 and his queen, Uasal, in 643, and we are justified in assuming that he himself most likely died in the period 635-45. Fáelán's successor in that Leinster king-list – Fiannamail mac Máel Tuile of the Uí Máil – did not die until as late as 680. The Annals of Ulster describe Crundmáel Erbuilg, son of Rónán, as king of the Leinstermen on his death in 656. The testimony of these annals is ultimately superior to that of the king-list, and so we must conclude that Fáelán was succeeded as king of all Leinster by Crundmáel Erbolg, and that on Crundmáel's death, Fiannamail ruled from 656 until 680. Fáelán's reign over the Leinstermen, therefore, extended from his victory at Áth Goan in 633 up to *c.*645 when he was succeeded by Crundmáel Erbuilg of Uí Cheinnselaig. There is another reason for placing the death of Fáelán close to 645. The Annals of Ulster record 'the battle of Colgu, son of Crundmáel Bolg Luatha, king of Uí Cheinnselaig' in 647. The implication of entries such as this is usually (but not always) to note the death of the participant. We do know from the Uí Cheinnselaig king-list, that Colgu son of Crundmáel Bolg Luatha was succeeded in that tribal kingship by Crundmáel Erbuilg who also ruled as king of all the Leinstermen. Colgu's battle therefore in 647 may have involved the Uí Cheinnselaig in a civil war to decide the succession to the kingship of all the Leinstermen on the death of Fáelán of the Uí Dúnlainge. The succession to the Leinster over-kingship at this period now reads as follows:

Table 2.7 Kings of the Leinstermen, A.D. 600-700

[6] (10)	Áed Cerr mac Senaig		Uí Máil
[7] (11)	Brandub mac Echach	+ 605	Uí Cheinnselaig
[8] (12)	Rónán mac Colmáin	+ 624	Uí Cheinnselaig
[9] (13)	Crimthann Cualann mac Áeda Cirr	+ 633	Uí Máil
[10] (14)	Fáelán mac Colmain	fl. 633	Uí Dúnlainge
[10A]	[Crundmael Erbuilg mac Rónáin]	+ 656	Uí Cheinnselaig
[11] (15)	Fiannamail mac Máeltuile	+ 680	Uí Máil
[12] (16)	Bran [Mut] mac Conaill	+ 693	Uí Dúnlainge
[13] (17)	Cellach Cualann	+ 715	Uí Máil

Numbers in square brackets indicate reconstructed order of succession. Numbers in round brackets indicate numerical order of succession as found in Leinster king-list in the Book of Leinster.

Fáelán's son, Conall, did not succeed his father in the kingship of the Leinstermen, for on Fáelán's death that kingship reverted first to the Uí Cheinnselaig and then back to the Uí Máil in the person of Fiannamail son of Máeltuile. The Leinster kingship was still in the grip of a tribal confederacy led by the Uí Máil and the Uí Cheinnselaig, and the province was not yet ready to accept the uninterrupted rule of one dynasty, however powerful. Yet Fáelán's role in establishing the future greatness of Uí Dúnlainge within Leinster is without question and it is significant that on the death of his grandson, Bran mac Conaill, in 693, the Annals of Ulster describe that king as 'Bran grandson of Fáelán, king of the Leinstermen'. This, as Dobbs observed, emphasised Bran's descent from his royal grandfather, and it was as if his father Conall, had not existed.[76] By the middle of the seventh century, the Uí Cheinnselaig were falling behind in the race for the over-kingship of the province, leaving the field dominated by the Uí Máil. From the death of Crundmáel Erbuilg in 656 until the opening of the eighth century, Leinster history is concerned with the overthrow of the Wicklow Uí Máil and with the triumph of the Uí Dúnlainge on the Kildare plains.[77]

There is a misplaced entry in the Annals of Ulster recording the death of Toca son of Áed, king of Cualu (*regis Cualann*) under the year 477. Given the rare form of the name and the association with Cualu, this can only refer to Toca son of Áed [Cerr] mac Senaich of the Uí Máil, who is mentioned in the Rawlinson genealogies of the Leinstermen.[78] This Toca was a brother of Crimthann Cualann, that king of Leinster who was slain by Fáelán of Uí Dúnlainge in 633. The notice of Toca became unaccountably misplaced in the Annals of Ulster and belongs somewhere in the period 615-650. While Crimthann ruled as king of the province, his brother Toca ruled as a tribal king of Uí Máil. Both kings had the nickname 'of Cualu' as also had their great-grandnephew, Cellach Cualann who ruled as the last Uí Máil king of all Leinster, and who died in 715. This emphasis on the name *Cualu* shows that the Uí Máil kings who ruled Leinster in the seventh century were based along the western and north-western foothills of the Wicklow mountains. Their territory controlled the Slige Chualann, or the ancient trackway which led from Bohernabreena down through west Wicklow into the Barrow and Slaney valleys. This was a long stretch of country with natural strategic advantages, and which provided a necessary defence for the Uí Máil who were coming under increasing challenge from the Uí Cheinnselaig and the Uí Dúnlainge on the fertile plains below them.

Fiannamail mac Máeltuile was the third Uí Máil king in just over half a century to rule the Leinstermen – proving that his people were still one of the dominant tribes in Leinster. Fiannamail was almost certainly involved in an attack on the Southern Uí Néill in 677. The Annals of Ulster record 'a battle between Fínsnechta and the Leinstermen in a place near Lagore in which Fínsnechta was the victor.' Fínsnechta Fledach ('Snow-Wine') was a king of Brega (county Meath) who ruled at this time as the Uí Néill high-king (675-695). Tara, which had long been abandoned since the sixth century at latest, had been replaced as a residence for the Southern Uí Néill kings of Brega by centres such as Knowth in the Boyne valley, and by the crannóg at Lagore (Loch Gabair) near Dunshaughlin. Since Fiannamail's death in 680 had been brought about by Fínsnechta, it is reasonable to assume that Fiannamail of the Uí Máil led the Leinster attack on Lagore in 677. The Annals of Ulster is a source biased in favour of the Uí Néill, and in spite of the statement that Fínsnechta repulsed this Leinster attack, the fact that it occurred at all is significant. This expedition, organised from the distant Glen of Imaal, and presumably involving numerous satellites of the Uí Máil king, shows that Leinster was still capable of mounting a serious challenge aimed at Uí Néill strongholds in the heartlands of the present county Meath.

The Annals of Ulster note 'the assassination (*iugulatio*)' of Fiannamail mac Máele Tuile, king of the Leinstermen in 680, while the *Chronicum Scotorum* adds that he was slain by Fochsechán, one of his own people at the instigation of Fínshnechta.[79] A gloss and a stanza of verse preserved in the Rawlinson collection of Leinster genealogies also implicates Fínshnechta in the slaying of Fiannamail by Fochsechán.[80] So Finshnechta had taken his revenge for the attack on his fortress three years before. A note in the Leinster king-list in the Book of Leinster acknowledges the tradition that Fiannamail was slain by Fochsechán 'of his own people' (*dá muintir féin*), and it also records a further tradition that the Uí Máil king was slain in the battle of Aife or Selga by the Uí Cheinnselaig.[81] This tradition locates Fiannamail's end in the Glen of Imaal – the heartland of his dynasty – which in turn would fit with the notion of a kin-slaying. Fiannamail was succeeded by Bran mac Conaill, the grandson of Fáelán, that all-important Leinster king of Uí Dúnlainge. It is clear, therefore, that here we have another instance of the succession of an Uí Dúnlainge king being facilitated, indirectly at least, by the intervention of the Uí Néill in Leinster affairs. Fáelán, it will be recalled, had come to power with the help of the Southern Uí Néill king of Mide who had assisted yet again in the overthrow of an Uí Máil king, back in 633. Ryan observed that the later Uí Dúnlainge kings of Leinster – however secure their hold on the province may have been – were not distinguished for their strong leadership.[82] The reason may lie in the possibility that their kingship was a puppet institution created and sustained by their powerful Uí Néill neighbours. This may explain how the Uí Dúnlainge quickly developed an Uí Néill type dynastic succession to the Leinster kingship, involving much tighter rules of succession confined within strict limits of kindred, and abandoning the older oscillating or rotating kingship which prevailed in the days of the Uí Máil and Uí Cheinnselaig confederacy. The Annals of Ulster have nothing to record for the reign of Bran grandson of Fáelán apart from the notice of his death in 693. It is significant, however, that when the Uí Máil recovered the Leinster kingship on his death, Uí Néill and other opposition immediately reappeared. It was as though a concerted attempt was being made to drive the Uí Máil from power.

Cellach Cualann (693-715) was the last Uí Máil king to hold the kingship of all the Leinstermen, and with the possible exception of Áed Mind of Uí Cheinnselaig (died 738), he was the last Leinsterman outside the Uí Dúnlainge dynasty to hold that kingship until Diarmait son of Máel na mBó seized it for the Uí Cheinnselaig in 1042. Clearly Cellach's reign marks a watershed in early Leinster history and deserves close study. If he was the last of his line to rule Leinster, he was also the greatest of Uí Máil kings. This is shown not only from the record of the annals but from the detailed information preserved on Cellach's immediate family in the genealogies. His marriage and family relationships placed him within the centre of an intricate network of alliances involving leading dynasties within Leinster and among the Uí Néill (tables 2.5 and 2.10). He was a first cousin, once removed, of Fiannamail, his Uí Máil predecessor in the Leinster kingship. Cellach's queen, Mugain, was of the neighbouring Uí Bairrche, and her mother in turn was Ethne, daughter of Crundmáel Erbuilg son of Rónán, the Uí Cheinnselaig king of Leinster who died in 656. Cellach's daughter to

Mugain was Conchenn, who married Murchad son of Bran Mut of the Uí Dúnlainge. Murchad was Cellach's immediate successor in the kingship of Leinster. Cellach's son-in-law, Murchad, was the founder of the three ruling branches of the Uí Dúnlainge which dominated Leinster history down to the late eleventh century and beyond (table 2.6). Murchad's son, Dúnchad, was the progenitor of the Uí Dúnchada or Mac Giolla Mocholmóc dynasty of north Kildare and south Dublin. His son, Fáelán, was the progenitor of the Uí Fáeláin or O'Byrnes who were later forced into Wicklow by the Anglo-Normans. Murchad's other son, Muiredach, was the ancestor of the Uí Muiredaig and later O'Tooles who also eventually settled in the Wicklow Hills.

Conchenn, the daughter of Cellach Cualann, lived until 743 to see her husband Murchad's family firmly established as permanent overlords of the Leinstermen. Muirenn, another of Cellach's daughters, is described on her death in 748 as 'the queen of Írgalach' (*regina Írgalaigh*) which identifies her husband as Írgalach grandson of Conaing (*nepos Conaing*), an Uí Néill king of Northern Brega who was slain in 702. Irgalach was a cousin of Fínsnechta Fledach, the enemy of the Uí Máil. The *Ban-Shenchus* or 'Historical Lore of [Royal] Women', claims that Fínsnechta was himself married to Derborgaill, yet another of Cellach's daughters. It is not chronologically impossible, or perhaps as unlikely as it might seem, for Cellach who died in 715 to have been the father-in-law of Fínsnechta who died in 695, for Cellach had become king of the Leinstermen by 692. Finally, the Annals of Ulster record the deaths of two further daughters of Cellach Cualann – that of Coblaith in 732 and Caintigern in 734. Caintigern was remembered in Scottish hagiographical tradition as St Kentigerna, a saint of Loch Lomond.[83] This remarkably detailed record of Cellach's immediate family, which is preserved not only in the genealogies but also in the Annals of Ulster, is without parallel for the seventh and early eighth centuries, and underlines the importance of Cellach and the Uí Máil at this time.

The feud with the Uí Néill continued unabated throughout Cellach's reign. Cellach defeated a combined invading force of Uí Néill at Clane (*Cloenath*), just west of the Liffey and some six miles north of Naas in county Kildare, in 704. Fogartach, the Uí Néill king of Brega was driven from the field and one Bodbcath Mide was slain. The nickname *Mide* ('of Mide' – the present Westmeath) suggests that Bodbcath had some connection with the Clann Cholmain dynasty of the Southern Uí Néill, three of whose leading members carried that name in the eighth century. Bobdcath Mide was the 'son of Diarmait', and therefore almost certainly the son of Diarmait Dian (+ 689) and the brother of Murchad Mide (+ 715), both of whom had been kings of Mide. We are told that

Fogartach, the grandson of Cernach, fled from the field. Fogartach was a descendant of Áed Sláine and he later ruled as Uí Néill high-king from 722 to 724. He was a cousin of Fínsnechta Fledach and a member, therefore, of the southern branch of the Síl nÁedo Sláine of Brega, who ruled from Lagore. Fogartach was eventually slain in 724 by Cináed son of Írgalach of northern Brega. That Cináed may have been the grandson of Cellach Cualann, if he were the son of Írgalach's queen, Muirenn. Cellach of Uí Máil, then, was caught up in a feud at Clane in 704, which went back at least as far as 677 when his predecessor, Fiannamail mac Máeltuile, was almost certainly the leader of an attack on the Uí Néill near Lagore. Yet again in 704, we have evidence for the strength of Uí Máil kingship within Leinster as shown by Cellach's ability to repel an attack, led by a future Uí Néill over-king, on the vulnerable fertile plains in the Liffey basin. The site of Cellach Cualann's victory cannot have been far from where his Uí Máil predecessor, Crimthann Cualann, was slain at Áth Goan back in 633. In that earlier encounter, Crimthann of the Uí Máil fell before the combined armies of the Uí Néill and Uí Dúnlainge. But in 704, the victory went to Cellach in the face of formidable opposition.

Cellach Cualann's victory over the Southern Uí Néill of both Mide and Brega in 704 drew the hostile attention of the reigning Uí Néill high-king, Congal Cend Magair of the Cenél Conaill (in county Donegal) in the far north. Congal Cend Magair also had old scores to settle with the Leinstermen. His grandfather, Domnall, had 'wasted' Leinster back in 628 to avenge the slaying of his father and his brother by the Uí Cheinnselaig. Now in 707, the Annals of Ulster record 'a hosting by Congal son of Fergus against the Leinstermen'. Such a raid was not just inspired by personal vendetta. It was politically advantageous for a reigning Northern Uí Néill over-king to be seen to be defending the honour of his southern cousins and of the entire Uí Néill alliance by punishing the traditional enemy in Leinster. Congal had only begun his reign in 705 and this Leinster expedition was his inaugural raid (*crech ríg*) against the Leinstermen – a punitive expedition in the heroic *Bóruma* tradition which virtually validated his position as high-king. The Four Masters record a stanza relating to this invasion of Leinster which, while adding little to our knowledge of the event, conveys some idea of how an Uí Néill audience expected a punitive raid to be carried out:[84]

> A hosting was made by Congal of Cend Magair, son of Fergus Fanaid, against the Leinstermen, and he obtained his demand from them. On returning home from this expedition, Congal spoke thus:

Bid me farewell, Plain of Liffey
Long enough have I been in your lap.
Beautiful the fleece [that was] on thee
You were safe except [for] your roof, O fort of Naas
The Plain of Liffey was so till now, today it is a scorched plain.
I will come to re-scorch it
That it may know a change.

The brunt of this attack, and the consequent payment of tribute, must have been borne by the Uí Máil. It was Cellach and his Uí Máil who defended the Liffey plain from the Southern Uí Néill at Clane in 704, and as overlords of the Leinstermen, they would have been expected to defend the same vulnerable region from Congal Cend Magair in 707. Although the Uí Máil centre of power was located in the Glen of Imaal, they would have controlled the Liffey basin directly or indirectly at this time.

The Annals of Ulster have no mention of any Leinster notables who were slain during Congal Cend Magair's invasion. If we can trust the general tone of the Four Masters' poem, it would seem that the Leinstermen prudently withdrew in the face of massed Uí Néill opposition, and the land was given up to a scorched earth assault. This may have had an adverse effect on the prestige and credibility of Cellach Cualann and his Uí Máil hegemony, and their Uí Dúnlainge and Uí Cheinnselaig rivals were swift to take advantage of any sign of weakness. Two years after the Uí Néill invasion, the Uí Cheinnselaig slew two of Cellach Cualann's sons in the battle of Selg in 709. The detail offered on this battle in the Annals of Ulster shows it to have been considered a major engagement at the time. It certainly marked a turning point in the affairs of the Uí Máil: 'The battle of Selg in the Fortuatha of the Leinstermen against the Uí Cheinnselaig, in which fell Fiachra and Fiannamail, two sons of Cellach Cualann. And Luirg with the Britons of Cellach [also fell]. And shortly afterwards, Coirpre son of Cú Coluinn was slain.'

The general location of this battle is given as the Fortuatha Laigen – among the tribal territories of the Wicklow mountains. It is clear from the saga of *Fingal Rónáin* that this *bellum Selggae* took place in the Glen of Imaal, so that the Uí Cheinnselaig had attacked the very centre of Uí Máil power about Kilranelagh. We note from the account in the Annals of Ulster that Cellach Cualann had enlisted the help of British warriors in an effort to save his tottering kingship. These Britons were part of wandering warbands – exiles from the north-western British kingdom of Rheged, recently conquered by the Northumbrian English.[85] We find Britons active in Ulster in 697 and 703. Írgalach, king of Brega, the son-in-law of Cellach Cualann, was slain by Britons on Ireland's Eye in 702. The location of that island off Howth Head suggests that Írgalach may have met his end while engaged in negotiations with these exiles, or he may have been held for ransom by them.

The loss of the two sons of Cellach Cualann in this battle at Selg was a major blow to Uí Máil fortunes. When Cellach died six years after this defeat in 715, Murchad mac Brain of the Uí Dúnlainge seized the kingship of the Leinstermen and his dynasty held on to that over-kingship for the next four centuries. Crimthann, yet another son of Cellach, was slain in battle at Belach Licce in 726. Crimthann was described as 'at a young age' (*immatura aetate*) when he fell, which suggests he was only a child or an infant when his father died in 715. The only other recorded son of Cellach Cualann who was capable of succeeding his father, was Áed, but he lost his life in an encounter (*congressio*) among the Leinstermen at the battle of Finnabair in 719. This battle which was clearly a struggle between the Uí Máil and the Uí Dúnlainge was fought either at Fennor, in the barony of Offaly and within two miles of the Curragh of Kildare, or perhaps at Finnore near Tallaght, county Dublin. In either case, the prize was control of the Liffey plain, and in this battle the Uí Máil finally lost their claim to the kingship of the province.

The fall from power of the Uí Máil was rapid. The next member of their dynasty to find a mention in the Annals of Ulster was Fianngalach son of Murchad whose death is recorded in 737. Significantly, he is described as king of Uí Máil (*rex Hu Máil*), the tribal kingdom of his own people, who from now on were to come under increasing pressure from the Uí Dúnlainge and later, in the next century, from viking Northmen along the Wicklow coast. Significant, too, is the fact that this Uí Máil king, Fianngalach, cannot be tied into the surviving genealogies of his tribe. The state of preservation of early Irish genealogical records for any given generation is often an accurate reflection of the political status of the people whose genealogies were being recorded. Just as extraordinary detail survives on the immediate family of Cellach Cualann, so in the generation after his death, the Uí Máil genealogies confine themselves to isolated and direct vertical lines of descent. Relevant, too, is the fact that the Uí Máil tribal king-list has not survived. It appears that even the kingship of Uí Máil passed away from Cellach Cualann's own sept after the downfall of his sons, and was held by another branch of the tribal aristocracy. Cellach's descendants, the Uí Cellaich Chualann, survived as a distinct group within Uí Máil, located in northern Cualu along the foothills of the Dublin mountains south of Tallaght and along the northern section of the Wicklow-Kildare border.

The kin-slaying of Rónán *(Fingal Rónáin)*: swansong of Leinster's heroic age

The fall from power of the Uí Máil left a lasting impression on the saga tradition of the Leinstermen. The *Fingal Rónáin* or 'kin-slaying of Rónán' survives in the language of the late Old Irish period and deals with a tale of jealousy and revenge which convulsed a royal court in seventh-century Leinster. The central characters in the story – Rónán and his son Máel Fothartaig – have been dubiously identified by Greene who, in his 1955 edition of this saga, followed Kuno Meyer's historical interpretation of events first put forward in 1892.[86] Meyer identified Rónán of the saga with Rónán mac Colmáin, that king of the Leinstermen who died in 624. By Meyer, and later by Greene, Rónán mac Colmáin of the annals was viewed as an Uí Dúnlainge king, whereas we may now identify that Ronan who died in 624 as a king of Uí Cheinnselaig. It so happens that Rónán of the Uí Dúnlainge did have a son, Máel-Ochtraig, and two other sons, Máel-cháich and Máeltuile, recalling Máeltuile, the son of Máel Fothartaig in the *Fingal Rónáin* saga. Rónán mac Colmáin of the Uí Cheinnselaig had two sons, Crundmáel Erbuilg, and Cummascach, both of whom ruled as kings of their tribe, and one of whom (Crundmáel) also ruled as king of the Leinstermen. As for Máel Fothartaig, the hero of the saga of *Fingal Rónáin*, he is stated to have been an *oenmac* or only son of Rónán, but such designations were inserted to heighten the tragic effect on a father who would slay such an only son. The Rónán of the Uí Cheinnselaig, like his namesake in the saga, had a grandson called Áed.

Rónán of the saga predicts the future greatness of this grandson, Áed, and it may or may not be coincidental that Áed, the grandson of Rónán of Uí Cheinnselaig, was the great-grandfather of the three brothers, Dondgal (+ 761), Dubcalgach (+ 769) and Cairpre (+ 793), all three of whom ruled as kings of Uí Cheinnselaig in their turn. The identification of Rónán of the saga with either the Uí Dúnlainge or Uí Cheinnselaig Rónán does not fit the chronological requirements very accurately, although given the vague chronological framework typical of Irish saga material, that in itself is not an insurmountable obstacle. Rónán of the Uí Dúnlainge had brothers Fáelán who flourished in 628 and Áed Dub who died in 639 – all of which suggests he died *c.*620-40. Rónán of the *Fingal Rónáin* married the daughter of Eochaid of Dunseverick (Dún Sobhairce) in Ulster. This Ulster Eochaid is identified in the *Three Fragments of Annals* with Eochaid Iarlaithe, a king of the Cruithin of Dál nAraide who died in 666.[87] According to the *Fingal Rónáin*, Eochaid and Rónán died as a result of the same family strife which was triggered by the slaying of Máel Fothartaig. But Rónán of the Uí Cheinnselaig died as early as 624, and it does not seem, going on strict chronological evidence, at least, that either the Uí Dúnlainge or Uí Cheinnselaig Rónáns qualify as candidates for the father of the saga hero.

Table 2.8 The family of Rónán mac Colmáin of Uí Dúnlainge

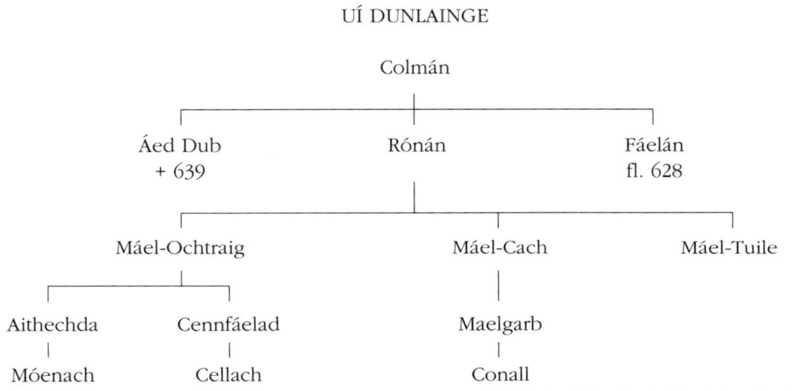

Table 2.9 The family of Rónán mac Colmáin of Uí Cheinnselaig Cf. table 2.4.

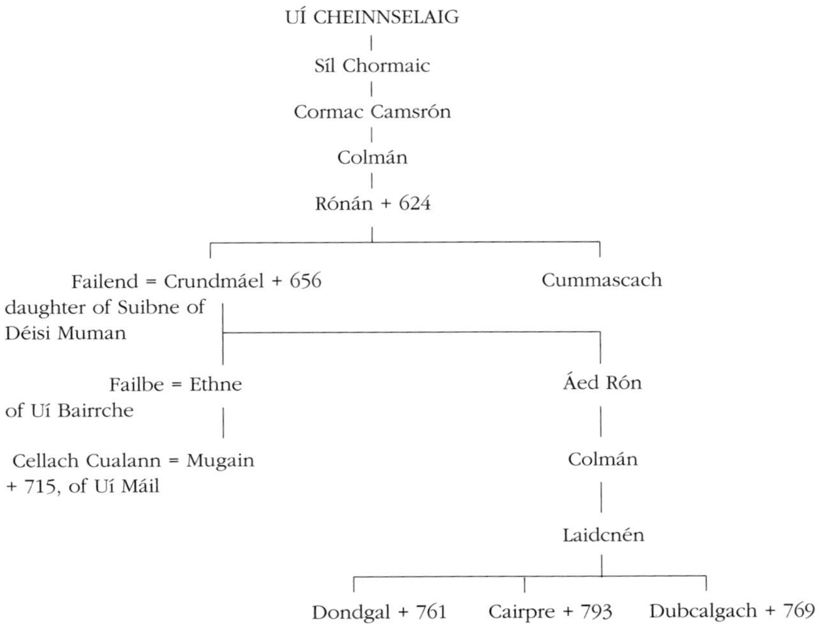

Table 2.10 Uí Máil Kings of Leinster. Cf. table 2.7.

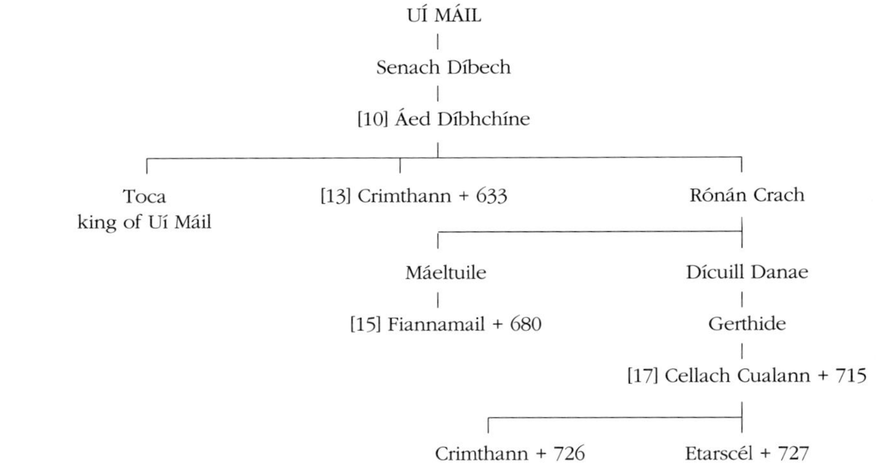

Numbers in square brackets indicate the order of succession to the Leinster kingship. This reconstructed order of succession is different from the original order as given in the Leinster king-list in the Book of Leinster.

There was never much justification for identifying the heroes of the *Fingal Rónáin* with kings of either Uí Dúnlainge or Uí Cheinnselaig. There is a note in the major genealogical collections to the effect that 'Rónán had a son, Máel Fothartaig. It is that Máel Fothartaig who was killed by his father through jealousy.' Other garbled manuscript readings claim that Máel Fothartaig was slain by his brother and refer to Máel Fothartaig's two sons, Máel Tuile and Áed, who slew their father's killer in the battle of Lara.[88] It was clearly this genealogical note which prompted Meyer to identify Rónán of the saga with Rónán son of Colmán of the Uí Dunlainge.[89] But the position of this note in the genealogical collections is ambiguous, and it is clear that the compilers were not themselves sure which Rónán it referred to. The note does not appear as an immediate gloss on the pedigree of Rónán of the Uí Dúnlainge. Instead, it is sandwiched between the end of the Uí Dúnlainge genealogy and the beginning of the genealogy of the Uí Máil.

A crucial point in the identification of Rónán of the saga of *Fingal Rónáin* is that he is nowhere called Rónán mac Colmáin in that saga. Yet the patronymic *mac Colmáin* is what we should expect as a first requirement for identifying him with kings of the Uí Cheinnselaig or Uí Dúnlainge. He is named instead, as Rónán mac Áeda, and as such he can be identified with Rónán Crach the son of Áed Díbhchíne of the Uí Máil. This Uí Máil Rónán, although given the rank of a bishop in the

Table 2.11 Dal Messin Corb Genealogy

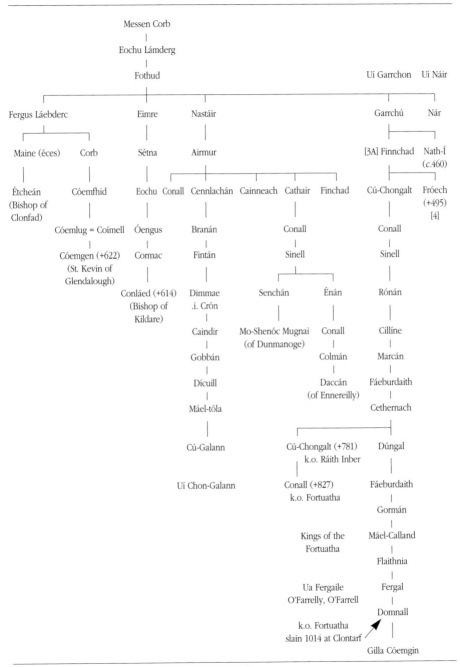

- Messen Corb
  - Eochu Lámderg
    - Fothud
      - Fergus Láebderc
        - Maine (éces)
          - Étcheán (Bishop of Clonfad)
        - Corb
          - Cóemfhid
            - Cóemlug = Coímell
              - Cóemgen (+622) (St. Kevin of Glendalough)
      - Eimre
        - Sétna
          - Eochu
            - Óengus
              - Cormac
                - Conláed (+614) (Bishop of Kildare)
      - Nastáir
        - Airmur
          - Conall
          - Cennlachán
            - Branán
              - Fintán
                - Dimmae .i. Crón
                  - Caindir
                    - Gobbán
                      - Dícuill
                        - Máel-tóla
                          - Cú-Galann
                            - Uí Chon-Galann
          - Cainneach
          - Cathair
            - Conall
              - Sinell
                - Senchán
                  - Mo-Shenóc Mugnai (of Dunmanoge)
                - Énán
                  - Conall
                    - Colmán
                      - Daccán (of Ennereilly)
          - Finchad
      - Uí Garrchon: Garrchú
        - [3A] Finnchad
          - Cú-Chongalt
            - Conall
              - Sinell
                - Rónán
                  - Cillíne
                    - Marcán
                      - Fáeburdaith
                        - Cethernach
                          - Cú-Chongalt (+781) k.o. Ráith Inber
                            - Conall (+827) k.o. Fortuatha
                              - Kings of the Fortuatha
                              - Ua Fergaile O'Farrelly, O'Farrell
                          - Dúngal
                            - Fáeburdaith
                              - Gormán
                                - Máel-Calland
                                  - Flaithnia
                                    - Fergal
                                      - Domnall (k.o. Fortuatha slain 1014 at Clontarf)
                                        - Gilla Cóemgin
          - Fróech (+495) [4]
        - Nath-Í (c.460)
      - Uí Náir: Nár

Numbers in square brackets indicate order of succession to the kingship of Leinster.
k.o. = king of

Table 2.12 Genealogy of Uí Enechglais

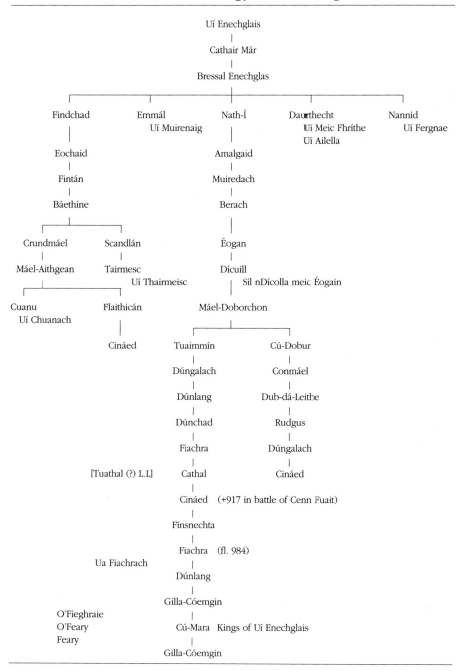

- Uí Enechglais
  - Cathair Már
    - Bressal Enechglas
      - Findchad
        - Eochaid
          - Fintán
            - Báethíne
              - Crundmáel
                - Máel-Aithgean
                  - Cuanu — Uí Chuanach
                  - Flaithicán
                    - Cináed
              - Scandlán
                - Tairmesc — Uí Thairmeisc
      - Ernmál — Uí Muirenaig
      - Nath-Í
        - Amalgaid
          - Muiredach
            - Berach
              - Éogan
                - Dícuill — Síl nDícolla meic Éogain
                  - Máel-Doborchon
                    - Tuaimmín
                      - Dúngalach
                        - Dúnlang
                          - Dúnchad
                            - Fiachra
                              - Cathal — [Tuathal (?) L.L]
                                - Cináed (+917 in battle of Cenn Fuait)
                                  - Fínsnechta
                                    - Fiachra (fl. 984) — Ua Fiachrach
                                      - Dúnlang
                                        - Gilla-Cóemgin
                                          - Cú-Mara — Kings of Uí Enechglais — O'Fieghraie, O'Feary, Feary
                                            - Gilla-Cóemgin
                    - Cú-Dobur
                      - Conmáel
                        - Dub-dá-Leithe
                          - Rudgus
                            - Dúngalach
                              - Cináed
      - Daurthecht — Uí Meic Fhríthe, Uí Ailella
      - Nannid — Uí Fergnae

Rawlinson genealogies,[90] was the son of a king of all the Leinstermen (Áed Díbhchíne), the brother of another Leinster king (Crimthann Cualann), and grandfather of another (Fiannamail mac Maeltuile – see Table 2.10). The Uí Máil Rónán's brother (Crimthann) died in 633 and his grandson Fiannamail in 680, all of which suggests a date *c.*620-40 for Rónán's own death, making him a contemporary of Rónán mac Colmáin of the Uí Dúnlainge and also of Rónán mac Colmáin of Uí Cheinnselaig. But since Rónán of Uí Máil is said in the genealogies to have been responsible for the wounding or slaying of his brother, Crimthann, then presumably he reigned over the Uí Máil in the period after 633, a circumstance which takes him closer in time to his supposed contemporary, Eochaid of Dunseverick who died in 666. Rónán of the Uí Máil had a son, Máeltuile, in the genealogies, as indeed had his contemporary Rónán of Uí Dúnlainge, all of which recalls Máeltuile the grandson of Rónán in the saga of *Fingal Rónáin.* A confusion between members of these neighbouring royal families whose sons had the same or similar names is understandable on the part of later generations of learned men who had a hand in the saga-telling process. So, we search in vain in the genealogies for a son of Rónán of Uí Máil called Máel Fothartaig, but it is significant that the Uí Máil Rónán is there remembered for a kin-slaying (or wounding) – that of his brother Crimthann, presumably at the latter's death in 633. Historians and linguists who demand exact genealogical information from saga writers, misunderstand the objectives and indeed the essence of the saga form – which was essentially to tell a good story, broadly reflecting a half-remembered tribal past and above all to entertain an aristocratic audience. It is important however, and also not impossible, to establish whether the *Fingal Rónáin* was originally intended for an Uí Dúnlainge or Uí Cheinnselaig audience, or whether the saga came into being elsewhere within Leinster. Not only has Rónán mac Áeda of the saga the same name as an Uí Máil ruler of the first half of the seventh century, but the topographical setting of the *Fingal Rónáin* is firmly rooted in the Uí Máil heartland of west Wicklow, and knows little or nothing of even the neighbouring Leinster world beyond. Indeed, rarely is an Irish saga so narrowly focussed topographically as the *Fingal Rónáin*, and it is part of the power of this piece to convey a brooding association with Kilranelagh and the surrounding hills of the Uí Máil heartland, which provided the backdrop to the tragic end of a great dynasty.

The tale *The kin-slaying of Rónán* opens abruptly.[91] We are told that Rónán son of Áed was a famous king who ruled over the Leinstermen and that his first wife was Ethne of the Munster Déisi. When she died, Rónán after a long time and against the advice of his equally famous and grown-up son, Máel Fothartaig, married a young girl, the daughter of Eochaid, king of Dunseverick (Dún Sobhairce) in Antrim. On the arrival of the girlish queen (who is never named) at the Leinster court, she instantly fell for the charms of her step-son, Máel Fothartaig, and charged one of her attendant maidens with the task of setting up a tryst for them. After numerous threats from the queen, her maiden eventually revealed to Máel Fothartaig that her mistress wished him to become her lover. Máel Fothartaig repelled her advances and left for Scotland to avoid his father's queen. In Scotland he distinguished himself as befitted a hero at the court of the Scots king. The Leinstermen threatened the ageing Rónán with death if he did not recall his illustrious son. Máel Fothartaig returned via Dunseverick, to find that the kin of his young step-mother were now also encouraging him to sleep with her. He still held aloof and on returning to his father's court continued to avoid her. Congal, the foster-brother of Máel Fothartaig, lured the queen to the Cows of Aife – great stones which looked like cows on the side of the mountain near the fortress of Rónán. Congal confronted the girl-queen several times on the mountain-side and drove her back to her quarters in disgrace, with help from his horse-whip. That evening, Máel Fothartaig remained aloof, hunting out of doors, reluctant to enter his father's court. Rónán lamented the absence of his son's company, and was taunted by the scorn of a rejected woman who accused Máel Fothartaig of having dishonoured and raped her, with Congal's connivance. At that point Máel Fothartaig entered and 'was drying his shins by the fire'. The queen appeared to prove Máel Fothartaig's guilt by tricking him into singing half a stanza of a song which he had previously sung every night to please her:

> It is cold against the biting wind
> For anyone herding the cows of Aife

To which the young queen replied:

> It is a vain herding
> With no cows and no lover to meet.

Rónán, convinced now of his son's guilt and overcome with jealous rage, commanded his attendant, Áedan, to drive a spear through Máel Fothartaig and another through his foster-brother, Congal, as they sat with their backs to the company by the fire. Máel Fothartaig's unfortunate jester, Mac Glass, was disembowelled in the ensuing carnage. Dond, another of Máel Fothartaig's foster-brothers, then went north to Dunseverick and returned with the severed heads of King Eochaid, his wife and their son – and he threw them into the lap of Rónán's queen. That lady, overcome with remorse and grief at the death of her own kin, slew herself with her own knife. The tragic tale ends with the death of Rónán, lamenting the loss of his only son, and apparently beleaguered in his fortress as a battle rages on the plain round about. The reader is left with the sense of ultimate tragedy and the complete destruction of Rónán's dynasty, although there is a hint that dynastic fortunes may revive under the leadership of Máel Fothartaig's son, Áed.

The action of the saga of *Fingal Rónáin* is confined to the fortress of the Leinster king and to Máel Fothartaig's hunting place at the Cows of Aife (*Bae Aife*) on a nearby mountain-side. This is unquestionably the same place, *Aife*, as appears in the *Bóruma* saga in the Glen of Imaal region. In that saga, Rón Cerr, son of Dubánach, yet another king of Uí Máil, went to spy out the Uí Néill camp near Kilbaylet, when the Uí Néill leader, Áed mac Ainmerech, dispatched the troops of Airgialla to hold a position further south in the Wicklow foothills at *Bun Aife* ('the base or foothills of Aife').[92] The final battle at Dún Bolg was fought close by, and if we accept that Dún Bolg was the ancient name of Brusselstown Ring, then Kilranelagh Hill is located only a mile to the south. Price identified the Cows of Aife in the Saga of *Fingal Rónáin* with great rocks on the side of Kilranelagh Hill which look indeed like a herd of cows from afar, and he further identified Kilranelagh Hill with 'White Cow Hill' on the Down Survey map of 1655.[93] In all of this he was supported by the detailed information supplied in the *Fingal Rónáin*, which says of the Cows of Aife:

> [They are] rocks which are on the side of the mountain. They are like white cows from afar. They stand on the *Aife* of the mountain.[94]

The identification of Aife with Kilranelagh Hill, and the vicinity of the chief fortress of Uí Máil is supported, too, by other evidence relating to the fortunes of the Uí Máil dynasty in the seventh and early eighth-century. Fiannamail, the grandson of Rónán son of Áed of the Uí Máil, was slain by one of his own people in 680, and the Leinster king-list in the Book of Leinster names the place of his slaying as the battle of Aife or Selgg.[95] One interpretation of this note is that Aife and Selgg were the same place, and if so, then it was here, too, that Cellach Cualann's two sons met their deaths in 709. A notable feature of early Irish political history is the regular recurrence of battles at key locations, usually at border-crossings, in a strategic pass, or in the vicinity of royal strongholds. The recurring references to battles involving the overthrow of the Uí Máil in the seventh century make best sense if we accept that Selgg and Aife were in the Glen of Imaal and in the immediate vicinity of the Uí Máil stronghold at Kilranelagh. Cummascach son of Áed mac Ainmerech was said in the *Bóruma* to have been slain near the Green of Kilranelagh by the warden of that monastery. A poem in the Book of Leinster supporting that tradition opens with the invocation: 'I entreat the Mighty Lord, the Protector of Kilranelagh, it was He that took revenge on Cummascach.'[96]

The metrical account of the burial places of the kings of Leinster claims that Áed mac Ainmerech was also buried at Kilranelagh,[97] and we know he met his death while attempting to avenge the slaying of his son in that same place. It would seem, then, that the identification of Aife with Kilranelagh Hill is secure, and that being so, the Uí Máil dimension of the *Fingal Rónáin* must also be beyond question. A saga cannot be expected to convey much more than a general outline in relation to the accuracy of historical events it describes. The *Fingal Rónáin* conveys a powerful image of a dynasty doomed by internecine strife – dragged down in this case by the powerful emotions of sexual desire and jealousy, culminating in disastrous strife in the Glen of Imaal, in the seventh century. The historical realities which brought this tale into being did indeed centre on the dynasty of Uí Máil which ran into serious trouble at that very time, and collapsed under pressure from without and destructive kin-slayings from within. If we are to believe an early genealogical tradition, then Rónán mac Áeda slew his own brother, Crimthann, in 633, while his grandson Fiannamail fell at the hands of one of his own kindred at Aife in 680. The final overthrow of the house of the great Cellach Cualann came in 709 when two of his sons and would-be successors fell in a disastrous battle at Selg which was also most likely at Aife or Kilranelagh Hill beside the stronghold of the Uí Máil. As Uí Máil power rapidly waned, those events were remembered by all Leinstermen in the evening of their Heroic Age and recorded in a saga, immortalising a family tragedy on the wind-swept slopes of Imaal.

The triumph of Uí Dúnlainge

Murchad son of Bran of the Uí Dúnlainge enjoyed several key advantages when he seized the kingship of the Leinstermen in 715. His great-grandfather, Fáelán, who died *c.*645 had first raised his dynasty into the ranks of contenders for the kingship of the province, and had annexed the prestige and power of monasteries such as Kildare and perhaps also Glendalough. Murchad's father, Bran Mut, had ruled the province as the 'grandson of Fáelán' and the rise to power of both men had been facilitated by the support of the powerful Uí Néill. The geographical position of the Uí Dúnlainge in central Leinster also gave them an advantage over both their Uí Cheinnselaig and Uí Máil rivals, who were less centrally placed and confined to less fertile hilly countryside. Uí Máil power had been steadily challenged and weakened by sustained Uí Cheinnselaig aggression since the time of Brandub, while the Uí Cheinnselaig, in addition to their cumbersome mode of tribal succession, were distracted by internal strife in the early eighth century. Both the Uí Máil and Uí Cheinnselaig, in addition to being rivals of each other, were relentlessly opposed by the Uí Néill, who regularly invaded and wasted their province. On the other hand, there is sustained evidence to show that the Uí Néill helped to establish the eventual dominance of the Uí Dúnlainge over all other rivals within Leinster. Murchad of the Uí Dúnlainge was ruling at the head of a tightly-knit dynasty, and was married to the daughter of the reigning Leinster king, Cellach Cualann. On Cellach's death in 715, Murchad stepped into the kingship of the Leinstermen and thereby became the progenitor of no less than thirty-five kings of the province. With the reign of Murchad mac Brain, the kingship of the Leinstermen emerged from the leadership of a tribal confederacy to that of a dynastic kingship, where royal power was confined within narrow lines of family succession. The heroic age of the Leinstermen was at an end.

References

NOTE: When dates are cited in the text from the Annals of the Four Masters (A.F.M.), Annals of Tigernach or Annals of Ulster (*Ann. Ulst.*), such entries will be found under the appropriate dates in the editions given under *Abbreviations.*

1. For a discussion of the early medieval landscape of Wicklow see A.P. Smyth, *Celtic Leinster: towards an historical geography of early Irish civilization a.d. 500-1500,* pp 50-8, with a discussion on coastal territories on pp 52-4.
2. L. Price, 'Glendalough: St. Kevin's Road' in *Féil-sgríbhinn Eóin Mhic Néill: essays and studies presented to Professor Eoin MacNeill,* (ed.), J. Ryan (Dublin, 1940), pp 249-50.
3. Ibid., p. 250.
4. Ibid. Cf. *Corpus Gen. Hib.*, pp 20-1 under Rawl. B. 502, 118.a.39-40, with additional readings from L.L. For the Dindsenchus of Dún Másc and Ráth Nuí, see L.L. ed., Best and O'Brien, iii, 704 (L.L. 160.a.25).
5. A.B.E. Hood (ed.), *St Patrick: his writings and Muirchu's life* (Chichester, 1978), p. 66.
6. Ibid.
7. Price, *Placenames* , vii, p.xv.
8. *Corpus Gen. Hib.*, Rawl. B. 502, 120.b.27-8.
9. C. Plummer (ed.), *Vitae Sanctorum Hiberniae* (Oxford, 1968 reprint of 1910 edn.), i, 236, 241.

10. *Corpus Gen. Hib.*, Rawl. B. 120.b.45 (citing alternative readings from Book of Ballymote, Book of Leinster and Book of Lecan).
11. *St. Patrick: his writings* (ed.), Hood, p. 66 (for Muirchú); K. Mulchrone, (ed.), *Bethu Phátraic: The tripartite life of Patrick* (Royal Irish Academy, Dublin, 1939), i, 20-3.
12. Ibid., i, 113.
13. Ibid., i, 20.
14. Ibid., i, 113.
15. Ibid., i, 19.
16. T.F. O'Rahilly, *Early Irish history and mythology* (Dublin, 1964), p. 29; Price, *Placenames*, iv, 240.
17. C. Plummer (ed.), *Venerabilis Baedae Opera Historica* 2 vols. Oxford, 1969 reprint of 1896 edn. (*Historia Ecclesiastica*, Bk. V, xii), i, 310; ii, 297-8.
18. *A.U.* A.D. 660.
19. R.I. Best, and H.J. Lawlor (eds.), *The martyrology of Tallaght* (London, 1931), under 3 May.
20. *A.U.* A.D. 790.
21. Smyth, *Celtic Leinster*, p. 89; *Ann. Ulst.* A.D. 783.
22. *A.U.* A.D. 833.
23. Plummer, *Vitae SS Hib.,* i, 245-6.
24. Ibid., i, 246.
25. D. Greene (ed.), *Fingal Rónáin and other stories* (Dublin Institute for Advanced Studies, Medieval and Modern Irish Series, xvi (1955)), pp 45-7; L. Price, 'Historical Note on Lagore' in H. O'Neill Hencken, *Lagore Crannóg, R.I.A. Proc.*, liii, C, 32 (1950); P. Walsh, *Irish Book Lover*, xxviii, 74-80.
26. The text of *Orghuin Trí Mac Diarmata mic Cerbaill* is edited by Greene op. cit, pp 48-51; an earlier edition and translation is found in K. Meyer (ed.), *Hibernica Minora: being a fragment of an Old Irish Treatise on the Psalter ... and an appendix containing extracts hitherto unpublished from Manuscript Rawlinson B 512 in the Bodleian Library* (Anecdota Oxoniensia, Oxford, 1894), pp 70-5.
27. W. Stokes (ed.), *On the calendar of Oengus* (Dublin, 1880). Notes under 21 May.
28. The text of *Aided Máelodráin* is edited by Greene, op. cit., pp 51-4, with an earlier text and translation in Meyer, op. cit., pp 76-81.
29. Greene, op. cit., p. 51.
30. L.L. (eds.), Best, Bergin and O'Brien i, 181.
31. P. Walsh, 'Leinster states and kings in christian times', *Irish Ecclesiastical Record* (Fifth Ser.), liii (1939), 57.
32. A. Smyth, 'Húi Failgi relations with the Húi Néill in the century after the loss of the Plain of Mide', *Études Celtiques* XIV, ii (1975), 503-23.
33. L.L. (eds.), Best, Bergin and O'Brien, i, 184-6. J. Ryan, 'The Ancestry of St. Laurence O'Toole', *Reportorium Novum*, i (1955) 71, was among those who believed that Brandub was the last Uí Cheinnselaig king to have held the kingship of Leinster before the revival of that people in the eleventh century. Price is also of this opinion (*Placenames*, iii, 142).
34. *A.F.M.*, A.D. 586.
35. Price, *Placenames*, iii, 118-22; iii, 162-5.
36. Ibid., iii, 140-2.
37. S.H. O'Grady (ed.), *Silva Gadelica: a collection of tales in Irish with extracts illustrating persons and places* (2 vols., London and Edinburgh, 1892), i, [Irish text] 359-69; ii, [translation] 401-6.
38. Ibid., i, 370-2; ii, 408-10.

39. Ibid., i, 372-81; ii, 410-18.
40. P. Ó Riain (ed.), *Corpus Genealogiarum Sanctorum Hiberniae* (Dublin, 1985), p. 46 (285), p. 140 (707.19).
41. F.J. Byrne, *Irish Kings and High-Kings* (London, 1973), pp 145-6.
42. Plummer (ed.), *Vitae SS Hib.*, i, 244.
43. Ibid., i, 253.
44. Ibid., i, 254.
45. Byrne, *Irish Kings and High-Kings*, p. 144.
46. Byrne (ibid. p. 145) was rightly sceptical of the presence of the Ulaid in a Northern Uí Néill army in the late sixth century. While the presence of the Ulaid on the expedition against Leinster was most likely a later invention, nevertheless the tale of their defection reflects a tradition of friendship which existed between the Laigen and the Ulaid from the earliest historical times. I have referred to the ties between Cormac king of Uí Bairrche and the monastery of Bangor, and there were others. The Leinsterman, Columbanus, studied at Bangor before embarking on his continental mission. These ties between the Ulaid and the Laigen were no doubt facilitated through contacts by sea. We know from Adomnán's *Life* of Columba, for instance, that contacts between Iona and the Leinster coast were frequent throughout the seventh century. A.P. Smyth, 'The Earliest Irish Annals: their first contemporary entries and the earliest centres of recording.' *R.I.A. Proc.*, lxxii (1972), 37-41.
47. *A.F.M.*, A.D. 601 claim that Brandub was slain by Sarán 'and by his own kindred (*deirbhfine*)'.
48. Smyth, 'Húi Failgi Relations with Húi Néill', *Études Celtiques*, XIV, ii (1975), 505-8.
49. Walsh, loc. cit.; Ryan 'The ancestry of Laurence O'Toole', *Reportorium Novum*, i (1955), 67.
50. L.L. (eds.), Best, Bergin and O'Brien i, 184-5. There is great confusion at this point in the Uí Cheinnselaig king-list in the Book of Leinster. The order in the L.L. MS as it stands is as follows:

    [16] Rónán mac Coluim
    Crundmáel mac Rónáin
    Cummascach mac Rónáin
    [17] Colgu mac Crundmáel
    [18] Crundmáel Erbuilg mac Rónáin
    [19] Cummascach mac Rónáin.

    There is a marginal instruction opposite the first entry for Crundmáel mac Rónáin to delete that name. Opposite the three following entries there is the marginal ordering *c, a, b* to show that the first entry for Cummascach is also out of place and should come after the name of Crundmáel Erbuilg (no.[18]).

    The correct ordering, therefore, is indicated by my numbering in square brackets – [16], [17], [18], and [19].
51. Plummer, *Vitae SS Hib.*, ii, 102-3. The source of the anecdote on Colum son of Cormac of Uí Cheinnselaig is incorrectly described as the *Life* of Fintán or Munnu of Taghmon (Tech Munnu in Wexford) in Byrne *Irish Kings and Highkings*, p. 136, and in my *Celtic Leinster*, p. 65 and n.23. The correct source is the *Life* of Fintán of Clonenagh.
52. Plummer, *Vitae SS Hib.*, ii, 16, 102.
53. Ibid., ii, 102.
54. M.E. Dobbs, 'Women of the Uí Dúnlainge of Leinster', *Irish Genealogist*, i, no. 7 (1940), p. 205 and n. 76.
55. Ibid., pp 199, 205.

56. J. P. Migne, *Patrologiae ... series Latina*, (Paris, 1844-64), LXXII, 775-90.
57. *A.U.*, A.D. 639.
58. *Corpus Gen. Hib.*, L.L. 316.a.26.
59. Ibid., L.L. 316.a.24.
60. *A.F.M.*, A.D. 965.
61. Ibid., A.D. 814.
62. Ibid., A.D. 819.
63. Plummer, *Vitae SS Hib.*, i, 251.
64. Ibid., i, 252.
65. Ibid., i, 250.
66. Ibid., i, 251, 252.
67. *Corpus Gen. Hib.*, Rawl. 124.b.35.
68. C. Plummer (ed.), *Bethada Náem nÉrenn: lives of Irish saints*, (2 vols., Oxford, 1922), i, 128-9, ii, 124-5; i, 151, ii, 147; i, 164, ii, 158-9.
    In the Latin *Life* of Kevin (*Vitae SS Hib.*, ed., Plummer, i, 235-6), a woman tries unsuccessfully to seduce the youthful Kevin in a wood. The motif, which is a commonplace in saints' *lives* may have become confused in modern folklore with Kevin's encounter with Fáelán's wicked step-mother.
69. Fáelán was succeeded on his death by Crundmáel Erbuilg of Uí Cheinnselaig, and on Crundmáel's death in 656, by Fiannamail of Uí Máil. See table 2.7.
70. *A.F.M.* follows Tigernach in naming Crimthann's opponents in this battle.
71. S. Mac Airt (ed.), *The Annals of Inisfallen: (MS Rawlinson B.503)* (Dublin, 1951), A.D., 637.
72. W.M. Hennessy (ed.), *Chronicum Scotorum: a chronicle of Irish affairs from the earliest times to A.D. 1135* (London, 1866), A.D. 641.
73. See 'Geography and Inter-tribal Marriage' in Smyth, *Celtic Leinster*, pp 78-83.
74. Smyth, *Celtic Leinster*, p. 54.
75. E. Hogan, *Onomasticon Goedelicum, Locorum et Tribuum Hiberniae et Scotiae* (Dublin and London, 1910), p. 186.
76. Dobbs, 'Women of Uí Dúnlainge', *Irish Genealogist*, i, no. 7 (1940), p. 205.
77. The eighth-century Uí Cheinnselaig did succeed in promoting a candidate for the kingship of Leinster in the person of Áed Mind (table 2.4) who died in 738.
78. *Corpus Gen. Hib.*, Rawl. 125.a.3.
79. *Chronicum Scotorum*, ed. Hennessy, A.D. 676.
80. *Corpus Gen. Hib.*, Rawl. 125.a.25.
81. L.L. (eds.), Best, Bergin and O'Brien, i, 181-2.
82. Ryan, 'Ancestry of Laurence O'Toole', *Reportorium Novum*, i (1955), 69-70.
83. D. Kirby, A.P. Smyth, and A. Williams, *A biographical dictionary of dark age Britain* (London, 1991), under *Kentigerna* and *Fáelán*.
84. *A.F.M.*, A.D. 705.
85. A.P. Smyth, *Warlords and holy men: Scotland A.D. 80-1000* (Edinburgh, 1989), pp 25-6.
86. Greene, *Fingal Rónáin*, p.1; K. Meyer, 'Fingal Rónáin', *Revue Celtique*, xiii (1892), 368-9. Meyer's edition of the text and translation of *Fingal Rónáin* is found on pp 372-97 (ibid.).
87. J. O'Donovan, (ed.), *Annals of Ireland: three fragments* (Irish Archaeological and Celtic Society, Dublin, 1860), pp 65-7.
88. *Corpus Gen Hib.*, Rawl. 124.b.50; L.L. 316.a.15.
89. Meyer, 'Fingal Rónáin', *Revue Celtiques* xiii, 368-9.
90. *Corpus Gen. Hib.*, Rawl. 125.a.11. O'Brien, in his edition of the genealogies

(ibid.), was undecided as to the identity of Bishop Rónán son of Áed, and provided him with an entry in his *Index* which was separate from that of Rónán Crach. It does seem clear, however, that the genealogists were referring to the same person.

91. The text was edited by Greene in 1955, and earlier it was edited and translated by Kuno Meyer. See notes 25 and 85 above.
92. O'Grady, *Silva Gadelica*, i [Irish Text], 378; ii, [translation] 415.
93. Price, *Placenames*, iii, 118-20, 122-4.
94. Greene, *Fingal Rónáin*, p. 5.
95. L.L. (eds.), Best, Bergin and O'Brien, i, 181-2.
96. Price, *Placenames*, iii, 121.
97. L.L. (eds.), Best, Bergin and O'Brien, i, 207.

Glendalough (Bartlett).

Chapter 3

EVIDENCE OF SCANDINAVIAN SETTLEMENT IN WICKLOW

COLMÁN ETCHINGHAM

Discussion of the Scandinavian settlement in Ireland has tended to focus on the urban centres of Dublin, Limerick, Waterford, Cork and Wexford. This is partly due to the relative wealth of evidence available for some of the towns but may also reflect a failure to appreciate the amount of rural settlement which occurred, as argued recently by John Bradley. His reassessment distinguishes between occupation of the countryside around the major centres – which were economically dependent on the agricultural output of these areas – and more isolated rural communities.[1] His view that Dublin included in its sway the Scandinavians of county Wicklow is in keeping with the assumptions of previous scholars regarding the wide extent of the so-called Dyflinarskíri.[2] Whether this was the case or whether Arklow and Wicklow towns should be seen as the foci of settlement in the county is one of a number of fundamental problems which are difficult to resolve on account of the limitations of the sources available for this study. The scope of this paper is necessarily restricted by the slim body of rather tantalising impressions which emerge from the material assembled and such conclusions as can be ventured are generally tentative in character. It is proposed to consider first the annals and other contemporary documentation together with the evidence of archaeology, the contribution of which is limited by the fact that no excavation of a county Wicklow site with Scandinavian associations has as yet taken place. Anglo-Norman and later records and placenames are then examined for the retrospective light they shed on Scandinavian inhabitation.

Contemporary records and material remains

The beginnings of Viking activity in Wicklow are in fact better documented than its subsequent history. The earliest relevant evidence is found in the annal for 827, some thirty years after the first appearance of Vikings in Ireland, when recorded raids on churches and battlefield encounters with the Irish were increasingly frequent.[3]

A.U. for 827 reports the destruction of an encampment of the Leinstermen 'by heathens' ('do gentibh') who slew Conall mac Conchongalt, king of the 'Fortuatha Laigen' or extern peoples of Leinster. The Uí Garrchon dynasty to which he belonged had provided kings of Leinster in the fifth century[4] but had long since been confined to the coastal area of county Wicklow between Newcastle and Ennereilly[5] (see fig. 3.1). *A.U.* does not reveal where the attack in which he was killed took place; *A.F.M.* locates it at an unidentified 'Druim' which, however, may refer to a different event as the account is conflated with another entry through a scribal slip.[6]

Raiding intensified during the 830s and the Vikings began to overwinter at coastal bases from which more ambitious penetration of the hinterland was undertaken.[7] They had evidently established themselves on the Wicklow coast by 836 when 'heathens' from 'Inber Deaae' attacked Kildare and burned half the church settlement ('leth na cille').[8] 'Inber Dée' has been variously identified with Bray, Wicklow and Arklow, the latter being the preference of Hogan, Price and Smyth.[9] This would place it in the lands of Uí Enechglais, a dynasty which like Uí Garrchon had once held lands in the north Leinster plain but was at this time restricted to a coastal portion of south-east Wicklow and north-east Wexford.[10] The location of 'Inber Dée' is not beyond dispute, however, as the tenth-century *Tripartite Life of St. Patrick* associates it with Nathí I son of Garrchu the eponymous ancestor of Uí Garrchon.[11] Uí Garrchon kings of the 'Fortuatha Laigen' – a title normally given to Uí Garrchon dynasts like the aforementioned Conall mac Conchongalt[12] but which perhaps denotes an over-king of the county Wicklow seaboard as it is borne by two Uí Enechglais dynasts in the later tenth century[13] – may have been considered ultimate overlords of the Arklow area. The most telling point adduced by Price in favour of locating 'Inber Dée' at Arklow is the statement in a Latin *Life of St. Kevin* that Glendalough was formerly known as 'Gleand De', 'Dée' being the Avonmore River which after its confluence with the Avonbeg is designated the Avoca River and, of course, enters the sea at Arklow[14] (see fig. 3.1).

Wherever it is to be located, 'Inber Dée' has the distinction of being the first Viking base identified by name in the annals, although the sequence of recorded raids after 831 implies that there was a base somewhere between the north Dublin coast and Carlingford Lough in the early 830s.[15] An expedition as far inland as Kildare in itself argues the existence of a Viking haven on the Leinster coast and the pattern of reported activity between 834 and 836 accords well with the proposed siting at Arklow. There were raids on Glendalough in 834 and again, possibly, in 836, on Clonmore, county Carlow on Christmas Eve 835 or

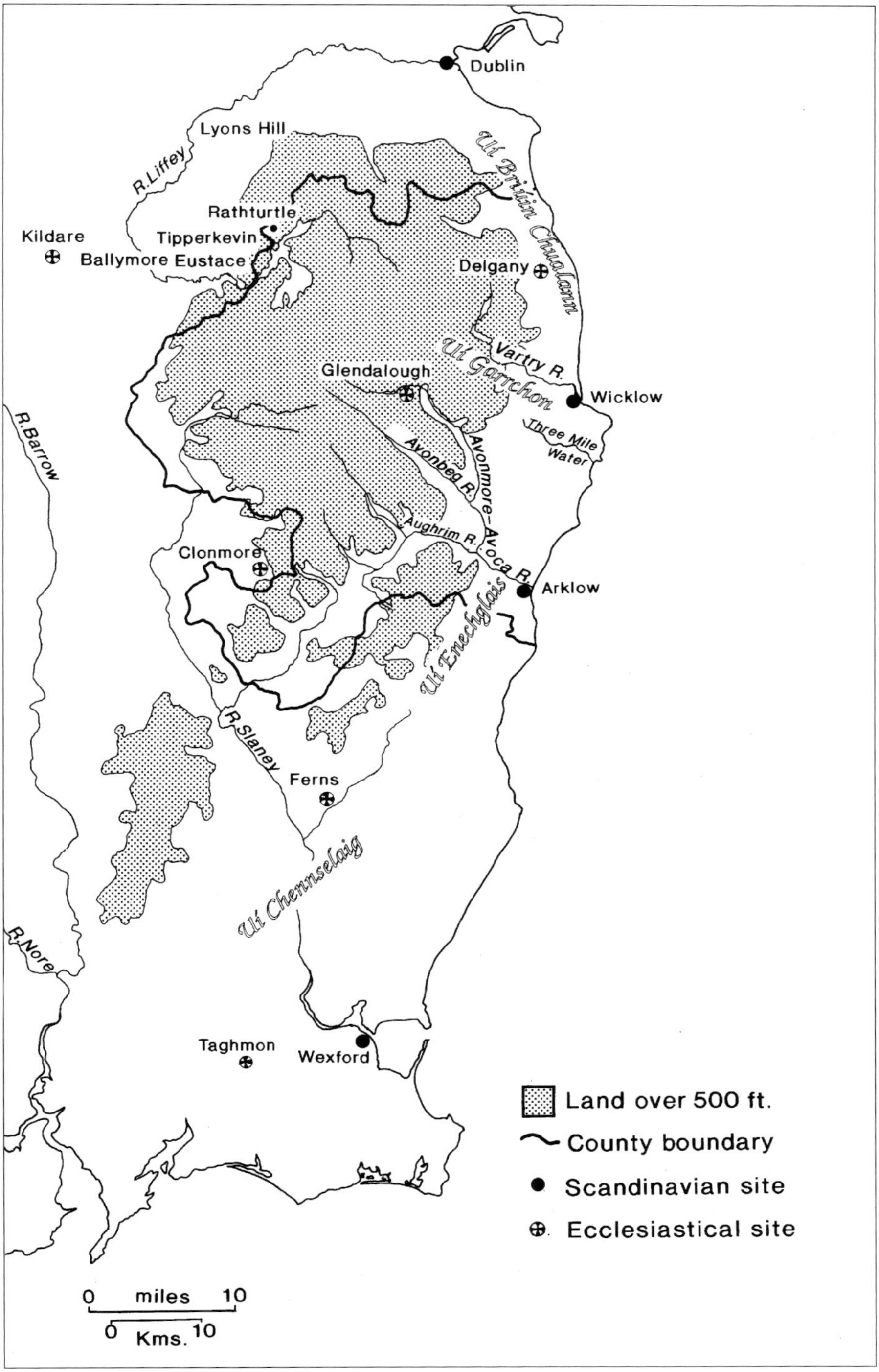

Figure 3.1 The Study Area.

836 – when many were slain and more captured – and on Ferns in 835.[16] The attack on Clonmore is the earliest documented instance of what appears to have been deliberate timing to coincide with a major church festival, doubtless in order to maximise the element of surprise and, conceivably, the haul of captives, though the importance of captives as potential slaves in early Viking raiding is controversial.[17] Familiarity with the native ecclesiastical routine must be inferred and the raiders were obviously over-wintering in Ireland.

Clonmore was presumably an Uí Chennselaig church as it lay within the territory of the Uí Fhelmeda Túaid branch of that dynasty and Aghowle, county Wicklow some five miles south is linked by the genealogies with a segment of the Uí Fhelmeda.[18]

The assault on Ferns in 835 may be connected with the capture in the same year of Cairpre mac Cathail, king of Uí Chennselaig – noticed only in *A.F.M.* and not expressly attributed to Vikings – whose father had made himself vice-abbot of Ferns by force in 817. In 828 Cairpre, in alliance with the community of his local church of Taghmon, had defeated Vikings in battle and his capture seven years later is the last mention of him in the annals before his death in 844; he seemingly escaped or was ransomed in or after 835.[19] While the attribution of the raids on Glendalough, Clonmore and Ferns to the Vikings of 'Inber Dée' is no more than surmise, all would have been eminently accessible from an Arklow base and the locations of the first two suggest routes by which Kildare could have been reached in 836, either directly over the mountains via Glendalough or by traversing the southern foothills in the vicinity of Clonmore (see fig. 3.1). In any event the raid on Kildare shows considerable daring and self-confidence on the Vikings' part in mounting such an overland operation from a coastal bridgehead apparently in county Wicklow.

After the events of 834-6 a raid on Ferns in 839[20] is the only other recorded action of this period which may have been the work of the Vikings of 'Inber Dée'. Indeed, despite the relatively early indication of a presence in Wicklow, the annalistic record of subsequent events up to the Norman invasion sheds precious little light on Viking activity or Scandinavian settlement in the region. This may be due in part at least to a lack of interest in the area east of the Wicklow mountains which, apart from the church of Glendalough, was always of marginal significance in Leinster affairs.[21] The establishment in 841 of a stronghold ('longphort') at Dublin[22] which was occupied throughout the rest of the century may have overshadowed any existing county Wicklow base. It is noteworthy that the reasonably full coverage afforded Glendalough in the annals includes only two Viking raids after the 830s, in 889 and 983, the latter being attributed to the 'Foreigners of Áth Cliath'.[23]

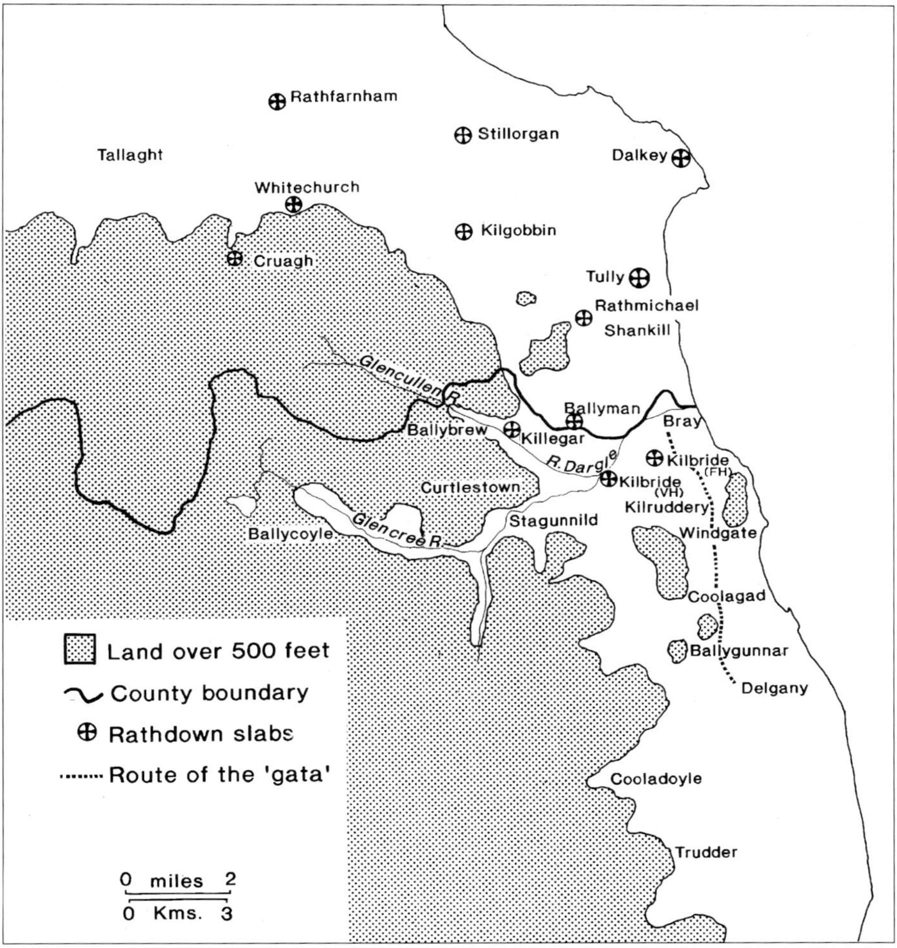

Figure 3.2 Dublin – Wicklow Borderlands.

There is no indication as to whether or not the 'Inber Dée' base marks the beginning of permanent inhabitation of the county Wicklow coast. The problem resembles that posed by other centres of attested settlement at a later stage such as Limerick, Waterford, Cork and Wexford, with which Scandinavians are occasionally associated in the ninth-century annals.[24] The expropriation of Dublin by the Irish in 902 heralded more than a decade of annalistic silence regarding Viking activity in Ireland and only after the arrival of a substantial new fleet at Waterford in 914 and the re-establishment of Dublin three years later can continuous occupation of some of the above-mentioned sites be postulated with confidence. Even the recent Dublin excavations failed to unearth material of earlier than the tenth century, though in this instance the annals together with the Kilmainham and Islandbridge cemeteries demonstrate beyond doubt a ninth-century occupation.[25] A regular ninth-century presence in county Wicklow after the 830s is a possibility which the evidence to hand neither proves nor refutes, but two finds of Scandinavian artifacts are probable indicators of settlement in the region before the later tenth century.

The first consists of two bronze oval brooches with silver decoration, and a silver wire chain with attached silver needle case, discovered in the nineteenth century somewhere between Three Mile Water south of Wicklow town and Arklow[26] (see fig. 3.1). While the precise location and circumstances of the find are unclear the brooches are typical of female Scandinavian burials elsewhere and have been dated to the tenth or earlier eleventh century.[27] A female burial betokens settlers rather than Vikings while deposition of grave goods is of course characteristic of pagan burial, the present example being one of only a dozen or less discovered in Ireland outside the Kilmainham and Islandbridge cemeteries.[28] Since Dublin, Limerick and Waterford were apparently being christianised by the second half of the tenth century,[29] the county Wicklow burial seems unlikely to belong to a period much later than this. The second find mentioned is the lower crossbar of an iron sword with remains of the tang and blade, much corroded and with vestiges of silver decoration; fourteen fragments of the sword were allegedly recovered from peaty earth on the low-lying coastal shingle-spit north of Wicklow town known as the Murragh (see fig. 3.3) about 1888, all but the crossbar having now disappeared.[30] While fragmentation might have occurred naturally, it is striking that a number of swords in the Kilmainham and Islandbridge graves had been deliberately bent or broken as part of the interment practices.[31] It is possible that the Murragh find also represents a pagan Viking burial of the ninth or earlier tenth century.

A suggested material trace of the settlement at Wicklow is the Round Mount, an earthwork on the hill at the northern end of the town (see fig. 3.3) which resembles a Norman motte and which seems to be the site of the 'castellum' entrusted to Strongbow in 1173. Price's supposition that the structure was originally the Scandinavians' assembly mound is credible in view of its proximity to what is perhaps the earliest extant ecclesiastical site in the town[32] of which more anon. Another monument which perhaps testifies to a settled stage of the Scandinavian presence in the Arklow and Wicklow region is a grave slab at Glendalough which bore an inscription, now obliterated, to Muirchertach Ua Cathaláin, supposedly a dynast killed in Munster in 1151, and to one 'Gutnodar' who was probably the carver of the slab.[33] The latter seems to be a Norse name and if so the slab may serve to

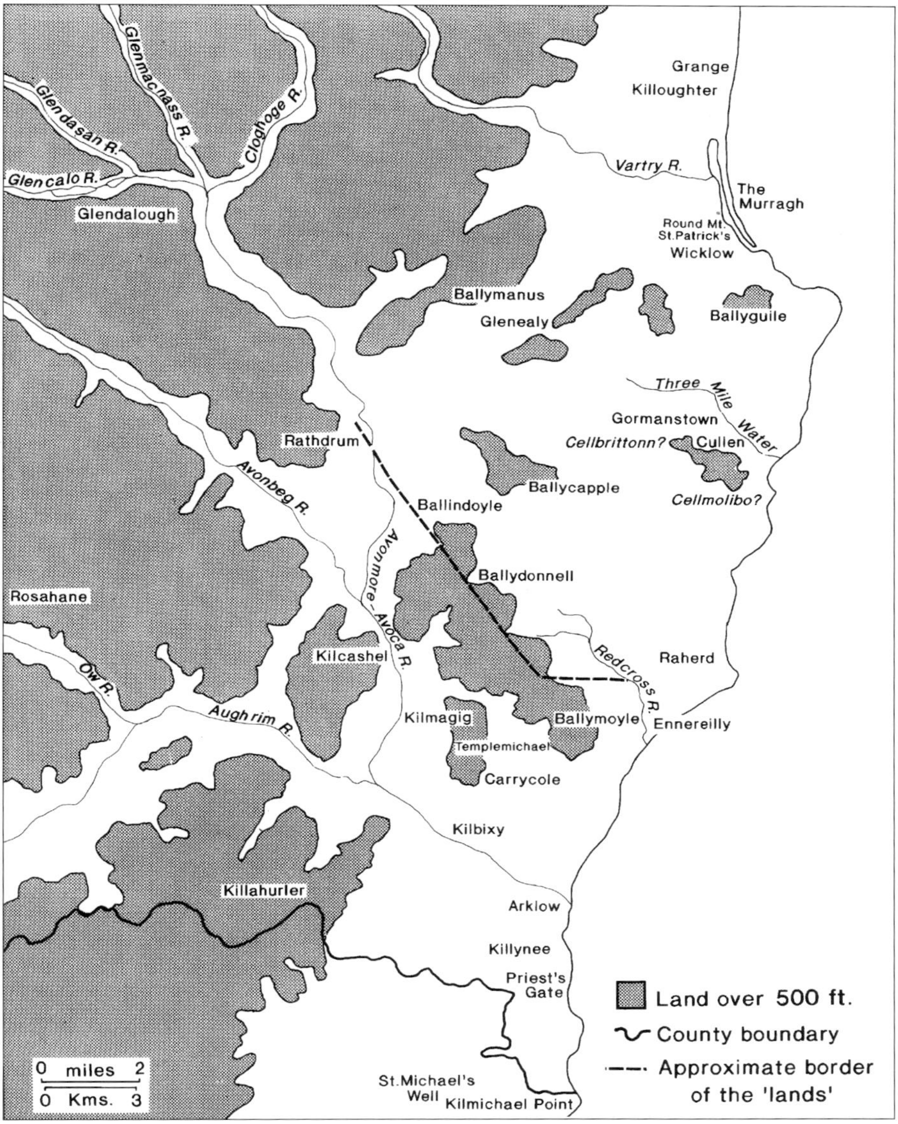

Figure 3.3 The 'Lands' of Arklow and Wicklow.

illustrate how far Glendalough, once the target of Viking raids, had come to terms with the Hiberno-Norse settlers by the twelfth century. A similar inference is probably to be drawn from a lost hoard of Hiberno-Norse coins deposited at Glendalough about 1090 and now known only from Ware's illustrations of six coins which he published in 1654.[33]

Both Price and Smyth maintain that the Arklow and Wicklow enclaves had a marked impact on the adjacent native polity and that the Uí Enechglais suffered particularly as a result of the occupation of Arklow, the larger stronghold according to Price, who proposes that its establishment followed the death of an Uí Enechglais king at the battle of Cenn Fúait in 917 when the Leinstermen were crushed by the second wave of Viking invasion.[34] Smyth conjectures further that the Uí Garrchon in contrast survived by coming to terms with the Scandinavians, as exemplified by the involvement in 984 of Fiachra mac Fínshnechta, king of the 'Fortuatha Laigen', in killing a dynast of the Uí Dúnchada, whose lands abutted the Dublin settlement on the southwest and whose claim to the kingship of Leinster seems to have ended with the tenth century.[35] However, Smyth's interpretation must be rejected since Fiachra was in reality one of two Uí Enechglais kings of the 'Fortuatha Laigen' in this period.[36] Thus the Uí Enechglais were still a force to be reckoned with at the end of the tenth century but their seizure of a kingship previously associated with the Uí Garrchon may nevertheless reflect the pressure of the Norse on the Uí Enechglais, which conceivably induced them to attempt to compensate themselves by subjugating their Uí Garrchon neighbours to the north. If so the attempt failed as the Uí Garrchon invariably provided kings of the 'Fortuatha' in the eleventh and twelfth centuries who are distinguished by the family name Úa Fergaile.[37]

Kings of Uí Enechglais are not recorded in the eleventh century but their eclipse by the Arklow settlers – if such it was – cannot have been complete for, as Price and Smyth observe, their dynasts reappear in the twelfth century under the family name Ua Fiachrach.[38] The first of these is Mac Íarainn Úa Fiachrach, king of Uí Enechglais (d. 1103), whose name is rare if not unique in Irish sources and whom Price plausibly suggests may be a Hibernicised Scandinavian, perhaps a product of intermarriage between the Arklow settlers and the Uí Enechglais.[39] The name is reminiscent of Glún Íarainn, a direct translation of Old Norse Jarnkné (Iron knee), and both Norse and Irish versions are found among the Dublin leaders mentioned in the ninth-century annals.[40] It is of course possible that the Uí Enechglais simply adopted a name current among the settlers, a practice which is well-documented from the mid-eleventh century,[41] though the rarity of the name Mac Íarainn tells against this. A contemporary reflex of the Arklow settlement is arguably discernible in the eleventh- or early twelfth-century *Book of Rights* which includes the king of the 'Fortuatha' alongside 'rí an Indbir' ('king of the Estuary') among recipients of stipends from the king of Leinster.[42] Price identifies 'rí an Indbir' with the king of Uí Enechglais whom one would expect to be mentioned here and, indeed, his particular stipend largely corresponds to the endowment of Bressal Enechglas in the earlier Leinster text *Timna Cathaír Máir*.[43] However, since the 'inber' concerned is evidently the estuary at Arklow, it is possible that this is an oblique reference to a Hiberno-Norse ruler of Uí Enechglais territory based at Arklow.

To date the discussion has concentrated on the limited contemporary evidence of Scandinavian settlement in the vicinity of Arklow and Wicklow towns. There are also intimations of a presence in the north of the county. The first such is in *A.U.* for 1021 which reports the defeat of Sigtryggr son of Óáfr king of Dublin by Augaire mac Dúnlaing, king of Leinster, at Delgany. This has been linked with the burning of Glendalough in 1020, but only the late and unreliable *Ann. Clon.* attributes this to the 'Danes'.[44] Price conjectures that Sigtryggr had a stronghold in the neighbourhood of Delgany and the seemingly implicit assumption that Augaire was the aggressor is credible since *A.F.M.* states that the battle was accompanied by 'a slaughter of the Foreigners in Uí Briúin Chualann' ('ár Gall i nUibh Briúin Cualand').[45] The territory of Uí Briúin Chualann extended from south county Dublin into the Wicklow coastal lowlands as far as Newcastle[46] (see fig. 3.1), and if the wording of *A.F.M.* reflects a contemporary account it may signify that Norse settlers dispersed through the region – and not merely Sigtryggr's warriors or the garrison of a putative outpost at Delgany – were slaughtered. Nothing further in the annals is indicative of Scandinavian inhabitation of the area. Like the Uí Garrchon and Uí Enechglais dynasts to the south, kings of Uí Briúin Chualann are noticed on occasion up to the twelfth century.[47] Sometime after 1130 their territory was taken over by the Uí Dúnchada of south-west Dublin and north-east Kildare who in turn had evidently succumbed to pressure from the Dublin colony; the Uí Dúnchada magnate Muirchertach Mac Gilla Mo-Cholmóc is called lord of the 'men of Cualu' ('Fir Chualann') in 1141.[48] A passage from a genealogical tract on the Uí Dúnchada found in the additional leaves of the *Book of Leinster* states that the 'Fir Chualann' were customarily subject to onerous levies by successive kings of Dublin in return for tenure of their lands and the aforementioned Muirchertach is credited with inducing the 'Foreigners of Áth Clíath' and Diarmait Mac Murchada – king of Leinster and ultimate overlord of Norse Dublin – to relax this burden.[49] While this remarkable text does not constitute evidence for settlement as such, it does suggest that a region which included north-east county Wicklow was in some sense subject to Dublin in the first half of the twelfth century and for some time prior to the advent of Muirchertach Mac Gilla Mo-Cholmóc.

The Uí Dúnchada tract and the record of the battle of Delgany together bear the inference that whatever Scandinavian settlement occurred in northeast Wicklow is likely to have been a direct extension of the Dublin colony. This interpretation finds support in a body of material remains known as the Rathdown slabs, which are almost entirely confined to the two half-baronies of Rathdown in south Dublin and north Wicklow. The highly distinctive character of the motifs carved on these granite monuments – cup-marks, concentric circles, herringbone patterns, medial bands, radiating lines, semi-circular loops, semi-spherical bosses and vestigial cross-arms – were long ago recognised and have been analysed in detail by Pádraig Ó hÉailidhe in his catalogue of the slabs.[50] Parallels with some of the designs have been discerned in the prehistoric epoch, including Neolithic art at Newgrange and Lough Crew, but as several slabs are cross-inscribed and all are found at ecclesiastical sites, they have generally been supposed to belong to the earliest phase of the Christian era.[51] However, in a more recent study of the material Ó hÉailidhe shows that the style of decoration corresponds to Viking-age carving outside Ireland – notably in Northumbria, where Hiberno-Norse influence was considerable – and finds a particular reflex in bone and antler work found in the Scandinavian levels of the Dublin excavations.[52] The distribution of the slabs (see fig. 3.2) accords with the proposition that they are relics of the christianised Hiberno-Norse. A number are found at Tully near Cabinteely which – as an Anglo-Norman document discussed below clearly shows – had ties with the Dublin Scandinavians, while the largest collection is at Rathmichael near Shankill where substantial remains include an elaborate enclosure and the stump of a round tower.[53] The dedication of this church to St Michael the Archangel has been discounted on the grounds of its rarity in Gaelic Ireland,[54] but as a patron of seafarers the saint was favoured by the Christian Hiberno-Norse, as witnessed by the two pre-Norman churches of St. Michael at Dublin and similar dedications at Waterford.[55] There is also evidence that a cult of Michael had developed by the ninth century at Tallaght, an important church in the territory of Cualu.[56] Both Rathmichael and Tully are of course in county Dublin as are most of the sites where Rathdown slabs have been found, but Killegar between the Scalp and Enniskerry, Kilbride (Violet Hill) and Kilbride (Fairy Hill, properly Killarney[57]) – both near Bray – lie within county Wicklow. Killegar is the location of one of the most intricately-carved slabs in the series and both it and Ballyman – a nearby repository of slabs which is within a hundred yards of the Wicklow border – were evidently attached to Glendalough,[58] an intriguing consideration when one recalls the postulated presence at Glendalough in the mid-twelfth century of the Hiberno-Norse stone carver 'Gutnodar'.

It seems a reasonable inference from all of the above that in north-east Wicklow at least the Scandinavian presence was closely connected with Dublin. It is not to be assumed, however, that Dublin was the immediate lord of Norse settlers here; rather, if reliance be placed on the Uí Dúnchada tract such settlers may be supposed to have been the direct subjects of a native mesne lord of Cualu who was himself in turn a tributary of the Dublin rulers.

Dublin's proximity was also seemingly of paramount importance in northwest Wicklow where a probable vestige of the Norse is Rathturtle ringfort in the townland of Deerpark Demesne near Blessington (see fig. 3.1), the name of which commemorates in garbelled form the Mac Torcaill dynasty of twelfth-century Dublin.[59] This impressive site located on a hill at an altitude of 900 feet consists of a massive approximately 'D' shaped rampart, 1 metre to 1.5 metres high internally and dropping 3.5 metres to 4 metres to the bottom of an external fosse, outside of which there is a second, lower, bank; the area enclosed by the inner rampart measures 49 x 36 metres.[60] The configuration of the rampart bears a resemblance to 'D' shaped Danish and Anglo-Saxon earthworks of the Danelaw frontier in ninth- and tenth-century England.[61] The fortification lies about eight miles south of Lyons Hill on the Dublin-Kildare border, once the seat of Uí Dúnchada kings of Leinster but apparently a stronghold of the Dublin Norse when the *Book of Rights* was compiled.[62] Rathturtle therefore appears to be a relic of the Dubliners' expansion at the expense of the Uí Dúnchada in this area in the eleventh or early twelfth century, but without excavation it is impossible to know whether it was simply a defensive outpost or, as its dimensions and the association with the Mac Torcaills might suggest, a royal residence and perhaps the focus of wider Hiberno-Norse settlement in the region.

Later records and placenames

Documents of the Anglo-Norman period and later reveal something of the surviving Hiberno-Norse population therein termed Ostmen (Old Norse 'austmadr', plural 'austmenn', 'easterner', 'Norwegian'), but this evidence like that of the pre-Norman sources is unevenly distributed among the places they inhabited in a way which is doubtless a crude indicator of the relative importance of these centres. Thus there is substantial material on the Ostmen of Dublin and the 'villa' of Ostmantown to which they were principally confined in the twelfth and thirteenth centuries, and a smaller body of references to similar communities outside Waterford, Limerick and Cork, while the Ostmen of Wexford were still a recognisable group in the Rosslare area in the late thirteenth century.[63] The Ostmen of county Wicklow are ill-served by the post-conquest records as by the earlier sources, but scattered references in the later documentation supplemented by placenames show that their identity was not submerged before the arrival of the Anglo-Normans. The Norse origin of the names of Arklow and Wicklow is not disputed. That of Arklow consists of the personal name 'Arnkell' or 'Arnketill' – which is found in the Dublin Roll of Names of *c.*1200 A.D. – combined with 'ló', which denotes a low-lying meadow near water.[64] In the case of Wicklow the first element is unlikely to be the common noun 'víkingr' (a Viking) but rather the same word used as a personal name – witness 'Willielmus Wiking' in the Dublin Roll of Names or the plural form meaning 'the people from Vík'. The possibility that the first element is simply 'vík' (a bay) is not supported by the forms attested by the earliest post-conquest documents, almost all of which have '-ing'.[65] In any event it is remarkable that these and not any Irish designations were used from the first by the Anglo-Normans to describe not only the towns but their surrounding lands, implying that the newcomers' informants were Hiberno-Norsemen, though the survival of the placenames does not of itself prove that Norse was still spoken in Arklow and Wicklow as has been suggested.[66]

The existence of an identifiable Ostman community at Wicklow town in the immediate post-conquest period is to be deduced from the mention in 1185 of 'a carucate of land at Wicklow which belonged to the Ostmen' ('una carucata terre apud Wichinglo que fuit Ostmannorum') which was granted by John, Lord of Ireland to St Thomas's Abbey, Dublin.[67] The ultimate fate of this community is not disclosed as both Wicklow and Arklow lack a body of material like that on the Ostmen of Dublin which is preserved in particular abundance in the records of St Mary's Abbey.[68] However, the past tense 'fuit' in the above indicates that the new settlers had acquired Ostman lands adjacent to the town of Wicklow, whether by seizure or other means. In 1188 Pope Clement III confirmed the possessions of St Mary's Abbey, Dublin, including a burgage in Wicklow ('Wikinlof') together with seven acres 'of the gift of Reginald the Palmer' ('ex dono Reinaldi Palmerii'), and in the same 'villa' another burgage with its land 'ex dono Bridni'. These were doubtless the 'burgagia sua apud Wikingelo', ownership of which had been confirmed to St Mary's by John, Lord of Ireland in 1185.[69] Strongbow himself retained Wicklow after the invasion and his chaplain Reginald, who was granted the churches of the Wicklow district by the bishop of Glendalough, is identified by Price with the above; one may also note that a 'Reginaldus Palmer' appears in the Dublin Roll of Names.[70] The background of Strongbow's chaplain is unclear, but in the form 'Ragnall' (Old Norse 'Ragnarr' or 'Rögnvaldr') the name is common among the Hiberno-Norse from the tenth century onwards; another 'Reginaldus' in the Dublin Roll of Names bears the Norse epithet 'utlag' ('út-lagi', 'outlaw').[71] Reginald the

Palmer's son, 'W. de Wykingelo', later conferred rental income in Wicklow on Llanthony Priory in Gloucestershire – which had considerable property in the area – in acquittance of his father's will.[72] Whatever about Reginald's origins, it seems likely that 'Bridnus' or 'Bridinus', St Mary's other benefactor mentioned above, was a Wicklow Norseman, as the name is found among the Dublin Ostmen and in form resembles 'Polin', 'Padin', 'Christin' and similar names favoured by them.[73] As St Mary's was a pre-Norman foundation[74] it is not inconceivable that Bridin's was a pre-conquest endowment.

Only one comparable hint of surviving Hiberno-Norse inhabitants of Arklow has come to light in the Anglo-Norman documentation. This is a grant of about 1260 by which 'Thomas clericus' endowed the Hospital of St John Baptist at Dublin with an 'area' ('site') 'in villa de Arclo' contiguous to the 'area' of one 'Gilleboth', with provision for payment of rent by the Hospital to 'Gilleboth' and his heirs. Gillaboth is clearly Irish in form, but given the known predilection of the christianised Norse in the Gaelic world for the 'Gilla' element it is plausible that this thirteenth-century Arklow proprietor was an Ostman.[75]

It has been suggested that burgages at Wicklow mentioned in the preceding documents were Strongbow's creation, but since continuity of property boundaries from the pre-Norman period is demonstrated by excavation at Waterford and Wexford – though not as yet at Dublin,[76] – the same may be true of both Wicklow and Arklow. Only excavation can test this and the related hypotheses that the layout of the main street in Arklow is of Scandinavian origin and that the Butler castle there occupies the site of the pre-Norman citadel.[77] Several Anglo-Norman records notice the church of 'Baccnaseri/Bakenes/Bachneser' – evidently 'Bacc na sóer' ('Creek' or 'Angle' of the craftsmen)[78] – which appears to be an Irish name for the Scandinavian settlement on the bend of the Vartry estuary at Wicklow. Price relates this to the Ostmen's renown as shipbuilders,[79] and craftsmanship in other fields such as is disclosed by the Dublin excavations and perhaps exemplified by 'Gutnodar' the reputed twelfth-century stone carver of Glendalough may also have given rise to the name 'Bacc na sóer'. The church here is seemingly distinct from the 'ecclesia Sancti Patricii de Wykingelow' which was in existence in Strongbow's time, adjacent to the castle which may be identical with the Round Mount mentioned above; it is probable that the Church of Ireland on Church Hill is the site of St Patrick's, since it appears to be the location of an earlier burial ground. On the other hand, it has been suggested that the existing ruins of Black Castle on the headland outside the harbour occupy the site of both the Norman 'castellum Guikingelonense' and its presumed

Hiberno-Norse predecessor.[80] John Comyn, the archbishop of Dublin, assigned the church of St Patrick to Llanthony Priory in a charter dated 1185/1188 which is witnessed by, among others, 'Osbernus clericus' – perhaps Old Norse 'Asbjörn' – but there is no indication that he was connected with the Wicklow church.[81]

The boundaries of the lands associated with Arklow and Wicklow are not detailed in the early Anglo-Norman grants, suggesting that they were already well-defined territories and most likely co-terminous with pre-existing Hiberno-Norse lordships.[82] The border between them seemingly ran south-east from the vicinity of Rathdrum along the high ground and then followed the lower reaches of the Redcross river, as Strongbow's charter to Glendalough listing churches and property in the 'lands of Arclo and Wyglo' includes in the former Ballymoyle ('Ballivmeill'), east of the hills and west of the river.[83] (For these and the following locations see fig. 3.1). The same document shows that the 'land of Arclo' encompassed Killynee to the south of the town and to the north and west Kilbixy, Carrycole, Kilmagig and Kilcashel in addition, perhaps, to Rathdrum and Rosahane.[84] The 'land of Wyglo' included Ennereilly, Cullen, 'Cellbrittonn' (perhaps near Ballinameesda), 'Cellmolibo' (possibly Castletimon), Glenealy and 'Ruba Scolaige', which may be the same as 'Rosculli' of the Llanthony records and has been identified with Grange near Killoughter.[85] Killoughter does not figure in Strongbow's charter but appears in the Llanthony documents; its name ('Cell Uachtar', 'Upper Church') may imply that it was at the northern extremity of the Hiberno-Norse territory of Wicklow.[86]

There is a dearth of placenames indisputably reflective of rural Norse settlement in the 'lands' of Arklow and Wicklow, though the grave goods found south of Three Mile Water suggest such inhabitation at quite an early stage. The townlands of Ballymanus Upper and Lower, extending from Carrick Mountain to Glenealy, contain the Norse name 'Magnus' which, however, was widely adopted by the Irish including the later medieval O'Byrnes.[87] Ballyguile Beg and Ballyguile More just south of Wicklow seem to represent 'Baile Mhic an Ghaill' ('Homestead of the foreigner's son') and is taken to refer to an Anglo-Norman settler but an allusion to an Ostman is not impossible. Ballindoyle, about two miles north-west of Redcross, apparently reflects Irish 'Dubgilla' ('dark lad' or 'servant') – which gave rise to the family name 'Ua Duibhghiolla' – rather than 'Dubgall' ('dark foreigner') which has specifically Scandinavian associations. Gormanstown, some three miles south of Wicklow, is also ambiguous and could represent Norse 'Gormr', or 'Gormundr' or Irish 'Gormán'. In the case of Raherd near Ennereilly, Price rejects O'Donovan's suggested 'Ráth Aird' ('Rath of the hill') on the basis that there is no high ground in the vicinity and proposes that it contains a Norse personal name such as 'Siward' (perhaps 'Sigurr' or 'Sigvatr').[88] The above would all have been in the 'land' of Wicklow. In the 'land' of Arklow, Killahurler, about six miles west of the town on the slopes of Croghan Mountain, perhaps incorporates a name like 'Thóraldr' or 'Thórhallr'. Templemichael, about three miles north of Arklow, bears a dedication to St Michael the Archangel which, as previously contended, may betoken Hiberno-Norse origin. The same can be said of Kilmichael Point and St Michael's Well in the adjacent north-east corner of county Wexford. Finally, Priest's Gate near Arklow Rock possibly includes the Norse word 'gata' meaning a path or road.[89]

Price points to what he considers a reflex of Hiberno-Norse settlement in the hinterland of Wicklow found in the records of Llanthony Priory, which refer to churches at 'Balimaccapel' and in the land of 'Duuenaldi Maccapel'. The former is the townland of Ballycapple about six miles south-west of Wicklow where there is a possible early ecclesiastical site. The latter is preserved in the name of Ballydonnell townland adjoining Redcross; Ballydonnell was the original designation of the parish of Redcross, where the graveyard is the site of Ballydonnell church (see fig. 3.3). Both places are connected with Domnall mac Capaill who was evidently lord of the whole area before the Norman conquest. Derivation of a proper name from 'capall' ('horse', generally a work-horse as distinct from 'ech', a saddle-horse) is extremely unusual in Irish but since Old Norse 'hestr' ('horse', 'stallion') is known to have been used as a personal name, Price suggests that Capall here is a translation from Norse and that Domnall mac Capaill was a Gaelicised Scandinavian magnate.[90] An apposite parallel is the translation of Jarnkné as Glún Íarainn, noticed heretofore.

With the possible exception of Priest's Gate the above placenames are Irish in form, for even where they may contain Norse personal names these are governed – according to Irish syntactical rules – by common Irish placename elements like 'baile' and 'cell'.[91] Thus while some of these names may reflect Scandinavian settlement they also bespeak a process of Gaelicisation which is likely to have affected the rural settlers in particular and may well account, in part at least, both for the scarcity of recognisably Norse placenames in the region and the limited traces of the Arklow and Wicklow Ostmen in the Anglo-Norman records.[92] However, in the case of Arklow this material can be supplemented by evidence from the later sixteenth and earlier seventeenth centuries which shows that almost all the tenants of the Butlers around Arklow were called 'Dowell', 'O'Dowle' or 'O'Doylle', denoting descendants of 'Dubgall' ('dark foreigner'). Notwithstanding the late date of these documents Price may well be right to suggest that they reflect a strong settlement of Gaelicised Scandinavians left in place by the resurgent O'Byrnes of the later middle ages who overran much of the territory further north, as Dubgall is attested as a personal name among the Dublin Norse in the early eleventh century.[93] In view of the relatively dense distribution of the name in the hinterland it could be significant that there are only two recorded O'Doyle tenants in the town itself and that only one of the burgesses of Arklow listed in 1571 was a 'Dowell' whereas the rest bear English names.[94] While it would be wrong to read too much into such late evidence, it is possible that the Ostmen of Arklow, like those of the better-documented centres, were largely excluded from the town itself by the Anglo-Normans. It is also worth noting that two of the O'Doyle tenures were at Killahurler and Templemichael, placenames which it has been proposed are of Scandinavian origin. (For the locations of O'Doyle tenants see fig. 3.4.)

Anglo-Norman documents and placenames also corroborate contemporary evidence of Norse settlement in north Wicklow. Material in this category relating to the Rathturtle neighbourhood in the north-west of the county is limited to three personal names. One is 'Downall son of Helge' (Old Norse 'Helgi') who, according to King John's charter of 1202 confirming many earlier benefactions of Christ Church by named Hiberno-Norsemen, granted 'land between Kealmuatamoch and Ballimore Abbot'; the former is unidentified but the latter may be Ballymore Eustace, county Kildare, about four miles south-west of Rathturtle[95] (see fig. 3.1). Also connected with this place is 'Turstinus ('Thorsteinn') de Balimor', evidently a canon of St Patrick's who had property in Dublin and is mentioned several times in records of St Mary's Abbey dating to the first half of the thirteenth century.[96] Another possibly Ostman landowner in the area was 'John Gormund son of John Gormund' who, as late as 1316, held twenty-two acres in the tenement of Tipperkevin, county Kildare, about two miles south-west of Rathturtle[97] (see fig. 3.1). 'Gormund' may represent Norse 'Gormundr'; the same name is perhaps preserved in that of the 'Porta Gormundi', one of the gates of medieval Dublin.[98] Rathturtle apart, however, no placenames indicative of a Scandinavian presence in this region have come to light.

Anglo-Norman documents and placenames reveal rather more about the Ostmen of north-east Wicklow. After the conquest Strongbow granted Walter de Ridelesford 'Brien and the land of the sons of Turchil' together with the 'house and messuage of Christin the Ostman' in Dublin.[99] The precise extent of what De Ridelesford received is uncertain and it would appear that 'Brien' did not include all the territory of Uí Briúin Chualann, but it is not disputed that the 'land of the sons of Turchil' was the patrimony of the Dublin Norse family of

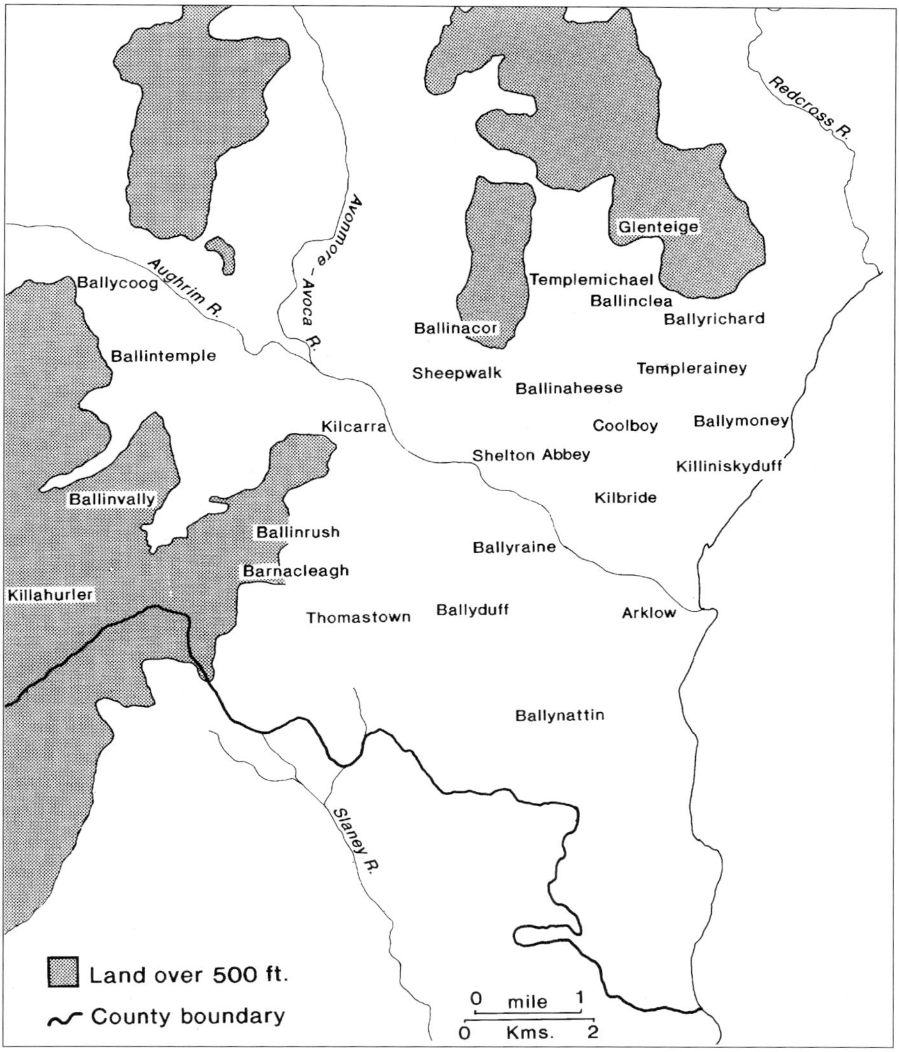

Figure 3.4 O'Doyle tenures in the Arklow district.

Mac Torcaill in south Dublin and north-east Wicklow.[100] The dynasty's origins are obscure, its eponym being perhaps the 'Turcall mac Éola' who, together with Rhys ap Tewdwr, king of south Wales, was killed by the Normans in 1093, according to *Ann. Inisf.*[101] The Mac Torcaills provided rulers of Dublin in the twelfth century, the last being Asgall or Hasculf ('Asgell' or 'Höskuldr'?) son of Torcall ('Thorkell') who was executed after the Ostmen's failure to retake Dublin from Myles de Cogan in 1171; they held extensive lands in north county Dublin apart from those in the Dublin-Wicklow border area with which the De

Ridelesford charter is concerned.[102] These latter stretched from the vicinity of Tully near Cabinteely – which John's 1202 charter to Christ Church states was granted to the latter by 'Sigraghre son of Thorkyll' before the Norman advent, and which has been mentioned as a repository of Rathdown slabs – apparently to the Dargle river. Within county Wicklow they included probably Ballybrew in Glencullen and certainly Curtlestown near Powerscourt which preserves a version of the family's name.[103] (For these and the following placenames see fig. 3.2.)

Records of the archbishop of Dublin's court at Shankill relating to the first half of the thirteenth century reveal a mixed community of Irish, English and Ostmen in the area. Establishing a claim to Ostman status could bring the benefits of English law, but resistance to this by the English colonists was facilitated by the extent to which the Ostmen had become Hibernicised; the records mention 'Macduel de Rathmichael que fuit Estmane' and 'Hodo Mac Foyde, Ostman'.[104] Rathmichael, it may be recalled, has the largest extant collection of Rathdown slabs. The archiepiscopal court records do not specify the nationality of a number of individuals who, judging by their names, could be Ostmen rather than Irish, including 'Omerthach/Ofinercach Mac Dowyll', 'Kilcrist Mac Soynne' and 'Kylchrist Mac Beain' of Glencree, the last of whom at least dwelt within the boundary of the modern county Wicklow. Another possible Ostman from this area was 'Reginald Mac Kause', a betagh-tenant of the archbishop whose land in the tenement of Shankill is noticed in 1304.[105] Documents of St Mary's Abbey show that in the first half of the thirteenth century land in Glencullen was held by one 'Shitterich Macahegan' – presumably 'Sigtryggr' – and his brother 'Lathegan'. St Thomas's Abbey was endowed in the earlier thirteenth century with one third of Ballybrew ('Baliobedan'), 'namely that part which Blevinus held', according to a series of charters in the Abbey's register, one of which is witnessed by three De Ridelesfords as well as 'Clemens de Bre' and 'Gillerod de Bre' It may be conjectured that 'Gillerod' was an Ostman and 'Blevinus' resembles names like 'Bridin', 'Polin', 'Padin' and 'Christin' which were common among the Dublin Ostmen.[106] In another document of the earlier thirteenth century Diarmait Mac Gilla Mo-Cholmóc, heir of the Uí Dúnchada lords of Uí Briúin Chualann, disposed of his land of Kilruddery ('Kilrotheri') except for that which he had assigned to 'Hamoni Ruffo'. While 'Hamo' is a name found among the Norman settlers one wonders if it could represent here 'Hamundus' (Old Norse 'Hámundr'), since one 'Hamundus Ruffus' appears as witness to several charters relating to St Mary's Abbey, twice in conjunction with the probable Ostman 'Ricardus Gillemichel'. This supposition is prompted by Price's suggestion that what may be another early name for Kilruddery 'Baliurodrach', contains the Norse name 'Rothrekr'.[107]

In addition to this example and the more decisive one of Curtlestown, there are several placenames in the county Wicklow portion of the region which may bear witness to Scandinavian settlement. The church site in Powerscourt Demesne appears to be the 'Stagunnild/Tachgunnild' of early post-conquest documents which possibly incorporates the Norse woman's name 'Gunnhildr', although some forms indicate rather 'Tech Conaill' or 'Tech Ua Conaill'.[108] The proposition that the 'sta' element here and in 'Stamoling' (Kilmalin, west of Enniskerry) – as well as in other placenames outside county Wicklow represents Old Norse 'star' ('place', 'dwelling', 'stead') does not seem warranted, however. As O'Rahilly points out, 'sta' and 'stach' replacing Irish 'tech' ('house') is a post-conquest phenomenon attributable to the difficulty for Norman-French speakers of pronouncing the initial palatal 't' in Irish; the distribution of the form also seems more consistent with a Norman than a Norse origin.[109] The townland of Ballycoyle is thought to commemorate late medieval Gallowglass settlers called 'Mac Dubhghaill' or reflect an earlier 'Baile Meic Gilla Comgaill', though one might point to the occurrence of 'Macduel' and 'Mac Dowyll' among the proven or putative Ostmen of the area previously noticed. Further south Windgate and Coolagad may contain the Old Norse term 'gata', meaning a path or road and referring to the old roadway linking Bray and Delgany. An obsolete placename seemingly to be located in Bellevue Demesne townland near Delgany is Ballygunnar, containing the Norse name 'Gunnarr'; the parish of Ballygunner, barony of Gualtiere, county Waterford, is also an area of known Scandinavian occupation.[110] The possibility of such settlement close to Delgany is particularly significant in view of the suggested implications of the battle there in 1021. Finally, the townlands of Cooladoyle and Trudder, in the neighbourhood of Newtownmountkennedy, bear names which are perhaps of Hiberno-Norse origin; the latter might be derived from Old Norse 'tro' ('a fold') but could equally well represent Irish '(an) tsruthair' ('stream').[111]

As in the Arklow and Wicklow areas, few of the placenames in the northeast of the county can be said to be truly Norse in form. At most they incorporate a Norse personal name or – in the case of 'gata' in Coolagad – a common noun governed by an Irish placename element. Windgate is perhaps the most likely instance of a purely Scandinavian placename and Trudder would also qualify if it is not in fact an Irish name. Stagunnild does not fit this description, however, in view of the interpretation adopted above and because the form of the compound is Irish; if it were Norse the order of the components would be reversed, i.e. 'Gunnhildarstar'. Thus while a number of placenames in the region appear to reflect an Ostman presence they also suggest either that the settlers were isolated among a predominantly Irish-speaking population which coined the placenames or that they were themselves substantially Gaelicised, an explanation which accords with the hybrid or even purely Irish personal names attested among the Ostmen of county Wicklow and elsewhere.

Conclusion

The outcome of this study of the evidence for Scandinavian settlement in county Wicklow is necessarily inconclusive in many respects. The principal object has been to assemble the available material, the nature of which ensures that interpretation is a decidedly hazardous undertaking, as observed at the outset. Few of the questions one would wish to ask can be answered satisfactorily. What little has emerged by way of general conclusions may be briefly summarised. There is direct and circumstantial evidence of an early Viking raiding base on the Wicklow coast, probably at Arklow, in the mid-830s. Pagan burial south of Three Mile Water and perhaps also on the Murragh at Wicklow seems to imply more regular inhabitation of the Arklow-Wicklow region before the second half of the tenth century. Rathturtle ringfort suggests that Dublin's sway extended into north-west Wicklow by the twelfth century if not before. In the north-east of the county the Mac Torcaill holdings, the Uí Dúnchada tract and the Rathdown slabs bear a similar interpretation and the battle of Delgany points to Scandinavian influence if not settlement here by the early eleventh century.

The haphazard survival of records and the effect of Gaelicisation in obscuring the identity of the Hiberno-Norse in both documentation and placenames are factors the impact of which is difficult to measure when attempting to assess the extent and character of the settlement. Bradley points to a comparable problem in seeking to identify distinctively Scandinavian sites and monuments, and his hypothesis that the difference between Norse and Irish was not so much cultural but primarily related to spheres of political control and in some respects to the economic function of the urban nuclei in relation to the wider Scandinavian settlement[112] is one which seems applicable to the situation in county Wicklow, as far as it can be determined. However, the specific inference that this region was part of the Dyflinarskíri, with Dublin as its political and economic focus, must be treated with greater caution in the light of the evidence to hand. In the realm of politics the nature of relations with the native dynasties of Uí Enechglais, Uí Garrchon, Uí Briúin Chualann and Uí Dúnchada remains largely unclear. However, it appears that the Hiberno-Norse presence did not involve expropriation but rather a more complex pattern of tributary relations and coexistence. The settlement in north Wicklow can probably be safely regarded as part of the Dyflinarskíri but it is not self-evident that the immediate influence of Dublin stretched further south. One wonders if the 'gata' or roadway which seemingly extended to Delgany may have gone further, linking the north-east of the county with the Wicklow enclave; the likelihood of this would be enhanced if the possible Scandinavian origin of the placenames Cooladoyle and Trudder – the latter only about three miles north of Killoughter, the postulated northern extremity of the Wicklow colony – were less doubtful. If the twelfth-century extents of the 'lands' of Arklow and Wicklow are at all reliable indicators there must also have been a considerable rural agriculture-based settlement in this region, for which it is conceivable that Arklow and Wicklow were themselves the urban nuclei. The degree to which these were true towns like Dublin with a trading economy and professional craftsmen is indeterminable, though the name 'Bacc na sóer' associated with Wicklow may carry some significance. Only excavation at Wicklow and Arklow and at other promising sites such as Rathturtle offers hope of illuminating this and other unresolved questions about Scandinavian settlement in county Wicklow.

References

1. John Bradley, 'The interpretation of Scandinavian settlement in Ireland', in Bradley (ed.), *Settlement and society in medieval Ireland* (Kilkenny, 1990), pp 49-78.
2. Bradley, op. cit., pp 56-62; Charles Halliday, *The Scandinavian kingdom of Dublin* (2nd. edn. Dublin, 1884), pp 138-40; Edmund Curtis, 'The English and the Ostmen in Ireland', *E.H.R.* xxiii (1908), pp 209-19: 209; idem, *Med. Ire.*, pp 34, 67 (but see idem, 'Norse Dublin', *Dublin Hist. Rec.* iv (1942), pp 96-105: 100); Annie Walsh, *Scandinavian relations with Ireland during the Viking period* (Dublin, 1922), pp 22-3; J.I. Young, 'A note on the Norse occupation of Ireland', *History* xxxv (1950), pp 11-33: 14 note 19; A.P. Smyth, *Celtic Leinster* (Dublin, 1982), p. 44.
3. *A.U.* (here and hereafter referring to Seán Mac Airt and Gearóid Mac Niocaill (ed.), *The Annals of Ulster (to A.D. 1131)* (Dublin, 1983) and not to Hennessy's edition) 821, 823, 824, 825, 827, 828; *Chron. Scot.* 822; annals are cited by year and not page numbers of the editions; for the correct dates in the latter see Paul Walsh, 'The dating of the Irish annals', *I.H.S.* ii (1940-1), pp 355-75.
4. F.J. Byrne, *Ir. kings*, p. 138; A.P. Smyth, 'The Huí Néill and the Leinstermen in the Annals of Ulster 431-516 A.D.', *Études Celt.* xvi (i) (1974), pp 127-36.
5. Liam Price, 'The placenames of the barony of Arklow, county of Wicklow', *R.I.A. Proc.* xlvi C (1941), pp 285-6; idem, *The placenames of County Wicklow* (7 vols., Dublin, 1945-67) vii, p. 494; Smyth, *Celt. Leinster*, pp 51-6 and plates V, VIII, XI; K.W. Nicholls, 'The land of the Leinstermen', *Peritia* iii (1984), pp 535-58: 544-5, 552.

6. *A.F.M.* (s.a. 825).
7. Hughes, *Ch. in early Ire. soc.*, p. 199; idem, *Early Christian Ireland* (Cambridge, 1972), p. 157; Donncha Ó Corráin, *Ireland before the Normans* (Dublin, 1972), pp 89-90; P. H. Sawyer, *Kings and Vikings* (London, 1982), p. 84.
8. *A.U.;* for the significance of 'cell' here see A.D.S. MacDonald, 'Notes on terminology in the Annals of Ulster 650-1050', *Peritia* i (1982), pp 329-33: 332.
9. Edmund Hogan, *Onomasticon Goedelicum* (Dublin, 1910), pp 457-8; Price, *R.I.A. Proc.* xlvi C, p. 274; idem, *Placenames* vii, p. vi; Smyth, *Celt. Leinster*, p. 51 and plates XII, XVI.
10. Smyth, *Celt. Leinster*, pp 19, 54-6 and plates V, VIII, XI; Nicholls, *Peritia* iii, pp 545-6.
11. *Trip. Life,* ed. Mulchrone, pp 19, 20 lines 292-4, 312-14; Price, *R.I.A. Proc.* xlvi C, p. 275; for the date of the *Tripartite* see most recently Gearóid Mac Eoin, 'The dating of Middle Irish texts', *Brit. Acad. Proc.* lxviii (1982), pp 109-39: 127-34; K.H. Jackson, 'The date of the Tripartite Life of Patrick', *Z.C.P.* xli (1986), pp 5-45, and works cited there.
12. *A.U.* 827, 1014, 1043; *A.F.M.* 1039, 1072, 1095, 1170.
13. *A.F.M.* (s.a. 972) 974, (s.a. 983) 984; Price, *R.I.A. Proc.* xlvi C, pp 285-6.
14. Plummer, *Vitae SS Hib.* i, p. 237; Price, *R.I.A. Proc.* xivi C, p. 274; but cf. Nicholls, Peritia, pp 543-5.
15. *A.U.* 831-6.
16. *A.U., Chron. Scot.,* 834, 835, 836; *Ann. Clon.* (s.a. 832, 833) 835, 836; *A.F.M.* (s.a. 834, 835) 835, 836.
17. Smyth, *Scandinavian kings in the British Isles 850-880* (Oxford, 1977), pp 155, 167; idem, *Scandinavian York and Dublin* (2 vols. Dublin, 1975-9) ii, pp 130-2; Poul Holm, 'The slave trade of Dublin, ninth to twelfth centuries', *Peritia* v (1986), pp 317-45: 318-31.
18. Smyth, *Celt. Leinster*, plates XV, XVI; O'Brien, *Corpus geneal. Hib.*, p. 354; C. Dohery, 'The Irish hagiographer: resources, aims, results' in T. Dunne (ed.), *The writer as witness: literature as historical evidence* (Cork, 1987), pp 10-22.
19. *A.U.* 817, 819, 828; *A.F.M.* (s.a. 834, 842) 835, 844.
20. *A.U., Chron. Scot., A.F.M.* (s.a. 838).
21. Byrne, *Ir. kings*, p. 130; Smyth, *Celt. Leinster*, pp 50-8.
22. *A.U., Chron. Scot., A.F.M.* (s.a. 840).
23. *Ann. Tig., A.F.M.* (s.a. 886) 889; *Chron. Scot., A.F.M.* (s.a. 982) 983.
24. *A.U.* 845; *Chron. Scot.* 848, 887; *A.F.M.* (s.a. 858, 865, 888) 860, 867, 892; see Ó Corráin, *Ire. before the Normans*, pp 94-5.
25. *A.U., Chron. Scot., A.F.M.* (s.a. 897) 902; *A.U., Chron. Scot.* (s.a. 913-18), *A.F.M.* (s.a. 912-17) 914-19; Smyth, *Scand. York and Dub.* i, pp 60, 64-71; ii, pp 18-35; Ó Corráin, *Ire. before the Normans,* pp 104-5; Breandán Ó Ríordáin, 'The High St. excavations', Bö Almquist and David Greene (ed.), *Proceedings of the seventh Viking congress* (Dublin, 1976), pp 135-40; J.A. Graham-Campbell, 'The Viking-age silver hoards of Ireland', ibid., pp 39-74: 39-40; Pat Wallace, 'The origins of Dublin', B.G. Scott (ed.), *Studies in early Ireland* (Belfast, 1981), pp 129-43.
26. Johannes Bøe, 'Norse antiquities in Ireland', Haakon Shetelig (ed.), *Viking antiquities in Great Britain and Ireland,* iii (Oslo, 1940), pp 73-4; George Coffey, 'A pair of brooches and chains of the Viking period recently found in Ireland', *R.S.A.I. Jn.* xxxii (1902), pp 71-3.
27. Coffey, loc. cit., p. 72; D.M. Wilson, 'Scandinavian settlement in the north and west of the British Isles: an archaeological point of view', *Royal Hist. Soc. Trans.* xxvi (1976), pp 95-113: 99.

28. Graham-Campbell, loc. cit., pp 40-2; Wilson, loc. cit., pp 97-100, 104-9.
29. See Young, *History*, xxxv, pp 27-9; *Ann. Inisf.* 975 (Limerick); *Chron. Scot.* (s.a. 978), *Ann. Tig., A.F.M* (s.a. 978) 980 (Dublin); *A.U., Chron. Scot* (s.a. 981), *Ann. Tig., A.F.M.* (s.a. 982) 983 (Waterford); 'genti' is used of the Hiberno-Norse only once after 943 in *A.U.*
30. Bøe, loc. cit., pp 83-4.
31. George Coffey, E.C.R. Armstrong, 'Scandinavian objects found at Islandbridge and Kilmainham', *R.I.A. Proc.* xxviii C (1910), pp 107-22: 108.
32. Office of Public Works, *Sites and monuments record, County Wicklow* (Dublin, 1986), p. 49; Price, *Placenames* vii, pp xxii, xxvii; M.V. Ronan, 'The ancient churches of the deanery of Wicklow', *R.S.A.I. Jn.* lviii (1928), pp 132-55: 142-3.
33. Macalister, *Corpus inscriptionum* ii, pp 84-6, plate XXXVI; James Ware, *De Hibernia et antiquitatibus ejus disquistiones ...* (London, 1654), pp 129, 130; R. H. M. Dolley, *The Hiberno-Norse coins in the British Museum* (London 1966), pp 75-6; Richard Hall, 'A check-list of Viking-age coin finds from Ireland', *Ulster Jn. Arch.* xxxvi-xxxvii (1973-4), p. 81; cf. Bradley, 'Scandinavian settlement', p. 54, and the eighty-four coin hoard deposited at Baltinglass about 1050 (Dolley, op. cit., p. 69; Hall, loc. cit., pp 80-1).
34. Price, *R.I.A. Proc.* xlvi C, pp 274, 283-6; Smyth, *Celt. Leinster*, pp 51, 54-6; *Chron. Scot.* (s.a. 916), *A.F.M.* (s.a. 915).
35. Smyth, *Celt. Leinster*, pp 43-4, 55-6; *A.F.M.* (s.a. 983); but for a reputed Uí Dúnchada king of Leinster in the late eleventh century see Nicholls, *Peritia* iii, p. 537, note 2.
36 See above, note 13.
37. *A.U.* 1014, 1039, 1043; *A.F.M.* 1039, 1043, 1072, 1095, 1170; see Price, *R.I.A. Proc.* xlvi C, p. 286 and Smyth, *Celt. Leinster*, p. 54.
38. *Chron Scot.* (s.a. 1099) 1103; *A.F.M.* 1154, 1170; Price, *R.I.A. Proc.* xlvi C, p. 285; Smyth, *Celt Leinster*, p. 56.
39. *R.I.A.Proc.* xlvi C, p. 285; for a possible example of the name see O'Brien, *Corpus geneal. Hib.*, p. 436.
40. *A.U.* 852, 883, 886, 895; *Chron. Scot., A.F.M.* (s.a. 891) 896; Alexander Bugge, *Contributions to the history of the Norsemen in Ireland* (Christiania, 1900) i, pp 12-3; see also *A.U.* 989 and Smyth, *Scand. kings*, p. 155, *Scand. York and Dub.* ii, pp 309-10.
41. See *A.U.* 1045.2, 1049.5, 1074.5, 1080.7, 1102.6, 1103.4, 1119.4, 1128.3,7.
42. *Bk. Rights*, ed. Dillon, p. 106, lines 1557-64.
43. Ibid., p. 154 and see Price's notes on the map ibid., under 'Lagin'.
44. G.D. Scott, The stones of Bray (Dublin, 1913), p. 66; *A.U., Chron. Scot.* (s.a. 1018); *A.F.M.* (s.a. 1019), *Ann. Clon.* (s.a. 1013) 1020; On the other hand, there is evidence that Augaire mac Dúnlaing's kinsmen, the Uí Muiredaig, had links with Glendalough by the earlier eleventh century; see A. S. Mac Shamráin, '*Prosopographica Glindelachensis*: the monastic church of Glendalough and its community, sixth to thirteenth centuries', *R.S.A.I. Jn.*, cxix (1989), pp 79-97: 85, and additionally *A.U.* 1014.3 in the light of *Bk. Leinster* i, p. 183 line 5474.
45. *A.F.M.* 1021; Price, *Placenames* v, pp 320-1; Smyth, *Celt. Leinster*, p. 54; however the phrase 'i nUibh Briúin Cualand' could be a misplaced gloss explaining the location of Delgany.
46. Price, *Placenames* v, p. 338; vii, p. 395; Smyth, *Celt. Leinster*, pp 52-3 and plate XI; Nicholls, *Peritia* iii, p. 538 note 2.
47. *A.U.* 788, 881; *A.F.M.* (s.a. 868) 870, (s.a. 889) 894, (s.a. 890) 895, (s.a. 955) 957, 1027, 1048, 1061, 1130.

48. *A.F.M.* 1141; see Price, *Placenames* v, pp 337-8; Smyth, *Celt. Leinster*, p. 44.
49. J.T. Gilbert, *History of the city of Dublin* (3 vols. Dublin, 1859) i, pp 403-8: 407 (see also pp 231-2); *Bk. Leinster* (facs.), pp 388-9; Nicholls, *Peritia* iii, p. 537.
50. 'The Rathdown slabs', *R.S.A.I. Jn.* lxxxvii (1957), pp 75-88; see P. J. O'Reilly, 'The Christian sepulchral leacs and free-standing crosses of the Dublin halfbarony of Rathdown', *R.S.A.I. Jn* xxxi (1901), pp 134-61, Scott, *Bray*, pp 60-2.
51. O'Reilly, loc. cit., pp 149-52; Scott, *Bray*, p. 61; Ó hÉailidhe, loc. cit., pp 87-8.
52. 'Early Christian graveslabs in the Dublin region', *R.S.A.I. Jn.* ciii (1973), pp 51-64: 53, 56-9 (I am grateful to the Society's Council for permission to reproduce figures 3 and 4 from pp 56 and 58 of the above); this interpretation of the slabs is accepted by Bradley, 'Scandinavian settlement', p. 60.
53. Scott, *Bray*, pp 57-64; Kathleen Turner, *If you seek monuments: a guide to the antiquities of the barony of Rathdown* (Rathmichael Hist. Soc., 1983), no. 46 (I am indebted to Pádraig Patridge of Bord Fáilte Éireann who referred me to this work); for slabs which have come to light since 1973 see Ó hÉailidhe, *R.S.A.I. Jn.* cxii (1982), pp 139-41; cxiv (1984), pp 142-4; Ó hÉailidhe and Ellen Prendergast, *R.S.A.I. Jn.* cvii (1977), pp 139-42; T.C. Breen, *R.S.A.I. Jn.* cxi (1981), pp 120-1.
54. O'Reilly, *R.S.A.I. Jn.*, xxxi, pp 152-4; Scott, *Bray*, pp 57-8; Turner, *Monuments*, no. 46; on foreign dedications see Pádraig Ó Riain, 'Conservation in the vocabulary of the early Irish church', in Donnchadh Ó Corráin, Liam Breatnach and Kim McCone (eds.), *Sages, saints and storytellers: celtic studies in honour of Professor James Carney* (Maynooth, 1989), pp 358-66: 360, 364 note 31.
55. John Ryan, 'Pre-Norman Dublin', *R.S.A.I. Jn.* lxxix (1949), pp 64-83: 80-1; Patrick Power, *The placenames of Decies* (2nd. edn. Cork, 1952), p. 229; see M.V. Ronan, 'The ancient churches of the deanery of Arklow, Co. Wicklow', *R.S.A.I. Jn.* lvii (1927), pp 100-16: 115.
56. Gilbert, *Hist. of Dublin* i, pp 404, 407; *Fél. Oeng.*, pp 12-3; see E.J. Gwynn and W.J. Purton (ed.), 'The Monastery of Tallaght', *R.I.A. Proc.* xxix C (1911), pp 115-79: 129§ 6, 130§8, 137§28, 138§30.
57. Price, *Placenames* v, pp 330-1; however, Ó hÉailidhe upon reconsideration feels that the Kilbride (Fairy Hill) slab may not in fact belong to the *genre R.S.A.I. Jn.*, cxii, pp 139-41.
58 *Alen's reg.*, p. 2; Gilbert (ed.), *Crede Mihi* (Dublin, 1897), p. 46; for the Killegar slab see fig.1, no. B15 and Ó hÉailidhe, *R.S.A.I. Jn.* lxxxvii, pp 81-2, no.12.
59. Price, *Placenames* iv, p. 263; O.P.W., *S.M.R. Wicklow*, p. 7, no. 012 and sheet 005 of the accompanying maps.
60. I am indebted to Anna L. Brindley of the Archaeological Survey for details of her assistant Eoin Grogan's report on visiting the site in the summer of 1989.
61. J C. Dyer, 'Earthworks of the Danelaw frontier', P. J. Fowler (ed.), *Archaeology and the landscape* (London, 1972), pp 222-36.
62. *Bk. Rights*, ed. Dillon, pp ix, 118-9 lines 1737-40, 1761-4; Smyth, *Celt. Leinster*, pp 43-4.
63. Curtis, *E.H.R.* xxiii, pp 209-19; idem, *Med. Ire.*, passim (see index under 'Ostmen'); Bradley, 'Scandinavian settlement', pp 62-5.
64. Price, *R.I.A. Proc.* xlvi C, p. 273; idem, *Placenames* vii, p. 477; see *Hist. & mun. doc. Ire.*, pp 6, 19, 32 ('lohannes filius Arcaill', 'Adam filius Arkil', 'Radulfus filius Anketalli').
65. See Price, 'The placenames of the barony of Newcastle, county of Wicklow', *R.I.A. Proc.* xliv C, pp 171-2; Magne Oftedal, 'Scandinavian placenames in Ireland', *Proc. 7th Viking cong.*, pp 125-33: 129-31; *Hist. and mun. doc. Ire.*, p. 44.

66. See Price, *Placenames* vii, pp xxvii-xxxiii, 494, and for the earliest post-conquest documents relating to Arklow and Wicklow see *Gormanston reg.*, p. 193; *Ormond deeds 1172-1350*, p. 8.
67. Curtis, *Med. Ire.*, p. 55 note 1; for the full text of this document see Bugge, *Bidrag til det sidste afsnit af Nordboernes historie i Irland* (Copenhagen, 1905), pp 286-7 note z.
68. *Chartul. St Mary's, Dublin* i, especially pp 83-4, 129-34, 181, 207, 216, 227-39, 246-9, 346-52, 363, 430, 471-9, 486-9, 495-513.
69. *Cal. papal letters 1417-31,* pp 129-30; *Chartul. St Mary's,* i, pp 85-6.
70. Price, *Placenames* vii, pp xxvi-xxviii; *Ir. Cartul. Llanthony,* pp 253-4; *Hist. and mun. doc. Ire.*, p. 9.
71. *A.U.* 914, 918, 921, 980, 994, 1005, 1035, 1087; *A.F.M.* 1133, 1146, 1167; *Hist. and mun. doc. Ire.*, p. 21.
72. *Ir. Cartul. Llanthony*, p. 256.
73. *Hist. and mun. doc. Ire.*, pp 3, 5, 9, 11, 12, 26, 32, 37, 43; *Cal. papal letters 1417-31,* pp 129-30; *Chartul. St. Mary's* i, pp 32-3, 84, 207, 246, 347-9, 489, 495, 505; *Reg. St. John Dublin*, pp 85-6, 132.
74. Aubrey Gwynn, 'The origin of St. Mary's Abbey, Dublin', *R.S.A.I. Jn.*, lxxix (1949), pp 110-25.
75. *Reg. St. John*, p. 237; Smyth, *Scand. York and Dub.* ii, pp 309-11.
76. Price, *Placenames* vii, p. xxviii; Wallace, 'Anglo-Norman Dublin: continuity and change', Ó Corráin (ed.), *Irish Antiquity* (Cork, 1981), pp 247-68: 263-5; E.C. Bourke, 'Two early eleventh century Viking houses from Bride Street, Wexford, and the layout of properties on the site', *Wexford Hist. Soc. Jn.* xii (1988-9), pp 50-61: 57-60.
77. Price, *Placenames* vii, p. xxii; P. J. Power, *The Arklow Calendar* (Arklow, 1981), pp 17, 22.
78. *Alen's reg.*, p. 2; *Crede Mihi,* p. 46; *Ir. Cartul. Llanthony,* pp 255, 257, 259.
79. Price, *R.I.A. Proc.* xliv C, p. 172; idem, *Placenames* vii, p. 423.
80. A. B. Scott and F. X. Martin (eds.), *Expugnatio Hibernica: the Conquest of Ireland, by Giraldus Cambrensis* (Dublin, 1978), pp 120-1, 142-3, 170-1, 330 note 288, and cf. G. H. Orpen, 'Motes and Norman castles in Ireland', *E.H.R.* xxii (1907), pp 228-54: 250-1. The details in the Llanthony grant seem to favour this identification of St Patrick's, rather than the belief that the Church of Ireland occupies the site of the chapel of St Thomas, attached to St Thomas's Abbey Dublin; see *Ir. Cartul. Llanthony,* p. 274; *Reg. St. Thomas Dublin,* pp 292-3; Ronan, *R.S.A.I. Jn.*, lviii, pp 142-3; Frank Mc Phail, *Guide to Wicklow town and district* (Wicklow, 1913), pp 4-5; Michael Clarke, *Wicklow parish,* 1844-1944 (Wexford 1944), pp 10-11, 15-20.
81. *Ir. Cartul. Llanthony,* p. 542.
82. Price, 'The Byrne's country in county Wicklow in the sixteenth century: and the manor of Arklow', *R.S.A.I. Jn.*, lxvi (1936), pp 41-66: 52-3; idem, *Placenames* vii, pp xxvii, 417.
83. Price, *R.I.A. Proc.* xlvi C, p. 257; idem, *Placenames* vii, pp 457-9; Smyth, *Celt. Leinster, p.* 131 note 17; *Alen's reg.*, p. 2; *Crede Mihi,* p. 46.
84. *Alen's reg.*, p. 2; *Crede Mihi,* p. 46; Price, *R.I.A. Proc.* xlvi C, pp 261, 267, 268, 277; idem, *Placenames* i, p. 14; ii, pp 62-3; vii, pp 465, 469, 473-4, 480.
85. *Alen's reg.*, p. 2; *Crede Mihi,* p. 46; Price, *R.I.A. Proc.* xliv C, p. 174; xlvi C, pp 243-4, 249, 258; idem, *Placenames* vii, pp 411, 439, 444, 446, 458.
86. *Ir. Cartul. Llanthony,* pp 255-9; Price, *Placenames* vii, p. 417.
87. Price, *Placenames* vii, p. 438.

88. Ibid., pp 429, 434, 448, 459; idem, *R.I.A. Proc.* xlvi C, pp 239, 242, 251, 259.
89. Price, *Placenames* vii, pp 484, 490; Ronan, *R.S.A.I. Jn.*, lvii, p. 115.
90. *Ir. Cartul. Llanthony*, pp 255, 257, 259; Price, *R.I.A. Proc.* xlvi C, pp 244, 253; idem, *Placenames* vii, pp xxii, 452-3; O.P.W., *S.M.R. Wicklow*, p. 58, no. 027 and sheet 030 of the accompanying maps.
91. See Oftedal, 'Scandinavian placenames', p. 127.
92. Price, *R.I.A. Proc.* xlvi C, p. 285; Curtis, *E.H.R.* xxiii, pp 215-17; idem, *Med. Ire.*, pp 196-9.
93. Price, *R.I.A. Proc.* xlvi C, pp 54, 59, 63-6; idem, *Placenames* vii, p. xxxii; *Ormond deeds 1547-84*, pp 211-15; *1584-1603*, pp 8-9; *P.R.I. rep. D.K.*, 17, pp 270-1; *A.U.* 1014.
94. *Ormond deeds 1547-84*, pp 211-2; *1584-1603*, p. 9; *P.R.I. rep. D.K.*, 17, p. 270.
95. *Alen's reg.*, p. 28; Bugge, *Bidrag*, pp 297-300; Bradley, 'Scandinavian settlement', p. 57.
96. *Chartul. St. Mary's* i, pp 222, 242, 430-1, 461.
97. *Alen's reg.*, pp 165-6; Nicholls (*Peritia* iii, p. 539 note 1) observes that the parishes of Tipperkevin and Ballymore were in county Dublin before 1837.
98. *Hist. and mun. doc. Ire.*, pp 238-9.
99. E. St. John Brooks, 'The De Ridelesfords', *R.S.A.I. Jn.* lxxxi (1951), pp 115-38: 118.
100. James Mills, 'The Norman settlement in Leinster: the cantreds near Dublin', *R.S.A.I. Jn.* xxiv (1894), pp 160-75: 163-4; Scott, *Bray*, pp 208-17; Brooks, loc. cit.; Price, 'The grant to Walter de Ridelesford of Brien and the land of the sons of Turchil', *R.S.A.I. Jn.* lxxxiv (1954), pp 72-7.
101. See Curtis, *Dublin Hist. Rec.* iv, p. 103.
102. Curtis, *Med. Ire.*, pp 21, 35, 41 note 2, 54-5, 62-3, 67, 80-3, 196.
103. Price, *R.S.A.I. Jn.* lxxxiv, p. 74; ibid., *Placenames* v, pp 283-4, 287; for the grant of Tully see *Alen's reg.*, p. 28; Bradley, 'Scandinavian settlement', p. 56.
104. *Alen's reg.*, pp 112-3; see Curtis, *E.H.R.* xxiii, pp 211-5, 219; idem, *Med. Ire.*, pp 195-9; I am indebted to Pádraig Patridge who first drew my attention to these records.
105. *Alen's reg.*, pp 112-3, 158-9.
106. *Chartul. St. Mary's* i, pp 106-8, 387; *Reg. St. Thomas Dublin*, pp 144-7; for examples of these names see note 73, above.
107. *Reg. St. Thomas*, p. 150; *Chartul. St. Mary's* i, pp 207, 250, 518; Price, *Placenames* v, pp 328, 331-2.
108. Scott, *Bray*, pp 183-4; Price, *Placenames* v, pp 296-8; Bradley, 'Scandinavian settlement', p. 56.
109. Bugge, *Bidrag*, pp 301-3; Price, *Placenames* v, pp 291, 297; Smyth, *Celt. Leinster*, p. 55; T.F. O'Rahilly, 'Notes on Middle Irish pronunciation', *Hermathena* xx (1926), pp 152-95: 161-2 (I owe this reference to Liam Breatnach of T.C.D.).
110. Price, *Placenames* v, pp 284, 318-20, 325; Power, *Placenames of Decies*, pp 185-6.
111. Price, *R.I.A. Proc.* xliv C, pp 158, 160; *Placenames* vii, pp 398, 400.
112. 'Scandinavian settlement', pp 60-2.

Chapter 4

THE 'UNITY' OF CÓEMGEN AND CIARÁN: A COVENANT BETWEEN GLENDALOUGH AND CLONMACNOIS IN THE TENTH TO ELEVENTH CENTURIES

A. S. Mac SHAMHRÁIN

Scarcely had a century elapsed from the time of the monastic founders, before the religious communities established by them had acquired extensive grants of land, complete with tenantry. These monastic estates produced an agricultural surplus which, in many instances, was enough to support a sizeable population. Through royal patronage, some foundations including Glendalough, developed into ecclesiastical centres, attracting pilgrims, penitents and refugees in sufficient number that permanent residences grew up around the monastic limits. Such foci of population in time attracted trade and commerce, so that in some cases they assumed the characteristics of prototowns.[1] Their value as sources of revenue, centres for recruitment and locations for billeting troops was duly recognised by local and regional rulers, who sought to subject these ecclesiastical settlements to dynastic interests.

Perhaps as early as the eighth century, as argued above by Professor Smyth, the foundation of Glendalough had expanded into the lower valley and the monastic *civitas* had commenced to develop. The century that followed witnessed the emergence of *principes* or princely abbots, men whose very tenure of office suggests dynastic interests.[2] By this time, Glendalough was developing as a commercial centre, having assumed an economic and political importance almost certainly never envisaged by its founder, St Cóemgen.[3] The ecclesiastical settlement *c.*900 consisted of a religious community some of whom were celibate, even ascetic, while others married. The religious formed the nucleus of a greater community, which included the monastic tenants and other permanent residents, officially classified as *manaig* (from the Latin *monachus,* a monk). All were under the spiritual and temporal jurisdiction of an abbot, who may have been ordained priest or bishop, or may merely have been in minor orders.

The combined evidence of the annals, genealogies and hagiography would seem to suggest that, prior to the turn of the tenth century, the dominant dynastic interests at Glendalough included those of Uí Máil and Uí Dúnlainge, the lineage which then provided the kings of Leinster. No doubt this level of royal patronage helped to promote the status of the foundation. It is clear from the above-mentioned body of sources that Glendalough had established a wide network of contacts with other foundations at quite an early date. One might expect the size and relative prestige of the foundations involved to be a factor in determining how relationships developed; lesser establishments generally submitted to greater ones, while centres of comparable status often arrived at some mutual agreement.

Hagiographical literature provides an important lead here. In all probability, reference in the Life of a saint to transactions involving other founder-patrons does reflect later relationships between the foundations concerned.[4] It may be noted that the Latin Life of St Cóemgen indicates a range of relationships There are express claims that the holy abbot Crónán personally submitted to Cóemgen, while Eógan and his companions feature as tutors to the young saint, performing a service for him, as it were; later sources make it clear that the south county Dublin sites of Clondalkin and Kilnamanagh were subject to Glendalough. In contrast, the alleged dealings between Cóemgen and the patrons Munnu, Cainnech, Comgall and Colum Cille seem to suggest that Taghmon, Aghaboe, Bangor and the Columban federation recognised the paruchial rights of *Familia Coemgeni*.[5]

In most cases there is not sufficient data available to facilitate inquiry into what these agreements actually involved. A relationship between Glendalough and Clonmacnois, however, represented in hagiographical tradition as a personal treaty between the patrons Cóemgen and Ciarán mac int sáir, receives considerable focus and may therefore have had particular significance. The Latin life of St Cóemgen which, although it survives only in later medieval compilations, is clearly based on a work of relatively early date,[6] includes an episode in which the patron of Glendalough is made to visit Clonmacnois. Prior to his arrival, Ciarán had already departed this life but, undeterred, Cóemgen entered the mortuary chapel whereupon the deceased was temporarily restored to life and the two saints engaged in dialogue. At the request of Ciarán, they agree to exchange vestments as a sign of everlasting friendship. The following morning, on opening the door of the basilica, the monks find that Cóemgen and Ciarán are wearing each other's garb.[7] The episode is alluded to but not related in detail in the Vita Sancti Ciarani; its introduction here is probably another instance of the thirteenth-century redactor of the compilation making editorial comment, various examples of which are highlighted by Sharpe.[8]

It has long been agreed that the Lives of the Saints, certainly in the Irish context, are not biographies but paradigms relating to the period of composition.[9] Leaving aside the miraculous content of the story as contained in the Latin Life, the episode discussed above does seem to suggest that an arrangement was made between the two foundations, and at a period considerably later in time than that of the patron Cóemgen. The hagiographer is apparently concerned to convey the message that no surrender was made on the part of Glendalough; on the contrary, what took place was a mutual agreement. The key motif in the episode is that of an exchange of habits; nothing is bestowed by one saint on the other and the pledge made is one of friendship, not obedience.

Many years ago, Ryan remarked on the forms of voluntary relationship that are known to have existed between certain ecclesiastical centres. He referred to *fraternitas* (brotherhood), the *óentad* (union) and the *cotach* (covenant); through such arrangements, foundations shared in each other's prayers and merits, and helped each other when their rights were endangered. He alluded to the existence of an arrangement between Glendalough and Clonmacnois, citing a version of the 'visit' episode from the Irish Life of Ciarán in the Book of Lismore.[10] The language of the *Betha Ciaráin* contained in this fifteenth-century compilation betrays many modernising features, yet preserves enough older forms to suggest original composition in the Middle Irish period. In this version, as in the Latin Life, the saints converse in the mortuary chapel and exchange garbs. This source, however, expressly uses the term *óentad* (union) to describe their agreement. The account continues with the claim that Cóemgen administered communion to Ciarán, who in turn presented his visitor with a bell. The hagiographer hastens to add that this gift was given *'i comurtha a n-óentad ocus i screpul a chomnae'* (in commemoration of their unity and in payment for his communion).[11] Nonetheless, one is left with the distinct impression that the community of Glendalough was in some way beholden to Clonmacnois.

In the final analysis, however, the Lives of the Saints are a genre of literature rather than an historical record. Although often reflecting property claims and assertions of privilege on the part of ecclesiastical foundations, these accounts have no chronological framework. Moreover, as the situations represented were presumably well known in the writer's time, there was no perceived need to explain how or why such arrangements came about. For a guide to chronology or historical context, one must rely upon the annals. Indeed, Ó Briain considered an appeal to this latter source essential for the task of interpreting hagiographical accounts.[12]

Turning to the compilations of annals, it emerges that the Annals of Ulster, generally viewed as the most reliable, do not even preserve a complete list of obits for the senior clergy of Glendalough.[13] Certainly, this collection contains no indication of a link between Glendalough and Clonmacnois. For many obits of the *familia Coemgeni* and, importantly, for incidental references to interaction between the two foundations concerned, we are dependent on the seventeenth-century compilation of Míchél Ó Cléirigh and his companions, known as the Annals of the Four Masters.[14] This is the only source in which certain abbots and bishops of Glendalough are recorded; it also provides the sole testimony to various interactions between the Wicklow foundation and Clonmacnois. Perhaps the most significant of these notices is the obituary of Abbot Ferdomnach Ua Maenaig. An entry in *A.U.* merely records in a typically laconic formula that this man passed away in the year 952; he is titled *comarba Ciarâin* (successor of St Ciaran), indicating that he was abbot of Clonmacnois.[15] It is only in *A.F.M.* that Ferdomnach is credited with a dual abbacy involving Glendalough. On the surface, the entry certainly appears authentic. Transliterated in form into the Early Modern Irish of the compilers' day, it reads:

> Ferdomnach abb Ua Maonaig, abb Cluana m Nois & Gline dá Locha do Corca Moga a cenél. (Abbot Ferdomnach Ua Maonaig, abbot of Clonmacnois and of Glendalough of the kindred of Corco Mocchae).[16]

The additional information linking this abbot to an obscure subject population of the Connachta, whose territory of Corcamroe was apparently located in the parish of Kilkerrin, barony of Killian, county Galway, seems quite in order for a midland ecclesiastic.[17]

The question, however, concerns the reference to Glendalough. Is it reasonable to accept as authentic a notice preserved only in a late source when there is no other record elsewhere of a dual abbacy between Clonmacnois and Glendalough? This is not to suggest that Ó Cléirigh and his collaborators were guilty of deliberate efforts to mislead; they were, however, compiling a vast bulk of data from a wide range of sources under extremely difficult and pressurised circumstances. It can be shown that, on occasion, they made mistakes. At least three *A.F.M.* entries regarding Glendalough are demonstrably erroneous, with one involving the not altogether uncommon scribal oversight of homoeoteleuton, whereby two separate annal entries containing similar elements become telescoped into a single notice.[18] As shall emerge in due course, however, the Four Masters carry two other entries linking Glendalough and Clonmacnois, which would suggest that they are relaying data from a lost Clonmacnois source. Apparently, none of these three items was available to Mageoghegan, who compiled his Annals of Clonmacnois in 1627, or to Mac Firbisigh who was working on his Chronicon Scotorum in the mid-seventeenth century.[19]

Although the record for Glendalough, as noted above, preserves no other reference to a dual abbot apart from the *A.F.M.* notice of Ferdomnach, nor indeed any intimation of a relationship with Clonmacnois prior to that date, an indicator may perhaps be discerned in the record of the latter foundation. The obit of a certain Dunchad mac Suthenéin is entered for the year 942 with the title 'episcopus Cluana m. Nóis.'[20] The personal name of this bishop, while not exactly rare, has strong Leinster connotations. At least four members of the North Leinster dynasty of Uí Dúnlainge, the over-lordship of which extended across the modern counties of Kildare and Wicklow, were called Dúnchad.[21] The name of the bishop's father, however, is highly unusual. The sole recorded bearer of this *praenomen* is Suthenén mac Artúir, a dynast of the Uí Muiredaig lineage of Uí Dúnlainge (see fig. 4.1), record of whom is preserved for the year 858 only by the Four Masters; it would be chronologically quite feasible for this dynast to have had a son living until 942 if, as seems likely, he was still a youth at the time of recording.[22]

The presence at Clonmacnois in the early tenth century of a bishop belonging to a Leinster royal lineage, which ruled a patrimony in south Kildare and west Wicklow and had an established interest at Glendalough, could indeed account for how a relationship between the *familia* of Cóemgen and that of Ciarán developed. However, the reason for his taking office there and the probable motive for the voluntary acceptance of a Clonmacnois abbot at Glendalough, if this is in fact what did happen, remains to be considered. The explanation should perhaps be sought through reconstructing the political maelstrom that was north Leinster in the ninth to tenth centuries.

It has been quite adequately demonstrated that the overkingdom of Uí Dúnlainge came under increasing pressure from the mid-ninth century onwards as the power of Norse Dublin expanded.[23] With the rise to power of the family of Sitric Gale after 917, it is clear that the lordship of Dublin extended southwards and westwards across the patrimonial kingdom of Uí Muiredaig.[24] The point raised by Byrne, however, that the impact of Osraige ambitions was ultimately more detrimental to the Uí Dúnlainge overkingship, is important to the present inquiry.[25] These kings of the Munster marchlands and their allies from the Barrow Valley region gradually extended their power into northern Leinster from the mid-ninth century onwards. It was

Cerball mac Dúngaile king of Osraige who, in 858, took the young Suthenén mac Artúir and his cousin Cairbre mac Dúnlainge as hostages. Cerball exercised considerable influence over north Leinster affairs until his death thirty years later. His son Diarmait celebrated the Oenach Carman in the early tenth century, thereby staking a claim to the overkingship of Leinster. Dublin Norse power may have faded in the years that followed the battle of Tara in 980, but a dynast of the line of Cerball, Donnchad mac Gillapátraice, ensured that Osraige ambition was kept alive into the following century to see down the overkingship aspirations of Uí Dúnlainge.

It seems clear that the principal dynasty of north Leinster remained weak throughout this period. Ailill mac Dúnlainge of the Uí Muiredaig lineage (fig. 4.1), claimant to the overkingship of Leinster, was slain in 871 by the Norse.[26] Many of the Uí Dúnlainge kings, as Byrne has observed, carried lesser titles or had short reigns, implying that they exercised little effective control; only Cerball mac Muirecáin of the Uí

Fig. 4.1 Uí Muiredaig Lineage of Uí Dúnlainge

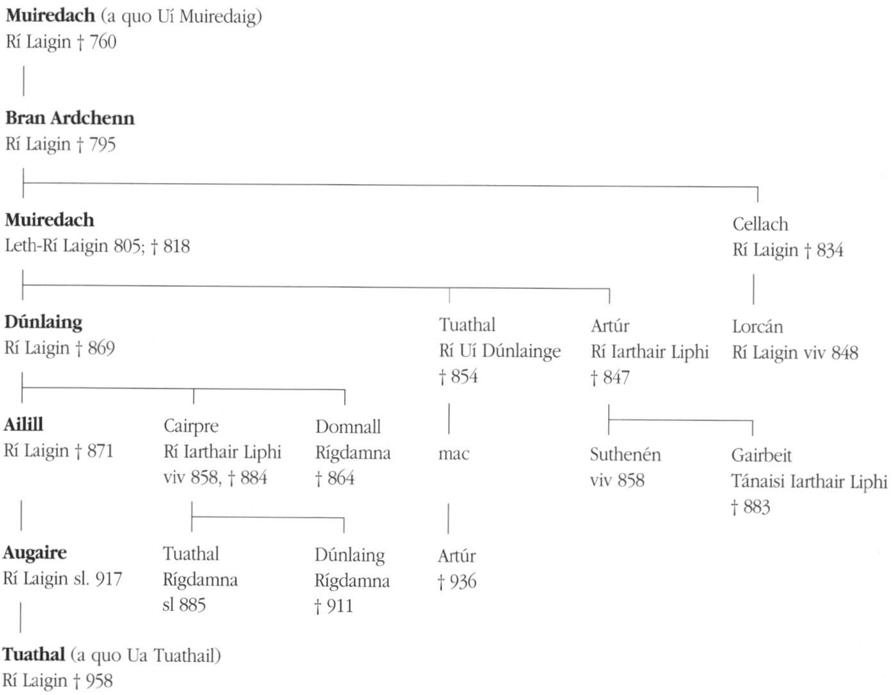

Pedigree of Ua Tuathail from the Pre-Norman genealogies in bold type; see also chapter 2, A. P. Smyth, 'Kings, Saints and Sagas', Table 2.6; Rawlinson B 502, 117 e, LL 337 d; *Corpus Genealogiarum*, pp 12-13; *Book of Leinster*, VI, p. 1480; Additional information from the annals.

Faeláin lineage († 909) stands out as a strong Leinster overking.[27] Following the death of Augaire, son of the above mentioned Ailill, slain by the Norse at the battle of Cenn Fuait in 917, it appears that the very patrimony of Uí Muiredaig was under threat; succession to the local kingship at this point is uncertain, until Augaire's son in turn, Tuathal (eponym of the Ua Tuathail line later established in county Wicklow), asserted his position just before mid-century.[28] It seems that the only Uí Muiredaig dynasty recorded at this time is a certain Artúr ua Tuathail (perhaps a grandson of Tuathal mac Maíle Brigte; fig. 4.1) whose obit, in which he is not accorded any royal title, is entered for 936 by the Four Masters.[29]

In the ecclesiastical sphere, a dilution of Uí Dúnlainge dominance may likewise be detected. At Glendalough, the abbatial record for the tenth century includes several clerics, notably Cormac mac Fitbrain and Flann ua hÁeduccáin, whose names appear to fit comfortably into the Osraige or 'west Leinster' context; the name of a subsequent abbot Crunnmael, which as this writer previously noted, occurs in the genealogies of Uí Cheinnselaig, is also found among the Osraige.[30] It may be significant that during the abbacy of Flann ua hÁeduccáin, an abbot of the Osraige foundation of Saigir died on pilgrimage at the establishment of Cóemgen.[31] An even more pointed indicator, however, could well lie in the obit of Dublitir mac Selbaig. This man, who died in 932 as *fer léginn* (head of the monastic school) of Glendalough was, significantly, abbot of Tech Moling in the Barrow Valley. He was probably a brother of Guaire mac Selbaig, who died in 945 as abbot of Castledermot, a foundation which was clearly subject to Glendalough.[32] It may be noted that the personal name of their father, Selbach, occurs among the genealogies of Osraige and Uí Dróna. The association of these west Leinster clerics with the *familia Coemgeni* provides a reasonable explanation for the otherwise curious episode in the Vita Sancti Moling which claims that the patron of St Mullins succeeded to the abbacy of Glendalough.[33] Significantly, Price gives the Irish form of Glasnamullen in the parish of Derrylossary (where there is an ecclesiastical site with a St Kevin's well adjacent) as Glaisne Moling.[34]

There is ample evidence, therefore, that the north Leinster region including the modern county of Wicklow and adjacent parts of Kildare and Dublin was experiencing severe political pressure in the tenth century. The Norsemen were undoubtedly a major factor in this; however, the Osraige rulers of the Barrow-Nore Valley clearly capitalised on the weakness of the Uí Dúnlainge dynasty and sought to extend their overlordship across the Leinster heartland. It appears that, parallel to this political expansion, strenuous efforts were made to establish a 'west Leinster' ecclesiastical ascendancy at the expense of

Uí Dúnlainge interests at Glendalough. As Hughes pointed out, dual abbacies are generally associated with difficult times; it is understandable that a foundation when threatened by politico-ecclesiastical interests within its own region, might seek to strengthen its position through affiliation with a more benign centre elsewhere.[35] The validity of the Four Masters' claim of dual abbacy notwithstanding, the motive for the *óentad* between Glendalough and Clonmacnois, reflected so clearly in hagiographical sources, should probably be understood in the context of the tenth-century political situation outlined above.

The relationship between the two foundations would seem to have continued into the eleventh century. In 1030, an abbot of Glendalough named Flann Ua Cellaig (who may have belonged to a segment of Uí Bairrche) died on pilgrimage at Clonmacnois while, almost a generation later, Daigre Ua Dubatáin *anmchara Cluana* (confessor of Clonmacnois) died at Glendalough.[36] By this time, however, dynastic politics within Leinster had undergone extensive reshaping and succession to St Coémgen was dominated by local interests and increasingly by the Uí Muiredaig lineage of Uí Dúnlainge.[37] There is no further record of contact between the *familia* of Cóemgen and that of Ciarán. As a final consideration, however, in view of the strong case for a Clonmacnois connection which apparently spanned more than a century, it seems reasonable to suggest that the church at Glendalough known as Cró Ciaráin, probably commemorated the patron of Clonmacnois rather than any other saint of that name.[38]

Acknowledgements

The writer is grateful to Dr Katharine Simms and to Dr Seán Duffy of the Department of Medieval History, Trinity College Dublin, for helpful comments on this paper; he is also obliged to Fr Fennessy, O.F.M., librarian and archivist at the Franciscan Library Killiney, for permission to consult the manuscript of the Annals of the Four Masters.

References

1. Doherty, C. 'The Monastic Town in Medieval Ireland,' in *The comparative history of urban origins in Non-Roman Europe,* ed. H.B. Clarke and A. Simms (Oxford, 1985), esp. pp 60-62.
2. See above Alfred P. Smyth, 'Kings, Saints and Sagas'; also A.S. Mac Shamhráin, 'Prosopographica Glindelachensis: the monastic church of Glendalough and its community, sixth to thirteenth centuries,' *R.S.A.I. Jn.*, cxix (1989), esp. pp 82-3.
3. The Irish Life of St Cóemgen, Betha Chaemgin 11§ 11, 111§ 22, probably a twelfth century product, refers to an *Óenach* or fair at Glendalough; Charles Plummer (ed.), *Bethada Naem nErenn,* 2 vols (Oxford, 1922), i, pp 144-5; pp 140-1; note that a market cross stood in a flat open space beside the river

adjacent to the hotel car-park at Glendalough; see Charles Doherty, 'Exchange and trade in early medieval Ireland,' *R.S.A.I. Jn.*, cx (1980), 83, Katharine Simms, *From kings to warlords* (Woodbridge, Suffolk, 1987), p. 63.

4. See James F. Kenney, *Sources for the early history of Ireland: ecclesiastical* (Columbia, 1929), p. 299; Kim R. McCone, 'An introduction to early Irish saints' Lives,' *Maynooth Review,* 11 (1984), 56.

5. Vita Sancti Coemgeni, §§1, 4, 21, 27; Plummer, *Vitae SS Hib.*, 1, pp 234-5, 244, 248; features Crónán, Eogan (later associated with Ardstraw, county Derry) and Munnu of Tech Munnu. Note the episode in which Cainnech, Comgall and Colum Cille meet with Cóemgen at Uisnech and apparently accord him recognition. The subject status of Clondalkin and Kilnamanagh seems confirmed by the inclusion of Mo Chua Cluana Dolcáin (hypochoristic form of Crónán) and the bishops of Cill Manach Escrach among the *familia* of Cóemgen in the Litany of Irish Saints; LL 373 b 40; *Bk. Leinster*, pp 1698-99.

6. R., Sharpe, *Medieval Irish saints lives* (Oxford, 1991), esp. pp 15, 19, 320-4, 329, argues quite convincingly, with reference to the decline of Latin as a literary medium and to the preservation of Old Irish forms, that most saints' lives in the medieval compilations were originally cast in the eighth or ninth centuries; cf J.F. Kenney, *Sources,* p. 404, argued for a tenth century date for Vita Sancti Coemgeni. As will emerge from the ensuing discussion, it is unlikely that the Clonmacnois espisode formed part of the original vita; it may, however, have been introduced at an intermediary stage, prior to the end redaction which Sharpe would place in the thirteenth century.

7. Vita Sancti Coemgeni, §28; Plummer, *Vitae SS Hib.*, 1, pp 248-9.

8. Sharpe, *Medieval Irish saints lives,* pp 223, 359, considers that formulaic topographical expansions found throughout the Dublin manuscript of the Vitae Sanctorum and also some references to Uí Chennselaig within the Vita Sancti Coemgeni represent editorial additions; The Vita S. Ciarani §32, Plummer, *Vitae SS Hib.*, 1, p. 215, provides a four line synopsis of the Cóemgen visit and adds 'Hoc iam diligenter longa sententia in vita ipsius Coemhgeni narratur,' clearly the comment of one who was in a position to make comparisons.

9. Kenney, *Sources,* pp 300-1; Máire Herbert, 'Beathaí na Naomh,' in P. Ó Fiannachta (ed.), *Ár nDúchas Creidimh, Léachtaí Cholm Cille viii* (Maynooth, 1977), pp 5-6; McCone 'Early Irish saints' lives,' 56; Charles Doherty, 'The Irish hagiographer: resources, aims, results,' in Tom Dunne (ed.), *The writer as witness: literature as historical evidence, Historical Studies xvi* (Cork, 1987), p. 11 f.

10. J. Ryan, *Irish monasticism* (Dublin, 1931), p. 326; significantly, the episode was considered by Ryan to represent a tenth or eleventh century situation.

11. Betha Ciaráin, II. 4459-71; *Lives of the saints from the Book of Lismore* (ed.), Whitley Stokes (Oxford, 1980), pp 132-3.

12. Felim Ó Briain, 'Irish hagiography: historiography and method,' in S. O'Brien (ed.), *Measgra i gcuimhne Mhichíl Uí Chléirigh* (Dublin, 1944), p. 127.

13. *A.U.,* vol. 1. There is no record of abbots Flann Ua Anaile (†950), Coirpre Ua Corra (†972), Flann Ua Cellaig (†1030) and Conaince Ua Cerbaill (†1031), or bishops Nuada (†930) and Maelbrígde Ua Maeilfind (†1041). This leaves aside the questionable case of Muiredach Ua Mancháin whose connection with Glendalough is uncertain; A.S. Mac Shamhráin, 'Prosopographica,' 83-4, 90.

14. *A.F.M.*

15. *A.U.* s.a. 951.

16. *A.F.M.,* s.a. 950; Franciscan Library Killiney, M.S. A 13, f. 382 r.

17. J. O'Donovan, makes this identification in *A.F.M.*, 1, p. 667, note n; followed by Edmund Hogan, *Onomasticon Goedelicum* (Dublin, 1910), p. 295.
18. *A.F.M.* s.a. 781, 785 duplicates the obit of Maelcombair (giving Maelconchubhair the second time), omits Ceithernach s.a. 794 (= 799) through homoeoteleuton, at 1031. Cathasach Ua Cathail is mistakenly called Comarba Fingin (= Cóemgin).
19. Mageoghegan in *Ann. Clon.* s.a. 947 (= 952) simply records 'Ffeardownagh O'Mooney abbot of Clonvickenos died'; *Chron. Scot.*, s.a. 951 has 'Ferdomnach h. Maonaig abb Cluana Muc Nois quievit i. i nGlinn dá Locha motuus [sic] i. do Corca Moga'; however, this is a gloss in Mac Firbisigh's autograph manuscript (T.C.D. H.1.18) and was incorporated into the text (and transposed) by Fr. John Conry, who was responsible for the mid-eighteenth century copy of *Chron. Scot.* (R.I.A. P.23.5); see W.M. Hennessy in *Chron. Scot.*, pp 210-11, n. 4.
20. *A.U.* s.a. 941 has 'Dúnchad mac Suthainéin'; *A.F.M.* s.a. 940, Franciscan Library Killiney, Ms A 13, f. 376 v, has 'Duncadh eps Cluana mc Nois' in hand 1 with 'i.mc Sutanien' added in the margin.
21. Hence we find Dúnchad mac Murchada (†728; *A.U.* s.a. 727) and Dúnchad mac Lorcáin viv. late 10th C.; see Rawl. B.502, 117 c28, d31, d38; *Corpus Genealogiarum Hiberniae*, ed. Michael A. O'Brien (Dublin, 1962), pp 13-14; note also Lorcán mac Dúnchada viv. 913 (*A.F.M.* s.a. 909) and Dúnchad mac Dúnlainge put to death 1037 (*A.F.M.*; he is called Donnchad in the other annals).
22. *A.F.M.* s.a. 856; Suthenén mac Artúir, nephew of the then king of Uí Dúnlainge, Dúnlaing mac Muiredaig, was taken hostage along with the latter's son Cairpe, who lived until 884. Suthenén's brother, Gairbeit, died as Tánaisi Iarthair Liphi in 883; see below.
23. Francis J. Byrne, *Irish kings and high kings* (London, 1973), p. 162; Donnchadh Ó Corráin, *Ireland before the normans* (Dublin, 1972), p. 101; Alfred P. Smyth, *Celtic Leinster: towards an historical geography of early Irish civilization A.D. 500 to 1600* (Dublin, 1982), pp 43-4.
24. Alfred P. Smyth, *Scandinavian York and Dublin: the history and archaeology of two related Viking kingdoms,* 2 vols. (Dublin & New Jersey, 1977, 1979), ii, pp 18-19, 22, 24, 33, 118, 120-1.
25. F.J. Byrne, *Irish Kings,* pp 162-3.
26. *A.U.* s.a. 870; *A.F.M.* s.a. 869; *Chron. Scot.* [871].
27. F.J. Byrne, *Irish Kings*, pp 163-4.
28. *A.U.* s.a. 916; *A.F.M.* s.a. 915; *Chron. Scot.* [915], for record of Auguaire's death at Cenn Fuait; the career of Tuathal mac Augaire, ancestor of the Ua Tuathail line, is charted in *A.F.M.* s.a. 935 (= 937), 937 (= 939), 950 (= 952), 951 (= 953), 955 (= 957); his obit at 958 (*A.F.M.* s.a. 956) is recorded in all the annals.
29. *A.F.M.* s.a. 934 (= 936) has 'Artuir ua Tuatail dég.'
30. *A.U.* s.a. 926, 956, 971; *A.F.M.* s.a. 925, 955, 970; *C.S.* [956]; A.S. Mac Shamhráin, 'Prosopographica', 84.
31. *A.F.M.* s.a. 951 (= 953); Franciscan Library Killiney, Ms A 13, f. 382 v.
32. *A.F.M.* s.a. 930 (= 932), 943 (= 945); Franciscan Library Killiney, Ms A 13, f. 371 v; A.S. Mac Shamhrain, 'Prosopographica,' 93; note that Castledermot features among the later properties of Glendalough; see *Alen's reg.*, p. 5.
33. Vita S. Moling §6, Plummer, *Vitae SS Hib.*, ii, p. 192.
34. Price, *Placenames*, i, p. 52.
35. Hughes, K., *The church in early Irish society* (London, 1966), pp 165-6; see also Kim R. McCone, 'Clones and her neighbours in the early period,' *Clogher Record,* 2, no. 3 (1984), esp. 314, 323, discusses different forms of alliance between ecclesiastical foundations, pointing to a 'Sletty syndrome,' whereby foundations

reach an accommodation (in the case of Sletty involving submission) with a far away centre to avoid unwelcome political pressures.

36. *A.F.M.* at 1030, 1056; Franciscan Library Killiney, Ms A 13, ff. 415a r, 433 r.
37. A.S. Mac Shamhráin, 'The Uí Muiredaig and the abbacy of Glendalough in the eleventh to thirteenth Centuries,' *Cambridge Medieval Celtic Studies,* xxv (Summer 1993), esp. 61-3.
38. Harold G. Leask, *Irish churches and monastic buildings,* 2 vols, 2nd ed. (Dundalk, 1977), i, pp 77-8, discusses the site of St Ciaran's at Glendalough.

St Saviour's Priory, Glendalough (Bord Fáilte).

Round tower, Glendalough (O.P.W.).

Chapter 5

MEDIEVAL WICKLOW – 'A LAND OF WAR'

J. F. LYDON

In the middle ages two facts had a decisive bearing on the politics of Wicklow. The first was that it was administered as part of the county of Dublin. Before the county of Wicklow was created in 1606, the last part of Ireland to be shired, it formed a section of the sprawling area for which the sheriff of Dublin was responsible. In 1297 an Irish parliament had decided that this area was 'too much scattered and the parts thereof too far removed from each other and dispersed ... whereby it less competently obeys the lord the king in his precepts and those of his court, and also his people is less adequately ruled or governed'.[1] In other words Wicklow suffered from a lack of good governance which had an important bearing on the fate of English settlers there and consequently contributed to the success of the so-called Gaelic revival in the area. For although the 1297 parliament enacted a statute which greatly reduced the size of the sprawling county Dublin, its effect was minimal and Wicklow was still left as part of the jurisdiction of the sheriff of Dublin.[2]

The second fact which is important was the character of the territory of Wicklow. Broadly speaking it consisted of highlands and lowlands. It has long been accepted that English settlement in Ireland was for the most part confined to lands below the 600 feet level. Stretching southwards from within a short distance of the city of Dublin, the great mass of the mountains which dominated much of the county was largely unsettled by English and thus for the most part effectively outside the jurisdiction of the Dublin government. Below the mountains, to the east and west, lay the settled lands through which ran the roads communicating with the south. When Strongbow in 1170 accompanied Dermot Mac Murrough (Diarmait Mac Murchada) to lay siege to the Ostman city of Dublin, he escaped the traps which Rory O'Connor (Ruaidrí Ó Conchubair) had set for his army by avoiding the normal route northwards to the west of the highlands and instead successfully followed a high route through the mountains.[3] No one expected an army to travel through what was then not only difficult, but largely uninhabited, terrain, so that Strongbow was able to get behind the Irish line. For the rest of the middle ages this highland-lowland division remained.

There were really two Wicklows, then, and this was reflected in the pattern of settlement which followed the Anglo-Norman invasion. Land above the 600 foot level was not suitable for the kind of new intensive agriculture introduced by the newcomers on their manors. In Wicklow this meant that new settlements were confined to the perimeters of the modern county. In west Wicklow, for example, the manor of Hollywood, a sub-manor of the archbishop of Dublin's manor of Ballymore Eustace, marked one limit. Immediately beyond lay the mountains.

This division is also well illustrated by the distribution of religious houses within the modern county boundaries. In fact, there were surprisingly few religious communities, which reflects the poverty and instability of even the lowland areas. Glendalough in the mountains was an exception, though even that ancient and prestigious monastic community fell on hard times in the later medieval period. The Arrouasian house (canons regular of St Augustine) there had a fitful existence after the thirteenth century and we know very little about it. Elsewhere the religious communities were few and all lowland. In Wicklow town the Franciscans arrived in the late thirteenth century and there was also a hospital for lepers there. In Arklow there was another Franciscan friary. In west Wicklow the Cistercians had come to Baltinglass in 1148 and founded a large monastery which survived the invasion. And that was all: five religious communities in the whole county, of which only one lay outside the area of English settlement.[4] It is also significant that only six boroughs are known to have existed in medieval Wicklow, none of them in the highland area.[5]

The official terminology used in thirteenth century governmental records explains this division in another and even more meaningful way. The mountains, for reasons which will become clear later, are always referred to as a 'land of war' (*terra guerre*), while the settled lowlands were in the 'land of peace' (*terra pacis*) or the 'march' (*marcia*), that frontier area in between. These terms vividly describe, from the perspective of Dublin, the realities of life in medieval Wicklow. They were in common use all over the lordship, instantly recognisable for what they represented. A well-known petition to the king, probably to be dated 1274-5, from one Roger Owein, brings this out well.[6] He refers to the royal manor of Saggart 'beside the land of war' (*iuxta terram guerre*), while less than five miles away another royal manor, Newcastle Lyons, was in 'the land of peace' (*in terra pacis*). Saggart was near the foothills of the mountains and was in an area which by the 1270s had become dangerous to man and beast; Newcastle, only a few miles away, was not in anything like the same danger. Saggart was in the march; Newcastle was not.

This same polarisation found expression in another way. Possibly the most important single political action in the troubled history of medieval Wicklow was the expulsion of two important Irish families, whom we know as the O'Byrnes and the O'Tooles, from Kildare at an early stage of the invasion. Eventually settled in the mountains, they were to become a dominant factor in perpetuating the almost continuous state of war which existed between the areas they controlled and the settled communities backed by the Dublin government. As 'Irish enemies' (*Hibernici inimici*) these two families created an enclave in the mountains which not only provided a refuge for dissidents fleeing from the land of peace, but proved a constant threat to those unfortunate enough to be living within striking distance.

Most of medieval Wicklow, then, was land of war or marchland. Even where strong manors had been created, guarded by stone castles, the character of life was that of the march rather than the land of peace. Along the fertile coast the settlers were hemmed in between the sea on one side and the mountains on the other, vividly expressed by Hugh Lawless in 1316 when he explained that he lived 'in a confined and narrow part of the country' with the sea 'for a wall on one side, and the mountains of Leinster and divers other wooded and desert places' as a barrier on the other. The Lawlesses were therefore empowered to negotiate with those who attacked them and to treat with them 'in the manner of the marchers', in other words according to the law of the marches and not the king's law of Ireland.[7]

Communication was difficult and dangerous, even by sea which increasingly became infested by pirates and foreign enemies of England. Travelling light, it was possible to get from one side of Wicklow to the other using old tracks which even today are still passable. Otherwise the traveller had to use one of the three great passes which bisected the mountains, so that protection was necessary and not always effective.

For the most part, then, east Wicklow, with its settled coastal plain, was cut off from west Wicklow, where the settlements in places like Imaal and Hollywood were more associated with Ballymore and the modern county Kildare. This had some repercussions politically. It meant that the Dublin government was not able to deal with problems in Wicklow on a global scale, as it were, and military expeditions tended to be focussed on one side of the mountains or the other. Politically the mountains were dominated by two leading Irish families, which also reflected this east-west division. The O'Byrnes were pre-eminent in the east; the O'Tooles were dominant in the west. But, as we shall see, O'Byrnes and O'Tooles could often engage in joint military action, particularly in destructive raids on the manors bordering the fringes of the mountains to the west.

There was a further complication which transcended this east-west political division. After the Anglo-Norman invasion the Mac Murroughs became confined to their own ancestral lands of Hy Kinsella (Uí Cheinnselaig) in south Leinster. Here they became in time the dominant political force in north Wexford, south Carlow and south Wicklow. They also reassumed the kingship of Leinster, with corresponding claims to some kind of lordship over the O'Byrnes and O'Tooles, as well as lesser families. In 1295, for example, when 'Maurice Macmuryarthi Macmurchoth with all his nation and following' was received into the king's peace, hostages had to be handed over not only for the Mac Murroughs but for the O'Tooles as well, and Maurice had also to guarantee (even to the extent of making war against them) that the O'Tooles would observe the terms of the agreement.[8] Later still, the Mac Murroughs were able to assert some sort of hegemony over a much wider range of important Leinster families, such as the O'Mores of Leix, O'Connors of Offaly, Mac Gillapatricks of Ossory, O'Nolans of Carlow and O'Brennans of north Kilkenny. Inevitably, then, under the leadership of the Mac Murroughs, the great Wicklow families were from time to time involved in wider Leinster politics which transcended their own more localised interests in east or west Wicklow.

It is clear, then, that the history of medieval Wicklow necessarily ranges well beyond the boundaries of the modern county if it is to be meaningful. The mountainous region running south from the outskirts of Dublin was one area and was so regarded by successive Dublin governments to the end of the middle ages. Indeed records commonly speak of the 'Irish of the Leinster mountains' (*Hibernici de montanis Lagenie*) without distinguishing between O'Byrnes, O'Tooles or Mac Murroughs.[9] In attempting, therefore, to delineate the history of Wicklow, it can only be done in a meaningful way as part of that larger area.

It is important, too, that a significant part of the modern county had been included in the diocese of Glendalough. But in the late twelfth century it had been incorporated into the diocese of Dublin and it was the archbishop, then, who was responsible for initiating many feudal settlements. Even before 1200, Archbishop John had introduced his nephew Geoffrey de Marisco into west Wicklow by granting him Hollywood, as well as Donard and other adjacent lands.[10] The archbishop himself had manors at Ballymore, Tallaght, and in other places bordering the mountains. But strategically the most significant for the future was Castlekevin. This was appreciated from early in the thirteenth century. The manor of Swords (which became far and away the wealthiest of all the archiepiscopal manors) was granted to the archbishop in 1216 'in aid of making and maintaining a castle at his manor of Castlekevin'.[11] As we shall see, this castle became of great importance in the recurring war against the Irish of the mountains in the late thirteenth and fourteenth centuries.

In February 1216 the union of Glendalough and Dublin was formally confirmed by Innocent III.[12] It is clear that this was not in any way an example of Anglo-Norman aggression at the expense of Gaelic Ireland, but was in fact a continuation of a policy adopted by the pre-Norman church reformers who had recommended the amalgamation of other Irish dioceses. It seems, too, that conditions in the diocese of Glendalough had reached an all-time low. Archbishop Felix Ó Ruadhain of Tuam, who was one of the Irish prelates attending the fourth Lateran Council in 1215, reported that Glendalough 'had been held in great reverence from ancient times because of St Kevin who lived the life of a hermit there, but now was deserted and desolate for almost forty years, so that the church had been made a den of thieves and a pit of robbers, and more murders are committed in that valley than in any place in Ireland because of the deserted and vast solitude'.[13] The introduction of respectable settlers into part of that 'solitude' was seen as beneficial and an antidote to disorder.

The history of Anglo-Norman expansion into and settlement of Wicklow is far too complex to be briefly narrated.[14] But, as elsewhere, it necessarily involved some dislocation of the native population. For example, when Strongbow granted twenty knights' fees in Omurethi in south Kildare to Walter de Ridelesford, it meant that the resident O'Toole lords were driven into the Wicklow mountains.[15] There we lose sight of them, except for incidental references to individuals, for a couple of generations. Their leaders, like those of the O'Byrnes and the Mac Murroughs, no longer enjoyed the status which great Irish lords elsewhere in the lordship continued to enjoy. In 1244, for example, when Henry III summoned all the leading Irish lords to join his expedition to Scotland, none of those three is listed among those who received military summonses.[16] So, whatever happened to the scattered O'Tooles, there is no doubt that their leaders lost status and ceased, for a time, to enjoy the rank of their ancestors. But like the O'Byrnes, who similarly were pushed out of north Kildare into Wicklow when Maurice fitz Gerald received a grant of Offelan, the O'Tooles never forgot their ancestral homelands or the glory of their pre-Norman past. Even at the very end of the middle ages, their poets frequently harked back in their eulogies to those pre-Norman times in Kildare.[17]

In the east of the modern county Henry II had reserved for himself, as part of the royal demesne, the lands settled by pre-Norman Norse as far south as Arklow. Subsequent grants, the most important to Maurice fitz Gerald, and consequent subinfeudation do not seem to have caused any serious dislocation of the pre-Norman population. This was probably because the Ostmen (the indigenous Norse), who occupied the best land, were granted the status of subjects with access to the common law and so found some measure of protection under the crown. The Irish, too, seem to have remained on the land, even if (as happened elsewhere) many of them were reduced to the status of unfree betaghs.[18]

Further north, where the royal manor of Obrun was created, followed at the end of the twelfth century by another royal manor based on Newcastle Mackynegan (on the borders of the older dioceses of Dublin and Glendalough), the same stability is discernable. In the early thirteenth centuries both manors were productive. In his account for Michaelmas term 1212, the sheriff of Dublin accounted for rent for Newcastle, as well as rents from the betaghs of Othee and Obrun.[19] Another sheriff accounted in 1228-29 for the farm of Newcastle, with its mill, plus an increment (or increase in rent), together with the betagh rents, with increments, of Othee and Obrun.[20]

For the most part the sources are silent about the Irish who survived on such manors, or those, like the O'Tooles and O'Byrnes, who migrated to Wicklow after the Anglo-Norman settlement. Clearly such Irish presented no real problem in Leinster, unlike in other parts of the lordship where what the king in 1225 called 'the threatened raids of foes' required the appointment of special bailiffs who would 'see to the safety of the land'.[21] No such officials, apparently, were required in Wicklow. The Irish there had seemingly been absorbed without too much trouble. As well as the unfree betaghs, there were free Irish tenants on the manors. In 1228, for example, a 'Maclauchelin' O'Toole was amerced in one mark [or as we would say fined] for game taken' – clearly a poacher in the royal forest who had been brought to court, which means that he must have had access to the common law.[22] The O'Tooles, certainly, had settled down within the feudal society which had emerged in Anglo-Norman Wicklow. This is evidenced, for example, by their adoption of christian names through contact with the settlers: names like Walter, Hugh, Meiler, Richard, Robert were common. Some remained on ancestral lands as tenants: in the early fourteenth century, for example, no fewer than seven were paying rents in the manor of Imaal.[23] In 1299 a Walter O'Toole was one of a jury inquiring into the 'state of the archdeaconry' of Glendalough in the archdiocese of Dublin and was clearly a man of substance.[24] This may even be the same Walter who in July of that same year appeared before John Wogan, the justiciar, claiming to have been unjustly disseised of land in Kildare. The accused refused to answer the charge because Walter, he said, was Irish (*Hibernicus*) and therefore 'not of such blood as they ought to answer'. In other words Walter did not have the use of English law, the law of the land of Ireland. But Walter then produced a charter which testified that no less a person than the great William Marshal, lord of Leinster, had in 1209 enfranchised his great-grandfather Gillepatrick and his heirs 'land granted to them that they might use English laws'.[25] Another O'Toole, Elias, was prominent on the archiepiscopal manor of Castlekevin. He, and a Simon O'Toole, were jurors on the famous mid-thirteenth century inquisition into the archbishop's juridical rights in his manorial court, and the evidence produced showed that Elias had even acted as 'serjeant of the county' in the time of Archbishop Luke.[26] Yet another O'Toole, Meiler, must have been an important tenant. Not only did Archbishop Luke 'with the consent of both chapters' grant him ('for his homage and services') substantial lands and rents which his father, Laurence, had held of the archbishop, but he later sold the wardship and marriage of his daughter Agatha for the large sum of £20 a year.[27] On another archiepiscopal manor, Ballymore, two other O'Tooles were enfeoffed of substantial tenements.[28]

It was Archbishop Fulk who made what was undoubtedly the most important single grant of land to an O'Toole at some stage during his episcopate (1256-71). This was the land of Glenmalure, which thus became, as it were, the headquarters of the O'Toole clan and provided, in the long defile which ran into the heart of the mountains, a refuge which proved virtually unassailable.[29] Fulk's charter was witnessed by some of the most important people in the diocese, such as his brother John de Sandford (a future archbishop) and Thomas de Cheddesworth (described as the archbishop's 'official'). Why such an extensive area of land was granted to the O'Tooles at this time has never been satisfactorily explained. Fulk has been depicted as a vigorous archbishop, anxious to 'regularise the position of the Irish who were in occupation of lands belonging to Glendalough'. Part of his plan was to instal Muriertagh O'Toole (the recipient of the land of Glenmalure) 'as a kind of overseer' of the Irish.[30] But it may also be that Luke was acknowledging the family of his great predecessor Laurence O'Toole, canonised as recently as 1225 and installed as patron saint of the diocese. A Muriertagh O'Toole, very likely the same man, had earlier inherited a substantial tenement, land which he granted 'in fee and inheritance' to Archbishop Fulk for 1d. a year, payable at Michaelmas at St Patrick's in Dublin.[31] Glenmalure, in fact, may thus have been part of some kind of elaborate exchange of lands.

Whatever the reason behind it, the grant was a disaster for the archbishopric and government alike, not to mention the settlers on manors which were to be subject to raids, destructive of property and human life alike, for years to come. For by the 1270s the O'Tooles, based on Glenmalure, had emerged as an organised clan (or extended lineage), under dynastic leaders of the old pre-Norman kind, strong enough not only to raid successfully the land of peace beyond the mountains, but even to defeat strong government forces led by the justiciar himself. They were in the forefront of what was technically a rebellion against the authority of the English king. Together with leading O'Byrnes and Mac Murroughs they were to become a scourge which no medieval government, whatever the investment of men and money, was ever able to contain permanently. Fear of 'the Irish of the mountains' became normal, especially at harvest time. In his harvest account for 1344, the bailiff of the Holy Trinity grange of Clonkeen in county Dublin was allowed 4d. paid to 'two men watching upon the tops of the mountains through fear of the Irish for two nights'.[32]

What exactly caused the trouble in the first place is impossible to discern. Why should those Irish who had been absorbed into the feudal structure of Leinster and been anglicised through a seemingly inevitable process of acculturation, suddenly by the early 1270s be in open rebellion? If Archbishop Fulk de Sandford had been so vigorous in pushing archiepiscopal rights to the limit, an earlier reaction might have been expected.Yet, so far as we know there was no trouble of a serious nature before 1270. Nor is it likely that the long vacancy which occurred after his death in 1271 was a major cause. The trouble had started by then, though undoubtedly the royal agents who exploited the situation, pressing rights to the full in order to procure as big a profit as possible for the exchequer during the vacancy, didn't help matters. It is probable that the shortage of food which resulted from the bad weather at the time had something to do with it. A heavy fall of snow early in 1270 was reported in the annals and this must have caused considerable distress from food shortage in the mountains. A year later one of the worst famines to hit Ireland in the middle ages was reported when 'multitudes of poor people died of cold and hunger and the rich suffered hardship'.[33] The easy pickings to be found on the rich manors, so conveniently located within striking distance of the mountains, must have seemed irresistible.

Clearly by 1270 something was afoot. In a letter from Westminster in July the English government orderd the justiciar and other officials to help the archbishop to repress what it called 'malicious rebellion' so that he might exercise his office.[34] By the summer of 1271 at least five hostages were in custody – three O'Tooles, one O'Byrne and one Harold.[35] Castlekevin was also provisioned and sums of money were forwarded to the keeper, suggesting that an attack was feared.[36] Late in the following year, 1272, three hostages were removed to Newcastle, suggesting a deterioration in the situation.[37] The justiciar, James de Audley, lost a horse 'in the pass of Glendalough' before he died in June 1272, almost certainly in some action since the record blames the Irish and he was allowed the large sum of twenty-five marks in compensation.[38] He may, indeed, have been travelling to or from Arklow, where a large quantity of wine had been sent, presumably for an armed force of some kind.[39] And his successor in office, Maurice fitz Maurice, seems to have led an army to Glemalure.[40] New O'Toole and O'Byrne hostages were in custody from 1 May 1273.[41]

These are tantalising references and it is not until 1274 that there is incontrovertible evidence for a major military engagement in Glenmalure. The Dublin chronicler expressed it starkly: 'William fitz Roger, Prior of the Hospitallers, and many others are captured at Glyndelory and many are killed in the same place.'[42] There is evidence that the Mac Murroughs were involved in this affair, which may explain why losses were so heavy.[43] It would also explain why the government of Geoffrey de Geneville reacted so positively. He had been appointed justiciar and assumed office on 19 August 1273.[44] A friend of King Edward I, with whom he was on crusade in the east, he seems to have been chosen because of his experience in dealing with the widespread disorders which had swept the lordship in 1265.[45] The fact that de Geneville came straight to Ireland from the Holy Land is a measure of how serious the situation was.[46] He was given wide powers, was well supplied with money, and straight away had to face the problem of the Wicklow mountains.[47]

There is some confusion over the events of 1274. As we have seen, there was a massive defeat of the army at Glenmalure and important prisoners were taken by the Irish. But it is clear that de Geneville also led an army into the mountains: in his enrolled account the escheator was later allowed for paying wages 'to constables and guards of the force going in the first advance made by the justiciar against the king's enemies of Glyndelory' in 1274.[48] He seems to have approached from the east, having enclosed Wicklow, left a force under Theobald Butler 'in the march of Arklow', and enclosed and provisioned Newcastle on the way.[49] He also brought hostages from Dublin castle, probably in exchange for the important men held prisoner by the Irish.[50] It may well be, therefore, that de Geneville mounted a rescue mission, to free the prior of Kilmainham and the others captured at Glenmalure.

But there was no peace afterwards. In January 1275 the manor of Ballymore 'and the parts adjacent' had to be protected, one suspects from the Irish of the mountains. Later in the same year, Ballymore was guarded again, as were Dunlavin and Baltinglass.[51] The 'marches of the vale of Dublin' had to be protected and Newcastle Mackynegan had to be fortified.[52] The capture of 'Morydech' Mac Murrough at Norragh, in county Kildare, in that same year is another indication of raiding parties from the mountains.[53] Yet another army had to be raised and led again to Glenmalure. It must have been large, since it included contingents from Connacht.[54] Maurice fitz Maurice was once again prominent. But it was led by de Geneville and seems to have been well supplied.[55] There was certainly some action in the mountains, but once again there seems to have been nothing to show for all the expenditure of time, money, resources, and possibly human life.[56]

The situation now seemed out of control. In August 1275 the king was roused to action. He sent letters to Ireland to all the leading men in the lordship, including the bishops, reminding them that it was now plain to all that Ireland was impoverished by 'discords and wars' and told them that he was anxious and disturbed by this.[57] Such a letter was unusual in Ireland and is some indication of how worried the English government was by the Irish situation. Early in September the king ordered the justiciar to suspend normal procedures and to take money 'and other necessaries' as required, wherever he was, because the king now realised 'that the perturbation of those parts is of long standing and not yet settled'.[58] On 11 September he sent his own agent to inspect the state of affairs in Ireland and to report in person to the king on his return. On the same day he urged everyone to help the justiciar to do as the king had ordered, namely 'to attend diligently to the custody and defence of Ireland, and to deal vigorously with the Irish and the king's enemies'.[59]

A major intervention was plainly called for if the mountains were to be brought under control. First the land of peace had to be protected. Guards were established at Baltinglass, Dunlavin, Ballymore, Saggart and in the vale of Dublin.[60] Some of these places were attacked: tenants at Dunlavin had to be compensated for losses, and horses were lost at Ballymore. Next, and seemingly for the first time during these Glenmalure campaigns, a subsidy was raised in Kildare, Kilkenny, Carlow and Wexford to help raise troops.[61] Then the justiciar was provided with very special help when Thomas de Clare, a brother of the earl of Gloucester and a close friend of the king's, was persuaded to join the justiciar with troops and his own special expertise in war. He was granted Thomond and on 26 January he was promised a royal service to help make good that grant 'after the men of Glenmalure shall have come within the king's peace or his rule'.[62] Thomas certainly supplied men for the campaign and had to borrow money from merchants. He was also later compensated for horses lost at Glenmalure.[63]

The army which de Geneville led to the mountains must have been huge. He himself led 2,000 foot from his own lands in Meath.[64] Maurice fitz Maurice (now the father-in-law of de Clare) led another force from Connacht.[65] Newcastle, which seems to have been used as a base, was well supplied.[66] But that is as far as our knowledge extends. We do know that de Geneville, despite all his preparations, suffered yet another disaster in the mountains. An Irish annalist graphically described how many of his men were killed, de Geneville himself wounded, that others had to eat their horses 'from famine' and many hostages were taken.[67]

What went wrong? The scale of the disaster was such that more than sixty years later the tenants of Saggart appealed back to the 'time of the war of Art Mac Murrough' and losses sustained then as an excuse for non-payment of debts.[68] Even before the expedition was mounted, de Geneville was worried about the possible outcome. He wrote to the king and said that while he was willing to try to raise the troops required, he would need help from the magnates of Ireland. He went further: far from solving the problem of the Wicklow mountains, he feared that the expedition might not only fail, with heavy losses, but might even result in what he called 'great danger to the land'[69] In another letter, de Geneville warned the king against lies which were being carried to England by some, arising from 'secret and malicious' opposition, and asked that the king should not listen.[70] We can only speculate on the nature of this opposition, which may have been a hangover from his involvement in Irish politics at the highest level during the traumatic disturbances of the 1260s, or may have been the result of local envy of a foreigner who not only had won the richest prize in Ireland (the lordship of Meath), but was also head of the government and garner of the opportunities which that high office presented. We shall never know the reason. But certain it is that de Geneville's attempts to cope with the problem of the Wicklow mountains were completely frustrated. It was time for another change.

Robert de Ufford was the man chosen to replace de Geneville and to deal with the Glenmalure problem once and for all. Ufford had already served as chief governor in Ireland and had first-hand experience of Irish warfare in Connacht in 1269.[71] Now he was to test his skills against a different enemy. The extent of the threat from the mountains was well appreciated and right through 1277 from January to November, the marches of Newcastle, Glenmalure, Saggart and the vale of Dublin were well guarded.[72] What that threat represented is vividly expressed in a petition to the king from the tenants (Irish as well as English) of the royal manor of Saggart: burnt out of their homes, with 'many of our fathers, brothers and relatives killed', for the past seven years they have had to seek refuge where they could, so that their lands lay waste and uncultivated. They specifically list the 'goods' which they have lost –

3,000 sheep, 200 cattle, 100 heifers, 200 pigs, not to mention crops burned or seized, as well as silver, clothing, household utensils and more, to the value of over £100. Rather pathetically they end by wailing that as they are 'the nearer to the mountains' they always suffer the first.[73]

The army was carefully prepared by Ufford and was not ready for action until Michaelmas 1277.[74] The force was a large one, with Thomas de Clare once again closely involved and with contingents provided by magnates 'from divers parts of Ireland'.[75] Ufford must have succeeded, where his predecessor had failed, in getting the cooperation of the magnates of Ireland. This time Castlekevin was used as the base of operations, and there is evidence of massive bulding works there, as well as the unusual presence of crossbowmen with the justiciar.[76] While details are lacking, there is no doubt that Ufford and his army enjoyed a great victory. He wrote to the king in July 1278 and reported that the 'thieves' who had been in Glenmalure had left, many of them 'to another strong place, to their damage, if God be pleased'.[77] The king accepted Ufford's assurances. On 29 July he fulfilled his promise to Thomas de Clare and gave him a royal service (the royal service owed to the king) for Thomond. In doing so, he wrote that the 'men of Glindelore have now been pacified and quelled'.[78] Whatever about that, and the future was to show that Glenmalure was far from deserted by the Irish, Ufford certainly had forced the rebels to come to terms. Not only were O'Toole hostages housed in Dublin Castle, but both the O'Byrnes and the O'Tooles were recorded in the sheriff of Dublin's enrolled account as owing a 'fine' of 260 marks, possibly for having peace.[79] New English tenants were introduced into Obrun and Othee, and it was probably at this time that Eustace le Poer got that land which subsequently became Powerscourt.[80] Rents began to flow again from Newcastle.[81] The castle there was rebuilt.[82] The government even went to the trouble of bringing fourteen carpenters all the way from Drogheda 'to execute works' there.[83] Castlekevin, too, quickly showed the good effects of the Ufford success. In the period after the campaign, to January 1279, over £118 was received, a spectacular increase on the miserable receipts for the period just before.[84] All now seemed well, so much so that a letter from Ireland could carry the news that 'in no part of the land is there anyone at war or wishing to go to war, as is known for sure.'[85]

But appearances were deceptive. Quite early in 1279 there must have been another outbreak of trouble. In his account for 15 January to 28 April 1279 the escheator answered for nothing for Castlekevin which, he said, 'was waste' and that no tenants could be found to occupy the empty land 'on account of the war of the Irish'.[86] This must have been the result of raids led by Mac Murroughs. When Roger Bigod, earl of Norfolk, came to Ireland to visit his lands early in 1280, he was told by the Dublin government that the Mac Murroughs (whom Bigod, remarkably, called 'my cousins') would have to be treated with care 'lest any disturbance of the peace be plotted by them'.[87] Bigod did his best. Not only did he make gifts of money to the two brothers, Art and Murtough, but he also gave the former the more intimate gifts of a robe, furs, a cap, and even a cask of wine.[88] But the two brothers continued to cause trouble. By 1281 Murtough was a prisoner in Dublin castle and in 1282 the 'betaghs and other men of the king in the valley of Dublin' were compensated for 'the depredations of Art McMumrith and his accomplices'.[89] So the government decided to get rid of the problem, once and for all, by arranging for the murder of the two brothers at Arklow on 21 July 1282, while they were actually travelling under the king's protection. Contemporaries were shocked and the event passed into folklore. As late as 1305 a man knew his daughter's birthday because she was born 'on the day when Art McMurth was slain . . . And it is known in the whole country that twenty-three years are passed since Art McMurgh was slain'.[90] In 1317 this same murder was one of a number of crimes produced as evidence of English perfidy in the famous Irish remonstrance addressed to Pope John XXII.[91] But if the crime horrified contemporaries, it certainly achieved the desired effect. Peace was restored to the mountains.

It lasted for years and the government must have become quite complacent about Wicklow. It was the other, western, side of Leinster which caused worry. In 1289 John de Sandford was busy trying to bring the Irish of Leix and Offaly to the king's peace. A series of parleys failed and eventually he had to resort to force. In planning for a major military intervention, he went from Ballymore to Baltinglass on 10 September 'and there', the record tells us, 'caused to be summoned before him as well the English as the Irish of the Dublin mountains and adjacent parts, who all promised at his request to be ready to attack the rebels'.[92] This was an astonishing turnabout from the turbulent 1270s. But, as before, troubles soon broke out again. By 1295 there were so many raids and so much stock and goods stolen, that licences were being issued to treat with Irish 'malefactors' for their return. In June 1295, for example, the abbot of Baltinglass was licensed, as was St Mary's abbey in Dublin, and a Ralph Patrick (to treat with the O'Byrnes).[93] There is plenty of evidence to show that such raids for booty which could then be held for ransom were on the increase and soon became commonplace.[94] The 'custom of Ireland' was quite clear that 'it is not allowed to any person despoiled of his goods by his and the king's Irish enemies to treat with those enemies.'[95] But increasingly, long-suffering tenants had little option but to negotiate the restoration of stolen goods, licence or no licence, even though the risk of harsh punishment under the law was always a danger. A woman might act as such a negotiator, or even as a spy for the malefactors, having greater freedom of movement than a man, especially if she bore an English name. In 1302, for example, Isabella Cadel in Kildare was accused 'that she had art and parts with the said felons (of the mountains) and is a spy of the country for them'. But because her deceased father, William Cadel, had often done 'praiseworthy service to the king' and also because 'of the simplicity of the women in this affair', Isabella and Fynewell, her maid (who was also involved) were pardoned.[96] Not so lucky was another woman spy. In December 1305 the wife of Andrew le Deveneys, Grathagh, was accused of being involved with O'Toole robbers. But the jury said that she was innocent. She herself was an O'Toole and was accustomed, they said, 'at the request of faithful men of peace, to go the parts of the mountains where she stays with women of the parts of peace, to see and search for cattle carried off by her own race', so that stolen cattle might be recovered. The jurors were explicit: 'But she does not go there for the purpose of doing any evil, but for the good of the peace'.[97] But years later Grathagh was in court again, accused of being 'a common spy'. This time the charge was sustained that 'by her spying the men of Saggart were robbed by the Irish of the mountains of divers goods' and she was also found guilty of other crimes. She was then summarily hanged.[98]

But in 1295 there was more going on than raids for booty. In the spring of that year the Dublin chronicle reported that the Irish had 'wasted Leinster and burnt Newcastle and other vills'.[99] Something like this had been anticipated. In the summer of the previous year Saggart and Newcastle had been guarded 'against the Irish of the mountains'.[100] As before, lack of food may have been one agent. On 20 July 1294 there was a great storm which destroyed the crops. The effect was devastating. Friar Clyn of Kilkenny recorded that as a result 'many people perished of the hunger'.[101] But it is more likely that the near civil war between the two leading magnates in Ireland, the earl of Ulster and John fitz Thomas, may have inspired the Irish of the mountains to take arms again. The seneschal of Wexford certainly feared repercussions of the affair on the Irish and took care to stock the castle of Ferns in case of attack.[102] Indeed the impact of this affair was such that throughout the winter and spring of 1294-5 members of the king's council in Ireland had to go 'to various parts of Ireland with an armed force to establish the king's peace which had been disturbed by the caption [capture] of Richard de Burgh, earl of Ulster'.[103]

Whatever the cause, the Irish of the mountains rose in rebellion again and the situation was so serious that the government had to prepare for a major campaign in 1295. It is a measure of how desperate the situation was that on 25 April Peter le Petit, and thirty-four others (including some Irish), who remained by order of the Irish council guarding Castlekevin and Newcastle Mackynegan against the O'Byrnes and their accomplices, were to have the king's peace for all offences up to 16 May following.[104] A royal service was proclaimed for Castledermot and strategic places around the mountains were carefully guarded: Ballymore, Castlekevin, Newcastle Mackynegan and what the account vaguely calls 'the parts of Dubin and the adjacent parts during the war'.[105] Perhaps the most significant indication of the dangers posed by the new rebellion is the fact that Dublin castle was well stocked and fortified because of the war.[106]

This time the army was led by Thomas fitz Maurice, chosen by the Irish council to fill the vacancy caused by the sudden death of William de Oddingseles on 19 April 1295.[107] The army was large. Fitz Maurice brought a force from Munster, the earl of Ulster another from Connacht, and two other great magnates, John fitz Thomas and Theobald Butler, also led troops. These magnates served for twenty days, which was the period of action; the chief governor, however, was engaged for thirty-one days, which included the time spent in negotiating with Mac Murrough to come to the king's peace.[108] This he did on 19 July. The terms agreed by Mac Murrough have fortunately survived, a unique record which is worth close analysis. First of all when Fitz Maurice on Tuesday 19 July received Mac Murrough the record tells us that it was 'with all his nation and following', a clear indication that the Irishman was submitting not only on behalf of himself and his clan but also of those who had followed him into rebellion. These certainly included the leaders of the O'Tooles and O'Byrnes, as the record later makes clear. The terms agreed were as follows:[109] on the following Sunday three named hostages were to be handed over at Castlekevin for the Mac Murroughs, O'Tooles and O'Byrnes. On the same day they were to provide sureties for the payment of 600 cows in compensation for 'depredations done by them'. It was also agreed that the Irish would 'make satisfaction for damages done to the betaghs and other tenants of the king, or the archbishop, or elsewhere' – clearly the royal and archiepiscopal manors had suffered most – and, most interestingly, it was agreed that the betaghs and others would make like satisfaction to the Irish. Finally, Mac Murrough swore, 'under forfeiture of his hostage', that he would make war on anyone who should 'attempt anything against the king or infringe this covenant', yet another indication that Mac Murrough was heading a confederation of Irish clans. He also put his seal to the instrument containing the agreement, a reminder to us that the concept of the 'wild Irishman', soon to become so prevalent, was a distortion of the true situation in Gaelic Ireland.

This impressive achievement of the Dublin government seemed to inaugurate a new era of peace in the mountains. But it was not to be. No record has survived of hostages in custody or of compensation being paid as agreed.[110] And before too long there was trouble in the mountains again. At Castlekevin, for example, hardly more than £3 was received in rents from tenants in 1295 and 1296; and at Newcastle Mackynegan John de Stratton was allowed for the loss of rent of two and a half carucates (a large area) of the demesne, where much of the best land was, 'because they were untilled and nobody would take them'.[111] By 1301 the Dublin chronicle was reporting serious trouble again – the Irish 'made war' and burnt Wicklow, Rathdown and other vills in that area. But, the chronicler wrote, 'they did not escape unpunished, because the greater part of their sustenance was burnt and their arms were lost in the plundering; and almost (all) the same Irish would have been destroyed in Lent had not the dissension of certain English prevented it'. It is hard to know what the writer had in mind, But he follows immediately with a report of an O'Toole attack on a 'small gathering' (*conventulum*) in which almost 300 'thieves' were killed.[112] Whatever about that, the government reacted by guarding the perimeters of the mountains as usual. In the south, where the liberty of Wexford was in the king's hands, the keeper was ordered to guard the borders 'to resist the malice of the Irish of the mountains of Leinster who set themselves at war'.[113] There was certainly trouble around Newcastle Mackynegan: in January 1302 the chief governor had to cancel his plans for holding court there and hearing pleas because 'there was a state of war by the Irish'.[114] Instead he organised an expedition which lasted from 18 January to 14 March 1302.[115] Where he found the necessary troops is impossible to tell. In 1301 the justiciar, John Wogan, had led a large army of over 2,200 men to Scotland, with most of the leading Irish magnates involved.[116] His deputy in Ireland, facing a winter campaign in the mountains, would find it hard to attract men to service. Yet despite the enormous cost of the Irish contribution to the war in Scotland, and the resultant strain on meagre exchequer resources, an army was found and a large sum, not far short of £1,000, was made available by the treasurer for what his enrolled account calls 'the preservation of the peace in Leinster'.[117]

As always, no sort of permanent peace was secured by military intervention. When the king wished to reward John fitz Thomas with lands in the royal demesne worth £60 a year, the full Irish council debated the matter in 1305 and decided that 'it would be least damage to the king, of all the places which they know in Ireland, if he should give to John his tenants at Newcastle Mackynegan, where there is a castle very weak and in a strong march'.[118] In the same year an inquisition revealed that land on the borders of Kildare and Dublin were worth 'in time of war nothing, because the issues are not sufficient for half the cost of keeping them, and that is a land of war among the Irish, who are more often at war than at peace'.[119] Soon the records use the term 'common war' – in 1306 a tenant at Kilbride, on the fringes of the mountains to the west, had to maintain a hobelar and a fully equipped horse to help protect the manor because of 'the great necessity on account of the common war'.[120] The situation was so desperate that in 1305 four criminals who had been found guilty of extortion were allowed to make fine to keep the peace in the future because, the jurors said, they were 'hateful' to the Irish of the mountains and were often successful in harrying them.[121] Pardons for service against the Irish of the mountains became more frequent, even for homicide. When Roger le Poer and John Fraunceis were charged with the murder of Maurice de Rupe in the justiciar's court at Castledermot on 13 October 1306, they were pardoned for their good service 'in the company of the justiciar, fighting the Irish felons of the mountains of Leinster'. Not only that, they were also pardoned 'for all other trespasses and felonies' to that day.[122] It was becoming increasingly difficult to maintain the rule of law and the government seemed more than anxious to turn a blind eye to misdemeanours if defence against the Irish of the mountains was at stake. When some of the Lawless family were charged in the justiciar's court in June 1306 that not only were they party to robberies, but that they were actually 'of the affinity of the Irish, and are sworn to them', they were pardoned because they 'are very useful in fighting the felons of the race of Ototheles, when they have a good leader and captain'. One, indeed, was pardoned simply because he lived in a dangerous area 'near the Irish'.[123]

To the east of the mountains, then, disorder was growing and lands had to be protected in whatever way possible, even if this meant that criminal activity was tolerated. But more orthodox methods were also used. For example. Edmund Butler paid well for the service of men at arms, as well as footmen, in defending lands in the vicinity of Arklow against the Irish.[124] The situation worsened. In the autumn of that year the justiciar, John Wogan, was engaged 'in fighting the Irish felons of the mountains of Leinster', in which he was joined by at least one force of Irish.[125] In the south the seneschal of Wexford was killed in 1305. The following year Ballymore was burned and Henry Calf (of the family later better known as Veel, lords of Norragh) was killed.[126] The Dublin chronicler links this with the start of a general war between the Irish and English of Leinster and with the summoning of 'a great army from divers parts of Ireland to curb the malice of the Irish of Leinster'. A royal service was proclaimed for Ballymore and the justiciar began preparations for a massive intervention in the mountains.[127] Judging by the large sums of money paid out of the exchequer to the clerk of the wages – £200 in June, £400 and £600 in August, £600 in October – this was by far the largest army led against the mountain Irish since the 1270s.[128] To meet the sustained demand for pay, money had to be regularly brought from the security of Dublin castle to the exchequer and to Holy Trinity, despite the risks.[129] There is evidence, too, that Irish soldiers were involved again: a 'Mahoun Mcarran' and his kern served with Wogan and a large contingent received protection from actions in the Royal Courts while on service with Walter de St Albino.[130]

Just what this formidable army achieved is not known. The Dublin chronicler lauds the deeds of one magnate, Thomas de Mandeville, 'an excellent knight', who had a serious encounter with the Irish near Glenealy, in which he fought manfully 'until his destrier was killed under him', and also praises him for the many lives he saved in battle.[131] Later another was awarded £20 compensation for his horse lost in battle with the Irish near Ballymore.[132] It seems, then, that the bulk of the fighting was concentrated in the west. But beyond that, and the fact that the campaign was mounted in the autumn, we know nothing.

Still the problems continued. In April 1307 the O'Tooles were posing such a serious threat that the government agreed that an extra 30 hobelars and 80 foot should be added to the garrison already manning Castlekevin.[133] Large supplies of wheat and oats, as well as 1,000 quarrels for crossbows, were also despatched to the castle. On the instructions of the justiciar, Nigel le Brun maintained a large force of 13 men at arms, 5 hobelars and 146 foot in an emergency operation fighting certain O'Tooles between 18 and 22 April.[134] Indeed the government was so desperate that in the same month it was decided by the council that a Murhuth O'Byrne was to receive land which had formerly been in O'Toole hands and this was done, we are told, 'that by this dissension may be moved between the said families'.[135] For the first time, too, we hear that the danger from the Irish was now so serious that they threatened the road south to Carlow, so that it was impossible to risk sending money.[136] By now the Mac Murroughs were again involved and the government resorted to the old practice of paying head money (*capitagium*); such a reward was offered to anyone who would get rid of the leader.[137] Forty marks were also given to John de Stetton, to be used for head money and for what was called 'secret parleys' with some Irish.[138] In 1308 Newcastle Mackynegan had to be heavily guarded with a force of men at arms, hobelars and foot 'to resist the malice of the Irish felons of those parts invading both the castle and the town there and the adjacent parts'.[139] In May the O'Tooles burned Castlekevin, the vill of 'Courcouly' and killed some of the garrison.[140] There was nothing for it but to mount yet another expedition into the mountains.[141] The focus initially was Newcastle, but soon shifted to Glenmalure where on 8 June the full army was assembled. But once again that valley proved fatal to the government forces and many were killed.[142] The immediate result, on 16 June, was that the Irish burned Dunlavin, Tobber, and other towns. Ironically, around that same day, the infamous Piers Gaveston, having been banished from England, arrived in Ireland, 'with ostentatious pageantry,' to head the government.[143] He was later to make a momentous impact on Wicklow.

But meanwhile there was need of urgent action. A terrible revenge was exacted from at least one Irishman, a William Macbaltor, who was brought before the justiciar in Dublin, condemned, and on 21 August was drawn by horses and then hanged.[144] On 23 October William de Burgo, deputy to Gaveston, led yet another army into the mountains.[145] Care was taken to recruit men from Connacht and Meath to swell the ranks and a formidable force of 38 men at arms, 158 hobelars and 614 foot was assembled. This served in the mountains until 18 November and its most interesting feature is that the majority of those who led contingents were Irish, most notably O'Connors and O'Kellys from west of the Shannon. It was augmented by local recruits. William de Burgo himself led a large contingent of 200 hobelars and 500 foot and a Richard le Neyr was also paid for the wages of 125 foot serving with the deputy at Newcastle.[146] But once again we are in the dark about what, if anything, this impressive army achieved. We know that Castlekevin was attacked by the Irish and the castle knocked down, but nothing more.[147]

The troubles continued and in 1309, almost inevitably it seemed, the government was forced to move against the Wicklow Irish again. This time the new chief governor, Piers Gaveston, personally led the army – a strange experience for a Gascon accustomed to the high society of the English court. As befitted his rank, Gaveston seems to have been able to employ larger forces than usual.[148] Between April and June his clerk of the wages accounted for more than £800 spent on wages and on repairs to Castlekevin which 'had been knocked down and destroyed' by the Irish. The Dublin chronicle, which had earlier shown some hostility towards Gaveston, gave him credit for not only rebuilding Castlekevin and Newcastle, but also for cutting a pass through the wilderness between Castlekevin and Glendalough. It also credits him with overcoming the O'Byrnes and subduing them.[149] On the face of it, then, this was a successful intervention.

But as always, appearances were deceptive. The O'Byrnes were almost immediately involved in the rebellion of Maurice de Caunton in south Leinster and John Wogan, back in office as justiciar, had to lead expeditions against them in the summer and the autumn.[150] Even though that rebellion was successfully put down, the escalation of trouble in the Wicklow mountains soon began to threaten the Dublin area itself. In December 1310, John fitz Thomas was in charge of a guard, based at Rathmore, to defend the land between Saggart and Ballymore, 'because of the rebellion of the Irish felons of Leinster'.[151] In July 1311, Geoffrey le Bret was retained with 10 men at arms at Rathfarnham 'to guard the march of those parts against the Irish felons of the king'.[152] Dublin city was only just down the road and the danger to the suburbs was now very real. Expeditions into the mountains, expensive at a time when the Irish exchequer was chronically short of money, and time-consuming for a hard pressed Dublin administration, seemed to be able to achieve little – certainly nothing permanent. Yet there was no alternative. In 1311, Wogan led yet another 'great army' to Glenmalure after the O'Byrnes and O'Tooles attacked Saggart and Rathcoole on 29 June.[153] The following year his deputy, Edmund Butler, blockaded the O'Byrnes in Glenmalure, supposedly forced them to capitulate and then threatened to destroy them unless they returned to the king's peace. This major intervention, which was decided upon not only by the council, but also by the magnates 'of the march of Leinster',[154] was not just because the O'Byrnes were committing 'robberies and murders, burnings and other evils without number ... from day to day in divers parts of Leinster', but also (and most sinisterly) because their example induced 'other Irish of parts adjacent to perpetate similar crimes'.[155]

To some extent this spread of O'Byrne influence was counter-balanced by the government's ability to employ Mac Murroughs in the service of the king at this time. Why exactly the Irish should now accept the king's penny, as it were, is not clear. It may simply be that they resented the obvious growth in prestige and power of the O'Byrnes. But as early as 1313 the exchequer was recording that by ordinance of the Irish council Mac Murrough was in receipt of an annual fee of 40 marks for his expenses 'in repressing the malice of the felons of the Leinster mountains'.[156] There is some evidence that the decision to employ him was taken at a special meeting of south Leinster magnates at New Ross.[157] What is certain is that Mac Murrough was paid £20 in reward for capturing a leading O'Byrne and handing him over to be imprisoned in Wexford castle, and that he was paid other sums for 'resisting the Obrynnes', or 'subduing the Irish felons of the Leinster mountains' between June and August in 1311.[158] It may also be of some significance that when Edward II in March 1314 attempted to recruit Irish chieftains into his service in Scotland (no fewer than 26 were contacted), Mac Murrough was among those who received the royal request.[159] But so did O'Toole and O'Byrne, and they can hardly be considered likely candidates at that particular time for service in Scotland. What is important is that now, unlike in 1244, their status as 'captains of their nations' was formally recognised. This is one tangible result of their success in rebellions since the 1270s.

That success, too, had made them feared and hated by the inhabitants of the land of peace beyond the mountains. Nothing illustrates this better than an incident which occurred on a night in 1312, when a gang of locals robbed some residents of Haughstown, near Moone in county Kildare. According to the evidence presented in the justiciar's court, they ran into the town and 'of malice they shouted in a loud voice fennok abo, fennok abo (fionnachta abú), which is the war cry of the O Totheles'. This caused the inhabitants to fly out of their houses in terror and the gang then proceeded with their robbery.[160] The terror is palpable, even in the cold record of the court. As we have seen, the manors close to Dublin in the land of peace had long since become inured to raids and murders. A tenant on the royal manor of Saggart in 1313 was allowed by the treasurer and barons of the exchequer to pay his arrears of rent in instalments because he was 'altogether impoverished and oppressed by reason of the robbery and burnings which the Irish of the mountains of Leinster, felons of the lord king, have lately made in the aforesaid town'.[161] The threat to Dublin itself was so real that in 1316 the government appointed Martin de Fyssacre, with crossbowmen, 'to keep vigil in the exchequer' against the Irish 'commencing to burn the houses of the said exchequer'.[162] With the special assent of what the record calls 'the community of county Dublin in the parts of Fingal and Leinster' (probably meaning north and south of the Liffey), the Irish council ordered that a special guard of 20 men at arms, 40 hobelars and 80 foot should be set up, supported by a subsidy of 2s. on each carucate of land in Fingal and 40d. in Leinster, to protect the land from attack by the Irish of the mountains, with William Comyn as captain.[163] On 22 May the guard under Comyn was in action, killed Donough O'Byrne and twelve of his followers, and brought their heads to be publicly displayed in Dublin.[164] On the night of 6 September David O'Toole with eighty men secretly hid themselves in the woods at Cullenswood and next morning came to Dublin. But the same William Comyn and his 'fellow citizens' came out of the city, put them to flight, followed them for about six leagues, killed about sixteen of them, mortally wounded many 'and the vile men fled.'[165] Even as late as 1325 the same Comyn was still active, when he was paid £70 for his wages in 'spying the exits of the Irish from the mountains', killing one of the leading O'Tooles, capturing nine other leading Irishmen (including five O'Tooles) and, significantly, a Stephen Petyt, and bringing them back to Dublin where they were imprisoned in the castle.[166]

Those were particularly dangerous times. In 1315 the Scots under Edward Bruce invaded Ireland and there was a marked reaction in Leinster. Hugh Lawless, to whom the king's lands at Bray had been committed in July 1314, complained in the exchequer that he could receive no profit from them. Because the Scots had come to Ireland, he said, the Irish of the Leinster mountains had gone to war against the king and had 'hostilely invaded, burned and altogether destroyed' not only his lands at Bray, but 'all other lands and tenements of divers faithful of the king in those parts'.[167] Later, while the Scots were ravaging the midlands, the O'Tooles and O'Byrnes burned Arklow, Bray, Newcastle Mackynegan and all the vills in that country.[168] More sinister was the new confederation which followed, including the same two kindreds together with the Archbolds and Harolds. They 'devastated' (the word used by the chronicler) the town of Wicklow and all the country round about.[169] Later, in 1317, the new chief governor, Roger Mortimer, led an expedition against the Irish of the mountains, into Imaal and then Glenealy and had a major engagement with them in which many on both sides were killed.[170] The Archbolds and the O'Byrnes came into the king's peace as a result, which seems to have lasted long enough to make the government complacent about Wicklow once again for a time. And not only the government: in 1319 a new stone bridge was built across the Liffey at Kilcullen in county Kildare by a canon of Kildare cathedral, almost an invitation to the Irish to attack.[171]

In 1327, however, an event occurred which perhaps more than anything else symbolises the success of the Gaelic revival in the mountains, when the Irish of Leinster, we are told, 'came together and made a certain king, that is Donald the son of Art Mac Murrough'. As soon as he was inaugurated, he ordered that his standard should be placed within two miles of Dublin and that 'afterwards it should travel throughout all the lands of Ireland'.[172] There is more than a hint here that not only was Mac Murrough asserting his kingship over Leinster to within two miles of the capital, and that with the assent of the Irish of Leinster, but was also reviving older ambitions to the kingship of Ireland – at least that is how it must have appeared to some in Dublin.

But God, the chronicler commented, soon checked his 'pride and malice' and allowed him to be taken prisoner by a Henry Traharn, who brought him to Leixlip and was paid £100 'of ransom', inferring that the government had been sufficiently alarmed by the whole affair to put a high price on Mac Murrough's head. The new king was brought to Dublin and lodged in the castle, there to await the judgement of the king's Irish council.[173] Clearly there was more in this than meets the eye, because the same chronicler reports that as a result of Mac Murrough's capture 'many misfortunes happened to the Irish of Leinster', including the capture of David O'Toole and the deaths of many Irish. The following year the same David (described as a 'strong thief, enemy of the king, burner of churches, destroyer of people') was brought before the justices of the bench in the Tholsel of the city, judged, and given over to be drawn by horses through the city to the gallows and there publicly hanged.[174] Interestingly, too, Adam Duff O'Toole was convicted of heresy in 1327. He denied the Incarnation of Christ, said that there could not possibly be three persons in one God, asserted that the Blessed Mary, mother of the Lord, was a prostitute, denied the resurrection of the dead, insisted that the sacred scriptures were nothing more than a collection of fables, and denounced as false the Holy See. On 11 April 1328 Adam was burned as a heretic on Hoggen Green in Dublin.[175] Some years later, when the Irish government was responding to the famous remonstrance addressed by O'Neill to Pope John XXII, O'Toole's heresy was produced as evidence of the depravity of the Irish. It was said that because of his 'perverse doctrine ... many souls among the Irish were lost and damned'.[176]

A horrific event in 1332, when the Irish of Leinster 'plundered the English and burned churches', seemed to confirm what the Dublin government complained of to the pope. The Dublin chronicler specifically records how they burned the church in Freynstown in west Wicklow, with eighty men and women inside. He writes that when 'a certain chaplain of the said church, clothed in sacred vestments' wished to leave the building with 'the body of the Lord', they drove him back with their lances and burned him with the others. It was as a result of this incident that the pope ordered the archbishop of Dublin to excommunicate the Irish later that year.[177] It is a fact that the exchequer paid half a mark to Brother Richard McCormegan 'to execute the sentence of excommunication pronounced against Otothel and his accomplices, enemies and rebels of the king.'[178]

Despite the best efforts of successive governments, then, the mountains close to Dublin remained disturbed and the Irish of Leinster were still a problem. So by 1324 the round of military expeditions into the mountains began again. The need was obvious to all, not least to the inhabitants of the manors skirting the trouble spots. Inquisitions into the state of the archiepiscopal manors provide a dramatic insight into how bad conditions were in places. On the manor of St Sepulchre, close to the city, some betaghs were living in the march, 'near evildoers', where they would not stay at night for fear of the Irish, and so their 'duty labour' was of no value. Even tenements in the city of Dublin itself were lying waste.[179] Lands in Tallaght were valueless, because 'no tenants will stay as it is near the Irish'. Some lands on the manor were lying waste now because they were actually 'among the Irish'.[180] The same story was repeated at Rathcoole, Clondalkin, Ballymore and Shankill (where all the burgesses had fled 'on account of the Irish').[181] The royal manors fared no better. In Saggart, for example, arrears of rents were running at over £1,311 in 1342.[182] In the same year the burgesses at Newcastle Mackynegan informed the king that '80 years ago the said manor was destroyed by the Irish felons of that locality so that for ten years it lay uncultivated and devastated and no profit could be obtained therefrom'; now 'the said manor is situate in a March and on divers occasions has been burned and devastated by the said Irish enemies and felons ...the burgesses now dwelling there are constantly plundered and injured by fires caused by said felons and enemies so that they can scarcely live there.' So the king pardoned arrears of rent.[183]

From 1324 hardly a year went by without an expedition (and occasionally more than one) to try to provide a remedy.[184] Most of these were ineffective, even if, as with Lucy in 1332, large forces were involved. Places like Ballymore, Dunlavin, Baltinglass in the west, or Newcastle and Arklow in the east, were regularly guarded to offer some protection to the manors, especially when the government was militarily engaged in the mountains and there was a danger of attack in the absence of the local militias. Everyone had to play a part in such operations. In 1338, for example, when Newcastle Mackynegan was guarded, the Holy Trinity priory in Dublin had to provide its quota.[185] But with war virtually endemic and little being achieved by orthodox military methods, new ways of coping had to be tried. In 1350 the council in England discussed Irish affairs and amongst other matters on the agenda was a plan to plant conquered lands in Ireland with new English settlers, instead of wasting, as the record of the meeting puts it, 'all the issues of the land on war with no conquest or profit'.[186] But there is no evidence that in Wicklow at least this imaginative scheme was ever attempted. Instead governments tried to maintain some semblance of order in the old-fashioned way of campaign, forcing the Irish into submission, taking hostages and lodging them in Dublin castle or some other secure place. More and more, too, attempts were made to buy off, as it were, dangerous Irish. As we have seen Mac Murrough was regularly paid an annual fee. Exploiting internal Wicklow politics, governments were sometimes able to employ one Irish chief against another. In 1334 Mac Murrough fought O'Byrne on behalf of Dublin and was rewarded by the council for capturing Philip O'Byrne and handing him over to prison.[187] If the leading O'Byrnes were more often than not in rebellion, from time to time they too served with government forces. Indeed Tadhg O'Byrne was actually made a knight during the 1360s.[188] A 'Murghut' O'Toole brought a contingent to serve in Darcy's 1329 expedition against the O'Byrnes.[189] They might even be prepared to serve in government armies outside Leinster, as Mac Murrough did in Munster in 1345 and 1352.[190]

Elsewhere in Ireland as the middle ages wore on governments had to withdraw from regular and active intervention in the localities and leave it to the local supremos to deal with the Gaelic and Anglo-Irish 'captains of nations' in order to preserve some semblance of order and control. But Wicklow was too close for comfort and no Dublin government was ever able to delegate the problem of peace-keeping to the nobility, as was done elsewhere.[191] Indeed, as has been remarked, the head of the Irish government when dealing with Wicklow was very much in the position of a local lord elsewhere. All the government could hope to achieve was to force the rebellious Irish chieftain into formal submission, such as we have already seen in the case of Mac Murrough in 1297. After defeating the O'Byrnes in 1335, the leader promised the justiciar to compel his followers to obey the king, compensate those damaged by their rebellion, and take hostages from his important kinsmen who, presumably, would be handed over to the justiciar.[192] Because of an ordinance made at the Westminster parliament of 1331, such hostages would now have to meet their own costs while in custody. The same ordinance added ominously that 'if they who have given such hostages observe not the conditions and conventions which they shall have made, the justiciar shall execute justice and judgement upon such hostages.'[193]

From time to time the regular routine was broken by some catastrophe which necessitated the application of a more vigorous hand than usual. The Black Death, which struck Ireland and devastated Anglo-Irish communities in the autumn of 1348, was such a disaster. When a new chief governor, Sir Thomas de Rokeby, was appointed in the following July, the English government seems to have recognised that the situation in Ireland was indeed grave – 'because the land of Ireland is not in good plight or in good peace' was the excuse for sending an armed force with him, the first such English troops to be employed here.[194] By 23 April 1350 he had met with such success in

Wicklow that not only did the gaelicised Harolds choose a captain of their nation in his presence, but so too did the Archbolds and the O'Byrnes.[195] The captain elected swore not only to keep the king's peace, but also to seize any of his 'progeny or following (*parentela*)' who committed a felony and hand them over to the king's prison. On paper this was a remarkable achievement for de Rokeby. To preside over, and therefore presumably to influence, the election of a chieftain, seemed to provide a new guarantee that peace would be maintained. But it did not work. Aedh O'Toole may have been retained, at a fee, to proceed with the justiciar 'against Irish rebels and for the safety of the marches',[196] but it was impossible to control either the inhabitants of the marches intent on conducting their own defence, or some O'Byrnes determined to maintain their age-old prerogative of attacking convenient manors. When a raiding party led by the Dowdings of Ballymore came into conflict with some O'Byrnes they were handsomely rewarded by the government for wounding one senior O'Byrne, killing another, and taking yet another prisoner and handing him over to Dublin castle. The latter was called 'Shaan son of Donald Mor Obryn', almost certainly the same John who had been elected captain in the presence of de Rokeby.[197] By 1358 the areas around Leighlinbridge had to be warded because they were 'in the march near the Mac Murroughs and O'Byrnes'.[198] In August 1358 John O'Byrne, 'captain of the O'Byrnes' was described as 'recently a rebel' and was handed over to the justiciar at Carlow.[199] The following January, 1359, Walter Harold and others were rewarded for 'rescuing' a prey taken from Tallaght by the O'Byrnes and O'Tooles and for killing five of them in the process.[200]

So, despite all, the troubles of the Wicklow mountains continued. When Lionel son of Edward III, later duke of Clarence, came to Ireland as chief governor in 1361, like every one of his predecessors he could not avoid tackling the same old problem of the mountains. That the situation had even worsened is certain, if we are to believe what a meeting of the great council in Kilkenny in July 1360 told the king: Ireland was then on the point of being lost, unless a swift remedy was provided. The Irish, he was told, 'of one assent' have commonly gone to war, which on the face of it seems unlikely, if not impossible.[201] Yet in 1359 the government, in letters to all the most important ports in Ireland, stated categorically that 'confederacies have been made between the Irish of Leinster and elsewhere that each Irish captain in his own march shall make war at a certain time, so that by this each one might conquer by continuous war the lands of the liege people in his country (*patria*).'[202] Whatever the reality, the expedition of Clarence was the result, a major investment of men and money by the English taxpayer to try to pacify Ireland, including Wicklow.[203] The very fact that soon after his arrival the new chief governor shifted the exchequer from Dublin to Carlow is a good indication of how serious a view was taken of the situation in Wicklow. Clarence arrived on 15 September and by the 28th he was engaged in Wicklow. Within a short time he had dealt successfully with the O'Byrnes, though the O'Tooles were still making war in 1363 and 1364. In the end Clarence successfully pacified the area south of Dublin: eventually both O'Byrne and O'Toole, as well as Mac Murrough, were retained at a fee by the government.[204]

The great French chronicler Jean Froissart relates a true story from this period of the Clarence campaign which is worth recounting because it shows that there was what we might call a 'hidden Wicklow' behind all the war and the killing.[205] A man called Henry Crystede told him that serving with the earl of Ormond they were ambushed by the Irish and he was taken prisoner. His captor, a man called Brin Costerec, took him to his fortified house in the woods and kept him with him for seven years. He also gave Henry one of his daughters in marriage and they had two daughters. During the course of the Clarence campaign the Irishman was involved in fighting William of Windsor who had led an attack on the mountains. He was captured and was promised his freedom only if he would release Crystede, his Irish wife, and their two daughters into the hands of the English. 'He was most unwilling to make this bargain, for he was very fond of me, and of his daughter, and of our children.' But in the end he agreed, painful as it was. Crystede eventually went to live near Bristol, leaving one daughter behind in Ireland where she had married. In England the other daughter soon married and gave him four grandsons and two granddaughters. 'And because the Irish language always comes as easily to my tongue as English ... I have always gone on speaking it with my wife and have started my grandchildren on learning it as well as I have been able.' This charming story, unique in Ireland, provides clear evidence that not all was war and that even in a disturbed area like Wicklow there was room for the kind of cultural assimilation which might have led to peace.

But as always, there was no permanent peace. After Clarence had left the situation continued to deteriorate. When next there was another major expedition from England, the Leinster mountains were so threatening that it was against the Irish there that the full force of the invading army was directed. This army, the greatest ever to arrive in Ireland during the middle ages, was led by King Richard II in person.[206] One measure of how great an ascendancy had now been achieved by the Irish in Wicklow is that before Richard arrived the Irish annals, for the first time, mention their chieftains by name. In 1368 David O'Toole and in 1376 'Dalbach' O'Byrne are recorded. By 1376 Aedh O'Toole is actually called 'king' of Imaal by an annalist. Even more interesting, in 1378 Bran O'Byrne is called 'king of Uí Fhaeláin', the old Kildare dynasty from which they were descended and which had been expelled by Strongbow.[207] The high status of these chieftains is also reflected in the treatment they received from the king after the successful conclusion of his Leinster campaign. In the course of that campaign the Irish suffered terribly, particularly at the hands of the English archers. Many were killed, great preys of cattle were seized, and much property was destroyed.[208] Richard himself in a letter refers to the 'great burnings' in the lands of the Irish, as a result of which Mac Murrough, O'Byrne and OToole submitted to him. They came into his presence, he wrote, 'to make obeisance to us, bare-headed, disarmed, their girdles undone, holding their swords by the points, with the pommels erect, and put themselves unreservedly at our mercy, without any conditions'. The king then brought O'Byrne and O'Toole to Dublin, where, 'moved with pity and compassion, we received them into our grace'.[209] On 18 February 1395, in a room in Dublin castle, in front of a gathering of witnesses which included the archbishop of Dublin, the bishop of Lismore and Waterford, the chancellor, treasurer, the mayor of Dublin, and many more, and carefully recorded by a public notary, Donnchadh O'Byrne approached the king, 'and swore on the holy gospels, which he touched with his hands and kissed, to be from that time henceforth faithful liegeman to our lord the king'. Then, having sworn to keep the laws and do all that 'a faithful liege subject and vassal is bound and held to do . . . he did fealty and homage'.[210] Much later, on 29 March, Felim O'Toole similarly did homage to the king at the Franciscan abbey in Castledermot.[211]

King Richard, through these submissions, confirmed the high status of these new subjects from Wicklow. One measure of the rank they now held is the amount of money which they pledged to forfeit for breaking the oath of fealty, no less than 20,000 marks in the case of O'Byrne and £1,000 by O'Toole.[212] That both these chieftains took seriously the new relationship with the king and accepted his overlordship is not to be doubted. When they felt the need to protect their interests in Wicklow it was to him that they naturally turned looking for redress.[213] So that by the time the king left Ireland, not only had Wicklow been pacified and a new relationship established between the king and the leading chieftains there, it seemed that as a result the problem which caused successive Dublin governments so much trouble had at last been solved.[214] Early in February 1396 Donough O'Byrne travelled to England. In August of the same year he paid a second visit, with a Kavanagh representing Mac Murrough and with ten other Irishmen. At court they were joined by O'Carroll of Ely and from there in December they accompanied the king overseas to Calais.[215]

All seemed well and the king's settlement of the Wicklow problem seemed to be holding. Yet appearances were deceptive. As happened elsewhere in Ireland, the Anglo-Irish took the opportunity to reassert old landed claims and even old claims to overlordship. O'Byrne wrote to Richard, even before he left Ireland, complaining of the earl of Ormond who 'claims divers lands and tenements by ancient right within the said (my) country, about which right I know nothing, and that he is threatening me by his messengers for occupation of the said lands and tenements.'[216] As early as the summer of 1396 the annals record an O'Toole victory 'over the Anglo-Irish and Saxons of Leinster, in which the English were dreadfully slaughtered; and six score (of their) heads were carried for exhibition before O'Toole, besides a great many prisoners, and spoils of arms, horses and armour'.[217] By 1399 Richard II was back in Ireland again, his earlier settlement in ruins. In a letter he describes what he calls 'a very good beginning' when his nephew, the duke of Surrey, made 'a prey of a great number of beasts' and also attacked Mac Murrough, O'Byrne and other Irish 'to the discomfiture of the enemy, wherein we have killed of them 157 armed men and kerns'.[218] And so the round of raids and counter-raids began again. In 1402 the mayor of Dublin led the citizens against the O'Byrnes and on 11 July, near Bray, engaged them in battle and, if we are to believe the chroniclers, slew 493 of them.[219] In a raid on Ballymore in 1419 the O'Tooles took a prey of 400 cattle and in retaliation the justiciar, accompanied by the mayor and citizens of Dublin, attacked and destroyed Castlekevin, the headquarters of the O'Tooles.[220] In a long letter of 1427, Archbishop Swayne of Armagh, who had been asked by the king to report on the state of Ireland, vividly described how conditions in Leinster had deteriorated. On one occasion Mac Murrough, O'Byrne, and O'Toole had destroyed Castledermot, burned most of the houses, took its lord, Sir Thomas Wogan, prisoner, ravaged all the countryside, and finally had to be each paid an annual fee in exchange for peace.[221] Such a device, the equivalent of those 'black rents' which were becoming increasingly common throughout the lordship, did little or nothing to preserve the peace. The government was now almost powerless. It was only when a special effort could be made, and extra resources provided, that a chief governor could intervene in Wicklow, as Richard duke of York was able to do in 1449. He made a great show, brought both O'Byrne and O'Toole back into the king's peace, and made them swear 'to be the king's true servant and to bear tribute to the king'. In a curious anticipation of what was to become official policy later, when the government tried to teach the Irish 'civility' (thus 'civilising' them), O'Byrne also swore that he, his children, and his leading followers 'shall wear English array and learn English'.[222] But this was all unreal, the Irishmen simply agreeing to whatever was demanded, so long as it did not interfere with their power locally.

When an Irish parliament in 1455 solemnly enacted that barriers were to be erected on the bridges at Lucan and Kilmainham, and that all fords across the Liffey between Lucan and Dublin bridges were to be 'stopped', with trenches if necessary, then it was obvious that the government had more or less lost all control over Wicklow. Parliament was told that these drastic measures were necessary because Irish enemies (and indeed English rebels) used these crossings at night to 'rob, kill and destroy the liege people of the king' in Fingal.[223] Communities now had to look after themselves. Tenants on the royal manor of Saggart had actually put themselves 'into the truce and protection' of Esmond O'Toole, until parliament in 1470 ordered that the tenants 'be compelled to surrender their truce' and return to the old practice of guarding the manor 'with lookers-out and watchers'. This was not only for their own protection, but also of 'the country thereabout'; otherwise the whole of the county of Dublin would be destroyed in a short time. More realistically, the parliament decided that if this attempt to revive the older practice should fail, then it would 'be lawful for all others of the said county residing very near thereto to put themselves into truce in like manner'.[224] But in the very next parliament, in 1471, legislation had to be enacted that large numbers of labourers were to be pressed into service, with barrows, spades and pickaxes, for three days, to help in the construction of adequate defences for Saggart. The reason for such drastic measures was that the town had recently been burned by O'Byrne and O'Toole and many of the inhabitants had fled. And as Saggart, according to parliament, was a 'great defence' of county Dublin, if it were not adequately protected much of the county would be destroyed.[225] Ballymore, too, called 'the key between the counties of Dublin and Kildare against the Irish enemies of our sovereign lord the king, the Obrynnes, the Otooles', was in a perilous condition.[226] And in 1467 a Crumlin tenant petitioned parliament for help: he had been captured by the O'Byrnes and held to ransom, the payment of which had crippled him. He also complained that he could not find tenants because 'of the great oppression of the borderers adjoining'.[227]

In some ways the situation was almost surreal. A parliament in 1450 heard a petition from Sir Edward Mulso, seneschal of the liberty of Meath, for permission to build a town (to be called, rather grandly,

Mulsoescourt), establish as many burgesses there as he liked, who would annually elect a portreeve and two bailiffs, and who would have jurisdiction, exactly as the city of Dublin had, in the franchise to be created within the new city, together with all profits of justice. There would be a hierarchy of city officials, a free market every Tuesday and an annual fair, a system of customs on merchandise to finance murage and pavage, and other privileges besides. This exciting plan for a new town was designed for land in Fercullen, which parliament was told was 'situated in the frontier of the marches, and is the key and protection for the whole county of Dublin, and the county of Kildare'.[228] What no one, seemingly, told the assembled lords and commons was that Fercullen was then, and remained, firmly occupied by the O'Tooles. Little wonder that Mulsoescourt never became a reality.

The famous 1515 report on the state of Ireland and 'Plan for its Reformation' was more realistic. Among the 60 'countrys' listed, 'where reigneth more than 60 Chief Captains ... and that liveth only by the sword, and obeyeth to no one other temporal person, but only to himself that is strong', are both O'Byrne and O'Toole in Wicklow as well, of course, as Mac Murrough further south. Only half of county Dublin, it said, was in any real sense subject to the king's laws; Wicklow was not.[229] On 26 June 1536 the deputy, Leonard Grey, and the Irish council bluntly told the king that to 'have your dominion defended from Irishmen' would demand 'great charges' every few years. The only answer to the situation inherited from the middle ages would be to conquer Mac Murrough, O'Byrne, O'Toole 'and their kinsmen, which inhabit beteen Dublin and Wexford'.[230] Such notions of 'conquest' were new and beyond the capacity of Dublin governments of the time, though they were to be given effect not long afterwards. Until then, Wicklow remained a 'land of war', mostly controlled by the great Irish chieftains who continued to terrorise the inhabited countryside almost up to the gates of Dublin itself.

References

1. *Stat. Ire., John-Hen.V,* p. 197.
2. A substantial part of the country surrounding Arklow was, for historical reasons which need not concern us here, administered as part of county Kildare; J. Otway-Ruthven, 'The medieval county of Kildare', *I.H.S.*, xi (1959), pp 183-5 and map p. 196.
3. Orpen, *Normans*, i, 209. Strongbow seems to have kept to the high ground over Glendalough and may also have followed the route of the later military road through the Sally Gap and on to Rathfarnham. For an alternative route see Price, *Placenames*, vii, p. xxvi.
4. Aubrey Gwynn and R. N. Hadcock, *Medieval religious houses* of *Ireland* (London, 1970).

5. B. J. Graham, 'The documentation of medieval Irish boroughs', *Bulletin of the Group for the study of Irish Historic Settlement,* no. 4 (1977), p. 17.
6. Richardson and Sayles, *Admin. Ire.*, p. 230.
7. Robin Frame, 'War and peace in the medieval Lordship of Ireland', in James Lydon (ed.), *The English in medieval Ireland* (Dublin, 1984), pp 126-7; Hand, *Eng. law in Ireland*, pp 36-7.
8. *Cal. justic. rolls. Ire., 1295-1303*, p. 61.
9. For example, in 1315 crops from the manor of Shankill were carried off by 'the Irish of the Leinster mountains' *(per Hibernicos de montanis Lagenie), Hist. and mun. doc. Ire.*, p. 372.
10. Price, *Placenames*, vii, p. xliii.
11. *Alen's reg.*, p. 161. This valuable property was to revert to the crown 'if the castle were not made or maintained', no idle threat as the archbishop was to discover in the future.
12. Sheehy, *Pontificia Hib.*, i, no. 93.
13. Ibid., p. 172, n. 3; *Alen's reg.*, p. 40.
14. The best accounts are still Orpen, *Normans,* i-ii; Price, *Placenames,* under particular names as listed and in his 'historical background', introduction to vol. vii.
15. Orpen, *Normans,* i, 386; iv, 10-11. And see the long note by O'Donovan in *A.F.M.* 1180 (vol. 3, pp 53-4).
16. *Cal. doc. Ire.1171-1251,* no. 2716. Earlier, when the king wrote to the 'magnates' of Ireland about his new justiciar, the list was headed by six Irish (two of them addressed as 'kings'), none of whom came from Leinster – ibid., no. 1001.
17. Alfred P. Smyth, *Celtic Leinster* (Dublin, 1982), p. 49.
18. Price, *Placenames,* vii, p. xxii.
19. *Pipe roll Ire. 1211-12,* p. 11.
20. *P.R.I. rep. D.K. 35,* p. 32.
21. *Cal. doc. Ire. 1171-1251,* nos. 1114, 1124.
22. *P.R.I. rep. D.K. 35,* p. 31.
23. *Red Bk. Ormond,* p. 20. Among the witnesses to a charter of 1225, granting land in Imaal, was a 'Dovenald O Douigill' – *Alen's reg* , p. 46.
24. *Cal. justic. rolls Ire., 1295-1303,* p. 270.
25. Ibid., p. 271.
26. *Alen's reg.*, pp 110, 111.
27. Ibid., pp 81-2, 114. There is no doubt that Meiler had been a substantial landholder. Of particular interest is the fact that he had to do homage for his lands.
28. Ibid., p. 121.
29. Ibid., p. 136.
30. Price, *Placenames,* vii, pp. xlix, liii.
31. *Alen's reg.*, p. 141.
32. James Mills (ed.), *Account roll of the Priory of the Holy Trinity, Dublin* (Dublin, 1891), p. 64. R. F. Frame, 'The Dublin government and Gaelic Ireland 1272-1361' (Ph.D. Dublin University, 1971) is invaluable not only for information on the logistics of the different campaigns, but also for its insights into government policy regarding Gaelic Ireland in general and Leinster in particular.
33. *Ann. Inisf.*, p. 371; Robin Flower, 'The Kilkenny Chronicle', *Anal. Hib.* ii (1931), p. 339: 'There was a great famine in Ireland ... and many died.'
34. *Hist. and mun. doc. Ire.*, p. 183. This may not refer to armed rebellion, but to some internal trouble with clerks refusing to accept ecclesiastical discipline exercised by the archbishop. But in that same year, 1270, an inquisition

described Castlekevin as 'on the frontier of the whole march' (*in frontura tocius marchie*) – N.A.I., RC 8/41,. p. 368.

35. *Cal. doc. Ire. 1252-84,* p. 313.
36. Ibid., p. 312.
37. Ibid., p. 313.
38. Ibid., p. 148.
39. Ibid., p. 149.
40. Ibid., p. 313. The calendar actually reads 'fitz Gerald', which is obviously a mistake for fitz Maurice, who acted as justiciar from June 1272 to April 1273 – Richardson and Sayles, *Admin. Ire.*, p. 81. The keeper of the vacant archbishopric was allowed £13. 19. 0. for 60 cows delivered to fitz Maurice 'for supply of the expedition led to Glyndelore' – Sir William Betham, 'Account of Thomas de Cheddesworth, custodee of the temporalities of the Archbishopric of Dublin, from 1271-1276', *R.I.A. Proc.* v, (1850-51), p. 160.
41. *Cal. doc. Ire., 1252-84,* p. 171.
42. *Chartul. St Mary's, Dublin,* ii, p. 318. In his chronicle Clyn is even more stark:'The killing of the English at Glandelory' – Richard Butler (ed.), *The Annals of Ireland by Friar John Clyn,* (Dublin, 1844), p. 9. The fact that the sheriff of Limerick was also among those taken prisoner may indicate that he had brought a contingent of men from the west – *P.R.I. rep. D.K. 36,* p. 37.
43. Flower, *Anal. Hib.* ii, p. 332. As Dr Williams has now demonstrated, this chronicle is not only contemporary, but actually belongs to Castledermot (and not Kilkenny), where the friars would have been very much aware of what was happening in the mountains – Bernadette A Williams, 'The Latin Franciscan Anglo-Irish annals of medieval Ireland (Ph.D. Dublin University, 1991), ch. 4.
44. His enrolled account as justiciar commences 19 August 1273 – *P.R.I. rep. D.K. 36.* p. 40.
45. James Lydon in *N.H.I.*, ii, 183-4.
46. *Chartul. St Mary's, Dublin,* ii, 317.
47. Lydon, *N.H.I.*, ii, 189-90. It is possible that he engaged in some sort of military action straight away. Not only was the keeper of the vacant archbishopric ordered, in September 1273, to give de Geneville all the issues 'to expedite the king's affairs', he was also 'to assist the justiciar with all the posse of the archbishopric' – *Cal. doc. Ire. 1252-84,* no. 977. He was later allowed the large sum of over £900 which he had given de Geneville 'for certain arduous business of the king's' – Betham, 'Account', *R.I.A. Proc.,* p. 160.
48. *P.R.I. rep. D.K. 36,* p. 33.
49. Ibid., pp 40-41.
50. The expenses of the prior of Kilmainham and the sheriff of Limerick 'when they came out of the prison of Glyndelur' were subsequently allowed to the keeper of the archbishopric – Ibid., p. 37.
51. Ibid., p. 33.
52. *Cal. doc. Ire. 1252-84,* pp 237, 241. The justiciar was worried about his lack of resources and wrote to the king asking that help promised at Easter should be made available sooner – G. O. Sayles, *Documents on the Affairs of Ireland* (Dublin, 1979), no. 11.
53. *Chartul. St Mary's, Dublin,* ii, 318. He was captured by Walter le Enfent, who was in charge of the guard at Ballymore during that summer (Betham, 'Account' *R.I.A. Proc.*, p. 159) and who was also a member of the justiciar's household (*Cal. doc. Ire., 1252-84,* pp 238, 287).

54. *P.R.I. rep. D.K. 36*, p. 33: payments to 'constables and guards of the force of Connacht'.
55. *Cal. doc. Ire., 1252-84*, no 1180, pp 235, 236. It is strange, however, that this army does not figure among the allowances on the justiciar's enrolled account for 1275.
56. What is called 'a valuable horse' was lost at Glenmalure – Ibid., p. 238.
57. *Cal. pat. rolls , 1272-81*, p 134.
58. Ibid., pp 103-44.
59. *Cal. doc. Ire., 1252-84*, nos. 1160-61.
60. Ibid., pp 157, 160; *P.R.I. rep. D.K. 36*, pp 33, 37.
61. See the note added to the Kildare account in *P.R.I. rep. D.K. 36*, p. 74.
62. *Cal. doc. Ire. 1252-84*, no. 1191.
63. Ibid., pp 256, 257; *P.R.I. rep. D.K. 36*, p. 33.
64. *Cal. doc. Ire., 1252-84*, p. 257.
65. Ibid., p. 258.
66. Ibid., pp 258, 259.
67. *Ann. Clon.*
68. Robin Frame, 'The justiciar and the murder of the MacMurroughs', *I.H.S.*, xviii, (1972), p. 37. Mac Murrough was certainly involved in this war – *P.R.I. rep. D.K. 36*, p. 37.
69. *Facs. nat. MSS Ire.* ii, plate lxxix, no. 3.
70. Sayles, *Affairs*, no. 41.
71. Otway-Ruthven, *Med. Ire.*, p. 199.
72. *Cal. doc. Ire.,1252-84*, pp 284-5.
73. Sayles, *Affairs*, no. 41.
74. *P.R.I. rep. D.K. 36*, p. 36 – the enrolled account of Ufford. He was allowed the large sum of nearly £1,200 'expended in collecting the force which the said justiciar, Thomas de Clare, and other magnates led to suppress the rebels and enemies at Glyndelur at Michaelmas'.
75. *Cal. doc. Ire., 1252-84*, p. 267.
76. Ibid. Over £154 was spent on the wages of labourers.
77. Sayles, *Affairs*, no. 18; *Cal. doc. Ire., 1252-84*, no. 1400. It was in this same letter that Ufford reported that what he called the king's 'business' in Ireland was now much better, and that the Irish 'communally' (*communalement*) had offered 7,000 marks for a general grant of English law. It may be, then, that there is some connection between the defeat of the Irish of Wicklow and the offer of money for law.
78. *Cal. doc. Ire., 1252-84*, no. 1476.
79. Ibid. pp 316, 317. *P.R.I. rep. D.K. 36*, p. 45. The 'fine' was still owing in 1282 (ibid., p. 69), 1292 (ibid., *37*, p. 49), and indeed for long after.
80. Orpen, *Normans*, iv, 18-19.
81. *Cal. doc. Ire., 1252-84*, pp 361, 382.
82. Ibid., pp 309, 310, 422-3, 440, 441, 535-6; *P.R.I. rep. D.K. 36.*, pp 36, 53, 59.
83. *Cal. doc. Ire., 1252-84*, p. 502.
84. *P.R.I. rep. D.K. 36*, p. 42.
85. P.R.O., S.C. 1/31/169.
86. *P.R.I. rep. D.K. 36*, p. 46.
87. Frame, 'Murder of the MacMurroughs', p. 229.
88. Ibid., p. 225.
89. *Cal. doc. Ire., 1252-84*, pp 401, 440.
90. Frame, 'Murder of the MacMurroughs', p. 224.

91. Edmund Curtis and R. B. McDowell, *Irish historical documents 1172-1922* (London, 1943), p. 42. *Ann. Inisf.*, pp 381-3 calls Muirchertach 'king' and reports that they were 'treacherously slain by the foreigners in violation of the peace of the king of England' and added that they had 'the greater part of Leinster under their own rule'.
92. *Cal. doc. Ire., 1252-84*, p. 272.
93. *Cal. justic. rolls Ire., 1292-1303*, pp 71-2.
94. It wasn't only Irish who raided in this manner: the records of the courts show that the practice was common in the land of peace.
95. *Cal. doc. Ire., 1252-84*, no. 1068.
96. *Cal. justic. rolls Ire., 1295-1303*, p. 368.
97. Ibid., *1305-7*, pp 480-81.
98. N.A.I., KB, 1/2, m.1.
99. *Chartul. St. Mary's, Dublin*, ii, 324.
100. *Cal. doc. Ire. 1293-1301*, p. 83.
101. Clyn, *Annals*, p. 10. The Dublin chronicle also recorded 'great scarcity and pestilence throughout Ireland in this year and the two years following' – *Chartul. St Mary's*, ii, 323.
102. *Cal. justic. rolls. Ire., 1295-1303*, p. 148. The seneschal took his action 'for fear of the disturbance ... in Ireland on account of the taking of the earl of Ulster'.
103. *Cal. doc. Ire., 1293-1301*, p. 123.
104. *Cal. justic. rolls Ire., 1295-1303*, p. 4. Peter le Petit had earlier been involved in an incident near Castleknock, while coming with others from Uriel 'by counsel of the king ... to fight the king's enemies in the mountains' – Ibid., p. 29. See also *Cal. doc. Ire., 1293-1301*, p. 144.
105. Ibid., pp 124, 221, 259, 284, 302, 635; *P.R.I. rep. D.K. 37*, p. 75.
106. *Cal. doc. Ire.*, 1293-1301, p. 123.
107. Richardson and Sayles, *Admin. Ire.*, p. 82.
108. *Cal. doc. Ire., 1293-1301*, pp 121, 123-4. As the keeper was hearing pleas at Cork on 14 June and was back in Dublin on 8 July, the campaign must have fallen between those two dates – *Cal. justic. rolls Ire., 1305-7*, p.v.
109. Ibid., 1295-1303, p. 61.
110. See the enrolled accounts of the Irish treasurer in *Cal. doc. Ire., 1293-1301*, nos. 273, 346.
111. *P.R.I. rep. D.K. 38*, p. 47. He was also allowed for expenditure on works at the castle, including the wall, in 1295 and for building a moat and new wall in 1298.
112. *Chartul. St. Mary's, Dublin*, ii, 330. Dowling in his annals says that it was 'inferior Leinstermen' who rose and that because of the devastation they caused, their goods and chattels were confiscated for the use of the king – Richard Butler (ed.), *The annals of Ireland by ... Thady Dowling* (Dublin, 1849), p. 17.
113. *Cal. justic. rolls Ire., 1305-7*, p. 87. This happened when the prior of Kilmainham was deputy justiciar, that is between August 1301 and March 1302 – Richardson and Sayles, *Admin. Ire.*, pp 9, 83.
114. *Cal. justic. rolls Ire., 1305-7*, p. 383.
115. *P.R.I. rep. D.K. 38*, p. 87: the enrolled account of Nigel de Penystoun, clerk of the wages. Unfortunately the calendar gives no evidence of the numbers engaged.
116. Lydon, *N.H.I.*, ii, 200.
117. *Cal. doc. Ire., 1302-7*, p. 5.
118. *Cal. justic. rolls Ire., 1305-7*, p. 28.
119. Ibid., p. 30.
120. Ibid., p. 356.

121. Ibid., p. 483.
122. Ibid., p. 293. For another pardon for murder see p. 359. For other cases see pp 187, 359, 501 (when more than 43, mostly Irish, were pardoned), 504.
123. Ibid., p. 503.
124. Ibid., p. 242.
125. Ibid., p. 501. The need of men was so great that at a special council at Carlow it was agreed, 'for the utility of the state', that anyone who lost a horse in fighting the Irish should be compensated by the local community – Ibid., pp 325-6.
126. *Chartul. St. Mary's, Dublin*, ii, 333.
127. Jocelyn Otway-Ruthven, 'Royal service in Ireland', *R.S.A.I. Jn*., xcviii (1968), p. 43.
128. *Cal. doc. Ire., 1302-7,* nos. 549, 556, 561, 567; on the exchequer issue roll (P.R.O., E.101/234/17) £1799. 1. 4 was paid to the clerk of the wages, out of a total issue of £2238. 17. 5. The clerk of the wages actually accounted for a total of £2050. 18. 7., which included some receipts from subsidies – *P.R.I. rep. D.K.* 39, p. 24. See also *Cal. justic. rolls Ire., 1305-7,* pp 282, 501.
129. P.R.O., E.101/234/17.
130. *Cal. justic. rolls Ire., 1305-7,* pp 293, 501.
131. *Chartul. St Mary's, Dublin,* ii, 333.
132. *Cal. justic. rolls. Ire., 1305-7,* p.325.
133. Ibid., p. 353.
134. Ibid., pp 353, 355; *P.R.I. rep. D.K. 39,* p. 54.
135. *Cal. justic. rolls Ire., 1305-7,* p. 354.
136. Ibid., p. 392.
137. Ibid., *1308-14,* p. 22; 100 marks was allotted to Edmund Butler, who killed 'Morghuth Ballagh' Mac Murrough. See also *Chartul. St Mary's, Dublin,* ii, 335.
138. *Cal. justic. rolls Ire., 1305-7,* p. 353.
139. Ibid., *1308-14,* p. 77. The castle, in fact, was in a disastrous state: the constable complained in June 1308 that 'the houses and walls of the castles in divers places are split asunder . . . and are greatly in need of being improved and repaired' – ibid., p. 85. John le Dene was also paid £64, not only for the guard at Newcastle, but also 'elsewhere along the coast to resist the malice of the Irish felons' – P.R.O., E. 101/235/13.
140. *Chartul. St Mary's, Dublin,* ii, 336.
141. In Trinity term 1308 the rolls had to be carried back and forth from the castle, each day, 'because of the imminent war of Leinster – P.R.O., E.101/235/13.
142. *Chartul. St Mary's, Dublin,* ii, 336; *P.R.I. rep. D.K. 39,* p. 34.
143. *Chartul. St Mary's, Dublin,* ii, 337.
144. Ibid.
145. *P.R.I. rep. D.K. 39,* p. 34. A transcript of the orginal full text has survived in the N.A. and has been edited by Philomena Connolly, 'An account of military expenditure in Leinster, 1308', *Anal. Hib*., xxx (1982), pp 3-5.
146. *Rot. pat. Hib*., p. 8, nos. 41-3.
147. Ibid., p. 9, no. 3 – money was allowed for the repair of the castle 'which had been knocked down by the Irish'.
148. *P.R.I. rep. D.K. 39,* p. 34; James Lydon, 'The enrolled account of Alexander Bicknor, treasurer of Ireland, 1308-14', *Anal. Hib*., xxx (1982), p. 31; P.R.O., E/101/235/20. Another indication that special care was taken is the appointment of purveyors at Drogheda to provide corn, wine and other provisions – *P.R.I. rep. D.K*., p. 38.
149. *Chartul. St Mary's, Dublin,* ii, 338.
150. P.R.O., E.101/235/20; 235/24; *Rot. pat. Hib.,* p. 12, no. 9.

151. Lydon, 'Bicknor's Account', p. 30.
152. Ibid., p. 32.
153. *Chartul. St Mary's, Dublin*, ii, 339.
154. There is a record of a meeting of magnates at New Ross in support of Butler, where it was also agreed that Wicklow and Arklow were to be guarded against the O'Byrnes with the substantial force of 20 men at arms, 30 hobelars and 26 foot in each place – Philip Herbert Hore, *Old and New Ross* (London, 1900), p. 17.
155. P.R.O., E.101/236/6; Lydon, 'Bicknor's account', pp 29-30. Well over £1000 was paid to the clerk of the wages, a good indication of the magnitude of the effort by Butler.
156. P.R.O., E.101/236/7. When the fee was paid in 1315 it was said to be granted to him by the king and to last as long as the king should wish – Lydon, 'Bicknor's account', pp 32-3.
157. Hore, *Old and New Ross*, p. 177.
158. N.A.I., RC 8/9, pp 325-6; *P.R.I. rep. D.K. 39*, p. 49. It is interesting that the pipe roll records that Mac Murrough was guarding the southern marches 'as ordered by the justiciar and council in the parliament at Kilkenny'. This, presumably, refers to the 1310 parliament, but there is no reference to Mac Murrough in the surviving record – *Stat. Ire., John-Hen.V*, pp 258-77.
159. F. Palgrave (ed.), *Parliamentary writs and writs of military summons* (London, 1827), i, 423. no. 12.
160. *Cal. justic. rolls Ire., 1308-14*, p. 244. The Dublin chronicle records that in 1316 after the Irish of Imaal came to Tallaght 'and began a war', 400 of them were killed and their heads sent to be exposed in Dublin. 'And afterwards miracles were seen there, that the dead arose and fought together and exclaimed Fennok Abo, their cry (*signum*)' – *Chartul. St Mary's, Dublin*, ii, 296, 350-51.
161. R.I.A., Ms 12. D.8., p. 201. On 8 December 1315, 80 foot and 6 men at arms were posted at Saggart 'to keep watch against the Irish there every night' – *Hist. and mun. doc. Ire.*, p. 372.
162. P.R.O., E101/237/5.
163. *Hist. and mun. doc. Ire.*, p. 381.
164. *Chartul. St Mary's, Dublin*, ii, 350.
165. Ibid., p. 297.
166. *Rot. pat. Hib.*, p. 31, no. 79; P.R.O. E.101/238/17.
167. *Hist. and mun. doc. Ire.*, p. 457. Other tenants at Bray were also allowed a reduction in rents to be paid because 'divers wars of the Irish' made their tenements 'untilled and uncultivated' – N.A.I., RC 8/9, pp 506-7.
168. *Chartul. St Mary's, Dublin*, ii, 348.
169. Ibid., p. 349.
170. Ibid., p. 356.
171. Ibid., p. 361. A policy of warding was continued. In May 1325, for example, the new earl of Kildare was paid for two guards at Baltinglass and Dunlavin against the O'Byrnes and others – *Rot. pat. Hib.*, p. 32, no. 83.
172. Ibid. pp 365-6.
173. He was not held prisoner for long. In January 1330, with the help of a rope supplied by Adam Nangle, he escaped from Dublin castle. Nangle was later 'drawn and hanged' for his trouble – *Chartul. St Mary's, Dublin*, ii, 372.
174. Ibid., pp 366-7.
175. Ibid., p. 366.
176. J. Watt, 'Negotiations between Edward ll and John XXII concerning Ireland', *I.H.S.* x (1956), p. 20.

177. *Chartul. St Mary's, Dublin*, ii, 376.
178. P.R.O., E.101/239/29.
179. *Alen's reg.*, pp 170-71.
180. Ibid., p. 181.
181. Ibid., pp 184, 186, 189, 191, 195.
182. *P.R.I. rep. D.K. 53*, p. 22.
183. Ibid., p. 23.
184. There were far more expeditions into this region than any other part of Ireland – see the map in Robin Frame, 'Military Serice in the Lordship of Ireland', in Robert Bartlett and Angus McKay (eds.), *Medieval frontier societies* (Oxford, 1989), p. 103.
185. *Act. roll Holy Trinity*, pp 9, 13, 17 and 154n. On 21 February the prior entertained William de Assheburne, captain of the guard at Newcastle, to dinner in Dublin.
186. Sayles, *Affairs*, p. 193.
187. *Rot. pat. Hib.*, p. 38, no. 37.
188. Frame, 'Military service', p. 122.
189. *P.R.I. rep. D.K. 43*, p. 28.
190. Frame, 'Military service', p. 121.
191. Robin Frame, 'English Officials and Irish Chiefs in the Fourteenth Century', *E.H.R.* xc (1975), p. 749 and passim.
192. Ibid., p. 759.
193. *Stat. Ire., John-Hen. V*, p. 325.
194. Jocelyn Otway-Ruthven, 'Ireland in the 1350s: Sir Thomas de Rokeby and his successors', *R.S.A.I. Jn.*, 97 (1967), p. 47.
195. Edmund Curtis, 'The Clan System among English Settlers in Ireland', *E.H.R.* xxv (1910), pp 116-20. Six named Harolds, two Howells, one Lawless, Archbold and Walsh elected Walter Harold as *capitaneum progenie des Harolds;* unfortunately the surviving record does not recount who participated in the election of John Byrne and Matthew Archbold as captains.
196. *Rot. pat. Hib.*, p. 59, no. 11. He served for 40 days, with 20 hobelars and 40 foot, defending Tallaght 'against hostile O'Byrne invaders'; his brother John explored Imaal for the government and his chaplain Caan spied on the Irish – Ibid., p. 63, no. 129.
197. Ibid., p. 59, no. 33.
198. Ibid., p. 66, no. 5.
199. Ibid., p. 66, no. 7.
200. Ibid., p. 66, no. 17. For the continuing trouble see Otway-Ruthven, 'Ireland in the 1350s'.
201. Richardson and Sayles, *Parl. and councils med. Ire.*, pp 19-21.
202. *Rot. pat. Hib.*, p. 77, nos. 26-7.
203. For the expedition in general see Philomena Mary Connolly, 'Lionel of Clarence and Ireland, 1361-1366' (Ph.D., Dublin University, 1977).
204. Ibid., pp 134-8, 140-41, 160. The O'Byrnes and O'Tooles certainly served against 'Irish enemies' and John O'Toole was actually made a knight – Ibid., p. 144.
205. The full Henry Crystede story may be read in translation in Geoffrey Brereton, *Froissart chronicles* (Penguin Books, 1968), pp 409-16.
206. Edmund Curtis, *Richard II in Ireland, 1394-5* (Oxford, 1927); J. F. Lydon, 'Richard II's Expeditions to Ireland', *R.S.A.I. Jn.*, xciii (1963), pp 135-49; D. B. Johnston, 'Richard II and Ireland, 1395-99' (Ph.D., Dublin University, 1976).
207. Price, *Placenames*, iii, pp lxvii-lxviii.

208. The English used guns during the second expedition in 1399, but there is no evidence that they used them during the first – Johnston, 'Richard II', pp 441-2.
209. Edmund Curtis, 'Unpublished letters from Richard II in Ireland, 1394-5', *R.I.A. Proc,* xxxvii, C (1927), p. 291.
210. Curtis, *Richard II,* pp 152-3.
211. Ibid., p. 187.
212. Ibid., pp 167, 168. O'Byrne was classed on the same level as Mac Murrough, O'Neill, O'Connor, O'Brien and the other most important Irish chieftains; O'Toole with second-rank chieftains such as O'More and O'Connor Faly – Johnston, 'Richard II', p. 65.
213. Curtis, *Richard II,* pp 206-7, 220. It is very significant that in his letter O'Byrne refers to his Wicklow lands as *patria mea.*
214. Dorothy Johnston, 'The interim years Richard II and Ireland, 1395-99' in James Lydon (ed.), *England and Ireland,* pp 175-95.
215. Ibid., p. 178.
216. Curtis, 'Letters of Richard II', p. 298.
217. *A.F.M.*
218. Curtis, 'Letters of Richard II', p. 298.
219. *The chronicle of Ireland by Henry Marleburrough* (Dublin, 1809), p. 18. Dowling gives the year as 1401 and the number slain as 400 – Butler, *Dowling,* p. 25.
220. *Marleburrough,* pp 27-8.
221. Gilbert, *Viceroys,* p. 576.
222. Edmund Curtis, 'Richard Duke of York as viceroy of Ireland, 1447-60', *R.S.A.I. Jn.,* lxii (1932), pp 166-7. Both made 'presents' of cattle to York, O'Byrne 400 and O'Toole 40. In a touching gesture O'Byrne also gave a special gift of two hobbies to York's young wife. More significantly, he also swore to allow the escheator to take possession of any ship or boat wrecked along the shoreline, a clear indication that by then he controlled the whole coast from Bray to Arklow.
223. *Stat. Ire., Hen. VI,* p. 315. That this would certainly have an adverse effect on trade was a price that had to be paid.
224. *Stat. Ire., Ed. IV,* i, 665. The watchers were to be paid with 'smokesilver' levied on all tenants.
225. Ibid., p. 809.
226. Ibid., pp 583-5.
227. Ibid., p. 321.
228. *Stat. Ire., Hen. VI,* pp 215-9
229. *S. P. Hen. VIII,* part III, pp 3, 8.
230. Ibid., p. 339.

St Kevin's church, Glendalough (O.P.W.).

Chapter 6

ANGLO-NORMAN SETTLEMENT IN UÍ BRIÚIN CUALANN, 1169-1350

LINZI SIMPSON

For the purpose of this account the confining limitations imposed by county boundaries have been discarded in favour of a more topographical region bounded by the sea on the east and the Dublin/ Wicklow mountains on the west. Known as Uí Briúin Cualann, it represented the coastal lands south of Dublin extending into county Wicklow. It stretched from Dalkey in the north, to Powerscourt and Glencullen in the west, and as far south as Newcastle McKynegan.[1] Thus it included some of the most fertile lands of Dublin's southern hinterland and a good section of the eastern coastline (fig. 6.1). Its close proximity to the city of Dublin ensured it was always to play an important role in the safeguarding of the colony and, from the early stages of the Anglo-Norman conquest, the securing of these lands became of primary importance.

The region has been chosen as a study area for several different reasons. Topographically the large mountain range, which cuts county Wicklow in half, provides a natural barrier which separates the settlements on the eastern and western sides of the mountains. Secondly the county border creates an artificial line at Bray which did not exist in the medieval period since Wicklow was not formed into a county until the early seventeenth century. Prior to this most of it formed part of county Dublin and was administered through crown officials.[2] Finally and most importantly, Uí Briúin Cualann represents an Irish territorial area, a pre-existing political entity, which was adopted by the incoming Anglo-Norman settlers. It continued as a recognisable unit of land south of Dublin after the invasion although it was adapted and modified to some degree.

This account does not attempt to provide a history of the region, but rather represents an effort to list the Anglo-Norman archaeological sites and to fit them into the historical framework which has been reconstructed by earlier writers[3] for the period in question.[4] The documentary sources for the main political events are comparatively rich. Furthermore much information can also be gleaned, through these

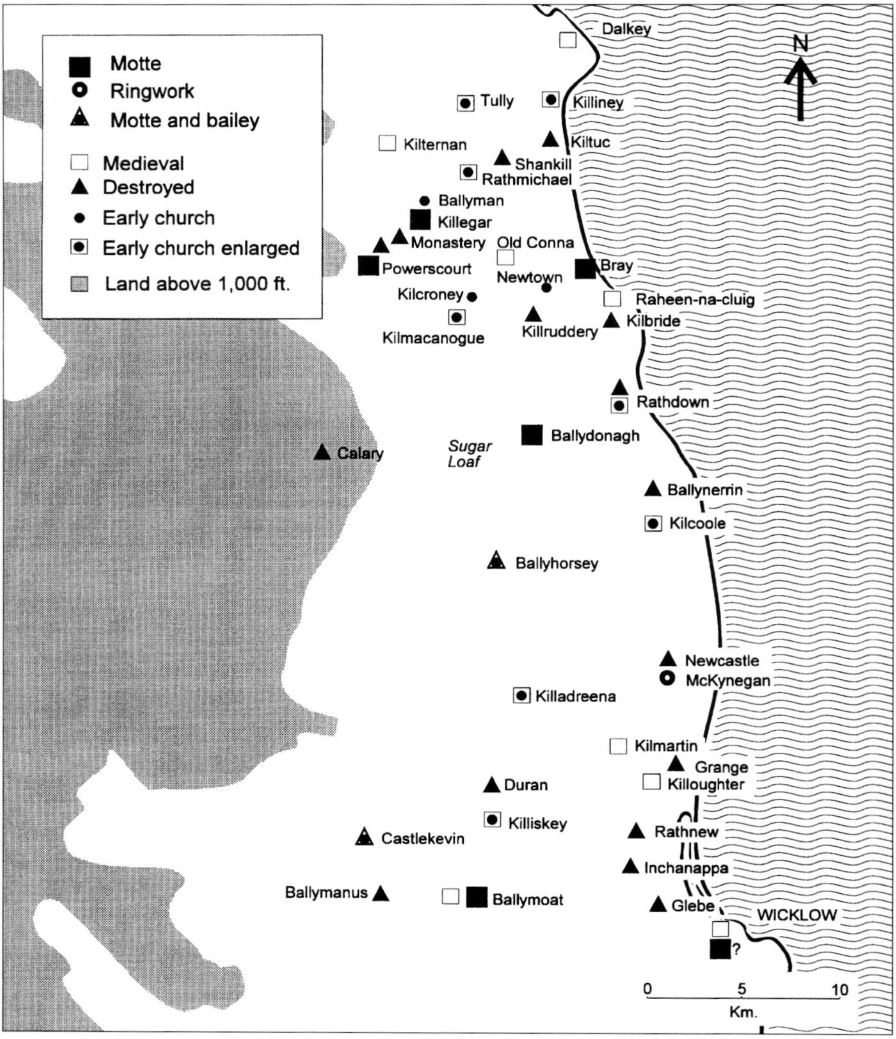

Figure 6.1 Primary Military Earthworks and Churches of Uí Briúin Cualann.

sources, about the everyday mechanics of land administration. The surviving sites in the field complement this information.

Pre-Norman Uí Briúin Cualann

In the early period the lands of Uí Briúin Cualann were inhabited by a powerful Irish sept the Uí Théig. By the eighth century, however, the sept of Uí Briúin had conquered the district, giving their name to the lands, and the Uí Théig were forced further south. When the Viking raids began in the ninth century the Uí Dúnchada, Uí Fáeláin and

Uí Muireadaig tribes were controlling the lands around Dublin and beyond.[5] The Scandinavians established trading bases at Dublin and probably further south at Wicklow and Arklow. The coastal fringe between Arklow and Dublin was settled to some degree.[6] Some surviving placenames in Uí Briúin Cualann suggest as much; Ballygunner (Delgany) and Stagonil (Powerscourt) being derived from the Norse personal name 'Gunnhildr' and Curtlestown taking its name from the Hiberno-Scandinavian Mac Torcaill family.[7] When the Anglo-Normans invaded in 1169 the latter family were controlling Dublin and some of the surrounding lands.[8] To the south lay the lands of the Irish dynasty the Uí Dúnchada, the principal family among whom was the Mac Giollamocholmóg.[9]

Some documentary evidence exists which indicates the land-holding pattern on the eve of the invasion in the area around Dublin. A confirmation charter dated 1202 records lands granted to the priory of the Holy Trinity (Christchurch) before the invasion and contains a list of original grantors.[10] From it we learn the Mac Torcaill family had granted lands at Tully, Ballyuacharan, and Tirodran; they also probably held lands at Balitober, Ballyogan and Dromin[11] as well as extensive lands in North Dublin.[12] The Mac Giollamocholmóg family also endowed ecclesiastical establishments, primarily the abbey of Glendalough. In another charter dated 1192 some of the possessions of the latter are described as being 'in the lands of Macgilleholmoche'; these included Killegar, Ballyman, Delgany, Kilmacberne and Ballydonagh.[13] Thus the region of Uí Briúin Cualann was extensively occupied, with the abbey of Glendalough, the priory of the Holy Trinity, the Mac Torcaill and the Mac Giollamocholmóg families being the recorded principal landholders.

The Anglo-Norman invasion

It is against this background that the Anglo-Norman intrusion into the area took place in 1169. The attack on Dublin by Asculf Mac Torcaill in 1171 and his subsequent defeat resulted in the remaining Ostmen being banished to an area north of the Liffey later known as Oxmantown.[14] Domnall Mac Giollamocholmóg, by siding with the Anglo-Norman leader Miles de Cogan and submitting to the English king at a later date, fared better under the new regime. He received lands in Uí Briúin Cualann at Rathdown with a considerable holding at Newcastle Lyons in south-west Dublin.[15] He probably held these lands prior to the invasion.[16]

Uí Briúin Cualann was included in Dermot Mc Murrough's kingdom of Leinster. In 1171 however, on Dermot's death, the lands passed to his son-in-law Strongbow as had been previously agreed,[17] but there was one crucial exception: the king was to hold in his own hand the town of Dublin and the adjoining cantreds, including Uí Briúin Cualann. The king also retained the towns and fortresses along the coast including the ports of Wicklow and Arklow.[18] In 1173 Strongbow did receive the castle of Wicklow[19] and Wexford as part of his fief but the most important port, Dublin, remained firmly under the king's control.[20] Wicklow was subsequently granted to Maurice FitzGerald although the town itself remained in Strongbow's hands.[21]

The Anglo-Norman settlement of Uí Briúin Cualann, which followed the invasion, can be divided into three distinct phases. The first phase marks the initial granting of lands and the military occupation of the region. Phase two involves the subinfeudation process, the establishment of manors, boroughs, and markets and the economic expansion generally associated with the colonisation of new lands. The third phase is one of contraction and retreat and one which saw the gradual re-establishment of dispossessed Irish tribes in Uí Briúin Cualann.

Church lands in Uí Briúin Cualann

The documentary sources for the land-holding pattern improve after the invasion, mainly concerning the confirmation of lands already held and the granting of new lands. The abbey of Glendalough held a sizeable amount of land especially in the Wicklow mountains but also along the plain at Ballyman, Kilmacberne and Killegar. In the late twelfth century these lands were confirmed to the abbey.[22] However in 1216 the sees of Dublin and Glendalough were united and many of the abbey's former lands passed into the hands of the archbishop of Dublin.[23]

By this date the archbishop was the greatest land-holder in county Dublin with approximately 53,200 acres of land under his control.[24] For administrative purposes his vast lands were grouped into manorial centres, two of which were south of Dublin, at Shankill, county Dublin and Castlekevin, county Wicklow. The manorial centre at Shankill dominated the plain south of Dalkey. The external lands attached to it, however, ranged much further afield. A fourteenth century extent[25] reveals the considerable lands attached to the manor, at Rathmichael, Killegar, Ballydonagh and Powerscourt, with two large vills at Dalkey and Kilmacberne. The lands in total amounted to 1,560 acres.[26]

Further south in the mountains at Annamoe lay the manor of Castlekevin where the archbishop held lands mostly encompassing the property formerly held by the abbey of Glendalough. Documentary sources of the mid-thirteenth century give details of this property, some of which may be identified as being along the coastal strip, for example at Killiskey and at Killadreena.[27] Other property included houses at Wicklow[28] but the bulk of the estate was mountain including lands in the Fartry district.[29] The priory of the Holy Trinity also held substantial lands in Uí Briúin Cualann, some antedating the invasion. Its grange was situated at Clonkeen, county Dublin, from where it controlled the fertile lands in the surrounding area.[30] These holdings included Killiney, Killegar, Kiltuc, Tully,[31] Dromin[32] and Tibradden.[33] They also held lands at Brennanstown, Foxrock and Murphystown, which in all amounted to 2,578 acres.[34] Dalkey, Ballyogan and Carrickmines were also part of their possessions.[35] The relatively late date of the elevation of the church of St Patrick's to prebendal status, 32 years after the invasion, in 1191,[36] accounts for the small amount of land in its possession. It held only 748 acres at Shanganagh and Rathsallagh and Killegar church with appurtenances. At a later date it held two carucates at Ballyogan.[37]

From the foregoing it can be seen that the bulk of the lands north of Bray were in ecclesiastical hands, the archbishop holding a block around Shankill extending southwards with St Patrick's and the priory of the Holy Trinity holding a tract of land that stretched from Ballyogan to Killiney.

Secular holdings in Uí Briúin Cualann

Domnall Mac Giollamocholmóg, lord of Uí Dúnchada, remained a very important land-holder in Uí Briúin Cualann. Married to Dervogilla, daughter of Dermot Mac Murrough and therefore brother-in-law to Strongbow, he was very influential and, unusually for a Gaelic lord, was quickly assimilated into the Anglo-Norman hierarchical system. He held his lands at Newcastle Lyons and Rathdown as a feudal tenant, rendering a nominal rent of two otterskins and liable for military service.[38] The centre of his lands in Uí Briúin Cualann lay at Rathdown where he held at least eight carucates.[39] Attached to this manor were lands at Killruddery, Tilseachan (Kilternan), Loughlinstown, Old Conna,[40] Glencullen and Newcastle McKynegan. In 1207 his son Dermot received a grant from King John to hold the lands in fee for the service of one knight.[41]

The continuity of the land holding pattern, as evident in the retention by the priory of the Holy Trinity and the Mac Giollamocholmóg family of lands formerly under their control, meant a considerable amount of the lands of Uí Briúin Cualann was not directly affected in the few years immediately following the invasion. However Mac Torcaill, arguably the most important overlord in the region, had been dispossessed and effectively removed. His lands around Dublin and Wicklow were now administered by crown officials.

The de Ridelesfords and Bray

Land in Ireland was being granted in vast tracts as fiefs, usually in appreciation of services rendered during the invasion. In *c.*1173 Strongbow, ostensibly on behalf of the king, made what at first sight appears to be a large grant of lands in Uí Briúin Cualann to Walter de Ridelesford who was a staunch supporter of his. De Ridelesford received 'Brien and the lands of the sons of Thorkill with appurtenances'.[42] The lands encompassed five knights' fees to be held by the service of two knights. This probably represents twenty to forty carucates if not more.[43] He also received other lands including some at Donnybrook, Ballymaice, and Knocklyon.[44] De Ridelesford therefore might have been expected to dominate land-holding in the region, but this is not the case. Instead he emerges as holding Bray and a few mountainous carucates at Glencullen.[45] De Ridelesford's lands were confirmed by King John but the confirmation is far more specific than and presents a much curtailed version of Strongbow's earlier charter.[46] The lands referred to are identified by placename: at Brien he received two carucates with lands at seven other unidentified places.[47] The total number of carucates, however, is only fourteen, which represents a considerable reduction in the lands intended for him by Strongbow.

Stongbow's grant was obviously not specific enough, and was in conflict with the royal policy of directly controlling the lands surrounding Dublin, and securing the coast-line. The problem may hinge on the placename 'Brien'. It is difficult to assess whether it represented the smaller area of Bray or the far larger territory of Uí Briúin Cualann. In the original charter it may have denoted Uí Briúin Cualann and represented a vast tract of land, some of which had been held by Mac Giollamocholmóg. By the late twelfth century however, King John, possibly taking advantage of this ambiguity, could claim it represented only Bray.[48] The 'lands of the sons of Thorkill', mentioned in the same grant, presumably represents an area in Uí Briúin Cualann not in ecclesiastical hands but held of the Mac Torcaill family prior to the invasion. The king, wishing to regain direct control of the land, took advantage of the vagueness of Strongbow's charter and when Walter's son, a second Walter, attempted to receive confirmation of the lands he inherited through his father's death *c.*1200, he was refused 'because the king suspects Walter's charter'.[49]

The lands controlled by de Ridelesford still represented a sizeable grant,[50] stretching north beyond the river at Bray. Before 1207 he granted to the nunnery of Graney the churches of Derdach (St Paul's, Bray), Kilmohud (Kilmacud?), Killesocalter (Killarney, Bray) and the tithes of his mill at Bray.[51] Richard de Cogan, on marrying Basilia, daughter of Walter de Ridelesford I, before 1213, received lands at Balibedan (Ballybrew) and Glencullen.[52] De Ridelesford's fate is but one example of the way in which the crown could be totally unscrupulous in the formation of demesne lands, especially with the early grants. It compares, for example, with the actions of Philip of Worcester who revoked grants made by Hugh de Lacy in north Dublin. These were restored as demesne lands of the crown.[53] By 1200 it was royal policy to extend the king's demesne lands and in 1222 the justiciar was ordered to extend, specifically, the king's land of Obrun.[54] The important coastal town of Bray remained in de Ridelesford's hands however as it had been specifically named in the original grant and the crown did not regain control until the late thirteenth century.[55]

Further south lay the property granted to Maurice FitzGerald by Strongbow. Myler FitzHenry who subsequently received it is probably responsible for its settlement. Because they were not royal lands few records survive of the subinfeudation process. However, FitzHenry did grant lands at Killoughter, Grange and Castletimon to the priory of Llanthony.[56] In 1216 he entered a religious order, and by 1229 the lands had reverted to the barons of Naas, the FitzGeralds.[57] Wicklow town, however, on Strongbow's death passed into the hands of William FitzAudelin, whom the king had instructed to take over Strongbow's lands.[58]

The royal demesne

The royal demesne lands on the south of Dublin, formed mainly from de Ridelesford's original grant, were administered through manorial centres. In the study-area, there were three large manors, Obrun, Othee, and Newcastle McKynegan. Further north, other lands formed part of the king's demesne but these were accounted for under the title 'the Vale of Dublin'. In the manor of Obrun the lands are scattered throughout Uí Briúin Cualann and not necessarily grouped topographically together; thus it included Cork near Bray, Ballycorus, parts of Kilmacanogue, Ballytenned (Powerscourt), and Carricgolyn near Shankill. Little is known about the territory of the manor of Othee, which was probably of equal size if not larger than Obrun.[59] It included lands west and south of Newcastle McKynegan, most of which were along the mountainous strip. By 1290 it was described as being in the marches of 'Glindelury'[60] although it included lands as far south as Glencap.[61] The manor of Newcastle McKynegan, by the early fourteenth century, had an area of 1,900 statute acres. Most of the placenames listed in an extent dated to this period are unfortunately obsolete but they presumably surrounded the village of Newcastle and the castle there.[62]

Unfortunately the archaeological records are not as prolific as the documentary sources; in some cases entire medieval villages have disappeared without a trace. The evidence of habitation sites prior to the invasion is limited, and little is known about the living conditions of the tenantry of the Mac Giollamocholmóg and the Mac Torcaill families. However, the settlement pattern was probably similar to that of the later Anglo-Norman colony, for which we have some evidence. The mountain range, which dominates central county Wicklow, contains large areas of rock and rough pasture suitable only for stock-rearing. The Anglo-Normans were, to a great degree, more interested in arable farming and this is reflected in a concentration of settlement sites along the lowlands on either side of the mountains.[63] The strategically placed manor at Castlekevin was the highest Anglo-Norman settlement but even here a sheltered location and good drainage and soils made it useful arable land. The distribution of the early church sites is perhaps the best indication of the pre-invasion population. Figure 6.1 shows densities around Bray with a scatter along the coastline, thinning out north of Newcastle (which was heavily wooded), and avoiding the lowlands of the coastal region which were very marshy. A network of roads and mountain paths gave access to Glendalough, the main focus of settlement in county Wicklow. The monastery, founded in the sixth century, was originally centred around the upper lake. The sheer extent of the surviving monuments bears testimony to the importance of this ecclesiastical settlement, and justifies the use of the term 'city of Glendalough'.[64]

Military earthworks of Uí Briúin Cualann

The conquest of Ireland was a military conquest, a campaign designed to take over lands and subdue the inhabitants, by force where necessary, and this is reflected in the surviving archaeological sites in the field. The military conquest of Uí Briúin Cualann proceeded in much the same way as elsewhere in the country. A series of military strongholds was established, mostly along the coast, to subdue and hold the land. By 1176 Strongbow was making grants on behalf of the king, the land having been secured by this date.[65]

The motte and bailey is perhaps the best known Anglo-Norman military earthwork castle type.[66] Erected mostly in the late twelfth/early thirteenth century, the castle consisted of a large mound artificially raised or scarped from a pre-existing natural feature. The summit was flat, crowned by a palisade with a wooden tower or bretesch. Around the base of the mound was a fosse, sometimes water-filled, with an external bank. A secondary earthwork, the bailey, was often associated with the motte. This was lower in height but larger in area and housed the administrative and domestic buildings. The distribution of mottes in Uí Briúin Cualann follows the coastline, avoiding the Wicklow mountain range (fig. 6.1). A corresponding pattern may be observed in west Wicklow and along the Meath and Kildare border. The Anglo-Normans pushed south from Dublin along the coast but there are few mottes marking this progression possibly because they met little resistance in this area.

In Uí Briúin Cualann the largest example of a motte is at Powerscourt near Enniskerry. This formed part of the royal manor of Obrun and it may represent the manorial centre. It stands some distance north of Powerscourt House and is 28 metres in diameter at the summit. The mound appears largely natural and was probably simply re-used as a convenient site for a castle. It stands within a roughly D-shaped field enclosure with no indication of a bank or a fosse, although the area is very overgrown. No associated earthworks are visible. The placename Powerscourt has been identified with Ballitenned, first mentioned in 1290 and described as being in the king's manor of Obrun.[67] The land probably formed part of the original grant to de Ridelesford and he may have been responsible for its construction. A similar motte type survives at Newtownmountkennedy demesne, although it is smaller in height. This motte has a diameter at the summit of 16 metres with a circumference of approximately 1,000 metres but neither is there any indication of a surrounding fosse or bank. It also appears scarped from a natural hillock since there are several in the vicinity. A rectangular mound to the north-east of the motte, lower in height and measuring 92 metres by 40 metres, represents all that is left of a bailey.[68] There is no mention of this castle in the documentary sources. The neighbouring townland of Ballyhorsey suggests that it was held by the de Horseye family at some stage.[69] The size of the motte and bailey implies that it was probably built soon after the invasion. The area around Newtownmountkennedy formed part of the manor of Newcastle McKynegan and so was in royal hands. The castle appears not to have been rebuilt in stone.

Castlekevin at Annamoe, the centre of the archbishop's manor, represents one of the most striking examples of a motte and bailey in county Wicklow. The motte, which is square in shape, is 8 metres high and 30 metres square and is scarped from a natural gravel ridge; to the east lies a large bailey. The site bears much evidence of re-building in mortared stone and the motte itself is revetted by masonry which is especially visible at the southern side. The entire motte is surrounded by a deep fosse approximately 10 metres wide with massive banks 4 metres high. The fosse continues around the north side of the bailey, where the remains of a stone footing indicates the bailey was originally surrounded by a stone wall. The fosse may have been water-filled, since there is a stream running east-west with a dry leat extending from the north-west corner. An old road runs along the northern side of the site. The sheer size of the fortification of Castlekevin indicates its strategic and vulnerable location facing high Wicklow. The land belonged originally to the abbey of Glendalough; however, it formed part of the archbishop's holdings from an early date. John Comyn, the first Anglo-Norman archbishop, appears to have had few dealings with church property in this area, and it was probably Henry de Londres who was responsible for the construction of the castle.[70]

The remaining five sites have been tentatively identified as possible motte sites.[71] The initial fortification at Wicklow town, a site known locally as the 'Roundmount' and commanding a powerful view of the river, is traditionally ascribed to the Scandinavians. However, it may represent the castle mentioned by Giraldus in 1173.[72] It displays the characteristics of a typical Anglo-Norman motte. The summit measures 16 metres in diameter but the sides have eroded considerably. Faint traces of a fosse and bank can be seen on the north and eastern side. This was probably water-filled with a leat running from the north-east corner down to the river. At Ballydonagh, close to Greystones, O'Curry in the nineteenth century, recorded a 'fine moate',[73] but all that remains today is a small mound 6.5 metres high with a flat summit. The site has unfortunately been badly damaged by a gravel pit which has resulted in most of it being quarried away. The identification of this site as a motte rests on the meagre documentary evidence which identifies Ballydonagh as having had an Anglo-Norman presence. It has been tentatively identified with Villa Uduread given by the Mac Giollamocholmóg family to the priory of the Holy Trinity in 1172-6.[74] By 1326 it formed part of the archbishop's manor of Shankill, where 60 acres were held by Jordan Walrant.[75]

Close by at Killegar, Price identified what he thought may have represented a motte; it stood approx. 4 metres high with a circumference of 150 metres and a diameter on the summit of 25 metres. The sides were almost vertical.[76] Unfortunately this area has also been extensively quarried and nothing remains of the site. Killegar formed part of the archbishop's manor of Shankill and by 1219 the church was assigned to St Patrick's Cathedral.[77] There was probably a small vill associated with the motte and church. Further south at Glenealy a 'moate' was recorded by O'Curry which had been cleared away by the local people.[78] No further information is given but it was probably a motte built by Myler FitzHenry after he received a grant of Wicklow from Maurice FitzGerald. De Ridelesford's castle at Bray was also probably a motte. The Down Survey of 1654-6 depicts the castle perched on top of a large mound.[79] The traditional site of the castle is on the ridge overlooking the Dargle river on the north; however, it would have been exposed and vulnerable to attack on its southern side.

Perhaps the best documented military earthwork is still to be seen at Newcastle McKynegan. Built before 1190[80] the scale of the surviving remains is an indication of its importance in the overall defensive strategy along the eastern coast. Its sheer size makes classification of the site difficult. It consists of a roughly circular mound with a massive summit 62 metres in diameter. It was carved from a natural ridge which continues eastwards and may have formed part of a bailey similar to that at Castlekevin. Around the base of the mound traces of a fosse can be seen especially visible at the eastern side where it is 4.4 metres wide by 1.2 metres deep. A small stream which probably fed the fosse runs along the northern boundary. In 1908 the remaining stone walls of a gaol could be seen a little to the north of the site and according to tradition a gallows was situated to the north-west.[81]

The large area encompassed at Newcastle McKynegan is more reminiscent of the ringwork castles of England and Wales than of a motte. The ringwork castle was a second type of military fortress introduced by the Anglo-Normans. It consisted of an area completely surrounded by large banks and a fosse, the main defensive element being a strong gate-house. In England and especially Wales, the ring-works are well represented in the field at a ratio of one ringwork to every three mottes,[82] but in Ireland the situation is complicated by the similar morphology of the native rath which was usually circular with an external bank also. To date, only forty-five examples of ringworks have been tentatively identified.[83]

Newcastle McKynegan, from its very large summit, may represent a ringwork which has been subsequently filled in.[84] On the western slope stand the remains of a large stone building. At first glance this appears to be a late medieval building though it incorporated the fabric of a much earlier structure.The remaining structure may represent all that is left of the original gate-house; in 1279-82 works are recorded which include the building of a tower and a hall.[85] The ringwork may have been filled in at this date to facilitate the construction of the great hall.

In general it can be seen that Uí Briúin Cualann was militarily well secured at an early date. De Ridelesford received his grant of Bray, and built a strong castle which acted as a buffer between the native Irish and the vulnerable but valuable lands south of Dublin. The royal strongholds at Newcastle and Wicklow protected the coastline which the crown sought to control throughout the medieval period.[86] Inland the mottes at Newtownmountkennedy and Powerscourt commanded the areas closest to the Dublin/Wicklow mountains, the smaller mottes at Ballydonagh and Killegar belonging to individual sub-tenants leasing the lands. Graham in his study of the distribution pattern of mottes in Meath concluded that the larger mottes indicated a frontier position while the smaller mottes were normally manorial centres.[87] However, in Wicklow the distribution pattern is dominated by the mountain range. The coastal lands formed part of the lands granted in the early years after the invasion areas which were secured very quickly. The even but sparse distribution from Dublin to Arklow indicates a policy of maintaining control along the coast rather than resistance shown by the native population.

SETTLEMENT OF UÍ BRIÚIN CUALANN

By the twelfth century Uí Briúin Cualann was settled extensively, especially along the coast where much of the land is fertile. The inhabitants probably occupied very flimsy house structures which have left little trace on the ground, or lie beneath the subsequent medieval occupation, since the Anglo-Normans re-used, to a great degree, existing foci of settlement and incorporated them into their own manorial systems.

The tenantry of Uí Briúin Cualann

The settlement of the lands of Uí Briúin Cualann was relatively peaceful and developed rapidly. This was due, to a large extent, to the acquiescence of Domnall Mac Giollamocholmóg in the Anglo-Norman domination. His holding at Rathdown must have facilitated the peaceful assimilation of the native Irish who had been inhabiting the lands and continued to do so. The manors of Obrun and Othee appear to have been extensively occupied, at an early date by 'betaghs'[88] or native Irish who provided the framework of the settlement of Uí Briúin Cualann.[89] There are no known manorial centres for either manor, suggesting the tenantry was already *in situ*, the bulk being Irish. Obrun[90] appears as a fragmented manor with lands spread across Uí Briúin Cualann. The manorial names were more administrative than topographical, although originating in Irish territorial areas. Yet the fact that the names of the pre-existing tribal regions were adopted – Obrun representing the Uí Briúin and Othee representing Uí Théig – suggests that a great number of Irish remained on the lands, especially the lands of Mac Giollamocholmóg.[91] Elsewhere the Anglo-Normans imposed new territorial units which bore little resemblance to the existing settlement pattern.[92]

This dominance by the Irish of the royal manors of Obrun and Othee is evident in surviving manorial accounts. At Bray, where the town was held by de Ridelesford, the settlers were, for the most part, typically English, and they out-numbered the Irish. At Obrun and Othee, however, the reverse was true.[93] In 1235 the rent of the betaghs, at an estimated rate of 6d an acre, accounts for 1,007 acres at Obrun and

1,288 acres at Othee, representing a considerable amount of land.[94] As a work force they were much in demand, especially by the king, who went to great lengths to safeguard his interests. When William de Deveneys complained of betaghs fleeing his lands in the Vale of Dublin, the king gave him leave to recover them, provided they were not residing on royal lands enjoying tenure under the king.[95] Similarly, on granting other land he ordered that the Irishmen dwelling there be shifted elsewhere on demesne lands.[96] Conversely, in some cases a grant of land could include the betaghs. When the bishop of Glendalough received ten carucates of land in Wicklow the betaghs were included as part of the grant,[97] and lands granted by St Thomas's abbey at Killiskey also included the use of the 'betaghs'.[98] The betaghs are recorded as paying rent directly to the crown. At Obrun, in 1235, they paid £25. 3s. 6d.[99] On the manor of Othee the Irish paid 2d an acre,[100] the low rent indicating it was probably rough pasture land. But not all betaghs were holding inferior land; by 1382 the betaghs were paying 6d an acre (2.5 statute acres) in the archbishop's manor of St. Sepulchre.[101]

Ostmen in Uí Briúin Cualann

Little evidence survives of the fate of the Ostmen who must have inhabited some of the lands south of Dublin. After the death of Mac Torcaill they probably continued to occupy lands and were incorporated, at a higher level than the Irish, into the Anglo-Norman system.[102] In the Vale of Dublin thirty-six rents are accounted for from 'the Ostmen', suggesting some recognisable group remained in possession of lands, the small amount indicating the low numbers.[103] Because they were assimilated into the system they become lost in the documentary sources but there are occasional later references to surviving Scandinavians. A Reginald Klause, possibly an Ostman, held considerable lands at Shankill under the archbishop of Dublin in 1304.[104]

Archbishop's manor of Castlekevin

At the archbishop's manor of Castlekevin the integration of the Irish was at a much higher level, probably because of the isolated position of the manor and the predominantly Irish tenantry living there. The manor at Castlekevin, for a century after the invasion, had a strong Anglo-Norman presence.[105] However, the lands there were previously controlled by the abbey of Glendalough and were well settled. The archbishop, who was well experienced in setting up manorial centres, had shown an interest in settlement of lands in the area, especially in west Wicklow.[106] The Anglo-Norman presence at Castlekevin reflects the economic necessity of utilising pre-existing concentrations of population. The Irish were left *in situ* and were integrated into the system at a high level. They not only held large amounts of lands and had access to English law,[107] but also fulfilled royal functions. In an inquisition dated 1257-63 Elias O'Toole is recorded as being 'sergeant of the county.'[108] In the same reference eight of the jurors had Irish names.[109]

Settlement and administration

It is difficult to assess where the Irish tenantry actually lived. Many presumably lived at or close to the manorial villages, especially the 'unfree' who worked the lord's demesne lands. However, some betaghs had considerable holdings[110] and there is evidence to suggest that they may have occupied separate settlements in the outlying parts of the manor.[111] At Duleek, *c.* 1620, land is described as being the 'land of the betaghs of Duleek'.[112] At an earlier date at Finglas, in 1326, farmers are recorded as holding 'betagh's land', suggesting a unit of land which was held collectively by betaghs.[113] Surviving placenames such as Ballybetagh, Ballynametagh and Betaghton, Betaghford[114] may be survivals of such settlements. At a later date 'Ballybetagh' denoted a specific area of land containing 960 Irish acres and this usage may have been derived from nucleated settlements of the betaghs.[115] Ballybetagh, near Kilternan, had a series of linear earthworks possibly representing such a settlement: unfortunately they leave little trace today.[116]

The manors, both of the archbishopric and the crown, were administered similarly. The manorial centre, located at the lord's motte or castle, acted as a focal point of settlement. A weekly market was usually granted, and a manorial court established. Surrounding the fortification were the lord's demesne lands, which could vary in acreage but were normally two carucates. The lands were worked by the lord's tenants as part of services owed. At Shankill, in the late thirteenth century, the services of the tenants were worth £19.7s.7d., a sizeable sum. Other revenue was generated through the lord's mill, a tax on brewing and on prize fish, and the delivery of the customary cow.[117] Pleas and perquisites of the manor court added to this revenue.[118] Against this was set expenses incurred in the running of the manor throughout the year; these included repairs of houses, mills and the wages of the bailiffs. The manors operated a mixed economy, both arable and stock-rearing. At Newcastle McKynegan sheep and cattle were important, but corn, which was a major export, was also grown.[119] Common grazing was the usual practice, especially in the mountain regions where it was relatively cheap at 1d to 2d an acre.[120] The manor of Clonkeen, in 1330, displays a diversity of produce which could be expected at any big manor. The crops included wheat, barley, oats, beans and peas. At harvest time some eighty-eight people were employed, presumably in the demesne lands of the grange.[121]

Development of Uí Briúin Cualann

The settlements developed rapidly along Uí Briúin Cualann, and 'vills' or small villages sprang up around the fortifications and established manorial centres. Markets[122] were granted at Castlekevin, Stagonil, Bray,[123] Newcastle McKynegan,[124] and Glannor,[125] and a network of roads linked the outlying settlements. The vills of Shankill, Dalkey, Bray, Kilmacberne, Newcastle McKynegan, Kilbla[126] and Wicklow received borough status.[127] This social status was designed to act as an inducement to attract new settlers by offering favourable tenurial conditions. The burgesses held a 'burgage plot' for a fixed rent (usually one shilling);[128] they also belonged to their own 'court of the hundred' and had a right to tax themselves. In other parts of Ireland some of the larger boroughs became important nucleated centres which developed urban characteristics. However, smaller villas, while given borough status, were never more than agricultural villages.[129] In Uí Briúin Cualann the distribution pattern of the boroughs and markets reflects the coastal spread of the Anglo-Normans. In all there were seven boroughs and five markets. This mirrors the overall distribution map where densities along the Dublin and Kildare border follow the line of the mountains.[130]

The social structure of the manors was comprised of different types of tenants. In Bray in 1311[131] at the summit of the social scale were the thirty-two 'burgesses' who held their burgage plots for 31s.[132] The three 'free-holders' were tenants holding lands and paying rents but not liable for military service; they held considerable lands amounting to around 1.5 carucates. The 'firmarii' leased their lands for a specific rent, sometimes owing military service; at Bray only one Irishman holding twenty acres was recorded. Beneath him were the two Irish 'gavillers' who owed labour services and suit of court, while the seven 'cottagers' held their cottages with rent and labour services. The three betaghs held only a small amount of land.[133]

External lands of the manors

The external lands of the manors were granted out as the conquest progressed, some to ecclesiastical establishments. The abbey of St Thomas had considerable interests at Killiskey, Kilruddery, Newcastle and Glencullen.[134] It also received a plot of land at Bray on the river from which to trade.[135] St Mary's was granted a similar plot 24 feet wide by 10.5 perches long.[136] The abbey also held extensive lands at Carrickbrennan and Glencullen.[137] The Knights Hospitallers held four caracutes at Carrickdolygn (Carrickgollagan), as did the Knights Templars.[138] The latter also held half a carucate at Bray.[139] English tenants, attracted by the favourable tenurial conditions, began to settle on the manors, marking the secondary phase of settlement. Parts of Obrun were leased out in vast tracts. In 1243, for example, Reymund de Careve held a carucate of land that stretched from Dundrum to Shankill.[140] At Powerscourt, by the thirteenth century, lands were held by the de Poer family, Ralph le Maresechal held Ballycorus,[141] and Fulk de Cantilupe had a large holding at Corkagh, all within the manor of Obrun.[142]

Medieval church sites

The distribution pattern of the small vills throughout Uí Briúin Cualann can be best traced on the ground by the distribution of churches in use during the medieval period. The earlier churches were usually too small to service the new community and its dependants and the surviving sites often show evidence of having been enlarged. This was usually done by the insertion of a simple chancel arch in the west or east gable of the original nave. The addition was usually wider and longer and the nave itself often had additional windows inserted. A classic example of this type can be seen at Tully, county Dublin. Here the new chancel is attached to the east end of the nave. The nave walls only survive to a height of 60 cm but above the later chancel arch is a small slit-window with the splay on the east side indicating it is the original east gable of an earlier structure. The new chancel displays steeped gables and four round-headed windows with wide arched embrasures and is twice the width of the original nave. A similar addition, although probably later in date, can be seen at Killadreena where the chancel measures 8.3 metres east-west by 5 metres north-south.

At Killiney there is a variation in the method used. Here the addition was tacked on very haphazardly to the side of the church. The northern wall of the nave was simply broken through at intervals, then arched to give access to the addition. This resulted in the windows of the nave being completely blocked. The church at Kilcoole also had a large extension added; this included an upper storey that is clearly of later date. In some cases the churches were built during the medieval period. At Raheen-na-Cluig, for example, the surviving church is a medieval structure which originally had two smaller buildings attached. It was also reputedly surrounded by a moat.[144] The church, measuring internally 13 metres long by 5 metres wide, is in a very good state of preservation, and a fine sandstone round-headed window survives in the eastern wall.

The medieval church at Kilmartin further south is unfortunately not in as good condition. It measures 14 metres east-west by 6.6 metres north-south with walls 1 metre thick. A square headed doorway survives in the south wall. A graveyard was recorded lying to the south of the church but this has since been ploughed out. Its outline is still clearly visible. Killoughter, lying to the west of Kilmartin, also displays medieval features, but is very badly overgrown. Measuring 10.6 metres by 5.2 metres, the twelfth-century doorway is in the west gable. Pointed arched windows were recorded in the nineteenth century although little is visible today.[145]

Royal forests of Uí Briúin Cualann

To the west lay the vast royal forest which covered the entire valley of Glencree. There were many disputes concerning the royal forest, especially with the archbishop of Dublin who also held forests in Wicklow.[146] However, in 1229 he managed to get a disafforestation charter for his vast forest at Coillacht.[147] The royal forest at Glencree was enclosed by a deep fosse and bank, traces of which can still be seen near Curtlestown church. In 1913 it was recorded as a bank standing 3 metres high by 3 metres wide with the fosse 4 metres wide and 1.6 metres deep.[148] Today, the bank and fosse is still visible although it has eroded considerably; a large stone wall runs along the top of the bank. The medieval earthwork was probably constructed to prevent the royal deer from wandering,[149] and, because of the severe laws on poaching, to delineate the precise boundaries of the forest. Timber was an important commodity in medieval Ireland, especially oak for which Ireland was renowned.[150] The port of Dublin depended completely on the hinterland to provide the large quantities of wood required for industrial and domestic uses as well as for building.[151] Timber was also exported. In 1290 Queen Eleanor established a large timber works at Glencree. A second royal forest at Newcastle McKynegan also had timber works at this date. From here she exported timber for her castle in Haverford in Wales.[152] A third royal forest is recorded at Glarfoun in the manor of Obrun somewhere between Powerscourt and Kilmacanogue.[153]

The royal and archiepiscopal manorial centres catered for a large population who were settled peacefully and the various religious houses had set up centres from which to exploit the trade route. Easy access to the sea, especially at Newcastle McKynegan, made transportation easier. The conquest and settlement of Uí Briúin Cualann had been achieved quickly and peacefully and this was conducive to the rapid expansion of the Anglo-Norman settlement. However, the political situation was to change radically by the end of the thirteenth century.

THE CONTRACTION OF THE COLONY

The O'Byrnes and O'Tooles

The first indication of the changing political climate is usually cited as being an order by Prince Edward in July 1270 instructing the justiciar to aid the archbishop in quelling a rebellion in his lands.[154] The lands are not specified but from subsequent events it is obvious that it is the tenants of the manor of Castlekevin who are causing the trouble. The O'Byrne and O'Toole clans occupied much of the mountainous country around Castlekevin. Little is known about the circumstances of their arrival in county Wicklow. It is possible that they were deliberately settled in the Glen of Imaal by the Geraldines anxious to clear the fertile plains of Kildare,[155] or that on dispossession in county Kildare by Walter de Ridelesford they sought refuge at Glendalough and Glenmalure where their kinsman Laurence O'Toole, abbot of Glendalough, had a powerful presence. The O'Tooles received a grant – later to have a disastrous impact on Anglo-Norman settlement – of Glenmalure between 1256-71.

The causes of the rebellion have never been firmly established; it coincided with a vacancy in the archbishopric (1271-79) which resulted in crown officials controlling all the lands.[157] Situated as they were high in the mountains far from Dublin, the O'Byrnes and O'Tooles had remained independent. The lands surrounding the manor were really only suitable for stock-rearing which they practised extensively.[158] The large sums of money coming out of the manor in the early years is an indication of the numbers of tenants. It was far more profitable to leave the Irish *in situ* and the trouble may have arisen through contact with crown officials wishing to exploit this revenue. The tenants of Castlekevin, especially the Irish, were isolated and very vulnerable to economic disasters. The political situation was exacerbated by bad weather and famine which must have resulted in starvation in the mountains.[159] The exposed manors proved easy targets; they also had stores of food.[160]

War in the Wicklow Mountains

War broke out in the Wicklow/Leinster mountains between 1271 and 1277. Expeditions were speedily mounted with varying success. In 1274 the Irish soundly defeated the government forces at Glenmalure. Successive campaigns under de Geneville, the justiciar, in 1275 and 1276 met with little success. Robert de Ufford replaced de Geneville, and immediately mounted another series of campaigns. However, the strategy he used was slightly different. His priority was not just to defeat the rebels but to protect the surrounding settlements. De Ufford based his campaigns on strategically placed castles and wards around the base of the mountains. He managed to drive the Irish out of Glenmalure in 1277 and, for more than a decade, there was relative peace.[161] Hostilities broke out again in 1294 which resulted in the establishment of a more concentrated series of wards. The wards consisted of men-at-arms assigned to protect an area from a defensive base and represented a new policy of partial offensive/partial defensive which was to be repeated throughout the fourteenth century.[162]

Contraction of settlements in Uí Briúin Cualann

The worsening political situation can be traced through the surviving documentary sources especially in the manorial accounts. Castlekevin was in the most vulnerable position and this is reflected in its accounts. Between 1271-77 it produced a total of £609. 9s. 1d,[163] a sizeable amount, but for the year 1281 it produced nothing 'on account of the war of the Irish'.[164] The manor was recovering somewhat by 1295[165] but by 1326 in a general survey of the archbishop's lands it is not even listed.[166] Further north in the king's manor of Othee by 1284 the rent was 'uncertain'.[167] Twelve years later only 8s 4d was received.[168] At Newcastle McKynegan watchers and armed men were employed,[169] and by 1284 the revenue was uncertain due mainly to the external lands of the manor lying waste.[170] However, the strong military fortress did protect the settlement to some degree. Burgesess are still recorded as holding lands at Newcastle McKynegan in 1343.[171]

The late thirteenth century heralded the beginnings of the disintegration of the Anglo-Norman dominance in Uí Briúin Cualann and the gradual concentration of lands in individual hands, a situation which was far more profitable to the crown. Obrun was leased out for a block number of years to various individuals. Thomas Godfrey and Ralph Marshall, for example, held parts of Obrun from 1285[172] to 1293.[173] Othee was held by William Burnell who also held extensive lands in the Vale of Dublin and in Obrun.[174] However, the revenue from the royal lands becomes increasingly uncertain, with the accounts of the manors falling into arrears. This was probably due to the landholders exploiting the political climate and damage caused by raids. At Obrun it was claimed that the king had many losses while the tenants of the manor had great profit.[175] An extent of Newcastle in 1305 shows a vill which was still functioning,[176] perhaps suggesting that the level of devastation is, to some degree, exaggerated. The situation fluctuated; there were periods of relative peace which allowed the new English tenants to grow their crops. The rent was collected even as late as the early fourteenth century at Newcastle, Othee and Obrun.[177]

As the fourteenth century progressed the situation worsened and law and order seems to have all but broken down. The outbreak of the Black Death in 1348 did little to bring stability and the food shortage that followed must have hit the Irish.[178] We know that William de Deveney's betaghs in the Vale of Dublin deserted because of the warlike conditions.[179] To curb endemic absenteeism lands were granted on condition that a dwelling be built and inhabited.[180]

Prominent families, such as the Lawlesses and Archebolds who held the lands in large blocks and at a cheaper rent dominated ownership. The Lawless family appear at an early date at the archbishop's manors at Ballymore and Castlekevin,[181] and by the fourteenth century they held extensive lands around the manor of Shankill. Sir Hugh Lawless was appointed constable of Bray castle in 1314,[182] but by 1350 his stronghold at Kilcommon had been deserted.[183] The Archebolds settled around Delgany, Bray, Kilruddery and Newcastle. They occupied Kindlestown castle by 1315 and may have been sub-tenants under Albert de Kenley.[184]

Such families found their position increasingly precarious with their homesteads isolated in a dangerous march. Their problems were compounded by the devastations of the Bruce invasion in 1316 which affected the entire country. The O'Byrnes and O'Tooles were quick to take advantage of the confusion caused to increase their raiding expeditions. Hugh Lawless complained that his lands around Bray were worthless because the Irish rose against the king when the Scots came to Ireland.[185] The castle at Bray was burnt as were Arklow and Newcastle Mckynegan.[186] Additional damage was also caused by the king's armies attempting to halt Bruce's progress.[187]

The extents made of the archbishop's manors in 1326 show the state of the delapidated settlements. The manor of Shankill was derelict and deserted, the demesne lands lying untilled and all the buildings thrown down. At the neighbouring vill of Kilmacberne the lands were in a similar state. Rathmichael is deserted, the lands at Dalkey having no tenants; Killegar is waste as is Stagonil and Carrickmines.[188] Even the lands at Rathdown fared little better. The Mac Giollamocholmóg family had decreased in importance and by *c.* 1305 had sold the last of their lands amounting to some eight carucates to Nigel le Brun.[189] Le Brun only gained possession of the lands for a very short period; by 1310 the lands are described as being waste.[190] A complaint from the burgesses of Newcastle McKynegan reveals how serious the devastation was by 1343. The manor is described as being situated in the march and was so often burnt that they (the burgesses) could scarcely live there; they also claimed the manor was lying waste and had gone uncultivated for ten years.[191]

The changing political climate had an enormous impact on the settlers in Uí Briúin Cualann. In less than fifty years the lands went from being *terra pacis* to being *terra guerre* in a dangerous frontier march.[192] This had a disastrous effect on the settlement sites south of Dublin and resulted in the desertion of some sites and the re-fortification of others.

Stone castles of Uí Briúin Cualann

The natural progression in the castle building sequence was the re-fortification of the earthen castles in stone. Motte and baileys hurriedly built in the early years of the conquest could now be re-built in a more durable form. One of the first to be rebuilt in stone was probably the royal castle of Newcastle McKynegan described in the late thirteenth century as 'almost the strongest in Ireland'.[193] In 1279-82, Hugh de Crus was engaged in the re-fortifying of the castle,[194] and David de Offyntoun received £74 6s. 9d. for building a tower.[195] In 1295 the castle is under re-construction again but the works appear far more extensive probably because it had been burnt earlier in the year.[196] This included the building of a wall around the castle. Other works were carried out on the great hall and other houses.[197] The hall was probably located on the summit of the mound enclosed by a wall with an entrance on the west side through the gate-house.[198] Orpen re-interprets what had previously been translated as a 'moat' as 'motte', giving one of the few instances where the 'motte' is distinguished from the castle.[199] The castle did have a moat, however, with John de Stratton diverting water around the base of the motte.[200] The castle is probably distinguished from the motte because of the latter's unusually large size.

The surviving stone building at Newcastle McKynegan represents a medieval structure which has been considerably altered. It is roughly constructed of local uncoarsed stone with extensive red-brick additions. The remaining structure is clearly a large gate-house with a massive barrel vault, 4.20 metres wide, orientated east-west. On the northern side lies a small chamber, 2.70 metres wide with a low groin vault. A small blocked doorway on the southern side indicates that a similar chamber lay on the other side. The steep staircase, in the northern wall of the gate-way, is clearly a later insertion since it blocks a small doorway, 1.30 metres wide, in the east wall. The latter gave access to the small chamber, possibly a guard-room. Fragments of badly decayed tufa mouldings are also visible. The staircase leads to an overhead chamber probably contemporary with the gate-house but extensively re-modelled. This chamber displays a large seventeenth-century fire-place, a slop-stone, and three large windows. The southern chamber, which is 1.50 metres higher, is mostly constructed of red brick as are the two upper storeys. An early date for the core of the building is suggested by the remains of the plank shuttering used in the construction of the barrel vault of the gate-way. Similar imprints can be seen in the small vault of the guard-room. The blocked doorway in the eastern wall may also suggest an earlier date. The size of the gate-house suggests that the fortifications at Newcastle McKynegan were very extensive; little remains of the massive curtain wall which must have surrounded the castle precincts.

At Castlekevin it was imperative to refortify the castle as quickly as possible because of its relatively exposed position. By 1277 it was being used as a base from which to mount expeditions against the Irish. The accounts of Robert de Ufford as justiciar show the amount of money spent on the refortification. The documentary evidence probably refers to the revetting of the motte in stone and the building of the corner towers and the gate-house.[201] By 1308, however, Castlekevin had been burnt,[202] but was quickly rebuilt by Piers de Gaveston. The works included some rebuilding in stone since payments to stone quarriers were included in the accounts.[203] The site still bears the evidence of the massive refortification works of the thirteenth and fourteenth centuries. The entire motte is revetted in masonry, giving it a vertical face; this is seen clearly on the southern side. On the summit are the foundations of corner towers at the north-west and north-east angles, roughly 5 metres square. Midway on the eastern side are the remains of a substantial structure, probably a gate-house. This was 8 metres wide and originally extended over the fosse towards the bailey. The structure is of a local slate and is roughly coursed, the base displaying a pronounced batter; this has collapsed entirely, however, with only the very base still in position. In 1908, when Orpen visited the site, the gate-house was still standing with a small guard-room attached.[204] Strong as the castle was, it was constantly under attack and by the early fourteenth century it was badly damaged.[205]

Black Castle at Wicklow has a strategic coastal site. Situated on a rocky out-crop, only the foundations survive in part, with a good portion of the south wall still standing. The plan of the castle is determined by the topography of the site and appears as a somewhat haphazard enclosure roughly triangular in shape. The large fosse is rock-cut,[206] 11 metres wide, with a section of the headland enclosed by a bank and fosse forming an outer bailey.[207] At the south-west corner are the remains of a rectangular tower, built of shale, measuring internally 4 metres by 2.3 metres. The surviving wall stands to a height of 2.4 metres and is 1.8 metres in width; it displays a pronounced external batter. Two loophole windows are also evident; in the north-west angle the window moulding is Dundry probably of the thirteenth

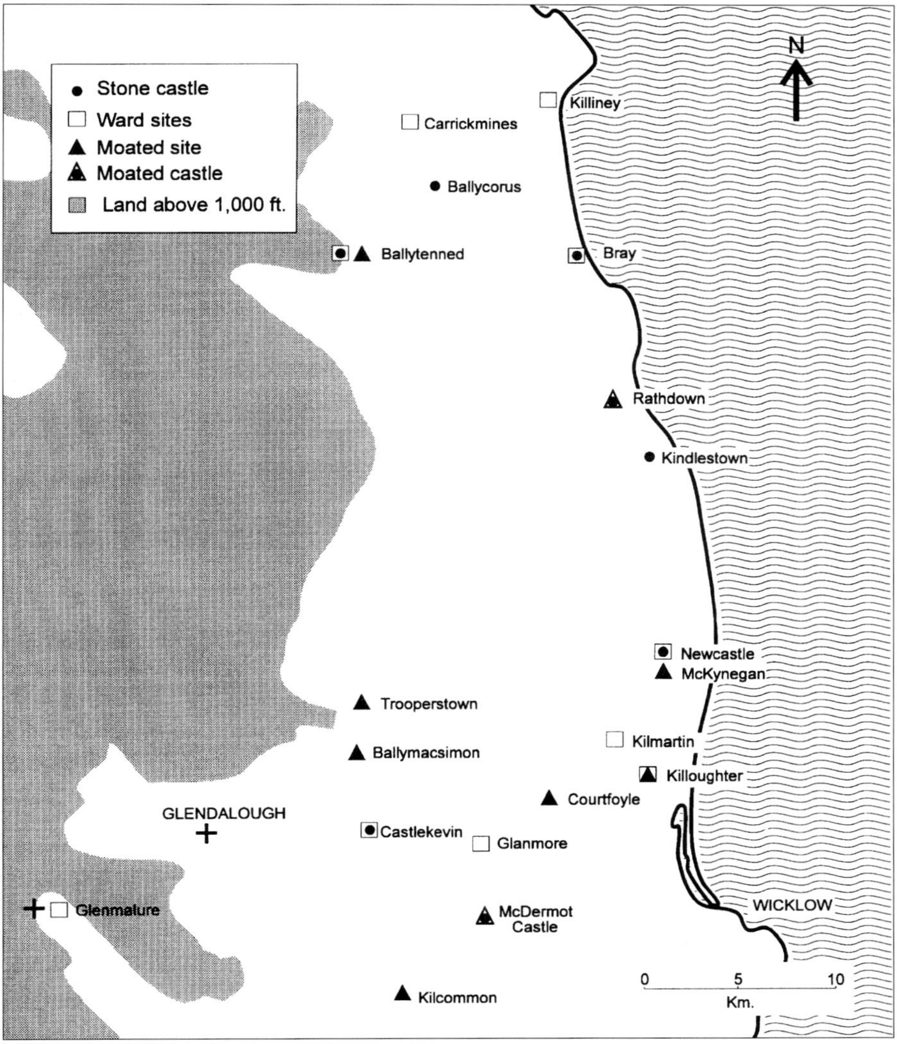

Figure 6.2 Fortifications *c.*1250-1350 and ward sites of Uí Briúin Cualann.

century.[208] A second tower can be seen in the east angle but this appears smaller in size; a garderobe chute discharges into the sea through a rough gully cut into the rock. On the seaward side a series of rock-cut steps gave direct access to the sea. Black Castle was a very strong castle, probably built in the thirteenth century as part of the coastal defensive line stretching from Bray to Arklow. In 1229 the castle was in Geraldine hands,[209] but by 1339 it was held, in conjunction with Arklow, Newcastle and Powerscourt, by a royal constable with a garrison of soldiers.[210] The O'Byrnes seized the castle temporarily in

1370, though it was soon re-built. A William Fitzwilliam was then constable and he received 40 marks for this purpose. The rebuilding was to include the completion of the wall at the front of the castle which was to be 5 perches in length and the building of three towers with stone and cement. The towers, two of which were to be 30 ft high, were situated over the gate and chapel; the third tower was termed the garret.[211] The Down Survey depicts the castle as a three-storey crenellated building with two visible square towers on either side.[212] The depiction is somewhat stylised but the castle may have been partially rebuilt. In 1410 Edward Perrers is recorded as being the constable,[213] but by the end of the fifteenth century it was in disrepair.[214]

De Ridelesford's castle site at Bray bears no evidence of the castle type. The Down Survey depicts it as a square tower crenellated with a single slit-window.[215] In 1334 Geoffrey Crumpe received the manor of Bray on condition that he rebuilt the castle. From this date on the castle at Bray became an important garrison post. In 1356 there were 20 light horsemen with 40 archers stationed there.[216] All these castles – Black Castle, Bray and Newcastle – reveal the influence of government policy because they were royal castles, as did Castlekevin because it was used as a base by the government troops. However, there were other castles in Uí Briúin Cualann built by the local land-holders as part of a defensive strategy.

At Kindlestown the remains of a large castle still survive but there is no evidence of a motte. Situated close to Delgany, the castle has been ascribed to Walter de Beneville,[217] but it was from Albert de Kenley that it took its name. De Kenley, sheriff of Kildare,[218] probably received the lands of Ballygonner (Delgany)[219] as part of a dowry when he married the wife of Ralph, son of John Mac Giollamocholmóg, in the early fourteenth century.[220] De Kenley died in 1343 with the lands reverting to the king.[221] The castle was definitely in existence in 1377 when it is cited as being seized by the O'Byrnes.[222] It was a halled-type castle with the lower chamber divided in two and can be compared stylistically to Rathumney castle in county Wexford.[223] Both have two storeys with a corner tower at one end. There are substantial remains still visible on the site. The north wall survives almost intact to its full height with portions of the east and west wall also evident Internally, the springing of a barrel vault is visible with remains of plank-shuttering similar to that at Newcastle McKynegan. The east wall, however, which is 3 metres thick, displays evidence of wicker-shuttering. At the upper level, square-headed rectangular slit windows, 1.20 metres long by 15cm wide with deep embrasures, provided meagre light to the upper chambers. One well-preserved example has a window-seat. The castle dimensions are 18 metres long by 6.6 metres wide, with a square tower at the north-west end. Two garderobe chutes are visible on the outer face of the wall, one presumably from the upper chamber, the other from the parapet. A squinch arch bridges the gap between the tower wall and the external face of the castle. The building has been badly damaged, possibly during the Cromwellian exploits in the area, but the remains suggest the original scale and strength of Kindlestown.

The castle site at Ballycorus may also date to the late thirteenth or early fourteenth century. Ralph le Mareshal received the lands which formed part of the king's manor of Obrun in 1281.[224] John de Wallop had held the lands previously, receiving them on condition that he built a dwelling; for which purpose he received timber from the royal forest of Glencree.[225] In a nineteenth-century map the castle is named 'Cromwell's Castle' and has associated earthworks on the eastern side.[226] It is depicted as being square in plan with the eastern wall completely missing. Today only faint earthworks mark the site of the castle. The outline can be seen measuring roughly 20 metres by 9 metres with an internal dividing wall. Ballycorus castle from its hilltop site commanded a clear view of the Vale of Dublin; there are no associated earthworks in the surrounding fields which are in pasture. It may have resembled Kindlestown, being a hall-castle type.

At the archbishop's manor of Shankill a castle survives relatively intact. It has been modified in recent years and has a residence attached. The roof is flat-topped with a round-headed doorway at the eastern side. It displays a distinct batter with double square-headed windows; at the lowest level rectangular red-brick windows have been inserted. Internally the castle is vaulted and has several fireplaces. The castle resembles a tower-house type in size, usually dated to the fifteenth and sixteenth centuries. However, the siting of the castle at the centre of the archbishop's manor and home to the prominent Lawless family may indicate it was built on the site of the earlier manor-house or that it incorporates the fabric of an earlier structure. A similar late castle can be seen at Shanganagh. Only a small portion survives but it was vaulted with two massive fireplaces. It was destroyed by fire in 1763.[227]

Some of the castles built in the period unfortunately leave little trace. The Down Survey depicts Rathdown castle as a large structure,[228] and when O'Donovan visited the site in 1838 the remnants of the castle could still be seen.[229] There was a great quantity of cut stone, described by O'Donovan as being 'all very fine', lying around on the site. Parts of the wall were still intact. The south wall stood 2.6 metres high and was 18 metres long while the eastern wall only stood to a height of 1.6 metres. Only a small fragment of the north wall was still *in situ*. The Down Survey depicts a tower two storeys high with crenellations and a rectangular building attached, probably a hall.[230] By 1936 the site had been badly damaged by the insertion of a lime-kiln; today the site is occupied by a sewage plant.

Moated sites of Uí Briúin Cualann

It became increasingly difficult to maintain any form of settlement in Uí Briúin Cualann especially south of Newcastle McKynegan during the later fourteenth century. The castles along the coast kept the fringes under Anglo-Norman control but the settlers inland suffered badly. Some simply did not have the finances to build large castles like Kindlestown and resorted to a cheaper form of defensive homestead, the moated site. First recorded in Ireland by Orpen[231] and later by Westropp,[232] they usually consist of a platform, rectangular in shape, and are surrounded by a deep water-filled moat with external and internal banks. The general consensus of opinion is that the sites were a settlement feature, representing defended farmsteads dating to the late thirteenth or early fourteenth century.[233] The type is well represented in England where between 3,000 and 4,000 examples are known, but unlike England where they are most often associated with a church or castle, in Ireland they tend to be situated in more rural locations.[234]

Because of their relative lateness in the chronology there are few examples of this settlement type in the study area. By the fourteenth century many of the settlers had been driven out of south Wicklow. Ballinapark, in Rathnew parish, is the best surviving example of the typical defended farmstead. The site, although very overgrown, is relatively complete. The internal platform which is raised by 2 metres, is square in shape, measuring 30 metres. The fosse, which is still intact, is 7 metres wide in places and 1.8 metres deep. An internal bank still survives in part with the typical build-up of upcast on the north-west corner; this bank stands 1 metres high by 5 metres wide. There are no visible signs of an external bank, although slight traces were recorded in 1952. At that date a small raised circular area on the platform may have represented some sort of structure which has since disappeared.[235] The moat is fed by a small leat taken from a nearby stream on the northern side. Nothing is known about Ballinapark, which was probably held by a sub-tenant of Myler FitzHenry.

At Courtfoyle, in Killiskey parish, a similar type of site can be seen, unusually situated on high ground. It is rectangular in shape, 55 metres long by 18 metres wide, with a small internal bank. The moat is water-filled but has been eroded considerably by stones which have been dumped in. It shows some evidence of having been revetted with masonry. Courtfoyle formed part of the lands granted to St Thomas's

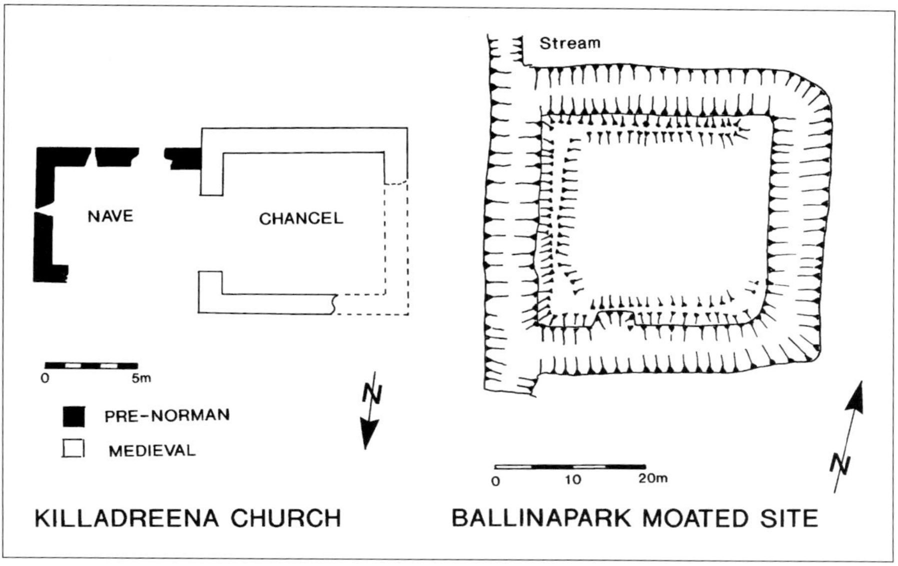

Figure 6.3 Killadreena Church and Ballinapark moated site.

Abbey at Killiskey in 1215-55.[236] The moated site was, however, probably built by William Lawless who received the land on condition that he built a suitable dwelling there.[237] A second Lawless stronghold existed at Kilcommon called 'Stump of the Castle'. Here the remains of a large moated site 40 metres square survive with a moat 3 metres in width. The moat is missing on the south-east side but a large external bank 3.2 metres in height is evident on the north-west side. The site has been much disturbed by the building of roads and a farm-house. There are also remains of a castle on the south-east side of the site but only one small tower survives. It was originally one of four which were still traceable on the ground in 1839.[238] Kilcommon was abandoned soon after Lawless's death in 1350. The remaining castle may date to 1581 when a garrison was placed there during the wars with Feagh McHugh O'Byrne.[239]

At Newcastle McKynegan, Orpen recorded a square enclosure lying to the north of the castle.[240] It measured 80 paces by 50 paces and had a narrow moat; there were also small banks. No further information is given and the site could not be located in the field by this writer. A second site may have existed at Clonmannan where an aerial photograph picked up the outlines of several square enclosures;[241] this field has since been ploughed. Similar crop-marks can be seen at Ballyloughlin near Leabeg and Coolagad.[242] Further south, moated sites have been recorded at Ballymacsimon and Trooperstown.[243] At the former the site measured 36 yards square with a raised internal platform. It was surrounded by a moat 8 feet wide by 8 feet deep.[244] The site at Trooperstown is marked as a square enclosure surrounded by a fosse or moat on the six-inch Ordnance Surveys maps of 1838 and 1908 respectively. Both these sites have since been destroyed.[245]

Moated castles in Uí Briúin Cualann

There are several other examples of sites that are moated in the study area but there are problems with their classification. Hadden, in his study of county Wexford, noted the existence of two distinct moated site types, the heavily fortified type which he dates to 1170-1200 and the smaller type site representing the defended farmstead of the late thirteenth or early fourteenth century.[246] In county Wicklow, however, a third type emerges which is in fact a hybrid of both, a square moated defensive castle type dating to the late thirteenth or early fourteenth century.

In 1953 Price described a moated enclosure measuring 50 metres square surrounding the castle at Rathdown. He compared its morphology to Ballinapark and Courtfoyle and discounted O'Curry's observation that the castle stood within an earlier rath.[247] Traces of this moat can still be seen at the site especially on the southern side. Thus we get a stone castle which is situated within a large moated site. This differs in respect to a classic moated-castle such as Drimnagh castle, Dublin, where the moat only encompasses a very small area around the base of the castle. It is not known whether the Mac Giollamocholmóg family or its successor Nigel le Brun who acquired the lands in 1305 were responsible for the moated enclosure. It was probably the former since at Knocktopher some of the moated sites have been attributed to the Irish population.[248]

A similar type of site can be seen at Ballynagran south of Wicklow town in Glenealy parish. It is known locally as 'McDermot's Castle' and, although very far south, is also associated with the Mac Giollamocholmóg family.[249] It lies north of Kilnamanagh, possibly the Klymanch mentioned in association with Rathdown in 1301.[250] The enclosure is 40 metres square surrounded by a fosse which was originally 10.3m wide and between 2 to 3 metres deep. The platform had a small internal bank 1.3 metres wide but only surviving to 60cm in height. A causeway gave access on the south side. Within the platform a large portion of a stone building survives 8 metres long by 5.5 metres wide, with an internal width of 3.5 metres. The structure, with such narrow confines, may represent all that is left of a gate-house. On the eastern side are the remains of an adjoining wall although there is no corresponding wall on the western side. The only internal features are two small wall cupboards. At Killoughter the moated site may also have been a moated castle which was re-used as a ward site.

Establishment of wards

When the political situation changed in the late thirteenth century there were few militarily secure strongholds to cope with the situation. A lack of military fortifications meant that there were in fact few stone castles which could be refortified and re-occupied. Newcastle McKynegan and Castlekevin were hurriedly rebuilt; so possibly was Bray castle which had come into the king's hands by 1280.[251] Wicklow castle became a royal stronghold but this defensive line along the coastline was simply not adequate to cope with the guerilla tactics of the Irish. The moated castle represents a succession from the defensive moated farmstead to the partially offensive stronghold for the few settlers that were left; a surrounding moat was a further defensive feature particularly effective in withstanding the sudden raids which were a feature of medieval warfare. The few examples are close to the Irish stronghold at Glenmalure, with only two north of Newcastle McKynegan. The crown officials were quick to realise that the containment of the rebels depended on strategic strongholds which could be speedily garrisoned. The potential of the existing moated castles was realised and some were re-fortified.[252] Robert de Ufford had enjoyed some measure of success in repressing the rebels but he depended largely on the castles of Newcastle McKynegan and Castlekevin.[253] By the late thirteenth century wards had to be established at Newcastle McKynegan,[254] Brownstown and, surprisingly, as far south as Glenmalure.[255] At Newcastle McKynegan reinforcements were added to the large garrison stationed there.[256]

The brutal murder of the McMurrough brothers at Arklow in July 1282 restored peace for over ten years but by 1294 war had broken out again.[257] In the years following the situation changed little and mostly consisted of Irish raids followed by government campaigns. In 1355-7 Thomas de Rokeby, as justiciar, made a determined effort to deal with the rebels by changing tactics. By a policy of buying off the O'Byrnes and the O'Tooles and placing them in control of certain lands, de Rokeby, for a short period, quelled the trouble in the area.[258] A far more extensive programme of wards was established in a ring around the Wicklow/Leinster mountains at this date. In the study area Bray, Newcastle McKynegan, Carrickmines and Ballycorus, Kilmartin, Killoughter, Balyteney, and Killiney are all listed as being warded.[259] Castles were in some cases refortified, as at Bray, Newcastle McKynegan, Carrickmines and Ballycorus. However, some sites were constructed from the existing moated sites and others constructed anew.

Ward sites in Uí Briúin Cualann

A good example of a ward site can be seen at Kilmartin in Killiskey

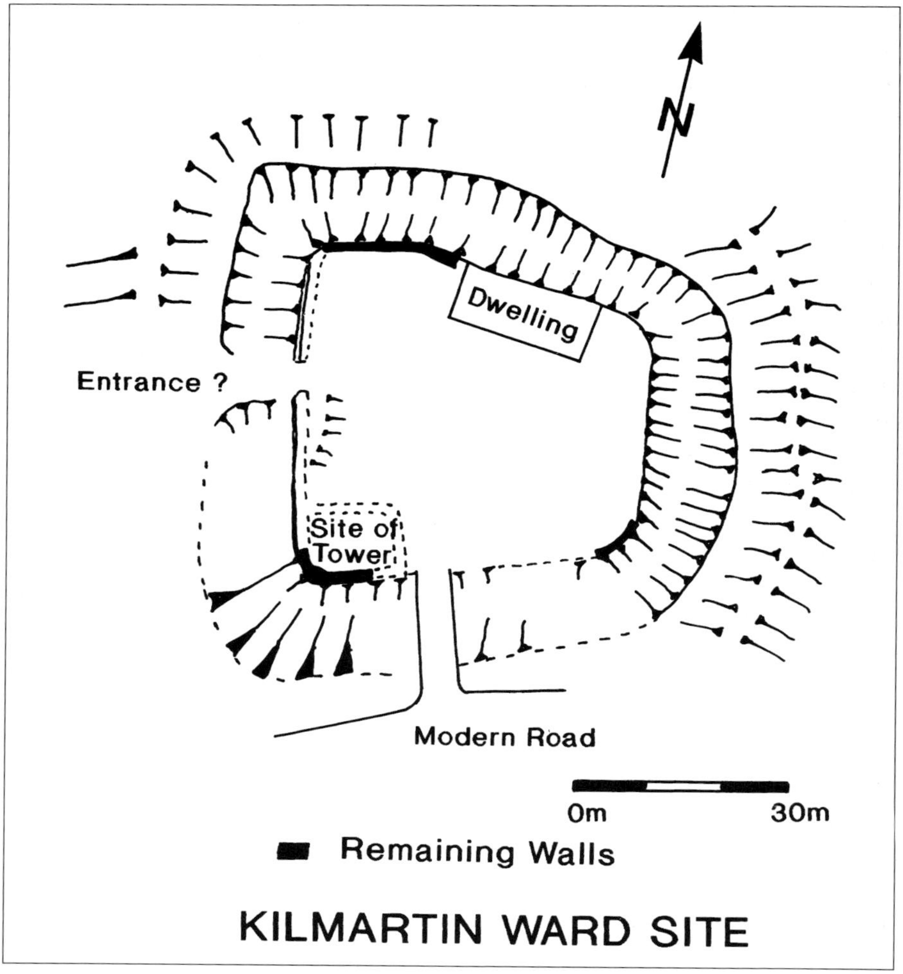

Figure 6.4 Kilmartin ward site.

parish. It consists of a five-sided fortification with a deep fosse and an external bank. The dimensions are roughly 32 metres by 38 metres; on the north side a wall survives 1.2 metres thick to a height of 3.2 metres. This originally encompassed the whole site; traces of a stone footing can be seen along the western side. In 1931 there were traces of stone corner towers in the south-east and north-east corner with a possible gate-house to the south; the entire site is now badly overgrown.[260] The fosse is 5 metres deep on the north and eastern side but only a faint trace is discernible on the western side; the external bank survives to 5 metres in height on the eastern side. The moat was water-filled; a tunnel with a stone arch originally conducted water from a nearby stream into the fosse.[261] There are few documentary sources concerning Kilmartin. Geoffrey Trivers accounts for rents of 'Kilmart' in 1298 but this could be Kilmartin, Mulhuddart, county Dublin.[262] The castle may have been constructed in the mid-fourteenth century specifically as a ward castle.

Close by at Killoughter was a second ward site, where the partial remains of a large moated site still survive. It appears to have had two platforms side by side, the southern site being the earliest. This has a small internal bank on the eastern side measuring 80cm high with a possible external bank on the northern side. A small spring feeds the moat. The site to the north is much larger in area and was extended by enlarging the moat. The external bank was continued on the eastern side where the surviving moat is 7.5 metres in width.[263] A farmhouse occupies the platform of the northern site but the moat, although not complete, is still water-filled in places. It is up to 8.5 metres at its widest with a recorded depth of 1.7 metres. Killoughter probably represents a moated defended farmstead which was enlarged in the mid-fourteenth century when the site was used as a ward. The neighbouring ward castle of Kilmartin, because of its small size, may have proved inadequate to cope with large garrisons.

Balyteney has been identified as Powerscourt.[264] At Powerscourt the large motte was not apparently rebuilt in stone but some form of castle was erected close to the site. By the sixteenth century Powerscourt along with Fassaroe and Rathdown are cited as being the strongest castles in the area; however, these were probably tower-houses, another castle-type datable to the fifteenth and sixteenth centuries.[265] Parts of this later castle are possibly incorporated within Powerscourt House built in the eighteenth century,[266] but there must have been some type of castle still existing at Powerscourt in the late thirteenth or early fourteenth century. In 1316 a crown official was responsible for the repair of the castle and there are references to constables in the succeeding years. By 1398 the castle was said to be in disrepair.[267] It was not rebuilt until the fifteenth century, when the eighth earl of Kildare had possession of the surrounding lands. It is difficult to assess what type of castle existed at Powerscourt in the late thirteenth or early fourteenth century as there is no known site. A rectangular enclosure recorded as lying to the south of the castle and now unfortunately destroyed may be all that remains of a late ringwork type similar to Kilmartin and Killoughter.[268] Further north the site of the ward at Killiney is unknown. The present train station is reputedly on the site of a fort but this may refer to the defensive fortifications of the late eighteenth century.[269] It was probably a small fortification similar to that at Kilmartin.

The surviving military fortifications tell us much about the overall defensive strategy of the colony. Ward sites were based on pre-existing military strongholds. Where there was a strong castle it was used but Wicklow had few strongholds from the early years of the conquest and so was forced to rely on less defensive sites, which were small and not capable of catering for large armies.[270] The castles were not intended to act as strong bases from which the surrounding land could be conquered. To a great degree their type was dictated by successive guerrilla tactics. Descending from the high boggy ground the Irish could quickly waste the lands along the plain, forcing the government to take the campaign where they were at a distinct disadvantage.[271] The primary function of the wards was to combat these raids and this can be seen clearly in their distribution pattern. The wards were located in areas which were still, in the fourteenth century, nominally under Anglo-Norman control. In 1297 it was decided that persons holding lands in the march hinterland but not inhabiting them had to provide wards. The surrounding landholders were to provide the men; in 1349 the grange at Clonkeen provided two mailed horsemen and six hobelars for the garrison in Bray.[272] One of the problems cited is a lack of horses with which to chase the perpetrators.[273]

Despite the seriousness of the situation there was no real expenditure on new stone castles or military strongholds apart from Castlekevin and Newcastle McKynegan. Finance was spent on paying the wages of the large armies sent into the mountains. The ward-castles were a last ditch attempt to create a military presence and to prevent the gradual encroachment of the Irish into the lands immediately south of Dublin. This problem became more acute when the port of Dublin was rendered useless due to the silting up of the mouth of the Liffey in the late fourteenth century.[274] This caused the level of water in the river to drop with the result that there was no anchorage or berthage for the merchant ships. There were ports at Howth and Malahide but it was Dalkey that became the main port for Dublin city. Every effort was made to safeguard it. It was included in the Pale and the archbishop could produce two hundred men-at-arms to protect it.[275] By the fifteenth and sixteenth centuries there were at least seven towerhouses within Dalkey.[276]

Deserted medieval villages

Collapse of the de Rokeby strategy by 1355 brought war to the area and the military following was summoned to Newcastle.[277] The O'Byrnes and O'Tooles were not retreating but were occupying the lands. The O'Tooles, by this date, had complete control of the Castlekevin district and had settled extensively around Powerscourt,[278] the O'Byrnes occupying the lands to the east. The former villages and towns which had once flourished in east Wicklow under Anglo-Norman control now lay waste and deserted. In some cases only earthworks in the ground give any indication of what were once large settlements. Such sites have been noted across the country, for example at Newtown Jerpoint, county Kilkenny and Kiltinan, county Tipperary where linear earthworks show clearly the outline of medieval settlements.[279]

A classic example of such a site can be seen in Delgany parish. It is situated off the king's highway at Windgate close to the sea.[280] In 1534 the manor consisted of 20 messuages, 218 acres, a watermill, and a castle;[281] by 1668 there were only eighteen houses in the area.[282] However, surrounding the castle site and in the field to the north is a complex of rectilinear earthworks and sunken ways indicating the extent of the medieval settlement. These probably represent house platforms and associated plots. To the south lie the remains of a late church with possible foundations of an earlier church visible. A second documented church has completely disappeared. The linear earthworks extend to the east of the church indicating that it was within the medieval settlement. No above-ground remains of the mill are now visible although a much reduced mill-race runs through the site.

In cases where there are no visible signs of medieval habitation tradition and documentary evidence become all important. The location of Kilmacberne, the satellite vill of the archbishop's manor at Shankill, had up until recently not been known. It has since been identified with the village of The Downs, the name being preserved in the townland 'Killickabawn'.[283] All that now remains of the site is a church of late medieval date and a large hillfort. A trackway which possibly represents the old medieval highway runs through the site. In the later medieval period it became an O'Byrne stronghold.

Even the vill of Shankill, the very centre of the archbishop's manor, became totally deserted. It was on the main route; a land grant dated *c.*1243 describes the great straight road which led to Shankill.[284] Today the village of Shankill has shifted two kilometres to the east. In the fourteenth century it consisted of seventeen burgage plots, a church, a manor house with an attached garden, a rabbit warren, and a park of oaks. It also had a mill.[285] All that survives is the castle and a possible roadway to the east of the castle. Two small streams which cross the site may represent all that is left of the mill-race. The documentary sources state that the vill had a gate in the thirteenth century which suggests that it was walled, possibly similar to the archbishop's second manor at Swords.[286] A church of Shankill is mentioned in the thirteenth century but the site is now unknown.[287] It probably lies north of the castle where a small stone cross marks the path of an old roadway leading to Rathmichael church. The latter may be marking the sanctuary boundaries.[288] At Stagonil all that was left in the early nineteenth century was the remains of a church, medieval in date. It had been granted a weekly market and must originally have been a large settlement. By 1482 the market was transferred to Dalkey.[289]

A great number of smaller settlements and those which never received borough status disappeared entirely. At Tinnapark demesne the entire medieval settlement lies beneath the derelict Holywell House.[290] At Killruddery the vill held by St Thomas's Abbey had a house, mill and a garden as well as 'walls and ditches of the court',[291] the latter perhaps indicating a moated site of some description. When part of the present house was under construction a large quantity of human bones were disinterred, possibly from a graveyard. At Kilmartin all that remains are the church and the fort; in the early twentieth century a small medieval smelting works was discovered a short distance from the fort.[292] Similarly at Killoughter all that remains are the fort and church.

Generally the larger settlements survive in some form to the present day. Bray town, although burnt occasionally, survived the rigours of the medieval period. By the late thirteenth or early fourteenth century the Butlers had a considerable interest in Bray,[293] as did Geoffrey Crumpe.[294] De Ridelesford's castle was pulled down, chiefly to supply stone for a barracks, and the mill of the castle, which was situated beneath it, has been superseded by an eighteenth-century mill.[295] At Newcastle McKynegan a small village survives but the emphasis has shifted eastwards along the old road to Rathnew. The church probably lies beneath the present church directly opposite the castle. The stream running to the south of the church presumably powered the two medieval mills; there is no indication of the 'fosse' for the repair of which some of the burgesses retained their rent in 1344.[296]

Irish re-occupation of the Uí Briúin Cualann

By the late fourteenth and early fifteenth centuries the Anglo-Norman[297] colony south of Bray had been completely destroyed, the settlers having abandoned their homesteads. The O'Byrnes and O'Tooles occupied much of the lands, the only colonial presence being a military one. In contrast to other parts of Ireland, the initial years of Anglo-Norman settlement were characterised by peaceful assimilation, followed by consolidation and expansion. Domnall Mac Giollamocholmóg's acceptance of the Anglo-Normans resulted in no great displacement of the lower stratum of tenantry and no organised resistance at the higher level. In the first years after the invasion mottes were constructed as elsewhere in the country, but quickly fell into disuse and few were refortified in stone. In colonising the lands the Anglo-Normans re-used the centres of population already in existence on their arrival. The Irish continued to inhabit the lands south of Dublin throughout the thirteenth century, making up the bulk of the tenants of the large royal manors.[298]

Similarly, at Castlekevin, the Irish remained the dominant presence. However, the land-holding pattern did change. Anglo-Norman colonists, lured perhaps by the fertile lands and attractive tenurial conditions, began to settle the lands. The political situation which developed rapidly in the late thirteenth century coincided with this natural secondary phase of settlement and the sites in the field become dominated by the political climate. The inherent weaknesses of having large amounts of land administered by government officials became apparent in the absence of strong castles and large magnates ready to defend their property should the need arise. Some of the larger sites were re-fortified in stone but these were militarily inadequate to deal with the situation. The few moated defended farmsteads recorded is an indication of the few settlers left by the late thirteenth /early fourteenth century. The moated sites gave way rapidly to garrisoned castles and ward sites as the few remaining settlers were forced out.

The O'Byrnes and O'Tooles had, to a great degree, been ignored in the early years because the lands of Glenmalure were unsuitable for the type of agriculture practised by the Anglo-Normans and it was more profitable to leave the Irish as tenants. The archbishop of Dublin was left trying to control a growing Irish population which had been seriously underestimated and allowed to go its own way. The irony of the situation is that the O'Tooles and the O'Byrnes, in re-conquering Uí Briúin Cualann and forcing the Anglo-Normans out had, in effect, forced out the original occupiers of Uí Briúin Cualann.[299] The discontent of the Irish in the mountains, harnessed to the strong leadership of the Mc Murroughs who were only too willing to exploit that discontent, made for an explosive situation which was effectively to undermine the Anglo-Norman presence in Dublin. It was eventually to cause the virtual abandonment of lands within ten miles of Dublin city and left a legacy of discontent which was to haunt the administration in Dublin.

Acknowledgements
Sincere thanks are due to various people who helped in the writing of this chapter. Firstly my father, Arthur Simpson, for his work in reading and editing the account. Also Seán Duffy for his many helpful suggestions and corrections. Geraldine Stout for all her help in consulting the files in the Sites and Monuments Record office and

finally the Kenny family, especially Alicia and Lorna, for their help and enthusiasm in completing the field-work.

References

1. Price, *Placenames*, v, p. 338, vii, p. 395; K.W. Nicholls, 'The land of the Leinstermen', *Peritia,* iii (1984), p. 538, note 2; Alfred Smyth, *Celtic Leinster* (Dublin, 1982), pp 52-4.
2. The rest of county Wicklow belonged to counties Kildare, Carlow and probably Wexford. See Nicholls, 'The land of the Leinstermen', p. 540.
3. The most notable being Liam Price and more recently, Kenneth Nicholls and Robin Frame.
4. I have also included sites not actually in Uí Briúin Cualann, especially those south of Newcastle as far as Wicklow, in an attempt to obtain a more complete overview.
5. Gearóid Mac Niocaill, *Ireland before the vikings* (Dublin, 1972), p. 26; Liam Price, *Placenames,* vii, p. xx.
6. See John Bradley, 'The interpretation of Scandinavian settlement in Ireland', *Settlement and society in medieval Ireland, Studies presented to F.X. Martin* (ed.) John Bradley, pp 49-78; A.P. Smyth, *Celtic Leinster* (Dublin, 1982), p. 44.
7. Price, *Placenames*, vii, pp xxii-xxiii.
8. John Bradley, 'Scandinavian settlement in Ireland', p. 56.
9. See Nicholls, 'The land of the Leinstermen', p. 538.
10. *Alen's reg*., pp 28-9.
11. De Ridelesford is recorded as granting these lands to Christchurch probably having received them in his grant of the 'lands of the sons of Thorkill'. *Alen's reg.*, pp 257-8.
12. *Chartul. St Mary's, Dublin*, i, no. 61.
13. *Alen's reg*., p. 21.
14. Orpen, *Normans*, i, p. 269; Michael Dolley, *Anglo-Norman Ireland* (Dublin, 1972), p. 71.
15. *Cal. doc. Ire., 1171-1251*, no. 356.
16. *The song of Dermot and the earl* (ed.) G.H. Orpen (Oxford, 1892), p. 321; *Expugnatio Hibernica: the conquest of Ireland by Giraldus Cambrensis* (eds.) A.B. Scott and F.X. Martin (Dublin, 1978), p. 95.
17. Orpen, *INormans*, i, p. 91.
18. Scott and Martin, *Expug. Hib*., p. 89; See Orpen, *INormans*, i, p. 251.
19. Strongbow is recorded by Giraldus as receiving the castle of Wicklow but from his subsequent grants in the area he must have received the lands of Wicklow also.
20. Scott and Martin, *Expug. Hib*., p. 288; Orpen, *The song of Dermot*, ii, p. 120.
21. Orpen, *The song of Dermot*, ii, p. 143; Price, *Placenames*, vii, p. xxviii.
22. *Alen's reg*., p. 21.
23. M.V. Ronan, 'The union of the dioceses of Glendalough and Dublin', *R.S.A.I. Jn*., lx (1930), pp 56-72.
24. A.J. Otway-Ruthven, 'The medieval church lands of county Dublin', J.A. Watt *et al.* (eds.) *Medieval studies presented to Aubrey Gwynn, S.J.* (Dublin, 1961), p. 56.
25. An extent is an administrative account which records the lands of a manor and how much they were worth.
26. *Alen's reg*., pp 194-6.

27. Ibid., pp 123-4.
28. *P.R.I. rep. D.K., 36*, p. 36.
29. *Alen's reg.*, pp 123-4. Now known as Vartry, county Wicklow.
30. James Mills, 'Norman settlement in Leinster; the cantreds near Dublin', *R.S.A.I. Jn.*, xxiv (1894), p. 163.
31. Kiltuc was situated near the modern Shankill.
32. *Alen's reg.*, p. 13 for location of Dromin somewhere between Leopardstown and Ballyogan.
33. In 1306 the grange of Clonkeen had seven carucates of land, two at Bray with a mill which was being farmed, one carucate worth £4.10s.1d at Tully, one unspecified and three around the grange at Clonkeen. They also held other lands: see 'A calendar of the Liber Niger and Liber Albus of Christchurch Dublin' (ed.) H.J. Lawlor, *R.I.A. Proc.*, xxvii (1908), p. 68. One carucate is approx. 320 modern acres. However, it could vary considerably according to the fertility of the land.
34. Otway-Ruthven, 'Medieval church lands', p. 59.
35. A sixteenth-century reference lists these lands but they were granted by Walter de Ridelesford, presumably in the late twelfth or early thirteenth century, *Alen's reg.*, pp 256-7.
36. St Patrick's received lands at this date; see *Alen's reg.*, p. 18. In 1219, on being given cathedral staus it received more lands. *Alen's reg.*, p. 42.
37. Otway-Ruthven, 'Medieval church lands', p. 61; M.V. Ronan, 'History of the Diocese', *Reportorium Novum*, i (1955), p. 39.
38. *P.R.I. rep., D.K., 47*, p. 17.
39. *Chartul. St Mary's, Dublin*, i, pp 32-7.
40. K.W. Nicholls, 'Anglo-French Ireland and after', *Peritia*, i (1982), pp 382-3, footnote no. 3.
41. *Cal. doc. Ire., 1171-1251,* no. 356.
42. E. St. John Brooks, 'The de Ridelesfords', *R.S.A.I. Jn.*, lxxxi (1951), p. 118.
43. George D. Scott, *The stones of Bray* (Dublin, 1913), p. 210.
44. For list of de Ridelesford's lands see Brooks, 'The de Ridelesfords', pp 117-9.
45. *Cal. doc. Ire., 1171-1251*, no. 469, for the king inspecting Walter de Ridelesford's charter to see if certain 'vills' are in the king's demesne. The latter were probably in the Vale of Dublin. However, Walter is given land in exchange for these lands.
46. Brooks, 'The de Ridelesfords', p. 121.
47. Baliconeli, Balialleridan, Balivendum, Balimakelli, Balikin, Balimaclivan and Balimelguiry.
48. Liam Price, 'The grant to Walter de Ridelesford of Brien and the lands of the Sons of Turchill', *R.S.A.I. Jn.*, lxxxi (1951), p. 77.
49. *Chartul. St Mary's, Dublin,* i, no. 301.
50. In 1248 Walter de Ridelesford held four carucates and twenty-five acres in the Vale of Dublin, also a further three and a half carucates with a mill; for this he owed one knight's service. *Cal. doc. Ire., 1171-1251,* no. 2970.
51. Brooks, 'The de Ridelsfords', p. 125.
52. *Chartul. St Mary's, Dublin*, i, no. 387. A later grant to St Thomas Abbey mentions Balisenechil, Fenebo and Balimakelli none of which have been identified but which were all in the 'honour of Bre'; *Reg. St Thomas, Dublin*, nos. 153, 155.
53. Philip of Worcester was sent over in 1184 by the king to replace de Lacy who had alienated the lands in contradiction to the charter he was granted. See Orpen, *Normans,* i, p. 368; J. Otway-Ruthven, *A history of medieval Ireland* (2nd ed., London, 1980), pp 64-5.

54. '... the land of Obrun as it may be extended by the Justiciar and those ordered to extend the King's demesne'. *Cal. doc. Ire., 1171-1251*, no. 1070.
55. Ibid., no. 1798, when Christina de Marisco, grand-daughter of de Ridelesford, exchanged the lands for lands in England.
56. *The Irish chartularies of Llanthony Prima and Secunda* (ed.) E. St. John Brooks (Dublin, 1953), pp 254-8.
57. *Alen's reg.*, p. 62.
58. Price, *Placenames,* vii, p. xxix.
59. Othee was worth more than Obrun in yearly rents. Othee was worth £56.11s.6d, while Obrun was only worth £51.1s.1d: *Cal. doc. Ire., 1252-84*, no. 2329.
60. Ibid., *1171-1251*, no. 622.
61. Ibid., no. 2329. These were granted to William Burnell in 1284, ibid., no. 2199.
62. *Cal. doc. Ire.,1302-7*, no. 335.
63. None of the Anglo-Norman manors were located above five hundred feet; Anngret Simms and Patricia Fagan, 'Villages in county Dublin: their origins and inheritance', p. 114, in *Dublin city and county from pre-history to present,* Studies presented to J.H. Andrews, F.H. Aalen and Kevin Whelan (eds.), (Dublin 1992).
64. *Alen's reg.*, p. 40; See H.G. Leask, *Glendalough, Official historical and descriptive guide* (Stationery Office, Dublin).
65. Brooks, 'The de Ridelesfords', p. 118.
66. See R.E. Glasscock, 'Mottes in Ireland' in *Chateau Gaillard,* vii (1975), pp 95-110; T.E. McNeill, 'Ulster mottes, a checklist', *U.J.A.*, 3rd series, xxxxviii (1975), pp 49-56.
67. Liam Price, 'Powerscourt and the territory of Fercullen', *R.S.A.I. Jn.*, lxxxiii (1953), p. 122.
68. The construction of the present house may have partially damaged it.
69. See John de Horseye, member of a jury at Castlekevin in 1257-63. *Alen's reg.*, p. 110.
70. G.H. Orpen, 'Castrum Keyvini: Castlekevin', *R.S.A.I. Jn.*, xxxviii (1908), p. 17.
71. There are problems with identifying any raised mound with a motte since an eroded motte can resemble many other sites in the field. An indication of a motte is, however, a site in which Anglo-Norman occupation has been attested by documentary sources, although many sites go completely undocumented.
72. Scott and Martin, *Expug. Hib.*, p. 121.
73. M. O'Flanagan, O.S. letters, p. 39.
74. Price, *Placenames,* vii, p. 318.
75. *Alen's reg.*, p. 196.
76. N.M.I., Liam Price, Collection of handwritten field-books on temporary deposit with Sites and Monuments Record, Office of Public Works, 15 Hatch St. Lr, Dublin, 27 vols, vol. 26, pp 35-6.
77. *Alen's reg.*, p. 42.
78. O'Flanagan, O.S. letters, p. 119.
79. Down Survey (1654-6), parish and barony maps, m. 2506, f. 55, N.L.I., Ms.
80. M.V. Ronan, 'Killadreena and Newcastle', *R.S.A.I. Jn.*, lxiii (1933), p. 174.
81. Goddard H. Orpen, 'Novum Castrum McKynegan, Newcastle, county Wicklow', *R.S.A.I. Jn.*, xxxviii (1908), pp 126-40.
82. D.C. Twohig, 'Anglo-Norman ringwork castles', *Bulletin of the Group for the Study of Irish Historic Settlement,* v (1978), p. 5.
83. T.B. Barry, *The archaeology of medieval Ireland* (London, 1987), p. 52.
84. Compare, for example, Aldingham in Lancashire, where the existing motte was originally a ringwork which was filled in: *Current Archaeology,* 12 (Jan 1969) p. 23.

85. *P.R.I. rep. D.K.*, 36, p. 53.
86. The sea-coast was under the maritime jurisdiction of the mayor of Dublin in the fourteenth century. In 1375 all the customs of the ports from Skerries to Arklow belonged to the city of Dublin: *Calendar of ancient records of Dublin* (ed.), J.T. Gilbert, i (Dublin, 1889), p. 144.
87. B.J. Graham, 'The mottes in the Norman Liberty of Meath', in *Irish Midland Studies* (Athlone, 1980), pp 39-56.
88. For 'betaghs' see Gearóid Mac Niocaill, 'The origins of the betagh', *The Irish Jurist,* new series, i (1966), pp 292-8.
89. 'The Irish pipe roll of 14 John', (eds) O.Davies and D.B. Quinn, *U.J.A.*, iv (1941), Supplement, p. 13.
90. In 1226 Archbishop Henry surrendered a vill called 'Obrun' which is described as being in the king's demesne (*Cal. doc.Ire., 1171-1251*, no. 1461); this is not the manor of Obrun but Brownestown near Bohernabreena; see Liam Price, 'The manor of Bothercolyn', *R.S.A.I. Jn.*, lxxiv (1944), pp 107-9; Walter de Ridelesford held land there originally. *Cal. doc. Ire., 1171-1251*, nos. 1641, 2200.
91. Anngret Simms, 'The geography of Irish manors: the example of the Llanthony cells of Duleek and Colp in county Meath', in Bradley (ed.), *Settlement and society in medieval Ire.*, ed. Bradley, pp 291-92.
92. R.E. Glasscock, 'Land and people *c.*1300', *N.H.I.*, ii, p. 213.
93. See the extent of Bray dated 1311 *Red bk Ormond*, p. 24.
94. See Mills, 'Norman settlement in Leinster,' p. 173, where the betaghs of Obrun accounted for £25.3s.6d and Othee accounted for £32.13s.4d.
95. *Cal. doc. Ire., 285-1292*, no. 622, p. 309.
96. *Cal. doc. Ire., 1171-1251*, no. 1264.
97. *Alen's reg.*, p. 36.
98. M.V. Ronan, 'The ancient churches of the deanery of Wicklow', *R.S.A.I. Jn.*, lviii (1928), p. 136.
99. Mills, 'Norman settlement in Leinster', p. 173.
100. *Cal. doc. Ire., 1285-92*, no. 622, p. 309.
101. James Mills, 'Notices of the manor of Sepulchre, Dublin, in the fourteenth century', *R.S.A.I. Jn.*, xix (1889), p. 31.
102. The Ostmen were probably too valuable as traders to suppress completely; Edmund Curtis, 'Norse Dublin', *Medieval Dublin, the making of a metropolis* (ed.) Howard Clarke (Dublin, 1990), p. 106; in 1234 the king took the Ostmen of Waterford into his protection: *Cal. doc. Ire., 1171-1251*, no. 2198.
103. *P.R.I. rep. D.K.*, 35, p. 30.
104. *Alen's reg.*, p. 158. Reginald is described as 'betagh' having lost the distinction of Ostman. Some betaghs held more land than others; at Swords in 1326 a distinction was made between 'betaghs' and 'poor betaghs'. Ibid., p. 176.
105. *Alen's reg.*, pp 110-12.
106. Archbishop Comyn established his nephew Geoffrey de Marisco at Hollywood and made grants at Donard and Rathsallagh; Price, *Placenames*, vii, p. xliii.
107. Ibid., p. 111.
108. Elias is recorded as being sergeant in 'Archbishop Luke's time' (1228-55).
109. *Alen's reg.*, pp 110-112.
110. Nicholls, 'Anglo-French Ireland', p. 379.
111. Kenneth W. Nicholls, *Gaelic and gaelicised Ireland in the middle ages* (Dublin, 1972), pp 112-3.
112. Simms, 'Geography of Irish manors', p. 302.
113. *Alen's reg.*, p. 173.

114. Twenty-three betaghs held land at 'Betaghford' in the manor of Clondalkin in 1326; *Alen's reg.*, p. 188.
115. Edmund Curtis, 'The rental of the manor of Lisronagh 1333 and notes on betagh tenure in Ireland', *R.I.A. Proc.*, xlii c (1936), p. 72.
116. O'Flanagan, O.S. Letters, pp 33, 35; Sites and Monuments records, Sheet 26 (Dublin), site no. 34.
117. W. Betham, 'On the account of Thomas de Chaddisworth, custodee of the temporalities of the Archbishop of Dublin from 1221-56, *R.I.A. Proc.* v (1850-3), p. 156.
118. Obrun and Newcastle had separate manorial courts, *P.R.I. rep. D.K.*, 36, p. 59.
119. Ibid.; see Timothy O'Neill, *Merchants and mariners in medieval Ireland'* (Dublin, 1987), p. 20.
120. *Cal. doc. Ire., 1285-92*, no. 622.
121. *P.R.I. rep. D.K.*, 20, p. 78.
122. The presence of a market could indicate an undocumented borough; see J. A. Otway-Ruthven, 'The character of Anglo-Norman settlement in Ireland', *Historical Studies,* v (1965), pp 75-84.
123. For Castlekevin see *Cal. doc. Ire., 1171-1251,* no. 1351, for Stagonil, ibid. no. 2209, and Bray, ibid. no. 471.
124. Newcastle McKynegan is not documented as having had a market; however an account by David de Offyntoun includes revenue generated by the sale of 'corn, cows and cow-hides etc.' suggesting there was one. *P.R.I. rep. D.K.*, 36, p. 59.
125. *Cal. doc. Ire. 1171-1251*, no. 471; This belonged to the archbishop and is probably Glanmore near Ashford.
126. Little is known about Kilbla. Price identifies it with Ballybla near Killiskey; Price, *Placenames,* vii, pxlvi.
127. For Dalkey, Shankill, Kilmacberne see *Alen's reg.*, p. 195; for Bray see *Chartul. St Mary's, Dublin,* i, p. 29; for Newcastle McKynegan, see *Chartul. St Mary's, Dublin,* i, no. 226; for Ballybla and Wicklow see Price, *Placenames*, vii, p. xlvi.
128. *Alen's reg.*, p. 43.
129. Glasscock, 'Land and people, *c.*1300', p. 237; for discussion on burgesses see Gearóid Mac Niocaill, 'The colonial town in Irish Documents', *The comparative history of urban origins in non-Roman Europe* (1985), British Archaeological Reports, International series, 255, pp 373-8.
130. For distribution map see Barry, *Archaeology of Ireland*, p. 119.
131. *Red bk. Ormond*, p. 24.
132. See *Alen's reg.*, p. 43 for details of burgesses paying 12d a burgage plot and for the law of 'Brytoylle' at Rathmore dated 1220.
133. See Curtis, 'Rental of Lisronagh', pp 46-76; see also *Alen's reg.*, p. 176 where the betaghs are obliged by custom to watch the lord's 'nags and kine'.
134. They held five carucates (*Reg. St Thomas* p. 166), two of which were at Killruddery. In 1240 Nicholas de la Felde held lands at 'Kylrethelin' probably Kilruddery. There was a dispute between the latter and the abbot of St Thomas at this date. *Cal. doc. Ire. 1171-1251*, no. 2495.
135. They received a plot 50 feet frontage to a depth of 30 perches opposite the castle and next to the plot of St Mary's; *Reg. St Thomas*, p. 170.
136. *Chart. St Mary's, Dublin,* i, p. 29.
137. *Chart. St Mary's, Dublin,* i, pp 78-83, 158; See C. Ó Conbhuí, 'The lands of St Mary's Abbey, Dublin', *R.I.A. Proc.*, lxii (1961-3), p. 62; the lands at Glencullen were in dispute; only settled in the 1230s. For details of this dispute, see ibid. pp 56-62.

138. *Alen's reg*., p. 91.
139. *Cal. doc. Ire., 1252-84*, no. 2340.
140. *Alen's reg*., p. 69.
141. *Cal. doc. Ire., 1252-84*, no. 2070.
142. *Cal. doc. Ire., 1171-51*, nos. 128, 129, 322. This land was later leased in 1234 to the priory of the Holy Trinity; ibid. no. 2123.
143. Simms and Fagan, 'Villages in county Dublin, p. 80.
144. *R.S.A.I. Jn*., xxxv (1905), p. 428; there are traces of a moat to the north approx. 3 metres in width but no trace on the southern side.
145. Ronan, 'The ancient churches of the deanery of Wicklow', p. 139.
146. There was obvious friction; in 1225 a grant was made to archbishop Henry stating that the forests would remain in the same state for five years and that the men and the vills would not be disturbed: see *Cal. doc., Ire., 1171-1251,* no. 1317. *Alen's reg*., p. 62.
147. This covered most of the barony of Lower Talbotstown, county Wicklow. *Alen's reg*., pp 25-6.
148. J.T. Westropp, 'Earthwork near Curtlestown, county Wicklow', *R.S.A.I. Jn*., xliii (1913), p. 118.
149. In 1244, 60 does and 20 bucks were sent to Dalkey to stock the forest; *Cal. doc. Ire., 1171-1251*, no. 2671.
150. Glasscock, 'Land and people *c.*1300', p. 209.
151. Bradley, 'Scandinavian settlement in Ireland', p. 52.
152. *Cal. doc. Ire. 1285-92*, nos. 149, 251, 631, 641, 741, 796.
153. This forest was at the centre of a dispute between the king and Walter de Ridelesford. De Ridelesford had possession of the lands which the king claimed formed part of the manor of Obrun. *Cal. Doc. Ire., 1171-1251*, no. 2409.
154. *Alen's reg*., p. 134.
155. K. W. Nicholls, 'Anglo-French Ireland and after', *Peritia*, i (1982), p. 374.
156. *Alen's reg*., p. 136.
157. Price, *Placenames*, vii, p. xlix.
158. Glasscock, 'Land and people *c.*1300', p. 211.
159. J.F. Lydon, 'A land of war', p. 158 below.
160. At Shankill the Irish carried off the meadow crop; *P.R.I. rep. D.K*., 39, p. 65.
161. *Cal. doc. Ire., 1252-84*, nos. 1400, 1412.
162. Robin Frame, The Dublin government and gaelic Ireland, 1272-1361' (Ph.D., unpublished, Trinity College Dublin, 1971), pp 92, 94.
163. Betham, 'Account of Thomas de Chaddisworth', p. 157.
164. *P.R.I. rep. D.K*., 36, p. 60.
165. *P.R.I. rep. D.K*., 38, p. 47. Only £3.1s.10d was collected from the 'free tenants' of Castlekevin.
166. *Alen's reg*., pp 170-198.
167. *Cal. doc. Ire., 1252-84*, no. 2329.
168. *Cal. doc. Ire., 1293-1301*, no. 2329.
169. *P.R.I. rep. D.K*., 36, p. 59.
170. *Cal. doc. Ire., 1252-84*, no. 2329.
171. *P.R.I. rep. D.K*., 53, p. 23.
172. *Cal. doc. Ire., 1285-92*, no. 149.
173. *Cal. doc. Ire., 1293-1301*, no. 4. The fragmented nature of the lands of Obrun can be clearly seen in the number of people holding 'Obrun' without any distinction being made of where exactly the lands were located.
174. *Cal. doc. Ire., 1252-84*, nos. 2199, 2329.

175. Ibid., no. 2329.
176. *Cal. doc. Ire., 1302-1307*, no. 355.
177. *P.R.I. rep. D.K.*, 38, p. 55; In total £105.12s.6d. was paid. The grange at Clonkeen appears to be functioning normally in the mid-fourteenth century suggesting that the devastation is perhaps limited in this area, see *Chartul. St Mary's, Dublin*, i, no. 266.
178. Otway-Ruthven, *Medieval Ireland*, p. 268.
179. *Cal. doc. Ire., 1252-84*, no. 622.
180. For example John de Stretton received lands, in 1285, described as 'waste' at Newcastle Mckynegan. He was granted the lands on condition he built a dwelling there and inhabited it. *Cal. doc. Ire., 1285-92*, no. 7.
181. *Alen's reg.*, p. 120, p. 123.
182. *Hist. & mun. hoc. Ire.*, pp 456-62.
183. Price, *Placenames*, vii, p. lxiii.
184. *Cal. justic. rolls Ire., 1308-14*, p. 319.
185. *Hist. & mun. hoc. Ire.*, p. 381.
186. F.E. Ball, *History of Dublin*, iii (Dublin), 1905, p. 101; Scott, *Stones of Bray*, p. 121.
187. J.F. Lydon, 'The Bruce invasion of Ireland', *Historical Studies*, iv (1963), p. 112. See also Robin Frame 'The Bruces in Ireland 1315-18', xix (1974), pp 22-4, 34-6.
188. *Alen's reg.*, pp 194-6.
189. *P.R.I. rep. D.K.*, 39, p. 21. A list of Le Brun's lands at this date amounts to approx. twenty carucates, *Cal. justic. rolls Ire., 1308-14*, pp 112-3. Some are recognisably in Uí Briúin Cualann and therefore originally held by the Mac Giollamocholmóg family. At Glencapy (Glencap) he held three and a half carucates with a further two carucates at Glencry (Glencree) and Mondelouch (Mundelay of later documents). At Balimakcorris (Ballycorus) he held one carucate with a hundred and ten acres. This accounts for nearly all of the eight carucates.
190. *P.R.I. rep. D.K.*, 39, p. 60.
191. *P.R.I. rep. D.K.*, 53, p. 23.
192. See Lydon, 'A land of war', p. 151 below.
193. *Cal. doc. Ire., 1285-92*, no. 622.
194. *P.R.I. rep. D.K.*, 36, p. 53; *Cal. doc. Ire., 1252-84*, no. 1935.
195. Ibid., 36, p. 59; *Cal. doc. Ire., 1252-84*, no. 2169.
196. Orpen, 'Novum castrum Mckynegan', p. 132.
197. *P.R.I. rep. D.K.*, 38, p. 47.
198. By 1308 the constable complained that 'the house and walls of the castle in divers places are split asunder', *Cal. justic. rolls Ire., 1308-1314*, p. 85. The house is probably the hall surrounded by the wall.
199. Orpen, 'Novum castrum McKynegan', p. 133.
200. Ibid.
201. Orpen, 'Castrum Keyvini', p. 21.
202. *Chartul. St Mary's, Dublin*, ii, p. 336. See Orpen, 'Novum castrum McKynegan', p. 135.
203. *P.R.I. rep. D.K.*, 38, p. 47. He also cut a path through from Castlekevin to Glendalough; Orpen, 'Castrum Keyvini', p. 22.
204. Ibid., p. 17.
205. *Rot. pat. Hib.*, no. 3.
206. The castle-builders probably took advantage of a natural fault in the rock and modified it for their own use.
207. G.H. Orpen, 'Mottes and Norman castles in Ireland', *E.H.R.*, xxii (1907), p. 251.

208. D.M. Waterman, 'Somersetshire and other foreign building stones in medieval Ireland, 1175-1400', *U.J.A.*, xxxiii (1970), p. 71.
209. Wicklow reverted to the Geraldines. They presumably held the castle at some stage; see *Alen's reg.*, pp 2-3.
210. Price, *Placenames*, vii, p. lxiv.
211. *Calendar of ancient deeds and muniments preserved in the Pembroke Estate office* (privately printed, Dublin, 1891), p. 34.
212. Down Survey, sheets 84 and 85.
213. *Rot. pat. Hib.*, no. 89.
214. Price, *Placenames*, vii, p. lxxiii.
215. Down Survey, sheets 85 and 86.
216. F.E. Ball, 'Rathmichael and its neighbourhood', *R.S.A.I. Jn.*, xxxii (1902), pp 121-2.
217. Price, *Placenames*, v, p. 322.
218. *P.R.I. rep. D.K.*, 38, p. 101.
219. *P.R.I. rep. D.K.*, 47, p. 44.
220. See *P.R.I. rep. D.K.*, 38, p. 38, where de Kenley held two parts of the manor for John, son of Ralph, who was a minor.
221. *P.R.I. rep. D.K.*, 47, p. 44. The land is listed as 'Ballygonner, county Dublin'.
222. Price, *Placenames*, vii, p. lxviii.
223. Maurice Craig, *The Architecture of Ireland from the earliest times to 1880* (London, 1982), p. 100.
224. *Cal. doc. Ire., 1252-84*, no. 2069.
225. Ibid., nos. 1466, 1633, 2002, 2083.
226. O'Flanagan, O.S. letters, p. 40; S.M.R. file, Sheet 26 (Dublin), site no. 44.
227. Ball, *History of Dublin*, iii, p. 89.
228. Down Survey, sheet no. 81.
229. O'Flanagan, O.S. letters, pp 39-41.
230. Down Survey, sheet no. 81.
231. Orpen, *Normans, 1169-1333*, ii, pp 343-4.
232. T.J. Westropp, 'The ancient forts of Ireland: being a contribution to our knowledge of their types, affinities and structural features', *Transactions of the Royal Irish Academy*, xxxi (1897), pp 702-3.
233. See T.B. Barry, *Medieval moated sites of south-east Ireland*, British Archaeological Reports, no. 35 (Oxford, 1977); P. David Sweetman, 'Excavations of a medieval moated site at Rigsdale, county Cork, 1977-78', *R.I.A. Proc.*, lxxx c (1981), pp 193-205.
234. Barry, *Archaeology of Ireland*, p. 84.
235. Price, Fieldbooks, vol. 24, p. 93.
236. *Reg. St Thomas*, p. 288.
237. Ronan, 'Churches of the deanery of Wicklow', p. 136.
238. Liam Price, 'The O'Byrne's country in county Wicklow in the sixteenth century and the manor of Arklow', *R.S.A.I. Jn., lxvi* (1935), p. 49.
239. Price, 'The O'Byrnes in county Wicklow', p. 50.
240. Orpen, 'Novum castrum McKynegan', p. 126.
241. S.M.R., sheet 25 (Wicklow), site no. 4.
242. S.M.R., sheet 13 (Wicklow), site no. 34.
243. S.M.R., sheet 25 (Wicklow), site no. 21; S.M.R., sheet no. 24 (Wicklow), site no. 4.
244. O'Flanagan, O.S. letters, p. 120.
245. See T.B. Barry, *Moated site research group*, ed. C. J. Bond, vii (1980), p. 31. Trooperstown is recorded on the first edition of the Ordnance Survey (1838), and the second (1908), six inch, sheet no. 24.

246. G. Hadden, 'Some earthworks in county Wexford', *Journal of the Cork Historical and Archaeological Society*, lxix (1964), pp 118-22.
247. Price, Fieldbooks, vol. 25, p. 18.
248. Nicholls, 'Anglo-French Ireland', p. 392; see C.A. Empey, 'Medieval Knoctopher', pp 329-42.
249. Price, 'The O'Byrnes in county Wicklow', p. 47.
250. *P.R.I. rep. D.K.*, 38, p. 78; see Price, 'The O'Byrnes in county Wicklow', p. 48. However 'Ralph de Rathdowne' did have land at 'Kilmanaghe' in Tallaght in 1306-7. Kylmanach may refer to this: *Alen's reg*., p. 161.
251. *Cal. doc. Ire., 1252-84*, no. 1798.
252. In about 1327 Hugh and Walter Lawless are recorded as supplying victuals to five stone houses in the district which were probably the major strongholds in the area; Price, *Placenames*, vii, p. lxiii. These were possibly McDermot's castle, Killoughter, Kilmartin, Kilcommon and Powerscourt.
253. Frame, 'The Dublin government', p. 83.
254. See *Cal. just. rolls Ire., 1308-14*, pp 67, 77, for details of garrisons.
255. *Cal. doc. Ire., 1252-84*, no. 1496; Frame, 'The Dublin government', p. 79. A ward was established at the 'ville of Obrun'; this was probably at Brownstown; see footnote no. 90.
256. *Cal. just. rolls Ire., 1308-14*, p. 67.
257. Robin Frame, 'The justiciar and the murder of the Mc Murroughs in 1282', *I.H.S.*, xviii (1972-3), p. 38.
258. Frame, 'The Dublin government', p. 36.
259. Price, *Placenames*, vii, p. lxvi.
260. Price, Fieldbooks, vol. 24, p. 96.
261. Price, Fieldbooks, vol. 11, p. 47. The site possibly incorporates an earlier 'rath' since a pennanular brooch dated to the tenth century was reputedly found in the fosse; this may account for its peculiar shape. See Liam Price, *R.S.A.I. Jn*., xlvii (1936), p. 145.
262. *Cal. doc. Ire., 1293-1301*, nos. 289, 613.
263. On clearing the northern side of the site for a new barn the ground was made up of 'fill'; this may have been the continuation of the moat on this side.
264. Price, 'Powerscourt and Fercullen', p. 122.
265. Walter Fitzgerald, 'The Manor and Castle of Powerscourt, County Wicklow in the sixteenth century, formerly a possession of the Earls of Kildare', *Kildare Arch. Soc. Jn*., vi (1910), p. 127.
266. Price, 'Powerscourt and the territory of Fercullen', pp 120-21.
267. Ibid., p. 122.
268. M. Reynolds, 'A Preliminary Report on the monuments of archaeological interest in County Wicklow' (An Foras Forbartha Teoranta, Conservation and Amenity Advisory Service, 1973).
269. Arthur Flynn, *History of Bray* (Dublin, 1986), p. 33.
270. They bear little relation to the large earthwork castles which were erected in an attempt to subdue Wales in the eleventh and twelfth centuries; see E. Neaverson, *Mediaeval Castles in North Wales* (London, 1947).
271. In 1297, it is stated that the Irish escaped 'because of the density of the woods and the depth of their morasses', 'Cal. Liber Niger and Liber Albus', p. 44.
272. *Chartul. St Mary's, Dublin*, ii, p. 266.
273. 'Cal. Liber Niger and Liber Albus', p. 43.
274. *Alen's reg*., p. 233; see petition made by the merchants *c*.1396, in which Dalkey

is described as being 'six leagues from the city' and as being the only port large enough to accommodate the ships in the area.

275. Ibid., p. 247.
276. Some of these probably acted as warehouses to protect the goods that were being landed at the small harbour of Bullock.
277. Price, *Placenames*, VII, p. lxvi.
278. See Price, 'Powerscourt and territory of Fercullen', pp 123-4.
279. Barry, *Archaeology of Medieval Ireland*, pp 75-6; Glasscock, 'Moated sites and deserted boroughs and villages', pp 168-75.
280. The king's highway at 'Windgate' is mentioned in the thirteenth century; *Reg. St Thomas*, p. 4.
281. Fitzgerald, 'The manor of Powerscourt', p. 129.
282. Liam Price,'The hearth money roll for county Wicklow', *R.S.A.I. Jn*., lxi (1931), p. 168.
283. Identified by Kenneth Nicholls; see Turner, 'Rathmichael', pp 82-3.
284. *Alen's reg*., p. 69.
285. *Alen's reg*., p. 196.
286. For detailed description of Swords manor see *Alen's reg*., p. 175.
287. Ibid., p. 112.
288. Scott, *Stones of Bray*, p. 69.
289. *Alen's reg*., p. 66.
290. S.M.R., sheet 13 (Wicklow), site no. 16.
291. *Reg. St Thomas*, pp 175-7.
292. Price, Fieldbooks, vol. 24, pp 95-6.
293. See Scott, *Stones of Bray*, appendix v, pp 222-30 for details of the manor of Bray in the late thirteenth century.
294. F.E. Ball, *History of Dublin*, iii, p. 101.
295. The tithes of the medieval mill were granted to the convent of St Mary of Graney priory in 1207, *Cal. doc. Ire., 1171-1251*, no. 355. Mill sites often display a remarkable continuity in their locations; the site of a late mill is sometimes situated over its medieval predecessor, probably because of the complexities of building mill-races.
296. *P.R.I. rep. D.K*., 53, p. 23. See petition dated 1343.
297. By this date it is more accurate to refer to the Anglo-Irish as opposed to the Anglo-Normans.
298. As late as 1293 the 'betagii of Mundelay' still paid rent. Mundelay was possibly somewhere in Obrun (See *Cal. doc. Ire., 1293-1301*, no. 21) and the betaghs held it exclusively since it is always accounted for in connection with them. It may have been located at Monalin, south of Bray.
299. In 1282 the 'betagii' and other men of the king are recorded as being paid £19.0s.2d. in part payment of compensation for 'the depredations of Art Mc Murrough and his accomplices'. *Cal. doc. Ire., 1252-84*, no. 1935.

Glendalough (O.P.W.).

Chapter 7

Three settlements of Gaelic Wicklow 1169-1600: Rathgall, Ballinacor and Glendalough

HARRY LONG

Introduction

The predominant form of settlement in pre-Norman Ireland was the ringfort. A ringfort can be defined as a circular, sub-circular or oval-shaped area enclosed by a bank or ditch with a diameter generally within the 15m-35m (*c.* 45ft-115ft) range. Ringforts functioned as enclosed homesteads, or in the case of smaller examples as animal enclosures. Examples of excavated ringforts in county Wicklow at Burgage More and Ballyknockan were, according to the excavator, used as cattle pens.[1] Three other ringforts in the townland of Lackan yielded datable evidence to the period 800-900 A.D.[2] These are the only ringforts in Wicklow that have been excavated to date. All were rescue excavations, carried out in the 1940s before the flooding of the Liffey-King's river valleys to form a reservoir. Hillforts, which can sometimes be simply larger ringforts located on a hill-top or promontory and usually more than one rampart, may also have been occupied in the early medieval period (*c.* 500-1169). Examples can be seen at Brusselstown ring, Baltinglass hill and Rathgall.[3] Ecclesiastical enclosures, often of similar size and shape to ringforts and crannogs or lake-dwellings were also important types of settlements in pre-Norman times. The larger ecclesiastical settlements were known as monastic cities, Glendalough in county Wicklow being one of the most important of these 'cities' in Ireland.[4]

Much debate has centred on the continued occupation of pre-Norman settlements or the building of new ones. There is a paucity of documentary sources on this subject compounded by a severe lack of excavated sites from this period compared to the Anglo-Norman sites for which evidence is relatively abundant. Excavations at Shannon airport[5] and field-work in south Donegal[6] provide firm evidence that ringforts were at least being occupied in the west and north-west of Ireland in the late medieval period. The O'Neills of Ulster retained their traditional centre at the rath of Tullahoge until the fourteenth century.[7]

Crannogs were also occupied long after 1169, as evidenced by a drawing of *c.*1600 showing a crannog under attack.[8] In Wicklow the hillfort at Rathgall, ringforts at Ballinacor and the monastic city of Glendalough provide evidence of either occupation or building at some time in the period from 1169 to 1600. This evidence is examined in some detail for each site. All three sites are in areas which were not consistently held by the Anglo-Normans or English from the late twelfth century to the late sixteenth century. Indeed from the 1270s onwards, Ballinacor and Glendalough were in the heart of the mountainous country which nurtured the Gaelic Revival in Wicklow. A brief examination of other sites known to have been occupied by the Gaelic Irish illustrates the significant point that sites built by the Anglo-Normans also formed part of the Gaelic settlement pattern in Wicklow.

Rathgall

Rathgall is located 6km east of Tullow near the modern boundary of counties Carlow and Wicklow. Excavations there unearthed evidence of significant late medieval occupation.[9] The site has been classified as a hillfort because it defends rather than encloses a hill-top. Rathgall consists of four roughly circular, concentric ramparts. The three outermost ramparts are not as prominent as the innermost one, but all are of drystone construction. The innermost is a dry-built wall of granite boulders, some of considerable size. Although this central enclosure appears to be circular, it is constructed in a series of straight lines and would be more accurately described as polygonal. The entrance is a simple break in the walls slightly to the north of west. On the southern side there is a small, unroofed chamber measuring 2.3m (7ft 7in) by 3.9m (14ft 10in). The thickness of the wall varies from 7m (*c.*23ft) in the south-east to 1.5m (*c.*5ft) in the north. Rampart 3 is faced with granite boulders on the inside, and has only one opening roughly aligned to that of the central enclosure on its north-western side. The overall diameter of the site is approximately 310m (1,017ft). The outermost rampart encloses an area of about 7 hectares (18 acres).

There were some indications of activity at the site in neolithic times, but the finds from the Late Bronze Age (*c.*800 BC-*c.*500 BC) make Rathgall the most extensive settlement yet discovered from this period in Ireland. There was some evidence of a brief re-occupation in the Iron Age (around the second or third century AD) but a more substantial re-occupation took place in the later middle ages. Raftery found a small trench, rectangular in outline, outside the central enclosure at a distance of about 15m (50ft) to 20m (66ft) to the east. In this trench he found medieval pottery which dated the structure to the thirteenth or fourteenth century. The presence of post holes indicated that it was probably of wattle-and-daub construction with building methods similar to that of houses in medieval Dublin where walls consisting of upright posts interwoven with horizontal layers of wattles were plastered with mud and probably thatched.[10] Circular examples of a similar type of structure were excavated at an early medieval rath at Deer Park Farms in Antrim.[11] The structure at Rathgall measured 12.5m (41ft) by 8m (26ft). This is considerably larger than the Dublin houses, which ranged in size from *c.*8m (26ft) by *c.*4.75m (15ft) to 5m (16ft) by 3.5m (11ft).[12] Raftery found no traces of a hearth within this structure. Later spade cultivation, which destroyed much of the upper layers in the area excavated, probably destroyed traces of a hearth.

The pottery found in the trench of the house-plot was part of a total of about 2,000 sherds which were found inside and outside the central enclosure. Two types of pottery were found: Leinster Cooking Ware and an assortment of glazed wares. The glazed wares were not of the Saintonge type, and cannot be identified as any of the known imported pottery types of thirteenth or fourteenth century Ireland.[13] Leinster Cooking Ware has been found on many attested Anglo-Norman sites. Some sites where it has been found, including Rathgall, may have been native settlements.[14] Spouts from what were probably wine vases were found amongst the glazed wares. The pottery finds at Rathgall which dated the construction of the wattle and daub structure and occupation inside and outside the central enclosure to the thirteenth or fourteenth century were complemented by the finding of two silver coins. One was a penny of Edward I (king of England 1272-1307) minted in Dublin, the other a penny of Edward III (1327-1377) minted in London. These coins were found with the pottery in the central enclosure.

The stratigraphy of the central enclosure's uppermost layers was badly destroyed by what Raftery assumed was spade cultivation in comparatively recent times. It is possible that the medieval occupants built houses within the central enclosure. It is also possible that the dry-stone wall of the central enclosure and the reinforcing wall of rampart 3 were built in medieval times, but they could be later. Raftery removed a section of wall in the eastern part of the central enclosure. Medieval pottery was found both inside and outside this wall, but none was found underneath it. Prehistoric layers were found under the basal stones of the wall. Raftery observed that the foundation stones of the walls were seen to lie only a few centimetres under the surface, and in places seemed almost to rest on it. He concluded that the central enclosure was built in the medieval period or later.[15] The shallow foundations may indicate that the walls were built hastily, perhaps by medieval occupants wishing to fortify the existing ramparts.

It is possible that other evidence of medieval occupation exists at

Rathgall. Raftery's excavations took place over a very limited area of what is overall a very large site. The pottery finds and the wattle-and-daub structure indicate definite occupation and construction in the thirteenth and fourteenth centuries whereas the coins indicate a possible date-span of 1272 to 1377. While the occupation period may have fallen with this time-span or even some years outside it, the coins do provide a useful indicator of dates which fall within range of the more broadly dated pottery finds.

It is difficult, on the basis of the archaeological evidence alone, to state definitively whether the medieval occupants of Rathgall were Anglo-Normans or Irish. While Leinster Cooking Ware has been found on attested Anglo-Norman sites, it is as yet by no means certain that this type of pottery was not also in use amongst the Gaelic population.[16] Research currently being carried out may reveal more about the origin of the glazed ware found at Rathgall.[17] Given the large quantities of Saintonge found at Anglo-Norman centres, notably Dublin,[18] one would expect that Anglo-Norman occupiers of Rathgall would have used this or another imported pottery. The lack of any imported wares amongst the 2,000 or so sherds of pottery could suggest a Gaelic occupation. The silver coins of Edward I and Edward III could quite easily have passed into Gaelic hands through normal trading contacts or may have been part of the spoils of war. Given the tentative nature of the archaeological evidence regarding the identity of its occupiers it is worthwhile to look at the site in the more general context of the history of other settlements in Wicklow. Before 1270, there is little evidence that the process of colonisation and establishment of Anglo-Norman settlements was under any significant threat. On 25 July 1270, Edward, first-born son of the king of England (later Edward I) commanded the justiciar and his officers 'to aid the archbishop of Dublin against those rebelling against his authority.'[19]

After years of intermittent warfare the O'Byrnes and O'Tooles submitted 'to the king's peace' and handed over hostages, a MacMurrough, an O'Byrne and an O'Toole, to the king's men at Castlekevin and paid compensation for damages done. The O'Byrne hostage who was handed over was 'a son of John son of Ger Obryn (O'Byrne) senior'.[20] A certain John O'Byrne, 'son of the chaplain,' held lands of the earl of Ormond in the manor of Lismacloman in 1303.[21] Rathgall is located within the civil parish of Liscolman, and would have been within the manor of Liscolman in 1303. Without further evidence, it is impossible to be certain that the John O'Byrne, whose son was handed over at Castlekevin in 1295, is the same man who held land of the Butlers at Liscolman before 1303. John O'Byrne held lands at a place called 'le Conyngier' ('the rabbit-warren'), but the name is now obsolete. Another

O'Byrne held half a carucate (*c.*60 acres) of land in the manor of Liscolman.[22] Again the placename 'Authethulte' is obsolete, but was somewhere in the immediate vicinity of Rathgall. 'Tothel Oconil' also held half a carucate of land within the manor of Liscolman.[23] These are the only three landholders in the extent of 1303 who have Irish names. In respect of Conor O'Byrne and 'Tothil Oconil', the tenancies are new. Conor O'Byrne's lands were formerly held by two men by the name of 'Tawly'. The lands of 'Tothil Oconil' had formerly been held by the betaghs and cottagers of Liscolman and Verteri Grangia (Butlerstown, Carlow).[24] The latter are described as being 'waste'. The combined effects of famine, bad harvests and war with the Irish began a process of decline in Anglo-Norman settlements from the 1270s onwards. This led to many manors becoming 'waste' and it is apparent in the case of Tothil Oconil that what was formerly a substantial plot of land worked by betaghs and cottagers had been secured by him as a single tenant because no other tenants were available. While no place which is identifiable as Rathgall is mentioned in the extent, the presence of two O'Byrnes and 'Tothil Oconil' in the immediate vicinity around 1303 may well be linked to the re-occupation of the site. The Anglo-Normans are unlikely to have occupied a disused hillfort in an area where betagh and cottager holdings were becoming waste. For the Irish expelled from Glenmalure in 1277, the triple ramparts of Rathgall would have provided immediate shelter and security.[25] When the justiciar reported to the king that many of them had gone to 'another strong place,' he may well have been referring to Rathgall.[26]

The presence of Tothil Oconil and the two O'Byrnes as substantial landholders in the Rathgall area in 1303, when viewed in the context of an overall decline in Anglo-Norman settlement, points towards a Gaelic occupation at Rathgall. During the fourteenth century the O'Byrnes and O'Tooles continually raided the Wicklow lands of the archbishop of Dublin and the king's manors on the coastal strip and in south county Dublin. The role of Rathgall must be viewed in the wider context of south-east Ireland. There is also evidence, however, of an increasingly strong O'Byrne-McMurrough alliance in the area of south Wicklow-Wexford-Carlow during the fourteenth century. In 1331 and 1336, the O'Byrnes and MacMurroughs were allies in Wexford. Two hundred of them were recorded as being killed 'at Wexford' in 1331.[27] In 1336, they killed Lord Matthew Fitzhenry and 'around 200' other faithful subjects of the king in county Wexford.[28] The O'Byrnes of Duffry in north-west Wexford, to the south of Rathgall, were also at war at this time. In 1334, James Lord Ormond plundered and burned their lands.[29] The 1336 killing of the archdeacon of Ossory, Howles de Bathe, and Andrew de Bathe by the O'Byrnes of Duffry provides firm evidence that Ormond's action two years previously had not destroyed their power base.[30] Carlow, only ten miles from Rathgall, became a crucial centre in the crown's attempts to defend English settlements against the rising power of the Gaelic alliance of south Leinster. In 1346 the justiciar directed officials at Wexford, Kilkenny and Carlow to combine for the purpose of subduing the O'Byrnes, O'Tooles, MacMurroughs and O'Nolans.[31] John O'Byrne, 'captain of his nation', submitted to the justiciar in 1358, not at Castlekevin or Newcastle, but at Carlow.[32] The exchequer and the common bench, the only fixed institutions of colonial government, were at Carlow instead of Dublin from 1361 to 1394.[33] Attempts by the government to curb the rising power of the Gaelic alliance had little success and in 1392 the MacMurrough, O'Byrnes, O'Tooles, O'Mores ... 'and other Irish enemies ... assembled a great host and came to the town of Carlow, which town together with the other part of the county of Carlow, and great part of the county of Kildare, they gave up to fire and flame ...'[34]

Rathgall commands fine views of counties Wicklow, Wexford and Carlow. In the context of the decline in Anglo-Norman settlements in the late thirteenth and fourteenth centuries, there is no basis for assuming its occupation by the hard-pressed colonial settlers. The balance of historical evidence points firmly towards the occupation of Rathgall by the Irish. The O'Byrnes gained great power and prestige in the fourteenth century. By 1378 they were recorded in the annals under their ancient title 'Kings of Uí Fhaeláin.'[35] In 1395, when the Wicklow chiefs and MacMurrough submitted to Richard II, the O'Byrnes regarded themselves as being as powerful as the king of Leinster; for on that occasion both MacMurrough and O'Byrne bound themselves to forfeit the same sum, 20,000 marks each, if they broke their agreement with King Richard.[36] Given the geo-political context outlined above it seems reasonable to suggest that Rathgall was re-occupied by the Irish who were defeated at Glenmalure.

Ballinacor

Although many ringforts have been identified in county Wicklow, there is as yet no archaeological evidence of their occupation or construction in the post-Norman period.[37] In 1946 Price observed in relation to the Gabhal Raghnaill, O'Byrne's settlement at Ballinacor in Glenmalure, that 'There is nothing to indicate that the house at Ballinacor was a stone castle; it was probably of wood surrounded by earthen ramparts, the word used in the Four Masters is *baile* not *caisleán*'. Price also noted that the traditional location of the O'Byrne settlement was somewhere in the immediate neighbourhood of Ballinacor House, south east of Glenmalure.[38] The Annals of the Four Masters describes how the chief justiciary and his men arrived in 'Baile-na-Curra' in the month of January, 1595:

> but before they had passed through the gate of the rampart that surrounded it, the sound of a drum was accidentally heard from the soldiers who were into the castle. Fiagh (MacHugh O'Byrne) with his people took the alarm, and he rose up suddenly and sent a party of his people, men, boys and women out through the postern-doors, and he followed them, and conveyed them all in safety to the wilds and recesses where he considered them secure.[39]

The term used for castle is, as Price observed, *baile* and not *caisleán*. Price was assuming that *caisleán* would be used if the structure was made of stone. The use of *baile*, meaning 'homestead, farmstead' [40] and not *caisleán* implies that this was not a stone castle. More recent research demonstrates that *caisleán* did not necessarily refer to a stone castle, as the Irish annalists used the word to refer to pre-1169 Irish fortresses and Norman earthworks as well as Irish and Norman stone castles.[41] Nonetheless, closer scrutiny of other Irish terms used in this passage provide significant evidence of the type of structures that existed at Ballinacor. The Irish for 'through the gate of the rampart that surrounded it' is *tar dorus an dúnchlad baoi ina timpeall.*[42] *Dúnchlad* in middle and early modern Irish described not simply 'rampart' but more precisely, 'earthen dyke or rampart entrenchment'.[43] The distinction made in the translation between *dorus an dúnchlad* ('the gate of the rampart') and *doirsib élaid* ('the postern door') is correct; *élaid* in Irish encompasses the meanings 'escape, abscond, make-off.'[44] The annals clearly state that the O'Byrne homestead at Ballinacor was surrounded by an earthen rampart with an entrance gate and a separate postern-gate to allow the residents to escape.

A report from Russel at Ballinacor just after the incident described above tells how he 'cutte down the plashed wood near the house of Fiagh.'[45] The verb 'to plash' means the same as 'to pleach,' that is 'to construct or repair (a hedge) by interlacing the shoots (fourteenth century *plechen*, from the Old North French *plechier*, from Latin, *plectere*, to plait, to weave, plait ...).'[46] Shakespeare (d.1616) used the word 'pleached' to mean fenced or overarched with intertwined boughs.[47] Hedges planted on the top of earthen banks increased the defensive capabilities of a settlement. The rath at Tullahogue in the O'Neill's country was still inhabited around 1600, and Bartlett's picture shows tall trees growing from an encircling bank.[48] It is clear that precisely this kind of structure existed at Ballinacor in 1595 and that Russel destroyed the defensive capabilities of the rath at Ballinacor by cutting down the hedge that surrounded it.

In April 1581, Ballinacor had been burned by Sir William Stanley.[49] Sir Nicholas White, Master of the Rolls, in 1584 described Fiach MacHugh O'Byrne's residence as being 'at the mouth of the Glynn.'[50] At the mouth of Glenmalure, just over 1km (.625 of a mile) from the present Ballinacor House, the Ordnance Survey map of 1839 shows two circular enclosures.[51] 'Baile na Corra' as the name appears in *Leabhar Branach*, the poem book of the O'Byrne's (written *c.*1550-*c.*1630) means 'the townland of the slope.'[52] The two circular enclosures in the townland of Ballinacor were located on the gentle slopes of Ballinacor mountain, about .75km from the Avonbeg river and over 300m (854ft) apart. One of these enclosures has survived although it is extremely overgrown and difficult to view. Another structure marked on the 1839 map and still extant is a sub-circular enclosure located about 300m (854ft) to the east of the surviving circular enclosure.[53]

The ramparts of both enclosures are constructed of earth with stones loosely mixed in. Their height varies, but is around 1m in most places. The eastern enclosure has trees growing around its banks and is reasonably clear on the inside. From the north-west, it appears to be circular, but the bank on the south-east is almost straight. There are three openings in the bank, the widest of which, on the north-west, appears to be an entrance. The enclosed area is *c.*35m (115ft) at its widest. The western enclosure is somewhat larger, but is badly overgrown with trees and bushes. Two breaks are discernible in the banks, one facing up towards the peak of Ballinacor mountain to the south-west, the other opening on the north-east. Both are located on a ridge overlooking the Avonbeg river commanding fine views of the approach to Glenmalure from Rathdrum, north-eastwards to the opposite side of the steep valley, and northward up the valley pass towards Glendalough. There are no traces of stone structures within these enclosures. Lord Grey, reporting Sir William Stanley's action in 1581, stated that he had 'burned Fiach's house at Ballincor,'[54] suggesting it was a wooden structure. The very use of the term 'house' as opposed to 'castell' (castle) in the English sources implies a wooden structure. Fiagh McHugh continued to live at Ballinacor after 1581, and Sir Nicholas White on his circuit of Leinster in 1584 states: 'I was at Ballynecor, Feagh McHugh O'Byrne's chief house ....'[55] The term 'castell' is again avoided, but was used by Grey in 1581 to describe 'Castle Kevan' and 'Castle Comin' (or Kilcommon),[56] both of which have traces of stone structures to the present day.

The combined Irish and English sources suggest that the sixteenth century residence of the O'Byrnes at Ballinacor was a wooden house surrounded by an earthen rampart planted with trees or a hedge. The two circular or sub-circular enclosures described above are the only such structures within the townland of Ballinacor. The *Leabhar Branach* (The Book of the O'Byrnes) contains a poem composed on the desolation of Ballinacor at the time of Fiagh McHugh. Mac Airt suggested that this poem was written possibly after the burning of Ballinacor by Stanley in 1581.[57] As Ballinacor was re-occupied by Fiagh after this and he was not finally expelled from there until 1595, the poem may in fact be later. The poem laments the desolation of:

> The enclosure (*lios*) of the hostages
> The comely enclosure (*lios*) of the womenfolk
> The bright bank of the slender spears
> The house of the guests (*teagh na n-aoigheadh*)[58]

The stanza following laments the fact that the poet cannot see '... the house where Fiach himself used to be.'[59] The term *les* (*lios*) was used in Old and Middle Irish to describe 'the space about a dwelling-house or houses enclosed by a bank or rampart.'[60] Riordan noted that *lios* and *ráth* are terms which are usually used to describe earthen ringforts, while *caiseal* and *cathair* are used for the stone type.[61] While allowances must be made for the poetic nature of this description, and the metrical and rhetorical concerns of its author, the use of the term *lios* in relation to Ballinacor concurs with the historical sources. A settlement consisting of more than one *lios* is confirmed by the presence of three enclosures on the map of 1839.

On 24 September 1596 Russel described in his diary how he approached Ballinacor with his men from the direction of Rathdrum: '... and drawing near the ford, the rebels (Fiagh's men) raised the cry and made show on the hill by Ballencor ... (and) drew down to the ford to meet us there at the bridge.' The lord deputy's men, presumably crossing the river, '... drove them from their stand and recovered over the ford with a small loss and some hurt.'[62] The description matches perfectly the sites of the present enclosures at Ballinacor and the bridge at Greenan (where the townlands of Ballinacor and Greenan Beg meet), the road from Rathdrum leading over this bridge and up the hill to the enclosures. One of the structures that survives here, however, would appear to be a *ráth* of Fiagh's settlement reconstructed by the lord deputy after Fiagh's abandonment of the site in January 1595. For Russel, between 5 February and 22 February 1595 '... caused to be made a verie strong ffortification in Bayliennecorre (Ballinacor) which is the Chieff House of Feach make Hews.'[63] He was assisted in his work by 100 of Fiagh's churls who, on 11 February '... came out of O'Birne's

Figure 7.1 Brusselstown ring.

Figure 7.2 Rathgall.

Figure 7.3 Model of monastic 'city' of Glendalough (Bord Fáilte).

country, to work at the fort.'[64] An English garrison was left at the newly fortified Ballinacor. Having held the site for almost a year and a half, they lost it again 'by the treachery of a serjeant' to Fiagh MacHugh, who 'razed the fort to the ground.'[65] It is some indication of the significance of Ballinacor, renamed 'Mount Russel,'[66] to the English that the serjeant and two others were executed 'for treachery in yielding up the fort.'[67] Russel fortified the church at Rathdrum and eventually built another new fortification there.[68]

While the re-fortification of Ballinacor by the English in 1596 is important in understanding the site, the survival of what was clearly a rath settlement into the sixteenth century requires some explanation. Gaelic chieftains in other parts of Ireland had constructed stronger stone tower-houses to increase their security. Glenmalure, however, was secure in its isolation and the inaccessibility of the steep mountains around it. Shortly after the defeat of the English forces under Lord Grey by Fiagh MacHugh O'Byrne at Glenmalure in August 1580 Sir William Stanley wrote: 'The places was such so very ill that were a man never so slightly hurt he was loste, because no man was hable to help him upp the hill. Some died being so out of breath that they were hable to go no further, being not hurte at all.'[69] The rough terrain around Glenmalure had proved too difficult for many Anglo-Norman and English armies throughout the middle ages. Russel succeeded in defeating and killing Fiagh Mac Hugh O'Byrne (in May 1597) only after a long campaign which involved moving garrisons inland from Wicklow and Arklow to the refortified castles at Kilcommon and Castlekevin;[70] clearing passes at Drumkitt[71] and Kilcommon;[72] reconstructing Ballinacor itself after its capture in 1595 and, after losing it again, building new fortifications at Rathdrum.[73] It is hardly surprising, then, that in such a remote and naturally secure valley the O'Byrnes of Gabhail Raghnaill had no need to construct a stone tower-house before the end of the sixteenth century.

Glendalough

The valley of Glendalough lies to the north-east of Glenmalure. Here in the sixth century, St Kevin established a small community of ascetic monks. In the following centuries the settlement at Glendalough flourished and expanded. The early ninth century *Martyrology of Oengus* described its significance in the following words:

> Emain's burgh it hath vanished
> Save that its stones remain;
> The ruam of the west of the world
> is multitudinous Glendalough.[74]

Emain Macha, the capital of Ulster in pre-Christian times, is portrayed by Oengus as having been superseded by Glendalough. The word *ruam* which he uses to describe the latter is derived from the Latin *Roma* or Rome. In this context it means a monastic settlement or a monastic city.[75] The term emphasises the importance of these 'cities' in pre-Norman Ireland.[76] They developed into large settlements with a lay, as well as a religious, population. Alongside the development of Christian spirituality, artistic, educational and commercial activities flourished.[77] Control over the abbacy of a settlement such as Glendalough assumed great political significance, and caused direct intervention by the dynasties of south Leinster from as early as the eighth century.[78] By the early twelfth century, the diocese of Glendalough covered most of modern county Wicklow and parts of counties Kildare and Dublin.[79] Contacts with Europe meant that the significance of this monastic city went beyond Ireland. In the decade before the Anglo-Norman invasion, for instance, Gilla na Naem Laighnech retired from office of bishop of Glendalough to go to Wurzburg. He died there as head of the Schottenkloster *c.*1160.[80]

The physical remains of Glendalough's early medieval settlements are scattered along 5km of the valley floor. To the east of the lower lake lies the largest settlement or the monastic city. It consists today of a double-arched gatehouse, a cathedral, a round tower and a number of other churches. These were originally surrounded by an inner and an outer enclosure, the latter measuring approximately 400m (1,312ft) by 200m (656ft).[81] To the west of the monastic city, beside the upper lake, are the remains of Temple-na-Skellig and Reefert Church. To the east are Trinity Church and St Saviour's Priory. All of these churches would appear, from their architectural style, to have been constructed before the arrival of the Anglo-Normans.

Glendalough was, in ecclesiastical and political terms, one of the most important settlements in pre-Norman Leinster and control over its bishopric and abbacy would be important to the Anglo-Normans. Both offices were subsumed by the Anglo-Norman ecclesiastical administration in Dublin by the middle of the thirteenth century.[82] 'Under the impact of the feudal system,' wrote Leask, 'the great days of Glendalough passed away. The place sank into relative obscurity but the fame of St Kevin lived on.'[83] A combination of architectural, documentary and archaeological evidence, however, suggest that while the 'great days' may have gone, settlement continued at Glendalough for 400 years after 1169. While the evidence is somewhat fragmentary, there is no doubt that far more than the fame of St Kevin survived the feudal system.

In the decades immediately following the Anglo-Norman invasion, building continued at Glendalough. Located within the monastic city in its cemetery, is a small building known as 'The Priests' House'. Although reconstructed in the nineteenth century, it retains many of its original architectural features. It is a single-chamber structure with a doorway in the south wall and a window in the east. The latter consists of a narrow aperture surrounded by an arched recess. The voussoirs of the arch are carved with chevrons which have a single trefoil infill. Comparable infills are found at Baltinglass Abbey (Wicklow) and Jerpoint Abbey (Kilkenny). These have been dated to *c.*1148-1180 and *c.*1160-1200 respectively.[84] The period *c.*1148-1200 saw the beginnings of a transition from Romanesque to Gothic style architecture. Some carved details in 'The Priests' House' have parallels at St Saviour's Priory, Glendalough, a Romanesque church dated to *c.*1152-1162.[85] These include foliate patterns on the bases of pillars, rows of pellets and a capital consisting of a moustached face whose hair is intertwined with an interlace pattern. Other details from the pillars of the arch, however, indicate that 'The Priests' House' is later than St Saviour's. Keeled mouldings are found on the arris roll and under the face of the north capital. Keeled mouldings were an influence from English architecture and the earliest examples in Ireland are found at Inch Abbey (founded 1187), Christchurch Cathedral, Dublin (*c.*1186-1200) and Corcomroe Abbey (1205-1210).[86] All of these were established by the Anglo-Normans. As their influence is likely to have spread to Glendalough through ecclesiastical contacts with Dublin, 'The Priests' House' can hardly pre-date Christ Church Cathedral; *c.*1186, then, would be the earliest possible date at which 'The Priest's House' was constructed.

The name 'The Priests' House' is not medieval but derives from the custom of burying local parish priests within the walls of this building in the eighteenth century.[87] The building is aligned east-west and this, combined with the fact that it is located within the monastic city's cemetery, suggests that it served as a mortuary chapel.

The cathedral at Glendalough, located close to 'The Priests' House', also displays elements of a transition from Romanesque to Gothic architecture. It consists today of a nave, a chancel and a sacristy. The nave was originally built in the early medieval period and there may also have been an early chancel.[88] A substantial re-building of the cathedral took place in the late twelfth or early thirteenth century. A door was built in the north wall of the nave along with a new chancel and sacristy. A type of stone which had not been used in the earlier buildings at Glendalough can be found in the doorways, windows and chancel arch of this phase of the cathedral. Leask, following Cochrane, observed that this stone 'to all appearances an oolitic limestone, is actually a soft and fine-grained granite.'[89] The Department of Geology at Trinity College Dublin has confirmed that it is, in fact, an oolitic limestone which comes from the Dundry quarries near Bristol.[90]

Dundry limestone has been identified at thirty-eight sites in south-east Ireland.[91] It has been found in considerable quantities in Dublin, where its earliest known use was in Christchurch cathedral *c.* 1186.[92] Anglo-Norman masons favoured the use of Dundry freestone for dressed work and it was easily transported by boat to Dublin and other parts of Ireland.[93] It may have been transported from Bristol to Glendalough via Dublin, Wicklow or Arklow.

Limestone is used in the chancel arch, although this was constructed on earlier pillars where plain blocks of local granite and mica-schist were used. The arch is incomplete but was obviously rounded in Romanesque style rather than pointed in the Gothic style. It is executed in three orders, the second of which is carved with chevrons. Chevrons are also found in the east window. A capital carved with trumpeted scallops survives on the north side of the chancel arch. Chevrons and scallops were both common features in Romanesque architecture, but are also found in transitional buildings. The mouldings of the Romanesque period were rounded and while fillets were used; their widespread use in engaged columns and arch mouldings were Gothic, not Romanesque, features.[94] The fillets, which appear in the north door and arch mouldings of the cathedral, are indicative of a transition to the Gothic style. While the chancel's east window is rounded, its long, narrow opening and wide splay are features more common in Gothic than in Romanesque architecture.[95]

This phase of construction at the cathedral represents a curious blend of features. The pillars of the chancel arch appear to be pre-Romanesque while the features of the arch itself, the north door and the east window belong to a period of transition from Romanesque to Gothic architecture. The construction of the arch on plain pillars suggests that either the job was rushed or insufficient limestone was available to allow for the building of new pillars. The use of Dundry limestone at Glendalough is unlikely to have preceded its use at Christchurch Cathedral in Dublin, the earliest known cathedral which the Anglo-Normans re-built in Ireland. The reconstruction of Christchurch began in *c.* 1186 in Romanesque style.[96] By the time it was completed in 1240, a transition to the Gothic style had been made.[97] The cathedral at Glendalough, then, was not built before *c.* 1186. The unusual combination of features makes it difficult to date and it could have been anytime from *c.* 1186 into the early thirteenth century.

Under Anglo-Norman influence, a number of Irish cathedrals were re-built in the late twelfth and early thirteenth centuries.[98] The reconstruction work at Glendalough, however, is not on the same scale nor as finely executed as at other diocesan sees such as Dublin, Waterford and Kilkenny.[99] The Anglo-Norman ecclesiastical administration in Dublin had clearly intended to unite the diocese of Glendalough with the archdiocese of Dublin as early as 1185.[100] They did not succeed in doing so, however, until 1216.[101] All four bishops of Glendalough in the period 1169-1216 were involved in exchanging or granting properties and witnessing Anglo-Norman charters.[102] These contacts explain how Dundry limestone and English architectural influences found their way into Glendalough at that time. Some degree of stability and control over considerable financial resources must have existed to allow for the undertaking of building 'The Priests' House' and rebuilding the cathedral. Both may represent the final architectural flourish of a diocese whose Irish bishops struggled to survive against incorporated into the archdiocese. Just as Glendalough's diocesan status was destined to disappear, however, so the reconstruction of its cathedral lacked the scale and splendour of other cathedrals where status was retained.

The abbacy of Glendalough survived until sometime between 1228 and 1255.[103] It was then granted to the archbishopric of Dublin and a priory was established in the 'Great Church' at Glendalough.[104] This can only refer to the former cathedral. The priory here survived until the early fourteenth century.[105] The prior and canons were granted 'pasture of their beasts in the mountains nearest them' and 'fallen timber for firewood' by Fulk, archbishop of Dublin (1256-1271).[106] The prior of the 'Great Church' also served as a juror at an inquisition on the archiepiscopal manor of Castlekevin sometime between *c.*1257 and 1263.[107] In 1263 there is also reference to 'the canons of the Disart of St Keyuin [Kevin].' 'Díseart Caoimhghin' was identified by Price as the settlement at Reefert Church on the north side of the Upper Lake.[108] The canons here had been granted lands by Laurence O'Toole, archbishop of Dublin (1162-1180)[109] and the 'desertum' of St Kevin was mentioned in a grant of 1198 as an appurtenance of the abbot of Glendalough.[110] These monastic houses at Reefert and the 'Great Church' clearly became incorporated into the Anglo-Norman system, as were two others in Glendalough whose priors participated in the inquisition at Castlekevin (*c.*1257-1263).

One of these was St Saviour's Priory, located about 1km to the east of the monastic city.[111] It was founded *c.*1152-1162 and, after 1216, became subject to the Arrouasian Priory of All Saints, Dublin. In the grant of St Saviour's to All Saints, the archbishop stated that 'we have obtained a prescript from the Holy See on this matter to the effect that we shall subject to the regular discipline of the one house and prelate those canons that are scattered and not so well governed.'[112] This probably refers to the canons at 'Díseart Caoimhghin' whose agreement with the archbishop of Dublin in 1263 was sealed by the latter and 'at the canons' insistence, by the prior of St Saviour's.'[113] Another group of canons who were 'scattered' across the valley were those at the priory of 'Rupe'. The archbishop's intention *c.*1216 was apparently to gather the three houses at Glendalough together under the control of All Saints in Dublin.

'Donohu, prior of Rupe, near Glendalough' was the third prior from the valley to attend the Castlekevin inquisition.[114] *Rupe* is Latin for 'cliff,' the Old Irish word being *sceillic*, steep rock, crag.[115] It refers to the place now known as Temple-na-Skellig,[116] located on the south side of the upper lake at Glendalough. The site is surrounded by steep cliffs and is only accessible, with any ease, by boat. A series of steps lead up from the shore to a platform cut out of the mountainside. This is the first of two such platforms and on it are the remains of a small, single-chamber church. To the east is a second platform, somewhat larger than the first. Steps lead up to it on the east and west sides and the remains of a paved causeway run towards the centre of the platform from the eastern slopes. The church has an undecorated west doorway with inclined jambs and a flat lintel. The structure is clearly pre-Romanesque, although the two-light east window suggests a partial reconstruction in Romanesque times. The early medieval or pre-Romanesque churches at Glendalough do not have two-light windows. The only parallel to the east window at Temple-na-Skellig is to be found in St Saviour's Priory.

The second or 'settlement' platform was excavated by Henry in 1956-1958.[117] She found, in the earliest phase, evidence of wattle huts connected by paved paths. They were built in a period when iron was in use, but no dating could be deduced from finds at this level. It seems likely that they were early medieval remains of a monastic settlement.[118] The huts had been destroyed by a large avalanche of slabs. These slabs were later cleaved away. In the middle of the platform a wooden house resting on a base of stones was built. Pottery and coins dated its period of occupation from the late twelfth century to the late fourteenth century or the fifteenth century. It was destroyed by an avalanche of slabs.[119]

In 1198 'Scelec' was listed as one of the appurtances of Glendalough confirmed to Abbot Thomas by Pope Innocent III.[120] The wooden structure which was occupied from the late twelfth century may have served as domestic quarters for a monastery which was controlled by Abbot Thomas. By 1257-1263, when Prior Donohu of Rupe attended the inquisition at Castlekevin, control over the monastery had passed into the hands of the archbishop of Dublin.[121] This is the only reference we have to the priory at Rupe or Temple-na-Skellig. Despite its disappearance from Anglo-Norman records, occupation continued at the site for over a century afterwards.

Later excavations at a site in Glendalough which was located between the monastic city and Trinity church provided evidence of quite an extensive iron-working industry.[122] Pottery dated the iron-working activity to the thirteenth or fourteenth century.[123] Glendalough thus retained something of its economic significance long after 1169. A desire to control the iron-working industry, as well as the monastic houses, ecclesiastical offices, and lands of Glendalough, must have generated an Anglo-Norman interest in the 'monastic city.' While the bishopric and abbacy eventually disappeared under the impact of the feudal system, monasticism and industrial activity continued to be significant aspects of Glendalough's settlement for well over one hundred years after the Anglo-Normans arrived. The archdiocese of Dublin had some success in asserting its authority over Glendalough's priories up to the late thirteenth century. As war broke out in the Wicklow mountains and control over the area slipped away from the colonial government in Dublin, Glendalough became part of 'the land of war.' The deanery of Wicklow (within the archdiocese of Dublin) received no taxes from the prebend of Glendalough in 1294 because of war.[124] The tax levied on the priory at the 'Great Church' was received by the deanery in 1322.[125] This, however, is the last record we find of Glendalough's priories. Monastic life may have continued outside the control of the archdiocese. This is suggested by archaeological evidence of settlement at Temple-na-Skellig over a century after it was last mentioned (in 1257-1263) in administrative records. We should not, therefore, assume that the disappearance of Glendalough from Anglo-Norman records necessarily meant that settlement there ceased.

The O'Byrnes and O'Tooles met with increasing success in pushing back Anglo-Norman settlement on the fringes of the mountains throughout the fourteenth century. Apart from Temple-na-Skellig, there is no evidence of what sites in Glendalough were occupied in this century. In 1398, both the Annals of Clonmacnois[126] and the Annals of Connacht[127] mention the burning of Glendalough by the English during the summer. Settlement still existed in the valley and this rare fourteenth-century reference to the former 'monastic city' in the Gaelic annals implies that the burning was an event of considerable importance. Neither annalist gives a reason for the burning, but in June of the same year the O'Byrnes and O'Tooles had killed 'the earl of March and many other Englishmen' near Carlow.[128] The earl was Roger Mortimer, lord deputy of Ireland and heir to the English throne.[129]

Having entered into an agreement with Richard II only three years earlier, this action by the O'Byrnes and O'Tooles was bound to provoke retaliation. As Glendalough was in the heart of the mountainous country, which they controlled, its burning in the summer of 1398 may have been retaliatory.

From the end of the fourteenth century the O'Byrnes attempted, with some success, to establish themselves in the office of archdeacon of Glendalough.[130] In 1468 the archbishop of Dublin complained of the effects of 'continual war of the Irish enemies and English rebels' on 'the revenues of the precentorship, treasureship and the archdeaconry of Glendalough.'[131] Five years later the archbishop moved to suppress attempts at reviving the 'corbanate' (apparently the bishopric) of Glendalough.[132] Despite this a Dominican friar, Denis White, held the office of bishop of Glendalough from 1481 to 1497.[133] It appears that the Irish had turned their attention to establishing Glendalough as a separate diocese again.[134] The possibility of restoring Glendalough to its former glory as a diocesan see must have seemed very real for the sixteen years that Bishop White held office. It is apparent from documents relating to these events that a settlement of some size existed at Glendalough in the late fifteenth century. The 1473 pastoral letter was addressed to 'the clerks, vassals, betaghs and other inhabitants of the vill and whole lordship of Glendalough.'[135] 'Vill' was a territorial division under the feudal system which consisted of a number of houses or buildings with their adjacent lands.[136] Later in the letter the archbishop appoints a 'custodian of the vill and church of Glindelach.'[137] We cannot be sure which church of Glendalough is being referred to here, and there is no further detail available on the type or number of houses and other buildings which made up the vill. What is clear, however, is that a populated settlement existed in the valley in 1473. While the archbishop of Dublin still held titular control over this settlement, it is apparent that effective control had been lost due to the activities of the 'Irish enemies and English rebels'.

The continued presence of Gaelic chieftains hostile to the English led to a major series of military campaigns in the late sixteenth century. Lord Deputy (August 1580-September 1582) Grey de Wilton led an English army into the mountains in 1581. In the early stages of his campaign, while 'Castle Comin' and Castlekevin were being refortified in June, 1581, the lord deputy wrote: 'I searched all the mountaines and fastnes adjoyning, and took from the rebels stoare of their leane and weak cattel and slew divers in those roads and burned their villages and places of relief as Clandelough and suche like.'[138] The 'vill and church' over which the archbishop of Dublin still hoped to establish control in 1473 had clearly become part of the 'rebel' country of Fiagh MacHugh O'Byrne and his allies by 1581. The monastic city of pre-Norman times one thousand years after its foundation by St Kevin had become but a small part of the Gaelic struggle to survive the Tudor conquest. Located in the heart of 'the land of war' since the late thirteenth century, Glendalough nonetheless survived as a settlement into early modern times. From the early thirteenth to the end of the sixteenth century, no new structures in stone were built at Glendalough. Many of the lands and revenues which formed the economic base of Glendalough's status had been lost to the archdiocese of Dublin. The aspiration to diocesan status for Glendalough did not, however, die out until the late fifteenth century.

Other sites

The hillfort at Rathgall, the ringforts at Ballinacor and the monastic city at Glendalough are important as pre-Norman settlement forms which continued to have significance in Wicklow after 1169. The settlement history of county Wicklow cannot, however, be reduced to a simplistic notion of displaced Gaelic septs living in ringforts and eking out an existence which involved raiding the Anglo-Norman mottes, moated sites and stone castles. The MacGiolla Mo Cholmoc, who controlled lands in south Dublin and north Wicklow before 1169 co-operated with the Anglo-Normans in their early years in Ireland.[139] They became anglicised as the Fitzdermots and were accepted into the Anglo-Norman aristocracy. There is considerable evidence of the O'Tooles securing legal title to lands within the Anglo-Norman system in the first centuries of the conquest.[140] Even Glenmalure was held legally of the crown down to *c.*1290.[141] From the 1270s Irish attacks on colonial settlements began a process of Anglo-Norman decline.[142] This, combined with the problems caused by bad harvests, famine and plague from the late thirteenth into the fourteenth century, led eventually to increased Irish control over lands which were formerly Anglo-Norman.[143] What had been called the 'Gaelic Reconquest' of Ireland would more aptly be termed the 'New Conquest' in Wicklow. The lands in the north, east and south of the county and the mountainous regions, where the O'Tooles and O'Byrnes emerge so strongly in the fourteenth and later centuries, were not being reconquered by them. These lands, before 1169, were controlled by tribes whose prominence was lost with the coming of the Anglo-Normans.[144] There is considerable evidence that in the 'New Conquest' the O'Tooles established important settlements at Ballytened (now Powerscourt) and Castlekevin, both originally Anglo-Norman settlements from the thirteenth century onwards. The O'Tooles who established themselves at Castlekevin and Powerscourt appear to have done so initially through co-operation with the Crown.[145] The O'Byrnes established important settlements at Kiltimon[146] and possibly Kilcommon[147] some time after the middle of the fourteenth century. Both Kiltimon and Kilcommon were previous Anglo-Norman settlements. There is no evidence that raths were constructed at Powerscourt, Castlekevin, Kiltimon or Kilcommon. At Powerscourt there was a castle which appears to have been incorporated into the later mansion.[148] A motte-and-bailey survives at Castlekevin, where there is also evidence of later stone structures. There is a tower-house at Kiltimon[149] and at Kilcommon there was a moated site with a later stone castle beside it.[150] The occupation of these formerly Anglo-Norman settlements by Gaelic Irish families was an important element of the 'New Conquest' from the fourteenth century onwards.

Conclusion

Although defined as settlements generally associated with pre-Norman times rather than the period 1169-1600, Rathgall, Ballinacor and Glendalough are in other respects very different. Rathgall, originally settled in the Bronze Age, obviously provided some enticement to late medieval settlers by virtue of its location and, probably, the existence of ramparts there. Ballincor's raths represent the remarkable survival of a settlement form which, originating in the Iron Age, could still be used in early modern times in a remote, inaccessible location such as Glenmalure. Glendalough, founded in the sixth century, appears to have had continuous settlement down to the late sixteenth century. Building continued there in the decades immediately succeeding the invasion of 1169. Monasteries still existed at four separate sites in the valley in the mid-thirteenth century and possibly at Temple-na-Skellig for over a century later. The thirteenth or fourteenth century iron-working in Glendalough meant that something of its economic significance also survived the Anglo-Norman invasion. Despite loss of diocesan status and much of the lands controlled by its bishops and abbots, Glendalough became the focus of a serious attempt to re-establish its former glory in the fifteenth century. A settlement of some size appears to have existed there at the same time and in the late sixteenth century was important enough to be burned by the lord deputy campaigning against the Gaelic 'rebel' Fiagh MacHugh O'Byrne.

It would be simplistic to describe Glendalough throughout the period 1169-1600 as a 'Gaelic' settlement. Despite differences between Rathgall, Ballinacor and Glendalough, however, they were all pre-Norman settlement forms which were part of Gaelic Wicklow at some time in the late medieval or early modern eras. The occupation of Anglo-Norman sites was also significant from the time of the Gaelic

Revival and if we can begin to speak of a 'Gaelic settlement pattern' in Wicklow, we must start by recognising the complexity of the site types involved. There can be no doubt that as the last Gaelic septs of the Wicklow mountains struggled to hold on to their lands and their way of life in the sixteenth century, an awareness of sites associated with pre-Norman Ireland reinforced their sense of having a distinct identity to the English. One poem contained in the *Leabhar Branach* celebrates the similarities between Ballinacor and Emain Macha (Navan Fort), the seat of the prehistoric kings of Ulster.[151] Emain Macha, Tara, Rathcroghan and Dún Ailinne form a special group of sites which functioned as tribal and ceremonial centres during the Celtic Iron Age.[152] While the comparison of Ballinacor to Emain Macha in the sixteenth century may be somewhat anachronistic, it illustrates the symbolic significance which pre-Norman sites had in Gaelic Wicklow. Other branches of the O'Byrnes might reside in castles at Kiltimon and Kilcommon which were built by the 'Gall.' But the raths of the O'Byrnes of Gabhal Raghnaill at Ballinacor, a settlement form which originated in the Iron Age of the *Tâin* and *Emain Macha*, could more realistically evoke a sense of identity with the Celtic past.

Rathgall, Ballinacor and Glendalough all had some connection with Ireland's pre-Norman past. They should be viewed as a distinct group of site types within a Gaelic settlement pattern which also included the motte-and-bailey and stone castles originally built by Anglo-Norman colonists.

References

1. R.A.S. MacAlister, 'Two ringforts submerged by Poolaphuca reservoir,' in *R.S.A.I. Jn.*, lxxiii (1943), pp 145-149.
2. M. O'Connor, 'The excavation of three earthen ringforts in the Liffey Valley' in *R.S.A.I. Jn.*, lxxiv (1944), pp 53-60.
3. For a general account of hillforts, including details of their classification and the sites in county Wicklow, see B. Raftery, 'Irish hillforts' in *The Iron Age in the Irish See Province*, C.B.A. Research Report 9, (London, 1972), pp 37-58.
4. On the significance of the 'monastic cities' in general see C. Doherty, 'The monastic town in early medieval Ireland' in H.B. Clarke and A. Simms (ed.) *The comparative history of urban origins in non-Roman Europe* (British Archaeological Report 5255, 2 vols, 1985). For Glendalough in particular see H.G. Leask, Glendalough (Dublin, no date) and L. Barrow, *Glendalough and Saint Kevin* (Dundalk, 1984).
5. E. Rynne, 'Some destroyed sites at Shannon Airport, Co. Clare, in *R.I.A. Proc.*, lxiii (1963), C, pp 245-77.
6. See A.F. Barrett, The ring-fort: a study in settlement geography with special reference to southern Donegal and the Dingle area, county Kerry (Ph.D. Thesis, unpublished, Queen's University Belfast, 1972). This work is referred to and its results discussed in the context of 'Land and people, *c.* 1300' by R.E. Glasscock in *N.H.I.*, iii, pp 227-8.

7. See T.E. MacNeill, *Anglo-Norman Ulster* (Edinburgh, 1985), p. 115. Although abandoned as the O'Neills' main settlement for Dungannon at this time, there is evidence that the rath at Tullaghoge continued to be occupied up to the early seventeenth century. It may have been occupied at that time by the O'Hagans, hereditary guardians of Tullaghoge. The site continued in use as an inauguration centre for the O'Neills until September 1602, when Lord Deputy Mountjoy broke to pieces 'The Stone of Kings' there. See Hayes-McCoy, *Ulster and other Irish maps c. 1600*, pp 8-9 and plate v.
8. See Hayes-McCoy, op. cit., plates v and xi.
9. B. Raftery has published the following partial reports of the excavations at Rathgall: 'The Rathgall hillfort, co. Wicklow in *Antiquity* 44 (1970), pp 51-54; 'Rathgall, co. Wicklow: 1970 excavations' in *Antiquity* 45 (1971); 'Rathgall: a late Bronze Age burial in Ireland' in *Antiquity* 47 (1973), pp 293-295; 'Rathgall and Irish hillfort problems' in D.W. Harding (ed.) *Hillforts: later prehistoric earthworks of Britain and Ireland* (London, 1976), pp 339-357, 478-482, 532-539; 'Rathgall Hillfort' in *Ogham: Tullow's Historic Magazine* (6th edition), 1990, pp 19-27. Most of these articles deal with the prehistoric evidence from Rathgall in detail. For greater details on the medieval evidence I have relied on personal communication with the excavator. The interpretation of the archaeological and historical evidence as pointing towards a Gaelic occupation is my own.
10. P. Wallace, 'The archaeology of Viking Dublin' in Clarke and Simms, *Urban origins*; i, pp 117-125. Little has survived in Dublin in the Anglo-Norman period compared to the tenth and eleventh century houses and Wallace in vol ii of the same book writing on 'The archaeology of Anglo-Norman Dublin' states (p. 390) that '... most town houses may have been of traditional post-and-wattle construction,' although there was some evidence of other types of structure.
11. C. Lynn, 'Deerpark farms, Glenarm, co. Antrim' in *Arch. Ir.* i (1987), p. 14.
12. See P. Wallace, 'The archaeology of Viking Dublin,' p. 125. The 8.5m x 4.75m is described by Wallace as an 'average' measurement for Type 1 houses. These houses are pre-Norman.
13. Caroline Sandez, Department of Archaeology, U.C.D. is currently working on the medieval pottery found at Rathgall.
14. R. Ó Floinn, 'Handmade medieval pottery in S.E. Ireland – Leinster cooking ware' in *Keimelia: Studies in medieval archaeology and history in memory of Tom Delaney* (Galway, 1988), pp 326-348, particularly p. 333.
15. These details have been published by Raftery in his 1976 article, pp 340-348.
16. See Ó Floinn, op. cit., p. 333.
17. Ibid.
18. For Saintonge pottery in Anglo-Norman Dublin see P. Wallace, 'The archaeology of Anglo-Norman Dublin', pp 395-396.
19. *Alen's reg.*, p. 134.
20. *Cal. justic. rolls Ire.*, 1292-1303, p. 61.
21. *Red Bk. Ormond*, p. 2.
22. Ibid., p. 6.
23. Ibid., p. 6.
24. Price, *Placenames*, vi, p. 362.
25. After unsuccessful campaigns in 1274 and 1276, a new justiciar, Robert de Ufford, led a successful expedition against the Gaelic Irish in Glenmalure in 1277. *Cal. doc. Ire.*, 1252-84, no. 1400.
26. In 1277, de Ufford reported to the king that: 'The affairs of the latter are much improved. The thieves who were in Glindelory are departed, many of them

having gone to another strong place' *Cal. Doc. Ire. 1252-84*, no. 1400.

27. *The annals of Clyn*, 1331.
28. Ibid., 1336.
29. Ibid., 1334. The Duffry or 'Dubhthir' was a thickly wooded district between the river Slaney and the mountains. Just before the Anglo-Norman invasion Murchad Ua Brain (O'Byrne) of the Duffry was an underlord of Dermot Mac Murrough. See *N.H.I.*, ii, p. 63. The Duffry, a district mainly in the barony of Scarawalsh, was intensely colonised after the Anglo-Norman invasion. For details, see E. Brooks *Knights fees in counties Wexford, Carlow and Kilkenny (thirteenth to fifteenth century)* (Dublin, 1950), pp 129-141.
30. *The Annals of Clyn*, 1336.
31. *Rot. pat. Hib.*, p. 47.
32. Ibid., p. 66.
33. See A.J. Otway-Ruthven, *Medieval Ireland* (London and New York 1968), pp 160 and 287.
34. *A Roll of the Proceedings of the King's Council in Ireland ... 1392-3*, ed. J. Graves (London, 1887), p. 41.
35. *A.U.*, p. 556.
36. E. Curtis, *Richard II in Ireland 1394-5* ... (Oxford, 1927), pp 166-167.
37. For a full list of sites see *Sites and Monuments Record, Co. Wicklow* (Office of Public Works, Dublin, 1986).
38. Price, *Placenames*, ii, p. 57.
39. *A.F.M.*, vi, p. 1956.
40. *Dictionary of the Irish language based mainly on Old and Middle Irish texts* (Compact edn., Dublin, 1983), ed. E.A. Quin, p. 63.
41. B. Graham 'Medieval timber and earthwork fortifications' in *Medieval Archaeology*, xxxii, (1988), p. 115. Graham is here referring to the twelfth and thirteenth centuries, but it is well to beware of assuming that *caislen* in the Irish Annals always refers to a stone castle.
42. *A.F.M.*, vi, p. 1955.
43. *Dictionary of the Irish language* ... p. 256.
44. Ibid., p. 270.
45. H.F. Hore, *History of the town and county of Wexford* 6 vols (London, 1900-1911), vi, p. 424.
46. *Collins dictionary of the English language,* ed. P. Hanks (London and Glasgow, 1979), p. 1124.
47. *The shorter Oxford English dictionary on historical principles* (Oxford, 1973), ii, p. 1605.
48. Hayes-McCoy, *Ulster and other maps c. 1600,* Plate v.
49. *Cal. S.P. Ire.*, ii, p. 296.
50. Ibid., p. 531.
51. O.S. 6-inch series (surveyed 1839), sheet 29.
52. See Price, *Placenames*, ii, p. 57 and S. Mac Airt (ed.), *Leabhar Branach* (Dublin, 1944), p. 416 for 'Baile na Cora' and p. vii for dating of poems contained in the book.
53. O.S. 6-inch series (surveyed 1839), sheet 29.
54. *Cal. S.P. Ire.*, ii, p. 296.
55. Ibid., p. 531.
56. Grey's letter to the Privy Council, quoted in Hore, *Wexford*, i, p. 402. Grey found Castlekevin and Kilcommon abandoned but employed masons and carpenters to rebuild them and left garrisons in both.

57. *Leabhar Branach*, p. 378.
58. Ibid., p. 146, lines 3845-3848. This is a translation of the original for which I must thank Peadar Smyth M.A.
59. Ibid., line 3849.
60. *Dictionary of the Irish language*, p. 429 under LES.
61. S.P. Ó Riordáin, *Antiquities of the Irish countryside* (5th edn. London, 1979), p. 30.
62. *Cal. Carew MSS*, ii, p. 249.
63. Russel recorded the work of building the fort in various entries in his diary between 5 Feb. 1595 and 22 Feb. 1595: see *Cal. Carew MSS*, ii, pp 226-32. The quotation comes from a report by Captain Price on the expedition: see Hore, *Wexford*, vi, p. 424. There is no evidence, archaeological or documentary, that Russel built new structures at Ballinacor. He probably simply re-fortified the existing structures after cutting down the 'plashed' wood that existed there. In 1601 at Mount Norris, county Armagh, Lord Deputy Mountjoy built a new fort around the nucleus of an old ringfort. See *Ulster and other maps*, *c.*1600 plate ii and pp 3-4.
64. This is apparent from various reports received by Russel from Ballinacor, most notably on 19 April 1595 and 2 Sept. 1596. See *Cal. Carew MSS*, ii, pp 247-248.
65. *Cal. Carew MSS*, ii, p. 248.
66. *Cal. S.P. Ire.*, vi, (1596-1597), p. 53, where Ballinacor is described as '... the fort of Mount Russel which he (the Lord Deputy) took from Feagh.'
67. *Cal. Carew MSS*, ii, p. 249.
68. Ibid., pp 249-250.
69. Hore, *Wexford* vi, p. 402.
70. This happened in Lord Grey's time, in 1581: see Hore, *Wexford* vi, p. 402.
71. *Cal. Carew MSS*, ii, p. 227; work was in progress on 17 Feb. 1595.
72. Idem.
73. Ibid., p. 250.
74. *The martyrology of Oengus the Culdee*, ed. W. Stokes (London, 1905), p. 25.
75. *Dictionary of the Irish language*, 512.107.
76. *Ruam* can also mean 'burial place, cemetery' and can be found as *Ruam* meaning simply 'Rome', *Dictionary of the Irish language*, 512.107.
77. See Doherty, 'The monastic town'.
78. A. Mac Shamhráin, 'Prosopographica Glindelachensis: The monastic church of Glendalough and its community cxix sixth to thirteenth centuries' in *R.S.A.I. Jn.* cxix (1989), p. 79. Also A. Mac Shamhráin, 'The Ui Muiredaig and the abbacy of Glendalough in the eleventh to thirteenth centuries', in *Cambridge Medieval Studies*, xxv (summer 1993), pp 55-75.
79. See Smyth, *Celtic Leinster*, p. 146 for a map showing the extent of Glendalough diocese. The Synod of Rathbreasil, 1111, named Glendalough as one of the bishoprics of Leinster; see M.V. Ronan, 'The union of the diocese of Glendalough and Dublin in 1216,' *R.S.A.I. Jn.*, lx (1930), pp 56-7.
80. A. Mac Shamhráin, 'The monastic church of Glendalough', p. 91.
81. L. Swan 'Monastic proto-towns in early medieval Ireland: the evidence of aerial photography, plan, analysis and survey', in Clarke and Simms (eds), *Urban Origins*, pp 77-102, particularly p. 95 and p. 98.
82. The union of the dioceses of Dublin and Glendalough received papal confirmation on 25 Feb. 1216; *Alen's reg.*, p. 38. 'Tadeus Otothyll, abbot of Glendalough' is the last known person to hold that office and the latest reference to him is *c.*1228-1255; *Alen's reg.*, p. 76.

83. Leask, *Glendalough* , p. 7.
84. R. Stalley, *The Cistercian monasteries of Ireland* (London and New Haven, 1987), p. 242 and p. 247.
85. Stylistic links with Baltinglass Abbey coincide with documentary evidence that St Saviour's was founded by Laurence O'Toole, Abbot of Glendalough *c.* 1152-1162; C. Plummer, 'Vie et Miracles de St. Laurent, archeveque de Dublin' *Anal. Boll.*, xxxiii (1914), 135 and Stalley, *Cistercian monasteries*, pp 273-4.
86. R. Stalley 'Corcomroe abbey, some observations on its architectural history' *R.S.A.I. Jn.*, cv (1975), pp 25-46, particularly pp 26-27. Thanks to R. Moss, whose unpublished research on the Priests' House helped with comparison to other sites and dating.
87. W. Wilde, *Journal of the Royal Historical and Archaeological Association* (1874), p. 466. The tombstones can still be seen, dating from 1759 and 1772 with a later one, from after the building was restored, dated 1893.
88. H.G. Leask, *Glendalough*, p. 27.
89. Ibid., p. 30.
90. Dr Patrick Wyse-Jackson of the Dept. of Geology. T.C.D., identified the stone as oolitic limestone from Dundry quarries. Professor Roger Stalley, Dept. of Art and Architecture, was also consulted.
91. D.M. Waterman, 'Somersetshire and other foreign building stone in medieval Ireland, *c.* 1175-1400,' *U.J.A.*, xxxiii, pp 63-75.
92. Ibid., p. 63, where the use of Dundry at Christchurch is given at *c.*1175. R. Stalley, *Architecture and sculpture in Ireland c. 1150-1350* (Dublin, 1971), p. 584, suggests that the first phase of Anglo-Norman building at Christchurch began soon after 1181, but his 1975 article (op. cit., n. 86) dates the first phase at Christchurch to *c.* 1186-1200.
93. Waterman, (op. cit.), p. 65.
94. R. Stalley, *Cistercian monasteries*, p. 92.
95. Ibid., p. 92.
96. Stalley, *Architecture and sculpture*, p. 58.
97. Ibid.
98. Ibid., pp 58-59.
99. Ibid., pp 58-68 (Christchurch), p. 71 (Waterford), pp 71-74 (Kilkenny).
100. *Crede Mihi*, ed. J.T. Gilbert (Dublin, 1897), p. 31; Chapter to 'John (Comin) archbishop of Dublin, and his successors: the episcopate of Glendalough, with all its appurtanances.'
101. *Alen's reg.*, p. 38.
102. For summary and sources see Mac Shamhráin, 'The monastic church of Glendalough', pp 91-2.
103. See n. 80 above.
104. *Registrum prioratus omnium sanctorum juxta Dublin*, ed. R. Butler (Dublin, 1845), xi, for grant of abbacy of Glendalough (and bishopric) to archbishop of Dublin, A. Gwynn and R. Hadcock, *Medieval religious houses in Ireland with an appendix to early sites*, (London, 1970), p. 177 suggest that the abbey may have become Arroasian at the time of Benignus or Thomas (i.e. *c.* 1162-1213).
105. Taxation of 1302-07 on the 'Priory of the great church de Glydelagh' received 1322; *Cal. doc. Ire.*, 1302-7, v, p. 241.
106. *Alen's reg.*, p. 142.
107. *Alen's reg.*, p. 110.
108. For 1263 mention of canons see *Alen's reg.*, p. 97; identification of site in Price, *Placenames*, i, p. 22.

109. *Alen's reg.*, p. 8.
110. Ibid., p. 24.
111. Ibid., p. 110, 'Thomas, Prior of St Saviour's of Glendelache,' listed as a juror at the Castlekevin inquisition.
112. *Registrum prioratius omnium sanctorum*, p. 100.
113. *Alen's reg.*, p. 97.
114. Ibid., p. 110.
115. *Dictionary of the Irish Language*, 524.80.
116. 'Teampull na Skellig first recorded in 1786; Price, *Placenames*, i, p. 40.
117. Council for Old World Archaeology (COWA), *Surveys and bibliographies British Isles, Area 1*, No. 11 (1960), p. 13 contains the only published account of Dr Henry's excavation. This paragraph is a paraphrase of the very brief report found there.
118. The report of the excavation states simply of this phase, 'It may be of Early Christian date.'
119. COWA report, p. 13.
120. *Alen's reg.*, p. 24.
121. Ibid., p. 110.
122. C. Manning, 'Excavations at Glendalough,' *W.H.A.S. Jn.*, xvi (1984), pp 342-7.
123. Ibid., pp 346.
124. Cal. Christ Church Deeds, no. 150 in *P.R.I. rep. D.K. 20.*
125. See n. 103 above.
126. *Ann. Clon.*, 321.
127. *Ann. Conn.*, 1398.9.
128. *Ann. Clon.*, 320. see also *N.H.I.*, ii, p. 392.
129. *N.H.I.*, ii, p. 392.
130. Ronan, *Union of the dioceses* ... pp 66-67 contains a list from the annals of archdeacons from 1399 to 1491. Five O'Byrnes and one O'Toole are listed as archdeacons in that time.
131. *Alen's reg.*, p. 244.
132. Ibid., p. 245. See n. 130 on 'corbanate' meaning 'bishopric.'
133. *Alen's reg.*, pp 253-4 for Denis White's resignation; *Cal. papal letters* xiii, 744 for the provision of 'Denis Fuyt' (White) to the see at Glendalough in 1481.
134. *Alen's reg.*, 254 has a note added to this document by Archbishop Alen in 1530 stating: 'This is in favour of the king, when the see is vacant and against McMorrow altogether.' This suggests that in 1530 it was believed that McMurrough was behind the move to re-establish the 'corbanate' (from this note apparently the bishopric) of Glendalough.
135. *Alen's reg.*, p. 245.
136. *The shorter Oxford English dictionary on historical principles*, ed. C.T. Onions (Oxford, 1990), p. 2475.
137. *Alen's reg.*, p. 245.
138. Hore, *Wexford*, vi, pp 402-3 contains a full transcript of the letter.
139. Strongbow's brother-in-law was one of the Mac Giolla mo Cholmoc and submitted to Henry II at Dublin in 1171-2; see *Expugnatio Hibernica by Giraldus Cambrensis*, ed. F.X. Martin (Dublin, 1978), p. 94. In 1207 Dermot Mac Giolla mo Cholmoc had a grant from King John of all lands held by his father i.e. Liamhain or Newcastle Lyons and the manor of Rathdown, near Bray: see *Cal. doc. Ire., 1171-1251*, no. 356. Dermot's son John (John FitzDermot) married into a leading Norman family, his wife being Claricia, daughter of Gilbert Fitzgriffin, who was a nephew of Raymond le Crois: see Price, *Placenames*, vii, p. xxxv.

140. See grants in *Alen's reg.*, pp 8, 97, and 136 for grants relating to the same lands in the Glendalough-Glenmalure area dated to 1162-80, 1263 and 1256-71. On the identification of these lands see Price, *Placenames*, i, pp 21 . Two of the grants (1162-80 and 1256-71) are specifically to O'Tooles. See also *Alen's reg.*, pp 81-2 and p. 114 for grants relating to Meyler O'Toole in 1228-55 and 1264 respectively. See *Red Bk Ormond*, pp 19-20 for an extent of the early fourteenth century showing that several O'Tooles held lands of the Butlers in Imaal by free tenure.

141. *Cal. doc. Ire., 1285-92*, p. 313, a petition by John de Ufford to the king dated *c.*1290 to enfeoff him of land in the 'marches of Alindelury which the Irish inhabit and hold of the king.'

142. This process can be seen, for example, on the archbishop of Dublin's lands in county Wicklow. In 1270 the justiciary was commanded to aid the archbishop against those rebelling against his authority: see *Alen's reg.*, p. 134. By 1279 the archbishop's manor of Castlekevin was waste on account of war with the Irish, *P.R.I. rep. D.K.*, 36, p. 42. The last traceable accounts of the manor were produced in 1295, *P.R.I. rep. D.K.*, 38, p. 47.

143. *The Annals of Clyn* record plague in 1271, bad weather, food scarcity and hunger in 1294, famine in 1318, storms in 1329 and 1337 and heavy snows which led to damage and hunger in 1334.

144. The lands of the Uí Briúin Cualann and the Uí Théig, for example, were partly incorporated into new royal manors called Obrun and Othe in the area between Bray and Wicklow. The Uí Briúin Cualann and Uí Théig never regained control over these lands. See Price, *Placenames*, vii, 'Historical background.'

145. The O'Tooles appear to have gradually established themselves at Castlekevin by co-operating with the Anglo-Normans *c.*1257-1263, 'Elias Othothel was sergeant of the country' around Castlekevin; *Alen's reg.*, p. 111. By 1343, however, Castlekevin had been destroyed by the Irish. The O'Tooles appear to have taken over Castlekevin around this time. In 1419 the lord lieutenant led an expedition to destroy the castle there apparently in retaliation for an O'Toole raid on Ballymore-Eustace (a manor of the archbishop of Dublin). Under the 'Surrender and Regrant' policy the O'Tooles received legal title to the manor of Castlekevin. See G.H. Orpen, 'Castrum Keyvini: Castlekevin' in *R.S.A.I. Jn.*, xxxviii (1908), pp 17-27. The campaigns of the 1580s and 1590s saw the establishment of English garrisons at Castlekevin.

146. Kiltimon, an anglicisation of 'Coill tSiomóin,' was called 'Symondeswode in O'Bryns contre' in 1449. It was here that O'Byrne submitted to Richard Duke of York in that year: E. Curtis, as viceroy of Ireland, 1447-1460; *R.S.A.I. Jn.*, lxii (1932), *Richard Duke of York*, p. 166. For the Anglo-Norman background see Price, *Placenames*, vii, pp 407-9.

147. A genealogy of a branch of the O'Byrnes who were in occupation of Kilcommon in the sixteenth century reads: 'Clann Sheamuis mic Cathaoir i tighearna Bhaile na Coille and in Bhaile Fhiothaid oile Cille Commain.' 'The family of Seamus son of Cathaoir, this is, Lord of Ballinakill (literally, 'the townland of the wood') and three other wooded townlands at Kilcommon'. (Quoted by Price from *Leabhar Branach* manuscript in 'The Byrnes' country in county Wicklow in the sixteenth century,' *R.S.A.I. Jn.*, lxiii (1933), p. 188. This may be the origin of the O'Byrne occupation of the site.

148. In 1355 the justiciar agreed with Odo O'Toole that he would defend English settlements in south county Dublin from the hostile invasions of the O'Byrnes. Odo O'Toole was based at 'Balytyn' (Powerscourt). See *Rot. pat. Hib.*, p. 59,

nos 11 and 127. The O'Tooles were granted Powerscourt under the 'surrender and regrant' policy in 1540, although the castle there had been rebuilt by the Earl of Kildare in 1482. For details on 'Balytyn' (Powerscourt) see Price 'Powerscourt and the territory of Fercullen' in *R.S.A.I. Jn.*, lxxxiii (1953), pp 117-32. The seventh viscount of Powerscourt in *A description and history of Powerscourt* (London, 1903), stated: 'I feel sure that the old castle was incorporated in the present home, because in the two central rooms, both on the ground and first floors, the walls are of great thickness, the embrasures of the windows in these two rooms being some 8 feet (2.44m) deep.'

149. Now known as Duncan Castle. The Down Survey map of 1654 shows Duncan Castle standing on top of a hill surrounded by thatched houses. The present castle is lower down the hill and may be an imitation or reconstruction of the original one.

150. Only slight remains of a corner-tower of this castle now survive. When O'Curry visited the site in 1839, however, there were the remains of two round towers and traces of two others, the four enclosing an area of 13.4m square. These may have been the corner towers of a tower-house. There is also an enclosure *c.* 60m square on the north-western side of the 'castle' which, in 1839, has 'a wide, deep fosse and mound of great depth, breadth and height' around the south, west and northern sides. See Ordnance Survey letters Wicklow (typed copies in T.C.D. library), pp 375-376.

151. *Leabhar Branach*, poem 56, pp 197-203.

152. See B. Raftery, n. 3 above.

Castle Howard (Bartlett).

Chapter 8

SETTLERS' UTILISATION OF THE NATURAL RESOURCES

ROLF LOEBER

The extraordinary beauty of the Wicklow forests has been captured in paintings, displaying wooded glens, rugged rocks, long valleys, and waterfalls. Images of Wicklow's landscape prior to the 1680s are not known to have survived.[1] However, that landscape probably was even more primeval and inaccessible than is depicted in the surviving paintings.

Englishmen settling in the area in the sixteenth and seventeenth centuries were often entrepreneurs. The settlers in county Wicklow established timber and iron industries, quickly profiting from the forests that covered large parts of the county. The industry brought innovations in technology to the county, and certainly extended its links, through inland rivers and maritime commerce with other countries such as England, the Northern Netherlands, France, and Spain. The settlers' appreciation of the landscape, however, was not solely mercantile. By creating several deer parks, they derived pleasure from their environment as well. This chapter reviews settlers' utilisation of natural resources in the county, especially during the seventeenth century.

Deer parks

The development of deer parks in county Wicklow in the seventeenth century reflected a propensity among the wealthy settlers in Ireland to hunt deer in the 'protection' of their park rather than in the open countryside. In the preceding century, only two deer parks are known to have existed: the earl of Ormond's at Kilkenny and the earl of Kildare's at Maynooth.[2] In the early seventeenth century, the trend for settlers to establish deer parks had been initiated by Sir Arthur Chichester, the lord deputy, who by 1611 had created a deer park at Belfast with a diameter of three miles. Others settlers followed Chichester's example, laying the foundation for the walled-in deer parks of the gentry.

In Ireland, as in England, deer parks could only be established by a licence from the crown. In contrast with England where the number of deer parks increased in the sixteenth century, and only further substantially increased after 1660, Ireland saw a considerable rise in deer parks during the first four decades of the seventeenth century.[3]

In county Wicklow, the earliest deer park was created at Carnew by Calcott Chambre I, descended from a Welsh family, who migrated to Oxfordshire. (Several members of the family had the same first name, Calcott.) Some time before 1611, Chambre had moved to Ireland, and had purchased the manor of Shillelagh. In 1635, a traveller described the deer park at Carnew as 'about seven miles in compass, and wherein are both fallow and red deer [in] good store.'[4]

A second deer park was created by the lord deputy Sir Thomas Wentworth (later first earl of Strafford), who purchased the lands of Cosha in 1637 from William Graham, son of the original settler in the area. In the next year, he acquired the half barony of Shillelagh, north of Carnew, from Calcott Chambre's brother of the same name (Calcott Chambre II), thus forming a huge contiguous holding. At that time, he wrote from 'Cosha, the Park of Parks,'[5] a heavily wooded area east of the village of Shillelagh, which he later called Fairwood (figs. 8.1 and 8.3).[6] He explained the new name for the estate, 'it is considered, that [a] crow takes her own birds to be ye fairest and thence it is I am resolved to call it Fairwood Parke.'[7] In a letter to King Charles in March 1637, Wentworth wrote that he had 'found [there] that which I did not believe had been in Ireland a place which ... affords Sports to pass over a grass-time [i.e., the time of year that animals are at grass] in as great measure, and with as much delight, as most that are in England. Indeed the finest mountain country I ever saw ...' Later he wrote, 'here I may have a place to take my recreation for a month or two in a year ... keeping myself, if so please God, a little longer in health.'[8]

The manor of Fairwood consisted of about 10,000 acres, equally divided between profitable and unprofitable land, with the deer park probably situated in the latter. It seems likely that Fairwood Park consisted mostly of pasture, allowing the deer to graze. Wentworth, writing in 1638 to Sir Peter Middleton, expressed his delight and indicated that he was already planning to expand the park: 'I could shew you fifteen hundred deare and should have yr advise for a parke wch I am inlarging (sic).' In another letter, he described how on some evenings, he saw as many as five hundred [deer] feeding near his hunting lodge. And to the king, he extolled the 'pleasure of buck hunting'. It is not clear whether at that time the park was already enclosed. In another letter from Cosha, he stated that 'I am playing the Robin Hood, and here in the Country and Mountains and Woods I am chacing all the out-lying Deer I can light of.' The pleasure, however, was not undivided. 'I met with a very shrewd Rebuke the other Day:

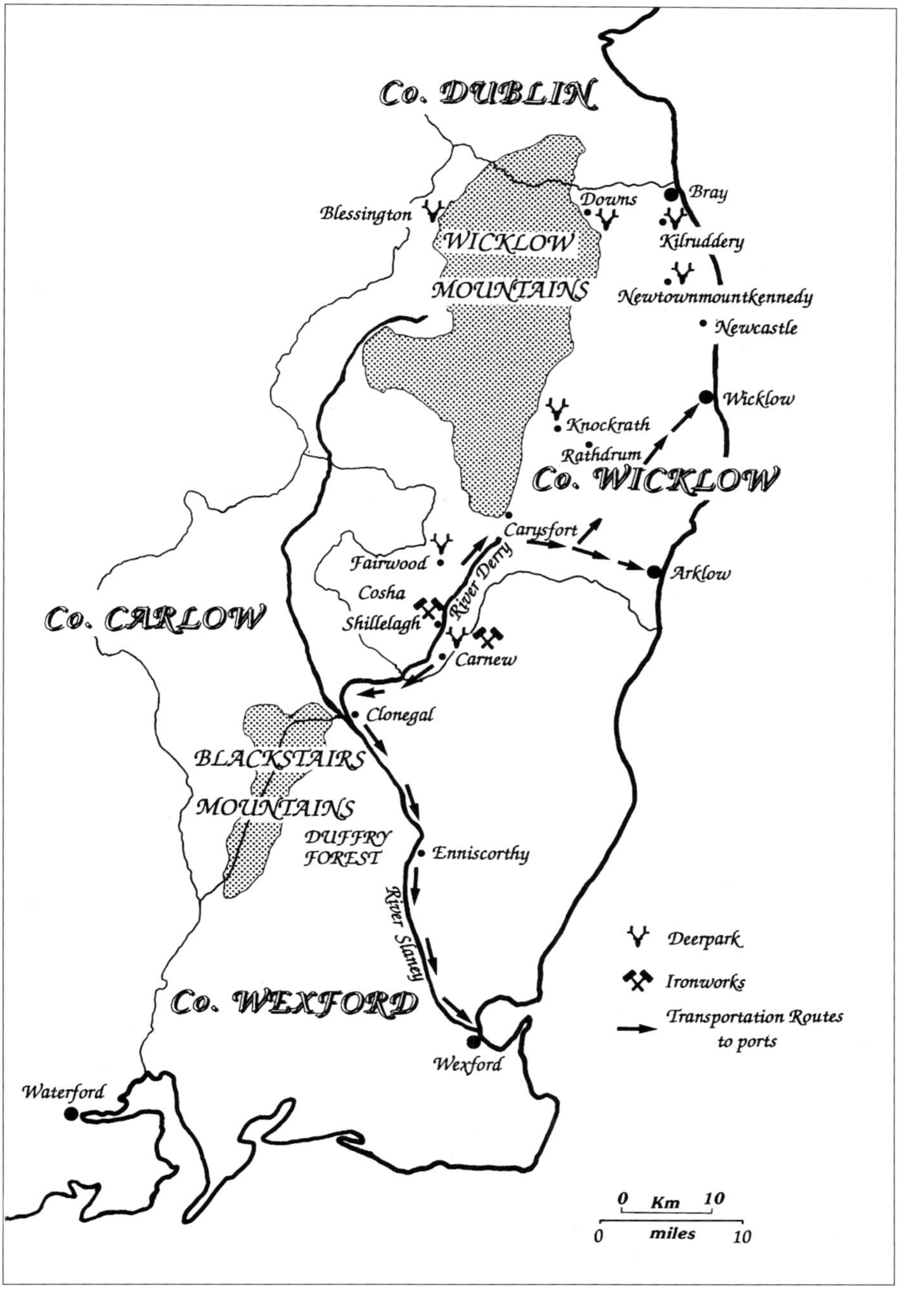

Figure 8.1 The study area.

For standing to get a Shoot at a Buck, I was so damnably bitten with Midges, as my Face is all mezled over ever since, itches still as if it were mad ... I never felt or saw such [mosquitoes] in England. Surely they are younger Brothers to the Muskitoes the Indies brag on so much.'[9] In all likelihood measures were taken to protect the deer and other animals from poachers; Wentworth had protected the game adjacent to his seat at Jigginstown (county Kildare), where people were forbidden to shoot any living thing within a radius of five miles, but this may also have been a security measure. A statute to prevent the unauthorised hunting of deer was not instituted until much later. However, as early as the reign of Henry VII, a statute was on the books to prevent unlawful hunting, which could very well have been enforced under Wentworth's lord deputyship. It stipulated: 'Any being suspected of hunting unlawfully in chases, warrens or forrests, in the night time, or with painted faces or other disguisings, may by a warrant be brought before a Justice.'[10]

It is probable that several forms of hunting took place at Fairwood Park, because Wentworth liked pursuing both partridge and deer. When he arrived in Ireland in 1633, he complained about the scarcity of partridges around Dublin. Instead, he hunted blackbirds there with hawks, a pastime which drew a large number of spectators from the local gentry. 'It is an excellent sport,' he wrote, 'there being sometimes two hundred horse on the field looking upon us.'[11]

Horses were an absolute requirement for the hunt as well as for travel. Wentworth planned in 1638 to breed horses at his estate of Fairwood, presumably as an alternative to the smaller Irish horses. The Irish native breed of 'hobby,' called a 'dainty breed,' which had been exported to England and other countries because of their desirable qualities, had become extinct or very uncommon by 1630. That horse breeding was started by Wentworth on this estate is confirmed by an account of 1641-2, which noted that the rebellion spread to 'Sillealy, where the earle of Strafford kept his breed of horses'.[12] In this period, deer hunting in England was practised in various forms, sometimes with bow and arrows or firearms, but in its most esteemed form with buck hounds, which Wentworth preferred. The deer were sometimes driven into nets or 'pales' where they could be shot without the trouble of the chase, which is what Wentworth must have done when he was badly bitten by the mosquitoes.[13]

Since Fairwood Park was probably two days' journey from Dublin, it was necessary to provide accommodation in the form of a hunting lodge. In England, it was quite common for landowners to have lodges in deer parks, specifically built to better enjoy the hunt. For that purpose, they were often tall with large windows, so that those who did not partake in the hunt could view it at ease, a forerunner of the belvedere.[14] The location of a lodge had to optimise the observation of the hunt. This was facilitated by the cutting of alleys in the forest in a radiating fashion with the lodge at the centre, which enabled the viewers to observe glimpses of deer, hunters and dogs in pursuit when they crossed the alleys. Wentworth, who also owned a park in North Yorkshire, had a hunting lodge there, which on the outside was more like a small country house. Inside, however, Wentworth had planned a chapel and a gallery, to make it truly 'commodious'.[15]

In Ireland, only a few examples of seventeenth-century lodges in deer parks are known. In 1648 Lord Mountgarret had one at his park at Ballyragget in county Kilkenny. The earl of Cork also completed a hunting lodge at his deer park at Lismore (county Waterford) in 1625, which contained a dining room and sleeping accommodation.[16]

In September 1637, Wentworth contracted for the building of 'a frame of wood' at Fairwood at a projected cost of £1,200, which he called a 'handsome lodge. The former owner of the estate, Sir Richard Greame (also Graham), had built a castle at Cosha in 1620, but it is unclear whether Wentworth ever used it. If it was a typical defensive tower house, it would have lacked the comforts of a hunting lodge. In September 1638, Wentworth wrote that 'Here I am in my hermitadge,' indicating that his lodge served as a retreat from worldly affairs.[17] No other details about the structure are known. What type of building is indicated by the anticipated cost of £1,200? Prior to 1622, Sir William Stewart built one of the best plantation castles at Aughentaine in county Tyrone for the same amount of money. This included the main stone castle of three storeys, a bawn, and minor buildings.[18]

In comparison, Wentworth's timber lodge was presumably a comfortable and larger structure, especially since the construction price probably did not include the cost of timber which could be obtained from the Wentworth estate. Unlike other hunting lodges close to a manor house, the building would have to be a complete residence with dining or banqueting room, kitchen, hall, and bedrooms, as well as auxiliary buildings such as a guard house, kennel, and stables. The work at the site was overseen by Wentworth's architect, the Reverend John Johnson, an 'ingenious man', who was also involved in the building of Wentworth's palatial country house at Jigginstown, county Kildare.[19]

Wentworth's park was formerly occupied by the Byrnes, and was far from safe. The closest English garrison was at Carysfort, almost ten miles from Fairwood, built to protect settlers at the 1620s Ranelagh plantation. This fort was described in 1638 by Wentworth to the king as 'ye poorest yt ever was seene, and in truth of noe use'. To safeguard himself and his hunting guests from a possible attack by the Byrnes, he formulated plans for the building of a large fort around his hunting lodge (Plate 8.1, for a reconstruction). The fort was to consist of a quadrangle of 300 by 130 yards, surrounded by a wide trench 8 feet deep, 40 feet wide at the top (and 24 at the bottom). Adjoining the trench, the rampart was to be 12 feet high, with a base of 24 feet and a top of 19 feet. It was to be surrounded by a stone parapet 5 feet high. At each corner, Wentworth projected a 'handsome bullworke' to protect the two flankers; outside the main ditch of the fort he planned a hornwork (an outwork consisting of four faces forming two salient angles) and a ravelin (an outwork of two faces forming a single salient angle). The fort itself was to be double trenched, approached by a drawbridge, because a river was to be diverted through the trench. The estimated cost was £1,400 for the fort alone, not including the building of the lodge. Ten or twelve 'fine field pieces' were to give additional protection. Wentworth sought to finance the project by charging the first rents that would come in from the plantation around the Byrne country in north county Wicklow. Soon afterwards, the king approved the building and financing of the fort.[20]

There are some remains of Wentworth's house and fort at a site locally known as Black Tom's Cellar, in reference to Wentworth's habit of training his own troop while clad in black armour and mounted on a black horse.[21] A brick foundation, surviving up to one or two feet above the ground, has an entrance to a vaulted cellar in the centre, on which the timber lodge may have rested. According to the architect David N. Johnson, large ditch cuttings into the bedrock suggest 'the beginnings of a rectangular rock cut fosse for a defended residence'. The lodge was probably one of the very last timber residences built for a settler outside the towns.[22]

Wentworth was only one of several Englishmen who sought out county Wicklow for the creation of deer parks, particularly in the 1630s. The earl of Meath received a licence in 1634 to lay out a park at Kilruddery, south of Bray, and impale it with a circuit of 3,000 Irish perches, amounting to almost twelve statute miles (fig. 8.1).[23] One of the earliest Irish hunting paintings, dating from the early eighteenth century, still survives at Kilruddery, showing riders and hounds enthusiastically chasing deer.[24] Wentworth's former secretary, Sir George Radcliffe, Master of the Rolls in Ireland, created a deer park at Downs, east of Kilruddery. Lastly, Sir Adam Loftus of Rathfarnham, who was one of the grantees in the Ranelagh plantation, established a deer park at Knockrath, west of Wicklow. This park was stocked by twenty deer provided by the earl of Cork, who in return in 1637 received 'a fat Buck' from Loftus's park. This was the only deer park created in the Ranelagh plantation during this period.[25] After the Restoration, at least

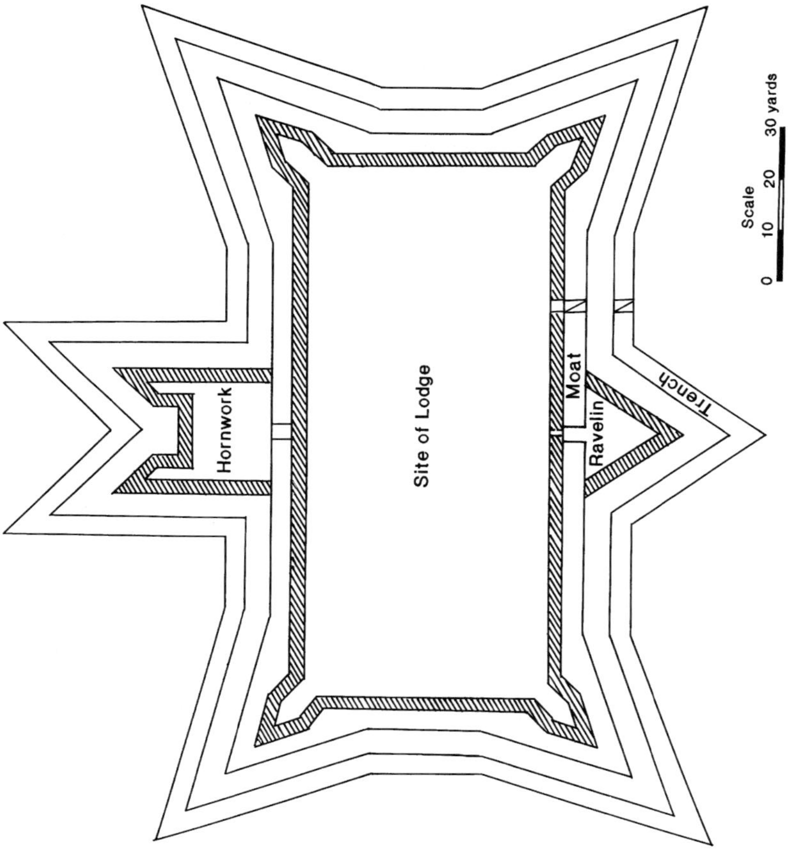

Plate 8.1 Plan of Black Tom's Castle at Tinahely, 'Fairwood Park'

two other deer parks were licensed, at Mountkennedy (1664) and at Blessington (1669). In 1678, at the latter site, we find Michael Boyle, archbishop of Dublin, taking 'a litle ayre ... as physick to prepare mee against the next terme'.[26] Almost all of the deer parks were situated close to a settlement. The economic basis for these settlements did not lie in the deer parks, but usually was founded on the exploitation of forests for the production of timber and the manufacture of iron.

Timber industry

An extensive timber industry evolved under the English, starting probably before 1600, and accelerating in the late 1630s, especially in the woods at Shillelagh. Contemporary records show that this was more than a merely local business for it had a spin-off to Enniscorthy and to the nearby coastal towns of Wicklow and Arklow, and also to Wexford and Dublin. Through these towns, timber products were exported to England, the Northern Netherlands, France and Spain.

One of the earliest English settlements in eastern county Wicklow took place in the reign of Edward VI (1547-53), when Lord Deputy Bellingham made provision for settlers in the barony of Shillelagh. However, very little is known about this plantation, and it is unclear whether the timber industry was founded at that time. The Wicklow woods saw some exploitation in the 1560s when boards were shipped through the ports of Wicklow, Arklow, or Dublin to Scotland for the building of galleys. In 1568, the lord justices forbade this export in order to prevent the earl of Argyle from making such ships. This order probably did not prevent the export of pipe staves or barrel staves.[27] The first largescale mapping of Shillelagh took place in 1571, when the surveyor Robert Lythe visited the area and incorporated it in his map of Ireland.[28] Seven years later, the lands of Shillelagh were granted for twenty-one years to Sir Henry Harrington, seneschal of the O'Byrne and O'Toole country; to whom they were soon afterwards granted in fee-farm. In addition, he became searcher of the customs in several ports in 1577, including Dublin, Wexford, and Waterford.[29] He probably contracted with Sir Walter Raleigh's partner Henry Pine to develop the timber at Shillelagh. Most of Raleigh and Pine's joint business was situated in Munster, but Pine also produced pipe staves in Shillelagh for export. His enterprise is mentioned in 1596 by Sir Henry Wallop, who noted that Pine and his partners exported a great quantity of ship planks and pipe staves to Spain, but that this trade had been prohibited sometime before 1593 because of the war. Pine, however, obtained a licence in that year to export pipe staves and hogshead boards to the island of Madeira, the Canaries, Bordeaux, and La Rochelle.[30] In partnership with Wallop, this trade originated from Enniscorthy, where he had his estate. The timber was to be transported in Dutch ships, presumably from Wexford.[31]

In 1586 Wallop wrote that he planned to make the river Slaney more navigable up to five or six miles above Enniscorthy in order to 'bring downe with more ease greate store of shipp planks and shipp tymber, pipe boards and barrel boards ... to the porte or haven of Wexforde, whereof there is as faire and as greate store, strong good and sounde as any is to be founde in any place of the World'. This made good sense, since he had a received a grant of one-thirteenth of the customs of all timber passing through Enniscorthy.[32]

In Wexford, further down the Slaney, warehouses and cranes were an absolute necessity in order to keep the costly loading time of ships to a minimum. Records show that timber was indeed shipped from Wexford to Cornwall at this time, and to Milford Haven and Cardiff in Wales, where ship-building wharves flourished (fig. 8.2). The size of the boats carrying the ship timber could be quite small, as in the case of the *Saviour* of Wexford, a mere six tons, carrying such a load of one hundred boards and one thousand lathes to Milford Haven in 1586.[33]

The sawing of timber may have been introduced into Ireland sometime in the late sixteenth or early seventeenth century; prior to that boards and larger timbers had be cleft with an axe, as is known from Munster and Wexford records. Robert Payne, advertising the advantages of plantation lands in Munster in 1589, wrote that 'a single workeman with a beake axe will cleave a great o[a]ke to boardes of less than one ynche thicke, 14 ynches broad and 15 footes in length, [and] such a board there is usually sold for 2½d.' The first known record of a licence for saw mills in Ireland was issued to a planter from county Armagh in 1619.[34]

Wallop's letters show that he did not own much timber land, and had to rely on acquiring the trees from native freeholders.[35] This may have exerted more pressure to exploit timber further up the rivers Slaney and Derry as far as the large woods of Shillelagh in county Wicklow, situated on both sides of the river Derry.

The government realised that timber was not just a strategic commodity for England's enemies, but also for the English navy. A first step in ascertaining how much wood was suitable for this purpose was the sending over of a surveyor to Ireland to take stock of the woods. In 1608 a surveyor reported first on the woods in Munster and later visited Shillelagh, but his account is not known to have survived. Following an order by Lord Deputy Chichester in 1611, another survey listed the number of oak trees reserved for the crown on the rivers Slaney and Barrow.[36]

The survey did not include parcels of timber from the Harrington estate of Shillelagh, which in 1608 had been leased by Sir Henry Harrington to a Richard Mitten or Mytten and his partners for sixty-two years. A 1607 inquisition of the boundaries of Shillelagh survives and may be associated with this transaction. Perhaps significantly, the inquisition was held at 'Mynmore' [Minmore] which subsequently became the site of ironworks (fig. 8.3). Records show that Mitten's partners were merchants, some from London, including Richard Gilbert, by profession a cooper, who took a quarter share in the venture.[37] Mitten, who came from a Leicester family, was undoubtedly the leader of the partnership, and he may have been related to Harrington.[38]

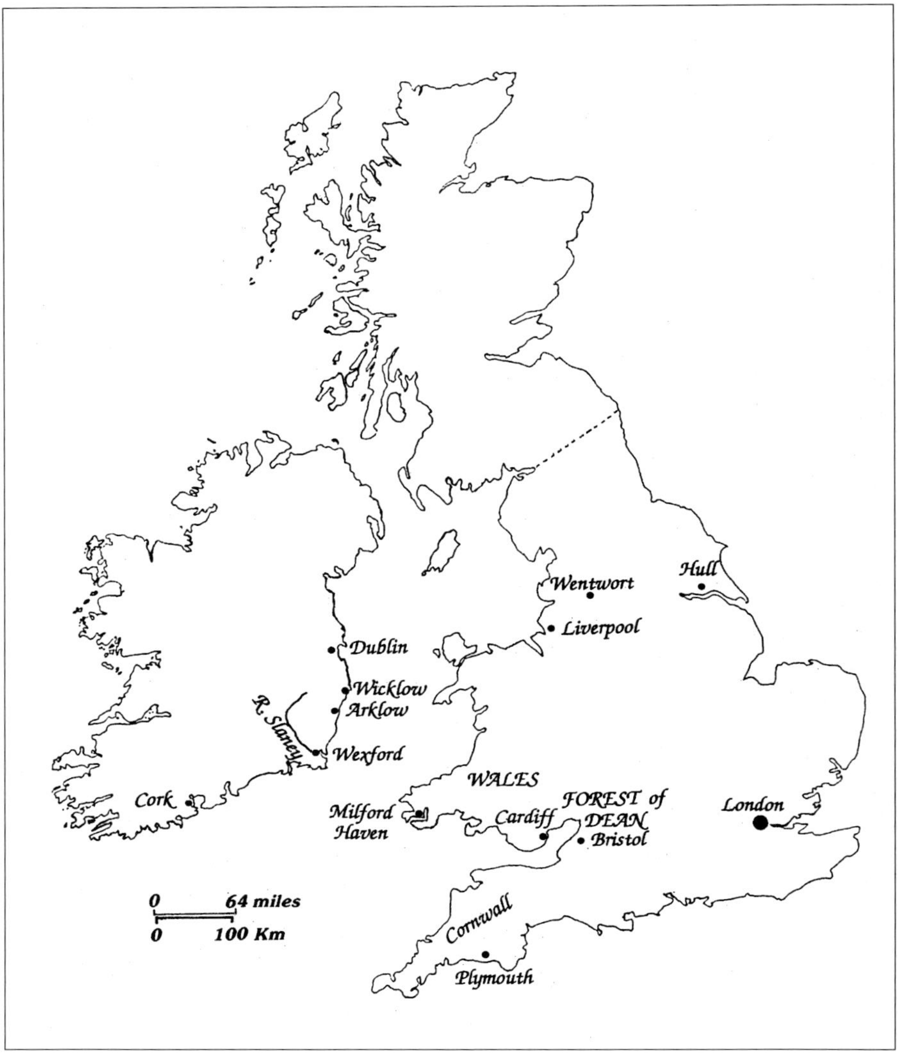

Figure 8.2 Timber trail *c*.1590.

Harrington renewed his letters patent of the property in 1609; these carried a new stipulation, requiring him to build a 'castle or stone fortress, with a portcullis [a fortified gate] for the defence of the country'. Prior to his death in 1612, Harrington erected the castle at Carnew and another castle at Knockloe in the western part of the barony of Shillelagh, where the road to Tullow in county Carlow crossed the river Derreen.[39] Lord Deputy Chichester considered Byrnes' country, including Shillelagh, as dangerous territory for an Englishman. He characterised Shillelagh as a 'strong, fast, and remote country, the

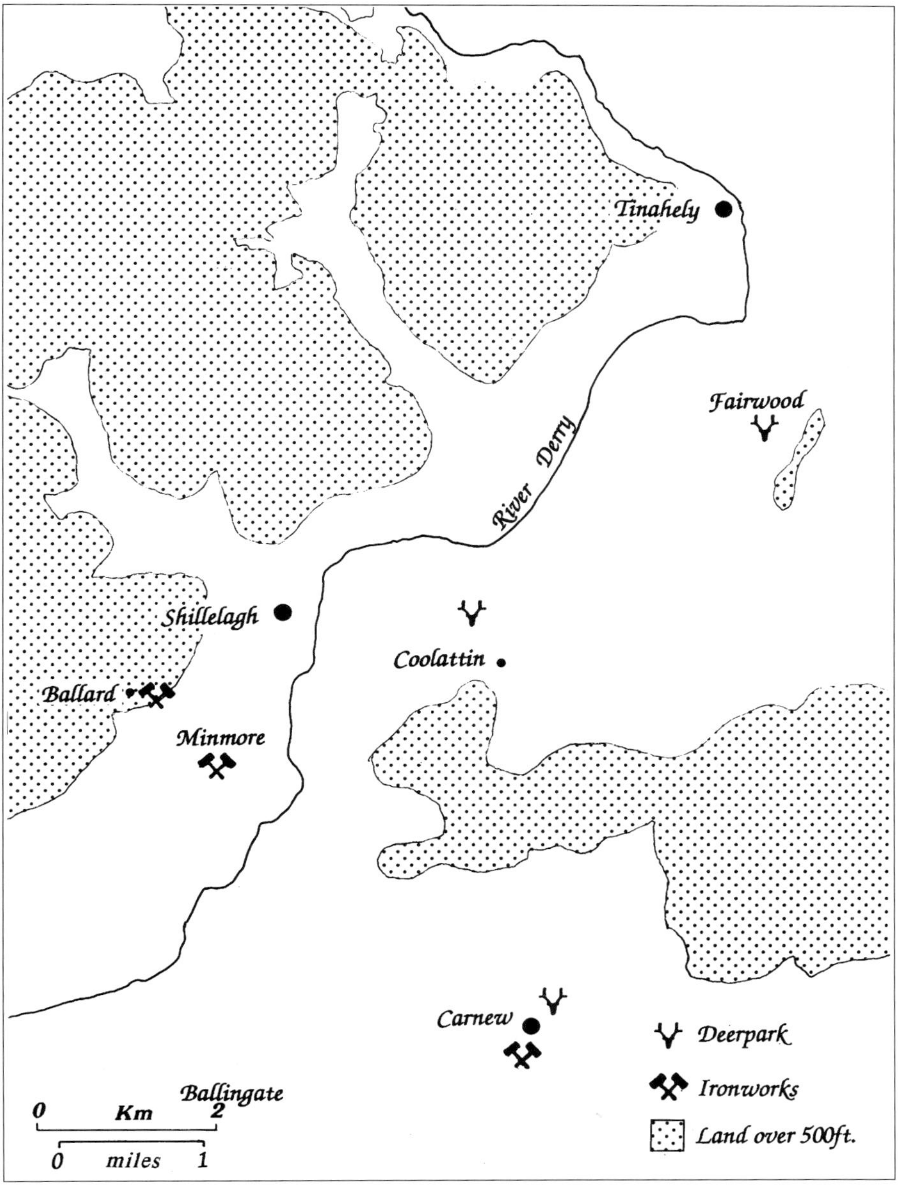

Figure 8.3 Deerparks and Ironworks in the upper Derry valley in the seventeenth century.

common receptacle and shelter of the thieves and ill-disposed members of those parts of Leinster'. Mitten offered to build a 'strong' castle for the government, possibly an improvement of Carnew Castle built by Harrington. Soon afterwards he was made constable of Carnew

Castle and was given a ward of twelve soldiers for the protection of himself and his workmen.[40]

Mitten's plans were to produce pipe staves and ship timbers; given that his partners, presumably, had access to the London financial market for necessary funds, the products were destined for the London market. According to Lord Deputy Chichester, the ship timber was to be used in Ireland or to be exported to Milford Haven for the building of ships for the English navy. In 1612 Mitten was appointed keeper of the customs at the ports of Wexford and Arklow,[41] again showing a link between inland timber production and governmental port excise. A possible conflict of interest occurred because he continued his involvement in the timber trade, probably through these ports. In 1617 he obtained a licence to cut timber (except those marked by the king's officers for the English navy) and an export licence for twenty-one years for pipe and hogshead staves, clapboards, and other 'cloven' ware.[42] He probably died soon afterwards, for the licence was renewed twice in the next year by Henry Mitten, possibly a son. The second licence renewal took on the proportions of a monopoly, in that it stipulated 'a prohibition against others cutting or exporting such timber' during its twenty-one years. The arrangement, however, lasted only three years, after which a vacillating policy prevailed.[43]

During the tenure of the Mitten family, the production of pipe staves and related products must have increased. This is indirectly corroborated by a surge in the export of pipe staves from Wexford harbour in Dutch ships. Documents from the Municipal Archive in Amsterdam show that between 1608 and 1614 an Amsterdam merchant, Jan Vechtersz, freighted nineteen ships for fairly long journeys, which included loading timber products at Wexford. One contract, concluded in 1614, involved Vechtersz's sale of 50,000 pipe staves to other Amsterdam merchants. Other ships chartered by Vechtersz were to bring the pipe staves to Spain and France.[44] According to one of the notarial contracts, the ship *La Catalena* of Calais was to depart from Amsterdam in 1608, sail to Romsdal in Norway to load deal, and carry the cargo to Dublin. From Dublin the ship was to sail to Wexford town, under ballast. At Wexford it was to load pipe staves, to be transported to Santa Maria de Porto (near Cadiz) in Spain. Subsequently, the ship was to sail to Marseille, prior to returning to Middleburgh in the Northern Netherlands.[45]

After Mitten's death, the Welshman Calcott Chambre I purchased the lordship of Shillelagh from Harrington's heir and obtained letters patent from the crown in 1618. According to a survey made almost forty years later (1656), more than one fifth of the lordship (5,609 plantation (Irish) acres, or about 9,087 statute acres) contained woodland,[46] but the wooded area must have been much larger at the time when Chambre acquired it. He continued to exploit the timber with the main production site situated close to the river Derry, so that the timber could be rafted down that river and thence to the river Slaney, to Enniscorthy and Wexford. The manufacture of pipe staves probably slowed down during the period 1625-30, when England waged wars with France and Spain, but at the resumption of peace with each country (1629-30), the export of wood products must have accelerated again. In 1635, Sir William Brereton visited the estate and noted that there was:

> an abundance of woods, more than many thousand acres; and some of those parts through which we travelled, the ground was so thronged with wood which was fallen and lay upon the ground, as the ground was thereby made of no use. Out of this part of the wood the best hath been made use of for pipe-staves, which were sold for £6 a 1000; upon every 1000 of these there is now a custom imposed of £3, which doth so much deduct as there is no valuable advantage, the charge of hewing being £1. 10s., besides conveying them down by water to Ennerscoff [Enniscorthy], which is twelve miles, at which time there is required the aid and endeavour of a hundred men to conduct and guide them in this narrow, shallow and crooked river [Derry], which runs through this Wood.[47]

In the 1630s the Irish export in pipe staves was seen as detrimental to English interests in the manufacture of pipe staves and an embargo was, therefore, instituted by Lord Deputy Wentworth. Wentworth, however, created a licensing system to control the trade in order to increase the Irish revenue. The hefty cost of the licences, to be granted by himself, plus an additional custom duty, and an export ban beyond half a million pipe staves annually, considerably discouraged the production of pipe staves in Ireland and caused a dilemma for those producers who had a large stock. As a result, Calcott Chambre I was left with nearly 250,000 staves on his hands.[48]

Prior to this set-back, Chambre's estate may have gone through a financially difficult time, forcing him in 1629-30 to mortgage it to James and Nathaniel Fiennes, first and second sons of William Viscount Say and Seale, and John Crewe, son and heir of Sir Thomas Crewe. The conveyance is curious, because it obliged the lenders to use the profits of the estate to pay all of Chambre's debts, legacies, and the cost of his funeral.[49] When Chambre redrafted his will in 1632, he may have allocated more money than he actually owned. He assigned £5,000 to his daughter as a dowry upon her marriage to the earl of Meath, gave his eldest daughter an additional £1,000, and left his son of the same name his estates in Ireland and England.[50]

When Calcott Chambre I died in 1635, the estate was burdened by debts and basically had already been conveyed to the creditors according to the agreement concluded in 1629-30. He left a son, Calcott Chambre III, who probably was under age, because his uncle Calcott Chambre II signed an indenture in 1637 to settle the estate. He and the creditors agreed to lease the lordship of Shillelagh for twenty-one years to Sir Philip Perceval at a payment of £3,490. Perceval, who was bound to keep up the buildings and maintain the 'game of deer' in the park, was a paper purchaser. He represented the interest of Lord Deputy Wentworth and Lady Carlisle, who had a share in the transaction. It was Wentworth, however, who had beneficial control of the woods.[51] Further deeds of sale were signed in the next year, when the 24,000 acre estate was sold for £13,200.[52] Calcott Chambre II, possibly using the residue of the sale of the estate, purchased or leased Sir Adam Loftus's plantation lands of Knockrath, west of Wicklow town in 1639, thus moving closer to the coast. Chambre II's death in 1640 and the outbreak of the rebellion in 1641 inevitably thwarted the development of this property.[53]

By purchasing the half barony of Shillelagh, Wentworth acquired vast and valuable timber lands on terms which probably had become more favourable than would have been possible if he had not instituted the licensing system for pipe staves. Wentworth had been willing to grant exemptions to some favoured individuals (probably excluding Chambre), and, not surprisingly, exempted his own industry in Shillelagh from the duties. This was ratified by the king in 1641, allowing him to export 'crooked and knee timber ... both for pipe staves and for the navy...'. It is likely that Wentworth felt forced to sell timber in order to deal with the large debts he had incurred.[54] There is little doubt that Wentworth's timber licensing system was highly controversial. One of the charges levied against Wentworth in 1639 was his ill treatment of Robert Esmond, a timber merchant of Wexford, who had refused to ship Wentworth's timber and who had died in Dublin Castle.[55]

In 1641, Wentworth, by then earl of Strafford, was put on trial at Westminster Hall in London on a variety of charges, including his monopolies, and was eventually beheaded in that year. His monopolies in Ireland helped to enrich him and to build his extravagant country house at Jigginstown outside Naas. It is probable that the Shillelagh woods provided the necessary timber for its roof structure, because the Jigginstown estate was devoid of woods.[56] According to tradition, Shillelagh oak was used in the roof of Westminster Hall. We know for certain, however, that Calcott Chambre II donated two hundred tons of oak timber from the Shillelagh woods for building projects at Trinity College, Dublin, in January 1636.[57] That Wicklow timber was used for building projects in Dublin was nothing new: in 1598, a letter addressed to the Dean of Christ Church Cathedral mentions that timber was due to the Church out of their wood near Arklow, which must have referred to the repairs which were then underway to the fabric of the cathedral.[58]

Timber production in county Wicklow, of course, was not solely concentrated in Shillelagh, although that is the best documented site. The Wentworth estates in that county were vast and included separate holdings at Rathdrum, and at Newcastle on the coast. It appears that timber production in Shillelagh was the only site directly managed by Wentworth's agents; at other sites, leaseholders may have had the right to cut and export timber. For example, one of the tenants at the Newcastle estate also manufactured timber products; a report of his losses in the 1641 rebellion included 6,000 barrel staves.[59] A similar report of losses survives for Francis Sandford, an engineer and brother-in-law of Calcott Chambre III, who incurred the loss of approximately 8,000 barrel staves at Wexford to the value of £49, apparently lying there ready for shipping. Calcott Chambre (II or III) lived at this time at Minmore in a house which he considered indefensible, forcing him and others to flee to Carnew.[60] Chambre's losses did not include pipe staves or iron wares, indicating that he was no longer involved at Minmore in such commercial activities at that time.

In 1641, after a siege of twelve weeks, Carnew Castle fell into the hands of Luke Birne [Byrne].[61] The production of timber from the woods at Shillelagh and elsewhere in county Wicklow may have been interrupted as a result of the rebellion. It is possible, however, that the timber industry was revived by the Irish until the area came into the hands of the Parliamentarians. By the middle of the seventeenth century the production at the Wentworth estate in Shillelagh had recovered and the woods produced an income of £1,000 per annum from the manufacture of pipe staves and other timber products. These included building timber necessary for the rebuilding of houses damaged or destroyed during the rebellion and the ensuing wars. Possibly to aid in the rebuilding, the exportation of building timber from Ireland was prohibited in 1656.[62] It is likely, however, that exportation of pipe staves continued.

In 1661, Wentworth's son, the second earl of Strafford, was able to contract with ship builders for timber.[63] A volume among the Wentworth papers, probably dating from the 1660s, gives many details of the projected exploitation of timber on the Shillelagh estate.[64] The plan called for production of two million pipe staves 'and of cooperware of the like kinde ...,' while two 'good' English shipwrights were to select the timber to be cut for ship-building. Table 8.1 shows a comparison of the projected costs of timber production at Shillelagh and at the Wentworth estate at Wentworth Woodhouse in England, with the cost in Ireland amounting to about half of that in England.

The further plan formulated at this time was to introduce two 'good sawing engines' in Ireland of a similar type as were used at Lambeth Marsh, near London, which were driven 'by water or by winde', which needed to be attended by ten workmen. Mechanisation was far from complete, however, for 130 sawyers were thought necessary to be brought over from England as well.[66]

Despite the report of poor quality timber at Shillelagh, the woods provided 1,000 tons for the rebuilding of Phoenix House outside Dublin in the early 1660s, and 40 tons of squared beams in 1671 for the making of the new roof of St Patrick's Cathedral in that city. In the meantime, the production of pipe staves at Shillelagh continued in the 1660s.[67] In 1671, the estate was surveyed twice, once by Peter Bronsdon who reported to the navy commissioners in England, and once by Richard Clifton. Bronsdon reported that the Shillelagh woods were nine or ten miles long and contained a large quantity of 'great' timber. Most of it was straight, but that which was big enough to make three- or four-inch planks was 'very much shaken, and some full of small worm-holes'. The estate steward listed the costs of production, which are shown in Table 8.2. Felling, squaring and sawing made up

Table 8.1

Comparison of the cost of sawing of wood at Wentworth Woodhouse (Yorkshire) and at Shillelagh (county Wicklow) in the 1660s

	England			Ireland		
	£.	*s.*	*d.*	£	*s.*	*d.*
Squaring of wood at 3 roods per tree			8			1
Sawing per rood		10			2	6
Carriage per mile	1				2	6
Carriage by sea per ton	1			1		
Rate of loading at Hull/Ireland			8			8
Rate of loading in London			8			8
Rate of insurance			6			6
	£2	12*s.*	6*d.*	£1	6*s.*	11*d.*[65]

Source: Strafford Ms 34, ff. 9-10.

only a small proportion of the total cost, which amounted to £2 14s. per ton.[68]

According to Bronsdon's report, the best timber was situated at Ballingate, east of Carnew on the border of county Wexford, which was also the nearest location of the woods to Enniscorthy (at eighteen Irish miles distance or twenty-four statute miles). Rafting of the timber in the rivers Derry and Slaney was no longer feasible in 1671 and, instead, the timber had to be carried over land to Enniscorthy, and then loaded in small boats to be ferried to Wexford town, where the timber was reloaded in larger boats for export. The town must have had large storage facilities for this purpose as was first noted by Wallop in 1586. After the siege of the town by Oliver Cromwell in 1649, he found there 'great quantities of iron, hides, tallow, salt, pipe and barrel staves'. Wexford's prominence as an export port for timber, after a drop in the mid 1660s, was regained afterwards; in 1682-3, Wexford, of all the Irish ports, had the largest export of pipe staves.[69]

Thus, the critical stumbling block in furthering exploitation of the woods was the high cost of land carriage caused by the impossibility of rafting logs through the rivers. It is unclear whether this was caused by a gradual clogging of the upper rivers Slaney and Derry or because the water level had become lower. In 1674-5, Andrew Yarranton, an English engineer, surveyed the river Slaney with an eye to making the river navigable upstream (fig. 8.4). He reported that the river could be made navigable at a cost of £10,000, which would facilitate the transportation of timber from Shillelagh and from Lord Arran's woods at Sherwood in county Carlow.[71] Nothing was done, presumably because of the high cost of clearing the river.

Table 8.2

Cost of production of timber at Shillelagh (county Wicklow) in 1671

	Cost per ton	
	s.	*d.*
Felling and squaring	2	6
Sawing into planks	3	(per 100 ft.)
Price of the timber	8	6
Land carriage to Enniscorthy (10 miles)	10	
Carriage by boat from Enniscorthy to Wexford	2	
Sea carriage	28	
Total	£2 14*s.*[70]	

Source: *Cal. State Papers Dom., 1671*, p. 207

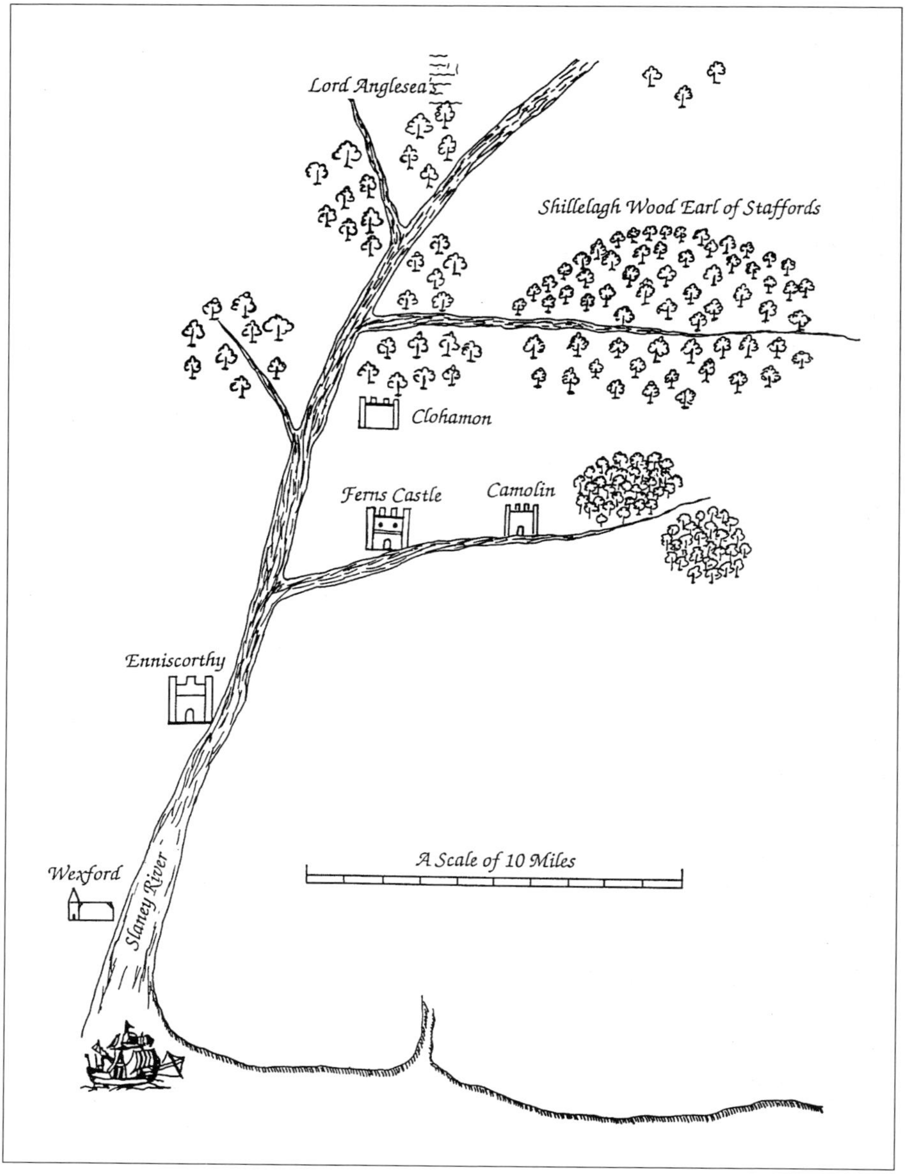

Figure 8.4 The Shillelagh woods drawn by Yarranton in 1670.

In 1671 Bronsdon, relying on information from the steward of the Shillelagh estate, pointed out that small timber could be exported through the harbours of Wicklow and Arklow, but this was equally costly because of the necessary land carriage, presumably using horses, from the woods to the harbours. The animals could carry iron ore or bars from the coast to Shillelagh and small timber on the return journey to the coast. The limitation of these harbours was that vessels above twenty to thirty tons could not land there, while the harbour of Wexford, although more commodious, could not accommodate vessels above fifty to sixty tons. Thus, two to three times as many ships were needed for the import of the same quantity of iron ore to the ports of Arklow or Wicklow as to Wexford. Shipping to or from the towns of Arklow and Wicklow was complicated by the presence of sand banks in front of the coast. These bank are visible on a Dutch sea chart, published in Amsterdam in 1612 (fig. 8.5). The chart contained specific directions to help skippers navigate to these two harbours, and warned that a pilot was needed to get in and out of Wexford harbour. These transportation factors were a great disadvantage to the exploitation of the Wentworth's woods. In comparison, the Kenmare woods owned by Sir William Petty in county Kerry were much more accessible and advantageous.[72]

The pipe stave trade was closely related to the trade in Irish provisions because many products were casked in barrels. The prohibition of the export of live Irish cattle in the mid-1660s was followed by an increase of salted meat, pork, butter, cheese and tallow, for all of which barrels were required.[73]

The second survey of Shillelagh in 1671 by Richard Clifton summarised income from the estate. It stated that the total area of wood consisted of 3,905 acres (i.e. approximately 6,326 statute acres). Given that these probably were plantation acres, this meant that between 1656 (when the woods covered 5,609 plantation acres) and 1671, the woods had been reduced in size by almost a third. As to the value of the remaining woods, the report mentions that:

> The 3,905 acres of woods, allowing the threescore tunn to every acre amounts to 234,000 tunn of timber which at 10¼d. per tunn comes to £10,006 14s. 2d., which wee humbly conceive to be full value worth and purchase thereof by reason of the many great falls of late yeares made, and a great p[ar]t of the biggest tymber Trees soe fallen, besydes those standing very rotten & much decayed.[74]

Thus, the Shillelagh woods had been badly neglected, but even in that state they were a valuable property. Given the transportation problems of timber from Shillelagh, it is not surprising too that other woods, situated closer to the ports, were exploited. For example, eight wood cutters were noted at Rossahane in 1669 on the Knockrath estate, near Rathdrum, the property of Calcott Chambre II. Judging from their names, they were all Englishmen: William Byrd, William Scott, William

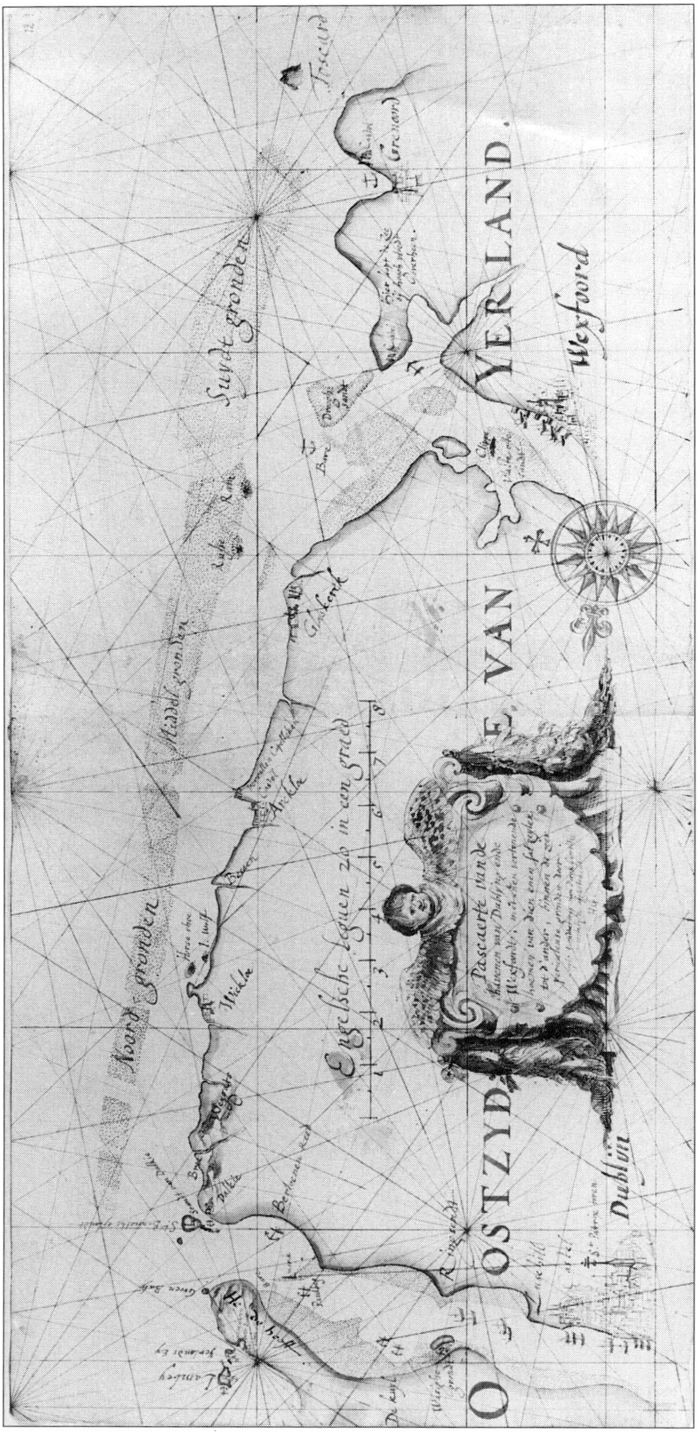

Figure 8.5 Dutch sea chart 1612 showing approaches to east coast ports including Wexford, Arklow, Wicklow and Dublin.

Jenkinson, Edward Groves, Henry Cox, Thomas Harding, Ralph Dayton, and Henry Page. Their temporary accommodation must have been frugal; only two of them had a dwelling with a single chimney; the others were not taxed because their abode lacked a chimney.[75] Rossahane was close to Wicklow town; compared with Shillelagh, it must have produced timber at a cheaper rate because of the lower transportation cost.

An important auxiliary industry in the Wicklow woods was leather tanning, for which oak bark was particularly suitable. Presumably, the Wicklow valleys had ample grazing lands for cattle, whose hides could provide the leather much needed in seventeenth-century Ireland, particularly for shoes. One of the first known tanneries is noted in 1620, when Christiaan Bor, a naturalised Dutchman living in Dublin, was given a licence, stipulating that he could keep 'tan-houses' in the town of Wicklow for a period of thirty-one years.[76] The licence constituted a form of monopoly for that area; the fact that the tan houses were situated in Wicklow town must have been advantageous as a collection point for the hides, and as a distribution point from which the tanned leather could be transported to Dublin, or perhaps exported. References to tan houses also occur at other locations; Calcott Chambre (II or III) counted among his 1641 losses a well stocked tan house at Minmore, near the village of Shillelagh.[77] It is quite likely that tanned hides were manufactured for export, aside from inland consumption; the yearly export figure for hides in 1640 was 67,741 hides exported from Ireland to England and another 59,269 hides further abroad.[78]

The practice of the leather tanners was to strip the bark of oak trees. Complaints about this practice already featured in a 1622 report by commissioners sent to inspect the state of affairs in Ireland. They complained about the 'great waste & spoile that is daily made of timber by such as for tanning of leather doe strip of the barke when the leaves are greene, and so distroy the whole body of the tree.' Bronsdon wrote in 1671 that much of the Irish woods was spoiled by the brogue-makers, who stripped off the bark three or four feet from the root, leaving the rest of the trees to be cut down and converted into barrel staves.[79]

Those parts of the forest that were not suitable for timber production could still be used to fire the forges set up to produce iron. Most of the latter industry was based on the importation of iron from England, subsequently either re-exported back to England or exported to the continent.

Ironworks

An iron industry was probably first established in the sixteenth century by settlers in county Wexford rather than in county Wicklow. In the

1560s Colonel Roberts founded an ironwork at Enniscorthy, which must have been quite sophisticated since it produced sword blades. Eventually, ironworks were established in western parts of the county Wicklow near Carnew, and at Minmore and Ballard near the village of Shillelagh.[80] Aside from Carnew, all other seventeenth-century ironworks were situated on the north bank of the river Derry (fig. 8.1).

The forge at Carnew was probably the earliest known ironworks in county Wicklow operated by Englishmen. It was founded prior to 1635 by Calcott Chambre I, and was situated about a quarter of a mile from his castle at Carnew. The exact location of these works is not known, but because of the need for water power, it was probably situated on one of the tributaries of the river Derry. Since iron ore was not mined in Ireland, it must have been imported from south Wales or Cornwall, where it was smelted into sow iron; this iron was then transported to Bristol, subsequently shipped to county Wicklow, and transported overland to Carnew, where it was refined into bar iron. Sir William Brereton described this in 1635:

> the sows of iron [pig iron], which are brought from Bristol are melted into iron-bars. They stand in 5l. a ton, being laid down at the door, and are worth in bars xxx l. a ton.[81]

Thus, the manufacture of the iron, by means of the ample supply of cheap wood necessary for charcoal, increased the value of the iron six-fold, not counting the cost of production near Carnew. However, the quantity of charcoal needed for the production of bar iron was large: two and a quarter tons of charcoal went into producing one ton of bar iron (charcoal was prepared in the forests close to the site where the timber was cut).[82] That sow iron was imported from Bristol seems surprising, because Liverpool, a port from which iron mined in Lancashire was shipped, was much closer to Shillelagh.

The description of Chambre's ironworks in 1635 does not mention how the sow iron, once landed in Ireland, was transported to Carnew. The most logical route would have been via the nearest harbour at Arklow. However, Kinahan found traces of an 'iron trail' between Shillelagh and Wicklow town, the iron being carried in panniers on horseback, which may indicate that Wicklow rather than Arklow was the prime harbour for import and export.[83] It may well be that the harbour of Wicklow was favoured by Wentworth, since he had acquired the manor of Wicklow. (The manor of Arklow, on the other hand, although closer to Shillelagh, was not for sale as it was owned by Wentworth's adversary, the earl of Ormond.)[84]

It is also likely, however, that iron was brought into west county

Wicklow via the port of Wexford, and then transported along the river Slaney and by road to the Shillelagh forges. Whether through this route or via the Wicklow to Shillelagh route, regular land carriage of the iron must have seriously affected road maintenance, especially in winter.

The towns of Arklow and Wicklow probably benefited from the iron and timber trade in several ways. The trade must have attracted merchants willing to undertake the transportation by land and by sea. The individuals employed in transportation and at the wharf must have needed provisions for themselves and their families. And lastly, when foreign ships were not available, vessels had to be built and equipped. In 1644 Richard Dickson, an Arklow mariner, reported that as a result of the rebellion, he had lost 2,500 feet of 12-inch planks intended for ship building.[85]

Profits in the iron industry could only be generated by the infusion of much capital. According to Sir Thomas Ridgeway in 1610, the minimum figure for the setting up of ironworks was £3,000, while one of those founded by Sir Richard Boyle (later earl of Cork) in Munster required an initial investment of £1,660. The start-up costs included construction of one or more forges, usually circular in form and eighteen to twenty feet high, specially built to withstand the extreme sustained heat of the fire fed by charcoal. In addition, iron-works required water mills (to provide power), storehouses, and housing for craftsmen and labourers.[86]

As Boate in his *Ireland's Naturall History* (1652) explained, iron-works demanded:

> [a] great number of workmen and labourers of severall sorts ... [such as] wood-cutters, who fell the timber; sawyers, to saw the timber; carpenters, smiths, masons, and bellows-makers, to erect the iron-works, with all the appurtenances thereof, and to repair them from time to time; water-leaders, or water-course-keepers, to steer the water-courses, and to look to them constantly; basket-makers to make baskets for to carry the oar and other materials; boat-men, and boat-wrights to make the boats, and to go in them; diggers, who work in the mine; colliers, who make the char-coal; corders, who bring the char-coal to the work; fillers, whose work it is from time to time to put the coals in the furnace; keepers of the furnace, who look to the main work, rake out the ashes and cinders, and let out the molten metell at convenient times; finers, who look to the works where the iron is hammered; hammerers, whose work it is to see the iron hammered out; besides severall other labourers, who have no particular task, must help to put their hand to every thing.[87]

Using Boate's estimate, more than 800 individuals worked at a given ironworks in the early part of the seventeenth century; this may be an exaggeration, but it must have included the many people responsible for transportation.[88] Boate does not mention the technological innovation which had led to improvements in iron production on the continent in preceding centuries. Although contemporary Irish sources are silent about this, a few aspects can be deduced. First, improvements consisted of building a blast furnace with a large leather bellows about twenty feet long to fan the flames in the hearths. In England, the bellows were usually driven by a high overshot water wheel, fed by water led through a wooden trough to a point over the wheel. Water power was also used to drive mechanised hammers to forge the metal into bars.[89] For these reasons, water mills became an intrinsic part of the manufacturing process, with even small forges usually having at least two water mills (and redirected streams, artificial ponds, and dams). Another innovation was the refining of the brittle cast iron into wrought iron that a smith could forge. For this pig-iron was re-melted in oxidising conditions where carbon was burnt out. The resulting bloom was then hot hammered, for which a water mill produced the power.[90] In order to profit from these improvements, it was necessary to attract foreigners as they often were more knowledgeable about modern techniques, especially for the manufacture of cannons. For example, Walloons from the city of Liège (a major iron industry centre) were employed at the ironworks at Ballynakill in county Laois, where cannons were manufactured in the early 1630s.[91]

There is no evidence, however, that labour from the continent was used in the Wicklow iron industry. The ironworks outside Carnew probably continued to operate until the outbreak of the 1641 rebellion.[92] In 1638, Wentworth first mentioned his plans for setting up an ironworks, when he purchased the half barony of Shillelagh from Calcott Chambre II through Sir Philip Perceval.[93] In all likelihood he referred to either the Carnew works or the ironworks eventually established at Ballard and Minmore, south of the village of Shillelagh (fig. 8.3).[94]

Five years before broaching plans for the founding of ironworks in Shillelagh, Wentworth had dabbled in the production of iron ordnance in Ireland. Instead of erecting his own ironworks, he invested money in an ironworks founded by the ironmaster, Richard Blacknall, a former farmer of the earl of Cork's ironworks in Munster. It is very likely that these ironworks were situated on the Ridgeway estate at Ballynakill in county Laois. These ironworks did not flourish and soon Wentworth thought he would be £600 out of pocket; Blacknall's death at Ballynakill in 1634 may have further contributed to the decline of the works there.[95] It is therefore surprising to see Wentworth take up the ironworks project in 1638. Careful analysis of the anticipated costs of the ironworks were noted in a volume which, unfortunately, is not known to have survived.[96] The Shillelagh area also produced its own iron ore, which sometimes was mixed with imported ore. Sites for such ore could be found at Ballinaclash and the Vale of Avoca, but also in Shillelagh. A 1629-30 conveyance of the Shillelagh lands included the mining rights, which may indicate the potential for opening a mine, or the presence of existing mines for the exploitation of local ore.[97]

Wentworth eventually again lost money establishing his Shillelagh ironworks. His death in 1641 and the outbreak of the rebellion probably further stifled production at the site. However, the works were revived, possibly during the interregnum, by Wentworth's son, the second earl of Strafford, and they continued to perform at least as late as 1668, when they were noted at the townland of Ballard, south of the present village of Shillelagh on the river Derry (see fig. 8.3).[98] The economic benefits of iron production in the woods of Shillelagh was extensively documented in a surviving manuscript volume of the 1660s. It details the careful preparations of all aspects of the project. Several chief officers of the work were to be appointed: a comptroller, a treasurer, a surveyor of the wharf, a surveyor of the wood works, a clerk of the ironworks, a surveyor of the mine (in England), a factor to conduct sales, and a register of the work. For each of these functionaries, extensive job specifications were drawn up. The plans called for the production of 1,000 tons of bar iron, 'if there bee waters convenient to beare so many workes there'. This figure, presumably, is per year, which would have made these several forges the largest ironworks in the country.[99] In order to facilitate the landing of English ore at Arklow, a wharf, cranes and several houses were to be built. Another wharf to receive the refined iron was to be leased or built at 'Redriff' (Rotherhithe) in London (the city served as a store house for the iron trade).[100]

Not surprisingly, the plans called for the hiring of trained craftsmen, including bellows makers, founders, finers, and hammer men who were to be attracted from England, and would be paid at about half the English rate. One of the benefits for them of working on the Shillelagh estate would be to obtain a farm, presumably to cultivate food produce and fatten cattle. The Wentworth estate would benefit reciprocally from this arrangement, because the tenant was to be charged a rent for his farm.[101]

Minute comparisons were made between the production costs of iron in England and Ireland, to show the financial advantages of the latter. One of these comparisons for the production of charcoal has been summarised in Table 8.3. It shows that the projected cost of production of charcoal in Ireland was ten times lower than in England, but the figures for each country are not very comparable: much of the production costs consisted of purchasing the wood to be cut, which were not included in the calculations for Irish charcoal since the Irish woods were already owned by the earl of Strafford. As is known from other sources, Irish charcoal was also exported to the iron industry in England.[102]

The actual production costs were sometimes vastly different from those projected. For example, whereas the projected cost of cutting one cord at Shillelagh was 4p. per cord, the actual cost in 1668 was three times as high and amounted to 1s., as is evident from a lease to James Bacon of the land of Minmore. He was a member of a family who in 1640 had come from England, and established in Shillelagh a dynasty of ironmasters, continued by the Chamneys, one of whom married his only daughter. Bacon, who had an interest in the Forest of Dean in England, imported ore from south Wales and used local charcoal to smelt it.[103]

Nothing has come to light about the destination of the iron produced at Shillelagh, with the exception of the 1660s plans which called for transportation of iron to London. Earlier in the century, the Dutch were seeking iron from Ireland, and Sir Richard Boyle exported iron to Amsterdam in 1622. Another equally important market for iron had developed in Ireland, particularly in Dublin.[104] The ironworks in Shillelagh in 1668 consisted of fourteen houses with one hearth, and 33 widows' houses, probably as a charitable gesture to the widows of

Table 8.3

Comparison of the cost of the production of charcoal for one ton of bar iron in England and in Shillelagh in Ireland in the 1660s

	England			Ireland		
	£.	*s.*	*d.*	£	*s.*	*d.*
Purchase of wood for cutting 26 cords	5	4		No charge*		
Cutting of 26 cords of wood	1	19			8	
Cording the same		8	8		2	6
'Coaling' the same	1				5	
Carriage of 10 dozen 'Coales'	1	10			5	4
	£10	1*s.*	8*d.*	£1	0*s.*	10*d.*

* Since the woods were owned.
Source: Strafford MS 34, ff 13-15

ironmasters or labourers on the estate. The ironworks continued to function until 1756, showing that the clearance of the woods progressed at a slow rate.[105]

The costs and profits, and the volume of production of iron in Wicklow, are not known. It is also unclear to what extent and for what length it remained competitive on the international market. From other sources, we know that the price of iron rose slightly during the seventeenth century,[106] but much depended on its quality, and here the known documentary sources of the Wicklow ironworks are silent. The diplomat Sir William Temple, in an essay on Irish trade written in 1673, critically commented that:

> Iron seems to me the manufacture that of all others ought the least to be encouraged in Ireland; or if it be, which requires the most restriction to certain places and rules. For I do not remember to have heard that there is any ore in Ireland, at least I am sure the greatest part is fetched from England; so that all this country affords of its own growth towards this manufacture is but the wood, which has met but with too great consumptions already in most parts of this kingdom, and needs not this to destroy what is left. So that ironworks ought to be confined to certain places, where either the woods continue vast, and make the country savage; or where they are not all fit for timber, or likely to grow it; or where there is no conveyance for timber to places of vent, so as to quit the cost of the carriage.[107]

Connections made

The timber and iron industry linked county Wicklow more firmly to the outside world than had ever happened before. The two industries were interlocking in that some of the shipping of ore into Ireland depended on the availability of return cargo for which timber products were ideal (aside from the finished iron). The mercantile contacts between Ireland, England, and the continent were organised by a relatively small group of entrepreneurs and merchants; given the employment of English craftsmen ('men of mystery') at the works,[108] the industry is less likely to have employed Irishmen in the highest paying positions. In the early seventeenth century, a small but probably significant contingent of Dubliners became property owners in the town of Wicklow, including the master, warden and company of Taylors.[109] Also, the Dutch merchant Christiaan Bor received a licence in 1620 to keep tan-houses in the town. The harbour of Wicklow was improved sometime before 1625 when a quay was built into the river, possibly by Sir William Ussher, who was constable of Wicklow castle.[110] The quay's function is unclear, because it is not known that either cots or rafts were used on the river.[111]

This chapter focused on the iron and timber industry as founded by Englishmen. However, one should not underestimate native enterprise, although such references rarely occur in contemporary English documents. The lord deputy Sir Henry Sidney, while travelling from county Wexford to Dublin in the late sixteenth century, reflected favourably on the native inhabitants, and commented on the fact that they supplied Dublin with firewood.[112] The fact that in county Kerry, native Irish owned and operated at least one iron mill in the early seventeenth century,[113] indicates that the Irish were not excluded from this industry. Whether they participated, other than as labourers, in the rise in the iron and timber industry in county Wicklow, however, is far from clear.

The study of the iron and timber trade is incomplete without a better knowledge of the merchants in ports of entry where the merchandise was unloaded, whether in England, Northern Netherlands, France, or Spain. For example, Irish timber used for the building of the Guildhall at Plymouth in 1606-7 appeared to have been imported by Sir Richard Hawkins.[114] He was a son of the famous mariner Sir John Hawkins, and accompanied his father to the New World, of which he left a famous account. Sir Richard later became vice-admiral of Devon, and at the time he was mayor of Plymouth he was also a member of parliament.[115] The study of the lives of merchants such as Hawkins can only illustrate better the nature of Irish manufacturing and external trade.[116]

The contacts with the wider world, however, were not without risks since both timber and iron were sensitive to price fluctuations on the international markets and vulnerable to foreign wars or political interventions. For instance, iron prices rose particularly at times of high demands and during war, and fell when overproduction flooded the market. The export of pipe staves to Spain was restricted during the English-Dutch war at the end of the sixteenth century. Similarly, the Anglo-Dutch war brought timber exports in 1665 to an abnormally low level. By that time, however, the direction of the timber trade had changed from a strong reliance on continental customers to a predominance of Irish exports to Scotland and England.[117]

Both timber and iron production were exploitative industries which could lead to the deforestation of large tracts of land in the absence of planting. However, ironworks did not need to destroy mature woodland, if the woodland was well taken care of.[118] Reforestation was more in the interest of individuals who both owned the forests and the ironworks, than for leaseholders who were more likely to more permanently strip the land. Little is known about the reforestation of

Shillelagh woods under the ownership of the earls of Strafford during the seventeenth century. One document, however, mentions in 1671 that 'the non improvement of the saplings for 30 years past, has been observed by knowing men, many of them [the saplings] ... being rotten.'[119] This comment indicates that saplings were already nursed prior to 1641. The private papers of Sir Philip Perceval, who bought the Shillelagh estate for Wentworth, show that Sir Philip was already grafting trees in 1637, and engaged in planting the 'tops of willows' in low wet ground, presumably on his own estate in Munster or county Kildare.[120] That at least one commercial tree nursery was in existence during the interregnum is clear from the will of Garatt Nugent, a nursery man from Dublin, who left 100 trees from his nursery to Sir Robert Meredith in 1650.[121]

It is certain that from the 1660s onward the cultivation of trees, including evergreens, oaks, and chestnuts, had become more common on other Irish estates.[122] Sir William Petty, in one of his grandiose schemes to employ the Irish people, recommended in 1672 a vast reforestation scheme for 'planting 3 million of timber-trees upon the bounds and meers of every denomination of lands at 3d. each' at a total cost of £360,000. This would then, according to his calculations, return a investment of 3d. into a profit of 10s. per ton of timber, but he did not take into account whether the market might be flooded by this massive supply![123]

By the early eighteenth century coppice management on the Shillelagh estate had become a regular practice. As a result, a 1728 survey of the deer park at Coolattin (the successor to Fairwood Park) counted 2,150 oaks, characterised as 'The glory and ornament of the Kingdom of Ireland', which were valued at £8,317. The protection of the coppices was then in the hands of a clerk and a small team of coppice keepers or woodrangers and woodmen, overseen by the resident land-agent in his capacity of woodward. Each individual coppice, had its own coppice keeper, who was supervised by area coppice keepers. The woodmen on an individual coppice included woodcutters, squarers, sawyers, cleavers, barkers, and carters. In addition, ditchers and hedgers were employed who were responsible for the construction of ditches and banks, and the planting of whitethorn hedges, protecting the coppice's saplings against grazing animals. A book on the cultivation of trees, written by William Boutcher, and published in Dublin in 1786 (entitled *A Treatise on Forest Trees*), contained the warning, 'To plant without inclosing, is not only amongst the idlest ways of throwing away money, but is laying up a fund of remorse and discontent that will necessarily follow, from the devastations of cattle and sheep ... Let this then be your first care to perform in the most substantial manner, with double ditches or hedges'.[124] This book, together with Samuel Hayes' *A Practical Treatise on Planting and the Management of Woods and Coppices* (Dublin, 1794), helped to inform improving landlords and estate agents on how to take care of the forests in their charge.

In the beginning of the eighteenth century, the intervals between successive cutting of the timber in the Shillelagh woods varied from sixteen to thirty-three years, with a mean of twenty-five years.[125] To make this possible, long-term planning and care was necessary. The cultivation of saplings was a necessary requirement in order to produce coppice for harvesting. One cannot but agree with the estate agent of Shillelagh, who wrote in 1730: 'I look upon planting to be the chiefest improvement in Ireland by reason most of the woods in Ireland are destroyed, and wood to posterity will be a valuable jewel'.[126]

Acknowledgments

Portions of this chapter were presented at a seminar at the department of Geography, UCD in October 1991. The author is grateful for the comments and inspiration provided by the attendees there, and by Lucille Stark, who read an early draft of the chapter. The author also received much help from Dr Kevin Whelan, who provided several of the sources. He is much indebted to Dr Magda Stouthamer-Loeber for her continuing support in writing the chapter. Stephen Hannon of the Department of Geography, UCD kindly drew the maps.

References

1. J. Hutchinson, 'Intrusions and representations: The landscape of Wicklow' in *Irish Arts Review* (1989-90), pp 91-99; E. Malins and The Knight of Glin, *Lost demesnes, Irish landscape* gardening 1660-1845 (London, 1976), pp 12ff.; A. Crookshank and The Knight of Glin, *The painters of Ireland c.1660-1920* (London, 1978), chapter 7. One of the earliest representations of county Wicklow are two views of the town of Wicklow, possibly by Thomas Phillips, and dating from around 1685 (B.L., King's Maps 55, ff. 48-49).
2. In the thirteenth century, a deer park was created at Glencree, four miles west of Enniskerry (M. Gibbon and T. Clarke, 'Deerparks' in *Carloviana* (1990-1), pp 4-5); G. Benn, *A history of the town of Belfast* (London, 1877), pp 86-7.
3. J. Thirsk (ed.), *The agrarian history of England and Wales, v, pt. II, 1640-1750: agrarian change* (Cambridge, 1985), pp 366-7. In Ireland, outside of county Wicklow, examples were Lord Esmond at Limerick (county Wexford); Sir Edward Fisher at Phoenix Park, outside Dublin; Henry Warren, probably at Ballybrittan (county Offaly); Sir William St. Leger at Mallow, and Sir Philip Perceval in Duhallow (both in county Cork); Sir Richard Boyle at Lismore (county Waterford); George Courtney at Newcastle (county Limerick); Sir Robert King, probably at Boyle (county Roscommon); Lord Conway at Lisburn (county Antrim); and Lord Grandison at Ballymore (county Armagh). In addition, native magnates made or improved their parks, including Lord Clanricard at Portumna (county Galway);

Lord Thomond at Bunratty (county Clare); Lord Kildare at Maynooth (county Kildare); Lady Ormond at Dunmore and Lord Mountgarret at Ballyragget (both in county Kilkenny); and, Lord Muskerry at Blarney (county Cork).

4. Nottingham University Library, Ms Mi Da 57/1 (z), Rathfarnham, 26 June 1611, Call. Chambres [sic] to [Sir Thomas Ridgeway?]; E. Hawkins (ed.), *Sir William Brereton. Travels in Holland, The United Provinces, England, Scotland, and Ireland 1634-5* [London, 1844], p. 146. This park is also referred to as lying in the lordship of Shillelagh (*Egmont MSS* (H.M.C.), i, p. 98). In a survey of 1655, it is listed as containing 1,306 acres 'without distinction of woods', while the 'Low Parke' contained 1,810 acres (Sheffield City Library, Strafford Ms 41, later referred to as Strafford Ms). One source mentions that Calcott Chambre I came from Denbigh in North Wales, west of the port of Chester, but without providing any evidence (Hawkins, *Brereton*, p. 146, n. 1), a sometimes inaccurate family genealogy mentions ancestors at Llewenni, Denbighshire (*Burke's Irish family records* (London, 1957), p. 221. However, both he and his grandfather, Walter Calcott, were styled of Williamscote, Oxfordshire (*Egmont MSS* (H.M.C.), i, p. 97); *Burke's Irish family records* (London, 1957), p. 221). Calcott Chambre I in his will left donations to the poor in Bunbury (probably in Cheshire, south-east of Chester) (P.R.O., London, PROB 11/171, ff. 77v-78). He married first Lucy, daughter of John Gobert, of Coventry, and secondly, Mary, daughter of Edward Villiers, of Howthorpe.
5. H. Kearney, *Strafford in Ireland 1633-41* (Manchester, repr. 1961), p. 175; W. Knowler (ed.), *Letters and dispatches of the Earl of Strafford* (London, 1737), ii, p. 209, 18 Aug. 1638, Wentworth to Lord Clifford. For the earlier history of Cosha, see L. Price, 'The case of Phelim MacFeagh O'Byrne and the lands of Ranelagh' in *R.S.A.I. Jn.*, lxxiii (1943), pp 50-59; L. Price, 'The Byrnes' country in county Wicklow in the sixteenth century' in Ibid., lxiii (1933), 224-42. The lands were surveyed, and a plan of Cosha (not known to have survived) was sent by Sir Thomas Wentworth to Sir William Parsons in 1638 showing the villages, parishes and names of the landowners (Strafford Ms 18, f. 103).
6. *Ormonde MSS* (H.M.C.), n.s. i, p. 40.
7. Strafford Ms 10, f. 192-3, 12 Sept. 1638, Wentworth to Sir Peter Middleton.
8. Knowler, *Letters*, ii, p. 60, 31 Mar. 1637, Wentworth to the King; Knowler, *Letters*, ii, p. 105, 27 Sept. 1637, Wentworth to the Archbishop of Canterbury.
9. Kearney, *Strafford*, p. 175-6. The purchase money for the estate was £8,000 (J. Cooper, 'The fortune of Thomas Wentworth, Earl of Strafford' in *Ec. Hist. Rev.*, 2nd ser. xi (1958-9), p. 243; C. V. Wedgwood, *Thomas Wentworth, first earl of Strafford 1593-1641: A revaluation* (London, 1961), p. 225; Strafford Ms 11, f. 123-7, 29 Aug. 1638, Wentworth to the King; Knowler, *Letters*, i, p. 173, 23 May 1638, Wentworth to Laud.
10. *Cal. S. P. Ire. 1633-47*, p. 262; *The office and authority of a justice of the peace for Ireland...* (Dublin, 1727), pp 71, 180.
11. Knowler, *Letters*, i, pp 162-3.
12. Strafford Ms 10, ff. 192-3; *Cal. S. P. Ire., 1625-32*, p. 536; *Cal. S. P. Ire., 1647-60*, p. 177; J. Gilbert (ed.), *History of the Irish Confederation* (Dublin, 1882), i, p. 24.
13. Lady Burghclere, *Strafford* (London, 1931), i, p. 22; M. Vale, *The gentleman's recreations: accomplishments and pastimes of the English gentleman 1580-1630* (Cambridge, 1977), p. 26. For a general text on hunting, see J. Cummings, *The hound and the hawk: the art of medieval hunting* (New York, 1988); Knowler, *Letters*, i, p. 173, 23 May 1638, Wentworth to Laud.
14. See e.g., the hunting tower at Chatsworth, Derbyshire (M. Girouard, *Robert*

Smythson and the Elizabethan country house (New Haven, 1983), p. 119 and colour plate VII.

15. See drawing of New Parks Lodge, Huby (N. Yorkshire) in M. W. Barley, 'Rural building in England' in J. Thirsk (ed.), *The agrarian history of England and Wales*, v, pt. II, p. 618; Knowler, *Letters*, i, p. 85.
16. J. T. Gilbert (ed.), *Aphorismical discovery of treasonable faction ...* (Dublin, 1878-80), iii, p. 209; A. B. Grosart (ed.), *Lismore papers* (London, 1886-8), ii (ser. 1), pp 125, 156; iv (ser. 1), pp 25, 121; ii (ser. 2), p. 156; *Egmont MSS* (H.M.C.), i, p. 252; information kindly provided by Mr Patrick Bowe.
17. *Cal. S. P. Ire., 1615-25*, p. 289; Knowler, *Letters*, ii, 105, 27 Sept. 1637, Wentworth to Archbishop Laud; *Various collections (H.M.C.)*, vii, p. 419-10, 8 Sept. 1638, Wentworth to Sir Gervase Clifton.
18. N.L.I., Ms 8,014 (ix), Survey of Aughentaine in 1622.
19. R. Loeber, *Biographical dictionary of architects in Ireland* (London, 1981), p. 62.
20. Strafford Ms 11, ff. 123-7, 29 Aug. 1638, Wentworth to the king; *Cal. S. P. Ire., 1633-47*, p. 199, 24 Sept. 1638, King to Wentworth.
21. Burghclere, *Strafford*, i, p. 222.
22. D. Johnston, The medieval fortifications of county Wicklow. Unpublished M.A. thesis, University College, Dublin (1982), p. 101.
23. N.L.I., Ms 24, f. 75. In this calculation the Irish perch is taken as amounting to 21 feet (J. Andrews, *Plantation acres* (Belfast, 1988), p. 17). The park at Kilruddery was modest in size in comparison with that founded by Sir Richard Boyle, earl of Cork, at Lismore (county Waterford), with a circumference almost three times as large (T. C. Barnard, 'Gardening, diet and "improvement" in later seventeenth-century Ireland', in *Jn. Gard. Hist.*, x (1990), p. 78).
24. Reproduced in Malins and The Knight of Glin, *Lost demesnes*, pl. 14.
25. *Ormonde MSS* (H.M.C.), n.s. i, p. 148, [1650] listing of deer parks in county Wicklow; Grosart, *Lismore papers*, series 1, v, p. 10; T.C.D., f. 201. The manor of Knockrath was sold by Loftus to Calcott Chambre I in 1639, and subsequently, through Chambre's daughter came into the hands of the Temple family. The estate, however, was probably leased to Jaobe [sic] Ward, who is noted there in 1641 and in 1650. The killing of deer from this park is mentioned after the outbreak of the 1641 rebellion (Price, *Byrnes' country*, p. 240; T.C.D., Ms 811, ff. 197, 201v).
26. *Cal. S. P. Ire., 1663-5*, p. 438; *Cal. S. P. Ire., 1666-69*, pp 720-722; 20 May [1678], Archbishop Boyle to Orrery (E. MacLysaght (ed.), *Calendar of the Orrery papers* (Dublin, 1941), p. 200).
27. Pipe boards or staves refer to the staves of which twenty five made up a pipe or butt of 105 imperial gallons.
28. J. H. Andrews, 'Robert Lythe's petitions, 1571,' *Anal. Hib.*, xxiv (1967), p. 236.
29. D. White, 'The reign of Edward VI in Ireland: some political, social, and economic aspects' in *I.H.S.*, xiv (1965), p. 204; A. K. Longfield, *Anglo-Irish trade in the sixteenth century* (London, 1929), p. 120; *Fiants Ire., Eliz.*, nos. 3060, 3372; J. Morrin (ed.), *Calendar of the patent and close rolls of chancery* (vol. ii) (Dublin, 1862), p. 17.
30. Hogshead boards are parts of a barrel slightly smaller than a pipe.
31. The income from the customs of Wexford town were extremely low during the period 1586-1593 (B.L., Lansdowne Ms 156, f. 304); E. McCracken, *The Irish woods since Tudor times* (Newton Abbot, 1971), p. 100; P. H. Hore, *History of the town and country of Wexford* (London, 1901), vi, p. 438-9, 438n.2, 1596, Sir Henry Wallop to Sir Robert Cecil; *Salisbury MSS* (H.M.C.), iv, p. 464, [1593?],

Trade in pipe staves from Ireland; Longfield, *Trade*, pp 123-4.

32. K. Whelan, 'Irish historic towns: Enniscorthy', Thomas Davis lecture, Radio Éireann, June 1991.
33. Hore, *Wexford*, vi, p. 411, 1586, Wallop to Walsingham; E. McCracken, 'The Irish timber trade in the seventeenth century' in *Irish Forestry*, xxi (1964), p. 14; Longfield, *Trade*, p. 120; J. De Courcy Ireland, 'County Wexford in maritime history' in K. Whelan (ed.), *Wexford: history and society* (Dublin, 1987), p. 493.
34. Cited in Longfield, *Trade*, p. 122. In 1586, Sir Henry Wallop mentioned that he 'caused great store of tymber to be felled and clefte'. (Hore, *Wexford*, vi, p. 411, 1586, Wallop to Walsingham); *Cal. pat. rolls Jas. I.*, p. 412.
35. For a listing of owners of timber lots along the River Slaney in 1611 see Hore, *Wexford*, vi, p. 456.
36. *Cal. S. P. Ire. 1608-10*, pp 21, 93, 96; Hore, *Wexford*, vi, p. 456, Schedule of timber trees marked for H. M. in the woods of Leinster near the Rivers Slane[y] and Barrow by warrant from the lord deputy, dated 27 July 1611.
37. *Inq. cancell. Hib. repert.*, i (Dublin, 1826-9), county Wicklow, James I, no. 1; *Cal. pat. rolls Jas. I*, p. 253. Aside from Richard Mitton of Mitton-Mowberie in Leicester, gent. (one eighth share), the partners were Gifford Watkins of Draston, Northamptonshire, merchant of the staple of England (one quarter share); Thomas Garway (?Garraway) of London, draper and merchant of the staple (who sold his quarter share to his son Timothy); Richard Gilbert of London, cooper (one quarter share); and Brian Watkines, citizen and grocer of London (one eighth share).
38. Sir Henry Harrington was the son of Sir John Harrington of Exton, while his mother was Elizabeth, heir to Sir Robert Motton, knt., of Pickleton, Leicestershire (J. Fetherston (ed.), *The visitation of the County of Leicester in the year 1619* (London, 1870), p. 59). Irish sources refer to Richard Mitten or Mytten, which may have been variant spellings of Motton.
39. *Cal. S. P. Ire., 1608-10*, p. 88, 27 Oct. 1608, Sir Arthur Chichester to Salisbury; *Cal. pat. rolls, Jas. I*, p. 127; *Inquisitionum*, county Wicklow, James I, no. 11.
40. *Cal. S. P. Ire., 1608-10*, p. 508.
41. *Cal. S. P. Ire., 1608-10*, pp 88-90, 27 Oct. 1608, Sir Arthur Chichester to Salisbury; 8 Nov. 1608, Sir Arthur Chichester to Privy Council; J. Hughes, *Patentee officers in Ireland* (Dublin, 1960), p. 91. The customs of Wicklow were incorporated into those of Dublin.
42. *Cal. pat. rolls Jas. I*, p. 316. The term 'cloven ware' is not listed in the *Oxford English Dictionary*, and may refer to wood split by axe.
43. *Cal. pat. rolls Jas. I*, pp 410, 422; H. O'Grady, *Strafford and Ireland* (Dublin, 1923), i, p. 296.
44. Municipal Archive, Amsterdam, examples of documents are: 111/178v-179v; 116/11-12; 118/127-128; 128/202-203; 131/172v-173; 134/134 (all notary J. F. Bruyningh). I am very grateful to Mrs E. J. Bok-Cleyndert and the staff of the Municipal Archive for communicating these sources to me.
45. Municipal Archive, Amsterdam, 111/178v-179v.
46. *Cal. pat. rolls Jas. I*, pp 360, 362. Chambre obtained this grant through Thomas Freeman and John Dawson who, as assignees of Sir William Harrington, received letters patent of the territory of Shillelagh in 1617, when it had been surrendered by Sir Adam Loftus and Sir William Ussher. Harrington before his death probably mortgaged the property to Sir Patrick Barnwall, Sir Christopher Plunkett, John Sarsfield, and Thomas Allen, while Loftus and Ussher may have acted as the discoverers of concealment of this alienation to the crown (*Cal. pat. rolls Jas. I*,

pp 176, 325, 327); M. Jones, 'Coppice wood management in the eighteenth century: an example from county Wicklow', in *Irish Forestry* (1984), pp 21-2.

47. Hawkins, *Brereton*, p. 146.
48. McCracken, *Timber trade*, p. 5; O'Grady, *Strafford*, i, pp 297-8.
49. N.L.I., Ms 24, pp 93-4, 18 August 1629, deed of sale by Calcott Chambre of Williamscote, county Oxford, on the one part, and James and Nathaniel Fynes, first and second sons of William Viscount Say and Seale and John Crewe, son and heir of Sir Thomas Crewe knt., lands of Shelelowe, etc., to hold from the death of Chambre for 200 years, with liberty to dig for mines and to cut timber; provided that they would use the profit to pay for all of Chambre's debts, legacies, and cost of his funeral, and the making good and performance of all such leases, etc., with the power to make this lease void during his life time, 16 June 1630.
50. P.R.O., London, PROB 11/171, ff. 77v-8, will of Calcott Chambre, probated 1636; for the inquisition after his death, see *Inq. cancell. Hib.*, county Wicklow, Charles I, no. 20.
51. 5 November 1637, Indenture between Calcott Chambre of Carnew, county Wicklow, Esq., James Fines [Fiennes], son and heir of William, Viscount Say and Seale, Nathaniel Fines, second son of Viscount Say and Seale, and John Crewe, Esq., son and heir of Sir Thomas Crewe, serjeant at law, deceased, of the one part and Sir Philip Percivalle, of Dublin, of the other part (*Egmont MSS* (H.M.C.), i, pp 97-8, 177; ii, 515-6, 552; B.L., Add. Ms 27,988, f. 29). Lady Carlisle's investment appears to have amounted to £4,000; in return she was to receive £500 per year for the duration of the lease (J. P. Cooper, 'Wentworth and the Byrne's country' in *I.H.S.*, xv (1966), p. 19n. 85).
52. 3 Nov. 1638, Conveyance by Calcott Chambre of Carnew, county Wicklow, esq., to Joshua Carpenter, Henry Wentworth, George Carr, Thomas Little, and William Billingsley, all of Dublin, Esqs., for £13,200; of the lordship of Shillelagh (N.L.I., Report on Private Coll., vol. xii (Meath papers), p. 2521). 3 Nov. 1638, Agreement between Josua Carpenter, etc. (as in preceding deed); and Calcott Chambre, Ralph Leycester of Taft, Cheshire, esq., Job Warde of Newbawne, county Wexford, esq., and Foliott Chambre of Minmore, county Wicklow, esq., Provides for payment of residue (£12,000) of the purchase money (N.L.I., Report on Private Coll., vol. xii (Meath papers), p. 2521). According to Kearney, the estate consisted of 16,000 acres profitable and about another 8,000 acres waste (Kearney, *Strafford*, p. 179), while Cooper estimated that the estate of Shillelagh contained 17,400 acres (and 6,600 acres unprofitable) (Cooper, 'Fortune,' p. 243).
53. Price, *Byrnes' country*, p. 240; Calcott Chambre III married Mary, daughter of Ralph Leycester of Tofts in Cheshire. Calcott Chambre II's will was proved in Ireland in 1640, when he was styled of Carnew. The published family genealogy, which is somewhat inaccurate, mentions that Calcott Chambre (II) married Edith, daughter of John Ward, which may have been the Ward family of Knockrath: (*Burke's Irish family records* (London, 1957), p. 221; A. Vicars, *Index of prerogative wills of Ireland, 1536-1810* (Dublin, 1897), p. 84).
54. *Cal. S. P. Ire. 1633-47*, p. 250. Knee timber were pieces of timber with a distinct bend used in ship building. In 1636, the English Privy Council also requested an exemption for Samuel Neale of Wexford to export 40,000 pipe staves to London, and a further exemption for 190,000 of various types of staves (*Cal. S. P. Ire. 1633-47*, p. 125; see also Ibid., p. 220); Wedgwood, *Wentworth*, p. 333; Cooper, *Fortune, passim.*
55. *Cal. S. P. Ire., 1633-47*, p. 214.

56. Strafford Ms 10, f. 49, 12 Sept. 1637, Naas, Thomas Wentworth to [Viscount Loftus]; R. C. Simington (ed.), *The Civil Survey a.d. 1654-56, viii, County of Kildare* (Dublin, 1952), pp 47, 66-7. The assumption is that between the 1630s and the 1650s little wood would have been spoiled in this location.
57. *A guide to the county of Wicklow* (Dublin, 1835), p. 97; J. W. Stubbs, *The history of the university of Dublin* (Dublin, 1889), p. 80; *Burke's records*, p. 221.
58. Representative Church Body Library, Christ Church Ms 'Law Proceed', f. 24 ; Sir J. Gilbert (ed.), *Calendar of ancient records of Dublin* (Dublin, 1889), ii, p. 340.
59. T.C.D., Ms 811, f. 97, deposition by John ffenn of the city of Dublin.
60. T.C.D., Ms 811, f. 79; deposition by Calcott Chambre Senior's grandson (T.C.D., Ms 811, f. 175); N.L.I., Report on Private Coll., vol. 12, p. 2521. Calcott Chambre III's uncle ffolliott Chambre resided at Minmore in 1638.
61. J. T. Gilbert (ed.), *A contemporary history of affairs in Ireland from 1641 to 1652* (Dublin, 1879), i, part 1, p. 16.
62. Cooper, 'Fortune,' p. 243, n. 7; T. C. Barnard, 'An Anglo-Irish industrial enterprise: Iron-making at Enniscorthy, county Wexford 1657-92' in *R.I.A. Proc.*, lxxxv (1985), C, p. 106.
63. See also B.L., Sloane Ms 856, f. 115, Order to stay the cutting of timber in 'Shelleh' to preserve it for the English navy, but sold by the Earl of Strafford to some merchants, *c.*1661.
64. Strafford Ms 34. The volume lacks introductory pages and a date.
65. Incorrect figures in ms. are £2 12s. 0d., and £1 6s. [pence illegible].
66. In 1667 Sir Hugh Middleton was authorised to have a monopoly of saw mills in Ireland for fourteen years (*Cal. S. P. Ire. 1666-9*, p. 358).
67. Undated estimate for building works at the Phoenix House (N.L.I., Ms 2,487, f. 119); St. Patrick's Cathedral, Dublin, Chapter Minutes 1671-77, f. 8; McCracken, *Woods*, p. 102.
68. *Cal. S. P. Dom. 1671*, p. 207; for other sources showing governmental interest in the Shillelagh woods, see Barnard, 'Enterprise', p. 140, n. 160.
69. T. Carlyle (ed.), *Oliver Cromwell's letters and speeches* (New York, 1845), i, p. 390; Barnard, 'Enterprise', p. 111.
70. Total of 56*s.* in original.
71. A. Yarranton, *England's improvement* (London, 1677), p. 39.
72. *Beschrğvinghe van de Zeecusten ende Havenen van Yerlandt* (Amsterdam, 1612); *Cal. S. P. Dom. 1671*, p. 207; McCracken, *Woods*, pp 50, 123.
73. McCracken, 'Timber trade', pp 6, 8, 12; *The works of Sir William Temple* (London, 1740) i, p. 115.
74. A survey of the Strafford estate, county Wicklow, 1671, by Richard Clifton, directed to Sir George Rawdon (Huntington Library, San Marino, California, Ms HA 14, 245).
75. G.O., Ms 667, Hearth money roll, county Wicklow, 1669, p. 34 (This is a fuller transcript than that published by L. Price in his 'The hearth money rolls for county Wicklow' in *R.S.A.I. Jn.*, i (1931), pp 164-78); NAI, Book of Survey and Distribution, county Wicklow.
76. *Cal. pat. rolls Jas. I*, p. 483 (on the Bor family, see Family of Bor of Holland and Ireland, *Miscellanae Genealogica*, Dec. 1911). A sixteenth-century scheme by a member of the Ussher family to found a leather manufacture for export may be associated with county Wicklow (the family owned property on the coast, close to Wicklow town) (*Anal. Hib.*, xiii (1943), pp 69-78).
77. TCD, Ms 811, f. 175, deposition by Calcott Chambre III.
78. *Cal. S. P. Ire. 1633-47*, p. 311.

79. B.L., Ms 4756, f. 32v; *Cal. S. P. Dom., 1671*, p. 184.
80. R. Loeber, *The geography and practice of English colonisation in Ireland from 1534 to 1609* (Athlone, 1991), p. 20. The name of the village of Shillelagh dates only from the nineteenth century; formerly it was called The Forge. According to tradition, the forge was situated close to the bridge across the River Derry (L. Price, *Placenames*, vi, p. 339).
81. Hawkins, *Brereton*, p. 146.
82. McCracken, *Woods*, pp 92-3.
83. Perhaps another trail from Arklow to Shillelagh has not been investigated yet.
84. Cooper, 'Fortune', p. 243. Around this time, Wentworth attempted to create a plantation in the two baronies of Ormond (county Tipperary), claimed by the earl of Ormond. Wicklow, compared with Arklow, was much larger: in 1668, Wicklow had about twice as many houses as Arklow, indicating a higher degree of prosperity (there were 140 houses in Wicklow town, compared to 68 in Arklow (G.O., Ms 677).
85. T.C.D., Ms 811, f. 177.
86. E. McCracken, 'Charcoal-burning ironworks in seventeenth and eighteenth-century Ireland' in *Ulster Jn. Arch.* xx (1957), pp 124, 126; H. Kearney, 'Richard Boyle, ironmaster' in *R.S.A.I. Jn.*, lxxxiii (1953), p. 157; Barnard, 'Industrial enterprise', pp 121-2, calculated that a much larger investment was necessary to start the ironworks near Enniscorthy in the late 1650s; H. Cleere and D. Crossley, *The iron industry of the Weald* (Leicester, 1985), pp 242-59.
87. G. Boate, *Ireland's naturall history* (London, 1652), p. 110.
88. Boate, *Naturall history*, pp 110-11.
89. J. U. Nef, 'The progress of technology and the growth of large-scale industry in Great Britain, 1540-1640' in E. Carus-Wilson (ed.), *Essays in economic history* (London, 1954), i, pp 88-107.
90. Cleere and Crossley, *Iron industry*, pp 121, 176-77, 219-220.
91. W. Nolan, The historical geography of the ownership and occupation of land in the barony of Fassadinin, Kilkenny, *c.* 1600-1850. Ph.D. thesis, University College, Dublin (1975), p. 76; Safe conduct for Richard Rowley and Jacquisse Lagasse and sixteen Walloons whom they have brought over from beyond the seas to make ordnance, bar-iron and other things at the King's ironworks in Ireland (*Anal. Hib.*, ii (1931), p. 77).
92. Judging from a deposition by John Mallington of Minmore, who in mentioning his losses blames one John Garrett of Carnew, 'a man employed in the Ironworks' (T.C.D., Ms 811, f. 80).
93. Strafford Ms 10, f. 192-3, 12 Sept. 1638, Cosha, Wentworth to Sir Peter Middleton.
94. N.L.I., Report on Private Coll., vol. 12, p. 2521 (Meath papers) 3 Nov. 1638, Conveyance by Calcott Chambre of Carnew, county Wicklow, esq., to Joshua Carpenter, Henry Wentworth, George Carr, Thomas Little, and William Billingsley, all of Dublin, esqs., for £13,200; of the lordship of Shelelowe als. Sheleloe als. Shelelagh als. Shelely in the counties of Wicklow, Dublin, Wexford, and Carlow. 3 Nov. 1638, Agreement between Josh Carpenter, etc. (as in preceding deed); and Calcott Chambre, Ralph Leycester of Taft, Cheshire, esq., Job Warde of Newbawne, county Wexford, esq., and Foliott Chambre of Minmore, county Wicklow, esq., Provides for payment of residue (£12,000) of the purchase money on or before 1 Nov. 1645; and for conveyance of the premises, in the meantime, to Warde, Leycester, and Foliott Chambre, in trust for payment of an annuity of £100 to Calcott Chambre; with remainder to Mary Chambre, his wife and his heirs. The transaction does not only fail to mention

Strafford, but also the Countess of Carlisle, who had an interest in the estate valued at £4,000 (*Egmont MSS* (H.M.C.), i, p. 515).

95. Knowler, *Letters*, i, pp 128, 145, 163, 181; Grosart, *Lismore papers*, series l, iii, p. 209; Kearney, *Boyle*, p. 161; Vicars, *Wills*, p. 37.
96. Referred to in Strafford Ms 34, p. 9. In 1637 Sir Philiberto Vernatti and Capt. Thomas Whitmore concluded an agreement with the king to sell iron at a specified price from their ironworks in England and Ireland (*Cal. S. P. Dom. 1637*, p. 576). It is unclear whether Wentworth was involved in these works.
97. P. Lennon, 'Eighteenth century landscape change from estate records: Coolattin estate, Shillelagh, county Wicklow.' B.A. dissertation, Department of Geography, Trinity College, Dublin, 1979, p. 82, citing G. H. Kinahan, 'Irish metal mining' in *Jn. Royal Geol. Soc. Ire.*, n.s. iii, 1886, p. 64; N.L.I., Ms 24, pp 93-4,
98. Cooper, 'Fortune', p. 245; Price, 'Hearth money roll', p. 166; L. Price, *Placenames*, vi, p. 339.
99. Strafford Ms 34. In comparison, the Monart works in county Wexford initially produced 1250 tons of refined iron in its first three years of operation (Barnard, 'Industrial enterprise', p. 110) .
100. Cleere and Crossley, *Iron industry*, p. 161; Strafford Ms 34, f. 7.
101. Strafford Ms 34, f. 19.
102. For other comparisons between charcoal production in England and Ireland, see J. Andrews 'Notes on the historical geography of the Irish iron industry' in *Ir. Geog*., iii (1954-8), p. 142; McCracken, *Woods*, 1971, p. 95.
103. Andrews, 'Irish iron industry', pp 141, 148 n. 11; McCracken, *Woods*, p. 95.
104. Kearney, *Boyle*, p. 158; Barnard, 'Enterprise', p. 126.
105. Price, 'Hearth money roll', p. 166; McCracken, *Woods*, pp 50, 94.
106. McCracken, *Woods*, p. 125.
107. *The works of Sir William Temple* (London, 1740) i, pp 119-120.
108. Strafford Ms 34, f. 13.
109. *Cal. pat. rolls Jas. I*, p. 521. The individuals from Dublin owning property in the town were Daniel Birne and Garret FitzDaniel Birne. Others, probably from Dublin were Thomas Bee and William Harrington. A Michael Bea from Dublin had built White's Castle prior to 1580 (C. Lennon, *The lords of Dublin in the age of the Reformation* (Dublin, 1989), pp 230-1). James Bee held the castle at his death in 1626. In 1620, another Michael Bee was subconstable of the castle, while Thomas Bee was its occupant (*Inq. cancell. Hib*., i, county Wicklow, James I, no. 21; Charles I, no. 5).
110. *Cal. pat. rolls Jas. I*, p. 521; N.L.I., Ms 24, p. 36, 1 June 1626, Charles I, grant to Sir William Ussher, as assignee of Sir Dudley Norton, including three messuages and quay lately built on part of the strand in or near the Creek or River of Wicklow, extending into the sd Creek or River East to Peter White's land West & to other parts of the strand south and north, 1 June 1626. Ussher had an estate called Grange on the coast north of Wicklow.
111. A survey by William Brooke, following 1633, gives detailed descriptions of Irish harbours, but, inexplicably, does not describe either the harbours of Wicklow or Wexford (B.L., Add. Ms 70,521).
112. H. F. Hore, 'Sir Henry Sidney's memoir of his government in Ireland' in *Ulster Jn. Arch*., viii (1860), pp 179-180.
113. Massari, 'My Irish campaign' in *The Catholic Bulletin*, vi (1916), p. 218.
114. E. Welch (ed.), *Plymouth building accounts of the sixteenth and seventeenth centuries* (Torquay, 1967), pp 23, 56.

115. J. Williamson, *Hawkins of Plymouth: A new history of Sir John Hawkins* (New York, 1969), p. 331.
116. As another example, among the commercial notes in 1635-6 of Christopher Lowther of Whitehaven (Cumberland) are references to his contacts with Lord Deputy Wentworth (D. Hainsworth, 'The commercial papers of Sir Christopher Lowther, 1611-1644' in *Surtees Soc.*, clxxxix (1977), pp 159, 194).
117. McCracken, *Woods*, pp 107-8.
118. Barnard, 'Enterprise', p. 140, n. 160.
119. A survey of the Strafford Estate, county Wicklow, 1671, loc. cit.
120. B.L., Add. Ms 47,016, f. 106-106v, 1637, Instructions concerning Sir Philip Perceval's estate.
121. *Anal. Hib.*, xx (1958), p. 147.
122. T. C. Barnard, 'Gardening', pp 78-79; E. C. Nelson, '"This garden to adorne with all varietie:" The garden plants of Ireland in the centuries before 1700' in *Moorea*, ix (1991), p. 48.
123. Petty, *The political anatomy of Ireland* (London, 1691), p. 14; Marquis of Lansdowne, *The Petty papers* (London, 1927), i, p. 127; see also P. Kelly (ed.), 'The improvement of Ireland' in *Anal. Hib.*, xxxv (1992), pp 64, 75.
124. W. Boutcher, *A treatise on forest-trees* (Dublin, 1786), p. 294. This book contains a section entitled 'Some hints on planting. By a planter. Printed at Newry, in Ireland.' This pamphlet was originally published in 1773.
125. Jones, 'Coppice management', pp 22-5.
126. Cited in Lennon, 'Landscape change', p. 60.

Chapter 9

THE BYRNES OF BALLYMANUS

CONOR O'BRIEN

St Kevin, St Laurence O'Toole, Feagh McHugh O'Byrne, Billy and Garrett Byrne of Ballymanus, Michael Dwyer and Charles Stewart Parnell are the names synonymous in the popular mind with the history of county Wicklow. But whereas there are biographical works relating to Dwyer, Parnell and the two saints, nothing concrete is available about the two most renowned O'Byrne families other than passing references in accounts of the Elizabethan conquest of the country and the 1798 rebellion. The essay that follows is based on the primary documentary sources relating to the Byrnes of Ballymanus with the objective of elucidating who they were and what became of them.[1]

The surname O'Byrne is derived from Bran mac Maolmórdha, a king of Leinster who was deposed in 1018 and who died in 1052. In pre-Norman times the O'Byrnes and the O'Tooles, then known as the Uí Fhaeláin and Uí Muireadaig septs respectively, inhabited the rich Kildare plains.[2] With the progress of the Anglo-Norman conquest these septs were compelled to migrate to the poorer lands and the mountainous country eastwards, in due course appropriating the lands of the ancient tribes who occupied this region, later to be denominated as the county of Wicklow. By the early 1200s the O'Tooles are to be found well entrenched in the northern part of this territory with the remainder mainly under the control of the O'Byrnes, apart from small pockets such as the towns of Arklow and Wicklow. The paucity of records from the period does not permit a comprehensive assessment of how the territory was ruled. However, by the beginning of the fourteenth century a division of the clan into two principal branches was apparent. The senior branch, usually described as the Crioch Branach, ruled the district east of the Avonmore from Delgany to the outskirts of Arklow. The semi-autonomous junior branch held the mountainous country east of Imaal between Glendalough and Shillelagh and was called the Gabhal Raghnaill, the name deriving from Raghnall Ó Broin, a scion of the family placed ninth in the line of descent from Bran in the ancient genealogies.

Its territory, centred around the chief's principal residence at Ballinacor at the mouth of Glenmalure, became known by various anglicised versions of this name such as Colranell or the Ranelagh.[3] The relative strengths of the two branches may be inferred from an English document of about 1480 enumerating the armed forces maintained by the Gaelic chiefs. A 'batayle' of 60 to 80 galloglasses, a further 60 horsemen and 88 kern, each category with its complement of servants to carry armoury, are attributed to 'O Brin Lord of ybranaght' while 'Redmond McShane Lord of Gowllranel' is listed with the rather smaller force of 8 horsemen and 40 kern.[4] That situation altered with the accession of Hugh McShane O'Byrne, grandson of Redmond, as chief of the sept around the middle of the sixteenth century. While the Crioch Branach apparently submitted to the lord deputy's rule, the Gabhal Raghnaill aggressively pursued a policy of resistance to anglicisation until the final collapse of the old Gaelic order at the battle of Kinsale. Under Hugh McShane's leadership the Gabhal Raghnaill became a formidable force, regularly carrying out raids and expeditions against the contiguous English settlements. When Hugh died in 1579 his son Feagh (Fiacha) was chosen to succeed him as chief of Gabhal Raghnaill.

Feagh's reputation as a redoubtable opponent of the Dublin regime continued until 'unwieldy and spent with years,' as Lord Deputy Russell had described him in 1596, he and four guards were cornered by the lord deputy's armies in Glenmalure and slain in the vicinity of Feagh's residence at Ballinacor on the morning of Sunday, 8 May 1597.[5] On his return to Rathdrum from the victorious expedition the exultant lord deputy bestowed knighthoods on three of his company commanders in front of the heavily fortified church in Rathdrum and despatched news of his achievement to the privy council in London. Feagh's pickled head was then sent by messenger to Queen Elizabeth. She, however, was not impressed and 'was much troubled with the late knights that were made' and displeased that 'the head of such a base Robin Hood is brought so solemnly into England', concluding that 'if it be true his son be still out, his youth will better his father's age'.[6] This son, Phelim, Feagh's successor as chief, and Raymond, the other surviving son, maintained the war against the Pale for a few more years.

An inquisition held in Ballinacor on 16 January 1606 to determine his estate concluded that when Feagh was killed he was seized in fee of several named townlands in the Ranelagh and also some tracts of land in territory formerly held by the Crioch Branach in the baronies of Arklow and Newcastle and the district known as Cosha – essentially the basin of the Derry Water, comprising the parishes of Kilcommon, Kilpipe, Preban and part of Moyne – which Feagh had acquired through mortgage.[7] The estate, deemed forfeit to the Crown, was divided by royal grant some months later between Phelim and

Raymond, while disposal of the remainder of the clan lands was left undecided.[8] This sparked off a rapacious campaign by influential persons aligned to the government to oust the O'Byrnes. Their machinations were aptly described by John O'Donovan, as affording 'an appalling picture of human depravity and perfidy in those murderous times'.[9]

In response to his insecure situation Phelim pursued a temporising policy with the government while maintaining *de facto* possession of his territory until his death in 1631. In his will there are several references to 'my son and heir, Bryan McPhelim'.[10] Since there are no specific bequests to Bryan it was apparently believed that his nomination as chief of the clan would suffice for an inheritance. Phelim divided amongst his other sons, Hugh, Garrett, James, Turlough, Cahir and Art, what he regarded as his personal estate held under English law, since the townlands listed were much the same as specified in the royal grant of 1606. The Down Survey shows that the disposals made by Phelim in his will were generally held by his sons in 1641, and that his brother Raymond and the latter's son, Luke, were deemed also to be in possession of various lands. Tenure of all these holdings came to an end following the forfeitures in the wake of the 1641 rebellion and when the Books of Survey and Distribution were compiled later in the century no member of either Phelim's or Raymond's families is shown in possession of any land at all in the county.[11]

Little is known of what became of these families. Bryan McPhelim is mentioned *circa* 1648 as being in command of the Gabhal Raghnaill troops in the Catholic Confederacy in which Bryan's son, Seán, also served with the rank of colonel.[12] Hugh McPhelim, addressed as a lieutenant-general of the Confederate Catholics, was appointed governor of county Wicklow in 1648.[13] According to the writer of the contemporary polemic, *An Aphorismicall Discovery,* Bryan afterwards went to Ulster and thence to Inisbofin, while Hugh went into exile in Spain.[14] Another brother, Fr Laurence Byrne, is mentioned by that writer as being guardian of the Franciscan Friary at Ballinabarney.[15] Phelim's other sons, Garrett, James, Turlough, Cahir and Art are, along with Hugh, listed in the outlawries of 1641-47, and likewise Raymond McFeagh and his sons Luke, Phelim and Shane.[16] Presumably they all fled into exile. With the exception of Cahir's children, one of whom, Don Arturo O'Bruin, became a general in the Spanish navy and a Knight of the Order of Calatrava, the fate of this generation of the Gabhal Raghnaill has not been elucidated.[17]

According to the genealogist O'Hart, the Ballymanus Byrnes were descended from Raymond McFeagh.[18] O'Hart is at odds with the more distinguished genealogist John O'Donovan, who notes in his edition of the *Annals of the Four Masters* that, according to tradition in the country, Garrett was not descended from Feagh but a branch of Feagh's sept who became spies and informers to ruin the great Ballinacor family.[19] O'Donovan concluded that the tradition pointed to Cahir McHugh Duffe O'Byrne of the rival Knockrath branch who was closely associated with Lord Esmond in a scheme aimed at having Phelim's sons convicted of murder and their lands confiscated.

There would seem to be more substance in the tradition recorded by O'Donovan than in the ancestry outlined by O'Hart. The source of O'Hart's information seems to have been a genealogical table constructed by Edward Joseph Colclough Byrne of Rathmines, a grandson of Edward Byrne of Ballymanus, brother to Garrett and Billy of '98 fame. As a twenty-two year old temporary employee in the excise branch of the Inland Revenue he conceived the idea that he might have been heir to the Ballymanus estates and spent much of his free time during the summer months of 1867 researching his family history with the objective of establishing a claim to the ancestral lands. He kept a diary and this along with several items of correspondence relating to his ancestry are fortunately extant.[20] Amongst the correspondence is a letter somehow acquired from the papers of Luke Cullen, the Carmelite monk of Clondalkin and well-known authority on 1798. It appears to be a reply written to Brother Cullen in 1855 by Mary Ann Byrne of Kilcullen on behalf of her ninety year old father, Garrett Byrne of Ballycapple. In it the old man asserted that the Ballymanus family and other branches of the O'Byrnes were descended from Feagh's son, Raymond.

Edward refers to this letter in his diary and tells of an evening spent discussing these matters with Father C.P. Meehan of Saints Michael and John's parish. Meehan, a writer on historical topics with an established reputation, had mentioned that he and the late John O'Donovan had had long discussions on the pedigree of the Ballymanus Byrnes but had been unable to establish any connection between the family and Feagh McHugh. Undaunted by the failure of such eminent scholars, Edward asserted that John Byrne of Kiltimon was a son of Raymond, Feagh's son, and 'having purchased Ballymanus about 1620 removed the family seat thence from Kiltimon'. Nothing in Edward's papers indicates how he formed this idea and no documentary evidence supporting the contention has come to light. Young Edward died in 1870 but some time before his death he had become acquainted with Reverend John Edge, the incumbent of Calary, who had planned to publish a history of the Byrne families. Edward provided his pedigree to Mr Edge for this purpose but in the event it was not used. Only one part of Edge's history appeared in print and this consisted largely of extracts relating to the O'Byrnes from O'Donovan's *Annals of the Four Masters*.[21] Edge remarked that O'Donovan had been misled by tradition in regard to some families and that this would be rectified with respect to the Byrnes of Ballymanus. However, since the first issue of the history met with disappointing support, another was not published. O'Hart's pedigree bears such close resemblance to that prepared by Edward that it seems very probable that it was supplied to O'Hart by Edge, thereby leading to the repetition of the errors.

Apart from the unsupported assertion that the family descended from Raymond McFeagh O'Byrne, Edward's researches were otherwise painstaking and productive. His discovery in the Registry of Deeds of conveyances executed in 1817 and 1821 by his granduncle, Garrett Byrne of Ballymanus, to which his own grandfather and his grand-aunts, Frances and Eleanor Byrne were parties, put paid to his hopes of a title to the Ballymanus property.[22] One of these deeds of sale cited the original conveyance of the lands of Ballymanus, Macreddin and Clohernagh to Garrett Byrne of Ballymanus by Sir Laurence Esmond of Clonegal on 13 January 1700 for ever at a yearly rent of £12.[23] The granting of a lease in perpetuity to the Catholic Byrne family before the passing of the notorious 1704 Act 'to prevent the further growth of popery' enabled them to hold on to the estate during the period of the penal code.

It seems not improbable that Garrett's ancestors were tenants on these lands long before the lease referred to was obtained from Sir Laurence Esmond, then under some financial pressures. After an abortive effort by Esmond's great grandfather to secure Ballymanus along with numerous other townlands in the county by grant from James I in 1622, his ambition was better satisfied in 1628 by King Charles I with a grant of nearly 5,000 statute acres in the territory of Ranelagh, the lands to be called the manor of Castle Laurence.[24] Since Ballymanus was never named in the numerous commissions of inquiry on land ownership as having been in the possession of Feagh McHugh or his sons, the troublesome question of dispossessing influential tenants would not have arisen. It is likely that Esmond, by then raised to the peerage as Baron Esmond of Limbrick, regranted the townland to the sitting tenant whose descendants remained in possession for the next two centuries.

The appearance in the records of the Ballymanus Byrnes as a family of some standing first occurs towards the end of the seventeenth century when Hugh Byrne Esq. was elected as MP for the Borough of Carysfort (i.e. Macreddin) in the short-lived parliament convened by James II in 1689.[25] He is no doubt the same Hugh Byrne esquire of Ballymanus who was listed amongst the persons subsequently outlawed for treason by William III. These lists also include a 'Gerrald Byrne, Ballymanus, gent', most likely the Capt. Garrett Byrne, gent, listed among the ajudications on 4 July 1694 under the articles of Limerick and Galway.[26] This implies that he had been pardoned by the Irish Privy Council and allowed to keep his property intact. Garrett was Hugh's son and heir. A further indication that Hugh was a person of substance is revealed by the list of claims under the Act of Resumption of 1700.[27] Included in this list are claims for the rectorial tithes of Kilpipe, Kiltegan and Killinor, described as formerly the property of Hugh Byrne esquire by virtue of leases executed in 1687 but who had forfeited it 'being attainted of High Treason'. Assuming that Hugh Byrne of Ballymanus was head of a family long established on these lands the question arises of where he and his forebears had lived.

On the Ordnance Survey map of 1840 the presumed site of Castle Laurence is shown about 200 yards west of Ballymanus House. It is traditionally thought to have been built by Laurence Esmond, the grantee of these lands in 1628.[28] Esmond died in 1646 and, because his son and heir, Sir Thomas, had fought with the Confederate Catholics in 1641, difficulties were encountered in establishing title to his father's estate and lengthy litigation ensued before the Esmonds regained possession.[29] However, there is no record of the family having resided at any time in Ballymanus and if the castle was ever completed it seems likely that it suffered the same fate as many other castles – Arklow, Kilcommon, Knockrath, Ballinacor and Killaveny – in this part of the county during the wars of the 1640s. The Down Survey recorded 'a church in ruins' on the lands of Ballymanus but there is no other evidence of a church ever having existed in Ballymanus.[30] Petty's surveyors, working in hazardous conditions in hostile country, had either mistaken the castle ruins for a church or else confused the location with the church ruins in nearby Rosahane which are not shown on Petty's maps. The remaining archival source that might lead to information about the Byrne family's abode is the Hearth Money Roll of 1668-69 for the county but, unfortunately, it leaves the question unsettled.[31] Neither castle nor house befitting a gentleman of property is indicated in Ballymanus. Indeed in the whole district comprising Ballymanus and the adjoining townlands of Askakeagh, Cappagh, Coolballentaggart and Kiladuff only five of the thirty-six habitations in this district possessed hearths and of the sixteen householders named Byrne only one, John Byrne of Coolballentaggart, aspired to such comfort.

It is possible that the Byrnes resided outside Ballymanus and that the house there was not built until late in the 1600s. A residence in the vicinity of Rosahane is suggested by the fact that it was their traditional burial ground. Garrett Byrne of Ballymanus who died in 1714 requested in his will that he be buried with his ancestors in Rosahane.[32] This implies that his connection with the place went further back than his father's generation. A Mary Byrne of Rosahane died intestate in 1685.[33] Further information about her was lost in the Four Courts fire in 1922 but the fact of her estate requiring legal proceedings suggests a woman of substantial property residing in Rosahane. She may have been the mother of Hugh.

Complete copies of the wills of both Hugh Byrne and his son Garrett perished in 1922 but fortunately some scholars had previously transcribed essential particulars. An abridged version of Hugh's will, preserved in the Genealogical Office, shows that it was made on 1 March 1696 and proved in 1707.[34] He left his interest in the farm of Ballymanus and Macreddin to his son Garrett, he to pay for the 'schooling of testator's two little boys Simon and Hugh'. To his son Edward he left the benefit of the lease of Cappagh 'after Mr Thady Byrne's debt is paid'. Cows were left to his wife Mary and ten sheep to 'Joan Talbott or her mother'. The guardian and friars of Wicklow were left 20 shillings but if Hugh recovered his tithes they were to receive £10 per annum out of the benefits of the lease while he held it. Likewise his wife was to receive £10 per annum should the lease be recovered. The convent of Arklow was given 10 shillings; Fr Charles Byrne got 10 shillings and Fr Edward Byrne 20 shillings, presumably for masses. Charles Byrne was parish priest of Rathdrum at the time while Edward is probably the then parish priest of St Nicholas Without in Dublin who succeeded as archbishop of Dublin in 1707; he may have been related to Hugh.[35]

Before its destruction in 1922, Garrett Byrne's will had been synopsised by Dr Stanley Lane-Poole, an historian and orientalist who settled for some years earlier in the century in Dunganstown, county Wicklow, and planned to write a history of the county. His notes indicated that the will was made on 21 February 1714 and proved about six weeks later, Garrett devising the lease of Ballymanus and Clohernagh to his eldest son and namesake (whom we shall refer to as Garrett Byrne II). Unspecified references were made to his wife Catherine, his second son, Thomas, and his daughter Joan. His brother Hugh was given two cows. Instructions were issued for the woods in Ballymanus and Glenmalure to be sold. The executors appointed were his brother, Charles Byrne of Clone, and Walter Byrne of Killoughter who was described as his cousin.[36] Some particulars from the will had also been abstracted by Sir William Betham, Ulster King of Arms, who had made a copy of the devices apparently used on Garrett's seal. This shows a shield bearing a chevron between three right hands as is usually associated with the Clan O'Byrne but with the difference that the crest surmounting the shield consists of the head of a hound rather than the customary representation of a mermaid holding a mirror in her right hand and a comb in her left.[37]

An unabridged copy of the will of Garrett's brother, Charles of Clone, survives and is of considerable interest because it reveals contemporary practices and values.[38] Made on 18 April 1728 and admitted to probate a few weeks later, it provides at the outset for the appointment of three neighbouring gentry, Thomas Brownrigg, Thomas Pyers and Francis Hatton, as advisers to his wife and young children. They were asked to arrange the sale of his livestock and corn, the proceeds to be divided equally between his wife Ellinor and his six children, Mary, Frances, Elizabeth, John, William, and Ambrose, 'share and share alike'. Special provision was made for another daughter, Catherine (presumably a natural daughter), to be put out to a trade by leaving £10 for the purpose with another £10 to be paid by the family when her apprenticeship had been served. The main bequest was his 'right title and interest in and to the farms of Clone and Tomenerin and to the lease made to me by Thos. Bunbury Esqr.' to his sons John and William along with the residue of all cash, notes, bills, bonds and debts due to him. The Bunbury lease, dated 20 November 1723, comprised two-thirds of the rectorial tithes of the parishes of Kilpipe and Kiltegan in county Wicklow, and Killinor in county Wexford.[39] Out of this income John and William were to pay £10 per annum to Ambrose during the continuance of the lease. In addition to his cash disbursement Ambrose was left a mare and foal. Charles's daughter Mary, who seems to have been his eldest child, was bequeathed the profits of his malt house and mill until John had reached the age of twenty-one or until the time of her marriage if earlier.

A bequest surely fraught with the possibility of domestic tensions was Charles's disposal of the family home. To his wife he left 'the large room upstairs with the furniture thereof'; to his sons John and William 'the parlor, blew room and the furniture thereof equally between them, together with all my plate except my plate spurs which I leave to my said son John as also my new boots, my watch, black britches and my new wigg' with William being left 'my new hatt, saddle and bridle'. Complicating the allocations in the house at Clone was the bequest to his widowed sister, Ann Byrne, of £4 along with 'lodging and dyett in the dwelling house at Clone until my son John shall be of age'. Charles's brother Francis was also provided with food and lodging in Clone until John's majority along with 'my new black coat and wastecoat, my double breasted coat and black waste coat, with my new black and white britches'. Some family retainers were catered for too: 'to Terrence or Turlough Byrne my old boots, wigg, hat and one shirt' and 'to John Ugan my black and white sarge coat and vest'. His spiritual bequest had a somewhat ironic touch: to Father Philip Furlong he bequeathed the rectorial tithes of Curraghlawn townland in Kilpipe parish during the minority of his son John, together with one barrel of malt.[40] A further direction given was 'that the sume of twenty or thirty pounds whatsoever it be that was left to my said wife by her father be divided equally between my said wife and my daughter Frances'. All of the bequests to his children were governed by the stipulation that none of them was to marry without the approval of their mother and two of the three family advisers, while if his wife remarried during the minority of Ambrose she was to forfeit all legacies except that left to her by her father. Charles appointed his wife and daughter Mary in trust as executors until his son John had become of age, he then becoming sole executor.

An unusual feature of the will was Charles's division of the main part of his estate equally between his two sons, John and William, with John being named as if he were the principal of the two. A possible explanation may be that Charles felt William had not long to live. William's name does not feature as co-heir in any surviving documents concerning the estate. John himself came of age in 1735. However, he does not seem to have made a success of his inheritance. A deed dated 18 May 1747 concerning the disposal of Thomas Bunbury's estate and naming Ambrose and John Byrne as parties reveals that Ambrose had sold the annuity charged on the Bunbury tithes to John and that John in turn had assigned the lease to his cousin Garrett Byrne of Ballymanus for £100.[41] Rather significantly, however, the domicile of both John and Ambrose is now given as Tomcoyle rather than Clone. The townland of Tomcoyle comprised part of the Wentworth estates in the county inherited by the marquess of Rockingham, and the head tenant at the time was Jacob Coates.[42] John presumably had by then lost Clone and become an undertenant to Jacob Coates. Further deterioration in John's fortunes emerges from a deed poll he executed on 4 October 1766 providing for the transfer of all his rights and property to his brother Ambrose in return for food and lodgings and the other necessities of his remaining lifetime.[43] His domicile at that time is given as Killalisk, county Wicklow.[44] Finally, the intestacy of Ambrose Byrne of Knockboly, county Wicklow, in 1776, is the last reference noted to this once relatively well-off family.[45]

It is convenient at this juncture to note the associations between the Coates and Byrne properties. Jacob Coates died sometime before 1763, his son George taking over the remaining period of the lease of Tomcoyle. However, George failed to obtain a renewal of the lease in

1763. The principal objection to him, as expressed in Rockingham's agent's correspondence, was that Jacob Coates 'marrying a Papist wife had issue by her the said George Coates and two other boys and two girls who are brought up rigid Papists'.[46] Given that rank and social status were important considerations in marriage choices at the time and that the Byrnes were one of the few if not the only Catholic family of rank in the district it is not inconceivable that Jacob Coates had married one of the Ballymanus family.

Jacob's kinsman, Charles Coates, had acquired the lease of the neighbouring townland of Rednagh on the Rockingham estate on the death of his father in 1751.[47] Three years later he acquired the lease of the estate formerly held by Charles Byrne. The deed, dated 29 May 1754, refers to 'the lands of Cloan and Timonering now in the possession of said Charles Coates and his undertenants except that part of Timonering which is in the possession of Mich. Carey'.[48] In 1785 he brought back Tomcoyle into the Coates family, with whom it remained until recent times.[49] Tankersley House in Tomcoyle is synonymous with the Coates family and probably attests to Yorkshire origins but Clone House was where Charles Coates lived. It was here that Billy Byrne of Ballymanus was given refuge one night in 1798 when escaping from the Hacketstown yeomen. Clone House was later burnt by the rebels and Coates family tradition has it that Charles's elderly wife refused to leave her bed whereupon Billy Byrne had her carried down carefully in her bed and deposited on the lawn.[50]

Garrett Byrne of Ballymanus inherited the Ballymanus estate from his father Hugh. In June 1713 he added the lease of Ballymorris, a property of around 420 statute acres, obtaining it for thirty-one years at £33 per annum from Robert Johnson of Kirktown, county Down.[51] Johnson was the husband of Lucy Magill, eldest daughter and devisee of Capt Hugh Magill who is listed in the Books of Survey and Distribution as the person to whom Ballymorris was disposed following its confiscation from Raymond McFeagh McHugh O'Byrne, its proprietor in 1641.[52]

In Garrett's will of 1714 his second son, Thomas, is named. While nothing definite is known about the provisions made for Thomas he may well have secured a lease of the interest and title to the lordship of Glendalough and Strangeen and the lands of Drummin in 1747.[53] The deeds of conveyance recite that a judgment had been obtained in the court of exchequer by Garrett Byrne, gent. (address not given) against Thomas Sherwood and that on foot thereof the sheriff of county Wicklow had sold Sherwood's interest in the Glendalough and Drummin estate to John Hetherington of Callan, county Kilkenny, 'for the use of Thos. Byrne of Larah, Co Wicklow, gent.' Witnesses to the transactions include Thomas Hugo but perhaps more significantly 'Ally

Byrne sister to Garrett Byrne of Ballymanus, gent'. Her involvement would suggest a close family association with the beneficiary and points to her brother as the instigator of the suit to secure the Drummin estate. Thomas Byrne died a few years later and appears to have been childless. The Betham abstract of his will names John, Simon and Thomas Hugo as his nephews, and Jane Hetherington, Margaret Robinson and Sarah Simpson as nieces, all presumably legatees.[54] Thomas Hugo was appointed executor. Sometime subsequently he became proprietor of Drummin. Hugo's son Thomas developed a close friendship with Billy Byrne of Ballymanus later in the century which may have originated from this family connection. The friendship soured, however, and Thomas Hugo became one of the chief state witnesses against Billy at his treason trial in 1799.[55]

The little information we have on Garrett Byrne II is derived primarily from the diary of Edward Byrne. In June 1867 he travelled on a rail excursion to Wicklow and visited Fr Molony of Kilbride who had been recommended to him by Fr Meehan. Fr Molony suggested that he should call on Colclough Byrne of Ballycapple. The ensuing discussion at Ballycapple led to the discovery that he and Colclough had a common ancestor in Garrett Byrne II, Colclough's father, Garrett, being a son of John Byrne, second son of Garrett II, while Edward's grandfather was a son of the same forebear's eldest son, Garrett III. Another interesting discovery for Edward was that Colclough had in his possession in Ballycapple the will of Garrett II.[56] Edward noted in his diary that the will was dated from Hacketstown on 17 January 1767 and that the names mentioned included Garrett, the eldest son, who was described as having been provided for by his marriage articles, two other sons, John and Colclough, a daughter Margaret, a cousin Luke Masterson and his wife Frances, and a Jemmy Kavanagh whom Edward assumed to have been a natural son. The only detail of legacies that Edward noted at the time was one that particularly fascinated him – a feather bed.

In the genealogical table for the family compiled by Edward he ascribes a 'Miss Colclough of Tintern, aunt to Caesar Colclough' as being the wife of Garrett II. Efforts to locate documentary evidence substantiating this have been unsuccessful but the assertion if valid would account for the adoption of Colclough as a forename in subsequent generations. It is tentatively suggested that she was Katherine Colclough, a sister of Dudley Colclough of Duffrey Hall who married Mary Barnewall in 1691 and whose eldest son, Caesar, born in 1696, inherited Tintern Abbey in 1723.[57] He is usually known as 'The Great Caesar'. Katherine Colclough had another brother, Adam of Boley, who married Margaret Masterson of Monaseed, county Wexford, in 1701. Margaret's brother, John, was the father of Luke Masterson who is described in the will of Garrett Byrne II as his cousin. The term cousin was used rather loosely in former times and Luke Masterson might more accurately be described as Garrett's wife's sister-in-law's nephew. The friendship was close in any event. Luke Masterson was one of the trustees to the marriage settlement of Garrett's eldest son, Garrett III, in 1755 while both Garrett and Luke acted as arbitrators in May 1746 in the settlement of a dispute between Patrick Colclough of Duffrey and the 'Great Caesar'.[58] Both the Mastersons and the Ballymanus Byrnes had social links with the wealthy Juliana, countess of Anglesey, whose seat was at Camolin, county Wexford, and who in her will dated 12 December 1776 left small bequests to four of Luke Masterson's daughters and the unnamed 'eldest daughter of Garrett Byrne of Ballymanus Esq'.[59]

The possibility of a second marriage for Garrett II is suggested by the name and description of a witness to a deed of settlement executed on the occasion of the marriage of Garrett III in 1757.[60] References to the two Garretts, father and son, occur in the document but there is also mention of a third Byrne of that name, described as 'Garrett Byrne ye Elder now of Ballymanus afores'd Gentleman Uncle to the s'd Garrett Byrne ye Son'. While this could suggest that a sister of Garrett II had married his namesake it could also mean that a second wife to Garrett had a brother of the same name living in Ballymanus.

Garrett Byrne II had three sons. The two younger, John and Colclough, apparently moved from Ballymanus to Hacketstown with their father at the time of their brother Garrett's marriage in 1755. Both signed his marriage articles, giving Hacketstown as their address. John Byrne was, as discovered by Edward on his visit to Ballycapple, the progenitor of that particular branch of the Ballymanus family, which still flourishes. The details of John's descendants compiled by O'Hart in 1887 are likely to be accurate since they would in all probability have been supplied by reliable family sources.[61] John's younger brother, Colclough, settled some time later in Drumquin, near Hacketstown. According to Edward's genealogical researches, Colclough married a Miss Galwey of Cork, a sister of Lady Esmond and a great grandniece of James, first duke of Ormond.[62] Edward's urge to record such a remote connection with a titled person reveals the abiding interest in even the most tenuous aristocratic links.

In 1774 Colclough is recorded as mortgaging for £239 the remainder of a twenty-one year lease he had obtained on 25 March 1770 of the lands of Killacloran and Balleeshal (townlands adjoining Aughrim) to John Tate of Fananierin.[63] However, he lost the opportunity to redeem the lease as the property was sold to Tate in March 1778 by the high sheriff of the county on foot of a court decree.[64] Sometime after that Colclough went to reside in London where he subsequently died. He had two sons, Garrett and William Michael. Garrett lived for a while in Kilkenny and then returned to Carlow, residing in Inch Cottage where he died in 1839 aged sixty-eight. William Michael lived in Park Hill, Glen of the Downs. He was deeply involved in the preparations for the '98 rebellion and attended the United Irishmen county foundation meeting held at Annacurra in the house of his cousin John Loftus. He was arrested at a provincial committee meeting of the United Irishmen in Oliver Bond's house in Dublin on 12 March 1798, convicted of high treason and hanged outside the Courthouse in Green Street on Wednesday, 25 July.[65] The dignified manner in which he faced his execution left a lasting impression. *The Dublin Magazine* reporting on his trial said he 'met his fate with a degree of courage perhaps unequalled'.[66] He was survived by his wife, mother and young daughter. It is probable that John Loftus of Annacurra was a son of one of the two daughters of Garrett II listed by Edward Byrne on his genealogical chart. An unnamed one was noted merely as marrying 'Graham' and the other as Bridget Loftus 'from whom descends Tom Doyle'. The precise links between those mentioned have not been established.

Garrett Byrne III, the eldest son of that particular Ballymanus generation, is often referred to in the literature of the '98 rebellion as 'Old Garrett' to distinguish him from his better known namesake son. He married, in 1755, Christian Jans, daughter of a Dublin surgeon, John Jans. For her marriage portion her father provided the sum of £1,200 in consideration of Garrett's father providing them with an annuity of £200 along with a lease of Ballymanus at the low rent of £22 per annum.[67] The couple had five sons, Garrett, John, Colclough, Edward and William, and two daughters, Eleanor and Frances. Garrett seems to have been a hard-living rumbustious type of country squire. Miles Byrne tells of Garrett's dexterity with arms and of how Miles' father had often seen Garrett shoot swallows from his hall door with a pistol ball.[68] The story of his horsewhipping Hunter Gowan of Mount Nebo for some perceived offence on the hunting field is recounted by Miles Byrne and is repeated by Mrs O'Toole, a native of Ballymanus, who in her eighty-fifth year in 1934 recorded on an Ediphone instrument accounts heard in her childhood from relatives who were alive in 1798.[69] Her version of the incident tells of Garrett's pack of hounds getting mixed up with Gowan's: in the ensuing confusion separating the hounds Gowan was discovered beating one of the Ballymanus pack with his whip, an action which provoked Garrett to deal reciprocally with Gowan. She related that Garrett lived in high style and kept only forty acres around the house for breeding horses and dogs. He did not farm the estate himself and depended on tenants for his income. Heavy gambling was another of his pastimes. It is likely that Mrs O'Toole met Edward Byrne the diarist, for it was surely this descendant of the Byrnes who 'had a good position in the Castle', whom she remembered calling to her father's house one Christmas day 'to inquire about his ancestral home and about how the title stood'. Garrett was predeceased by his wife Christian – presuming it is she who was the 'Mrs Byrne, lady of Garrett Byrne of Ballymanus, Co Wicklow, Esq.' whose death on 22 January 1778 is listed in *Walker's Hibernian Magazine*. This would indicate that several of the Byrne children were quite young when their mother died. Garrett himself died in Arklow between 18 July 1793, the date of his will, and 20 February 1798, the date it was admitted to probate.[70]

It was probably around the time of his eldest son's marriage that Old Garrett consigned the bulk of what remained of his dwindling inheritance to his eldest son and heir and moved from Ballymanus with his two daughters to live in Arklow. The original lease from Sir Laurence Esmond in 1700 comprised the townlands of Ballymanus, Macreddin and Clohernagh. However, it had now been reduced to the townland of Ballymanus, Garrett having mortgaged Macreddin and Clohernagh to the Reverend Edward Bayley who foreclosed on the mortgage in the court of chancery in 1774.[71] The loss of this part of the estate rankled with the family for many years to come. As late as 1867 a story was in circulation which probably had its genesis in this incident. Edward Byrne, to whom it was told by Matt Kavanagh, an old man in Ballymanus who had known the family early in the century, noted in his diary: 'Matt's father, Andy Kavanagh was sent by Garrett my great grandfather to Symes Bailey of Ballyarthur for a loan of some money on land (not known where) who sent back a paper supposed to be a mortgage for old Garrett to sign which he then refused to sign and never did.' There are other indications of Garrett's mismanagement of his affairs and extravagant lifestyle. A mortgage deed dated 29 May 1765 reveals that he then held the lease of Kiladuff, a property of 345 acres adjoining Ballymanus which should have yielded him a substantial profit rent.[72] The absence of further references to this property in the Ballymanus name would suggest that Garrett had failed to retain it.

Rosahane looms large in diverse Byrne sources and it is surprising to find this burial place highlighted so much when many important biographical details concerning the family went unrecorded. Both Garrett III and his wife are buried there though, strangely, not in the same tomb. Fr Redmond, the parish priest of Arklow, writing *circa* 1850 to Madden, the historian of the United Irishmen, reported that Garrett 'died in Arklow and was buried in the vault in Rosehane. His wife was buried also in Rosehane but not in the vault but by the side of it with a priest of the name of Fr Brennan from Rathdrum parish'.[73] Corroborating this is a note in the Rathdrum parochial records to the effect that the Rev Laurence Brennan, parish priest of Rathdrum (*c.* 1771-81) was 'buried in Rosehane near the Byrnes of Ballymanus'.[74] Edward Byrne also mentions it. In his diary account of an excursion he made to Ballymanus on 29 June 1867 with Matt Lambert, a local companion, Edward wrote that Lambert's mother thought she had seen many years previously 'a flag covering the entrance to the Byrnes' vault at Rosehane on which were some inscriptions, one of them giving the name of the first of the Byrnes who had been interred there; says that no one was buried there since my great grandfather in 1795, that some of the Loftus family who were intermarried with the Byrnes are buried in the vault'. Though her recollections may have been slightly confused, the octogenarian Mrs O'Toole had also something to say about it: 'there is (sic) fourteen skulls in it belonging to the family. They were all over six-foot men. Garrett (i.e. Garrett III) was married to Lady Folkes of King's County and she was called Lady Madame Byrne. She is buried outside the vault'.[75]

Rosahane burial ground lies on top of a flat hill overlooking the valley through which the river Ow flows on its passage to Aughrim, parallel to the modern road from Aghavannagh. About one mile below Rosahane on the south side of the Ow valley is Ballymanus House. The burial ground is today surrounded by forest which makes it a particularly peaceful and picturesque last resting place. The vestiges of what is possibly a twelfth- or thirteenth-century Romanesque church are visible but little concrete information is known about its history. The three ancient dioceses of Ferns, Glendalough and Leighlin meet in this district but there is evidence to suggest that their precise boundaries varied over the centuries. Ballymanus, placed in the Down Survey in the parish of Kilpipe and hence in the diocese of Ferns, may have earlier belonged to Rathdrum parish in Glendalough diocese, as did Rosahane. This may account for the Ballymanus-based family's allegiance to Rosahane rather than a parish church in Ferns though the Byrnes may have resided closer to Rosahane before Ballymanus House was built. Sadly there is no trace now visible of the Byrne family vault.

Finally we come to deal with Old Garrett's family of two daughters and five sons. Both daughters, Eleanor and Frances, were described as spinsters on a deed dated 1821 conveying their interest in their deceased brother William's farm to Daniel Tighe.[76] On Edward's genealogical chart, however, Eleanor is denoted as having married '– Anderson'. Both died in 1831 and are buried at Golden Bridge.

John, the second son, died in 1800. Like his brother Colclough, the third son, he had been a member of the Carlow Militia. There is some mystery about his activities at the time. In a letter written by Garrett Byrne on 11 April 1800 from exile in Hamburg to his sister Frances in Dublin he refers to the 'situation of my poor unfortunate brother John' and remarks that it may be a 'rather fortunate circumstance for himself and Family that he is no more'.[77] There is no indication given of what Garrett was referring to. William, who had been hanged some months previously, had apparently left fifty pounds to John and it was decided by Garrett that the sum should be appropriated to pay John's and William's debts. Captain Thomas King of Rathdrum, a most resolute discoverer of real and imagined rebel activities, and watchdog for the authorities in Dublin Castle, was confused by the brothers. In a letter written in 1803 to the Castle he refers to 'John Byrne now of Baltinglass, late a Lieut'n in the Carlow Militia' as being then engaged in seditious activities, probably confusing John with Colclough.[78] Colclough was commissioned a lieutenant in the Carlow Militia on 10 February 1796. He is said to have resigned his commission on William's being condemned to death.[79] He died aged thirty-six at Harolds Cross and was interred in the cemetery attached to St Michan's in Church Street on 5 July 1807.[80] He is not known to have married.

The fourth son of Garrett III was Edward, the diarist's grandfather. Prior to the rebellion he had a good business house in Tinahely but lost all his property during one of the yeomanry rampages in the town. In the immediate years after the rebellion he is reported by Thomas King of Rathdrum as working as a clerk in a distillery in Patrick Street, Dublin, and married to a sister of another Edward Byrne, a Rathdrum shopkeeper and prominent United Irishman.[81] She died around this time and he re-married on 17 February 1802 Maria Kavanagh of Ballyscarton, county Wexford,[82] with whom he had his four sons and two daughters. For a period (1813-17) he owned an hotel in Athy. He died there in 1824. Of his four sons, only Edward, married to Joanne Kennedy, is known to have had children. Edward was employed as a clerk in the Collector's Office of the Inland Revenue. He died on 19 July 1864 and was survived by his wife, his second son – our diarist Edward Joseph Colclough Byrne – and four daughters.[83] Edward III is therefore the last known descendant in the direct male line of Old Garrett Byrne of Ballymanus.

Garrett's youngest son was William, or Billy as he is more commonly known in ballad and book. Much of what has been written about Billy, as in the case of his brother Garrett, is inaccurate.[84] It is, however, outside the scope of this essay to deal with the details of their involvement in the 1798 rebellion. Well after the rebellion had subsided

William was arrested in Francis Street, Dublin, on 14 May 1799 and conveyed to Wicklow to be tried before a court martial. The trial commenced on 24 June and continued by adjournment to 2 July. The report of the trial proceedings would suggest that William had had a falling-out with his brother Garrett about 1795 and had gone to live with Thomas Hugo in Drummin.[85] He joined the Wicklow Yeomanry Cavalry, of which Hugo was lieutenant, during the latter part of 1797. In February 1798 he and three other Catholic members of the corps took exception to the wording of a test oath they had been asked to swear and were consequently expelled. William then returned to Ballymanus and joined in the preparations for the rebellion, subsequently taking part in various engagements. He was acquitted of the charge that being a member of a yeomanry corps he deserted to the rebels. He was likewise acquitted of having participated in several murders during the rebellion. However, the court convicted him of acting as a captain or principal rebel leader at the battles of Arklow, Vinegar Hill and other places, and sentenced him to death. While William undoubtedly acted in the capacity of an officer or person of rank on these occasions the testimony appeared insufficient to credibly establish that he was a principal leader, justifying the capital sentence which shocked many of the ordinary populace at the time.

Efforts to obtain a pardon were then set in train. His sisters presented a petition to the lord lieutenant, in a desperate attempt to impress him even resorting to the tactic of claiming a spurious relationship with the marchioness of Buckingham. In response to the petition, a report was prepared for Cornwallis, the lord lieutenant, by the commanding officer of the militia in Wicklow which revealed that revenge for the burning of Hugo's house and property, allegedly by William, and the burning of the Rev. Edward Bayley's house at Lamberton on the day of the battle of Arklow, influenced the death sentence. It was even suggested in the report that the motive for burning Bayley's house was that Bayley had some years previously purchased part of Billy's father's estate under a decree of the court of chancery. The sentence of death was affirmed by Cornwallis on 21 September 1799 and despite last minute efforts by his sisters (see Appendix C) William was executed on 26 September.

William was unmarried and aged about twenty-four at the time of his death, according to his nephew, Edward Byrne, who, in response to a questionnaire sent to him by Madden, the historian, replied that 'He was of very superior personal appearance and his character for humanity, integrity and industry the very best'.[86] The execution took place 'nearly a mile from the prison of Wicklow which distance he had to walk through the town'. Edward also noted that 'Rev Mr O'Toole attended him as spiritual director at his execution'.[87] Edward's knowledge of the family was scant so he referred Madden to Bridget Loftus as one who 'would know a great deal of all the family and of Billy's trial etc'. Bridget Loftus had given evidence at the trial and had said they were related, her father and Billy's being first cousins. Ironically we turn to Miss C.M. Doyle, a great granddaughter of Bridget Loftus's mother, who in an article published in *The Wicklow Star* in the '98 centenary year best dealt with the mystery concerning Billy's burial place: 'some people have asserted that his body was cast into the sea; others that he was removed from Wicklow Abbey to Rosehane by night. But I think, all things considered, that we may safely believe he was buried in the Abbey and left there.'[88]

Many others who paid the supreme penalty and had played more prominent roles in the rebellion are now virtually unknown but Billy Byrne's fame as a heroic figure has endured for two centuries. To some extent it is due to the ballad, inspired by the great esteem in which he was popularly held and the revulsion felt at his execution, which commemorates him. Father C.P. Meehan, who was a curate in Rathdrum for eighteen months after his ordination in 1834, took a special interest in the recollections of the local people about the Ballymanus family. He has relayed some of these in the preface to a semi-fictional history of the O'Toole clan which he wrote under a pseudonym and published some thirty years after his transfer from Rathdrum parish.[89] He quotes Father Grant, the parish priest of Wicklow, as recalling Billy as 'one of the finest men I ever saw. He stood more than six feet in his vamps, and was the best man in the county after the hounds ... Billy, poor fellow, ... was sacrificed to placate the Orange faction in this county .... Ah, poor Billy, I'll never forget the day I saw you marching handcuffed, with a priest at your side, past the Old Franciscan friary of the town of Wicklow to the gallows-hill.'[90] Meehan attributes a similar comment about Billy's wide popularity to an old man the historian met in Glenmalure while visiting the ruins of Crutchley's mansion, burnt by the rebels, as well as the information that Billy was courting one of Crutchley's daughters before the rising, and that she then never married.[91] Charles Dickson relates the remark passed by one of Billy's companions in arms: 'I wonder how any young lady could look on him without being in love with him.'[92] Dickson suggests that Billy may have frequented Hugos of Drummin because of the beauty and engaging manners of one of Hugo's daughters and that when he transferred his attention to Betty Crutchley of Ballyboy this led to a coolness with the Hugo family. Miles Byrne also comments on Billy's popularity: 'He was amiable and simple in his manners; handsome, powerfully strong and well-proportioned; six feet six inches in height, about twenty-four years of age.'[93]

Father Meehan was very attracted to the plaintive air of the ballad about Billy, the words of which he attributes to a hedge schoolmaster, Peter McCabe, who lived in Glenmalure. He implies too that Peter had compiled a manuscript abounding in songs and stories about the rebellion in which he had been an active participant. Meehan subsequently bought this from the late bard's brother, Driscol McCabe, for ten sovereigns. Fearing that some of its revelations would bring down vengeance on a number of the people implicated, a condition of the sale was that the manuscript should not be published for many years.[94] Meehan's intention that it should be published posthumously with his own memoirs was never realised and it is not known if the manuscript still exists.

William's heroic reputation was publicised in the United States by an eccentric clansman, one Oliver Byrne, who was born in Leyden, Holland, about 1810. He subsequently acquired some eminence in England as a teacher and writer of numerous innovative works on mathematics, engineering and military science. Byrne toured the United States in the 1850s and published from Boston in 1853 a treatise entitled *Freedom to Ireland* which advocated revolt from Britain and provided lessons in the use of small arms, field fortifications, pike exercises and street fighting. The book was dedicated 'To the memory of William Byrne, Esq., of Ballymanus, County Wicklow, Ireland', and to the fulsome list of qualities attributed to the dedicatee was the rather dubious claim that Billy 'by the dexterious use of the Pike destroyed two thousand of his country's enemy; and out of twenty-seven engagements in the open field, won twenty-one.'[95]

The only member of the Ballymanus family who seems to have been a registered member of the United Irishmen was Garrett IV, the eldest son and heir to the estate. According to Luke Cullen, Garrett was born about 1762. For part of his early education he was sent to France where, exposed to a new political philosophy, he became aware of the necessity for radical changes in the government of his own country. His first cousin was William Michael Byrne of Parkhill who was deeply involved in the councils of the United Irishmen while another 'near relation', as Billy described him at his trial, was Esmond Kyan, one of the Wexford leaders, whose family operated the copper mines in nearby Ballymurtagh.[96]

In either 1786 or 1788 Garrett married Mary Sparling, an adoptive child and niece of James Cullen, a wealthy distiller in Hacketstown. Luke Cullen mentions that the marriage disappointed Garrett's family because she hadn't much, if any, of a fortune. At all events, it did not prove to be a successful union, to judge by a deed of trust dated 9 April 1795 reciting that several disputes and differences had arisen

Genealogical Chart

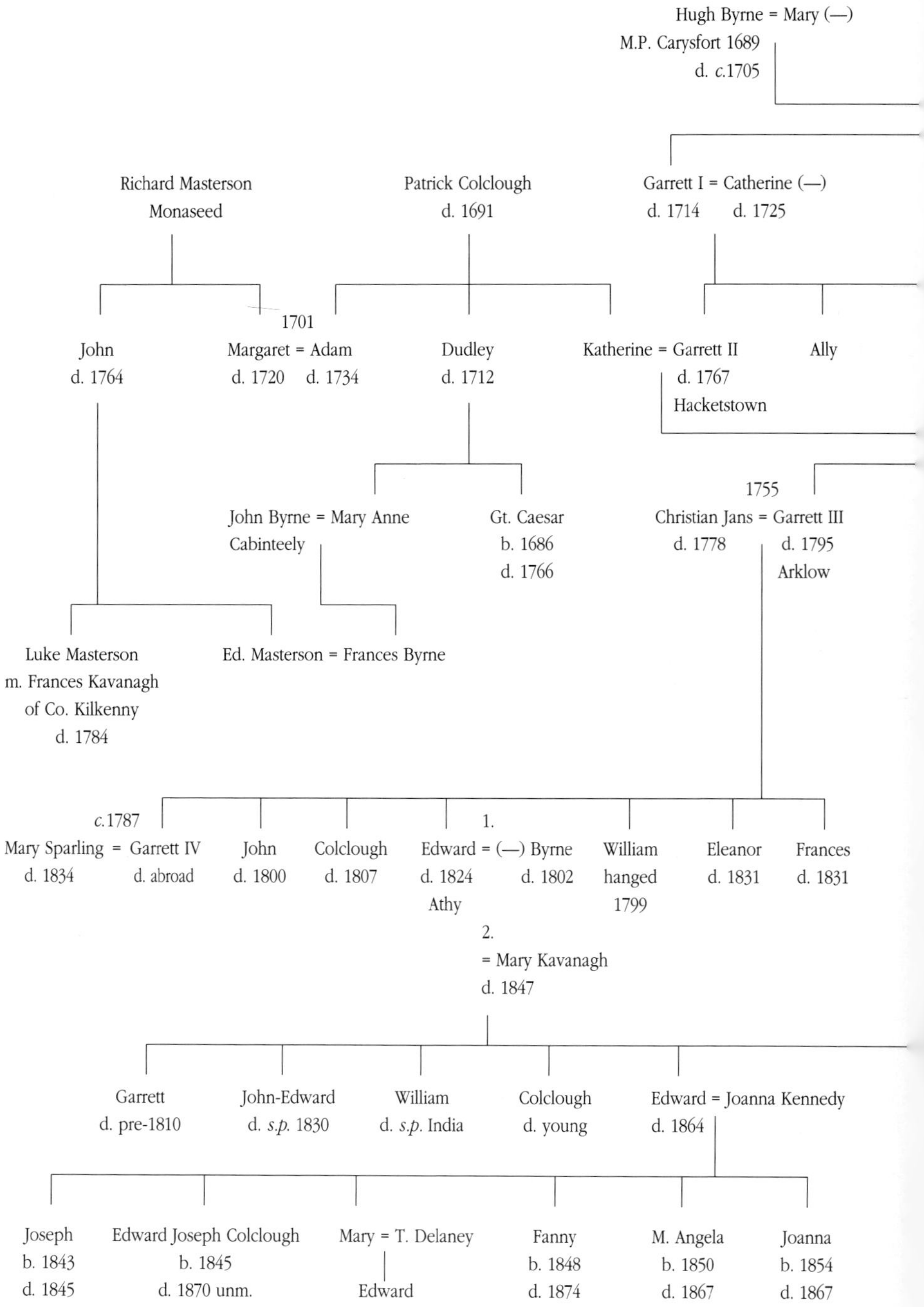
Hugh Byrne = Mary (—)
M.P. Carysfort 1689
d. c.1705
Richard Masterson
Monaseed
Patrick Colclough
d. 1691
Garrett I = Catherine (—)
d. 1714 d. 1725
1701
John
d. 1764
Margaret = Adam
d. 1720 d. 1734
Dudley
d. 1712
Katherine = Garrett II
d. 1767
Hacketstown
Ally
John Byrne = Mary Anne
Cabinteely
Gt. Caesar
b. 1686
d. 1766
1755
Christian Jans = Garrett III
d. 1778 d. 1795
Arklow
Luke Masterson
m. Frances Kavanagh
of Co. Kilkenny
d. 1784
Ed. Masterson = Frances Byrne
c.1787
Mary Sparling = Garrett IV
d. 1834 d. abroad
John
d. 1800
Colclough
d. 1807
1.
Edward = (—) Byrne
d. 1824 d. 1802
Athy
2.
= Mary Kavanagh
d. 1847
William
hanged
1799
Eleanor
d. 1831
Frances
d. 1831
Garrett
d. pre-1810
John-Edward
d. s.p. 1830
William
d. s.p. India
Colclough
d. young
Edward = Joanna Kennedy
d. 1864
Joseph
b. 1843
d. 1845
Edward Joseph Colclough
b. 1845
d. 1870 unm.
Mary = T. Delaney
Edward
Fanny
b. 1848
d. 1874
M. Angela
b. 1850
d. 1867
Joanna
b. 1854
d. 1867

– Byrnes of Ballymanus

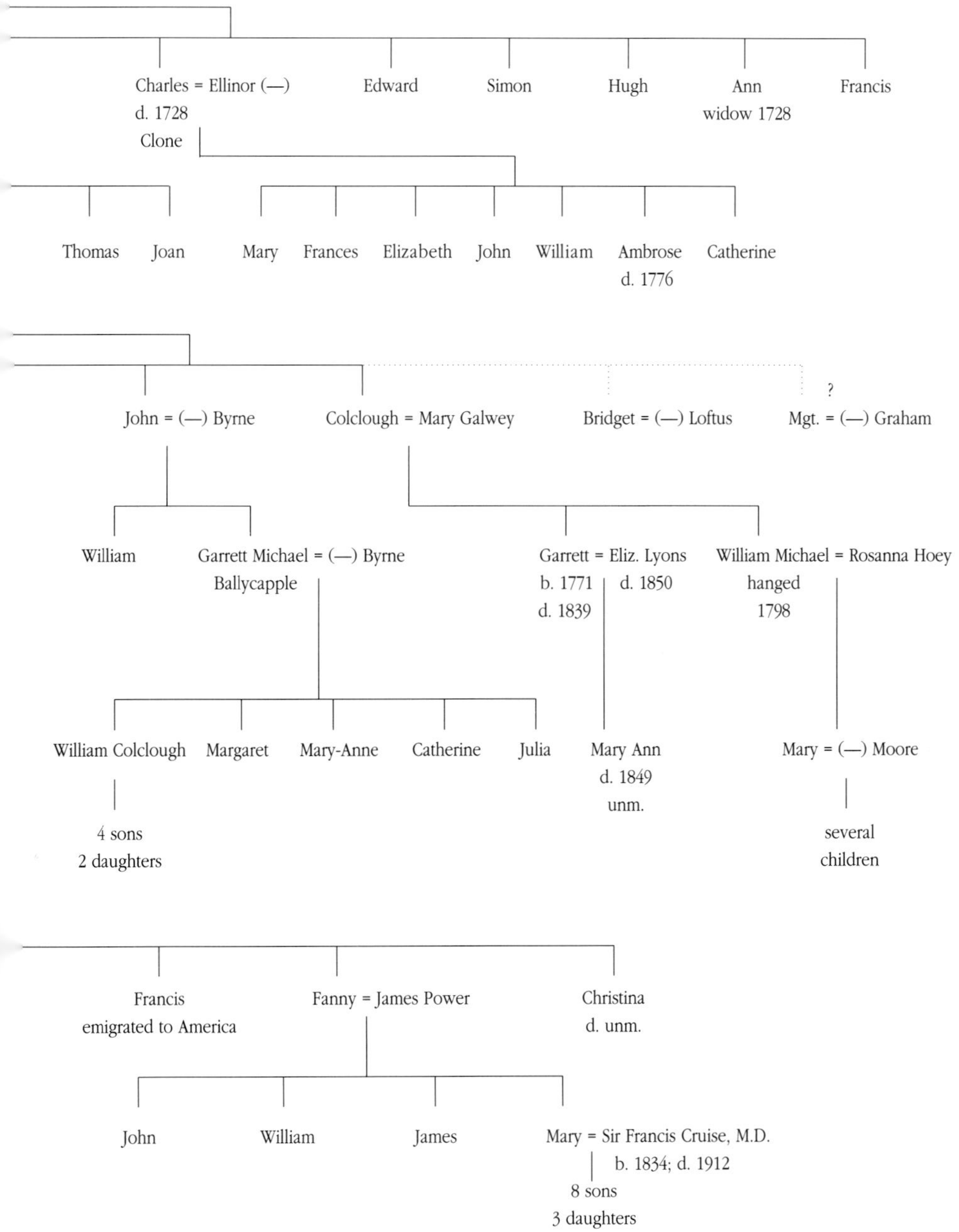
Charles = Ellinor (—)
d. 1728
Clone
Edward
Simon
Hugh
Ann
widow 1728
Francis
Thomas
Joan
Mary
Frances
Elizabeth
John
William
Ambrose
d. 1776
Catherine
John = (—) Byrne
Colclough = Mary Galwey
Bridget = (—) Loftus
?
Mgt. = (—) Graham
William
Garrett Michael = (—) Byrne
Ballycapple
Garrett = Eliz. Lyons
b. 1771
d. 1839
d. 1850
William Michael = Rosanna Hoey
hanged
1798
William Colclough
Margaret
Mary-Anne
Catherine
Julia
Mary Ann
d. 1849
unm.
Mary = (—) Moore
4 sons
2 daughters
several
children
Francis
emigrated to America
Fanny = James Power
Christina
d. unm.
John
William
James
Mary = Sir Francis Cruise, M.D.
b. 1834; d. 1912
8 sons
3 daughters

between James Cullen and Garrett relating to Mary's marriage portion and the title to certain lands at Hacketstown.[97] The outcome was that Walter Byrne, a merchant of Abbey Street, Dublin, was appointed a trustee of the settlement terms. As Walter also held property in Killoughter, county Wicklow, and was involved with the Catholic Committee and the United Irishmen it is likely that he was well known to Garrett. Sir Richard Musgrave, albeit a virulently hostile reporter of rebel activities, relays what was no doubt gossip circulating about the marriage at the time. In his account of the rebel attack on Hacketstown on 25 June 1798 led by Garrett Byrne and Edward Fitzgerald, Musgrave in reference to a house commanding the main street noted that: 'The family of Mr McGhee, all the protestant women of the town, and even the wife of General Byrne, (whom, it is said, he wished to get rid of), took refuge in it.'[98]

According to the Madden manuscripts, Garrett Byrne's house at Ballymanus was first sacked by the Tinahely Yeoman infantry on 8 May 1798 when 'his mother had gone to relatives at Hacketstown, never to return. His sisters went to Dublin and Garrett was with his sisters in Dublin when the Insurrection broke out, when he left to join the insurrection.' The reference to Garrett's mother is almost certainly a mistake for his wife. According to Luke Cullen, the house was built 'about 1650' by Garrett Byrne, great grandfather of William and Garrett, the family residing there until 1798 when 'the fine baronial house was burnt by the loyalists'.[99] Mrs O'Toole with her customary astonishing mix of fact and fancy recorded in 1934: 'the house itself was a four storey house and was burned in '99 (sic) on 8th May by the Tinahely yeomen. Then a landlord named Tadhg (sic) of Roseanna bought it from Colclough. He bought Ballymanus and Macreddin and Clorthna in Glenmalure and a townland named Bettyfield in Kildare. Tadhg had no right title as Colclough could not sell it, so he sold it to Col. Bayley, and he sold it to Guinness the Brewer in Dublin, and if anyone could make a title for it he could'.[100] While Luke Cullen is clearly wrong about the date of building of the house it was evidently a substantial edifice as it features prominently as a landmark on the Taylor and Skinner road maps of 1778.

Garrett's involvement in the rebellion concluded on 20 July with his surrender to General Moore in the Glen of Imaal. The terms required him to go into exile for ever. Towards the end of the year he and his close friend, Edward Fitzgerald of Newpark, the Wexford leader, were transported to Bristol where they remained until 22 March 1799 when they were removed to London and thence to Hamburg. Describing their arrest in Bristol the *Freeman's Journal* said: 'They each appear to be between thirty and forty years of age; Fitzgerald, a remarkably ill-looking man, of rough manners; Burne with rather a pleasing countenance, and of manners apparently mild and gentle.'[101] The interval between their surrender and departure from Ireland was used to arrange their affairs. Garrett made provision for his two spinster sisters, Eleanor and Frances, transferring to them by deed poll the 'dwelling house, out offices and gardens in the town of Arklow wherein the said Eleanor and Frances there lately dwelt.'[102] Presumably this was the house to which his father had retired. The sisters had by then moved to Dublin and were residing at No. 20 Bishop Street at the time of Billy's execution and it was to this address that Garrett directed two letters, which survive among Edward Byrne's papers, from Hamburg to Frances in April and May 1800. They poignantly convey a sense of the lonely and depressing situation in which Garrett and Edward found themselves, with occasional glimpses of humour and fortitude. Ballymanus and family affairs were uppermost in Garrett's mind:

> Edward also wishes me to send him an ac't of all money transactions between William and me. I will also do that soon, as I have providentially one ac't book left which will enable me to do it and have nothing to prevent me from sending it now but an unquiet mind. It is a task I am not equal to at present. I believe in my soul that all Edward's tenants and mine would be gratified in hearing of our being starved here, a circumstance they must suppose will be the case if they don't pay us. For what can we do in a country where we don't even understand the language.

A second letter, dated 30 May 1800, suggests the problems inherent in conducting family business from afar – it also conveys the special symbolic significance of the oak woods of Ballymanus to the Byrne family:

> I have sent the leases signed to Edward by Captain Crawford of the sloop William, who has witnessed them. He sailed from here last Sunday morning so I suppose he will arrive in Dublin as soon as this. Let Ew'd enquire for him at Mr George Casson, No. 9 Fleet Street, who is the owner of the vessel. He ought to sign them in the presence of Captain Crawford and keep the one that has the rec't for 5s on the back of it. Let them give the other copy to you to keep. Captain Crawford said he would return to Hamburg immediately. If he does I would wish Edward would get me half a doz'r handsome oak hand sticks from the neighbourhood of Ballymanus and send them by him. I fear they have made free enough with my wood in cuting sticks. Let him mind that I don't mean to give a sanction to

any person to cut them for me, only to get them from some of the people who already has them [see appendix B].

Luke Cullen (and Charles Dickson) states that Garrett Byrne died an exile in Hamburg.[103] It has not been possible during the course of the present study to establish exactly where Garrett died but it is highly unlikely to have been Hamburg in any event. While his banishment from Ireland may have been permanent, his period of exile in Hamburg seems only to have lasted a few years. This is apparent from a lease of part of the Ballymanus lands dated 21 October 1806, wherein Garrett's abode is designated as the City of London.[104] Another one of four years later gives his complete address in Camberwell.[105] From London he seems to have moved to the south-west of England, since two conveyances, one dated 4 October 1817 and the other 14 March 1821, give his abode as Sidmouth in Devonshire.[106] The outcome of these various transactions was that virtually the whole of the Ballymanus estate, comprising in the region of 1,600 statute acres, passed to the Tighe family of Woodstock, county Kilkenny, and Glenealy, county Wicklow. An idea of the value of these lands may be gleaned from the sale under a court of chancery decree made on 10 August 1805 of a part of Ballymanus known as Creerna and amounting to nearly 690 statute acres whereby the solicitor acting for William Tighe of Woodstock purchased the lands for £3,310.[107]

The date as well as the location of Garrett's death is also a matter of considerable confusion. The writer of a somewhat inflammatory review of *Memoirs of Miles Byrne* in *The Nation* in 1863 stated that Garrett was shot soon after surrendering in Glenmalure under promise of pardon.[108] This assertion prompted the then rather youthful Edward Byrne, our diarist, to pen responses under the pseudonym 'The Last of the Byrnes of Ballymanus' denying that his granduncle had been shot, that he had instead quit Ireland and resided for some time in Belgium, afterwards settling in Bath from which address he had written to his sisters Ellen and Frances as late as 1823.[109] Edward admitted that there was no information within the family as to Garrett's death. Another unlikely assertion was published in *The Wicklow Star* centenary article referred to earlier. In this, Miss Doyle, his kinswoman, relates that Garrett chose Caen in Normandy as the home of his adoption and died there in 1830. The credibility of this account is impaired by the writer's rather tall tale that the gentleman who had carried the terms of the 'treaty' between Garrett and Sir John Moore in Imaal in 1798 had on a subsequent occasion been touring through Normandy. Seeking directions one day he had called quite fortuitously to the very cottage where Garrett was ending his days and they both recognised each other!

A further unsubstantiated account of Garrett's death is given in Crone's *Dictionary of Irish Biography.*[110] The version here is that Garrett was born in Ballymanus in 1774 (making him a youthful twenty-four year old eldest son of a large family at the time of the rebellion) and that he was allowed retire to France after his surrender, dying in Paris and being interred in Montparnasse in 1832. The same biographical detail is recounted by the writer of an historical novel, *The Green Bough of Liberty,* published in 1979.[111] This is a fictionalised account of the life of Edward Byrne, Garrett's brother. The author, one David Rees, claimed that Garrett was his great-great-great grandfather.[112] Whatever about the veracity of that claim, it is not beyond the bounds of probability that Garrett had natural offspring during his life in exile though no evidence for this has hitherto been noted.[113] The assertion by both Crone and Rees that Garrett was buried in Paris in 1832 seems to have its origin in a note from a correspondent in Paris in 1856, preserved in Dr Madden's papers, informing Madden that there was a tomb in the cemetery of Vaugirard in Paris bearing the inscription: 'The Grave of my poor friend and brother Gerard Byrne. He was born in Ireland 1776 and died at Paris 1832. May he rest in peace. Amen'. Nothing here provides justification for the assumption that this was the grave of Garrett Byrne of Ballymanus.

Though spared the supreme penalty, Garrett Byrne paid dearly for his part in the '98 rebellion. Miles Byrne wrote that Garrett had been 'brought up with high notions of what he owed to his ancestors'.[114] The loss of his patrimony must therefore have wounded him deeply. However, it was possibly inevitable in any event. C.P. Meehan best summed up the family's problems in one of the fictional remarks he attributed to Fr Grant: 'Go visit Ballymanus and you will see the remains of the now solitary house where they lived, I fear very riotously, and beyond their means.'[115]

Appendix A

Billy Byrne of Ballymanus

Come, all you loyal heroes, I pray you'll lend an ear,
And listen to those verses I am going to declare,
Concerning Billy Byrne, of fame and high renown,
Who was tried and hanged in Wicklow as a traitor to the crown.

In the year of '98, brave boys, we got reason to complain,
We lost our chief commander, Billy Byrne was his name,
In Dublin he was taken and brought to Wicklow gaol,
And to our great misfortune for him they'd take no bail.

When he was taken prisoner the traitors all came in,
There was Dixon, Doyle, Toole, Davis, and likewise Bid Dolin,
They thought it little scruple his precious blood to spill,
And deprive the county Wicklow of the flower of Pleasant-hill.

Now that they had him taken, they home against him swore,
That he upon Mount Pleasant a captain's title bore,
And the king's grand army before his men he did review,
And with one piece of cannon marched on to Carrigrue.

It would melt your heart with pity how the traitors all agreed,
That at his father's table so frequently did feed
And in his brother's kitchen where many did him see,
Sure the Byrnes were well rewarded for their hospitality.

It would make your heart to bleed how the traitor did explain,
He swore Byrne worked the cannon on Arklow's bloody plain,
He swore he worked the cannon, that the pikemen he did drill,
And on his retreat to Gorey three loyalists did kill.

My curse on you Mat Davis, I will not curse your soul,
It was at the bench of Wicklow you swore without control,
You thought it little scruple his precious blood to spill,
That never robbed, nor burned, nor any man did kill.

Where are the odious traitors – why onward don't they come,
To prosecute those prisoners that now are in Rathdrum?
The devil has them fast in chains repenting for their sins,
In lakes of fire and brimstone, and sulphur to their chins.

When the devil saw them coming he sang a pleasant song,
Saying, you're welcome, Matthew Davis, ah! what kept you so long?
Where is the traitor Dixon, to the crown so loyal and true?
Sure I have a warm corner for cursed Bid Dolin too.

Success to Billy Byrne, may his fame for ever shine,
Through Holland, France, and Flanders, and all along the Rhine,
May the Lord have mercy on him, and all such men as he,
That stand upright for Ireland's cause, and die for liberty.

Several versions of the ballad exist. They differ in some textual details and arrangement but are essentially similar in theme. Some misdate the event to '98 instead of '99. The variant given above is attributed by C. P. Meehan to Peter McCabe. J. H. Fowler states that the ballad was written by a local rhymer named Jackey Aspel.[116] His version discreetly omits the names of the local witnesses, the relevant lines being rendered:

When a prisoner he was taken the traitors forward came
To swear our hero's life away, and well they're known by name;

Mrs O'Toole omitted reference to Toole from the version she recorded in 1934:[117]

When the informers they came in
There was Dixon, Doyle and Davis, and likewise Bid Doolin.

Another version omits both Doyle and Toole:[118]

The day his trial it came on, the perjurers came in:
There was Dixon, Matthew Davis, likewise Biddy Doolan.

The Carnew massacre and a reference to Joseph Holt, rendered in the vernacular pronunciation, is introduced in the 'Co Carlow Version' collected by P. J. McCall:[119]

Billy Byrne of Ballymanus he is valiant and he is stout;
Likewise that bould commander that we call Captain Hoult.
Twas in the year of '99, we got reason to complain;
For we lost our chief commander – Billy Byrne was his name.

The bloody Orange faction against us did combine;
Twas in the alley of Carnew where they shot thirty-nine;
They shot poor Lory Kirwan, our sorrows to renew;
They would crucify Our Saviour if they had Him in Carnew.

The remaining verses are similar to other versions.

Appendix B

The following two letters, preserved in Edward Byrne's papers, were sent by Garrett Byrne to his sister Frances at No. 20 Bishop Street, Dublin.[120] The house no longer exists. However, by a curious quirk of fate these letters now repose in the National Archives occupying virtually the same location in Bishop Street.

My dear sister,
Your letter of the 19th of February last I have only now rec'd on account of all communications between this country and England being stopped by the long continuance of frost. To be sure in winter it is a devil of a climate. I have also rec'd Ew'd's letter and the leases he sends me to be signed. Inform him from me I will not neglect the first opportunity of getting them witnessed by some person going to Ireland in order to prove my signature to have them registered. I will also have some alterations made in them but as the alteration will be for his advantage of course he won't dislike it.

I must own my dear Fanny considering every circumstance and the situation of my poor unfortunate brother, John, I think it rather a fortunate circumstance for himself and Family that he is no more. May God forgive him and he merciful to him. Edward says the fifty pounds which my very unfortunate brother William left John should be appropriated to the payment of their debts. I think so too and will as soon as possible give an Order for that sum to be paid him. Edward also wishes me to send him an ac't of all money transactions between William and me. I will also do that soon, as I have providentially one ac't book left which will enable me to do it and have nothing to prevent me from sending it now but an unquiet mind. It is a task I am not equal to at present. I believe in my soul that all Edward's tenants and mine would be gratified in hearing of our being starved here, a circumstance they must suppose will be the case if they don't pay us. For what can we do in a country where we don't even understand the language. I will drop the subject; it can't serve me and surely would be unpleasant to my Fanny.

You mention a woman of the name of McDonald telling you she seen us. She told you true. The poor woman was here in the greatest distress. We heard of her in the evening and was preparing to go in search of her next morning when she came to us. We exerted ourselves for her. I was so fortunate as to be able assist her to return to her country. She said she did not believe her family would assist me. That I thought of no consequence. I should detest myself if I thought myself capable of such mean prejudices. She mistakes in saying I shewd her a house I would take here. I certainly brought her out to walk with me, and I suppose shewed her many fine houses, and tho' I perceived her mean and awkward appearance, made many people laugh as we passed. Yet I for the time felt as happy in her company as I would in the company of the first duchess or princess here. It is also true that Edward and I were fools enough to spare a little out of our little to get our pictures drawn with an intention of sending mine to you and his to his relations. I believe he will send his but if I am of the same mind I am now I will break mine for two reasons: the first is I am not at present very fond of either the original or the picture; the second is, it is very ugly; the fellow finished it very soon after I heard of poor William's fate which I think makes it a bad likeness at any other time. Adieu my d'r Fanny. May every blessing attend you, my dear brothers and other sister etc, which is the constant wish of your affectionate brother, Garrett Byrne, Hamburg, April 11th, 1800.

As a postscript to the above Edward Fitzgerald added the following:

My D'r Girls,
Though Garret gave my comp'ts to you on the back of his last letter I do assure they are not from a person who is *cool* in his regards for you. I am surprised you did not mention a word of Bess in your last, I will write to her this post also. Should have wrote this time past but expected something pleasant to communicate from the other side of the water, which has not as yet arrived. We are sometimes in hope, at other times in despair, but trust in God that our misfortunes are almost at an end. The Lord knows if we have not had our share of them. I beg to be remembered to my good friends in Corn Market and all who may think it worth the while to enquire. Believe me my d'r Girls to be your sincere friend, Edw'd Fitzgerald. P.S. James is well.

My dear Fanny,
I rec'd your letter of the 3rd inst., which I assure you I longed much for, particularly as I have been very ill indeed since I wrote to you last and was so at the time I wrote to you, tho' I did not mention it to you nor would I now only that I can assure you (thank God) I am recovering fast. You say so much about my picture that I shall keep it for you and would have sent it to you by Mr Carpenter, who you mentioned to have come here with his daughter, but it may want some alteration in the drapery to make it palatable, which I will get done the first opportunity.

I have sent the leases signed to Edward by Captain Crawford of the sloop William, who has witnessed them. He sailed from here last Sunday morning so I suppose he will arrive in Dublin as soon as this. Let Ew'd enquire for him at Mr George Casson, No. 9 Fleet Street, who is the owner of the vessel. He ought to sign them in the presence of Captain Crawford and keep the one that has the rec't for 5s on the back of it. Let him give the other copy to you to keep. Captain Crawford said he would return to Hamburg immediately. If he does I would wish Edward would get me half a doz'r handsome oak hand sticks from the neighbourhood of Ballymanus and send them by him. I fear they have made free enough with my wood in cutting sticks. Let him mind that I don't mean to give a sanction to any person to cut them for me, only to get them from some of the people who already has them. I seen Mr Carperter when he was here and also his daughter. She has remained here after him with her husband. They have established themselves in some mercantile business in Hamburg. She is a very gay little body.

I had a letter some time ago from Mr Waters. Indeed his ac't of the conduct of the Ballymanus tenantry, as well as yours, distresses me beyond anything I can mention. He also sent me a list of the proposals he rec'd for the Demesne with the names of those who offered as tenants. Some of them were responsible tenants but all infinitely below the value. He also mentioned he again set it for one year but he forgot to say to whom. I am sorry Colclough don't write and pay more attention to you than you say he does. All I shall say is, I can't help him. You mention your hopes that I have seen poor William's Tryal. I have not got it, and melancholy as the subject is I wish very much for it. You say my dear Fanny only for Hope you should have been lost long ago. Believe me Fanny a sincere confidence in the will of God, assisted by that pleasing but delusive idea, hope, will enable us to support many difficulties which otherwise we would fall victim to. You say my sister Elen is afraid I am angry at her not writing. She need not as I consider your writing all the same. She knows that was a point I settled before I parted you. I would wish very much to write to my brother Colclough but as I have already been so much the victim of misrepresentation I realy fear in the smallest instance to go beyond my priviledge. Edward desires his compliments. He would write a few lines to you but he has many letter to answer this day. From the manner Mr McCarty directed his last letter to Ew'd it was quite a chance we got it as saying to Ew'd Fitzgerald Altona is rather too general a direction for an obscure individual living in a hovel on the verge of the city. Tell him for the future to direct to the House of Tonnies & Hammond, Hamburg, and enclose them to his friend, Pollard & Cooper, London, which I think is the only safe way. I shall hope for no delay in your answering this or any other of my letters. Believe me my dear Fanny your truly sincere & affectionate brother while I am, Garrett Byrne.

May 30th, 1800

Appendix C

Two communications from the lord lieutenant's office, the first advising of the decision not to pardon William, and the second, probably a response to a request from Frances to be given her brother's body for burial.[121]

Phoenix Park
September 25th, 1799

Madam,
Since I saw you this morning I have had the honor to communicate to My Lord Lieutenant the anxiety of mind in which you and your sister discovered relative to the fate of your unhappy Brother William Byrne, and it is with extreme pain I am to acquaint you that His Excellency cannot alter the decision upon the case of your brother which is stated in the enclosed copy of a letter to Mr Garrett Byrne.

Having mentioned to my Lord Lieutenant that you received assurances from Lord Fingall that His Excellency was disposed to think favorably of the case of your brother I am desired to say that His Excellency informed Lord Fingall that he had not then seen the proceedings of the Court Martial upon him, and that he was in full hope and expectation that he was not capitally convicted, or that his guilt would admit of a mitigation of his punishment; the contrary upon mature investigation has most unfortunately been proved.

I have the honor to be, Madam,
Your most obedient humble servant, E. B. Littlehales

Miss Byrne
No. 20 Bishop Street.
L't Colonel Littlehales has this moment received and communicated to the Lord Lieutenant the contents of the note from Miss Byrne's and in reply Lieut. Colonel Littlehales has been directed by His Excellency to issue his commands to General Eustace to comply with their request.

The Lord Lieutenant will be happy to do anything in his power to alleviate the anxiety and distress of mind which Miss Byrne's must now experience.

Phoenix Park, Sept 26/99.

References

1. Many people helped me when gathering information for this essay but I wish very particularly to acknowledge my indebtedness to Gerard Lyne of the N.L.I. and Kevin Whelan of the R.I.A. for their assistance in numerous ways.
2. S. Mac Airt (ed.), *Leabhar Branach: the book of the O'Byrnes* (Dublin, 1944), pp viii-ix; A.P. Symth, *Celtic Leinster* (Dublin, 1982), pp 22, 49, 111-2; Price, 'The Historical Background' in *Placenames*, vii, pp v-lxxxiv.
3. L. Price, 'Notes on Feagh McHugh O'Byrne' in *Kildare Arch. Soc. Jn.*, xi (1930), pp 134-175; 'The Byrnes' Country in the 16th Century' in *R.S.A.I. Jn.*, 63 (1933) pp 224-42, and 66 (1936) pp 41-66.
4. L. Price, 'Armed Forces of the Irish Chiefs in the early sixteenth century' in *R.S.A.I. Jn.*, 62 (1932), pp 201-7; D.B. Quinn and K.W. Nicholls, 'Ireland in 1534' in *N.H.I.*, iii, p. 32, n. 3.
5. *Cal. Carew MSS, 1589-1600,* pp 258-9.
6. *Cal. S.P. Ire., 1596-7,* pp 286-9, 300, 310.
7. *Inq. cancell. Hib. repert.*, i, Co. Wicklow, Jac. I, no. 8; G.E. Hamilton, 'Fiacha Mac Aodha ... and Domhnall Spáinneach ...' in *R.S.A.I. Jn.*, 35 (1915) pp 109-14.
8. *Pat. rolls Ire. Jas. I* (Dublin, 1966), pp 90, 94.
9. *A.F.M.* vi, pp 2018-9.
10. The will perished in 1922. A copy had been transcribed in 1872 by Fr Richard Galvin into Archivium Parochiale de Rathdrum, Liber II, (MS. in custody of the parish priest of Rathdrum).
11. N.L.I., Bk. Survey & Distribution, county Wicklow.
12. *A.F.M.*, vi, p. 2018.
13. Mac Airt, *Leabhar Branach,* pp 441-3.
14. J.T. Gilbert (ed.), *A contemporary history of affairs in Ireland* (Dublin, 1879) iii, p. 126.
15. If the relationship stated for Laurence is correct (which it may not be) the absence of his name from Phelim's will and other contemporary documents could be accounted for if Laurence were a name taken in religion by the friar. The friary at Ballinabarney dated from about 1644. Fr Laurence Byrne was Guardian in 1650. The office was declared vacant in 1658 and the friary abandoned after 1675. See B. Millett, OFM, *The Irish Franciscans 1651-65* (Rome, 1964), p. 71; also Millett, 'the Friars Minor in County Wicklow, 1260-1982' in *Archivum Franciscanum Historicum* (Rome, 1984), An. 77, pp 110-36.
16. *Anal. Hib.* 23 (1966), pp 360-64. Two other sons of Phelim, who may have predeceased his will, are known, Feagh (anglicised to Luke) and Colla; see *A.F.M.,* vi, p. 2018. Four daughters are mentioned in Phelim's will: Grany Peppard, Ellenor, married to the son and heir of William Eustace of Castlemartin, Bise (al. Bysse), married to the son and heir of Teige Oge Byrne, and Sara, married to John Woolverstown.
17. M. Walshe (ed.), *Spanish knights of Irish origin* (Dublin, 1970), iii, pp 31-4. Two of Arturo's sons, Don Carlos Manuel O'Bruin and Don Fernando Silvestre O'Bruin, became Knights of the Order of Calatrava in 1695.
18. J.F. O'Hart, *Irish pedigrees* (New York, 1923) i, p. 619.
19. *A.F.M.*, vi, pp 2020-1.
20. NAI, M 5892a.
21. *The O'Byrnes and their descendants* (Dublin, 1879), no. 1, n.a.
22. Reg. of Deeds, 720/218/492153; 761/304/516839.
23. Ibid., 492153; see also 627/347/432522.
24. *Cal. pat. rolls Ire. Jas I.*, p. 521; *Cal. pat. rolls Ire., Chas I,* p. 357.

25. J.G. Simms, *The Jacobite parliament of 1689* (Dundalk, 1974), p. 26.
26. *Anal. Hib.*, 22 (1960), pp 38, 90. A Captain Garrett Birne was attached to Lord Westmeath's Regiment: J.T. Gilbert, *A Jacobite Narrative of the war in Ireland 1688-1691* (Dublin 1892), p. 308.
27. *List of claims entered ... at Chichester House ... before tenth August 1700* (Dublin, 1701), pp 40, 144, 168; see also Petition of J. Aylmer, prop. of rectorial tithes of Kilpipe, Kiltegan & Killinor (Marsh's Lib. Ms Z3.2.6).
28. L. Price, *Placenames*, p. 73.
29. See 'Under the shadow of Croghan' in *The People* (Wexford), 1 Nov. 1902.
30. N.L.I., Ms 726. Parish maps with terriers, showing forfeited lands in counties Wicklow and Carlow, commonly known as the 'Down Survey'.
31. L. Price, 'The hearth money roll for county Wicklow' in *R.S.A.I. Jn.*, 51 (1931), pp 164-178; see also NAI, M.4909; G.O. Ms 667.
32. S. Lane-Poole Papers (N.L.I., Ms 5359, p. 66).
33. NAI, Index to Prerogative Grant Books, 1595-1810.
34. G.O. Ms 290, abstract of wills proved in Dublin diocesan court 1560-1710.
35. For Dublin seventeenth century priests see: W.M. O'Riordan, *Reportorium Novum*, ii (1957-8), p. 120; ibid., iii (1962), pp 191-6.
36. See note 32.
37. NAI, Betham's Genealogical Abstracts (NAI, BET 1/3, p. 165).
38. Prerogative Will Book (1726-8, fol. 3A).
39. R.D. 115/361/80777; 117/276/80776. It will be recalled that Hugh Byrne, Charles's father, had forfeited his interest in these tithes as a consequence of his support for King James.
40. Philip Furlong was listed as a popish priest in the parish of Kilcommon in the Report on the State of Popery in Ireland, 1731; see *Archivium Hibernicum* iv (1915), p. 169.
41. R.D. 126/96/85824.
42. N.L.I., Ms 18521-14, Fitzwilliam papers.
43. R.D. 257/464/169386.
44. The townland has not been identified; the locale of the witnesses' addresses would suggest it lay on the Carlow-Wicklow border.
45. NAI, Index to Prerogative Grant Books, 1595-1810.
46. N.L.I., Ms 18521-14, Fitzwilliam Papers.
47. Ibid., Ms 6055.
48. R.D. 169/122/11304.
49. N.L.I., Ms 6004, Fitzwilliam Papers.
50. Communicated to the author by Mrs Shiela Forrest, London, a great-great-grand-daughter of Charles Coates.
51. R.D. 13/13/4450.
52. Magill had likewise acquired Clone (1641 proprietor, Donagh Byrne) and Tomanierin (prop., Luke Byrne). His grants were enrolled 16 October 1667. The rent for Ballymorris was £5.4s.10¾d; for Clone (364.5 statute acres) £4.11s.1¼d; for Tomanierin (664 acres) £8.0s.6d. See *P.R.I. rep. D.K. 15*.
53. R.D. 121/362/87220 and 171/550/116108.
54. Ian Cantwell, 'Glendalough estate and the Hugos' in *Roundwood Hist. & Folklore Jn. 4* (1991), pp 32-4.
55. Charles Dickson, *The life of Michael Dwyer* (Dublin, 1944), pp 58 *et seq.*
56. I have been unable to discover if this document survives.
57. I am indebted to Seán Cloney, Dungulph Castle, county Wexford, for this suggestion. For further information on the Colclough family see his essay in

58. R.D. 177/44/117454; see also Colclough Papers (N.L.I.).
59. Prerog. Will Book, 1777 (A-L), fol. 49a.
60. R.D. 183/498/123608.
61. O'Hart, pp 621-2. Note corrigenda, p. 791.
62. Sir Henry Blackall, 'The Galweys of Munster' in *Cork Hist. Soc. Jn.* lxxiv (1967), p. 30, nn 179, 180, states that Mary Galwey married *c.*1757 Colclough Byrne of Ballymanus, county Carlow, son of John Byrne of Cabinteely, by Mary Ann, d. of Col. Dudley Colclough, MP of Duffrey Hall. The claim is not sustainable nor is his statement that Colclough's brother John was enobled by Louis XV of France. There is clearly confusion between the Ballymanus and Cabinteely Byrnes.
63. R.D. 309/498/206543.
64. R.D. 320/249/215442.
65. W. Ridgeway, *Report of the trial of Michael-William Byrne* (Dublin, 1798). Ridgeway erroneously gives the date of execution as Wed., 28 July 1798; see *Correspondence of ... John Beresford* (London, 1854), ii, pp 163-5.
66. *The Dublin Magazine and Irish Monthly Register,* Aug. 1798, pp 92-9. The execution is erroneously given here as Wed., 17 July 1798.
67. R.D. 177/44/117454 and 183/498/123608.
68. S Gwynn (ed.), *The memoirs of Miles Byrne* (Dublin, 1906), i, p. 10.
69. P. Ó Tuathail, 'Wicklow traditions of 1798' in *Bealoideas,* Dec. 1935, pp 154-88.
70. Madden Papers, Luke Cullen's Ms.
71. R.D. 352/532/240170.
72. R.D. 232/524/154726.
73. T.C.D., Ms 873, Madden Papers.
74. Archivium Parochiale de Rathdrum, Liber I, fol. 244 (Ms in custody of parish priest of Rathdrum).
75. Ó Tuathail, *Béaloidars,* p. 181.
76. R.D. 761/304/516839.
77. See Appendix B.
78. Dickson, *Dwyer,* p. 210.
79. T.C.D., Ms 873, Luke Cullen's Ms, Madden Papers.
80. N.A. Ms 5892a, (8) xvii.
81. Dickson, *Life of Dwyer,* pp 166, 210.
82. N.A. Ms 5892a, (8), xvi, marriage certificate.
83. N.A. Ms 5892a.
84. Probably the most publicly visible example of such misinformation is the plaque which for many years has been mounted on the wall facing the 'Billy Byrne' monument in Wicklow. Amongst other inaccuracies it states that Billy was a Protestant landowning member of the establishment.
85. *The tryal of William Byrne of Ballymanus, county of Wicklow, Esq.* (Dublin n.d.).
86. Madden Papers, T.C.D.
87. This is probably Fr Patrick O'Toole of Annacurra. Fr Andrew O'Toole, parish priest of Wicklow, had died in the previous month.
88. 'Billy Byrne of Ballymanus' in *The Wicklow Star,* 26 Nov. 1898.
89. *The O'Tooles, anciently lords of Powerscourt, Fertire and Imale; with some notices of Feagh MacHugh O'Byrne* by John O'Toole, Esq., Chief of His Name (Dublin, n.d.).
90. Ibid., preface, pp xx-xxi.
91. Ibid., p. lxxvi. The name is often spelt 'Critchley'.
92. Dickson, *Dwyer,* pp 58-9.
93. Miles Byrne, *Memoirs,* i, p. 117.

94. O'Toole, *The O'Tooles*, pp lxxvii, xcvi.
95. Oliver Byrne, *Freedom to Ireland* (Boston, 1853). I am grateful to Dr Sidney Kolpas, California, for very helpful information on this publication and its author.
96. *The Tryal* ... p. 66. Billy's uncle, Colclough Byrne of Drumquin, William Michael Byrne's father, was married to Mary Galwey of county Cork whose sister Helen was married to Sir John Esmond of Ballynestragh, county Wexford. Esmond Kyan's mother was Frances Esmond, also of the Ballynestragh family. There may, however, have been another family connection, possibly a more direct one: Esmond Kyan's first wife was a Mary Ann Byrne. Unfortunately her family background has not been identified. *Burke's landed gentry of Gt. Britain & Ireland* (5th ed., 1875) p. 744.
97. R.D. 537/150/352380. It was not until six years later that the agreement was registered in the Registry of Deeds, Garrett then being in exile and apparently irreconcilably separated from his wife.
98. Sir Richard Musgrave, *Memoirs of ... rebellions in Ireland...* (Dublin, 1801), p. 513.
99. T.C.D., Madden Papers, Luke Cullen Ms.
100. Ó Tuathail, *Béaloideas*, p. 180.
101. *Freeman's Journal*, 2 April 1799. My thanks to Joan Kavanagh, county Wicklow Heritage Soc., for this reference.
102. R.D. 532/230/348818.
103. Luke Cullen, *Wexford and Wicklow insurgents of 1798* (Enniscorthy, 1959), p. 77; Dickson, *Dwyer*, p. 58.
104. R.D. 641/290/446698.
105. R.D. 627/346/432521; the address given was: Bellisle Cottage, Park Place, Southampton Street, Camberwell, London.
106. R.D. 720/218/492153 and 761/304/516839.
107. R.D. 593/205/402475; Price, *Placenames*, i, p. 73, states that 'Creenery' is the local name for the stretch of poor, wet and hilly land on the western boundary of Ballymanus.
108. *The Nation*, 28 March 1863, p. 490.
109. Ibid., 4 April 1863 and 18 April 1863. That Garrett was alive in 1825 is tenable if we accept the proposition that Daniel O'Connell writing to his wife from London on 3 May 1825 was referring to Garrett Byrne when he said, 'Darling the two ladies who made appointments with me are the one a Mrs Byrne whose great national business with me turned out to be the endeavour to get leave for an United Irishman of 1798 to return to reside in his native country'; M. O'Connell (ed.), *The correspondence of Daniel O'Connell* (Shannon, 1972), iii, let. no. 1216.
110. Crone, *Ir. biog*. (2nd ed., 1937). This source states that William was hanged near Wexford!
111. David Rees, *The green bough of liberty* (London, 1979). I am indebted to Stan O'Reilly of Rathnew for bringing this work to my attention and for providing information on the author.
112. The death of Rees in May 1993 has hindered investigation of this claim.
113. John O'Donovan, *O.S. Letters, Wicklow,* seems to have been in an uncritical mood during his hasty passage through the district in the bitter winter of early 1839. Reporting on the antiquities of the parish of Kilpipe, he wrote from Baltinglass on 3 January 1839 that Garrett Byrne of Ballymanus had been detained a state prisoner in England during his life. 'His brother William, also a man of most gigantic proportions, was taken in a battle and hanged at Wicklow. Their little property which, according to the old men with whom I have conversed, amounted to £300 or £400 a year, was confiscated. William was never

married, and Garrett left no male issue. One grand-daughter now living in Athy is the only representative of this splendid family.' It is of interest to note that Billy was the subject of a spurious ancestral claim in 1904 by one Professor W. Byrne. Byrne wrote to some newspapers at the time under the guise of being the only lineal descendant of Billy Byrne then alive, that his father, Billy's only son, had been a large mountain grazier near Delgany. Byrne's claims spurred a number of irate letters published in the columns of *Ireland's Own* in 1905. Eventually it was discovered that Byrne, a copper miner in Montana and son of a music hall entertainer, had been indulging his imagination during the course of a flying visit to Ireland. See *Ireland's Own*, 22 Feb., 15 Mar., 5, 26 Apr., 24 May, 28 June 1905.

114. Miles Byrne, *Memoirs*, i, p. 11.
115. O'Toole, *The O'Tooles*, p. xx.
116. J. H. Fowler, *Chapters in '98 History* (London, 1938).
117. Ó Tuathail, *Bealoideas,* pp 181-2.
118. G.-D. Zimmermann, *Songs of Irish Rebellion* (Geneva, 1966), p. 149.
119. Ibid., p. 150; McCall coll., N.L.I. For the air see P.W. Joyce, *Old Irish folk music and song* (1909), no. 374.
120. N.A. Ms 5892a. 5 (iii) & 5892a. 5 (iv). There has been no alteration to the original grammar.
121. N.A. MSS 5892a. 5 (i) & 5892a. 5 (ii). Neither has been altered.

Glendalough House, Annamoe, out-offices wing (The Irish Architectural Archive, Dublin).

Chapter 10

THE REBELLION OF 1798 IN COUNTY WICKLOW

RUAN O'DONNELL

Wicklow was one of the first counties in Ireland to experience the outbreak of rebellion in May 1798 and in the succeeding months suffered a level of destruction to property and the rural economy which was exceeded only in neighbouring county Wexford. Indeed, the amount of damage inflicted by the military on suspected rebel households both before the rebellion and in its aftermath was perhaps without parallel anywhere in Ireland.[1] Wicklow was also notable for the extreme militancy of its United Irishmen who fought on for six months after the general suppression of the rebellion, the remnants of whom kept the county unstable until 1804.

These facts are not generally appreciated because the harsh realities of the rebellion in Wicklow did not attract the attention of nationalist historians who from 1801 to 1898 were preoccupied with the anomalies and controversy posed by the conflict in Wexford. Defenders of the loyalist establishment in the post-rebellion period sought to make political capital by focusing selectively and often dishonestly on the disparity between the theory and practice of United Irishmen ideology in Wexford in 1798 which they generally misrepresented as sectarian. While Wicklow had its share of nationalist atrocities it lacked sensational conflagrations of the order of Scullabogue and the conduct of its rebels was not a bone of contention in the press between 1797 and 1804. Newspapers and private correspondence of that period relating to Wicklow is insignificant compared to that of Wexford, especially after 1798.[2] It is also significant that no account of the rebellion in Wicklow appeared until 1838 when Joseph Holt's autobiography received its first and last printing. The edited version presented to the public compounded the reticence of its author and the book did little to modify the orthodox model of the rebellion which apart from the brief French incursion in Mayo in August 1798 placed little or no emphasis on rebel combat after the battle of Vinegar Hill in Wexford on 21 June.[3]

The United Irishmen in Wicklow

Wicklow's geography was perhaps the key determinant governing the conduct of the county's United Irishmen during the rebellion in 1798 and this is particularly evident in the first week of hostilities when the organisation attempted to mobilise and wage revolutionary war in a pre-determined manner. With the benefit of hindsight the actions of the Wicklow rebels from 23 to 30 May appear futile and ill-conceived but when contemporary factors are considered it is clear that a logical and coherent plan, albeit an unsuccessful one, was implemented. Initial local reverses and the failure of other county and provincial organisations to carry out their assigned roles forced changes in subsequent strategy which of necessity became relative and *ad hoc*. It is significant that on 23-24 May, before the situation became confused, rebels in all six of Wicklow's baronies responded to the orders from Dublin to rise and participated in a series of attacks along the county's borders with Dublin, Kildare and Carlow. The speed and intensity of the response points to planned rather than spontaneous assaults on particular military outposts and it was only the lack of success and demonstrably poor tactics that have given rise to suggestions of rashness.[4]

The mountains which dominate central county Wicklow were an almost impenetrable barrier which greatly hindered cultural, commercial and political communications in the late eighteenth century and had a profound impact on county life. Rathdown in the north of the county gravitated towards its natural hinterland of south county Dublin while Arklow and Shillelagh were oriented towards north Wexford and east Carlow respectively. This tendency was reinforced by the siting of most towns of consequence on or near the county borders. Rathdrum was the main exception although it was a sizeable market town sustained by a thriving woollen goods cottage industry and connected by roads to the north and east. It did not, however, enjoy close and easy communications with the west of the county. Similarly, the county town in the barony of Arklow and Arklow town itself have virtually no practical or instinctive bond with the baronies of Upper and Lower Talbotstown in west Wicklow which faced Carlow, Kildare and Dublin. These constraints of geography had a marked effect on the way in which the United Irishmen established themselves in Wicklow after April 1797 and defined the role assigned to the county's organisation, ultimately the most numerically powerful in Leinster, in the Great Rebellion of 1798.

When the rebellion began in May 1798 Wicklow's highly structured United Irishmen organisation ceased from military necessity to be the semi-autonomous county entity its officer committees implied it was. From late 1797 the county organisation was theoretically in place and a constituent of a provincial and national body but only as this was deemed politically desirable and the most efficient way to promote the spread of the conspiracy while regulating the formation, control and utilisation of new societies. This county superstructure, as delineated in successive constitutional models, facilitated the holding of elections, dissemination of policy and propaganda, collection of funds and distribution of weaponry.[5] In operational terms the Wicklow rebels were not a county regiment or brigade to be handled as a regular army formation but rather several distinct company and battalion level groupings which could act independently of county level command or combine with others regardless of their county of origin or pre-rebellion leadership. Indeed the natural strength of local as opposed to county allegiance created the partnership of the north Wexford and south Wicklow rebels who fought together for much of the rebellion while detached from other active elements of their own counties. This liaison had its roots in the spring of 1797 when the impetus to form United Irish societies came into Talbotstown barony from Kildare while another effort was made directly from Dublin to contact radicals in the Arklow area.[6] Although these early overtures were clearly influenced by the presence of recognised disaffected persons, such as elements of the Ulster settlers living in both baronies, the manner in which the approaches were made was also influenced by the road networks. Cross-border ties were subsequently very close and Arklow having been used as a base to organise the conspiracy in north Wexford, remained closely allied to that area's rebel leadership to the extent that the signal to rise in Wexford was expected to come through the Arklow network.[7]

Counter-insurgence in Wicklow

From early April until the outbreak of the rebellion the rebel infrastructure in Wicklow was subjected to a vigorous and brutal counter-insurgent policy directed by Major Joseph Hardy of the Antrim militia. This campaign severely disrupted the chain of command, which was of vital importance for the mobilisation of rebel forces in the crucial first hours and days of the rebellion. Hardy's tacit and explicit sanctioning of the use of torture, random floggings, house burning and other forms of state terrorism to elicit intelligence from rebel suspects resulted in the identification and neutralisation of many important rebel officers in the six weeks prior to the insurrection and the seizure of large quantities of hidden armaments.[8] Government estimates vary as to the numbers of arms seized in Wicklow during this period but Hardy himself put the figure at between 700 and 1,300 firearms and 4,000 to 4,500 pikes.[9] Firearms and ammunition were in short supply and this loss was of particular concern in Wicklow where the mountainous and difficult terrain generally ruled out the pike as an effective assault weapon.

The reign of terror experienced in much of west and south Wicklow prevented the United Irishmen replacing missing leaders through the mechanism of elections to which they were constitutionally bound and a partial breakdown of the organisation ensued. This difficult situation was exacerbated by compromised leaders like Michael Dwyer of Imaal and Joseph Holt of Mullinaveigue (Roundwood) being forced into hiding to avoid arrest. Their absence curtailed the effectiveness of the units within their areas of responsibility when the orders to rise were issued.[10] Others withdrew from the conspiracy altogether or defected to the government, exchanging information for clemency as did Thomas Murray of Sheepwalk in the barony of Arklow.[11] Matters were not improved by the promotion of ineffective substitutes such as Phil O'Neil in the key sector of Arklow and the enforced absence in Dublin of Garret Byrne of Ballymanus who commanded more respect and allegiance than any other acknowledged leader.[12] Hardy's programme ensured that only a fraction of the 14,000 Wicklow United Irishmen nominally committed to rebellion turned out on its outbreak. These were poorly armed and often led by substitute leaders of a lesser calibre than their absent officers. In Wexford where circumstances shielded the rebel officer cadre, to an extent, from the devastation visited on their comrades in Wicklow, orderly and rapid mobilisation was the norm, resulting in large concentrations of well-led and militarily successful insurgents.[13]

Rebel objectives

The precise role laid out for the Wicklow rebels by the Dublin leadership is unknown but some indications can be gleaned from contemporary documents and from observing where rebel activity actually occurred. At one point the county's rebels were charged with attacking the army reserve camp north of Bray at Lehaunstown, county Dublin, which had been established in 1795.[14] It was hoped that this tactic would pin down troops loyal to the government and prevent them reinforcing Dublin during the planned revolt by city rebels. It was also advocated on the grounds that it would afford United Irish infiltrators in the King's county militia and other regiments based in Lehaunstown the opportunity to defect. This plan, however, was devised by Henry and John Sheares who became estranged from the supreme command in early May and it may not have enjoyed the support of the dominant Lord Edward Fitzgerald/Samuel Neilson faction.[15] As no attack was made on Lehaunstown it appears likely that the plan was deemed too risky to attempt or was dependent on a simultaneous uprising in the city which failed to materialise. It seems probable that only rebels from Rathdown and possibly Newcastle would have taken part, given that the commotion and time required to mobilise further afield would have attracted the attention of the military. However, a well-placed informant of the spy master Samuel Sproule learned that 14,000 Wicklow rebels, the actual paper strength of the entire force in the county, were to 'draw off the army' in the Dublin district and then second the efforts of their comrades in the city.[16] This was reputedly the task entrusted to the rebel forces of Meath and Kildare and was clearly a variant of the Sheares' plan with more emphasis on the prudent aim of diversions and without a potentially suicidal attack on the three regiments which generally comprised the Lehaunstown reserves. A feint on Lehaunstown during the first hours of the rebellion may well have been contemplated. This would have required few rebels and was probably the intention of those whose camp fires in the Dublin mountains were visible in the capital for several days preceding the outbreak.[17]

The first phase of the rebellion in Wicklow was characterised by a wave of attacks on small towns in Kildare and Carlow. On 23-24 May the Wicklow rebels attempted to capture Ballymore-Eustace, Stratford-on-Slaney and Baltinglass and had a reasonable probability of success given that these garrisons, like many others in Wicklow, were numerically weak and heavily reliant on yeoman auxiliaries whose fighting ability was unproved. Attacking the border towns also held out the prospects of removing the surrounding districts from government control long enough to permit the orderly mobilisation of the local United Irishmen; success would undoubtedly have encouraged a higher proportion of vacillating United Irishmen to honour their oaths. In strategic terms these assaults served the useful purpose of obliging the commanders of the major garrisons at Rathdrum, Newtown Mount Kennedy and Arklow to retain their troops to await developments rather than assisting in the defence of Dublin city or resisting the mobilisation of rebel forces in the districts within their remit. Victories also entailed the probable release of prisoners, the capture of arsenals and the recovery of lost armaments, all of which would have rendered the insurgents more formidable in further engagements.

Control of towns, furthermore, equated to control of road networks which in the context of Wicklow was essential for the rapid deployment of the cavalry, artillery and military baggage the government could be expected to use in counter-attacks.[18] Possession of the towns along the Wicklow/Kildare border would have threatened communications between Dublin and south and central Wicklow and isolated all garrisons in the district. This had potentially catastrophic consequences for the administration if similar success was enjoyed in the east of the county. From the rebel perspective the seizure of border towns would enable them to effect a juncture with their comrades from neighbouring counties – an essential prerequisite to consolidating victory. Judging from the rapidity with which the rebels congregated in the last days of May at Clohogue, Blackmore Hill, the Devil's Glen and other sites it is evident that a second phase of rebellion was envisaged which involved the massing of larger forces to attack the stronger and strategically significant garrisons sedulously avoided at first.

The rebellion in west Wicklow

For some nights prior to the outbreak on 23 May loyalists in Dublin were alarmed by the sight of fires in the Dublin/Wicklow mountains which they assumed to be rebel signals emanating from the camps of disaffected country people.[19] As the specific date and timing of the rebellion remained a closely guarded secret from the authorities until the day of the rising and was unknown to most United Irishmen it is probable that the fires were not set, at least initially, by armed rebels anticipating revolt but rather by some of the hundreds of fugitives who had fled the conditions imposed by the army once martial law was declared. As early as 10 May a sizeable group of refugees camped in the Devil's Glen and on several occasions thousands had abandoned their homes overnight on hearing false rumours of massacres.[20] However, on the night of 23 May a rebel force up to fifty strong moved from Rathfarnham at the foot of the Dublin mountains towards Clondalkin, presumably expecting to find the city in rebel hands.[21] Earlier that day emissaries had visited parts of Wicklow and Kildare instructing the United Irishmen to rise immediately.[22] Consequently, the men who approached Clondalkin included some mobilised Rathdown men in addition to county Dubliners from the Rathfarnham/Bohernabreena area. It became obvious as they approached that the city remained under government control and as all plans were apparently contingent on this salient factor they retreated towards the relative safety of the mountains. One section had the misfortune at Fox and Geese to fall in with elements of Lord Roden's Fifth Dragoons and several yeomanry corps and suffered a small number of casualties before eluding their pursuers.[23]

The rebellion had nevertheless begun in Kildare on the night of the 23rd on orders from Dublin and because of the non-arrival of the mail coach which was the agreed signal to the provincial rebels to turn out. The Kildare men who left their homes and recovered their pikes from hiding places did so in the mistaken belief that the city rebels had risen as planned, whereas the yeomanry had prevented them congregating by occupying their assembly points and putting the garrisons on alert.[24] As a result the vital mail coaches were not detained and most of the attempts to stop them outside the city were bungled, leaving the formidable Ulster rebels and the organised parts of Munster and Connaught ignorant of the order to rise. The failure of the key element was the first news of the insurrection to reach the provinces and the prevarication and inaction this engendered ruined all prospects of a general outbreak.

The rebellion gathered momentum in Wicklow around nine o'clock in the morning of 24 May when large numbers of men began to assemble along the Kildare borderlands, collecting their arms and singing republican songs which terrified the loyalist community.[25] Contemporary estimates of the numbers involved are nearly all from the government and tend to be very unreliable. This is not surprising given that the sources were generally the junior officers who had borne the brunt of the rebel attacks and had a tendency to inflate figures in order to magnify the extent of their victory or mitigate their defeat. An estimate of thousands could well signify several hundred. It is known, however, that in the vicinities of Baltinglass and Stratford-on-Slaney across the Kildare border at Ballitore and Castledermot, a vast number of United Irishmen appeared in arms.[26] Rumours abounded of the fall of Dublin and rebel successes at Naas and Ballymore-Eustace. Naas withstood a concerted assault by rebels under the command of Michael Reynolds and Michael Murphy who drew their forces off to Blackmore Hill near Blessington after the attempt. Blackmore may also have attracted some of the Rathdown and county Dubliners who had approached the city the previous night.[27] Ballitore, Narraghmore and Kilcullen, however, did fall to the rebels and the Kildaremen might well have menaced the outskirts of the city had not Lt-General Sir Ralph Dundas checked their progress at Kilcullen Bridge.[28] The garrison of Ballymore-Eustace narrowly survived an attack which left seven of Lieutenant Beavor's Ninth Dragoons and a lieutenant of the brutal Tyrone militia dead. As a reprisal twelve captured rebels were summarily executed by the notorious Ancient British light fencible cavalry, or Ancient Britons, whose atrocities when stationed at Bray and Newtown Mount Kennedy in April made them the chief object of rebel 'fury'.[29]

According to Lieutenant Macauley of the Antrim militia four to five hundred rebels appeared in the Baltinglass area around one o'clock and approached Sratford-on-Slaney where the bulk of the fighting took place. The textile town was defended by only thirty Antrim militia and twenty of the Ninth Dragoons under Cornet Love. The cavalry seized the initiative afforded by the high ground by meeting the rebels on the Baltinglass road and driving them back towards that town. While this was in progress Captain Benjamin O'Neal Stratford attacked the rear of the rebel force with his Baltinglass cavalry, trapping them between his men and the better trained dragoons. Macauley claimed that the rebels were completely routed and it seems that a melee occurred in which men and women were killed and few prisoners taken.[30] Rebel losses were estimated at 200 men killed besides many wounded but this figure seems improbably high given the relatively small number of troops involved and their lack of cannon.[31] It is significant, however, that although at least twenty soldiers and yeomen were injured, including O'Neil Stratford, they suffered no fatalities. This infers extremely poor rebel tactics and mishandling of whatever firearms they possessed.

Luke Cullen, the Bray-born historian, discussed the rebellion with many veterans during the early 1800s and formed the opinion that the insurgents at Stratford carried out a wild and ill-conceived plan without leaders, order, or determination.[32] However, the plan itself was logical; only its execution invited disaster and the rebels learned that henceforth it was prudent to attack towns from at least two directions simultaneously while driving cattle in front of their columns to act as a buffer against cavalry. The leaders present at Stratford included Martin Burke of Imaal who had much influence in his home area and would later make a name for himself as Michael Dwyer's right-hand man.[33] The most important senior rebel in Talbotstown, however, was Thomas Kavanagh a wealthy farmer and a member of the county committee of United Irishmen. He was also enrolled in O'Neil Stratford's yeoman cavalry corps and appeared in uniform at one meeting of the county committee at the house of John Loftus in Annacurragh.[34] Kavanagh's predicament illustrated very well the confusion which reigned in the early days of the rebellion as the rebels grappled with the realities of waging war on government forces who were themselves reeling from the shock of facing a rebellion of unknown proportions. It seems that Kavanagh was on permanent duty with his corps when the rebellion broke out and found himself on 24 May opposing his own men outside Baltinglass. This suggests that he either did not realise the rising was imminent or more plausibly was unable to excuse himself from his yeoman duties to fulfil his true role as commander of the Talbotstown insurgents. After the rebellion it was alleged that Kavanagh had offered to perform guard duty at Baltinglass on 25 May with a view to admitting the rebels to the town to surprise the garrison, although it is unclear how this was to be effected.[35] If the Baltinglass plot did exist it suggests that contact was maintained between Kavanagh and his men before Stratford forced his hand. His defection during the battle was misinterpreted by Luke Cullen or his informants, who were apparently unaware of his rebel status, as an impetuous patriotic gesture. After the collapse of the attack Kavanagh escaped to the house of William

Valentine of Manger where he was betrayed, arrested and executed at Baltinglass. Due to Hardy's drive other important Talbotstown rebels such as Michael Dwyer were not only absent from Stratford but unaware of the plan of attack which was to be put into execution.

The massacre of over thirty-five rebel prisoners at Dunlavin was the most significant occurrence in Wicklow on 24 May. The town's garrison consisted of the light company of the Wicklow militia under Captain Richardson, detached from the rest of the regiment for service along the Kildare border, Captain Morley Saunders of the Saundersgrove yeoman infantry and Captain William Ryves' Dunlavin yeoman cavalry. The event which triggered the executions seems to have been the arrival of Charles Doyle of Merginstown, the young son of a strong farmer, who brought the first news of the attack on Ballymore-Eustace.[36] Shortly afterwards a party of Ancient Britons reached the town and a decision was made to kill the prisoners confined in the guardhouse. These Britons almost certainly came from Ballymore-Eustace to apprise the Dunlavin garrison of the encounter there and were probably elements of the same group who had put to death the twelve prisoners captured in Ballymore-Eustace. It has been suggested that the men were killed while the battle of Stratford was underway to obviate the possibility of a breakout in a follow-up attack, although the methodical way in which the condemned men were bound together and shot on Dunlavin fair green disabuses any contention that the garrison acted out of panic. It is more likely that the executions were a reprisal intended to intimidate wavering rebels in Talbotstown and to punish those whose comrades had inflicted heavy casualties on the garrison of Ballymore-Eustace. Four of those shot were senior Talbotstown rebels including John Dwyer of Seskin, Imaal, an uncle of Michael Dwyer. He was probably a baronial delegate.[37] Fourteen members of the Narraghmore and eighteen Saundersgrove yeomen infantry suspected of being rebel infiltrators were also executed. Several other prisoners were hanged at the Markethouse; only Daniel Prendergast of Ballinacrow survived, grievously wounded, by feigning death. Later in the day two to three hundred rebels in the vicinity of Dunlavin, a separate group from those repulsed from Stratford, may well have been about to attack before they were confronted by Richardson's militia and the mounted yeomen and driven off into the mountains. Some of those captured were issued with certificates of pardon and released in return for pledges of allegiance to the government, reflecting the urgent need felt by the garrison to defuse tension in the area through clemency.[38]

Few details are extant relating to the first battle of Hacketstown on 25 May but it is likely that the attack was predominantly the work of rebels from county Carlow.[39] It is probable that some from the highly organised contiguous Wicklow county took part in the attack. They were led by Edward Byrne of Liscolman, a cousin of Wicklow's most prominent rebel family, the Byrnes of Ballymanus. Edward Byrne unconvincingly claimed after his arrest to have been conscripted by the masses to take command.[40] The rebel forces failed to capture the town due to the level-headed conduct of its garrison and their strategic possession of a strong barracks. Having reconnoitred the advancing rebels and launched a pre-emptive attack to create confusion in their ranks Lieutenant Gardiner's Antrim militia and Captain William Hardy's Hacketstown yeoman infantry retreated to the safety of their barracks from which the rebels, lacking cannon, could not dislodge them. A well-timed cavalry charge by Captain William Hume's Lower Talbotstown or Humewood yeoman cavalry forced the rebels to withdraw with heavy losses, over-estimated by one defender as at least 300 fatalities.[41]

North Wicklow

In north Wicklow the failure of the Dublin insurrection to materialise did not deter the local United men from turning out in considerable numbers. Their main rallying point seems to have been a camp on Blackmore Hill which, although established by the Kildaremen under Michael Reynolds, who had been repulsed from Naas on the 23rd, may well have been a predetermined site.[42] Concerned loyalists in Dublin put the number of men in camp at 'not less than four thousand', although a quarter of this figure would seem more realistic.[43] A high degree of mobilisation in Rathdown is indicated by pre-rebellion reports that the men were 'bent on turning out' and the presence at Blackmore of at least two captains, Thomas Miller, a Protestant from the Powerscourt area who was a county committee man and Charles Gallagher of Castletown.[44] Active also were captains Charles Bryan of Hoeyfield near Bray who fought in Wexford in early June and possibly Jeremiah Delamere who was arrested sometime in May.[45] No attempt was made by the Blackmore rebels to attack Bray in north Wicklow or any of the towns within their reach in south county Dublin which suggests their intent to move on the capital. Perhaps they were unwilling to operate in low-lying areas while the nearby Lehaunstown reserves remained undefeated. It is also apparent that after the initial strategy of the United Irishmen went awry in Dublin there were no effective contingencies in place to restore a cohesiveness of purpose. The breakdown of communications which ensued was inevitable and enabled the shaken Dublin Castle administration to regain the initiative.

General Sir James Duff attacked Blackmore on 31 May with the Sixth

Dragoons and Dublin city militia to deter the rebels from approaching the city. By that time, however, it had been determined to relocate the camp deeper in the mountains and the rebels lost some requisitioned livestock and equipment with little loss of life.[46] Some took advantage of the surrender terms offered by the government and dispersed while others moved in small groups to other rebel camps in the south of the county and in Wexford where their comrades had achieved a greater degree of ascendancy. On 29 May several reports reached Major Hardy of rebel movements in north Wicklow unconnected with the Blackmore group. There was reputedly 'a large party'[47] near Roundwood, 'vast numbers'[48] in the Devil's Glen and other parties of insurgents in Dunran Wood and in the barony of Newcastle who unbeknownst to the army were preparing to attack Newtown Mount Kennedy. In the course of the day a series of bloody skirmishes in which the rebels came off poorly confirmed their disposition but not their intention. One group, up to 300 strong, was dispersed by the Britons and Newtown Mount Kennedy yeoman cavalry near Roundwood; these were the men that Holt was to command at Newtown the following day. There is much evidence to suggest that Holt himself was leading them on the 29th although this fact was obscured in his disingenuous autobiography.[49] The cluster of Clohogue was burned as a reprisal by its landlord, Thomas Hugo, a yeomanry officer and newly-appointed magistrate, whose home at Drumeen had been one of those attacked and robbed of arms by the rebels earlier that day. Luke Cullen related in his manuscript notes how he learned of the burning of Clohogue from 'the survivors and children of the butchered'.[50]

At around 1.00 p.m. on 30 May Thomas Maguire of Ballydonagh in the barony of Newcastle led a large force of rebels to attack Newtown Mount Kennedy from the Kilcoole side, seconding the efforts of a separate force, possibly composed of rebels from North Ballinacor, who approached the town from the west bringing the rebel force up to 1,000. Although Holt's third Roundwood column was unable to rally quickly enough after their defeat the previous day and failed to arrive *en masse*, the rebels at Newtown overcame whatever outer defences Captain Burganey placed around the town and broke into the centre where fierce fighting ensued. While twenty Antrim militia grenadiers and around forty supplementary yeoman infantry held off the rebels from the town's magazine, forty of Burganey's Britons supported by a similar number of Newtown Mount Kennedy yeoman cavalry counter-attacked.[51] Part of the town was fired upon, on Burganey's orders, to create a smoke screen to confuse the insurgents. This added to the conflagration caused by the rebels who burned the empty cavalry stables and other buildings. It seems that Maguire's men did not arrive in time to assist their comrades during the initial cavalry charge but their presence caused a fairly orderly retreat which included the evacuation of the wounded. Around thirty rebels and ten government troops, including Burganey, were killed during the fighting.[52] Major Hardy, however, directed an effective follow-up operation which greatly increased rebel losses, using troops diverted at Bray from their march to Wexford, principally the Dunbartonshire fencible infantry, together with the Wicklow town yeomanry corps. It was believed in government circles that Hardy had instructed the men to 'make examples'.[53] Dunran Wood was cleared of rebel fugitives as was the Devil's Glen, the Ballycurry side of which was burned in the process and its rebel occupants massacred. After Burganey's funeral on 31 May the Britons and local yeomen ran amok killing at least twenty suspected rebels and members of their families in the townlands of Callowhill, Ballyduff and Monalern. Among those killed was senior activist Michael Niall of Upper Newcastle whose family property was also razed, although the killing of ninety-year-old Laurence Cooney, to cite one case, indicates that the element of reprisal was uppermost in the minds of the troops.[54]

Defeat at Newtown and the savage response of the government wrested control of Wicklow's northern baronies from the rebels wherever they had gained a foothold. Consequently the approaches to the capital were safeguarded and a buffer was maintained between the city and the then victorious rebel armies of Wexford. Hardy's other major garrisons in the district at Rathdrum, Wicklow and Bray were also protected from the threat of being outflanked and besieged and it is notable that the rebels in the north of the county possessed neither the strength nor tactical opportunity to attack them at any time in 1798. After Newtown Mount Kennedy the belligerents of both camps focused their attention on Wicklow's southern border with Wexford where owing to the outstanding achievement at Oulart Hill on 27 May and elsewhere it was increasingly obvious that the decisive engagements would occur in that region before substantial reinforcements were received from Britain or available from Munster.

South Wicklow and north Wexford

One of the key issues of the rebellion in Wicklow is the absence of rebel activity in the southern baronies in its first days and the decision of the insurgents, once hostilities began there on 26 May, to throw in their lot with the north Wexfordmen. No serious attempt was made by the south Wicklowmen to capture territory in their home county and they were apparently either unable or disinclined to engage government forces. Yet in November 1797 the murder of an elderly magistrate,

Richard Nixon, during an arms raid at Killinure and a spate of other 'outrages' on yeoman families had marked Shillelagh as the most violent barony in Wicklow.[55] This hastened the early introduction of martial law and military forces to Wicklow county but by May 1798 what had been considered a highly disaffected barony appeared outwardly pacified. Arms-raiding was against United Irish policy and while indicative of a radical and militant rank and file it also revealed an ill-disciplined and disorganised hard core which was not provided with arms by their leaders.[56] The prevalence of such high profile activities made their practitioners especially vulnerable to informers and the determined loyalist backlash which ensued produced at least one well-placed defector in time for the March assizes.[57] If, as seems likely, organisational weakness of this kind did afflict the barony, it was exacerbated by the incompetence of one of their two delegates to the county committee, John Waters of Johnstown. In July 1798, Waters provided incriminating evidence to magistrate Rev. James M'Ghee concerning his kinsman and comrade Garret Byrne and may well have imparted intelligence on lesser subordinates before the rebellion.[58] Waters was at very least a weak and irresolute delegate who claimed, perhaps truthfully, to have 'never acted'.[59] Certainly the readiness of the authorities to utilise hard-line measures to combat the conspiracy bore fruit in Shillelagh to the detriment of its United Irishmen.

In the Arklow district Hardy's success in identifying simple cell leaders and captains in early May 1798 seriously disrupted rebel communications. Even though the barony's upper leadership was compromised only just prior to the rebellion, the early detention of Garret Graham, Phil O'Neil, Thomas Murray and several others at such a critical moment probably prevented attacks on the garrisons of south Wicklow.[60] The plans to attack Carnew and Arklow and the actual assaults during late May and June 1798 suggest that both towns were indeed prime objectives of the local rebels and were considered such by the many hundreds who crossed into Wexford or rallied at Mount Pleasant Hill when the rebellion began. They evidently intended to execute these attacks when sufficient manpower had been amassed to prevail in Wicklow's loyalist heartland.

By 26 May loyalist depredations in the Gorey and Monaseed area of north Wexford coupled with news of the massacre of rebel prisoners at Dunlavin seemed to confirm the most sanguinary black propaganda of United Irish agitators.[61] A consequence of the widespread terror was the creation of camps on high ground sites such as Kilthomas and Oulart Hill where refugees mingled with mobilising local rebel units and perhaps sought their protection. Victory at Oulart on the 27th over the grenadier company of the hated North Cork militia gave the rebel effort sufficient momentum for Wexford's largely intact officer cadre to rally their men.[62] As the pre-rebellion reign of terror in north Wexford was paralleled over the border in Wicklow's baronies of Arklow, South Ballinacor and Shillelagh, it is highly probable that some of those who initially joined the refugee/rebel camps on the Wexford side were Wicklow people. In theory United Irish structure should have minimised intimate cross border collaboration but the strong political and marriage ties between leading rebel families on both sides of the border, such as the Monaseed Byrnes and the Grahams of Arklow, ensured that co-operation was nevertheless forthcoming and potentially extensive. The transfer of armaments from simple societies in Wicklow's Ballycoog district to neighbouring townlands in Wexford in January 1797 further suggests that such associations were mirrored in the rank and file and would have been strengthened by their shared experience of counter-insurgency.[63]

No territorial concerns constrained the authorities. They readily granted Hunter Gowan of Mount Nebo an extension to his commission of the peace in early 1798 which enabled him to operate in Wicklow.[64] When hostilities first commenced in north Wexford yeoman cavalry from Carnew, Shillelagh and Tinahely, together with elements of the Antrim militia based in these towns, featured prominently in skirmishes with rebels on the Wexford side of the border and brought the few prisoners they took back to Carnew gaol on 26 May.[65] There is no doubt but that the Wicklow/Wexford borderlands were considered one operational district by both government and insurgent forces and this accounts to an extent for the peculiar inactivity of the south Wicklowmen. The aggressive patrolling of the south Wicklow yeomanry in Wexford, however brief, at a time when their counterparts in the north of Wicklow were facing imminent threat is telling and reflects a perceived lack of danger in their home towns and a determination to forestall its emergence. The towns of Carnew, Shillelagh, and Tinahely comprised the most staunchly loyalist district of south Wicklow. Here the Orange Order had first taken root in some of the nine official and supplementary yeomanry corps in the locality, producing the county's and perhaps Leinster's densest concentration of these auxiliaries.[66]

A specific reason for the failure of the rebellion to gather momentum in south Wicklow on 23 May, or when it broke out in Wexford, may have been that the orders to rise were not received or widely imparted and this is strongly indicated in the barony of Arklow at least by the mission of Miles Byrne of Monaseed. Byrne, acting for the rebels of north-east Wexford, expected the final details regarding the timing of the rising to come through his contacts in the disorganised town of

Arklow but they did not reach him on or before the 23rd and he was obliged to undertake an extremely dangerous mission into Wicklow and Carlow to ascertain the position.[67] By the time news of the rising was obtained the garrisons were similarly informed and prepared to resist attack. Ironically, the delay in the rising in south Wicklow and north Wexford, which occurred a full three or four days later than in the countryside around Dublin may well have contributed to its relative success as those who turned out were marginally better-informed regarding tactics and the true nature of the rebellion. Reference has been made by previous commentators to the impact which news of the Dunlavin massacre had in north Wexford but, quite apart from the emotive responses, it is evident that some home truths were also imparted regarding the utter futility of small lightly-armed forces attempting to capture stone buildings without cannon. Such attacks were sometimes successful but only under cover of darkness as in Kildare on 23-24 May. With the benefit of this knowledge the south Wicklow pikemen evinced no desire to allow patriotic fervour lead them to the same fate as their raw northern colleagues who attacked the towns on unequal terms. It is no coincidence that virtually all daylight battles won by the rebels in 1798 occurred in open ground where either gradient or complex field systems nullified the effect of cavalry and hampered the deployment of cannon. Indeed, it was success in the open countryside at Oulart Hill, Three Rock Mountain and Tubberneering rather than costly assaults on fortified barracks in the strategically important towns of Wexford and Enniscorthy that made their garrisons untenable. The obvious need for large rebel concentrations to exploit these successes soon became apparent and camps were organised at Carrigrew Hill, Vinegar Hill and Limerick Hill in the Gorey/Enniscorthy area, at Carrickbyrne Hill near Wexford town and at Mount Pleasant near Tinahely in Wicklow, with smaller staging camps elsewhere.[68] All of these high points became the focus of dispersed and hitherto inactive rebels and may be defined as the second phase of the Wexford rebellion which Wicklow failed to achieve other than briefly at Newtown Mount Kennedy.

Mathew Doyle of Polahoney (Arklow) entered Wexford on 29 May and formed a corps out of those sailors from Arklow who had not fled to Wales.[69] He was among the first senior rebel figures from south Wicklow to rally in Wexford, and given his impressive pre-rebellion standing in the region arising out of his proselytising with William Putnam McCabe, his presence is significant. Holt referred to Doyle holding the rank of colonel, and like Holt's possession of that title, it was probably an honorary promotion granted in recognition of his pre-rebellion seniority in the civil wing of the movement.[70] Doyle was followed over the next week by often intact rebel companies from Redcross, Ballinacor, Glenmalure, Ballymanus and the other brave Wicklowmen whom Miles Byrne noted had marched 'in groups of twelve, to join the camp at Vinegar Hill.'[71] The Wicklow contingent in north Wexford rallied their desperate elements at Mount Pleasant Hill near Carnew in their native county and assumed the name 'Ballymanus division' in honour of their absent leader Garret Byrne who resided there.[72] Byrne was their *de facto* adjutant general, even though not formally appointed to the rank, and was accorded that status in nineteenth-century folk memory. The position of adjutant general was only obtained through appointment by the provincial committee which apparently did not fill the offices in any Leinster county, although it is likely that Byrne was formally returned as a colonel in November 1797.[73] Michael Dwyer of Imaal reached Wexford alone on 29 May from Lugnaquillia mountain where he had been in hiding and immediately retraced his steps from Limerick Hill in Wexford to Mount Pleasant camp.[74] His movements point to a highly-orderly build up of forces in which unit cohesion on a county basis was promoted and perhaps demanded by Wicklow officers. As Dwyer was not an elected officer and there were few other Talbotstown men in the camp he joined James Doyle's company of Ballinacor rebels and enjoyed status approximating to the rank of lieutenant. The Ballinacor company was fifty to sixty strong when Dwyer joined and some of its members may have encountered him on the recruiting drives he organised in their home barony in late 1797.

Having secured control of most of county Wexford by the first week of June the rebels attempted to overrun the strong garrisons at New Ross, Newtownbarry and Arklow. These towns offered access to counties Waterford, Carlow and Wicklow respectively. The first attempt to effect the reactivating of the rebellion took place on 1 June when Fr Mogue Kearns attacked Newtownbarry, on the Carlow border, with a strong force but was repulsed and endured a bloody counter-attack.[75] Kearns, had he succeeded, intended establishing communications with rebel groups in Wicklow and Carlow and mounting attacks on Carnew and Dunlavin. It was fear of such an attack which prompted Lieutenant Patten of the Antrim militia detachment in Carnew to order the executions on 2 June of forty-one of the sixty-one rebel prisoners in the town's guardhouse.[76] Many of those confined in Carnew and probably killed had been acquitted of rebel involvement at the March assizes but were re-arrested on the advent of rebellion and sentenced to transportation by magistrates Henry and Francis Moreton and Rev. Charles Cope. Their deaths elicited a similar response to the massacre at Dunlavin and jeopardised the lives of all loyalist activists, yeomen, orangemen and suspected informers who fell into rebel hands and indeed the town of Carnew itself which was sacked by vengeful insurgents only four days later. The massacre, however, has obscured the militarily more significant defeat of the United Irishmen at Newtownbarry which contained the county's only effective rebel fighting force.

On 5 June Bagenal Harvey's Ross army suffered an even heavier defeat than that inflicted on Kearns when after initial success in capturing New Ross the army rallied and regained control.[77] Among those who took up positions at Corbet Hill prior to the attack were Joseph Holt and either William or more probably Garret Byrne of Ballymanus. These men were listed as rebel colonels supplied with provisions in the returns of commissary John Brennan.[78] Captain Charles Bryan of Bray who in all likelihood made his way south through the Wicklow mountains to the Wexford town area after the dispersal of Blackmore Hill camp is also listed. The presence of Holt and Garret Byrne at New Ross on the eve of the battle is not recalled either in the folk tradition or in interviews collected by Luke Cullen and John Thomas Campion in the mid-1800s but this is not altogether surprising given the concentration of these writers on west Wicklow between 1798 and 1804.[79] Holt and Byrne and their men were part of the group which contributed little to the battle on the 5th when Thomas Cloney's Bantry men were pre-eminent; and if they did not fight, the absence of information regarding them is more explicable. It is significant that two Dubliners on Brennan's list, Felix Rourke of Rathcoole and Colonel McClune of the city, both subsequently fought in the Wicklow mountains with Holt and may well have marched north with him just before or immediately after New Ross.[80]

In north Wexford the defeat at Tubberneering on 4 June of a strong relief column under the command of Colonel Walpole augured well for the rebels and while it is clear that the Wicklow contingent was not present in its entirety for this notable victory it is known that elements of at least James Doyle's group were.[81] During the five days following Tubberneering and preceding the battle of Arklow the Wicklowmen moved camp several times to better co-ordinate their planned attack. Although Mount Pleasant remained the principal base of operations a temporary camp was established on Kilcavan Hill, north-west of Carnew. When it was discovered on 5 June that the garrisons of Carnew, Shillelagh and Tinahely had fled to Tullow on being apprised of the fate of Walpole's men, Carnew was occupied by the rebels and 'burnt to ashes'.[82] On 8 June William Byrne of Ballymanus left his place of hiding with the Coates family at Clone and entered the camp on Kilcavan at the head of around 300 Wicklowmen.[83] The camp was quickly abandoned in order to concentrate on Gorey Hill and their arrival brought the strength of the Ballymanus Division of which Byrne assumed command up to at least 1,000 and possibly as many as 1,800.

Arklow

A crucial opportunity was lost on 5 June when the urgings of John Hay and Esmond Kyan to attack Arklow were disregarded.[84] Unknown to the rebels the town was undefended having been temporarily abandoned by its terrified garrison after the rout of Walpole. This simple failure of reconnaissance may well have cost the United Irishmen the rebellion, given the vital strategic importance of Arklow to the defence of Dublin and the psychological effect its capture might have had on the already badly shaken army.[85] Another proposal to send a strong force through the mountains to cut the Dublin road at Rathdrum was also rejected despite the availability of men and the propriety of preventing the reinforcement of Arklow. This over-confidence and error of judgement enabled Major General Sir James Needham to enter Arklow just prior to the battle with major reinforcements from Dublin city and Lehaunstown, bringing the strength of its garrison up to 1,360 infantry, 125 cavalry and six yeomanry corps.[86] The fact that military forces in Dublin city did not exceed 1,500 at this time is indicative of the importance placed on the successful defence of Arklow by Lord Lieutenant Camden's administration.[87]

The battle of Arklow is one of the best documented and most discussed events of the rebellion in Wicklow. Needham's men, unlike the garrisons of many other towns attacked by the rebels, fully anticipated an assault and prepared elaborate defences. Entrenchments were dug to protect carefully sited gun positions and undergrowth; fences and other obstacles were cleared to produce firing lanes where attacking rebels were vulnerable and visible.[88] The Ballymanus division led the combined north Wexford/Wicklow army on 9 June from their camp on Gorey Hill through Inch and Coolgreany towards Arklow. Having rested at Coolgreany, the rebels divided into two columns and advanced on Arklow on both the Coolgreany road and through the fishery district.[89] One Welsh trooper recalled after the battle that 'the appearance the enemy made was astonishing; they seemed to cover the face of the earth ... [and] advanced in most regular order each parish by itself and headed by its priest'.[90] This confirms the retention of the corps system under battle conditions by the rebels at Arklow with its attendant morale-enhancing camaraderie and facility for deployment which compensated to an extent for the relative lack of executive authority in such a large body.

Prominent among the rebels on the Coolgreany road were William

Byrne and Fr Michael Murphy of Ballycanew whose men encountered stiff opposition from the recently arrived battalion guns of Colonel Skerret's Durham fencibles and their infantry which shielded the emplacements. A series of pike charges on these positions resulted in very heavy casualties as grape and round shot reputedly 'tumbled them by twenties, making large gaps in the rebel lines which were as quickly filled up'.[91] Although many of the Durhams were killed and one of their cannon was destroyed by a direct hit from one of the two guns in rebel hands, the death of Fr Murphy at the point when the Ballymanus division exhausted its inadequate supply of ammunition caused the attack to falter.[92] The fisheries column also failed to make inroads and having withstood a cavalry charge gave ground during a concerted counter-attack by the Cavan militia.[93] As the insurgents failed to breach the town's defences and were unable to cut the garrison off from Dublin their heroism and fighting ability came to nothing. Rebel losses may have totalled several hundred casualties and would have been considerably higher had not the notoriously incompetent Needham judged the countryside 'too much enclosed' for a cavalry pursuit of survivors.[94] Those who fell into government hands were allegedly hanged in the grounds of the Protestant church in accordance with Lieutenant General Gerard Lake's policy of not taking prisoners and the common military practice of killing wounded irregulars.[95] The rebels withdrew to Gorey Hill where they waited two days for stragglers to arrive and contemplated their options.

Defeat at Arklow was an unexpected occurrence to the leadership of the Dublin United Irishmen who expected the insurgents to march on the capital. It seems that the Dubliners took pains to facilitate the anticipated attack on the city and sent at least one emissary, Fr John Martin of Drogheda, into north Wicklow and parts of Meath to 'hasten this march'.[96] Martin met Holt sometime between 6 and 8 June near his brother's home in Ballynascorney in the Dublin mountains overlooking Rathfarnham. Holt had by that time established himself as the strongest rebel leader in north Wicklow and was in contact with other groups under Francis McMahon and two other Dubliners named Doyle and Nugent who had rallied in the mountains following the failure of the citymen to rise.[97] On or just before 9 June the various rebel factions allied to Holt moved from their camps in the Dublin mountains to Clohogue above Roundwood while McMahon's Dubliners remained closer to their native county at Whelp Rock near Blessington.[98] This move was possibly in response to news of failure at Arklow which forced postponement of the planned assault. A further attempt to revive the plan was made on 12 June but failed due to the breakdown in communications which arose from the capture of emissaries and uncertainty surrounding the developing situation in Wexford.[99]

It was probably the frustration of this check that prompted Holt's raid two days later on loyalist properties which skirted the mountains above Roundwood from Derrybawn to Ballinastoe. The brunt of the losses was borne by active magistrates and yeoman families such as Thomas Hugo of Drumeen, the Hardings and Scarfs of Tomriland, Freemans of Willmont, Weekes of Annamoe and Critchleys of Derrybawn and Lara.[100] In all about twenty homes were burned, among them the Lord Mayor of Dublin's residence at Diamond's Hill and Lady Francis Beresford's Ballinastoe home, while another five were robbed of arms. It seems that an even greater amount of loyalist property was earmarked for destruction but was saved on the intervention of Rev. Christopher 'Wiggy' Lowe, parish priest of Derrylossary, who remonstrated with the rebels and at length convinced them to desist.[101] Rathdrum's Tom King claimed to have fallen in with a section of the rebels and killed many, although the Rathdrum garrison did not venture out of the safety of the town, perhaps fearing ambush.[102]

While based at Clohogue the rebels attempted to increase their strength by compelling reluctant United Irishmen to join them. Loyalists who fell into their hands were tried by kangaroo courts and generally released unharmed if no acts of atrocity were established against them.[103] Holt's men moved briefly on 17 June to Glendassan in the Glendalough area where they were joined by another hundred men, and two days later drove off a patrol of Reay Highlanders and Newtown Mount Kennedy yeomen at Ballinrush before crossing the mountains to Whelp Rock.[104] The whole force then returned to the Seven Churches on the 23rd where they were joined by a mixed force of Dublin and Kildare men and another group who were part of Edward Fitzgerald's north Wexford column.[105] The Wexford men were some of the survivors of Vinegar Hill and brought with them news of that defeat in Wexford and also of Garret Byrne's intention to capture Hacketstown. All the rebels, totalling several thousands, went to Glenmalure the following day and took up positions on the hills surrounding Hacketstown on the evening of 24 June.[106]

The remnants of the north Wexford army of which the Ballymanus division formed a part had undergone a gruelling series of battles and forced marches to join their comrades from north Wicklow, Dublin and Kildare at Hacketstown. Once rallied after Arklow the insurgents relocated to Mount Pleasant camp on 14 June while some others took up positions on Kilcavan Hill by 17 June.[107] On the 17th a strong army reconnaissance patrol led by generals Loftus and Dundas left their forward base at Tinahely which they had re-occupied, and probed rebel positions at Mount Pleasant. When challenged by the Ballymanus division Loftus and Dundas immediately retreated, fearing a repeat of Oulart Hill, and hastily abandoned Tinahely once more to the pursuing insurgents who on this occasion burned it as a reprisal for the murderous conduct of its yeomen. The rebels re-formed at Kilcavan, their positions were inspected by the army, this time under commander-in-chief General Lake in person and once again an attack was ruled out as 'too hazardous'.[108] Orders were received shortly afterwards from Rev. Philip Roche to fall back on Vinegar Hill outside Enniscorthy, which they reached on 20 June having marched through Camolin and Carrigrew Hill. After the battle of New Ross Roche displaced Harvey as the most influential rebel leader in the region and while his strategy of massing the insurgents at Vinegar Hill had provided unprecedented numerical strength and held great potential for eliminating the command level dissension which had hitherto so gravely weakened the rebel effort, the prompt action of the military ensured that this was never realised.

On 21 June Lake divided 10,000 troops into several columns led by his most successful commanders, John Moore, Johnson, Duff, Needham and Dundas who were ordered to simultaneously surround and advance on the camp of the rebel main force at Vinegar Hill.[109] The Ballymanus division did not fight on the Hill itself as they were instructed to check the progress of Johnson's column which advanced from the direction of Enniscorthy. A bridge over the river Slaney became hotly contested even before Lake's artillery commenced their preparatory bombardment of Vinegar Hill and the insurgents staggered and reeled from the stream of musket balls as they attempted to gain control of the crossing.[110] A section of the Ballymanus gunmen covered the advance of their pikemen, led by Daniel Kerevan, over the bridge, in an attempt to dislodge Johnson's infantry.[111] Kerevan's death and a shortage of ammunition recalled the fighting on the Coolgreany road two weeks before and it also proved to be the turning point of the action insofar as the Wicklowmen were concerned.

The remainder of Roche's forces fared no better and it was only due to an error on the part of Needham that Vinegar Hill was not completely surrounded, a fortunate circumstance which allowed the bulk of the rebels to escape.[112] At Darby's Gap the Ballymanus division finally met up with their absent commander Garret Byrne in company with Edward Roche's Shelmalier riflemen. Garret Byrne immediately succeeded his brother William at the head of the Wicklowmen. William obtained a certificate of pardon from Wexford yeomanry brigade's Major Fitzgerald and retired from the rebellion to Dublin.[113] At Three Rock mountain the rebels split along geographic lines into two divisions. The north Wexford division headed by Edward Fitzgerald of

Newpark, Anthony Perry of Inch and Garret Byrne went towards Peppard's Castle, and the south Wexford division under Fr John Murphy and the two Roches entered the barony of Forth.[114] In the confusion of the retreat and rearguard actions some Wicklowmen became attached to Murphy's division which, after Moore had recaptured Wexford town, went through Carlow into Kilkenny seeking recruits. Fitzgerald's men moved northwards through Gorey, White Heaps, Aughrim and Ballymanus and having eluded all the government forces in pursuit of them reached the hills east of Hacketstown on 24 June.[115]

Hacketstown and Ballyellis

Hacketstown united the rebel forces of north and south Wicklow for the first time for a battle intended to redress the chronic shortage of munitions by capturing the garrison's stock and thereby enabling battles of more strategic importance to be undertaken.[116] The second battle of Hacketstown differed greatly from the first in terms of rebel determination and tactics. To prevent the cavalry keeping them from the town the rebels drove cattle in front of them and had flanking parties led by Michael Reynolds and Michael Dwyer advance through fields adjacent to the road leading into the town.[117] When the anticipated challenge occurred the Humewood or Lower Talbotstown and Shillelagh yeoman cavalry were repulsed with four dead, a rebuff which caused them to retire behind Eagle Hill and take no further part in the battle. Skilled rebel gunmen from Wexford's Shelmalier district provided effective covering fire during the crossing of the Dereen river and drove the Antrim militia and Hacketstown infantry from their positions.[118] The retreating infantrymen gained the barracks with some loss where, supported by nine loyalist supplementaries under Rev. James M'Ghee in an adjacent building, they exacted a heavy toll on the exposed insurgents. In a desperate attempt to create a protective smoke screen the rebels set the town on fire, burning at least seventy-six houses. But even this temporary expedient failed to dislodge the defenders.[119] Indeed, it became apparent that nothing short of cannon could have eliminated the garrison with its stone buildings and after nine hours or so of incurring heavy losses to a near invulnerable enemy the rebels withdrew from Hacketstown and went to Whelp Rock.[120]

It was decided at Whelp Rock on 26 June to return towards Wexford to seek news of Murphy's column and to attack Carnew which had again become a centre of military activity.[121] The Dublin and Kildare contingents, who were so prominent at Hacketstown, decided to accompany the main body and could not be compelled owing to the informal command structure practised by the senior rebel commanders. At Ballymanus and Reddenagh Hill the rebels were augmented by a group of Wexfordmen under Edward Roche and a few others who had survived the debacle which befell Murphy's men in Kilkenny.[122] They moved on the 30th through Tinahely, Wingfield and Wicklow Gap and into Wexford's Monaseed where a 200-strong cavalry patrol of Britons and Fifth Dragoons under Lieutenant Colonel Richard Puleston closed with them. The rebels were aware of the grave threat posed by Puleston's troopers and when an ideal ambush site was discovered on the road at Ballyellis between Monaseed and Carnew, Holt devised a stratagem to exploit the enclosed terrain.[123] The road ahead was blocked around a blind bend by horse-drawn carts used to carry the wounded and was sealed behind by a large force of pikemen who remained hidden in dense thorn hedgerows until the soldiers had passed. The dragoons found themselves surrounded by the rebels on a small piece of road which ran through fields unsuitable for horses. At least forty-nine cavalrymen and a few yeomen were killed. There were no rebel fatalities. It was a battle of no real consequence other than a massive boost to rebel morale.[124] After this success a half-hearted attempt was made to take Carnew but its garrison had been alerted by the sounds of battle at Ballyellis and could not be reduced in their barracks.[125]

After Ballyellis rebel strategy again became unclear and as Wexford was then flooded with troops and suffering from the effects of six weeks of rebellion the north Wicklowmen under Holt decided to return to the less ravaged, more secure and familiar terrain of Whelp Rock which they reached after an arduous march.[126] Byrne and Fitzgerald fought an engagement at Ballyraheen on 2 July in which nineteen yeomen of the Wingfield, Shillelagh, Coolattin, Tinahely and Coolkenna infantry, including the captains of the latter two corps, were killed. A fruitless attempt to dislodge survivors from Major Chamney's mansion in which 'considerable loss' was incurred gave further emphasis to the total inability of the insurgents to assault stone buildings.[127] The rebels were joined at White Heaps on Croghan mountain and Ballyfad by more of their comrades who had fought with Murphy, although their experiences and lack of numbers 'greatly disappointed' the men.[128] A strong force of the military under Needham and Duff pursued the rebels from White Heaps to Ballygullen near Cranford on 4 July where they were eventually forced to give battle when the cavalry established contact. Initial success against the troopers, however, could not be driven home owing to the strength of Needham's infantry force and lack of ammunition.[129] This battle was not particularly bloody or decisive but it convinced the bulk of the insurgents who took part that further resistance was futile. Most of them availed of the amnesty terms introduced by the new liberal-minded viceroy Lord Cornwallis under which rank-and-file rebels who surrendered arms and took an oath of allegiance were pardoned. Brigadier General Grose alone issued 'near 1,600' certificates of pardon at Enniscorthy by 8 July to those who wished to retire from the struggle, while a few thousand who did not wish to made their way towards Glenmalure and other rebel strongholds in Wicklow.[130]

Meath expedition and Wicklow mountains, July and August 1798

Renewed but illusory expectations of assistance from France and from the Ulster rebels encouraged those who spurned the government's amnesty programme to fight on in the Wicklow mountains. Fresh plans were laid to attack the city and a major build up of forces was attempted in the mountainous parts of south county Dublin and north Wicklow. Staging camps at Castlekelly and Sorrel Hill dispatched rallying insurgents to Whelp Rock, giving rise to fears in the Castle administration that the rebels intended 'carrying on a kind of brigand war!'[131] To prevent this General Moore led a large body of light infantry on 12 July into what was believed to be the rebel headquarters at Glenmalure but found it free of rebels. Further operations ascertained that the rebels had left their camps in Wicklow and entered county Meath.[132] This decision had been taken on 7 or 8 July at a council of war at Whelp Rock which, despite the objections of several important commanders, agreed that an expedition into the midland counties to link up with rebel factions believed to be in hiding there would 'raise' them in preparation for an attack on Dublin.[133]

From 8 to 10 July the rebels marched through Blessington into Kildare and went through Newbridge, Prosperous, Kill and several other towns, menacing the small bodies of yeomen and soldiers they encountered but failing to attract recruits while constantly losing men from fatigue and disillusionment. The weakness of William Aylmer's Kildaremen whom they encountered on the 10th was a major disappointment and not all of them were prepared to accompany the rebels to Clonard the following day.[134] Clonard was another fiasco where only twenty-eight yeomen repelled a few thousand rebels with heavy losses and when a hundred reinforcements arrived from Kinnegad the rebels retired to Ryndville Hill burning Johnstown en route.[135] The rebels at Ryndville were surprised on 12 July when attacked by 200 dragoons under Lieutenant Colonel Gough, the Limerick city militia and several yeomanry corps.[136] The assault had not been anticipated and little resistance was offered before a disorganised retreat began, shielded by Holt's hastily improvised rearguard.[137] Most of the rebels fled towards Garristown where a disagreement arose which led to inter-county dissension. The Kildaremen split off and made for Timahoe Bog with Fitzgerald while the Dubliners attempted to reach Whelp Rock, the city and also Glenmalure where a small force had remained to protect the wounded.[138] Byrne led the rump of the Wicklow and Wexford men to Blacklion and Stackallen and then to Knightstown Bog where defeat in another skirmish on the 14th precipitated the near total dispersion of the insurgents.[139]

After the collapse of the Meath expedition Holt was the only surviving rebel leader of note willing to take command of the few hundred survivors who gained the Wicklow mountains. His officers included Michael Dwyer of Imaal, James Doyle of Ballinacor, Mathew Doyle of Polahoney, Andrew Hackett of Coolgreany, William Casey of Glenmalure, William Pluck of Ballycotton, Patrick Grant of Kirikee, Murtough Byrne of Aughrim and Michael Neil, James Hughes, James Ryder and Michael Dalton, who all hailed from west Wicklow.[140] The Wexfordmen, now in the minority, were commanded by the able Miles Byrne who had remained in Glenmalure with Dwyer during the Meath expedition and safeguarded the wounded in their care when Moore's troops and raiding yeomen entered the valley.[141] The few Kildaremen and many of the Dubliners still in the mountains attached themselves to the various Wicklow corps while their officers negotiated terms with the government and with the exception of McMahon would surrender on 8 August. On 20 July four Antrim militiamen defected to the rebels from Arklow and were followed before the end of the month by twenty-four of their comrades.[142] Similar defections from the Sligo, Leitrim and King's county militia brought almost 150 trained, equipped and determined recruits to Holt's force over the succeeding months whose total strength probably did not exceed 1,000. The militiamen tended to fight together under one of the two men called Antrim John but were also associated with 'captain' Collagan and Andrew Hackett. In keeping with all rebel forces, the men from a particular area generally retained a distinct identity in their appropriate corps and companies, which had been raised in their home parishes before the rebellion, and owed their first allegiance to their immediate commander. When circumstances and disagreements arose it was not unusual for corps to withdraw to their own neighbourhoods or operate independently of Holt, as Dwyer's Imaal faction often did, being reluctant to operate outside of west Wicklow. Major decisions of strategy were taken by officer committees in which Holt's authority, owing to his maturity, experience and recognised tactical skill, carried much weight and entitled him to use the widely acknowledged rank of 'general'.[143]

The campaign waged by Holt in the late summer and autumn of 1798 was necessarily defensive and modest in scope given the overwhelming superiority of numbers then enjoyed by the government which had by mid-July quelled organised rebellion in every other part of Ireland. The rebels hoped to survive long enough to spearhead a general insurrection whenever the French managed to effect their promised landing in force and to this end set about making their mountain sanctuaries more defendable.[144] This entailed destroying all the stone buildings and slated dwellings within their reach to prevent their conversion into barracks which could impinge on the rebel's freedom of movement.[145] Battle was given only on advantageous terms or if it could not be avoided. To prevent encirclement and being forced to a decisive battle they could not hope to win, the rebels frequently moved camps and traversed the length of the county in the highland and mountainous districts where cavalry, so devastating in the lowlands of Meath, were virtually ineffective. Whelp Rock, Blackditches, Oakwood, Glenmalure and Croghan mountain were the principal resorts of the insurgents and skirmishes with yeoman and small infantry patrols which chanced upon them in transit were common. But the unwillingness of both parties to engage in close-quarter battle on such terms kept casualties low. Fighting was almost always carried out at some distance from the enemy and conducted with firearms rather than pikes of which Dwyer remarked when in captivity were only useful for executing prisoners.[146] Powder shortages were made good by the manufacture of an impure and poorly granulated but otherwise adequate gunpowder known as 'Holt's mixture' at Whelp Rock.[147] These stocks were supplemented by blasting powder stolen or donated from the county's many mining operations and small quantities of munitions provided by sympathetic yeomen and militia. The rebels sometimes levied cash or 'blackmail' from wealthy loyalist families and commandeered their sheep and cattle whenever food was required but they did so only in accordance with their needs and without unnecessary violence, unlike the bandit factions whom they detested and denounced to the authorities on at least one occasion.[148]

Towards the end of July Henry Allen's large cotton printing factory at Greenan was burned by the rebels to prevent it being used by the army. The village was first occupied by the rebels who afterwards withdrew to Aghavannagh and Glenmalure and then by the military from Rathdrum who burned several homes, including that of the curate Fr Byrne, as a reprisal.[149] Raids on the yeomanry base at Humewood on 26 July and house burning attacks at Ballyconnell and Clonmore resulted in several fatalities before the end of the month. On 6 August General Moore again invaded Glenmalure with his light infantry and

German riflemen from Hesse-Darmstadt but despite converging his forces from Seven Churches, Fananierin and Rathdrum in the hope of trapping the rebels his men failed to prevent their escape.[150] After conducting the skilful withdrawal from Glenmalure, Holt marched across the mountains to the King's river valley and went through Oakwood to Knockalt. The rebels retraced their steps to Imaal the following day where it was decided to make for Croghan mountain to obtain supplies and avoid Moore.[151] En route they burned a military convoy at Killballyowen, killing several drivers and guards and upon arriving at Croghan learned of the renewed efforts of Moore to pacify the county by granting lenient amnesty terms from his camp in Imaal.[152]

Amnesty and the arrival of the French

Moore's integrity and the relative discipline of his troops impressed many rebel fugitives who were soon crowding in to obtain protection,[153] 4,000 of which were issued at Arklow by 13 July and a further 1,200 by Moore's own officers during the subsequent drive on Imaal.[154] The amnesty greatly reduced Holt's force as the majority of his men seized the opportunity to retire from the rebellion in time to take in the harvest. Garret Byrne, who had made terms with the government on 20 July, visited Moore's camp to add his influence to the process but was disappointed with the ineffectiveness this gesture produced; he had perhaps felt his authority would impress all of his former subordinates now with Holt.[155] It is probable, however, that the amnesty would have reduced Holt's fighting strength to an insignificant level had the amnesty legislation made provision for his complement of deserters and the unforeseen influence of what Moore described as the violence and atrocity of the Wicklow yeomanry.[156] Extreme loyalists in the yeomanry were opposed to any act of clemency however expedient to the government and provocatively murdered several rebels who had returned home with protections in August 1798.[157] One leading insurgent who obtained a protection was Michael Dwyer and it was this threat of loyalist revenge coupled with his unwillingness to seek refuge outside of his native county that obliged Dwyer to remain a fugitive for a further four years.[158]

Rebel activity declined steadily in the first half of August but experienced a revival in the days following 22 August when General Humbert landed at Killala, county Mayo with 1,100 French soldiers who formed the advance party of a much larger force at Dunkirk and Brest.[159] The belated arrival of the French in the west obliged Lord Cornwallis to immediately re-deploy the bulk of his available forces to that theatre to ensure that they did not have time to mobilise the region's disaffected inhabitants. Moore's camp was broken up and within an hour of his column marching through Blessington for the west the town was occupied by some of the rebels he had failed to bring in.[160] Holt sought to take advantage of the invasion crisis by gearing up his operation and taking offensive action against his old yeomen and militia adversaries who remained in Wicklow. He is reputed to have entered the Blackwater district of Wexford with Hackett in an unsuccessful attempt to encourage recruitment for an attack on the capital and he certainly fought a series of clashes with a large yeomanry force on 28-29 August in and around Aghavannagh and Clone Hill.[161] At least six loyalists and an unknown number of rebels were killed in these skirmishes from corps which included the Rathdrum, Tinahely, Hacketstown, Donard, Coolgreany, both Arklow corps and probably several other units.[162] They had evidently banded together in a bid to prevent the rebels running amok and defeating them piecemeal at a time when few regular or militia soldiers were available to bolster the county's garrisons. Dwyer, who had remained in west Wicklow with his group, also skirmished with the yeomen at this time and drove one raiding party led by Thomas Hugo out of Glenmalure and burned yeoman owned property at Colvinstown and Fendecoyle after a less successful encounter at Keadeen Bog.[163]

By 2 September Holt had relocated to the Seven Churches in north Wicklow where he was joined on that day by twenty-one King's county militiamen and 'above one hundred' civilians who had accompanied them from Arklow and were optimistic about the progress of the French.[164] They moved to Oakwood from which the town of Blessington was raided twice on and before the 5th, driving more than 400 cattle back into the mountains with them, some of which they may have slaughtered and carried to their camps at Ballynabrocka and then Imaal.[165] News of Humbert's defeat at Ballinamuck reached Holt on 9 September but neither this disaster nor the placing of a £300 reward on Holt's head curtailed insurgent activity to any appreciable extent.[166] Around this time Holt mounted a night raid to obtain provisions on the townlands adjoining Greenan and was ambushed at the Greenan bridge by the forewarned Rathdrum yeoman infantry. Miles Byrne paid tribute to Holt's brilliant conduct on this occasion in restoring order in the ranks of his disconcerted rebels and forcing the yeomen to retreat before serious losses were suffered.[167] Perhaps the most daring attack carried out by the rebels in this period was on Aughrim on 19 September when they marched from Oakwood and drove the notorious Hunter Gowan and Rathdrum's Tom King together with the three yeomanry corps under their control out of the town. During the night the rebels spent in the town a great deal of damage was done to the houses owned by yeomen.[168] This success troubled the government and gave credence to the declarations that Holt was in the habit of issuing, declarations such as the one which the Dublin press alleged he sent into Arklow informing the inhabitants that he would speedily be among them, and that he would not spare a single orangeman.[169] Unsubstantiated reports and rumours of further rebel victories were sent to the Dublin newspapers by their Wicklow correspondents which testified to the unease and insecurity felt at the time by the county's loyalist community.[170]

On 20 September a group of rebels met at the home of Nicholas Doyle of Ballnacuppogue and went to Ballinteshin where they killed a yeoman named John Leeson and proceeded to rob another of arms in Ballinalea. Having spent the night in Holt's camp at Oakwood they returned to their home area the following night and made an unsuccessful bid to kill several members of the Wicklow town yeoman cavalry who lived at Ballinalea and Rosanna.[171] It seems likely that it was this same group who returned to the Tighe estate at Ballynockan on the 22nd and killed three yeomen of the Bryan family.[172] Two other yeomen, privates of the Cronebane/Rathdrum yeoman infantry and the Wicklow town infantry, were also killed that night in separate incidents elsewhere in the county. This spate of assassinations was by no means extraordinary in the climate which prevailed in the autumn of 1798 in the Wicklow mountains and all loyalists known to have taken an active role against the rebels were in grave danger if they lived in or were seen alone outside garrison towns or yeomanry bases of Powerscourt and Humewood. The army and yeomen in particular responded to these outrages with further atrocities, feeding a spiral of violence. The cavalry of Rathdrum, Wicklow town and Newtown Mount Kennedy were regarded as being exceptionally brutal and it is probably not a coincidence that orange lodges were formed in these three corps by 1799, augmenting the previously established lodges in the Donard, Tinahely, Coolkenna, Carnew and probably Shillelagh corps.[173] According to *The Courier* of 26 September, 'for five miles [around Roundwood there was] not a single cabin to be met with', and that all had been 'levelled to the ground' by the military.[174] John Blachford, brother-in-law to Henry Grattan, surveyed the same scene and upon asking a Powerscourt yeoman to account for the bodies of the country people he saw lying in the fields his colleague allegedly could assign no reason.[175] Between June 1798 and March 1800 the triumphant Orange yeomen of Wicklow burned seventeen catholic chapels and killed at least two and possibly three priests, leaving several parishes in the south of the county with few or no clergy until 1802 when sectarianism subsided.[176]

A major military sweep to eradicate the surviving rebels was entrusted to General Lake. He left Dublin on 22 September with almost 2,000 troops in addition to a considerable cavalry force massed at Blessington.[177] A few days later command devolved on Lieutenant Colonel Robert Crauford who had distinguished himself at New Ross but found it impossible to trap the rebels and force them to battle. When Holt's men were finally located at Clone Hill on the 27th, 900 troops took up surrounding positions and waited for dawn to attack.[178] It was discovered in the morning, however, that during the night the rebels had used a clever ruse to break through the army cordon undetected and had escaped to Oakwood. Three hundred troops based at Blessington re-established contact with them at Knockalt around 1 October and were immediately ambushed and put to flight by insurgents concealed in trenches. Ten soldiers were killed in the retreat while the remainder were fortunate to evade a second rebel force led by Dwyer which almost trapped them in the King's river valley.[179] Dwyer played an important part in this modest victory and in the escape from Clone Hill and was now well established as one of the most intelligent and dynamic rebel leaders in Wicklow. His contacts within the yeomanry provided the rebels with detailed accounts of military dispositions and intentions.[180] It was apparent to the military even then that conventional infantry tactics were largely redundant in a county where the terrain gave considerable advantage to well-led and informed defenders. The inability of the administration to devise affective counter-insurgent measures further complicated the situation.

The end of the rebellion

In October/November 1798 violent incidents relating to the rebellion occurred over a greater area of Wicklow than before, giving the false impression of growing disaffection and instability. In fact, the trend arose from the increasing decentralisation of the rebel effort as several factions gravitated away from Holt's main force and towards their home districts. This process was due in part to dissatisfaction with Holt on the part of Dwyer and Hackett who mistrusted his ongoing and well publicised negotiation of terms with the government and resented his disciplinarian style of command.[181] Holt, however, enjoyed the support of the bulk of the insurgents and far from being deposed remained 'on very good terms'[182] with Dwyer after their distancing even if the two did not fight together as frequently as before. Indeed, despite his exploratory messages with the authorities Holt remained firmly committed to the rebellion and sent 'missionaries', as they were called, into neighbouring counties to encourage them to take up arms.[183] He maintained a channel of communication with the French Directory in Paris and conferred with the surviving members of the Dublin leadership in person and through emissaries. Holt was from the outset a serious-minded rebel with no interest in becoming a fugitive die-hard but rather wanted to play a part in overthrowing the government with French assistance.

Loyalist alarm peaked on 8 October when William Hume of Humewood, member of Parliament for Wicklow, magistrate and captain of the Lower Talbotstown cavalry was killed near his home in a skirmish with rebels who had sallied out from Imaal.[184] This incident was followed less than two weeks later on 16 October by daring attacks on property belonging to yeoman officers at Ballyteigue and Ballinderry near the invulnerable garrison of Rathdrum.[185] Dwyer's group burned the houses in reprisal for the acquittal in Dublin of a Newtown Mount Kennedy yeoman accused of murdering a protected rebel in Killincarraig.[186] Skirmishing took place for several days in Glenmalure where the army burned homes and shot 'such persons as they did not like', although their depredations were not unopposed and General Eustace had narrowly escaped death at the hands of Dwyer's men.[187] After this burst of activity Dwyer's group kept a very low profile and with the exception of a brief upsurge in early December shifted their emphasis from waging rebellion to surviving the winter in the mountains and glens of Talbotstown. From that time onwards there were rarely more than fifteen men with Dwyer at any time and generally only four or five.[188]

The onset of winter plagued Holt's force with illness and fatigue which weakened their effectiveness at a time when their movements were dogged by informers trying to obtain the £300 bounty on their commander's head.[189] It was decided that their only chance of remaining undetected was to divide into several groups which they did under amicable circumstances at Glenbride in the first week of October. In winter the harshness and exposed nature of the Wicklow mountains, then without most of the forest cover of the present day, militated against large concentrations of men as bivouacs and tents no longer provided sufficient shelter against the elements and all had to be accommodated indoors.[190] Much of the livestock they required to subsist was also removed from isolated pastureland to less vulnerable farm buildings. The viability of sizeable rebel congregations on any one townland was further reduced by the army's 'scorched earth' policy whereby farm buildings in the desolate areas of the mountains frequented by the rebels in summer and autumn, even those belonging to loyalist landlords, were razed to prevent them being used by the rebels.[191] Of the 300 men or so who remained with Holt before the split only 'about fifty'[192] were retained by him as a bodyguard after Glenbride and some of those were killed fighting their way out of a trap there on 10 October.[193] Within a few days of this narrow escape Holt ventured into Dublin city where he met rebel figures and was undoubtedly informed of the decision reached by United Irish heads on the 15th 'not [to] act without the French or [un]till the English troops are recalled'.[194] With the destruction of the Brest fleet by Admiral John Warren on 12 October, closely followed by Nelson's crushing of the French at the Battle of the Nile, it became evident that no French armies would be landing in Ireland in the foreseeable future.[195] Holt again conferred with other leading United Irishmen on 4 November in Thomas Street where the diminished prospects of foreign intervention must have been high on the agenda.[196] In this altered context further rebel activity was not only fraught with difficulty but militarily pointless and the pragmatic Holt had no hesitation on returning to Wicklow and dismissing his men at Ballylow before making his way to Powerscourt where he surrendered on 10 November.[197] His surrender brought about the end of organised rebellion in Wicklow in 1798 and in Ireland as a whole. James Hughes, James Ryder, Michael Dalton and many other former subordinates of Holt turned to brigandage but all had been killed or captured by 1800. Of the more politically motivated, Andrew Hackett was killed during an arms raid on 20 November 1798, Mathew Doyle was captured around the same time and Miles Byrne escaped to France.[198] The rump of the Talbotstown/Ballinacor rebels under Dwyer, Martin Burke and James Mernagh survived until December 1803 when the legal and tactical difficulties in countering their militarily slight but politically significant resistance were overcome and their demise brought about the total cessation of United Irish activity in the county.[199]

There is no doubt but that the intensity and importance of the rebellion in county Wicklow has been greatly underestimated. Wicklow fielded a high proportion of its United Irishmen in 1798 from every part of the county who at times threatened the security of the capital and remained in arms long after all vestiges of co-ordinated rebellion had disappeared elsewhere.

References

1. *Commons Journals, Ireland*, xix, pp clviii-cccxcviii and R.B. McDowell, *Ireland in the Age of Imperialism and Revolution, 1760-1801* (Oxford, 1979), pp 604-5.
2. Ruan O'Donnell, 'General Joseph Holt and the Historians' in Bob Reece (ed.), *Irish Convicts* (Dublin, 1987), pp 25-49 and L.M. Cullen 'The 1798 Rebellion in Wexford: United Irishman organization, membership, leadership' in K. Whelan (ed.), *Wexford: History and Society* (Dublin, 1987), pp 248-95.
3. Ruan O'Donnell, 'General Joseph Holt and the 1798 Rebellion in County

Wicklow', unpublished M.A. thesis (National University of Ireland, 1991), cited hereafter as 'Holt', Chapter Two; and Ruan O'Donnell and Bob Reece, 'A Clean Beast: Crofton Croker's Fairy Tale of General Holt' in *Eighteenth-Century Ireland, Iris an dá chultúr*, vol. 7, 1992, pp 7-42.

4. O'Donnell, 'Holt', pp 127-31.
5. 10 May 1797, Public Record Office, London, H.O., 100/70/245 and 1 February 1798, H.O. 100/75/199 and 27 August 1797, NAI, Frazer Ms, 1, item 17.
6. Information of Richard Turner, 9 July 1798, NAI, Rebellion Papers, 620/39/38, J. Smith to ____, 15 May 1797, 620/30/83, B. Senior to Edward Cooke, November 1797 and 6 December 1797, 620/18/3.
7. Miles Byrne, *Memoirs of Miles Byrne*, 2 vols (Paris, 1863), i, pp 28-9.
8. O'Donnell, 'Holt', pp 111-18.
9. Journal of Major Joseph Hardy of the Antrim Militia, Wentworth Wodehouse Muniments, Sheffield City Library, 31 May 1798 (N.L.I. microfilm, p. 5641) and Memorial of Major Hardy, n.d., N.L.I., Melville Ms.
10. 'They live [sic] and Adventures of Joseph Holt, Known by the Title of General Holt in the Irish Rebellion of '98', Mitchell Library, Sydney, Ms A2024, p. 21.
11. Holt Ms, p. 120.
12. Rev. James M'Ghee to ____, 7 May 1798, 620/37/31.
13. Cullen, '1798 Rebellion', p. 1290 and Luke Cullen, *Personal Recollections of Wexford and Wicklow Insurgents of 1798* (Enniscorthy, 1959), pp 10-11.
14. Samuel Sproule to John Lees, 19 May 1798, 620/51/27. cf. 20 May 1798, H.O. 100/76/270 and McDowell, *Ireland*, p. 603.
15. Tommy Graham, 'An Union of Power? The United Irish Organization' in Dickson, Keogh and Whelan (eds), *The United Irishmen, Republicanism, Radicalism and Rebellion* (Dublin, 1993), pp 252-3.
16. Sproule to Lees, 17 May 1798, 620/37/97.
17. Richard Musgrave, *Memoirs of the Different Rebellions in Ireland*, 2 vols (Dublin, 1801), ii, p. 267.
18. John Moore, *Diary*, 2 vols (ed.) J. T. Maurice (London, 1904), i, pp 308-10.
19. Thomas Pakenham, *The Year of Liberty, the bloody story of the Great Irish Rebellion of 1798* (London, 1969), p. 118.
20. 7 August 1797, NAI State of the Country Papers, SOC 3099 and Holt Ms, pp 21-2.
21. Ibid., p. 131 and Camden to Portland, 24 May 1798, H.O. 100/76/256.
22. Sproule to [Lees], 23 May 1798, 620/51/10.
23. _____ to Clarke, 23 May 1798, N.L.I. Ms 13,839.
24. Camden to Portland, 24 May 1798, H.O. 100/76/258 and Pakenham, *Liberty*, p. 117.
25. Luke Cullen cited in Charles Dickson, *The Life of Michael Dwyer with some account of his companions* (Dublin, 1944), p. 30.
26. Rev. Charles Robinson to Aldborough, 24 May 1798, 620/38/51.
27. *Faulkner's Dublin Journal*, 26 May 1798.
28. Pakenham, *Liberty*, p. 132.
29. Sproule to Lees, 22 June 1798, 620/51/36 and Aldborough to _____, 620/37/132/30.
30. Lt. Macauley to Hardy, 24 May 1798 in *Hibernian Telegraph*, 28 May 1798. cf. Petition of Hugh McClane, 26 May 1798, 620/51/64.
31. Macauley to Hardy, 24 May 1798 in *HT*, 28 May 1798. Cf. Catherine Carroll to Mrs Carroll, 29 May 1798 in *Historical Manuscripts Commission*, Report 3, Appendix 1872, p. 260.
32. Cullen cited in Dickson, *Dwyer*, p. 30.

33. Luke Cullen, *Insurgent Wicklow, the story as written by Bro. Luke Cullen O.D.C.* (ed.) Myles V. Ronan (Dublin, 1948), p. 81.
34. Information of Thomas Murray, 21 May 1798, 620/3/32/6.
35. Musgrave, *Rebellions*, cited in Dickson, *Dwyer*, p. 31.
36. O'Donnell, 'Holt', pp 129-30, Dickson, *Dwyer*, p. 34 and William James Fitzpatrick, *The Sham Squire and the Informers of 1798* (Dublin, 1866), pp 309-11.
37. Luke Cullen Ms, N.L.I. Ms 9762, p. 262 and Ms 8339, p. 56.
38. _____ to Cooke, 29 May 1798, 620/37/211A.
39. *Freeman's Journal*, 29 May 1798.
40. Thomas King to Alexander Marsden, 16 January 1803, 620/65/148.
41. James M'Ghee to _____, 25 May 1798 cited in R.R. Madden, *The United Irishmen, their lives and times,* 4 vols, 2nd ed. (Dublin, 1858), iv, p. 460.
42. Pakenham, *Liberty*, p. 184.
43. 7 August 1798, S.O.C. 3099.
44. *The tryal of William Byrne of Ballymanus* (Dublin, 1799), p. 118 and Castlereagh to _____ n.d., 620/18/11/6.
45. Information of Jeremiah Delamere, 10 April 1800, NAI, Prisoners' Petitions and Cases, PPC 346 and Luke Cullen papers, Trinity College Dublin, Ms 1472, p. 202.
46. Camden to Portland, 31 May 1798, H.O. 100/76/327, Information of John Boothman, n.d., 620/51/60 and George Parvisol to Cooke, 30 May 1798, 620/37/218.
47. Hardy to Loftus, 29 May 1798, 620/39/210.
48. Ann Tottenham to _____, 27 June 1798, N.L.I. Ms 3531, p. 35.
49. O'Donnell, 'Holt', pp 131-4.
50. Cullen Ms 8339, p. 57.
51. R.Marshall to Knox, 30 May 1798, N.L.I. Ms 56, p. 170, *Hibernian Telegraph*, 1 June 1798 and Musgrave, *Rebellions*, i, pp 385-6.
52. Cullen, *Insurgent*, p. 38 and John Edwards to Cooke, 30 May 1798, 620/37/217.
53. Shannon to Boyle, 30 May 1798 in *Lord Shannon's letters to his son* (ed.) by Esther Hewitt (Belfast, 1982), p. 105.
54. Cullen, *Insurgent*, pp 20-38 and O'Donnell, 'Holt', pp 136-7.
55. Hardy to Fitzwilliam, 27 November 1797 and 27 January 1798, N.L.I. microfilm, p. 5641.
56. 27 August 1797, Frazer Ms 1, p. 17.
57. Hardy to Cooke, 19 January 1798, 620/35/48 and Cullen, *Insurgent*, p. 30.
58. M'Ghee to _____, 7 May 1798, 620/37/31 and 11 July 1798, 620/39/51 and Hardy to Cooke, 22 May 1798, 620/37/123.
59. Information of John Waters, 11 July 1798, 620/39/51.
60. Hardy Journal, April 1797, Byrne, *Memoirs*, i, p. 28.
61. Hay, *History*, p. 106, Cullen Ms 1472, pp 202-3, 214.
62. Richard Foote to _____, 27 May 1798, 620/37/179 and Jane Adams Narrative in Thomas Crofton Croker, *Researches in the South of Ireland* (London, 1824), p. 348.
63. Information of Terence Kinshelagh, 28 May 1798, N.L.I. Ms 871 and O'Donnell, 'Holt', p. 122.
64. Hardy to Cooke, 27 May 1798, 620/37/184 and Byrne, *Memoirs*, I, p. 84.
65. O'Donnell, 'Holt', pp 137-8.
66. Hereward Senior, *Orangeism in Ireland and Britain, 1795-1836* (London, 1966), pp 97-8.
67. Byrne, *Memoirs*, i, pp 28-40.
68. O'Donnell, 'Holt', pp 138-42.

69. Byrne, *Memoirs*, i, p. 114.
70. Holt Ms, p. 235.
71. Byrne, *Memoirs*, i, p. 47. cf. 28 March 1798, 620/17/30/64.
72. *tryal*, pp 7, 30-1.
73. O'Donnell, 'Holt', p. 87.
74. Dickson, *Dwyer*, pp 36-7, 256.
75. Dickson, *The Wexford Rising in 1798* (Tralee, 1955), p. 102, *Catholic Telegraph*, 29 September 1856 and Camden to Portland, 2 June 1798, H.O. 100/81/7.
76. Wainwright to Fitzwilliam, 6 February 1800, N.L.I. microfilm, p. 5641 and Hay, *History*, pp 97-8.
77. Pakenham, *Liberty*, pp 230-1 and Thomas Cloney, *A Personal Narrative ... 1798* (Dublin, 1838), pp 35-40.
78. John Brennan list, n.d. [4 or 5 June] 1798, 620/51/225.
79. John Thomas Campion, *Michael Dwyer or the Insurgent Captain of the Wicklow Moutains, a Tale of '98* (Dublin, n.d.), p. 80.
80. Dundas to Castlereagh, 8 August 1798, 620/39/158.
81. O'Donnell, 'Holt', pp 139-40 and Archibald McClaren, *A minute description of the battles of Gorey, Arklow and Vinegar Hill: together with the movements of the army through the Wicklow mtns* (1798), pp 9-10.
82. McLaren, *Minute*, p. 12 and G. A. Hayes-McCoy, *Irish Battles* (London, 1969), pp 284-9, Lake to Wickham, 7 June 1798, H.O. 100/81/31.
83. Cullen, *Recollections*, p. 50 and Dickson, *Dwyer*, p. 60.
84. Cullen, *Recollections*, p. 30 and Byrne, *Memoirs*, p. 95.
85. Hardy Journal, 3-6 June 1798.
86. Camden to Pelham, 5 June 1798, H.O. 100/77/50 and McCoy, *Battles*, pp 286-7.
87. McCoy, *Battles*, p. 285.
88. Needham to Littlehales, 18 December 1799, 620/7/76/4 and Thomas Edwards to Cooke, 27 March 1800, 620/57/94.
89. Cullen, *Recollections*, pp 23-4 and McCoy, *Battles*, p. 290.
90. Sarah Tighe to _____, 10 June 1798, N.L.I. Ms 4813.
91. Henry Lambart Bayly to Edward Bayly, 9 June 1798, NAI, M.2464, cf. Needham to Lake, 9 June 1798, H.O. 100/77/122.
92. Cullen, *Recollections*, p. 124, McClaren, *Minute*, p. 18 and William Maume to Sylvester Shea, 15 June 1798, N.L.I. Ms 5006.
93. McCoy, *Battles*, pp 302-3.
94. H. Moore to Lake, 9 June 1798, 620/38/100A.
95. Cullen, *Recollections*, pp 125 and Cullen Ms, NAI, M.5892/8, p. xii.
96. Information of Fr. John Martin, 16 June 1798, 620/38/126, cf. Hardy to Lake, 11 June 1798, 620/38/126.
97. Ibid., cf. B. Senior to Cooke, n.d., 620/17/32 and 620/18/1 and O'Donnell, 'Holt', pp 149-50.
98. Holt Ms, pp 21-2 and Information of Bartholomew Connolly, 24 July 1798, 620/37/73.
99. Senior to Cooke, n.d., 620/18/1.
100. O'Donnell, 'Holt', pp 151-2, *Saunder's Newsletter*, 14, 20 and 30 June, 4 July, 7 and 8 August 1798 and John Giffard to Marsden, 14 June 1798, 620/38/145.
101. *SNL*, 20 June 1798, cf. Thomas Archer to Marsden, 7 July 1800, 620/57/44 and Cullen Ms 8339, p. 349.
102. *SNL*, 14 June 1798.
103. Information of Joseph Thompson, 27 June 1798, 620/38/243, Byrne, *Memoirs*, i, p. 115 and Cullen, *Recollections*, pp 28-9.

104. O'Donnell, 'Holt', pp 158-9, Holt Ms, p. 25 and H. Morrison to Rossmore, 20 June 1798, 620/38/192.
105. Holt Ms, pp 25-6, 19 August 1799, 620/17/30/85 and Camden to Pelham, 21 June 1798, 620/18/9/1.
106. 28 March 1799, 620/17/30/64.
107. Camden to Pelham, 13 June 1798 in J.T. Gilbert, *Documents Relating to Ireland, 1795-1804* (Dublin, 1970), p. 133, Cullen, *Recollections*, pp 29-30 and *SNL*, 20 June 1798.
108. Hardy Journal, 17-18 June 1798.
109. Lake to Castlereagh, 21 June 1798 in Madden, *United*, iv, p. 408 and Pakenham, *Liberty*, pp 293-5.
110. Cullen, *Recollections*, pp 35-6.
111. Byrne, *Memoirs*, i, p. 128 cf. 23 November 1798, 620/17/30/17.
112. Pakenham, *Liberty*, p. 293.
113. Cullen, *Recollections*, p. 37.
114. Hay, *History*, pp 215-7, Lake to Castlereagh, 22 June 1798, H.O. 100/81/161 and John Moore, *Diary*, i, p. 300.
115. O'Donnell, 'Holt', pp 157-8.
116. Cullen, *Recollections*, p. 42.
117. Ibid., p. 43, Dickson, *Dwyer*, p. 176, Hay, *History*, p. 247 and Thompson, 27 June 1798, 620/38/243.
118. Dickson, *Dwyer*, p. 176, 25 June 1798, 620/38/239 and Hardy Memorial.
119. 'Suffering loyalist' list, N.L.I. microfilm, p. 7665, *SNL*, 6 July 1798 and *Wicklow People*, 9, 16, 23 and 30 July 1938.
120. Cornwallis to Portland, 26 June 1798, H.O. 100/81/119 and Musgrave, *Rebellions*, i, p. 56.
121. Holt Ms, pp 27-9.
122. Cullen, *Recollections*, p. 81, *Catholic Telegraph*, 29 September 1856 and Asgill to Castlereagh, 27 June 1798, H.O. 100/81/201.
123. O'Donnell, 'Holt', pp 167-9, Detail Book of Camolin yeoman cavalry in H. Wheeler and A.M. Broadley, *The War in Wexford* (London, 1910), pp 208-9 and Holt Ms, pp 34-5.
124. Muster list of the Ancient British light fencible cavalry, 1798, P.R.O., London, W.O., 13/3732 and Camden to Portland, 6 July 1798, H.O. 100/81/227.
125. O'Donnell, 'Holt', p. 174.
126. Cullen Ms 8339, p. 80 and *Recollections*, pp 47-8.
127. Hay, *History*, p. 250.
128. Cullen, *Recollections*, p. 48.
129. *HT*, 9 July 1798 and Shannon to Boyle, 6 July 1798 in *Letters*, p. 137.
130. Hunter to Hewitt, 8 July 1798, 620/39/35 and *SNL*, 6 July 1798.
131. Moore, *Diary*, i, p. 304, cf. Cooke to Wickham, 9 July 1798, H.O. 100/81/239.
132. Moore, *Diary*, i, pp 305-8 and *SNL*, 11-12 July 1798.
133. Cullen, *Recollections*, p. 53.
134. Ibid., p. 54 and Holt Ms, pp 42-3.
135. 11 July 1798, H.O. 100/81/243.
136. Holt Ms, p.44 and Felix Rourke to Mary Finnerty, 27 July 1798 in Madden, *United*, iv, p. 546.
137. Lt-Col. Gough to Col. Verecher, 12 July 1798, 620/4/36/1.
138. Connolly, 24 July 1798, 620/39/73 and Byrne, *Memoirs*, i, p. 220.
139. O'Donnell, 'Holt', pp 187-8, Major-General Weyms to Taylor, 15 July 1798,

620/39/85 and Major-General Myers to Hewitt, 15 July 1798, 620/39/83.

140. O'Donnell, 'Holt', pp 193-4.
141. Byrne, *Memoirs*, i, p. 220 and James Critchley to Sir John Parnell, 21 July 1798, 620/15/198.
142. Holt Ms, p. 63 and Muster list of King's County Militia, 1798, W.O. 13/2574.
143. O'Donnell, 'Holt', pp 165-6.
144. Benjamin O'Neale Stratford to _____, 28 July 1798, 620/37/123.
145. Byrne, *Memoirs*, i, p. 203.
146. Information of Michael Dwyer, 11 January 1804, H.O. 100/124/26-301.
147. n.d., Sirr papers, T.C.D. Ms 869/8, f. 98 and Information of Daniel Doyne, 15 July 1798, 620/51/48.
148. *SNL*, 17 and 23 October 1798 and Mary Leadbeater, *The Leadbeater Papers*, 2 vols (London, 1862), i, p. 250.
149. Holt Ms, pp 90-93, 27 November 1799, 620/17/30/73 and Cullen, *Insurgent*, pp 76-7.
150. O'Donnell, 'Holt', p. 198 and Moore, *Diary*, I, p. 310.
151. Byrne, *Memoirs*, i, p. 223.
152. Ibid., pp 223-4 and Cullen Ms 8339, p. 162.
153. Moore, *Diary*, i, p. 309, cf. 11 October 1799, 620/17/30/97.
154. Ibid., and *SNL*, 13 July 1798.
155. Moore, *Diary*, i, p. 310, cf. Cornwallis to Portland, 7 August 1798, H.O. 100/78/20 and Garret Byrne to _____, 24 March 1799, H.O. 100/66/413.
156. Moore, *Diary*, i, p. 310.
157. O'Donnell, 'Holt', pp 202-3.
158. Cullen Ms 8339, p. 153 and Hardy Journal, 7 August 1798.
159. McDowell, *Ireland*, pp 645-50 and J. Stock, *A narrative of what happened at Killala* (Dublin, 1800).
160. Major Peyton to _____, 26 August 1798, 620/3/31/2.
161. *Courier*, 27 September and 30 October 1798 and Hay, *History*, pp 266, 326-7.
162. O'Donnell, 'Holt', pp 211-12, Holt Ms, pp 121-2 and *SNL*, 5 September 1798.
163. Cullen Ms 8339, pp 151-2 and Memorial of William Hume Steel, 14 October 1805 in Dickson, *Dwyer*, p. 121.
164. Col. L'Estrange to Eustace, 2 September 1798, 620/40/11, cf. 13 March 1799, 620/17/30/15.
165. *Hibernian Journal*, 7 September 1798 and *SNL*, 12, 14 and 21 September 1798.
166. Critchley to Parnell, 11 September 1798, 620/40/36.
167. Byrne, *Memoirs*, p. 223, cf. Cullen Ms 8339, p. 121.
168. Holt Ms, pp 101-2 and *SNL*, 24 September 1798.
169. *Courier*, 1 October 1798.
170. O'Donnell, 'Holt', pp 222-3.
171. 23 April 1799, 620/17/30/30, 1 June 1799, 620/17/30/81 and Cullen Ms 8339, p. 204.
172. *Dublin Evening Post*, 29 September 1798.
173. Senior, *Orangeism*, pp 97-8, Byrne, *Memoirs*, i, pp 24 and 84 and Luke Cullen to R.R. Madden, 27 July 1858, Ms 1472, p. 236.
174. *Courier*, 26 September 1798.
175. *Memoir of the Life and Times of the R.H. Henry Grattan by his son* (London, 1847), iv, pp 392-3.
176. William Hamilton Maxwell, *History of the Irish Rebellion in 1798* (London, 1845), p. 446, Cullen, *Recollections*, pp 92-3 and Archbishop Troy to Marsden, 15 February 1802, 620/63/65.

177. *SNL*, 21 and 24 September 1798, *Faulkner's Dublin Journal*, 21 September 1798.
178. Holt Ms, p. 68 and Cullen Ms 8339, p. 115.
179. *Courier*, 4 and 6 October 1798, Holt Ms, p. 76.
180. Holt Ms, pp 74-5.
181. O'Donnell, 'Holt', pp 228-31 and *Courier*, 7 November 1798.
182. Cullen Ms 8339, pp 206-7.
183. *Courier*, 4 October 1798.
184. Dickson, *Dwyer*, pp 398-90 and *DEP*, 11 October 1798.
185. Hardy Journal, 8 June 1798.
186. *The geniune trial of Hugh Woolaghan* ... (Dublin, 1798).
187. Cullen Ms 9761, p. 12.
188. Cullen Ms 8339, p. 201.
189. *DEP*, 11 and 24 September 1798.
190. Holt Ms, pp 146-60.
191. Petition of Abraham Critchley, 4 April 1801, 620/49/99.
192. Holt Ms, p. 151.
193. *HT* and *SNL*, 15 October 1798.
194. Sproule to Lees, 19 October 1798, 620/40/172.
195. McDowell, *Ireland*, pp 650-1.
196. O'Donnell, 'Holt', pp 236-8.
197. Ibid., p. 239 and *Courier*, 20-22 November 1798.
198. O'Donnell, 'Holt', p. 240, *SNL*, 8 November 1798 and Information of Francois Joseph, 5 July 1799, 620/56/110 and 15 February 1799, 620/17/30/3.
199. See Dickson, Dwyer, Kieran Sheedy, *Upon the Mercy of Government, the story of the surrender, imprisonment and transportation to New South Wales of Michael Dwyer and his Wicklow comrades* (Dublin, 1988) and Ruan O'Donnell, 'Michael Dwyer' in Bob Reece (ed.) *Irish Convict Lives* (Sydney, 1993).

Note:
Lehaunstown = Loughlinstown.

Chapter 11

'MASTERS OF THE MOUNTAINS': THE INSURGENT CAREERS OF JOSEPH HOLT AND MICHAEL DWYER, COUNTY WICKLOW, 1798-1803[1]

THOMAS BARTLETT

'You command in Montelepre but here we are in the mountains, and in the mountains I command.' Salvatore Giuliano, Sicilian Bandit (1923-50), to Giuseppe Calandra, Chief of the Carabinieri, quoted in Gavin Maxwell, *God protect me from my Friends* (London, rev. ed. 1972), p. 108.

I

The 1798 rebellion did not end with the defeat of the Wexford rebels at Vinegar Hill on 21 June. As the vanquished rebels poured out of Wexford, north to Wicklow or west into Kilkenny, furious skirmishes were fought in which hundreds of casualties were sustained, and these continued throughout the summer. Moreover, the nature of the fighting in the months of May and June had meant inevitably that there would be many scores to settle. Public ferocity would merely yield to private vengeance while those military depredations which had played so prominent a role in provoking the rebellion, now reappeared, reinvigorated and frequently sectarianised, to frustrate all efforts at establishing a lasting peace. General lawlessness, too, was endemic as criminal gangs, swollen by large numbers of military deserters, took advantage of the widespread disorder and preyed on the traveller and the isolated farmer.[2] In addition, despite the disasters of June 1798 a skeletal rebel command still remained; there were continuing hopes of a French intervention; and reports soon circulated of a planned second rebellion, possibly in the spring of 1799. Central to these expectations was the 'little war' waged by unreconciled rebels in the Wicklow mountains.

From June to November 1798, 'General' Joseph Holt, and from June 1798 to – astonishingly – December 1803, Michael Dwyer remained at large in the mountains and valleys of Wicklow, frustrating all attempts to capture them. As long as these men and their followers remained 'outstanding' so close to Dublin the rebellion would not be at an end. For their endurance alone, and what that tells us about the limits of state power in the years after Vinegar Hill, the careers of these two men would be worthy of study. But it may also be suggested that their successful defiance sheds light on a variety of other matters. It shows clearly, for example, the paradoxical situation of Wicklow – a rebel stronghold, a last frontier, yet located on the outskirts of the capital city. Again, consideration of their activities – particularly those of Dwyer – uncovers that potent fusion of memory and myth, that mixture of fact and fantasy, that selective amnesia that allowed pride to emerge quickly as the dominant legacy of the débâcle of '98. Finally, examination of the composition of both Holt's and Dwyer's bands, and of the forces that opposed them, reveals the shifting and blurring that occurred between public and private as soldier turned deserter turned rebel turned bandit turned informer. As military red and Scots plaid vied with Whiteboy white and republican green, these colours blended and merged with the ever-changing landscape while, above all, loomed the mountains. The emerging romanticist admiration for man in harmony with nature, at one with a wild landscape – not rendered savage by it – fixed on the careers of Holt ('the master of the mountains') and Dwyer ('this mountain general') and reinterpreted them in keeping with the new aesthetics.[3] Holt and Dwyer, in the end, were as much the creations of their enemies as of their friends.

II

The career of Joseph Holt has recently been subjected to detailed examination by Ruan O'Donnell and all students of the period are indebted to him for his painstaking reassessment of Holt's role in the rebellion and after in Wicklow.[4] It is now clear that Holt's campaign in the late summer of 1798 was a much more formidable one than had hitherto been supposed and that Holt himself – for reasons that had much to do with a determination on all sides to 'catholicise' the rebellion – has been unfairly ignored by subsequent historians. Holt's protestantism, unlike that of Wolfe Tone or Henry Joy McCracken, was unaccompanied by martyrdom, and this made him an unlikely entrant to the pantheon of Irish heroes. Suspicions that he may have given information concerning his accomplices on his surrender and recollections of his pre-rebellion career – 'I was deemed a good tory hunter in the county Wicklow', wrote Holt – further helped marginalise his memory.[5] T. Crofton Croker's two-volume edition of Holt's *Memoirs* published in 1838 did little to rehabilitate him for, as O'Donnell has shown, Crofton Croker fabricated nearly 20 per cent of the *Memoirs*, inserting incidents, conversations and even Holt's 'reflections' as the mood took him. Holt, himself, in his unpublished memoirs was also cavalier with the facts. In Crofton Croker's edition, Holt emerges as a reluctant rebel, a Byronesque hero, on the model of a Sir Walter Scott character. Arguably, Holt might not have been displeased at this.

Holt was born of Protestant settler stock in Ballydonnell, county Wicklow some time around 1759.[6] He seemed destined for a military career. 'I conceived that a martial disposition was imbibed at my earliest period', he later wrote and he enjoyed spells in the 1780s as a sub-constable, member of the local Volunteer corps and recruiting sergeant for the 32nd Regiment of Foot. By the early 1790s, however, the army had become only one of a number of career options. He became a deputy alnager with responsibility for inspecting cloth and woollen goods over a wide area of counties Wicklow, Wexford and Dublin; a road overseer in the same area; and a billet master 'for moving militias and army that passed through that part of the county [Wicklow]'. These occupations he found compatible with a little bounty-hunting: in 1794 he pursued a robber, Pat Rogers, for over 500 miles throughout the south east before capturing him.[7]

What is missing from this account is any indication of the motives that led him to shun the loyalist camp – he was never a Yeoman – and instead to opt for the United Irishmen. There are reports that he fell foul of Hunter Gowan's brother in Wexford, and that he was on bad terms with another equally important loyalist in Wicklow, Thomas Hugo: and these may be significant; but there is nothing to explain fully his (or his brothers') firm commitment to the United Irish cause. As O'Donnell comments, 'He and his brothers may well have become rebels to redress social grievances of a nature as yet unrevealed.'[8] However, he was clearly identified as an United Irishman in the months before the rebellion, and his house was burned in May 1798. He later claimed that it was at this point that he became an active rebel: 'I then roused my spirits and vowed vengeance on the wicked perpetrator', he wrote in his *Memoirs*.

He fought in Wexford but his manuscript memoirs glosses over his time there and his career as rebel commander really began in June 1798 on his return to Wicklow. At Whelp's Rock and at Seven Churches, Glendalough, he rallied the dejected rebels and turned them into an effective fighting force. A successful attack was launched on Hacketstown, county Carlow (25 June) and, thus encouraged, an attack on Carnew in south Wicklow was determined upon. On their way to

Carnew, the rebels led by Holt ambushed a pursuing squadron of cavalry and killed nearly fifty of them, but at Carnew itself the garrison, secure in their stone barracks, repulsed their attack (30 June). Holt then fell back to Whelp's Rock on Black Hill Mountain south of Lackan from where he was prevailed upon to 'invade' county Meath in an effort to rouse those counties to the north which had not yet participated in the rebellion. This proved a disaster and in the ensuing rout Holt was left for dead. After many adventures and close escapes, he made his way back to the Wicklow mountains. In these mountains, throughout the summer and autumn of 1798, he launched a relentless war against informers, loyalists – reportedly over 400 loyalist properties were burned – and local Yeomanry corps.[9]

Various sweeps involving thousands of troops were launched against him but somehow he always managed to elude them. Government spies – one, Sproule, was particularly persistent – likewise sought to pinpoint his location. In early November 1798, Sproule reported to his controller, Lees, that he had learnt that 'Holt slept last night but one in the back house of a widow poor woman [sic] who lets beds in Dirty Lane [Dublin]. To come nearer them is impossible as they now conduct things with such secrecy as none but 2 men of themselves know of the meeting till they are brought to the spot.' Sproule suggested a coordinated search of all suspect houses in the district, adding 'they will never be got by any other plan'. But this search, and others, drew a blank.[10]

In his camps 'General' Holt sought to maintain a firm military discipline; 'the robbing system' i.e. ordinary crime, was firmly discouraged; his men were regularly drilled; informers were flogged or shot; and on occasion Holt's men were encouraged to live at free quarters in areas like Rathdrum where he had encountered opposition from the local people. A military regime was not perhaps all that difficult to effect: Holt claimed to have 126 deserters from thirteen regiments in his band, most of them having joined him since the collapse of the rebellion in Wexford.[11] A further blurring of the distinction between public and private, state and locality occurred when General Craig offered a reward of £300 for General Holt's apprehension, only to find that Holt in response promptly offered £600 for Craig's capture. Similarly Holt offered 'protections' for sale on the model of those offered by the government to repentant rebels. (His were probably worth as little.)[12]

O'Donnell has conjectured that Holt continued his resistance in hopes of a French landing and that it was the failure of General Humbert and his French raiding party in September 1798 to capitalise on their initial victory at Castlebar that finally dashed those hopes.

Certainly from that point on, Holt began to consider carefully the terms he was likely to obtain from government; and the increasing lack of discipline among his followers as well as his own poor health undoubtedly concentrated his mind on this matter. Holt's wife was known to the influential La Touche family and their good offices were sought. Negotiations were set in train and on 10 November 1798, Holt surrendered to Lord Powerscourt. It is unclear what terms Holt surrendered upon:[13] certainly he was transported to the convict settlements in Australia but the fact that he was (eventually) allowed to bring his wife and son with him (a daughter was left behind) indicates that he was accorded special privileges; and Holt himself claimed that in contrast to the other convicts he was allowed the freedom of the ship during the voyage. Again, in marked contrast to other prisoners, he was allowed to return to Ireland in 1814. Dublin Castle, and the loyalist community in Wicklow, were by no means pleased at this, and for years he was subjected to petty harassment and close surveillance. He died in 1826 and was buried at Monkstown, county Dublin.

III

Holt makes little mention of Michael Dwyer in his memoirs but it cannot be inferred from this that he was unaware of his existence or that there was any great animosity between them. Holt's *Memoirs* were about Holt: others were admitted insofar as they had dealings with him; but he was not writing a history of the rebellion in Wicklow. And yet, notwithstanding the publication of Holt's two-volume *Memoirs*, it is Dwyer who is best remembered as the insurgent general of Wicklow. His lengthy resistance – over five years compared to Holt's six months – in the Wicklow mountains; his numerous adventures and especially his daring escapes; and his final surrender and transportation to Australia (from whence he did *not* return) earned him an enduring place in the canon of Irish resisters. Throughout the nineteenth century, his memory proved an inspiration for Irish nationalist groups while in his native Wicklow he passed quickly from history into ballad and folklore.[14]

Michael Dwyer was born in 1772 in the Glen of Imaal, county Wicklow. His family were small farmers, moderately prosperous, and when the 'United system' was introduced into the county in the spring of 1797, Dwyer became active in the organisation. He was quickly identified as 'more than a common man and was soon after voted to the office of lower baronial delegate', according to an informant of Luke Cullen, the nineteenth-century collector of eye-witness accounts of the rebellion years.[15] The United Irishmen were numerically strong in Wicklow but their leadership structure was ineffective and was quickly exposed when rebellion broke out.[16] Ill-conceived attacks were launched on Blessington and on Newtownmountkennedy, and when these proved unsuccessful, the Wicklow rebels, Dwyer and Holt among them, moved south into Wexford.

Dwyer apparently fought at Arklow and then followed the campaign through to Vinegar Hill. After the rebels' defeat there he made his way back to Glenmalure Valley, county Wicklow, but now his reputation had grown – Myles Byrne referred to him as 'the intrepid Dwyer' – and he assumed a leadership role in the valley.[17] For the next five years, with a notional break during the Peace of Amiens (March 1802-May 1803), he conducted a brilliant guerilla campaign which defied all the efforts of the authorities to quash.

As with Holt, various planned searches were organised to capture him. In June 1800, Lieut-Colonel George Stewart swept into Glenmalure at the head of his men and left small detachments dotted along the valley: it was no use – Dwyer and his band simply dispersed on their approach. In December 1801, the eager Major Tattam of the Somerset Fencibles was given leave to encircle Aghavannagh ('where it is supposed the rebels harbour') with units of his own regiment, local Yeomanry corps, and the Duke of York's Highlanders. The campaign was a complete fiasco; Dwyer and his men easily slipped the net and Tattam and his men were left to blunder about in freezing conditions on the mountains.[18] By 1803, however, Dwyer had had enough of living 'on his keeping'. He had always maintained that he would fight on until the French came but the failure of Emmet's rebellion brought home to him the hopelessness of the cause. Robert Emmet's father appears to have known Dwyer's father,[19] and contact was established between Robert and Michael through the agency of Arthur Devlin, Dwyer's cousin and one of the soldiers assigned to guard Emmet and the other state prisoners at Fort George in Scotland. Dwyer may not have been as sceptical of Robert Emmet's plans as he later claimed:[20] but in any case, the premature explosion at Emmet's Thomas Street munitions store put paid to the entire plot.

Over the years various atttempts had been made to talk Dwyer down from the mountains but they had all foundered on Dwyer's insistence on a free pardon for himself and his companions. In late 1803, however, alarmed by his involvement in the Emmet conspiracy, Dublin Castle sought to reopen negotiations. In November, the lord lieutenant, Lord Hardwicke, referring to Dwyer's 'extraordinary ascendancy over the inhabitants of those parts', offered him and his family removal to another country if he would surrender. When Dwyer rejected these terms a proclamation was issued outlawing him, offering a reward of £500 for his capture, and rendering all those who harboured him liable to martial law.[21] Within a few weeks there was a round-up of Dwyer's extended network of relations and of those likely to succour him[22], putting him under intense pressure to make terms.

Moreover, the Military Road which had been under construction since 1800 between Glencree and Aghavannagh was finally completed in the summer of 1803. In additon, barracks were to be constructed at Glencree, Imaal, Seven Churches and Glenmalure;[23] in the meantime, small parties of troops were to be billetted in the houses of suspected harbourers in Imaal and Glenmalure, at a stroke denying Dwyer shelter and increasing the pressure on his supporters, now saddled with the costs of feeding military 'lodgers'. A harsh winter added to Dwyer's troubles. One of Dwyer's band later recorded that on the 7th or 8th of December 'a sort of council of war on the subject of surrender' was held in a cave near the Wicklow Gap and, with one dissenting voice (John Mernagh), the rebels decided to give themselves up on condition of being sent to the United States. William Hoare Hume, member of Wickow and a liberal in his politics, brokered Dwyer's surrender which took place on 14 December. It was not, however, the United States that was to be Dwyer's distination: and it is unclear whether such a condition had been agreed upon before Dwyer came in. The *Freeman's Journal* in one of its early reports of his surrender was nearer the mark when it forecast that Dwyer would 'become a fellow subject with Holt in Botany Bay'.[24]

For well over a year Dwyer lay in Kilmainham and in July 1805 he was transported to New South Wales. As was the case with Holt, Dwyer was given preferential treatment on board ship, being neither ironed nor shaved. His wife and children joined him in Australia in 1806 and they farmed a 100-acre holding at Liverpool, near Sydney. Perhaps fittingly, Dwyer was made a district constable in the Sydney area in 1813 and he served the forces of law and order until his death in 1825.

IV

Why were Holt and Dwyer able to hold out for so long, so close to Dublin? It is evident that both enforced a strict discipline on their own men and a due obedience on the wider population by a judicious use of intimidation. Holt had an eleven-year old boy executed as a spy and he ordered the flogging of a woman with the cat-of-nine tales. He shot dead a man who answered him in an insolent manner and when a woman remonstrated with him as his men sacked her house and others in Rathdrum as a punishment for harbouring thieves, Holt's brusque reply was 'Madame, observe yon tree. Instantly disappear or it shall be your gallows.'[25] Nor was he above giving information to the authorities on thieves and robbers, especially those who claimed to act in his name. Dwyer too was well capable of firm action: it was reported that he killed by his own hand three men who had tried to desert from his band. In reality, however, there was little that could be done to resist him. In December 1800, Edward Byrne wrote to Lord Cornwallis concerning the conviction of his two sons for harbouring Dwyer and his men. Byrne protested that 'it was impossible for petitioner or family to prevent the robbers and plunderers [i.e. 'Dwyre and his associates'] who then infested the country from making any use of petitioner's house they thought proper and any person who should refuse them entertainment or should express any dislike of their outrageous conduct was instantly murdered.'[26] Dwyer also dealt harshly with informers: one of these latter reported anxiously in August 1798: 'Dwyre and his party is in all most every house in the glin of Emale. The inhabitans [sic] is so much his frend that aney person who the[y] think is not the same way dar not darnt [sic] speak one word but are in deanger of being kild ... I am in danger of my life I am so pinted at for liting the armey know ever thing I know about these robbers': and Byrne reported that 'every person they suspected of giving information was instantly put to death'.[27] Moreover, Dwyer could certainly be oppressive in his demands for food, drink and money. William Wickham, the chief secretary, wrote in 1804 that the people of Wicklow were glad that Dwyer was taken for he had made continual levies on them and had brought in the soldiers.[28]

It would be, however, entirely wrong to suggest that Holt and Dwyer survived because they conducted a reign of terror in the mountains. The secret to Dwyer's survival – and to an extent, Holt's – lay in popular support: 'The country wished to protect him [Dwyer] and I found it impossible to arrest him,' declared Captain Hume of the Baltinglass Yeomanry. Similarly, Captain Thomas King of the Rathdrum Yeomanry spent years trying to catch Dwyer but in the end was forced to concede that 'while he continues in Imale or the boggs about Rathdangan, he thinks himself and I have much reason to believe he is perfectly safe;' and he added 'while the inhabitants of Imale continue his protection nothing can be done there by any man from this side [of the mountains].'[29] In addition, Dwyer had the advantage of an extensive kinship network based in Glenmalure and Imaal which was able to offer succour with security. When Michael 'Red Mick' Dwyer was captured in 1803 the authorities were for a short time jubilant, believing they had caught Dwyer himself: 'Red Mick' however scornfully pointed out that 'he is not nearer related than second cousin to Michael Dwire, the noted rebble chief'.[30] This kinship network was vital to Dwyer and, accordingly, the arrest and imprisonment of around twenty of his relations in late 1803 dealt him a devastating blow, precipitating his surrender.[31]

It is clear that elements of the yeomanry were prepared to harbour Dwyer or at least to turn a blind eye to him, and this too explains his lengthy career. 'It is most confidently asserted,' Captain King wrote, 'that all the Yeomen resident in Imale ... make no secret of harbouring him ... Dwyer is as free in every Yeoman's house there (if I am rightly informed) as he can wish', and he went on to list those yeomen whom he particularly suspected. Evidence for these assertions is not lacking. John Jackson, a yeoman, was sentenced to 500 lashes for harbouring Dwyer, and one of the escort party that brought Dwyer into Dublin on his surrender had earlier been courtmartialled for giving him shelter. One reason for the yeomen's lack of enthusiasm in pursuit of Dwyer lay in the fact that so long as Dwyer remained outstanding, the Yeomanry would remain embodied: his apprehension would have caused them to be stood down, and thus suffer a loss in income.[32] But prudence also played a major role here. On one occasion, in June 1803, two of the Saunders' Grove Yeomanry – 'men ... distinquished for their loyalty during the rebellion' – actually had Dwyer in custody, 'but unfortunately', reported Captain Myers, 'there were a number of women in the house, relations of the yeomen, who were terrified at the apprehension of having their houses burned by the following of this daring ruffian and persuaded the men to let him go.'[33] One yeoman probably summed up the mixed views of his colleagues accurately enough: 'Several of the corps liked him very well and if they could in any way avoid it they would not go out to search for him. Others of them were afraid to say a harsh word of him unless in a certain place where it would be sure to pass off well. And some of them hated and never ceased to abuse him but we would all be glad not to have the good fortune to meet with him.'[34]

Dwyer himself exhibited great prudence in his career as a rebel leader. Unlike Holt, he was always wary of deserters who came to join his band and a lengthy probationary period had to be completed before they were accepted.[35] James Murray, a deserter from the Waterford Militia, revealed that he 'went directly to join Dwyer in the Glen of Imale who gave him no encouragement but permitted him to continue with the gang about ten days, at the end of which the whole party of about sixty dispersed in different directions, remaining only with Dwyer six or eight friends in whom he placed confidence'.[36]

Moreover, he sought to confine his sphere of action to the highlands of Wicklow. Myles Byrne later recalled that Dwyer 'could never be brought to march with us any distance from his native mountains'; and again, unlike Holt, he had little interest in forays into neighbouring counties.[37]

In his dealings with Emmet he also showed his caution. He took elaborate precautions before he met him in Butterfield Lane in 1803: he told Arthur Devlin, his cousin and go-between, that he 'never met any person at an appointed time', and when he finally reached the hideout where Emmet and his men were 'they remained together for three days during which time [Dwyer] never slept or lay down lest any of them should go out'. Dwyer was wary of Emmet's enthusiasm: 'If Emmet had brain to his education, he'd be a fine man,' he told his interrogators after his surrender. He also made it clear to Emmet that he, Emmet, had to instigate the action in Dublin. Dwyer would move only when 'he could perceive the green flag flying above the King's on the tower of the Castle'.

Moreover, Dwyer's fieldcraft and survival skills were of the highest order and help explain his continued evasion of the authorities. He had at his disposal a number of dugouts, caves and, especially, safe houses with false ceilings and secret compartments within adjoining turf clamps. In his examination in Dublin Castle, he revealed that 'his mode of evading pursuit was this: he never slept in a house; always in some hiding place or in the open air which by wrapping himself in such covering as he carried [he] was able to do in the severest weather. He had always a store of bacon and such kind of provisions in some concealment to which he never resorted but in case of absolute necessity. If it snowed, he made his way to his place of concealment while the snow was falling, still defacing the marks of his feet as he went. While the snow lay on the ground he never moved.'[38]

In his military operations too, Dwyer displayed an acute grasp of the principles of both regular and guerilla warfare. At the battle of Rathdrum in October 1798, the Dublin *Courier* reported that Dwyer 'drew up his men in regular order of battle';[39] but inevitably in the years that followed it was his conduct of the 'little war' that attracted most attention. 'Dwyer', explained an exasperated Hardwicke in 1803, 'has hitherto contrived to elude all pursuit ... by dispersing his men on the approach of the military and trusting to the protection which he is sure to find from the general attachment of the inhabitants of that wild part of the country'.[40] It was only when the army developed a comprehensive counter-guerilla policy – construction of a military road, a programme of barrack-building, billetting of troops on private houses and imprisonment of likely harbourers – that Dwyer's days were numbered.

Finally, Dwyer was lucky, and so too was Holt. On his way back from defeat in county Kildare – where he had been left for dead – Holt had many adventures which displayed his coolness in moments of danger. In the folklore records of county Wicklow, however, it is only Dwyer who features, coolly bluffing his way out of tricky situations – or even receiving due warning from the birds of the air. As Mrs O'Toole, whose grandfather had fought in the rebellion, recalled in 1934:

> So the four [Dwyer and three companions] awoke [in their cave], and they began to talk and they got up and struck their flints and steel 'cause there was no matches. Then they lit their pipes, each of them, and they commenced to smoke and to talk as happy as the day is long, when a robin came in – and a robin is unusual so high up in the mountain, you know – a robin flew in and she jumped around the quilt over them, and one grabbed at her, and another and she flew out from the whole of them and it wasn't two minutes till she came in again and when she came in she bustled and set herself just as if she was going to jump at them and she got wicked-looking and: 'O!' says they, 'there is something in this.' The four jumped to their feet and one of them put his head through the hole [of the cave] and he pulled back excited. 'O!' he says, 'the hillsides is red with soldiers'. 'Which will we, lie in,' says another, 'or will we get out? If they have bloodhounds we're found out'. 'That's right' says they, and they all jumped to their feet, and the bloodhounds came into the bed, but they dragged on their breeches and put their hats on them and out they went with their guns. Dwyer whipped [out] his sea-whistle and he whistled and he could be heard, I suppose, in Arklow and they fired off their three shots and the soldiers turned around and they ran for their lives and they never got time to look back till they fell over Lugnaquilla and they told when they got below that the hills was full of rebels.'[41]

In fact, the historical record is scarcely less dramatic. At Derrynamuck, Dwyer fled near-naked and barefoot from a cottage in which he and his men had been sleeping and which had been set on fire and surrounded by Scottish Highlanders and their dogs. Eight of his companions were taken, of whom six were subsequently executed. Dwyer alone escaped: as he burst through the Scottish line slipping and sliding on the ice and clambering desperately up the snowy slopes, a lucky stumble saved his life – a volley of musket balls discharged by the startled Highlanders whistled harmlessly overhead.[42] Dwyer ran to freedom. There were many other escapes from seemingly hopeless situations.

IV

Lastly, we turn to the question of motivation. It is clear that despite the frequent allegations that they were mere criminals neither Dwyer nor Holt fit easily into this category. Admittedly, Sproule, the informer, reported that 'Holt has no commission, nor ever had, commands robers [sic] only'; but in fact General Holt professed a hatred for robbers: 'As to those felons who have taken up robbery as their profession,' he declared, 'nothing but the bullet or the halter will cure them.'[43] Similarly with Dwyer: one yeoman later recalled that 'no man knew Dwyer better than I did and I never knew him to do a mean or unmanly act'; and Dwyer's biographer, Charles Dickson, while conceding that others may have used his name as a cloak for their misdeeds, concluded that 'I have found no evidence that Dwyer or any of his trusted companions were guilty of acts committed for private gain.'[44] And of course, had he been so minded, Dwyer had a great opportunity for financial gain by turning in Robert Emmet to the authorities. He did not do so, and neither he nor Holt in their 'informations' informed on their colleagues in a way that might have been expected from mere criminals. Holt in fact seems to have specifically targetted common robbers in his 'information'; and his rather hysterical parthian shot warning the authorities of a new rebellion was vague on the particulars.[45] Again, both Holt and Dwyer connected their resistance to the prospect of help from France; both maintained contact with the remaining United Irish leadership in the months and years after the rebellion; and each surrendered as they saw no hope of French aid. Finally, as we have seen, the authorities treated each of them rather differently to 'common' convicts, thus tacitly recognising their difference.

On the other hand, statements of lofty purpose, still less of revolutionary or republican purport, are extremely rare from either Holt or Dwyer. An eloquent claim by Holt in his published *Memoirs* that 'self-preservation was the motive' has been shown by O'Donnell to have been concocted by his 'editor', T. Crofton Croker.[46] In his manuscript *Memoirs*, Holt himself seems to trace his own motivation to the burning of his house by Yeomen, and to the conduct of that force who 'generally put an unfortunate man to death without requiring whether he was guilty or not'.[47] Dwyer too was similarly reticent: admittedly, Major Henry Sirr had it from an informer in 1803 that 'Dwyer stated he was fighting five yrs. for liberty and the sixth ... w[oul]d gain it';[48] but in general, there was a marked absence of an economic or political agenda in Dwyer's reported utterances. Perhaps one solution to this problem of motivation would be to consider Holt and Dwyer as 'social bandits'?

The concept of social banditry was first advanced by Eric Hobsbawm some thirty years ago in a book entitled *Primitive Rebels* and he followed that volume up with another, *Bandits*, published some years later but elaborating on the earlier work.[49] Social bandits, wrote Hobsbawm, 'are peasant outlaws whom the lord and the state regard as criminals but who remain within peasant society and are considered by their people as heroes, as champions, avengers, fighters for justice ... and in any case as men to be admired, helped and supported'; and he defined the phenomenon itself as follows:

> *Social banditry*, a universal and virtually unchanging phenomenon, is little more than endemic peasant protest against oppression and poverty: a cry for vengeance on the rich and the oppressors, a vague dream of some curb upon them, a righting of individual wrongs. Its ambitions are modest: a traditional world in which men are justly dealt with, not a new and perfect world. It becomes epidemic rather than endemic when a peasant society which knows of no better means of self-defence is in a condition of abnormal tension and disruption. Social banditry has next to no organisation or ideology and is totally inadaptable to modern social movements.

In further delineation of the social bandit, Hobsbawm described how 'the poor ... protect the bandit, regard him as their champion, idealise him and turn him into a myth', and he instanced Robin Hood as the archetype of the social rebel 'who took from the rich to give to the poor and never killed but in self-defence or just revenge'. Again, Hobsbawm noted that 'a man becomes a bandit because he does something which is not regarded as criminal by his local conventions [e.g. smuggling, revenge, or abduction] but is so regarded by the state or the local rulers,' and he pointed out that the standard end of the social bandit is brought about by betrayal, i.e. *only* the community or family or friends can destroy him, *not* the state. Finally, he claimed that 'the social brigand appears only before the poor have reached political consciousness or acquired more effective methods of social agitation. The bandit is a pre-political phenomenon'.[50]

Hobsbawm illustrated his analysis of social banditry with a wealth of examples culled from various European countries, but especially he drew on the bandit stories of Sicily, Corsica and Sardinia. Curiously, given the general phenomenon of tories and rapparees in seventeenth-century Ireland, the incidence of agrarian protest movements in the eighteenth century, and the number of well-known Irish bandits such as Redmond O'Hanlon, Dudley Costello and James Freney, Hobsbawm made no mention at all of the Irish experience.[51] From a certain perspective, it would appear that the examples of Joseph Holt and Michael Dwyer fit rather well into Hobsbawm's model of the social bandit. Both became bandits, brigands or rebels – the distinction is immaterial – largely by accident (so they claimed) and were forced by the action of authorities to take a stand; both enjoyed popular support; both claimed to abhor criminal behaviour; and one at least – Dwyer – generated an impressive body of story, folklore and ballad. In addition, they allegedly exhibited those qualities of good humour, generosity, cunning, valour, athleticism and courtesy – as well as being masters of disguise – that were always associated with the 'good thief', the 'noble bandit', the 'bandit of honour' rather than with the ignoble or mercenary bandit.[52] Neither, it is true, was betrayed: both surrendered; but this could be seen, at least in Dwyer's case, as a result of his anxiety for his extended family. In these respects, then, Holt and Dwyer seem to fit the model rather closely; but before reaching this conclusion, one should attend to Hobsbawm's warning that 'it is not my intention to encourage careless generalisation', and indeed take note of what his critics have written regarding the 'social bandit'.[53]

Later commentators who have sought to apply the concept of social banditry, as defined by Hobsbawm, to the bandits of other societies at other periods in history have not, in fact, been satisfied with his model. They have recognised the significance of the bandit, certainly: but Hobsbawm's definition of the phenomenon and his typology, even his very notion of the social bandit, have been severely criticised. In particular, Hobsbawm's emphasis on class has been challenged and his rather rosy picture of the social bandit has been overshadowed by an altogether grimmer terrorist bandit, sometimes the client, if not the creation, of regressive social elites intent on controlling or preventing change. Anton Blok in a sustained critique of the Hobsbawm thesis pointed out that Salvatore Giuliano, the notable Sicilian bandit, and one of Hobsbawm's models, massacred villagers gathered at a communist party rally in Sicily in 1947, enjoyed an ambiguous relationship with the Mafia, and certainly received elite as well as popular protection.[54] Similarly, Stephen Wilson in his study of banditry in Corsica writes that he found Hobsbawm's model to be 'of limited applicability' in his researches, and he comments that notions of 'Robin Hood' bandits 'derive almost entirely from popular songs and bandit laments, that is, from legends about bandits, rather than from direct experience of them'.[55]

Such cautions are well made for they emphasise the 'terror' rather than the 'goodwill' which enabled bandits to thrive, and they situate banditry in a more complex social structure, one in which competing elite groups rarely scrupled to afford protection to 'bandits' for their own regressive purposes. However, it must be said that this 'revisionist' view of banditry scarcely fits the Irish case. Admittedly, both Holt and Dwyer had elite contacts: witness Holt's pathetic letter to Mrs Peter 'Lettuce' [i.e. La Touche] and Dwyer had a connection of sorts with the Emmet family, and possibly with the Hume family of Wicklow; but they cannot be regarded as the stooges of such people. Moreover, both Holt and Dwyer had a political agenda, however ill-defined: Holt looked to French aid and Dwyer reportedly told his men that he rejected the overtures made to him by government 'for theirs and cause sake [sic]';[56] and this separates them from the cut-throat, like Schinderhannes, who preyed on the people for his own purposes or, like Giuliano, at the behest of others.[57] Ironically, this political vision or wider purpose of Holt and Dwyer also separates them from Hobsbawn's 'social bandit', with his first loyalty to the peasantry, his fierce defence of a threatened (or doomed) traditional world, and his silence on social issues. Perhaps the only real social bandits in Ireland in the late eighteenth century were the Defenders and the Peep of Day Boys.[58] In the end, while Dwyer and Holt may have been perceived by the Wicklow peasantry as 'social bandits' on the Hobsbawm model, they can more properly be seen as political partisans.

This conclusion does *not* mean that the study of banditry can make no contribution to our understanding of Holt's and Dwyer's careers. Brent Shaw has written that banditry raises problems of 'political legitimacy and the practical exercise of power' and he has identified one source of banditry as 'the imperfect control of the central state over whole geographic regions which were surrounded by its forces but which were otherwise inadequately penetrated by its institutions'.[59] Not surprisingly, banditry and a mountainous terrain tended to go together whether the theatre of operations was Corsica, Sicily, Sardinia, the frontiers of the ancient Roman world, or indeed Wicklow. Similarly, the idea of a military road and a chain of barracks built to contain and defeat Dwyer and his outlaw band, along with the arrest of suspected (or likely) harbourers, would have been familiar to Roman governors grappling with banditry on the outskirts of the empire.

Furthermore, the study of banditry has focussed attention on the fudging of the distinction between private men of violence (bandits) and public men of violence (soldiers): state sanction – a fluid, shifting concept on the frontier or in a colonial situation – made all the difference. It is clear, for example, that the yeomanry were extremely ill-disciplined during and after the rebellion and that individual members frequently engaged in criminal pursuits and violent behaviour that were indistinquishable from mere banditry.[60] On one occasion in

Wicklow, members of a yeomanry corps ambushed and killed a robber they had reason to believe was one of Dwyer's men. The dead man in fact turned out to be a yeoman himself: state sanction was withdrawn for his head was cut off and placed on a spike beside that of Andrew Thomas, one of Dwyer's outlaw band, killed (and decapitated) earlier.[61] A similar blurring of public and private violence took place with the large number of deserters who fled to Holt and Dwyer: public men of violence going private, these men highlighted the ambiguous nature of state authority. This ambiguity was reinforced when the state re-enlisted into its forces those who had deserted to the likes of Holt and Dwyer. Mathew Doyle, a United Irish captain, fought for the rebels in Wexford, then fled to Holt's band. He was captured but chose to enlist in the 87th regiment, the Royal Irish Fusiliers, dubbed the 'Croppy regiment' because of the number of ex-rebels in its ranks. Demobbed in 1802 on the signing of the Peace of Amiens, he then took part in Emmet's conspiracy but when that failed he joined the regiment of Dillon, formerly one of the Irish Brigade regiments in the service of France but now on the British establishment, and he served King George until the war's end in 1815.[62] Doyle's case was not unique: Thomas Halpin, one of Dwyer's band, subsequently became one of Major Sirr's chief agents;[63] Holt himself was a former Volunteer, soldier and constable and was offered a commission in the yeomanry on his surrender (which he refused): he did, however, assure the authorities that 'I hope I will be useful to my king and country.'[64] And, as we have seen, Dwyer ended his days as a law officer. Holt and Dwyer may not have been 'social bandits', but their careers like those of other bandits illustrate well the limits of state authority in this period.

Finally, Brent Shaw has noted how the notion, as opposed to the reality, of the social bandit was one of 'fearsomely compelling dimensions generated by people who desired that some such man could be found'.[65] The people wanted a saviour, and by clinging to the *idea* of a 'social bandit', a Robin Hood figure, who would right wrongs and curb unjust power, they were registering a modest social protest. Shaw, however, tends to overlook the way that elements within the governing elite, too, invented the social bandit for their own purposes, seeking to use him in order to make a critique of that corrupt state in which they found themselves or to suggest a way of escaping that stultifying conformity to which they were condemned. It may be argued, for example, that the adventures of those 'mountain generals', Holt and Dwyer, set many a writer's pulse racing and the romantic imagination at work in the writings of Maturin, Edgeworth and Lady Morgan surely drew some inspiration from their exploits.[66] Nor were the petty functionaries of Dublin Castle immune to the spell cast by the brigands in the mountains. When John Mernagh, Dwyer's 'lieutenant' who had refused to surrender with his chief, was captured some months later, Evan Nepean, a recently arrived under-secretary, penned the following remarkable lines in which were present determination but also admiration, regret, and longing:

> Mernagh would not say one word. He is a very fine young man, but hanged he must be. There is no blinking the business in times like the present.[67]

Moreover, as we have seen, Crofton Croker could not resist the opportunity offered by Holt's manuscript recollections to write what amounted to a romantic novel and to pass it off as Holt's *Memoirs*. In short, consideration of the insurgent careers of Holt and Dwyer opens a window onto a wide range of issues in early nineteenth-century Ireland. The 'masters of the mountains' may have been figures in a landscape but they also haunted the imagination.

APPENDIX I: DOCUMENTS RELATING TO JOSEPH HOLT, WICKLOW, 1798-99

1. Letter from James Critchley, Wicklow, to Sir John Parnell, 11 Sept. 1798

[NAI 620/40/36]

NAI, Rebellion Papers, published by permission of the Director, National Archives, Dublin.

Dear Sir,

I have the honour to inform you that large parties of rebels assembled last week in different parts of the county and searched several houses for arms in consequence of the advantages that were reported to have been gained by the French over his Majesty's troops; but the news of their defeat which arrived here last Sunday at four o'clock has for the present thrown a damp upon their operations.

Holt and his party (which have been lately joined by several deserters) still continue to infest the mountains and mark their rout [sic] with murder and robbery. You can't conceive the rapidity of their movements and the uncommon secrecy which attends them, but I trust from the exertions that we are now making they will soon meet the reward of their crimes.

As the limits of a letter will not permit to mention the many evil consequences which daily result from indiscriminately granting protections, I shall only say that not only persons of a suspicious appearance but those whose guilt is evident from a combination of circumstances are suffered to pass under them thro' the country unnoticed as the civil and military officers from recent circumstances are afraid that they would be severely censured, if not punished for apprehending them. You will therefore suffer me to say (without offense to government) that the country ought to have been divided into districts and magistrates appointed in them to grant protections who would know the determined and desperate rebel from the penitent one. Richd. Kelly, son of Edwd. Kelly of Glenmalure and James Kavanagh late of Roundwood, publican, were apprehended on charges of a treasonable nature and tried in this town by a courtmartial. Their guilt being manifest beyond doubt, they were sentenced to transportation and sent to Dublin for that purpose about two months ago w[h]ere they contrived the means to procure their liberty and are now at large. Kelly, I must inform you, was the most active and dangerous rebel in Glenmalure and such terror has his return created that several of our miners (particularly the agent) who stood loyal have left the county from vengeance being denounced against them by him and his partizans. As I wish to institute an enquiry concerning their liberation but am totally ignorant of the channel thro' which it ought to be prosecuted, I must beg the favour of you to point it out which I shall steadily pursue for the sake of publick justice.

No desertion has taken place from the King's County Militia quartered here since my last but ten of the Leitrim [Militia] deserted from Rathdrum last week (who carried off their arms and ammunition). One of them was taken soon after he deserted.

You will be so good when at leisure to enclose me the Amnesty Bill.

2. Letter from Sproule, a Castle spy, to Edward Cooke, Under-Secretary at Dublin Castle, 19 Sept. 1798. [NAI 620/40/76]

[no salutation]

On Saturday, my friend's journeyman return'd from Holt's army; quit it in disgust from want of subordination and robbery being the object. Holt's party reported to be so strong, consists of but 400 men attached to him, among which are 20 of the King's County Militia, all well arm'd. Holt has quit them on Saturday last and is gone to Carlow to recruit. He is riding out through the country everyday but sleeps in the town of Carlow every night.

A Frenchman of distinction commands Holt's men till his return which is to be on Sunday next.

McMahon, hitherto joyned with Holt has split from him; they disputed on Friday and quit on Saturday. McMahon is gone to Wexford to raise all he can there and if he succeeds is to make some attack near Dublin. McMahon is a Col[one]l. Holt has no commission, nor ever had, commands robers [sic] only. McMahon has a brother a Col[one]l in the French service, is nephew to Moore of Thomas Street and makes excellent gunpowder, all but glazeing.

Doyle, O'Neil and Neil are 3 of Holt's captains. McMahon is very well liked. Holt is not; his party have no subordination.

They assemble at the Whelp Rock and at Oaklands or Oakwood, forgets which it is called.

McMahon and Holt had equall command at Hacketstown. McMahon had 2 horses shot under him.

Seen a return of arms with these men; sent them from the north, amount of all sorts 65432.

My friend cannot be persuaded to come forward; is certain he would fall a sacrifice to it; will not on any account. Wishes to relinquish the business; he and his family say he has lost his customers and his trade by it, and for what? He looks to me for a reward which I must give him and to have done, as he sees no prospect of good from the business but perhaps destruction on himself and family in the end.

N.B. If General Craig manages this matter well he will get Holt in Carlow, as this information comes from Holt's own mouth on Friday last.

3. Letter from R. Cornwall Esq, Myshall Lodge, Leighlinbridge, to Wm. James Esq., 25 Sept. 1798 [NAI 620/40/105]

My dear Sir,

Holt has not been nearer the country than Hacketstown, but Dogherty, his colleague, came to near Ballon to try the pulses of the people but having got information I sent out a party in pursuit who were within a few minutes of surprising him. From the chain of information I have got it is impossible Holt can be anywhere in this country for a night without [my] knowing it and I trust you will believe that I will not be backward in doing my duty should an opportunity offer. We have had a number of robberys [sic] committed about the neighbourhood of Ballon. I have every reason to think that about three o'clock this morning one of my patrols apprehended two of the gang which I trust will lead to a discovery of the whole.

Take care not to let Regan back.

4. Letter from Sproule to John Lees, Postmaster-General, 18 Oct. 1798

[NAI 620/40/170]

[no salutation]

Holt has now done what I told you would be his plan when the mountains was [sic] no longer tenable.

He arrived in Dublin on Tuesday night last wounded. On Tuesday night last he slept in a cellar in Francis Street.

My man is after him ever since and I must be in the way if he makes him out. Burk a Col[one]l at the Hacketstown fight and others of the heads say they will make one desperate attempt this winter; say – there is [sic] now no patrols, guards or hindrance and that it will be easy for numbers to gather unknown to government. The Castle will be the first object.

5. Letter from Sproule to Lees, N.D. [c. Oct. 1798]. [NAI 620/40/198]

[No salutation]

I went to Mr Cooke's in the Park – did not meet him – waited on him at the Castle. He was too much hurryed to see me. I sent him the letter. Had I the honor to see him I meant to say what is here set down and I think he ought to get this immediately.

In my last letter but one [not found] I described him [sic] accurately. I here repeat it'. About 5ft 9 inches high. Smoothfaced, well-looking man, about 40 years of age. Well made, short black curly hair, generally wears an officer's scarlet coat. [mss. torn – Has?] a very poor address.

6. Joseph Holt, further informations, 16 Nov. 1798 [NAI 620/41/39a]

Dublin Nov. 16th '98

Lord Powerscourt and Mr Colthurst as magistrates examd. Holt in the Castle, not on oath, and recd. the following hints in addition to what he had given before.

[Marginal comments by Powerscourt and Colthurst are given in italics beneath the statement to which they refer]

OWEN BYRNE of Bone Valley, near Luggelaw – farmer. Holt heard from Long Peter Nowlan's wife on Saty. the 10th Ult., and whose daughter is married to Owen's son Terence that Owen stole the beds from Luggelaw House and brought them back again at a guinea each.

This fact I partly know to be true as I heard it from a person concerned in the matter of the beds – Wm. C.

Owen was at the first attack on Mr Hugo's house, but not at the burning because he was look'd on as so great a rogue to all parties as to have sold the pass and was trusted by no party.

This, I believe, as Mr Hugo's steward's watch I found in Andw. Byrne's pocket when I took him in the mountains – Wm. C.

Heard that Owen, his sons and others robb'd Smythe the innkeeper at Roundwood's House – Darby Carberry, Owen's son-in-law, a noted rogue for 15 years past.

I brought Smyth's wife to Dublin to prosecute Andw. Byrne for this robbery, hearing she knew the men and would do so. She positively told me she would swear to Owen, his two sons, and Darby Carberry, his son-in-law being present. She said so to Mr Hugo and others. Yet on the tryal of Andw. she denied every word. Owen, John his son and Darby Carberry are now in the Prevost [prison]. *We hope to get Mathew the uncle shortly and Terence Byrne with fresh evidence.* [Three lines deleted] *Andw. Byrne has been found guilty – sentence not known.*

A great gang of robbers about Roundwood viz

Thomas Harris*
John Harris* brothers
Valentine Browne* with a crooked eye

*These three keep in town viz Dublin except whilst robbing

Wm Repton to be found at Holly Park near Rathfarnham at the house of one Byrne
Michael Wafer
——— Wafer – these keep in town except whilst robbing, and others whose names he knows not.

I believe it and will look after them when they think matters are blown over.

MATHEW BYRNE, Owen's brother is a great robber and supposed to have amass'd a great deal of plunder to the amount of near £500 which he has concealed.

As to the sum I doubt it.

Owen Byrne was one of the most active men in the rebellion and used to stay 4 or 5 nights together drinking the money he recd. for pike heads. Terence Byrne was in Clohogue last Friday the 9th Ult.

Believes that about 14 or 15 good firearms are conceal'd about the 7 Churches

WM BRADY was a captain, supposed to be in Dublin

JAMES KAVANAGH near the Paddock on Long Hill, son of Andrew Kavanagh.

There is such a man. A Watch upon him; not at home at present. Wm C.

Jas. work'd mostly in Addown and work'd with Samuel Wallis of Old Court near Blessington. Could give most material evidence as he was deeply concerned in all the robberies in the Rebellion. He might be taken at Wallis's by a party from Blessington and is a soft fellow.

Informt. suspects that arms are concealed in stacks of corn and hay – Addown, Ballysmullen, and Ballylow, villages much frequented by the rebels.

Intend making an early search in these three villages in a few days at one instant. At present things have not cool'd since Holt's taking. Strongly think Holt is right as we have during the Rebellion found arms in that situation.

CHARLES NOWLAN, son of Shanogue about a month since had a large pistol. John Walsh, blind of an eye had a fowling piece. Andrew Byrne a musquet. John Byrne a handsome carbine. These all came to him in Addown this day five weeks ago, also Garret Nowlan had a musquet. They all marched with him to Oakwood.

There are such people

YOUNG CLASSON, the farmer near Roundwood was eager in the Rebellion at first; knows nothing of him lately.

REBELS not afraid of the Yeomen, very much of the army – the Militia ought to be look'd after.

THOS. SMITH is shot.

JOHN WALSH of Bona Valley could give as much information as anyone; his father's nickname Rockstown.

WM McQUIRK who robbed the Banquetting House at the Waterfall keeps in Ballysmullen. Old McQuirk who recd. the goods (his father) keeps at Glynebride near Oakwood

Wm. McQuirk fretted much at not finding inft. Holt the night the Powerscourt and Meath's corps lay at Addown and Shraunamock as he was in search of Holt to give him notice. Had Holt recd. the notice he would certainly have attack'd us with great success as he had then about 180 musquets with him.

This is only a remark made by Holt

RECOMMENDS great attention to our escorts on ammunition. 3 Hessians, the Leitrim and Sligo deserters brought him most ammunition. There is one keg of powder somewhere in Barnesky in the barony of Arklow near Arklow.

I believe Holt here from observations of my own in escorting ammunitions.

Had about two months since about 126 soldiers from 13 regts of Militia etc.

5	Cavan Militia
3	Hessians
22	King's County
8	D[own?] County
28	Antrim County
16	Leitrim County
9	Sligo County
5	Carlow County
5	Kildare County
5	Dublin
2	Durham Fencibles
1	Jos. Bigly, an Englishman
109	

Does not recollect at present the names of the others.

This exactly agrees with an acct. that Capt. Philip Armstrong of the King's County and I made out some time since. Wm. C.

On being ask'd what had become of these men and the deserters in general, he said many were killed, many hanged, and the most of the remainder exchanged their muskets with the rebels for pistols and were robbing their way in gangs to their own counties; sometimes not 2 together.

Col. Rochford of the Cty. Carlow [Militia] and others assured me this was the case. If so and the Cols. of regts. to whom these belong had persons ready to receive them on their going home much good would arise. Every deserter is known where to have come from: it would be easy to secure them.

THE DOGHERTY that was killed at Ballyfad: at the time it was said Hacket [who?] was kill'd belong'd to the Antrim. It was not the Carlow Dogherty.

[sense unclear]

THE TWO HARMANS, one Porter, John Haley, Andw. Thomas and John Byrne, all living in and about 7 Churches told him that Hatton, Burbridge and Freeman were easy for they were dead and brought him one Marks, a prisoner.

PATRICK WARDER, the hatter near Mooneystown beyond Roundwood would be a proper person to tell who kill'd Freeman and the others; has an house of his own there.

Informt. never had either directly or indirectly any communication with the State Prisoners in the different gaols in Dublin or with those prisoners hang'd. Had no commission; only the men in common call'd him General. The 4 instances he mentioned being at when murder was committed in cool [sic] blood were 1st. Hacket killed one Cooper at Newbridge, was not actually present; 2nd. The Antrim deserters shot one Jos. Tate, inft. was present but wanted to save both these men; 3rd.The King's Cty. took a man at Ballybeg, he had a sword cane, the King's Cty. shot him, was present; 4th. They were going to shoot a Protestant out of some prisoners, informt. said he should not be shot and after some altercation 1 Protestant and one Papist were shot in cool [sic] blood.

JAMES BUTLER, at Ballymoneen near the Divil's Glyn [sic], son of Walter Butler has one musquet. One Smullen whose father lives in the same place has another.

KATHY KINGSHELAGH, wife of Val Browne, a proper person for setting robbers, and her husband is a great robber also.

INFORMT. had much difficulty in saving Russborough House from being burn'd.

FATHER LOWE of Derrilossory parish, and our two priests very good men.

7. Letter from Joseph Holt, Duncannon, to Mrs Peter Lettuce [i.e La Touche], Dublin, 15 Jan. 1799 [NAI 620/56/97]

Dear Lady,

May it plase you to receive this my last pittison to Ireland. I hope you will through your bountyfull goodness yeld me the greatest comfort and pleasure that I can wish for at your request and the two noble Lords that i resined myself to and put myself under theire purtection. I thought I would be let to imagrait for life and that I would be let to bring my dear wife and childer with me whos lives are dearer to me than my owne. Know all that i wish for is that you and the noble lords may interseed to his Excellency for my wife and two childer to be let come along with me and if god and your goodness will grant me that favour you will make me happier than all the riches of the wourld cud make me. O noble lady, consider my dear wife and childer, luck [i.e. look] on them with compasion. It is in your power to make them happy or forever to breake theire harts and minds. For myself, if you dont get that favour granted, I hope I will soon yeld my last and painfull breath for I dont wish to live on the earth one moment if I am parted from my sweet family so I hope you will all take pitty on the innocent. Sepose you despise me. [sense and punctuation not clear] It would not so much [have] afflitted me if I had got too or three days notice that I might have the pleasure of taken my last fairewell of my dear childer and wife. O honoured Lady, if you and the noble Lords cant get the grant for them to come with me, get my time shortened that I may come for them when the wourld settles and bring them to some place that I will provide. O give me some hopes of living; it is in your power. Noble Lords, altho I was [forced?] to misfortune I has not changed my hart for I hope I will be usefull to my

King and country. All I know [and] can wish is that you may mind the very words that I told Mr Masdon [Marsden] for I declare the[y] are the truth and any one sais to the contrary the truth is not in them i am sorry that Alderman James did not get the last piece of rithing [ie. writing] that I roat in the tower and had no time to send it to him. It would be of use to your country and I dropped it in the sea for fear it would be seen. My Lord, I am still bolted, there is no differ[ence] between the robbers and others only the[y] cant be so much despise[d]. I have good hopes of god and my contrey. O may I beg and imploar of some of you to send me answer to relieve my destressed hart; if you do, direct to Waterfort, Passage, or elsewhere. Noble Lady pardon me if I have roat improper, it is hard for me to [indite?] and my person at passage and all my taught at home [sense unclear]. I remain your umble sarvant,

Joseph Holt
January the 15th 1799
Passage near the forth of Duncannon.

8 (a). Letter from Lord Cornwallis, Lord Lieutenant of Ireland to Duke of Portland, Home Secretary, 4 March 1799 [P.R.O. London, H.O. 100/86/19-22]

I have the honor to enclose to your Grace a copy of the important information voluntarily given at Cork by the rebel chief Holt to Major General Myers and Sir Charles Ross on his way to Botany Bay.

It is difficult to say what degree of credit may be given to this account but I have every reason to believe the agitators are at this time exceedingly active and busy throughout the whole kingdom.

I have the honor to be etc.

8 (b). 'Information of Joseph Holt, given voluntarily, and by his own desire' [Cove] February 27, 1799. [Published with tolerable accuracy in Marq. of Londonderry (ed.), *Memoirs and Correspondence of Viscount Castlereagh* (4 vols., London, 1848), ii, pp 186-7]

Says, that since the arrival of the convicts from Cork, viz., Dry, Desmond, Cox, Fitzgerald, and several others, they have held conversations, all of which tend to state positively that there are 20,000 rebels organized at Cork and its neighbourhood, and that they are determined to make a rising on the evening of Easter Sunday next, when they expect the French. A feint is to be made at Killala [co. Mayo], but the principal attack is to be made about Cork. That he has heard through those people, and from the conversations of several there, that the whole country is organizing with more activity than ever, especially in Munster, and is assured and believes that great numbers of the Militia soldiers are sworn and ready to join them, and expresses strongly a desire that the Government will be very attentive to the conduct of the Militia soldiers. He is certain they have given up meetings, but they carry on their plots by writing little notes to one another, and that they encourage the disaffected to enlist in the regiments of Militia. These are, on what they call the big day (Easter Sunday) to asassinate the well-disposed, and to secure their arms and ammunition. He is certain that the country will experience great disorder next summer, and recommends again and strongly the strictest watch of the Militia, who, he says, and is certain, are not to be trusted, and that the country is now preparing for rebellion more strongly than ever, and in greater numbers. The Dutch, and particularly the Spaniards, are expected to come to their assistance. With great anxiety he again entreats that Government may exert itself in time, and take measures to prevent a rebellion, that is certainly determined on, and that of the most universal nature. The common conversations are, that there is not a Catholic who would not kill a Protestant as soon as he would a rat. He is satisfied that if there were but five Catholics, they are determined and will pursue this principle and intent as long as they exist. Joseph Holt adds, that he is himself a Protestant.

9. Letter from Joseph Holt, Cove of Cork, to Wilm. Colthus Esq. [i.e. William Colthurst], Tinnahinch, Bray, County Wicklow, 18 May 1799 [NAI 620/47/38]

Sir,

Your well knowen humanity to me has imbolden me to troble you with these few lines. I am happy to hear that Mathew Doyle is taken; he is the only man can give the most information of any one in the County of Wicklow or Wexford or Dublin if he likes to do so. He allso can tell who shot Coper [i.e.Cooper] and who robbed Lord Waterford's housekeeper for he himself had 25 guineys and James has 25 more so he must know who toock the hole of it; and I must say he was the only man of his profession that always strove to save the lives of Protestants, but I am afraid he wont give a true information as there is hardly one of his sart ever does. There is a man of the name black Pady Murray; he lives in Crokey near Seven Churches. I luck on him to be very useful to take. He can give good information of arms for he is very handy in repairing [fire]locks and knows who has arms in all that country.

Sir, I am also happy to hear of the fate of Byrne and Nowlan and I hartly wish you may sarve mor [of] them so and I also wish that every county may dispence with theire own for I think there is no use in transporting them out of one countrey into another for the[y] say in this ship that the[y] will begin in Bottany the same business but I hope as I was deemed a good tory hunter in the County Wicklow I will I hope be very useful in Bottany to hunt both sorts and i wish every Protestant in the world new theire intentions as well as I do and if you take notice of my infermation you will find it will be of the greatest use. I main that [information] I left with Alderman Jaims for it is better for the Lords and Gentlemen of Ireland to have waist houses on their estates than to pursarve the lives of peopple that does intend to murder themselves.

Sir, I asure you I am very happy as a prisoner for our captain is a gentleman of the best morals i ever new and all his offisers to such as disarve indugence. I have nothing more to ad but my wife and son and myself are in good helth and ever will pray for the success of Lord Powerscourt and Lord Monk and you. Sir, I remain your sincere and truly devoted humble servant.

Joseph Holt

APPENDIX II: DOCUMENTS RELATING TO MICHAEL DWYER, 1803-1804

1. Letter from Captain Benjamin O'Neale Stratford, Dublin, to [Alexander Marsden?], 28 April 1803 [NAI 620/67/104]

Sir,

I take the earliest opportunity of enclosing you a letter this inst. recd. for your perusal and also to communicate to you the information of James Valentine, a yeoman in Captain Hume's Corps and his father-in-law, Wilson. They report that Dwyer has now with him forty one men arm'd; that they are plundering the loyalists of sheep and fowl and that they are certain they meditate some sudden mischief from the great stir now making in the Glin of Imale, near Stratford on Slaney, in wh. town there is on every Sunday a reward proclaim'd of ten pounds for [the] head of a Protestant.

I am etc.

2. Letter from Morley Saunders, Saunders Grove [Wicklow], to Alexander Marsden, 4 June 1803 [NAI 620/67/2]

Sir,

A report of Dwyer's being taken has lately prevailed in this neighbourhood which I think it my duty as a magistrate and Yeoman officer to report to you for the information of his Excellency.

Between the hours of four and five o'clock on Sunday morning some cars stoped at a place called Ballyroan (between Talbotstown and Kilbranla) at two of my Yeoman's houses. Whilst they were assisting the drivers in loading, two men, both armed, one of them with a blunderbus passed them. A gig with two gentlemen (one of them said to be Alderman Thorp's brother) had before passed. The two men stoped a boy, mounted his horse, pursued and stoped the carriage. The boy informed my two men (Wm Eager and Sandy Eager) that they went to rob it. They loaded their firelocks and in pursuing came up to a man on foot armed with a pistol. They triped him up, took him and draged him into Sandy Eager's house, took the pistol from him, sent word to Col. J.W. Greene but recalled the messenger before the message was delivered. This man turns out to be the noted Ml. Dwyer, the other men his associates, Martin Burke and Byrne. Upon hearing these reports on Thursday, I went directly with Captain Thos. Ryves and interogated my Yeomen who informed us that the prisoner informed them that his name was Taylor, that he was a Yeoman from Tinahely, upon which they discharged him. Notwithstanding which and that during the Rebellion these men's houses were burnt by the rebels, that Sandy Eager, who is a serjt. in my corps, was shot thro' the arm in an engagement agst. Dwyer and his party, tho' [sic: that] they are both Protestants and have hitherto behav'd well and loyally; yet from what I can collect I have reason to believe that they suffered him to escape knowing him to be the rebel that was proclaimed by government.

Capt. Hume's stewart, Kane, was shortly after stoped by Burke and Byrne and his stores taken. In following his horse (which he got afterwards) he walked with Dwyer after he had been liberated by the Eagers. Thus either by intention or mistake has this desperate man been again let loose upon the country.

It is further reported that a few days before he (Dwyer) was taken that he went up to Mr Taylor where he was overseeing the workmen at Leitrim Barracks in the Glin of Imaal and had a conversation with him, the particulars of which (if any) he, Mr Taylor, can best relate.

I am concerned to say that a degree of terror prevails thro' this country with all descriptions who live out of protection respecting this man and his associates. Something should be done. You will have the goodness to mention these circumstances to his Excellency, that he may give such directions or take such measures as his Excellency may approve to free the country of a man who from terror or goodwill has obtained a dangerous degree of authority and protection among the lower order of the People.

I have etc.

[postscript] The servant of the Revd. Edwd. Bayly who lives in Aungier Street, Dublin was present when the prisoner was taken by the Eagers and perhaps can give further information.

[Endorsed by Marsden] The servt. says it was not Dwyer.

[Further endorsed by Marsden] I think it would be worthwhile to ascertain whether the Eagers liberated their prisoner under an idea that he actually was Dwyer or from finding that he was not this man. If they took him for Dwyer and liberated him from fear or goodwill, they should certainly be dismissed the Corps, at least.

3. Letter from Capt. Myers, Inspector of Yeomanry, Monkstown, to Sir Edward Littlehales, Dublin Castle, 21 June 1803 [NAI 620/66/78]

Sir,

I had the honour to state to you the beginning of this month that I found every thing perfectly quiet in East Wicklow. I returned the day before yesterday from the Co. Kildare and West Wicklow. There are many reports of the lower order of the people holding meetings in different parts of the country but I think they are merely reports. I could not trace them to anything like respectable authority. I dare say you have long before this heard how unfounded in truth the report was that the Barracks that are building in the Glen of Imall were burned or destroyed by Dwyer. I was on my way there last Monday when I met Mr Tennison, a magistrate, on his return from there who told me that he had been there, seen the construction and that the whole of the injury done did not amount to a guinea. As far as I could learn, the workmen had got drunk, begun to fight and broke a window or door. It was said one Mernagh, an outstanding rebel, was of the party but there's no doubt but Dwyer is infinitely more publick than formerly, has frequently been at the Barracks, held conversations with the contractor and workmen and gave them to understand that they never would meet the least molestation from him; if times turned out well, he would want them for his own people. And it is equally certain he was taken by two yeomen, brought prisoner into the house of one of them and was in their custody for a considerable time. These men were distinguished for their activity during the rebellion but unfortunately there was a number of women in the house, relations of the yeomen, who were terrified at the apprehension of having their houses burned and their family murdered by the followers of this daring ruffian and persuaded the men to let him go. I sent for these Yeomen, one only came, he admitted all the circumstances but denied his personal knowledge of Dwyer. Should there hereafter, unfortunately, be any disturbance in this part of the country this fellow [Dwyer] will be found to be a troublesome and dangerous ruffian; the attatchment [sic] and fidelity of the country people to him is without parallel.

I have the honour etc.

4. William Hoare Hume, Humewood, Wicklow, to [Marsden?], 21 October 1803. [NAI 620/65/90] (Published in both M.V. Ronan (ed.), *Insurgent Wicklow* (Dublin, 2nd. edition, 1948), pp 119-20; Chas. Dickson, *Dwyer* (Dublin, 1948), pp 237-8

Dear Sir,

In course of a general search through this country on Sunday last there was one John Neil taken up who is married to a sister of Dwyers. He kept a dairy in Dublin and as I am informed left it the day after the insurrection in consequence of Major Sirr having been in search of him on some information. There is also in the neighbourhood, one

Murphy, a taylor, who left Dublin the same time with Neil (as I hear) on account of Major Sirr having information against him for making rebel uniforms and other acts of treason. He is not yet taken but I would wish to know whether Major Sirr has any information against either of these fellows. They bear a very bad character in the country. If there is any information against any fellows in the country I would be glad to hear it and I will use every exertion to have them apprehended.

I am certain that no consideration whatsoever will induce Dwyre [sic] or his associates to surrender. I have parties out continually day and night hunting after them, as yet to no purpose, owing to the protection he meets with from the people of the country and which will continue to be the case unless strong measures are made use of. I have written to Mr Wickham this day on the subject.

There is one Thomas Linnen in the Provost [prison] now who was taken up in Hacketstown some short time ago by Major Richardson of the Monaghan regt. for being in company with one Hauxy who was singing a seditious song, and both sent to Dublin. There are some friends of this Linnen in the Glen of Imaal who are giving me a good deal of private information and I think will be useful to me in that way. I therefore think it would be well and would wish to have that Thomas Linnen set at liberty, if there is not any other information or charge against him but that for which he was sent from Hacketstown.

I have the honour etc.

5. Letter from Capt. Benj. O'Neale Stratford, Stratford Lodge, Wicklow, to [Marsden?], 28 Oct. 1803 [NAI 620/67/108]
(Partially published in Dickson, *Dwyer*, p. 242)

Sir,

As I have not recd. an answer to my letter of 19th inst in which I enclosed you a copy of examination of Michl. Dwyer* then and still a prisoner in our guardroom, I again beg leave to request to know how govt. wish to dispose of him. As I am tormented with applications for his liberty and fear that some of the number of persons who come in here under that pretence have convey'd intelligence to the outlaw'd rebel of that name of the several times we have been since after him, as notwithstanding Col Ker's indevatigable [sic] exertions and the very vigilant search made by the several corps composing the garrison etc he has had some very extraordinary escapes. He has gained considerable credit and convidence [sic] with those before too ready to conceal and support his [sic] by his refusal of the great overtures he sais [sic] were made him by govt. and he for theirs and cause sake he rejected. I trust however we shall shortly give an acct. of him pleasing to govt.

I have the honour etc.

* Michael 'Red Mick' Dwyer was captured by Stratford in mid-October; in his examination he declared that 'he is not nearer related than second cousin to Micheal Dwire, the noted rebble chief': Stratford to [Marsden?], 19 Oct. 1803 [N.A.R.P. 620/67/107]

6. Letter from Alexander Marsden, Dublin Castle, to Peter Carew, 17 Jan. 1804
[P.R.O. London, H.O. 100/124/26-30]

I send you a copy of the examination of Dwyer. It is not in any good form and is not very important in the way of information but it contains some curious particulars of the history of this mountain general which you might like to see.

It is supposed that there is but one of his gang outstanding [i.e. Mernagh]. A courtmartial was assembled at Rathdrum in the county of Wicklow for the tryal of persons who harboured the associates of Dwyer. One man was found guilty and sentenced to be transported.

7. Copy of the examination of Michael Dwyer, 11 Jan. 1804, Dublin Castle [Copy in P.R.O. Northern Ireland, Redesdale transcripts T3030/12/1; another copy in P.R.O. London, H.O. 100/124/26-30; only partially published in Dickson, *Dwyer*, pp 253-6]

Michael Dwyer examined

When the prisoners were leaving Ft. George Arthur Develin was on board the ship they went in. Old Sweetman gave him a letter to his son a brewer and Arthur (Big) afterwards worked with him. He was in a club to which he became in debt six pounds. [Thomas] Russell sent for him and the party promised to pay his debt. He was then sent by Russell to W[itness] to desire an interview which Witness declined not knowing how far he could depend on him. After some time Develin returned, assured Witness they might be depended on and asked him to come to Butterfield lane. Witness never met any person at an appointed time and therefore told Develin he would go there perhaps in a couple of months. In three days after, Witness went, got to Ballinascorney about nine in the evening and to Butterfield by night. Burke and Byrne (now in Kilmainham) were with Witness. He desired Develin to let Emmet know that he was there and that no person who came into his company must leave it while he remained there. Witness was then introduced to Emmet and Russell. They remained together for three days during which time Witness never slept or lay down lest any of them should go out. There was a mattress in an inner room on which the other two occasionally slept. They drank brandy freely, Witness's constitution being too strong to be affected by any kind of punch. They talked chiefly of Emmet's plans: he [Emmet] said he had 60,000 men and intended to surprise and take Dublin, that he would astonish the Government (from which Witness concluded that some of themselves were to support him), that they intended to make Ireland independent of all the world. If Witness had known that he depended on the lower orders, Witness would have undeceived him. In 1798 the people were told the Orangemen intended to murder them and the loyal were assured they were to be massacred by the people; troops were sent into the country, on their approach the people fled, the houses were found empty and thus both parties were confirm'd in their belief. But they have since discovered the truth and in Witness's county the Protestants and Catholics are now as good friends as ever. Is not acquainted with Kildare, never was in that county but once. Witness promised to assist Emmet and Russell when they should be in possession of Dublin 48 hours: said he could engage for 800 men and that he thought he could in that event bring 5000. Witness was sure they could not perform their part and therefore thought he might promise anything. They did not tell Witness the names of the leaders but boasted of the secrecy with which they acted; if Emmet had brain to his education he'd be a fine man. They wanted Witness to come on the night of the attack and proposed to give him intelligence of it by fires on the mountains. He refused to take any signal but the noise of the cannon. Witness encouraged them tho' he knew they could not succeed because he thought the rebellion in Dublin would draw the troops about Dublin and leave Witness's county free and that he might then become a peaceable inhabitant.

Russell said his name would raise the North – thinks they did not like an invasion from France. They held Humbert in great esteem and wished him in Bonaparte's place – is sure many people promised to support Emmet who had no intention to do so –

thinks it would be now impossible to raise the County Wicklow – that if there was now an invasion they'd remain quiet and that even if Emmet had succeeded Witness could not have brought him 26 men. On the third day of Witness's stay at Butterfield, going to a window he saw a girl cutting paper and at every interval looking attentively at the window. He enquired if they knew her and being informed they did not, he said he must set off that night for that he would not remain in any house that had such a watch on it and he went off accordingly.

Just before he left Butterfield he saw two men there whose names he was informed were Hamilton and Dowdal, was with them about three quarters of an hour, took no notice of them and did not hear either of them speak. This was just after Emmet got the lease of Butterfield. Witness never returned to Butterfield and never saw Emmet or Russell after – was in Dublin on the 14th of March with [Jemmy] Hope in the Coomb and often before with a car. Hope then sent for him to give him some blunderbusses. Hope had before been in the mountains to excite the people; he told Witness they were organizing their army and waited only for that to begin and that 19 counties were to rise.

Witness first joined the rebels in the year 1798 at Limerick hill, then went to Mount Pleasant, then to Vinegar hill, was one of the Ballymanus corps of 1800 men, ran off from Vinegar hill alone – is 30 years of age – was once, while at Mount Pleasant for 8 days and nights that he never slept nor lay down nor eat [sic] and drank nothing but milk and water. Towards the latter end of that time Witness began to feel himself quite distracted. It seemed to him as if there were 1000 men round him all calling out his name. Thought during the peace that all idea of rebellion was given up; never knew a pike have any effect but against a prisoner; the people in the mountains were lately afraid to receive Witness in consequence of Capt. Hume's threats; was at the barracks when they were building it and saw the workmen. For the last fortnight Witness's party consisted of 8 men, Mernane [sic, Mernagh], Burke, Byrne, Cullen, Mulvany (Chas.), Kennedy (Tim) and Laurence Keeffe who is now in the prevot [i.e. Provost prison]. Arthur Develin was not with them since Nov. 1. Mernane [sic] is a leading man, has many friends in that country. Witness saw him the evening before he (Witness) surrendered but did not inform him of his intention. No two of their party ever travell'd together by day; believes their party did sometimes shoot soldiers.

Witness thinks if he was let go now for 6 hours all the soldiers in the empire could not take him in 6 years. His mode of proceeding was this: he never slept in a house, always either in some hiding place or in the open air which by wrapping himself in such covering as he carried he was able to do in the severest weather. He had always a store of bacon and such kind of provisions in some concealment to which he never resorted but in case of absolute necessity. If it snowed he made his way to this place of concealment while the snow was falling, still defacing the marks of his feet as he went. While the snow lay on the ground, he never moved. At other times he was accustomed to go to any cottage, always without any previous notice. With a cocked pistol in his hand, he compelled the owner to give him full intelligence of all that was passing in the country and to give him such provisions as the house afforded and as he chose to demand. Having done so, he went off, first recommending it to the owner of the house to go for his own safety and give immediate information of what he had done. Before any pursuit could be made witness was perhaps eight or nine miles off. Witness thinks he could live in this manner for many years. For arms, witness should wish to have a musket by day and a blunderbuss by night.

Arthur Develin remained at Butterfield on the 23rd [July] and told Witness that Emmet and his party were at Butterfield in three quarters of an hour after the attack began – the key of the letter which Emmet got from France was in Dowdal's trunk which Major Sirr took – [end of information]

References

1. I am grateful to Kevin Whelan for his advice on Wicklow sources, and to my colleague Niall Ó Cíosáin for references to banditry.
2. For lawlessness in the aftermath of the rising in Wexford, see the excellent article by Daniel Gahan, 'The "Black mob" and the "Babes in the wood": Wexford in the wake of rebellion, 1798-1806', *Wexford Hist. Soc. Jn.* (1992). The history of the aftermath of the rebellion from 1799-1803 remains unwritten: the events of those years may have had an even greater impact than the rebellion itself.
3. P.R.O.N.I., Lake Papers, Mic 67, Dundas to Hewett, 5 Sept. 1798; , P.R.O. H.O. 100/124/24, Marsden to Carew, 17 Jan. 1804.
4. Ruan O'Donnell, 'General Joseph Holt and the rebellion of 1798 in county Wicklow' (M.A. thesis, U.C.D., 1991). O'Donnell has discussed Holt's treatment by later writers in his 'General Joseph Holt and the historians' in Bob Reece (ed.), *Irish convicts: The origins of convicts transported to Australia* (U.C.D., 1989).
5. Mitchell library, Sydney, Ms A2024, Holt's manuscript. Peter O'Shaughnessy's copy was made available to me by Kevin Whelan.
6. Unless otherwise stated I have drawn freely on O'Donnell's excellent thesis. O'Donnell has published a short resume of Holt's career in R. Reece (ed.), *Exiles of Erin* (Dublin, 1990) 'General Joseph Holt', pp 27-56.
7. Holt Ms.
8. O'Donnell, 'General Holt', p. 93.
9. Ibid., pp 170-1, 179.
10. NAI, 620/41/12, Sproule to Lees, 4 November 1798. Two letters from Sproule are published in appendix I to this chapter.
11. NAI, 620/41/39a, 'Joseph Holt, further informations', 16 Nov. 1798. This document is given in its entirety in the appendix to this chapter.
12. Charles Dickson, *The life of Michael Dwyer with some account of his companions* (Dublin, 1944), p. 66.
13. He protested that he had been deceived: see the document published in the appendix to this chapter.
14. See Dickson, *Dwyer*, and for the folklore, see Pádraig Ó Tuathail (ed.), 'Wicklow traditions of 1798', *Béaloideas*, iml.v, uimh.ii, Noll. (1935).
15. Quoted in Dickson, *Michael Dwyer*, p. 369.
16. See L.M. Cullen below, 'Politics and rebellion: county Wicklow in the 1790s' for the United Irishmen in the area.
17. Quoted Dickson, *Dwyer*, p. 47.
18. Ibid., pp 222-3.
19. Ibid., p. 231.
20. See Dwyer's remarks in his information published as an appendix to this chapter.
21. P.R.O. H.O. 100/118/172-5, Hardwicke to Yorke, 14 Nov. 1803.
22. P.R.O. H.O. 100/118/199-202, Wm. Wickham to R.P. Carew, 30 Nov. 1803. Perhaps twenty family members were arrested; see M.V. Ronan (ed.), *Insurgent Wicklow: 1798* (2nd edition, Dublin, 1948), p. 125. For the Dwyer kinship network see Paul Gorry, 'The family of Michael Dwyer', *West Wicklow Hist. Soc. Jn*, i (1986), pp 30-36.
23. *Freeman's Journal*, 3 Mar. 1803: (I am indebted to Kevin Whelan for this reference).
24. Dickson, *Dwyer*, pp 239-50.
25. Holt Mss; in general, Crofton Croker suppressed or misrepresented such incidents.
26. Dickson, *Dwyer*, p. 394.

27. Ibid., pp 183-4, 394.
28. P.R.O. H.O. 100/122/25, Wickham to King, 14 Jan. 1804.
29. Ronan (ed.), *Wicklow*, p. 107.
30. NAI, 620/67/107, Stratford to Marsden, 19 Oct. 1803.
31. See note 21.
32. Dickson, *Dwyer*, pp 207, 252, 209.
33. NAI, 620/66/78, Myers to Littlehales, 21 June 1803: the letter is published in the appendix to this chapter.
34. I am indebted to Kevin Whelan for this reference from the Cullen Mss.
35. Dwyer had 51 known companions listed in February 1801 but only three of them are described as military deserters: Dickson, *Dwyer*, pp 287-8.
36. Ibid., p. 349.
37. Quoted ibid., p. 47.
38. Examination of Michael Dwyer, 11 Jan. 1804 (Redesdale Mss, Gloucester County Record Office; transcript in P.R.O.N.I., T3030/12/1; another copy in P.R.O., H.O. 100/124/26). Dickson, *Dwyer*, p. 253, states that he had access to a private copy of Dwyer's information which he published for the first time. However, for some reason he omitted about 15 per cent of the text and the full examination, based on a close comparison of two extant copies, is here published for the first time (Appendix to this chapter). I have not discovered Dickson's copy in private keeping.
39. Quoted Dickson, *Dwyer*, p. 83; see also the engagement described on pp 78-9.
40. P.R.O. H.O. 100/118/211-2. Hardwicke to Yorke, 7 Dec. 1803.
41. Ó Tuathail (ed.), 'Wicklow traditions', pp 174-5.
42. Dickson, *Dwyer*, pp 105-112.
43. NAI, 620/40/76, Sproule to Cooke, 19 Sept. 1798; Dickson, *Dwyer*, p. 92.
44. Ibid., pp 196-7, 220.
45. P.R.O. H.O. 100/86/19-22). Information of James Holt, 27 Feb. 1799. See appendix I.
46. O'Donnell, 'General Holt', pp 42-3.
47. Holt Ms.
48. Dickson, *Dwyer*, p. 191.
49. Eric Hobsbawm, *Primitive rebels: studies in archaic forms of social movement in the nineteenth and twentieth centuries* (2nd edition, New York, 1959); Idem, *Bandits* (London, 1969).
50. Hobsbawm, *Primitive rebels*, pp 5, 13-15, 23.
51. See T.W. Moody, 'Redmond O'Hanlon', *Proc. Belfast Nat. Hist. and Phil. Soc.*, 2nd Ser., i, part i, pp 17-33; Edward MacLysaght, *Irish life in the seventeenth century* (Dublin, 1979 edition), pp 271-2; S.J. Connolly, *Religion, law and power: the making of Protestant Ireland, 1660-1760* (Oxford, 1992), p. 210.
52. Florike Egmond, 'The noble and ignoble bandit: changing literary representations of West European Robbers', *Ethnologia European*, xvii, pp 139-56; Stephen Wilson, *Feuding, conflict and society in nineteenth century Corsica* (Cambridge, 1988). Surprisingly, Italian historians have proved reluctant to move beyond Hobsbawm's model: see P. Brunello, *Ribelli, Questuanti, e Banditti: Proteste contadine in Veneto e in Friuli, 1814-66* (Milan, 1981): but see now Elsa Gregori, 'Banditi e Banditismo nell' Europa Moderna', *Società e Storia*, n. 50 (1990), pp 879-90; G. Ortalli (ed.), *Bande Armate, Banditi, Banditismo* (Roma, 1986).
53. Hobsbawm, *Primitive rebels*, p. 5.
54. Anton Blok, 'The Peasant and the Bandit: Social Banditry Reconsidered', *Comparative Studies in Society and History*, xiv (1972), pp 494-503. In fairness, it

should be stated that Hobsbawm is not blind to Giuliano's imperfections.

55. Wilson, *Corsica*, pp 347-8.
56. NAI, 620/67/108. Benj. O'Neale Stratford, to [Marsden?], 28 Oct. 1803.
57. For Schinderhannes see Egmond, 'Noble and ignoble bandit', pp 144-5 and Hobsbawm, *Primitive Rebels*, pp 20, 22; for Giuliano see the evocative book by Gavin Maxwell, *God protect me from my Friends* (London, revd. edition, 1972).
58. On whom now see James Smyth, *The men of no property: Irish radicals and popular politics in the late eighteenth century* (London, 1992) and David Miller (ed.) *Defenders and peep of day boys* (Belfast, 1990).
59. Brent Shaw, 'Bandits in the Roman Empire', *Past and Present*, no. 105 (Nov. 1984), pp 3-52, quotations at pp 3, 30.
60. Thomas Bartlett, 'Indiscipline and disaffection in the armed forces in the 1790s' in Patrick Corish (ed.), *Radicals, rebels and establishments* (Belfast, 1985), pp 115-35.
61. Ronan (ed.) *Insurgent Wicklow*, p. 100.
62. Dickson, *Dwyer*, p. 317.
63. Ibid., pp 160-70; Halpin was still working under cover for Sirr in 1808: Thomas Bartlett, *The fall and rise of the Irish Nation* (Dublin, 1992), p. 319.
64. NAI, 620/56/97. Holt to [Mrs Peter Latouche], 15 Jan 1799.
65. Shaw, 'Bandits in Roman Empire', p. 51.
66. Tom Dunne, 'Haunted by history: Irish romantic writing 1800-50' in Roy Porter and Mikulas Teich (ed.), *Romanticism in national context* (Cambridge, 1988), pp 68-91.
67. P.R.O. H.O. 100/122/136. Nepean to King, 3 Mar. 1804. Mernagh, in fact, was transported to Australia some months after his capture. For the impact of Ireland on the English imagination in this period see Seamas Deane, 'Irish national character, 1790-1900' in T. Dunne (ed.), *The writer as witness* (Cork, 1987), pp 90-113.

Chapter 12

POLITICS AND REBELLION: WICKLOW IN THE 1790s

L. M. CULLEN

I. The general background

In contrast to Wexford Wicklow has scarcely featured in the post-rebellion literature. There was neither literature nor debate: Holt's account, published in 1838, was limited on the background, prompted more by Holt's personal circumstances than by post-rebellion controversy. The actual editing and publication of Holt's memoir, as shown by Ruan O'Donnell in his recent thesis, arose from the confused political concerns of Crofton Croker, and involved a significant doctoring of the original text.[1] Neither the original manuscript itself nor its final publication arose out of the circumstances of Wicklow nor in any direct way out of the political aftermath of the rebellion.

The lack of controversy resulted from the existence in the county of a powerful liberal establishment; there was no gulf, before or after the rebellion, of the type which accounted for the Wexford literature. In that county, debate revolved either around the political capital that could be made from the Wexford Bridge massacres and other atrocities and the role of the catholic clergy, or on the other side around damage limitation exercises that the same events imposed on rebels and liberals. This debate reflected existing party lines prior to '98, clearly visible in the 1790 and 1797 elections and in the many public debates of 1792 and 1795. No comparable confrontation had occurred in Wicklow. It may seem surprising to stress how liberal the Wicklow establishment was, because subsequently the county with the largest protestant rural community in southern Ireland became the most powerful rural outpost of the Orange Order outside Ulster. However, that shift was very much a case of *autres temps, autres moeurs*, and even in the 1790s the liberal ethos itself had been more evident among the county's gentry with a window on a wider world than among its more embattled middlemen and freeholders.

Moreover, Wicklow, not Wexford, suffered from oppressive administration of law and order measures before the rebellion broke out, and because the county's political establishment could not be trusted by Dublin Castle, the pace of events, as in Kildare for a similar reason, was set from Dublin. The thread of continuity was of a liberal county establishment before and after the rebellion. Its good reputation was never at risk from rebel propaganda; neither did its members have to defend themselves nor had they the urge to exploit an opportunity to condemn rebels and catholics. The fact that Dwyer in 1803 chose to surrender to Hume, son of William of Humewood and his successor as a member of parliament for the county, is a symbol of the acceptable face of the local establishment. The death of Hume's father in October 1798 in a clash with rebels was a accident of war; Hume himself had not been a hate-figure of the rebels.

Given government concern with Wicklow, the correspondence, though not voluminous, is richer and more informative than for Wexford. Because ruthless methods were applied to rebels in Wicklow as in Carlow and Kildare there were some particularly useful confessions which reconstruct the structure and progress of the movement. The single most arresting feature of the Wicklow correspondence is that much of it is from Joseph Hardy, the military officer made responsible for the county in late 1797; the other main correspondent was Benjamin O'Neale Stratford, a fanatic on the Kildare border of the county. His judgement was in doubt, and his significance may have been smaller than his letters suggest: six years after 1798 a marginal annotation on one of his letters in the Rebellion Papers dismissively reads 'whatever one may think of Mr O'Neale Stratford or of the reliance to be placed on him ...'.[2] However, with a borough seat in parliament and belonging to a family whose members held the commission of the peace in all three counties, Kildare, Wicklow and Carlow, his role gave him close and influential ties with conservative gentry in Kildare and Carlow.

Below these men can be perceived lesser gentry like King at Rathdrum, or still more lowly figures – on the western side Hornidge at Tulfarris or Cope and Moreton (Morton) in Shillelagh barony, on the eastern side Edward Bayly at Arklow, James Critchely at Laragh – who attached themselves to the government party, more particularly as it emerged as the dominant force nationally in the aftermath of the 1797 general election. In an epistolary sense the most significant of these figures was Tom King, and he was probably a man of ability.[3] The attention given to him in the Luke Cullen manuscripts underlines his impact. More obscurely, in conjunction with King, Hugo played a role at Rathdrum in creating a loyalist party within the county. But though Hugo's loyalist image was strong enough to survive in the folk memory, it is King, not Hugo, who broods over the region in the record compiled by Luke Cullen, and his role as a magistrate (Hugo was not one before the rebellion broke out) gave him an active place in 1798 on the committee of magistrates to receive 'private informations'. The confused character of tradition and the weight which King held in it is reflected in the fact that Luke Cullen who had read and was influenced by accounts of the rebellion (including Holt's) filled in the unidentified magistrate enemy in Holt's published account with the name of King.[4]

However, as in Kildare but in contrast to Carlow, the loyalist group as a county force lacked coherence. Of the three loyalist magnate families, Wingfield (Powerscourt) and Monck were on its northern fringe and the Stratfords were on its western frontier (Aldboroughs' seat physically even being in Kildare). Others like Proby and Whaley (whose sister was married to FitzGibbon) were absentee. Indeed, in regard to absentees, recollections in the Luke Cullen memoirs[5] hint at gentry being misled by their agents and lesser gentry on the spot, which may either be true enough or alternatively a facile way of explaining how some individuals once politically benign became in crisis basically supporters of law and order. Politically, liberal dominance of the county was unshaken and unshakeable, and hence it was Hardy, not a gentry faction, who made law and order an effective force. Colonel John Staunton Rochfort in Carlow in effect made the point when he observed to Dublin Castle at the outset of April 1798 that 'if the gentlemen in every other county conducted themselves as they have conducted themselves in this county (Carlow) rebellion would soon be stifled'.[6] The government was never taken in by the local political establishment in Wicklow or Kildare, as it was in Wexford. Not only were there no doubts about Wicklow's disloyalty, but there was active dislike of the county's liberal magnates. It was fear of the prospect of two disloyal counties on the major southern communication routes to the capital that accounted for alarm in Dublin and among loyalist gentry as 1797 wore into 1798. That fear in turn prompted systematic contact by government figures like John Lees and Edward Cooke with loyal gentry (for which there was no parallel in Wexford), the early appearance of the Orange Order, and heavy reliance on professional military officers for the maintenance of law and order.

II. The Rebellion Papers and Edward Cooke

The Rebellion Papers are ultimately deceptive; for Wicklow and other counties for the most part, they reveal only a fraction of the reality. Liberal magistrates did not write to the Castle either because they held government in contempt or because they had no illusions (in any event with some exceptions magistrates, liberal or loyalist, were not epistolary). A protracted correspondence from a liberal magistrate like

John Edwards of Oldcourt is therefore quite unusual, not simply for Wicklow but for any county. Indeed, Edward's correspondence is itself a counterpart to an anti-government pamphlet which he wrote: though a 'fragment' of a copy was known to Luke Cullen,[7] it no longer seems to survive.

More typically, surviving correspondence reflects the Castle's lines of party communication at work. Lord Downshire for Down is the key example, as well as being the most socially elevated figure in the regular network. Where correspondence does not reflect the government circuit of local management, it was often prompted simply by the urge of a magistrate to put himself in a good light or (in typical eighteenth-century fashion) to support a case for government favour. In consequence, the correspondents are sometimes odd individuals. In instances like that of Blayney (a landlord militia officer from Monaghan) who gave government liberal advice and later became a house burner, the correspondence is that of a temperamentally unstable and despised man. Caesar Colclough of Duffrey Hall is a better, and socially lower instance of a weak and favour-seeking man, only partly redeemed by his liberal outlook. His advice might in any event be construed by a hostile critic as mere complacency: the attorney general who had no time for liberal views was brutal in his appraisal of the value of Colclough's recommendation of dealing with people by 'fair means (rather) than by coercion'. He simply dismissed the letter by observing to Cooke that 'it probably will add nothing to your stock of information'.[8] Lord Mountnorris himself in Wexford was not dissimilar to Colclough. He had an agenda of his own for government favour: his political leitmotif was opposition to Lord Ely, and an ambition to replace him in the patronage of county Wexford. He was an active correspondent around October 1797,[9] and his pacifying campaign in Wexford, which influenced the government view and moderate loyalists within the county, was launched the following month. Letters from gentry not identified with the loyalist party have their value: precisely because they pursued different interests, they were less prone to imagine disloyalty, and their letters have a particular importance in underlining the fact that the United Irishmen did not exist simply in loyalist paranoia.

The Rebellion Papers are the largest single source for the study of the late 1790s. They have never been viewed however as an archive in their own right: they have simply been taken for granted as a rich quarry for isolated letters or references.[10] Yet if they are looked at as an archive they tell us much about the Castle administration, and above all its objectives and methods. The papers are in fact successor to the Miscellaneous Papers, running to 1789 and destroyed in 1922.[11] Dublin

Castle was casual in handling paper which did not arise directly from official business. Thus the Miscellaneous Papers, rich though they were for the first half of the century, became thin or non-existent for the remainder of the century, a few short intervals of revival excepted. For reasons which are not self-evident, practice in the administration in handling these papers changed after mid-century and, except where private papers became attached to official files, they were no longer retained. For the first half of the eighteenth century, it was the wealth of the Miscellaneous Papers which made for the remarkable raciness of the accounts of Irish social conditions by Froude and Lecky, just as the absence of comparable evidence for the second half of the century accounts for the often lacklustre quality of their later pages.

The Rebellion Papers were a revival of the practice of keeping the miscellaneous correspondence of the Castle, in a form somewhat modernised to correspond to the official preoccupations of the decade. The fact that they were accumulated at all is a tribute to the under-secretary Edward Cooke to whom most of the letters were addressed. He not only kept the papers but through his enquiries, actually generated much of the writing to the Castle. Already in 1795 he had made a remarkable digest of information on the Defenders.[12] As the crisis got more serious, the flow of information increased. His regular correspondents were either officials, acting beyond the call of their paid duties, or dedicated loyalists in crisis counties. They constituted a network which was systematised from 1796 onwards.

The Rebellion Papers did not consist exclusively of letters addressed to Cooke. Letters addressed to the lord lieutenant and to Pelham were as a matter of course regularly passed on to him. Equally some letters passed out of Cooke's hands into Pelham's or Camden's. If these letters were not passed back to Cooke, and standard contemporary practice for non-official papers was very clearly neither to copy them nor to send them back, they became scattered. First, some remained in the chief secretary's office. Second, some seem to have constitued something of a lord lieutenant's archive. Third, a few were referred to London and appear in the Home Office Papers. Fourth, some were to find their permanent home in the private papers which Pelham and Camden later took away with them, and now lie in well-known and accessible collections. The basic corpus was however the Rebellion Papers, out of which some letters passed at the time, but which in reverse received a much greater quantity of material from both chief secretary and lord lieutenant. The existence, survival and character of the main corpus is tribute to the vigour of the undersecretary Cooke who faced and responded to the challenge of the 1790s. Crisis over, the papers became an isolated curiosity, especially as in and after 1818, when a proper system of registering incoming correspondence emerged, no comparable runs of private letters for the years immediately prior to or subsequent to the period of the Rebellion Papers existed.

The earliest known general comment on the Rebellion Papers in 1890 harked back to 1853 when they were all stored in 'two very large chests carefully fastened down with the government seal and with these words written on them: "secret and confidential; not to be opened"'.[13] When sorted they filled sixty-eight cartons. They included, inter alia, the letters of Higgins, McNally and Collins, court martial and state prisoner papers, and seized correspondence. Many of these are technically official papers, pre- or post-1795. The bulk of the collection however relates to the years 1796-1805, and is incoming private correspondence, addressed to Cooke or passed on to him.

While Cooke controlled the machinery of security and the corresponding archives (which he built up), letters had of course to be shown to other officials. In many cases Cooke may have simply quoted from letters in conversation, or shown them on the spot to his colleagues; in other cases the exigencies of the office made it necessary for officials to take possession of them. If they did not then go into the private papers of chief secretary or lord lieutenant or eventually into the Home Office Papers, they were left lying around in the Castle apparently as part of the extensive and rather badly organised records of the chief secretary's office or in a smaller accummulation which preserved some of the character of having once been a lord lieutenant's collection. When the sorting of the public archives began in earnest in the 1870s a number of letters for the years 1796-1805 were in the early days transferred to the State Paper Office, and they were sorted before the listing of the main Rebellion Papers began.[14] Attached by the archivists to a series of military reports on the state of the country from 1808, they made up the artificially constituted State of the Country Papers. To distinguish them from subsequent discoveries, they later became designated as the State of the Country Papers, first series. Some further discoveries of papers however seem to have been incorporated into the main Rebellion Papers: 'a small collection contained in four cartons labelled "Selected Papers" had been at some former time taken from this series. As there seemed no good reason for continuing it as a separate class, the papers have been restored to their places in the principal series. A number of miscellaneous papers not hitherto classed have been examined and inserted in the classes to which they relate.'[15] The use of the terms Rebellion Papers and State of the Country Papers, even on the part of senior archivists, was hopelessly loose and imprecise in the office: reference to the principal series seems to imply that these papers were integrated into Cooke's 'Rebellion Papers'. The finding of these loose papers was later supplemented by another cache coming to light when, very late in the day, the work of listing and cataloguing the Official Papers, second series, got under way. In 1917 the Keeper of the State Papers reported that 'The State of the Country Papers, excluded from the Official Papers, second series, have been arranged in chronological order, and put in six cartons. They cover the period 1790-1808, and form an important addition to contemporary papers of this class'.[16] These are the so-called State of the Country Papers, second series, of which a list exists only in modern and still unfinalised catalogues, in part typescript, in part manuscript.

The letters in the so-called State of the Country Papers, first and second series, are, it cannot be stressed too strongly, simply papers which escaped in the course of administrative process from the Rebellion Papers, or to put it in more precise terms from Cooke's office. In some respects this is itself a measure of the level of attention particular matters merited. The letters either required action at the highest level, or the weight of the issues warranted either lord lieutenant or chief secretary mulling over their contents. In the case of the letters in the first series, for instance, they are intertwined with letters addressed to Littlehales, private secretary to Cornwallis. In other words, they were something of a lord lieutenant's informal series, which explains why they were not embedded in the chief secretary's files from which the so-called second series of letters was later made up. They are all identical with the Rebellion Papers, and many individual letters themselves fit into a more protracted correspondence which has survived in the Rebellion Papers, and which needs on occasion to be amplified by material in the Home Office Papers or in the private collections.

These circumstances help to explain why there are gaps within the Rebellion Papers. In addition, individual letters sometimes advert to preceding letters which no longer survive and cannot be found in the several sources in which letters found refuge; some letters which should logically survive in the papers even pop up outside both the public records and private collections of former Castle officers. Thus Cooke corresponded with Kemmis, the state solicitor, and some office correspondence lodged in Kemmis's office. The few letters from the spy Smith who visited Wickow in 1797 and whose circumstances are quite singular can be augmented only from the Frazer Collection. However, though unfilled gaps exist, the series seems to be a fairly complete *corpus* of incoming letters. Offsetting the value of a fairly complete incoming corespondence, is the lack for the most part of the outgoing letters. Significantly, and revealing of the somewhat slapdash administration in the Castle, replies were not systematically copied. Letter books of outgoing letters existed only for official correspondence, and hence the copying of replies to private correspondents was even more erratic than the keeping of the incoming letters themselves.[17] Pelham as chief secretary sometimes made copies in his own hand of replies, but surprisingly few letters exist in Cooke's hand in proportion to the vast correspondence addressed to him: he must have typically treated many replies as his private business, not as part of the daily routine of official duties. On the evidence of the Rebellion Papers, he must have corresponded closely not only with Kemmis but with John Lees, the post master general: a significant number of letters addressed to Lees which were then forwarded to Cooke are in the Rebellion Papers. Yet there are scarcely any copies of letters to Lees, and very few from Lees to Cooke. What seems to have happened is that Cooke felt some of his letters from Lees warranted their being shown to Pelham or the lord lieutenant. In that event they became part of the office correspondence. There was in all probability a Cooke private archive, just as there was also a Lees archive: had they survived, these collections would have completed the story.

The most important feature of the surviving correspondence is not the information, fragmentary and often slight, within the letters but the evidence, which the series as a whole constitutes, of the regular lines of communication which Cooke and Lees built up with key loyalists. Pelham as chief secretary fits into this framework, but he was not in good health and was sometimes absent. Essentially Cooke ran the security machine in the Castle. All relevant correspondence was handled by him, and analysed by him. The key element was the huge correspondence with individuals in relation to security. This was regular but small up to the end of 1795. Thereafter, as the threat to the state grew, the correspondence swelled out: the Rebellion Papers, extensive and varied though they be, are dominated by the great *corpus* of letters from 1796 onwards, and which from the internal evidence were held together more faithfully and systematically. Moreover, it was not a purely passive archive. In essence, it was less a mass of correspondence than a security machine, within which letters from spies like Collins, Higgins, and McNally were centralised under Cooke, or in the case of Smith sent to Kemmis when the key decision on arrests was being made in August-September 1796. In political terms many people corresponded with him first and foremost. Downshire, the key magnate in the north, wrote to him rather than to any one else in the Castle, for instance. Arthur Wolfe, the attorney general, corresponded with him regularly.

In months of growing crisis and mounting challenge to authority, Cooke and Lees built up a loyalist party for multiple purposes: partly electoral in sensitive counties in 1795-7 but in 1797 and 1798 more centrally directed to active endorsement – which required local political support – of a vigorous security policy at county level. Their role was evident in Kildare and Wicklow (which at first lacked a coherent loyalist party) and in Carlow, a divided county but one which had a cohesive loyalist force, destined to become the driving force of loyalism in south Leinster. Cooke's parliamentary seat was Leighlinbridge (with Patrick Duigenan, a fanatical loyalist, as his constituency mate) and his patron was the fervently loyalist Cleaver, bishop of Ferns. Complacency about Wexford, shared even by the county's loyalists, accounts for the surprise expressed in Cooke's much quoted words when news of the outbreak of rebellion there reached Dublin.[18] In contrast to Ulster and Leinster counties, liberal letters were as numerous as loyalist ones in the small *corpus* of Wexford letters. The Lees and Cooke machine made its appearance only on the Carlow borders of the county.

The uneven coverage by the archive is noticeable. It rested heavily on ties with individuals like a handful of loyal – and loyalist – regulars in disloyal Down and Antrim, Warburton in Armagh, Hill in Derry for instance, or the Wolfes in Kildare, the Stratfords, King and Hardy in Wicklow, or Cornwall and the Rochforts in Carlow, and correspondents in problem Cork. Recurrence of correspondents' letters refers to a specific purpose: they were the key men in the field. However, outside such districts the archive was limited: neither did a loyalist machine exist nor did Cooke even seek to build one up. The correspondence from these counties was a random and erratic inflow of letters, sometimes unhelpfully conveying deafness to, or forthright opposition to, the concerns of the Castle. In this context it is very important to understand Cooke himself. He was ruthless and above all intent on guaranteeing the security of the state. While he regarded catholics as a threat, he was not irrationally obsessed, as some, like the chancellor FitzGibbon, were with a threat from them. Hence if there was no *prima facie* proof of a threat, or no local evidence which identified one, he did not worry. Thus neither the west nor Wexford loomed large in his concern. Cooke's outlook is hinted at in a letter from General Nugent which implies what the general assumed his attitudes to be.[19] In contrast to FitzGibbon, Cooke under the Cornwallis administration was to show a pragmatic attitude on the matter of a settlement with catholics.

Even in problem counties Cooke was singleminded. Down received less of his attention than its problems might seem to warrant, because its responsibilities devolved on Downshire (who however kept in touch regularly with Cooke), and Louth featured less than equally disordered but politically divided Meath because the powerful and effective John Foster managed the county almost singlehandedly and in political terms with great success. The counties of Kildare, Wicklow, and Carlow were a different story. They were by their proximity a security risk, if things did not go well; the absence of a secure gentry interest in Kildare and Wicklow, or a delicate balance in Carlow, made them important.

III. County Wicklow and its high politics

Wicklow as a county presents geographical problems. It is dissected by the great spine of mountains, running north-east to south-west, which divides east from west. The county had no organic social or political unity: in proportion to its size and population, the county town was small and undistinguished. The west of the county looked towards Carlow and Kildare. The south-east ran into Wexford; and Carnew, the largest village in the extreme south-west, isolated as a wedge between Carlow and Wexford, had its closest social intercourse with Gorey by a broad gap in the mountain ranges.

The varied topography was compounded by its political geography. The Stratfords would have liked to represent the county, though they were powerless to do so on their own resources. As far back as 1760 they had contacts with Fitzwilliam, and even at that time Charlemont had been drawn into the politics of the county as a Fitzwilliamite advisor on Irish affairs. Twice, in 1776 and again in 1783, they had represented the county in the second half of the century. After a defeat in 1790 a petition was launched against the successful Fitzwilliam candidates, Westby and Hume, in the county which with Antrim had the most complete Whig triumph. It was frivolous and collapsed embarrassingly.[20] In December 1795 Aldborough, seeing himself as 'the second interest' in the county, canvassed FitzGibbon's support (FitzGibbon was married to a daughter of Whaley) in the hope of not letting 'our late, short-lived viceroy put the county Wicklow in his pocket'.[21] However, stresses and strains were growing between FitzGibbon and Aldborough. Calculation to gain the goodwill of Ftzwilliam was evident in 1797, when Aldborough, very late in the day, declined to join a newly created loyalist interest, and threw his support behind the Fitzwilliam candidates in the hope that, doing so on this occasion, 'I have a reasonable claim to your aid upon a future one.'[22]

The La Touche family in the north of the county, with the traditional ambivalence of the family which tried to look both ways, had not wholly revealed their real colours: in the neighbouring county of Kildare, the duke of Leinster's party did not contest the election, making it possible for the La Touches to gain the support of the Leinster interest. This may seem surprising in the light of county events in May 1797 in Kildare where a La Touche was high sheriff; but in May the pressure on high sheriffs not to allow county meetings came from the Castle, not from local circumstances. In the forthcoming elections any alternative to supporting the wavering La Touche interest would have thrown the county representation into the hands of the singleminded Wolfe camp, which for the duke of Leinster would have been unthinkable. John Wolfe had ambitions of again representing for the county, and the Leinster policy appears to have been guided by the prospect of ditching a more determined loyalist in favour of a less declared one. In Wicklow, likewise, the La Touches were not specified in Aldborough's summary of the government line-up in July 1797. In Carlow one of the La Touches, David junior, seems to have promised to run as an opposition candidate to the county's loyalists, and then to have withdrawn.[23] Significantly, the La Touches' calculation landed them in trouble even in Dublin: a La Touche candidate was an object of censure in 1801 by the redoubtable alderman James, master of an Orange lodge.[24] The duke's action, in typical eighteenth-century fashion, stymied Wolfe's ambitions to rise from a mere borough to the prestige of a county seat. Wolfe's plaintive letter to the Castle tells it all:

> Had I not relied on the postponement of the election until after the next session, and upon that supposition deferred registering my friends till October, or had I noticed of the dissolution of parliament in time to have formed adequate arrangements, or had any other person but Mr La Touche stood on the Duke's interest, I should have certainly succeeded. And had Mr La Touche united with me, we should both have succeeded, but he went to the Duke without holding any communication with me.[25]

In the 1790 and 1797 elections, the two members of parliament returned in Wicklow were Whigs, William Hume and Nicholas Westby, brought in by the Fitzwilliam interest. Supporters of Fitzwilliam included Samuel Hayes, Morley Saunders, and William Tighe. Lesser interests included John Jervis White, a self-declared lover of 'the true principles of all government' on the Wexford border of the Fitzwilliam estate who had nurtured a hope of running for the county in the forth-coming general election.[26] The ambitious, self-serving role of the Stratfords and the La Touches effectively undermined any possibility of building cohesive loyalist opposition to the Fitzwilliam interest; the withdrawal of the government candidate, Howard, on the very morning the hustings were to open on 31 July 1797 reflected crushing failure.[27]

The Howards themselves were a somewhat doubtful proposition from a loyalist perspective. One of them had supported the Relief Bill in 1795; in 1798 they never crop up in loyalist support, and in 1801 McNally reported them once more in communion with the Old Whigs.[28] Almost certainly the government party had counted on gaining a more positive response from the La Touche and Stratford interests: if they had responded to overtures or at least had 'plumped' for the sole loyalist candidate, the government might have breached the Fitzwilliam monopoly of county representation.

The Wicklow election was a humiliating failure for the government, conceded publicly on the very morning of the poll opening, and the more serious as it had been firm government policy not to run the risk of losing in open contest. The point had already been made to John Wolfe in Kildare: 'the lord lieutenant signifies to me his wishes, that there should not be a contest in this county, unless I had strong probability of success.'[29] Late in the day, anticipating failure in Wicklow, no doubt because of the self-interested calculation of the Stratfords and La Touches, the lord lieutenant had to put the best face on circumstances. Noting that the elections at large had gone well for the government, Camden conceded that 'this county (Dublin) and Wicklow will be contested, but the event is neither important nor interesting to government.'[30] Camden's view reflects both his disappointment and his recurring capacity to present events to London in a self-serving light. In writing to Fitzwilliam Aldborough, who had been approached by the loyalists for support, had referred to '*Government* aided by the interest of Lords Carysfort, Powerscourt, Wicklow, Meath and most of the independent* interests, *having set up* Mr Howard for the county of Wicklow to oppose your interests' (italics mine).[31] No doubt, despite the conservative company that the Stratfords frequented and the frustrated ambitions of the family,[32] Aldborough's dislike of FitzGibbon and his famous quarrel with the chancellor which was now coming to a head made it easier for him to support Fitzwilliam.

While losing in electoral terms, the government succeeded in the broader strategic sense; once the election was out of the way, the government party, profiting from the animosities sown among the gentry, could make greater strides in the county. With the La Touche interest now decisively behind the government, Peter La Touche played a key active role in the politics of the magistracy in the early months of 1798. Given a mere polite but dismissive acknowledgement from Fitzwilliam of their support and overtures, the Aldborough interests were likewise active in settling old scores with the Fitzwilliamites and

* 'independent' in the sense of free of Fitzwilliamite influence

building up the county faction in 1798. Their links in office and land with loyalists in Carlow and Kildare inevitably led them in that direction. To these should be added Monck of Charleville, one of the most active landowners in political terms in north-east Wicklow, and the Powerscourt family, whose political alignment was defined by their role as one of the leaders of the protest in the House of Lords against the Whig stand in 1789 on the regency question. Apart from the Howard family (Whig in background and whose loyalism seems to have been lukewarm), Monck, La Touche, Stratford, Powerscourt, and Meath were on the geographical fringe of the county. Indeed, when the county was proclaimed in March 1798, the region which concerned John Edwards (from Bray to Newtownmountkennedy), seems to have been proclaimed, by implication with his consent, merely 'from our desire to oblige the magistrates of the upper part of the county', who had problems on their own estates.[33] That meant Powerscourt and Monck, on whose estates United Irishman organisation seems to have been quite deep both in Glencree and on the Long Hill. Though there was strong United Irishman organisation in Newtownmountkennedy also, a gentry faction in favour of proclaiming seems to have been lacking there. Outside a small pocket of magistrates, an active loyalist interest was lacking at upper gentry level in the entire east of the county. The divides in the 1797 election had run deep. Edwards himself summarised them better than modern words can: 'county gentlemen have been disgruntled and either decline acting or what is worse, brood over their animosities to administration in a silence which not infrequently is construed into an approbation of seditious violence.'[34]

The strength of the Fitzwilliam interest is shown in the fact that in 1798, in contrast to other counties where gentry avoided the office or only loyalists came forward, a Fitzwilliamite, Walter Bagnel Carrol of Ballinure in Baltinglass parish, became high sheriff. He was a nephew of Beauchamp Bagnel of Carlow and cousin of Colonel Keatinge of Narraghmore, both leading figures in the Whig interest in their respective counties. At local level Carrol was related to Henry Harrington of Grangecon, who in turn was supported by two nephews James and Harrington Wall. One of the ironies of 1797-8 is that the Stratford family faced in their own bailiwick of Baltinglass and neighbouring parishes the largest resident Whig interest in the county: the Saunders in the parish, Westby and Hume just outside it added to its strength. Even elsewhere few loyalist magistrates can be identified. In the eastern region from Bray to Avoca, the only loyalist figures who stand out are King and Critchley, both of whom were magistrates, and Hugo who was not one. Edwards – and the Volunteer activist of 1780 was probably the same Edwards – was a central figure in the Charlemontite politics of the north-east. Other figures were either sympathetic or stood aside: Synge, Acton and Rossmore probably supported the Fitzwilliam line, Samuel Hayes and the Tighes certainly did, and Price in Roundwood was in Hardy's words 'sickly and *of course* inactive' (italics mine).[35] On the Fitzwilliam estate, the agent Wainwright dominated the scene: a government and law and order interest had to be created.

Apart from the Stratfords and from King, leaving Hardy aside as a military man sent to the county to command, few letters reached the Castle in 1797 and 1798. The county was otherwise even more silent than Wexford, a striking illustration of the extent to which the county's resident families were beyond the Castle machine. The Fitzwilliam estate was even more decidedly so. Despite subversion on the estate, the agent Wainright was not represented prior to the rebellion by as much as a single letter in the Rebellion Papers. In other words, there were no lines of communication between him and the Castle, and the government had the complex business of creating a loyalist faction among lesser gentry on the vast Fitzwilliam estate: a network of these lowly figures emerged slowly and belatedly out of Hardy's assiduous courting of minor figures in the county. When information was laid against two servants of a '*noble earl*' of being United Irishmen, Christopher Robinson, rector at Baltinglass and chaplain of Lord Aldborough (presumably of his yeomanry corps), triumphantly underlined the words.[36]

If Dublin or national politics invaded county Wicklow, Dublin's role was no less important at the economic level. Wicklow was a centre for wet nursing Dublin children.[37] It supplied the city with eggs, a traffic often overlooked, and its flannel merchants, with their trade at its secular peak, were a source of contact: at least one Dublin flannel merchant, Looby in High Street, supplied firearms to Wicklow United Irishmen in 1798.[38] The through traffic to Wexford passed close to the east coast, the route then moving inland to Rathdrum where one branch of the road continued south to Arklow and the other forked off across the lower passes in the southern hill ranges to the west and the south-west. Rathdrum's central position in the politics of the county derived both from Fitzwilliam's patronage and from its geographical location, making it the nearest thing the county had to a meaningful meeting point for east and west. The same circumstances made Rathdrum and its vicinity the centre of subversion for the county, and in countervailing action, of loyalism as well. Thus Rathdrum was the centre for the first loyalist meeting in the county in mid-1795 just as Annacurragh, to the south of the mountain ranges, and hence not approached by the watched paths over the Black Banks, the Wicklow Gap, and the high tracks from Rathangan through Aghavannagh and Macreddin to Rathdrum, was the seat of the first county meetings of the United Irishmen.

Likewise, communications from Dublin to Carlow and Waterford ran close to the western fringe of the county's mountain mass. Thus, while the county was sliced into eastern and western sections it was wide open to the personnel from Dublin who carried commodities, ideas and subversion further afield. Between Kildare, Carlow and Wicklow there were no natural frontiers, and virtually every town serving west Wicklow was in adjoining counties. The consequence was that intercourse at lower social levels was intense with Naas, Athy, Tullow and Carlow. Within the Wicklow lands, Baltinglass, a Stratford town and borough, was disproportionately important because it was close to the seats of the resident Stratford, Hume, Westby and Saunders families. This proximity ensured that the deepest county divide was in the west and that the electoral politics of 1797 had their bitterest aftermath in the same lands and within the few miles that separated the houses of a handful of both great and minor gentry.

Hume, Westby, Saunders, Carroll and Wall, the very personification of Fitzwilliamite politics in the county beyond the Fitzwilliam estate, all lived in the Baltinglass region. Moreover, this interest was supported by the presbyterian businessmen who had been attracted by Aldborough's sponsorship of the textile industry on his estate. The Orrs, Maxwell and Millar, were among the *bêtes noires* of the Stratfords in the late 1790s. William Putnam McCabe's brother had been a foreman in the Orrs' factory at Stratford,[39] a connection which may well have given him his knowledge of the county.

The landed class of the west had many ties with their counterparts in adjoining counties, ties which could frustrate as well as support the creation of a loyalist policy. When Benjamin O'Neale Stratford, not yet having received the commission of the peace for Kildare, presumed to act there, another magistrate Archbold with 'whom as I know his kidney I will have nothing to do', lost no time in pointing out that he was not a magistrate.[40] Robert Cornwall in Carlow was a magistate in Wicklow, and so influential was Colonel John Staunton Rochfort as a magistrate in Queen's County that, after a divide among the magistrates there on proclaiming the county, his presence was counted on for the reconvened meeting in January 1798.[41] In south Wicklow, an overlapping family network linked the protestant centres of Carnew and Gorey and further east one linked the catholics of Arklow and Gorey baronies. The most significant ties of these latter were between Byrnes on both sides of the borders. Byrnes at Monaseed were married into

Grahams as far afield as the Avoca, and the Doyles and the Esmondes were related. The interconnections are revealed in the will of the celebrated Juliana, countess of Anglesey, mother of Lord Mountnorris, whose tokens of remembrance embraced the Byrnes at Ballymanus as well as the catholic families south of the border.[42]

IV. Moderate and radical currents among the United Irishmen

One consequence was that when the United Irishmen emerged, the United Irishmen of south Wicklow had many Wexford ties, and in this region, the one district in Wicklow with anything approximating to a catholic middle-class, the leading faction revealed all the characteristics of the organisation's leadership in Wexford. Wicklow had made a colourless showing in the catholic politics of 1792 and 1795, partly because of the benign profile of the county establishment, partly because of its relatively weak middle class. They also made a poor showing in the early United Irishmen, as did the catholic families of Wexford. Apart from the Perry/Sweetman nexus (Perry a protestant married to a catholic; Sweetman, a catholic converted nominally to the established religion), whose main achievement was a United Irishman society in 1792 in protestant Gorey, the early United Irishmen in Wexford were protestant. Two Wicklow names do crop up in the Society, Richard Doyle of Lemonstown and Walter Byrne of Killoughter and Dublin (both of them members of the Catholic Convention also), but neither made any impact in the Society, and at the Convention were silent.[43] Catholics in Wexford and in Wicklow offered a contrast to the Ulster borders and to north Connaught where catholic United Irishmen had appeared early. In Wexford catholics, despite their political activism in the county and in Dublin, failed, Sweetman apart, to join the United Irishmen even during their sojourn in Dublin for the catholic convention in December 1792. Wexford radicalism was closely geared to political action, both among its early protestant United Irishmen and its politically militant catholics of 1792 and 1795. Edward Sweetman, closely linked to radical forces, was a lone catholic figure, and he frequented radical circles in Dublin more than he visited the county. Thus, when the opposition formally quitted both parliament and conventional politics in May 1797 and the great radical counties of Antrim, Down and Kildare were left uncontested by them in the subsequent general election, many Wexfordmen in sharp contrast failed to withdraw in like fashion. In the hard-fought Wexford election of 1797, participants included even actual or future United Irishmen like Thomas Cloney and Edward Hay.

The 1797 withdrawal of the radicals from politics acknowledged the failure of political action: it added to alienation, and prepared middle-class and gentry activists for more militant action later. Care must be taken not to read the past out of later events such as those which gave Wexford its notoriety. Primarily political in their interests, Wexford United Irishmen were closest to the 'moderate' elements in the several factions which made up the Dublin United Irishmen. These ties centered on Bagenal Harvey both in 1792 and in the reconstituted society in 1797, and as late as 1798 a communication intercepted in Wicklow was said to be intended for Harvey. In the early United Irishmen, Harvey, not a party to the absenteeism policy of the Neilson/ Tone faction in 1793, can be cast in the Sheares' interest; in the aftermath of the March 1798 arrests, Wexford gentry United Irishmen seem to have backed the Sheares' faction, who, while scarcely moderates, fell short of the more extremist Neilson interest.[44] The Dublin ties of the Wexford gentry United Irishmen in 1797 appear to have been with Mathew Dowling. It was he for instance who swore Perry into the reorganised society. Dowling, an acquaintance of William Drennan and an associate of Thomas Braughall, who was not a United Irishman at all, was to the right of United Irishman politics. From the outset Wexford United Irishmen, Sweetman excepted, were identified with those United Irishmen who saw the society as a group of masonic-style clubs of middle-class and gentry members geared towards overt political action rather than as an organisation spreading outwards and downwards to embrace the lower classes. When the security situation deteriorated in 1796-7, relative moderation acquired the further identifying characteristic of an emphasis on revolution after the French arrived, not on more recklessly launching it whether they arrived or not.

Such men lacked the evangelical force or drive to recruit the masses and to strengthen the clubs either by saturation rank-and-file membership at local level or by recruiting lower-class cadres if acceptable middle-class leaders were not to hand. Hence, if the United Irishmen were to spread rapidly and deeply in local society – and Wicklow even more than Wexford lacked a substantial catholic middle class – they would have to rely on the emissaries sent out by the radical wing. This wing in and after 1796 revolved around Arthur O'Connor and Lord Edward Fitzgerald, who had not been members of the society in its earlier years and who, quite apart from their flamboyant and self-chosen roles as aristocrats *déclassés,* previously had few if any associations with the moderate United Irishmen. Supported from 1796 by a number of Belfast radicals who remained in the capital to help to win the battle for the minds and hearts of Union men and would-be Union men, this wing became the real driving force of southern radicalism. The spread of the United Irishmen in Wicklow depended on them, and the only barony in which the United Irishmen failed to spread in depth – Arklow – was the sole one which possessed a real catholic middle-class. From these considerations derives the importance of William Putnam McCabe who appeared in Wicklow and in Wexford in the crucial period in late 1797 when the spread of the movement gathered pace and county organisation was perfected in Wicklow. The Perry confession in May 1798 seems to imply that in Wexford there had been both a cool response to McCabe and a reluctance or ambivalence on the part of Harvey, Colclough, and Edward Fitzgerald of Newpark in declaring themselves openly. Despite visits by both McCabe and Perry to Edward Fitzgerald, Fitzgerald avoided giving – or was unable to give – Perry an answer: he 'did not tell examinant whether the barony was organised but brought one Adams who told examinant it was and said to the best of his opinion the barony was armed'. The original scheme in Wexford as revealed in Perry's confession was characterised by an intent of organising the county from the top down by creating the county officers (who should have been elected from below) ahead of organisation in depth. The ineffectiveness of the leading Wexford figures is illustrated not only in Fitzgerald's coyness or ignorance but in Perry's statement that 'he (Perry) never swore any person'.[45] In other words, given the evidence in the Perry confession of membership growing around him, the implication is that recruitment proceeded independently under the aegis of McCabe and his associate Mathew Doyle of Pollahoney in Wicklow.

If McCabe failed with the east Wexford gentry, he was more successful elsewhere. His travels from Monaseed to Scarawalsh and Blackwater are illuminating. In Monaseed he had a ready response from Nicholas Murphy and from Miles Byrne, and if further south he did not make great headway with Fitzgerald in person, he must have had the satisfaction either of knowing that lower-class activism was well afoot in Blackwater by October 1797, or even of having promoted it. When Wicklow formed its county organisation, McCabe was present. In regard to Wexford, Miles Byrne stressed the role of both McCabe and Mathew Doyle of Pollahoney. Doyle had been present at some of the early meetings in Wexford, and it was he, not Perry, who had 'proposed to organise the county of Wexford in the same manner as the county of Wicklow'.[46] This dates his visits to Wexford, and puts them as late as October-November 1797. There is little evidence that Perry was a real force, and in Gorey barony the strength of the movement was to the west, around Monaseed, not in Perry's district at Inch in the east of the barony. The spread of the organisation depended less on local gentry than on lower-class activists, working in conjunction with Dublin emissaries. Mountnorris had commented on its progress in

March and again in October 1797. Handcock reported on its spread in Kilcormick and on the Dublin connections of local activists in May and September.[47] The diffusion of radicalism was inevitably helped by Kilcormick's location close to the main traffic route from Dublin to the south-east and by the presence of carmen (a circumstance which also accounted for an inn at a centre as forlorn as Oulart). King had singled out Rathdrum at an early stage precisely because of its location on the same main road. The spread coincided with a power struggle in Dublin, between moderates and the radicals supported by the northern allies who had come to Dublin to help ensure their victory. McCabe's role and that of the lower-class emissaries reflect extension further afield of radical influence, as it prevailed over its opponents in the capital.

V. Creation of a loyalist party

In the aftermath of the Dublin political débâcle in 1795, Fitzwilliam visited the county before his return to England. According to Luke Cullen, Garrett Byrne, the county's only resident catholic gentleman of consequence, met him in Dublin and may have done so again on his Wicklow visit.[48] The bitterness of the divide in Dublin politics combined with Fitzwilliam's Wicklow associations gave a new edge to county politics. The prospect of a general election in two years time was already in the foreground, and every action in 1795 has to be seen as calculated in terms of defining or creating electoral interests. That accounts for the fervour with which the battle of the Boyne was celebrated by a faction in Rathdrum on 12 July 1795: it would also have taken place just before the summer assizes. Our account of Rathdrum on that day relies on Sir Edward Newenham who was present for the occasion. According to him, every protestant house was decorated with orange lilies, and 'at church, men, women and children, except three democrats, had these loyal emblems affixed to their persons'. After the church service, apparently in response to this provocation, John Byrn (sic), thirty-year-old son of a principal shop-keeper, paraded in the village distributing white roses. He was confronted by Newenham and by Thomas King: in Newenham's words, 'Mr King (the active magistate that I formerly mentioned to you) being in the town I brought him to the square where these jacobins were.' The political flavour of the confrontation is well conveyed in Newenham's language: 'I then told them that as they had signed addresses to Lord Fitzwilliam expressive of their loyalty, they were rascally hypocrites as they now erected a standard of rebellion.' Supported by a crowd whipped up by his servant, Newenham, who seems to have been anticipating trouble, snatched a rose from another Byrne 'in order to have it to produce in case of any riot or tryal at the assizes'. The atmosphere of tension lasted for the rest of the day. In the evening, to follow Newenham's words, '32 protestants paraded in the market place opposite the Tavern where 18 of us loyalists dined, they then fired 12 rounds, afterwards marched around the town firing volleys, all dressed with orange ribbands'. At eight, ale was distributed to the loyalist crowd and after toasts the crowd danced till dawn. The select eighteen themselves left the tavern at midnight for fear of a confrontation with 'the white rose men'.[49] This account identifies a small loyalist coterie made up of the eighteen diners who organised the occasion (and who presumably had invited Newenham, who was ideal for Wicklow, because while anti-catholic he had past impeccable Volunteer and radical credentials). The presence of King was interesting, and one may surmise that another diner was Hugo, destined to be high sheriff in 1796.

In the aftermath of the 1797 election stresses and strains began to emerge, and friendships to break down. Holt in his memoirs is vague enough on his relations with Hugo: it is quite likely that Holt may have played a prominent role in 1797 electoral politicking for which his numerous small posts of responsibility made him a useful man, and that this, not the stated reason, strained for the friendship of Holt and Hugo, and led to the subsequent falling out. According to Cullen, Holt had been an intimate of Hugo's.[50] Likewise, the Byrnes' relationship with Hugo seems to have gone sour. The Luke Cullen papers paint a picture of Billy Byrne of Ballymanus having once been a close confidant of Hugo: indeed Byrne is said to have lent Hugo £100 and Hugo to have counted on Byrne marrying his daughter.[51] Such loans from tenant to landlord were commonplace, however, and the marriage proposition itself is scarcely credible. A quarrel at a Rathdrum dinner in mid-1797 in which Lieutenant Tomlinson of the Rathdrum yeoman cavalry taunted Byrne, a member of the Wicklow mounted yeomanry, and Byrne challenged him to a duel, takes the divide beyond a purely Hugo-Byrne framework.[52] The rather obscure quarrel between Byrne and Hugo, a counterpart to a similar progression on Holt's part from good relations to enmity, best makes sense in timing and causation in a political context.

We have now identified the hyper loyalist faction in mid-Wicklow revolving around two men, King and Hugo, neither of whom were established county figures, and who at the outset lacked backing from the county's premier gentry. While Hugo's background is surprisingly obscure, he was a very large landowner, and a rising one: although many gentry avoided the difficult job of high sheriff (especially with county divides in the offing) and those prepared to shoulder the task in crisis were frequently zealots in search of government favour, county gentry were never prepared to tolerate social inferiors in the position. Though less wealthy than Hugo, King was probably the real driving force in mid-Wicklow. Newenham's reference to having mentioned King in preceding correspondence with Pelham suggests that King may have organised the Rathdrum dinner in July 1795. The later approval of him in January 1798 by Joseph Hardy, military commander for Wicklow, and King's own letters hint at his central role in creating a loyalist party in Wicklow. Though Hugo had been high sheriff in 1796 and may have pursued a correspondence with Pelham (which suggests a follow-through from the King actions in 1795), he was not a magistrate, and therefore not a member of the standing committee of magistrates which played a vital role in 1798. Indeed, he did not feature in the story of the early months of 1798, though Hardy's recommending a commission for him in late May suggests that he was a known loyalist and that he was, though not a magistrate, an activist in the crisis weeks of May 1798.[53] However, an effective county loyalist party still did not exist at the end of 1797: of itself the Stratford hysteria on the Kildare border did not amount to one. Hardy's role in creating a county law and order faction and co-ordinating its actions seems to have been crucial in a way which was not paralleled by a single military man in any other county. His movements were frequent and widespread: over time it is possible to trace him as having covered all the main areas of the county. Moreover, he seems at the outset to have won the co-operation of both Edwards and Wainwright. Like Cooke with whom he corresponded regularly, he was ruthless but not fanatical. A post-rebellion report by him reveals a calm, clear mind, and in the light of his readiness to give protections without the surrender of arms, something which was anathema to loyalists at that stage, a detachment from party outlook.[54] For Wicklow, where government support was wanting at the outset, he was in a sense the loyalist counterpart of McCabe.

The evidence of correspondence with Pelham is especially significant, because it hints at the role of government in fomenting or organising a loyalist faction in Wicklow as in other liberal counties. Leaving aside a sole surviving letter on the theme from the egregious Newenham, there is much wider evidence of a government correspondence revolving around Edward Cooke, the undersecretary and John Lees, the postmaster-general, who were supplemented as far as Kildare was concerned, by the Wolfe family (of whom Arthur was attorney-general). Cooke himself was one of the office-holders dismissed by Fitzwilliam in January 1795 and triumphantly restored in the aftermath. The fact of Cooke and Patrick Duigenan sitting for Leighlinbridge borough may be more than a coincidence in the emergence of a powerful Carlow interest which interfered in the politics of surrounding counties and founded the Orange Order in south Leinster. That the government was privy to this is hinted at in June 1798 in a reference in a letter from William Elliot, military under-secretary at the Castle, to 'the Orange associations, which, *you will recollect*, were formed and promoted by Colonel Rochfort and some other gentlemen in the counties of Wexford and Carlow' (italics mine).[55] We are faced here with a hidden agenda in the Irish politics of the day.

The essence of Cooke, Lees and Wolfe's strategy was to create government support in the counties adjoining Dublin. While John Foster's Louth had a managed gentry and Meath a divided but broadly supportive one, Kildare and Wicklow were the great county bastions of grandee whiggery in Ireland. Moreover, Carlow had been a traditional power base of the Whig Burtons, and its radical focus had also been promoted by one of its borough-seated gentry, Beauchamp Bagenal, 'an inflexible patriot, but a singular man, and a zealous supporter of catholic claims'.[56] Likewise as late as 1794, Vesey Colclough, the whiggish patron of Enniscorthy borough, was content to let Robert Cornwall come in, in a by-election. However, the Fitzwilliam recall combined with the catholic question had unexpected consequences in the county, and a swing to the right in outlook by some Carlow politicians presaged the likelihood of a violently contested election in 1797.

In Wexford an opposition to the county's establishment, combining both radicals and an opportunist Mountnorris faction, did emerge in 1797, and it might at first sight appear to pose a threat to the repetition of the 1790 success of the Ogle-Ely interest in winning both seats. In reality it did not. Ogle, with his Volunteer associations and Ely with his independent stance on the regency, provided a novel – and Newenham-like – focus gathering the old Volunteer political tradition as well as loyalists. Moreover, while the election itself helped to fan the flames of local resentments, given an opposition less radical than in other counties (as the 'opposition' candidate John Maxwell Barry was scarcely an independent in any meaningful sense and failed to draw all the independent votes), the outcome was not in serious doubt. Government preoccupation did not fix its gaze on Wexford.

Antrim aside, Kildare,Wicklow and Carlow represented the area in which government electoral support in 1797 was weakest in Ireland. While the government could not hope to take Kildare and Wicklow in open contest, it had a large, though challenged, stake to defend in Carlow. The need for political management was first prompted by the proximity of the 1797 election. Events in Armagh were in mind too, because, despite the opportunistic Caulfield alliance with Gosford (in return for an assurance of support for Charlemont's son as a candidate in 1797), the outsider Cope with radical support had lost the by-election in January 1795 by only 30 votes. Moreover, after Fitzwilliam's departure, despite the bitter hostility of the new administration, the catholic bill had mustered 87 supporters in the division, a disturbing reminder that many protestants were prepared to make radical concessions (just as in the aftermath of the Fitzwilliam débâcle Charlemont himself finally came to back the concession of ultimate political rights to catholics). With so much evidence of a gain in radical strength in large swathes of the countryside, the 1797 election could well result in an alarming loss of ground by the government.

One answer to this was to beat the protestant drum (of which the Orange Order was a vehicle); another was to organise practical electoral support on the ground. Wicklow with its Fitzwilliam interest and Whig power was impregnable; Kildare was a prospect only from the time in May when the Leinster interest decided not to contest the county (an event which could not have been foreseen and which was a unique instance in county politics of a powerful independent interest rigidly following the electoral abstention policy of the radicals). Carlow, though in the government camp, was by no means certain. A change in the county's fortunes had been caused by defection of the Burtons from the Whig interest, and by a shift in position by the attorney gentleman, Robert Cornwall. The latter had not supported protestant machinations in 1792; in a by-election in 1794 the radical Vesey Colclough had, as already mentioned, given him a seat in his Enniscorthy borough,[57] and he supported the catholic bill in 1795. The result was an embittered contest in which two loyalist candidates beat two challengers to confirm the swing in the county.[58] The stresses and strains of this appalling contest in which Sir Edward Crosbie had played so prominent a part were reflected in the events a year later (which included a duel with young Robert Burton at the time of the spring assizes), and which were a prelude to his becoming on slight evidence, after the rebellion had broken out, the victim of his political enemies. His court martial and execution were a measure of the political traumatising of the county in a sequence of electoral and law and order issues.

Wexford was less in doubt. However, Mountnorris's courtship of the county's liberal faction promised to create a novel alliance between many, though not all, of the county's divided radicals and an interest hitherto not central to the county's politics. Ogle's withdrawal is significant because its timing and purpose were intended to make the catholic question an explicit one in the election and to embarrass the Mountnorris candidate (whose own bitter anti-catholic sentiments were on public record). While a favourable outcome for the government seemed certain, a particularly bitter campaign was fought on the Mountnorris estate and in the parts of Wexford bordering Carlow. It was in these districts, which were not radical enough to stand aside from electoral politics in mid-1797, that electoral rancours and the bitterness of defeat helped to prepare the way for the acceptance of the militant radicalism of the United Irishmen.

VI. Political issues and radicalisation

In the wake of withdrawing from parliament in May 1797 the radical decision not to contest the election left Kildare open. In Carlow and Wexford, with gentry locked in both counties in a bitter local struggle, external events did not decide the day. One consequence in Wexford was that a contest divided the radicals. Some, observing the radical call for abstention from politics, withdrew altogether, and this explains why Cornelius Grogan, in an analogy to the duke of Leinster's decision to support La Touche, contemplated at one stage giving his support to Ely. In true eighteenth-century fashion, if there was no radical contestant, support would be based on dynastic or family considerations (rather like the Caulfield family in Armagh in 1795), and would go to existing interests rather than to the creation of new and incalculable forces. Mountnorris was the outsider to county politics, and the entry of Colonel Rochfort into the field in 1797 illustrates a view among hyperloyalists that Ely was not advanced enough (and also served as a ploy for stealing the Maxwell or Farnham support on the borders of Carlow which can hardly have relished the public and opportunistic professions of good will to catholics by Maxwell Barry). That makes Grogan's wavering all the more comprehensible, and while he did not support Ely eventually, the episode seems to show that his patronage did not fall behind Mountnorris. This, combined with Rochfort stealing some of the Maxwell Barry votes, accounts for the downfall of his candidature, which, given a divide among the loyalists themselves in 1797, is otherwise inexplicable.

In 1797 the real radical Wexford wing (the Grogan interest) in effect followed the same line as the United Irishmen and political independents like the duke of Leinster. Others did not, and contested the election on behalf of the Mountnorris candidate. The support for Maxwell Barry came from individuals on the ground like Cloney in the north-west of the county, or Edward Hay in the Mountnorris lands in the east. Subsequently Hay (and Sir Thomas Esmonde) were identified with the anti-proclaiming campaigns of Mountnorris in November 1797 and April 1798. As Mountnorris's actions can be seen as self-interested (a concerted aim of proving his goodwill to government, and of maintaining a higher profile than Ely), it is not surprising that more advanced elements in the radical wing saw (or thought they saw) through him, and did not support him in his politically-inspired effort to oppose proclamation under the terms of the Insurrection Act. In any event, the real hotbeds of United Irish activity – Monaseed and Castletown – were left out of the proclaiming in November, reflecting the political clout the Grogan interest carried among their fellow-magistrates. This was an agreeable result, attained by a Grogan readiness not to jeopardise the interests of their estates and tenants by putting political principle first. The politics of the meeting of magistrates in November thus centred on the loyalist urge to oppose Mountnorris, and the districts proclaimed, apart from an isolated pocket at Clonegal on the Carlow border, devoid of liberal magistrates, embraced in political terms the anti-Whig Ram and Stopford enclave of Gorey and the politically obnoxious Mountnorris estates. Essentially, the November divides were part of the continuing fall-out from the electoral contest.

Behind the divide in the radical camp, as witnessed by the fact that some radicals joined Mountnorris and others did not, was the cleavage between political United Irishmen and others who were activists for mass-organisation. Ironically in the case of United Irishmen like Cloney, while they had participated in the election on behalf of Maxwell Barry, they were also linked to the more advanced wing of the United Irishmen. Cloney and others such as Kelly reflect not the politicised Wexford leadership group with its roots in the older movement of 1791-4 but the progress of the mass-organisation faction. It was this movement which spread across all south Leinster in 1797 and which, not having to cope with a prominent self-serving moderate group, advanced more rapidly in Wicklow and Carlow than in Wexford. Kildare, with Fitzgerald and Wogan Browne providing subversion from the top, was a special case in its success in recruiting the middle and upper classes to radical causes. It was even evident on the battlefield in 1798 and, in the wake of the battle at Rathangan on 29 May, Lieutenant-Colonel Longfield reported that 'all those I saw dead were of the better kind of people.'[59] Elsewhere, the movement spread most effectively in the areas where there was no existing upper-class leadership interest in the movement. In Carlow, for instance, the United Irishmen lacked upper-class leadership, and significantly there was conflict in the spring of 1798 between the one well-placed United Irishman in the county and others. It was in fact the absence of upper-class involvement in Carlow in contrast to Wicklow, Wexford and Kildare that accounts in part for the loyalist obsession that Sir Edward Crosbie was both a United Irishman and a military leader of the movement.

In Wexford, the movement acquired real strength in particular areas like Monaseed and Blackwater and marked time in intervening districts. The cleavage was to emerge dramatically at the battle of New Ross. The men under Harvey's direct control there – those at Corbett's Hill covered by 'commissary Brennan's book' and drawn from east and south Wexford – did not engage in the battle.[60] If the forty-seven captains in the list are a clue to the size of the units under them, they would at most have accounted for under 6,000 men. Those that actually engaged were separately organised under Cloney and Kelly. This cleavage – dramatically borne out by the fact, not only that Cloney and Kelly's forces had a separate combat structure, but that they alone bore the brunt of battle – accounted for the replacement of Harvey as commander-in-chief three days after the battle by Fr Philip Roche, latterly a resident of the district whence the combatants had come. The appointment of Roche may have been both recognition of his signal victory at Clough or Tuberneering on 4 June and of the prospect of compromise offered by his position as an east county man who had at least resided in the west of the county and who had on 4 June commanded a combined force of east and west county men in his victory. An east-west cleavage in the forces was evident over the remaining fortnight of Wexford's effective military threat. Philip Roche himself remained in the west and south of the county over the next twelve days, and the only actions involving mobility, the attack on Borris and the skilful retreat and hard-fought action at Goffs Bridge on 20 June, came from his forces. In other words the rebel forces were deeply fragmented in their leadership; the immobility of the forces in east Wexford reinforced the contrast.

As the prospect of rebellion grew, the aim of moderates, if they did not withdraw altogether or as in the case of Reynolds seek the insurance of offering his services as an informer behind the scenes, became the 'moderate' one of a bloodless revolution, contingent on the presence of French forces (which would make the revolution irresistible and therefore limit bloodshed and radical change). This wing included McNeven, Emmet, and according to McNally the men of property and profession. The opposing wing was led from 1796 by O'Connor and Lord Edward Fitzgerald. Their social position, greatly above that of any remaining United Irishmen, gave them both enormous prestige and an appeal to many ambitious men who thought that a new order would arise from the surge of support for the radical cause in 1797. Moreover, in the power struggle in Dublin between moderates and revolutionaries, they had northern allies in the capital. Emmet, the only really formidable figure among the moderates, was off the executive from May to November 1797 inclusive: O'Connor was on it without interruption to February 1798. That gave the revolutionary faction the opportunity to give an impetus to organisation and to early rebellion; it was in this period – before November – that the drive in the neigbouring counties acquired its real momentum.

VII. The spread of the United Irishmen: mass organisation

Impatient with the lack of spread of the organisation in the southern countryside, the ascendant advanced faction in Dublin sent out emissaries to organise a mass movement. The key organisers were northerners, primarily McCabe but also more briefly James Hope likewise from county Antrim and from the same milieu in the county who backed alliance with Defenders. This repeated a pattern of a rural radical apostolate conducted at an earlier date and to the north of Dublin by Tandy, Russell, Neilson, Charles Teeling and more briefly Tone. It now brought about the spread of the organisation in areas where no United Irishman presence had existed; in other areas it gradually built up a force on the ground under the nominal leadership of existing and ineffectual local leaders. Its effective strength depended not on local notables but on the new men recruited. Thus Monaseed, not the Perry district, provided the source of strength in Gorey barony. Gordon implied a lack of United Irishmen in and around Gorey itself which he saw 'as the least violent of all in the county of Wexford, in rising against the established authority'.[61] Further south in the Fitzgerald bailiwick, the strength lay in new recruits on the ground, embracing the Kilcormick men, Blackwater men, Shelmaleers, and the Castlebridge Dixons who were not to the liking of Edward Hay whose antipathy for north county men, while it might seem just a convenient label for pinning the blame on others, in reality reflects the political split and some of its local geographical focus.[62] Among the Hays the divide was evident even within the family itself, and can be sensed in Edward Hay's perfunctory attempt in his book to defend his brother. Edward Hay was a friend of Edward Fitzgerald of Newpark right up to the outbreak. On the other hand, there was bad blood between John Hay and Fitzgerald, and they had fought a duel.[63] John Hay was, if not in the Neilson camp, in the Sheares' camp, and thus opposed to the moderate Emmet interest, which was backed, we must suspect, by the highly politicised Edward Hay who had participated both in the 1797 elections and Mountnorris's subsequent loyalty campaigns, and by his friend Edward Fitzgerald. In a dim sense, one can see in Wexford town in its three-week occupation by the rebels a conflict between two different groups of United Irishmen, a divide which surfaced again in the politics of the tribunal which condemned the men who were massacred on Wexford Bridge on 20 June.

Wicklow and Kildare were likely to experience the new movement more powerfully than Wexford, Kildare because of the presence there of Lord Edward Fitzgerald himself, Wicklow in part because of its proximity to Dublin and Kildare alike. Carlow experienced organisation more quickly than Wexford, and one, though not the sole, reason was the lack of a vested interest in the form of an existing middle-class group of moderate United Irishmen on the spot. The contrast between two concepts of radicalism, a lower-class and an upper-class one, reflects the complexity of the real situation. Many modern accounts have attempted to solve the issues inherent in this distinction by claiming that there were two different currents of disaffection, one the Defenders, the other the United Irishmen. However, there were not two distinct currents in the late 1790s in mid- and south-Leinster, though the radical wing did gain strength by linking up with or absorbing radical clubs in the capital. Likewise in the countryside, they linked up with Defenders where they had existed, and where Defenders did not exist, the United Irishmen recruited lower-class elements for whom old-type moderate United Irishmen had little time or appeal. There is an interesting contemporary confusion of language especially in the months preceding the spring of 1798 when the term United Irishman became universal: the terms 'Defender' and 'United Irishman' were almost but not quite interchangeable. Instinctively or otherwise the term Defender tended to apply to those who were recruited in the mass-recruitment by emissaries from further afield. In contrast the term United Irishmen was applied to a more genteel element who saw organisation in terms of little more than a proliferation of mason-type lodges.

Prospects of radical contacts in Wicklow at popular level existed from the outset of the decade. Later accounts sometimes fixed on men at the Orrs' factory at Stratford-on-Slaney, attracted by Aldborough for his new estate village, as the vehicle which brought agitators into the county. Musgrave identified the first appearance of Defenders in the south of the county with the Ballymurtagh mines, though Cullen's informants later derided this idea.[64] Whatever the realities of the political story, the county was changing rapidly in the early 1790s. Mining in the southern mountains, the textile factory in Stratford, the short-lived gold-rush on Croghan, and a booming flannel trade carried on in the new cloth hall in Rathdrum (erected by Fitzwilliam in the 1790s) are all part of this movement which brought cash and thought to the county. As early as 1793 Collins, in reporting on Dublin meetings of the United Irishmen, adverted to an oath being administered to the 'common people' in Wicklow.[65] Significantly, there was a follow-up to this early contact. Newenham, on information picked up no doubt in his libations with his seventeen fellow-loyalists at dinner in Rathdrum had reported of the thirty-year old Byrne that 'this Byrne was a parish delegate to the Francis Street meeting – a great friend and correspondent with one Carolan in Carrickmacross in the county of Monaghan – a noted incendiary.'[66] The Carolans seem to have been attached to the Neilson or radical wing, and this is the first evidence of that wing acquiring a hold in Wicklow.

Camden in his key report of August 1796 to London adverted to the recent appearance of emissaries in Dublin, Meath and Kildare to inflame people against the outrages in Armagh.[67] Simultaneously, they reached the borders of Wicklow. Aldborough, writing from Belan three days after Camden's missive, reported 'three notorious vagabonds, defenders or as they now call themselves regulators in this vicinage of the names of Patrick and Thomas Corrigan and James Cane, who frequent each market or ale house, threatening to knock out the brains of every protestant, and to regulate the price of labour, rent of land and value of provisions ... If left here they will poison the minds of all the ignorant men about this neighbourhood, who hitherto have kept quiet.'[68] Another letter at about the same time from Powerscourt reported that at the appropriately named shebeen house in Glencree 'a number of disorderly people meet there frequently, but most especially on Sunday – and are supposed to be defenders.'[69] Cooke and Pelham were now receiving information from several sources. A magistrate, William Nixon, had arrested a man named Campbell who gave a long testimony about Defenderism in Armagh, Louth and Dublin. This testimony referred to earlier Defender meetings 'with Hamilton Rowan and Napper Tandy at the Man of War Inn on the road between Dublin and Drogheda where the said Rowan Hamilton and Napper Tandy made their intentions public, the object and reasons of which is easily guessed at.'[70] On his own declaration Nixon had not previously corresponded with Pelham, but significantly he declared himself 'influenced by motives of permanent attachment to government', and his letter which appeared out of the blue was almost certainly a result of concerted contact with others as it preceded by days a report on what was described as 'a general meeting of the gentlemen of Wicklow' held at Rathdrum on 30 December. Thomas Hugo, the high sheriff, rather officiously convened the meeting, and as chairman read the contents of a letter from Pelham (which does not appear to survive) addressed to the sheriff. While the resolution passed at the meeting culminated in a declaration of 'constant readiness' to attend when called on to suppress disturbances of the peace and to help the magistrates, its real substance was political:

> Impressed with the liveliest sense of loyalty to our beloved sovereign and the strongest zeal for the preservation of our happy

> constitution and government in church and state we declare our determined resolution collectively and individually at this alarming crisis to pursue such measures as will most effectively tend to evince our steady attachment to our king and the preservation of the peace and good order of our country.[71]

This is very much a follow-up to the sense of the meeting held in Rathdrum on 12 July 1795, and represents a further step, taking advantage of the alarm created by the presence of the French fleet in Bantry, to found a loyalist faction in the county with the forthcoming election in mind. Its support base can only have been quite narrow, and the strength of the meeting lay less in unanimity of the county gentry than in the fact that expressions of unqualified loyalty were in themselves unexceptionable at a time of threatened invasion.

The prospects for party were greatly enhanced by the multiplication of evidence of radical organisation of a new sort. It was first reported on from Kildare, when John Wolfe at Forenoughts on 5 January reported that 'there has been some appearances (sic) of this kind about Longwood, and also about Kilcock – and not *long* since, 6 or 8 weeks ago, an attempt to administer oaths was made in Kilcullen.'[72] The first appearance in Wexford was reported by Mountnorris in March 1797 when he conveyed information about 50 men who had assembled in Blackwater. Two of the members, one of them a man named Connor who was a member of a gang 'who styled themselves French republicans', were lodged in jail.[73] From later evidence we can identify this nucleus more clearly, with direct contacts with lower-level figures in Dublin, mainly in the seditious milieux of Thomas Street or Francis Street, a common theme of much of the evidence from all south Leinster. In May, even from Kilkenny, the mild bishop of Ossory (a friend of Edmund Burke's), in a letter so critical of government that it even drew the preparation of a defensive reply from Pelham (significantly endorsed as 'never sent' and abandoned in favour of a shorter letter), had reported information that two soldiers who had been billeted on a sick woman visited by one of his clergymen had been 'at a public house where two gentlemen from Dublin had been administering the United Irishmen's oath to them and to others'. More ominously he reported that

> nothing of the kind had been discernible amongst us as yet. But I hear from every quarter that the spirit of loyalty which shewed itself so generally at the period of the French attempted invasion is sinking from day to day, that there is a very great change observable in the temper and language of the Roman catholics, and that

> persons who were then the most active and forward now speak a language of discontent and shew manifest signs of disaffection.[74]

The first Wicklow reports are from mid-May. One was from John Smith about whom we will have occasion to say more later, who was lodged in west Wicklow and who had travelled from Hollywood to Wicklow town the previous day. On his way, in a public house 'in a mixed company', a man named Patrick Burk (sic) who kept a whiskey shop in Hollywood declared himself publicly 'to be up i.e. an U.I.M.' He heard from the same man an assertion than more than half the Dunlavin yeomanry were United Irishmen. He added that 'I understand farther that at Baltebois (sic), where I lodge, there is a club forming, and that emissaries are now preparing to travel the mountains and to form societies there.' Moreover, the contagion had spread to Wicklow town itself: 'The postmaster of this town (Wicklow) has just informed that a capital tradesman in this town has just got books to swear U.I.M. but he had not yet discovered his name.'[75] The guess would be that this man was John Lacy, who was party to organising the county in November 1797 and who, according to a later report from King, 'resides in Wicklow, is a tobacconist and of some consideration.'[76]

Thomas Grogan Knox, writing from Castletown in June, reported the affixing of seditious papers on the chapel in his neighbourhood. It was seen by him as the first step on the eastern border lands of Wicklow and Wexford.[77] On 19 May O'Neale Stratford had reported Patrick Hacket, a man who was formerly a nurseryman at Carnew and who, coming from Dublin, distributed papers at Baltinglass.[78] Taken 'with such avidity and secretly kept', they included a speech of that 'little rascal Grattan, and the resolution of the grand jury of Armagh calling for the king to dismiss his ministers'. Hacket was arrested and sent to Carlow. Such papers had never been seen before and had been distributed at the fair on 12 May. O'Neale Stratford expressed the fear that 'the contagion of the county Kildare is likely to creep into this part, to which I am sorry to say it is too near and that the magistrates of the nearer part (to) this have not been as alert as they should be is too risible.'[79] Thus with some confidence the spread of the organisation can be dated both to May 1797 in county Wicklow and to the apostolate of lower-class emissaries coming from Dublin more than to the county's prominent catholics. While patrols existed in Kildare as early as January, they were now instituted in Stratford's region. The evidence also points not only to direct spread from Dublin but to the percolation of ideas from Kildare.

VIII. Magistrate divides on law and order

Government support for loyalists is very evident in John Wolfe's letter of 5 January 1797, which points to his contacts with Stamer, a magistrate at Prosperous (and brother to the late sheriff of Dublin). Stamer wished to raise a loyal corps of yeomanry at Prosperous, but ran into opposition from the county liberals who sought to undermine his attempt by poaching his tenants into their corps of yeomanry:

> Great exertions have been made (as Stamer tells me) by Griffith and *Esmond** (who is Griffith's lieutenant) to get the people of Prosperous, who are all Stamers' tenants, to quit their landlord, and to join them. The people are disposed to stand by Stamer, but it is a matter of struggle, and nothing could so completely run Stamer down as government countenancing the efforts against him. The other consequences, in (sic) a political point of view, I know you are aware of and therefore I need not enumerate, but the best way to manage is to appoint Stamer at once, and put an end to the cabals.[80]

The political 'point of view' refers to the forthcoming general election. The political context of the outrages which emerged in Meath and Kildare from this time – the most serious ones were attacks on the property or persons of advanced loyalists – is illustrated at a later date in Stamer's house being attacked by a mob; two day later a boy watching his cattle was killed and his haggard was burned.[81]

In Kildare, Carbery barony had already been proclaimed in May 1797, following arms raids, an attack on the local charter school, and the murder of the high-profile loyalist, the Rev. George Knipe, across the border in Meath. In the proclaiming of Carbery, there were differences on the advisability of the step among the magistrates. Thus, Sir Fenton Aylmer of Donadea Castle, while going along with the decision, declared his opposition to proclaiming:

> I must confess I am an enemy to proclamation, although I signed my name yesterday with 21 other magistrates to have the barony of Carbery in this county declared out of the peace. As no other mode was proposed and that something immediate must have been done, I preferred it to suffering a continuation of the system of murder, assassination and robbery both of arms and money that pervaded that whole barony, *confident am I that there are means that would be more likely to keep down the flame.* (Italics mine) [82]

---

*underlined in original. John Esmonde from Wexford who had settled in Kildare and who was an early United Irishman.

Thus some who publicly supported the proclaiming were privately against it. Though only twenty-one supported the proclamation, there had been thirty-five magistrates at the meeting. Wogan Browne, one of the dissenting magistrates, observed to Pelham: 'twelve were againt the measure and several others declared that they voted for it only because no other specific measure was at that time subjected to their consideration.' The last sentence is clearly a reference to Fenton Aylmer, who was a prominent supporter of Fitzwilliam, and who as high sherrif in 1795 had summoned no less than two meetings of freeholders in the wake of the viceroy's recall. This had been an unprecedented level of county activism for the period. Wogan Browne also pointed out that the occasion should have taken the form of a session of the peace in open court. While notice of the meeting had indicated it as such, in practice the magistrates 'assembled in a private room, the grand jury room, where the magistrates and they only were admitted'. No evidence of any specific outrage was adduced on oath. Wogan Browne saw the occasion as a step in abandoning conciliation and as 'a political expedient used to prepare Leinster as Ulster has been for military proscription and execution'.[83]

This was clearly the view of the liberal party, and written on successive days, Fenton Aylmer and Wogan Browne's letters were presenting a concerted protest. Inevitably, given the strong liberal feeling in the county a meeting of freeholders was proposed. This was proscribed as were some similar Leinster meetings in May, reflecting a concerted government policy in the delicate counties near Dublin, though elsewhere as in Antrim and Down meetings went ahead. The petition of the magistrates, freeholders and inhabitants of county Kildare calling for the dismissal of the members of the Irish government, which it had been intended to put to the meeting, was instead circulated to collect signatures in the first half of June.[84] According to McNally, Wogan Browne was its author, and 1,000 copies were to be printed.[85] In all a total of 6,000 signatures was claimed. The government policy of preventing county meetings and more specifically the Kildare one was the catalyst of the radical decision both to withdraw from parliament and from the general election: the advocates of withdrawal from parliament were Lord Edward Fitzgerald, Arthur O'Connor and Lawless.[86]

Events in the county were now being watched closely, and even comparative moderates like Fenton Aylmer were under suspicion because of their associations. John Wolfe, in officiously enclosing a letter to Cooke on 23 June from Theobald Wolfe, a magistrate and first lieutenant of the Wolfe cavalry at Forenaughts, observed that 'he tells me that the Duke's yeomanry, (Wogan) Browne's and Sir Fenton

Aylmer's exercised together at Kilcock last Sunday, that Browne took the command or at least the lead and Sir Fenton remained quiescent; he does not say the Duke was there. I have thought this worth communicating to you, because I think it leads or may lead to something very mischievous.' The corps of another liberal, Griffith, also received attention.[87] Day, a law officer, attacked Wogan Browne. 'Why is Mr Wogan Browne left in the commission of the peace? Why is so ill-conducted a man left in the possession of power which is so inclined to abuse?' [88] Political alienation reaching into even the higher ranks and the activism of Edward Fitzgerald, with his populist flair in the county where he was accused by loyalists of walking beside the ploughmen in the fields, combined to accelerate United Irish recruiting in the county at a rate ahead of its progress elsewhere in Leinster.

Inevitably, given the proximity, this had implications for west Wicklow, and McNally, in one of his few specific comments on organising outside Dublin on 22 May 1797 observed that 'the county of Wickow is now ... organising.'[89] At one level the spread into Wicklow was fomented by the diffusion of ideas from Kildare. At another level it was fanned by the social contacts between the few and beleagured hardline gentry in Kildare and their counterparts in Wicklow. Thus John Ravel Walsh, an active magistrate close to the Wicklow border, after a visit to the Dunlavin area the preceding day, wrote critically on 6 June of Wicklow magistrates.[90] Benjamin O'Neale Stratford's fears as expressed in a letter of 9 June are not unlike those of Walsh in his letter.[91] Morover, like Walsh's, his letter referred to troubles at Dunlavin, and the two letters in close succession suggest that both men had been in contact and that their letter writing was concerted. Nor were the fears imaginary. Hardline figures were now subject to physical attacks. Walsh's letter of 6 June reported the attack on Stamer's property, and we may suspect that Walsh's probable contacts with Stratford involved some co-ordinating of security measures. Patrols were in evidence in parts of Kildare as far back as January, and Stratford in May seems to have been the first to institute night patrols in Wicklow. In August, the loyalist Robert Day, painting a picture of deep popular disaffection in the midlands, reported to Wolfe that 'gentlemen here and in the county of Kildare have converted their houses into garrisons.'[92]

Wild allegations against moderate magistrates now became an insistent refrain. Significantly, emphasising its political context, the theme first surfaced in the letters of both Walsh and Stratford on 6 and 9 June respectively, Stratford repeating with reference to Kildare magistrates what Walsh said in his letter of 6 June. Walsh declared:

> It would be well if some magistrates would restrain their

> compassionate feelings *and interferences** on the apprehension of suspected persons, which appears more from a wish to ingratiate themselves with the populace than humanity, and has one very bad effect, as it contrasts the conduct of the proper magistrate who does his duty and renders him the particular and marked object of resentment.

Walsh had seen 'the bad consequences of such conduct in many instances', and instanced the attack on Stamer's property as a case in point.[93] It was all the more galling for O'Neale Stratford that one of the easy going magistrates in west Wicklow was his own nephew Morley Saunders of Saundersgrove, who was on a different side in politics.[94]

John Smith, in reporting from both Kildare and Wicklow, re-echoed these sentiments on 16 June: as a follow-up to two earlier letters, one from Wicklow and another from Naas (the latter not surviving). He reported that 'the country is infamously neglected by the magistrates as it is, not *one* of whom in this part of the country makes the smallest attempt to preserve the peace, but on the reverse *to my knowledge* and in several instances have been instrumental in breaking it.'[95] A persistent loyalist belief was that members of Morley Saunders and Hume's yeomanry units were United Irishmen. Matters became ugly after an attack on some Carnew men, one of whom was a yeoman, near Humewood allegedly by United Irishmen, some of whom were recognised and 'one of the most active *Mr Hume's own man* (underlined in the letter) who declared himself to be "Paddy Doyle by night and by day winter and summer, that he lived at Humewood and did not care a pin for any one"'. Tutty, the assaulted yeoman, swore before the magistrate Cope at Carnew and the warrant was sent to Hume for execution. This was a calculated challenge to Hume, as the warrant was sent only after Cope had 'consulted the gentlemen of the neighbourhood'. The letter went on: 'but what does Hume do; betrays the trust committed to him, never does anything in the business at all.' The next step was for Captain Swayne of the Royal Cork Militia, already active in Kildare, and Lieutenant Blayney along with Tutty to go to Humewood, demand to see the man, and arrest him.[96]

Carlow had simultaneously experienced the phenomenon of United Irishman infiltration. An acknowledgment in Cooke's hand of a communication from Robert Cornwall of Myshal Lodge exists from 2 September: 'your information as to the present plan of the United Irishmen in your county is very curious, and I trust that you will not relax in endeavouring to detect the agents and emissaries.'[97] The fact

* a subsequent interpolation in the letter

that it survives in the State of the Country Papers, and not in the Rebellion Papers, is significant, as Cooke must have passed both the letter and his reply to his superiors. Cornwall's correspondence in fact began as far back as 1797.[98] Cornwall and the Rochforts were to swing into action, and from this time forward the largest block of correspondence received from Leinster came from this group. The associations with Cooke from the outset are significant.

At this stage the pressure for proclaiming – in modern language resort to special powers – under the Insurrection Act began to build up. The demand stemmed in part from the fear that infiltration came from further north: a theme evident in Meath, Kildare and equally in Carlow. Hence, from a Carlow loyalist perspective, firm law and order was as necessary on the ground in other counties as in Carlow itself. Specifically that amounted to pressure from Carlow for proclaiming in Kildare, Wicklow and the Wexford side of the Carlow border. As far as Wicklow was concerned, it related to the west of the county with its powerful and obnoxious Fitzwilliam interest revolving around Hume and Saunders in the Talbotstown baronies. The fact that Shillelagh and Ballinacor baronies were not proclaimed (while neighbouring Clonegal on the Wexford border and the two Talbotstown baronies were)[99] shows that within the Fitzwilliam estate the Fitzwilliam interest through its agent Wainwright was deaf to the representations of the Carlow gentry. While Carlow set the pace for the rest of south Leinster, political forces in Kildare, Wicklow and Wexford ensured that proclaiming in those counties was highly selective. In Carlow itself, unique at the time as the only Leinster county proclaimed in its entirety, proclaiming heightened the election divides, and Sir Edward Crosbie in particular still bitterly opposed the proclaiming as late as the time of the spring assizes in 1798 which he refused on principle to attend.[100] There is little doubt that in Wexford the clergyman James Gordon took a critical stand on law-and-order methods.

The earliest arrests in any numbers had occurred at the border village of Clonegal.[101] By 5 October Mountnorris wrote of 'Clonegal and Newtown Barry where I understand the United Irishmen have made many proselytes'. Further east at the heart of his own estates, one of his tenants, Hawtrey White, who had raised a corps of yeomanry, had made arrests.[102] In Carlow by the outset of November the situation was much uglier: an attempt had been made on the life of John Butler, first lieutenant in Cornwall's First Carlow cavalry, and there had been a number of raids for arms in the last week of October in one of which a man named Bennett of Leighlinbridge had been murdered.[103] Cornwall wrote of the 'spirit of rebellion that of late like a torrent, has spread itself over this hitherto peaceful county.'[104] In response to these fears the magistrates of the county assembled on 2 November. In the aftermath of the meeting, Colonel Rochfort reported to the Castle that 'almost all that part of this county betwen the counties of Wicklow and Wexford and the county Kilkenny is united, and that their number in this county now amounts to 3000 men.'[105] The request at that time was for extra troops. A week later (9 November) proclaiming of the county was requested, though in conveying the decision to the Castle, Burton and Rochfort requested that the use of troops be withheld to give time for an amnesty to have effect for those who would surrender with arms. While the Castle agreed to the amnesty provided it exempted captains and 'any persons who have come from Dublin', it found it simpler to defer the promulgation of the proclamation until 15 November.[106] The proclaiming of the two Talbotstown baronies in Wicklow was requested on the same day (9 November), and was acted on without delay. This points to the concerted nature of the Carlow-Wicklow loyalist campaign: in fact Benjamin O'Neale Stratford had been in Carlow on 9 November, and had therefore probably attended both the west Wicklow and Carlow meetings. The grounds for proclaiming in Wicklow lay in the fact that Nixon at Killinure had been murdered in an arms raid by men who, according to Benjamin O'Neale Stratford, 'are become more desperate from the idea that government will not proclaim.'[107] No attempt was made to proclaim the rest of Kildare or Wicklow outside the Talbotstown baronies, a recognition of the liberal political forces that stood against the measures. In Wexford likewise the districts proclaimed on 20 November were politically highly selective.

One of the galling things for loyalists in countryside and Castle alike was the failure of the Kildare gentry on whose estates trouble emerged first and ran deepest, to act. The first suspects in Carbury included artisans, farmers, labourers, and canal taskers.[108] However, in the spread of the contagion to the east of the county, men of a higher station were suspected, and at Kildare, Commins the apothecary was arrested in calling at the barracks by Captain Swain, he being 'a suspicious character'.[109] By August a number of men were in Naas jail, and Day, a government barrister, released some in August:

> The judges are relieved of much fruitless trouble, the county of the burden of maintenance and the fees of acquittal, and (what is more essential) the crown of the mortification and mischief of many defeats. Sixteen prisoners have been this evening discharged, each of whom I have no doubt would be acquitted, and who now instead of the triumph and audacity inspired by impunity, carry home with them impressions of the moderation

> and mercy of that government which they are taught to abhorr ... I have been forced to grope my way here for want of evidence, and much time has been wasted in dispatching expresses through this county for the justices.[110]

Trouble appeared in west Wicklow almost as quickly as in neighbouring parts of Kildare. In June 1797 information or suspicion hinged on the Dunlavin area. A report dated 16 June from Smith noted that 'a junta belonging to Ballymore Eustace, Dunlavin, Donard and Hollywood are continually promoting mobs under the pretence of cockfighting'. Emissaries from Dublin and the north attended to swear people in, and when rambling in the mountains Smith was applied to by two men who wanted to join the United Irishmen. He claimed that most of the catholic priests were 'up', and that one attempted in his house 'in a manner at once solemn and equivocal' to swear him.[111] According to Benjamin O'Neale Stratford the inhabitants of Stratford-on-Slaney, who had contact with emissaries from Kildare and Dublin, were suspected, 'and I fear not unjustly' of being United men. A number had been sworn: 'one Dempsey a baker from Dublin is I hear a principal agent with one Doyle a tailor.'[112] Smith later reported that a man named Hampton had been murdered at Blessington, and feared for his own safety. He doubted the loyalty of the son of the house he resided in, a Charles O'Reilly who had been nearly two months in Dublin, and who 'is this day gone to Wicklow no one knows for what'.[113] In this context it is easy to see how Michael Dwyer could have been sworn in: it is not necessary to speculate as Dickson does that he was sworn in by Garrett Byrne, which is inherently unlikely. Alarmist accounts continued to flow in through the hand of Benjamin O'Neale Stratford.[114]

The brutal methods applied in Kildare in April and May 1798 began to supply information not only on Kildare but on the organisation across the border in Baltinglass and Stratford-on-Slaney. In May 1798, information came to hand of 'Joseph Fox, a Stratford-on-Slaney baker, one of the first who swore united men in the county Wicklow. He has been committee man and secretary and can give information of how the fugitive rebels from Belfast, Lisburn, Hillsborough etc under the protection and influence of the Orrs first introduced uniting in Stratford and spread it through all parts of the adjacent neighbourhoods.' Another man, Roger McGuire, a smith at Stratford and a fugitive from Tyrone, was described 'as one of the first and a most active citizen; he has sworn more men and probably made more pikes than any other smith in the county Wicklow'. Although there were already northerners in Stratford in 1797, some originally brought in by the Orrs, others allegedly refugees who fled the north when the trail got too hot, the same source attributed their recruitment into the organisation not to their northern background but to 'one McCabe who had been the first to introduce uniting in Stratford'.[115]

IX. William Putnam McCabe and Wicklow

This brings us to the role of William Putnam McCabe. There is more reference to McCabe for Wicklow than for any other southern county, and his actions there must reflect the importance attached by the executive in Dublin to building up an organisation, comparable to Lord Edward's in neighbouring Kildare, another county bordering the capital. McCabe can be followed across Wicklow, and north and east Wexford. His role in Wexford may have been the crucial factor in recruiting both John Kelly of Killann and Thomas Cloney of Moneyhore, the only two Wexford colonels of real distinction in the actual fighting. Kelly, probably the first United Irishman of consequence in west Wexford, may have been first recruited in Dublin through the more moderate wing, and then re-recruited by McCabe. Caesar Colclough had later reported of Kelly, referring to June 1797, that 'I had got information he was sworn in Dublin and that he was to be an officer and was very active.' Colclough made him take the oath of allegiance at a time when he had already sworn in his first local recruit. Kelly's letter is dated 17 June. Apparently, in the light of Colclough's representations, Kelly persuaded the man to leave the area, and on Colclough's evidence, Kelly himself promised to give up.[116] This may be true, and his later reinvolvement may have been one of the fruits of McCabe's missions in the area. It seems fairly certain that Cloney was recruited by McCabe: this is implied in the denial by Cloney, a man with a track record of many lies in his later written account, that the fact that he was seen in Rudd's Inn in Enniscorthy at the same time as McCabe had no significance.[117] McCabe was the real driving force in Wicklow, but his visits were supplemented by others, such as a mission of Nicholas Butler and Laurence Tighe,[118] and numerous contacts with lesser fry from Francis Street and Thomas Street, nerve centres of the plebeian forces within the United Irishmen. County Carlow was certainly recruited by the same Dublin interests. With his good information Robert Cornwall had observed as early as November 1797 that 'great attention ought to be paid to the cars that set out from the Sun Inn, Francis Street, for this county and Wexford.'[119]

Later sworn evidence confirmed that the county organisation in Carlow was already functioning long before the regular three-monthly elections which became due in February 1798: in other words the organisation could have been perfected as much as a quarter earlier, a fact which coincides neatly with the outbreak of loyalist alarm in

Carlow at the beginning of November. It would thus have been not far behind the Kildare organisation, which seems to have been a functioning one when Thomas Reynolds was elected a colonel in the early spring. At that time Kildare was unique in south Leinster in not only having a large-scale organisation, but in having reached the point of electing colonels for its military organisation.[120] There were many Carlow ties with Kildare: on the Wexford border Fr Mogue Kearns had Kildare assocations, and Colonel Rochfort in Carlow had reports in November 1797 that a letter had been received from Lord Edward Fitzgerald.[121] McCabe was present at the meeting in early December which presided over the organising of Wicklow. Both the perfection of organisation in Carlow and the recruitment of Kelly and Cloney in Wexford may plausibly be dated to much the same period. The presence of emissaries from the north was mentioned in Carlow. McCabe himself may have been one of them.[122]

The creation of a McCabe-inspired organisation in Carlow seems to be reflected in a hint of social divide. Remarkably few people of real social rank were recruited in Carlow and reports of the involvement of Dr Fitzgerald, a lieutenant in the Carlow militia and a medical doctor there, were regarded as ill-founded.[123] Here as elsewhere a conflict can be detected betwen the McCabe wing and other interests as at a county meeting in February 'a person of the name of Morgan Kavanagh of the Barony of St Mollins had taken upon him to represent himself in Dublin as a representative for said barony and had written to have money collected to be remitted to him for the use of the said society ... Resolved that a letter sent to the barony of St Mollins by a Mr Kavanagh from Dublin had been false, injurious, tending to injure the business ... that said Morgan Kavanagh shall be excluded the Society unless he shall come forward and acknowledge his errors and promise his amendments (sic).'[124] The influence of the Neilson wing is reflected in the fact that the Carlow county committee unanimously accepted the provincial decision of 25 February 'that the people should arm immediately and that the business would immediately commence without the assistance of any foreign aid'. When rebellion came, a greater forwardness can be seen in McCabe recruits than others. For instance men like Miles Byrne and Nicholas Murphy of Monaseed, and George Sparks lost no time in congregating at action points. Equally Cloney and Kelly were effective: they led large cohesive groups of men from their own districts, they headed them in person from the very outset, and their bands entered into action at New Ross (in contrast to the failure of other Wexford groups to engage). The later contemporary apologetic claim that the Wexford leaders were slow to join their men has an element of truth in that some of them favoured the moderate wing or had held purely civilian office, and their actions, as in the case of Bagenal Harvey or Edward Hay, betray ambivalence at the outset. The contrast between Edward Fitzgerald's hesitancy and John Hay's more spirited role in the course of 25 and 26 May spells out the story equally.

McCabe's role and that of more lowly minions was crucial in the United Irishmen. He both promoted organisation in depth, and spear-headed the final stage of structuring the movement, that of converting the civilian structure into military form. The range of his movement was necessarily limited by time, and his penetration towards the south does not seem to have reached beyond Carlow and mid-Wexford. That may help to explain why Kilkenny and Tipperary, although both counties had more organisation than has been believed (and in Kilkenny at least was on paper a large force), may have remained ineffective. It may explain too why Queen's County was unable to collect funds to defend prisoners, a fact which led McNally to conclude, probably wrongly, after the spring assizes in 1798 that there was no organisation in the county.[125] Indeed the contrast was known at the time, and the information of one McCarthy, though in the main more hearsay than fact, may have repeated a truism held by local United Irishmen: 'he had been told that the counties Tipperary and Kilkenny were the weakest counties in Ireland with respect to United Irishmen'.[126] McCarthy's information, while doubtful in relation to individuals, repeated facts confirmed from other evidence: he reported 16,000 men in Kildare, and 14,000 in Carlow with no less than 900 in the town itself. They had been 8,000 to 9,000 in Carlow at the end of February.[127] Schoolmasters were an important source of recruiting. Thus in Newcastle, John Murphy of Knockrobbin, a schoolmaster, reported on recruiting in his district to the prospective head of the baronial organisation. And in the small number of Wicklow depositions printed by Musgrave, no less than two have reference to schoolmasters swearing in United men.[128] Schoomasters occur elsewhere such as Peter McCabe of Gleniban near Glendalough, and James Ryan of Powerscourt.[129]

X. The County Wicklow United Irish leadership

Ineffective top leadership usually came from the moderate wing, tempted into United office by a vanity which sought titles, or impelled by the belief that events were moving irresistibly in favour of the United Irishmen. As Samuel Neilson of Belfast, the driving force in mass recruitment, later observed, 'many people joined the United Irishmen, supposing them to be the strongest party in the state.'[130] Thomas Reynolds in Kildare is a classic illustration; Morgan Kavanagh in Carlow, and Anthony Perry at Inch, a man apparently, like

Kavanagh, in financial difficulties, are other instances. At lower levels similar cases abounded such as John Maccowen, a cotton manufacturer, holding the lowly rank of private in the Carlow yeoman cavalry, but who 'was using every exertion to be made a captain in the United Irishmen.'[131]

Wicklow, in contrast to Carlow, had an involvement by comfortable middle-class types. As in Wexford one can trace the presence of prominent United Irishmen, recruited in Dublin and hence probably through the Emmet-McNeven wing of the movement. William Michael Byrne, John Lynch of Roundwood and Garrett Byrne are all described in the Luke Cullen manuscripts.[132] How effective they were is another question: the conduct of another of the Wicklow baronial leaders, Richard O'Reilly, in accepting an assurance from Tom King that the seal would not be broken on a letter whose contents led to the consequent raiding of a United house in Dublin, provides a revealing example of utter ineffectiveness. Garrett Byrne in particular seems to be greatly exaggerated by Luke Cullen, aware of his social position and moved by the tragedy of his brother, Billy Byrne. Quite in contrast to Kildare or Wexford, he was the only member of real social standing on the county executive; his role has however much of the vagueness which characterised Perry, Fitzgerald and Harvey in neighbouring Wexford. Moreover, he was out of the county from February 1798: the strength of the organisation lay in the activists below him, who had not been recruited by him. For all the south Leinster counties except Kildare, there seems to have been some slowness in appointing colonels, and the work had not been executed in time for the elections in February. Only in March or later was the task completed, and the fact that the posts were created in the interval between regular elections in February and the next elections due in May, seems to have cast some shadow over their authority or legitimacy. How the conflicting balance between imposing socially well-connected figures on the baronies and respect for the rule of election by the captains was resolved, it is hard to say. In Carlow Kavanagh seems to have been a colonel by May 1798, and, in Wicklow, Byrne seems to have become adjutant general in the same month.

In addition to the close Dublin ties of some like William Michael Byrne and John Lynch, other prominent Wicklow United Irishmen had Wexford links. Thus Richard O'Reilly, a miller at Mount Kennedy, 'where he gave great reason to suspect he was disaffected', and who was related to William Michael Byrne, was in touch both with the movement in Arklow and with Harvey in Wexford. In March, Thomas King had arrested him on his way to Philip O'Neil in Arklow and to Bagenal Harvey in Wexford: suspicion was all the greater because no papers were found on him and 'the mountain road which O'Rielly (sic) says he travelled was the longest to Arklow but the most private.' According to King, 'Philip O'Niel (sic), son of Miles O'Niell of Arklow with whom O'Rielly says he has but a slight acquaintance and where he intended to lie at night is generally reputed to be treasurer to the county Wicklow committee of United Irishmen – it is unnecesary to say anything to you of Mr Bagenal Harvey.'[133] Hardy had already commented in January 'on a bigoted catholic shopkeeper of considerable opulence (Miles Neal) whose son is under strong suspicion.'[134]

The Byrnes of Ballymanus were given much attention in Luke Cullen's account: Garrett himself was seen as leader of the United Irishmen in the county. While Billy Byrne is said by Charles Dickson not to have been a United Irishman, this is doubtful: the balance of evidence suggests that he was.[135] As regards Garrett Byrne himself membership is not in question: the real question is his effectiveness. For Luke Cullen there was no doubt, and he even claimed a large role intended for him in the strategic deployment of the United Irishman forces of both Wicklow and Kildare.[136] However, he had fled the county as early as February, fearful no doubt that he might be taken up in the arrests which were already taking place. According to Hardy, 'Mr Byrne of Ballymanus has fled, he has never publicly appeared since I stationed the sergeant's party under his nose at Aughrim ... The county is well rid of him. You see I was not mistaken in my information about him.'[137] Hardy had said that he had fled to England, but a magistrate informant in May, searching a house in Hacketstown whose occupants were suspected of treasonable correspondence with him, reported that 'Garrett Byrne is secreted in the house of a widow Caulfield at Booterstown.'[138] Later evidence from the same source suggests that a Major McDermott of the Irish Brigade 'was constantly with Garrett Byrne at Mrs Caulfield's in Booterstown.'[139]

King was already active in Avoca-side in January 1798, and several highly informative statements made by witnesses before him survive.[140] Others which do not survive were made as well, and the hearsay in them is obviously the basis for Hardy's statement in the same month that 'the men of opulence sworn against are a Mr Doyle, near relation of Sir Thomas Esmonde, and a Mr Morne of the county of Wexford near Gorey.'[141] These men are James Doyle and Mort Mernagh. Mernagh on Byrne's telling was an activist. Hardy in May was to report that with Esmonde 'the Doyles who are people of substance and connection .... have been the head of this cursed rebellion in the borders of the county Wexford, joining Wicklow.'[142] Indeed it was evidence collected in the Arklow district which provided the grounds for arresting Perry in Wexford.

Activists south of the Wicklow border like Nicholas Murphy and Mort Mernagh were reinforced by the support of Mathew Doyle in Wicklow who was a member of the McCabe circuit. On both sides of the county border the Doyle-Mernagh-Murphy axis seem to have represented an antithesis to a more moderate – or more ineffective – O'Neil-Perry axis. The Perry sector was the least well-organised part of the barony of Gorey, just as across the border Arklow barony, despite the efforts of Mathew Doyle, under the direction of O'Neil was the worst organised Wicklow barony. The inadequacy of O'Neil is strongly hinted at in 'the private information of A.B. sworn before Rev. Edward Bayly 'on 21 May, which threw doubts on the figure of 2,400 United Irishmen for Arklow barony given in the Wicklow United Irishman report of January: 'very few men enrolled in Arklow barony since the finding of the report of 22 January. (I) could not explain the figures in that report but believe there were not at that time above 200 pikes in Arklow barony.'[143]

'A.B'.'s information is the clearest we have on the growth of the organisation in south-east Wicklow. He has been identified by Ruan O'Donnell as Thomas Murray of Sheepwalk.[144] He had been sworn in in May 1797 by Garrett Graham, son of Richard Graham of Arklow. Thereafter 'A.B.' with Garrett Graham and Phil O'Neil formed societies of thirty-six men.[145] In October they were reorganised into groups of 12 men 'by order of one McCabe who acted by direction of the executive directory'. Indeed, this is the first firm dating of McCabe's appearance in the county, and appears to coincide with his activity in Wexford which is described in the Perry confession. In the context McCabe's work implies not civil organisation but the introduction of military organisation. McCabe must have simply sought to convert the civil structure directly into a military one. According to 'A.B.' the heads of sections (groups of 120) were simply 'latterly called captains'. This practice is in fact borne out by McNally, who had reported earlier in relation to the basic cell that the terms chairman and secretary were 'the fictitious terms for sergeant and corporal'.[146]

The timing of military organisation itself depended on the existence of prior civil organisation. At the lower levels the task of conversion proceeded smoothly. With the lower committees of the military structure in place, the real problem arose at the point when the colonels came to be elected: the question then was whether the colonels would be freely elected by the captains, or whether colonels with little real interest in military organisation would in effect be imposed on a barony. The problem was that military office was elective but that except in Kildare, military organisation had not been advanced enough for the posts to be filled in February in the regular quarterly elections to all offices. Yet with no elections due until May and with the pressing preparations in immediate prospect for an early rising, offices had to be created. That explains how offices were filled, without regular elections (or perhaps any election), in March or later: the divide can only have added to tensions. It also illustrates a different issue, but one which makes the conflict more intelligible. In Dublin the Leinster executive committee had broken down by May: *ad hoc* structures, not provided for in the constitution (which envisaged quarterly elections) had already been implemented, and in May, when elections became due, an attempt to regularise things brought rivalry between different interest groups into the open. Indeed in Dublin competing directories seem to have been elected in May.

In Wexford tension may have existed between the Perry-Colclough-Fitzgerald-Harvey interest, undistinguished in organising and interested more in radical politics, and the McCabe interest, which on the Wexford and Wicklow evidence was concerned with arming, i.e. turning the movement into an effective military structure. King later noted that McCabe 'has been often in every part of the county.'[147] In fact McCabe was present not only at county meetings in Wicklow but, as in Wexford, at other gatherings. Thus on the later information of a schoolmaster informer John Murphy of Knockrobbin 'a Mr McCabe from Belfast' was present at a meeting of the Newcastle baronial committee at Ballinalea on 8 November.[148] At that time, at least at baronial level the organisation was already far forward, and with a county meeting in prospect Richard O'Reilly of Newtownmount-kennedy had already written to Murphy to ascertain the number of United men in his district: he reported 160 of whom only 84 contributed financially. This was an interesting meeting because the attendance included William Michael Byrne of Drumban, gent, and also John Lynch of Roundwood who seems to have attended as a delegate from Ballinacor. The purpose was to elect baronial officers to the first county meeting. The date is significant, because it was in the wake of the new constitution of 27 August 1797, which raised the minimum number of baronial committees necessary for a county organisation from three to four. The fact that Wicklow (unlike Wexford) was anticipating county organisation, apparently without problems, emphasises the momentum of the movement in the county. Given the doubts we may entertain of the competence of William Michael Byrne and Richard O'Reilly, we may be tempted to attribute the success of arming the barony to McCabe: the fact that in a January report to the county executive, there was an admission of dissatisfaction in the barony of Newcastle in regard to the pace of arming is itself illuminating.

The county meeting followed hard on this gathering (and presumably similar ones in other baronies) 'in or about December'. There were delegates present from six baronies. This suggests both that Wicklow organisation, already well forward, became formal in December. By way of contrast Wexford reached this stage only in February. The first meeting of the county committee took place at John Loftus's at Annacurragh in December. Loftus according to King was a relation to O'Reilly and William Michael Byrne, 'a poor fellow and keeps a little whiskey house'.[149] The meeting reconvened the following Sunday in the Sun Inn in Dublin to complete the county organisation. Thus the structure was perfected not only in close association with Dublin representatives such as McCabe, but the first full meeting of the county organisation actually took place in Dublin.

It is possible from the detail of 'A.B'.'s testimony, combined with other evidence to reconstruct the composition of organisation at the time of the Annacurragh meeting with some confidence:

Rathdown	William Michael Byrne
	Thomas Miller[1]
Newcastle barony	Richard O'Rielly (sic)
	John Byrne[2]
Ballinacor	William Young
	John Lynch[3]
Talbotstown	Kavenagh, 'a yeoman in uniform'
	'a lame man'
Shillelagh	John Waters
	Garrett Byrne[4]

1. A. B. mentioned only 'an elderly man'. However, he also mentioned the election of a William Byrne to office for another barony. Recalling the meeting months later, confusion between two Byrnes (William Michael and John) is quite natural. Ruan O'Donnell suggests with evidence to support his claim that William Martin Byrne and Miller represented Rathdown (op. cit., p. 79).William Michael Byrne's seat – Park Hill, Glen of the Downs, the most northerly known location of any member of the county executive – makes the identification with the barony all the more plausible.
2. Both are identified in N.A., R.P. 620/38/188. 'A.B.' had given the name as William Byrne.
3. The second delegate is described as 'a young man with red whiskers'. As John Lynch is elsewhere described as a delegate from Ballinacor (N.A., R.P. 620/38/188), it seems likely that he was the whiskered man.
4. 'A.B.' said that he 'did not know the delegates from Shillelagh'. Another source suggests that John Waters was a delegate (N.A., R.P. 620/39/51). The fact that he was said to be 'the intimate friend' of Garrett Byrne may imply that Byrne was the second delegate. See also O'Donnell (op. cit., p. 80), drawing on the Ridgeway account of the trial of William Michael Byrne which suggests that a Byrne of Tinahely attended county meetings.

Arklow	John Lacey Phil O'Neal (sic)[5]

John Waters, according to later testimony in July 1798, gave information of the committee of 'delegates that were to sit at either 15 or 18 Francis Street in December, and that he was appointed grand secretary for the half barony of Shillelagh', but had never acted.[150] The information is a little garbled. First, it seems to be contradicted by 'A.B'.'s information which suggests that two Shillelagh delegates attended. Secondly and more importantly, it seems to imply that he was actually giving information as far back as December. The Wicklow authorities were in considerable ignorance about the real structure then and later, and the information in July really must arise from a much later deposition giving retrospective information reaching back to December. In other words it is quite manifest that there was no spy on the committee in the months following its inception.

John Lynch from near Roundwood in Ballinacor barony, William Michael Byrne (of Rathdown barony) and Richard O'Reilly, who became secretary for the barony of Newcastle, seem to have represented a small coterie, connected by blood or marriage, who were a driving force in seeking to perfect the organisation in Wicklow. The fact that, though they were from three different baronies, they were all present at the meeting to elect a baronial committee in Newcastle in November suggests as much.[151] Information from 'A.B.' in the following May brings out the importance of this trio. He said that William Michael Byrne and O'Reilly were nominated as the first representatives to the provincial meeting in December: in March we know, because they were arrested, that the delegates from Wicklow were William Michael Byrne and John Lynch whom 'A.B.' recognised to be later, 'a provincial committee man'. What is puzzling is that 'A.B'.'s information suggests that in the interval either O'Neil and Lacy on his own attended provincial meetings.[152] O'Neil's importance was somewhat inflated in public repute. Thus, while King represented O'Neil as having the repute of being the county treasurer, another source gave Lacy as holding this post.[153] Whatever the precise detail, if we add Lacy and O'Neil to the trio of William Michael Byrne, Richard O'Reilly and John Lynch, we seem to have a central force in creating the structures of county organisation as opposed to creating a real force on the ground.

5. 'A.B.' did not know what barony Lacy represented. However, as Lacy lived in Wicklow, he should have represented Arklow barony, NAI, SOC, 2nd. series, no. 3060, in pencil *c.*1796, said to be head treasurer).

A puzzling thing also is the vagueness about Garrett Byrne's position: 'A.B.' certainly could not later recall him by name; the lack of impact made at the time by the man who was later the military leader is striking. Despite his social position, he attained at this stage no prominence and no high office, considerations which suggest that subsequent to March he was imposed on the county as adjutant general.

The detail in the January return, which first came into the possession of the government because a copy of the paper had been dropped at Dunganstown on the road from Wicklow to Arklow, implies that either at the Sun Inn meeting or in its wake the Wicklow organisation had been further subdivided, by the creation of a second baronial committee, both in the Talbotstown and the Ballinacor baronies. This would reflect a growth in membership and a restructuring or 'splitting' into further baronial committees. Already in the January returns there were separate returns for Talbotstown and Lower Talbotstown and for Upper and Lower Ballinacor. In fact this seems to have been but the first stage in a larger reorganisation of the county. Wicklow's membership was as large as that of Carlow or Kildare, and would warrant subdivision of existing baronial structures to create further baronial committees. A later undated document gives Wicklow twelve colonels, which would put it on a par with Carlow and Kildare.[154] It is doubtful whether these extra posts had been filled in practice, though the bureaucratic task of re-organising and filling offices without elections in the difficult months from February to May can only have added to tensions within the organisation. This restructuring, if it took place, could conceivably account for the title of colonel attributed in some sources to Holt and to Mathew Doyle. It could also, as in Holt's case, arising from the lack of proper elections, account for the controversy that his assumption of the style certainly caused.

A disturbing hint of organisational weakness lies in the fact that Garrett Byrne himself remained a shadowy figure, in the background rather than an active organiser. Little less serious was the fact that, despite ambition and a local notoriety, the effectiveness of O'Neil is in doubt. He had not attended the meeting in December, and his barony must already have been lagging because, at the meeting in the Sun Inn, the barony of Arklow was singled out for comment: 'The organisation of Arklow barony was then recommended to be forwarded as soon as possible, and it did proceed rapidly.' A divide between moderates and radicals clearly existed in Arklow as 'A.B.' resigned – or so he claimed – his command soon after 22 January, 'being disgusted at the business getting into very low hands'. Such conflict was a major problem in Wicklow as the report of the county Wicklow committee on 22 January observed that 'your county committee again earnestly recommends it to their constituents to pay no attention to idle reports as they certainly know emissaries are encouraged to disseminate such news as may create distrust, disunite them and lead them astray.'[155] A cynic might also feel that the first arrests had prompted a rethink among the faint-hearted. 'A.B.' never acted in any official capacity afterwards, but still 'continued of the body and was made acquainted with the subsequent proceedings'. His evidence singled out the names of Lord Edward Fitzgerald and Arthur O'Connor – which suggests the source of contacts in Dublin – and also mentioned the circulation of the *Union Star* in the committees. It also identified the dominance of the radical view as 'A.B.' said it was 'understood that it was resolved that even if the French did not come it was intended to rise and risk everything to prevent the execution of Bond and the other prisoners in Dublin'. Colonels seem to have been appointed only in March, but one was not apparently appointed for Arklow, as according to 'A.B'.'s report O'Neil was still in expectation of becoming one. Given either election or, failing that, nomination of colonels in other baronies, protraction of a decision can only suggest an impasse at local level.

The forwardness of organisation in Kildare was evident in the fact that colonels existed in February, and six colonels were returned for the county in March. At this stage, despite problems such as the conflict in St Mullins barony in Carlow, or the initial reluctance of leaders to come forward in Wexford, the military organisation, already taking shape in the arming of the lower committees, began to acquire its formal leadership or colonelcies at baronial level. By the time of the rebellion, Morgan Kavanagh, after having had 'the entire managment at the last assizes of the concerns of the rebels prisoners' and, perhaps because of the prominence that that conferred, seems to have become a colonel in Carlow and 'was the person deputed from Dublin on the 23rd of May to order this county to rise'.[156] In Wicklow, on 'A.B'.'s authority, colonels were appointed in March. Garrett Byrne became one, and subsequently became adjutant general for the county. In this way his ascent is similar to that of Kavanagh in Carlow or O'Neil in Arklow. While Byrne was certainly suspected of deep involvement in the county's affairs, so obscure was his role at the top of the organisation that Hardy was taken by surprise by news of his actual position. In a letter on the eve of the rebellion to Castlereagh he observed, 'I have not been able to discover their leaders or chief but in one instance and on that subject I write privately to Mr Cooke.'[157] To Cooke he was more explicit, observing that 'I find the character I have often spoken to you of, Mr Garrett Byrne of Ballymanus deeply implicated', and he asked Cooke whether he had details of his location.[158] Wicklow entered the rebellion with a strong organisation on the ground, but an ineffective leadership at the top (although that hardly differentiated it from other counties, if we bear Fitzgerald of Newpark in Wexford, Kavanagh of Carlow or Simms of Antrim in mind).

XI. United Irishman numbers in Wicklow

Nonetheless organisation in Wicklow had spread apace. At its peak Wicklow had the largest numbers of United Irishmen of any county in Leinster. In proportion to population, it would have been much the same as Carlow or Kildare, and was on paper a formidable force. In an account of arrears due the strengths are set out in the late spring of 1798:[159]

Wicklow	14,000
Kildare	11,919
Carlow	11,300
Meath	11,110
Dublin City	8,396
Dublin County	7,412
Kilkenny	6,700
King's County	6,500
Westmeath	5,250

The figures mirror the basis for government concern with what was happening in the counties around Dublin. The January figures for Wicklow were 12,794 men, divided beween the various baronies as follows:[160]

Talbotstown	2,974
Lower Talbotstown	700
Arklow	2,400
Rathdown	1,200
Newcastle	1,800
Upper Ballinacor	1,800
Lower Ballinacor	840
Shillelagh	1,080
Total	12,794

Arms were listed for Talbotstown, Arklow, Rathdown and Newcastle, showing how, though the organisation had not yet proceeded to select its colonels, McCabe's work in 'arming' the lesser groups below the baronial committees was already advancing. Ignoring the doubtful return for Arklow, the largest returns were for Talbotstown (which included the highly politicised north-west Wicklow region), Upper Ballinacor (which included Roundwood, Laragh and Rathdrum) and Newcastle (which included Newtownmountkennedy, Glenealy and Wicklow). For Rathdown, Lower Talbotstown, Lower Ballinacor (which included Ballymanus, Aughrim and Tinahely) and Shillelagh, the returns were smaller. Though these baronies had smaller populations, the lower number of United Irishmen in Lower Ballinacor and Shillelagh may also reflect a relatively large protestant population: in these baronies, despite the liberal mantle of Fitzwilliam, many failed to support the United Irishmen. This region moreover was the bailiwick of Garrett Byrne; he sat on the Shillelagh committee but lived at Ballymanus in Lower Ballinacor. Whether organising weaknesses on the part of individual United Irishman leaders compounded other problems is hard to say. Newcastle on the other hand had a large number of United Irishmen, and apparently militant ones. The county committee was obliged to record that 'your committee hear with regret the dissatisfaction expressed by their brethren in the barony of Newcastle with respect to their not being as yet fully supplied with arms, and your committee assures them that every exertion in their power has been made to that purpose and that a number of pikes are now ready for delivery but would at the same time recommend to have as many as possible made in each barony'.[161] The largest concentration of United Irishmen in the county was probably in the region running from Roundwood in Upper Ballinacor to Newtownmountkennedy in Newcastle. That seems to explains also why the scarce new troops brought to the county in April 1798 were garrisoned in Newtown, and lost no time in launching the county's first reign of terror.

How numerous were protestants in the organisation? Given the liberal ethos of the county and its active politicking one would expect many, and in fact Hardy on the eve of rebellion distrusted all except for 'some few staunch protestants'.[162] Around Stratford-on-Slaney, loyalist suspicion fingered the presbyterians in the textile industry. Of the county's protestant United Irishmen, Holt is the best-known example; two brothers of his were also rebels.[163] More highly placed in the organisation was William Young, one of the representives for Lower Ballinacor, arrested in early 1798 on Cooper's evidence and rearrested near Tinahely in May. Some other protestants are identified by Luke Cullen.[164] Given the fact that up to one third of the population of the county was protestant, the impression is that they were not proportionately well-represented in the organisation. Tellingly, Kemmis, the state solicitor, having moved in late March 1798 from the Wicklow to the Wexford assizes, recorded that juries were more reliable in Wicklow than in Wexford.[165] The magistrate Rev. Edward Bayly related how the seven or eight protestants among the 200-300 fishermen at Arklow resisted being recruited into the organisation.[166] Of the members of the Wicklow county committee, Young seems to be the only protestant. Impressionistically, protestant membership was strongest in the lowlands of Upper Ballinacor barony, and in Newcastle and Rathdown Some twenty of Edward's yeomanry were catholic;[167] the number declining to take the test, a proof of radical or United sympathies was thirty-three. Nor was Edward's the sole recalcitrant corps. Members of Lord Meath's yeomanry also refused to take the oath.[168]

There are reasons why a divide existed or could deepen. Old sectarian tensions existed in the county. Buck Whaley's father's nickname of Burn-chapel points to something, although not necessarily an event quite as colourful as the shooting up of the image in Greenane chapel, related in the tradition collected by Cullen.[169] Protestant settlement was extensive on and under the eastern shoulder of the mountain ranges from Delgany and Enniskerry to Templetown (Roundwood) inland, and to Dunganstown near the coast. It was strong in pockets on the western slopes. Further afield, protestant settlement was large in Rathdrum, Arklow itself and around Tinahely and Carnew. In the southern districts, moreover, the memory of the illegal wresting of their lands from the Byrnes in the 1630s was still alive, as testified to in Miles Byrne's account; that memory could be fanned in time of crisis into still greater resentment on the catholic side and greater fear on the protestant side. The memory of the Byrne lands ran deepest in the liberal bailiwick of the Fitzwilliam estate, and thus created a gulf which loyalists could seek to widen: it was in this region that Hardy seems to have had his greatest confidence in protestant loyalty.[170]

XII. Political issues in 1798: spring assizes and yeomanry test

Carlow and Wicklow presented ample evidence of involvement in the United Irishmen by the early spring. In Carlow arrests went on apace in the wake of proclaiming the county in November and a stream of reports came into the Castle. Cornwall sent some men summarily to Duncannon in January without waiting until the assizes, as the jails were already full.[171] At the Carlow assizes in March, there were 170 men on trial, in addition to men sent either by legal process or summarily to Duncannon.[172] If the numbers sent to Duncannon, a stream which was already a subject of note on the route,[173] were added, the total arrests would be very sizeable indeed in comparison to other Leinster counties. In Wicklow arrests commenced at the beginning of the year, either mainly or even solely on the evidence of the informer Cooper, though Hardy from the outset had doubts about the value of his testimony.[174] Some Wicklow men were in jail in February in Carlow, and others were in jail in Wicklow town. According to the United Irishman county committee on 22 January, there were forty-five in jail: five from Arklow barony, eight from Shillelagh, fifteen from Ballinacor, fifteen from Talbotstown, two from Newcastle.[175] In fact the number held in Wicklow jail eventually rose to at least ninety. Writing on the second day of the assizes Hardy was in no doubt about the seriousness of the situation after conversation the preceding day with Kemmis: 'Cooper's evidence not being supported and his own character doubtful if not worse'. They expected that those whose arrest depended on Cooper's testimony would be enlarged.[176] Four of the defendants were acquitted at the outset, and the cases against the remaining eighty-six prisoners seem to have been quashed by direction of the liberal and larger-than-life Yelverton.[177]

The conduct of the assizes in Wicklow, and in Wexford where crown cases also collapsed, contrasted with the Maryborough and Carlow assizes presided over by Robert Day, an old confidant of Arthur Wolfe's, raised to the King's Bench as recently as January. Day's indulgence for the symbols of loyalty and laxity in regard to the behaviour of the court can be measured by the atmosphere of the Maryborough assizes, which were indicted by no less a figure than McNally.[178] Day's partiality can be measured in a reference in a letter of his on 21 March, days ahead of the Carlow assizes at which he was to preside, to 'a Jacobin attorney from Carlow noted for lying'.[179] The outcome in Carlow was more satisfactory from a government point of view than either Wicklow or Wexford: eleven were convicted capitally and seventy were bailed.[180]

The Wicklow assizes provided the occasion on their first day for twenty-eight magistrates unanimously calling for proclaiming of the county.[181] The news was reported to Cooke by Monck, chairman of the meeting. The political tone of the meeting is reflected, however, in the meeting's instruction to Monck, to wait on Edwards, 'the commanding officer of the Bray infantry and to tell him that as thirty-three of his men are strongly suspected of being United Irishmen, and will take no test to prove their innocence, they conceive it highly dangerous, in the present state of the country, to suffer persons of that description to retain his majety's arms and ammunition in their hands'.[182] Two issues almost simultaneously damaged the credibility and appearance of fairness of the loyalist party: collapse of the prosecution case at the assizes, and partisan insistence on dismissal from the yeomanry on mere suspicion of United Irishmen membership. An added partisan feature of the assizes was the fact that, despite acquittal, in their aftermath (on the authority of O'Neale Stratford) Hardy merited 'the thanks of the loyalists in the highest degree as he prevented the rascally batch of United men being turned loose "at the last assizes".'[183] Some or many must however either have been released later or have succeeded in securing their own release, as they were among rebels re-arrested close to the outset of the rebellion.

The question which loyalists harped on was the 'supiness' of magistrates, a phrase which became a catchcry on loyalist lips in 1797 and 1798. A theme which first appeared in this region in Kildare, it was repeated in Wicklow almost immediately, and it gathered pace in 1798. Loyal magistrates were contrasted with the disloyal and inactive. As early as January, Hardy praised 'two of the most active magistrates in that part of the country Mr King and Mr Hunter Gowan whose exertions to preserve peace is (sic) highly laudable.' He recommended a commission of the peace in Wicklow for Hunter Gowan in addition to his Wexford one to make his work more effective. At the same time he commented adversely on a magistrate Thomas Bolger of St Austin's who had admitted James Doyle and Mort Mernagh to bail, and requested that Bolger be deprived of his charge in Wexford as had already occurred in Wicklow.[184] As late as May, Hardy complained to Cooke that 'two or three of the temporising magistrates of this county are cramping my exertions here, by granting protections to people *without surrendering arms* (underlined in text). I have written to one of them to desist; if he does not I trust you will on my application prevent his acting.'[185]

At the same time the loyalist faction began to spread the belief that the yeomanry corps of their political opponents were disloyal. La Touche claimed in January that he had information that most of Isaac Cornock's Scarawalsh corps were United, and 'positive proof' against several members of Knox Grogan's Castletown corps. Both corps were commanded by highly liberal gentlemen on the Wexford side of the county border. This news, communicated by Hardy to Cooke on 19 January, was the first salvo in the campaign against catholics in the yeomanry.[186] By mid-February the corps of Jervis White, a Fitzwilliamite gentleman near Carnew, had been disbanded.[187] Though Peter La Touche was not high sheriff, he was a central figure in these events. He and Cooke had entered into correspondence as far back as January.[188] He presided at the secret session of the peace in Wicklow (presumably the secret committee for getting information, set up by the grand jury) at which the nineteen magistrates present recommended disarming the Castlemacadam cavalry and Ballymurtagh infantry, 'as being almost entirely composed of seditious and disaffected persons, and as being in general unattended by their officers'.[189] This meeting, presided over by

La Touche, seems one of the fruits of the channels of communication with Cooke opened up by La Touche in January: the government was being kept closely informed of what was afoot. The letter from La Touche intimated that publication of the oath and of the lists of corps which had taken it would be deferred until the decision of the government was made known. Musgrave asserts that the oath was devised by the officers of a number of corps in Wicklow, Dublin and Wexford, and published in the *Dublin Journal*. He also seems to suggest that the oath originated with King.[190] The fact that Billy Byrne was removed from the Wicklow yeomanry is a comment on the local politics of Rathdrum and the continued deterioration of the relations between King and the Byrnes in the spring of 1798. The oath itself was very much a political act directed against the corps of the liberal gentry. It was strongly resisted, and some of the corps never administered it. It is significant that Byrne applied to Hume for admission to his corps, and Hume's reply, while perhaps a diplomatic reason for refusal – that his corps was full –[191] implies that the oath was not for Hume an issue, a fact which other evidence confirms. Edwards, whose later pamphlet touched on Wicklow issues, was probably the spokesman for the liberal magistrates, and he may have been singled out at the meeting on 19 March for that reason. He was already the most articulate – or at any rate the most epistolary – of the liberal magistrates, and was later to write a pamphlet – now lost – on Wicklow events.

As far as the test was concerned, Edwards' correspondence opened in early March. He professed not to be opposed to it, and took it himself. But to his surprise – or so he claimed at any rate – he found that his corps were divided on it. Edwards and seventeen took the test; thirty-three with the second lieutenant, Litton, refused to take it. He claimed that 'to dismiss these men, for refusing to take an oath *not prescribed by law* (underlined in text), is, as I conceive it, not in my power, although some have exercised that authority.'[192] He was still hopeful in late March that the matter would be solved 'without reprobation or making enemies of the men'.[193] By April he was pleased with the outcome or compromise in which the men took the test as individuals, and he was confident that 'with a little management' every thing would go well.[194] Taking the test as individuals meant that the oath was administered to each man in private. This signified of course that Edwards, in avoiding a collective public ceremony, was making a concession to his men who had said that they would take it only on formal demand by government (which it in turn could not do as it did not have statutory authority to make such a demand). Moreover, in taking this conciliatory approach, he was publicly holding out against his political enemies. However, whatever his political delicacy, Edwards was no fool, and when the situation reached crisis point he excluded thirty from his company, 'not from any proof of guilt, but having at first refused the test, I was doubtful of their sincerity, and thought it a step however severe, yet due to the necessity of the times'.[195] More than the test divided Edwards from his fellow-magistrates. He had maintained to Hardy, that contrary to the decision of the magistrates on the preceding day, the stationing of troops in the Bray district was unnecessary. Hardy was quite dismissive of him, claiming that 'the man who shuts himself up in a cloister can not be a judge, particularly a man who imagines such terror from the appearance of the military'.[196] The liberals had never been inactive in support of law and order; they were mindful of legality. When Hardy was appointed, Wainwright, Fitzwilliam's agent, co-operated closely with him, and Edwards, though aware of allegations of the army having run amock in Aughrim, actually extolled Hardy's 'unremitting exertions, *tempered by the principle of justice* (underlined in text)'.[197] Hume was likewise foreman of the grand jury in March when it sought to protect Cooper's security and to provide for him.

The issue of the yeomany test was political, in essence an attack both on the moderate magistrates and on the presence of catholic yeomen. Hume and Saunders, both of whom held out against the oath, were an object of persistent attack. A letter in May from the Rev. Christopher Robinson in Baltinglass to Cooke went so far as to ask 'if he ever heard that Mr Saunders was sworn an United Irishman by Mr Maxwell of Stratford-on-Slaney near twelve months ago'. He had declared that 'I hear this morning that 6 men of Mr Saunders' yeomen are discovered of to have conspired some time back to assassinate him; he need have expected no better faith from the villains that he enrolled; it is terrible to think how he temporises and cringes to those rebels, and (to) the priest the *blessed chaplain of his whole* corps except (for) 3 or 4' (italics are Robinson's). This letter seems to imply both that nearly all Saunders' men were catholic and that catholics were *ipso facto* disloyal. As well as attacking Travers, Hume came in for hostile comment in this venemous missive: 'Mr Hume of Humewood (tho' his corps of yeomen are most of them loyal good men) is himself wonderfully prone to liberate and exculpate the men concerned in this bloody confederacy; it is most scandalous and weak of country gentlemen, if they exert themselves in this manner through a motive of gaining such filthy popularity; but if it be in consequence of their political creed bearing a similar tincture, they ought to sink in eternal dishonour.'[198]

In an earlier letter Robinson had already excoriated 'noblemen, and gentlemen who wished to make themselves appear of consequence in the eye of government, to muster up a set of poisoned papists in their corps'.[199] It remained to set in motion a campaign against those gentlemen who had held out against the test. Saunders and his corps were in the eye of the storm, both because his corps was largely catholic in its composition and because Saunders was a less formidable target than the powerful figure of Hume. Stratford confronted Saunders' corps and his servants on a number of occasions in the course of May: despite Stratford's efforts, 'he has not as yet satisfied me: the worst are still in his house.' Stratford went on to describe a stormy confrontation with the local priest, Travers, an object of deep distrust by both Robinson and O'Neale Stratford. Stratford was proud of his information 'and in every instance it has turned out the best in this country'. He asserted that 'nothing but coercion will bring them forth. I have informed Major Hardy to no purpose, and had he agreed or I had the power I would have made the earth ere this vomit up its hidden pikes.'[200]

The campaign thus centred on the Aldborough faction. One of Robinson's letters even included a detailed map of the victims of arms raids in Baltinglass parish.[201] Robinson had an acute sense of being beleaguered: he believed with some justification that the parish 'exceeded any other parish in that county in its number of United Irishmen'. To add to his mortification, the district's gentry and near-gentry figures alike – Saunders, Walter Carroll the high sheriff, Harrington, and Harrington's relatives James and Harrington Wall – were all liberal in their politics. Moreover, they lived in his immediate vicinity, and perhaps his paranoia explains why they are all noted on his map. Robinson was anxious not to have his letters to the Castle left around, and warned Cooke to be 'so good never to let one line of my writing go to the commander-in-chief's office, or anywhere but from your own hand to the fire'.[202] Far from going to the fire, the methodical Cooke kept the letters, though he took care to cut out Robinson's name. We can identify Robinson from the accident of a letter of Robinson's having been forwarded by Aldborough to the lord lieutenant.[203] When it passed down, the usually attentive Cooke did not remove the name. In all no less than seven letters survive from Robinson in May and early June. As long as Camden set the tone in the Castle, Robinson could apparently count on a friendly audience. Thereafter, under a Cornwallis openly contemptuous of advanced loyalists, there was no further scope for his letter writing. Indeed he was reduced to writing a real anonymous letter from 'a county Kildare farmer', and Cooke duly filed it away without breaking confidence, endorsing it as an 'anonymous letter as to the state of Kildare'.[204]

Robinson's letter of 14 May was the most detailed of his communications and the most politically revealing. He and O'Neale Stratford were working closely together in collecting arms from United Irishmen who were suitably frightened by the oppression afoot in neighbouring Kildare into surrendering them. He described negotiations for a protection for 'about 100 men with their democratic landlord and neighbour Mr Henry Harrington of Grangecon', adding that 'if the leaders and instigators of this accursed murderous conspiracy are not now fully made known of, it must be the fault of the magistracy.' He commented in particular on two other men, James Wall of Knockrigs as well as his brother Harrington Wall and advised that in no circumstance should they be given the commission of the peace: 'their principles are too well known and felt in this neighbourhood.' Here again the political context came in: 'I fear our high sheriff Mr Carroll is too much infected with the whiggishness of his uncle Bagnell, and the liberty and equality of his cousin Keatinge.' Harrington of Grangecon was criticised for granting protections without discriminating between the innocent and the guilty. His worse venom however was reserved for Saunders:

> It is shameful to see how Mr Saunders of Saundersgrove still labours to nurture and screen that hellish group of republican assassins, the heads and leaders of Stratford-on-Slaney; it is also unpardonable how he connived at and cherished them, and those of his own corps and every other description of rebel, since the first outset of this abominable system; and how he and William Travers the parish priest of Baltinglass, with them fiery jacobins of Stratford-on-Slaney, humbugged, browbeat, and cajoled by turn the inhabitants of their own neighbourhood and one another into a motly but inveterate union of arms, bloodshed and anarchy.

He launched also into an attack on William Hume: 'I wish Mr William Hume of Humewood was (sic) properly cautioned for screening the disaffected of his own neighbourhood. I think it should be insisted on that everyone who do (sic) not give arms, should give *information* who are their treasurers, secretaries, captains etc.' Even Captain Stratford, 'pretty loyal but ... vain and wavering in such a good and great cause', was not quite good enough for this loyalist, and Captain Ryves was condemned because 'in examining a man to get information he sticks too much to the quibbles of courts of law, and forgets the now necessary roughness of the soldier.'[205]

Not having being dismissed by their commander from their corps, several of Saunders' men were jailed in Dunlavin on uniting charges which had been pressed against them. The arrest of Dunn, a corporal in the unit, on 21 May resulted in information against other members and their detention on 22 May in Dunlavin.[206] They were there when the rebellion broke out on the night of 23 May, and they were massacred in cold blood the following morning. While further south a saga of jail massacre repeated itself on 25 May in Carnew, the local circumstances of the preceding weeks made the Dunlavin event particularly chilling. Even in the aftermath of defeat of the rebels on the Kildare borders, loyalist impatience with the liberal outlook of Saunders and Hume knew no bounds: 'it is therefore much to be wished for in that quarter that Morley Saunders Esqr would entirely desist from interfering so incessantly with the other magistrates in favour of rebels or from inrolling such men in place of those of his corps of yeomen that were shot for traison (sic) or from embodying a multitude of the men of Stratford-on-Slaney whom he must know were *United Irishmen*, or that William Hume Esqr would not exert himself so earnestly in favour of such men; or seem to draw no distinction between the protestant and the papist.'[207]

XIII. The rise of the Orange Order

The growth of a government interest in Wicklow in the spring of 1798 was seen in two forces which were closely intertwined: the spread of the Orange Order, and the emergence of a committed magistrate group who actively endorsed firmer methods in support of government. Hardy was the lynchpin of the group in Wicklow, where higher gentry opinion at large was hostile to the government. Appointed commanding officer in Wicklow around October 1797, in the following month he obtained the commission of the peace not only for Wicklow but for Wexford, Carlow and Kildare as well.[208] The essential vehicle for this work was the secret committee of magistrates for receiving confidential information, dominated by Peter La Touche. With Hardy's support, it had acquired an entrenched position by March when the new Whig high sheriff took up office. As Robinson's letter above hinted, Carroll was related to Bagnel in Carlow, a determined opponent of the ruling faction in that county, and to Colonel Keatinge of Narraghmore in Kildare. Keatinge too was liberal and in June 1798 his yeomanry corps was damned as 'a corps unworthy of existence'.[209] Either by process of exclusion or by his own disinclination on Fitzwilliamite principles to participate (shades of Crosbie in Carlow perhaps), Carroll seems to have played no part in the security events as their pace accelerated from March.

The magistrate committee was a vehicle for running a security policy that was not that of the gentry at large. From the outset Hardy and Cooke corresponded regularly, and one letter, which refers to repeated conversations on a particular subject, implies that they were also in frequent personal contact. In January Cooke mentioned as a matter of course 'some additional information from Major Hardy which I daily expect'.[210] In February Hardy's declared concern in a letter to the Castle was: 'to carry both your wishes and the commander in chief's into effect': in other words he had a dual political and military brief.[211] He was already disbursing government money for the 'subsistence of informers etc.' He established communication with both Hunter Gowan and King by January. Later he had particular praise for Shillelagh which had a small group of activists 'who have not only preserved the peace of their own district but have on all occasions showed the laudable spirit of protecting their neighbours even at considerable distance from all assailants'.[212] He travelled widely and repeatedly across the county; on 3 May he was in Dunlavin in conjunction with William King (not to be confused with Thomas King) and Stratford at the outset of the confrontation with Saunders and the priest William Travers.[213]

Cooke not only played a vital role in setting up policy for the region but may have had a part in setting up Orange lodges there. The order may have begun in Carlow with Colonel Rochfort in January: one of the early rumours related not to Orangemen in general as they usually did but specifically to 'the Orange protestants of Carlow'.[214] Nor was the establishment of the Orange Order an isolated phenomenon of south Leinster. George Holdcroft, postmaster at Kells, a regular correspondent of John Lees – and the fact that the letter is addressed to Lees is itself significant – noted on 6 February, when the Order was beginning in county Meath that 'the Orange associations formed and forming in different parts of the kingdom give great uneasiness to the seditionists.'[215] Three lodges were set up in Meath.[216] The Order spread rapidly and by May there were ten lodges in Carlow, three in Wicklow and one in Wexford[217] (though one of the Carlow lodges was in the hands of the Derensy family who held property in Wexford and the commission of the peace in Wicklow). Elliott in June indicated his awareness of the key role of Lieut-Colonel J.S. Rochfort, one of Cooke's correspondents, in setting up the order there. In fact all three of Cooke's Carlow correspondents, John Staunton Rochfort, Robert Rochfort and Robert Cornwall, as well as Patrick Duigenan, Cooke's fellow MP for the episcopal borough of Leighlinbridge, became members of the Order that spring.

The Rochforts had links with the Keatings of Millicent (not to be confused with Colonel Keatinge); and the Montgomerys, another family which provided an early member of the Orange Order, had ties with the Faulkners at Castletown in Carlow (who incidentally were also agents for Ogle's estates). Members of the Keating and Montgomery families became members of lodge 176 in Dublin, and in turn a number of gentry in the region, Cornwall, John Staunton Rochfort, Robert Burton and Benjamin O'Neale Stratford became members of the same lodge, at various dates from February onwards, introduced for the most part by the two Kildare members of the lodge. The pressure or at least a patronising readiness to make decisions for others, was evident in the case of Henry Faulkner of Castletown, who was in the rather special and vulnerable position of being estate agent for Ogle: he was nominated a member of Lodge 176, but quickly resigned. The first meeting of the grand lodges of Ireland in Dublin on 9 April coincided with these events, and Robert Rochefort and Hunter Gowan were present.[218] Two other grand masters, captain William Blacker of Armagh and John Maxwell Barry of Cavan, had interests in north-west Wexford as well (Blacker certainly visited Wexford in person in the spring of 1798, and Maxwell Barry with some absurdity had run as a candidate supposedly sympathetic to catholics and political reform in the 1797 election). With their estate interests in the region they may well, Blacker in particular, have played a part in setting up the Order in the county. In other words it was well-established, even though it was only in April with the arrival of the North Cork militia and its flamboyant Orangeman colonel (and longstanding friend of Ogle, a frequent visitor to the King house in Henrietta Street) that it made its public appearance in Enniscorthy. The regiment had its own lodge. In April there was reputedly only one Orangemen in Enniscorthy; their number began to grow in the aftermath of Kingsborough's regiment arriving, though probably more as coincidence than as direct cause. The emergence of the Order in the region was a phenomenon of a particular group located on or close to the overlapping borders of Carlow, Wexford, and Wicklow. In addition to Kildare the Order also made its appearance in King's County politics. The True Blues, evident in Birr as well as in Carnew seem to have been an Orange manifestation: in Birr they were in conflict with Sir Laurence Parsons. In Queen's County in the spring assizes the extent of Orange symbols shocked McNally.

The spreading nature of the movement, and participation beyond gentry figures in it, is evident from the only letter relating to the Order in Kildare: a letter bearing the initials only of its four signatories from Naas and addressed to Willam Kane Blackwood: 'Our society in Naas is very strong. We meet at Connel's in Naas twice a week. We have a great many of the militia in our society. The last night we met at your house there was great talk of it in Naas a few days after.' Blackwood seems to have founded a society elsewhere as the authors wrote that 'I(sic) hope your society is getting strong as the day will soon come that we will get the better of our ends of the papist rascils (sic).' The letter also seems to imply a society at Edenderry. Blackwood got himself sworn as an United Irishman: 'the last letter we got from you we sent to Dublin: they approved how you are acting.'[219] The letter is endorsed with the name of John Atkinson, presumably 'our brother Orange Atkinson the shopkeeper in Naas', and a statement that it had been 'found in the drawing room of John Hart 27 March 1798'. What this means is that it had been intercepted by the United Irishmen, and ended up among the papers of the United Irishman John Hart whose house in 18 French Street in Dublin had been raided in late March. The suspicions of the authorities had first been drawn to Hart, when King arrested Richard O'Reilly near Rathdrum. Assured by King that a letter to someone in Dublin would be delivered 'safely from any examination', he had written to Hart. The letter itself passed into Cooke's papers, and Hart's house was raided.[220]

O'Neale Stratford must be suspected of playing a role in the spread of the Order into Wicklow. He already had close links with both Kildare and with the Rochforts, and it is hardly surprising that he became a member of Lodge 176. The three early lodges (Tinahely, Carnew, Coolkenna) in Wicklow were all on the Fitzwilliam estate, representing a challenge to the noble earl, to his agent and the moderate gentry. They probably are represented also in Tinahely in the 'society called the True Blues under the direction of the magistrate here (which) are night and day at work guarding and bringing in prisoners.'[221] Hunter Gowan's prominence in the movement was evident by April; and he was far from being the sole Orangeman in Wexford. The small local gentleman magistrate, John James, resident at Ballycrystal between the border village of Clonegal and Bunclody, who wrote with alarm in April, was probably an adherent.[222] A William James, who had already been in touch with Cooke with news, having looked over 'some memorandums from the county of Wexford', wrote again at the end of March.[223]

XIV. Intelligence activities

One of the problems of the security forces was an awareness that they were not penetrating radical circles as fully as they wished. That explained the interest by the Orange Order in the radical county of Kildare. Kane Blackwood was told that 'you are the only man in that county that we can depend upon to give us all the intelligence', and he had himself accepted as an United Irishman. The same problem accounted for the employment of John Henry Smith in Wicklow. Smith was an Englishman who had originally come to Belfast in September 1795. He had become a frequenter of the United Irishmen circle in Belfast. In financial difficulty, resentful of their not supporting him in his need, and of their suspicions which he temporarily dispelled, he offered his services as an informer. His cover blown in August 1796 – he found the United Irishmen 'jealous of strangers' – he fled to Liverpool. Needing money and proposing new schemes, he unfolded to Cooke 'designs of importance which I will explain when I have the honour of seeing you ... and which I am willing to run the hazard of executing if you'd condescend to support me in it'.[224] His attraction for Cooke was that he had close ties with the United Irishmen in the immediate aftermath of their reorganisation in May 1795 and when they had put an emphasis on cementing their links with the Defenders. Smith even provided a remarkable series of vignettes of the leading Belfast United Irishmen, and summaries of their new structures at the very moment when the government was still uncertain of what was afoot and of the extent and success of their Defender relationships. Cooke was haunted by the Defender threat. Smith was the only informant at the centre of things at the very moment when these issues were central to Cooke's preoccupations, and to the government's, in the critical month of August 1796. The fact that the correspondence has survived in the Frazer papers means that it had been referred to Kemmis for action, and that it may well have been the decisive factor in overcoming hesitations within the Castle, and thus led to the key northern arrests in September 1796.

It seems that Cooke hoped that, having been so much at the centre of things in Belfast, Smith might perform similar services in Kildare and Wicklow. While the Belfast correspondence with Cooke survives in the Frazer letters (because Cooke passed it over to Kemmis), all that survives of Smith's later role is three letters in the Rebellion and State of the Country Papers. It was harder for an outsider to pass himself off as a confirmed radical in rural Ireland than as a textile businessman in commercial Belfast. He was dieted and lodged in Dublin from 9 September to 23 November. His Wicklow/Kildare services began subsequently, and some bills were settled apparently retrospectively like the £9.2.0 to William Patrickson 'for diet, lodging etc in the county of Wickow for Smith and wife, 4 weeks', and £14.4.4½ to Ben Eves of Blessington, for what he advanced to 'Johnston, alias Smith'.[225] While in mid-May, prepared to continue 'under a more extensive service if you dare upon confidence in me than any other man here can do', he engaged 'to trace out every step they take', four months later he was in alarm. He had been identified, he was said to be a spy, and was writing for money and wanted to leave.[226] A somewhat boastful tone, a need for money, and the suspicions he prompted repeated an identical pattern to that of 1795-6 in Belfast. The fact that Smith's cover was blown within four months and that the letter to Kane Blackwood ended up in the house of a United Irishman raided in Dublin shows how efforts to penetrate the union had themselves a high failure rate.

XV. Free quarters and law and order

Abercromby's famous critique of law-and-order methods and his emphasis on centralising his forces for military purposes rather than for local security represented a challenge to a growing mood among loyalists who wanted sterner methods. Later defence of free quarters claimed that they were not oppressive, and that their weight fell only on the better off. The real issue, however, was not free quarters, politically notorious though the issue was, but the effort to disperse the military so that they would be available to support strong-handed measures at local level. These measures were themselves debatable, quite apart even from the central legal issues of the extent of proof required to justify action and the degree of magistrate supervision. The mood corresponded to the new prominence of the Orange Order in Leinster in February, and which became even more marked in and after the holding of the assizes in the second half of March. The new mood, tolerated by the egregious Judge Day, was most dramatically perceived in the Maryborough assizes, at which Orange colours and symbols were flaunted. New-style methods were confirmed in the order of 30 March, and heralded a new, ruthless and, in counties with suspect magistrates, an army-officer directed drive. Abercromby himself, in preparing the detail of putting free quarters by the military into effect, was not initiating policy: the arrangements which he had to superintend clashed with his earlier perception of the proper use of manpower, and ran counter to his military conception of the use of troops. It was a case of a military man having to bow to civil power, and of civil power in turn being in the hands of a group who wanted to impose stern methods on the countryside. The emphasis on free quarters was primarily political, because it meant that the forces were dispersed rather than concentrated. The underlying issue was less free quarters (and significantly many loyalist gentry themselves opposed the implementation of free quarters), than the methods which a *dispersed* military would pursue in execution of ends chosen for them by civil authority.

Such methods were already foreshadowed at an earlier date (February) in Carlow in three episodes involving a half hanging and the burning of two houses, in which three local gentry, Cornwall, Butler (probably Cornwall's yeomanry lieutenant) and Kavanagh were implicated. Nine affidavits were collected in Carlow to open the case in these proceedings, and it must have been of some consequence in Dublin for McNally, privy to the small-talk of Dublin United Irishmen, to be aware of and report it.[227] After 30 March such methods became more general. The politically most notorious instance was in Tipperary, where they were conducted under the supervision of the high sheriff Judkin Fitzgerald. Fitzgerald was rabidly anti-catholic. As brother-in-law to John La Touche,[228] he was in the ambivalent La Touche circle with the growing government identification of its members. His language was colourful and absurd; his reports exaggerated. His eccentricity was evident early on, as for instance in a proclamation dated 20 April calling on all who had left their homes to return within forty-eight hours.[229] Munster was claimed with some imagination to have been quieted by General Duff with the help of the high sheriff of Tipperary and 'some necessary severity, timely though sparingly applied'.[230] Anxiety to secure a baronetage was also a motive of his actions, and helps to account for their continuance even when active rebellion was at an end and when they no longer served a military purpose. Fitzgerald was already a political embarrassment even within the county. However, when his methods became a subject of legal attack, his defence was to exaggerate the scale of the threat and even of his actions. What would have been impossible to defend as isolated actions were more easily defended as measures which, given the extent of the threat, were themselves on the scale of acts of war. The case against Fitzgerald in 1799, which absorbed much public attention, was backed by the radicals as part of the campaign against the anti-Cornwallis reactionaries in Irish political circles. For that very reason Fitzgerald had to be defended on Lord Denning-like principles of warding off perspectives of the failure of justice which were too awful to contemplate.

Before the outbreak of rebellion the key areas for the new methods were Kildare and Wicklow where the authorities held the easy-going magistrates in contempt, and where in contrast to Carlow or Tipperary the methods were in the main pursued, not by local gentry (as in the case of Judkin Fitzgerald), but by military men with no local ties at all. The steps were also coloured by desperation because it was clear in April that the authorities had not really penetrated the United Irishman cells. Immediately after the arrival of the Ancient Britons in April Edwards had occasion to complain of events at Newtownmountkennedy:

> We never have had here the smallest appearance of disturbance, nor are we likely to have the least ... I deprecate dragooning such people. It is a bad system except in open rebellion. Those already enemies to government it exasperates. Of those who are wavering and timid it makes decided enemies and it tends to disaffect the loyal. Where is the man whose blood will not boil with revenge

> who sees the petticoat of his wife or sister cut off her back by the sabre of the dragoon, merely for the crime of being green, a colour certainly with them innocent of disaffection.

With his eighteen years experience as a magistrate and Volunteer officer, Edwards wished to have responsibility for the preservation of peace in Bray district entrusted to him: 'I should not promise the trophies of burned houses etc.' He wanted no military in Bray, and warned that 'should this military power not be repressed, I and my corps are ready to lay down our arms, and in such case I cannot but think it most advisable for us so to do.'[231] While mildly worded, the demand for the supervision of the Bray district was in effect throwing down the gauntlet in front of Hardy. Hardy's response was bound to follow and to be ruthless.

On Sunday 13 May Hardy issued orders for arms to be surrendered in twenty-four hours.[232] This was not a general order in the county, and it was issued moreover by an officer who was very clearsighted. It was the final stage in a power struggle in Bray intended to isolate and defeat Edwards. Edwards' protest predictably followed immediately, 'when I find that in other places a week or ten days has been allowed from the first coercion of the military.' As a result his attempts were nullified, he claimed, to get arms surrendered in a United Irishman stronghold on the Long Hill on the Monck estate, where the United men preferred, he asserted, to surrender to him rather than to the other magistrates. On Monday orders were issued to recommence arms searches on Wednesday 'with increased assiduities and where necessary with rigid severity'. Edwards' mood can be detected in his declaration that 'it is certainly true that we have not yet burnt houses nor strangled their owners, as not withstanding all my pains I had not been able to get informations to authorise me to such proceedings'.[233] It had added point because it was Hardy himself, not Hugo, who later sanctioned the burning of Holt's house.[234]

Edwards was now subject to a captain and the lieutenants of the King's County militia,[235] and was even superceded in his duties as magistrate by Capt. Armstrong. John Beaumann, a liberal Wexford magistrate to whom Edwards had given a pass over Bray bridge, was turned back by a lieutenant; Edwards was prevented from speaking to him and could not get redress from Captain Armstrong, 'and this in the most public manner'.[236] He seems to have been restored to the exercise of his functions by Lord Cornwallis, and his letters are full of sentiments of the need for reconciliation.[237] His comments about Charlemont in one of his letters are interesting: 'it delights my very soul to find dear and valuable friend Lord Charlemont in his (Cornwallis's) intimacy with sentiments similar to his own, through whom I hope to possess some share of attention from an administrator so cordial to my feelings as a man and a soldier.'[238] It is likely that his pamphlet was written at some time in the months following these events, pursuing the liberal line of support for the Cornwallis administration that animated personages as varied and as far apart as Gordon and Alexander in Wexford and Stock in Mayo.

The contrast between Carlow and other counties – Tipperary, Kilkenny, Wexford, Wicklow and Kildare – was that the leading body of gentry magistrates in Carlow were in agreement on stern methods. While the February irregularities were probably untypical at the time, magistrates were active in arresting people in large numbers. Rochfort's smug comparison of Carlow magistrates with those in surrounding counties simply reflected the readiness to proclaim the entire county and to arrest large numbers of suspects.[239] The legal basis for the arrests was probably slight: the apparent success of the magistrates was based less on the quality of their information than on the fact that as the only county in the region which was proclaimed in its entirely at an early date, the light burden of proof resting on determined magistrates meant that they could effect at will a policy of almost indiscriminate arrests. Indeed, despite the number of arrests, they had not by any means swept up all the leaders even in late spring, and from the tone of letters from Carlow in May and later it is clear that Cornwall and Rochfort were not aware of the full dimensions of the movement and of the identity of many of the leaders until May; the important arrests were made only in that month. However, with a proclaimed county and an active magistracy, fear was evident by late spring among the Carlow United Irishmen. Farrell's account was simply an effort written in later years and intended for publication, to justify his abandonment of the men whom he as a captain had helped to bring together.[240] Farrell's fear was evident enough. In his effort to make light of the movement his account blatantly ignored the anti-catholic feeling and the political tensions in Carlow, and represented participation in the United Irishmen as a lighthearted activity which people did not take seriously.[241] Only in May did a real breakthrough in information take place. With the help of a schoolmaster informer, Cornwall reported that there were 'now in custody a captain, a secretary, a treasurer, three sergeants and nine others of the chief promoters of rebellion in this neighbourhood'.[242] More important still was the confession, apparently in May, of John Kelly, a land surveyor 'in consequence of which we were able to come at all the heads, and more than twenty leaders were brought to punishment through his means.'[243]

There were no free quarters in Carlow,[244] and neither is there evidence of them in Wicklow. It is possible of course that they were resorted to unofficially, as in Wexford by the Camolin yeoman cavalry.[245] However, there is no evidence of this, and O'Neale Stratford also testifies to their absence as late as May. In Kildare on the other hand they were a prominent feature of military action, intended more to harass the property of prominent radicals such as Lord Edward Fitzgerald, Thomas Reynolds who had leased Kilkea Castle from Lord Edward and Thomas Fitzgerald of Geraldine (reputed in at least one confession to be a United leader in the county) than as a coherent intelligence measure. As early as 2 May a Monasterevin miller sought protection for his premises, adding that 'I should not be so troublesome but it is on Lord Edward Fitzgerald's estate which is said will be laid waste'.[246] Thomas Fitzgerald of Geraldine paid dearly for his radical reputation by having officers with 100 cavalry and forty horses living at free quarters on his property for twenty-four days.[247] In Fitzgerald's case, seditious papers, uncovered in the course of the occupation, provided the grounds for arresting him. The prospect of getting hands on his papers, was in the view of Colin Campbell, the value of the free quarters.[248] Stratford like Campbell regarded free quarters as useful, but may have been simply parroting Campbell's opinion.[249] In fact they were an expensive and inefficient method of uncovering proof, and a tough and hardworking officer like Hardy significantly did not work for their introduction in Wicklow.[250] In any event, there is no evidence that they afforded information on the membership of the conspiracy, or on its subordinate leaders and rank and file.

From widespread and indiscriminate resort to house burning and more directly from flogging came the sudden flow of information in the course of May. Given liberal magistrates and yeomanry units – in contrast to Carlow with its activist magistrates and zealous yeoman commanders – action by way of house burning or flogging necessarily depended in Kildare and Wicklow on the army and militia. The methods as followed in Kildare were a direct, logical and intended outcome of the loyalist victory over Abercromby. In Kildare the real point of the campaign was less free quarters, than unrestrained methods of terror enjoying an official tolerance amounting to sanction or connivance. Their premeditated and co-ordinated nature can also be detected in their introduction at the same time in Wicklow and Kildare.

In Kildare, there were accounts of discontent among the militia men even as early as 27 April over these methods.[251] With its well-connected liberal establishment, there was powerful opposition in Kildare to these excesses as well. In mid-May, 'complaints were to have been urged by men of influence against Captain Erskine and Cornet Love of the the 9th Dragoons, for their exertions ... at Ballitore, and the *rebelly* petitioners hoped to have them broke'.[252] Very precise confessions now began to appear.[253] The discoveries made by a smith, William Brennan and his apprentice in Kildare caused alarm in Baltinglass and many fled.[254] The evidence and the alarm it caused in turn then provided the justification for increased frenzy in action as the campaign wore on. According to one loyalist, Cornet Love's 'temper and manner is peculiarly adapted to make a successful impression on the hardened feelings of these barbarous rebels'.[255] Colonel Colin Campbell reported on 14 May his success after burning 'a few' houses in Athy and neighbourhood 'together with a little military discipline'.[256] Even an officer of as high rank as General Dundas was witness in the four days to 16 May to 'many very affecting scenes'. He complacently assured Cooke that 'the head of the hydra is off, and the county of Kildare will, for a long while, enjoy profound peace and quiet'.[257]

The distinguishing feature of Kildare and Wicklow was the use of the army rather than reliance on the machinery of justice in the hands of magistrates. In Wicklow the first intimation of force came from the behaviour of troops at Aughrim in January when the actions of the soldiery were so 'terrible as to drive the people to desperation and some (actions) lately done in that neighbourhood were named to me'.[258] However, as that evidence rests in a complaint by a liberal, at the time satisfied with Hardy himself, the pattern in Wicklow – similar to that of Kildare in the exercise of force by external military units – really began with the Ancient Britons in Newtownmountkennedy in April. Luke Cullen's assembling of local recollections provides a very substantial account of their actions. Indeed, Hardy's admission, made at the height of the campaign in south Wicklow, was startlingly frank: 'where I am by violence obliged to compel by rigour I employ the whole.'[259] Unlike Kildare, however, there were a number of magistrates who were prepared to supplement army action on a scale that was impossible, given the absence of local zealots, in Kildare. Benjamin O'Neale Stratford had resorted to house burning by 12 May when a letter of his instanced a case. He was sanguine that these methods would make the free quarters employed in Kildare unnecessary, though he admitted that what happened there was useful as an example: 'I must however add that it is to those measures I am certain that we are indebted for the very sudden and pleasing change here and of which we have taken every advantage by informing the people that they were the most likely to expect the like unless they surrendered arms.'[260]

Before April there was no break-through in intelligence in Wicklow. While their local knowledge had left Stratford and King suspicious of individuals – in Stratford's case obsessively; in King's case more shrewdly – detailed information came only in May. Arrests had of course been numerous in the early spring: around a hundred were jailed. The arrests, based on Cooper's doubtful testimony, afforded no in-depth insight into the structure of the movement. In the west of the county, the first intelligence came in the form of the confessions in Kildare, which provided information on the United Irishmen in west Wicklow, and encouraged a resort to like methods. In the east of the county the real break-through came with the informations provided by 'A.B.', a captain in Arklow barony, which were taken down on 21 May. While 'A.B'.'s information seems to have been voluntary, brutal methods, now resorted to in a frenzy as in Kildare, and in contrast to Kildare by some magistrates as well as army officers, produced results. A local magistrate reported that 'I have just heard that the districts of Coolattin, Carnew and Coolakenney are in the same pleasing situation and the peasantry of the county are now the most humble creatures alive'. Why they were amenable is all too clear. After prisoners had sworn they were not United men, 'two being well flogged the others looking on, they all confessed, some turned approvers and by that means the whole plot came out'.[261] Information now flowed in on the movement, according to Hardy 'faster than it can be taken down and I shall endeavour to select such as is of a serious nature against their principals.'[262] As a result of it 'full informations against their secretaries and treasurers, some of whom are in custody, and captains appears (sic). The latter and some of the former I detain as principals'.[263] Indeed the information was said to prove that all but two of those indicted by Cooper were United Irishmen, and after Morton and Cope had been sitting for two days, twenty-one smiths and principals were sent to Duncannon on 23 May (in other words had been condemned to transportation).

Hardy was surprised at the extent of the conspiracy, confessing that despite months in Wicklow 'he had no idea the evil had so generally spread, and pervaded the whole mass ... military excepted and even they not totally untainted'.[264] Moreover 'from the very extensive informations got here we are enabled to have sent informations to our neighbouring magistrates, particularly to the barony of Gorey and county Wexford.'[265] Ironically even Hardy, like Dundas, fell into the trap of complacency and fatuity. On 22 May he assured Castlereagh that 'our information is now so frequent and good, that all hope is fled, and distrust of one another has occasioned many to leave their houses, and carry away any valuables easily removed'. Sergeants were bringing in pikes, and blacksmiths were giving information of those to whom they supplied pikes. Houses were required to have the names of their male inhabitants posted on the door (a similar or wider requirement in

Carrick-on-Suir and in Dublin city provided information for a population census to attentive observers in both places). The requirement in Wicklow, apparently a general one in the county, had originated in an order by Hardy, as a letter of 9 May claimed that it would not be known 'how many or who have fled from their houses for want of having taken a correct account of the names of all the inhabitants in due time'.[266]

XVI. The rising itself

The machinery of starting the rising is fairly clear. In Wicklow advance notice had been sent through the county some days beforehand. Hardy, in the light of the information coming in, reported that 'information on oath proves they sent such emissaries through all this county about the middle of the week to make them resist, but I trust it was the last effort of an expiring party.'[267] In fact as Hardy was writing on Tuesday 22 May and referring in effect to events a few days earlier, it is likely that there were both final instructions for the rising (probably settling the precise day and hour) and preliminary advice. If the middle of the week refers to the preceding week, it could imply that the fatal decision on a rising had been taken around Tuesday or Wednesday, 15 and 16 May. That explains why Miles Byrne and others in Wexford were expecting instructions to rise, and also why some reports exist which seem to suggest that the countryside was to rise a few days earlier than the capital. The complexity of getting the final news to the countryside explains lags in the actual rising outside Dublin. Morgan Kavanagh had been sent to Carlow with the final news, and the town rose on the night of 24 into 25 May. In Wexford for whatever reason the news was a little later in coming, and it reached Wexford town only in the course of 26 May. In Wicklow we do not know what happened at county level. It cannot have helped that Garrett Byrne the adjutant general was in Dublin, and only joined the rebels later. The arrests were also wholesale in these days, and included figures like William Young, released after the assizes and rearrested in Tinahely district. His rearrest ensured his death in the massacre of the Carnew prisoners.

The rebellion broke out in west Wicklow at the same time as in Kildare. By 9 am on 24 May rebels were seen all along the border with Kildare: 'they sung (sic) horrible songs and never before heard by any loyalist, to excite the rebellion'. They were dispersed by the yeomanry of Dunlavin, Baltinglass and Hacketstown as well as the Wicklow militia. Dispersal put an end to the plans the rebels had of taking the garrison towns of Dunlavin and Baltinglass which were basic to the grand design of an advance by the victorious rebel forces on Dublin.[268] The rebellion took the loyalists by surprise on the morning of the 24th:

Christopher Robinson had gone to Castledermot on business. His house was burned down, and both he and his family had various adventures on the eventful day.[269] Scattered and defeated on the plains, some of the defeated Wicklow and Kildare men withdrew to the camp on Blackmore Hill. This camp seems to have been created as part of the strategy at the very outset of the rising. One of the accounts makes it clear the fugitive rebels 'joined their camp in the hills'. Michael Dwyer later commented that the rebels should not have chosen to confront government forces in the plains but should have gone in the first instance to the Bog of Allen or the Wicklow hills: 'I would prefer the former but in either case I would have a natural defence by encamping on the heights near Blessington.'[270] In fact by 30 May, at least in that quarter the rebels were said to be gaining strength every hour: 'Blackmore Hill near Blessington and about that quarter is where they are situate'.[271] An account noted that 'there they have encamped in such tents as are seen at fairs', and sent out foraging parties.[272] The camp was about 1,000 strong, and 'very well supplied with all kinds provisions and all the carpentry and heads of the houses they had plundered'.[273] Depending on the source, the rebels seem to have been either dispersed from Blackmore Hill or driven to its summit on 1 June.[274] However, it certainly was not defeat. Blackmore Hill which commands the east side of Blessington is simply a shoulder of Sorrel Hill. What the reports mean is that, disturbed on Blackmore Hill, vulnerable with its easy gradients to a cavalry attack, they retreated to the more impregnable slopes of Sorrell. The rebels seem to have remained in the more sheltered location of Whelp Rock under neighbouring Black Mountain, with the possibility of easy refuge in the hills. Thus they remained at Lackan, which shows that in the early days at any rate the loyalists did not have much command of the lower ground. A Dublin report of 5 June noted that outside of Wexford the country was quiet apart from Blackmore Hill.[275]

The priest Martin, taken on 11 June, confirmed that he had been employed to communicate with the United Irishmen at Blackmore. He said that he had been instructed by a committee in Thomas Street to make contact with several persons at 'Dunboyne' in Kilbride (i.e. Manor Kilbride) on the borders of counties Dublin and Wicklow 'to cooperate at a fixed time, and to excite the people to act'. He made visits on two occasions after the dispersal of the rebels in the first days of the rebellion, apparently making contact with Holt in person. Holt had 300 men 'just behind the hill', and another two captains Nugent and Doyle had men 'just over the way'.[276] Holt's men would have been well on the far side of Duff Hill in the Cleevaun range gathering for an attack on Newtownmountkennedy. Doyle and Nugent would have been variously

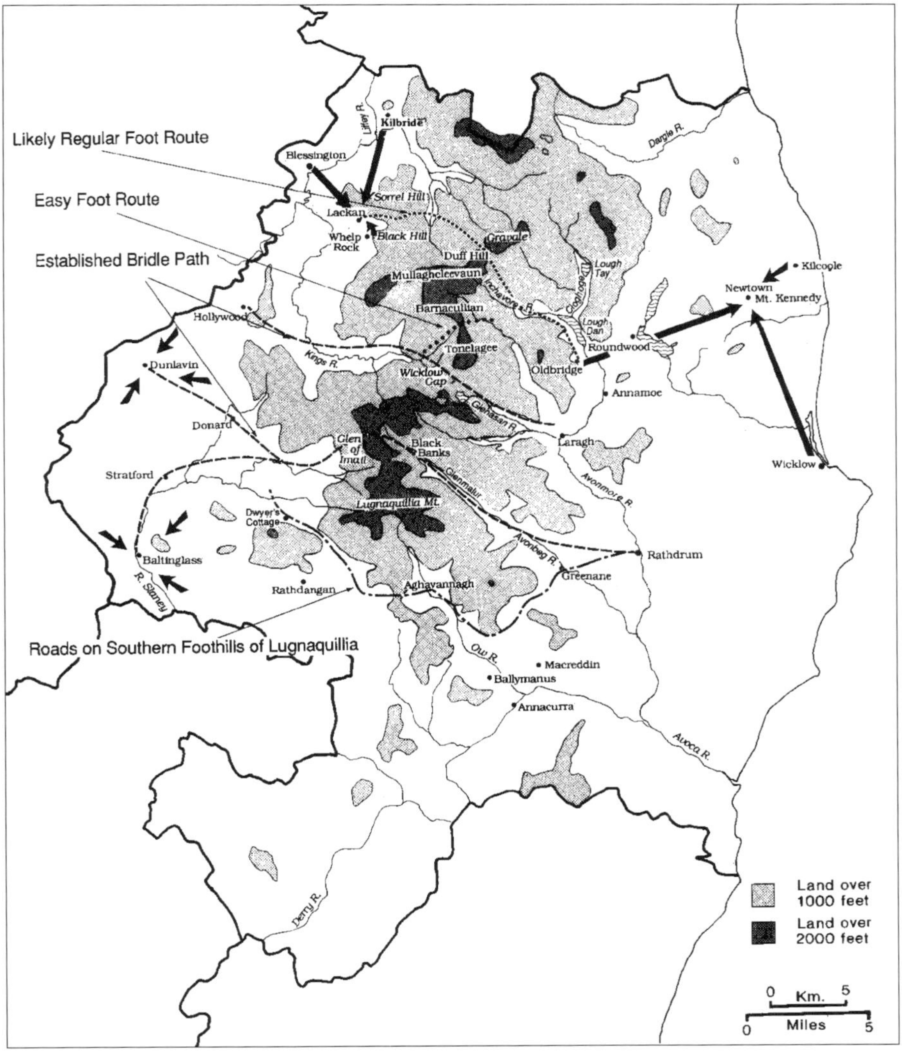

Figure 12.1 United Irishmen's routes in county Wicklow in 1798.

on Sorrel Hill or sheltered at Whelp Rock, and significantly it was these men only that were promised for an attack on Dublin.

One of the problems of Wicklow, a combined consequence of the county's difficult geography and of the ineffective Byrne leadership, was that the concerted plan for the county, in so far as one existed, broke down. It is possible to visualise the plans. On the east side of the hills forces gathered at several points, one of them Cloghoge (safer from attack than Oldbridge); on the west side, at Blackmore. In both cases the purpose was to back the strategy of attacking the garrison towns. As the only two mountain passes with bridle paths (the Black Banks pass from Glenmalure, and the Wicklow Gap) were watched by patrols, communication with Old Bridge near Roundwood must have been kept by a trek over the high plateau watered by the Cloghoge and Inchavore rivers and across the northern shoulder of Duff Hill to Sorrell. This is the easiest and quickest route northwards across the Cleevaun range. Holt's visit to Rathfarnham and probably Blackmore fits into a strategy already in some uncertainty and beginning to fall apart. While east Wicklow began to gather early, it was slow to act, and only on 29 May did they decide to launch the attack on Newtownmountkennedy. There may have been uncertainties in communication between the different groups in the east which were to join in a three-pronged attack on the garrison: the Ancient Britons, who had ruthlessly broken the back of the United Irishmen in the key hinterland of Newtown in 1798 may have undermined morale and lowland communication facilities alike. In these circumstances Holt's appearance at the far side of the mountain range in the days before the attack is less likely to point to an interest in concerting the larger strategy for the county than to sheer desperation. That strategy was of course one later criticised by Dwyer (and one that may already have become, in the light of the failures of the first week, a bone of contention among the United Irishmen in the county) of fighting in the plains with a view to taking the garrison towns, Dunlavin and Baltinglass in the west; Newtownmountkennedy in the east. If they were taken, it left the way clear for the United Irishmen to advance on Dublin. The central place that that plan held in their strategy is illustrated by the Wexfordmen's attack on Arklow on 9 June, and also by the expectations of rebels in the capital of support from the south. Sproule, who was well informed on Wicklow, in a letter which could have been written on any date from 17 May, described a plan for the rising to the north to begin two days early and, with its defenders lured out, for the forces of counties Kildare, Dublin and Wicklow to pour into the city.[277] The plan, one of several floated in these days of internal struggles among the Dublin leadership, was modified in favour of a general rising on a single day, but the principle of an advance to Dublin seem to have remained part of it.

The plan was in tatters from the opening days not only in Wicklow but in Kildare. In the east of the county it had still to be launched. The intention was to mount an attack on Newtown from three directions. Newtown dominated the low land of east Wicklow, and its Ancient Briton garrison was the most formidable military presence in the county: it would have to be crushed if the United Irishmen were to take over east Wicklow. However, one of the three columns, amounting to 300 men and including Holt, which had intended to approach Newtown from the west, was dispersed on 29 May by the Ancient Britons and the Newtown yeomanry near Roundwood 'just as they were commencing their depredations'. Twenty-four of the rebels were killed and the village of Cloghoge, 'whence these people principally came was burned'.[278] The consequence was that only two columns attacked Newtown, the third was either late or delayed. The town was attacked at 2 am on the morning of 30 May by 500 to 1,000 rebels. While they succeeded in forcing their way into the town, they failed to take the market house and were driven out with a loss of sixty. Another sixty of the attacking force who took refuge in the Devil's Glen were killed.[279]

Thus successive disasters overcame the Wicklow forces. Dispersed in the western plains on 24 May, the eastern rebels in turn were crushed at Newtownmountkennedy. It was a decisive defeat, and Holt lost no time, if the commissariat document at the rebel camp at New Ross is correct, in going to Wexford.[280] While north Wicklow had mobilised on both sides of the mountains and failed in the field, south Wicklow did not mobilise at all. There was no point of concentration of rebel strength in south Wicklow, no action of any consequence took place, and local rebels were already finding their way in small detachments into Wexford, some of them to play an important role there.[281] The absence of planning for action or of visible massing of men turns Holt's presence at New Ross or Three Rock Mountain into a commentary on the situation near his home base. As Byrne was the adjutant general, his presence in Wexford, bereft of troops (the commissariat document reveals, Holt apart, no other Wicklow officers), is comment both on his incapacity and on confusion in south Wicklow. After the battle of Ross, he must have returned north to make contact with his own men, a move prompted by the failure of the rebels at Ross and by the prospects of success in Wicklow for the still victorious north Wexford army in its advance to attack Arklow. As Miles Byrne has noted, a plan of creating a large skirmishing force under Garrett Byrne was entertained and abandoned in the days before the battle of Arklow.

Holt probably for similar reasons withdrew to Wicklow, and in fact we know very little about either his movements or Byrne's in the ten days after Ross. On the instructions of a committee in Thomas Street, Martin made a final visit to the south of the county to encourage an attack on Dublin to take place on 12 June. He was finally arrested at the mines at Cronebane.[282] He had probably left Dublin when prospects of a rebel advance on Dublin were still alive and hence before the defeat at Arklow. Martin's answers in the questioning after his apprehension at Cronebane mines at the end of a circuitous route that took him to Roundwood, then back to the coast, and inland again to Cronebane reveals that he had no contact with rebels, and was drawn south to the Arklow region by a vague directive given to him to make contact with men in the Arklow region (probably as it was a Thomas Street committee Mathew Doyle was in mind, hardly the worthless O'Neil).[283] Mathew Doyle had been among those who went into Wexford in late May, and later when rebellion was extinguished in Wexford he was among Holt's companions in the hills (he was in fact one of the few for whom Holt expressed a high regard).[284]

After defeat at Arklow, any real hopes lay with the large rebel armies in Wexford rather than in advance to Dublin. With the retreat to Wexford, Wicklow men, now with even less hope on their home ground, continued to drift south to Wexford, in a patchy saga. Martin's final visit to Wicklow was simply a bold but forlorn hope by a very marginal figure. After the defeats in Kildare and at Newtown, any prospect in Wicklow existed only in the south of the county, as the instructions for Martin's last visit recognised. But initial organisation there was less effective than further north, and moreover after Arklow government military presence began to assert itself. The organisation, such as it was or survived in south Wicklow, was also undermined by the move into Wexford where the rebel forces were still powerful. The fact that three camps under the captains Holt, Nugent and Doyle, are mentioned in the Martin court martial documents, may point to little, or to fragmented, command structure.

Moreover, the United Irishmen were in conflict among themselves. Holt's assumption of the title colonel was a subject of contention with fellow-United Irishmen who from the outset attached bureaucratic importance to hierarchy and election. He already held the style in the commissary record on 5 June at the time of his fleeting presence in Wexford. Holt, a man 'with a very poor address',[285] might seem an improbable figure for a colonel, but the many arrests in May combined with attempts to fill offices in an expanded structure may have resulted in the creation of office in an informal and hence contentious way. Evidence of tensions comes not only from the later informants of Luke Cullen, but from contemporary sources. There was friction even within June: an informant testified that Holt was only a captain: 'Holt who was called colonel, but informant heard he was no more than a captain.'[286] In September, a report to Cooke stated that 'McMahon is very well liked. Holt is not.' Francis McMahon held an undisputed rank of colonel in Dublin, and significant resentments over rank were hinted at in a report that 'Holt has no commission nor ever had.'[287] The bad blood between Holt and others including Dwyer, much commented on by Luke Cullen and evident in Holt's coyness in his later account in not referring to Dwyer at all, may variously reflect, in some form or other, pre-rising internal politics, resentment released by the vagaries of United Irishman office-making in the highly confused March-May period, and differences over tactics in the difficult days after 24 May. Dwyer also came from the west where rank and file were more radical; Holt, with his background of minor public offices and his proximity to the Byrne presence in the affairs of Rathdrum, may have fitted into recruitment through the politicised east Wicklow leadership. If he was included in the commissariat which looked after the Harvey forces, that suggests that he had no ties with the Cloney-Kelly axis, and that he may have been a member of the 'moderate' faction. Dwyer by contrast may have been recruited through the strong Francis Street-oriented links that ran through west Wicklow into Carlow and into the Cloney-Kelly districts in Wexford. Tensions with Dwyer may thus have reflected politics more than personality, and Holt's friction with the Dublin colonel McMahon who also held out in the Wicklow hills would tend to support this conclusion.

The south of the county furnishes no evidence at any time of a coherent gathering of men. Dwyer and Holt, from the Glen of Imaal and from Roundwood respectively, where organisation had been effective and where a military structure had existed, reflect some of the capacity of their districts, in each of which there had been an impressive initial turnout of the order of 1,000 men. Both men moreover were to prove their personal worth. Garrett Byrne, on the other hand, leader of the county United Irishmen and adjutant general, is a shadowy and ineffective figure, present at much of the later action in both counties, but never showing the leadership qualities that might be expected from his elevated social position or his military office.That helps to explain the uncertainties and ambiguities of teasing out his precise locations before the final and painful retreat to the midlands.

XVII. Contrasts with Wexford: initial success, firearms, clergy role

One of the problems of the Wicklow United Irishmen was their limited supply of firearms. Some 600 had been seized in Baltinglass district in November 1797 when the two Talbotstown baronies were proclaimed; 600 to 700 stand of arms were acquired in the blitz in May; over 3,000 pikes were also taken.[288] In contrast, Wexford was well armed, partly because the drive against rebels had begun only in the week before the rebellion, but above all because a series of victories provided arms. Oulart had given them over a hundred, Camolin was raided in the night of the 27th into the 28th, and victories at Enniscorthy and Tuberneering yielded futher weapons for the rebels.[289] Michael Dwyer, according to the Cullen manuscripts, thought that the Wexford men were twice as well armed. He gave a figure of 1,200 guns for the Wicklowmen.[290]

Priests were not active in the actual rebellion in Wicklow, whereas they were in Wexford both as members of the United Irishmen, and as leaders in the field. In Wicklow they were suspected of course by zealot loyalists. Stratford in particular was predictably obsessed by the 'priests of this town, and Dunlavin who I believe to be at the head of whole'.[291] Yet despite some suspicions before the rebellion of their loyalty, they did not play a role. The reason for the contrast is essentially a consequence of the liberal profile of the county. They were not under pressure as they were in Wexford. There, priests were pressurised not only by loyalists but by their friend Mountnorris, by catholics such as Edward Hay and Esmonde, and by their own bishop. This caused resentment, and Kilcormick, John Murphy's parish, signed the second declaration administered in April only under protest. Almost certainly, it was the process of conflict between priests and their own lay and ecclesiastical hierarchy which isolated some priests in Wexford. In Wicklow, perhaps because the Dublin archdiocese was so large, its loyalist archbishop was effectively impotent. In other words in Wexford, Caulfield's hyperactive role, augmented by the officious Mountnorris role to declare the loyalty of catholics, caused some priests to rebel against pressures from their own side. That may not be the whole story, but simultaneously they were subject to the intense McCabe-inspired organisation around them, and apt to resent the persistent lay and clerical pressure less from their enemies than from catholics and friends of catholics.

The Mountnorris loyalty campaigns did not reach to north-west Wexford, but in that region the stresses of the 1797 election when John Maxwell Barry was run by Mountnorris and supported by some prominent catholics, could have put impossible pressures on some priests and laymen who can hardly have failed to advert to the cynical (and commented-on) process of running a religious bigot of no known reform principles, whose mother was a sister of John Foster, as an anti-government candidate. The only priests involved in the United movement or in the rebellion can be identified with well-defined regions. One of these districts was in the north-west of the county where the influence of Maxwell Barry as a local landlord was strong and the election pressures had been intense; the other to the east of the Slaney on or close to the Mountnorris estate where the influence of the earl was paramount and where he launched his campaigns of November and April. The priest Thomas Dixon was in trouble for uniting in 1797; the others may have been officers, like Edward Sinnot, Philip Roche or Mogue Kearns from as early as 1797 or in the case of the Murphys

(John and Michael) from April 1798. With no such pressures Wicklow clergy were not forced to make an agonising decision either to buckle under or to consciously reject lay and ecclesiastical directives; they probably remained in a fluid position wavering around points between poles reaching from loyalist to strong rebel sympathies.

XVIII. Conclusion

The Wicklow rebellion is an important case, precisely because it has not entered into the realm of subsequent polemics and as a consequence remains more obscure than Wexford. Study has also been bedevilled by reliance on the Holt document and on the accounts of Dwyer in the Cullen manuscripts, though both sources relate primarily to the post-July period; they also imply that because the two individuals were capable, organisation in the preceding rebellion itself had been more effective than it actually was. Luke Cullen gives undue emphasis to Garrett Byrne's position and importance: in fact there is a singular lack of any convincing testimony of real capacity. He was stated by McGhee to have been closeted in Dublin with an Irish brigade officer who was 'a principal leader in the attack intended on the capital'. This might suggest a large role for Byrne in the grand design, and Luke Cullen claims as much. However, Luke Cullen's testimony is not corroborated by McGhee: both opinions may re-echo a common source. All United Irishmen in the adjoining counties were in a manner of speaking involved in this task, and this aspect of his role may be exaggerated, given his role as adjutant general: his duties were not accompanied on the ground either by good organisation or by lines of command reaching to trustworthy subordinates in Wicklow. In any event McGhee himself was hardly a precise reporter, and was to declare wildly in August that 'not a night passes without one or two loyalists being murdered.'[292]

The growth in the organisation was helped by the liberal profile of the county. Many of its United Irishmen undoubtedly were drawn into the movement by the active politics caused by the intensity of government opposition to the Fitzwilliam monolith. The lack of confidence in the gentry led to the government interest being put into the hands of an army officer, who maintained close links with Cooke, four months before a comparable event took place in any other southern county; it also resulted in the notorious yeoman test, originating in the county and devised in association with the Castle. The deep divide helped to radicalise opinion and to lead to an easy growth of the United Irishmen. On the other hand, many were superficial in their commitment, and there were strong links both with the Dublin moderate wing and the corresponding Perry-Harvey group in Wexford.

On paper the United Irishmen in Wicklow were strong, and Putnam McCabe and Mathew Doyle were to the fore in building up a radical force below the anaemic leadership. However, several offsetting considerations have to be taken into account. First, the impact of arrests was especially serious. The Cooper arrests had put many, including some leading figures, out of circulation for several months. Garrett Byrne's own departure, occurring in the midst of this wave, must clearly have been prompted by fear. In addition, the two important figures of William Michael Byrne and John Lynch, delegates to Dublin, were arrested at Oliver Bond's on 12 March. Finally, the numerous arrests on the eve of rebellion crushed the remaining top leadership capacity. In Arklow the ineffective Philip O'Neil surrendered, himself.[293] That resulted in the removal of all the leading figures before the rebellion broke, plus an unknown but probable large proportion of the captains. The wretched O'Neil apart, Garrett Byrne was the only holder of high office in the county organisation of earlier months still known to be at large by 24 May, and he was out of the county.

Second, we have to allow for the importance of the moderate wing, whose heart was not fully in rebellion ahead of a French landing. Garrett Byrne probably belonged to this group, and like Harvey had little stomach for a rebellion whose success was not guaranteed by prior French invasion; like Harvey too he was probably one of those ambitious and vain men who had not clearly thought out in advance their course of action. In Wexford by contrast four of its seven colonels were at large at the very outbreak of rebellion; two of them (Cloney and Kelly) were to prove highly effective; the other two (Roche and Keugh) has some qualities of competence as well, more particularly Keugh whose bearing later impressed the English general Moore and whose running of a three-week republic in a county town, full of rebels themselves divided into two revolutionary schools, merits real recognition. The only totally ineffective colonels were Perry and Fitzgerald, two of the three colonels who were prisoners in the early days. Fitzgerald, the adjutant general for Wexford, was the counterpart in rank and colourlessness of Garrett Byrne. More of the captains survived as well. These circumstance plus above all the run of dramatic successes from 26 May to 4 June created an impression that the Wexford movement was invincible. At the outset, it was the absence of all three of the colonels for east Wexford north of Castlebridge (Perry, Kyan and Fitzgerald) which made John Murphy a leader in that region. That combined with some incapacity of Roche and astonishing successes on 27 and 28 May gave Murphy a real standing. In regard to Fr Philip Roche's victory at Clough (Tuberneering), it does not seem to

Lough Bray Upper.

N.N.E. from Aughrim.

Ow valley, s.w. of Lugnaquillia.

Coastline north from Wicklow.

W.N.W. from Glendasan – through Wicklow Gap.

Blessington sand quarries.

Turf banks near Sally Gap (Bord Fáilte).

Glen of the Downs.

Glenmacnass (Bord Fáilte).

Brittas Bay.

Luggala and Lough Tay.

S.W. from Baltinglass.

Powerscourt waterfall (Bord Fáilte).

Greystones (Bord Fáilte).

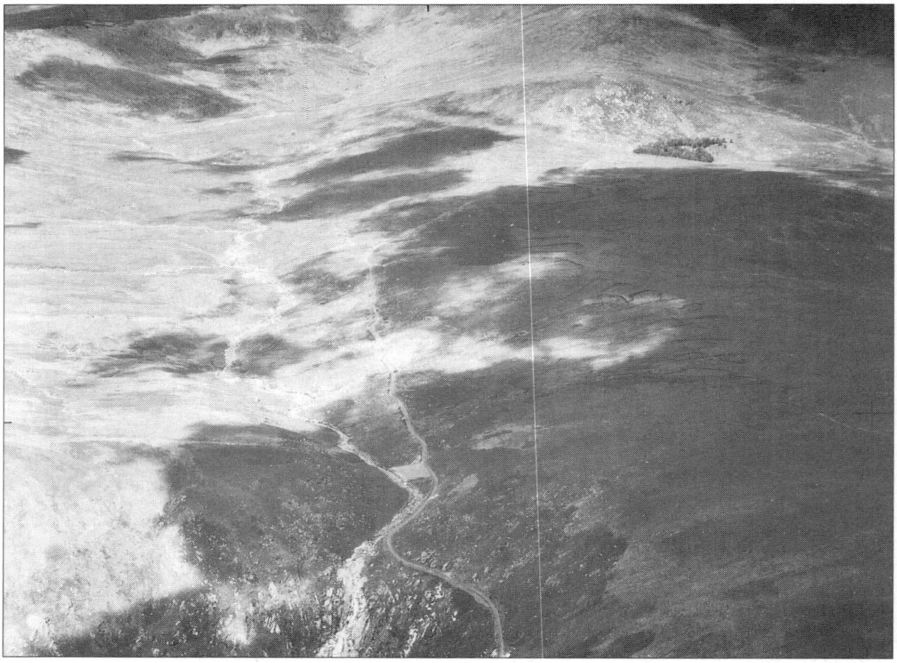

Glenmacnass.

N.N.E. from Avoca.

Ring-fort, Toor, west Wicklow (F. Aalen, 1992).

Newcastle castle.

Kilruddery House.

Vernacular house, Ballinguile, Wicklow.
(C. Ó Danachair, 1949, courtesy of Dept. of Irish Folklore, U.C.D.)

Powerscourt Garden looking towards Sugarloaf (Bord Fáilte).

Stone wall at Ballyknockan.
(C. Ó Danachair, 1952, courtesy of Dept. of Irish Folklore, U.C.D.).

Russborough.

Dwyer-McAllister Cottage, Glen of Imaal (Bord Fáilte).

Avondale demesne.

Muckduff village.
(C. Ó Danachair, courtesy of Dept. of Irish Folklore, U.C.D.).

Mount Usher gardens, Ashford (Bord Fáilte).

Stratford-on-Slaney.

Townhall, Bray.

Vernacular house, Arklow.
(A. Eskeröd, 1935, courtesy of Dept. of Irish Folklore, U.C.D.).

Stone fence-post, Ballyknockan.
(C. Ó Danachair, 1970, courtesy of Dept. of Irish Folklore, U.C.D.).

Sheep, drovers and dogs near Ashford (Bord Fáilte).

have rested totally on east Wexford forces. The west Wexford forces after they gathered on Vinegar Hill on 29 May provided most of the mobility of the rebels. Some of them attacked Newtownbarry on 1 June: others wheeled north to meet Walpole's advancing force, and those that advanced from Three Rocks Mountain bore the brunt of action at Ross. This record allied to Roche's success at Tuberneering on 4 June, the last real rebel victory in Wexford as it proved, paved the way for his election to the post of commander-in-chief on 8 June.[294]

The combination of massive arrests beforehand, lack of military victories in the vital first days, and the singular ineptitude of the sole colonel (and certainly the sole uncontested one) free to take charge of the movement doomed the Wicklow rebellion. Even with vicissitudes of this sort, it could still have been possible to mount a rising as events in neighbouring Kildare proved, and one reason for Kildare's failure was, that with the deep government fear of its United Irishmen, far more of the army was to hand. Wicklowmen gathered in numbers at Blackmore Hill and around Newtownmountkennedy. Victory at either location (or in Kildare) would have altered the story. The really striking thing is the failure of the United Irishmen to gather in force in the south of the county, just across the borders from insurgent Wexford. There was no large-scale mobilisation, despite the fact that for ten days, apart from a set-back at Newtownbarry on 1 June, the neighbouring Wexford rebels, often connected to them moreover by blood and marriage, carried all before them. It was here in the south of the county that the real failure in Wicklow lay.

References

1. Ruan O'Donnell, 'General Joseph Holt and the rebellion of 1798 in County Wicklow', unpublished MA thesis, University College, Dublin, 1991; see also Ruan O'Donnell and Bob Reece, '"A clean beast". Crofton Corker's fairytale of General Holt', *Eighteenth-Century Ireland,* vii (1992), pp 7-42.
2. NAI, Rebellion Papers 620/13/181/20, 24 July 1804. His name was over time variously rendered as O'Neill Stratford, and O'Neale Stratford.
3. Few King letters exist for 1797-8, but for his later correspondence see C. Dickson, *Life of Michael Dwyer* (Dublin, 1944), pp 199-219. See also the plaque to him in Rathdrum parish church.
4. Dickson in his account was unaware of the identity of Holt's enemy, though in fact the author was identified (incorrectly) in the Cullen Mss as King. This illustrates a dimension of Cullen's manuscript which is not always sufficiently adverted to: it is less a collection of folk tradition than an account by a man who, though untutored, had read all the literature published up to the 1840s. Cullen and his account are themselves part of popular politicisation in the nineteenth century, and his own account arose from a quickening interest in the 1830s and 1840s in the rebellion. What makes it particularly interesting, in contrast to apologetic writers such as Cloney or the novelist Banim, was the explicit acceptance of revolutionary aims: he thus anticipated the view developed

publicly in the 1840s by Madden and Davis, and he lost no time in making contact with Madden in response to the appearance of the first stage of Madden's work.

5. Mss Room, Library, T.C.D., Ms 1472, p. 137.
6. NAI, 620/36/110 bis, J. S. Rochfort, I April, Carlow.
7. T.C.D., Ms 1472, p. 201.
8. NAI, 620/34/14, undated but endorsed 24 May, Wolfe to Cooke, enclosing letter of Colclough of 18 Aug.
9. NAI, OP, 1st series, 33/22, 7 Oct. 1797, to Pelham.
10. See L. M. Cullen, 'The United Irish rebellion in Wexford ...' in Whelan, *Wexford history and society*, p. 262.
11. On the Miscellaneous Papers, see Wood, *Guide to the Public Record Office* (Dublin, 1919), p. 208, and *Deputy Keeper's Report* (D.K.R.) 1873, no. 5, pp 30-31. The Calendars to the Miscellaneous Papers to 1759 and 1760-89 survived the conflagration, but not the papers themselves.
12. See T. M. Bartlett, 'Select documents xxxviii: Defenders and Defenderism in 1795', *I.H.S.*, xxiv, no. 95 (1985).
13. NAI, SPO, Search book no. 2, 1889-1898, pp 54-5, Sir Bernard Burke, March 1890. The note was written at the request of Lecky. The earliest contemporary description of them is the brief note in *P.R.I. rep. D.K., 9*, 1877, p. 17 (1877).
14. Compare *P.R.I. rep. D.K., 8*, p. 23 and *P.R.I. rep. D.K., 9*, 1877, p. 17.
15. *P.R.I. rep. D.K., 36*, p. 21.
16. *P.R.I. rep. D.K., 49*, p. 13; *50*, p. 11.
17. The casual methods persisted even later when all incoming correspondence was registered. When letters later passed to other officials or to London, no record was kept of their movement, and the series is now riddled with unaccounted-for gaps.
18. E.g. Lecky, *Ireland*, iv, p. 402. These words are very interesting, because their tone of surprise reflects the extent of Cooke's involvement and his surprise at being taken unawares. It is worth bearing in mind Burke's scorching comment, though hardly unprejudiced, on him as 'a shallow, hotheaded puppy, proud and presumptuous, and ill-behaved'. *Burke correspondence*, ed. T.W. Copeland, vol. ix, p. 339, to French Laurence, 12 May 1797.
19. NAI, 620/38/185, General Nugent to Cooke, 19 June 1798.
20. *Journals of the house of commons*, vol. 14, pp 32, 68, 341.
21. P.R.O.N.I., Fitzwilliam papers, T.3300/13/12/7, 30 Dec. 1795. I am indebted to Miss Ann Kavanagh for this reference.
22. P.R.O.N.I., Fitzwilliam papers, T.3302/2/99, 29 July 1797. I am indebted to Dr Malcomson for a number of extracts from the Fitzwilliam papers.
23. I am indebted to my student Miss Lindsay for information about the Carlow election.
24. NAI, 620/10/118/20, 15 Dec. 1801, Leonard McNally. See also 620/10/118/21, 21 Dec.
25. NAI, OP 34/8, Forenaughts, 28 July 1797.
26. P.R.O.N.I., Fitzwilliam papers, T.3302/2/96, John Jervis White to Fitzwilliam, 2 Aug. 1796.
27. P.R.O.N.I., Fitzwilliam papers, T.3302/2/100, William Hume to Fitzwilliam, 1 Aug. 1797.
28. NAI 620/10/118/20. 15 Dec. 1801.
29. NAI, OP 34/8, Forenaughts, 28 July 1797.
30. P.R.O., London, H.O. 100/70, ff. 73-5, to Portland, 18 July 1797. I am indebted to Dr Malcomson for this reference.

31. P.R.O., Fitzwilliam papers, T.3302/2/99, 29 July 1797.
32. E.M. Richardson, *Long forgottten days* (London, 1928) is very informative on the Stratford circle, though unfortunately the record seems to be deficient for the years immediately preceding 1798.
33. NAI, 620/36/176, 16 April 1798, Edwards to lord lieutenant.
34. NAI, 620/35/47, 14 Jan. 1798, to the lord lieutenant.
35. NAI, 620/37/184, 27 May 1798.
36. NAI, 620/37/43, 9 May 1798, to Cooke. Robinson's name was removed from the letter.
37. For a very revealing comment, see TCD, Ms 1472, p. 72.
38. NAI, 620/38/188, John Murphy, 20 June 1798.
39. O'Donnell, op. cit., p. 83.
40. NAI, State of the Country Papers, 1st series, SOC 1017/66, to John Stratford, undated.
41. NAI, 620/35/28, 9 Jan. 1798, Harvy Fitzmaurice to Col. Rochfort.
42. NAI, Prerogative Will Book, 1777, ff. 49-51, will of Juliana countess Anglesey, 12 Dec. 1776.
43. R. B. McDowell, 'The personnel of the Dublin Society of United Irishmen', *I.H.S.*, vol. 2, no. 5 (March 1942), pp 25, 32.
44. See L. M. Cullen, 'The internal politics of the United Irishmen 1791-98', in *The United Irishmen*, ed. D. Dickson, D. Keogh, K. Whelan, pp 176-96.
45. C. Dickson, *The Wexford rising in 1798: its causes and course* (Tralee, 1956), pp 45-7.
46. Dickson, op. cit., p. 45.
47. Cullen, 'The United Irish rebellion in Wexford ...', pp 275-6.
48. T.C.D., Cullen Mss, Ms 1472, p. 63. The Cabinteely branch of the Byrne family had land and some electoral influence in the county, but did not reside there.
49. NAI, 620/22/16, Rathdrum, 14 July 1795, Sir Edward Newenham to Pelham.
50. NAI, Cullen Mss, MS 1472, p. 217.
51. T.C.D., Cullen Mss, pp 111, 118; Dickson, *Dwyer*, pp 58-9.
52. T.C.D., Cullen Mss, pp 112-113; Dickson, *Dwyer*, p. 58.
53. NAI, 620/37/184, Hardy to Cooke, 27 May 1798.
54. NAI, SOC 1017/64. Undated and unsigned, but the handwriting is clearly Hardy's.
55. John T. Gilbert, *Documents relating to Ireland 1795-1804* (Dublin, 1893, 1970 ed., Shannon), pp 125-6.
56. H.M.C. *Charlemont Mss*, vol. 1, p. 65.
57. M. L. Duggan, 'Co. Carlow 1791-1801, a study in an era of revolution', U.C.D., M.A., thesis 1969, pp 55, 67n.
58. I am indebted to my student Ms Deirdre Lindsay for information on the Carlow election.
59. NAI, 620/37/208, to Dundas.
60. NAI, 620/51/225. The endorsement refers to it as a list drawn from the commissary's records of 'rebel captains ... having been supplied with provisions out of his stores'. If they were present, and the names include those of four east Wexford colonels (though one of them is not given the rank of colonel), then the collective failure of Harvey and the incapacity of his leading officers is even more devastating, and hence makes more understandable the division and resentments that it stirred up. But see note 280 below regarding the interpretation of this document. On either interpretation, however, it confirms the separate character of the Cloney/Kelly force.
61. J. Gordon, *History of the rebellion* (London, 1803), p. 125. Gordon's own political stance is very clearly implied in his comments on *A narrative of the*

apprehension, trial and execution of Sir Edward Crosbie (Gordon, p. 94).
62. E. Hay, *History of the insurrection of the county of Wexford* (Dublin 1803), pp 89, 136, 220.
63. Gordon, op. cit., p. 141.
64. R. Musgrave, *Memoirs of the different rebellions in Ireland*, 3rd ed. (Dublin, 1802), vol. 1, pp 372, 378. T.C.D., Cullen Mss, Ms 1472, p.175.
65. R. B. McDowell, 'Proceedings of the Dublin Society of United Irishmen', *Anal. Hib.*, xvii, pp 80-1.
66. NAI, 620/22/16, Newenham to Pelham, Rathdrum, 14 July 1795.
67. NAI, 620/18/11/1, Camden to Portland, 6 Aug. 1796. The fact that a copy survives in the Rebellion Papers undelines its significance: Cooke would have been consulted on its terms.
68. NAI, 620/24/97, Aldborough to Cooke, 9 Aug. 1796.
69. NAI, SOC 3055, Mr Winder to Cooke, *c.*1796, Curtlestown (Cuddlestown).
70. NAI, SOC 3053, William Nixon to Pelham, 20 December 1796. He corresponded with the Castle later as well. See R.P. 620/30/240, 30 May 1797.
71. NAI, 620/26/189.
72. NAI, 620/28/44, to Cooke.
73. NAI, SOC 1016/49, 25 March 1797.
74. NAI, 620/30/136, 21 May 1797.
75. NAI, 620/30/89, John Smith, 16 May 1797.
76. NAI, 620/3/32/6, 22 May 1798.
77. NAI, 620/31/38, 5 June 1797.
78. NAI, 620/30/108, 19 May 1797.
79. NAI, 621/31/ 65, Benjamin O'Neale Stratford, 9 June 1797.
80. NAI, 620/28/44, John Wolfe to Cooke, 5 Jan. 1797. Griffith's residence was at Millicent. John Esmond or Esmonde is of course the brother of Sir Thomas Esmonde, who, having made a good marriage, lived in Co Kildare and was executed in 1798.
81. NAI, 620/31/45, John Ravel Walsh, 6 June 1797, Strawberry Lodge, post town Naas.
82. NAI, 620/30/38, 8 May 1797.
83. NAI, 620/30/46, to Pelham, 9 May 1797. According to McNally, Wogan Browne was a correspondent of Tandy's. NAI, 620/10/121/41, 17 Jan. 1797.
84. See NAI, 620/31/103, Stephen Sparks to Pelham, enclosing a copy, Carbery, 15 June 1797. It was a much admired document, which is reproduced in C.H. Teeling, *Sequel to the history of the Irish rebellion* (I.U.P. ed, Shannon, 1972), pp 162-3. See also *Personal recollections of the life and times with extracts from the correspondence of Lord Cloncurry* (Dublin, 1849), pp 51-4.
85. NAI, 620/10/121/62, 29 May 1797. In July he was a signatory of a document calling for an aggregate meeting in Dublin. NAI, 620/10/121/70, 28 July 1797. Though Wogan Browne was a protestant, his brothers and sisters were catholics, and William Aylmer of Painstown, the Kildare rebel later to hold out longest, was a tenant of his. William Aylmer's father was said to be worth £1,600 a year. See Fenton Aylmer in NAI, 620/38/44, 4 June 1798.
86. See especially *Personal recollections of the life and times with extracts from the correspondence of Valentine Lord Cloncurry* (Dublin,1849), p. 54.
87. NAI, 620/31/141, to Cooke, 23 June 1797.
88. NAI, 620/34/14, Naas, 16 Aug. 1797, Day to Wolfe.
89. NAI, 620/10/121/58, McNally.
90. NAI, 620/31/45, Strawberry Lodge, post town Naas.

91. NAI, 620/31/65.
92. NAI, 620/34/14, Philipstown, 19 Aug. 1797, Robert Day to Wolfe.
93. NAI, 620/31/45.
94. NAI, SOC 3099, 7 Aug. 1797.
95. NAI, SOC 3086, 16 June, endorsed contemporaneously 16 July either in error or reflecting the delays in its transmission to the Castle.
96. NAI, SOC 3120, Carnew, 26 Sept. 1797, second sheet missing, letter addressed to 'dear uncle'.
97. NAI, SOC 3107.
98. NAI, 620/34/18, 18 August, with many to follow. See also Duggan, op. cit., which makes much use of his letters, and provides convenient access to the content of his correspondence.
99. Luke Cullen erroneously says that the county was proclaimed in November 1797.
100. *An accurate and impartial narrative* ..., quoted Duggan, op. cit., p. 173.
101. NAI, 620/34/20, Alex Durdin, Huntingdon, near Clonegal, 20 Sept.
102. NAI, SOC 1016/50a, 5 Oct. 1797; 1016/ 50b draft reply, 9 Oct. 1797.
103. NAI, 620/33/9, William Burton, 2 Nov. 1797; 620/33/3, Walter Kavanagh, Borris, 1 Nov.; *Finn's Leinster Journal*, 22 -25 November 1797.
104. NAI, 620/34/27, 9 Nov.
105. NAI, 620/33/8, J.S. Rochfort to Pelham, 2 Nov. 1797.
106. NAI, 620/33/29, Burton and Rochfort, 9 November, reply of lord lieutenant to Burton, 10 Nov. 1797. See endorsement on letter of 10 November, 620/33/32.
107. NAI, 620/33/32, O'Neale Stratford (9 Nov., answered 10 Nov.).
108. Sworn testimony of Stephen Hyland, blacksmith, 10 May 1797, enclosed with letter of William Lambert, Edenderry, 10 May 1797, NAI, 620/30/47.
109. NAI, 620/30/147, 22 May 1797, Naas, Mr Nevill. On Commins, see also James Alexander, *Some account of the first apparent symptoms of the late rebellion in the county of Kildare* (Dublin, 1800).
110. NAI, 620/34/14, Naas 16 Aug. 1797, Robert Day to Arthur Wolfe.
111. NAI, SOC 3086, 16 June 1797.
112. NAI, SOC 3099, no date, recd. 7 Aug. 1797.
113. NAI, SOC 3111, 15 Sept 1797.
114. NAI, SOC 3133/1, rec. Nov. 1797, enclosing examination of Ed. Webb against 13 Stratford men committed to Wicklow, dated 11 Nov.
115. NAI, 620/37/43, 9 May 1798, enclosing 'list of persons'.
116. NAI, 620/34/14, Kelly, Killann, 17 June 1797 enclosed in Colclough to Wolfe, 18 Aug. 1797. This is the only known letter in Kelly's hand. See also Colclough, 15 June, NAI, 620/31/101, whch refers to the same episode.
117. T. Cloney, *Personal narrative* ... (Dublin 1832), p. 6. On McCabe, see O'Donnell, op. cit., pp 63-4.
118. McDowell, 'Personnel of the Dublin Society ...', pp 23, 51. On Nicholas Butler see NAI, 620/10/121/143, n.d., McNally.
119. NAI, 620/34/27, Cornwall, 9 Nov.1797.
120. NAI, 620/37/37, testimony of Luke Brannick, 8 May 1798.
121. Cullen, 'The United Irish rebellion in Wexford.,' p. 277; NAI, 620/33/93, Clogrenane, 26 Nov. 1797, J. S. Rochefort to Pelham.
122. Duggan, op. cit., p. 83.
123. NAI, 620/37/67, Colin Campbell, Athy, 14 May 1798.
124. NAI, 620/37/191, sworn testimony of John Kelly of Moneybeg, 28 May 1798.
125. NAI, 620/10/121/97, n. d., NcNally.
126. NAI, 620/37/27, Daniel McCarthy, 5 May 1798, copy given to Col. Campbell, 9 May.

127. NAI, 620/37/191, sworn testimony of John Kelly of Moneybeg, 28 May 1798.
128. NAI, 620/38/188; Musgrave, op. cit., vol. 2, pp 318-9.
129. O'Donnell, op. cit., pp 88, 89.
130. *Journals of the house of commons*, vol. 17, app. dccccxxvi.
131. NAI, 620/37/27, Daniel McCarthy, 5 May 1798.
132. T.C.D., Cullen Mss, Ms 1472; Dickson, *Michael Dwyer*, passim.
133. NAI, 620/3/51/1, 25 March 1798, Rathdrum. According to the *Dublin Evening Post* of 29 March, O'Reilly was the holder of 'extensive corn mills', and on his arrest was brought to Dublin.
134. NAI, 620/35/48, 19 Jan. 1798, Baltinglass, Hardy to Cooke.
135. Dickson, *Michael Dwyer*, p. 58; O'Donnell, op. cit., p. 88.
136. T.C.D., Cullen Mss, Ms 1472, pp 71-2.
137. NAI, 620/35/115, Hardy to Cooke, Hacketstown, 4 Feb. 1798.
138. NAI, 620/37/31, Rev. James McGhee, Clonmore Lodge, 7 May 1798.
139. NAI, 620/39/51, Rev. James McGhee, Hacketstown, 11 July 1798.
140. NAI, SOC 1017/62, sworn statements of Hugh Ollaghan of Ballymurtagh, 2 Jan., John Tyson of Croneban,17 and 20 Jan.
141. NAI, 620/35/48, Hardy to Cooke, 19 Jan. 1798. I am indebted to Dr Kevin Whelan for the identification of James Doyle who is not to be confused with Mathew Doyle.
142. NAI, 620/37/127, Hardy to Cooke, 22 May, 1798.
143. NAI, 620/3/32/6, enclosed under cover of letter from Thomas King.
144. O'Donnell contains a substantial amount of information about Murray and his contacts. O'Donnell, op. cit., pp 75-7.
145. The evidence confusingly telescopes this into 'societies of 12 ... in parties of 36'.
146. NAI, 620/10/121/45, 11 Jan. 1797, McNally.
147. NAI, 620/3/32/6, 22 May 1798.
148. NAI, 620/38/188, John Murphy, 20 June 1798. This testimony has much detailed information on the composition of the Newcastle baronial committee.
149. NAI, 620/3/32/6.
150. NAI, 620/39/51, Rev. James McGhee, Hacketstown, 11 July 1798.
151. NAI, 620/38/188, sworn testimony of John Murphy, 20 June 1798.
152. NAI, 620/3/32/6. 'A.B'.'s information under cover of Thomas King's letter of 22 May 1798.
153. NAI, SOC 3060, undated. A pencil mark indicates the date as '*c*.1796', but it is in fact later. In the text the highly variable spelling has been standardised as O'Neil and O'Reilly.
154. NAI, 620/52/105.
155. NAI, 620/35/55.
156. NAI, 620/40/90, Walter Kavanagh, 23 Sept. 1798.
157. NAI, 620/37/128.
158. NAI, 620/37/127.
159. NAI, 620/37/29. Wexford and Queen's are missing, and Louth and Monaghan which are also not given of course belonged to Ulster province. The document is undated but is inserted between the pages of a letter of 6 May, and with other letters of May. Hence it may refer to a late spring estimate.
160. NAI, 620/35/55.
161. Ibid.
162. NAI, 620/37/128, 22 May 1798.
163. O'Donnell, op. cit., pp 59-60.
164. T.C.D., Cullen Mss, Ms 1472, pp 159, 197. See also O'Donnell, op. cit., p. 85.

165. NAI, 620/36/92, Kemmis to Cooke, 28 March 1798.
166. NAI, 620/18a/6, 21 Sept. 1797, Bayly to Sir John Parnell, and forwarded to Cooke.
167. T.C.D., Cullen Mss, Ms 1472, p.194.
168. NAI, SOC 3165, 5 March 1798.
169. See Cullen's account as given in Myles Ronan, *'98 in Wicklow* (Wexford, 1938), p. 49.
170. See Wainwright's letters to Fitzwilliam, quoted in O'Donnell, op. cit., p. 104. See also letter of Hardy in May, quoted above, footnote 212.
171. NAI, 620/35/41, Robert Cornwall, 17 Jan. 1798. See also Cooke to Major General Fawcett, 30 Jan. 620/35/84. He had probably also acted under the influence of Foster Archer, inspector of prisons, Carlow, 3 Jan. 620/35/11.
172. NAI, 620/36/76, Cornwall, 26 March.
173. J. Alexander, op. cit., p. 25.
174. NAI, 620/35/48, Hardy to Cooke, 19 Jan. 1798.
175. NAI, 620/35/55.
176. NAI, 620/36/32, Hardy, 20 March 1798.
177. *Finn's Leinster Journal*, 24-28 March, 28-31 March, 31 March-4 April 1798. Interestingly Yelverton as a young barrister had been one of the defence team retained by Edmund Burke to defend propertied catholics accused of treason in Munster in 1766. He was a judge in the Orr trial in the north.
178. NAI, 620/10/121/97, McNally.
179. NAI, 620/36/104, Judge Day to Sir John Tydd, 21 March 1798.
180. *Glasgow Courier*, 12 April 1798; NAI, 620/10/121/97, McNally.
181. NAI, 620/36/27, Monck to Cooke, 19 March 1798. Monck, though a magistrate in neighbouring Wexford, is not on the list for Wicklow in *Watson's Almanack*.
182. Ibid.
183. NAI, 620/36/186, 10 April 1798.
184. NAI, 620/35/48, Hardy to Cooke, 19 Jan. 1798.
185. NAI, 620/37/127, 22 May 1798.
186. NAI, 620/35/48, 19 Jan. 1798.
187. NAI, 620/35/159, 26 Feb. 1797, Hardy to Pelham.
188. NAI, SOC 3152, Cooke to Peter La Touche, 16 January 1798.
189. NAI, 620/35/146, 20 Feb. 1798.
190. Musgrave, op. cit., vol. 1, pp 373-5.
191. Dickson, *Dwyer*, p. 60.
192. NAI, SOC 3165, 5 March 1798.
193. NAI, 620/36/87, 27 March 1798.
194. NAI, 620/36/115, 2 April 1798.
195. NAI, 620/39/118, 25 July 1798.
196. NAI, 620/36/123, 4 April 1798, Hardy to Cooke.
197. NAI, 620/35/47, 14 Jan. 1798, Edwards to lord lieutenant. This is the most informative single letter on Edwards. He had resigned as magistrate three years previously, and sought (and obtained) reinstatement at the outset of 1798. The facts are confirmed in a later letter in which he refers to eighteen years as magistrate and volunteer. On Hardy's relations with Wainwright, see O'Donnell, op. cit., pp 101-103.
198. NAI, 620/37/109, I9 May 1798, Rev. Christopher Robinson to Cooke.
199. NAI, 620/37/43, to Cooke, 9 May 1798
200. NAI, 620/37/133, O'Neale Stratford, 23 May 1798.
201. NAI, 620/37/35, 7 May 1798. This letter is reprinted in *The rebellion of 1798: facsimile documents* (P.R.O.I.), no. 3.

202. NAI, 620/37/109.
203. NAI, 620/38/51, Aldborough to lord lieutenant, 3 June 1798.
204. NAI, 620/40/69, 18 Sept. 1798. The handwriting is more disciplined, but there is little doubt about the identity.
205. NAI, 620/3/32/5, 14 May 1798.
206. For details see Musgrave, op. cit., vol. 1, p. 383.
207. NAI, 620/37/211A, Rev. Christopher Robinson, 29 May 1798.
208. Hardy said in May 1798 that he had been eight months in Wicklow in a civil and a military capacity. NAI, 620/37/128 to Castlereagh, 22 May 1798. His appointment seems to go back to September 1797. O'Donnell, op. cit., p. 101.
209. NAI, 620/38/23, Colin Campbell, Athy, 2 June 1798. On Colonel Keatinge see also Musgrave, op. cit., vol. 1, pp 336-7.
210. NAI, SOC 3152, E. Cooke, 16 Jan. 1798.
211. NAI, 620/35/159, Baltinglass, 20 Feb. 1798.
212. NAI, 620/37/190, Glenmalure camp, 28 May 1798, Hardy to General Loftus. Hardy was referring to the role of both the Antrim militia and the Shillelagh yeomanry in Wexford.
213. NAI, 620/37/133, Benjamin O'Neale Stratford, 23 May 1798.
214. News from Carlow, 6 Jan. 1798 in *Faulkner's Dublin Journal*, 13 Jan. 1798. The suggestion in Pakenham, *The year of liberty* (London, 1969), p. 379, fn. 22, that a lodge was set up in Carlow in January 1798 is not quite borne out by the quotation, though it is otherwise quite plausible.
215. NAI, 620/35/119, 6 Feb. 1798. He had already broached the subject in some specific detail in a letter of 14 February 1797. See 620/28/268.
216. J. G. Kerrane, 'Background to the 1798 rebellion in Co. Meath', unpublished MA thesis, U.C.D., 1971, p.119n.
217. A. McClelland, *The formation of the Orange Order* (n.d.), p. 13.
218. See Duggan, op. cit., pp 129-35; N.L.I., Ms 5398.
219. NAI, 620/36/I, 4 March 1798. The letter had an postscript enjoining 'burn this letter as soon as you reed(sic) it'. The reason the injunction was not acted on was that it was intercepted by the United Irishmen, and was later found among papers seized by the authorities.
220. NAI, 620/36/105. Richard O'Reilly's letter is undated, but may be dated by reference to King's account.
221. NAI, 620/37/139, Tinahely, 24 May. According to Gordon, there were 151 True Blues led by Henry Morton, the magistrate. Gordon, op. cit., p. 162. The Shillelagh yeoman infantry was led by James Morton. The name is variously rendered as Morton or Moreton.
222. NAI, 620/36/202, Ballycrystal, Clonegal, 23 April 1798. A report, probably from James, appeared in *Faulkner's Dublin Journal*, 14 Oct. 1797.
223. NAI, 620/36/96, 29 March 1798. It was probably a brother. There was an alderman James, master of an Orange lodge in Dublin. NAI, 620/10/118/20, 15 Dec. 1801, McNally. Alderman William James had been the loyalist candidate for the Dublin mayoralty in the violently disputed and protracted electoral contest of 1790, which had involved open confrontation with the government.
224. NAI, Frazer papers, no. 36, undated (after August 1796). He had first been brought to the attention of Cooke by C. Skeffington, MP for Belfast, in April 1796, and wrote regularly to Cooke from then on. On his background and circumstances, see especially letter of Thos. Whinnery, Post Office, Belfast, 18 Aug. 1796, no. 32, and his own letter of 19 April 1796, first of four enclosures to Skeffington's letter (no. 17) in April, in a series of letters in the Frazer papers,

from or relating to Smith, 2/17-40 (no. 17 has four enclosures). The numbering of the letters is confusing and also differs from the numbering in the report in the Deputy Keeper's Reports.

225. NAI, 620/30/89, 16 May 1797; SOC 3111, 15 Sept. 1797; 'Account of secret service money, Ireland, 1797-1804', pp 4-10, various entries in J.T. Gilbert, *Documents relating to Ireland 1795-1804* (reprint, Shannon, 1970). William Patrickson reported to Cooke on occasion. See e.g. NAI, 620/33/161-3, Blessington, 18 Dec. 1797.

226. The sum of £11.7.6 'to send Smith to bring him to town' on 31 October suggests that Cooke acted on his plea. He and his wife were still being maintained in some comfort into February 1798: the fact that there is no later entry (and the final entry on 2 February refers to a balance, not to recurring expenditure) suggests that his expensive services had at last been dispensed with.

227. NAI, 620/10/121/92, 28 February 1798; 620/10/121/93, 4 March 1798. See also undated McNally letter, NAI, 620/7/74/7, which seems to go back to February 1798.

228. NAI, OP 43/15/5, 5 Feb. 1798.

229. Dublin news, 4 May, quoted *Glasgow Courier*, 10 May 1798.

230. Dublin news, 28 May quoted in *Glasgow Courier*, 2 June 1798.

231. NAI, 620/36/176, 16 April 1798, to lord lieutenant.

232. See Edwards' letters to lord lieutenant, NAI, 620/37/99, 17 May; 620/39/118, 25 July 1798.

233. NAI, 620/37/99, 17 May 1798. A rather detailed account of some of the Wicklow events appeared in *Faulkner's Dublin Journal,* 20, 22 May 1798. See also *Glasgow Courier,* 26 May 1798, for some information from Dublin 21 May on arms surrenders at Powerscourt.

234. On relations between Hugo and Holt see O'Donnell, op. cit., passim.

235. NAI, 620/37/217, 30 May 1798, to Cooke.

236. NAI, 620/38/63, 6 June 1798.

237. NAI, 620/39/63, 12 July; 620/39/66, 13 July: 620/39/118, 25 July 1798.

238. NAI, 620/39/63, 12 July 1798.

239. NAI, 620/36/110 bis, John Staunton Rochfort, 1 April 1798.

240. *Carlow in '98: the autobiography of William Farrell of Carlow*, ed. Roger McHugh (Dublin, 1949).

241. Dr Pádraig Ó Snodaigh was the first person to detect the weakness of his account. See his *'98 in Carlow: a look at the historians* (Coiste Éigse Ceatharlacha, 1979), which deserves to be more widely known.

242. NAI, 620/37/108, 19 May 1798.

243. NAI, 620/40/191, 27 Oct. 1798, J. S. Rochfort and R. Cornwall to Cooke. There is reference in a letter of Cornwall's on 9 November 1797 to a deposition by a man named Kelly, but it would appear to be a different man: the deposition certainly did not provide information of consequence.

244. NAI, 620/37/65, Cooperhill, 13 May 1798, W. Cooper to William Cope, Dublin.

245. See detail book of Camolin cavalry in H. F. B. Wheeler and A. M. Broadley, *The war in Wexford* (London, 1910), p. 82.

246. NAI, 620/37/6, Monasterevin, 2 May, Robert Kelly to John Carleton. He was apparently a protestant. NAI, 620/37/34, Mountnorris to Cooke, 7 May; Kelly to Mountnorris, 4 May.

247. NAI, 620/37/118, 21 May (but redated 24 May at end of letter), Thomas Fitzgerald. One report had suggested that Thomas Fitzgerald along with Lord Edward was to command the county. NAI, 620/37/66, 14 May 1798.

248. NAI, 620/37/67, Athy, 14 May 1798.
249. NAI, 620/37/63, 12 May 1798.
250. O'Donnell, op. cit., p. 101.
251. NAI, 620/10/121/97, 27 April 1798, McNally.
252. NAI, 620/3/32/5, 14 May 1798, Rev. Christopher Robinson.
253. NAI, 620/37/37, examination of Luke Brannick, 8 May; 620/37/66, information of Jas. Kelly, 14 May.
254. NAI, 620/3/32/5, 14 May 1798.
255. Ibid.
256. NAI, 620/37/67, Athy, 14 May, Colin Campbell.
257. NAI, 620/37/90, Castlemartin, 16 May 1798, Gen Dundas to Cooke.
258. NAI, 620/35/47, 14 Jan. 1798, Edwards to lord lieutenant.
259. NAI, 620/37/128, 22 May 1798, Hardy to Castlereagh.
260. NAI, 620/37/63,12 May 1798.
261. NAI, 620/37/125, 22 May 1798, William Morton to John Lees. Morton's brother, Hugh, was a magistrate.
262. NAI, 620/37/127, 22 May 1798, to Cooke.
263. NAI, 620/37/128, 22 May 1798, Hardy to Castlereagh.
264. ibid.
265. NAI, 620/37/139, Tinahely, 24 May 1798, William Morton to Lees.
266. NAI, 620/37/43.
267. NAI, 620/37/128, 22 May 1798.
268. NAI, 620/37/211A, 29 May 1798, Robinson; 620/38/51, letter of Robinson enclosed with letter of Aldborough's.
269. See description of events in letter of 3 June from Christopher Robinson, chaplain of Aldborough's corps, sent by Aldborough to Elliott, 5 June. NAI, 620/38/51.
270. *Personal recollections of Wexford and Wicklow insurgents of 1798 as collected by Rev. Br Luke Cullen* (Enniscorthy, 1959), p. 112.
271. NAI, 620/37/218, 30 May 1798, Geo. Percival to Cooke.
272. *Glasgow Courier*, 5 June 1798, quoting a Dublin report of 31 May.
273. NAI, 620/38/15, 1 June 1798, E. Linde to Mary Linde.
274. The suggestion of being driven to its summit and of encirclement is contained in a Dublin report of 2 June quoted in *Glasgow Courier*.
275. Dublin news, 5 June in *Glasgow Courier*, 9 June 1798.
276. NAI, 628/38/126, Rathdrum, 11 June 1798, Hardy to Lake. Dunboyne has been taken to be Dunboyne in Co. Meath. In fact Dunboyne seems to be an error for Blackmore Hill, and the Kilbride mentioned was said to be '10 miles from town near Blackmoor Hills'. See evidence of Thomas Hawkins, in NAI, 620/38/126. There is an account also of Martin in Musgrave, op. cit., vol. 1, pp 390-1, which repeats mention of Dunboyne and gives the date of his arrest incorrectly as 24 June. Elsewhere there is reference in the court martial testimony to 'Dunamore Kilbride' which is clearly a garbled rendering of Blackmore pronounced in the Irish fashion as 'Blackamore'. The court martial account was very tersely and sparingly written. Its detail has to be interpreted with care. On Martin, see Daire Keogh, 'Fr. John Martin: an Augustinian friar and the Irish rebellion of 1798', *Analecta augustiniana*, vol LI (Rome, 1988), pp 227-46.See also Daire Keogh, '"The most dangerous villain in society". Fr John Martin's mission to the United Irishmen of Wicklow in 1798', *Eighteenth-Century Ireland,* vii (1992), pp 115-35. Holt's account of his own movements for the first month of the rebellion is brief, vague and incomplete.
277. NAI, 620/37/97, Sproule to Cooke.

278. NAI, 620/37/210, Wicklow, 29 May, Hardy.
279. NAI, 620/37/224, 30 May, 11 p.m., Hardy to Loftus, See also for an account, O'Donnell, op. cit., pp 133-7. O'Donnell suggests that Holt himself may have fought at Newtown.
280. NAI, 620/51/225, Commissary Brennan's book. The balance of probability is that this book contained the names of officers not only at New Ross, but at Three Rocks, prior to division of the force.
281. O'Donnell, op. cit., pp 141-2.
282. NAI, 620/38/126, Rathdrum, 11 June 1798, J. Hardy; Giffard, King and others, court martial, 11 June.
283. NAI, 620/38/126, court martial, 11 June 1798.
284. O'Donnell, op. cit., p. 39. Holt described Doyle as a colonel, but there seems to be no positive evidence for this rank. It is possible that if the six Wicklow regiments had been restructured into twelve at least on paper, he was designated as one of the extra colonels.
285. NAI, 620/40/198, to Lees, endorsed with name of Sproule and month of October. Sproule was relatively well-informed on Wicklow.
286. NAI, 620/38/243, 27 June 1798, William Colthurst.
287. NAI, 620/40/76, 19 Sept. 1798, to Cooke.
288. NAI, 620/37/128, 22 May 1798, Hardy to Castlereagh. The earlier report is in NAI, 620/33/102, 29 Nov. 1797.
289. Several accounts refer to 800 arms taken at Camolin. This must be an over-estimate. The origins of this version rest with Gordon. He referred to the rebels being armed with 800 guns on their attack on Enniscorthy, and his footnote reference on the same page, mentioning 'a large quantity of firearms' seized at Camolin, has been taken to imply that they had all been acquired there. Gordon, op. cit., p. 111. Lecky in fact so interpeted it, and stated that the rebels found '700 or 800 guns' in Camolin. Lecky, *History of Ireland*, vol. iv, p. 357. It is inherently unlikely that there were that many guns in Camolin.
290. *Personal recollections of Wexford and Wickow insurgents of 1798* (Enniscorthy, 1959), p. 113.
291. See Benjamin O'Neale Stratford in NAI, 620/36/186, 10 April 1798, and in undated letter in NAI, SOC 3119/1, and 620/37/133, 23 May 1798.
292. NAI, SOC 1017/3, 22 Aug. 1798.
293. Pakenham, *The year of liberty* (London, 1969), p. 145.
294. There is, contrary to what has been written, no doubt about Philip Roche not having been present at the Battle of Ross. Miles Byrne regrets his departure from the forces in the north of the county at this stage. (*Memoirs*, Paris, 1863, i, p. 126).

Enniskerry (Bartlett).

Chapter 13

THE POOR LAW IN COUNTY WICKLOW

EVA Ó CATHAOIR

INTRODUCTION

The Poor Relief (Ireland) Act of 1838 was the British government's first major response to Ireland's considerable social problems. The poor law was to have a profound impact on Ireland, up to and even after its formal abolition in 1923. This chapter deals with the poor law in relation to county Wicklow and explores the building and development of five workhouses, their administration, their policy concerning work, education and training, diet and discipline, religion and health care during the early years, the Famine- and post-Famine periods. It is based primarily on the records of the Wicklow poor law unions, British parliamentary papers and other contemporary sources.[1]

1.1 Poverty in pre-Famine Wicklow

In comparison with many other parts of Ireland in the nineteenth century, Wicklow was comparatively prosperous and peaceful. Resembling Ireland in microcosm, the county's wealth was concentrated in the north-east. A major cause of poverty was lack of regular employment: in west Wicklow, for instance, twice as many labourers as needed were eagerly competing for wages and potato plots. As alternative foods were too expensive for the poor, their chief diet consisted of the potato. Each summer, after the old crop had been eaten and until the new one was ripe, families went out begging or ate weeds. The poor inquiry commissioners noted that this was 'a season of great distress and trial for the poorer labourers and the destitute part of the population. For them it amounts, in fact, to an annual return of a temporary half famine'. Occasionally, a local potato failure, as for instance in the barony of Upper Talbotstown in 1829, increased the seasonal distress.[2]

Progressive landlords, such as Lord Fitzwilliam, began to consolidate farms before the Famine. At least 800 persons of an estimated 1,530 people served eviction notices in the county were evicted on the Coolattin estate in 1830. The dispossessed speedily used up remaining assets to feed their families and drifted to the towns: about 1837 a German traveller noted crowds of half-naked men at work as casual porters in Kingstown Harbour. Touring county Wicklow, von Hailbronner considered the peasantry wretched in comparison with their German counterparts. In Little Bray, speculators let cabins to the poor. Similarly in Arklow, the underprivileged consisted of unemployed labourers and fishermen, who experienced periodic hardship: in 1824, for instance, the absence of herrings from their coasts forced the men to sail north, leaving their families behind. Out of a population of 3,000, the *Freeman's Journal* considered upwards of 1,200 'totally destitute'.[3]

Baltinglass, in west Wicklow, had slums inhabited by the chronically ill, widows and their children, the unemployed and the elderly. The poor inquiry commissioners inspected over fifty of these hovels. A typical example: 'occasional labourer, wife and four children; cabin with two rooms, floor very damp; no chimney; no window; all but bare walls, most miserable'.[4]

Potatoes were grown on marginal land, where 'cultivation ... has been gradually extended far up the mountains'. The evicted also settled on common land in Rathnew. On their 1840 tour the Halls described a similar settlement on a commons near Roundwood: 'a few miserable hovels now and then skirting the wayside with wretched patches of shrivelled potatoes planted in bits of land, the forcing of which into comparative cultivation can scarcely recompense the very extreme poverty'.[5]

Although Wicklow respondents to the poor inquiry generally considered that there had been very few deaths from starvation, Catholic clergymen stated that poverty and malnutrition were the cause of fever and cholera mortality. Local food shortages had occurred in Wicklow in 1824, 1826 and 1827. There had been distress in Baltinglass in 1829, 1832 and 1835; twenty-two deaths from cholera were reported in Arklow in 1832, while this epidemic claimed fifty-four victims in Bray between 1832 and 1833. Mrs Smith of Baltiboys recorded an outbreak of fever in the Blessington area in 1841. Undoubtedly there were many others, which went unnoticed by contemporaries because they were commonplace.[6]

1.2 Organised private charity before 1840

The poor inquiry commissioners summarised the customary attitude of ordinary Irish people, who freely shared food and shelter with those in need, thus: 'The humanity of the poor is very great towards one another.' While Mrs Smith and Mrs Asenath Nicholson on her Irish travels were critical of the better-off Irishwoman's lack of interest in the underprivileged, considerable organised charity existed in Wicklow before the 1838 poor law. The upper and middle classes contributed to education and health services and assisted in the building and maintenance of Catholic chapels and presbyteries.[7] By the standards of the 1830s, Wicklow enjoyed good healthcare facilities. The east of Ireland with its resident gentry was favoured by a system which decreed that these institutions were established first by private subscriptions before receiving state funding. To extend the benefits of the county infirmary (1766) in Wicklow town, a western branch was established in Baltinglass in 1817. As the infirmary dispensaries remained inaccessible to many poor people, local dispensaries were founded (date of establishment in brackets): Arklow (1821), Aughrim (1831), Blessington, Bray (1811), Carnew, Calary, Dunlavin, Enniskerry, Kiltegan, Newtown Mount Kennedy (Newcastle) with Delgany branch, Rathdrum (1812), Redcross/Dunganstown, Shillelagh, Stratford on Slaney (1817) and Tinahely. Treatment was free for the poor and because many of the doctors regarded malnutrition as a cause of illness, fever patients in the county's six fever hospitals, Arklow (1818), Bray (1817), Enniskerry (1814), Newtown Mount Kennedy (1814), Stratford on Slaney (1817) and Wicklow (1836), were given wine and additional food. Some accounts also mention Blessington and Carnew (1841) fever hospitals administered by voluntary committees. These establishments employed competent doctors. The situation of psychiatric patients, however, was grim: overcrowding in Dublin's Richmond District Lunatic Asylum meant that some would continue to be confined in Wicklow Jail.[8]

Landlord contributions to these rudimentary social services can be found in the Coolattin estate papers: in 1831, for instance, Lord Fitzwilliam donated £25 for the poor in Newcastle parish, £20 for those in Wicklow, £10 for those in Rathdrum and £10 towards establishing Aughrim dispensary. Schools operated by landlords, for example, the Putlands, sometimes also fed and clothed poor children. Those funded by Col. Howard (Parnell's ancestor) and Grattan in the Enniskerry area in the 1820s were conducted on non-sectarian lines. Others, however, used schools to proselytise poor children. The evangelical Rev Robert Daly was accused of this practice in Powerscourt parish. Such episodes contributed to a distrust of establishment institutions, which was to spread to the future workhouses, despite the poor law commissioners' efforts to remain non-denominational.[9]

Wicklow's poor benefited from church-funds, coal and blanket funds, almshouses, charity events, legacies and the occasional, additional collection during hard times. Savings' banks allowed the thrifty to plan for the rainy day, while loan funds offered opportunities to improve one's circumstances. The latter sometimes had a charitable dimension. Some places also had associations employing the poor, ladies' Dorcas societies or poor shops. Here, savings could be accumulated until sufficient purchase money had been saved. The Coolattin poor shop records (1830-1838) show that shillings and pence were deposited to buy clothes, blankets and shoes. A premium was given as encouragement.[10]

Established by John Tate, Tate's Charity had an annual income of £100, derived from lands in Knockrath, of which £50 p.a. went to Rathdrum dispensary, while the remainder was utilised in small loans of up to £5. Recipients had to repay these, interest-free, within a year. In cases of hardship caused by illness or misfortune, the trustees could donate small sums for which the elderly or the very poor with five or more children also qualified. Tate's Charity benefited the 'industrious poor', who had been residents of Rathdrum for at least three years. The fund was non-denominational and trustees were elected by resident parishioners with an income of £50 upwards. People owning £100 p.a. in land or £1,000 in personal property in the Rathdrum district were eligible for trusteeships. Tate's Charity is still active and recently, for instance, gave loans to families who would otherwise find it difficult to send their offspring to college.[11]

2 THE WORKHOUSES: ADMINISTRATION

2.1 Building the workhouses

Although the Commission of Inquiry into the Conditions of the Poorer Classes in Ireland, established in 1833, had recommended dealing with the root causes of Irish destitution, this was rejected by the British administration. George Nicholls, an English poor law commissioner, was appointed to conduct a brief investigation in 1836. He supported a system of workhouse relief, based on the English poor law of 1834. The Poor Relief (Ireland) Act of 1838, which divided the country into 130 poor law unions, was the first major piece of social legislation for this country. At a meeting in April 1838 Wicklow gentry and farmers, while supporting 'the principle of a poor law', rejected the legislation as 'totally unsuited to the condition of the country'. Lord Fitzwilliam, Wicklow's largest landlord, was also reported as opposing it, on the grounds that the country was too poor to afford it.[12]

The new Irish unions were collections of parishes grouped into electoral divisions, which sent representatives to the boards of guardians. Unions were to be composed of a 'compact, convenient, and accessible' district, with, if possible, a market town at its centre. Union size varied considerably; for instance, the Rathdown Union had a population of 44,214 in 1841, while 110,408 people lived in the Armagh Union. Electoral divisions were formed on the basis of enough

Table 13.1 Wicklow Charities 1820–1840[13]

Arklow
miscellaneous
harbour improvements offer employment
Baltinglass
poor shop
in Stratford Lodge demesne
miscellaneous
private subscription list (1835)
government loan £60
Blessington
charity fund/loan fund
Protestant rector distributes small sums
ladies' Dorcas society
informal, Mrs Smith & family
miscellaneous
Smith tenants given money, clothes, food
Bray
charity fund/loan fund
loan fund
legacy
Adair bequest £60 p.a.
charitable/employment training
Putlands employ 40 women in wool and flax manufactory, clothes made given to poor
annual events
gents' committee runs boat race to benefit fishermen
miscellaneous
collections in times of hardship, coal etc. given by some landlords
Carnew
charity fund/loan fund
loan fund (est. 1834) run by gents' committee, profits go to charity
charitable/employment training
ladies supervise weaving and spinning association
Coolattin
poor shop
est. 1830
Delgany
charity fund/loan fund
parish and church funds, poor apply to gentry committee
legacy
Adair bequest
poor shop
yes
Donoughmore parish (Upp. Talbotstown barony)
charity fund/loan fund
loan fund est. 1824
legacy
£20 p.a. for Protestant poor; interest on £200 stock for 5 Protestant and 5 Catholic poor
miscellaneous
private subscription list in times of hardship
Dunganstown
legacy
interest of 2 legacies of £100 each, £6 p.a.
charitable/employment training
ladies' association for employing female poor
Enniskerry/Powerscourt
legacy
Adair bequest
poor shop
yes
almshouse
for 6 old and infirm women
ladies' Dorcas society
makes and sells nightcaps
Castle McAdam/Redcross parish
annual events
£20 p.a. collected for widows and orphans; committee donates blankets and clothes at Christmas
miscellaneous
increased efforts during times of hardship
Drumkay and Kilcoole parish
charity fund/loan fund
Kilcoole eligible for Delgany parish and church funds, s. a.
almshouses
8 Protestant widows supported in Wicklow town
Newcastle barony
annual events
Protestant gentry contributes at annual charity sermon
Killiskey parish & Ashford district
legacy
Tottenham bequest, £10 p.a.
miscellaneous
charity sermon for poor and indigent; Before 1834 Mrs Tighe of Rosanna supported, educated and gave dowries of £27 each to some destitute girls
Rathdrum
charity fund/loan fund
Tate's Charity £50 p.a. available in loans and donations
charity/employment training
charitable association to assist the poor in their own homes and to encourage industry, supported by subscriptions
Wicklow town
charity fund/loan fund
loan fund, sick, coal and blanket funds, £500 p.a. spent on poor
almshouses
for 15 aged men and widows, supported by subscriptions and weekly church collections
charitable employment/training
school of industry
miscellaneous
cargo of rice donated by Ld. Fitzwilliam; ball held, profits for poor

property to support poverty through local poor rates. It was therefore in the ratepayers' best interests to have as many wealthy and as few poor people as possible in their electoral division, thereby keeping rates low. Prior to the formation of the Rathdown Union, a representative of the poor law commission explained the arrangements to a meeting of the principal landlords, tenants and residents. There were strong objections to Bray and its poor being placed with Delgany, which already included the impoverished village of Kilmacanogue. The future ratepayers protested vigorously and petitioned Nicholls at the Dublin Custom House. The point was taken: Delgany and Bray became separate electoral divisions.[14]

Five poor law unions incorporated parts of Wicklow: the prosperous Rathdown Union, established 10 August 1839, consisted of ten electoral divisions, of which three (Bray, Delgany and Powerscourt) were in north Wicklow, the remainder in south county Dublin. Kingstown and Bray were its largest towns. It was decided to site the workhouse in Loughlinstown, county Dublin, in a central location. A proposal to adapt Glencree barracks was rejected as impractical and expensive; access would have been difficult for the poor and suppliers alike. The chosen location was objected to by Judge Robert Day and Sir Compton Domville, the occupier and owner of Loughlinstown House respectively. They feared proximity to a workhouse would reduce the value of their mansion but relented when the board suggested they pay the re-location expenses. The board rented eight acres at an annual rent of £49 from a local farmer. The workhouse was intended for up to 600 inmates and cost £9,683 to build, which would be repaid from future poor rates. It opened on 12 October 1841.[15]

The adjoining Rathdrum Union, established on 30 October 1839, consisted of twelve electoral divisions in central and south-east Wicklow (Newcastle, Arklow, Killiskey, Kilbride, Dunganstown, Wicklow, Rathdrum, Glendalough, Roundwood, Glenealy, Aughrim and Castlemacadam). Arklow and Wicklow were the largest towns in this union. Rathdrum, like many Irish workhouses, was built on the outskirts of the town. Unlike Ireland's fine eighteenth-century hospitals, for instance, Dr Steevens' or the Rotunda, poorhouse buildings were strictly utilitarian. The Rathdrum guardians rented five acres, paying a rent of £10 p.a. Here, too, the institution was intended for 600 inmates. It cost £8,363 to build and opened on 8 March 1842.[16]

The Baltinglass Union, established 30 November 1839, had eleven electoral divisions, eight of these (Baltinglass, Stratford, Kiltegan, Rathdangan, Donard, Hollywood, Donaghmore and Dunlavin) in county Wicklow, the remainder in counties Carlow and Kildare. The poorhouse was intended for 500 people, cost £7,848 to build, was located outside Baltinglass on seven acres at a rent of £23 p.a. and opened on 28 October 1841.[17]

Originally conceived as the 'Tinahely Union', the formation of the Shillelagh Union encourages speculation, as it was not based on a town such as Carnew or Tinahely, but was conveniently situated in the centre of Lord Fitzwilliam's Wicklow estate. Shillelagh Union included south-west Wicklow and east Carlow. Established on 20 July 1839, fifteen of its nineteen electoral divisions (Tinahely, Carnew, Ballingate, Killinure, Cronolea, Shillelagh, Coolattin, Coolboy, Ballybeg, Ballinglen, Kilballyowen, Kilpipe, Coolballintaggart, Munny and Aghowle) were in county Wicklow. Sited on six acres of land at a rent of £8 p.a., the poorhouse on the outskirts of Shillelagh village was planned for 400 inmates, cost £7,394 to erect and opened on 18 February 1842.[18]

Blessington and Baltiboys were among the twenty-three electoral divisions of the Naas Union, established on 18 February 1839. Naas workhouse on five acres (£26 rent) accommodated 550 people and opened on 4 August 1841.[19]

The poor law commissioners employed George Wilkinson, the architect of some Welsh poorhouses, to design their Irish institutions. His symmetrical plans were readily adaptable for various sizes. An Irish workhouse consisted of three horizontal blocks: the admissions building, containing porter's office, probationary wards and the guardians' boardroom; the main building with dormitories, school and dayrooms and master and matron's accommodation; the third building housed the infirmary and lunatic wards. The dining hall, which doubled up as chapel, formed a vertical axis connecting the main building with the infirmary. Kitchen and washrooms were in an annex behind the main workhouse. The complex was segregated into male and female sides and surrounded by high walls. Loughlinstown was exceptional insofar as the admissions department adjoined the Dublin to Bray road; the remainder of the poorhouse was located on a hill.[20]

Soon after completion, the poor law commissioners received numerous complaints of poor workmanship from Wicklow guardians: walls, windows and roofs let in rain, the mortar floors were unsatisfactory and the water supply was out of order. On 23 September 1839 the Naas guardians, convinced that their contractor's sand was 'totally unfit' for building work, informed the commissioners who suspended him until he provided better material.[21]

2.2 Boards of guardians and staff

Ultimate authority over the administration of Irish workhouses was initially vested in the English Poor Law Commission. One of its members, George Nicholls, who advocated a system of minimum relief, supervised the creation of the Irish poor law. In a major legislative change in 1847, a separate poor law commission for Ireland was established, which assumed the powers and duties of the English commissioners. As their communications to the Wicklow boards of guardians testify, the commissioners exercised rigid control. In 1872 the Irish Poor Law Commission became part of the Local Government Board.[22]

Every owner/occupier of a land holding paid poor rates and was entitled to elect poor law guardians; in the case of large holdings additional votes accrued. Occupiers with a rateable valuation under £4 did not vote, as they paid no rates. With polling by 'open voting papers', a landlord could pressurise tenants in favour of his candidate; on the other hand, Mrs Elizabeth Smith claimed that the parish priest of Boystown (now Valleymount) harassed parishioners supporting her husband against the Catholic clergy's candidate for poor law guardian.[23]

A property qualification reserved guardianships for the well-off. Moore's 1850 work illustrates the sliding scale from east to west: the highest rateable valuation of £30 was required for guardianship of the North and South Dublin Unions, representatives of, for instance, the Rathdown, Naas and Baltinglass Unions needed to have a minimum valuation of £25, while the Rathdrum and Shillelagh Unions' requirements were on the lower £20 scale. No Wicklow union was listed on the lowest level of £10 applicable to the Ballinrobe Union in county Mayo, for instance. Boards comprised elective and *ex officio* members: the poor law guardians for Wicklow Unions in 1852 were[24]

Baltinglass (16)	Naas (20)	Rathdown (19)	Rathdrum (27)	Shillelagh (15)
37	50	43	57	39

Wicklow guardians were landlords, strong farmers, merchants and, in the Rathdown union, professional men. (For detailed lists of guardians see appendix I). Feingold states that the landlord/*ex officio* section dominated boards of guardian for the first forty years of their existence, virtually monopolising chairmanships. This was the case in Wicklow, where the officers of the first Rathdrum board were landlords: Acton of Kilmacurragh, Parnell of Avondale and Synge of Glanmore. Lord Fitzwilliam, who owned 89,891 acres, headed the Shillelagh board in 1848. Saunders, a west Wicklow landlord, chaired the Baltinglass guardians' meetings in 1848. Sir George Hodson was *ex officio* chairman of the Rathdown board for almost 50 years and was succeeded by a fellow landowner, Lord Powerscourt.[25] As the nineteenth century progressed tenant farmers' influence increased. Some Rathdrum guardians, particularly active between 1869-73, joined the Wicklow Tenants Association, calling for land reform. The Local Government

Board reprimanded them on 28 October 1873 for reading circulars from Isaac Butt's Home Rule Association at board meetings as 'altogether foreign to the business of the guardians'.

Although by 1882 a Rathdown guardian served on the Central Land League Committee, the county was not in the forefront of land agitation. Women, who became eligible for guardianships in 1896, were elected to office in Rathdrum and Rathdown. The change-over from *ex officio* to elective chairmen occurred in county Wicklow only after the Local Government Act of 1898.[26] Attendance at board meetings fluctuated considerably. At the first meeting after the annual election of guardians on or near 25 March, officers were chosen and this usually meant a 'full house', not to be repeated until the following year. Although three guardians constituted a quorum, Rathdrum meetings of the early years were irregular. This is instanced by the minutes of 29 September 1857 – thirteenth failure of board to meet that year; 4 May 1858 – ninth meeting missed. Occasionally guardians reversed poor law commissioners' decisions: on 31 December 1842 the master in Loughlinstown refused to admit an urgent case following his dismissal by the commissioners, the board re-elected him. Similar incidents of guardians protecting officials are recorded for Rathdrum.[27]

While unremunerative and time consuming, guardianships offered prestige and opportunities of patronage when selecting officers and contracts. A Rathdown guardian held the union's pre-Famine contract to treat fever patients; relatives of other guardians supplied goods to the workhouse. In 1856 a company complained that their tender had been rejected because of 'local interest influenced by friendly feelings'. In 1899 former Loughlinstown boards were accused of having run a 'closed shop.' The situation in Rathdrum was similar; for instance, one guardian's son became a poor rate collector, another held the Indian meal contract. In 1899 the Shillelagh coal contract 'had for a longtime past appeared to be a sort of family arrangement', according to the *Wicklow News-Letter.*[28]

Workhouses were managed by paid officials, selected by the guardians and vetted by the poor law commissioners. The master had overall responsibility, while the matron was the most important female officer. Rathdrum and Rathdown boards liked to appoint married couples, in the sometimes futile hope of harmony. (An independent matron's salary was also higher.) In keeping with the regimented system, military men were preferred in the early years, as having experience of accountancy and crowd control.[29]

Before the Famine, Loughlinstown had the largest and best-paid staff among the Wicklow workhouses. Nevertheless, its officials were not of superior calibre. Although Loughlinstown and Rathdrum were the same

Table 13.2 Salaries of Workhouse Officers

Workhouse	Clerk	Master	Matron	Porter	Medical Officer	Chaplains C. of I.	Chaplains RC	School-master	School-mistress	Nurse	Maximum number of places
	£ p.a.	£ p.a.	£ p.a.	£ p.a.	£ p.a.	£ p.a.	£ p.a.	£ p.a.	£ p.a.	£ p.a.	
Rathdown	80	60	60	15	60	30	50	15	10	8	600
Rathdrum	40	46	25	12	50	30	50	15	12	8	600
Naas	52	50	25	10	50	20	50	20	15	10	550
Baltinglass	70	40	25	12	40	25	–	12	8	8	500
Shillelagh	70	40	25	12	50	25	40	12	8	8	400

Workhouse	shoemaker	tailor	servant	cook	sweep	No.	rate collector	vaccination	No.	wardmaster	wardmistress		Total number of officers
	£ p.a.	£ p.a.	£ p.a.	£ p.a.	£ p.a.			£ p.a.					
Rathdown	15	20	—	10	—	4	6d in £ each	1s for each case	11	10	8	Every union employs a valuator of property	31
Rathdrum	—	—	—	7	5	8	6d in £ each	1s for each case	8	—	—		29
Naas	15 12s	16	—	—	—	5	6d in £ each	1s for each case up to 200 vaccinations, 6 d each for further cases	5	—	—		23
Baltinglass	1s 4d per day	1s 4d per day	4	—	—	4	5d in	1s for each case	4	—	—		21
Shillelagh	1s per day	1s per day	—	6	—	4	5d in £ each	1s for each case up to 200 vaccinations, 6 d each for further cases	4	—	—		22

(*Source:* H.C. 1843 xlvi pp 78-88)

size, Rathdrum guardians were slow to raise salaries, which resembled those of the smaller Baltinglass and Shillelagh Unions. During the Great Famine wages and staff increased temporarily. In 1873 the Rathdrum master's salary, which had remained at £60 p.a. for 22 years, was increased by ten pounds.[30]

Gerard O'Brien's contention that the pre-Famine workhouse did not function effectively, can be confirmed from the Rathdown and Rathdrum records: by 1845 the Loughlinstown master, matron, clerk and porter had each been replaced once, the schoolmistress and nurse three times and the schoolmaster four times. By 1844, after two and a half years in operation, the Rathdrum workhouse had its second clerk and its third master and cook respectively. For the 1845-70 period the poor law commissioners' order books record the dismissal of seven Shillelagh, six Rathdrum, five Baltinglass and three Rathdown officials. (This does not take into account those who resigned after misdemeanours to remain eligible for employment in another poorhouse.) Except for the doctor, clerk and chaplains, officers lived in, separated from their families. This rule was often ignored by officials on Rathdrum and Rathdown boards. From 1860, the Rathdrum guardians' liberal approach to staff holidays/family visits resolved the problem of illegal workhouse residents. By contrast, abuses associated with illicit family residents still occurred in Rathdown.[31] Working conditions in the pre-Famine workhouse contributed to tensions: the master's duties began at 6 am and ended at 9 pm. Retaining a satisfactory schoolmaster in Rathdrum and Rathdown was difficult for similar reasons. Male teachers were paid £15 p.a. with rations and lodgings, sometimes close to the lunatic cells. The schoolmaster supervised the boys at all times, besides acting as understudy to the master. Mrs Smith's national school teacher in Baltiboys had the same salary with more free time, while the Rathdown teacher's wages compared unfavourably with the tradesmen. In 1848 the Rathdrum guardians had to double the schoolmaster's wages to £30 to attract applicants. Nevertheless, at least six male teachers absconded, died or were dismissed between 1842-72.[32]

Rapid staff turnover and accusations of inefficiency, drunkenness, embezzlement, violence and sexual immorality were characteristic of the first 25 years of the poor law in Wicklow. To give representative examples: between April and July 1844 Rathdrum provided no weekly returns; the Rathdown minutes of 3 September 1844 record dissatisfaction with the state of the union records and quarrelsome personnel; some weeks later an inquiry in Baltinglass Workhouse accused officers of pilfering from sick inmates; in 1848 the Rathdrum matron gave birth to an illegitimate child in the poorhouse; the following year Loughlinstown's staff intrigues, culminating in the married matron's affair with a colleague, featured in the *Freeman's Journal*. The minutes of 1 August 1848 record the stabbing of two people by a jealous Rathdown shoemaker. In 1853, the missing master was found in a Dublin brothel, while the schoolmistress's husband beat a Loughlinstown inmate with a poker the following year.[33] Staff relations became more stable during the 1860s, in particular, in Rathdrum Workhouse. Nevertheless, sporadic incidents occurred: in 1879 a Baltinglass relieving officer was dismissed after pocketing outdoor relief, while a Rathdown official, who disobeying his board, jammed a suicide victim into too small a coffin and interred him in waste ground, was forced to resign. Throughout the remainder of the nineteenth century, Wicklow unions received occasional, negative publicity: for instance, in 1899 the Shillelagh nightnurse was dismissed after neglecting a dying patient, while she had an affair with a married contractor in the workhouse. Allegations that she had concealed the birth of her illegitimate child, led to the constabulary searching the poorhouse, albeit unsuccessfully.[34]

The poor law system depended on effective rate collection, but collectors were often inefficient and sometimes dishonest. Reminiscent of the west of Ireland rather than county Wicklow, Baltinglass Union collectors in 1843 needed police protection. Regular complaints about Rathdrum collectors featured in the minutes well into the 1880s. In 1845 a Rathdrum official absconded, another fled with £400 of union funds in 1849, as did a Shillelagh collector in 1852, while a member of the Baltinglass collecting staff arrested in 1854 had a ticket purchased to America and £30. In 1879 the Rathdown Union lost £213 in a similar incident.[35]

The minutes of an organisation usually attempt to present the positive side, but occasionally we get a glimpse of a divergence between poor law theory and practice: long-established Rathdrum officials developed a tradition of acting without the guardians' authority; for instance, when the master transported inmates to hospitals and lunatic asylums prior to the board's deliberations. The frequent repetition of the order to take children and mentally ill inmates for walks, encourages the suspicion that Loughlinstown officials ignored inconvenient orders.[36]

Relatives of workhouse officers were sometimes appointed to minor positions as a matter of convenience; for instance, in Rathdown in 1857 the porter's wife became the 'female searcher' at a salary of £5 p.a. In Rathdrum, a workhouse officials' dynasty emerged: Isaac Flower, master from 1850 to 1899, married the matron's daughter, who succeeded her. His son was appointed assistant clerk of Rathdown, having first helped Isaac in Rathdrum. Several guardians and officials named 'Manning' feature in the Rathdrum records; they were local Protestants and probably related. In 1899, during an inquiry into Shillelagh poorhouse, it was stated that three key staff members were relations and that it was unwise to oppose them. When appointing a seamstress to the county home in 1922, the *Wicklow News-Letter* reported the comment 'you may take it there is some friend to give the job to'.[37]

Some competent officials however spent their working lives in poor law administration: a schoolmaster left the small Rathdrum workhouse school for the more prestigious one in Loughlinstown, eventually becoming master; Isaac Flower had been assistant master of the North Dublin Union. Joseph Cope started as assistant master in Shillelagh, went to Celbridge Union and eventually died as clerk of Rathdown poorhouse. This point is also illustrated by superannuation records. In some instances former officials became inmates; for instance, an ex-master of Loughlinstown, a native of Enniskerry, who had failed in business in England, was repatriated to spend his old age in his former workhouse in 1879.[38]

The Local Government Act of 1898 opened up membership of local authorities to a larger section of the population. By summer 1899, twenty-three mayors and chairmen of urban district councils belonged to the Irish Republican Brotherhood. This secret society had decided on a policy of infiltration which was only sporadically successful in county Wicklow. By the 1890s nationalists began to compete for workhouse appointments: Laurence Murphy, the Roundwood IRB leader, became a relieving officer of the Rathdrum Union. Clerk Cope of Loughlinstown, who had founded a workhouse officials' trade union, which improved working conditions, died in 1899. There were thirteen candidates for the clerkship, including such advanced nationalists as John Wyse Power, whose wife Jenny, incidentally a native of Baltinglass, was a prominent Dublin guardian and future senator: and Tom Clarke, the first signatory of the 1916 Proclamation, whose candidature was supported by a Fenian on Bray's UDC. A Wicklow teacher with a Fenian past was elected.[39]

2.3 Inmates

The criteria for admission were destitution as a result of old age, illness or handicap or because the applicants were children. Adults, destitute through unemployment, came next on the list of priority. Should there be more applicants than places, locals were to be preferred. During the pre-Famine period unpaid district wardens recommended applicants, but in 1847 relieving officers were introduced. These inspected candidates on application, deciding on temporary admission, which had to be confirmed at the next board of guardians' meeting. The master could admit urgent cases conditionally, especially when these had been recommended by a figure of authority.

On arrival the 'pauper' was bathed and dressed in the workhouse uniform, consisting of jacket, waistcoat, shirt, trousers and cap for male and cotton dress, shift, petticoats and cap for female inmates. Clothing clearly displayed the union's name and thus the wearer's social status, adding to the poorhouse stigma. The newcomer was inspected by the medical officer and, if necessary, transferred to the workhouse infirmary or fever hospital. Until his admission had been confirmed, he remained in a probationary ward, a precaution designed to reduce the spread of infections to the main building. In practice, however, Rathdrum officials tended to ignore these safeguards.[40]

The Loughlinstown indoor register 1841-5 confirms that only the most disadvantaged sections of society entered the institution before the Famine. Of the first 120 (legible) admissions from 12 October 1841 to 30 November 1841, 61 were classified as disabled by disease, while 59 were healthy. Nevertheless, only nine of the latter could be seen as potential wage earners. The largest number of inmates came from the Bray electoral division. Diseases recorded on admission were not specific to the Rathdown Union, but similar to those noted in the South Dublin Union and, presumably, Ireland as a whole.[41]

Table 13.3 Examples from indoor registers
Loughlinstown indoor register 1841-5

Origin of Inmates		**Diseases on Admission**	
Electoral division	*Number of Inmates*		
Bray	22	rheumatism	12
Union at large	21	lameness, only one leg etc.	12
Glencullen	15	bad sight, blind	7
Delgany	12	paralysis, paralytic	5
Killiney	11	deafness	3
Kingstown	10	general debility	3
Rathmichael	9	asthma	3
Stillorgan	9	'idiot'	3
Powerscourt	5	palsy	2
Blackrock	4	'decline' (TB?)	2
Dundrum	2	epileptic	2
		unmarried pregnancy	2
		unspecified pains	2
		others	3
Total	First 120 Inmates	Total	61

Status of Healthy Inmates

Category	*Number*
Child of Inmate	12
Orphan	10
Healthy Adult	9
Widow	6
Deserted Child	5
Person over 65	5
Deserted Wife	3
with Child	6
Unmarried Mother	1
with baby	1
Unaccompanied illegitimate baby	1
Total	59

Occupations of Inmates

Occupation	*Number*
None	44
Servant	40
Labourer	20
Dealer	3
Dressmaker	2
Blacksmith	2
Schoolmistress	2
Shoemaker	1
Thatcher	1
Silkwinder	1
Messenger	1
Nurse	1
Quarryman	1
Parish clerk	1
Total	120

There are indications that a surviving Rathdrum indoor register (*circa* 22 March 1842 – 10 December 1852) contains long-stay inmates. Among the first 120 entries were 82 children and 23 sick people. Throughout their history, workhouses sheltered more women than men, here 71 of 120 patients were female, 49 male.

Rathdrum indoor register *c*.1842-52

Occupations of Inmates

Occupation	*Number of Inmates*
None	93, including 82 children
Servant	7
Labourer	6
Knitter	5
Nurse	2
Charwoman	2
Shoemaker	1
Tailor	1
Fisherman	1
Dairywoman	1
Plainworker	1
Total	120

Diseases on Admission

infirm	8
bad sight, blind	4
'idiot, insane, imbecile'	3
cripple	3
delicate (TB?)	2
deafness	1
epileptic	1
lameness	1
Total	23

Analysing similar samples admitted to Rathdrum between 23 November and 10 December 1852 the following pattern emerges:

Origin of Inmates

Electoral division	*Number of Inmates*
Union at large	37
Wicklow	22
Brockagh	8
Rathdrum	7
Glenealy	5
Ballyarthur	5
Ballinderry	4
Aughrim	4
Newcastle	4
Arklow	3
Trooperstown	3
Glendalough	3
Ennerreilly	3
Cronebane	3

Elect. div.	*Number*
Ballinaclash	3
Dunganstown	2
Killiskey	1
Avoca	1
Oldtown	1
Knockrath	1
Total	12

(Rathdrum electoral divisions were rearranged in 1850)

Occupations of Inmates

Occupation	*Number*
None	56
Servant	23
Charwoman	22
Labourer	18
Shoemaker	1
Total	120

Diseases on Admission

Healthy	100
Fever	9
'Sick'	5
Infirm	3
Idiot	2
Smallpox	1
Total	120

Status of Healthy Inmates

Category	*Number*
Child of Inmate	30
Orphan	—
Healthy Adult	44
Widow	5
Deserted Child	6
Person over 65	1
Deserted Wife with accomp. Child	no longer filled in
Unmarried Mother with baby	7; 7
Unaccompanied illegitimate baby	—
Total	100

(*Source:* Rathdrum Union Indoor Relief Register 1842-1852; last 120 patients admitted between 23 November and 10 December 1852)

The table clearly shows the post-Famine pattern in Rathdrum, with mostly healthy, able-bodied people being admitted. By comparison, the Rathdown Union Indoor Relief Register 1870-74 between 30 September and 19 October 1870 demonstrates that a large number of inmates had migrated to this union from elsewhere. The random sample confirms that the poor were drawn to towns, in this instance, Dublin, Rathdrum, Kingstown and Bray. The last place of residence before admission is, however, no indication of an inmate's origin.

Rathdown Indoor Register 1870

Origin of Inmates

Electoral division	*Number*
Union at large	82
Bray	13
Kingstown	12
Dundrum	4
Killiney	3
Delgany	3
Rathmichael	2
Glencullen	1
Total	120

Occupations of Inmates

Occupation	*Number*
None	37
labourer	31
servant	22
sailor	5
shoemaker	4
tailor	3
carpenter	2
boilermaker	2
pensioner	2
nailor	1
trouser maker	1
moulder	1
dealer	1
brushmaker	1
gardener	1
cardriver	1
porter	1
sawyer	1
weaver	1
clerk	1
cutler (?)	1
Total	120

Origin of Union at large Inmates
(i.e. inmates from outside the union)

Last residence before admission	*Number*
Dublin	21
Rathdrum	15
Kingstown	11
Bray	10
Wicklow	9
Ballymore	6
Swords	2
Calary	1
Bahana	1
Newtown Mount Kennedy	1
Balbriggan	1
Old Connaught	1
Killiney	1
Fermanagh	1
Rathnew	1
Total	82

Diseases on Admission

healthy	76
sick	23
sore legs, feet or lame	5
infirm	3
'hurt'	3
no entry	3
bad sight, sore eyes	2
sore arm	1
broken thigh	1
paralysis	1
epilepsy	1
unmarried pregnancy	1
Total	120

Status of Healthy Inmates

Category	*Number*
Child of Inmate	8
Orphan	3
Healthy Adult	50
Widow	3
Unaccompanied child	1
Person over 65	—
Deserted wife with child	not filled in
Unmarried mother with baby	5; 5
Accompanied illegitimate child	1
Total	76

(*Source:* Rathdown Union Indoor Relief Register 1870-1874)

The workhouse was often the only refuge open to the unmarried mother and her child. There are occasional indications that they became inmates of Magdalen homes in the second half of the nineteenth century, leaving their babies in the poorhouse.[42]

Table 13.4 Women with illegitimate children in Wicklow workhouses on 1 Jan. 1854

Name of Union	*No. of women with illegitimate children*	*No. of other women*	*Total no. of women*	*No. of illegitimate children of these women*
Baltinglass	12 (18)	118	130	12 (32)*
Naas	21 (19)	168	215	40 (26)*
Rathdown	18 (19)	186	204	20 (22)*
Rathdrum	67 (26)	121	188	89 (44)*
Shillelagh	19 (23)	73	92	21 (40)*

In brackets are the number of women with illegitimate children and also the number of these children (with asterisk) who were inmates between March and September 1845.[43]

3 LIFE IN THE WORKHOUSE

3.1 Diet and Discipline

The administration of the pre-Famine workhouse was inspired by the 'less eligibility' principle – inmates were to be less comfortable than employed labourers. This concept was reflected in the discipline, work and diet of the poorhouse. Food was to be sufficient for survival, but less than the local diet. In many instances this 'less eligibility' directive could not be implemented, as it would have endangered inmates' health.

The pre-Famine diet in Wicklow workhouses (and elsewhere) consisted of potatoes, oatmeal stirabout, brown bread, milk and buttermilk. Cheap meat and white bread were used in the poorhouse infirmary. Inmates ate two meals a day; children, however, received a small supper. Rathdown and Baltinglass, like the Dublin and Lisburn Unions, used an 'improved diet' by including soup in their somewhat monotonous menu (see 1841 Loughlinstown dietary, based on that of the South Dublin Union). The poor law commissioners recommended minimum food allowances for the guidance of boards. Officers received rations of bread, meat, tea, milk and butter besides the workhouse fare.[44] The Famine forced the replacement of the diseased potato with alternatives, such as Indian meal, oatmeal and brown bread.

The Rathdown post-Famine dietary of 1851 is based on the 1849 poor law commissioners' recommendations:[45]

	breakfast	*dinner*
Healthy men	8 oz. Indian meal & ½ pt. milk	14 oz. brown bread & 2 pts. soup
Healthy women	7 oz. Indian meal & ½ pt. milk	12 oz. brown bread & 1½ pts soup

The food served was similar to the Wicklow Jail diet of 1848:[46]

	breakfast	*dinner*
adults	8 oz. mixed meal & 1 pt. mixed milk	16 oz. brown bread & 1 pt. mixed milk

Rathdrum guardians, in particular, resisted increasing their poor rates, despite the poor law commissioners' urgings to improve the insufficient quantity of food. After a five-year correspondence with the latter, the board introduced an improved dietary in 1859.[47] A comparison of diets in Wicklow unions and an adjoining county Wexford workhouse confirms that Rathdown operated on a more generous scale than Rathdrum.

During the Famine contractors began to send meat into the workhouse after dark to disguise its poor quality and to evade the board's

Table 13.5 Comparison of Average Cost of Dietary (Rathdrum minutes, 8 January 1859)

	Rathdown		Shillelagh		Gorey		Baltinglass		Rathdrum	
	s	*d*	*s*	*d*	*s*	*d*	*s*	*d*	*s*	*d*
general average	2	4	1	8	1	8½	1	11¾	1	9
infirmary avg.	5	8	2	1	2	2½	2	4	2	3½
fever hospital	2	3	2	6½	3	4¼	5	8	2	7½
Total	10	3	6	3½	7	3¼	9	11⅗	6	7½

inspection. Complaints about the oxheads and trimmings for the inmates' soup and the staff meat continued into the 1860s in Rathdown and Rathdrum, where the master reported: 'the meat is supplied in an unsatisfactory manner as regards time and quality. I had to return some three times last week.' Rathdown officers, in a memorial to their board, stating that the meat rations endangered their health, demanded a money allowance instead. (A disgruntled Rathdown schoolmaster claimed in 1856 that his meat had been rotten.) Reports of poor quality beef, milk and bread delivered at odd hours recurred in Rathdrum in the 1880s.[48]

Parsimonious guardians contracted cheap goods and services. Sub-standard articles were sometimes retained, at a discount. As a result twenty-one complaints about poor or adulterated food appear in the Rathdown minutes from 1841 to the end of 1845, while there are twenty-eight references to unsatisfactory food during the next decade. In the sometimes less detailed Rathdrum records twenty complaints were noted between 1842 and 1855. Late nineteenth century communications from Local Government Board and contractor alike suggest that Rathdrum supplies were too cheap and below quality.[49]

By 1868, all but the small category of able-bodied adults had three meals, while eggs and butter became part of the infirmary diet from the 1870s. Chemical analysis of the frequently diluted workhouse milk now became possible, leading to successful prosecutions. Tobacco and alcohol, once strictly forbidden, except as medicine, began to be issued to the elderly on a regular basis, usually as a medical 'extra'. Pauper assistants, too, were rewarded with whiskey and tobacco by the 1880s. As Rathdown had the largest infirmary population of the Wicklow workhouses, its consumption of porter, whiskey, wines and gin cost £540 in 1880.[50]

Although the simple Christmas and Easter meat dinners of the early years had grown more elaborate, with charitable people and guardians sending Christmas trees, children's toys (and by the beginning of the twentieth century snuff and tobacco into Rathdown, Rathdrum and Shillelagh, the workhouse diet ultimately failed to improve on par with general living standards. (The Rathdrum minutes of 29 February 1876 indicate that food allowances were more generous in Wicklow Jail). The Wicklow unions of 1887 still used oatmeal, Indian meal, milk, buttermilk, bread and soup. This lack of improvement is also reflected in a Rathdown guardian's condemnation of the stew as 'unfit for human food' in 1899, sentiments echoed by the medical officer in Rathdrum, while at that time an improved diet was rejected as too expensive by the Shillelagh board, which served the cheap combination of Indian meal, oatmeal and buttermilk first introduced during the Famine.[51]

The conduct of inmates was regulated by the workhouse rules. On admission inmates were separated into groups according to age and sex. No contact was permitted between married couples. Parents were to have reasonable access to their children, without inconveniencing the poorhouse administration.[52]

Early Wicklow boards enforced the rule that the whole family must enter and leave the institution together. This did not allow fathers to search for jobs while dependants sheltered in the workhouse. Despite the poor law commissioners' objections, the pragmatic Loughlinstown guardians allowed selected inmates out on 'passes' on the understanding that the family would follow if employment was found. In the pre-Famine period guardians were eager to discharge the able-bodied during the summer. Attempts were made to charge men who had evaded admission for their families' support in the workhouse or have them remove dependants. Under the 1838 Act the unmarried mother was solely responsible for her child. In cases of desertion the guardians had her arrested and prosecuted; for instance, in 1844 the Loughlinstown board offered £5 reward each for the identification of the mothers of two foundlings. From 1862 on legal changes allowed the prosecution of fathers for the support of their illegitimate children in the workhouse. Rathdrum officials at times read inmates' mail and received anonymous communications identifying fathers in order to obtain maintenance orders.[53]

Inmates' misdemeanours were divided into disorderly and refractory. The former consisted of refusing to keep silent, using foul or threatening language, refusing to work or wash, shamming illness, playing cards, misbehaving at prayers, entering an out-of-bounds part of the workhouse, dawdling on an errand outside or disobeying a workhouse officer. If the disorderly behaviour was repeated, or if the 'pauper' smuggled in alcohol or tobacco, attempted to assault anybody, was drunk or indecent, disturbed a religious service, damaged or tried to steal union property or tried to leave by climbing over the workhouse wall, he was considered refractory.[54] Most of the above offences are recorded for Rathdrum and Rathdown, notably pilfering, acts of vandalism and burglaries, as well as occasional fights between inmates and attacks on staff. Incidents declined sharply from the 1870s on.[55]

Disorderly behaviour was punished by extra work and loss of milk allowance. Those refractory could be confined in the punishment cell, known in Rathdrum as the 'black hole', for up to 24 hours. Bad cases could be committed to jail. Absconding in the union clothes, which constituted theft, was common before and during the Famine. In 1842 two Rathdown escapees were advertised in the *Hue and Cry*, a reward of ten shillings being offered for the capture of each man. Rathdown guardians' desire to get back union outfits cooled, when experience demonstrated the expense and trouble of legal proceedings. Corporal punishment, which could not be inflicted on girls, was standard practice for boys. The 1844 Rathdown minutes recorded the following punishments: John Dempsey, scribbling over his copy – four pandies; Michael Cullen and Patrick Reynolds quarrelling – each four pandies; Philip Roache and John Dempsey, terrifying William Doherty at night – six pandies and to carry the night bucket until further orders.[56] Boys were involved in theft, in Rathdrum and Loughlinstown, and tended to escape from these institutions. Although children were not to be deprived of food as a punishment, during a drive to restore discipline after the Famine, Rathdown guardians ordered absconding youths to be deprived of their milk and in cases of repetition, to be flogged. But the evidence of the minute books, as no punishment books of the Wicklow unions have survived, suggests that this was unusual. While the Rathdrum schoolmaster was summoned to court for 'harsh treatment of a pauper girl' after an unspecified incident in 1845, four cases of child abuse recorded in Loughlinstown workhouse were committed by pauper aides.[57]

Misdemeanours could also lead to dismissal of the culprit and his family from the poorhouse. This practice, although illegal, continued in the post-Famine period. Disturbances in Loughlinstown Workhouse occurred over food, clothing and work. During the first 20 years women acted as ringleaders in two of three major incidents: in 1844 the female inmates boycotted the sewing of a particular type of workhouse cap, and strike leaders were brought to court; when a woman refused to work in 1857, her peers made two efforts to rescue her from the punishment cell, attacking the poorhouse officers. The constabulary was called to restore order; in 1848 the men refused to go to work and, on being deprived of their milk, threatened the master and damaged union property.[58]

Although no records of strikes survive in the other workhouses, it is likely that conditions were similar. Discipline improved gradually from the late 1850s on; the relative monotony of the minutes of the 1870s and later decades is due to a combination of reasons; lower numbers of inmates, more space and a generally more liberal application of the poor law.

3.2 Work, education and training

The expectation was that constant, tedious work combined with strict discipline would deter the poor from seeking admission. Throughout the history of the workhouse system its inmates performed maintenance tasks, while women also helped in the kitchen, laundry, nursery and infirmary. In Wicklow and elsewhere poorhouse grounds were planted with potatoes and vegetables, a practice continued in the twentieth-century district hospitals. In the early years in Rathdown and Rathdrum adults and boys had to break stones, a practice revived on an Arklow relief scheme of 1881.[59]

During the pre-Famine period the unsatisfactory Loughlinstown water supply resulted in the few healthy inmates having to carry water from the Shanganagh river. In later years the water pump was operated by a treadmill. This controversial mechanism, which meant that men and boys drudged incessantly in a circle, was used in Wicklow Jail as a punishment. Its use was discontinued in Loughlinstown in 1858 after several accidents.[60]

From the beginning of operations the poor law commissioners acknowledged the difficulties of providing work in a country of high unemployment. In 1845, a Rathdown inmate instructed his companions in the making of cocoa fibre mats. He had acquired this skill in Kilmainham Jail. These mats were also assembled in Rathdrum. In the 1840s workhouses employed permanent tradesmen, such as tailors, shoemakers and weavers. Guardians hoped to involve as many inmates as possible in work schemes aimed at self-sufficiency. The Rathdown minutes show that from 1848 on, oats, wheat, barley and flax were grown, bread baked, yarn and thread produced, stockings knitted, frieze and tweed woven and clothing and shoes made by the 'paupers', while surplus vegetables were sold to reduce union expenses. A similar range of activities was carried on in Baltinglass, Naas and Shillelagh in 1852. In addition, inmates of Baltinglass manufactured clogs and tinware and embroidered fine table linen, while Naas inmates 'painted' – presumably the workhouse – and were engaged in mantua making. The very modest level of activity in Rathdrum suggests continuing disorder after the Famine crisis on 1 July 1852.[61]

The Rathdown minutes show that inmates' products featured at the

Table 13.6 Inmate statistics 1852-1853

Name of Union	*Number of Inmates*	*Number employed in workhouse*	*Aged, infirm or sick in workhouse*
Baltinglass	751	528	70
Naas	1,156	273	140
Rathdown	475	267	217
Rathdrum	834	92	279
Shillelagh	664	261	168

(*Source: BPP* 1852-1853 (513) lxxxiv 299)

1853 Dublin Industrial Exhibition. Nevertheless, there were repeated complaints that the bread was inedible and that better, cheaper shoes could be bought outside the workhouse. A review in 1852 found that these efforts at self-sufficiency were uneconomical, because of the high cost of raw materials and instructors' wages. Indiscipline and pilfering also contributed to failure. During the 1850s falling numbers led to a scaling down of work projects, as the Rathdown board stated: 'the circumstances of the present time [are] so different ... [that they] do not warrant their continuing a large and useless expenditure ...'.[62] A poor person, while an inmate of a workhouse, could work only for the benefit of his poor law union. Nevertheless, this tenet of the commissioners was occasionally flouted in Rathdrum prior to 1860. In 1850, for example, the board attempted to let three acres of unused workhouse ground inclusive of manure and 'pauper' labour; in 1857 a poor law commissioners' inspector found the poorhouse in a filthy, disorganised state, while inmates sewed a patchwork quilt for the master, Isaac Flower, and embroidered dresses for the matron and schoolmistress. The board proceeded to protect their officials from the criticism of the commissioners'.[63]

Workhouse staff was assisted by selected inmates, who were given responsibility as ward attendants, nursing aides, ambulance drivers, lunatic keepers, assistant tailors, clerks or teachers, barbers, child-minders and sewerage workers. Lack of supervision combined with the sometimes unsatisfactory conduct of pauper assistants' led to a fatal burning accident in Rathdrum in 1870: a three-year-old orphan had been left in a ward without fireguard, while his minder, his grandmother, attended Mass; the ward maid, the child's aunt, was absent without explanation.[64]

As the poor law commissioners prohibited any reward for inmates' efforts, the lack of incentives for additional, more responsible work was a major stumbling block to the efficient running of the institution. The

Loughlinstown men, ordered to guard the crops from marauders at night, had to patrol without food from 3 p.m. to 9 a.m. the following morning.[65]

Only one category of 'pauper' aide could be given an officially approved, increased diet: the nurses, whom the poor law commissioners believed would steal their patients' food, should they not be more generously fed themselves. The Rathdown guardians, in particular, realised the effectiveness of extra food for extra labour, despite the commissioners' resistance. Incentives finally became accepted practice in the 1860s.[66]

Although the Rathdown minutes (22 June 1850) record a draconian regime of rising at 5.30 a.m. for the able-bodied, who worked from 6.30 a.m. until 6 p.m. with an hour off for each meal, there are also indications that inmates were reluctant to work. During the late 1850s the Arklow Manure Works used Rathdrum Workhouse children to strip rotting meat off bones, while inmates were occasionally hired as seasonal labourers. The lack of references to work in the minutes of the latter decades of the nineteenth century indicates that only routine tasks were carried out, while semi-invalids and the sick spent long dreary hours in the poorhouse wards. In the twentieth century Rathdown and Rathdrum, whether as workhouse, county home or district hospital, provided locals with paid employment.[67]

Workhouses operated separate boys' and girls' primary schools under the nominal supervision of the National Board of Education. Besides a basic curriculum suitable for future labourers and servants, teachers were to be 'successful moral trainers'. The Rathdown boys' day of 1850 was typical for Wicklow unions: three hours instruction in the three Rs, followed by agricultural labour and trade training with an hour for play and half an hour for dinner.[68]

Selected Baltinglass, Rathdown, Shillelagh and Naas boys learned shoemaking, tailoring, weaving and, in some cases, baking, while girls were taught needlework, spinning and knitting. Naas and Baltinglass girls also learned embroidery. Rathdrum, alone among Wicklow workhouses in 1853, offered no industrial training for boys and little besides knitting and sewing for young women. In 1854, of 134 Irish workhouses inspected, 54 had no trade training, 47 had no agricultural instruction and in 26 the boys were 'kept in idleness'. When conditions improved during the 1850s, many young people left the poorhouses, industrial and agricultural training was scaled down and tradesmen became part-time instructors, who also mended the bought-in stock. While a few Loughlinstown boys had been groomed to assist the union's clerk during the 1840s, the 1899 board decided that some of the juveniles should learn to operate the recently purchased typewriter.[69]

Reports by educational inspectors were generally positive: on 5 June 1852 Rathdown girls' school consisted of 40 knitting, 20 straw plaiting and 28 spinning pupils. Children were placed in 'service' in Rathdrum, Naas and Baltinglass Unions before 1845, often earning only their keep. Loughlinstown became more enterprising in this respect, as the chairman and other guardians employed workhouse children. From March to September 1851, for instance, 31 girls went into service. Relieving officers' reports on 17 placed locally were generally satisfactory, although the occasional child was unable to settle and absconded. Falling numbers during the mid 1850s and the boards' cost-cutting drives led to a decline in standards in Rathdown and Rathdrum. It is also possible that rising educational aspirations contributed to complaints about the poor pupil teacher ratio, low academic standards, an over-emphasis on agricultural work and the workhouse officers' custom of sending the boys on errands during school hours.[70]

In 1853 the poor law commissioners confirmed that embroidery should replace agricultural instruction for girls, endorsing the Rathdown matron's conviction that more needlework would lead to better employment prospects. The Rathdown girls had rebelled against work on the poorhouse farm on at least one occasion. Fine needlework and singing were taught in Wicklow's workhouse schools from the late 1850s onward. The commissioners firmly opposed instruction outside the poorhouse.[71]

Schooldays in those institutions seem to have improved in the second half of the nineteenth century, a visit to the circus, a magic lantern show, fireworks, annual gifts of Christmas toys and donated fruit in summer being mentioned. Nevertheless, the segregation of workhouse children from ordinary schools continued. A proposal to integrate Rathdrum youngsters into local schools proved unacceptable, as '... the parents of the children attending the national school would object to the pauper children ...'. In 1897 Lady Meath offered £2,000 to establish a Catholic and a Protestant training school for workhouse girls to become domestic servants, thereby circumventing the stigma of belonging to the very poor and being forced to live, separated from family and friends, in regimented surroundings on minimum relief. Because of the Roman Catholic hierarchy's opposition, the scheme was abandoned.[72]

In 1907 the Rathdown board, at the request of the Gaelic League, appointed an Irish teacher for the children. This may well have been a unique initiative. Not until 1918 did the Rathdrum guardians finally send their last child inmates to national schools, while the Loughlinstown educational establishment survived until the closure of the workhouse in 1920.[73]

3.3 Religion

The commissioners' resolve that the poor law system should be non-denominational, was difficult to maintain in a sectarian age. Inmates' spiritual needs were attended to by the workhouse chaplains, who held Sunday services and administered the sacraments. 'Paupers' were provided with cheap devotional books and rosary beads in Rathdrum and Rathdown, where the board considered appointing a full-time chaplain in 1850, for 'the improvement of the inmates in morality and religion in which they are at present most lamentably deficient ...'. Clergymen appointed to workhouse positions were instructed to concentrate on spiritual matters and not to interfere in the management of the institution; they were not eligible to serve as guardians.[74]

The chaplains' mutual fear of proselytising generated an atmosphere of distrust. During the first twenty years of the poor law in Ireland, charges of proselytising were made in Rathdown, Rathdrum and Baltinglass workhouses. These usually related to vulnerable inmates, such as children and the mentally ill. Between 1842 and 1862 at least eighteen items of sectarian controversy featured in the Rathdrum minutes: in 1844 the poor law commissioners dismissed the master, after complaints by the Roman Catholic chaplain that he had made sectarian remarks were upheld; in 1845 allegations of proselytising children were made against the schoolmaster; in 1848, the Protestant chaplain accused his Catholic counterpart of poaching his flock, while the priest alleged that three child inmates were being kept in quarantine to facilitate their conversion to Protestantism.[75] The Loughlinstown board, at pains to avoid controversy, insisted that conversions take place outside the poorhouse. Inmates therefore discharged themselves, converted and were registered under their new denomination on return to the institution. The strained relationship between the Rathdown chaplains culminated in 1863 in the board's order that the medical officer should ascertain the sanity of potential converts to Rome. During sectarian tensions in Baltinglass Workhouse in 1851, the Protestant chaplain complained of an inmate burning Bibles, as well as feeling intimidated by the Catholic 'paupers'. The Catholic priest concerned counter-charged by publicising the Protestant minister's visits to the poorhouse accompanied by proselytisers and stated that religious literature had been burned by an insane inmate, irrespective of denomination. Further tensions developed in Baltinglass in 1855.[76]

Although inmates were overwhelmingly Catholic, key workhouse officers tended to be Protestants. This was the situation in county Wicklow. Archbishop Cullen, a persistent opponent of the poor law, consecrated Rathdrum's new Catholic church in September 1859. Eighteen months later he criticised the nearby Rathdrum poorhouse as having '339 inmates, of whom 30 only are Protestants', while the master, matron, clerk, two doctors, three relieving officers, apothecary and five further doctors on contract to the union were Protestants. Listing Catholic staff, he mentioned the chaplain, the schoolmistress, two nurses and the porter. Cullen continued: 'so you have £985 paid out of the poor rate to 15 Protestants'. (The combined salaries of Catholic employees amounted to £127.) The future cardinal concluded: 'the officials get more than £1,000 for starving some 300 poor people'. Occasionally accusations that appointments were made on sectarian grounds surfaced: in 1878 the chaplain of Shillelagh workhouse objected to the election of a 'coalyard clerk' as schoolmaster, claiming that he was chosen as a Protestant.[77]

There is also evidence that boards of guardians voted along sectarian lines. During an 1844 Baltinglass inquiry into allegations of sexual immorality and the withholding of food from inmates, Sally Nolan, the cook, admitted having done the latter on the master's orders. When the board moved to reprimand her, the *Freeman's Journal* recorded the following voting pattern: 'ten (Conservative Protestants)' voted in favour of reprimanding, while 'seven (Catholics)' voted against. A long drawn-out Rathdown controversy concerned a Protestant orphan who wanted to attend Catholic worship. Repeated discussions and votes suggest that, except on a brief occasion, the board's Protestant majority prevailed. Prior to 1875, Rathdown Union's Kingstown electoral division operated a compromise by electing an equal number of Catholic and Protestant guardians to the board, which consisted of approximately 42 Protestants and 12 Catholics.[78]

The poor law commissioners' legal ruling of 1842 that foundlings, whose religious background was unknown, were to be brought up in the (Protestant) state religion, caused widespread controversy. The Rathdrum board acquiesced in deserted babies sometimes being baptised as Catholics before admission to the poorhouse. When this practice was rejected by the poor law commissioners, two months of objections by the board followed. The Rathdrum Guardians resisted the commissioners' order, as they were apprehensive '... of much angry discussion amongst the guardians which it is essential to avoid'. On another occasion, a foundling had been baptised in both denominations under different names. Tired of such controversies, the poor law commissioners dropped the foundling rule in 1862.[79]

Sectarian disagreements dwindled in the Wicklow workhouses in the second half of the nineteenth century, aided in Loughlinstown by an unusual ecumenical spirit between the chaplains, the celebrated Fr James Healy of Little Bray and Rev Frederick Burton of Rathmichael, during the 1870s and 1880s. Wicklow workhouses also demonstrated the growing influence of the Catholic Church: while the evangelical John Parnell, father of Charles Stewart, Anna and Fanny, had attempted to obstruct the purchase of Catholic vestments when chairman in 1857, a more cordial relationship between board and chaplain developed, culminating in an episode in 1888, when Lady Meath presented prints to brighten the workhouse wards, but only after these had been approved by the Catholic clergyman.[80]

In an effort to keep poorhouses strictly non-denominational, nuns were not allowed access in the early years; for instance, the Rathdown guardians refused the Sisters of Mercy's request to console Catholics in the workhouse in 1844. But with a mainly Protestant board deciding for mostly Catholic inmates, in Loughlinstown and elsewhere, such refusals were open to charges of anti-Catholic bias. In Rathdrum, where the master visited the Protestant inmates of the infirmary to pray with them, this rule had been abandoned by 1876. In 1899, the Rathdown guardians welcomed a religious order as matron and nurses, the master and matron having retired. The now predominantly Catholic board and inmates alike felt that this would improve the institution both materially and spiritually.[81]

According to Rathdown and Rathdrum minutes, only Protestant chaplains attended at the graveside. To lessen the stigma of burial in the 'paupers' plot', inmates led by a workhouse officer were permitted to attend funerals. Despite sporadic efforts, Wicklow's poorhouse graveyards tended to be ill-kept: in 1850, for instance, the Rathdown board ordered 'to have the heap of manure removed ... to a pit at the burial grounds', while in Rathdrum a carelessly interred body was disturbed by a dog. Altogether 8,024 people were buried in Rathdrum. Interments continued here until 1944, and up to 1939, in Loughlinstown.[82]

3.4 Health care

Workhouse infirmaries made health care accessible to a greater number of people. They were, however, primitive and had the cheapest equipment available. The chronically ill and handicapped were among the first patients. Occasionally an operation took place in the workhouse infirmary. Babies, many of whom were illegitimate, were also born there. Although it was possible from 1843 to transfer inmates to specialist hospitals, Wicklow guardians made no use of this legislation until the 1850s. In exceptional cases consultants could be called in: the Rathdown board summoned a Dublin surgeon to investigate an outbreak of ophthalmia, a eye infection caused by malnutrition, highly contagious in unhygienic conditions, which could lead to blindness. Tuberculosis, on the other hand, was not considered infectious and carriers were not isolated in the mid-nineteenth century.[83]

From 1840 on legislation enabled Irish boards of guardians to set up vaccination districts with local doctors employed at the rate of one shilling per successful inoculation. Smallpox vaccination of children became compulsory in 1864. This service was available outside the poorhouse, foreshadowing future health-care developments.[84]

In the early years guardians began to convey the seriously ill to the workhouse on simple carts. Later there are references to the Rathdown Union fever cart and a Rathdrum ambulance van of the 1860s. In 1879 the Baltinglass board's practice of bringing smallpox and fever patients to the workhouse on open carts, which had to be 'begged or borrowed', was exposed by the *Freeman's Journal*. Patients were said to have died after such a journey in winter. Raising the issue in parliament, Charles Stewart Parnell was told that the board had since purchased two vans. As the son of a Rathdrum poor law guardian, Parnell, conscious of the fear of contagion which made people reluctant to lend horses, suggested that the union purchase their own team.[85]

The Medical Charities Act of 1851 replaced the previous system of voluntary dispensaries with one controlled by the poor law commissioners. There were occasional cases of negligence: in 1858 a Bray labourer's broken thigh, which a dispensary doctor had failed to bandage, bled for the duration of the journey to Loughlinstown; another doctor's failure to attend a woman in childbirth led to her own and her child's death and the medical practitioner's removal from office. In December 1854 a sick man was exposed to the elements on an open cart in transit to the Rathdrum workhouse. As patients of public institutions were not considered destitute in a legal sense, no direct transfer from the County Infirmary to Rathdrum poorhouse was possible when discharging the homeless. In 1875 a destitute man was discovered dying in a Wicklow yard. Although too weak to reach Rathdrum, he had been released from the infirmary.[86]

The most disadvantaged inmates were the mentally handicapped, the psychologically disturbed and epileptics, who were kept in cells and wards for 'lunatics and idiots'. Because of lack of space they were also mixed with other categories of patients in Rathdrum and Rathdown. Although county Wicklow belonged to the Richmond Lunatic Asylum's catchment area, overcrowding limited transfers from the workhouses to 'dangerous lunatics'. Wicklow boards of guardians and the poor law commissioners were unanimous about the lack of treatment in the poorhouse; nevertheless, violent, mentally ill inmates had to be committed to jail to await a vacancy in the Richmond.[87]

Cold and damp affected their health in the overcrowded workhouse cells and lead to security breaches: thirteen of Rathdown's 31 lunatics broke out in 1845 and remained at large for some weeks. There were other, less spectacular escapes. A mentally ill Rathdown inmate stabbed five people in 1861. A Shillelagh 'pauper' killed her baby in 1878. In Rathdrum, insufficient space and personnel culminated in a deranged inmate killing the second occupant of her cell in 1883, while in 1920 a 'pauper' ward-maid sustained serious injuries when attacked by a disturbed inmate, who then turned his razor on himself. Those who attempted to commit suicide were usually jailed for some weeks.[88] Despite some improvements and generally favourable reports from the lunatic inspectors conditions in Rathdrum and Rathdown remained poor. By 1881 Baltinglass still had 13 'lunatics' (seven women), Naas housed 35 (24 female), Rathdown 80 (56 women), Rathdrum 26 (20 of them female) and Shillelagh ten, of whom seven were women. Although there was a general desire to see these inmates in asylums, such cases continued in Wicklow's and other workhouses into the twentieth century.[89]

The philanthropic Lady Meath criticised the unsuitable way in which epileptics were 'cared for' in these institutions in 1901: 'recreation there was none, and the requirements of a quiet, peaceful life, free from mental excitement, were secured by putting them into the workhouse cell in the immediate vicinity of lunatics'. In 1920 Rathdrum still contained 13 mentally handicapped or disturbed women, one man and an epileptic child. The board regretted that ambulant cases among the above could only have one cold bath a month. Similarly in Naas, mentally ill people remained there until the closure of the poorhouse.[90]

4 THE FAMINE IN WICKLOW WORKHOUSES

The Famine years of 1845 to 1849 represented the greatest emergency in the history of the poor law. While Wicklow experienced little of the extreme suffering of the south and west of Ireland, the crisis affected the county's poorhouses well into the 1850s. Food disimproved, the number of inmates increased dramatically, discipline and cleanliness declined. Infectious diseases broke out among inmates and staff; the death rate increased; people wandered the roads looking for food and work, gaining temporary admittance to the workhouses as 'night-lodgers'. Although the poor law commissioners dissolved thirty-nine insolvent boards of guardians and replaced them with paid administrators, no Wicklow board was disbanded.[91]

4.1 Diet during the Famine

The partial failure of the potato crop in 1845 led to a scarcity of this staple food of the poor. Flour and other alternatives became increasingly expensive from July 1845 on, so that the Rathdrum board's bread

Plate 13.1 Admissions building, Rathdrum workhouse, the boardroom was upstairs (Kevin Byrne).

Plate 13.2 Catholic chapel in Rathdrum workhouse (Kevin Byrne).

contractor faced ruin and successfully petitioned the guardians to be released from an unrealistic contract. In November the poor law commissioners authorised the replacement of the potato with oatmeal or tea and bread. The commissioners' suggestion to convert existing potato stocks attacked by blight into starch and pulp or potato flour led to the Loughlinstown board experimenting with a potato grinding machine, in the misplaced hope of extracting food from rotting tubers. In Rathdown, decaying potatoes had to be thrown out at intervals. Here, as well as in Rathdrum, potatoes were abandoned as part of the basic workhouse diet by April 1846. Although Rathdrum introduced an officially recommended diet in March 1847, which granted inmates doing onerous work a small supper and suggested the use of nutritious soup with salt fish or cheap beef, a close scrutiny of provisions accounts confirms that no fish and little meat were purchased. The latter could well have been officers' rations or for hospital consumption. There is no mention of a Christmas dinner in Rathdrum in 1846, while with 1,055 inmates in December 1849 the board decided against the traditional treat that year. In both institutions Indian (yellow) meal, oatmeal, rice, brown bread, milk and buttermilk were extensively used. By 1848 the Rathdown fare, which consisted of an adult's dinner of 16 oz bread and soup with vegetables, to counteract scurvy, was superior to the Rathdrum diet, where an adult's main meal consisted of less than 12 oz brown bread. Reductions in the quality and quantity of food took place; in Loughlinstown cheaper meat was used in the soup, which was subsequently discontinued in summer; Rathdrum resorted to contracting the cheapest provisions available. The brown bread in Loughlinstown did, however, make inmates in poor health ill, so that both there and in Rathdrum half brown and half white bread were ordered.[92]

4.2 Number of inmates

The Famine created an unprecedented demand for poorhouse places. Although the Rathdown board had urged legislation to build Irish railways as early as 1845, railway construction at Bray lasted from autumn 1847 to summer 1848, when 70 men were dismissed. Increasing destitution in Bray led to 40 poor men staging a sit-in protest at Loughlinstown Workhouse in April 1846. The board received a delegation and explained that no assistance was possible until they became destitute and thus eligible for the poorhouse.[93] People streamed into these institutions in late 1846. Baltinglass was the first of the Wicklow workhouses to be declared full on 14 November 1846, followed by Rathdrum on 12 December and Naas and Shillelagh on 10 January 1847. Considerable hardship was experienced, as the 1846 potato harvest was completely destroyed by blight, while in Arklow the herring fishery had also failed. The winter of 1846/7 was particularly harsh; in Bray the homes of fishermen were flooded. In February 1847 the *Freeman's Journal* noted the 'deplorable state of the once cheerful peasantry of this part of county Wicklow'.[94]

The crisis forced boards to adapt and expand existing accommodation by converting dayrooms, stables and sheds. The Naas guardians rented an auxiliary workhouse in February 1847, while Rathdrum hired the brewery with 60 places in November 1846 and parts of the Flannel Hall, which offered an additional 200 places in February 1847. Loughlinstown was to build an extension for 600.[95]

The poor law commissioners restricted admissions, fearing an epidemic in overcrowded conditions. On one occasion the Loughlinstown board turned down 138 applicants. Boards discharged batches of able-bodied 'paupers' to make room for those more wretched. On 9 and 16 February 1847, for instance, the Rathdrum guardians refused all requests for admission because of 'the crowded state of the house'; on 30 March 40 poor persons were rejected, on 27 April there were again no admissions and on 8 June it was reported that of 40 'paupers' compulsorily discharged the previous week, several 'have been lying under the hedges ever since'. Admissions peaked in spring 1847, gradually declined, then rose to a second high point later that year. A pattern of high numbers of inmates in winter/early spring developed, which continued until at least 1856 in Rathdrum and Rathdown. 1847 and 1848 were the worst years of the Famine, when Arklow in the Rathdrum Union and Baltinglass acquired the reputation of 'the two great seats of misery in Wicklow'.[96]

After losing up to 40 per cent of its potato crop in 1845, Wicklow experienced the total failure of 1846, which resulted in reduced planting and a smaller, if healtier potato harvest in 1847. The following year blight recurred in some parts of the county and the resulting social disruption ensured that the people's rush into the workhouse continued. Admissions were to rise still further and reached an all-time high in February 1850, but declined gradually thereafter:[97]

Table 13.7 Persons receiving relief on 28 February 1850

Name of Union	*Number of males over 15 years*	*Number of females over 15 years*	*Number of children under 15 years*	*Total*
Baltinglass	121	304	479	904
Naas	324	468	716	1,508
Rathdown	223	212	361	796
Rathdrum	213	471	590	1,274
Shillelagh	95	234	501	830

Persons on outdoor relief

Name of Union	*Males*	*Females*	*Total*	*Total Indoor & Outdoor Relief*
Baltinglass	250	384	634	1,538
Naas	11	14	24	1,533
Rathdown	3	2	5	801
Rathdrum	48	62	110	1,381
Shillelagh	—	—	—	803

Persons receiving relief on 1 February 1851

Name of Union	*Extent of available accommodation*	*Number in Workhouse on that date*	*On Outdoor Relief on that date*	*Total*
Baltinglass	1,100	955	7	962
Naas	1,386	1,443	5	1,448
Rathdown	1,280	631	5	636
Rathdrum	1,290	1,132	28	1,160
Shillelagh	1,030	853	(Additional accommodation for 200 has been taken)	853

4.3 Nightlodgers

Before the Famine the occasional travelling stranger had been treated reasonably generously in Loughlinstown Workhouse, where he was given accommodation, supper and breakfast. During the Famine years, however, the number of 'nightlodgers' increased considerably: from 22 October to 22 November 1848, for instance, 242 short-term admissions were recorded, while between 16 October and 21 December 1849, 323 'nightlodgers' feature in the register. Applicants included single people, the elderly and family groups, often led by the mother or eldest sibling. The travelling poor put pressure on many workhouses at this time, but the problem was more acute in Loughlinstown because of its location on the main road from Dublin to Arklow, close to Kingstown and Bray. As the Rathdown area was prosperous, it would also have attracted poor people from elsewhere.[98]

The board attempted to reduce the workload and expenditure, because the poorhouse administration was already under pressure from the large number of regular inmates. A Rathdown guardians' committee recommended that 'nightlodgers' should receive only one meal during their stay, in return for work performed. The master was to admit selectively and no later than 9 p.m., except in emergencies. The committee's report at this time of social turmoil in November 1849 rejected past leniency as 'it encourages and tends to perpetuate those baneful habits of vagrancy and idleness to which many of the Irish peasantry are addicted'.

Soon after these cutbacks had been implemented, the master refused admission to a group of poor travellers, who camped outside all night in December and became so ill by morning that they had to be admitted to the infirmary. The board's attitude towards these unfortunate people is also illuminated by an episode in early 1850, when the workhouse bread, which had been considered inedible by staff and inmates, was given to the nightlodgers 'on condition that they do not return'. Local tradition suggests that some of the travelling poor died by the roadside and that their remains were found during the building of Dun Laoghaire's Mounttown estate.[99]

The number of travelling strangers declined to a manageable size when normality returned. Migrant labourers, discharged soldiers, the homeless and the occasional eccentric continued to be treated with distrust when admitted to the workhouses during the second half of the nineteenth century. They began to feature in statistics as 'tramps' and 'casuals', having been previously ignored, and were still among the denizens of the Wicklow poorhouses in the twentieth century, when they caught the literary imagination of J.M. Synge.[100]

4.4 Outdoor relief

The Poor Law Amendment Act (1847) provided that under certain conditions the guardians could grant relief outside the workhouse. Although the Rathdown board opposed outdoor relief on 'moral' grounds as removing the spur to struggle ceaselessly to survive and as 'eventually ruinous to property', the overcrowded conditions of 1847 forced its introduction; 1,660 people received outdoor relief in the Rathdrum Union in January 1848, numbers rose to 2,282 by August and, as the crisis abated, were scaled down to 361 for 1850.[101]

West, central and south-east Wicklow were badly affected, although pressure on the workhouse system was generally greater in Wexford and Kildare. For the period 29 September 1847 to 29 September 1848, the situation had improved to some extent: 12.1 per cent of the population of Enniscorthy Union, 7.4 per cent of Gorey Union, 5.6 per cent of Naas Union, 4.6 per cent of Baltinglass Union, 4.2 per cent of Rathdrum Union, 3.9 per cent of Rathdown Union and 1.9 per cent of Shillelagh Union received outdoor relief.[102]

4.5 Workhouse administration during the Famine

1846 to 1851 was the period of greatest turmoil for the poor law administration. In September 1846 dirt and confusion reigned in

Rathdrum, where the commissioners considered officers' performance to be 'very unsatisfactory'. The following year the auxiliary establishment in the Flannel Hall was found to be in a state of 'disorder and filth'. Although the 1846 Rathdown records are lost, it is likely that conditions were similar.[103]

The recruitment of additional staff did not result in greater efficiency, as personnel often fell ill in the unhygienic, overcrowded institutions. The Famine mercilessly exposed any weaknesses in the administrative apparatus, which in turn increased inmates' discomfort. In July 1847 a Loughlinstown 'pauper' complained about the dirty state of bedding and the staff's rough behaviour. The Rathdown board, however, considered that conditions were tolerable under the circumstances. While greater demands than ever before were made on the administration, it became obvious in Rathdrum and Rathdown that their workhouse masters were both unable to maintain discipline and incapable of keeping accurate accounts. The Rathdrum master permitted inmates to go on outings to the town in 1849, which the board considered particularly reprehensible in the case of women, some of whom stayed out all night. In Loughlinstown 'paupers' forged passes to attend Bray fair, which was said to surpass Donnybrook for drunkenness, fighting and gambling. On paying a surprise visit to the poorhouse one night, a Rathdrum guardian found staff absent, the building lit up and the inmates in possession of a master key. Idle hours were filled with card games. The situation in the Flannel Hall was similar: entrance doors were discovered to be open in the middle of the night on several occasions.[104]

When stocktaking, Rathdrum guardians noted that their master's records rarely tallied; in 1849 for instance 686 loaves of bread were listed in his books, but only 18 were found in store. Loughlinstown inmates were ordered to share any spare clothes with more scantily clad peers. The guardians of both unions refused to issue workhouse socks and shoes to youngsters admitted barefoot. Waste caused by officials' carelessness was therefore galling. The board alluded to one such disappearance of linen at the time when 'the 1,000 yards of clothing materials was found on the roof of the poorhouse'.[105]

The Rathdrum master of 1847 combined dishonesty with inefficiency. He was dismissed after allowing officials and guardians to 'borrow' inmates to bring in their harvest or otherwise assist them, which was in complete contradiction of the workhouse rules. The medical officer, the Roman Catholic chaplain and the respected Gilbert and Manning guardians were among the beneficiaries of this Victorian forerunner of social welfare fraud. The figures of authority escaped lightly with the poor law commissioners' reprimand being entered in the minutes, the 'paupers' concerned, however, were discharged. The commissioners disapproved 'as it was but right for them to obey the orders of their superiors'. In March 1847 the commissioners expressed their dissatisfaction with the equally disorganised Naas poorhouse.[106]

Pilfering from kitchen and store became endemic; meal, potatoes, shoes, clothing belonging to the union and officers' own blankets, tradesmen's materials and tools and even the lead off the roofs were stolen and smuggled out. There are indications that some of the proceeds, at least, were spent on drink. Enterprising inmates in Loughlinstown attempted to return with tea, sugar and tobacco. 'Paupers' escaped, abandoning their families in the workhouse. Others used the general confusion to scale the walls and eat raw turnips in the adjoining fields. Incidents of vandalism occurred, for instance, when 20 Rathdown boys broke workhouse windows in 1849. There were fights between inmates, who sometimes refused to work. There were occasional attacks on staff: in 1849 some Rathdrum men incited a group of boys to attack the schoolmaster with mud and stones. Coming out of the boardroom after the guardians' investigation of the case, he was again assaulted by a male 'pauper'. During the Famine a few officers assumed the behaviour of inmates: in 1849 the Rathdrum schoolmistress climbed out of the compound at nightfall, while an assistant master attempted to win allies against colleagues by holding a meeting of male inmates, who were promised additional food. Accused of fomenting insubordination, the officer was forced to resign.[107]

Boards found it difficult to restore discipline. In January 1848 the despairing Rathdrum guardians insisted that henceforth inmates would only be allowed visitors four times a year and threatened key officials with dismissal, because of 'the extensive plunder of clothing that has been going on for some time and the irregular and dirty state' of the institution. As the porter had either lost or defrauded inmates of their clothes, Rathdrum 'paupers' tended to keep 'a great quantity of their own filthy clothing' in the beds. Ordering the locks to be changed and purchasing a watchdog proved ineffective. Rathdown guardians decreed that inmates' register numbers were to be sewn on to their workhouse outfits, to identify culprits instantly. In Loughlinstown male 'paupers' patrolled the grounds by night and roll calls were held in the small hours to discourage absconding. These measures proved futile and the board longed for the establishment of a police station in Louglinstown. With falling numbers during the 1850s, especially after more than 1,000 inmates of the Wicklow workhouses had been sent to North America as poor law emigrants, more orderly conditions gradually prevailed.[108]

High numbers of inmates between 1850 and 1852 made Rathdrum

difficult to administer. Isaac Flower's appointment as master in 1850 signalled a return to strict discipline. Troublesome inmates were incarcerated in the 'black hole', boys were flogged and those guilty of vanishing over the walls sent to jail for four weeks. Warrants were issued to arrest absconders, who had abandoned their families in the workhouse. The practice of rewarding responsible 'paupers' with extra food, which had crept in during the Famine, was discontinued. Accusations by a disgruntled official that the master ignored the commissioners' rules and treated inmates harshly, were ignored by the board.[109]

4.6 Famine-related illness in the Wicklow workhouses

Wicklow boards of guardians did not provide union fever hospitals before the Famine, as inmates suffering from infectious diseases were cheaply and conveniently treated in local fever hospitals. These arrangements proved adequate until May 1846 in Rathdrum and until June 1847 in Rathdown. Capable of taking about 30 patients each, Wicklow and Arklow Fever Hospitals soon became overcrowded during the summer of 1846. In May the Rathdrum guardians authorised Dr Wright, of Arklow Fever Hospital, to treat poor people ill with infectious diseases. Within weeks, however, the board returned some of the Arklow bills as exorbitant. The guardians also delegated two Arklow members to move the temporary fever hospital, located 'in the centre of the Main Street to the danger and inconvenience of the inhabitants'. In June Dr Wright reported that fever was on the increase in Arklow, while Dr Nolan, of Wicklow Fever Hospital, became the Rathdrum Union's medical officer for Wicklow town in July. Both doctors filed regular reports to be read in the boardroom until the winding up of the relief commissioners on 1 September 1846. While on average 46 poor fever patients were treated in Arklow per week, 18·6 such cases were attended to in the Wicklow district.[110]

The Rathdrum guardians learned in October that Famine fever had failed to decline in Arklow, where the fever hospital had been forced to go into debt. In November the board rented the New Brewery, converting it into a temporary union fever hospital. Doctors Wright and Nolan were requested to hand over equipment purchased for their institutions at the expense of the union. Renewed calls for assistance came from Arklow Fever Hospital in March 1847. 'The prevalence of fever in that town and the neighbourhood during the last six months' had exhausted finances to the point that no further patients could be admitted. As the Rathdrum Union Fever Hospital in the Brewery had no free beds left either, the board decided to pay for the treatment of the destitute and ill in Arklow Fever Hospital, as if these had been admitted to the workhouse. The obituary of Captain Hore, Lord Carysfort's agent and also a prominent Rathdrum guardian, records that during the worst of the Famine an eerie silence fell on Arklow, as the town's children ceased to play.[111]

Generally speaking, the Rathdown Union was less affected during 1846. By February 1847, however, the Rathdown poorhouse infirmary had become badly overcrowded. Half the stables built for the guardians' horses and carriages were converted into an emergency hospital. An event in June signalled a rise in infectious diseases in the union: an inmate suffering from fever was taken on a round trip to Rathdown Fever Hospital in Monkstown, county Dublin, and to that in Bray, both of which were full. The board began to erect fever sheds in the grounds, which were at first unheated. As they tended to let in the rain during bad weather, patients had to be evacuated occasionally. These shed were in use in Loughlinstown in 1847 and 1848, containing a record 91 patients in February of that year. An attempt to install such temporary facilities for fever patients in fashionable Kingstown foundered on the opposition of middle-class residents.[112]

Dysentery, diarrhoea, fever, relapsed fever, typhus, scurvy, measles, ophthalmia and smallpox were among the infectious diseases recorded in the Rathdown minutes between 1846 and 1852. The young and the elderly suffered most: on 16 February 1847, for instance, the Rathdrum medical officer reported nine deaths from dysentery, adding 'the cases are all old and infirm'. Both poorhouse doctors commented on the sickly state of children in the overcrowded workhouse nurseries. In 1850, the Rathdrum medical attendant insisted that the girls in the auxiliary building be given stockings, shoes and bonnets, as there had been an outbreak of ophthalmia. It was thought that fresh air and exercise would improve the youngsters' health and contain the spread of infection. The board obliged after pressure from the poor law commissioners, but ignored requests that a small, separate house be hired for smallpox patients. The Rathdrum children recovering from fever remained in danger of contracting smallpox, then potentially fatal, while in the union fever hospital.[113] Cholera broke out in Bray on 5 September 1849, lasting until 28 October; 68 out of 176 patients died. The Rathdown board relieved 493 cholera sufferers and their dependants, including 72 orphans. The Naas board assisted 71 people, while the remaining Wicklow unions remained almost cholera free.[114]

County Wicklow mortality rates doubled during the Famine. The number of deaths from infectious diseases in the county's workhouses was highest in the most populous Rathdrum Union, followed by Naas and Rathdown. Central and south-east Wicklow suffered more deaths than the adjoining Gorey Union. By comparison, the mortality rate of

Table 13.8 Impact of the Famine on the Wicklow Workhouses

Union (original accommodation)	*occupied week ending* 17 Oct. 45	17 Oct. 4	*last week* 6 Nov. 46	5 Dec. 46	9 Jan. 47	30 Jan. 47	13 Feb. 47	6 Mar. 47	27 Mar. 47	3 Apr. 47	17 Apr. 47	1 May 47
Baltinglass (500)	265	430	540	555	620	618	618	621	606	602	594	611
Rathdown (600)	311	449	550	581	650	689	700	672	687	693	676	670
Rathdrum (600)	297	399	567	636	728	842	819	789	865	876	879	870
Shillelagh (400)	232	254	311	339	391	406	424	476	504	505	531	504
Naas (550)	351	374	463	496	605	646	641	723	767	762	766	762

(*Source:* IUP BPP reprint, Famine (Ireland) 1)

AVERAGE NUMBER RELIEVED IN THE WICKLOW WORKHOUSES DURING 1848

A = average number of inmates in workhouse; B = average number on outdoor relief.

	March			*May*			*July*			*October*			*November*			*December*		
Name of Union	*A*	*B*	*Total*	*A*	*B*	*Total*	*A*	*B*	*Total*	*A*	*B*	*Total*	*A*	*B*	*Total*	*A*	*B*	*Total*
Baltinglass	736	1,733	2,469	836	1,665	2,501	868	1,725	2,593	836	980	1,816	882	1,204	2,086	892	1,357	2,249
Naas	1,072	2,694	3,766	1,005	2,727	3,732	866	1,861	2,727	778	435	1,213	1,008	466	1,474	1,223	1,092	2,315
Rathdown	710	1,589	2,299	569	905	1,474	512	574	1,086	468	266	734	561	312	873	599	362	961
Rathdrum	841	2,288	3,129	798	2,331	3,129	701	2,242	2,943	614	1,370	1,984	725	1,196	1,921	865	396	1,261
Shillelagh	636	561	1,195	626	634	1,260	580	559	1,139	478	330	808	568	367	935	647	415	1,012

(*Sources:* IUP BPP reprint Famine (Ireland) 3; 4)

the Ennistymon Union, county Clare, one of the worst-hit districts in Ireland, was four times that of Rathdrum. Famine fever, smallpox, influenza, dysentery, diarrhoea, scarlatina and whooping cough were among the causes of death listed.[115]

Table 13.9 Deaths from infectious diseases in workhouses, auxiliary workhouses and workhouse hospitals from 6 June 1841 to 30 March 1851

Name of Union	*Population in 1841*	*Deaths*		*Total Deaths*	*General Total**
		Male	*Female*		
Baltinglass	40,687	206	215	421	815
Naas	52,228	261	232	439	1,224
Rathdown	44,214	250	209	459	1,162
Rathdrum	56,709	392	341	733	1,167
Shillelagh	34,800	194	141	335	727
Gorey	39,054	303	318	621	1,197
Enniscorthy	61,816	310	277	578	1,440
Ennistymon	49,935	1,434	1,379	2,813	3,843

* Includes deaths from other causes.

One hundred and sixty four workhouse officials died of fever during the years 1847 to 1849, including two Rathdrum schoolmasters and a porter, the master of Naas poorhouse and the Rathdown porter and tailor. A carpenter erecting sleeping galleries in Rathdrum also caught the fever and died. Many other workhouse officers and their dependants residing in the staff quarters became ill, but recovered.[116] While guardians' minutes of the Famine period are valuable, they do, however, depict the crisis from the poor law administrators' perspective. Few among the anonymous masses at the receiving end of the workhouse system had the income or education to record their experiences.[117]

The Famine had a profound effect on Irish society in loosening family ties, as evident from the deserted wives and children in the poorhouses. It also disrupted customs, such as wakes, and broke down traditional patterns of behaviour, for instance, hospitality towards strangers and the poor. This was demonstrated by an incident in September 1848, when a sick, unaccompanied boy died at the roadside in Shillelagh, nobody daring to approach him for fear of fever. The Famine also copper-fastened hatred and shame of the workhouses in folk memory. Mrs Smith, a writer and the wife of a Naas guardian, agreed with a poor west Wicklow woman, risking her children's lives in a ditch rather than exposing them to 'the wickedness of the poorhouse'.[118]

5 THE EFFECT OF THE FAMINE ON WICKLOW WORKHOUSES

5.1 Emigration

The Famine forced the poor law to change. Hitherto guardians had been unwilling to assist inmates to emigrate. After the crisis years of 1847-1849, however, solvent unions, including those in county Wicklow, began to send emigrants abroad, instead of relieving them in the workhouses, perhaps for years to come. Poor law emigration from county Wicklow was relatively well organised; Rathdown emigrants, for instance, were provisioned, had their clothes made in the poorhouse and were allowed farewell visits to relations. The unions provided landing money, usually one pound per adult and 10 shillings per child, on arrival in the New World, to help ex-inmates in their search for work. This precaution proved sensible; some of the 1850 Baltinglass 'paupers', having received their landing money on embarkation, spent it on food and luxuries on board the 'Washington'.[119]

There are discrepancies in the emigration figures: the poor law commissioners noted the departure of 235 Baltinglass 'paupers', but the emigration agent in Quebec recorded the arrival of 275 in June 1850. The commissioners' figure of 110 emigrants leaving Rathdrum Workhouse in 1850, is contradicted by 124 inmates being discharged in the Rathdrum records. The low number of emigrants from Shillelagh Union was due to extensive landlord assisted emigration from the Fitzwilliam estate between 1847 and 1856. About 850 families, mainly from south Wicklow, left. Empty cabins were levelled and potato gardens amalgamated into larger holdings. There has been little follow-up research into the subsequent lives of these emigrants, who were sent to

Table 13.10 Emigration from the Wicklow workhouses

Aug. 1849 Apr. 1850	May 1850 Mar. 1851	Apr. 1851 Mar. 1852	Apr. 1852 Mar. 1853	Apr. 1853 Mar. 1854	Apr. 1854 Mar. 1855
Baltinglass 3, America	235, Quebec	1, Australia 7, Quebec	194, Quebec 14, New York	3, Ohio	2, Van Diemen's Land
Naas 305, Canada	—	1, Canada	62, Quebec 4, New York	176, Quebec 6, New Orleans 1, Philadelphia	6, Quebec
Rathdown 154, Canada —	—	4, Australia-	—	—	—
Rathdrum —	110, Canada	139, Canada 6, New York	144, Canada 31, New Orleans	9, Melbourne	75, Upper Canada
Shillelagh —	—	60, Quebec	—	—	—

Canadian ports as the cheaper alternative to New York. Many probably used their landing money to cross into the United States.[120]

The poor law and emigration commissioners initiated a scheme to send Irish workhouse girls to Australia in 1848. While there was a shortage of women in the Antipodes, Irish orphans left in the poorhouses faced a bleak future. The arrangements were advantageous to ratepayers, as the unions had to pay for girls' outfits and transport to Plymouth emigration depot only. Promises of good employment prospects in Australia (and of 'delicious' food on the voyage out) resulted in eager competition for places. Rathdown guardians followed the guidelines that girls should be Christian, clean, industrious, aged between 14 and 18 and with a basic education. Emigration agent Lt Henry, RN, however, imposing his own random selection, included girls between 13 and 20 and rejected a number of local candidates.[121] (See appendix II).

The Australian colonists believed that prostitutes had been included on an early ship. Publicity of abuses, anti-Catholic prejudice, growing Australian self esteem and the girls' lack of training for pioneer life combined to lead to the abolition of this scheme in 1850. Nonetheless, 4,175 girls were brought out, including 22 from Shillelagh, 19 from Rathdown, 16 from Baltinglass, 15 from Rathdrum and 15 from Naas. Wicklow boards began assisting inmates to join families abroad, sometimes supplementing passage money received from relatives in the US, while dependants of convicts were sent to Australia.[122]

During the Famine some desperate adults fled abroad, abandoning their children. Having established new lives, parents requested the return of ten Rathdown child inmates from the mid-1850s on. Two girls, for instance, who were reunited with their father in 1855, had been left in Loughlinstown in 1848, aged one and three respectively.[123]

5.2 Outdoor relief and population trends

The Famine had broken the authorities' resistance to outdoor relief. Although eager to discontinue it, when the crisis receded, a precedent had been set. Indicating growing compassion and perhaps also an awareness that it was cheaper, outdoor relief became established practice during the second half of the nineteenth century. In 1860 the Rathdrum board decided to apply the workhouse test, that is, only those unable to leave their homes without endangering their health qualified. In April 1860, 66 people out of a population of 47,861 in the Rathdrum Union were in receipt of outdoor relief, but by April 1865 there were 341 poorhouse inmates with 309 eligible for outdoor relief. This trend continued. Four years later 647 were outdoor relief recipients with only 419 in the workhouse. By 1884 only 277 people remained in

Rathdrum, in contrast with 850 people assisted outside. Similar, gradual changes also occurred in the other unions. By 1908 the poor law in Wicklow had developed into a dual system.[124] (See appendix IV).

The Famine reversed population trends. Between 1841 to 1851 Wicklow lost 21.53 per cent of its people, and up to 1891 a decline of about 10 per cent was recorded in each decade. From a record 126,143 inhabitants in 1841, Wicklow's population declined to 60,824 by 1901, with emigration peaking between 1851 and 1854. The enumeration of Irish emigrants to the US by county began in May 1851; figures do not exist for the shorter route to Britain. More than 11,173 Wicklow people boarded the emigrant ship between 1851 and 1861. Those figures are an underestimate, as many refused to reveal their place of origin.[125]

Furthermore, these statistics mask considerable, regional differences. The population of the Baltinglass, Shillelagh and Rathdrum Unions declined between 1841 and 1861, and the value of property fell. By 1865 the Baltinglass rateable valuation continued to decline, Shillelagh's remained static, but Rathdrum's had begun to increase. In contrast to south-west Wicklow the north-east suffered only a temporary setback, its property was rated at record heights by 1865, as can be seen in the figures below. The Rathdown Union's main town, Kingstown, was among the few places which continued to expand during the Famine, while numbers in the whole union remained static.

Table 13.11 Population and valuation 1841-1865

Population					**Valuation**	
	1841	*1851*	*1861*	*on Sept 1846*	*on Sept 1851*	*on 29 Sept 1865*
				£	£	£
Baltinglass*	40,687	27,324	22,032	90,934	76,157	73,309
Rathdown	44,214	48,240	53,298	189,069	154,134	214,867
Rathdrum*	56,709	47,932	43,402	153,538	121,105	126,545
Shillelagh*	34,800	24,172	19,183	64,485	50,032	50,092
Naas*	52,228	44,863	47,598	134,419	131,499	151,228

*Boundaries adjusted in 1850[126]
(*Source:* Published censuses of population, Valuation office records)

6 THE WORKHOUSE IN THE POST-FAMINE PERIOD

6.1 Health care

The Famine had increased the poor law commissioners' involvement in health care: the Wicklow boards of guardians, for instance, had augmented their workhouse accommodation and built union fever hospitals. Faced with extended buildings, but falling numbers of inmates, guardians began to enlarge their infirmaries, especially as many post-Famine inmates were chronically ill. As economic conditions improved, the sick, the young, the old and the mentally ill tended to be left behind in these institutions.[127]

Table 13.12 Post-Famine Accommodation of the Wicklow Workhouses on 29 September 1865

Name of Union	*No. of places available in Workhouse Infirmary*	*Fever Hospital*	*Other Accom.*	*Total*
Baltinglass	135	56	609	800
Rathdown	222	61	1,001	1,284
Rathdrum	90	80	653	823
Shillelagh	75	50	806	931
Naas	74	32 (+13 in WH)	857	97

(*Source:* BPP 1866 (309) lxii 93)

Proportion of sick to healthy inmates in 1861 and 1871

Name of Union	*in 1861*	*in 1871*
Baltinglass	1 in 6.7 inmates was sick	1 in 5.7 inmates was sick
Naas	1 in 4.6	1 in 4.7
Rathdown	1 in 2.1	1 in 1.7
Rathdrum	1 in 5.8	1 in 9.3
Shillelagh	1 in 6.4	1 in 3.7

(*Source:* Census of Ireland, 1861 and 1871, Part III, Vital Statistics)

Indicating poor health in the post-Famine period, in 1855 and 1858 ophthalmia recurred among the Rathdown children. There were also sporadic deaths from fever, diarrhoea and smallpox. Between September 1853 and March 1854, 271 cases (108 of measles, 102 of fever, 44 of scarlatina and 17 of smallpox), of whom 22 died, were treated in Rathdown. A few instances of cholera occurred in county Wicklow in late 1854. Guardians responded by cleansing and lime washing poor quarters. In Bray Fever Hospital 'pauper' nurses from the Rathdown Union attended patients. This small local institution was closed in 1857, having been superseded by the workhouse fever hospital.[128]

The last significant outbreak of cholera occurred in Wicklow between September and December 1866. In the Rathdrum Union the epidemic was centred on Arklow, where 88 of 148 cholera patients died. Panicking staff deserted Arklow Fever Hospital, people blocked the road to the workhouse fever hospital and stoned the relieving officer's van. The guardians attempted to restrict outdoor relief to families whose sick members entered the fever hospitals. The parish priest assisted Mercy nuns to care for cholera patients in their homes, while some gentry families provided soup. A cholera house on the Murrough in Wicklow remained empty, while two nuns attended the sick in the Ashford area. Dispensary doctors cared for cholera patients in the Bray district, where people's reluctance to enter the Rathdown Union Fever Hospital was respected. Charitable fund-raising also took place. In the second half of the nineteenth century diphtheria and scarlatina superseded other infectious diseases as potentially life threatening.[129]

Between 1848 and 1878 the importance and functions of boards of guardians increased considerably: the 1848 and 1849 Nuisance Removal and Diseases Prevention Acts enabled guardians to have places like Little Bray and Arklow cleansed to reduce the spread of infection; the 1851 Dispensary Act replaced the voluntary dispensary service with a centrally controlled outpatient system; the 1866 Sanitary Act strengthened the poor law commissioners' power in health matters, authorising the provision of clean water supplies. The 1878 Public Health Act saw the poor law commissioners, since 1872 the local government board, as having replaced the grand jury system.[130]

Gradually the poor law became more lenient after the Famine. During the 1850s the Rathdown board began to concern itself with the comfort of the inmates by measures such as the creation of a little privacy in the infirmary. Rathdrum, on the other hand, made a habit of postponing all improvements and attendant expense. Since the Famine patients had been admitted to the hospital without their families entering the workhouse; this practice was legalised by the poor law commissioners in 1862. Poor, though not destitute, persons could now become 'paying patients', who were exempt from wearing the workhouse uniform. The Rathdown guardians' generally more generous attitude may have been influenced by the growth of Catholic relief organisations in the barony of Rathdown after 1860. These included: St Columcille's branch of the St Vincent de Paul Society, Bray; St Kevin's Burial Society, Bray, where members saved regularly for a respectable funeral; and St Michael's Hospital, Kingstown.[131]

There are indications that many people preferred local health-care facilities, like the pre-1857 Bray Fever Hospital, the Newtownmount-kennedy Fever Hospital, where sick children were admitted with their mothers, or the 1918 temporary influenza hospital in Bray.[132]

6.2 Child care

There had been repeated complaints about the cold, unsuitable nurseries of the early Wicklow workhouses. Foundlings, in particular, were often admitted in a wretched condition. They were invariably illegitimate and often given stigmatising names. In Loughlinstown poorhouse one such infant was baptised 'John Loughlinstown'; a baby girl named 'Shankhill Claremont' – having been found at Claremont in Rathmichael electoral division – however had it amended to 'Jane Claremont'. In Rathdrum, too, infants were called after whatever place they were found in; for instance, 'Frances Field', 'James Field', 'John Walk', 'Mary Green', 'John Woods' and 'Matthew Church, found in the porch of the Rathdrum Church'.[133]

In the 1860s a Wicklow poor law inspector concluded that pauper aides could not be induced to handle these delicate babies with 'affection and tenderness'. The poor law commissioners' growing conviction that an institution was unsuitable for motherless children, as, for instance, expressed to the Rathdrum board on 26 June 1855, resulted in a boarding-out scheme in 1862, which was considered successful in Wicklow by contemporary standards. The foster families were usually of the labourer and small-farmer class. The Naas board initially held no annual inspection of children and foster mothers, unlike Rathdown and Baltinglass, while the Shillelagh guardians insisted on four such appearances before their board during the year. Such demonstrations of the guardians' interest in the children had positive results and were to become compulsory for boards. Relieving officers also visited the children's foster homes. The 1868 Rathdrum board paid foster mothers £5 p.a. and clothed their charges, nine infants placed were either deserted or orphaned, while siblings were fostered together.[134]

Table 13.14 Orphan and deserted children fostered in Wicklow unions

Name of Union	*Number of children from 7 Aug. 1862 – 12 July 1869*	*Number of children from 12 July 1869 – 18 Jan. 1873*
Baltinglass	—	16
Naas	37	8
Rathdown	—	17
Rathdrum	10	20
Shillelagh	12	22

(*Source:* 1st Irish Local Government Board Report, 1873)

In 1869 the boarding out of unaccompanied children under five years of age, authorised by the 1862 Poor Law Amendment Act, was extended to include those up to the age of ten. The 'children at nurse' scheme would eventually outlive the poor law, as indicated by Rathdown foster records extant for the 1925 to 1936 period. It is the ancestor of modern foster care. Guardians also used their powers to transfer handicapped children to special schools and hospitals.

The transformation from workhouse infirmary to district hospital for the poor was painfully slow. The disparity of inmates, which included the sick, the elderly, accident victims and the unfortunate, as well as a tough vagrant element, made a specialised, caring approach difficult. When the Rathdrum chairman, Col. Tottenham, proposed planting shrubs to make the workhouse yards less prison-like in 1898, he echoed the Young Irelander John Mitchel's condemnation of the 'poor law jails'. Despite improvements, the workhouse stigma clung to these institutions. In the words of J.M. Synge, old people talked about 'the three shadowy countries that are never forgotten in Wicklow – America (their El Dorado), the Union and the Madhouse'.[135]

7 THE LEGACY OF THE POOR LAW SYSTEM

The workhouse remained essentially unchanged in the early years of the twentieth century, despite well-meant efforts by, for instance, the Irish Workhouse Association, which hoped to improve the system 'with due regard to the interests of the ratepayers'. Lord Meath and Sir Henry Grattan Bellew were among its leading officers, promoting conferences of guardians, the study of the 'workhouse question' and the 'enlistment in the service of the ... poor of women', as inspectors, poor law guardians and ladies' visiting committees.[136]

With steadily declining numbers, the amalgamation of unions became certain. After transferring their remaining inmates to the Dublin Union in 1920, the Rathdown guardians converted their workhouse into a district hospital. Likewise the Naas poorhouse was wound up in 1921 and its Wicklow inmates sent to Shillelagh.

During the War of Independence, British military commandeered Shillelagh Union Fever Hospital and Baltinglass Workhouse, the latter becoming the 'workhouse camp'. (Inmates were transferred to Shillelagh.) Wicklow boards of guardians, like their colleagues outside of north-east Ulster, now boycotted the 'English' local government board to take their instructions from the alternative Dáil body. In 1921 Lawrence Murphy, the Rathdrum relieving officer and Roundwood Fenian, applied for further leave of absence, as he was being detained in Kilmainham Jail. The Rathdrum guardians' compliance is symptomatic of the nationalistic change in attitude. The Rathdown board's assistant clerk, Farrell, was also a prominent IRB man, who secreted records to hamper British control over local administration. A Dáil local government board inspector was arrested in January 1921, after examining Shillelagh workhouse records. Having been repeatedly vandalised by crown forces, Baltinglass poorhouse and its records were burned sometime between late 1922 and early 1923.[137]

The Free State abolished the poor law system by enacting the Local Government Act of 1923, but it remained a symbolic gesture due to lack of funds. Although the Wicklow County Scheme Order dissolved the four main unions, the county infirmary and the Arklow, Newtown Mount Kennedy and Wicklow Fever Hospitals, the spirit of the Victorian poor law continued to permeate the system. Rathdrum workhouse, now the 'county home' for the whole of Wicklow, was to provide relief for the old and infirm, chronic invalids and expectant mothers. In 1936 a TB unit was added. The traditional focus of north Wicklow's poor was changed from the Dublin direction to central Wicklow. In the west, Baltinglass people objected to having to cross the mountains for hospital care, as had been the case before 1817. In 1970 the antiquated, unhygienic Rathdrum workhouse complex was demolished and a modern St Colman's geriatric hospital erected on the site. Rathdown continued to function as St Columcille's Hospital, a programme of renovations began after 1944. The order of the Poor Servants of the Mother of God, in Loughlinstown since 1899, took over Rathdrum in 1922. Foundress Fanny Taylor had nursed with Florence Nightingale in the Crimean War and both were to introduce trained nurses into the workhouse infirmaries. The order withdrew from St. Columcille's in 1991, due to falling vocations.[138]

The Baltinglass ruins were cleared during the 1940s and a new district hospital was built. The Shillelagh Union Fever Hospital became the county fever hospital, but in 1947 the poorhouse buildings, with the exception of the chapel, were demolished. Extended and renovated, it became Shillelagh's Catholic church in the parish of Carnew. Naas County Hospital incorporates parts of Naas workhouse. Medical, surgical and maternity cases continued to be treated in the Wicklow county hospital – the successor of the infirmary – now Wicklow District Hospital.[139]

The records of these institutions show a remarkable continuity: patients continued to be elderly people without family support, the chronically ill and unmarried mothers. Staff and patients alike considered the abolition of the poor law a pleasant fiction well into the 1940s. Among illuminating episodes documented is the 1945 application of a Wicklow woman for hospital admission as 'a poor law patient'. In 1937 Rathdrum was the destination of the 'Bray Hunger Marchers' – unemployed workers – who demanded adequate relief or employment, reminiscent of the Bray men who had demonstrated outside Loughlinstown workhouse in 1846.[140]

7.1 Loughlinstown's Literary Legacy

As this essay demonstrates, the number and variety of people involved in the poor law in county Wicklow amount to a canvas of Tolstoyan proportions. While Asenath Nicholson mentions Rathdrum poorhouse in *The Bible in Ireland* and Baltinglass has been described in reminiscences, Loughlinstown is probably unique. Among its visitors were the founder of the poor law system, George Nicholls, and Maud Gonne, when supporting Clarke's political campaign in 1899. Countess Markievicz conducted a Fianna Éireann training camp in the grounds in the summer of 1921. Mother Taylor was prevented from seeing 'Rathdown Union Workhouse at Loughlinstown' because of her approaching death, while Louie Bennett, the Irish trade unionist, was one of its many patients. It is said that Louisa Greene's Victorian novelette *The Grey House on the Hill* was based on Loughlinstown. It features in Hugh Leonard's autobiography *Home before Night* as 'the union'. Rathdown poorhouse also made an impression on the imagination of the young James Joyce, who was to list it among Irish antiquities in *Ulysses*, concluding: 'all these moving scenes are still there for us today rendered more beautiful still by the waters of sorrow which have passed over them and by the rich incrustations of time'.[141]

Conclusion

The administration of the poor law in Wicklow, as elsewhere, was flawed from the beginning. Although the famine was less cataclysmic on the east coast, the poor suffered much, particularly in the Rathdrum Union and in west Wicklow. Punitive regulations gave the workhouses a negative image, which clung to them despite later improvements. They remained the last refuge of the very poor in the post-famine period and even after the official dissolution of the poor law system in 1923.

Appendix I: Boards of Guardians

The following were present at the first meeting of the Rathdown Board of Guardians on 16 September, 1839:

Name	Status	Profession	Address
Sir George Hodson	Chairman ex-officio	Landlord	Hollybrook, Bray.
Sir William Betham	Ex-officio	Genealogist, Ulster King of Arms	Stradbrook Hse., Newtownpark, Stillorgan and Office of Arms, Dublin Castle and Kildare St.
Cornelius Sullivan	Ex-officio	Agent to Sidney Herbert	Mount Merrion Hse., Stillorgan Rd.
Arthur Burgh Crofton	Ex-officio	'Esq.'	Roebuck Castle, Dundrum.
Christopher FitzSimon	Ex-officio	Landlord	Glencullen, Co. Dublin.
Bryan Molloy	Ex-officio	Major	Belvedere Place, Dublin.
Isaac Weld	Ex-officio	Travel writer, statistician	Ravenswell Hse., Bray.
Robert Sandys	Ex-officio	Agent to Lord Powerscourt	Dargle Cottage, Enniskerry.
G. Hatchell	Elective	Several listed, probably of or possibly Dr. G. W. Hatchell (?)	Ludford Park, Dundrum
Henry C. Field	Elective	Medical doctor	Baggot St. and Field Villa, Blackrock.
John Gilman	Elective	'Esq.'	Bellevue, Cross Ave., Booterstown.
William Plant	Elective	Medical doctor of Rathdown Fever Hospital	Plantation, Monkstown Rd.
Bargeny McCulloch	Elective		Not found.
Barry Edward Lawless	Elective	Solicitor, landlord	Harcourt St., Dublin.
Thomas M. Scully	Elective	Barrister	Airfield, Dundrum.
John Byrne	Elective	Several listed, not identified	
John Warren	Elective		Sidney Pl., St. George's Ave., Blackrock.
Benjamin Grant	Elective	'Esq.'	Monkstown Cottage, Monkstown.
George Seymour	Elective	Coal and timber merchant	Seapoint Hse., Bray.
John Quin, Jun.	Elective	Hotelier, property investor	Quin's Hotel, Bray.
Phineas Riall	Elective	Landlord	Old Conna Hill, Bray.
William Sherrard	Elective	Land agent and valuer of estates	Blessington St., Dublin.
Thomas Thompson	Elective	Solicitor	Harcourt St., Dublin.
William Hopper	Elective	'Esq.'	Shanganah House, Co. Dublin.
George Kennan	Elective	Not found	
Richard Fox	Elective	Not found	
Arthur Jones	Elective	Auctioneer, valuer or solicitor	Stephen's Green or Dominick St., Dublin.
Henry Keegan	Elective	Not found	

(*Source:* Pettigrew & Oulten's Street Directory 1840, 1842).

The following were present at the 3rd May, 1899 meeting of the Rathdown Board of Guardians:

Name	Profession	Address
William Rafferty, J. P. (Chairman)*	'Esq.'	Springfield, Golden Ball.
Charles B. Jennings	Surgeon, Lieut.-Col. M.S.	Nutley, Southhill Ave., Blackrock.
John F. Colohan	Medical doctor	Woodvillw, Rock Rd., Blackrock.
Cecil W. Betham		Belgrave Sq., Monkstown.
Francis D. Murphy	'Esq.'	Ardravinia, Killiney.
Capt. Lewis Riall	Landlord	Old Conna Hill, Bray.
D. G. Beamish	Colonel	Eglington Park, Kingstown.
Thomas W. Robinson	Chemist	Upper George's St., Kingstown; Clarinda Park North, Kingstown.
Lady Rosa Gilbert (Rosa Mulholland)	Writer	Villa Nova, Mount Merrion Ave., Blackrock.
Thomas Clarke	'Esq.'	Newstead, Avoca Ave., Blackrock (?)
John Cullen	Several listed, not identified	
Mrs. Mary Hogan	Not listed	
Miss Catherine Hamilton	Several listed, not identified	
Isaac W. Usher	Medical doctor of Dundrum Dispensary	Laurel Lodge, Dundrum.
A. Armstrong, J.P.	Paper merchant and wholesale stationer	Lower Abbey St., Dublin and Hollywood, Carrickmines.
William Connolly	Doctor, Deputy Inspector-General of hospitals and fleets, R.N. (?)	Crosthwaite Park West, Kingstown (?)
John Swift Hyland	Several listed, not identified	
J. H. North, J.P.	F.I.A.	Garfton St., Dublin and Haddington Park, Glenageary.
James Collins		Janeville, Merrion.
C. O'Connell FitzSimon	Landlord	Glencullen, Co. Dublin.
James Byrne	Hotelier (?), several listed	Shanganah Hotel, Ballybrack (?)
Michael Bourke	Not listed	
J. J. Reilly	'Esq.'	Laurel Villa, Ballybrack.
Mary P. Sinnott	Not listed	
Thomas J. Callaghan, J.P.	Saddler, tailor and military outfitter	Dame St., Dublin and Farmhill, Roebuck.
Sir Henry Cochrane, J.P.	Drinks manufacturer	Kildare St., Dublin and Woodbrook, Bray.
Sir Rowland Fanning	Late Deputy Inspector-General R.I.C.	Rosslyn, Bray.
John F. Lacy.	Hotelier	Bray Head Hotel and Fontenoy Tce., Bray.
Thomas Lawless	Publican	'The Hotel', Delgany.
Miss Ellen Griffin	Not listed	
Walter T. Bryan	'Esq.'	Holyrood, Bray.
Philip Condrin	Member of Bray Urban District Council	

Name	Profession	Address
William Bourke	Not listed	
C. Cullen	Not listed	
Andrew U. O'Farrell	Not listed	
William George Morris, J.P.	'Esq.'	Windgates Hse., Windgates.
Francis Buckley	Hotelier	Powerscourt Arms Hotel, Enniskerry.
Michael Tallon	Not listed	
S. J. Doyle	Not listed	
J. Murphy	Several listed, not identified	
Alfred Sexton	'Esq.'	Purbeck Lodge, Brighton Ave., Monkstown Rd.
Henry Darby-Dowman, J.P.	'Esq.'	Knoyle Lodge, Brighton Ave., Monkstown.
John Masterson	Several listed, not identified	
James Triston	'Esq.'	York St., Kingstown.
Thomas Brown	Several listed, not identified	
William Keegan	Spirit merchant (?)	Lower George's St., Kingstown or Bahana, Enniskerry.
Thomas M. Corbett	L.R.C.S.I.	Upper George's St., Kingstown.
John McDermott	'Esq.'	Beechmount Ave., Merrion (?).
James Joseph Kennedy	Several listed, not identified	
Thomas Lowry	'Esq.'	Clarinda Park East, Kingstown.
John Ennis	Farmer	Rathdown Upper, Greystones.
Norman Thompson	Medical doctor	Kendalstown Hse., Delgany.
James Evans	'Esq.'	Spencer Rd., Kingstown.
P. Byrne	Not listed	
S. Doyle, Sen.	Not listed	
Robert Wogan	Not listed	

*Reported as present by WNL on 29 April, 1899).
(*Sources:* Thom's Directory 1899; 1900; Slater's Royal National Directory of Ireland, 1894; Wicklow Newsletter, 6 May, 1899).

The following were present at the first meeting of the Rathdrum Board of Guardians on 5 November, 1839 were:

Name	**Status**	**Profession**	**Address**
Col Thomas Acton, M.P. (Chairman)	Ex-officio	Landlord	Kilmacurragh (Westaston).
John Dick	Ex-officio	'Esq.'	Belfield, Newtown-Mount-Kennedy.
Capt. Samuel Hore	Ex-officio	Agent to Lord Carysfort	Lambarton, Arklow.
John Parnell	Ex-officio	Landlord	Avondale, Rathdrum.
Admiral Hon. G. L. Proby	Ex-officio	Lord Carysfort's heir	Glenart Castle, Arklow.
John Synge	Ex-officio	Landlord	Glenmore Castle, Ashford.
William T. Bookey, J.P.*	Ex-officio	Landlord	Derrybawn, Rathdrum.
Thomas Mills King, J.P.	Ex-officio	'Esq.'	Kingston, Rathdrum.
Capt. George Bury	Ex-officio		Cassino, Rathdrum.
Joseph Dickson	Ex-officio	'Esq.'	Ballyfree, Glenealy.
James Byrne	Elective	Provision dealer (?) or tenant of tenant of C. Tottenham in Upper Newcastle (?)	Back Lane, Rathdrum (?).
Christopher Byrne	Elective	Tenant of C. Tottenham in Upper Newcastle (?)	
J. J. Byrne, J.P.	Elective	'Esq.'	Kilpatrick, Arklow.
Peter Byrne	Elective	Crushing Mill tenant	Ballinacor.
Laurence Byrne	Elective	L. Byrne, landlord of Cronybyrne or tenant farmer of Upper Newcastle and Ballinacor	
James Comerford	Elective	Miller	Glassneyet, Rathdrum.
Charles Case	Elective		Not listed.
Francis Cullen	Elective		Not listed.
William Ellis	Elective		Not listed.
Matthew Ellis	Elective	'Mr.'	Uppertown, Rathdrum.
Laurence Graydon	Elective	Landlord	Tooman, Kilcoole.
Robert Hudson	Elective	'Esq.'	Spring Farm, Delgany.
William Gilbert	Elective	'Esq.' property owner in Rathdrum	Prospect, Rathdrum.
William Heatley	Elective	Schoolmaster	Elton House Boarding & Day School, Lamberton, Arklow.
James Jones	Elective		Not listed.
Simon Moran	Elective	Miller	Milltown Mills, Ashford.
Thomas Murray	Elective	'Esq.'	Cooladangan.
Dr. Gerard Macklin	Elective	'Esq.'	Lake Park, Lough Dan
Joseph McGrath	Elective		Not listed.
Francis Russell	Elective		Not listed.
Robert Roe	Elective	Tenant and property owner in	Newtown-Mount-Kennedy.
Robert Sharpe	Elective		Not listed.
Peter Walshe	Elective		Not listed.
Charles Herne	Elective		Not listed.

* Noted among Guardians listed in *F.J.*, 21 October, 1839. (*Sources:* Slater's National Commercial Directory of Ireland, 1846; Burke's Landed Gentry; Griffith Valuation).

The following were reported as present at the Rathdrum Board of Guardians meeting reported in *WNL* on 6 May, 1899:

Name	Profession	Address
Col. Charles G. Tottenham* (Chairman)	Landlord	Ballycurry, Ashford.
Col. William Kemmis, R.A., J.P.	Landlord	Ballinacor, Rathdrum.
Laurence Wolohan	Farmer	Castlemacadam.
J. Clarke	Spirit dealer	Leitrim Place, Wicklow.
William Coleman		Not listed.
Edward Cullen	Hotel keeper and grocer	Ashford.
Henry Delahunt	Grocer or farmer	Arklow or Dunganstown.
John Richardson		Not listed.
P. Neill		Not listed.
Owen Byrne		Not listed.
Garret Short		Not listed.
James Turner		Not listed.
M. Byrne	Several listed, blacksmith or farmers	Castlemacadam or Wicklow or Dunganstown (?)
Thomas Byrne	Farmer	Rathdrum.
Patrick Padin, J.P.		Bay View Cottage, Wicklow.
Michael Giffney		Not listed.
Michael Miley		Not listed.
P. Kavanagh	Several listed, grocer or tailor	Arklow or Ashford.
Peter Tyrrell	Farmer	Glenealy.
M. Loughlin		Not listed.
Edward Cullen	Farmer	Season Park, Newtown-Mount-Kennedy.
William Byrne	(Member of Wicklow County Council, 1903)	Coolbeg, Wicklow.
M. Cullen		Not listed.
B. Brady		Not listed.
Peter Brennan		Ballyknockan Lr., Rathdrum.
M. Doyle	Several listed, farmer (?)	Arklow.
G. P. Healy		Not listed.
Morgan Travers		Not listed.
P. R. Fogarty	Coal merchant	Rathdrum.
James Byrne		Tinnakilly Lr., Aughrim.
John Turner		Not listed.
Maurice Mernagh	Farmer	Rathdrum.
B. Doyle		Not listed.
D. M. Doyle		Not listed.
Edward Ellison	Farmer	Rathdrum.
Capt. Higgins	Identical with James H. (?) agent, Tigroney Mines	
Mrs. Teresa Dargan	'Private resident'	Mill Mount, Avoca.
Miss O'Brien		Not listed
Daniel Condon		Arklow

*Not present on that date. (*Sources:* Wicklow News-Letter 22 April, 1899; Slater's Royal National Directory of Ireland, 1894).

Appendix II

ORPHAN EMIGRATION FROM THE RATHDOWN UNION TO AUSTRALIA

Name	Age at Admission	Religion	Origin (Elect. Div.)	Trade	Condition on admission	Last admission	Discharged for Australia
Eliza Sharp	18	RC	Union at large	Servant	Clean	27th June, 1849	15th August, 1849
Mary Golden	16	Protestant	Delgany/Union at large	Servant	Clean	27th June, 1849	15th August, 1849
Mary Byrne	18	RC	Kingstown	—	Clean	4th July, 1849	15th August, 1849
Catherine Kernan	13	RC	Union at large	—	Deserted, clean, healthy	16th July, 1849	16th February, 1850
Anne McEvoy	15	RC	Delgany, Glencormick	—	Clean, healthy	22nd July, 1849	15th August, 1849
Teresa Keogh	14	RC	Union at large	—	Deserted, sickly, clean	9th August, 1849	15th August, 1849
Essy Dempsey	18	RC	Powerscourt	—	Healthy, clean	25th August, 1849	16th February, 1850
Sarah Murphy	15	RC	Union at large	—	Sickly, clean	9th December, 1849	16th February, 1850
Mary Hamilton	20	Protestant	Scalp (Union at large)	Servant	Clean, healthy	24th March, 1849	15th August, 1849
Rebecca Byrne	19	RC	Union at large	Labourer	Healthy, ragged	29th October, 1848	15th August, 1849
Eliza Rossiter	12	RC	Union at large	—	Healthy, clean, mother dead, father in America	24th October, 1848	15th August, 1849
Catherine Byrne	13	RC	Killiney	—	Healthy, clean	1st August, 1848	15th August, 1849
Charlotte Basset	14	Protestant	Union at large/ Rathmichael	—	Healthy	19th July, 1848	15th August, 1849
Jane Roony	13	RC	Delgany/Powerscourt	—	Healthy	5th July, 1848	15th August, 1849

(*Source:* Indoor Relief Registers of the Rathdown Union, 1847-1850).

Appendix III

INMATES SENT FROM RATHDOWN UNION WORKHOUSE TO NORTH AMERICA IN 1850

(from Wicklow electoral divisions and Union at Large)

Name	Age	Occupation	Health Status	Origin	Last admitted	Discharge for North America
Robert Fox	38	Labourer	Not disabled	Little Bray	22nd October, 1849	12th April, 1850
Sarah Fox	39 or 42	His wife	Not disabled	Little Bray	14th February, 1850	12th April, 1850
Robert Fox	14	Child of above	Not disabled	Little Bray	22nd October, 1849	12th April, 1850
Jane Fox	12	Child of above	Not disabled	Little Bray	22nd October, 1849	12th April, 1850
Joseph Fox	10	Child of above	Not disabled	Little Bray	22nd October, 1849	12th April, 1850
James Fox	8	Child of above	Not disabled	Little Bray	22nd October, 1849	12th April, 1850
Robert Dalton	41	Tailor	Not disabled	Town of Bray	29th November, 1849	12th April, 1850
Thomas Dalton	13	—	Not disabled	Town of Bray	16th January, 1850	12th April, 1850
John Dalton	10	—	Not disabled	Town of Bray	16th January, 1850	12th April, 1850
James Dalton	3	—	Not disabled	Town of Bray	16th January, 1850	12th April, 1850
Robert Dalton	7	—	Not disabled	Town of Bray	16th January, 1850	12th April, 1850
Rachael Dalton	40	Wife	Not disabled	Town of Bray	4th March, 1850	12th April, 1850
Mary Ann Dalton	17	Servant	Not disabled	Town of Bray	1st April, 1850	12th April, 1850
Jane Dalton	19	—	Not disabled	Town of Bray	13th March, 1850	12th April, 1850
Kevin Lennon	50	None	Not disabled	Town of Bray	16th January, 1850	12th April, 1850
Anne Lennon	14	Child of above	Not disabled	Town of Bray	16th January, 1850	12th April, 1850
Mary Lennon	12	Child of above	Not disabled	Town of Bray	16th January, 1850	12th April, 1850
John Lennon	10	Child of above	Not disabled	Town of Bray	16th January, 1850	12th April, 1850
Betty Lennon	50 or 33	Wife of Kevin	Not disabled	Town of Bray	20th February, 1850	12th April, 1850
Catherine Healy	29	—	Not disabled	Bray	17th December, 1849	30th April, 1850
Catherine Williams	1½	Her illegitimate child	Not disabled	Bray	17th December, 1849	30th April, 1850
Mary Byrne	28	Deserted wife	Healthy	Bray	16th August, 1848	30th April, 1850
Catherine Harris	25	—	Healthy	Town of Bray	19th December, 1848	30th April, 1850
John Salmon	16	—	Healthy	Bray	3rd October, 1848	30th April, 1850
Catherine Byrne	28	—	Sick	Bray town	23rd February, 1850	30th April, 1850
Thomas Wilson	48	Labourer	Not disabled	Bray town	27th March, 1850	12th April, 1850
Bridget Wilson	37	His wife	Not disabled	Bray town	27th March, 1850	12th April, 1850
William Wilson	16	Son of above	Not disabled	Bray town	27th March, 1850	12th April, 1850
Matthew Wilson	11	Son of above	Not disabled	Bray town	27th March, 1850	12th April, 1850
Mary Murphy	22	—	Not disabled	Town of Bray	13th March, 1850	30th April, 1850
Thomas Lennon	16	Labourer	Not disabled	Town of Bray	5th April, 1850	12th April, 1850

Name	Age	Occupation	Health Status	Origin	Last admitted	Discharge for North America
Michael Kelly	19	Labourer	Not disabled	Bray	22nd April, 1850	30th April, 1850
Eliza Byrne	24	—	Healthy	Bray	14th November, 1848	30th April, 1850
Henry Purcell	Not found	—	—	Powerscourt	—	—
John Purcell	10	Half orphan	Not disabled	Powerscourt/Union	27th June, 1849	30th April, 1850
Ann Purcell	12	Half orphan	Not disabled	Powerscourt/Union at large	27th June, 1849	30th April, 1850
Anastasia Purcell	44	—	Not disabled	Powerscourt	27th June, 1849	30th April, 1850
Mary Purcell	19	Child of above	Not disabled	Union at large	27th June, 1849	30th April, 1850
Eliza Roach	22	Servant	Not disabled	Powerscourt/ Enniskerry	13th March, 1850	30th April, 1850
George Roach	16	—	Not disabled	Powerscourt/ Enniskerry	10th October, 1849	30th April, 1850
James Hand	Not found	—	—	—	—	—
Margaret Mullen	20	—	Not disabled	Powerscourt/ Enniskerry	19th December, 1849	30th April, 1850 Unclear, did she sail?
Ellen Flynn	27	—	Not disabled	Powerscourt/ Enniskerry	19th December, 1849	30th April, 1850
Catherine Hamilton	20	Servant	Healthy	Powerscourt	21st March, 1849	12th April, 1850
Catherine Costello	20	—	Not disabled	Powerscourt/ Glencree	23rd January, 1850	30th April, 1850 Unclear, did she sail?
Mary Williams	20	—	Not disabled	Long Hill, Powerscourt	23rd January, 1850	30th April, 1850
Essy Neyland	17	—	Not disabled	Powerscourt	15th December, 1849	30th April, 1850
James Dolan	Not found	—	—	Powerscourt	—	—
John Dolan	Not found	—	—	Powerscourt	—	—
Ellen Bellew	Not found	—	—	Powerscourt	—	—
Ellen Hopkins	Not found	—	—	Powerscourt	—	—
Mary McGrath	13	Orphan	Not disabled	Powerscourt/ Enniskerry	6th February, 1850	30th April, 1850
Pat Neyland	24	—	Lame, sickly	Union at large	20th August, 1849	30th April, 1850
Nanny Bellew	30	Nursetender	Not filled in	Union at large	4th January, 1848	30th April, 1850
Mary Purcell	18	Servant	Not disabled	Powerscourt	26th March, 1850	30th April, 1850
-- Doran	8	-- boys, sons	Not disabled	Powerscourt	18th January, 1842	30th April, 1850
-- Doran, Jun.	3	of Wm. & Bridget Doran	Not disabled	Powerscourt	18th January, 1842	30th April, 1850
Dorah Campbell	19	—	Not disabled	Union at large	25th August, 1849	30th April, 1850
John Lynch	18	—	Sore leg	Union at large	18th January, 1850	30th April, 1850

Name	Age	Occupation	Health Status	Origin	Last admitted	Discharge for North America
John Jenkins	Not found	—	—	Union at large	—	—
Mary Jenkins	37	—	Healthy	Union at large	11th January, 1848	12th April, 1850
John Jenkins	13	Her son	Healthy	Union at large	11th January, 1848	12th April, 1850
Ralph Jenkins	11	Her son	Healthy	Union at large	11th January, 1848	12th April, 1850
George Reilly	Did not emigrate					
Catherine Reilly	20	—	Not disabled	Union at large	8th April, 1850	12th April, 1850
Mary Reilly	44	—	Healthy	Union at large/ Sallynogging	26th January, 1849	12th April, 1850
Richard Reilly	12	Child of above	Healthy	Union at large/ Sallynogging	26th January, 1849	12th April, 1850
Richard Reilly	Not found	—	—	—	—	—
Bernard Hanavin or Hanivan	16	—	Not disabled	Union at large	20th February, 1850	12th April, 1850
Mary Purcell	18	Servant	Not disabled	Powerscourt	26th March, 1850	30th April, 1850
Eliza Jenkins	10	Child of Mary Jenkins	Healthy	Union at large	11th January, 1848	12th April, 1850
Charles Jenkins	3	Child of Mary Jenkins	Healthy	Union at large	11th January, 1848	12th April, 1850
Jane Butler	Not found	—	—	—	—	—
Ann Leary	50	Widow	Not disabled	Union at large	9th January, 1850	30th April, 1850
William Leary	17	Labourer, her son	Not disabled	Union at large	9th January, 1850	30th April, 1850
Thomas Leary	19	Labourer	Healthy	Union at large	23rd January, 1849	30th April, 1850
Pat Leary	15	Servant	Not disabled, healthy	Union at large	7th November, 1848	30th April, 1850
John Neill	32	—	Healthy	Union at large/Bray	25th May, 1849	30th April, 1850
Ann Neill	8	His child	Healthy	Union at large/Bray	25th May, 1849	30th April, 1850
Jane Neill	27	—	Not disabled	Union at large/Bray	25th May, 1849	30th April, 1850
Biddy Sharky	19	—	Healthy	Union at large	27th September, 1848	30th April, 1850
Rose Croghell	23	—	Not disabled	Union at large	20th June, 1849	30th April, 1850
Mary Faulkner	23	Servant	Not disabled	Union at large	20th February, 1850	30th April, 1850
Ellen Thackaberry	17	—	Not disabled	Union at large	23rd August, 1849	30th April, 1850
Ann Kavanagh	20	Servant	Healthy	Union at large/ Dalkey	16th May, 1849	30th April, 1850
Julia Kennedy	50	Widow, servant	Not disabled	Union at large	12th January, 1850	30th April, 1850
Catherine Nolan	Not found	—	—	Union at large	—	—
Essy Tuite	20	—	Not disabled	Union at large	29th August, 1849	30th April, 1850

Name	Age	Occupation	Health Status	Origin	Last admitted	Discharge for North America
Eliza Ward	17	—	Not disabled	Union at large	1st December, 1849	30th April, 1850
John Ward	22	—	Not disabled	Union at large	1st December, 1849	30th April, 1850
James Allen	16	Shoemaker	Not disabled	Union at large	13th December, 1849	30th April, 1850
William Drout	18	—	Not disabled	Union at large	23rd January, 1850	30th April, 1850
Edward Neill	19	Tailor	Not filled in	Union at large	12th January, 1850	30th April, 1850
William Ears	44	Labourer	Not disabled	Union at large	17th October, 1849	30th April, 1850
Thomas Devitt	40	Labourer	Not disabled	Union at large	10th October, 1849	30th April, 1850
Mary Devitt	35	His wife	Healthy	Union at large	4th July, 1849	30th April, 1850
Catherine Devitt	13	—	Healthy	Union at large	4th July, 1849	30th April, 1850
James Higgins	22	—	Not disabled	Union at large	23rd January, 1850	30th April, 1850
Jane Rorke	25	—	Sickly	Union at large	21st March, 1849	30th April, 1850
Sarah Rorke	2½	Her child	Healthy	Union at large	21st March, 1849	30th April, 1850
Mary Grannon	32	Widow	Not disabled	Union at large	10th October, 1849	12th April, 1850
William Grannon	14	Her child	Not disabled	Union at large	10th October, 1849	12th April, 1850
Ellen Grannon	12	Her child	Not disabled	Union at large	10th October, 1849	12th April, 1850
John Grannon	2	Her child	Not disabled	Union at large	10th October, 1849	12th April, 1850
Mary Ann Grannon	5	Her child	Not disabled	Union at large	10th October, 1849	12th April, 1850
Biddy Heffernan	20	—	Not disabled	Union at large	2nd January, 1850	30th April, 1850
Biddy Chambers	Not found	—	—	Union at large	—	—
Phillip Rourke	16	—	Not disabled	Union at large	23rd January, 1850	30th April, 1850
John Byrne	16	Labourer	Not disabled	Union at large	6th March, 1850	30th April, 1850
Bernard McCann	18	Servant	Sick	Union at large	6th March, 1850	30th April, 1850
Ellen McGuirk	20	—	Not disabled	Union at large	6th March, 1850	30th April, 1850
Eliza Hand	25	Servant	Not disabled	Union at large	21st March, 1850	30th April, 1850
Stephen Connolly	13 months	Her illegitimate child	Not disabled	Union at large	21st March, 1850	30th April, 1850
Ann McGuirk	25	Not filled in	Not disabled	Union at large	27th March, 1850	30th April, 1850
Martin Purcell	22	Labourer	Not disabled	Union at large	1st April, 1850	30th April, 1850
John McCann	16	—	Sick	Union at large	3rd April, 1850	12th April, 1850
Ann McCann	52	Widow, servant	Not disabled	Union at large	11th April, 1850	12th April, 1850
Charles McCann	19	Shoemaker and clerk, son of above	Not disabled	Union at large	11th April, 1850	12th April, 1850
Jane McCann	14	Child of above	Not disabled	Union at large	11th April, 1850	12th April, 1850
Richard Kelly	45	Labourer	Healthy	Union at large/ Sallynoggin	28th March, 1849	12th April, 1850
Julia McGrath	24	Servant	Not disabled	Delgany	15th October, 1849	30th April, 1850

Name	Age	Occupation	Health Status	Origin	Last admitted	Discharge for North America
Anne William	18	Servant	Not disabled	Delgany	25th August, 1849	30th April, 1850
Mary Williams	40	Widow	Not disabled	Delgany	22nd December, 1849	30th April, 1850
Henry Williams	13	Her child	Not disabled	Delgany	22nd December, 1849	30 April, 1850
Mary Williams, Jun.	Not found	—	—	—	—	—
Mary Aspeill	19 or 18	—	Not disabled	Delgany/ Kilmacanogue	27th February, 1850	30th April, 1850
Maria Dooragan	30	Servant	Not disabled	Delgany/Bellevue	10th November, 1849	30th April, 1850
Patrick Cromeen	11 (?)	—	Healthy	Union at large	23rd January, 1849	30th April, 1850
John Flynn	14	—	Healthy	Union at large	28th November, 1848	30th April, 1850
William Corrigan	Not found	—	—	—	—	—
Frederick Corrigan	15	—	Healthy	Union at large	19 December, 1848	30th April, 1850

Total of emigrants from North Wicklow and Union at large **117**

Overall number of emigrants **154**

(*Source:* Rathdown Union Indoor Registers 1841-1850).

Appendix IV

ADMISSIONS TO THE WICKLOW WORKHOUSES 1842–1912

	For the year 1842				For year ended 29th September, 1847				
Name of Union	Remaining on 1st January, 1842	Admitted and born	Discharged and died	Remaining on 1st January, 1843	Remaining at beginning of year	Admitted and born	Total relieved	Discharged and died	Remaining at close of year
Baltinglass	157	655	493	319	359	919	1,278	729	549
Naas	377	967	866	478	336	1,121	1,457	962	495
Rathdown	163	696	577	282	401	2,914	3,315	2,696	619
Rathdrum*	–	767	444	323	380	1,594	1,974	1,442	532
Shillelagh*	–	550	294	256	230	997	1,227	824	403

*Unions opened during 1842

TOTAL NUMBERS RELIEVED DURING YEAR ENDED

	29th September, 1852			29th September, 1857			29th September, 1862		
Name of Union	in Workhouse relief	Outdoor relief	Total number	in Workhouse relief	Outdoor relief	Total number	in Workhouse relief	Outdoor relief	Total number
Baltinglass	1,753	10	1,763	999	16	1,015	1,618	163	1,781
Naas	2,586	60	2,646	1,503	383	1,886	2,175	414	2,589
Rathdown	2,837	91	2,928	1,812	15	1,827	4,075	13	4,088
Rathdrum	2,194	288	2,482	1,346	143	1,489	2,173	544	2,717
Shillelagh	1,432	–	1,432	575	–	575	575	–	576

TOTAL NUMBERS RELIEVED DURING YEAR ENDED

	29th September, 1867			29th September, 1872			29th September, 1877			29th September, 1882		
Name of Union	In Workhouse relief	Outdoor relief	Total number	In Workhouse relief	Outdoor relief	Total number	In Workhouse relief	Outdoor relief	Total number	In Workhouse relief	Outdoor relief	Total number
Baltinglass	2,019	494	2,513	1,709	700	2,409	499	819	1,318	997	760	1,757
Naas	3,538	1,556	5,094	2,416	1,114	3,530	2,252	1,209	3,461	6,097	1,354	7,451
Rathdown	3,424	117	3,541	3,266	71	3,337	2,998	194	3,192	8,591	965	9,556
Rathdrum	2,386	1,712	4,098	2,000	1,248	3,248	1,987	1,113	3,100	3,556	1,514	5,070
Shillelagh	607	5	612	846	26	872	1,063	24	1,087	2,458	29	2,487

TOTAL NUMBERS RELIEVED DURING THE YEAR ENDED

Name of Union	29th September, 1887 in Workhouse relief	Outdoor relief	Total number	29th September, 1892 Number at beginning of year	Number of births	Number of admissions	Outdoor relief	Total number
Baltinglass	952	680	1,632	147	7	539	632	1,325
Naas	6,536	1,545	8,081	287	2	5,520	1,695	7,504
Rathdown	6,766	1,602	8,368	491	23	2,153	1,026	3,693
Rathdrum	2,871	1,373	4,244	234	7	1,929	1,209	3,379
Shillelagh	2,446	130	2,576	153	4	991	295	1,443

TOTAL NUMBERS RELIEVED DURING THE YEAR ENDED

Name of Union	29th September, 1897 Number at beginning of year	Number of births	Number of admissions	Outdoor relief	Total number	31st March, 1902 Number at beginning of year	Number of births	Number of admissions	Outdoor relief	Total number
Baltinglass	118	4	405	459	986	165	7	577	551	1,300
Naas	282	7	5,036	1,172	6,497	318	13	4,864	789	5,984
Rathdown	536	20	2,740	2,141	5,437	534	19	3,381	1,500	5,434
Rathdrum	231	12	2,073	853	3,169	251	10	3,050	930	4,241
Shillelagh	138	5	1,273	237	1,653	100	2	1,589	171	1,862

TOTAL NUMBERS RELIEVED DURING THE YEAR ENDED

Name of Union	30th September, 1907 Number at beginning of year	Number of births	Number of admissions	Outdoor relief	Total number	30th September, 1912 Number at beginning of year	Number of births	Number of admissions	Outdoor relief	Total number
Baltinglass	160	10	586	674	1,430	110	4	1,467	426	1,007
Naas	302	14	5,266	926	6,508	297	14	4,969	1,152	6,432
Rathdown	511	13	3,902	2,223	6,649	497	32	3,109	1,364	4,002
Rathdrum	237	13	4,824	1,082	6,156	198	19	2,854	978	4,049
Shillelagh	94	3	2,150	153	2,400	75	3	2,420	128	2,626

No further statistics were found for each union, the following giving a more detailed breakdown of inmates:

NUMBER OF INMATES

25th March, 1844

Name of Union	Able-bodied			Others (sick, infirm etc.)			Total numbers		
	Males	Females	Total	Males	Females	Total	Males	Females	Total
Baltinglass	18	59	77	124	120	244	142	179	321
Naas	41	56	97	165	163	328	206	219	425
Rathdown	31	103	134	163	150	313	194	253	447
Rathdrum	9	57	66	180	221	401	189	278	467
Shillelagh	4	25	29	133	128	261	137	153	290

NUMBER OF INMATES

25th March, 1846

Name of Union	Able-bodied			Others (sick, infirm etc.)			Total numbers		
	Males	Females	Total	Males	Females	Total	Males	Females	Total
Baltinglass	22	58	80	143	156	299	165	214	379
Naas	32	76	108	203	199	402	235	275	510
Rathdown	34	94	128	170	140	310	204	234	438
Rathdrum	18	51	69	170	244	414	188	295	483
Shillelagh	6	27	33	112	99	211	118	126	244

Appendix V

Number in receipt of relief at any time during the year ended 31 March, 1908

Type of relief	Men	Women	Children	Total
Indoor relief	170	116	60	346
Outdoor relief	141	266	275	682
Both in and out	28	16	2	46
Total	339	398	337	1,074
Indoor relief	635	362	181	1,178
Outdoor relief	138	319	484	891
Both in and out	20	20	13	53
Total	793	701	628	2,122
Indoor relief	553	389	289	1,231
Outdoor relief	305	631	977	1,913
Both in and out	31	32	31	94
Total	889	1,052	1,297	3,238
Indoor relief	322	171	81	574
Outdoor relief	218	481	339	1,038
Both in and out	16	16	8	40
Total	556	668	428	1,652
Indoor relief	74	67	26	167
Outdoor relief	24	70	37	131
Both in and out	9	3	2	14
Total	107	140	65	312

Acknowledgements

I am deeply grateful to Eva Natt, my grandmother, who awakened my love of history while visiting the graves of Hessian ancestors; Colbert Martin (Bray), Brian Cantwell (Greystones), Kathleen Turner (Rathmichael) and Pat Cahir (Clare), who helped to transfer this fascination to Ireland – may they rest in peace.

I am also indebted to the Old Bray Society, which first suggested this subject to me in 1985; Bray Public Library, especially the indefatigable Michael Kelleher; the National Library of Ireland; the National Archives; the Gilbert Library; Wicklow County Library Services; Wicklow Heritage Centre and Dr Tom McGrath of Ballingarry, county Tipperary, whose reading of the second draft was encouraging.

A final word of thanks to my husband, Brendan, and to my children, Emer, Pat and Katharina Ó Cathaoir, who often felt themselves to be the last victims of the poor law in county Wicklow.

References

1. The records of the Rathdown Union are in the keeping of the National Archives (NAI, BG 137); Naas Union documentation is in the care of Kildare County Library; an early register and one 1850s minute book of the Shillelagh Union are among the pre-1880s fragments now extant, a large collection of minute books of this union survives from 1880 on; a number of minute books and registers of the Rathdrum Union from 1839-59 exist, records are almost complete from the 1860s onwards. Shillelagh and Rathdrum documentation is in the care of Wicklow County Library Service. Baltinglass records, however, perished when the workhouse was burned in the 1920s (6076, 7 Feb. 1923, Burning of the Old Workhouse, books etc. at Baltinglass, D/LG 1923 Guardians and County Boards of Health Correspondence Register in NAI).
2. *First report of inquiry into the conditions of the poorer classes in Ireland, appendix E,* H.C. 1836 [37] xxii 1 Barony of Talbotstown Upper entry; *Third report of the commissioners for inquiring into the conditions of the poorer classes in Ireland,* H.C. 1836 [43] xxx 1, p. 13; Lewis, *Topog. dict. Ire.* (London, 1837), county Wicklow and separate town and village entries; *First report of inquiry ...* appendix D, H.C. 1836 [36] xxx 1.1.
3. *Freeman's Journal,* 12 Nov. 1830; 18 Nov. 1830; 2 June 1836; Karl von Hailbronner, *Cartons aus der Reisemappe eines deutschen Touristen* (Stuttgart, 1837), relevant section translated by E. Ó Cathaoir in 'Victorian cutbacks' in *Bray Historical Record* 3, 1989; *F.J.*, 8 July 1824; Isolde Moylan, 'The development of modern Bray' in *The Book of Bray* (Blackrock, 1989), p. 50; *First report of inquiry ... appendix E,* H.C. 1836 [37] xxii 1. Bray, Old Connaught and Rathmichael entry.
4. *First report of inquiry ... appendix E,* H.C. 1836 [37] xxii 1, p. 89.
5. Lewis, *Topog. dict. Ire.* I, p. 451; Geraldine Lynch, *Cill Mhantáin* (Wicklow, 1983), p. 35; *Hall's Ireland, Mr & Mrs. Halls' tour of 1840* (ed.) M. Scott (London, 1984), pp 248, 259.
6. *First report of inquiry ... appendix A,* H.C. 1835 (369) xxxli Part I 1, Kilquade & Kilmurry, Baltinglass entries (testimony of Fr. Kennett, PP; of Fr. Lalor, PP); *F.J.* 8 July 1824; 25 Sept.1826; 23 May 1832; *First report of inquiry ... appendix E,* H.C. 1836 [37] xxxii 1., Barony of Talbotstown Upper; *First report of inquiry ...*

appendix A, H.C. 1835 (369) xxxii 1, Castlemacadam entry; *First report of inquiry ... appendix B*, H.C. 1835 (369 cont.) xxxii 1, Bray entry; D. Thomson and M. McGusty (eds), *The Irish journals of Elizabeth Smith 1840-1850* (Oxford, 1980), p. 33.

7. *First report of inquiry ... appendix C*, part II, H.C. 1835 [35] xxx 35, p. 107; *Irish Journals*, p. 6; A. Nicholson, *Lights and shades of Ireland* (London, 1850), p. 234; *F.J.*, 8 Oct. 1830; 5 Nov. 1829; F. Seymour, *A hundred years of Bray and its neighbourhood* (Blackrock, 1978), pp 40, 42, 47; see also E. Ó Cathaoir, 'Priests and people' in *Holy Redeemer Church 1792-1992: a Bray parish* (ed.) B. Ó Cathaoir (Bray, 1991).
8. Helen Burke, *The people and the poor law in nineteenth-century Ireland* (n.p., 1987), p. 9; *Census of Ireland for the year 1851*, part iii; *abstract of returns relating to infirmaries, fever hospitals and dispensaries in Ireland*, H.C. 1840 (59) xlviii 229; Lewis, *Topog. dict. Ire.*, Arklow, Bray, Blessington, Carnew, Enniskerry etc. entries; *First report of inquiry ... appendix B*, H.C. 1835 (369 cont.) xxxii Part II, 1; R. B. McDowell, *The Irish administration 1801-1914* (London, 1964), pp 172-174.
9. Memoranda dealing with tenancies on the estate of Earl Fitzwilliam in county Wicklow, 1796-1841', Coolattin estate papers MS 4948, in NLI; *F.J.*, 8 Oct. 1830; 24 Sept. 1831; Dr Nicholas Donnelly in *Bray Catholic Monitor*, May 1899, in Bray Public Library; Arthur Moore, *Compendium of Irish poor law* (Dublin, 1850), pp 37-38.
10. *F.J.*, 8 July 1820; 18 Oct. 1838; 12 May 1838; Lewis, *Topog. dict. Ire.*, Baltinglass, Carnew, Delgany, Donaghmore, Dunganstown, Enniskerry and Bray entries; *First report of inquiry ... appendix E*, H.C. 1836 [37] xxxii 1, Bray, Old Connaught and Rathmichael, Castlemacadam, Newcastle barony entries; appendix A, H.C. 1835 (369) xxxii Castlemacadam, Drumkey & Kilcoole, Newcastle, Delgany, Kilmacanogue & Kilcoole entries; F. Seymour, *A hundred years of Bray*, p. 47; Book recording transactions carried out with the poor shop operated in connection with the estate of Earl Fitzwilliam in county Wicklow, 1830-1838 Coolattin estate papers Ms 4962, in N.L.I.
11. Lewis, *Topog. dict. Ire.*, Rathdrum entry; Brian Cantwell, *Memorials of the dead in county Wicklow*, Rathdrum entry; records of Tate's Charity in Representative Church Body Library; interview with Rev. Halliday, rector of Rathdrum, 4 Jan. 1994.
12. McDowell, *Irish administration*, pp 175-176; *F.J.*, 5 Apr. 1838; 14 Apr. 1838.
13. Lewis, *Topog. dict. Ire.*, Baltinglass, Carnew, Delgany, Donaghmore, Dunganstown, Enniskerry, Bray, Killiskey, Rathdrum and Wicklow entries; *First report of inquiry ... appendix A*, Castlemacadam, Drumkey & Kilcoole, Delgany, Kilmacanogue & Kilcoole, Powerscourt, Granebeg & Kilbeg entries; Mrs Francis Seymour, *Bray*, p. 47, *Guide to the county of Wicklow* (Dublin, 1834), p. 64; *F.J.*, 19 Dec. 1821; 25 Sept. 1826; 15 Sept. 1829; Smith, *Irish journals*, pp 18, 24-25.
14. G. Nicholls, *A History of the Irish Poor Law, in connection with the condition of the people* (London, 1856), p. 178; *return of every poor law union in Ireland, stating the population, area, number of landholders, and extent of holdings*, H.C. 1845 (593) xxxviii 209; *Saunders News-Letter*, 25 July 1839.
15. *Date of the formation of each union under the poor relief act in Ireland, together with the dates of admission of the poor*, H.C. 1843 (627) xlvi 601; *sum advanced on loan on the security of the poor rates in Ireland, for the building of workhouses*, H.C. 1847 (157) lv l; Rathdown Minutes, 16 Sept. 1839; 23 Oct. 1839; 2 Mar. 1840; Liam Clare, *Loughlinstown Workhouse in the 1840s*, Foxrock Local History Club, Publication No. 16, p. 3.

16. *Date of the formation of each union under the poor relief act in Ireland ...; Sum advanced on loan on the security of the poor rates in Ireland.*
17. Ibid.; ibid.
18. *Resolution passed by boards of guardians in Ireland, relative to the suppression of mendicancy in Ireland,* H.C. 1840 (168) xlviii 357; *Date of the formation of each union under the poor relief act in Ireland ...; Sum advanced on loan on the security of the poor rates in Ireland.*
19. Ibid.; ibid.
20. *Fifth annual report of the poor law commissioners,* 1839, contains a bird's eye view of the basic workhouse on p. 144; Plans and elevations of Rathdown, Rathdrum (fever hospital only), Baltinglass and Shillelagh workhouses in Irish Architectural Archive.
21. *Correspondence between the poor law commissioners and the guardians of unions relative to poorhouses (Ireland),* H.C. 1843 (275) xlvi 5. 153, p. 33 (Baltinglass); pp. 232-234 (Rathdown); pp 238-240 (Shillelagh); Rathdown Minutes, 17 May 1842; C.F. Coleborn 'Naas Workhouse' in *Kildare Arch. Soc. Jn.*, 14 (1968), pp 312-322.
22. Nicholls, *Irish Poor Law*; for a contemporary account see McDowell, *Irish administration,* pp 181-182, 188 or Burke, *The people and the poor law,* pp 38-47.
23. F.S.L. Lyons, *Ireland since the Famine* (London, 1971), p. 31; *Irish journals,* pp 10-11.
24. *Moore's compendium,* pp 713, 717.
25. William L. Feingold, 'Land League power: the Tralee Poor Law election' in *Irish peasants violence and political unrest 1780-1914* (eds), S. Clark and J.S. Donnelly (Manchester and Madison, 1983); *Wicklow News-Letter,* 8 Apr. 1899; 26 Dec. 1848; T.W. Moody, *Davitt and Irish revolution 1846-82* (Oxford, 1982), p. 445; Seymour, *Bray,* p. 62.
26. *F.J.*, 9 Dec. 1869; Moody, *Davitt,* p. 573; *W.N.L.*, 22 Apr. 1899; 29 Apr. 1899; 16 Dec. 1899.
27. Rathdrum Minutes, 19 Mar. 1844 ff.; 16 Apr. 1872.
28. Rathdown Minutes, 27 Jun. 1843, 17 Sept. 1844; Rathdrum Minutes, 26 June 1855; 24 July 1855; Rathdown Minutes, 15 Nov. 1856; *Wicklow Star,* 11 Feb. 1899; *W.N.L.*, 27 May 1899.
29. Rathdown Minutes, 6 June 1843 ff.; Rathdrum Minutes, 10 June 1873.
30. For duties of workhouse officers see *Moore's compendium,* pp 448-457.
31. Gerard O'Brien, 'Workhouse management in Pre-Famine Ireland' in *R.I.A. Proc.*, 86, C. (1986); Poor Law Commissioners' Order Books, in NAI; Rathdrum Minutes, 7 May 1844; 15 Oct. 1844; Rathdown Minutes, 1 Feb. 1860; 8 Mar. 1842; 4 Apr. 1843; 13 Dec. 1842; *W.N.L.*, 28 May 1898; 'Rathdown schoolmaster works from 6 a.m. to 9 p.m., has had no holiday for 5 years'.
32. *Moore's compendium,* p. 450; Rathdrum Minutes, 19 Sept. 1848; Clare, *Loughlinstown Workhouse,* pp 15-16.
33. *F.J.*, 6 Nov. 1844; 20 Nov. 1849; Rathdrum Minutes, 25 Jan. 1848 ff.; Rathdown Minutes, 8 Jan 1853; 7 Jan. 1854.
34. *F.J.*, 5 Sept. 1879; 9 Oct. 1879; 2 Jan. 1879; *W.N.L.*, 15 July 1899.
35. *Return of the dates on which and the places where the military and police have been employed in enforcing the collection of poor rates in Ireland, between 1 Jan. 1843 and 1 Jan. 1844,* H.C. 1844 (186) xl 78; *F.J.*, 6 Mar. 1849; 8 Nov. 1854; 19 June 1879; Shillelagh Minutes, 4 June 1852; Rathdrum Minutes, 18 Nov. 1845; 20 Jan. 1846; 9 Apr. 1880; 22 Apr. 1881; 8 June 1883.
36. Rathdrum Minutes, 10 Nov. 1857; 10 Nov. 1863; 21 Feb. 1865; 19 July 1872 ff.;

16 Sept. 1873; 14 Oct. 1873; 24 Dec. 1880; Rathdown Minutes, 18 June 1844; 2 July 1844; 4 Feb. 1845; 23 Dec. 1845; 31 July 1861 ff.

37. Rathdown Minutes, 6 Dec. 1856 ff.; *Wicklow Star*, 1 Apr. 1899; Rathdrum Minutes, 15 Sept. 1863; 13 Oct. 1882; *W.N.L.*, 24 Apr. 1899; Rathrum Minutes, 13 July 1847; 9 Oct. 1847; *W.N.L.*, 15 July 1899; 30 Sept. 1922.
38. Rathdrum Minutes, 25 Jan. 1859; *W.N.L.*, 15 Apr. 1899; *F.J.*, 23 Oct. 1879.
39. CBS 19079/S, 10 Apr. 1899; 19203/S, 4 May 1899, in NAI; *W.N.L.*, 15 Apr. 1899; *Wicklow Star*, 3 June 1899; CBS 19286/S, 18 May 1899; greater detail on this subject is to be found in E. Ó Cathaoir 'Revolutionary undercurrents in Wicklow and South Dublin, 1867-1916' in *Bray Historical Record* 5, 1992; Fenian photographs, FP 101 in NAI; James MacSweeny 'The fight in the Bray area' in *Dublin's fighting story* (Tralee, n.d.), p. 188.
40. G. O'Brien, 'Workhouse management', pp 114, 125; *Moore's compendium*, p. 430; Burke, *The people and the poor law*, p. 47; Rathdrum Minutes, 10 Nov. 1857; 18 Dec. 1866; 11 May 1852.
41. Burke, *The people and the poor law*, p. 77.
42. Rathdown Minutes, 21 Jan. 1860.
43. *Return of the number of females having illegitimate children, inmates of workhouses in the poor law unions in Ireland, on 1 January 1854*, H.C. 1854 (183) lv 747; *Number of women having illegitimate children and the number of illegitimate children relieved in each of the several poorhouses of Ireland during the half-year ending Sept. 1845*, H.C. 1846 (79) xlii 273.
44. G. O'Brien, 'Workhouse management', pp 117-120; Rathdown Minutes, 20 Sept. 1842; 11 Sept. 1841; *Moore's compendium*, pp 433-436.
45. Rathdown Minutes, 1 Nov. 1851.
46. *27th Report of the inspectors general on the general state of the prisons of Ireland*, 1848; communicated to me by Joan Kavanagh, Wicklow Heritage Society.
47. Rathdrum Minutes, 24 Nov. 1857; 6 Apr. 1858; 4 May 1858; 26 Apr. 1859.
48. Rathdown Minutes, 2 Mar. 1847; 25 Jan. 1848; 2 May 1858; Liam Clare, *Loughlinstown workhouse*, p. 12; Rathdrum Minutes, 4 May 1858; 1 May 1860; (illegible) Apr. 1869; Rathdown Minutes, 25 Nov. 1857; 8 Nov. 1856; Rathdrum Minutes, 7 May 1880; 9 July 1880 ff.; 23 June 1882.
49. Rathdown Minutes, 30 Aug. 1842; 4 Oct. 1842; to give some samples of unsatisfactory food: Rathdown Minutes, 26 Dec. 1841 – milk unfit for consumption; 4 Oct. 1842 – potatoes unfit for use; 10 Jan. 1843 – both milk and meat bad; 7 Feb. 1843 – milk bad; 4 Apr. 1843 – potatoes bad; 31 Oct. 1843 – potatoes mixed with clay; Rathdrum Minutes, 14 May 1844 – oatmeal very bad; 8 June 1852 – half-baked bread returned; 10 Aug. 1852 – buttermilk returned as diluted with soda; 31 Oct. 1854 – milk returned three times during last week; 13 Mar. 1855 – Indian meal and milk bad; 16 Mar. 1883; 30 Apr. 1884.
50. *Return of the names of unions in Ireland in which a third meal is not allowed daily*, H.C. 1867-68 (322) lxi 61; Rathdrum Minutes, 28 Apr. 1868; 26 Nov. 1880; 27 Feb. 1884; 8 Aug. 1876 ff.; 23 Dec. 1881; *Return of the average number of sick persons, lunatics, idiots etc. in each union workhouse in Ireland ... showing how tended*, H.C. 1881 (433) lxxix 199.
51. Rathdown Minutes, 4 Oct. 1899; Rathdrum Minutes, 2 Jan. 1884; *W.N.L.*, 5 Jan. 1918; 6 May, 20 May, 16 Dec. 1899; *F.J.*, 30 Nov. 1876; *Dietary in force in each workhouse in Ireland on 25 Mar. 1887*, H.C. 1888 (83) lxxx vii 75.
52. *Moore's compendium*, pp 431-33; Rathdown Minutes, 24 Mar. 1858; 25 Sept. 1858.

53. Rathdrum Minutes, 7 May 1844 ff.; 17 Sept. 1844; 28 June 1864 ff.; Rathdown Minutes, 7 May 1844; 6 Mar. 1850; 8 May 1852; 29 May 1852; 14 Aug. 1852; 4 June 1844.
54. *Moore's compendium*, pp 441-3.
55. Rathdrum Minutes, 22 Feb. 1848; 13 Apr. 1852; 17 Aug. 1869; 14 Sept. 1869; 29 Mar. 1864; Rathdown Minutes, 7 May 1844; 6 Mar. 1850; 8 May 1852; 29 May 1852; 14 Aug. 1852; 4 June 1844.
56. *Moore's compendium*, pp 442-6; Rathdrum Minutes, 31 Mar. 1852; Rathdown Minutes, 19 Apr. 1842; 15 Oct. 1844.
57. Rathdown Minutes, 17 June 1845; 15 Oct. 1844; 16 July 1853; 30 Mar. 1853; 20 May 1857; 26 Nov. 1862; Rathdrum Minutes, 2 Sept. 1845; 31 Oct. 1848.
58. Rathdrum Minutes, 9 Mar. 1844; 6 Apr. 1852; Rathdown Minutes, 12 Mar. 1844; 15 Jan. 1857; 28 Dec. 1848.
59. O'Brien, 'Workhouse management', pp 115-7; Rathdrum Minutes, 9 Apr. 1844; 2 Nov. 1847; 31 Dec. 1880 ff.; Clare, *Loughlinstown Workhouse*, pp 9-10; Letter dated 25 May 1940 from Rathdown board of assistance to farm superintendant, St Columcille's Hospital, indicates that the grounds were still used to grow crops for the patients, in NAI; 1945 'Hospitals' file, dated Baltinglass District Hospital, 11 Sept. 1945: 'make somebody responsible for closing the hospital gate at night to prevent stray animals from damaging the vegetables that are sown for the patients in the hospital', in Arklow Public Library.
60. Rathdown Minutes, 28 May 1844; 20 Dec. 1842; 7 Mar. 1843; 14 Aug. 1858 ff.; 16 Oct. 1858 ff.; Patrick Fahy and Joan Kavanagh, 'A study of nineteenth-century prison life with particular reference to Wicklow Gaol' in *Wicklow Hist. Soc. Jn.*, iv, 1991, p. 40.
61. *Eighth Annual report of the Poor Law Commissioners*, as quoted in O'Brien, 'Workhouse management', pp 116-7; Rathdown Minutes, 14 Mar. 1845; 26 July 1851; 1 Nov. 1851 ff.; 10 Jan. 1852; 7 July 1849; Rathdrum Minutes, 10 Nov. 1857; *Return from each of the poor law unions in Ireland, showing what kinds of employment are carried on in the workhouse or on the land attached* ... H.C. 1852-3.
62. Rathdown Minutes, 8 Aug. 1857; 25 Aug. 1860 ff.; 18 Dec. 1852; 21 Oct. 1854; 27 Nov. 1852.
63. Rathdrum Minutes, 19 Feb. 1850; 10 Nov. 1857.
64. Rathdown Minutes, 24 Sept. 1844; 20 Dec. 1842; 14 Mar. 1845; 12 Jan. 1847; 15 July 1850; 8 Oct. 1853; 23 May 1855; 9 Nov. 1854; 20 May 1857; Rathdrum Minutes, 7 May 1844; 14 June 1864; 9 Nov. 1875; 24 May 1852; 21 Nov. 1865; 5 Dec. 1883; 19 June 1860; 22 Feb. 1870 ff.
65. O'Brien, 'Workhouse management', p. 117; Rathdown Minutes, 6 June 1855 ff.; 11 June 1853; 18 May 1847.
66. *Moore's compendium*, p. 844; Rathdown Minutes, 24 Aug. 1850: the board proposed to serve 1 pt. tea and 6 oz. bread for the pauper nurses' breakfast, 1 pt. soup and 6 oz. bread for their dinner and ½ pt. of milk and 4 oz. bread for supper; Rathdrum Minutes, 9 Nov. 1875.
67. Rathdown Minutes, 28 Dec. 1848 ff.; Rathdrum Minutes, 28 July 1855; 12 June 1860; R. Meath, *Memories of the nineteenth-century* (London, 1923), p. 222; about 1881 Lady Meath founded the Brabazon Employment Society to provide interesting occupations for the old and ill in workhouse infirmaries; P.J. Power, *The Arklow calender* (Arklow, 1991), p. 125; Local employment in Loughlinstown as recalled by Mrs Janet Meaney, Bray, and Mr Magee, Ballybrack.
68. O'Brien, 'Workhouse management', pp 121-2; Rathdrum Minutes, 9 Oct. 1855; Rathdown Minutes, 28 Sept. 1850.

69. Return relative to the industrial employment of the juvenile inmates of the workhouses in each union in Ireland in September 1853, H.C. 1854 (77) lv 739; O'Brien, 'Workhouse management', p. 122; J. Robins, *The lost children: a study of charity children in Ireland 1700-1900* (Dublin, 1980), p. 242; Rathdown Minutes, 29 Apr. 1854; 25 Aug. 1860; 30 Aug. 1899; Rathdown Union Indoor Registers.
70. Rathdown Minutes, 30 Aug. 1851; 27 Sept. 1851; 4 Oct. 1851; 11 Jan. 1862; 4 July 1857; 23 Feb. 1861; 4 Jan. 1862; 30 Sept. 1854; Rathdrum Minutes, 31 Dec. 1867 ff.: workhouse school had 102 pupils, later rising to 120, and one teacher; 22 June 1852; *A return in provinces of the number of children sent out to service from the union workhouses in Ireland in the years 1842, 1843 and 1844*, H.C. 1845 (351) xxxviii 189.
71. Robbins, *The lost children*, p. 242; *Sixth annual report of the Irish poor law commissioners*, H.C. 1852; Rathdown Minutes, 14 Aug. 1858; 8 Nov. 1851; 26 Apr. 1856; Rathdrum Minutes, 18 Aug. 1863; Poor law commissioners' order book no. 1, Baltinglass Union, in NAI.
72. Address of gratitude to Sir George Hodson of Hollybrooke House, county Wicklow, from the pupils of Rathdown Workhouse Schools, signed by Robert Stanley, Christmas 1883, Hodson Papers, MS 9,154, in N.L.I.; Rathdrum Minutes, 31 May 1859; 14 Apr. 1882; 9 Jan. 1877; 1 Jan. 1878; *W.N.L.*, 30 Dec. 1899; M. O'Malley, 'Killruddery, the Brabazons and Bray' in *Bray Historical Record* ii, 1986, p. 32.
73. *W.N.L.*, 7 Nov. 1908; 14 Nov. 1908; 12 Jan. 1918; 1 May 1920; Rathdown Minutes, 3 Apr. 1920.
74. *Moore's compendium*, pp 14, 457; Rathdrum Minutes, 9 Apr. 1844; Rathdown Minutes, 30 Nov. 1841; 4 May 1850.
75. Rathdrum Minutes, 27 Aug. 1844 ff.; 30 Sept. 1845; 6 Jan. 1846; 22 Aug. 1848 ff.
76. Rathdown Minutes, 7 May 1844; 23 Aug. 1851; 8 Aug. 1863; *F.J.*, 28 Aug. 1851; 11 May 1855; *Saunders News-Letter*, 13 Aug. 1851.
77. *F.J.*, 21 July 1859; D. Bowen, *Paul Cardinal Cullen and the shaping of modern Irish catholicism* (Dublin, 1983), p. 160; *W.N.L.*, 2 Feb. 1878.
78. *F.J.*, 6 Nov. 1844; 16 Mar. 1875; Clare, *Loughlinstown workhouse*, p. 13; Rathdown Minutes, 31 May 1842.
79. Joseph Robbins, *Lost children*, p. 246; Rathdrum Minutes, 12 June 1855; 11 & 18 Sept. 1855; 21 Aug. 1855; 23 Oct. 1855; 24 May 1852.
80. K. Turner, *Rathmichael, A parish history* (Rathmichael, 1987), p. 33; Rathdrum Minutes, 1 Sept. 1857; 6 Oct. 1857; *W.N.L.*, 22 Sept. 1888; Meath, *Memories of the nineteenth-century*, p. 222.
81. Ignatius Murphy, *The diocese of Killaloe* (Dublin, 1993) Part III, pp 150-2; Rathdown Minutes, 23 Apr. 1844; Rathdrum Minutes, 28 Mar. 1876; F. C. Devas, *Mother Mary Magdalen (Fanny Margaret Taylor) foundress of the Poor Servants of the Mother of God* (London, 1927), pp 331-4.
82. Rathdown Minutes, 19 July 1856; 14 July 1855; 28 Aug. 1850; Rathdrum Minutes, 2 Apr. 1859; 22 Jan. 1878 ff.; O'Brien, 'Workhouse Management', p. 128; the plaque in Rathdrum reads: 'Sacred to the memory of the 8024 poor interred in this cemetery from 1844 to 1944 ...'; Rathdown Union Record of Deaths, 1939, in NAI; on 12 Oct. 1991, the 150th anniversary of the opening of the Loughlinstown workhouse, the present writer attended the unveiling of a memorial in the paupers' graveyard, which was blessed during an ecumenical ceremony.
83. Rathdown Minutes, 10 Aug. 1841; 21 Dec. 1841; 24 July 1861; 16 Feb. 1859; 1 Nov. 1842; 6 Mar. 1858; Rathdrum Minutes, 8 Mar. 1864; interview with Dr Bill Roche of St Columcille's Hospital, 8 May 1988.

84. *Moore's compendium*, An Act to extend the practice of vaccination, pp 222-4; Burke, *The people and the poor law*, p. 278.
85. Rathdown Minutes, 4 May 1847; Rathdrum Minutes, 21 Nov. 1865; 18 Dec. 1866; *F.J.*, 4 Apr. 1879.
86. Burke, *The people and the poor law*, pp 153-4; Rathdown Minutes, 3 Feb. 1858 ff.; 11 Jan. 1860 ff.; Rathdrum Minutes, 12 Dec. 1854; 2 Jan. 1866; 21 Feb. 1865; 2 Nov. 1875.
87. Robbins, *Fools and mad*, pp 63-4, 89; Rathdown Minutes, 5 Mar. 1844; 2 Apr. 1844; 29 June 1850; Rathdrum Minutes, 8 Feb. 1859.
88. Rathdown Minutes, 18 Feb. 1845 ff.; 21 Sept. 1855; 19 Mar. 1853; 20 Nov. 1861; *F.J.*, 25 Oct. 1876; Rathdrum Minutes, 30 Mar. 1883 ff.; *W.N.L.*, 17 Apr. 1920; Rathdrum Minutes, 10 Jan. 1860; 6 & 20 Feb. 1866; Rathdown Minutes, 24 Jan. 1852.
89. Rathdown Minutes, 2 Apr. 1853; 18 Feb. 1845 ff.; 26 Oct. 1847; 19 Mar. 1853; Rathdrum Minutes, 14 June 1859; 10 Nov. 1863; 2 May 1871; 11 Nov. 1881; *Return of the average number of sick persons in each workhouse in Ireland during the year ... ; also, average number of lunatics, idiots etc., in each union workhouse in Ireland during the year, showing how tended*, H.C. 1881 (433) lxxix 199; Robbins, *Fools and mad*, pp 166-7; interview with Sr Austin, matron, St Colman's Hospital, Rathdrum, 4 June 1992.
90. Reginald Meath, *Memories of the nineteenth-century* (London, 1924), pp 34-6; *W.N.L.*, 16 Oct. 1920; *Leinster Leader*, 4 June 1921.
91. McDowell, *The Irish administration*, p. 184.
92. Rathdrum Minutes, 25 Nov. 1845; 4 Nov. 1845; 18 Nov. 1845; Rathdown Minutes, 18 Nov. 1845; 2 Dec. 1845; Rathdrum Minutes, 21 Apr. 1846; 9 Mar. 1847; 15 Dec. 1849; 22 Dec. 1849; 8 Jan. 1850 ff.; Rathdown Minutes, 27 Apr. 1847; Rathdrum Minutes, 6 July 1847; Rathdown Minutes, 13 Mar. 1850; Rathdrum Minutes, 2 Oct. 1849.
93. *F.J.*, 3 June 1848; 10 Apr. 1846.
94. *Return of the number of paupers in workhouses in Ireland for each week of the years 1844, 1845, and 1846, beginning with the last week in November; Correspondence relating to the state of union workhouses in Ireland for the week ended 9 Jan. following*, IUP Series Famine (Ireland) 1; M. E. Daly, *The Famine in Ireland* (Dundalk, 1986), p. 55; *F.J.*, 13 Feb. 1847; 10 June 1846; 9 Nov. 1846.
95. *Irish journals*, p. 311; Naas Minutes, 10 Feb. 1847; Rathdrum Minutes, 10 Nov. 1846; 15 Dec. 1846; 9 Feb. 1847; Rathdown Minutes, 14 Dec. 1847; 19 Mar. 1849; 27 June 1849.
96. Poor Law Commissioners' Order Book No. 1, Baltinglass Union, Limiting number in workhouse in 1847, 1848; Shillelagh Union, Limiting number in workhouse in 1849, in NAI; Rathdown Minutes, 19 Jan. 1847; 23 Feb. 1847; 9 Nov. 1847; 7 Dec. 1847; Rathdrum Minutes, 8 Dec. 1846; 8 June 1847; IUP Series Famine (Ireland), Boyle to Walker, 25 Feb. 1847.
97. Daly, *Famine*, p. 55; *F.J.*, 25 Aug. 1848; 4 Sept. 1848. *Number of persons receiving indoor and outdoor relief, on 28 Feb. 1850, in each union of Ireland; distinguishing males and females; and with regard to indoor relief, the children under 15 years old*; H.C. 1850 (377) 1 181; *Number of paupers in receipt of relief in the several unions of Ireland, on 1 Feb. 1851; distinguishing outdoor relief from indoor relief and the amount of workhouse accommodation*, H.C. 1851 (95) xlix 485.
98. Rathdown Minutes, 24 Nov. 1849; Rathdown Union Indoor Relief Registers, 1848-9.

99. Rathdown Minutes, 24 Nov. 1849; 17 Nov. 1849; 1 Dec. 1849; 9 Feb. 1850; 27 Feb. 1850; as recalled by Michael McNamara of Ballybrack; see also E. Ó Cathaoir, 'Victorian cutbacks: the nightlodgers in Loughlinstown workhouse' in *Bray Historical Record* iii, 1989.
100. P. Fahy and J. Kavanagh, 'A study of nineteenth-century prison life' in *Wicklow Hist. Soc. Jn.*, 4, 1991, p. 42; Rathdrum Minutes, 3 Apr. 1880; 10 Nov. 1882; J.M. Synge, 'The vagrants of Wicklow' in *Collected works* II (Prose) (ed.) Alan Price (Buckinghamshire, 1982).
101. Rathdown Minutes, 23 Feb. 1847; Rathdrum Minutes, 22 Jan. 1848; 17 Aug. 1848; *Fourth annual report of the Irish poor law commissioners*, H.C. 1851 (1381) xxvi 547 Appendix B I.
102. *Appendix to papers relating to the relief of distress ... Balance sheet for the year ending 29 Sept. 1848, proportion per 100 to the population of 1841, statement of the highest number on the outdoor relief lists at the close of any week during the year*, IUP Series Famine (Ireland) 4.
103. Rathdrum Minutes, 15 Sept. 1846; 20 July 1847.
104. Rathdrum Minutes, 26 May 1846 ff.; 24 Mar. 1847; 26 Oct. 1847; 2 Feb. 1847; Rathdown Minutes, 23 Feb. 1847; 2 Mar. 1847; 16 Nov. 1847; 1 Feb. 1848; 15 Feb. 1848; 21 Mar. 1848; 6 July 1847; 2 Feb. 1850; 5 Jan. 1850; Rathdrum Minutes, 4 Jan. 1848; 14 Mar. 1848; 16 Oct. 1849; Rathdown Minutes, 24 Sept. 1849; *Saunders News-Letter*, 18 Aug. 1848; Rathdrum Minutes, 9 Oct. 1849; 9 Apr. 1850; 17 Dec. 1850 ff.; 31 Oct. 1848.
105. Rathdrum Minutes, 9 Oct. 1849; 20 Nov. 1849; 11 Mar. 1848; Rathdown Minutes, 1 Feb. 1848; 8 Nov. 1845; *Wicklow Star*, 1 Apr. 1899; Rathdown Minutes, 5 Jan. 1850; 1 June 1850.
106. Rathdrum Minutes, 31 Aug. 1847; 14 Sept. 1847; 28 Sept. 1847; Naas Minutes, 10 Mar. 1847.
107. Rathdown Minutes, 2 Mar. 1847 ff.; 24 May 1847; 27 July 1847; 19 Oct. 1847; 15 Feb. 1848; 16 May 1848; 18 July 1848; 14 Nov. 1848; 27 June 1849; 17 Aug. 1850; 7 Dec. 1847; 15 Dec. 1849; Rathdrum Minutes, 4 Jan. 1848; 22 Feb. 1848; 24 Oct. 1848; 13 Mar. 1852; 23 Mar. 1852; 24 Nov. 1846; 1 Jan. 1850; 16 Apr. 1850; Rathdown Minutes, 25 Apr. 1848; 3 Oct. 1848; 16 May 1849; 2 May 1848; 15 May 1852; 6 Mar. 1850; 19 Feb. 1853; 19 Mar. 1853; Rathdrum Minutes, 19 May 1846; 8 Dec. 1846; 31 Mar. 1852; 26 Mar 1850; 24 Sept. 1849; 6 Nov. 1849; 19 Feb. 1850; 2 Oct. 1849; 11 Dec. 1849.
108. Rathdrum Minutes, 4 Jan. 1848; 22 Aug. 1848; 31 Oct. 1848; 24 Dec. 1850; 13 Apr. 1852; Rathdown Minutes, 11 July 1848; 18 May 1847; 22 Aug. 1848; 25 Apr. 1848; 21 July 1849.
109. Rathdrum Minutes, 12 Feb. 1850; 31 Mar. 1852; 16 Apr. 1850; 31 Dec. 1850; 18 Feb. 1851; 9 Apr. 1850; 12 Mar. 1850; 11 Mar. 1851.
110. Rathdrum Minutes, 26 May 1846 ff.; Rathdown Minutes, 8 June 1847 ff.; Rathdrum Minutes, 19 Jan. 1847; 9 June 1846 ff.; 26 May 1846 ff.; 16 June 1846; 14 July 1846; 9 June to 25 Aug. 1846.
111. Rathdrum Minutes, 20 Oct. 1846; 3 Nov. 1846; 24 Nov. 1846; 9 Mar. 1847; *F.J.*, 9 Dec. 1851.
112. Rathdown Minutes, 23 Feb. 1847; 8 June 1847; 6 July 1847; 21 Sept. 1847; 9 Oct. 1847; 21 Dec. 1847; 8 Feb. 1848; *F.J.*, 16 June 1847.
113. Rathdown Minutes, 29 Feb. 1848 ff.; Rathdrum Minutes, 7 May 1850; 30 Apr. 1850; 1 Mar. 1851, 18 Mar. 1851.
114. *Return of the number of persons who were attacked with cholera and were relieved ... by the guardians, in Ireland, from 29 Sept. 1848 to 25 Mar. 1850*, H.C. 1850 (459) li 241.

115. K. Hannigan, 'Wicklow in the famine years' in *Wicklow Hist. Soc. Jn.*, 5, 1992.
116. McDowell, *The Irish administration*, p. 182; Rathdrum Minutes, 30 Mar. 1847; 4 Jan. 1848; 4 Apr. 1848; 2 Feb. 1847; 24 Mar. 1847; 24 Oct. 1848; 11 Aug. 1847; Rathdown Minutes, 28 Mar. 1848; 24 Feb. 1848; 21 Mar. 1848; Naas Minutes, 11 Aug. 1847.
117. The Rathdown Union Indoor Relief Registers record the number of nightlodgers during the Famine period, but give no indication of their origins.
118. Shillelagh Union Indoor Relief Register, 25 Feb. 1842-13 Sept. 1867; Rathdrum Union Indoor Relief Register, 22 Mar. 1842-10 Dec. 1852; Robbins, *Lost children*, p. 192; *Irish journals*, p. 229.
119. Burke, *The people and the poor law*, p. 153; Rathdown Minutes, 12 Aug. 1854 ff.; 27 Mar. 1850; 6 Apr. 1850; *Papers relative to emigration to the British provinces in North America*, H.C. 1851 (348) xl 297, p. 31.
120. *Third Annual report of the Irish poor law commissioners: abstract of return from clerks of unions of the number of emigrants sent out by boards of guardians of unions in Ireland from the beginning of Aug. 1849 to the end of Apr. 1850*, H.C. 1850 (1243) xxvii 449; *Fourth annual report of the Irish poor law commissioners: abstract* ... H.C. 1851 (1381) xxvi 547; *Fifth annual report of the Irish poor law commissioners: abstract* ... H.C. 1852 (1530) xxiii 155; *Sixth annual report of the Irish poor law commissioners: abstract* ... H.C. 1852-3 (1645) l 159; *Seventh annual report of the Irish poor law commissioners: abstract* ... H.C. 1854 (1785) xxix 531; *Eighth annual report of the Irish poor law commissioners: abstract* ... H.C. 1854-5 (1945) xxiv 523; *Papers relative to emigration* ... H.C. 1851 (348) xl 297; Rathdrum admission and discharge book, 1850-1; Emigration books of the Fitzwilliam estate in county Wicklow, 1847-56, Coolattin Papers MSS 4974-5 in *N.L.I.*; *West Wicklow Hist. Soc. Jn.*, 1, 1983/84; 2, 1985/86; 3, 1989.
121. *First annual report of the Irish poor law commissioners*; Circular No. 58, H.C. 1847-8 (963) xxxiii 377; Joseph Robbin, *Lost children*, p. 204; Rathdown Minutes, 26 Jan. 1850; 9 Feb. 1850.
122. Robbins, *Lost children*, pp 210, 214-21; *Second annual report of the Irish poor law commissioners*, H.C. 1849 (1118) xxv 87; *Third annual report of the Irish poor law commissioners*, H.C. 1850 (1243) xxvii 449; Rathdown Minutes, 19 July 1851; 9 Aug. 1851; Rathdrum Minutes, 11 Sept. 1855.
123. Rathdown Minutes, 21 Apr. 1855; 5 May 1855; 29 Mar. 1856; 26 Apr. 1856; 28 Aug. 1861; 11 Sept. 1861; Patrick Fox, 14, reared in the workhouse, is given clothing by the guardians, as his relatives in California had sent his passage money; Rathdrum Minutes, 3 Apr. 1855; the grandmother of two orphans, inmates, requests that the board clothe the girls, as they are about to emigrate to New Zealand with her; *Third annual report of the Irish poor law commissioners: abstract* ..., the three Jackson children leave Baltinglass workhouse to join their father in the US.
124. *W.N.L.*, 7 Apr. 1860; Rathdrum Minutes, 7 Apr. 1860; 29 Apr. 1865; 17 Apr. 1869; 26 Apr. 1884; *Poor Law relief: return showing, for each poor law union in Ireland, the number who were in receipt of relief at any time during the year ended 31 Mar. 1908*, H.C. 1908 (306) xcii.
125. Vaughan and Fitzpatrick, *Irish historical statistics*, pp 261, 268, 296.
126. *Return for each poor law union in Ireland, of the population, valuation, and number of persons receiving relief in each union on the 29th day of Sept. in each of the years 1846, 1851 and 1865* ... H.C. 1866 (377) lxii 75.
127. *Ninth annual report of the Irish poor law commissioners*, H.C. 1856 [2105] xxviii 415; *Abstract of returns as to the medical charities in Ireland*, H.C. 1850 (758) li

505; Burke, *The people and the poor law*, pp 161-2; Rathdrum Minutes, 27 Feb. 1858; 378 inmates, 117 of these in the workhouse infirmary and 7 in the workhouse fever hospital; Rathdown Minutes, 24 Feb. 1855: 786 inmates, 106 of these in the infirmary and 36 in the fever hospital, an additional 286 inmates were on sick diet; 28 Feb. 1863; 519 inmates, 327 of these in the infirmary, 31 in the fever hospital.

128. Rathdrum Minutes, 26 Sept. 1871; 30 Mar. 1872; 19 July 1872; 25 Nov. 1854 ff.; Rathdown Minutes, 25 Mar. 1854; 3 Feb. 1855: 37 fever cases; 31 Jan. 1863; 35 fever cases; 14 Mar. 1863 ff.; 5 May 1855; 10 Feb. 1858; Rathdown Union Record of Deaths 1899-1900; Rathdown Minutes, 30 Sept. 1854-16 Jan. 1855; 28 Mar. 1857.

129. Rathdrum Minutes, 18 Sept.-18 Dec. 1866; 22 Jan. 1867; *F.J.*, 30 Oct. 1866; 11 Oct. 1866; 5 Dec. 1866; 22 Jan. 1867; Power, *The Arklow calender*, p. 97.

130. Burke, *The people and the poor law*, p. 285, 'the poor law tree', pp 274-8; Lyons, *Ireland since the Famine* (London, 1971), pp 66-8.

131. Robbins, *Lost children*, p. 283; Burke, *The people and the poor law*, pp 290, 295; Rathdown Minutes, 23 Aug. 1862; 14 July 1855; 5 Jan. 1856; 28 May 1862; Rathdrum Minutes, 14 Feb. 1860 ff.; 29 Feb. 1876; 24 Sept. 1880; 15 Oct. 1880; 21 Jan. 1881; 25 Mar. 1881; 11 Nov. 1881; *F.J.*, 27 Nov. 1872; information of Terry Doyle, Bray, whose granduncle was a founder member of St. Kevin's Catholic Burial Society in 1879.

132. Record book and accounts of the committee of management of the Newtown Mount Kennedy Fever Hospital, Apr. 1872-1918, MS 3237, in N.L.I.; Letter from Bray Urban District Council to Local Government Board, 21 Nov. 1918, in possession of E. Ó Cathacir.

133. Rathdown Minutes, 11 Mar. 1843; 10 Aug. 1847; Rathdrum Minutes, 11 May 1852; *First local government board for Ireland report*, statement of inspector Henry Robinson, H.C. 1873 [c 794] xxix 417; Rathdown Union Indoor Relief Register, 1841-45; Rathdrum Union Indoor Relief Register, 1842-52.

134. *First local government board for Ireland report*, H.C. 1873 [c 794] xxix 417; Burke, *The people and the poor law*, p. 230; Rathdrum Minutes, 19 May 1868; 9 June 1868; 13 June 1868; 1 Oct. 1880.

135. Burke, *The people and the poor law*, pp 231-2; Rathdown Union records, children at nurse, 1925-36, in NAI; Rathdown Minutes, 26 Jan. 1859 ff.; Rathdrum Minutes, 8 Mar. 1864; *W.N.L.*, 24 Sept 1898; J. Mitchel, *The history of Ireland* (Glasgow & London, n.d.), p. 178; J.M. Synge, *Collected works* II, p. 216.

136. Irish Workhouse Association, annual report for the year ending 31 Dec. 1906 (Dublin, 1907), pamphlet in N.L.I.

137. Rathdown Minutes, 7 Apr. 1920; *W.N.L.*, 1 May 1920; *Leinster Leader*, 23 July 1921; *W.N.L.*, 29 Jan. 1921; Amalgamation of unions, H.C. 1921 Cmd. 1432 xiv 781; *W.N.L.*, 16 Oct. 1920; 5 Feb. 1921; J. MacSweeney, 'The fight in the Bray Area' in *Dublin's Fighting Story*, p. 188; *W.N.L.*, 22 Jan. 1921; *Leinster Leader*, 18 June 1921; 16 July 1921; 17 Sept. 1921; 19 Nov. 1921; 3 Dec. 1921; 5 May 1923; A search in the Military Archives by Comdt. Young proved fruitless; see also 6076, 7 Feb. 1923 Burning of the Old Workhouse, books etc. at Baltinglass, D/LG 1923 Guardians and County Boards of Health Correspondence Register, in NAI.

138. Wicklow County Scheme Order 1923, Ministry of Local Government Order Book Index No. 5, in NAI; *Leinster Leader*, 28 Jan. 1922; *Wicklow People*, 10 May 1991, communicated to me by Mrs. R. O'Rourke; Interview with Dr Bill Roche, RIP, late of St. Columcille's Hospital, Loughlinstown, 3 May 1988; Francis Charles Devas,

Mother Mary Magdalen, pp 24, 33, 331-4; Cecil Woodham Smith, *Florence Nightingale* (Harmondsworth, 1955), pp 346-52.

139. Interviews with Phyllis Flanagan, *West Wicklow Hist Soc.*, 6 June 1992 and Josie Byrne, sacristan, Tinahely RC Church, 15 June 1992; *W.N.L.*, 4 May 1922.

140. Interview with Jim Brophy, RIP, late assistance officer, 3 June 1992; Interview with Sr Austin, matron, St Colman's Hospital, Rathdrum, 4 June 1992; Letter from Mrs Nellie Murphy, 31 Oct. 1945; Letter from Joseph Burke, ambulance driver, 11 Sept. 1945, file marked 'hospitals' in Arklow Public Library; Department of Justice registered files D 6137, 1937 in NAI.

141. A. Nicholson, *The Bible in Ireland* (London, 1847), pp 30-1; D. O'Donovan, *Kevin Barry and his time* (Dublin, 1989), pp 182-3; Rathdown Minutes, 10 Sept. 1853; K. Clarke, *Revolutionary woman* (Dublin, 1991), p. 26; *Wicklow Star*, 3 June 1899; Michael Burgess, Sligo, interviewed on 'Donncha's Sunday', RTE, 9 Jan. 1994; James Joyce, *Ulysses* (New York, 1961 edn.), p. 332.

Luggelaw (Bartlett).

Chapter 14

VERNACULAR RURAL DWELLINGS OF THE WICKLOW MOUNTAINS

F.H.A. AALEN

Until the present century most houses in the hill areas of Wicklow were modest, thatched, single-storey structures, oblong and narrow in plan and rarely more than one room in width. They were essentially similar to houses in other parts of rural Ireland, but had developed certain regional characteristics owing to the distinctive historical background and adjustments to the upland environment. While landlord policies, scattered industrial and mining growths and social class differences led to a variety of house styles within the region, the dwellings of the great mass of the peasantry were built in conformity with well established traditions and varied little in size, design and basic lay-out. Buildings whose form is regulated by regional peasant traditions rather than by trends in polite architecture are described by ethnologists and cultural geographers as vernacular or traditional. Until very recently, vernacular buildings were an important ingredient of the Irish rural landscape, sensitively mirroring the structure and way of life of local society and closely adjusted to the environment through use of locally available building materials and adaptation to climatic conditions.

Wicklow did not possess a rich or diverse vernacular. In the early nineteenth-century the bulk of the dwellings were humble and crudely constructed, lacking substantial outbuildings. Solid, improved farm-houses and steadings existed only on the largest farms. Pre-famine population growth, land subdivision and colonisation of waste land, especially on the edge of mountain commons, contributed to the profusion of small cabins or poorly constructed, single-room dwellings. Their number declined greatly in the second half of the nineteenth century owing to emigration, but primitive dwellings were inhabited in some localities until the 1930s and 40s and a few down almost to the present day.

Writing of county Wicklow in 1901, Robert Frazer states that 'the habitations of the lower tenants and cottars are in general extremely wretched', but the farmhouses of the principal tenants in the north and east of the county were 'in general of a superior style of accommodation and their offices roomy and convenient. In the southern and western parts, as well as those that had begun to be erected in the mountains, they have been almost wholly destroyed in the rebellion. They are, however, rebuilding them, in general on a more commodious plan than heretofore, and all of them with slated roofs where they were formerly only thatched'.[1] In 1843 J. G. Kohl, a German traveller, noted the wretched state of houses in Ireland and wrote 'especially wretched were the houses on the road south from Dublin through Blessington and Baltinglass'.[2] Also in the 1840s, the Halls referred to the miserable hovels skirting the road from Enniskerry to Roundwood[3] and Elizabeth Smith described the many one-roomed thatched cabins with wattle chimneys and earth floors on her Baltyboys estate in west Wicklow; she notes, however, that some better, two-storeyed slated houses were being introduced.[4]

Improvement in the average quality of houses during the nineteenth century was produced by building larger solid houses, progressive expansion and improvement of older ones and, not least, a rapid decline in the number of poor cabins owing to heavy emigration of the poorest classes. By the end of the century the typical dwelling in the area was a sturdy, stone-built, three-roomed structure and one-roomed cabins had become a minority. Growing prosperity increased the interest in house improvements and provided means to introduce them. Tradition as a regulator was thus progressively weakened and in the present century finally eliminated.

It is unclear how far changes in housing in the nineteenth century resulted from landlord policy or from the initiatives of the farmers themselves. Clearly there was a slow growth of concern for the living conditions of the rural classes in the nineteenth century but conditions and policies varied from estate to estate. Some Wicklow landlords undertook considerable housing projects for their tenants. Around 1800, for example, the Grenes of Kilranelagh consolidated rundale holdings and built 'comfortable dwellings and convenient offices' on the new farms.[5] The Cobbe family, landlords of Glenasmole and surrounding territory, extensively improved the rural housing there in the 1830s, providing 80 good stone and slate houses long referred to as 'Cobbes cottages'.[6] Considerable building also took place on the Downshire, Fitzwilliam, Powerscourt and Meath estates. Nevertheless, the survival of a recognisable regional vernacular suggests that general evolution of a deeply-rooted house style took place and that, taking the county as a whole, the landlord role, while influential, was not decisive.

Vernacular houses are still a significant element in the Wicklow landscape; they are most common on the west side of the mountains and these areas will be focussed on in this chapter. In the east of the county many of the farmhouses have evolved far from their vernacular progenitors, and polite forms which are a clear break with local building traditions were widely introduced in the nineteenth century both by well-to-do farmers and non-farming people. However, the higher ground and remoter glens of the east, such as Glenmacnass and Glencullen, retained many vernacular houses.

Building materials and construction methods

Until the 1930s and 40s most Wicklow hill farms were stone-built. Local granite provided the main building material, unlike the adjacent lowland where the underlying limestone or 'calp' was widely used as was also mud which could easily be obtained from the plentiful morainic materials. In the Wicklow hills, granite in a naturally fragmented form is abundantly available; boulders are scattered on the hillsides and in the fields, while cut stone could be readily acquired from the numerous small quarries which have long been a feature of the area. Granite is widely used in old bridges, walls and gate-posts as well as in houses, giving a distinct character to the cultural landscape. The schist belts on the eastern and western flank of the main granite mass are also a source of building material, providing thin flaky slabs suited for house and field walls and often used in combination with granite, sometimes serving as packing around poorly dressed stones. Volcanic rocks (tuffs and lavas) are extensively used as building material near Rathdrum and sandstones are used on the eastern edge of the Calary plateau.

The walls of old houses are thick and usually formed of either rubble or roughly dressed field stones; sometimes large boulders, which may be *in situ*, are incorporated at ground level (Plate 14.1). Cut stone was widely used for quoins, door and window lintels. Especially near major quarries, houses were built largely or entirely of ashlar. Perhaps the best examples are in and around Ballyknockan, where the largest granite quarry in west Wicklow is situated, and Barnacullia, a quarry settlement on the northern edge of the hills. Growan (sand and gravel from decomposed granite) was extracted from stream beds and used for mortar and for flooring. Clay floors were normal in poorer houses. The clay was renewed each year and we are told that in Imaal houses 'the children went around holding on to one another's "tails", singing and tramping it in.'[7] Fireplaces were generally paved by granite or schist flags and these materials were also used as flooring in the better houses and to form a solid base at the main entrance to the houses, although river cobbles were perhaps more commonly used for this latter purpose.

County Wicklow was one of the last areas to retain significant forests; sufficient in the seventeenth century to provide valuable oak and birch

1.

2. a.

2. b.

3.

4.

Plate 14.1 **Characteristic long, narrow steadings containing house, byre and shed**

1. There were frequently differences of roof level and roofing materials over various parts of the steading. Shown here is the rear wall, tucked into the slope and lacking windows. Annacarney, west Wicklow (Poulaphouca Survey, 1939).
2. a. This primitive thatched structure probably gives a good idea of the appearance of farmsteads in the eighteenth and nineteenth centuries. The back wall is without door or windows. Ballyknockan, west Wicklow.
2. b. Detail of walling and thatch (Poulaphouca Survey, 1939).
3. Front view of steading with doors to each section. Note the partly thatched gable wall of the house. Lackan, west Wicklow (Poulaphouca Survey, 1939).
4. This house is built into the slope, the back door without doors or windows. Corrugated iron covers the old thatch. Toor, west Wicklow (F. Aalen, 1986).

charcoal for the numerous ironworks in the south and east of the county.[8] Thomas Wentworth, first earl of Strafford, erected a large wooden hunting lodge in the 1630s in his deer park near Shillelagh,[9] and it is possible that timber and wattle structures were used widely and more recently in Wicklow than most other parts of Ireland. However, this was never to the exclusion of stone. Extant buildings are invariably of stone and there is no convincing evidence in them of any earlier tradition of timber framing or cruck structures of even the most rudimentary kind. That building in stone is deep-rooted in the hills is suggested by the survival of primitive, dry stone structures, some with circular plans and corbelled construction: these include well covers, lime kilns, herdsmen's huts, various farm buildings and a sweat house (Plate 14.12).[10] The old church of St Kevin at Hollywood (probably a seventeenth century structure on an ancient site) has a corbelled stone roof (now concealed by slates); the roof of Kevin's Kitchen, the well-known medieval church at Glendalough, is entirely of stone; so too is the roof of the (probably) twelfth century church at Kilcoole, and corbelled stone structures are found in the neolithic, mountain-top passage graves such as Seefin.[11] Presumably as local timber resources were finally cleared, stone-built houses became the rule, with the use of timber confined to rafters and beams to support roofs and chimney hoods. On the lowlands of south-east Ireland, mud as well as stone became a popular building material when timber resources dwindled, and it remained so until the present century. Wicklow, apart from its eastern lowland areas, has no strong tradition of mud construction and the use of mud was mainly confined to humble structures such as cabins or sheds.

Sometimes farm sheds and even the houses of poorer people were partially built with peat and layers of sod; not uncommonly the gable ends of cabins were constructed with sods (Plates 14.8, 14.9). Such buildings were not durable and often needed stone and timber supports, but some remained in use well into the present century.

Roofs are characteristically slated, but it is likely that slate has steadily replaced thatch since the late eighteenth century, a trend encouraged by high rainfall and exposure to strong winds on exposed hillsides. Oaten straw was widely used for thatching but also rushes where they could be obtained in ill-drained areas. Thatch was laid on a layer of sods or 'scraws' which together could approach two feet in thickness and rested on rafters attached to the walls or, in a few recorded instances on purlins. A layer of heather was sometimes placed between sods and thatch. Ceilings were not a feature of old houses and the rooms were open to the roof. Concealing the sods and rafters with wooden boards and other devices became common in the late nineteenth century. Around the same time, corrugated iron was introduced as a roofing material on inferior houses and often placed over the old thatch. Corrugated iron is still a common roofing material on farm outbuildings. Thatched houses survived in number until the 1950s but they are today rarities and thatchers are few. A survey in 1987 recorded only 15 thatched houses in the entire county and on some of these the thatch is a recent addition to superior houses for romantic effect.[12] Perhaps the best known vernacular thatched house is the Dwyer-Macallister cottage in Derrynamuck, Glen of Imaal, now preserved as a national monument: it is a two-roomed structure with hearths at the gable ends and built probably in the eighteenth century.

Stone gable ends are a very dominant vernacular feature in Wicklow and fully hip-ended thatched roofs seem to have been largely confined to the narrow coastal lowlands in the east and the western and southern margins of the hills. Is this a long-standing distribution pattern or could the gable end have recently replaced the hip in the hills, perhaps accompanying the spread of slated roofs or the introduction of stone flues and chimneys? The question cannot be answered decisively. On balance, however, general replacement seems unlikely. Existing houses and ruined structures do not suggest it; a number of old thatched houses possess a partially hipped roof at one end of the house away from the hearth and a gable at the other, but there is no evidence that one element is older than the other. Moreover, no tradition of a general transition has survived and thatch was common on gable-ended houses, suggesting some antiquity for both features.

House plans

Traditional Wicklow farmhouses commonly contained two or, more usually, three rooms (figs 14.1, 14.2; Plates 14.1, 14.2) separated by transverse load-bearing walls rising to the roof ridge. Windows were small and usually confined to the front wall. The back wall, sometimes dug into the hill slope, was generally featureless and where rear windows occurred they were smaller than front windows. Windows and doors never appear in the gable ends but sometimes a narrow slit in one gable ventilated and lighted an attic bedroom. Old farmsteads commonly formed a single, long range with house, byre and sheds joined together.

The kitchen, the largest and usually the central room of the house, was used for a variety of functions. One door served the house, invariably at the front; in many houses it was located at the end of the kitchen away from the hearth, permitting entry directly into the kitchen; but in others the door and the hearth lay together, forming a natural lobby entrance (figs 14.1, 14.2, Plate 14.1).

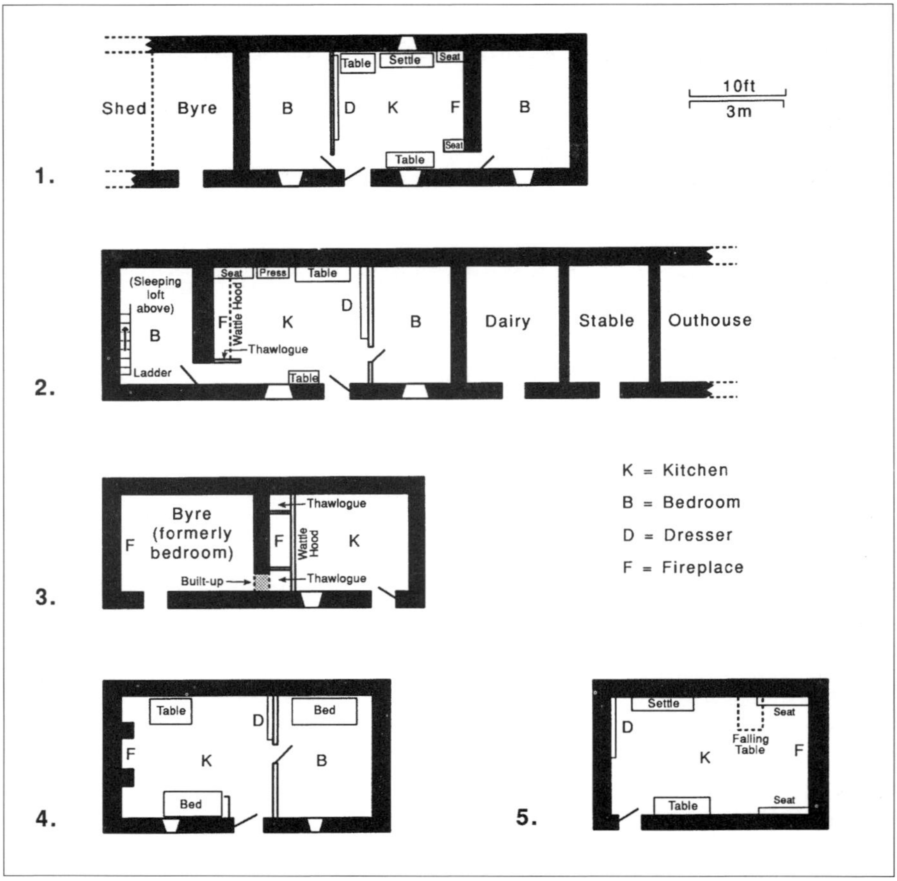

Figure 14.1 **Direct entry houses**

1. Valleymount, west Wicklow, 1939.
2. Monamuck, west Wicklow, 1939.
3. Lackan, west Wicklow, 1939.
4. Rathnew Commons, east Wicklow, 1935.
5. Ballinahown, west Wicklow, 1939.

Several scholars have used the relation of the door and hearth as a basis for classifying Irish vernacular dwellings into two fundamental plan varieties which possess complementary spatial distributions.[13] Houses with direct entry, where the hearth and doors are at separate ends of the main living unit, are characteristic of the west of Ireland and northern upland areas; they are usually regarded as derivatives of long-houses (or byre-dwellings) which originally accommodated animals and humans without internal divisions, an arrangement once widely found in Europe wherever livestock keeping was the basis of peasant economy. The byre end of Irish long-houses was eventually

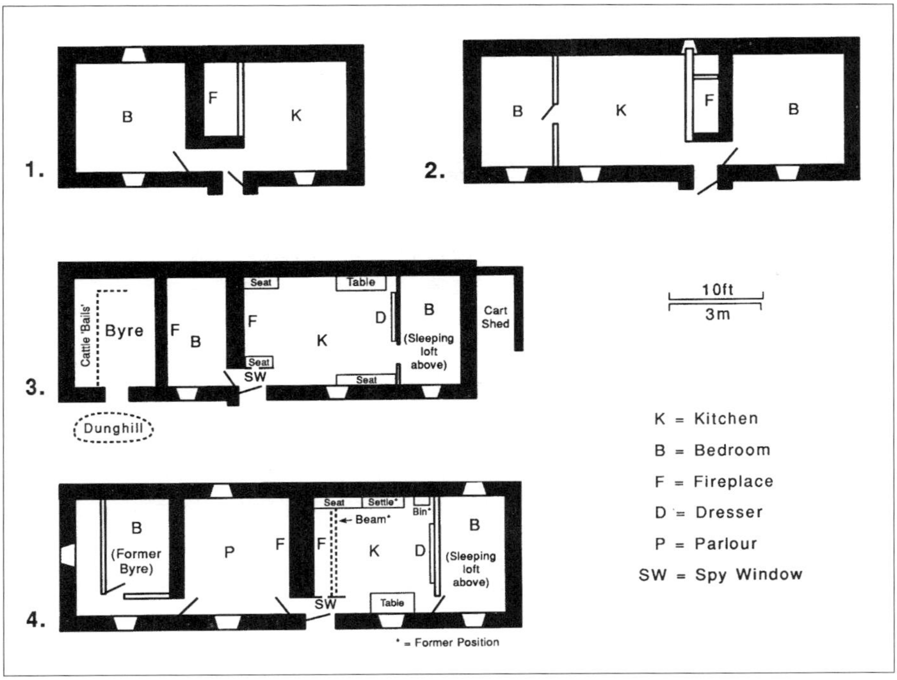

Figure 14.2 **Lobby-entrance/central-hearth dwellings**

1. Kilbaylet Upper, west Wicklow (after Danaher, *c.*1950).
2. Rostyduff Upper, west Wicklow (after Danaher, *c.*1950).
3. Baltyboys, west Wicklow (1939).
4. Tinnahinch, Imaal (1992).

converted into a bedroom and a further room developed behind the hearth at the other end of the house to produce a three-chambered dwelling frequently with opposite doors and a gabled roof. In contrast, the traditional houses of the east and south of Ireland commonly had their entrance adjacent to the hearth which is centrally located in the house and a lobby is formed at the side of the hearth; the terms 'central-hearth house' (Danaher) or 'hearth-lobby house' (Gailey) have been applied to these dwellings. 'The classic form was a two-roomed house with a hipped roof, the door in line with the hearth and the entrance screened by a jamb wall with a small window or 'spyhole' in it, permitting residents to survey the farmyard and identify visitors without leaving the fireside. There is no tradition that cattle were accommodated in these structures; indeed the internal layout of the house renders this arrangement unlikely and such houses are generally separated from farm buildings.

The high frequency in Wicklow of old houses conforming to the direct entry model is unusual in eastern Ireland but, as in several areas

Plate 14.2 **Direct entry houses**

1 Three-roomed thatched house. The projections on either side of the door formed an elementary porch often found in old houses. Boystown, west Wicklow.

2 Three-roomed thatched house, with attached byres. Lackan, west Wicklow.
(T.H. Mason, 1939)

of Ireland (such as the Ulster lowlands), they are intermixed with houses of the lobby-entrance type. 'The relationship between the two forms in Wicklow raises interesting issues which, unfortunately, cannot be conclusively resolved. Is one form older than the other? Has the lowland, central-hearth pattern perhaps infiltrated a pastoral society with an indigenous long-house tradition? Or does the direct entry form here represent an improvement which has largely replaced the lobby-entrance houses, perhaps being introduced in association with landlord improvements on the marginal hill lands and the spread of commercial sheep farming from the late eighteenth century. In that event, the direct entry house would not have direct long-house antecedents and the resemblance to long-houses may be essentially fortuitous.

It is tempting to see Wicklow as formerly an outlier of long-house territory, detached room the main north western long-house province. In the late medieval period, the pastoral community of the hills was distinct from that in the surrounding lowlands, indeed often in conflict with it, and could have possessed a separate dwelling-house tradition. However, with the shiring of the region in 1606, assimilation into the commercial hinterland of Dublin and incorporation into the framework of major landed estates, a long-house tradition could have been rapidly attenuated and eventually lost to folk memory. It is not therefore suggested that the existing traditional, three-roomed dwellings may have been long-houses built originally to accommodate humans and livestock together, but rather that their style could have been conditioned by rather remote long-house antecedents, and they are perhaps best described as 'derived long-houses'.

Clear evidence of a local evolution from long-houses to direct entry houses is not available, but suggestive circumstantial evidence can be adduced from the lay-out of older buildings. First, although opposite doors are absent, the tripartite division of many Wicklow houses and the relation of door to hearth accord with features of derived long-houses elsewhere in Ireland. Secondly, house, byre and other buildings are often linked together in a line (figs. 14.1, 14.2; Plate 14.1). Such linear steadings are common in the upland areas of Britain and Ireland and often indicative of the former presence of long-houses; the cattle byres were characteristically in a downhill position with internal access from dwelling to byre. Downhill position of the byre in Wicklow is common enough and an internal link is observable in a few abandoned steadings but this could be the result of recent conversion of the buildings for use as cattle sheds rather than an original arrangement. A farmstead in the Liffey valley (Plate 14.3) submerged by the Poulaphouca reservoir in the 1930s appears to have had an internal connection between byre and kitchen, but again it is difficult to decide

1. a.

1. b.

Plate 14.3 **Lobby-entrance/central hearth houses**

1. a. Single-storey, three-roomed house with byre attached.
   b. The lobby-entrance with spy window. Baltyboys, west Wicklow.

(T.H. Mason, 1939)

2. a.

2. b.

2. a. Single-storey house. The corrugated iron roof has replaced thatch; the end room (with gable-end window) was formerly a byre.
b. Entrance lobby with spy window. Tinnahinch, Glen of Imaal (see fig. 14.2).
(F. Aalen, 1992)

whether this was the original arrangement or a conversion.[14] Linear steadings were by no means universal in Wicklow. On the smallest farmhouses and labourers' cabins, for example, there were often no outbuildings apart from a lean-to fuel shed on one gable. Moreover, on progressive farms, outhouses were often separated from the house and relocated around a rudimentary farmyard.

There is little clear evidence of long-house arrangements in local tradition or written records, so if they once existed it was presumably a considerable time ago. It is clear that animals were kept in some of the houses either permanently or temporarily. Thus, a sow might farrow behind the settle and poultry be given a relatively free run in the kitchen, but this was commonplace in Ireland and not conclusive evidence of long-houses. A distinction must be made between dwellings constructed specifically for the purpose of accommodaling cattle and humans together in the long-house tradition, and those where animals were merely kept indoors from time to time. Elizabeth Smith in her diary in 1847 describes a farmhouse in Baltyboys, west Wicklow, where cattle lived in the bedroom which they entered through the kitchen.[15] Elizabeth was under the impression that this was simply the failing of a particularly ineducable family, but it may reflect a more deep-rooted and widespread custom – the bedroom may have been reverting to its original role. She also refers, approvingly, to the removal of dung heaps from cottage doors, an improvement which could have been connected with the terminal stages of long-house traditions.

Gable-ended, direct-entry houses are most common on the western flanks of the Wicklow hills and in the less accessible glens and valleys of the east such as Glenmacnass, Glencullen, and the Inchavore river valley above Lough Dan where there are numerous ruined farmhouses. Lobby-entrance, central-hearth houses seem to have been general on the eastern coastal lowlands of Wicklow and there are a few thatched, hip-ended examples surviving there, although often considerably modernised and mutilated.[16] In the hills the type appears to thin out, but there are scattered examples and their frequency again increases on the western edges of the hill area. The lobby entrance, central hearth model is well established in the Glen of Imaal, although not to the exclusion of direct-entry forms, and includes small single-storey and substantial two-storey houses. Imaal was extensively planted in the seventeenth century by Protestant families of English origin (e.g. Higginbotham, Heighington, Hanbidge and Hawkins) and some of the central hearth houses are in Protestant hands. There is however no conclusive evidence that the central hearth house is an intrusive feature. Catholic and Protestant lifestyles here are little differentiated and the planters could in time have adopted a native Irish house style.

Developing the traditional models

While new farmhouses were built in the nineteenth century, improvement of housing conditions was often owing to elongation and raising of the old houses and did not lead to general or sharp departure from basic vernacular forms. Elongation could be achieved simply by incorporating the flanking byres and sheds into the house, in which event new outbuildings were constructed, often separate from the house. But elongation of a house one-room in width clearly had its limits; not least it accentuated heating problems and might necessitate a second fireplace and chimney stack.

Two-storey farmhouses with slated roofs were in use in the eighteenth and early nineteenth-century but only for a relatively well-off minority. The fashion, however, eventually spread and upper-stories were often added to old single-storey houses, covering either the whole or part of the house (Plate 14.4). Sometimes only one end oF the house was raised and the end away from the fire was normally chosen. Here there was traditionally an attic bedroom, and thus a second-storey simply permitted an enlargement of this sleeping space and little change in the basic ordering of the house.

A complete upper-storey made a substantial addition to house space, permitting more privacy and rooms for specialised use. Moreover, the house could be largely consolidated around a single, central chimney stack. The room behind the hearth at ground level often became a parlour used only for special occasions, the kitchen remained fixed, and the room beyond it became either a storage area or a bedroom. Upstairs was used entirely for bedrooms, and usually the upstairs plan is essentially the same as the ground plan with the dividing walls continuing from ground to roof. Recent and incomplete emancipation from a single-storey tradition is suggested by the frequency of semi-attic bedrooms and downstairs ceilings so low that they can be easily touched. Stairs were usually placed at the end of the kitchen opposite the hearth where in the older houses the ladder to the attic had been placed. Lobbies are frequently found in association with the stairs but few were constructed until the second half of the nineteenth century. Projecting porches were added to some houses but only in the present century.

Addition of a new storey was often accompanied by some relaxation of vernacular patterns. For example, a slated roof replaced the thatch and there were attempts to create a symmetrical arrangement of door and windows in the facade in accordance with the dictates of polite architecture. But the tension between vernacular and polite arrangements was only slowly resolved. Since the upper-storey layout was largely determined by the lower, it was easy and practical for the upstairs and downstairs windows to be aligned but, owing to the chimney stack, it was awkward to locate the door centrally in the facade and its frequent retention towards the end of the house is a vernacular hangover. Moreover, the position and substantial size of the

1.

2.

Plate 14.4 **Developed vernacular forms**

Partial two-storied:
1. Gibstown, Glen of Imaal.
2. Crehelp, west Wicklow.
3. Lugglass, west Wicklow. (F. Aalen, 1992)

Two-storied:
4. Direct entry derivative, Lockstown, west Wicklow. (F. Aalen, 1992)
5. Central hearth/lobby-entrance derivative.
   Baltyboys Upper, west Wicklow. (Poulaphouca Survey, 1939)

3.

4.

5.

6.

7.

8.

9.

Plate 14.4 **Developed vernacular forms *(contd.)***

Two-storied, vernacular/polite threshold:

6. Gable-end chimneys. Ballinahown, west Wicklow.
7. Two centralised chimneys. Crosscoolharbour, west Wicklow. (Poulaphouca Survey, 1939)
8. Gable-end chimneys, Blessington.
9. Two centralised chimneys, Slievecorragh, west Wicklow. (F. Aalen, 1992)

main hearth and chimney can result in a wider gap between the window in the kitchen and the parlour than between the two parlour windows. Even when a second storey was added, the size of windows at the back of the house tends to remain smaller than those at the front and there is less emphasis on a symmetrical ordering of the fenestration.

As the nineteenth-century progressed, new two-storey houses with regular facades were built by an increasing number of better-off farmers. Two main types are found. In the first the door is located centrally and opens onto a hall and stairs and the chimneys are located at the gable ends. Another common type was a hip-ended house with two chimneys on either side of a central hall. Both types adopt features from grander houses, such as large windows and a 'Georgian' fanlight above the front door Clearly, vernacular influences have been much diminished. However, the houses still tend to conform to the old pattern of being one room in width.

Kitchen, hearth and furnishings

Fittings and furnishing in the houses were simple, even primitive.[17] Until the nineteenth-century most families slept on wads of straw on the floor and almost the only items of furniture were stools and the dresser In the second half of the century a range of furniture was increasingly introduced into the farmhouses. Cabins, however, remained relatively bare.

Hearth

The hearth was the hub of the house, both of domestic work and recreation, and the fire was always kept alight. Fire was used for cooking and the houses needed warmth throughout the year. Damp was everywhere a problem; the granite walls tended to 'weep' (ooze moisture) and damp rose through the earth and stone-flagged floors.

The fire lay on a flagstone at floor level, normally in front of an erect stone slab (the hob), on either side of which was a cavity formed by erecting stone slabs or leaving out stones at the base of the wall. One cavity was used to store peat, the main fuel, and the other (whose bottom was generally sunk below ground level) was a container for ashes. Suspended above the fire was the chimney canopy, made with wattles (woven sticks of hazel plastered with mud or cow dung and horse hair) and usually whitewashed on the outside. Some canopies, probably more recent features, were made with wooden boards (Plate 14.5). The canopy was supported on a horizontal wooden beam (a brace tree or breastsummer) either inserted in the kitchen walls and running right across the room or resting on a wooden pillar at one end.

1.

2.

Plate 14.5 **Chimney hoods**

1. Wattle chimney hood, 'thawluck' lofts on either side, suspended pot, keeping-holes on rear wall to right, falling table and 'creepy' on right.
   Valleymount, west Wicklow
2. Wooden chimney hood, fire on floor against hob stone, fuel and ash cavities. Lackan, west Wicklow. Valleymount, west Wicklow

Some old houses, including a number of those submerged in the 1930s by the formation of the Poulaphouca reservoir, never possessed chimney canopies; the smoke left the house through a hole in the roof, escaped through the doors or seeped through the thatch. Such primitive arrangements presumably represent a survival of conditions common before the general introduction of wattle chimney canopies.

Wattle chimney hoods were often superseded by fireplaces with stone flues set in large recesses constructed with stone (Plate 14.6) Substantial wooden beams, often of bog oak, span the recesses. Some of the better old farmhouses contained massive hearth recesses with

1.

2.

Plate 14.6 **Hearth alcoves**

1. Wooden supporting beam, steel crane, keeping-hole to right, ash and fuel alcoves to right and left of fire. Baltyboys Upper.
2. Crane with suspended pots, stone fireside seats, stone flagged floor, wooden bench to left. Baltyboys.

3.

4.

Plate 14.6 **Hearth alcoves *(contd.)***

3. Fire at floor level with crane and pots. Fuel cavities of carved stone, keeping-holes and mantelpiece above. Ballinahown. (Poulaphouca Survey, 1939)
4. Alcove with substantial curved beam of bog oak, preserved in modernised farmhouse, keeping-hole to right. Slievecorragh, west Wicklow. (F. Aalen, 1992)

seating and standing room for several people. Good examples occur in two neighbouring farmhouses in Hightown townland near Johnstown at the foot of the King's river valley. Here the recesses are built into the thick gable-end walls of single-storey and originally thatched dwellings which according to local tradition were formerly occupied by protestant families (Williams and Wilson). Hightown was formerly the property of the marquis of Waterford who planted a number of Welsh farmers (from Pembrokeshire) on his estates in the seventeenth century.[18] Could the fashion of building stone chimney recesses possibly have been introduced into the area by planters and, perhaps when stone blocks became readily available from granite quarries in the eighteenth century, copied in the houses of native rural people?

Around the hearth there was often a number of intramural 'keeping holes', sometimes shaped but in most cases formed by simply leaving a stone or two out of the wall. They were used for storage of a variety of objects including salt which needed to be kept dry. The small lofts or recesses at the side of the chimney canopy, referred to as thawlogue or thawluck (presumably derived from the Irish *tailleog*, a loft), were used mainly for storing pots and clothing but poultry occasionally nestled there (Plate 14.5).[19] Bigger lofts, which provided sleeping space, lay over the room at the end of the house opposite the hearth and were reached by a wooden ladder or open stairs.

As in most Irish farmhouses, a metal 'pot-rack' or 'crane' stood at the side of the fire in old Wicklow houses on which cooking pots were suspended over the fire (Plate 14.6).[20] Pots were also suspended on a metal hook and chain either pegged on the back wall of the fire or attached to a roof couple and hung down the chimney, and this arrangement may be the older one as it was usually found in association with the wattle canopy while standing cranes were fitted into stone recesses. In recent decades, old-style hearths and their equipment have been almost entirely removed and modern fireplaces inserted in their place. Wattle chimney hoods, however, sometimes survive beneath layers of wallpaper, boarding or plaster. 'The larger stone hearth recesses have occasionally been retained but today there is little interest among country people in old hearths and their fittings, nor concern to preserve them (Plate 14.6, 4).

Kitchen furniture

The main pieces of furniture were located in the kitchen and included the settle bed, falling table, open-fronted dresser, fireside seats and benches (Plate 14.7): most of these were familiar items in houses throughout Ireland.[21] Furnishings were placed in a more or less standard location around the kitchen walls, no article of furniture

1.

2.

3.

Plate 14.7 **Kitchen furniture**

1. Built-in wooden seat to left of fire and under chimney canopy. Burgage Moyle.
2. Falling table with settle bed to left and stone and wood bench to right. Ballyknockan.
3. Dresser against wall opposite hearth; to the left a long wooden table with two stretchers below, and tall wooden press. Monamuck. (Poulaphouca Survey, 1939)
4. Built-in dresser stretching from floor to ceiling. An unusually impressive example. Killybeg, Imaal. (C. Kinmonth, 1990)

4.

occupying the centre of the room. Folding furniture was common, ingeniously adapted to the confined narrow rooms.

A settle or long, high-backed wooden seat with arms often stood at a right angle to the fire, its high panelled back giving support and protection against damp walls. A settle bed, serving the dual purpose of seating and sleeping, might occupy the same position. At night, it could be opened out on the floor to form a double bed enclosed by wooden sides. Folding beds were also fitted into cupboards. Settle and cupboard beds were predecessors of the modern studio couch or zed-bed. Settle tables do not seem to have been used in Wicklow and may have been confined to well-off farm areas in the south-east of Ireland.[22]

A falling table was found in many houses and customarily placed at the foot of the settle. It consisted of a top made either of boards or a single piece of wood with a single leg which swung freely. When not in use, the table could be swung upwards and clipped to the wall. Free-standing tables are now used and tend to be placed against the wall where the settle and falling table stood: older versions are long and narrow with one or two stretchers beneath, a feature that enabled those sitting at table to rest their feet off the cold, damp floors. Campbell (1937) is almost certainly right when he observes that the table is not indigenous to Irish peasant culture; there are no ceremonies connected with it and it was invariably against the wall.[23]

The dresser was used for display of china and delph and of spoons which were slotted into the front of the shelves. An average dresser had three shelves in its upper portion but larger examples might have four or five (Plate 14.7, 3 & 4). Big dishes often stood on top of the dresser. The lower portion of the dresser was sometimes open and used for the storage of working pots, buckets and large utensils. However, drawers and cupboards became a feature of many dressers, perhaps following the popularisation of domestic hygiene in the nineteenth century. Cutlery was then transferred to drawers, and pots stored in the cupboard underneath. The dresser almost invariably stood facing the hearth and against the wall which divides the kitchen from the end room; indeed the dresser is sometimes a structural feature forming part of the wall itself and in some cases supporting the attic floor. The height of the dividing wall permitted the dresser to be taller than other items of furniture placed along the low side walls of the house. Apart from the settle bed, the dresser was the only piece that was decorated. Moulding along the dresser shelves was sometimes shaped, with perhaps a flourish or two along the top of the dresser, but there is no tradition in the area of elaborate carving. The lower portion of the dresser was characteristically divided by a 'fiddle-shaped' board. Pot racks were to be found in almost all houses often fixed on the wall beside the dresser, with cups, vessels and tools hung on the wooden or metal hooks. It is likely that these devices are older than the dressers.

Benches in the houses were sometimes formed with stone slabs or planks of wood resting on stone blocks. Stone benches often lay on either side of the fire but a typical arrangement was a stone bench on one side and a wooden seat on the other. Central-hearth houses with lobby entrances often had a wooden fireside bench or seat fitted into the jamb wall and structurally part of it. Ake Campbell noted this feature in his sketch of a fireplace in a house at Kyle, Ballinglen near Rathnew - one of the few published references to a Wicklow house.[24] Wooden chairs were eventually used but, save perhaps for the master of the house, they had no fixed place in front of the fire. Most houses possessed low wooden seats (creepies) which could be drawn up when needed and tucked away against the kitchen walls when not in use. Creepies usually had four splayed legs 'through-wedged' into the seat which was a solid block of wood.

High, wooden meal chests with a sloping lid were used in kitchens to store flour and oatmeal and to keep it safe and dry. Most of these were later transferred to outhouses and few survive. Wooden churns were also used and a wooden churn-dash with a wooden cross at the bottom. These, along with a variety of farm equipment, were also kept in the kitchen.

Sleeping arrangements and the number of bedrooms depended on the social level of the family. Wealthy households had separate bedrooms much earlier than the general populace. In small Irish farmhouses, the whole family traditionally slept on straw on the kitchen floor and only in the eighteenth and nineteenth centuries did separate bedrooms become a feature. In the nineteenth century metal bedsteads came to be widely used and rough wooden wardrobes. Given the large size of rural families, sleeping facilities were usually needed in each room and attic, and in the kitchen a settle bed was common. Farms often had a maid living in the house and while many farm labourers had their own cabins there were others who were accommodated in the farmhouse or a barn. It was common to keep Dublin orphans on the farms as maids or general workers.

Detailed reliable descriptions of traditional house interiors are few. However, in *The Memories of William Hanbidge* we are fortunate to have a classic account of a Wicklow farmhouse in the late nineteenth century.[25] Although not published until 1939, this account is based on the memories of William Hanbidge (1813-1909) recorded in his 93rd year by his daughter Mary. The Hanbidge house was a thatched, one-storey dwelling of three rooms built at Tinnahinch in the Glen of Imaal in 1795. Tinnahinch belonged to an old Protestant planter family but differed little from the general run of houses in the surrounding countryside. It survives today little changed from its original form (fig. 14.2, 4; Plate 14.3, 2). The kitchen was the central unit but there was a large end room behind the fireplace (a special place referred to as 'the room', where, among other things, the children were born) and a small bedroom at the other end with a loft above reached by a moveable ladder. 'There was no ceiling, only the roof; boughs or trees supported the thatch, black with age and turf smoke.' The bull's house beyond 'the room' was eventually incorporated into the house, in it 'a ceiling of pitch pine planks follows the slope of the thatched roof and hides it.' The house roof was covered by iron, not thatch. Mary Hanbidge gives the following description of the kitchen and its fireplace:

> The great fireplace survives where you can sit on benches beside the hearth fire right under the chimney and see the sky above you; the tiny cupboard for salt (salt was so dear) in the wall beside the fire; the long moveable irons hang from the cross bar,

with their hooks for the three-legged pots which swing over the fire heaped on the great stone hearth, coke, or turf when they can get it; and soda bread and potato cakes are still baked in the flat round iron vessel set on the hearthstone with the glowing coals heaped around it and on the cover. So had they cooked on the Irish hearths from time beyond memory and so my grandmother baked her cakes. Outside the fireplace is the long high-backed settle with a chest running under the whole length of the seat, the tall cornbin with sloping lid, the little shelves on the wall for spoons and mugs, the dresser with big shelves for crockery and spaces underneath which covers almost all the end wall, and under the little deep-set window the big deal table where the serving men eat; they sit on long four-legged deal stools, scrubbed like the table white with river sand. The master's large wooden chair stands in the front of the hearth; it was my father's seal in the later years. There are wooden chairs for others, and the whole life of the house has its centre in the kitchen.

Labourers' and smallholders' cabins

In nineteenth-century Ireland a deep social gulf existed between farmers and the landless labourers who worked for them. Most labourers lived in one or two-roomed cabins and their wretchedness induced a stream of adverse comment and official inquiries. Cottars or smallholders with only an acre or two of land often had equally inferior accommodation. In Wicklow almost all of these primitive dwellings have now been abandoned, although a handful were still inhabited down to the 1960s (Plate 14.8). Ruins and foundations survive in plenty, especially on the edges of mountain commonages, the homes of 'wild mountain squatters'.

John Millington Synge writes vividly of these wretched abodes at the end of the nineteenth-century. 'At every season heavy rains fall for often a week at a time, till the thatch drips with water stained to a dull chestnut, and the floor in the cottages seems to be going back to the condition of the bogs near it'. Channeled in the narrow glens, storm winds came 'with the congested whirl and roar of the torrent. At such times the people crouch all night over a few sods of turf and the dogs howl in the lanes'.[26] Synge believed that the inhospitable climate, primitive housing, the loneliness and dreariness of life, and the paucity of women owing to selective emigration, encouraged nervous depression and sadness in the hill people. Men were mournful and some had spent half their life in the madhouse, while intense nervousness was common in young women. Below the labourers, Synge reminds us, there existed a numerous class of homeless vagrants,

1. (a)

1. (b)

Plate 14.8 **Cabins**

1. Front (a) and rear (b) of single-room cabin on edge of mountain waste land. Lackan, west Wicklow. (W. Warham, 1965)

2. (a)

2. (b)

Plate 14.8 **Cabins *(contd.)***

2. Front (a) and rear (b) of cabin with turf gable. Glencullen. (F. Aalen, 1963)

tramps, tinkers and beggars, who frequented the roads and villages and found periodic refuge in the union workhouse and madhouse.

In the 1930s Kevin Danaher described a cluster of cabins on a small commonage near Rathnew, a haven for evicted families and other dispossessed people.[27] Still in their original form, the houses gave a picture of building styles perhaps a 100 years before. Most were small, two-roomed structures with the door in the middle of the front wall. Gable-chimney types predominated but a few houses had sloping thatch over the gable end opposite the fire. Walls were made with yellow clay mixed with rushes and roofs were thatched with straw and rush without a layer of sods. According to tradition these dwellings had been built very rapidly, each taking only three or four days to complete.

Detailed descriptions of the poorest type of dwelling in the 1930s are available from the Liffey Valley.[28] A house in Ballinahown is described as follows:

> The house is built on the bog, and was damp and dark within. Beside the fire in the kitchen was a stool, the supports of which were two round slicks driven through the bog floor. The house had a hole in the roof for the smoke to go out. Around the house on top a tardrum had recently been put up. There was no stone chimney as the upper part of the gable walls was of sod. Beside the wall was a table which had only one leg and was tied up against the side of the wall. The table rested on a wooden seat at the right-hand side of the fire. Below the table was a settle bed and against the lower gable end was a dresser.[29]

An interesting picture is also given of two primitive dwellings in Lackan.[30] In the first, which appears to have been built at the end of the nineteenth century, the walls were made of sods with the grass side down and marl between, and were the same height as the door to the living room (Plate 14.9, 2). At the back there was practically no wall. The living room was about 13 feet (4m) long with a floor of natural red clay like the ground outside. The fireplace was a flagstone placed on the open hearth with a canopy made of sacking and wicker plastered over with clay: the spaces beside the mantle were boarded over and used for storage space. Outside, the chimney was made of 'old tin buckets'. The roof was of sods laid directly on the purlins, thatched outside, coated with pitch inside. 'The roof beam, which runs along the top of the house from gable to gable, is a rough stem. At the other end of the living room it ran through the wall and through the chimney. The part which ran through the chimney was used as a support for the

1.

2.

Plate 14.9 **Sod walls**

1. Sod gable on dwelling house. Ballyknockan, west Wicklow.
2. House wall made of sods with marl and mortar in between. Lackan, west Wicklow. (Poulaphouca Survey, 1939)

"crane", which in this house was merely a long chain with pot hooks.' At the south wall was a settle bed and at the northern wall a table-cum-dresser. There were no windows. The writer comments 'this was the most primitive dwelling I ever saw.' A second house in the same townland was a single room with attached byre. The granite walls were plastered in the living area but bare in the byre. There was a boarded chimney hood and the roof was thatch over scraws.

In the late eighteenth and nineteenth century, improved housing was often provided for the workers on large estates. In Wicklow, notable examples of estate housing exist on the extensive Powerscourt, Fitzwilliam and Brabazon properties and at Mount Kennedy (seat of Lord Rossmore) and Belview (the demesne of the La Touche family). Usually the dwellings were built singly or in small groups or terraces on the edge of the demesnes; some are of high design quality and built in a 'picturesque' style with stone walls, slated roofs, and ornamental features such as quoins, door and window mouldings, and lattice windows. Ornamental gate lodges are recurrent features associated with demesnes and substantial houses (Plate 14.10), particularly numerous around Bray. Although provided in rural areas, most of these estate buildings are not part of the vernacular tradition; they were consciously designed to complement the polite architecture of the great estates.

Throughout Ireland little was done until the end of the nineteenth century to improve the housing of the great bulk of rural labourers, who worked not for landlords but for the small tenant farmers. Farmers usually engaged labourers by granting them small plots of land for short periods of six months to a year, on which a cabin was available or one could be built. Rent was paid for by labour for the farmer. Towards the end of the nineteenth century the wretched plight of labourers generated political pressure for improvements and in the 1880s the Labourers' (Ireland) Acts were introduced to enable local authorities to demolish primitive cabins and rehouse their occupants in solid 'cottages' each with a small allotment and at subsided rents. This legislation initiated a major public housing enterprise, the first in the British Isles, which continued for several decades.[31] Although cottage provision was more plentiful in more densely populated, neighbouring counties, the response in Wicklow was nevertheless significant and hundreds of compact solid dwellings were erected As elsewhere in Ireland, they were usually located on the roadsides either singly or in small terraces. By 1906, 339 cottages had been provided in the county, the majority in Rathdrum and Baltinglass No. 1 Rural Districts.[32] Thereafter, state financial provision for housing was considerably improved and the rate of cottage building quickened. By 1914, 847

1.

2.

Plate 14.10 **Gate lodges**

1. Humewood Castle, Kiltegan.
2. Laragh House, Annamoe. (F. Aalen, 1993)

cottages had been built and 35 more were under construction.[33] However, during the First World War all house building virtually came to a standstill and there was no significant renewal of cottage provision until the 1930s when large-sized schemes involving terraces of cottages became common.

Although modest, the new cottages were a considerable advance on the old cabins, sometimes placing labourers in better accommodation than the small farmers. The cottages were of stone with slated roofs and there had to be at least a kitchen and two bedrooms to every house with glass windows, concrete floors and a proper privy. Early styles vary, but cottages with two ground floor rooms, central chimney and attic bedrooms were common; this was a basic design widely used in eastern Ireland and not very different from the traditional pattern of small rural dwellings (Plate 14.11). Single-storey, roughly square cottages with small projecting porches are also numerous. Hanbidge writes of Imaal that 'the glen is largely unchanged and unspoilt, though empty compared with the glen of a hundred years ago. The crowds my father knew have gone, but so have the hovels which lingered on until almost 1900: I saw them, four mud walls, a rotting thatch, a door and no window at all. The labouring man now lives in a council cottage, sanitary, well built; of stone with slated roof and large windows.'[34] In recent decades, labourers' cottages have frequently been enlarged and much modified by their owners, the modern additions sometimes jarring with the original elementary forms.

Farmyard buildings and other traditional structures

Byres, barns and other outbuildings on most Wicklow farms were modest and often poorly constructed. On many small farms the only buildings were the cowhouse and the peat store, both attached to the house. In the nineteenth century, especially on bigger, progressive holdings, farm buildings were often separated from the house and relocated either at right angles to, or parallel with, the house to form a partially enclosed yard. The house, with few exceptions, was an integral part of the farmyard. However, small inner yards were sometimes formed against the house, separating it from the main yard and the livestock. It is only on the largest farms that farm buildings are arranged around regular, completely enclosed yards with the house standing apart. In such cases the houses are usually two-storied polite forms or developed vernacular forms.

Around farmyards there were often small paddocks used for various purposes such as vegetable growing and livestock sorting. The haggard is a small walled area alongside the farmstead used primarily for storage of hay and corn. It invariably contained one or more corn

1.

2.

Plate 14.11 **Labourers' cottages**

Some common styles built by Local Authorities under the Labourers' Acts since 1883.

Single-storey forms:

1. An early style, roughly rectangular with hipped roof, central chimney stack and small porch. Near Dunlavin.
2. Two chimneys with tiled hip-ended roof. A characteristic pattern of the inter-war period and later. Tomriland Crossroads, near Annamoe.

3.

4.

Plate 14.11 **Labourers' cottages *(contd.)***

With attic bedrooms:

3. Central-chimney house with two attic bedrooms and gable-end windows. A widely used pattern at the beginning of the century throughout the south and east of Ireland. Near Hollywood, west Wicklow.
4. Cottage with attic bedrooms. Tomriland Crossroads, near Annamoe. (F. Aalen, 1992)

stands (Plate 14.12, 4). These were formed usually with six upright granite pillars, some two feet (6m) high with stone caps arranged in a circle around a central pillar. Long narrow stones ('stretchers') connected the caps to each other and to the centre, providing a platform usually some 9 to 10 feet (2.7 to 3.0m) in diameter on which branches were laid and the corn stacked on top. This infrastructure was effective in protecting the crop from rodents which could not surmount the projecting capstones. Few complete corn stands can now be found, most having been demolished and their stones re-used in walls, buildings or rockeries. The hay-shed also stood in the haggard, its roof supported on tall wooden posts each standing on a stone base. An exceptionally large shed at Killybeg in Imaal has posts some 25 feet (7.6m) high and over 200 years old (Plate 14.12, 2).[35] This old type of shed has been almost completely replaced by metal structures. Hay-stands were low, rectangular, paved platforms usually located close to the hay-sheds. In the haggards there were occasionally long shelters thatched with a roof of scrub and rushes supported by widely-spaced wooden posts (Plate 14.12, 1). They were used for carts, livestock and turf. A few outhouses with walls constructed entirely of wooden uprights were recorded in the 1930s in the Liffey valley (Plate 14.12, 3); it is unclear whether this building technique was once more widespread.[36] Shallow granite feeding troughs were a common feature on farms. Wells and springs around the farm were sometimes protected with stone covers, a few of them roughly corbelled.

Scattered over the Wicklow countryside is a range of structures formerly integrated with the rural economy but now obsolescent. These include derelict lime kilns, cairns and other clearance features, sheep pens, various hut sites, and charcoal burning platforms (Plate 14.12, 5, 6).

The wide distribution of eighteenth- and nineteenth-century lime kilns, especially near the limits of improved land where almost every farm or farm cluster had a kiln, is evidence of the application of lime from lowland areas to the sour hill soils to permit an extension of upland farming. Kilns are usually substantial, circular stone structures which sometimes continued in use until the introduction of modern artificial manures. Stones and boulders had to be laboriously cleared from the land before it could be used for farming and they were eventually built into the field walls and ditches. It is likely that clearance was sometimes initially into small cairns. In a few places on the boundaries of improved land there are groups of cairns which may mark uncompleted reclamation projects.

Surprising in an area of sheep specialisation, distinctive fold and pen structures are neither numerous nor distinctive in their form. There is nothing equivalent to the circular stone hirsels of the Scottish borders

1.

2.

Plate 14.12 **Farmyard field structures**

Wood construction:

1. Shed with thatched roof on wooden poles against field wall. Near Valleymount, west Wicklow. (T.H. Mason, Poulaphouca Survey, 1939)
2. Hay shed. The posts in this large structure are some 200 years old. Killybeg, Glen of Imaal. (F. Aalen, 1992)

3.

4.

Plate 14.12 **Farmyard field structures *(contd.)***

3. Cart shed with log walls and hip-ended thatched roof. This is an isolated example but may represent a survival of older building techniques.
   Monamuck, west Wicklow. (Poulaphouca Survey, 1939)

Stone construction:

4. Corn stand. Annacarney, west Wicklow. (T.H. Mason, Poulaphouca Survey, 1939)

5.

6.

Plate 14.12 **Farmyard field structures *(contd.)***

5. Ruined lime-kiln. Slievecorragh, west Wicklow.
6. Corbelled spring cover. Lugglass, west Wicklow. (F. Aalen, 1990)

or the large T-shaped sheep shelters once characteristic of the Burren, which sheltered animals whichever way the wind blew. In Wicklow small enclosures were sometimes built in the corner of fields for the purpose of sorting sheep, and low openings formed in the stone field walls through which sheep could pass if required or which could be easily blocked. Few of these features have survived. Scattered circular and rectangular foundations occur in the hills which may be the remains of earlier animal pens but they are fragmentary and hard to interpret.

A number of derelict settlement sites occur above the present upper limits of improved land, a level which varies considerably but lies at approximately 800-900 ft (244 to 274m). Often associated with old potato ridges and small enclosures, it is likely that many of these sites are vestiges of a tide of peasant life which expanded uphill in the period of pre-famine population growth but in the last century and a half has ebbed away from the marginal hill zones. However, high level sites vary in size and shape (rectangular, oval and circular) and may have served a variety of functions. Some are abandoned dwellings, others were mere huts whose age and function are unclear. Many sites are merely heaps of stone or traceable only as low mounds or fern-free areas, and thus very difficult to interpret. Some may be old booley sites, i.e. the temporary habitations of seasonal, transhumant herders. Placenames, historical references and some vague local tradition attest that booleying was formerly a feature of the Wicklow hills and may have survived until a relatively recent date.[37] Hollywood parish, for example, was traditionally divided into Hollywood booleys and Hollywood lowlands.[38] Liam Price has discussed the placename Boleymushboy (James Boyes' Booley) in the Liffey valley, a name which indicates the site of the summer milking place of James Boyes' cattle.[39] Boyce or Boyes is identified as an influential retainer of the eighth earl of Kildare and probably lived in the townland of Boystown some 4 to 5 miles away. Bolenmanagh (*buaile na manach*), 'the monk's summer milking place' near Dublin and *Buaile na sagart* (now Saggart), 'booley of the priest' in Derrylossary parish indicate that booleying was part of the economy of local monastic establishments. A number of townlands abutting on the mountains had 'booley' elements in their placenames which later became 'bally', suggesting a transition from temporary to permanent settlement, perhaps resulting from long-term population growth and expansion of the improved land.

Oval or circular platforms, varying in width from approximately 15 to 30 ft (4.5 to 9m), have been noted in various places in Wicklow, often on steep slopes. Soil excavation from the upper part is used to build up the lower part and the platforms usually have a dry stone revetment on the downhill side and a rear retaining wall at the back. Various investigators have interpreted these platforms as sites for small huts, but few show traces of huts and most sites are probably charcoal-burning platforms associated with the local iron smelting industry of the eighteenth and nineteenth centuries.[40] Moreover, similar platforms have been recorded in Scotland and elsewhere which are unquestionably charcoal burning sites.[41] The features are very numerous (over 80 sites) around the western end of the upper lake in Glendalough, where they have been wrongly interpreted as Early Christian hut sites.[42] They are to be found also on Keadeen mountain in the Glen of Imaal and on the slopes above Lough Tay, and many other sites must remain to be discovered.

References

1. R. Frazer, *General view of agriculture and mineralogy, present state and circumstances of the county Wicklow* (Dublin, 1801), p. 219.
2. J. G. Kohl, *Travels in Ireland* [translated from the German (1843), p. 16.
3. S. C. Hall (Mr. and Mrs.), *Ireland: its scenery, character etc.* ii (London, 1842), pp 207-8.
4. D. Thomson with M. McGusty (ed.), *The Irish journals of Elizabeth Smith, 1840-50* (Oxford, 1980), p. 83.
5. R. Frazer, op cit, p. 92.
6. F. Power Cobbe, *Life of Francis Power Cobbe* (London, 1894), p. 26.
7. M. Hanbidge, *The memories of William Hanbidge*, private circulation (St Alban's, 1939), p. 170.
8. E. McCracken, *The Irish woods since Tudor times; distribution and exploitation* (Newton Abbot, 1971).
9. F. Loeber.
10. L. Price, 'Sweat house, Co. Wicklow' in *R.S.A.I. Jn.*, lxxxii (1952), p. 180.
11. R. MacAlister, 'A burial cairn on Seefin mountain, Co. Wicklow' in *R.S.A.I. Jn.*, lxii (1932), pp 153-7, viii (1937), p. 313.
12. Survey of thatched houses in county Wicklow, National Parks and Monuments Service, Office of Public Works (1987).
13. C. Ó Danachair, 'Traditional forms of the dwelling house in Ireland' in *R.S.A.I. Jn.*, cii (1972), pp 77-96; A. Gailey, *Rural houses of the north of Ireland* (Edinburgh, 1984), pp 140-63.
14. *Survey of the Liffey valley above Poulaphouca* by L. Price, F. Henry, S. O'Sullivan, *et al.* An unpublished survey of antiquities and folk culture undertaken in the late 1930s before the area was submerged by the Liffey hydro-electric scheme. The material is in the possession of the Department of Irish Folklore, University College, Dublin. Ms. vol. 654, pp 45-179. See description and plan of John Brennan's house, Lackan.
15. Thomson and McGusty, *Irish Journals*, p. 119.
16. Survey of thatched houses, *op. cit.*
17. F. H. A. Aalen, 'Furnishings of traditional houses in the Wicklow hills' in *Ulster Folklife*, 13 (1967), pp 61-9.
18. M. Girouard, 'Curraghmore, Co. Waterford, Éire – I' in *Country Life*, 7 Feb. (1963), p. 258.

19. A. J. Bliss, "Thallage, thawlogue and thawluck' in *Ulster Folklife*, 14 (1968), pp 28-33.
20. E. E. Evans, *Irish folk ways* (London, 1957), pp 66-8.
21. F. H. A. Aalen, op. cit.; A. Gailey, 'Kitchen furniture' in *Ulster Folklife*, 12 (1966) pp 18-31; C. Kinmonth, *Irish country furniture 1700-1950*, New Haven & London, 1993).
22. C. Kinmonth, 'Country seats' in *Country Life*, 17 August (1989), p. 58.
23. Å. Campbell, 'Notes on the Irish house' in *Folk Life*, i (1937), p. 234.
24. Ibid., p. 231.
25. Hanbidge, *Memories*, pp 19-21.
26. J. M. Synge, in *Wicklow and West Kerry* (Dublin & London, 1921), p. 12.
27. C. Ó Danachair, 'Old houses at Rathnew, Co. Wicklow' in *Bealoideas* (1935), pp 211-21; E. Kinsella and G. Lynch, 'Rathnew in the 1930s' in *Wicklow Historical Society*, 1, 5 (July, 1992), pp 10-13.
28. *Survey of Liffey Valley*, op. cit.
29. Ibid., Mathew Lennon's house, Ballinahown.
30. Ibid., Michael Carroll's house and John Brennan's house, Lackan.
31. F. H. A. Aalen, 'The rehousing of rural labourers in Ireland under the Labourers' (Ireland) Acts, 1883-1919' in *Jn. of Hist. Geog.*, 12, 3 (1986), pp 287-306.
32. Annual report, Local Government Board for Ireland, 1906. Parliamentary papers, *reports, commissioners*, cd. 3102, 23 (1906) xxxvi, p. 313.
33. Labourers cottages, Ireland. Parliamentary papers, *Accounts and papers* (1914) lxv, p. 13.
34. Hanbidge, *Memories*, p. 174.
35. Information (1993) from Mr. Sam Hawkins, farmer, Killybeg, Glen of Imaal.
36. *Survey of Liffey valley*, op. cit. (Old cart shed, John Quinn's house).
37. F. H. A. Aalen, 'Transhumance in the Wicklow mountains' in *Ulster Folklife*, 10 (1964), pp 65-72.
38. S. Lewis, *Topographical dictionary of Ireland*, ii (London, 1837), p. 7.
39. L. Price, 'Placename study as applied to history' in *R.S.A.I. Jn.*, Centenary volume (1949), p. 29.
40. P. Healy, 'Platforms', unpublished document, 1972.
41. A. Graham, 'A survey of the ancient monuments of Skipness' in *Procs. Soc. of Antiquaries of Scotland*, lii (1918-19), pp 76-118.
42. W. J. Hemp and C. Gresham, 'Hut platforms at Glendalough' in *R.S.A.I. Jn.*, lxviii (1938), pp 280-2.

Chapter 15

THE HOLY WELLS OF COUNTY WICKLOW: TRADITIONS AND LEGENDS

GERALDINE LYNCH

Introduction

In Ireland there has been a strong tradition of visiting and praying at holy wells. At least 3,000 such wells were to be found throughout the country with a number of these having special pattern days on the feast of the patron saint.[1] People gathered at the well on that day to seek cures and other favours and to give thanks. In addition to the religious observances the pattern day was a social occasion with singing, dancing and drinking. Towards the end of the eighteenth century the catholic clergy often voiced their condemnation of the drunkenness and faction-fighting which had become associated with the pattern day in many areas. In 1797 the archbishop of Cashel and Emly, Dr Bray, condemned the patterns held in his diocese.[2] Patterns which survived into the twentieth century were no longer characterised by fighting and riotous behaviour.

This survey of county Wicklow's holy wells and the traditions and legends associated with them focuses primarily on material collected from oral tradition in the 1930s which is in the archives of the Department of Irish Folklore, University College, Dublin. This source material is derived from the Irish Folklore Commission school's manuscript collection together with data from a more specific survey of holy wells in 1934.[3] In compiling the list of wells given in this study the Ordnance Survey six-inch maps (1st edition), letters and namebooks were also used. One hundred and six holy wells have been recorded in county Wicklow. Most of these are not now visited; indeed some had already fallen into disuse at the time of the Ordnance Survey in the 1830s.[4]

Names

The name of a place often remains long after its significance has been forgotten – the Ordnance Surveyors writing about the Quicken Tree Well (W.44) in Kilquade observed that the well was named after a large quicken tree which grew over it but which had already fallen thirty years before the survey took place. The names of the wells may however change with time, particularly when the original name becomes meaningless, as in the case of the Quicken Tree Well which later became known as St Patrick's Well.

The names of county Wicklow's holy wells can be divided into four main groups.[5]

Group	Commemorative of	No. of wells
A	Saints and Deity	62
B	People	4
C	Material culture	11
D	Function	3

Fifty-eight per cent of county Wicklow's holy wells belong to group A and can be broken down as follows:

13	St Brigid[6]
9	St Kevin,[7] St Patrick[8]
5	Our Lady[9]
3	St John[10]
2	St Michael,[11] St Boden,[12] the Deity (God, Trinity)[13]

Seventeen other saints are associated with one well each.

Tobar an Bhric (W.69) – the well of the trout – takes its name from the traditional belief that a fish resided in many holy wells. The Ordnance Survey namebooks report that several people had seen the trout in this well. Although healing was associated with a number of Wicklow holy wells, the name of only one well indicates the cure it was believed to possess, i.e. Tobersool *(Tobar na Súl)*, 'the eye well' (W.86). Nineteen of the holy wells listed below were known only as 'the holy well' or 'the blessed well'.[14] These would appear to be wells which have been neglected and almost forgotten in local tradition. In addition one well was recorded only as 'a neglected well'.[15]

Situation

Forty per cent of the wells are located near church property. Fraughan's Well, Trooperstown (W.23), is situated in a field called the 'Church Field' beside a Mass rock dating, it is said, from the penal times. A number of the wells are located in graveyards, others are near the ruins of churches or monasteries – or where these were said to exist formerly. Of the three wells in the Arklow Rock area of Arklow, one is situated near the ruins of an old church, another is near an old graveyard, while the third is located at the edge of a path known locally as a mass-path.[16] Some wells were near a *rath* or *dún*. The holy well dedicated to St Nicholas in the townland of Tornant (W.80) is situated near such an earthwork. This *dún* figures prominently in the origin legend associated with the well. Tradition says that the well was dug by local people and blessed by St Nicholas who needed water to baptise the inhabitants of the *dún*.

Cures

Cures were sought at holy wells. Some wells were believed to contain a cure for a variety of ailments; a cure for a specific ailment was associated with others. Ailments cured at county Wicklow's holy wells were said to include sore eyes, vomiting, colds, warts, skin diseases, deafness and lameness. The person seeking a cure went to the well, prayed, drank some of the water or bathed the afflicted area as appropriate. A cure for sore eyes was associated with St Kevin's Well, Ballinastoe (W.17); the patient had to visit the well at 9 a.m. on nine consecutive mornings and bathe his eyes. According to tradition St Brigid's Well, Ballinteskin (W.55) had a cure for vomiting provided you followed the procedure carefully; the water had to be collected, in a bottle, against the stream at a certain point. At Tobernacargy *(Tobar na Carraige)* (W.92) water taken with the stream was said to have cured one complaint while water taken against the stream cured a different complaint. In many places it was common for the person who visited the well to bring home a bottle of the well water – this could then be used by those who were unable to travel to the well, or put in holy water fonts. A report from Lady's Well, Arklow (W.3), states:

> This custom is still carried on for crowds of children and old people go out and say the rosary and tie pieces of ribbon on the tree and bring home [a] bottle of the water which is believed to be a cure for various ailments.[17]

People also visited the well as a preventative measure; they drank the water and prayed to be spared from illness during the coming year. In a time of high infant and childhood mortality parents brought their children to the holy well to prevent illness and to pray for health. Lord Walter Fitzgerald wrote of the practice of dipping children at St Nicholas' Well, Dunlavin (W.80):

> Father Shearman, C.C. of Dunlavin, in 1860 has left it on record that a curious custom was formerly prevalent at this well about St John the Baptist's Day (24th June), which was that of dipping children, Protestants and Catholics alike, in the water from the well to ensure a healthy growth.[18]

Water from a holy well was used in the prevention of accidents, as at St Patrick's Well, Tinahely (W.30), where a young boy described the procedure followed by local quarrymen. The boy, watching the men working in the quarry, was asked by one of them to fetch a bottle of water from the holy well. When he returned the water was poured into the blasting hole to ensure safety.

In addition to their curative properties certain holy wells were said to have special characteristics which indicated their holy or unusual qualities. It was said of St Laurence O'Toole's Well in the townland of Brittas (W.91) that the water was so cold in summer that it would cause toothache but very hot in winter. A similar claim was made for the water of the holy well in the townland of Mullinaveigue (W.19). St Patrick's Well, Arklow Rock (W.5), was believed to have sprung up on the point where St Patrick first set foot on the shore but despite its proximity to the sea the water of the well was always fresh.

Prayer

Prayer was important in the ritual of the well and the number and type of prayers to be said by those seeking cures were laid down by tradition as was the number of visits which the sufferer had to make in order to be cured. At St Boden's Well, Lacken (W.73):

> The acts of devotion or 'Rounds' according to the best authority were: (a) A visit to the well on each of three days. (b) On each day the patient walked round the well three times; at the end of each journey he (or she) knelt down and recited seven Our Fathers and seven Hail Marys, after which recitation the affected part was bathed in the water. (A separate part of the well was used for bathing purposes, as the water was also drunk.) The patient began the Rounds facing the North, and proceeding from left to right, completed each round of the well.[19]

Although prayer was undoubtedly an important aspect of visits to holy wells the accounts written by schoolchildren in 1937/8 – the main source used in this survey – pay very little attention to the devotional aspect even though information about the prayers said was specifically requested in the booklet sent to the schools.[20] There are many possible explanations. Perhaps on their visits to holy wells the children paid little attention to the silent prayers of the adults, becoming involved only in those instances in which the prayers were recited aloud – for example, the rosary at Lady's Well, Arklow (W.3), and Lady Well, Ballymoney (W.27), and the Litany of the Blessed Virgin at Lady Well, Ballymoney. It is also likely that the legends associated with the wells, the use of the water and the leaving of offerings held much greater appeal and attraction for children of this age than did the prayers. The importance of some form of religious observance of the well is recognised in an account written by a Roundwood child:

> There is another holy well in Mr John Lowe's field and it is unlucky to pass it by without making the Sign of the Cross because people who passed it by without taking any notice of it fell into some sickness, or had bad crops, or lost some of their stock.[21]

Offerings

Those who sought cures or who prayed for other intentions usually left offerings at the wells. Sometimes the piece of cloth used to bathe the eyes or hands was left, as at St Kevin's Well, Ballinastoe (W.17). St Kevin's Well, Glasnamullen (W.18), was said to have a cure for sore eyes:

> Every morning they used to go and bathe their eyes and the people that got cured tied the rag they bathed their eyes with on a little hawthorn that is growing beside it.[22]

The offering could also be a piece torn from the supplicant's garment. These rags were left not just in thanksgiving but were also believed to be of importance to the cure itself as it was believed that the patient improved according as the offering of cloth decayed. Other small objects such as medals, crosses, rosary beads, religious statues, scapulars, holy water fonts and holy pictures were left as offerings at wells. It was not necessary that these should be of religious significance; they could be small personal items such as hair-pins.

Cloth offerings were tied to the tree or bush at the well. Small religious or personal offerings could also be tied to the tree or bush, left by the well, thrown into the well itself or left in wall crevices. One informant recalled seeing crutches, walking sticks and pieces of cloth at St Nicholas' Well, Tornant Lower (W.80), in the 1880s. In the 1930s a Dunlavin schoolboy reported that there were rosary beads, crosses and statues at the well and that initials were carved on the sycamore tree nearby. It was considered unlucky to remove offerings from the wells. The building of a wall around St Boden's Well, Lacken (W.73), was not welcomed by local people but they particularly resented the fact that the two men who built the wall buried the crutches and other offerings which had been left there.

Trees

Cloths or rags left at holy wells were invariably tied to a bush or a tree close by. Reference to a specific tree or bush is found in 44 per cent of the Wicklow holy wells. Hawthorns or whitethorns are mentioned most frequently but ash, elder and sycamore also feature. While informants did not use the term 'sacred' it is obvious nonetheless from belief statements and legends that these trees or bushes 'were treated with a certain reverence which, normally, protected them from wilful damage' and so may be described as 'sacred'.[23] Near St Patrick's Well in the townland of Toberpatrick (W.32) there was a thorn-bush. Liam Price recounts the tradition of funerals pausing at this bush which was known locally as 'the corpse bush' and which was blown down early in 1945.

Patterns

Formerly patterns – *patrúin* – were held at 24 per cent of the Wicklow holy wells on the feast-day of the patron saint of the well. Some had already been discontinued when the Ordnance Surveyors toured the county in the 1830s. Most were held between June and September when the weather was warm and the days were long. One exception was the pattern at St Martin's Well (W.68) which was held on St Martin's Day, 11 November. The pattern here continued until the mid-nineteenth century. The feast of St Nicholas of Myra is on 6 December but the 'inclemency of the weather did not answer for the sports and the immersion of the children ...,' and so the pattern at Dunlavin (W.80) was held on 24-26 June.[24]

Although primarily a religious occasion the social aspect of the pattern day was pronounced. Music, singing and dancing were enjoyed and food and drink were consumed, leading at times to drunkenness and faction-fighting. The catholic church objected to what it considered abuses of the pattern occasion and in many instances put an end to the pattern itself. The parish priest, the Rev. John Hyland, terminated the three-day pattern at St Nicholas' Well (W.80) some time after 1827 because of drunkenness and serious faction-fighting. That the Glendalough pattern was more than a religious occasion can be seen from the following account by Sir William Wilde:

> Dancing, drinking, thimble-rigging, prick-o'-the-loop, and other amusements, even while the bare-headed venerable pilgrims, and bare-kneed voteens were going their prescribed rounds, continued. Towards evening the fun became 'fast and furious'; the pilgrimages ceased, the dancing was arrested, the pipers and fiddlers escaped to places of security, the keepers of tents and booths looked to their gear – the crowd thickened, the brandishing of sticks, the 'hoshings' and 'wheelings,' and 'hieings' for their respective parties showed that the faction fight was about

> to commence among the tombstones and monuments, and that all religious observances, and even refreshments, were at an end. Police and Magistrates were often required. What a change has taken place during the last twenty years! ... The Patron Saint's day at Glendalough on 3rd June is no longer celebrated.[25]

The pattern at St Colmcille's Well, Slieveroe (W.35), ended in 1833 while those held at Lady's Well, Glenealy (W.41) and St Kevin's Well, Dunganstown East (W.10), ceased near the end of the eighteenth century. The pattern at Trinity Well near Ashford (W.47) appears to have been one of the last to survive in the county. Two accounts from the Schools' Manuscript Collection speak of this. One reports that the pattern had ceased five or six years previously, while the other says that it was still being held. Both accounts emphasise the importance of dancing, singing and music during the pattern.

Holy well legends

Although some legends are confined to a certain well, most are common to wells all over the country. Caoimhín Ó Danachair divides these legends into seven types: (a) origin legends, (b) the preservation of the well, (c) respect for the ritual, (d) signs presaging future events, (e) wonders wrought at well, (f) supernatural phenomena and (g) treasure hidden at well.[26] This classification system is used below. There are no examples of legends dealing with signs of future events in the source material used in this study.

Origin legends

The origin stories relate either to the first appearance of the well or explain how an ordinary well became holy. St Patrick's Well, Arklow Rock (W.5), is said to have sprung up when the saint and his followers were thirsty. According to the legend, when St Patrick was returning to Ireland as a bishop they ran out of water on the long sea voyage; where St Patrick set foot on the shore water sprang up. Glasnamullen well (W.18) was said to have been made by St Kevin for the purpose of refreshing himself on his journey from the seven churches to Kevin's Port near Dublin. Another well in the same area (W.19) was said to have been made by St Kevin when he was carrying stones on his back from Enniskerry to Glendalough. He got thirsty, put down the stones and a well sprang up. St Columcille's Well (W.35) appeared when the saint needed some water to cure a man:

> The Saint, when in the locality, was asked by a man, who was afflicted by a terrible disease on the head and face, to cure him.

> He was blessed by the holy man and told to wash himself in water, but none was convenient; whereupon the saint took a stone from the ground and disclosed a gushing spring. The man bathed his head in the marvellous spring and was immediately cured.[27]

Sometimes an existing well was sanctified because of its association with a saint or holy person. Saint Kevin is refuted to have blessed the well of which he is patron in Dunganstown East (W.10) while journeying to Glendalough. St Kevin's Keeve in the parish of Derrylossary (W.20) was blessed by St Kevin who was said to have left a cure there. Tradition tells us that a well in Ballinastoe became known as St Kevin's Well (W.17) after the saint drank from it and blessed it.

Similar stories are told of St Patrick. In the townland of Toberpatrick there is a well called Patrick's Well (W.32) which St Patrick is said to have blessed when he stopped here for a drink on his way through county Wicklow. St Patrick is also reported to have blessed the holy well in the townland of Monaglogh (W.13) and St Patrick's Well in Tinahely (W.30). The well in Doody's Bottoms (W.79) was believed to have been blessed before St Patrick came to Ireland to preach Christianity. Legend says that St Patrick on arriving in Donard found that St Palladius had already baptised many of the inhabitants and so he continued his journey to Donaghmore where he built a church. On his way to Donaghmore he became very thirsty and stopped for a drink at Tobernacargy in the townland of Kelshamore (W.92). St Nicholas' Well in Tornant (W.80) was said to have been used as a baptismal well by St Nicholas.

According to legend the well in Bolinass (W.45) became known as St John's Well when it was blessed by a local priest, Father John Hickey. St Boden's Well in Lacken townland (W.73) was also known as Father Germaine's Well. Lord Walter Fitzgerald recorded a story of how the well became known by the priest's name from a local man, Pat Carr. While the parish priest was out driving on a calm day a gust of wind suddenly blew his hat off. He followed his hat until it stopped at St Boden's Well. Before leaving he blessed the well and it bore his name from that day on. This well was in the area flooded when the Electricity Supply Board formed an artificial lake by damming the river Liffey at Poulaphouca. In 1939 when Seán Ó Súilleabháin and others surveyed the Lacken area they were told that Father Germaine had blessed all the holy wells in the parish.[28] More recently St Boden's well, Lacken became the focus of national attention during the summer of 1978 when, because of the extremely dry weather, the level of water in the reservoir dropped and the well appeared once more. Traditional practices were revived and thousands of people visited the well before it was reclaimed by the waters of Poulaphouca Lake.[29]

On the Green Hill Road overlooking Wicklow town there is a holy well (W.15). An origin legend associated with it tells how St Patrick triumphed over pagan magic and christianised the well. When St Patrick visited Wicklow he heard that a woman sat by this well and offered a magic cup to those who requested a drink of water; whoever drank from this magic cup died immediately. St Patrick went to the well and asked for a drink but, when offered the cup, smashed it against a stone. The well has been known as St Patrick's Well ever since.

Eugene O'Curry, writing from Rathdrum on 24 January 1839, gave an account – including a local legend – of Tubber na Buadh in the parish of Drumkay (W.7). The legend told of a great battle between the Irish and the Danes. The hand of the Irish champion became so swollen from fighting that he could not take it out of the hilt of his sword. An old man showed him the way to the well, and he recovered after bathing his hand in the water. The well had never been seen before.

The preservation of the well

The holy well had to be treated with respect. Many legends are told of people who tried to pollute or defile a well and of what happened to them as a result. Some people interfered with the well through ignorance and these were not punished as severely as those who interfered with it through malice. The people of Rathdangan tried to pipe the water of *Tobar Eoin* (W.104) but this was unsuccessful; each morning the water would be red. Others tried to use the water for washing clothes but it turned the clothes 'iron mouldy'.[30]

Usually it was the landowners who interfered with the well, either because they did not approve of the 'superstitious' practice of visiting holy wells or because they did not like people entering their land and leaving offerings on the bushes at the wells. The names of landlords who interfered with the wells live on in legends. Edward O'Toole remarks about St Columcille's Well, Slieveroe (W.35), that there was doubt about its exact location. Each night some local landowners filled in the well but by morning the well was clean again. On one occasion they were determined that the well should remain filled in for at least one night, in order to disprove suggestions that the well was being cleared miraculously, and sat by the well throughout the night. A weird sound was heard coming from nearby Kyle Hill at midnight and the men looked in that direction. When they looked back the well was cleared.

> On another occasion, to show his contempt for the popular belief that some evil would befall any person who dared to interfere

> with a bush which grew over the well, he started to saw the bush down. Three versions of the result of his labour are given. One is that the bush fell on him; another is that the saw rebounded on him, as it had failed to penetrate the bark; and the third, that he heard a strange voice and looked around. All agree to the result – viz., that his head remained permanently turned sideways.[31]

O'Toole also recounted how soldiers tried to desecrate *Tobar Eoin* (W.104) by hanging a follower of Michael Dwyer's – John Moore – from the tree. The branch of the tree from which he was hanged rotted away. Although no-one would interfere with the tree while it was still standing, some of it was used as firewood when it fell. The wood exploded as soon as it was put on the fire. A similar story is told about the tree at Tubber Naghan Well in the townland of Ballyraheen in the parish of Mullinacuff (W.67). Here a local person saw that a branch from the tree had fallen and brought it home to burn. The pot of water over the fire would not boil until the branch was taken off the fire. A holy well may not tolerate even well-meaning interference as was the case at Lacken (W.73). The local priest decided to build a wall around the well having separate areas for drinking and bathing, but this was not a success as the water sprang up outside the wall.

Respect for the ritual

The ritual of the well had to be respected. The water of the holy well is blessed and so should not be used for any profane purpose. One of the most common legends deals with the belief that water from a holy well should not be used for household purposes and often incorporates a reference to the sacred fish which were said to inhabit certain holy wells. Indeed it is implied in the version of this legend given below, told of Tubber na Christamaun (W.99), that the family had used the water from the holy well, without incident, for household purposes on previous occasions. It was the presence of the two tiny fish in the water, in this instance, that prevented it from boiling:

> Some years ago, people by the name of Fenton, lived near the place, and they used the water of the well for churning and making tea. It happened one day, that Fentons were going to churn, and Mrs Fenton sent the workman to the well for two buckets of the nice, clean water. He brought the water home, and Mrs Fenton put it on the fire to boil, for the churning. They were waiting for the water to boil, and after half an hour they thought it should be boiled. The workman put on more sticks, and still they could not boil it. Mrs Fenton took off the lid, to look was it

> boiling, and it was as cold as when she put it into the kettle. She took off the kettle and put the water back in the bucket, and she saw two tiny fish in the water. They took back the water and the fish and put it in the well, and they never took any water out of the well after that. And anyone who took water out of Tobar Christamaun could not boil it.[32]

A Blessington schoolgirl recorded a version of this legend in 1938 told about St Boden's Well, Lacken (W.73). A woman from Lacken took some water from the well one day when her pump ran dry but although it was on the fire for two hours it would not boil. When she looked in the pot she found a fish. It was believed locally that the flooding of the Lacken valley would result in the sacred fish escaping from St Boden's Well and the well losing its powers.

It was forbidden to remove offerings from the wells. A story told about St Boden's Well illustrates this. A man who visited the well took a fancy to a nice walking stick which had been left as an offering at the well. He took the stick with him when he left but the illness which had crippled the former owner of the stick was transferred to him until he returned the stick and made three visits to the well. The informant adds: 'It is well known that it is neither safe nor lucky to remove anything that has been deposited at a blessed well.'[33]

Wonders wrought at wells

Although many informants state that people have been cured at the wells, and although many wells are said to have a cure in them for certain diseases, not many legends have been collected in county Wicklow which tell of immediate curing at the well. One legend tells how a man who wanted to destroy Tobersool, Knockenreagh (W.86), came to use the waters of the well as a cure himself. The farmer who owned the surrounding land got fed up with crowds of people breaking down his fences and tried to close up the well but his attempts were unsuccessful as the people re-opened it each night. Shortly afterwards the farmer suffered from sore eyes and was cured by the water from the well. He never interfered with Tobersool again.

Supernatural phenomena

Supernatural phenomena are mentioned in connection with only three wells in the county. They are Fraughan's Well, Trooperstown (W.23), St Laurence O'Toole's Well, Brittas (W.91), and St Kevin's Well, Ballinastoe (W.17). A report from Trooperstown N.S. says that the Blessed Virgin was once seen over the well. Spirits were seen on the road over St Laurence O'Toole's Well and a blue light was said to pass right over the well usually at eleven o'clock at night during February and March. According to local tradition people passing by St Kevin's Well, Ballinastoe, late at night heard footsteps following them for a certain distance and then turning back.

Treasure hidden at the well

This particular legend type was not mentioned in the questionnaire or in the booklet used by the schools in 1937/8 and this may account to some extent for the lack of references to treasure hidden at the wells. Priest's vestments were said to be hidden near Fraughan's Well, Trooperstown (W.23), in a cave under a thorn bush in the field.

Treasure was also said to be hidden near St Boden's Well, Kylebeg (W.72), in an underground passage which connected the well to either the hill to the north or the church ruins to the east. Stolen golden plates are supposed to be buried near the holy well on Church Mountain (W.78).

Conclusion

It is probable that in writing their school essays in the 1930s the children, whose information is used extensively in this study, were not primarily concerned with recording all the information on county Wicklow's holy wells which was available to them from the oral traditions of their parents and grandparents. In reading through the Schools' Manuscripts it is obvious that much thought was also given to the length and form of the essay, to sentence construction, to spelling and to handwriting. Nevertheless these essays contain valuable information, expressed concisely, on many wells throughout the county.

The legends told about the holy wells of county Wicklow in oral tradition are representative of those associated with holy wells throughout Ireland. It is difficult to assess the belief element in these legends as most are told in an abbreviated form having been collected by schoolchildren and summarised by them to fit neatly into an essay frame. Whether or not the legends were believed by the adults who told them or the children who wrote them down, they, like the other practices and rituals at the wells, undoubtedly reflect belief in and reverence for the holy wells.

The holy wells

The 106 holy wells listed below are those which have been included in this survey. They are arranged in alphabetical order of the baronies in which they are situated. Within each barony the wells are arranged in alphabetical order of the parishes and within each parish in alphabetical order of the townlands. The sheet reference number to the 6-inch

Ordnance Survey maps – for the townland in which each well is located – is given. Where the well is marked on the 1838 edition of the 6-inch maps this is indicated by an asterisk after the sheet number. References are given for the Ordnance Survey and IFC manuscript sources used in the preparation of this study together with a summary of their content.

Barony of Arklow

1. St Mary's Well; Tld. Ballyrooaun; Par. Arklow; O.S.6" 45
   IFC S 927: 46
   A small well on Ballyrooaun Farm, one mile west of Arklow is called St Mary's Well.
2. St Brigid's Well; Tld. Kish; Par. Arklow; O.S.6" 45
   IFC S 924: 45-46
3. Lady's Well; Tld. Rock Big; Par. Arklow; O.S.6" 45*
   O.S. letters, p. 423; IFC S 923: 143; IFC S 923: 201; IFC S 923: 206; IFC S 924: 42
   Our Lady's Well, Lady Well or Lady's Well is situated south of Arklow town near the ruins of Chapelhogan. In the olden times the people used to go out and whitewash all round the well for the Priest to go out and say the Rosary and they would tie pieces of ribbon on the tree and bring home a bottle of the water which is believed to be a cure for various ailments.
   (IFC S 923: 201)
4. St Diver's Well; Tld. Rock Big; Par. Arklow; O.S.6" 45
   O.S. letters, p. 423; *O.S. namebooks*, i, Arklow and Kilahurler parishes, p. 28; IFC S 924: 45
   Different versions of the name of the well are given. Although it had been visited in former times because of its curative properties, the Ordnance Surveyors reported that it had not been frequented for some time.
5. St Patrick's Well; Tld. Rock Big; Par. Arklow; O.S.6" 45*
   IFC S 923: 185-186; IFC S 924: 43
   The origin of the well is explained in a legend about St Patrick – where St Patrick stepped ashore a well sprang up. One account said that the well was frequented by local people while the other reported that although the well was well-known locally no visits were made. Water reported to be always fresh although it mixed with the sea-water.
6. Bride's Well; Tld. Ballintemple; Par. Ballintemple; O.S.6" 45*
   O.S. letters, p. 398; M. Ronan, 'The ancient churches of the deanery of Arklow, Co. Wicklow' in *R.S.A.I.Jn.*, LVII (1927), pp 107-8 note 20
   Located near churchyard, site of ancient church and fort.
7. Tubber na Buadh; Tld. Newtown; Par. Drumkay; O.S.6" 31
   O.S. letters, pp 362-4
8. Tubberaville; Tld. Tubberaviller; Par. Drumkay; O.S.6" 31*
   O.S. letters, p. 364; *O.S. namebooks*, iii, Kilpoole and Drumkay parishes, p. 42; IFC 468: 78
   Already neglected in the 1830s.
9. Holy Well; Tld. Cunniamstown; Par. Dunganstown; O.S.6" 30
   O.S. letters, p. 389
10. St Kevin's Well; Tld. Dunganstown East; Par. Dunganstown; O.S.6" 31*
    O.S. letters, p. 380; IFC 468: 77
    There is a holy well called after St Kevin in this townland, at which

> patterns were held 24th June till 1798. Children only are brought to be washed on that day. (*O.S. Letters*, p. 389)

Information re name, location, cures, tree, offerings. There had been a small fort nearby. The well had formerly been visited 'on every May morning'.

11. A neglected well; Tld. Kilnamanagh; Par. Dunganstown; O.S.6" 30
O.S. letters, p. 391; M. Ronan, 'The ancient churches of the deanery of Wicklow' in *R.S.A.I. Jn.*, lviii (1928), p. 150
12. Tobergall; Tld. Johnstown Hill; Par. Inch; O.S.6" 45*
IFC S 923: 36
13. St Patrick's Well; Tld. Monaglogh; Par. Kilahurler; O.S.6" 40
IFC S 923: 36
Well in the townland of Monaglogh said to have been blessed by St Patrick. Not visited by many but when visited piece of cloth hung on thorn tree over the well.
14. St Patrick's Well; Tld. Corporation Lands; Par. Kilpoole; O.S.6" 25
IFC S 926: 115
Story about St Patrick overcoming pagan magic at the well.
15. Bride's Well; Tld. Dunbur Head; Par. Kilpoole; O.S.6" 25*
O.S. letters, p. 358; *O.S. namebooks*, iii, Kilpoole and Drumkay parishes, p. 24
16. St Paul's Well; Tld. Kilpoole Lower; Par. Kilpoole; O.S.6" 31*
O.S. letters, p. 359; Ronan, 'Deanery of Wicklow', p. 147
Frequented up to 1789. Two raths were nearby.

Barony of Ballinacor North

17. St Kevin's Well; Tld. Ballinastoe; Par. Calary; O.S.6" 6,7,11,12
IFC S 918: 24; IFC S 918: 34; IFC 946: 61-2
Well, believed to be on the site of an old graveyard, blessed by St Kevin. Cure for sore eyes.
18. St Kevin's Well; Tld. Glasnamullen; Par. Calary; O.S.6" 12*
O.S. Letters, p. 202; IFC S 912: 163; IFC S 917: 245; J.D. Scott, *The Stones of Bray* (Dublin, 1913), pp 189-190
Well blessed by St Kevin and situated near the remains of an old church. The water was taken for its curative properties but not used for household purposes. Those who visited the well left offerings on the hawthorn bush beside the well. Large white stones surrounded the well.
19. St Kevin's Well; Tld. Mullinaveige; Par. Calary; O.S.6" 12,18
IFC S 917: 247; IFC S 918: 34; IFC S 918: 35
Well made by St Kevin. The well had a cure for vomiting in it. Story about the desecration of the well. The water was warm in winter and cold in summer.
20. St Kevin's Keeve; Tld. Brockagh; Par. Derrylossary; O.S.6" 23*
IFC S 917: 327; IFC S 1127: 42-3
A well

> which St Kevin blessed and in which he left a cure. Long ago on the 3rd of June every year people used to pray at this well and to be cured of disease. When leaving the well they used to tie a piece of cloth on a tree over the well. This tree went by the name of St Kevin's tree. (IFC S 917: 327)

Legend about a man who tried to cut down this tree.

21. St Kevin's Well; Tld. Derrybawn; Par. Derrylossary; O.S.6" 23*
O.S. namebooks, ii, Derrylossary parish, p. 50
Water always crystal clear.

22. Holy Well; Tld. Roundwood; Par. Derrylossary; O.S.6" 18
IFC S 918: 34; IFC S 918: 35
It was unlucky to pass it without making the Sign of the Cross.
23. Fraughan's Well; Tld. Trooperstown; Par. Knockrath; O.S.6" 18
IFC S 198: 155; IFC S 1127: 48
Holy well near where the priest said Mass in the penal days. Cures for sores and pains. Unlucky to interfere with holy well. The Blessed Virgin said to have been seen at the well.

Barony of Ballinacor South

24. Holy Well; Tld. Ballinacor; Par. Ballinacor; O.S.6" 29
IFC S 921: 24
> People came and danced around it and they put images around it. They bring sick people and they are supposed to heal them.

Water from the well used for household purposes.
25. Holy Well; Tld. Bahana (King); Par. Ballykine; O.S.6" 35
IFC S 921: 24-25
Said to have curative properties.
26. Loggies Well; Tld. Ballinatone; Par. Ballykine; O.S.6" 29, 35
IFC S 921: 25
Well named after man who found it. Not visited very often.
27. Lady Well; Tld. Ballymoney; Par. Ballykine; O.S.6" 34*
O.S. letters, p. 151; *O.S. namebooks,* i, Ballykine parish, p. 42; IFC S 918: 168; IFC S 918: 174; IFC 468: 61-2
Cures recorded there. A pattern was held at the well on 15 August. Water taken home. Small grotto at the well, flowers were placed there.
28. Holy Well; Tld. Threewells; Par. Ballykine; O.S.6" 34
IFC 1082: 229
29. Blessed Well; Tld. Ballymaghroe; Par. Hackettstown/Moyne; O.S.6" 33
IFC S 920: 91; IFC S 920: 97
30. St Patrick's Well; Tld. Tinahely; Par. Kilcommon; O.S.6" 38
IFC S 920: 6
It was believed that St Patrick drank from this well. The informant gives an account of the water from the well being used to prevent accidents.
31. St Bride's Well; Tld. Roddenagh; Par. Kilpipe; O.S.6" 34
IFC 1135: 96-7
> 'Rounds' were paid up to 50 years ago for cures, chiefly of toothache. Rags used to be tied to a *sceach* at the well ... The place is now planted over by the Forestry Dept. and the existence of the well mostly forgotten.

32. *Tobar Pádruig*; Tld. Toberpatrick; Par. Kilpipe; O.S.6" 44*
O.S. letters, pp 143-4; IFC S 920: 3; IFC S 922: 137-8; Price, *Placenames*, ii , p. 79
This well was blessed by St Patrick when he was travelling through county Wicklow. A woman with sore eyes who drank from the well was cured. No special visiting days. Liam Price gives an account of funerals stopping at a bush near the well.
33. St Gobbin's Well; Tld. Ballygobban; Par. Moyne; O.S.6" 28, 29, 33, 34
IFC S 920: 91; IFC S 920: 97; IFC S 921: 178; IFC 1135: 96-7
Blessed by St Gobbin.
> Even in the driest weather does not dry up and the water is always cool. I

> have heard it said that a drink of the water would keep off the hunger for a whole day. (IFC S 921: 178)

34. Holy Well; Tld. Coolballintaggart; Par. Moyne; O.S.6" 34; IFC S 920: 383
35. St Colmcille's Well; Tld. Slieveroe; Par. Moyne; O.S.6" 33*
    O.S. Letters, pp 149-150, *O.S. namebooks*, iii, Moyne parish, p. 29; IFC S 920: 92; IFC S 920: 382; IFC S 920: 383; IFC S 920: 384; L. Price, *Placenames*, ii, p. 88; E. O'Toole, 'The Holy Wells of County Carlow' in *Béaloideas*, iv (1933-34), pp 22-3; M. Comerford, *Collections relating to the dioceses of Kildare and Leighlin*, iii (Dublin, n.d.), p. 239
    There were many cures at the well and offerings were left there. Some people tried to close the well but it always reopened of its own accord. A pattern was held at the well in early June up to the early nineteenth century.

Barony of Newcastle

36. Holy Well; Tld. Carriggower; Par. Calary; O.S.6" 12
    J. Fisher, Mountmellick, 17.1.1977
37. Holy Well; Tld. Knockatemple; Par. Calary; O.S.6" 18
    IFC S 918: 34; IFC S 918: 35
    Prohibition against using the water for household purposes. There was a fish in the well which evaded all attempts to capture it.
38. St Kevin's Well; Tld. Moneystown; Par. Derrylossary; O.S.6" 24
    IFC S 918: 71
    It was said that St Kevin drank from this well.
39. St Lewis' Well; Tld. Moneystown; Par. Derrylossary; O.S.6" 24
    IFC S 918: 71
    > There is also a special cure attached to the well ... This well was supposed to have moved three times since its origin.
40. Coffey's Well; Tld. Ballymacsimon; Par. Glenealy; O.S.6" 24,25
    O.S. letters, p. 368, Ronan, 'Deanery of Wicklow', p. 138
    > It was still visited in the 1830s by those seeking cures for various ailments 'as the quantity of rags on the thorn over it testifies.' (*O.S. Letters*, p. 368)

    A pattern was held there in September.
41. Lady's Well; Tld. Ballymanus Upper; Par. Glenealy; O.S.6" 24*
    O.S. letters, p. 367; S. Burke, Glenealy, 1976
    A pattern was held on 15 August prior to 1798. Cure for colds in the water. The water was never used for household purposes. Hawthorn bush at the well.
42. Brideog's Well; Tld. Downs; Par. Kilcoole; O.S.6" 13
    O.S. letters, p. 191; J. Masterson, 'A Garden and A Grave' – Kilquade (Wicklow 1952), p. 40
    Patterns used to be held here.
43. God's Well; Tld. Holywell; Par. Kilcoole; O.S.6" 13
    O.S. letters, p. 193; *O.S. namebooks*, ii, Kilcoole parish, p. 17
    > At the holy well near Killickabawn, they are in the habit of performing devotions still, but those only troubled with the Shake (ague) are known to frequent it. There are three wells here triangularly situated, that at the south east angle only being considered blessed, and generally called God's Well. (*O.S. letters*, p. 193)

    IFC S 928: 62
    > Anybody threatened with Shake or Ague went there and performed devotions. When they left they usually left some offering at the well.
44. St Patrick's Well; Tld. Kilquade; Par. Kilcoole; O.S.6" 13*

O.S. letters, p. 191; J. Masterson, *A Garden*, p. 52

> They call the quicken tree well, from a quicken tree of great size which grew over it, but which fell from decay about 30 years ago.
> (*O.S. letters*, p. 191)

45. St John's Well; Tld. Bolinass; Par. Killiskey; O.S.6" 18
IFC S 927: 133
46. Tubber Patrick; Tld. Kiltimon; Par. Killiskey; O.S.6" 19*
O.S. letters, p. 236
47. Trinity Well; Tld. Newtownboswell; Par. Killiskey; O.S.6" 19*
O.S. letters, p. 231; IFC S 913: 76; IFC S 918: 23; IFC S 927: 36-7; IFC S 927: 96; IFC S 927: 132-3; C. Byrne, Glenealy, 1976; J. Fisher, Mountmellick, 1977.
Accounts of cures at the well. Pattern held on Trinity Sunday – dancing and singing. Many offerings at the well.
48. St Catherine's Well; Tld. Killadreenan; Par. Newcastle Lower; O.S.6" 19*
O.S. letters, p. 220; IFC S 927: 163-4; IFC S 927: 179-81; IFC S 927: 248; IFC S 928: 61
A whitethorn had marked the well but was cut down before the 1930s. The well had been frequented for the cure of many ailments, and offerings were left at the well. No memory of any pattern. An attempt was made to close the well with tragic consequences.
49. St Brigid's Well; Tld. Kilmacullagh; Par. Newcastle Upper; O.S.6" 13
IFC S 927: 248; IFC S 928: 62
Was visited at one time for cures. Water used for household purposes.
50. St Anne's Well; Tld. Kilmurray; Par. Newcastle Upper; O.S.6" 12,13,18
IFC S 927: 61-2; IFC S 927: 227; IFC S 928: 248; Ronan, 'Deanery of Wicklow', p. 150.
This well is called St Kevin's Well in one Schools' Manuscript account and Lady's Well in *R.S.A.I. Jn.* It was at one time frequented for cures. Offerings were left. Used in the 1930s for household purposes.
51. Holy Well; Tld. Ballybeg; Par. Rathnew; O.S.6" 25
IFC S 927: 36
Was frequented at one time but used in the 1930s for household purposes.
52. Tubber Brighde; Tld. Ballymacahara; Par. Rathnew; O.S.6" 25
O.S. letters, pp 247-8; Ronan, 'Deanery of Wicklow', p. 138.
Frequented for cures. Two ash trees over the well. Offerings left at the well.
53. Hemps Well; Tld. Friarshill; Par. Rathnew; O.S.6" 25
O.S. letters, pp 333-4
> . . . the water of which is occasionally used both by Protestants and Roman Catholics, as a cure for the bowel complaint.

Barony of Rathdown

54. Patrick's Well; Tld. Ballynamuddagh; Par. Bray; O.S.6" 8
O.S. letters, p. 68
Called the Church Well by some. Visited occasionally.
There is a faint tradition that St Patrick after making this well found that the spray from the sea sometimes had reached up to it, whereupon he opened another well a short distance to the west of the church.
55. St Brigid's Well; Tld. Ballinteskin; Par. Calary; O.S.6" 7
IFC 907: 154-7
> the water of it collected in a bottle by holding the bottle against the stream at a point where the water trickles into a rivulet is believed to be a cure for vomiting.

56. Bride's Well; Tld. Calary Lower; Par. Kilmacanoge; O.S.6" 7, 8, 12, 13
O.S. letters, p. 43; IFC 907: 151-3; IFC 907: 154-7
Patterns were held until near the end of the eighteenth century.

57. St Vallery's Well; Tld. Fassaroe; Par. Kilmacanoge; O.S.6" 7
O.S. letters, p. 55; IFC 468: 70; I. G. O'Malley, *The illustrated hand-book of Wicklow* (London, 1844), p. 25.
Frequented for cures. Offerings left at well.

58. St Croney's Well; Tld. Kilcroney; Par. Kilmacanoge; O.S.6" 7*
O.S. letters, p. 49; IFC S 913: 36; IFC 468: 69

59. Holy Well; Tld. Kilmacanoge; Par. Kilmacanoge; O.S.6" 7, 8
IFC 946: 57

> A holy well in the locality which was visited by the inhabitants until quite recently and kept neat and tidy by a local man who is now dead. The water of this well was taken for stomach troubles.

60. Holy Well; Tld. Annacrivey; Par. Powerscourt; O.S.6" 3, 7
O.S. letters, p. 12

> Up to a late period this well was much frequented by the devout, on the 25th March and 15th August, those meetings were not looked upon as regular patrons.

IFC 468: 68

> Occasionally visited, but no rag offerings are now to be seen. The old people remember seeing the bushes covered with such votive offerings.

61. The White Well; Tld. Ballylerane; Par. Powerscourt; O.S.6" 6, 7
IFC 468: 73
The water of the well had curative properties. Water collected using different methods to effect different cures. Not used for household purposes.

62. St Michael's Well; Tld. Cookstown; Par. Powerscourt; O.S.6" 7
IFC 468: 71
On May morning the water from this well was added to the domestic wells of the area.

63. Well of the Church; Tld. Killegar; Par. Powerscourt; O.S.6" 3*
O.S. letters, p. 5
Pattern said to have been held there formerly.
IFC 468: 72
As the late Father O'Dwyer got this well cleared out occasionally it got the name of Father O'Dwyer's Well.

64. Holy Well; Tld. Monastery; Par. Powerscourt; O.S.6" 3*
O.S. letters, pp 6-7

> An old well, now nearly choked up. The well some forty years ago, was frequented for the cure of headaches, &c.

IFC 468: 74

> It used to be visited seventy or eighty years ago for the cure of headaches. It is scarcely ever visited now.

65. *Tobar Melin*; Tld. Powerscourt Demesne; Par. Powerscourt; O.S.6" 7*
O.S. letters, p. 16

Barony of Shillelagh

66. Chapel Well; Tld. Killabegg; Par. Aghowle; O.S.6" 42
O.S. namebooks, i, Aghowle parish, p. 41; IFC S 918: 71

> There is a holy well in Aghowle in which is said to be a cure for many diseases. Some people still visit this well. There is a tree over it. IFC S 918: 71.

67. Tubber Naghan Well; Tld. Ballyraheen; Par. Mullinacuff; O.S.6" 43*
O.S. letters, p. 107; *O.S. namebooks*, iii, Mullinacuff parish, p. 38
Visited by people seeking cures. A pattern had been held up to 40 or 50 years before the Ordnance Survey.
IFC S 907: 159-160; IFC S 922: 131; IFC S 922: 137; IFC S 922: 138; IFC 468: 76-80
Well known as *Tobar na Gann* and also by some as St Brigid's Well. Water used for cures. Wood from the tree should not be used as firewood – story. Offerings left at well. Water brought home in bottles to those unable to visit well.

68. St Martin's Well; Tld. Cronelea; Par. Mullinacuff; O.S.6" 43*
O.S. letters, p. 108; *O.S. namebooks*, III, Mullinacuff parish, p. 45; IFC 683: 177-8; IFC 683: 186-7; E. O'Toole, 'The Holy Wells', pp 112-13; Price, *Placenames*, vi, pp 356-9
Patterns were held on 11 November up to the 1830s. Visits continued after the patterns ceased. Cures were sought and offerings left at the well. Water from well would not boil but it was much sought after for butter-making. Water taken home on St Martin's Day to drink that night.

Barony of Talbotstown Lower

69. *Tobar an Bhric*; Tld. Blessington; Par. Blessington; O.S.6" 5*
O.S. letters, p. 353; *O.S. namebooks*, i, Blessington parish, pp 27-8
Trout in well.

> The well is held in much veneration, few persons presuming to taste its water without putting a rag on the bush over it.
> (*O.S. namebooks,* i, Blessington parish, pp 27-8)

70. Scurlock's Holy Well; Tld. Crosscoolharbour; Par. Blessington; O.S.6" 5*
O.S. Letters, p. 353; *O.S. namebooks*, i, Blessington parish, pp 29-30
Visited on St John's Eve and from then until the pattern day on the first Sunday of August Cures sought and rags left on bush over well.
IFC S 913: 127; IFC S 913: 175; IFC S 913: 177; IFC S 913: 185
Cures sought at well; rags, crosses and medals left as offerings. One informant said that it was dedicated to the Blessed Virgin and that it was visited on May Day and during the month of May.

71. Holy Well; Tld. Ballyknockan; Par. Boystown; O.S.6" 10
IFC S 917: 22; IFC 654: 95
Small stone cross beside the well. Blessed by Fr. Rowan.

72. St Boden's Well; Tld. Kilbeg; Par. Boystown; O.S.6" 10*
Price, *Placenames*, iv, pp 239-40;
also called Mac's (blest) well after the man who owned the field.
IFC 468: 54-9
A comprehensive account of the practices and traditions associated with the well. Said to have underground connections with hill to the North or with church to the East – church valuables said to be buried there. Cures sought for all ailments particularly those of the head. Offerings left at well. Legends associated with well.

73. St Boden's Well; Tld. Lacken; Par. Boystown; O.S.6" 10*
IFC S 913: 131; IFC S 913: 138; IFC S 913: 175-6; IFC S 913: 177-8; IFC S 914: 331; IFC S 914: 538; IFC S 915: 185-6; IFC S 915: 188-9; IFC S 915: 190-91; IFC S 915: 192-3; IFC S 917: 24; IFC S 917: 29; IFC 468: 64-7; IFC 972: 543; Omurethi, 'Father Germaine's Well at Lackan, parish of Boystown (alias Baltyboys), in the county Wicklow' in *Kild. Arch. Soc., Jn.*, v (1906-1908), pp 203-4.
Origin legend of well. This well was frequented by people seeking cures and

offerings were left by supplicants. There was a lone whitethorn bush near the well. Prohibition against using the water from the well for household purposes. Two fish lived in the well and it was said that the fish would escape and the well would lose its power under Poulaphouca Lake.

74. St Michael's Well; Tld. Lacken; Par. Boystown; O.S.6" 10
IFC S 914: 285-286
Cures were sought for all kinds of diseases.

75. St Baoithen's Well; Tld. Burgage More; Par. Burgage; O.S.6" 5
O.S. namebooks, i, Burgage parish, p. 30; IFC S 917: 27; W. Fitzgerald, 'Burgage (formerly Donagh-emlagh), county Wicklow' in *Kild. Arch. Soc. Jn.*, vii (1912-1914), pp 416-18; W. Hawkes, 'Parish of Ballymore Eustace, 1791' in *Reportorium Novum*, ii (1958), p. 120
This well is called St Baoithen's Well in the *O.S. namebooks,* a 'holy well' in the Schools' Manuscript account and St Matthew's Well in the published accounts. It was frequented for cures.

76. St Mark's Well; Tld. Burgage More; Par. Burgage; O.S.6" 5*
O.S. letters, p. 316; *O.S. namebooks*, i, Burgage parish, pp 20, 30; IFC S 913: 175; IFC S 917: 26
There is some confusion about the name of this well in the Ordnance Survey material with St Mark's Well given on the map and recommended in the namebooks while St Baoithen's Well was given locally. In the Schools' Manuscript accounts the well is called St Mark's Well.

> It is said that it cures the toothache. People bathed in it up to fifty years ago. There are many relics in it like – a few medals, a piece of cloth, coins, etc. as a memory of some cure that the water had performed.
> (IFC S 913: 175)

77. Blessed Well; Tld. Lemonstown; Par. Crehelp; O.S.6" 9
IFC S 914: 331

78. Holy Well; Tld. Ballymooney; Par. Donard; O.S.6" 15*
O.S. letters, pp 324-5; IFC S 914: 6-7; IFC S 914: 251; IFC S 914: 299; IFC S 915: 5; IFC 973: 105-6; Price, *Placenames,* iv, pp 186-8
Well located near traces of foundation of a church on Church Mountain. The church was said to have been associated with St Palladius. A pattern was held here on 15 August

> At any time patients visit the holy well and when cured they leave souvenirs in acknowledgement. Many souvenirs were to be seen when I visited Church Mountain. (IFC S 914: 6-7)

Liam Price reports that the well was called St Gad's Well by some.

79. Holy Hill Well; Tld. Doody's Bottoms; Par. Donard; O.S.6" 15
O.S. letters, p. 326; IFC S 914: 2; IFC S 914: 558; IFC S 915: 188-9; IFC S 915: 192; W. Heighington, 'On Donard, county Wicklow' in *Kild. Arch. Soc. Jn.*, IX (1918-1921), pp 387-9
Story that St Palladius baptised hundreds of people there in one day. Pattern held on 15 August.

80. St Nicholas' Well; Tld. Tornant Lower; Par. Dunlavin; O.S.6" 5*
O.S. letters, p. 343; *O.S. namebooks*, ii, Dunlavin parish, p. 26
A pattern was held here on 24,25 and 26 June. It was stopped by the clergy because of serious faction fighting. Children were dipped in the water at this time. Offerings were left at the well.
IFC S 914: 78-80; IFC S 914: 80-83; IFC S 914: 83-4; IFC S 914: 109; IFC S 914: 112; IFC S 914: 115; IFC S 914: 167; IFC S 914: 173-4; IFC S 914: 331; IFC S 914:

539; IFC S 915: 182; IFC S 915: 190; IFC S 915: 194; IFC 946: 49-51; W. Fitzgerald, 'Dunlavin, Tornant, and Tober, county Wicklow' in *Kild. Arch. Soc. Jn.*, vii (1912-14), pp 229-30

The well was situated under a large sycamore tree. Origin legend. Stories of cures at well. Offerings were left at the well and those cured often carved their initials on the sycamore tree. The ordinary prayers were said – Lord's Prayer and Hail Mary. The water was never used for household purposes. Visiting days were 24 June and the Sundays before and after 29 June. Children were bathed in the well to ensure healthy growth.

81. Holy Well; Tld. Ballintober; Par. Hollywood; O.S.6" 9,10
Price, *Placenames,* iv, p. 209

> The well from which the townland gets its name is on a laneway on the west side of the road; it is said to have been a holy well.

82. St Kevin's Well; Tld. Hollywood; Par. Hollywood; O.S.6" 9
IFC S 914: 331; W. Fitzgerald, 'Hollywood, county Wicklow' in *Kild. Arch. Soc., Jn.*, viii (1915-1917), p. 196
Warts cured there. Offerings left.

> Situated in a small field at the back of the houses in Hollywood village to the north of the Church. (W. Fitzgerald)

83. Tubbernaboneen; Tld. Athdown; Par. Kilbride; O.S.6" 6
IFC S 913: 129

> Any person, how bad the attack of vomiting is, goes to Mrs Keogh and gets her to raise the water from the well, because she knows the prayer.

Offerings left at well.

84. St Kevin's Well; Tld. Kilbride; Par. Kilbride; O.S.6" 1*
O.S. letters, p. 311; *O.S. namebooks*, ii, Kilbride parish, p. 98

85. Holy Well; Tld. Tober; Par. Tober; O.S.6" 15
IFC S 914: 225; W. Fitzgerald, 'Dunlavin, Tornant', p. 229

Barony of Talbotstown Upper

86. Tobersool; Tld. Knockanreagh; Par. Ballynure; O.S.6" 26*
O.S. letters, p. 99; *O.S. namebooks*, i, Ballynure parish, p. 1; IFC S 917: 181-2; IFC 946: 49-51
A pattern had been held at one time but not in the memory of the oldest inhabitants of the area at the time of the Ordnance Survey. The eyes were bathed three times at the well. The water lost its curative properties if taken away. Story about the well being closed up but the man who closed it soon found that he had need of its healing powers.

> An old man Mick Griffin who died a short time ago and was well over 90 at the time of his death said he remembered people coming to *tobar na súl* to bathe their eyes. (IFC 946: 49-51)

87. Tobermacough; Tld. Lowtown; Par. Ballynure; O.S.6" 20*
O.S. letters, p. 99; *O.S. namebooks*, i, Ballynure parish, p. 4
Said to have had curative properties.

88. Tobergorry; Tld. Monatore; Par. Ballynure; O.S.6" 26*
O.S. letters, p. 99; *O.S. namebooks,* i, Ballynure parish, p. 2; IFC S 917: 182; O'Toole, 'The Holy Wells', p. 127
Said to have had curative properties.

89. Tobernaslige; Tld. Tinoranhill North; Par. Ballynure; O.S.6" 26*
O.S. letters, p. 99; *O.S. namebooks*, i, Ballynure parish, p. 3
Said to have had curative properties.

90. St Patrick's Well; Tld. Boley; Par. Baltinglass; O.S.6" 27*
O.S. letters, p. 277; *O.S. namebooks*, i, Baltinglass parish, p. 10

> A pattern held here about 80 years ago; pilgrimages made to it, but discontinued about 50 years ago. (*O.S. namebooks*, i, Ballynure parish, p. 10)

Edward O'Toole could find no trace of this well although its supposed site was pointed out to him.

91. St Laurence O'Toole's Well; Tld. Brittas; Par. Donaghmore; O.S.6" 22
IFC S 916: 7; IFC S 916: 75-7
According to tradition, St Laurence O'Toole drank from this well. Not visited in the 1930s. Water cold in summer and warm in winter. A blue light was seen over the well.

92. Tobernacargy; Tld. Kelshamore; Par. Donaghmore; O.S.6" 21*
O.S. letters, p. 167; *O.S. namebooks*, ii, Donaghmore parish, p. 42; IFC S 914: 430; IFC S 914: 558-9; IFC S 915: 186; IFC S 915: 188; IFC S 915: 190-91; IFC S 915: 193; IFC S 915: 194
Tobernacargy was said to have been frequented for cures. Said to have been blessed by St Patrick – by St Palladius in one account. Water taken with the stream cured one complaint while water taken against the stream cured another ailment.

93. Leitrim Well; Tld. Leitrim; Par. Donaghmore; O.S.6" 22*
O.S. letters, p. 169; *O.S. namebooks*, ii, Donaghmore parish, p. 20
A well frequented for cures at one time. Patterns had been held there on 25 July.

94. St Bridget's Well; Tld. Moorstown; Par. Donaghmore; O.S.6" 27*
O.S. letters, p. 171; *O.S. namebooks*, ii, Donaghmore parish, p. 29; IFC S 914: 560; IFC S 917: 171
Said to have been frequented for cures. Always a good flow of water. St Brigid was said to have visited – the stone at the well was known as St Brigid's elbow-stone.

95. Toberavoster; Tld. Randalstown; Par. Donaghmore; O.S.6" 21*
O.S. letters, p. 171; *O.S. namebooks*, ii, Donaghmore parish, p. 31
Well formerly frequented for cures.

96. St Briget's Well; Tld. Rostyduff; Par. Donaghmore; O.S.6" 21, 22, 27, 28
IFC S 914: 539; IFC S 917: 173
Said that a pattern used to be held there at one time on 1 February

97. St John's Well; Tld. Rostyduff; Par. Donaghmore; O.S.6" 21, 22, 27, 28
IFC S 914: 559

> There are seven springs, and if a person suffering from a pain in the stomach rises water out of the seven springs, he will be cured.

98. St Brigid's Well; Tld. Colvinstown Upper; Par. Kilranelagh; O.S.6" 27*
O.S. letters, p. 226; *O.S. namebooks*, iii, Kilranelagh parish, p. 39; IFC S 914: 560; IFC S 915: 194; IFC S 917: 169; IFC S 917: 218
Situated in a graveyard. Frequented for cures – headache, sores, pains. Offerings left at well.

99. Tubber na Christamaun; Tld. Talbotstown Lower; Par. Kilranelagh; O.S.6" 27*
O.S. letters, p. 228; *O.S. namebooks*, iii, Kilranelagh parish, p. 29; IFC S 914: 537; IFC S 915: 182-3; IFC S 917: 167; IFC S 917: 218
Many people were cured at well – offerings left. Story demonstrating that the water of the well should not be used for household purposes.

100. Holy Well; Tld. Talbotstown Lower; Par. Kilranelagh, O.S.6" 27
IFC S 914: 538
Well noted for cures. Story about clothes being washed in the well.

101. Tubbernathaunkill; Tld. Cornan East; Par. Kiltegan, O.S.6" 28*
O.S. letters, p. 238; *O.S. namebooks*, iii, Kiltegan parish, p. 21; IFC S 917: 178

> It is the belief of the people in the parish that the water of this well cures headaches and stops vomitings and retchings.
> (*O.S. namebooks*, iii, Kiltegan parish, p. 21)

102. St Brigid's Well; Tld. Cranareen; Par. Kiltegan; O.S.6" 28*
IFC S 920: 91; IFC S 920: 92; IFC S 920: 93; IFC S 920: 94; IFC S 920: 97; IFC S 920: 99; IFC S 920: 100
Frequented for cures. Bush growing over the well. Water used for household purposes. Also known as St John's Well by some.

103. St Tegan's Well; Tld. Kiltegan; Par. Kiltegan; O.S.6" 32
IFC S 917: 179

104. *Tobar Eoin*; Tld. Rathdangan; Par. Kiltegan; O.S.6" 28*
O.S. letters, p. 238; *O.S. namebooks*, iii, Kiltegan parish, p. 19; IFC S 917ff; IFC S 920: 91-2; IFC S 920: 92; IFC S 920: 93; IFC S 920: 94; IFC S 920: 94-5; IFC S 920:96; IFC S 920: 97-8; IFC S 920: 99; IFC S 920:100; IFC S 920:101; E. O'Toole, 'The Holy Wells', pp 122-3

> There was a station held near here formerly on St John's Eve and many cures said to have been performed; the station is discontinued about 26 or 30 years. (*O.S. namebooks*, iii, Kiltegan parish, p. 19)

A pattern was held at the well on 23 June up to 1798. John Moore, a companion of Michael Dwyer's was hanged from the tree at the well. The branch from which he was hanged withered. An attempt was made to pipe the water but it was unsuccessful. There was a cure in the well and offerings were left.

105. St Bernard's Well; Tld. Rampere; Par. Rathbran; O.S.6" 20*
O.S. letters, p. 93; *O.S. namebooks*, iii, Rathbran parish, p. 33; IFC 946: 49-51; E. O'Toole, 'The Holy Wells', pp 20-21
A pattern was held at the well on 20 August up to the late eighteenth century. The stations at the well ended at about the same time. The pattern was discontinued because a man was killed during faction fighting there. Many people had been cured at this well and many offerings had been left there

106. Tobermurry Well; Tld. Winetavern; Par. Rathbran; O.S.6" 21*
O.S. letters, p. 93; *O.S. namebooks*, iii, Rathbran parish, p. 40
A holy well formerly but at the time the *O.S. Letters* were written it was used for household purposes.

Acknowledgement
I would like to thank the Head of the Department of Irish Folklore, University College Dublin, for permission to use material from the archives of the Department.

References

1. C. Ó Danachair, 'Holy Well Legends in Ireland' in *Saga och Sed* (1959), p. 35.
2. T. Bray, *Statuta synodalia pro unitis diocesibus Cassel. et Imelac* (Dublin, 1813), p. 72 and pp 230-6.
3. During 1937-8 the Irish Folklore Commission (1935-71) in conjunction with the Department of Education and with the co-operation of the Irish National Teachers' Organisation undertook a major national folklore collection. As part of their schoolwork, children in the senior classes of primary schools collected folklore in their locality. A detailed account of the 1937-8 schools' scheme is given by S. Ó Catháin, '*Súil Siar ar Scéim na Scol* 1937-1938' in *Sinsear*, v (1988), pp 19-30. In 1934 a circular (9/34) from the Department of Education to all

national schools consisted of a questionnaire regarding holy wells. In contrast to the 1937-8 folklore collection this holy well questionnaire was aimed at teacher-collectors rather than child-collectors. Consequently more detailed information was sought regarding traditional observances at the wells.

4. Lady's Well (W.3) is still visited on the traditional visiting day, 25 March, which is known locally as Lady Well Day. A video recording of Lady Well Day 1990 was made by Bairbre Ó Floinn of the Department of Irish Folklore and is in the audio-visual archives of that department.
5. These groups are based upon those used by Francis Jones, *The holy wells of Wales* (Cardiff, 1954), pp 6-8.
6. Wells 2, 6, 15, 31, 42, 49, 52, 55, 56, 94, 96, 98, 102. Numbers refer to App. I.
7. Wells 10, 17, 18, 19, 20, 21, 38, 82, 84.
8. Wells 5, 13, 14, 30, 32, 44, 46, 54, 90.
9. Wells 1, 3, 27, 41, 106.
10. Wells 45, 97, 104.
11. Wells 62, 74.
12. Wells 72, 73.
13. Wells 43, 47.
14. Wells 9, 22, 24, 25, 28, 29, 34, 36, 37, 51, 59, 60, 64, 71, 77, 78, 81, 85, 100.
15. W.11.
16. Lady's Well (W.3) is situated near the ruins of Chapelhógan, St Iver's Well (W.4) is near a graveyard, and St Patrick's Well (W.5) midway along the mass path which was used to reach Chapelhógan from Clugga Strand.
17. IFC S 923: 201.
18. W. Fitzgerald, 'Dunlavin, Tornant, and Tober, county Wicklow' in *Kild. Arch. Soc. Jn.*, vii (1912-1914), p. 230.
19. IFC 468: 64-5.
20. How many holy wells are in the parish? Tell where they are (townland, name of field, if any). Do people still visit them on certain days? When? Are 'round' performed there and prayers said? Give an account of these.
    S. Ó Súilleabháin, *Irish folklore and tradition*, (Dublin, 1934), pp 18-19.
21. IFC S 918: 35.
22. IFC S 912: 163.
23. A.T. Lucas, 'The Sacred Trees of Ireland' in *Cork Hist Arch. Jn.*, LXVIII (1963), p. 16.
24. *O.S. namebooks*, ii, Dunlavin parish, p. 26.
25. W. R. Wilde, 'Memoir of Gabriel Beranger, and his labours in the cause of Irish art, literature, and antiquities from 1760 to 1780, with illustrations' in *R.S.A.I. Jn.*, xii, pp 449-50.
26. Ó Danachair, 'Holy well legends', p. 37.
27. E. O'Toole, 'The holy wells of county Carlow' in *Béaloideas*, iv (1933-34), p. 22.
28. S. Ó Súilleabháin's notes on this survey are in IFC 654:451-79. For a published account see S. Ó Súilleabháin, 'Beneath the Poulaphouca Reservoir' in C. Ó Danachair (ed.), *Folk & farm* (Dublin, 1976), pp 200-7.
29. See G. McClafferty, 'On the well which arose and was visited by many' in *Sinsear*, i (1979), pp 28-32.
30. IFC S 920: 95.
31. O'Toole, 'Holy wells', p. 23.
32. IFC S 914: 537.
33. Omurethi, 'Father Germaine's well at Lackan, parish of Boystown (alias Baltyboys), in the county Wicklow' in *Kild. Arch. Soc. Jn.*, v (1906-1908), p. 203.

Chapter 16

LAND AND LANDSCAPE IN COUNTY WICKLOW *c.*1840

WILLIAM NOLAN

The discovery of Ireland proceeded apace in the first half of the nineteenth century. Poet, travel writer, illustrator, celebrity and king came to Wicklow. In their wake followed policeman, surveyor, valuator and antiquarian who counted, measured, assessed and recorded. The first group mediated Wicklow's geography. 'Nowhere else,' wrote W.H. Bartlett in his *The Scenery and Antiquities of Ireland*,[1] 'is to be found assembled such a variety of natural beauties heightened and improved by the hand of art.' Fourteen of the one hundred and twenty engravings reproduced in his two volumes measure Wicklow's significance and highlight the inland cliffs and valleys where granite meets schist and water escapes the high ground. The familiar litany chants Enniskerry, Powerscourt from the Dargle, Powerscourt Fall, The Dargle, Bray, Glen of the Downs, Head of the Devil's Glen, Luggelaw, Glendalough, Round Tower at Glendalough, Head of Glenmalure, Castle Howard, Vale of Avoca, Meeting of the Waters and, the lone tourist outpost of west Wicklow, Poul a Phuca. Image was matched with apposite description. Powerscourt demesne, 'something like the composition of the Italian masters;' the waterfall was 'a beautiful semi-circular amphitheatre' where in winter 'the tumultuous fury with which the thundering cataract dashes at one solid bound down the frightful depths of descent fills the beholder's mind with wonder.' The Dargle 'like a shaft of silver through a dark landscape' contrasted with the view from the rectangular room of the La Touche mansion at Bellevue 'a scene of luxurious softness, combined with grandeur and significance'. Southwards lay ever more dramatic encounters with elemental forces. Glendalough 'a dim valley over which the Angel of Death seems to have spread the shadow of his dark wings' was the otherworld to the Victorian traveller, testimony in mist-shrouded ruins of man's fallibility. Earlier illustrations of the pattern day at Glendalough exhibit exuberance and gaiety strikingly vibrant and so different from this Gothic gloom.[2] No landscape, however, was beyond redemption and the 'savage grandeur of Glenmalure' served as a reminder of man's good works which created the waving woods, clear waters and vendant shores of Avoca. Wicklow was an open-air theatre, a place to be moulded and re-arranged, clothed or left in its nakedness. It was an escape, a place of seclusion where the natural world could be dramatised in a rural setting.

The blue of limestone is not found on Wicklow's geological map: the lone Irish county from which this fertile bedrock is absent.[3] Granite, quartzite, schist, slate and sand are the fundiments from which Wicklow draws its shape. The northern and southern extremities of Wicklow are marked by the residual peaks of long dormant volcanoes at Great and Little Sugarloaf [formerly and more appropriately Giltspur] and Croghan Kinsella mountain, respectively. Between the sea sand of the coast and the ice sand resting along the western hill flanks lies the solid highland granite core fringed by schist and slate. Interior Wicklow has more than a dozen broad convex summits whose toponomy symbolises a harsh, spectacular terrain. Kippure, Djouce, Mullaghcleevaun, Moanbane, Tonelagee, Table give way south to the high beads of Clohernagh, Carrowaystick, Croghanmoira, Lybagh and Slievemaan which circle the core of Lugnaquillia. Venerated Church mountain rises above Hollywood and Donard; Keadeen guards the southern approaches to O'Dwyer's country and Glen Imail. This impressive territory of the grey crow has its internal geography of massive, wide-rimmed basins dominated by tall, white grasses interspersed with quaking, pock-marked peat faces. Ice moraines in the mountains have left cold waters trapped in deep corries at Lough Bray Upper, Lough Bray Lower, Nahanagan, Ouler, Kelly's Lough and Cleevaun in its basket at 2,000 feet under the north summit of Mullaghcleevaun.

Along the eastern rim of the mountain massif, steep-sided, east-trending channels, excavated from the schist by trundling ice and deepened by rivers fed from the high ground, are Wicklow's great glens – Glencree, Glenmacnass, Glendasan, Glendalough and Glenmalure. At Glendalough and Cloghogue ice and water borne debris has restricted the rivers and created the Upper and Lower lakes of Glendalough and Tay and Dan respectively. At the glen heads, where water leaves granite for schist, Wicklow's cascades and waterfalls, Powerscourt, Glenmacnass, Glendasan, were born. Below the surface, mineral rich pipes were intruded to provide, along with the copper lodes of the ordovician volcanics in Avoca, raw materials for Wicklow's spluttering mining industry. Wicklow's west-facing glens along Liffey, King's river and Imail, are broad granite based and apart from Pollaphuca, where the Liffey leaves the mountains, they lack the sharp personalities of their eastern schistose counterparts. East-draining rivers along north Wicklow, such as the Dargle and Vartry, have short sharp courses and deep incised valleys providing a focus for the great demesnes and gardens. Further south in middle Wicklow the Potters, Three Mile Water and Redcross rivers follow a more lethargic course through the 'green grassy sod'.[4] Southwards again the Avoca draining into Arklow is the receptacle of Wicklow's mountain catchment which stretches from Sally Gap to Tinahely. Its list of tributary rivers is impressive: Cloghogue, Inchavore, Glenmacnass, Glendasan, Glenealo, Avonbeg, Avonmore, Ow and Derry Water. On the south face of Glenmalure the Carrowaystick, tributary to Avonbeg, epitomises the geography of water in the valleys. Rising at over 2,000 feet in Kelly's Lough it flows sluggishly through bog and rock-strewn moraine, then bursting over the granite rim of Glenmalure it cascades down 500 feet of spectacular cliff to join the Avonbeg coming west from Conavalla, through Glenmalure past Fananierin, Ballincor to become part of Moore's Meetings.

The Liffey rising on Kippure, hardly a mile from the east-flowing Dargle, is symbolic of the role of the mountains in dividing Wicklow. Its upper valley was the focus of one of the last pre-Famine bursts to reclaim the damp hills, both physically and spiritually. Further south it gave prospects to the Palladian mansion at Russborough before turning its back on Wicklow at Pollaphuca to become the river of Kildare and Dublin. Slaney issuing forth from the grim walls of the North Prison on Lugnaquillia knows the three Wicklows – the high summer sheep pastures, the middle cattle ground of Imail, the productive grain country around Baltinglass and the bumpy marchlands of Wicklow, Wexford and Carlow. Its major left-bank tributary – the Derry – bespeaks the oak woods of Shillelagh. The shaping of Wicklow was qualified by its physical geography. Communication, settlement and military followed the episcopal corridor on the west and the sea-facing lowlands to the east. Mountain Wicklow was no *terra incognita*. Gaps gave access at Sally, Wicklow, Black Banks, Ballinabarny. The search for lime brought carter to Kildare and Carlow, brought boatmen to Skerries and thence to Wicklow port. In winter, sheep and cattle followed the lime trail to Kildare.

County Wicklow's 499,837 statute acres ranked it seventeenth in size among the counties of Ireland.[5] Belonging by geography to the east, Wicklow's topography is more redolent of Ireland's western fringe. Apart from counting people, the enumerators in 1841 made a qualitative assessment of the land surface. By their calculations some 56 per cent of Wicklow was non-arable land: only Tyrone, Clare, Galway, Mayo and Donegal had a lesser proportion of arable land. Wicklow's rugged character places it apart in Leinster. All of its neighbours,

Carlow, Kildare, Dublin and Wexford had more than 80 per cent of their respective areas defined as arable. Little arable but many trees as the calculations found that some 3.5 per cent of Wicklow was covered with plantations: only Waterford had more woodland in 1841. When aggregated for the whole county, Wicklow had the second lowest population density [151] for each square mile after Kerry [145].

County Wicklow in 1841 was sub-divided into eight baronies which were made up of some sixty civil parishes (fig. 16.1) and 1,362 townlands. Fig. 16.2 provides a comparative assessment of population on a civil parish basis. The county's 126,000 people were unequally distributed. The middle hill country and great swathes of high ground north and south were almost empty. Forty of Wicklow's townlands had no recorded population in 1841: their identity shows the two wildernesses. Aghavannagh mountain (1,523 acres) in Moyne parish was empty but so also was Kilruddery Deerpark (438 acres) shared between the parishes of Bray and Delgany. Population followed the glaciers and the highest densities occur in the hinterlands of Bray, Arklow, Rathdown and Baltinglass. The only rural parish with a population density in excess of fifty people per square mile was Castlemacadam, a reflection of its mining history. Wicklow's population was invariably rural in character: only 15 per cent lived in agglomerations of more than twenty houses. Rathdown bordering Dublin was its most urbanised barony (26.5 per cent: 3031), followed by Arklow (23 per cent: 5844); Newcastle (16.7: 2760); Talbotstown Upper (14.3: 2546); Talbotstown Lower (12: 1969); Ballinacor North (12: 1232); Shillelagh (8: 1165) and Ballinacor South (4: 690).

Wicklow urban centres were relatively small in 1841 (Table 16.1). Arklow, Bray and Wicklow had populations of little over 3,000 respectively; Baltinglass in the mid-west had approximately 2,000 people. Rathdrum was the only other settlement with more than 1,000. The decayed cotton town of Stratford was still as significant as either Tinahely, Dunlavin or Carnew but Enniskerry, Donard and Blessington were little more than villages. Proximity to Dublin may have stunted Wicklow's urban growth and it is certain that the physical configuration of the county reduced the potential hinterlands of urban centres. The impact of military activity in 1798 and the subsequent desertion of the county, as even a temporary summer residence, by landlords such as Downshire of Blessington and Beresford of Hollywood had local significance. All of Wicklow's towns and villages were either created or remodelled by its gentry families: the Anglo-Normans left no walled towns nor does the county's surname geography suggest any large-scale immigration in medieval times. Although Wicklow seems on the surface to have been a poor county

Table 16.1

Census towns in county Wicklow 1841

Town	*Population*	*Number of houses*
Arklow	3,254	524
Wicklow	3,141	351
Bray	2,203	382
Baltinglass	1,928	282
Rathdrum	1,232	146
Dunlavin	990	143
Carnew	979	144
Newtownmountkennedy	823	113
Tinahely	640	99
Stratford	618	90
Donard	513	81
Blessington	466	66
Enniskerry	448	66
Ballinalea (Rathnew)	336	51
Redcross	310	46
Kilcoole	296	59
Delgany	201	32
Newcastle	196	28
Shillelagh	186	22
Killincarrig	179	30
Downs (Kilcoole)	172	30
Killiskey	157	23
Glenealy	148	27
Rathnew	118	20

Source: *Census of population, 1841.*

Landlords

County Wicklow's landed proprietors in 1838 are listed in the Ordnance Survey Name Books which are comparatively rich in information concerning ownership, tenure, rental, land productivity and general information about town and country.[6] The matter of ownership in the county was settled by 1700. Local elites were ruthlessly dispossessed and the O'Byrnes and, to a lesser extent, the O'Tooles were victims for the second time in their history. Little or nothing of Wicklow was beyond the remit of landlordism and by the period under review here, high and low Wicklow, apart from some scattered tenacious commons, were banded into the tight administrative net of estate, civil parish and county (fig. 16.3). Henceforth, gate lodge, rhododendron, dripping beeches, shooting lodge, demesne, deerpark, imperial garden were planted in receptive ground. Few of Wicklow's medieval lords had anything to do with modern Wicklow. Nowhere in the county do we find parallels with

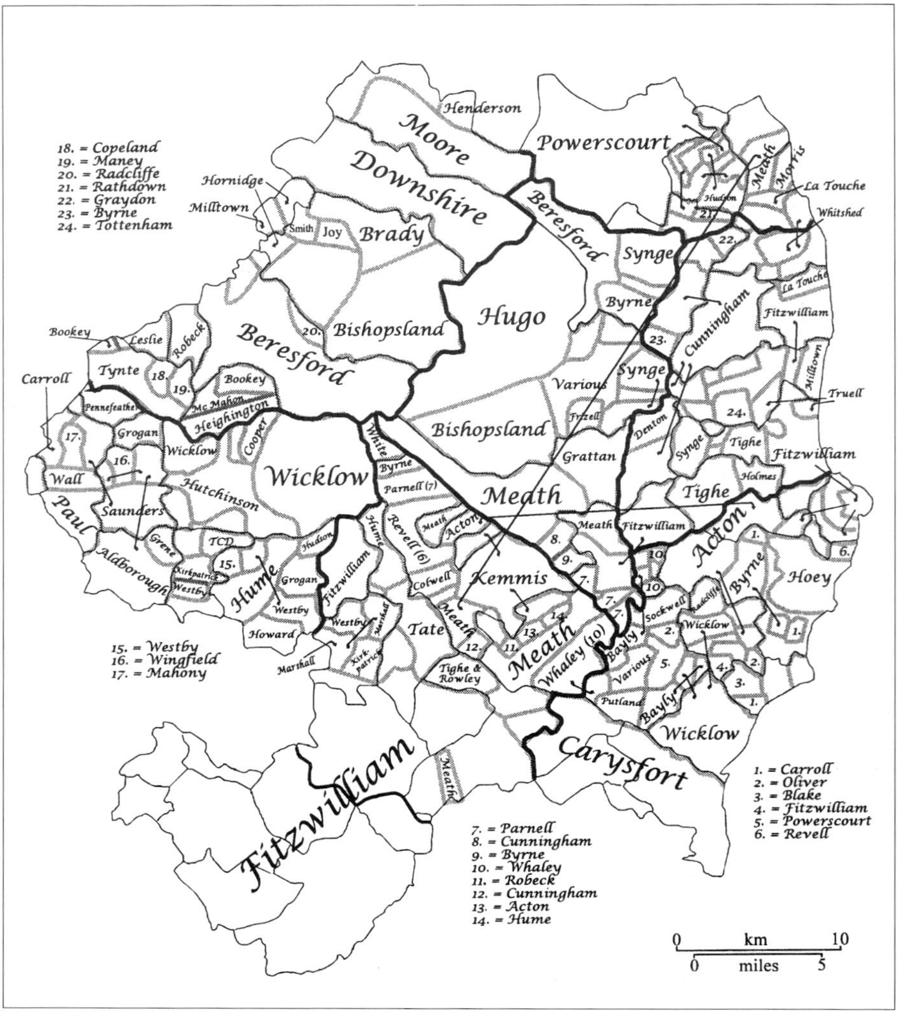

Figure 16.3 Landowners, county Wicklow *c.*1838.

the Butlers of Ormond or the O'Briens of Thomond. Wicklow planted late and was planted thoroughly as were north Wexford, north Kilkenny, north Tipperary and much of the province of Ulster. Two factors shaped the character of landlord settlement in Wicklow. One was the proximity of Dublin city. 'The districts on the sea coast,' wrote Wakefield in 1812, 'are very much divided, and abound with villas to which the citizens of Dublin retire to enjoy the pleasure of rural views, amidst all those comforts that flow from ease and independence acquired by industry.'[7] Dublin's urban entrepreneurs were involved in Wicklow but Wicklow landlords, such as Meath and Carysfort, owned large urban properties within the city. Secondly, many of Wicklow's landlords, such as Parnell and Powerscourt, derived secondary incomes from the exploitation of natural resources under and over their Wicklow domains, and the nascent tourism industry was significant in the north-east and along the Avoca.

Landlords of Wicklow

Table 16.2 lists landowners of county Wicklow in 1837 who held one thousand statute acres and over. Acreage, particularly in Wicklow where the land quality was so variable, is only a very general indicator of wealth but the hierarchical pattern which emerges is not radically altered when valuation as well as acreage is available in the government's listings of 1876.[8] Ten Wicklow estates were over 10,000 acres in 1837: three of these, See of Dublin, Hugo and Beresford, consisted mainly of barren mountain. Wicklow's largest estate, that of Fitzwilliam of Coolattin, was more than three times greater than the second largest property. From its administrative core in Coolattin's massive pile, Fitzwilliam governed *in absentia* almost one fifth of the county. The estate was born in the complex troubled times of the early seventeenth century, the offspring of the overweening ambitions of Thomas Wentworth, earl of Strafford and its magnificent woodland reserves.[9] It encompassed virtually all of Shillelagh barony and extensive tracts in Ballinacor South. This contiguous block in south Wicklow was complemented by a north-east, south-west trending stripe of land at Rathdrum, a strategic outlier on the coast south of Wicklow town, a stretch of fertile country between Rathnew and Wicklow and the northernmost outpost in the coastal tillage belt of Newcastle parish.

Wicklow's second largest estate, that of the See of Dublin, was a relict of medieval and perhaps earlier origin. Churchland was generally assigned on short-term leases which invariably became leases in perpetuity.[10] By 1838 the once more extensive ecclesiastical domain, now shorn of its more profitable lowlands (granted at times to relatives of the 'shepherd'), was confined to the rugged bogland edges and the empty mountain rims of north-west Wicklow. The families of Brabazon (Meath), Beresford (Waterford) and Howard (Wicklow) were each returned with some 23,000 acre estates. Sir William Brabazon of Leicester, an important government official and overseer of the great property transfers at the dissolution of the monasteries in the mid-sixteenth century, was the progenitor of the Meath family in Ireland.[11] The Meath estate in Wicklow was considerably fragmented. The demesne core and administrative centre was at Kilruddery House in Rathdrum barony incorporating part of the developing resort town of Bray. Further south Meath held the high ground skirting the military

Table 16.2

Wicklow's Landed Gentry 1838

Estate	Acreage
Over 75,000 acres	
1. Fitzwilliam	79,225
25-30,000 acres	
2. See of Dublin	26,469
20-25,000	
3. Meath	23,737
4. Beresford	23,163
5. Wicklow	23,081
6. Powerscourt	21,247
7. Hugo	20,360
15-20,000	
8. Carysfort	16,190
9. Downshire	15,780
10-15,000	
10. Cunningham	14,892
5-10,000	
11. Moore	8,664
12. Synge	8,488
13. Kemmis	8,179
14. Brady	5,880
15. Whaley	5,778
16. Hutchinson	5,712
17. Acton	5,381
3-5,000	
18. Aldborough	4,804
19. Westby	4,760
20. Hoey	4,398
21. Byrne (Croneybyrne)	4,067
22. Parnell	3,746
23. Hume	3,378
24. Howard	3,130
25. Saunders	3,083
2,000-3,000	
26. Paul	2,895
27. Tynte	2,868
28. Tate	2,826
29. Byrne (Cabinteely)	2,802
30. Revell	2,769
31. Grogan	2,758
32. Grattan	2,664
33. Bayly	2,604
34. Marshall	2,580
35. Radcliffe	2,453
36. Rowley	2,369
37. de Robeck	2,314
38. Blake	2,083
39. Sockwell	2,062
1-2,000	
40. Denton	1,811
41. Bookey	1,798
42. Whitshed	1,770
43. La Touche	1,721
44. Carroll (Dublin)	1,708
45. Kirkpatrick	1,682
46. Truell	1,669
47. Rathdown	1,667
48. Heighington	1,603
49. Joy	1,541
50. Hornidge	1,524
51. Carroll (Ballynure)	1,510
52. Tottenham	1,455
53. Leslie	1,423
54. Milltown	1,367
55. Oliver	1,346
56. T.C.D.	1,287
57. Maney	1,178
58. Frizell	1,148
59. Smith	1,142
60. Cooper	1,107
61. Mahony	1,103
62. Beatty	1,060
63. Copeland	1,057
64. Wall	1,051
65. White	1,043
66. Colwell	1,026
67. Wingfield	1,011

Source: *O.S. Name Books, Wicklow*, 3 vols., N.L.I.

road between Laragh and Drumgoff. This block extended east to the densely wooded Vale of Clara incorporating townlands on both banks of the Avonmore river. Below the high ground, Meath had a sizeable property in middle Wicklow including his secondary town of Aughrim and its hinterland extending east along the Aughrim river to the mining parish of Castlemacadam. A curious last fragment of the Meath estate lay embedded in two townlands deep in Fitzwilliam territory in Kilpipe parish.

Beresford of Stafford (manager for the Corporation of Londoners) and one of the transplantation officers administering the forced post-Cromwellian migration to Connacht, laid the origins of this family in Ireland. A descendant married into the Powers of Curraghmore, county Waterford, becoming enobled as earl of Tyrone and subsequently as marquis of Waterford. Beresford's Wicklow estate in 1838 was grafted onto the medieval manor of Hollywood. It consisted primarily of the broad, granite valley of the King's river extending east to encompass the strategic Wicklow Gap between Tonlagee mountain and Lough Nahanagan: a secondary outlier occurred at Ballinastoe above Lough Dan. The Howard connection with Wicklow was established in 1697 when John Howard, president of the College of Physicians in Ireland, acquired the estate of north Arklow from the duke of Ormonde. By 1830 the property comprised all of the parish of Kilbride, part of the contiguous parish of Castlemacadam which included the village of Avoca, and a northern arc based on Wicklow's newest planned town at Redcross. The Howards, now enobled with the title of earls of Wicklow, had augmented their lands by major purchases in the former Percy estate in Glen Imail. Wicklow's Imail lands were in two fragments – one block of highest Wicklow peaking at Lugnaquillia and taking in the rugged foothills west to the boundary with Hutchinsons of Coolmoney. Beyond the Hutchinson estate, Wicklow owned a stretch of fertile land at the entrance to the glen around the core of the Anglo-Norman settlement of Castleruddery.

Powerscourt symbolised the golden age of landlordism in county Wicklow. The Powerscourt title and estate was first granted to Sir Richard Wingfield, military adventurer who witnessed the articles of surrender of the Spaniard Don Juan D'Aquilia at Kinsale and quietened the O'Donnells and O'Dohertys of Donegal. Glencree was the heart of the sequestered O'Toole property granted in royal gratitude to Wingfield. It extended east to the mouth of the Dargle and west to the remote marchlands with Dublin and the neighbouring estates of Downshire of Blessington and Moore of Kilbride. Southwards, Powerscourt took in the spectacular mountain and lake lands as far as the townland of Clohogue. Powerscourt had a distant outlier, including the parish centre, in mineral-rich Castlemacadam in the Vale of Avoca.

Hugo's mountain domain, large in quantity and poor in quality, ranked him seventh of Wicklow's landlords in 1838. The name Hugo appears in rentals of the Protestant Archbishop of Dublin as early as 1700 when the family was granted the empty core of north Wicklow for a nominal rent.[12] Stretching from the jagged southern edge of Glendalough the estate was bounded in the east by the Avonmore and Clohogue rivers, northwards by the Powerscourt and Downshire lands and to the west its marches coincided with the watershed dividing east and west drainage systems. By the 1830s the more profitable edges of the Hugo lands were being detached and created into independent estates such as Bookeys of Derrybawn and Bartons of Glendalough House (Drummin). Carysfort and Downshire were compact properties aligned on parochial and older manorial divisions. Both families had come to Wicklow through marriage. The Carysfort estate coincided with the southern portion of the Ormonde manor of Arklow and was based in the civil parishes of Arklow, Inch and Killahurler, south of the Avoca river. Its title derived from the seventeenth century plantation town in the foothills north of Aughrim. The Carysfort or Proby family had extensive lands in south county Dublin around the coastal village of Blackrock. Downshire, one of Ireland's wealthiest landed magnates, owned the estate of Blessington in north-west Wicklow. Blessington represented the manor and borough created in the late seventeenth century by Archbishop Boyle whose daughter married into the family of Elizabethan soldier-adventurer Moyses Hill, later to be marquis of Downshire.[13] Both Downshire and Carysfort were permanent absentees from their Wicklow lands. The Blessington estate had the diversity typical of Wicklow: it included sandhill remnants of the Midlandian Glaciation, a swathe of grassy country in the lowland corridor to Dublin, the headwaters of the Liffey and the white meadows on the lower slopes of Duff Hill, Gravale and Mullaghcleevaun.

Seven Wicklow estates were in the size range from five to ten thousand acres in 1838. These were Moore of Kilbride and Kippure, Synge of Roundwood and Glanmore, Kemmis of Ballinacor, Brady of Kilboy, Whaley of Bahana, Hutchinson of Coolmoney and Acton of West Acton (Kilmacurragh). Apart from Acton and, to a lesser extent, Moore, these were invariably hill estates and the comparative poverty of their land is highlighted in the valuations returned in 1876. Valuation rather than scale is the more pertinent index of landlord ability to generate village or town settlement and none of this group fashioned any settlement more conspicuous than the Big House and its associated features. Their career paths to Wicklow landlord status were similar to those of their 'bigger' neighbours.

Moore of Kilbride held the Liffey lands north of Blessington up through Cloghleagh almost to the peak of Kippure and the marches of Powerscourt. Downshire, marked by a gamekeeper's cottage and the Scots' pines of newly planted Cornation Plantation, was at the opposite southern side of the Liffey. Moore began pushing upwards in the 1830s when a junior branch established a foothold at Kippure House on the north bank of the Liffey. A Protestant church and associated school-house at Cloughleagh served the spiritual needs of Wicklow's bravest planters. Their valiant attempts to reclaim the bog wilderness is marked by deserted stone houses within tidy farms, parcelled in parallel stone walled fields which run up the sloping ground below Seefin mountain. Synge, made synonymous with Wicklow by the landless poet who captured the melancholy vitality of his native heath, came to Wicklow through inter-marriage with the Hatch family, beneficiaries of the fragmentation of the earlier Temple estate around Roundwood. The Synge lands in 1838 were composed of three fragments of indifferent quality; the townland of Glasamullen in bleak, windswept west Calary, a couple of large townlands in Derrylossary below Roundwood and the home house and demesne at Glanmore, Killiskey in the rugged Devil's Glen demesne belt.

Kemmis, associated more with Laois, prospered at law and the high ground of Ballinacor and Knockrath may have been a therapeutic refuge for the incumbent in 1838 from the rigours of a busy law practice. Ballinacor House, commanding the middle ground before Glenmalure, had within its shrouded demesne the buried remnants of the older O'Byrne Wicklow. Actons of Kilmacurragh or West Acton are a good example of Wicklow's middle gentry families: resident, involved in local administration and military establishment, energetic promoters of silviculture and high farming. By the late seventeenth century the fine mansion house was being built on a north-facing site which commanded the route from Wicklow inland to Rathdrum. Ordnance field surveyors noted the tree nursery, deerpark and the three-storey residence with extensive out-offices to the west.

Brady of Clare, non-resident, had part of the Bishopslands in the bleak refuge country under Mullaghcleevaun. The most obvious landlord signature was The Lodge described by the field surveyors as:

> A neat House, the property of Mr Brady with about 30 acres of pleasure ground. It is kept by a gamekeeper and let for the shooting season to gentlemen, for which purpose it was built convenient to the mountains.

Hutchinson of Coolmoney, wedged between the Slaney and

Keadeen mountain, held Imail intermediate to the two blocks of Lord Wicklow's western lands. The Whaley property was fragmented between Castlemacadam and Ballykine parishes. Mining money probably helped in the construction of their big house at Bahana and in inculcating the gambling spirit which was to considerably reduce their Wicklow lands in the post-Famine era.

Fifty Wicklow estates were between 1,000 and 5,000 acres in area. These smaller properties dominated the barony of Talbotstown Upper, when we exclude the Hutchinson and Wicklow's Imail lands. They were also significant in the southern part of Talbotstown Lower around Donard and Dunlavin. Excluding the giant monolith of Fitzwilliam and the Wicklow, Carysfort, Acton, Synge, Cunningham and Meath blocks, the small estate is a pertinent feature all along the coastal lowlands of the county. Both the mining parish of Castlemacadam and the better endowed Killiskey exhibit a very fragmented ownership pattern. Estates in this category were invariably confined to single civil parishes but instances of fragmentation which include, as for example in the Parnell and Revell properties, a combination of lowland and more distant hill country may be a replication of the transhumance patterns evident lower down the scale.

Some owners were permanent absentees either elsewhere in Ireland or in England and others may be classified as impermanent absentees. In the first category were Denton and White who lived in England and were little concerned with their mountain estates: Aldborough of Belan, de Robeck of Straffan and Kirkpatrick of Celbridge were Kildare owners of Wicklow lands. Cooper resided in adjoining Carlow; Leslie was more distant in his estate at Glaslough in north Monaghan; institutional landlords such as Trinity College Dublin were by their very nature excluded from residence in Wicklow. It is more difficult to identify the impermanent absentees. Robert Saunders told the Devon Commission[14] that he went abroad in 1829 and didn't return until 1839 and the Ordnance Surveyors observed that counsellor Pennefeather of Dublin was agent to his own estate at Rathsallagh where he lived for part of the year.

This group had diverse origins: some such as the earl of Aldborough had ancestral links in the county back to the Williamite Wars when Robert Stratford had victualled William of Orange's army at Belan. The family subsequently laid the foundations of modern Baltinglass. Others like the La Touches had bought their way into landed society through the purchase of Ballydonagh, which later became Belle View (Bellevue), in 1753 from the dean of St Patrick's Cathedral, Dublin. Others again, such as David O'Mahony, one time MP for Kinsale, were newcomers to the county in 1838. O'Mahony, a great dealer in land

and a perceptive witness to the Devon Commission, profited from the ostentatiousness of Henry Harrington Esq. The Ordnance Surveyors gave an insightful summary of the transactions which brought O'Mahony the Grangecon property:

> Henry Harrington Esq [descendant of the Elizabethan grantee] 'till lately resided here; he erected two spacious galleries for the reception of paintings and curiosities of which he was an indefatigable collector but having gone beyond his means the lands of Grangecon have within the last few months being sold to D. Mahony Esq.

Byrne of Croneybyrne was the only major resident Catholic land-owning family in the county. Byrne's mansion house had been rebuilt in 1820 and the estate's 4,000 acres included well-wooded foothills in the vale of Clara and a detached block of high Wicklow at Barravore at the head of the Avonbeg. The family had branched into commerce, exploiting the native oaks for bark to use in the tanning and dyeing process and their Catholic status was recognised by their private oratory and a burial vault in the cathedral at Glendalough. Abraham Tate of Coolballintaggart owned almost 3,000 acres in the Ow valley north of Aughrim. He was optimistic in his evidence to the Devon Commission about the future. Tate was a working, farmer landlord – 'I dare say,' he stated in evidence, 'I have about 1,200 acres in my own land, but a great deal is rough ground. I rear all my own cattle and sheep. I never buy a bullock.' Tate preached the gospel of self-reliance; he employed thirty-five men and no pauper ever came from his estate to the workhouse where he was giving evidence.

The diminution in average size of estates from the seventeenth century onwards through the break-up of church lands probably accounts for the cluster of relatively small properties in the hinterland of Baltinglass and further north between Donard and Dunlavin. Bookey, Joy, Hornidge, Smith and more latterly, Barton, were engrossing the last of the see lands of Dublin. A similar process was evident in the Trinity College property in mid-west Wicklow where the Grenes of Kilranelagh had moved from Dublin brewers to Wicklow squires through the conversion of life leases to perpetuities. Institutions such as the see of Dublin and Trinity College were legally obliged to restrict tenures to leases of a maximum twenty-one years but such provisions were circumvented by the granting of renewals on payment of fines before the full term was expired.

Elizabeth Smith reveals much of the *mentalite* of Wicklow gentry.[15] Marriage to Colonel Smith brought her to Baltiboys below Blessington and from this vantage point she observed the minutiae of country life at a critical disjuncture between resources and population. Subsidised by Colonel Smith's Indian pension and her literary stipends, they built a fine mansion house which looked across the Liffey valley at Russborough. Rigorous management at Baltiboys, a prerequisite for survival on a relatively small estate of 1,200 acres which in bad years could only produce seven hundred pounds income, contrasted with the continuing extravagances of neighbours Milltown and Moore who Nero-like failed to trim their vanities. Elizabeth Smith's writings show the unspannable gulf which divided those who had from those who hadn't the land of Wicklow. Threatened by the reviled O'Connell's mass popularity, landlords such as the Smiths visited tenant supporters with revenge:

> The only one of our tenants who attended the immense meeting at the Curragh last Sunday was Pat Ryan. I am inclined to hope it was more curiosity took him there, but it was a very foolish proceeding and will prevent the Colonel adding to his farm as he intended, as he could not for the sake of example select for such a mark of approbation the only agitator on his property.[16]

Depopulation would produce a tidier landscape and a tidier people:

> Now we have larger farms, larger fields, some good fences, much finer cattle, a few sheep, even some turnips, five new slated houses, three of them two-storeys high, good clothing, meal and bread and bacon and a bit of hay by times. Draining a rage planting clearing, good schools, a night school, lending library, and much approach towards cleanliness.[17]

Freedom from the encumbrances of history would release landlords to begin the new shaping of Wicklow:

> What a revolution for good will this failure of cheap food causes. I wish there was not a tenant in Baltiboys; there will not be many by and by, no smallholders at any rate. When potatoes are gone a few acres won't be worth a man's time to manage.[18]

Leases, agents and rents

The landed estate was the fulcrum on which Wicklow was shaped. Management, tenure and rent were the primary determinants of landscape. Estates were sacrosanct domains but the sheer weight of population numbers and the impoverishment of estates to maintain the status of gentry families and their siblings were beginning to expose the frayed edges of landlordism. The gentry was a highly visible force in county Wicklow and the fact that the owners of some 200,000 acres, including Fitzwilliam, Downshire and Carysfort, were absentee, did not necessarily diminish the autonomy of the property. Resident agents – many Wicklow agents were absentee based in Dublin, Waterford, Belfast and Ballinasloe, county Galway – were the key estate officials.

The Devon Commissioners estimated that one-seventh of Ireland's land was held under tenure by lease for named lives subject to perpetual renewal on payment of a fine: land was also held on terminable leases and by tenure from year to year; but by far the largest proportion was occupied by tenants-at-will. A major distinction was between those who held their farms by a written instrument and those who did not. In the late eighteenth century, leases in Wicklow were for three named lives. Such a system was operable in a stable economic climate but the impact of the 1798 rebellion, and in particular the recession subsequent to the peace of 1815, depressed commodity prices and made it difficult for tenants to service leases made in good times. The earl of Meath gave a 2 per cent abatement in 1814 after 'the fall of Bonaparte' but the general pattern developing in Wicklow was for fixed-term leases of shorter duration than hitherto. Such leases gave certitude and solved the problems of trying to locate named lives, many of whom had emigrated. 'I have been searching,' John Quin of Bray told the Devon Commissioners, 'in vain for three months, to know whether two men are dead or alive; but I cannot find out any body who knows anything of them.'

Downshire writing in 1838 to his agent at Blessington was conscious of the changing political context:

> It appears that *lives* are no longer indispensable to confer an elective franchise on a tenant in Ireland and therefore that *years* only are required say 14 or 21. As to the size of holdings to be leased I shall prefer 40 to 50 acres in order gradually to accustom my tenants to enlarge their bounds and keep *them* so. I sh'd like the lease to contain a Clause that in case of any portion being let off either double rent or forfeiture sh'd be the penalty.[19]

Maguire in his analysis of the Downshire management policy concluded that it was precisely the absence of political considerations in the context of Blessington that led to the comparatively large leaseholdings which contrasted with the proliferation of small forty-shilling freeholders on Downshire property in county Down. Political considerations were very much part of the resident landlord's programme.

Robert Saunders of Saundersgrove placed much of the responsibility for the density of smallholdings in the 1840s on his predecessors:

> When the 40s Freehold Act was passed, landlords wishing to create for themselves a political interest in the county recognised and encouraged it without considering the results. That was the case I'm sorry to say upon my own property, and to this I trace most of the misery of the peasantry of this district.

Politicisation of tenants led to confrontation with the landlords and Saunders identified contested elections as the primary cause 'of destroying the relation' which would otherwise exist between landlord and tenant and the evictions which invariably followed.

It is certain that eighteenth-century leasing policy was firmly rooted in political religious considerations which may well have become more entrenched after the events of 1798. 'The majority of Tory landlords,' Simon Moran a tenant of Tighe of Dromana told the Commission, 'from some sort of party feeling, will give no leases, except to a few of their own sort and the consequence is that some of the best farms in the county Wicklow have no lease nor any security.' Rev Daniel Kavanagh the Catholic curate of Carnew in the heart of Fitzwilliam country was a little more circumspect when observing 'that very few Roman Catholics hold property directly from Lord Fitzwilliam but indirectly, through a middleman.'

Saunders considered leases as detrimental to the landlord's interest leading invariably to derogation of landlord authority, the creation of political conflict and the reduction of the value of the leasehold subsequent to its termination. Both he and Robert Chaloner, agent to Lord Fitzwilliam, believed that tenant confidence in the future of estates conferred a perpetual tenancy on tenants-at-will. Furthermore, tenants were now unwilling to pay the increased stamp duty which had driven the cost of a new lease to £11. Tenants had contrary views. John Norton, tenant to Chief Justice Pennefeather at Rathsallagh and 100 acres of fattening land in county Kildare, observed that a tenant with a lease would build a good slate outhouse whereas a tenant without a lease would build a house 'with mud walls, bad timber and roof it with potatoe stalks'. John Quin of Bray, landholder and hotelier, advocated the giving of long leases to solvent tenants but told the Commission that his own landlord Mr La Touche of Delgany was unable to grant him a lease in perpetuity because the estate was so entailed. There was also the distinction between a lease for a farm on which it was proposed to build and drain: a farm which was to be used for occupation only and a mountain farm requiring considerable capital investment. Direct tenurial

Table 16.3
Wicklow Houses valued at £40 and over in 1853

Owner	*Location*	*£ Valuation*
Powerscourt	Powerscourt Demesne	220
Meath	Kilruddery Demesne west	200
Monck	Charleville Demesne	130
Hodgson	Hollybrook	110
Milltown	Russborough	108
Ball	Newcourt	100
Putland	Oldcourt	100
Pennick	Bellevue Demesne	100
Wicklow	Shelton Abbey	90
Fitzwilliam	Coolattin	90
Gunn-Cunningham	Mountkennedy Demesne	80
Barton	Drummin (Glendalough)	74
Grattan	Tinnehinch	70
Synge	Ballymaghroe (Glanmore)	70
Tottenham	Ballycurry Demesne	66
Barrington	Fassaroe	65
Crampton	Fassaroe	65
Truell	Clonmannan	63
Darley	Wingfield	60
Brooke	Castlehoward	60
Evans (Tighe)	Rossana Upper	60
Kemmis	Ballinacor	60
Carawhaite	Stilebawn	55
Toombe	Ballydowling (Glenealy)	50
Hepenstall	Altidorel	50
O'Neill-Seagrove	Kiltimon	50
Proby	Glenart	50
Saunders	Saundersgrove	50
Peel	Oldcourt	50
Doyne	Ballyfree West	47
Westby	Highpark Upper	45
Crofton	Inchanappa South	45
Meath	Belmont Demesne	45
Eccles	Cronroe	45
West	Killarney	45
Smith	Baltiboys	44
Jackson	Killarney	42
Bookey	Derrybawn	42
Hutchinson	Coolmoney	42
Monck	Ballyorney	41
Tynte	Loughmogue Upper	41
Pennefeather	Rathsallagh Demesne	40
Byrne	Croneybyrne	40
O'Reilly	Kilquade	40
Bayly	Ballyarthur	40
Edwards	Oldcourt	40
Hore	Springfield	40
Jones	Killincarrig	40
Montgomery	Kindlestown Upper	40

Source: *General valuation ... county of Wicklow* (1853).

relationship between landlord and tenant was regarded by all witnesses as much more satisfactory than having a middle interest intervening. The court of chancery was the third Wicklow landlord and in his evaluation of the three – proprietor, middleman and court – Saunders observed that the condition of the tenant on the first 'is good, the second bad and the last pernicious and injurious to the land. It is let from 3 to 7 years. I have known five wheat crops one after the other. Some is constantly meadowed year after year without being broken up, or without any manure.'

The most radical and prescient solution to the question of land distribution in Wicklow and in Ireland as a whole was prescribed by Pierce Mahony, the new landlord of Grangecon and a man with considerable expertise in dealing with issues affecting property. He advocated that property be turned into the 'simplest form, namely that called fee simple, instead of the complicated form it now presents and to which English lenders particularly object'. Mahony, although a major landowner in Wicklow and Kerry, recommended 'the breaking up of large estates now encumbered almost to their full value, and only held on to gratify the pride and ambition of the holders at the expense of the country.' 'The farms I should prefer,' he told the Commission in a remarkably prophetic judgement, 'are, from twenty-five to forty acres; the labourers being protected by having their cottages and gardens, say one acre to each from the superior landlord.'

There was considerable variation in the geography of land tenure in county Wicklow. Robert Chaloner could only answer that 'There is a great quantity out of lease. The greater part is in lease,' when asked about tenure on Fitzwilliam property. Lord Wicklow's property was chiefly under lease except for town parks and smallholdings; Synge of Glanmore gave leases of twenty-one years, Fitzwilliam gave twenty-one year terms and the tenants' lives and the philanthrophic Abraham Tate of Coolballintagart behind Aughrim gave leases of three young lives in 1809. The possession of a lease gave a degree of discretionary control that was not available to the other categories of tenure. Because Wicklow leaseholdings were of considerable scale – some such as La Touche estate in Delgany, Grene of Kilranelagh and Bookey of Derrybawn had the status of estates – such a differential was likely to find expression in the landscape. Within estates, however, there were internal differences in tenure. On twenty-six selected townlands on the Carysfort estate the variety of tenures ranged from terms of twenty-one years, one life, three lives or thirty-one years, seven years and the freehold land of demesne and deerpark. The degree of discretionary control was qualified by stipulations described by Robert Saunders as:

against alienation, or dividing the farm amongst children at the death of the lessee; to repair; to till in a husbandlike manner; to reside; not to build more than one farm house on the land; power to enter and repair after three months' notice in writing having been given to the tenant, and he neglecting to do so; and not to till more than one-fourth of the land for the last four years of the lease.

One of the penal clauses attached to Fitzwilliam leases made the marriage choice of a widow with a lease subject to approval from the estate office so as to avoid the possibility of disputes over inheritance if the widow was to have a second family.

If the estate system was the fulcrum on which mid-nineteenth century Wicklow was shaped, the estate agent was the fulcrum on which the individual estates were organised. Table 16.4 lists the recorded agents either in the Ordnance Survey Namebooks or in the

Table 16.4
Land agents for some Wicklow estates

Estate	*Agent*	*Residence*
Fitzwilliam	Robert Chaloner	Coolattin, Shillelagh
Meath	Thomas C. Hamilton	Balbriggan (Dublin)
Beresford	George Meara	Maypark, Waterford
Wicklow (east estate)	Michael Hudson	Woodmount, Arklow
Wicklow (Imail estate)	Michael Fenton	Ballinclea, Donaghmore
Powerscourt	Robert Sandys	Balinagee, Donaghmore
Hugo	Lawrence Byrne	Croneybyrne
Downshire	Thomas Murray	Blessington
Hutchinson	Thomas C. Hamilton	Balbriggan, Dublin
Hume	Henry Humfrey	14 Park St., Dublin
Tynte	John C. Creamer	Cork
Marshall	Charles Coates	Tankerly, Tinahely
de Robeck	James Lynch	Whitlease, Kildare
Hawkins-Whitshed	Mr Moffett	Dublin
Synge	Charles Jetson Case	Clara
Brady	Mr Ebbs	Rathmore, Kildare
Paul	Sr Simon Newport	Brooklodge, Waterford
Aldborough	Major Hoey	Leeson St., Dublin
Carroll (Ballynure)	James Wall	Knockarigg, Ballynure
Carroll (Ashford)	Samuel Fenton	Gloucester St., Dublin
Leslie	Mr Murdough	Mountjoy Sq., Dublin
Denton	John Booth	Ballinabarny, Knockrath
Joy	John Jones	Baltinglass
Vavisour	John Jones	Baltinglass
Lee and Ratcliffe	John Jones	Baltinglass
Saunders	Charles Doyne	Blackrock, Dublin

Devon Commission for twenty-six Wicklow properties. Eleven resided outside county Wicklow, mainly in Dublin. Major Hoy of Leeson Street, Dublin was agent to Aldborough's Baltinglass estate; Frederick Joy of Belfast was agent to Baron Joy for Ballyknockan townland which had the important granite quarries; John T. Creamer of Cork represented Lady Tynte's interest in Dunlavin; Thomas C. Hamilton of Balbriggan managed both the Meath and Hutchinson properties; the two Waterford families, Beresford and Paul, had Waterford-based agents George Meara of Maypark and Sir Simon Newport of Brooklodge, respectively. Four of the twenty-six agents resided in Wicklow but not on the property they managed. John Jones, for instance, rented Newtown Saunders House near Baltinglass and was agent to middlemen proprietors, Lady Vavisour, Baron Joy and Lee and Ratcliffe in Baltiboys parish to the north. Others such as Ebbs of Rathmore or Lynch of Whitlease, agents to Brady of Baltiboys and de Robeck of Straffan lived across the county boundary in Kildare. Eleven of the twenty-six were resident, including some of Wicklow's most powerful land brokers: Robert Sandys, Ballingee (Powerscourt), Robert Challoner, Coolattin (Fitzwilliam), Thomas Murray, Blessington (Downshire), Charles Jetson Case, Clara (Synge of Glanmore, Tottenham of Ballycurry) and Michael Hudson Woodmount, Arklow (Wicklow). Michael Fenton of Ballinclea represented the gentleman farmer-cum-agent. In the Primary Valuation of Tenements he is listed as living in a house of £20 valuation which had a 303-acre farm adjoining.[20] He was agent in 1838 to the Glen Imail lands of Lord Wicklow as well as representing a number of smaller landowners. The Fenton family was one of the bigger claimants for government compensation for alleged damage to property in 1798. Henry Carroll's estate of Ballynure was looked after by a neighbour landlord, James Wall of Knockarigg, who was a kinsman and leasee. Robert Saunders, disenchanted with the financial downturn presided over by an agent, had assumed responsibility for managing his own property.

Robert Chaloner told the Devon Commission that the primary duties of agents were 'to view the farms, know the value of them and the ins and outs of every tenant: and I may say to regulate all disputes among them.' The working agent according to Michael Hudson should 'see that everything goes on properly pertaining to the valuation of land and encourage tenants to drain and build houses.' Robert Saunders, reflecting his own experience, was critical of agents, decrying absenteeism and observing that 'some only look to obtaining rents and never visit the farm. There are many agents who go to a public house, and get what rent they can and never visit the estate.' Resident agents in evidence to the Devon Commission naturally emphasised the demonstration impact of residency. 'I am a farmer myself,' Case of Clara said in evidence, 'by farming I live. I often go and advise the tenants, and I show them how to proceed and reason with them, and sometimes beg of them, but it is a hard thing to overcome their prejudices. They say 'we cannot afford to lay down the land, we must take another crop of it.' There are other agents who came down to receive the rent, and go back again to town. I am a resident agent.'

Although the centrality of the agent's role is well recognised little detailed study has been completed on these arbitrers of Wicklow lands. We know most about Thomas Murray, agent to the Blessington estate of the marquis of Downshire.[21] The Murray family had risen through surveying and valuing. Murray had a yearly salary of £650 out of which he had to pay his own clerk and other personal assistants but he had additional perks such as tenancy of prime fattening lands in Blessington demesne. Downshire, whose total gross rental was around £72,000 in 1845, was a taxing master who took a keen interest in the administration of all his property. Murray's role is exemplified in the context of Downshire's visit to Blessington in 1838. He had to prepare an inventory of tenants with an estimate of their personal status and financial solvency; list lands in out-farms held in rundale and commonage with a recommendation as to what should be done to regulate them; return the number of lime-kilns, assess the condition of the newly-planted Cornation Plantation, provide a register of Protestant freeholders and report on the state of the inn and school. On Downshire's arrival, reported in Elizabeth Smith's diary, Murray had to round up rent defaulters for a daunting private audience with their landlord creditor, make arrangements for a round of social calls, which also had a practical purpose, to neighbouring landlords such as Colonel and Elizabeth Smith of Baltiboys, Milltown at Russborough, Hornidge of Tulfarris and major leaseholders such as the rancher John Finnamore of Ballyward, who enjoyed special status as one of Downshire's money lenders.

Differential tenurial practices and the distinction between direct and indirect management are mirrored in the rent map of Wicklow but the primary economic tenet of supply and demand is the key criterion (figs 16.4 and 16.5). County Wicklow, according to Griffith's estimate, had 130,000 acres above 1,000 feet and 201,000 acres of unimproved land. Rent was not always directly related to either demand or even land quality as the chronology of leases was another significant element in the mosaic. The rental returns on which fig. 16.4 is based are derived from the Ordnance Survey Namebooks which are rich, but not uniformly so, in such detail for county Wicklow. Gaps in the Ordnance Survey data have been filled by using the evidence of land

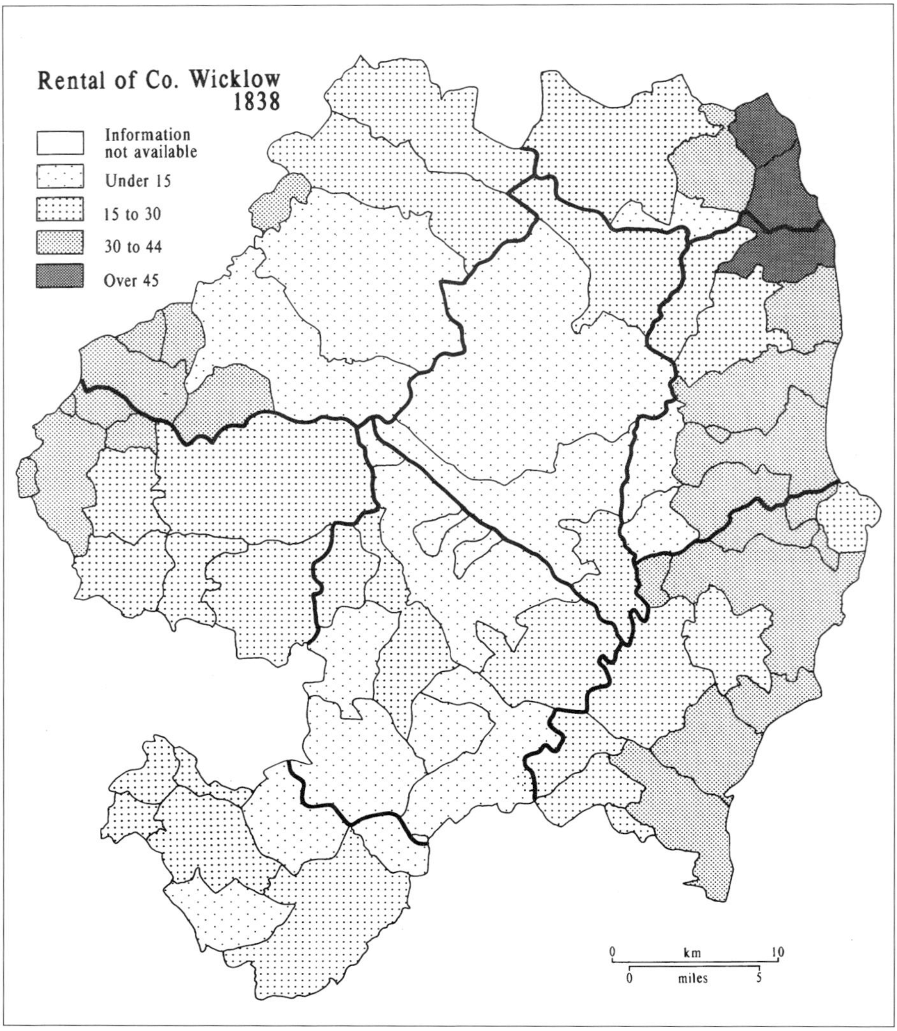

Figure 16.4 Rental of Wicklow, 1838.

agents and farmers in the Devon Commission and the manuscript rentals of estates when these were available. A number of factors need to be highlighted when analysing fig. 16.4. Because of the configuration of Wicklow's parishes the marginal, sometimes empty, lands in the high country tend to deflate parish rents when these are aggregated according to townlands, such as, for example in the parishes of Blessington, Donaghmore and Derrylossary. Therefore the *intra* parish differences which are often more crucial for understanding the landscape pattern are obscured. Secondly Wicklow rents were

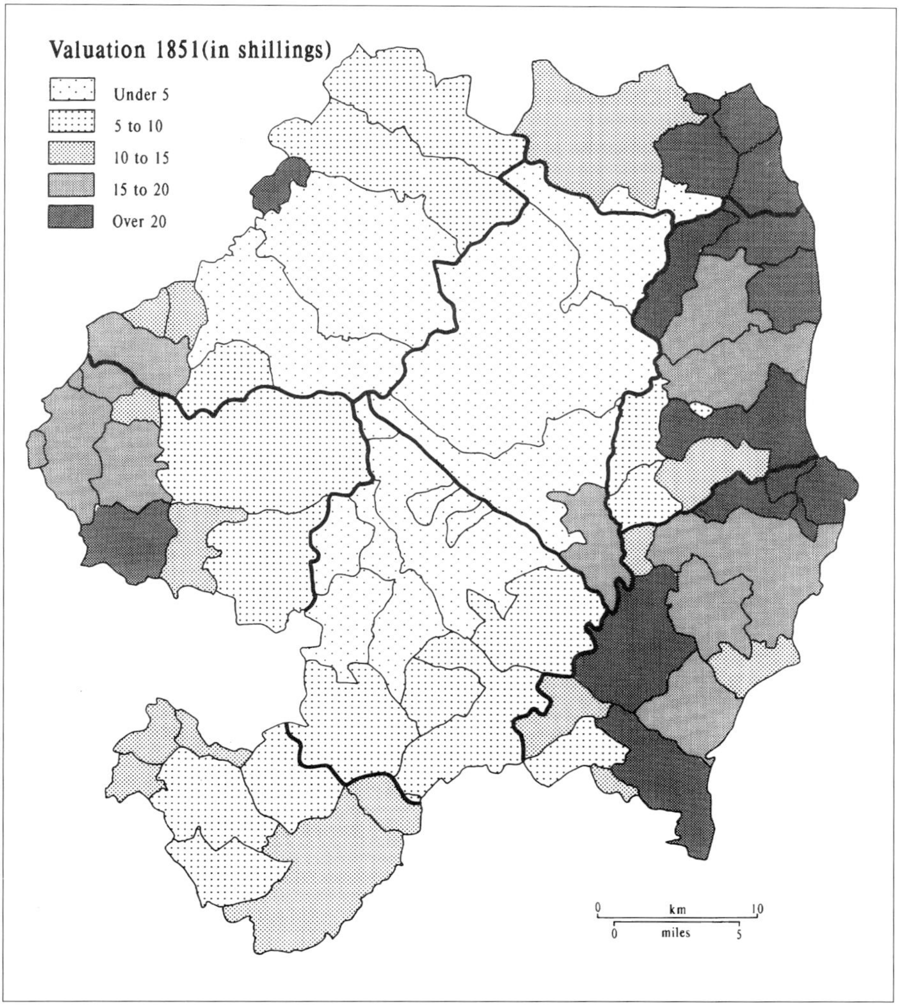

Figure 16.5 Average valuation per acre of Wicklow's civil parishes, 1851. Source: *Census of population, 1851*.

calculated in different ways. Rent on the good land or what Westby of High Park termed 'the low country' was acreable but in the uplands it was assessed, usually for letting to middlemen, by bulk or the gross sum. Tate of Coolballintagart, a working landlord-farmer, explained the method employed in renting such land to tenants: 'Rent was acreable upon the enclosure but upon the mountain lands there are collops grazing giving on the hill sufficient to graze the stock the enclosures will give hay for.' Sometimes, as in the large hill townland of Laragh East, collops were assigned in the ratio of one collop to every one pound rent paid. On the bigger estates rents were based on formal valuations, such as that undertaken on the Fitzwilliam lands in 1834 by a Mr Bingley, brought over from England.

In Arklow barony a noted dairy district, farms were rented not by quantity or quality but on the number of cows they would support:

> the farms are in a great many instances let off a portion to a dairyman, the general run is what will keep twenty cows summer and winter – less than two Irish acres will be sufficient to keep each cow summer and winter for which they never charge less then £6.5s.0d or in some instances £6.10s.0d. Revell of Ballymoney had let to dairymen land capable of sustaining one hundred and thirty milch cows for which he receives eight hundred pounds a year.[22]

The acreage proportion of the county paying highest rents of over 45 shillings was 2.2 per cent: 19.7 per cent was rented at average prices of from 30 to 44 shillings; 41.5 per cent between 15 and 30 shillings and 36 per cent at rents under 15 shillings.

The highest rents, over 45 shillings per acre, in county Wicklow were paid in the three north-eastern parishes of Bray, Delgany and Kilcoole. Inherent land quality, proximity to urban markets, the utility of the area for alternative land uses such as 'pet land' for Dublin-weary industrialists and professional classes and the beginnings of the tourist industry were all factors in raising rents here. Furthermore, the high proportion of land not available for agriculture reduced supply. John Quin, in evidence to the Devon Commission, estimated that the average rental of an Irish acre in Bray was from '£5 to £6, and some a great deal higher,' 'handsome, cottage residences in Bray let at £8 to £10 per acre.' Rents in the second highest category, 30 to 44 shillings, were more or less continuous along Wicklow's coastal parishes with the exception of Kilpoole where the leasing arrangements on Fitzwilliam property reduced charges. This was Wicklow's early land with good access both by road and sea to markets and manure, especially lime which was brought by sea from Skerries to Wicklow port. It had strong internal markets at Wicklow and Arklow and a high proportion of resident farming landlords such as Revel of Ballymoney. Highly specialised agricultural enterprises were recorded for Dunganstown parish by the field valuators:

> Some of the respectable farmers in Dunganstown parish carry on a great trade in rearing fed veal – they will get from £5 to £6 for a calf six weeks old in Dublin. Great numbers feed young lambs and when six weeks old they will get a guinea for each lamb from

> a Liverpool butcher by sending them into Dublin; they generally send in half a score at a time. They have plenty of lambs some a month old nearly; they were lambed the first week in January.[23]

Marl found in the low country near the sea was particularly favoured as a fertiliser for the sandy loam soils and there was no bogland in any of these parishes. Michael Hudson, agent to Lord Wicklow and resident close to Arklow, summarised the rental character of the estate for the Devon Commission:

> The highest lands we have are the town parks, which are let at £4 an acre. The highest land we have of farming land is two guineas and a half, and I believe there are but twenty acres at that rent on Lord Wicklow's property. I should say that the land lets generally from 45 shillings down to 15 shillings per Irish acre.

Rents in the second category were paid for a stretch of lowland in mid-west Wicklow contiguous to county Kildare in the parishes of Dunlavin, Tober, Crehelp, Rathsallagh, Ballynure and extending to Donard and Freynestown and the detached parish of Burgage. This country beyond the hill, free of bog and close to lime-rich Kildare was part of the great midland cattle-fattening belt. It was full of speculative middlemen which may also account for the comparatively high rents required to satisfy the layers of interest. Anthony Allen of Logatrine, Dunlavin rented his farm of 251 acres for 30 shillings per acre from middleman Bookey of Derrybawn who in turn paid ten shillings per acre to Saunders of Saundersgrove, who represented the absentee Lady Tynte of Dunlavin and the agent John J. Creamer of Cork. Allen was a progressive, innovative farmer who:

> tills about 20 acres, the remainder under pasture, grazing sheep, black cattle and horses. Cattle are chiefly of the Durham and some of the Ayrshire breed: he has a superior breed of pigs brought from Buckinghamshire in England. He has a threshing machine, worked by 3 horses: sows around five acres of turnips and grass clover in large quantities.

The third category of rents, 15 to 30 shillings, picked out the land which skirted the mountains. It included all the borderland with Dublin in Kilbride, Blessington and Powerscourt, part of Calary, Newcastle Upper and detached Kilcoole. Southwards it picked out the hill fringes of Redcross, Castlemacadam, Ballykine, Ballintemple, Killahurler and Inch on Carysfort's estate. Almost all of Shillelagh barony was in this category and the parishes of Moyne, Rathbran, Kilranelagh, Kiltegan and Donaghmore in the shadow of Lugnaquillia. Middle-rent Wicklow was a varied county. 'Milk and butter, the rearing of young cattle and sheep is what the farmer mostly depends on,' the valuator noted in his field notes for Ballintemple in the Carysfort estate and these were the stable products of this grazing belt. Castlemacadam, 'the surface hilly and in the north a great portion of it is uncultivated and marshy, the southern position of it is much better land and capable of growing all kinds of grain and vegetables,' typifies the varied topography so evident in Wicklow parishes.' The 'ready sale for everything their farms produce and employment for their horses and servants at all times' in the copper mines helped ameliorate the problems of land quality. Much of this country was described as 'kind land'. Proximity to markets was stressed by the valuators as a major advantage: Redcross parish 'produces oats, wheat and is remarkable for hay and grazes well ... farmers have a ready market for their grain in Wicklow and for their potatoes and milk at the mines.' Specialist witnesses to the Devon Commission concurred with the assessments of the Ordnance Survey sappers and the field valuators. Abraham Tate estimated that the average rent of arable in Moyne was about 25 shillings: Robert Chaloner was uncertain as to the average rent paid in Shillelagh. 'In truth up here,' he told the Commission, 'we have so little good land I do not know. I think we have very little up here. £1 an acre is the highest.' Robert Saunders, referring to his own estate in Rathbran and to the hinterland of Baltinglass, observed that 'the average rent is twenty-five shillings per acre, the mountain 2s. 6d. and the best land £2.'

Wicklow's lowest rents were found in the narrow lands of the central spine with outliers north-west to Boystown and Hollywood and south to Preban and Kilpoole, the latter two belonging to the generally lower rent area of the Fitzwilliam estate. This was remote Wicklow, beyond the pull of towns, a land of oats, cattle, sheep and high summer pastures. Many of the hill communities were accessible only by old bridle paths and a complex tenurial system made the calculation of rent a difficult job for the surveyors. The patchwork mosaic produced by such a system is revealed in the surveyor's description of Laragh east, a townland of 2,202 acres in Derrylossary parish:

> Mr Burrowes holds a large part of the townland, lease is for ever, he has let some farms to tenants-at-will. Part is let by Captain Hugo to tenants-at-will. Land is let by the bulk, the mountain ground held in common: they reclaimed *c.*564 acres. Those holding reclaimed land hold one collop grazing free on the mountain for every £1.00 rent paid.

Landscape: some parish case studies

It is not until the Primary Valuation of Tenements was published for county Wicklow in 1853 that we have a qualitative uniform assessment of land and buildings in the county. The relationship between total valuation and total population was used in the late nineteenth century by the Congested Districts Board[24] as a measure of poverty and it is possible to use the published 1851 valuation returns for Wicklow to identify barony variations in the distribution of wealth. Arklow which had a valuation ratio of £2.53 for each person in 1841 was by this measure the wealthiest barony in Wicklow, followed by Newcastle (£2.46) and Rathdown (£2.27). Talbotstown Upper (£1.85) and Talbotstown Lower (£1.81) were strikingly similar; Shillelagh (£1.55) was ranked sixth while the people of the mountains in Ballinacor North (£1.43) and Ballinacor South (£1.30) had adequate space but limited wealth. When the relationship between recorded population and valuation is again assessed in 1851 it is clear that the differential population decline of the famine decade had altered the situation. Newcastle (£3.16) had now outstripped Arklow (£2.91); Rathdown (2.27) was in third place; Talbotstown Upper (£2.65) and Talbotstown Lower (£2.45) had benefited from comparatively steep population losses; Shillelagh (£2.11) had done likewise and Ballinacor South (£1.83) was now ranked above Ballinacor North (£1.54) reversing the 1841 placings. Wealthier areas had a wider resource base and better access to markets; they had a higher proportion of gentry seats and were generally better endowed.

Parish transects

Blessington and Baltiboys in Talbotstown Lower

A north to south transect of west Wicklow reveals less striking differences in land and landscape than the west to east path. The civil parishes of Blessington and Baltiboys are ideal sampling grounds for landscape analysis. Blessington encompassed 16,000 acres in thirty-one townlands which varied in area from 41 acres in Old Paddocks in the sandy lowlands to 3,613 acres in uncharted Ballynabrockey. Blessington was a rare example in county Wicklow of a carefully managed property complete with its classic estate town but shorn of its Big House. The ordnance surveyors recorded:

> Downshire House in ruins, four fishponds a little east of the house in bad repair, one of them almost dry. There is scarce a trace of any of the offices and the garden is converted to a haggard. The house and offices were burned in the year 1798 by the Rebels, before that time it used to be the seat of the Marquis during the

> summer quarter and was kept in high and splendid repair and never since rebuilt.

In the absence of the landlord agent the middle tenant reigned supreme in a cattle-based economy. The lowlands were as empty as the two-thirds of the parish on the high ground. Ballyward (345 acres) for example, in the bend of the Liffey, was occupied by John Finnamore who resided in a house valued at £17.10s. and, apart from the herd James Keogh who lived in a one pound house, had the townland to himself. Finnamore's house and its furnishings earned the approbation of the critical Elizabeth Smith, and his sprawling grazier portfolio is more clearly revealed in the valuation returns of 1853. The contiguous lowland townland of Oldcourt in contrast had 56 houses in 1841, five or six of which were clustered around a crossroads which had its pattern day each year on the first Sunday in August. By 1853 twenty-two of its flimsy cabins and their occupants, some 119 people, had vanished from its map. Crosscoolharbour exhibited a strikingly different pattern than its neighbour Oldcourt. Although comparatively similar in area (826 acres) there were only twelve houses here in 1841 and the same number remained in 1851. The explanation of this contrast may lie in the observation of the surveyors that whereas Oldcourt was 'all Catholic', the inhabitants of Crosscoolharbour, leased in 1837 by Murray the estate agent, were invariably Protestants such as Browne, Boothman, Fearis and Panton. Protestant tenants, enclosed fields, high rents and low population densities characterised the townlands of Holyvalley, Old Paddocks, Haylands, Edmondstown and Dillonsdown which neatly encircled the town of Blessington. Two-storey, slated sheltered, stone houses in tidy farms gave way to the Catholic, Bally lands on the high ground. Here in great open moorland spaces, low thatched houses built with black slate stone huddled in their damp clusters against the west-winds in Ballynabrockey, Ballysmuttan, Ballynatona and Ballynascullogue.

Boystown to the south had no primate landlord: its lowlands were dominated by small resident landlords in townland estates; its middle ground was characterised by thin farms on absentee middlemen ground and above was the domain of the quarryman, the gamekeeper and those seeking refuge. A cross section from west to east in this part of Talbotstown reveals the striking complexity of Wicklow's cultural landscape. Russborough, belonging to the nearly insolvent earl of Milltown, lay in splendid isolation atop a carefully composed terrace. 'The mansion,' observed the surveyors, 'is in the Grecian style erected after a design by Mr Cassels and consists of a centre and two wings connected by a semi-circular colonade of alternate Ionic and Corinthian pillars and presenting a noble facade of hewn stone 700 feet in extent.' This splendid Palladian pile looked down on the Hornidge house at Russellstown and across the Liffey at Elizabeth Smith's newly reconstructed mansion, 'a fine dwelling house and other buildings called after the townland with ornamental ground and gardens'. Above them to the north-east lay the crowded democracy of Lacken with 550 inhabitants in 91 houses in 1841. The village, noted the surveyors, 'contains about fifty houses very irregularly built, there is a Roman Catholic chapel in the village the only place of worship in the parish of Kilbeg, it contains about 300 litters.' It was a self-sufficient place. 'The inhabitants hold less or more land with the privilege of mountain pasture for a few sheep; they manufacture all their woollen clothes; they feed on a little more than potatoes and milk.' Baron Joy, lately deceased, had little more than £500 rental for his vast mountain leasehold of some 10,000 acres; perhaps it was the 'very fine granite quarry at the east side of the village (Ballyknockan) which first brought him here.' The surveyors observed that:

> the quarry is considered the best in this part of the kingdom and has been in use for the last 14 years. The proprietor, the late Baron Joy, lately took that part containing the quarry into his own possession and has it rented at £40 per year. At present there are about 160 men employed in the quarry, labourers' wages six to seven shillings a week, smiths and stonecutters have from fifteen to twenty-six shillings.

Ringed round the perimeter of the mountain, where thin drift afforded a spadehold, were the agricultural clusters of Kylemore, Ballynastockan, Middletown and Lugnaskeagh. Surprisingly, these upland settlements held their 1841 populations during the decade of hunger and Ballyknockan, the quarry village, became a town.

Written evidence, apart from state and estate records, is sparse for those below gentry status in county Wicklow. Mary Hanbidge's reconstruction of her father's nineteenth century Imail illuminates the world of Protestant hill communities:

> The homestead of Tinnehinch stands back from the road down Kelsha Hill; a long lane just wide enough for a cart leads to the yard. Outside the upper gate is the opening to the haggard with its stone supports for ricks. Inside the gate is the new well and on the left the house itself with the fowlhouses and cowhouses; on the right the car house for ass's cart, gig etc., the barn and the dairy. Beside the dairy three stone steps lead up to the garden

> with its gooseberry and currant bushes, cabbages, lilies, stocks and roses. Beside the lower gate is a shed for carts and just outside the yard the pigstyes; the bull's house is now at the back of the house at the site of the bacon curing sheds burnt down in 1798. Behind the house is the row of poplars planted by my grandfather: there are tall elms in all the hedgerows.[25]

Stratford-on-Slaney across the river was 'the cotton manufactory of Mr Orr who employed large numbers of cotton weavers with their fly shuttles, also bleachers, cutters and printers,' much addicted to 'drunkenness, prostitution, cursing and swearing.'[26] Traces of elder faiths lingered on in the valley:

> They got up early on Easter Sunday morning to see the sun dance; there was witchcraft, the Banshee wailed at Ballintruer, those ancient mounds the raths were haunts of fear, the hollows of old stones held magic water ... there was cock fighting, bull baiting and drunkenness.[27]

Knockrath and Ballinacor in Ballinacor South

Knockrath parish was in thirty-one townlands shared between nine landlords. It consisted of a rectangular block of high mountain extending south from Laragh along the military road to Drumgoff Bridge; fingers of valley floor and valley wall in Glenmalure south of the Avonbeg; a lowland core in the vale of Clara along the Avonmore and a stretch of middleground around Trooperstown. Lord Meath dominated landownership in the parish with 11,000 acres; Kemmis of adjoining Ballinacor, Henry Grattan of Tinnahinch, a Mr White of London and the earl of Essex were also present. None of the proprietors in fee was resident. Knockrath suffered greatly in the military activity of 1798: the Chritchley mansion in Ballyboy in Glenmalure was burned (John and Abraham Chritchley claimed four thousand pounds compensation for the loss of the house, furniture and cattle);[28] Henry Allen's woollen manufactory in Grenane, 'said to be the best in Ireland but at that time it was burned and the machinery destroyed,' met a similar fate. Factory was replaced by military barracks at Drumgoff facing the valley of Glenmalure. By 1838 the mountains were quiet and the barracks had been sold 'by the present proprietor to miners working in Glenmalure', a Catholic chapel was being built at Claramore and Henry Hodgson was working the lead mines at Ballinafunshogue. Grass, minerals and timber were the shaping elements of Knockrath in 1838.

The middlemen of Knockrath were miners and cattlemen. Access to the high ground had improved dramatically when military road succeeded bridle-path in 1801. Henry Hodgson paid £60 rental to the earl of Essex for Ballinafunshogue where he employed forty men. Mining created the twenty-six houses listed in this remote place in 1841. John Edge, another mining speculator and proprietor of Newtown Collieries, county Carlow, held three townlands – Knockrath, Knockrath Little and Ballard. We know that he paid Lord Meath £76.14.0. rent for Knockrath Big and Little and that he had a profit rent of £111 from his sixteen undertenants. Edge's interest in Ballard may be related to the timber plantations in that townland and the interaction of mining and timber interests is a pertinent theme in the economic history of Wicklow.

The more localised middlemen afford interesting insights into how newcomer and native were integrated at the level of rent management. Invariably the locals were people of substance who may have links to the pre-plantation occupying families, thereby providing the ethnic affiliation with undertenants which facilitated rent collection. In Knockrath, Larry Byrne of Croneybyrne had such a role for the Meath estate. He rented over 600 acres of peripheral land by a variety of tenures for little more than £100. Most of this land was sub-let by him by the lump and the evidence suggests that he derived over £300 profit rent from his transactions.

The other middlemen identified in Knockrath parish were Wicklow's capitalists who linked rural production and urban consumption. These were the cattlemen – either originating further east in the county as did Sam Manning, Mr Ford of Ballinderry and John Sutton, or coming from the traditional core of ranching as did Henry Cottingham of Oldbridge and Mr Burridge, both from county Meath. The tenurial system was by no means uniform. Sometimes townlands were leased, as for example Ballysheeman Upper which was held 'by Mr Ford of Ballinderry who has let five holdings for £67 without leases'. In Meath's townland of Ballyboy which contained 1,000 acres, 'about one half is let to Mr Sutton at £7, the remainder is let to different tenants.' Henry Cottingham of Oldbridge had the grassy hillsides of Kirakee and Ballinabarny, some 1,200 acres from Lord Meath for £20.

Ballinacor parish adjoined Knockrath. Wedged between the Ow and Avonbeg rivers, Ballinacor encompassed the sharp east face of Lugnaquillia and much of Glenmalure valley. In west Wicklow, the mountain lands were invariably in large compact blocks in single ownership but here in Ballinacor and along almost all the eastern mountain fringe the pattern of ownership was greatly fragmented. Ballinacor's 17,000 marginal acres was shared between eleven landlords in 1837 as if the Wicklow gentry was engaged in a scramble for the high ground in the pre-Famine era. A transect from Barravore in Glenmalure along the Avonbeg river brings us successively through the properties of Byrne of Croneybyrne, Parnell of Avondale, Acton of Kilmacurragh, Kemmis of Ballinacor, Byrne of Cabinteely and Guinness, the rector of Rathdrum. Below along the Ow we encounter Lord Meath, Gunn of Newtownmountkennedy, Colwell of the same place, Reeves of Naas and Revell of Ballymoney. Significantly the mountain divide is reflected in the absence of any west Wicklow landlords in the parish. Kemmis was the only resident landlord. There is no apparent explanation for the fragmentation of ownership in these marginal lands. It may be related to the gentry penchant for the grouse moor and shooting lodge but it is more likely related to the opening up of the north-south routes by the military road which linked Aghavannagh with Dublin. Lime came from distant Carlow across the Ballinabarny gap, the land transport adding significantly to cost. Perhaps it is the mineral rich core at the junction of schist and granite which best explains the complex ownership geography of Ballinacor.

Ballinacor's peripheral lands afforded little scope for middlemen; furthermore, the resident landlord Kemmis who controlled some 6,000 of its thin acres may have restricted land speculation. Neither were the administrative cores of Byrne of Croneybyrne nor Parnell of Avondale too far distant from their Ballinacor lands. Aghavannagh's damp lands belonging to Revell of Ballymoney near Wicklow town were let in eight holdings for a rent of £262; Parnell had only four tenants on some 2,000 acres rented by bulk. On his townland of Ballinaskeagh the surveyor observed 'the uncultivated portion of this townland used as pasture during the summer season'. Colwell who owned Aghavannagh Ram had a resident agent, Mr Lambe, on the lands which were 'let in farms to the tenants each of whom holds their part by bulk; the houses are all low thatched cabins.' There is little evidence in the settlement context of the house clusters which proliferated in west Wicklow. The cluster of Mucklagh, one of the few referred to, on the high ground north of the Ow river below Aghavannagh, was on the property of Mrs Reeves of Naas, 'let to Mrs Valentine by bulk and she in like manner by bulk to some of the tenants and others at 15 shillings per acre and 8 shillings for the grazing of each collop or cow for six months'. Mucklagh cluster, the ruins of which are now buried in sitka spruce plantations, accounted for many of the 37 houses and 195 people recorded here in 1841. Famine decimated this settlement on the margins and the 1851 census recorded a total of 13 houses and 64 people in the townland.

Ballinacor House was the administrative core of the parish. The surveyor gave an appropriate summary:

> Ballinacor House has a square form, two storeys high. A great part

planted. There is an excellent farmyard, offices and garden a little north of the cottage. There is a splendid coach walk from the House to the north and south entrances at each of which there is a gate house. There is a Roman Catholic chapel near the north-west corner in the village of Grenane. Grenane chapel is a long time built.

The chapel village faced southwards to the newly built Protestant church at Ballinatona.

Carnew in Shillelagh barony

From the late seventeenth century onwards the greater part of Shillelagh barony was administered as a single estate.[29] This administrative continuity was reinforced by the longevity of resident agents: in the period from 1748 to 1848 the estate had only four agents and Robert Chaloner, who gave evidence to the Devon Commission, had succeeded his father as controller of the Fitzwilliam property. There is little evidence that any major changes in estate management were introduced when Fitzwilliam acquired the property through marriage in 1783. Fitzwilliam, a permanent absentee, devolved control to Protestant leaseholders in the well-founded belief that they would become instruments of landlord policy to the mutual benefit of both. Such a policy had obvious impact on land and landscape in town and countryside. In the first instance these leaseholders were more likely, than their counterparts in the rugged terrain of Ballinacor to the north, to be resident. Furthermore, covenants in leases stipulated that head-tenants should build substantial houses and out-offices or forfeit money. The ordnance surveyors carefully observed these townland houses. Archibald Mountfort of Killenure had recently (1834) built a 'large fine two-storey house, solid modern style of architecture ... good offices, a walled-in garden and handsome lawn with about 30 acres of plantation attached to it'. Similarly Fairwood House in Boleybawn townland, Crosspatrick parish, was 'in good repair, two storeys high and slated with good outoffices and well sheltered with trees. Land well fenced and arable part produces light crops of hay, oats and potatoes.' The surveyor noted that 'the remainder of the houses are held by cottiers or labourers holding from a rood to three acres at *c.* £1 yearly from the principal inhabitants whom they labour for.'

Resident middlemen farmed the greater part of their leaseholdings and sub-let the remainder. In Carnew parish, for example, townlands close to the town were held by Protestant tenants such as in Umrigar – Blayney, Tombreen – Swan, Ballingate – Braddle, Upper Croneyhorn – de Renzy. John Swan, who leased Tombreen, a townland of 1.187 acres, worked 621 acres and sub-let the remainder in fifty-three holdings with an average size of 17 acres. Andrew de Renzy, a graduate of Trinity College, magistrate and firm advocate of draining, reclamation and turnips, leased 416 acres, had 395 in his own possession and sub-let the remainder to thirteen tenants. Head-tenant and tenant did not share religion. In Crosspatrick parish 'the respectable leaseholders being Protestant and Methodists, the small farmers and labourers are Roman Catholics.' Social segregation was replicated spatially: Protestants though nowhere in the majority, formed strong minorities in lowland townlands, as elsewhere in Wicklow, around the three landlord towns of Tinahely, Shillelagh and Coolattin.

Segregation on religious lines was particularly evident in the town of Carnew.[30] Substantially rebuilt after its destruction in 1798 the town mirrored in its social morphology the dominant role of Protestants who occupied the strategic high-value buildings in Main Street and Brunswick Row. Catholics were found in more peripheral locations, huddled on the steep slopes of Mill Street close to the brewery or in the landlord-inspired Coolattin Row, built in the 1830s to replace thatched cabin suburbs. At least they were at home:

> in Coolattin about eight years ago (*c.*1837) there were a number of people turned upon the road in order to make way for a large farm or they were sent to America with a small recompense.

Castlemacadam

Castlemacadam with its 11,000 acres, divided into forty-four townlands, was shaped by fifteen landlords including Putland, Parnell, Sockwell, Powerscourt, Wicklow, Whaley and Bayly. Mineral-rich deposits underground and the flourishing overground landscape industry promoted so grandly by Thomas Moore had attracted money to this well-watered place. Wicklow's most distinctive demesne belt stretching from Avondale south to Shelton and contiguous Glenart with intermediate landmarks at Castlehoward, Cherrymount and Ballyarthur, was juxtaposed with rural slums housing the miners of Ballymurtagh, Connary and Cronebane. Paradoxically the waters so sung by Moore were sullied not only by pollution from Avoca but by mining works further west at Glendalough and Glenmalure, all flowing into Wicklow's major conduit to the sea. Ventilation chimneys, sturdy engine houses, stamp wheels and copper reservoirs were juxtaposed with crenellated Gothic mansions and new hotels. Castle Howard was 'a castellated mansion commandingly situated a short distance to the east of the junction of the rivers Avonmore and Avonbeg, having a view to the north up the Avondale and to the south down the Vale of

Avoca.' Mining defeated, but only short-term, the isolation of the hill. Barravore in Glenmalure, Ballyknockan on the granite and Brockagh above Glendalough, together with the sprawling settlements in Castlemacadam, exemplify this. Brockagh, where 100 men were employed in the lead mines, typified these impermanent industrial clusters: 'neither public house nor grocers in it nor any public road except an old bridle path for the accommodation of the inhabitants'.

Population transfer either through farm rationalisation, demesne creation or attempted avoidance of responsibility for pauper tenants under the new poor law legislation must have been a significant feature in pre-famine Wicklow. We get faint intimations of the process with the strongly divergent views of Simon Moran, a strong farmer from Milltown, between Ashford and Rathnew and Samuel Fenton, solicitor and land-agent to Samuel Carroll, proprietor of Ashford. Moran told the commissioners of the 'comfortable class of labourers living in the estate of Mr Carroll of Ashford who had their houses thrown down three or four years ago, that was when the new poor law was coming into operation and that was the reason for it as we supposed. The settlement consisted of a street of houses from eight to ten; it had evolved through subdivision and the provision of sites for siblings: 'one man had a daughter, and got her married to a nice labouring boy and the father-in-law let them build upon his land.' They were turned out – 'some of them have gone into the commons of Rathnew, a refugium peccatorum for these men. There are hundreds of them there and it was very fortunate for the country that it was there.'

In Rathnew Commons, the ordnance surveyors observed:

> are a great number of mud cabins inhabited by the lowest dregs of society; a police station is just outside the boundary for the purpose of checking the lawless inhabitants.

Samuel Fenton, agent to Mr Carroll, stated that Carroll had demised the lands to Thomas Byrne with strict covenants against sub-letting. 'We wished,' he told the commissioners, 'to prevent any disgraceful appearance of the buildings and also receptacles of filth ... but a great number of rough cabins being erected in this beautiful village of Ashford, Mr Carroll's attention was drawn to it in 1835, long before the poor law and not with any view to evade the poor law.' Carroll resumed the lands after compensating Byorn and his sub-tenants. 'It was,' continued Fenton, 'a receptacle for rogues and very bad characters indeed. A great many thefts were traced home to that place. Mr Carroll's woods were much plundered by the inhabitants of this place. They occupied about 200 yards along the road and not more than six to eight yards deep. One tenant had a field in the rere about one acre, and with that exception the others had no land but merely an enclosure behind with a pigstye.'

North-east Wicklow

Judged by any criteria the north-east quadrant between the hills and the sea was Wicklow's most prosperous. Wright, in his celebrated guide, equalled prosperity with 'Englishness'.[31] 'This neighbourhood (around Bray) is quite English,' he wrote, 'cultivation being carried to such a height of excellence and the peasantry, owing to the constant residence of the gentry in the precise vicinity, being in a state of comfort and happiness.' Topographically the countryside varied from lowlying flatlands to shingle beaches along the coast; higher drier ground on which prosperity and settlement were long based, and the highest ground marked by Great Sugarloaf which gave a natural focus to landscape architecture. Beyond Sugarloaf to the west the land levelled out at around 1,000 feet and here were the great dreary expanses of commonages only recently incorporated into the civil administration. Six townlands in the civil parish of Kilmacanogue had the suffix 'commons,' refuges of the demesne dispossessed, the casualties of industrial recession and the casualties of 1798. The most conspicuous expression of triumphant landlordism in county Wicklow was the unbroken demesne swathe which began at Kilruddery and extended west encompassing Wingfield, Bushy Park, Tinnehinch, Powerscourt and Charleville before ebbing at the eastern head of Glencree in Ballyorney. Here in almost 3,000 acres of countryside girdled by trees and bounded by crafted walls, lay the grandeur and statuary of imperial Wicklow.

It was not all one uniform piece. Delgany, the elegant showpiece of the La Touche family, had 400 inhabitants mainly Protestant, in its 100 houses.[32] 'Gaelic patronymics,' wrote Tom Jones Hughes, 'were rare among the camellias of Delgany.'[33] Enniskerry and its enveloping townlands was the domain of demesne and Protestant tenant: Catholic lay upslope or beyond to the north in the stone quarries of Glencullen. Kilcoole, on the Scott of Ballygannon property, was quite different and much older. In 1851, 40 of its houses were valued at less than £1, whereas Delgany had only one such tenement. Kilcoole on the old medieval commonage was home to a Catholic population. The poorer in this countryside were consigned to the crossroads and cul-de-sac, away from the landlord's eye at Blacklion, Kindleston and Windgate. The Downs, formerly a fair village, was left stranded on its high ridge when by-passed by the new road.

Land tenure outside the sacrosanct demesnes was not very different from low Wicklow: Tithewer, above the estate town of Newtownmountkennedy, is the residence of Mr Nuttall: the land about is neatly planted with fir trees. The inhabitants are all Mr Nutall's menials and of the Roman Catholic belief. Mr Nutall is a Protestant.' Richard Fox leased the townland farm of Coolagad in Delgany parish from the earl of Meath.[34] He resided in a house valued at £23.10s, and occupied 231 of the 285 acres. On the remainder he had eleven undertenants, eight of whom had less than one acre. Rising tourism sponsored by the gentry, such as Powerscourt who let summer houses, and property developers, such as John Quin of Bray, was influencing landscape tastes.

Fassaroe townland above Bray symbolises the villa-studded countryside of north-east Wicklow. Its 568 acres were owned by Judge Crampton:

> whose house St Valory is located on the south-west side near the Dargle. The demesne contains 20 acres. The whole east side is held by Mr Strong at £2.10s per acre on a long lease; part of the north-west side by Mr Barrington on which is a handsome cottage called Maryfield. On the south-west is Fassaroe Cottage let as a bathing lodge to a tenant for the season.

Conclusion

To distill the essence of early nineteenth-century Wicklow into a single analysis is an impossible task. County Wicklow is an elusive entity: its internal geography is so fractured that it must always remain an administrative convenience. The topography of the county has effectively shunted traffic on a north-south rather than east-west axis, thereby creating corridors of commerce along the margins of a comparatively deserted central core. Nineteenth-century ownership patterns and the scale of estates owe their genesis to reformation and plantation in the sixteenth and seventeenth centuries. Blocks of Wicklow were given as rewards for military and church service and the properties then established maintained remarkable spatial integrity. Scale was a significant pre-requisite for both continuity and settlement sponsorship and, by the nineteenth century, the fruits of these earlier grafting processes were displayed in splendid demesnes and a variety of 'pet' villages and estate towns. Such creative manipulations were encouraged by Wicklow's evolution as a place of literary pilgrimage and its inherent suitability for landscape engineering on a grand scale.

Landlords strode imperiously across early nineteenth-century Wicklow. Their remit encompassed the now heavily garrisoned high ground which they sought as adjunct to lowland home farm. The scramble for the hills is mirrored in the fragmentary nature of ownership along the east face of the mountains: it was further fuelled by the lure of gold and game. Few east Wicklow estates, apart from that of the earl of Wicklow, extended beyond the mountain crest which marked the drainage divide but it would be misleading to view the mountains as an impenetrable barrier. There were many gaps and passes which served as drover roads for sheep and cattle and conduits for the lime trade: the military road brought the capital city closer to the highland heartland.

Land agents and estate leasing policy were crucial elements in shaping nineteenth-century Wicklow. The role of the agent needs sharper elucidation but he was the effective facilitator of landlordism at ground level. There is a well-documented bias towards Protestant leaseholders at the scale of townland farm and this was significant in determining the shape and contents of the countryside particularly in the precincts of estate towns and villages, which were invariably sited in Wicklow's best endowed lands. Leases created middlemen and, surprisingly, these featured as much in the well-managed estates of Meath and Fitzwilliam as in the more marginal uplands. The evidence suggests that rents were comparatively higher in districts controlled by middlemen.

Access to land varied in response to management policy but it is certain that the existence of empty demesnes and uninhabitable mountain forced the landless to the edge of town and estate. Parish transects reveal the impracticality of making generalisations for areas greater than townlands. They bring us back to basics and reveal for Wicklow, at any rate, the differential impacts of topography and landlordism.

Appendix I

Wicklow's landed gentry 1876

		Acreage	*Valuation*			*Acreage*	*Valuation*
1.	Fitzwilliam	89,891	46,440	45.	Truell	1,663	1,708
2.	Powerscourt	36,693	8,890	46.	Hepenstall	1,568	926
3.	Waterford	26,035	4,621	47.	Grene	1,559	837
4.	Wicklow	22,103	10,763	48.	Smith	1,558	461
5.	Hugo	17,937	1,246	49.	Mahony	1,547	860
6.	Carysfort	16,291	11,856	50.	Barton	1,542	483
7.	Downshire	15,766	5,018	51.	Carroll (Coote)	1,519	1,149
8.	Meath	14,717	6,012	52.	Smith	1,518	1,091
9.	Cunningham	10,479	5,809	53.	Cooper	1,506	294
10.	Moore	8,730	11,595	54.	Guinness	1,493	384
11.	Kemmis	8,041	1,437	55.	Heighington	1,475	565
12.	Brady	5,837	587	56.	Byrne	1,410	125
13.	Acton	4,845	2,730	57.	Hodgson	1,402	257
14.	Dick	4,770	2,534	58.	Salkeld	1,355	344
15.	Parnell	4,678	1,245	59.	Radcliffe	1,353	523
16.	Hutchinson	4,671	1,202	60.	Cogan	1,348	802
17.	Mining Co Irl	4,409	262	61.	Carroll (H)	1,346	1,159
18.	Synge	4,298	1,825	62.	Keogh	1,319	470
19.	Wade	4,055	3,694	63.	Hudson	1,294	343
20.	Whaley	3,956	1,919	64.	Cherry	1,291	343
21.	Westby	3,874	1,179	65.	T.C.D.	1,287	409
22.	Grogan	3,761	2,106	66.	Booth	1,250	230
23.	Tighe	3,459	2,538	67.	Hodson	1,211	1,186
24.	Monck	3,434	1,556	68.	Hume	1,203	48
25.	Byrne	3,202	842	69.	Colwell	1,201	335
26.	Saunders	3,143	2,059	70.	Ellis	1,197	1,315
27.	Bayly	3,026	1,872	71.	Snell	1,178	25
28.	Kirkpatrick	2,976	1,196	72.	Vavasour	1,175	195
29.	Bourne	2,684	660	73.	Jones	1,159	79
30.	Paul	2,894	1,836	74.	Aldborough	1,155	803
31.	Radcliffe	2,847	761	75.	Frizell	1,148	442
32.	Courtney	2,827	451	76.	Graydon	1,148	442
33.	Fishbourne	2,820	269	77.	Whitshed	1,142	1,357
34.	Bookey	2,684	1,099	78.	Duckett	1,096	881
35.	De Robeck	2,638	1,655	79.	Day & Guinness	1,077	304
36.	Tottenham	2,540	1,410	80.	Scott	1,066	1,443
37.	Tynte	2,532	1,410	81.	Drought	1,064	381
38.	O'Byrne	2,363	2,118	82.	Humphys	1,048	394
39.	Esmonde	2,088	426	83.	Edge	1,028	189
40.	Pennefeather	2,088	426	84.	Sweetman	1,027	796
41.	Heytesbury	1,902	1,163	85.	Nixon	1,010	114
42.	La Touche	1,798	2,964	86.	Revell	1,000	375
43.	Mahony	1,769	1,434	87.	Finnamore	972	528
44.	Bookey	1,745	268				

References

1. W.H. Bartlett, *The scenery and antiquities of Ireland illustrated in one hundred and twenty engravings from drawings by W.H. Bartlett with historical and descriptive text by J. Stirling Coyne*, N.P. Willis, etc., 2 vols (London, n.d.). Wicklow is covered in chapter 7, vol. i, pp 108-124.
2. See, for example, the painting of the patron or festival of St Kevin at the *Seven Churches*, Glendalough 1813 by Joseph Peacock.
3. J.B. Whittow, *Geology and scenery in Ireland* (Harmondsworth, 1974), pp 260-72; W.P. Warren, *Wicklow in the ice age, an introduction and guide to the glacial geology of the Wicklow district* (Dublin, 1993).
4. This reference is from the topographical poems of Giolla na Naomh Ó hUidhrin 'Tuilleadh feasa ar Éirinn óigh.' The allusion is to the green grassy sod of the Mac Giollamocholmóg. See J. O'Donovan (ed.), *The topographical poems of Sean Mór O Dubhagain and Giolla na naomh Ó hUidhrin* (Dublin, 1862), p. 89.
5. *The census of Ireland for the year 1851, Part 1, showing the area, population and number of houses by townlands and district electoral divisions. Vol. 1, province of Leinster* (Dublin, 1852), pp 341-66; *Appendix to minutes of evidence taken before her majesty's commissioners of inquiry into the state of the law and practice in respect to the occupation of land in Ireland.* Part iv (Dublin, 1845), p. 273.
6. Ordnance Survey Name Books, Wicklow, 3 vols., typescript copies N.L.I. The Ordnance Survey Name Books are abridged typescript copies of the originals. Parishes are listed in alphabetical order.
7. Wakefield, *Account of Ire.*, i, 284.
8. Return of owners of land of an acre and upwards, in the several counties, counties of cities, and counties of towns in Ireland (*c.*1492), HC 1876, lxxx, 61, Wicklow county, pp 98-102.
9. J.P. Cooper, 'Strafford and the Byrnes' country', in *I.H.S.*, xv (1966), pp 1-20; T. Ranger, 'Strafford in Ireland: a revaluation', in *Past and Present*, xix (1961), pp 26-45.
10. For a discussion on this aspect of church lands and Trinity College estates see: R. MacCarthy, *The Trinity College estates 1800-1923* (Dundalk, 1993), pp 1-21.
11. Genealogical data on landlord families has been derived from J. Lodge, The peerage of Ireland, or a genealogical history of the present nobility of that kingdom with engravings of their paternal coats of arms collected from public records by J. Lodge, revised, enlarged and continued to the present time by Mervyn Archdall, Vol. i-vii (Dublin, 1789).
12. R.C.B., Rentals of the archbishop of Dublin 1700.
13. For a scholarly analysis of the Downshire estates in Ireland see W.A. Maguire, *The Downshire estates in Ireland 1801-1845* (Oxford, 1972).
14. *Appendix to minutes of evidence taken before her majesty's commissioners of inquiry into the state of the law and practice in respect of the occupation of land in Ireland*, part iv (Dublin, 1845), pp xxx-xxxi, lists the witnesses from county Wicklow who gave evidence to the Devon Commission. There were twenty-one Wicklow witnesses in contrast to sixty-seven for Tipperary and thirty-one for Waterford: Westmeath had the same number as Wicklow. The Wicklow evidence was published in part iii of the Devon Commission and the witnesses, their occupations and no. of evidence were as follows: Edward Burke, farmer (955); Charles Jetson Case, farmer and agent (1020); Robert Chaloner, agent (953); Thomas de Renzy, physician (958); George Douglas, farmer (963); Robert Dowse, farmer (957); Samuel Fenton, solicitor and agent (1049); Michael Hudson, agent (1019); Rev Daniel Kavanagh, Roman Catholic curate (956);

Simon Moran, farmer (1023); William Thomas Mould, solicitor (1060); John Nolan, farmer (1021); John Norton, farmer (964); John Quin, land proprietor (1024); James Roche, farmer (961); Robert Francis Saunders, land proprietor and farmer (952); James Arthur Wall, barrister (1082); Peter Walsh, farmer (1022); William James Westby, land proprietor (962).

15. D. Thomson and M. McGusty (ed.), *The Irish journals of Elizabeth Smith* (Oxford, 1980).
16. Ibid., p. 63.
17. Ibid., p. 83.
18. Ibid., p. 102.
19. W.A. Maguire (ed.), *Letters of a great Irish landlord, a selection from the estate correspondence of the third marquess of Downshire, 1809-1845* (Belfast, 1974), p. 145.
20. *General valuation of rateable property in Ireland, county of Wicklow, valuation of the several tenements*, published by barony (Dublin, 1853).
21. Maguire, *Downshire estates*, p. 204, *et seq.*
22. Valuation Office, Ely Place, Dublin, Field books of the surveyors, Arklow barony.
23. Ibid., Parish of Dunganstown.
24. W. Nolan, 'New farms and fields: migration policies of state land agencies 1891-1980' in W.J. Smyth and K. Whelan (ed.), *Common ground – essays on the historical geography of Ireland presented to T. Jones Hughes* (Cork, 1988), pp 296-8.
25. M. Hanbidge, *The memories of William Hanbidge* (St Albans, 1939).
26. Ibid.
27. Ibid.
28. *List of persons who have suffered losses in their property in the county of Wicklow and who have given in their claim on or before the 6th of April, 1799, to the commissioners for inquiry into the losses sustained by such of his Majesty's loyal subjects as have suffered in their property by the Rebellion.*
29. P. Lennon, Eighteenth-century landscape change from estate records – Coolattin estate, Shillelagh, county Wicklow, unpublished B.A. dissertation submitted to Dept. of Geography, T.C.D. (1979), pp 5-6.
30. M. Byrne, Religion in south-west Wicklow: a spatial and social analysis, unpublished B. Ed., dissertation submitted to Dept. of Geography, Carysfort College, Blackrock, Dublin (1984), pp 42-7.
31. Wright, *Guide to county Wicklow*, p. 48.
32. K. Rahill, A reconstruction of the landscapes of the civil parishes of Delgany and Kilcoole in the mid-nineteenth century, unpublished M.A. Qualifier dissertation presented to Dept. of Geography, U.C.D. (1985).
33. T. Jones Hughes, 'A traverse of the coastlands of county Wicklow and east county Wexford' in *Baile*, Jn. of the Geography Society, U.C.D. (1983), p. 5.
34. Rahill, Delgany and Kilcoole, pp 14-8.

John Brennan's house, Lackan, West Wicklow, 1939 (H. G. Leask).

Chapter 17

SYNGE AND WICKLOW

NICHOLAS GRENE

I. The Synges of Wicklow

> '... And, begging your pardon, may I ask your name?' I told him. 'There are two families of the Synges', he said, 'one with a place up above here by the glen of Imaal, and the other down by the Devil's glen and it['s] many's [the] day I have seen them at the fair of Wicklow.' 'It is out of that family I come myself.' I said. He stooped and pointed to my bicycle – 'It's on something higher than that the likes of you should be riding, and it is the truth I'm telling you.'[1]

The Synges of Glanmore, like so many landed Anglo-Irish families, had indeed come down in the world by the time of the playwright at the end of the nineteenth century. Their Wicklow property had been established in the eighteenth century following marriages with the Hatch family and was at its heyday in the time of Francis Synge (1761-1831). He owned not only Glanmore, with its fifteen hundred acres of demesne including the Devil's Glen, but Roundwood Park as well, an estate in all of over 4,000 acres. It was Francis who had the older house of Glenmouth enlarged and redesigned by Francis Johnson as Glenmore Castle, described in all its glory in Lewis's *Topographical Dictionary* (1837):

> Glenmore, the splendid residence of J. Synge, Esq., is a handsome and spacious castellated mansion, with embattled parapets, above which rises a lofty round tower, flanking the principal parapet, in the centre of which is a square gateway tower forming the chief entrance; it was erected by the late F. Synge, Esq., and occupies an eminence, sloping gently towards the sea, near the opening of the Devil's Glen, and surrounded by a richly planted demesne, commanding a fine view of St George's Channel, and the castle, town, and lighthouses of Wicklow, with the intervening country thickly studded with gentlemen's seats.[2]

Unfortunately, this idyllic picture of natural beauty and civilised power was not to last. Francis's heir John (1788-1845), known in the family as 'Pestalozzi John' because of his enthusiastic advocacy of the Swiss educationalist Johann Heinrich Pestalozzi, became increasingly indebted and on his death the estates were bankrupt.[3] His son Francis Synge managed to buy back Glanmore but not Roundwood Park from the Commissioners of Encumbered Estates in 1850. Although in his lifetime the reduced estate of Glanmore was relatively prosperous, after his death in 1878 his widow, Editha, and her second husband Major Theodore Gardiner only lived in the house intermittently and the property suffered under erratic management. This was the state of the family fortunes which the adult John Millington Synge (1871-1909) would have known.[4]

He himself came from a younger branch of the Glanmore family. His father John Hatch Synge (1824-72) was the seventh child of 'Pestalozzi John', a barrister by profession, who died when John Millington was only one, leaving his widow with five children to bring up. With an income of £400 a year derived from land investments, Mrs Synge did not live in poverty, but rather in what were known as 'reduced circumstances'. Her older children all became comfortably settled in middle-class professions. Edward was a land-agent to (among others) Lord Gormanstown and, from 1884 on, to the Synge estates in Wicklow. He was, it seems, regarded by the tenants as a hard man, at least to judge by one incident reported by Mrs Synge: 'He heard them talking among themselves and one said "it would take a Synge to do that"' (Stephens MS f. 478). Robert trained as a civil engineer, and emigrated to Argentina where for a number of years he ranched with cousins on his mother's side. Samuel, with qualifications both in divinity and medicine, served as a medical missionary in China. Annie married a solicitor Harry Stephens and lived with her family close to her mother. Only the youngest, 'Johnnie', proved a problem, horrifying the family with his aspiration, on graduating from Trinity College, of becoming a musician. 'Harry had a talk with him the other day,' Mrs Synge wrote Robert in January 1890, 'advising him very strongly not to think of making it a profession. Harry told him all the men who do take to drink!' (Stephens MS f. 586). Johnnie persisted, all the same, at first studying music in Germany, and then equally unsatisfactorily from the family's point of view, and equally unrewardingly, living in Paris with some ill-defined aim of becoming a writer. In Mrs Synge's letters to her other sons, her youngest is a constant source of worry: 'My poor Johnnie is my failure' (April 1894); 'Johnnie is vegetating in Paris. He calls himself very busy, but it is a busy idleness, in my opinion' (November 1896) (Stephens MS f. 931, f. 1148).

John Synge was troubling from his family's point of view not only because of his failure to find a respectable and respectably paid profession. There was also his loss of faith, deeply disturbing to his mother. On both sides of his family, his religious heritage was one of evangelical protestantism. His grandfather John Synge and his uncle Francis had both been members of the Plymouth Brethren which had its origins in Wicklow. His mother's father Robert Traill was a clergyman from Antrim who felt that he had been denied preferment in the church because of his strongly evangelical views. Mrs Synge shared those views and it was a real grief to her when John, at the age of 18, declared that he no longer believed, and refused to attend church any more. Again and again over the years her letters record her prayers for him and her yearning for him to accept Jesus as his Redeemer.

Politically also, Synge grew at odds with his family. Although he canvassed for an Anti-Home Rule Petition in 1893,[5] and as late as 1895 was of the view that Home Rule would provoke sectarian conflict,[6] by 1897 he was prepared to join Maud Gonne's Association Irlandaise in Paris and, like most Irish nationalists, he took a strongly pro-Boer position in the Boer war (Stephens MS f.1602). He was not only nationalist but socialist in principle. 'A radical', he told his young nephew Edward Stephens in an unusual outburst, 'is a person who wants change root and branch, and I'm proud to be a radical' (Stephens MS f.1663). Such ideas were hardly likely to be acceptable to his family. 'He says', reported Mrs Synge indignantly to Samuel in 1896, 'he has gone back to Paris to study Socialism, and he wants to do good, and for that possibility he is giving up everything. He says he is not selfish or egotistical but quite the reverse. In fact he writes the most utter folly...' (Greene and Stephens, p. 62).

There is nothing very unusual about a writer or artist from a conventional middle-class family diverging from their political, social and religious views. What is striking about Synge's case is that he continued to live in such close relations with the family in spite of his dissidence. From 1893 to 1902 he spent his winters on the Continent, but his home remained with his mother in Kingstown (Dún Laoghaire) and, with the exception of two brief periods when he took rooms in Dublin, he went on living with her until her death in 1908, not long before his own. He shared also the prolonged family holidays in Wicklow. Thoughout Synge's youth and adolescence Mrs Synge had taken a holiday house each year in Greystones and lived there as part of the tightly knit Greystones protestant community. From 1892 on, the houses she rented were in the Annamoe area, close to Glanmore, most frequently Castle Kevin. Most years the Wicklow stay lasted from June through September, providing a family base for Robert or Samuel Synge when they were home from abroad, for the Stephens, for cousins and missionary friends visiting Ireland. It was from these summer periods spent with his family around Annamoe that Synge formed the impressions of Wicklow which served as the basis for his essays and plays.

The Synges came to Annamoe as something between urban summer visitors and members of the local landowning family. They no longer stayed at Glanmore, as they had in the lifetime of Francis Synge; Francis's widow Editha and her second husband, Major Gardiner, when they were resident, lived on the hill farm of Tiglin for economy and rented out Glanmore Castle. The houses that the Synges rented were suggestive of their social position. Castle Kevin, a substantial early nineteenth-century house, home of the Frizell family, was vacant and could be rented cheaply because it was boycotted. The Synges spent in all seven summers there from 1892 to 1901. They did not seem to be troubled by the boycott, though Synge found on the doorpost of Castle Kevin (and later published) a triumphalist verse celebrating the departure of the Frizells.[7] When Castle Kevin was not available, Mrs Synge rented Avonmore, a big eighteenth-century house on the Castle Kevin property, lived in by Henry Harding, a local farmer and caretaker for the Frizells. It was quite large enough to accommodate the Synges as well as the Hardings, but it had the disadvantage of a mad lodger, a retired army captain, John J.A. Drought.[8] 'These are the robbers', was his greeting as the Synge family party arrived one summer; 'they've been in gaol for a year' (Stephens MS f. 1035). For the month of August 1897 they stayed on the Parnell estate at Avondale, but not in the big house, only in the steward's house, 'Casino', something which Harry Stephens felt as a social indignity. In other summers they had to be content with still less grand places to stay. In 1895 it was Duff House, a farmhouse with a beautiful situation on the southern side of Lough Dan. 'It was with some misgivings that Mrs Synge brought her future daughter-in-law [Robert's fiancée] there, for, as the house was owned by Roman Catholics, she feared that it would not be free from fleas' (Stephens MS f. 1022). Tomriland House, where the Synges stayed in 1902, 1903 and 1904, was just as unpretentious, but the farmers who owned it were Protestant.

In her holiday homes, as in Dublin, Mrs Synge preferred to have to do with people of her own religion. There were the Hardings with whom the Synges stayed at Avonmore; there were the Colemans who owned Tomriland; there was Willie Belton who acted as carter for the Synges when they travelled down from Kingstown and who aroused Mrs Synge's extreme anger by getting drunk on an outing to Glendalough with her maids. 'Is it not a dreadful thing', she wrote to Samuel, 'for one of our few protestants in this place to be going on in such a way?' (Stephens MS f. 2015). One exception was their close neighbour old Mrs Rochfort, known to the family by her favourite tag 'Avourneen', whose talk Synge incorporated into his essay 'The People of the Glens' (*CW* II 219-220) Still it must have been a significant part of Synge's Wicklow experience that so many of the people around him were of his family's religion. It adds a different dimension, for example, to the famous story of Synge listening in to the talk of the servant girls. In the Preface to *The Playboy of the Western World* he wrote defending the authenticity of his language:

> When I was writing *The Shadow of the Glen*, some years ago, I got more aid than any learning could have given me, from a chink in the floor of the old Wicklow house where I was staying, that let me hear what was being said by the servant girls in the kitchen. (*CW* IV 53)

The impression of the gentleman eavesdropper was unfortunate. But would the impression have been improved if he had added the detail that the girls whose talk so inspired him in Tomriland House in 1902 were Ellen the cook and Florence Massey the maid, both of whom had been brought up in a protestant orphanage and did not necessarily come from Wicklow at all (Stephens MS, f. 1974)?[9]

If the range of Synge's social acquaintance in Wicklow was limited, his knowledge of the countryside was not. Within a radius of some fifteen miles from Annamoe, he walked and cycled every hill and valley, generally in company with his relations or with friends of the family. He spent most of July 1898, for example, on excursions with Robert who was a passionate fisherman and who recorded their outings in detail in his diary. On 8 July they 'climbed Lugnaquilla – starting on foot from C[astle] K[evin] at 1.45, reaching the top at 7.45 – back to the [Glenmalure] Hotel at 10 and then walked home,' or again on 30 July, 'cycled Hollywood, Blessington, Liffey Valley, Sallygap and Roundwood – 53 miles' (Stephens MS f. 1416). In other summers he was with Samuel: Samuel's diary for 23 July 1894, for example, records 'Walked to the Meeting of the Waters to-day with John, going through Parnell's place, and then walked home to Annamoe.'[10] The guests at the Synges' holiday houses at different times included a number of younger women, Annie and Edie Harmar, sisters of Samuel's wife, and friends of theirs, Madeleine Kerr and Rosie Calthrop. These too were Synge's companions on long walks or cycle-rides and, interestingly, there never seems to have been any sense of impropriety at his going off unchaperoned for a day at a time with an unrelated woman of his own age. In the Wicklow essays Synge virtually always gives the impression of being alone on his journeys, but this was often not the case. Where, for example, in 'An Autumn Night in the Hills' he tells the story of going to fetch a pointer dog from the cottage where it had been recovering after a shooting accident, the essay ends most effectively with a description of his solitary walk back down Glenmalure (though it isn't named as such). What he does not reveal is that the dog in question belonged to his brother-in-law Harry Stephens who had rented shooting rights in Glenmalure and that Harry was with him on the mission to fetch the dog home.[11]

In his summers in Wicklow Synge lived a double life, the social life of the family in which he played a full part (attendance at church always excepted), and the life of the imagination slowly transmuted into writing. The Synges remained a close and united family, and John Synge never tried to escape from the closeness of those bonds. As Stephens commented on John's relations with Robert: 'The brothers differed about almost every subject, but they never quarrelled about their differences' (Stephens MS f. 1412). This is borne out also by Synge's own remark on Samuel, in a letter to his fiancée Molly Allgood: 'he is one of the best fellows in [the] world, I think, though he is so religious we have not much in common'.[12] It was Synge's deliberate strategy to avoid subjects of dissension. Thus he adopted a 'rule against talking to us [his nephews Edward and Francis Stephens] about religious or political theory, with which our parents would not have agreed' (Stephens MS f. 1828). He remained deeply attached to his mother and she to him for all their lack of understanding. So, for example, she was prepared to accept the prospect of Molly Allgood as daughter-in-law, though an ill-educated, nineteen-year-old Roman Catholic, a former shop-girl turned actress, must have offended nearly every prejudice she had. The rest of the family were less tolerant of the proposed marriage, but once again there was no outright quarrel.

Silence, repression, instinctive family loyalty kept the Synges together. John Synge walked with Samuel, fished with Robert, shot with Harry Stephens, cycled with his in-laws and his in-laws' cousins. Yet he looked at Wicklow as they would never have done. He was an internal drop-out within a class which he, but not they, saw as defeated and obsolete. His most telling evocation of that state is the essay 'A Landlord's Garden in County Wicklow'. The essay was based on a real incident in the walled garden of Castle Kevin in the summer of 1901 when Synge set himself to guard some ripening cherries against the depredations of the local boys, ending up chasing one of them round and round the garden. 'John sent us into fits of laughter telling us the story', Mrs Synge commented in her account of the matter in a letter to Samuel at the time (*My Uncle John,* p. 144). In writing the essay Synge turned the cherries into apples, more traditional fruit for orchard robbing, and made the garden into an eloquent emblem of the decaying fortunes of the landowning class:

> A stone's throw from an old house where I spent several summers in county Wicklow, there was a garden that had been left to itself for fifteen or twenty years. Just inside the gate, as one entered, two paths led up through a couple of strawberry beds, half choked with leaves, where a few white and narrow strawberries were still hidden away. Further on was nearly half an acre of tall raspberry canes and thistles five feet high, growing together in a dense mass, where one could still pick raspberries enough to last a household for the season. Then, in a waste of hemlock, there were some half-dozen apple trees covered with lichen and moss, and against the northern walls a few dying plum trees hanging from their nails. Beyond them there was a dead pear tree and just inside the gate, as one came back to it, a large fuchsia filled with empty nests. A few lines of box here and there showed where the flower-beds had been laid out, and when anyone who had the knowledge looked carefully among them many remnants could be found of beautiful and rare plants. (*CW* II 230)

This sounds a circumstantially precise description, but the substitution of the apples for the real-life cherries makes it clear that it is not literally accurate. Synge is in fact piling up the details to compound the sense of dereliction: the etiolated strawberries, the rank growth of the raspberries and thistles, the apple-trees neglected and mossed with age, the abandoned nests in the fuchsia, the '*waste* of hemlock', the fine and exotic cultivated flowers only to be found by connoisseurs in the wilderness. It is no wonder that he entitled one draft of this essay 'The Garden of the Dead'.[13]

In this one essay, Synge allowed himself a measure of the class nostalgia traditionally associated with the image of the crumbling big house – in this essay only, and a measure of it only.

> Everyone is used in Ireland to the tragedy that is bound up with the lives of farmers and fishing people; but in this garden one seemed to feel the tragedy of the landlord class also, and of the innumerable old families that are quickly dwindling away. These owners of the land are not much pitied at the present day, or much deserving of pity; and yet one cannot quite forget that they are the descendants of what was at one time, in the eighteenth century, a high-spirited and highly-cultivated aristocracy. The

> broken green-houses and mouse-eaten libraries, that were designed and collected by men who voted with Grattan, are perhaps as mournful in the end as the four mud walls that are so often left in Wicklow as the only remnants of a farmhouse. (*CW* II 230-1)

Synge is commenting here, and passing judgement, on his own class and his own family. 'Many of the descendants of these people have, of course, drifted into professional life in Dublin, or have gone abroad; yet, wherever they are, they do not equal their forefathers' (*CW* II 231). His most telling condemnation he omitted from the published essay: 'Still, this class, with its many genuine qualities, had little patriotism, in the right sense, few ideas, and no seed for future life, so it has gone to the wall' (*CW* II 231).

The essay makes it clear how deliberately Synge turned away from his own class and its situation as a subject for his writing:

> The desolation of this life is often of a peculiarly local kind, and if a playwright chose to go through the Irish country houses he would find material, it is likely, for many gloomy plays that would turn on the dying away of these old families, and on the lives of the one or two delicate girls that are left so often to represent a dozen hearty men who were alive a generation or two ago. (*CW* II 231)

This was not the material from which Synge was to create his plays, though his first drama *When the Moon has set* is concerned with something very like the country house subject he here rejects. Instead he turned to areas of local life outside the compass of his social background and brought to them attitudes very unlike those of his family. And yet we can see in the Wicklow essays and plays, refracted and transposed, the conditioned habits of mind of his own social situation. He is relatively little concerned with the rural community as a community, with its history and evolution. He remains someone from outside looking in, looking on, interested by those on the social margins or at the extreme peripheries of the region. He effaces, in so far as is possible, himself, his family, his class, and sees value and significance in what his own people would least regard. The wildness and primitiveness of local life represent a welcome contrast with the genteel repressions of middle-class protestant late Victorianism. Still the melancholy strain in his observation of Wicklow, his tendency to focus on and treasure what is at social vanishing point, are in some sort of emotional correspondence with his position as alienated member of a declining class.

II. In Wicklow: the essays

The eight essays included in the section 'In Wicklow' of Synge's *Works* had a relatively long evolution.[14] They seem most of them to have been originally drafted in the period 1900-1 and many of the incidents and impressions they record derive from this time. Synge had made his first visit to Aran in 1898 and almost immediately conceived the idea of writing a book about his experiences there. With a draft of what was to become *The Aran Islands* largely completed in the winter of 1900-1, he turned to doing something similar for Wicklow. The paradox of Synge's creative development was that it took the visits to the unfamiliar landscape of Aran to enable him see what there was in the Wicklow countryside which he had known all his life. The strangeness of Aran, and his strangeness in it, freed him from a social self-consciousness which would have been much stronger in Wicklow where he, or at least his family and family name, would have been well known and easily placed. From 1900 on he began to write up descriptive notes, interesting encounters of his Wicklow summers, and in 1901-2 he made a point of visiting fairs and races to collect material.[15] By 1902 he seems to have had the idea of trying to gather together a book on Wicklow life.[16]

However, Synge found difficulty in publishing his Wicklow essays, as he did indeed *The Aran Islands*. In February 1902 *The Gael* in New York turned down 'The Oppression of the Hills' (though it was to publish 'An Autumn Night in the Hills' the following year); the same month an early version of 'The Vagrants of Wicklow' was rejected by *The Cornhill Magazine*. Most of the essays were not in fact published until 1905-8 when Synge had begun to be established as a dramatist. The Wicklow essays may well have been hard to place because they did not seem to fit into any recognisable genre nor to be aimed at a specific audience. They are not, for the most part, lyrical descriptive pieces conjuring up the beauty of the Wicklow glens; they are not social reportage like Synge's later articles on Connemara, commissioned by *The Manchester Guardian* as an investigative account of the western 'congested districts'; they are not humorous/anecdotal sketches, nor yet collections of popular folklore, both models available at the time. Instead they are mood pieces of understated impressionism following their own individual logic with no obvious purpose or motivation.

As a record of Wicklow life of the time, they need to be read cautiously. The principle by which the essays were put together was one of collage. Synge would amalgamate incidents from different times and places, re-order or fictionalise his actual experiences to suit the needs of the essay. Thrifty of his material, he would cannabalise earlier drafts, noting which passages were already 'used'.[17] The result is that the published essays are a patchwork of bits and pieces derived from experiences over a number of years, often very difficult to track back to their origins. Apart from anything else, Synge was careful to omit or falsify the names of people and places, no doubt to avoid giving the sort of offence which some of the Aran islanders had taken at his published descriptions of them.

A useful example of Synge's practice here is the old man encountered in 'The People of the Glens' (quoted at the beginning of this essay) who felt that it was *infra dig* for a Synge to ride a bicycle. That passage, from a TS draft of the essay, Synge characteristically omitted from the published text. He also eliminated details of the time and place of the encounter: 'One evening, at the beginning of harvest, as I was walking into a straggling village, far away in the mountains, in the southern half of the county, I overtook an old man walking in the same direction with an empty gallon can' (*CW* II 220). The straggling village was in fact Aghavannagh, the date was (probably) 24 August 1901, and the old man was Patrick Kehoe, but Synge tells us none of this.[18] He calls the old man Kavanagh instead of Kehoe, and omits the name of the M.P. with whom Kehoe had the dispute over local history which forms a set-piece of story-telling in Synge's essay:

> One day I was near striking him [the M.P] on this stretch of the road. I was after telling him about two men were piked beyond that corner at the time of the Rebellion, and when I came to an end, 'It's all lies you're telling,' says he, 'there's not a word of it true.'
>
> 'How's that,' says I, 'what in the name of God do you know of the histories of the world?'
>
> 'It's all in my history book,' says he, 'and another way altogether.'
>
> 'Go home, then,' says I, 'and burn your history book, for it's all lies is in it, and you're the first man ever thought he knew the history of these places better than old Cavanagh – that's myself.'
>
> 'Well,' says he, 'I'm going home tomorrow, and I'll find out in the city of Dublin whether it's you is right or the book. Then when I come back in a twelve month – if we both have our health by the grace of God – I'll tell you about it.'
>
> A year after he came back late in the evening to my little dwelling. I wasn't in at that time, but with the rage he had to see me he came down again at the dawn of day. 'Ah, Cavanagh,' says he, 'you're the finest man for histories ever I seen. It's you were right and the book was wrong.'
>
> Would you believe that? (*CW* II 223).

This has all the hallmarks of oral narrative, whether heightened by Synge or not: the remoteness of 'the city of Dublin' as source of authority, the year and a day absence between the two meetings, the authenticating detail of the old man not being in the first time the M.P. called. But the story's triumph of oral over printed tradition is enhanced when we realise that Patrick Kehoe was in fact illiterate.[19] And it is interesting to discover that his antagonist was the veteran Parnellite M.P., William Joseph Corbet who was only six years younger than Kehoe and a Wicklow man himself, a farmer from the Newtownmountkennedy area.[20]

Tact and discretion aside, Synge avoids the specifics of historical time and place in his essays. Though he meets people like Kehoe, part of whose attraction is their folk memories of stories of the '98 Rebellion, he does not give the stories themselves. Likewise, he ignores details of regional social change, such as the striking depopulation of Glenmalure from a thriving lead-mining community in the earlier part of the nineteenth century. In the townland of Baravore, for example, where in 1854 there were twenty-six tenanted houses, by 1901 there were just two, one of them providing Synge with the setting for 'the last cottage at the head of a long glen in County Wicklow' in *The Shadow of the Glen*.[21] What absorbed Synge was the image of the desolate glen and the few people who lived there, not how it came to be thus desolate or what it had been like some years previously. Though his concern is to represent a life which he saw as disappearing, it is as something timeless, archaic, primitive, rather than as a given stage in a historical continuum of time.

'All wild sights appealed to Synge,' said Jack Yeats, 'and he did not care whether they were typical of anything or had any symbolical meaning at all'.[22] The wilder, the rougher the sights were, the better Synge liked them. Compare, for example, his account of an occasion such as the horse-races in Arklow in August 1901 with that of the *Wicklow News-Letter*. The *News-Letter* was the Unionist county paper, and its report on the races made them a very sedate affair. Headed 'Arklow Races', after a full list of the organising committee, the article continued:

> Favoured with delightful weather, the above races came off on Thursday, on The Green, Arklow, in the presence of an enormous multitude of holiday-makers from all parts of the country, including many from North Wexford and Dublin. The meeting was held under the Irish Racing Association rules, and it was pleasing to find that both the executive and stewards discharged their duties so satisfactorily that not a hitch occurred in the arrangements, which were excellent, and a most enjoyable day's

> racing resulted. A few minor details were wanting, such as a telegraph board, refreshments saloon, &c., while a little more attention might have been paid to the levelling of a short piece of the course. However, everything passed off well, and the stewards are to be congratulated upon the grand success they achieved.[23]

The article concluded with a formal list of results ending with the Farmers' Plate. Here is Synge on the same event:

> The races in Arklow [...] are singularly unconventional, and no one can ... watch them on the sand-hills in suitable weather, when the bay and the wooded glens in the background are covered with sunshine and the shadows of clouds, without thrilling to the tumult of humour that rises from the people.
>
> A long course is indicated among the sand-hills by a few scattered flag-posts, and at the portion nearest the town a rough paddock and grandstand – draped with green paper – are erected with about a hundred yards of the course roped off from the crowd.

This is Synge's version of the 'stewards discharging their duties so satisfactorily':

> Some half dozen fishermen, with green ribbons fastened to their jerseys or behind their hats, act as stewards [...] and as they are usually drunk they reel about poking the public with a stick and repeating with endless and vain iteration, 'Keep outside the ropes'.

It is the crowd and the sideshows rather than the racing that takes Synge's eye:

> At either side a varied crowd collects and straggles round among the faded roulette tables, little groups of young men dancing horn-pipes to the music of a flute, and the numerous stalls which supply fruit, biscuits and cheap drinks. These stalls consist merely of a long cart covered by a crescent awning which rises from one end only, and gives them at a distance a curious resemblance to the cars with sails which the Chinese employ. They are attended to by the semi-gypsy or tinker class, among [whom] women with curiously Mongolian features are not rare. All these are extraordinarily prolific, and at a few paces from each stall there is usually a pile of hay and sacking and harness that is literally crawling with half-naked children.

Finally, Synge gives us what are no doubt the about-to-be contestants for the Farmers' Plate:

> In the centre of the course there are a number of farmers from up the country riding about on heavy mares, sometimes bare-backed, sometimes with an old saddle tied on with rope, and often with a certain dignity of costume that is heightened by the old-fashioned rustic tall hat. (*CW* II 197-8).[24]

The *News-Letter* description aims to regularise the event to its readers, turn the races into Fairyhouse in little; Synge's object is to make them strange and, in his account, Arklow races are well on their way to becoming the mule-race in *The Playboy*.

Again and again in the Wicklow essays Synge's admiring attention is given to those whom the community disregard or dislike. It is significant that the old story-teller of 'The People of the Glens', Kehoe/Cavanagh, is disparaged by the publican:

> 'That's the greatest old rogue in the village,' said the publican, as soon as he was out of hearing; 'he's always making up to all who pass through the place, and trying what he can get out of them.' (*CW* II 224)

It is such people who attract hostility for their difference from the social norm whom Synge attends to with special interest. The central essay here is 'The Vagrants of Wicklow'. The essay begins with a comment on the number of vagrants to be found in Wicklow, and takes issue with the standard tendency to deplore this:

> Their abundance has often been regretted; yet in one sense it is an interesting sign, for wherever the labourer of a country has preserved his vitality, and begets an occasional temperament of distinction, a certain number of vagrants are to be looked for. In the middle classes the gifted son of a family is always the poorest – usually a writer or artist with so sense for speculation – and in a family of peasants, where the average comfort is just over penury, the gifted son sinks also, and is soon a tramp on the roadside. (*CW* II 202)

The nature of Synge's interest in the vagrants is here made clear. He is obviously thinking of himself when he speaks of 'the gifted son of a family' in the middle classes; with 'forty pounds a year and a new suit when I am too shabby',[25] he was much the poorest of the Synges. It is not, however, a matter of naïve or sentimental identification with the vagrants but of a precise analogy. They are the outcasts of their class as he feels himself to be of his.

All through the essay the vagrants described evoke a variety of Synge's imaginative preoccupations. The centenarian tramp, whom E.M. Stephens says was well-known around Castle Kevin as the 'Honest Tar' (Stephens f. 1442), supplied Synge with some of the features of Martin Doul in *The Well of the Saints*, particularly in the story of his quarrel with his wife (whom he married at the age of ninety) and his fierce complaints at having had his long white hair cut off in Kilmainham where he was committed for assaulting her:

> All his pride and his half-conscious feeling for the dignity of his age seemed to have set themselves on this long hair, which marked him out from the other people of this district; and I have often heard him saying to himself, as he sat beside me under a ditch: 'What use is an old man without his hair? A man has only his bloom like the trees; and what use is an old man without his white hair?' (*CW* II 203)

The same grotesque yet irrepressible sense of self-dignity reappears in Martin Doul's imagination of himself with 'a beautiful, long, white, silken, streamy beard' and his fierce determination not to allow the Saint to take this illusion away from him. Several other of the vagrants in the essay illustrate the antagonism between these figures and the settled community, the tramps and tinkers from the West with their 'curious reputation for witchery and unnatural powers', or the drunken flower-woman squaring up to the police, 'Let this be the barrack's yard, and come on now, the lot of you' (*CW* II 207). While Synge is exhilarated by the flash-points of defiance between the vagrants and the representatives of social order, he could find also the reflection of his own more melancholy strain:

> In these hills the summer passes in a few weeks from a late spring, full of odour and colour, to an autumn that is premature and filled with the desolate splendour of decay; and it often happens that, in moments when one is most aware of this ceaseless fading of beauty, some incident of tramp life gives a local human intensity to the shadow of one's own mood. (*CW* II 204)

This has Synge's special plangent awareness of the pressure of mortality upon life, and he acknowledges that it is the 'shadow' of this mood of his which allows him to see the 'local human intensity' in the figure of the young tramp 'suffering from some terrible disease' that he goes on to describe. The vagrants of the essay come alive imaginatively as they correspond in their very independent being to the thoughts and feelings of the man who watches them.

Synge in Wicklow was preoccupied with the old, the odd and the mad. Many of the people who figure most prominently in the essays, like Patrick Kehoe or the 'Honest Tar', in their extreme old age represent a life that is past or passing. The vagrants, in their difference, stand for the 'variations which are a condition and effect of all vigorous life' (*CW* II 208). In 'The Oppression of the Hills' Synge sought to classify the several sorts of mental disturbance which he thought specific to the Wicklow mountains and also saw as significant. The 'peculiar climate', he argues, with its alternation between prolonged periods of rain and an occasional 'morning of almost supernatural radiance', 'acting on a population that is already lonely and dwindling, has caused or increased a tendency to nervous depression among the people, and every degree of sadness, from that of the man who is merely mournful to that of the man who has spent half his life in the mad-house, is common among these hills' (*CW* II 209). With all his passionate feeling for the landscape of the hills and glens, Synge knew how little idyllic life in these desolate places might be. He quotes 'one old man who may be cited as an example of sadness not yet definitely morbid':

> 'I suppose there are some places where they think that Ireland is a sort of garden,' he laughed bitterly, 'and I've heard them say that Wicklow is the garden of Ireland. I suppose there's fine scenery for those that likes *(sic)* it, but it's a poor place in the winter and there's no money moving in the country'.[26]

Such glum cynicism, however, is the least of the mental troubles which Synge saw besetting the people of the glens. He describes the hysterical fears of a young girl convinced her two sisters had been drowned in the bogs, based on an incident which took place at Castle Kevin in June 1899 (Stephens MS f.1545), or the terrors of an older woman living alone: 'There's nothing I fear like the thunder. My heart isn't strong – I do feel it – and I have a lightness in my head, and often when I do be excited with the thunder I do be afeard I might die there alone in the cottage and no one know it' (*CW* II 210). 'The three shadowy countries', Synge tells us, 'that are never forgotten in Wicklow' are 'America (their El Dorado), the Union (the Poor House) and the Madhouse' (*CW* II 216). Madness is a threat to old and young alike. One victim is the woman Synge calls Mary Kinsella in 'An Autumn Night in the Hills':

> 'She was a fine young woman with two children' [Synge is told] 'and a year and a half ago she went wrong in her head, and they had to send her away. And then up there in the Richmond asylum maybe they thought the sooner they were shut of her the better, for she died two days ago this morning, and now they're bringing her up to have a wake.' (*CW* II 188)

The essay (originally entitled 'The Body of Mary Kinsella'[27]) ends with the sight of her coffin after a walk through the wild desolation of the glen which suggests the causes precipitating the madness. For Synge neurosis and dementia are associated with the mental exposure of those in lonely places to the oppressive emptiness of nature, its menacing power.

The essays contain some genre studies such as 'At a Wicklow Fair' in which Synge describes a typical rural event, evoking the fair's sights, sounds and customs. His tone is sometimes that of the social commentator, drawing together observations into generalising statements: 'The older people in county Wicklow, as in the rest of Ireland, still show a curious affection for the landed classes wherever they have lived for a generation of two upon their property [...] The younger people feel differently' (*CW* II, 211-12). But his real interest is not in the representative or typical among people or social phenomena. He pays little attention to villages and towns, to the ordinary work of farming or marketing, to politics, money or religion. His imagination is held by individuals and incidents on certain margins: the tinkers, tramps and story-tellers at the rough edges of their community, the isolated shepherds of the remote hills, situations of mind and place close to alienation. These are the preoccupations of the essays fully dramatised in the plays.

III. Plays and places

If his first autobiographical piece, *When the Moon has set*, is included, Synge set four plays in county Wicklow. Three of them are located, by the placenames mentioned, in the valley of the Avonbeg from Glenmalure (*The Shadow of the Glen*), through Greenane (Acts I and III of *The Well of the Saints*) to Ballinaclash (*The Tinker's Wedding* and Act II of *The Well*). All three were written quite close together in time, *The Shadow of the Glen* and the first draft of *The Tinker's Wedding* in the summer of 1902 (Synge's *annus mirabilis* as a playwright when he also wrote *Riders to the Sea*); *The Well of the Saints* started the year following. It is not clear why he should have so concentrated his plays in the one valley. E.M. Stephens conjectures that it may have been in the month spent on the Avondale esate in 1897 that he got to know the area well (Stephens MS ff.1243-4). Glenmalure he certainly visited often, as Kelly's Lake was a favourite fishing place of his, and there are several references to him walking or cycling through Ballinaclash.[28] But it may well be that he set his plays in an area some distance away from the Annamoe district which he knew best in order to be less suspected of using familiar local people as models. In any case, he is circumspectly vague in the settings he attributes to each of the plays: *The Shadow of the Glen* is in an unspecified 'long glen in County Wicklow', the scene of *The Well of the Saints* is given even more vaguely as 'Some lonely mountainous district on the east of Ireland, one or more centuries ago', *The Tinker's Wedding*, most indefinitely of all, 'a roadside near a village'.[29] And yet all three plays are given quite precise locales within the texts. One of the intriguing features of Synge's Wicklow plays is their combination of specificity and universality, of the locally realised and the purely imagined.

The story of *The Shadow of the Glen* originally had nothing to do with Wicklow at all. It was a folk-tale which Synge heard on Inishmaan from a storyteller called Pat Dirane and which he recorded in *The Aran Islands* (*CW* II 70-72). In the first draft of the play which is extant, there is no sign that Synge had a Wicklow setting in mind. The story is dramatised very much in the spirit of the original, the tale of the cunning old man pretending to be dead to catch out his wife, the comedy of the obviously unfaithful wife and her vigorous young lover.[30] A number of quite distinct Wicklow experiences had to coalesce in Synge's mind to make *The Shadow of the Glen* the subtle and complex tragicomedy of mood it was to become.

The setting appears to have been suggested by memories of the visit to Glenmalure to collect Harry Stephens's pointer dog in August 1897, the episode described in 'An Autumn Night in the Hills'. Harry Stephens, along with a friend, Willie Ormsby, a judge retired from India, had taken grouse shooting from 'the two old Harney brothers who lived with their sister in the last cottage at the head of Glenmalure and grazed their sheep on the slopes of Baravore' (Stephens MS f.1238). It was here that the dog was left when it was accidentally wounded out shooting, and here that Synge and his brother-in-law came to collect it. Pierce Harney's, a hundred years before, had figured in the '98 Rebellion as a hold-out position for the rebels Dwyer and Holt.[31] The Harneys of Baravore in Synge's time, Michael (b. 1840), Esther (b. 1843), James (b. 1846) lived in a house too large to be called a cottage and, with hill-grazing over 1,200 acres, must have been comfortably off.[32] In the essay Synge describes the house as 'the cottage of an under-keeper or bailiff', though what he enters – 'a long low room with open rafters' – does not sound quite like a standard cottage kitchen.

What evidently struck Synge was less the actual details of the house and its people as the idea of its situation at the head of the glen. There was the 'old woman' (presumably Esther Harney) with her folklore of Lough Nahanagan and its evil spirit. There was the 'finely made girl', quite possibly a niece of the Harneys,[33] with her devotion to the pointer dog: 'it's herself will be lonesome when that dog is gone' (*CW* II 191). The men were absent on their mission to escort home the coffin of Mary Kinsella whose death in the asylum for the insane was another suggestive element. The loneliness and need for companionship of women much left to themselves with the men out at work, the fears of haunting and enchantment associated with desolate places, the danger of madness, these are the imaginative impressions which carried over from 'An Autumn Night in the Hills' to *The Shadow of the Glen*. Nora Burke, in the original folk-tale a traditionally unfaithful wife, became in the setting of the glen a figure of melancholy and deprivation: 'It's in a lonesome place you do have to be talking with someone, and looking for someone, in the evening of the day' (*CW* III 49). The Tramp won't touch Dan's body for fear of the old man's curse – 'I wouldn't lay my hand on him for the Lough Nahanagan and it filled with gold' (*CW* III 35) – and when left alone with the 'corpse' asks for a needle as a talisman: 'there's great safety in a needle' (*CW* III 41). Even Dan Burke, the stock jealous husband, was turned into a creature of his situation: 'He was an old man, and an odd man [...] and it's always up on the hills he was, thinking thoughts in the dark mist' (*CW* III 35).

The most spectacular terror of *The Shadow of the Glen* is the madness and death of Patch Darcy. This too Synge took from a real event, though one quite unconnected with his visit to Glenamalure in 1897. It was in August 1901 on the road from Aghavannagh to Glenmalure that he was told the story which he later recounted in 'The Oppression of the Hills':

> Not long ago in a desolate glen in the south of the county I met two policemen driving an ass-cart with a coffin on it, and a little further on I stopped an old man and asked him what had happened.
>
> 'This night three weeks,' he said, 'there was a poor fellow below reaping in the glen, and in the evening he had two glasses of whisky with some other lads. Then some excitement took him, and he threw off his clothes and ran away into the hills. There was great rain that night, and I suppose the poor creature lost his way, and was the whole night perishing in the rain and darkness. In the morning they found his naked foot-marks on some mud half a mile above the road, and again where you go up by a big

> stone. Then there was nothing known of him till last night, when they found his body on the mountain, and it near eaten by the crows.' (*CW* II 209-10)

What Synge suppressed from this published version of the story he was told, apart from the details of place, was a suggestion that the man was mentally handicapped, 'a sort of half innocent':

> 'They say he was a poor weak minded sort of a creature'.[34]

The facts as recorded in the report of the inquest and the newspaper accounts of it (which Synge may well never have read) make for a more detailed but no less mysterious account.[35] The man was John Winterbottom, a small farmer who lived with his wife and three young children in Sheeanamore above Aughrim.[36] He left his home early on the morning of Thursday 15 August 1901 to go to work at hay for a Mrs Byrne who lived two miles away. He seems to have drunk a good deal in the course of the day – the local tradition was that a barrel of porter was supplied at a hay-drawing – and by the evening he was 'the worse of drink'. His fellow-workers suggested to Mrs Byrne that 'she should get the car to send him home, but she said he would be able to walk'. The last one witness saw of him he was kneeling in the road outside Mrs Byrne's gate. This was where his clothes were discovered early the next morning, when Mrs Winterbottom went to look for her husband who had not returned home. His body was only found a week later, on Thursday 22 August, five miles away from his clothes, on Slievemaan Mountain at Aghavannagh. The body was so disfigured that it could only be identified by a shirt button sewn with black thread on a small piece of shirt left on the body.[37]

The evidence of the inquest leaves much unclear. There was money missing from Winterbottom's clothes, eleven pence of the shilling's wages he had been given by Mrs Byrne, and nowhere apparently that he could have spent it. Different opinions were expressed about his mental state on the day. Mrs Byrne 'considered he was strange in his manner all day at the work, talking to himself'; Joseph Doyle, who worked with him, thought 'there was nothing peculiar about him'. Whether John Winterbottom suffered from any more chronic mental disability is equally doubtful in the reports. On the one hand it is said that 'he suffered from paralysis in his side, but there was nothing peculiar considered about him'; on the other, Dr O'Gorman of Aughrim who 'knew the deceased well ... always thought he was a little peculiar in his mind'. Reports of an inquest proceedings in a case like this may well not contain the whole truth and nothing but the truth. According to one family tradition, John Winterbottom was much bullied by his wife and, coming home drunk from the hay-drawing, was shut out of the house by her, and lost his way in the mountains.[38] This would not explain the abandoned clothes or the considerable distance to where the body was found, two of the strangest features of the case, but it suggests that there may have been aspects of the story which did not emerge at the inquest.

Whatever the truth about John Winterbottom and his sad end, Synge transforms him in *The Shadow of the Glen* into the crucial figure of Patch Darcy whom both Nora and the Tramp remember. 'If myself was easily afeard, I'm telling you,' says the Tramp,

> it's long ago I'd have been locked into the Richmond Asylum, or maybe have run up into the back hills with nothing on me but an old shirt, and been eaten with *(sic)* crows the like of Patch Darcy – the Lord have mercy on him – in the year that's gone. (*CW* III 37)

Patch had been a close friend of Nora's (suspected by Dan as a lover): 'God spare Darcy, he'd always look in here and he passing up or passing down, and it's very lonesome I was after him a long while' (*CW* III 39). The Tramp praises him to the inadequate Mike Dara as the very type of the hill-shepherd:

> That was a great man, young fellow, a great man, I'm telling you. There was never a lamb from his own ewes he wouldn't know before it was marked, and he'd run from this to the city of Dublin, and never catch for his breath. (*CW* III 47)

The terms of the eulogy here, which Synge puts into the mouth of a tinker in the essay 'At a Wicklow Fair' (*CW* II 228), he in fact heard from Willie Coleman, owner of Tomriland, in a conversation about mountain herds (Stephens MS f. 2022). By bringing in this admiring awe of the lowland or foothill farmer for the true 'mountainy man', Synge makes of Patch Darcy a heroic figure whose mad death is associated with his exceptional skills and his life of lonely isolation.

In this metamorphosis of the real-life John Winterbottom into the fictional Patch Darcy, there are a few details suggestive of a literalist strain in Synge's imagination. The Tramp remembers Darcy's death 'in the year that's gone' (*CW* III 37).[39] Winterbottom died in 1901, Synge was writing the play in 1902: he is thus imagining the Tramp in a contemporary present recollecting an event of the actual recent past. The Tramp claims to be the 'last one heard [Darcy's] living voice in the whole world.'

> I was passing below on a dark night the like of this night, and the sheep were lying under the ditch and every one of them coughing, and choking, like an old man, with the great rain and the fog ... Then I heard a thing talking – queer talk, you wouldn't believe it at all, and you out of your dreams, – and 'Merciful God,' says I, 'if I begin hearing the like of that voice out of the thick mist, I'm destroyed surely.' Then I run, and I run, and I run, till I was below in Rathvanna. I got drunk that night, I got drunk in the morning, and drunk the day after, – I was coming from the races beyond – and the third day they found Darcy. (*CW* III 39)

'I was coming from the races beyond' – an odd detail that; why should it be included? Maybe as an explanation of why the Tramp had the money to get drunk? But look at the dating. Arklow races, which Synge attended, took place on Thursday 15 August; that was also the day that John Winterbottom went missing. The Tramp is conceived to have walked over from Arklow to Glenmalure (a long walk by most people's standards but not by Synge's), and in the rainy night on the road to Aghavannagh is imagined hearing the voice of the fictional Darcy close to where the real body of Winterbottom was finally found.

In an instance such as this, Synge seems to be re-creating in his play the exact circumstances, the precise location, of a real event. But he is equally prepared to change what is literally authentic if it suits his aesthetic or imaginative purposes. This is especially noticeable with placenames. In the passage just quoted, the Tramp describes how he ran from the voice in the mist 'till I was below in Rathvanna'. If this were Aughavannagh, it would make perfect geographical sense in terms of the actual events of John Winterbottom/Patch Darcy's death, and in an earlier draft of the play, 'Aughavanna' is what Synge originally wrote.[40] It was only at the stage of the final typescript that this was changed to 'Rathvanna', not only here but consistently everywhere the name turned up in the play.[41] Now there is no such name as Rathvanna in Wicklow, and by the alteration Synge changes a real place into a fictional one. It is very unlikely that the motive here was the discreet disguising of the actual which we come across in the essays. Elsewhere in *The Shadow* he uses all real names, Glen Malure, Glen Imaal, the Seven Churches, which gives to the setting a definite locality. It seems rather that Rathvanna suited the rhythm of his language better, sounded better to his ear, than Aghavannagh, and this was why he made the substitution.[42] Synge's imagination, though it needed the real as starting-point, was not like Joyce's in re-creating a literal reality as bedrock.

In Synge's other Wicklow plays, there is a similarly mixed practice in the use of placenames. He evidently did like to have a particular setting in mind. Even in *When the Moon has set*, where the name of the house is allegorical, 'Kilgreine' ('Church of the Sun'), representing the pantheistic creed with which the liberated young hero Columb woos the nun Sister Eileen, references in the text locate the house at the head of Glenmacnass: Columb tells Eileen to 'look at [the] light on that little cloud above Tonagee'; later when he is recovering from an accident it is a measure of his convalescence that he has been able to walk 'to that white stone you can see above the Inchavor'.[43] Allowing for Synge's idiosyncratic spelling of the mountain Tonelagee which stands between Glendassan and Glenmacnass, and the Inchavore river which runs into Lough Dan, these are plausible landmarks for orienting the location of the play. Yet when drafting his plays initially, Synge did not seem to care about placing them with accuracy. Thus in early versions of *The Tinker's Wedding*, there are scattered references to Arklow, to Kilquade and to the (made-up) Killacree which don't seem to add up at all topographically.[44] However, in the published text all the indicators of place centre around Ballinaclash, though Synge includes his fictitious 'Rathvanna' and another favourite invented name 'Ballinacree' which may well stand for Ballinacor, a townland convincingly close by but hardly euphonious enough.

Just as the setting of Synge's plays is somewhere between a fictive and a real world, so they move in and out of real time. The death of Patch Darcy may have been based on an actual event which took place shortly before the play was written; *The Tinker's Wedding* derived from a story told Synge at the fair of Aughrim in 1901 as something which had happened recently nearby. But there is nothing in either play to date the action, beyond a reference by Sarah Casey to a half sovereign 'with a view on it of the living king's mamma' (*CW* IV 15). No doubt much of the currency in the reign of Edward VII would still have had the familiar head of Queen Victoria on the coins. He did not try to make the Wicklow plays set in his own time identifiably *of* his own time.

Correspondingly, when he wrote the fable-like *The Well of the Saints*, set back 'one or more centuries ago', he did not differentiate the life in it from his nominally more modern pieces. In fact, one of the characters of *The Well*, Timmy the Smith, seems to have been suggested by a real blacksmith living in Ballinaclash (again the play's setting) in Synge's time. George Smith had a forge in Ballinacarrig, just beside the mill on the Avonbeg river, about half a mile out of Ballinaclash on the road to the Meeting of the Waters. His situation did not correspond to Timmy's in the play insofar as he was an older man (67 in 1901), with a wife of his own age still alive, and several grown-up children.[45] In looks he

Plate 17.1 George Smith, the blacksmith of Ballinaclash.

seems rather to have resembled the Martin Doul of Martin's own imagination with 'a beautiful, long, white, silken, streamy beard', at least to judge by the charcoal drawing of him which survives. But it appears likely that the identity of name and trade of George Smith gave Synge the cue for Timmy the Smith, who is so addressed throughout the play. Family surnames frequently derive thus from occupations; Synge imagines a stage in this evolution from 'the smith' to 'Smith'.

In one respect, the real-life George Smith had some affinity with his dramatic counterpart. The story is still told in Ballinaclash of the tinkers' fight in which the tinkers took over the village. The men, who were all away working in the mines, were summoned to defend their homes. It was George Smith, as the story is told, who heated red-hot bars in the forge, and helped to drive the tinkers from the village.[46] Timmy in *The Well* is equally the representative of the settled community in its strength, when he expels the beggar Martin Doul from his forge:

> There's your old rubbish now, Martin Doul, and let you take it up, for it's all you have, and walk off through the world, and if ever I meet you coming again, if it's seeing or blind you are itself, I'll bring out the big hammer and hit you a welt with it will leave you easy till the judgement day. (*CW* III 121)

Violence is always potentially there in Synge's plays in the uneasy relationship between tramps, tinkers, beggars on the one hand, and the ordinary rural people on the other. The idea for *The Well* was taken from a fifteenth-century French *Moralité* but it was fleshed out with Synge's observations of the Irish country people. It is easy to imagine the initial plot device of the play, the local conspiracy to make the two blind beggars think they are beautiful, as a rough village joke. There is a measure of tolerance and practical charity for the beggars with their disability, but no disguising the social stigma that attaches to them. Molly Byrne, Timmy the Smith's vacuous, young fiancée, though she may flirt with Martin, is horrified that a mere beggar like him should seriously offer to make love to her:

> Go off now after your wife, and if she beats you again, let you go after the tinker girls is above running the hills, or down among the sluts of the town, and you'll learn one day, maybe, the way a man should speak with a well-reared civil girl the like of me. (*CW* III 123)

When Martin chooses 'a wilful blindness' for himself and Mary, knocking the miraculous water out of the hands of the Saint, the people are appalled at his blasphemous challenge to the orthodoxy by which they live.

> PEOPLE [*all together*]. Go on now, Martin Doul. Go on from this place. Let you not be bringing great storms or droughts on us maybe from the power of the Lord. [*Some of* them throw things at him.] (*CW* III 149)

Religion here supports a social status quo, and those who refuse to accept either or both are ultimately at risk of violent expulsion.

The Tinker's Wedding was never produced in Synge's lifetime because it was considered, as he wryly remarked, 'too immoral for Dublin'.[47] It was feared that the incident of the priest being bound and gagged by the tinkers would have provoked outrage from the largely Catholic audience of the Abbey Theatre. The Preface Synge wrote when the play was finally published in 1907 is defensive in tone:

> In the greater part of Ireland [...] the whole people, from the tinkers to the clergy, have still a life, and view of life, that are rich and genial and humorous. I do not think that these country people, who have so much humour themselves, will mind being laughed at without malice, as the people in every country have been laughed at in their own comedies. (*CW* IV 3)

It is hard to imagine that this would have soothed many potentially ruffled feathers. Certainly Synge did well to emend his final sentence which in an earlier draft read, 'I do not think these country clergy, who have so much humour [...] will mind being laughed at for half an hour without malice, as the clergy in every Roman Catholic country that had real religion were laughed at through the ages' (*CW* IV 3-4). Clearly for Synge the age he lived in, and the country, did not any longer have 'real religion'.

Yet Synge's plays are not truly anti-clerical or anti-Catholic, for all his satiric picture of the hardships of the Priest's life as he complains of them to Mary in *The Tinker's Wedding*:

> What would you do if it was the like of myself you were, saying Mass with your mouth dry, and running east and west for a sick call maybe, and hearing the rural people again and they saying their sins? (*CW* IV 19)

Synge, in the Wicklow plays as in his other work, ignores rather than mocks or denigrates the Catholic belief of the people. The opposition between those who conform and those who do not, between the villagers and the vagrants, has its origins in his lapsed protestantism rather than any animus against the majority faith. The conflict is secularised insofar as, with the arguable exception of the Saint in *The Well*, there are no serious spokesmen of religious orthodoxy in the plays. Instead what the Tramp in *The Shadow*, Martin and Mary in *The Well*, Mary Byrne in *The Tinker's Wedding*, stand for is some sort of independent individuality of vision at odds with the social consensus that surrounds them. They are laicised, small-p. protestants who protest, directly or indirectly, against seeing the world as their neighbours see it.

In this they are Synge's own representatives, for he saw the Wicklow which his imagination needed to see. Authenticity in this context has to be considered an irrelevant or discredited criterion. It obviously mattered to him that his imaginative works were based in the actual, and when criticised for inauthenticity he defended himself against the charge (unwisely as it turned out) in the preface to *The Playboy*. Though they are impressionistic, some of the insights of his Wicklow essays have value for the historian.[48] But in the end the imagination has to tell its own stories, however much or little they may correspond to verifiable facts. In the case of Synge and Wicklow, coming from where he did socially, there were areas of the local experience of the time which were not available to him as material for literature or drama: politics, religion, the social revolution of changing landownership. Instead he sought what could be represented as outside or on the edge of these historically conditioned circumstances. The natural world, particularly as it declared itself most essentially in the desolation of the glens, was the defining reality. Those who lived at the boundaries between it and the social community, marginal and alienated, offered figures for ultimate enduring patterns of human experience. The very specificity of the local underwrote the universal, and what Synge could imagine against the background of the desolate Wicklow mountains, inspired by the people he saw living among them, constituted its own form of compelling truth.

References

1. T.C.D. MS 4335, f.36, fragmentary typescript draft of material subsequently used in Synge's essay 'The People of the Glens'. See J.M. Synge *Collected Works*, General editor, Robin Skelton (Oxford, 1962-8): Vol. II *Prose*, ed. Alan Price (1966), pp 216-224. All quotations from Synge's published work, unless otherwise stated, are taken from the *Collected Works* cited within the text as *CW* I, II, III, IV. Unpublished manuscript material is from the collection in Trinity College Library: see *The Synge Manuscripts in the Library of Trinity College Dublin* (Dublin 1971). In transcribing from the manuscripts I have silently corrected spellings, punctuation, and typographical errors, adding accidentally omitted words in square brackets.
2. Samuel Lewis, *A topographical dictionary of Ireland* (London, 1837), ii, p. 144.
3. The fortunes of the Synges seem to correspond almost exactly to the pattern of rise and decline of the landed gentry traced by L.M. Cullen in *The emergence of modern Ireland 1600-1900* (London, 1981), pp 128-31, who posits a highpoint in landlord incomes in 1815. Interestingly, he associates the increasing troubles of the landlord class in the years following to an increased concern with

education on their estates, provoking resistance from tenants. Again John 'Pestalozzi' Synge seems a striking case in point.

4. Much of the biographical material here, as throughout this essay, is derived from the account of Synge's nephew, Edward Millington Stephens. His enormous manuscript *Life* of his uncle (now in Trinity College Library MS 6189-6197) has been used in two published works: David H. Greene and Edward M. Stephens, *J.M. Synge 1871-1909* (New York, 1959, rev. ed. 1989) and *My Uncle John*, ed. Andrew Carpenter (Oxford, 1974). There remains, however, much that is valuable in the (still largely unpublished) manuscript. For readers' convenience I have given references in the text to the published works where possible (Greene and Stephens; My Uncle John); manuscript references are given as (Stephens MS).
5. Recorded in Mrs Synge's diary 28 Feb 1893, quoted by Samuel Synge, *Letters to my Daughter* (Dublin and Cork, 1931), p. 193.
6. 'Le premier resultat de l'application de Home-Rule en Irlande serait une guerre, ou du moins un grand conflit social entre Catholique et Protestant'. Letter to unidentified correspondent of mid-July 1895. See *The collected letters of John Millington Synge*, ed. Ann Saddlemyer, (Oxford, 1983), i, 1, p. 29.
7. In the days of rack-renting
And land-grabbing so vile
A proud, heartless landlord
Lived here a great while.
When the League it was started,
And the land-grabbing cry,
To the cold North of Ireland
He had for to fly. (*CW* II 212)
The 'proud, heartless landlord', at the time of the Synges's residence in Castle Kevin, was Rev. Charles W. Frizell who lived in Belfast as secretary to the Bishop of Down and Connor.
8. The Census return of 1901 lists him as a 'boarder' with the Hardings. He died in 1905 and is buried in the Church of Ireland graveyard at Glenealy in the Drought of Glencarrig vault.
9. Florence Massey, who was already with the Synges in 1901 at the time of the Census returns, is listed as born in Dublin.
10. Samuel Synge, *Letters to my daughter*, p. 81.
11. The incident took place on 27 August 1897. See Stephens MS f.1262.
12. Saddlemyer (ed.), *Letters of Synge*, p. 224.
13. See *The Synge manuscripts*, p. 25.
14. The essays are 'An Autumn night in the hills', 'The vagrants of Wicklow', 'The Oppression of the Hills', 'On the road', 'The people of the glens', 'At a Wicklow fair', 'A landlord's garden in county Wicklow', 'Glencree'. To these Alan Price, editor of the *Prose* volume of the Oxford *Collected Works*, added 'People and places', a composite piece made up from unpublished passages in Synge's papers.
15. E.M. Stephens claims that the earliest drafts of the Wicklow essays date from as far back as 1897-8. Although undoubtedly some of the incidents used in the essays come from this time, I have found no evidence in the manuscripts of anything definitely written before 1900.
16. The notebook MS 4396 contains a plan for a projected 'Wicklow book' (ff4v-5). In the catalogue of the manuscripts (for which I was partly responsible) this notebook is said to date 'from the spring and summer of 1907', *The Synge Manuscripts*, p. 46. Though it was used at this later date, the Wicklow material in it may well be from 1902, as E.M. Stephens maintains.

17. *The Synge manuscripts*, p. 24.
18. In a TS draft of the essay Synge gives the place as Aughavanna and mentions the name as Kehoe (MS 4335, f.37). Because the old man gives his age precisely as 82 in the essay, it is possible to identify him certainly as Patrick Kehoe (or Keogh) of Aghavannagh Revell, the only person of that name and age in the area listed in the Census returns of 1901. He died in 1906 at the age of 87 and is buried in Macreddin Upper graveyard. In the draft of the essay, Synge records the meeting with Kehoe as taking place on the same day as the inquest on John Winterbottom (see below), that is, Saturday 24 August 1901. Although he may have merely put together the two incidents which took place at different times, as he frequently did in the essays, the encounter with Kehoe must have been in this summer of 1901.
19. His mark is attested by a witness on his 1901 Census return form.
20. Once again Synge includes Corbet's name in the TS, though removing it from the published text, MS 4335, f.37. Born in 1825, W.J. Corbet of Spring Farm, Delgany, was nominated as a candidate for Wicklow on Parnell's insistence in 1880, served as M.P. for Wicklow 1880-85, and for Wicklow East from 1885-92. Defeated as a Parnellite in 1892, he was re-elected in 1895, ending his parliamentary career in 1900.
21. See Richard Griffith, *Valuation of the several tenements comprising the Union of Rathdrum* (Dublin, 1854), p. 165, as against the Census returns for the townland of 1901.
22. E.H. Mikhail, *J.M. Synge: interviews and recollections* (London, 1972), p. 34.
23. *Wicklow News-Letter*, Saturday 17 August 1901.
24. This description is in fact taken from a draft which Synge never used in one of his published essays but which appears in 'People and Places', the editor's compilation, in the Oxford *Collected works.*
25. Lady Gregory, *Our Irish theatre* (Gerrards Cross, Bucks., 3rd ed. 1972), p. 77.
26. This is a passage from a TS draft of 'The oppression of the hills' which Synge omitted from the published text, MS 4335, f.24.
27. See MS 4421, Synge's 1902 diary, entry for 12 January.
28. See, for example, Samuel Synge, *Letters to my daughter*, pp 164, 215.
29. An early draft of *The tinker's wedding* specifies that 'the scene is in a Wicklow village far away from the sea', MS 4336, f.2.
30. The brief fragmentary draft, apparently entitled *Dead man's deputy* at this stage, is to be found in a notebook which also contains dialogue for *Riders to the sea* and *The tinker's wedding*, MS 4348, ff14-17.
31. See *Memoirs of Miles Byrne*, ed. Stephen Gwynn (Dublin, 1906), i, p. 221, and Charles Dickson, *The life of Michael Dwyer* (Dublin 1944), p. 119.
32. I am grateful to Joan Kavanagh of Wicklow County Heritage for the dates of birth, taken from the Baptismal Register of Rathdrum parish; the extent of the Harneys' land-holding is derived from the Valuation Office records, and the size of their house from the 1901 Census return. The ages of the Harneys on the Census return are given incorrectly as 50 (Michael), 42 (Esther), and 40 (James).
33. E.M. Stephens remarks that the unmarried Harney brothers and sister were 'without the company of any young people except when one of their nieces or nephews came to stay'. Stephens MS, f.1250.
34. See MS 4335, f.40.
35. The inquest was held under the coroner Thomas B. Doyle on 24 August 1901 with full reports in *The Wicklow News-Letter*, 31 August 1901 and *The Wicklow People*, 31 August 1901.

36. In the Census return of 1901 his age is given as 36, his wife Charlotte's as 35, and the three children Sarah (5), John (4), Richard (3).
37. This was a detail remembered by Thomas O'Neill of Ballinanty, Ballinaclash, who first suggested to me that the original of Patch Darcy was John Winterbottom. See my *Synge: a critical study of the play* (London 1975), p. 190.
38. For this information I am indebted to Jimmy Winterbotham of Avoca, who was told it by his father, a younger half-brother of John Winterbottom.
39. In the TS draft of the play Synge had originally written 'in the spring of the year' and then altered it. MS 4339, f.33.
40. MS 4339 f.33.
41. See MS 4339, ff9, 19, 63.
42. In *The tinker's wedding* again the fictitious 'Rathvanna' replaced the equally real 'Rathdangan'. See MS 4336, f.63.
43. *When the moon has set* was never published in Synge's lifetime, but a number of drafts of it were left among his papers. Quotations here are not from the one-act version published in the *Collected Works,* edited by Ann Saddlemyer (*CW* III 155-77), but from an earlier two-act draft edited by Mary King in *Long Room,* 24-25 (Spring-Autumn 1982), pp 24, 28.
44. MS 4336, ff8, 11, 12.
45. Only two sons, George, a postman, and William, an apprentice, were living at home at the time of the 1901 Census, but there were several other children including James (1874-1964) who was at this time in Glasgow and was to return home and set up a forge in another part of the village in 1909. I have to thank Canon James Hartin, Rector of Ballinatone, and Jim Smith of Ballinclash, for help with information on the Smith family.
46. The story was told me by Tom Cullen of Bahana Whaley who said that his father could remember some of the tinkers with their wounds coming to the Cullens' farm after the fight.
47. *Collected letters,* I, p. 148.
48. Louis Cullen, for example, cites Synge several times and always respectfully in *The emergence of modern Ireland,* pp 107, 131, 137.

Powerscourt Fall (Bartlett).

Chapter 18

A SURVEY: SOME WICKLOW MAPS 1500-1888

PATRICK POWER

Despite cultural borrowings and adaptations Gaelic society never developed the concept of depicting landscape or its surface features in a diagrammatic form.[1] Accounting by oral tradition in which the controlling caste of the sept described orally and embedded in folk memory the complex details of territory, land division, obligation and sept law of property was commonplace.[2] Such a system is only possible within an unchanging and relatively stable social structure. Maps were a rarity among all sections of early modern society, from highly organised institutions like the church to the great territorial lords of the Pale.[3] Even within the embryonic Tudor Irish civil service the use of maps appeared so rarely as to be a novelty.

County Wicklow's maps began far beyond its boundaries as early as *c.*150 A.D., in all probability as a navigational aid for merchants plying the fringes of the Roman empire. The celebrated, reconstructed Ptolemy map, though sparse in detail, places the Wicklow region fairly accurately in its Irish context.[4] The county is however inaccurately positioned in relation to Britain.[5] Of the geographer's sixty recorded placenames, four may have Wicklow connotations; the sept districts of Menapii, the fortress of Dunum, the river names Modonnos and Oboka. Of the four, only the last was adopted into common usage as a district feature name. There is still controversy over the precise locations of the other three. The naming of the lower reaches of the Avonmore as the Ovoca river dates to the late sixteenth century when the first maps and geographies of Ireland were being compiled by Englishmen with access to various Ptolemic constructions, such as the 'Schweinheim Bucknick' version published in various editions from 1478 to 1508.[6]

The technological skill required to survey and make maps for land transactions or military use appears to have eluded Anglo-Norman society in Wicklow even though a crude technique of one dimensional cartography was known to some of them.[7] It relied on clearly discernible geographical features which were tabulated in written form on legal documents. Rivers and their valleys, lakes, mountains and impassable bog were more likely to fossilise as permanent boundary features not only as part of the external frontier but also as internal borders between various vested interests within the county. Such rivers, valleys and mountain glens were to give geographical definition to O'Byrne's Country and Gabhal Raghnaill.[8] Almost from the first century of Norman settlement, Wicklow's baronial divisions found expression in the natural obstacles of the upper Slaney, the Liffey and Dargle rivers, the mountain region, its lakes, intercutting glens, and the low ground of the coast.

The utility of Wicklow's coast to external maritime societies, who themselves used and issued maps through the late Middle Ages, has resulted in a stark imbalance in the cartographic story of Wicklow.[9] The era of the portolan maps, more properly charts as they were devised for and by mariners seafaring from port to port, was from 1327 to 1552. Beautifully wrought Italian and Spanish portolans are the only maps of Wicklow (and Ireland) in existence for the late medieval period. Invariably, they give little inland geographical information other than representations of a widely distorted Slaney, while the Barrow and Nore rivers appear on some. In spite of shortcomings, these maps do throw some light on developing coastal towns. Bray, Wicklow, Arklow and an unidentified placename, possibly Kilcoole,[10] frequently appear, implying that sufficient external trade existed to tempt foreign merchants to these outposts of the Pale. Prominently depicted on several portolans is the series of off-shore sandbanks reaching from Wicklow head to Blackwater in Wexford, a fearful gauntlet to run for ships of the fourteenth and fifteenth centuries.[11] There was no inland equivalent to portolan maps. Property leases and tenancies, feudal dues, land divisions and related matters appear to have been compiled without supporting cartographical documents.[12] Church land was likewise beyond the realm of mapping. Land holdings by the archbishop of Dublin and monastic orders throughout the county were extensive and diverse but antiquity of ownership, along with bureaucratic efficiency, made maps superfluous. Diocesan clerks and the heads of religious houses, imbued with a long tradition of accurate clerical recording, knew exactly the extent and location of their assets.[13]

It is not true to say that there were no maps of the study region made before the seventeenth century. A small number of general Irish maps began to appear which revealed some cartographical detail within Wicklow. Gerard Mercator's map 'Angliae, Scotiae et Hiberniae Nova Descriptio' published in Duisburg in 1564 was the first to depict with some accuracy the courses of the Liffey, Dargle, Vartry, Avonmore and Avonbeg, and the political spheres of the O'Byrne and the O'Toole septs. Settlements such as Castlekevin, Glendalough, Newcastle, and the seaports of Bray, Wicklow and Arklow are named.[14] The accuracy of the Mercator map suggests it was surveyed by those who had actually visited the area, or who had first hand knowledge of some now lost earlier survey. Portolan maps, on the other hand, bear all the hallmarks of repeated copying of very limited originals based on little surveying. Mercator's map was followed by others. Within three years of its publication, John Goghe issued a detailed improved map of Ireland in 1567. While in many ways similar to the Mercator copy, Goghe's map locates the mountains much more accurately. In addition he includes woodland features in Arklow barony. This is probably an attempt to position the upper portion of the Duffrey forest, a traditional refuge of the Kavanaghs, which was then receiving attention in official reports.[15]

War, its prosecution, consequences and aftermath, was the catalyst which brought Ireland into the sphere of European map science. Centralised involvement by the British government from 1570 onwards demanded accurate information from its troubled colony. While no specific county survey was undertaken by the Tudors, several general maps covering Ireland and peripheral areas of Wicklow produced

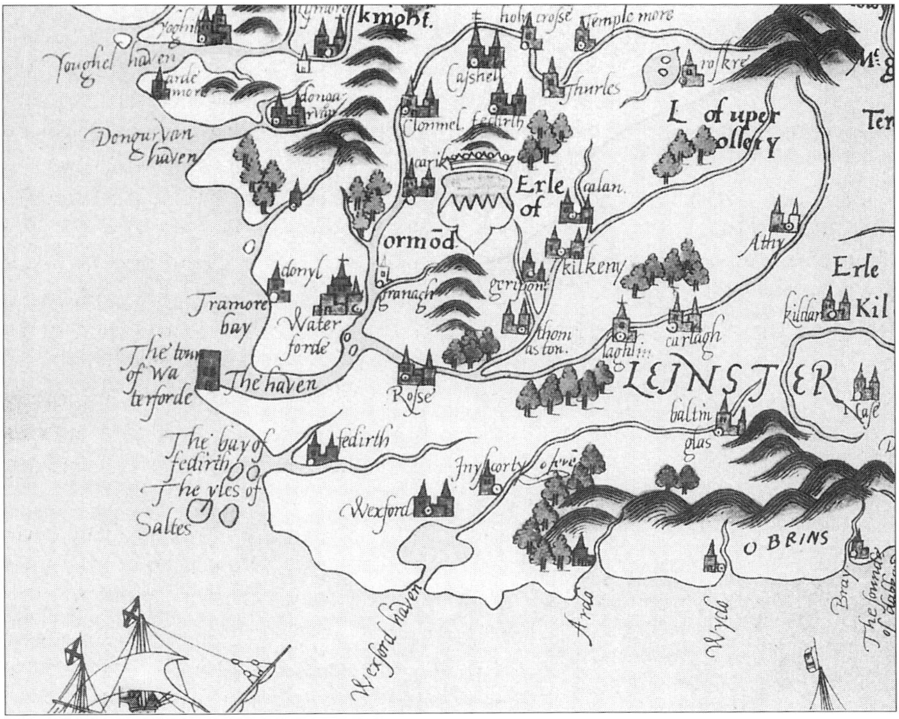

Figure 18.1 Extract from John Goghe's Map of Ireland 1567.

sufficient cartographic knowledge for the needs of the times. The paucity of Wicklow maps contrasts with the comprehensive mapping programme for contemporary Ulster.[16] This may be explained by virtue of the fact that Wicklow's terrain was well known to the Dublin military officials whereas Tyrone's was not. Impressive as the military successes of Feagh McHugh O'Byrne may be in folk memory, his Elizabethan adversaries perceived the Wicklow clan revolt as essentially a local disturbance and a costly military survey of their territory was deemed unnecessary as both its limits and economic worth were well known.[17] John Goughe's map of Ireland in 1567, Robert Lythe's map of the barony of Udrone (embracing parts of west Wicklow and county Carlow) of 1569 or 1571, and the map of the newly proposed county of Wicklow or Ferns in 1579, were sufficient to chart the military campaigns of Wicklow from 1580 onwards.[18] Special circumstances at times warranted a more local map such as that drawn up in 1599 by Captain Charles Harrington to explain the ignominious retreat by Sir Henry Harrington in 1599. This interesting vellum plan poses the question of what can be defined as a map, for the main thrust of the work suggests an early form of strip cartoon with a cartographic purpose.[19]

In the post-war era of 1605, surveys and maps of the new county of Wicklow were included in all-Ireland maps such as, for example, those by Baptista Boazio in *c.*1609, and John Speed's *Theatre of the Empire of*

Figure 18.2 Extract from *Irlandiae accurata descriptio* by Baptista Boazio, *c.*1609.

Great Britaine 1610. Speed's map was widely adapted as the bestseller of its time and remained the standard Irish map for almost fifty years.

Irish surveying in the Stuart era was generally confined to plantation regions. In county Wicklow no mapping projects were undertaken (or have survived) for the early seventeenth century despite major shifts in land ownership. Evidence from the earl of Strafford's estate and the O'Toole petitions shows that traditional oral inquisition without maps was generally used in property transactions.[20]

The use of military maps by either side in the wars of 1641-50 does not feature in the historical record for Wicklow county. The common-wealth army under Cromwell relied on local guides as they traversed the county in September 1649, while the forces of the confederation, drawn primarily from native residents, had even less use for a map of Wicklow. Ironically, it was the war's aftermath that produced the most significant of Wicklow's land maps. The Civil Survey and Down Survey were instituted by parliament in 1652 to search out the land and property of those who were designated rebellious subjects, Irish or otherwise, in the late wars. It was proposed – and subsequently carried out with great ruthlessness – to sequester attainted property by commission and use these assets to pay ex-soldiers and to honour loans made to parliament by sympathetic institutions who helped defray the cost of the Irish wars. The vicissitudes of the original Civil Survey is outside the scope of this essay. Inventories and parish maps for county Wicklow for the Down Survey have not survived. The barony maps have fared better.

Wicklow's barony maps were surveyed and drawn under the direction of Sir William Petty (1623-87). They comprise the half-barony of Rathdown and the baronies of Newcastle, Ballinacor, Talbotstown and Arklow. Each map was drawn to the scale of one hundred and sixty perches (a half Irish mile) to one inch. In no instance are the actual surveyors or their methods recorded though possibly William Farrand was involved in some or all five of them. The original manuscripts of the barony maps are now in the Lansdowne papers, as well as contemporary copies in the Bibliotheque Nationale in Paris.

Petty's maps of Wicklow afford a rare glimpse of the seventeenth century landscape and the first tangible insight into the county since its formation a half century previously. Parishes within the county are delineated as are contemporary townlands, many of which are now obsolete. Unforfeited lands are not described but the unfilled map spaces indicate those parts of the county in the hands of loyalists. There were five barony maps compiled in 1654.[21] Rathdown half-barony, as it is described, gives prominence to Oldcourt Castle. Five townlands of Bray parish are shown and a castle site, most likely the fortification of

Bray town. Beyond Oldcourt and the coast, over 80 per cent of the map area, little detail is shown except some 'boggy mountains' and 'Glencree', the hereditary (and fortified) lands of the O'Tooles.[22]

Newcastle barony extends from Delgany to Wicklow Head and inland to the 'Blackwater' (the Avonmore). Large tracts adjoining the coast were defined unforfeited. Such distribution patterns indicate that Elizabethan and other loyalist settlements were not extirpated during the Wicklow wars and that rebellious Wicklow septs used the mountain vastness of their ancient homeland as their base of operations. Castles and fortified positions are illustrated at Kilcoole and Kiltimon; the Broad Lough is described as 'Wicklow Lough' and its outlet as 'Newrath Water'. Lands within and adjoining Wicklow town are named as 'Churchlands' and 'Abbeylands'. A little to the north of the county town lie the 'New and Old Granges' (Grange and Grange North). The ubiquity of features associated with the church suggests that less than a century before Petty's survey, the pre-Reformation Church and religious orders were the county's biggest landowners. Wicklow's 'Black Castle' is depicted in its true situation on the sea promontory. A pair of towers and a curtain wall may well be an exact representation of how this citadel looked before its partial destruction. Except for one instance, Petty's anonymous surveyors did not show roads on the barony maps. In the exceptional example a portion of track across Dunbur townland is designated 'Highway from Dublin to Wicklow'. Land, not communications, was the surveyor's prerogative.[23]

Talbotstown typifies more than other baronies the complex political structure of seventeenth-century Wicklow. Extensive areas were delineated as lordships instead of parishes. Replete with castles, it proclaimed that here was marcher land; a troubled countryside where military considerations were paramount. Beneath the obvious martial trappings is evidence of west Wicklow's historical incorporation in the great lordship of Naas, under the tutelage of the abbey of Baltinglass. Enshrined in placenames such as Talbotstown, Boystown, and Humphreystown are echoes of once independent Norman manors.[24]

Ballinacor barony, where almost all the lands were forfeit, was from 1000 A.D. heartland of the O'Byrne sept.[25] It was, like Rathdown, only partially mapped. In all probability, the vast wastelands of Glen Imaal and Lugnaquillia sapped the surveyors' zeal as the comments 'Parts of 2 or 3 parishes,' 'Unprofitable bogge and mountain,' 'Aghavanagh,' 'Boggy mountain,' '5 great glins,' suggest. Much of Ballinacor's terrain was assessed unprofitable except that strip adjoining the Avonmore river valley. In their majestic solitude, the ancient ruins of Glendalough appear to have made a stark impression. In a rare departure from the severity of the barony maps, there is an attempt to fill in some detail on

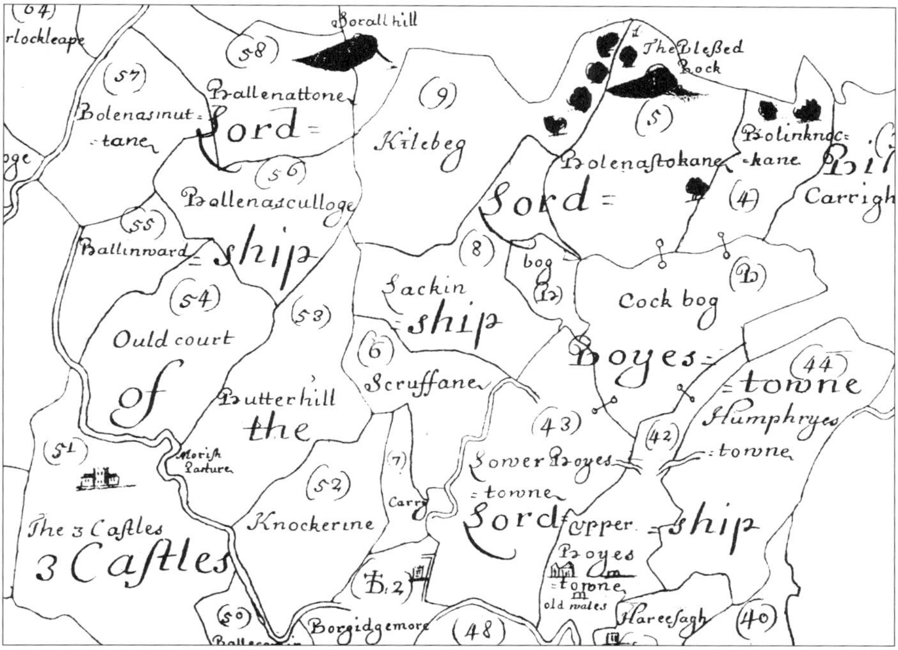

Figure 18.3 Extract from Down Survey map of Talbotstown barony.

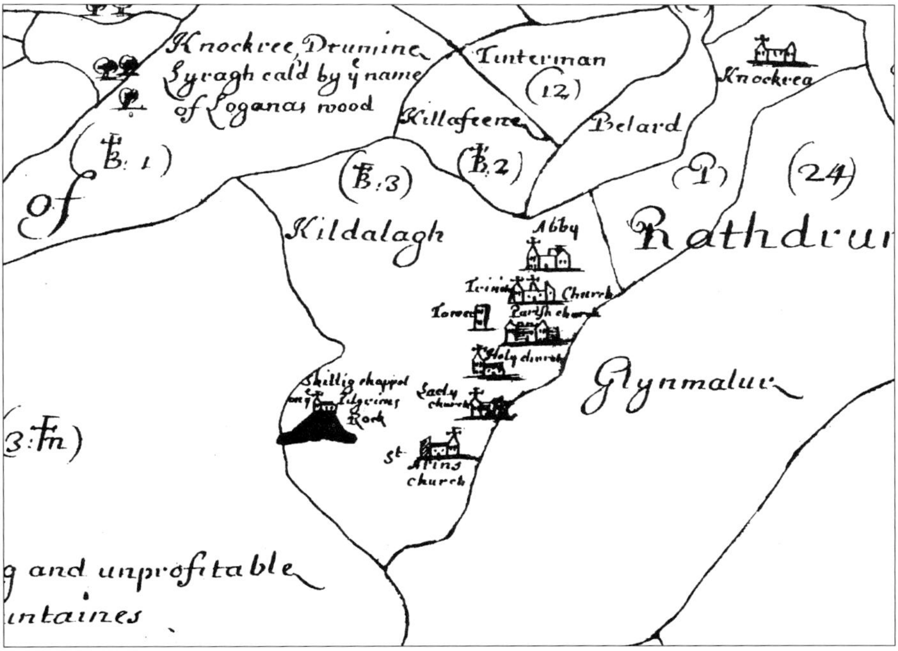

Figure 18.4 Extract from Down Survey of Ballinacor barony showing Glendalough.

the seven churches. Clearly indicated are 'The Abby,' 'Trinity Church,' 'Parish Church,' 'Holy Church,' 'The Round Tower,' 'Lady Church,' 'Skillig Chappel on ye Pilgrims Rock,' and 'St Kevin's Church'. The only feature comparably mapped on the Talbotstown map is the Bishop's Lordship where a hill described as 'The Bishop's Rock' is given some prominence.[26]

A considerable area adjoining Arklow was declared forfeit. The town itself and surrounding lands, the old Norman cantred called 'The Shires' remained, due to some deft political work on his part, in the hand of the pro-royalist duke of Ormonde. As they were unforfeited, the shires remained undelineated and are almost blank on an otherwise interesting map. Though it was not Petty's intention, parts of the

Figure 18.5 County Wicklow from Sir William Petty's *Hiberniae Delineatio* 1685.

barony maps show boundaries and townlands of some early seventeenth-century Roman Catholic parishes.[27] As many of these were rendered obsolete in the next century, the parish outlines now throw valuable light on the pre-Penal Law Roman Catholic Church in the county. Early Church of Ireland boundaries followed some of these same outlines before they, too, were drastically re-organised in the following century.[28] Embellishment on the Arklow map is scarce. The only man-made structure clearly shown is ruined Dunganstown Castle. It was originally built *c.*1610 by Sir John Hoey on a site confiscated from the Hospitallers of St John of Jerusalem. Like Glendalough, it must have impressed the surveyor enough to merit the inscription 'Dunganstown Great House demolished'.[29]

In 1685 Sir William Petty produced a bound thirty-eight page *Atlas of Ireland*, his celebrated 'Hiberniae Delineatio'. Map 15 of the volume is a coloured rendering of Wicklow county on a scale of four Irish miles to two inches. It is, in essence, a composite of the barony maps of 1655 though with much placename detail removed. However, some blank areas on the original barony sheets have been filled in, presumably from the now lost Wicklow parish maps. A second version of the atlas was issued in collaboration with Francis Lamb in 1689 with the Wicklow map scaled at eight miles to seven-eighths of an inch. For over fifty years this survey, reissued with few variations, was the definitive county map.

From the first decade of the eighteenth century, new maps of county and country were published, invariably from outside Ireland. In 1728 Herman Moll, a cartographer of German descent, produced an atlas of twenty Irish maps. County Wicklow was mapped in part. Much of Moll's work rests heavily on the Down Survey map of Wicklow, but he includes some additional placenames and road routes. Moll's venture may not have been a success. Trinity College Library has only one copy of his Irish atlas. From this scarcity of surviving examples, it is probable that the maps were not considered as a great improvement on Petty's county map.[30] Bernard Scale's 'Hibernian Atlas' was first issued in 1788 and subsequently in 1798. Wicklow on plan no.10 was plotted on a scale of six miles to one inch. This map supplanted all previous efforts for general purposes and was popular until the publication of the Ordnance Survey maps in 1840.

In 1760, Jacob Nevill, a mathematics teacher and surveyor produced the first detailed map of county Wicklow since Petty. With his dedication to the 'Nobleman, Knights of the Shire and Gentleman of the county,' Nevill clearly had the grand jury in mind, if not their actual commission. His map is scaled at seven miles to one inch and carries a flamboyant cartouche of cherubs with surveying instruments and a

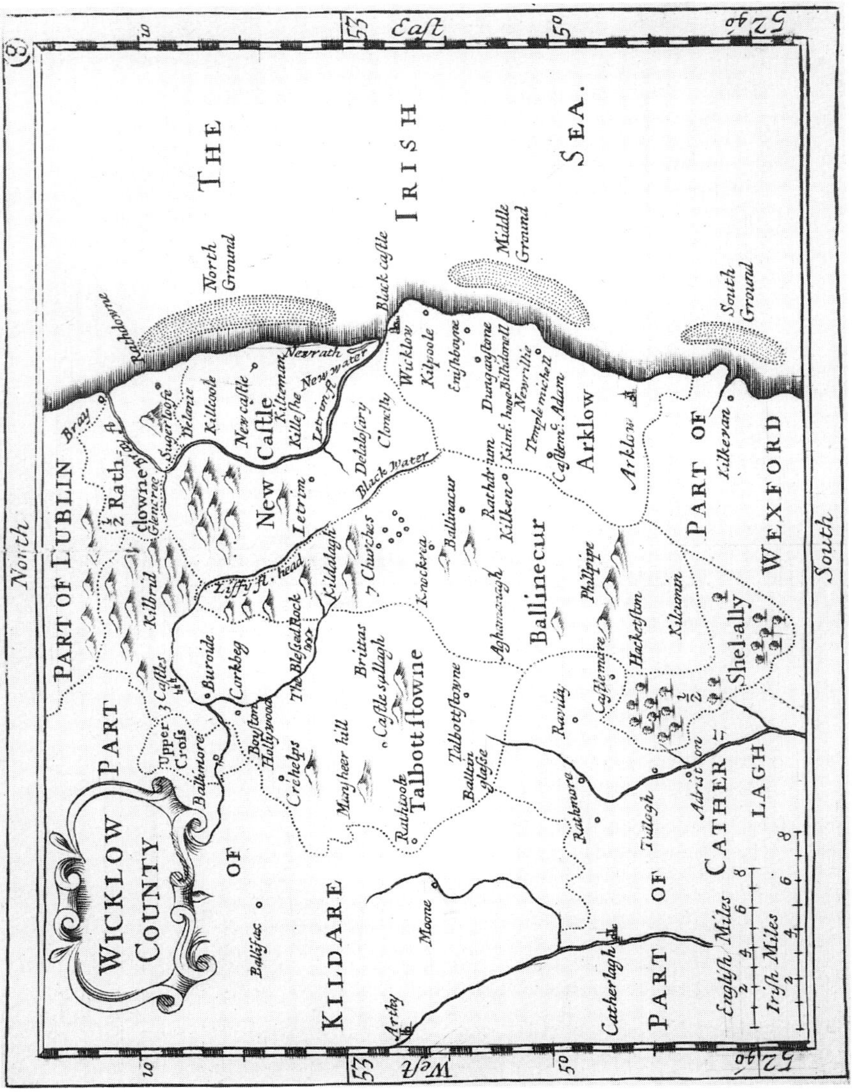

Figure 18.6 County Wicklow 1700 from *Geographical description of Ireland*.

representation of men engaged in stone breaking which may be a depiction of either quarrying or mining. There is much detail included on the map. Most county roads are shown, for their upkeep and maintenance was the essence of grand jury business. Churches of main denominations were plotted and an indication as to the state of repair. Places of worship of the smaller religious groups were noted such as the Quaker Meeting Houses at Redcross, Wicklow town, and Shillelagh. Schools were shown. At Tinahely, Shillelagh and Carnew the marquis of Rockingham's (later Fitzwilliam's) property shows a discernible estate type of layout with free schools prominent in these three locations. Local industry was also mapped, for Nevill surveyed the position of water mills. He also plotted bleaching greens in the villages of west Wicklow and quarries of granite and slate. There is a generous inclusion of placenames, some appearing for the first time in print. Other detail of interest to the county gentry, such as the racecourses at Baltinglass and Donard, was located. Detailed as Nevill's survey was, it had its glaring errors. The major one was placing Hacketstown and other county Carlow towns in Wicklow. A curiosity on the map is the segregation of Ballycore townland from the rest of the county with the following note: 'Tis said this part belongs to County Dublin.' Here is a reference to the old anomaly which placed Ballycore as a manor of the dean of Christchurch cathedral who, in 1760, retained considerable power in matters of local administration outside the grand jury's control.[31]

Portions of county Wicklow, especially its seaboard, were mapped, with a judicious use of colour, as part of the great unfinished survey by Colonel Charles Vallancey in 1776. Unfortunately, no reproduction of its Wicklow segments has been made to date, due to the unwieldy size and condition of the few originals which exist. There is much detail on Vallancey's map, despite its military overtones, such as boundaries, roads, strategic features and antiquities. The accompanying field reports, known as military itineraries, together with the maps represent a largely untapped source of county history of the late eighteenth century.[32] The main roads of Wicklow were surveyed with those of the rest of Ireland in 1777 by George Taylor and Andrew Skinner, whose work was published in an atlas of strip maps, two to a page, in 1778. Such road maps reflect an improved national communication system. Taylor and Skinner's format, which was an adaptation of John Ogilby's road routes of 1675, published in England, was a commercial success and was repeatedly imitated in a variety of Georgian almanacs, directories and roadside companions on both sides of the Irish Sea.[33] *A new map of Ireland, civil and ecclesiastical* by the Rev. D.A. Beaufort, produced in 1792, set an exacting standard for a national map. The county Wicklow segment is clearly and precisely engraved and was widely adopted by the public up to the introduction of the six inch to the mile Ordnance Survey maps. The county map produced for Fraser's *Statistical survey of Wicklow* in 1805, is essentially a redrawing of Jacob Nevill's 1760 plot.

Many of the errors in Nevill's 1760 map were corrected by his nephew Arthur Richard Nevill, city surveyor of Dublin, in his 'Map of said County of Wicklow, taken from actual surveys' and first published

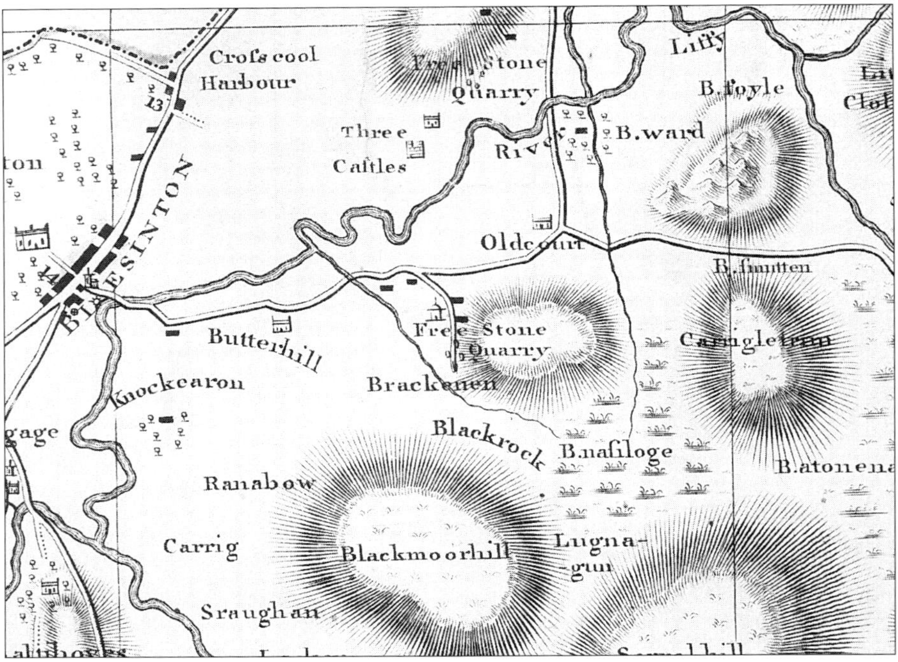

Figure 18.7 Extract from A.R. Nevill's map of county Wicklow showing Blessington (T.C.D.).

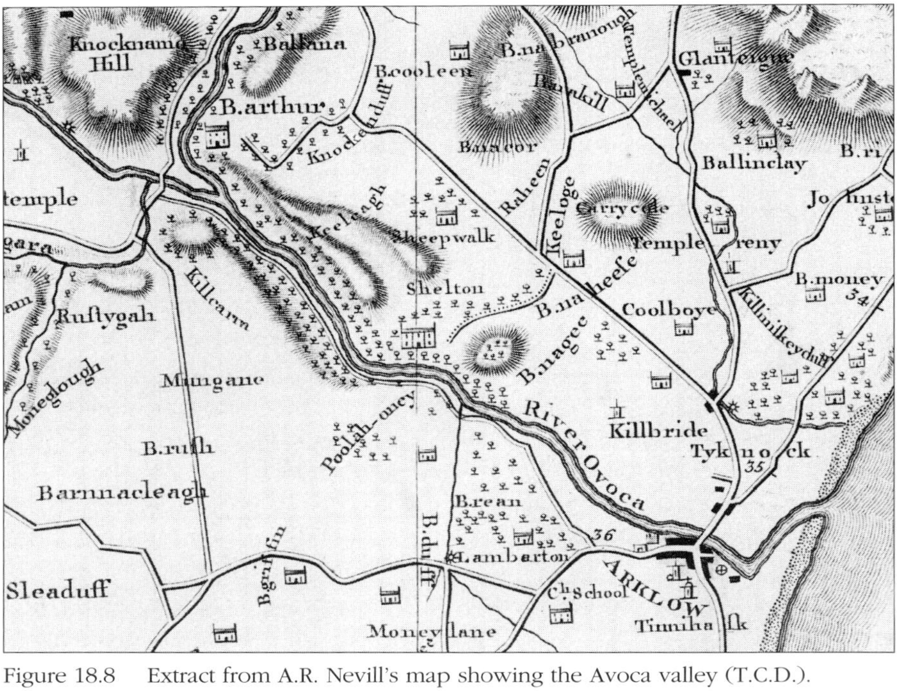

Figure 18.8 Extract from A.R. Nevill's map showing the Avoca valley (T.C.D.).

in 1798. This map adopted the same scale and format as its predecessor a half century earlier and included an elaborate cartouche – an engraved illustration of two wagons drawing what appear to be large boulders but may be bales of wool. New detail carried by the survey includes the route of the military road from Glencree to Drumgoff Barracks. Rathdown woollen exchange is shown and the site of Greenane cloth factory, a showpiece of county industry until its destruction in the rebellion of 1798. The granite quarry at Aughrim and the slate quarry at Kilcandra are given prominence; both industries were mapped as a guide to the grand jury in their road maintenance programme. Placename spellings have almost all been adapted to modern usage. Some names appear for the first time; for instance, Avondale as opposed to its former name of Hayesville and Ballytrasna, as it was described on the 1760 Survey. An accurate county boundary is drawn and the misplacement of Hacketstown and environs is corrected, yet curiously the disputed area is still included on the map. It is the only portion of another county plotted. As on the earlier Nevill map, parliamentary boroughs are outlined and the baronies hatched in.[34] Tourism to Wicklow, becoming extremely fashionable in the late Georgian period, received a nod in 1814 when a new edition of A.R. Nevill's map carried a printed terrier within the plan advising on beauty spots, inns and hotels.[35]

Samuel Lewis' *Topographical dictionary of Ireland*, published in 1837, contains the last private county map before the Ordnance Survey. In it, county Wicklow is scaled at eight miles to one inch. Most of the cartographic information included on the map is, in essence, an edited version of Arthur Nevill's 1798 survey.

The mapping of Arklow 1578-1910

Though Arklow is frequently named on the various portolan maps from 1327 onwards, no other detail or topographical information survives until 1578 with the production of an Elizabethan map entitled 'The Proposed County of Ferns', the single copy of which is in the Public Record Office at Kew. This interesting Tudor work, partially coloured on thin paper, is twenty-eight inches long by eleven wide, scaled at two inches per mile. Arklow's segment traces the valley of the Avonmore from Ballinacor to the sea and embraces the whole barony of Arklow. Four churches are depicted which suggest that the archbishop of Dublin's visitation itinerary may have formed a basis for some of the map's detail. The inclusion of the Island of Arklow in its approximate correct position on the river estuary also indicates familiarity and first hand knowledge of the area. Though lacking a cartographer's name, the 1578 map represents a significant if isolated development.[36]

An examination of the Ormond deeds, where they relate to Butler's Arklow estate, shows that property transactions in this vast lordship, between master, tenants and clergy were all conducted without the service of maps. This highlights the apparent efficiency of the system where boundaries were stable geographical features known and passed down through the generations.[37] Local maps were irrelevant until the Butlers (and similar county magnates) began to alienate their lands permanently, or when outside political considerations intervened, such as the Cromwellian and Williamite land settlements.

Petty's Arklow barony survey, though scaled at one hundred and sixty perches to the inch, has no detail of the shires of Arklow. Even the prominent Avonmore river and its outlet are ignored. The exception is a tiny insert for the town. On it are marked 'Arklow Castle,' 'Abbey' and 'Abbeylands 60A(cres).'[38] Even blank spaces when approached with diligence can serve useful research purposes and it has been possible to plot and identify some of the now obsolete townland names from the late sixteenth century Ormond deeds in relation to Petty's map with some accuracy.[39]

In 1726, a survey was made for the Arklow estates of Viscount John Allen but the original map of this survey was subsequently lost. A settlement of marriage between John Proby and Elizabeth Allen, in 1750, led to an inventory of the Arklow estate in the same year. As part of this stock-take, a new map based on the 1725 survey was made. This is a four foot by two foot wide paper sheet. It is a coloured representation of two of Arklow's three shires, 'Thouhemoyalyn,' and 'Thouhecowlenegleraghe,' on an approximate six inch scale plotted by Garret Hogan. Boundaries follow the course of the Avonmore river as far as Kilcarra (now Wooden) Bridge. Plantation, arable and boglands are depicted along with the tenant's names and their holdings. A coastal tract of rabbit warrens covering fifty acres acknowledges the understated role of the humble rabbit as an important meat source. Arklow parish church, the militia barracks, an eight-arched bridge, and nineteen houses are illustrated in a layout consonant with the true position of the urban building circa 1750.[40] The only ornament of note on the map is a beautiful rendering of a flotilla of ships offshore.

While George Taylor's and Andrew Skinner's 'Maps of the Roads of Ireland' surveyed in 1777 belong to the context of county maps, they merit observation in a more localised setting. Arklow's coach road network depicted on the sheets had an important bearing on Wicklow's military history during the 1798 rebellion.[41] Taylor's and Skinner's atlas also indicates those who were considered the end users of Wicklow's cartographic services, the landed gentry. These strip maps are replete with names of local landowners who held large and middle sized estates.[42]

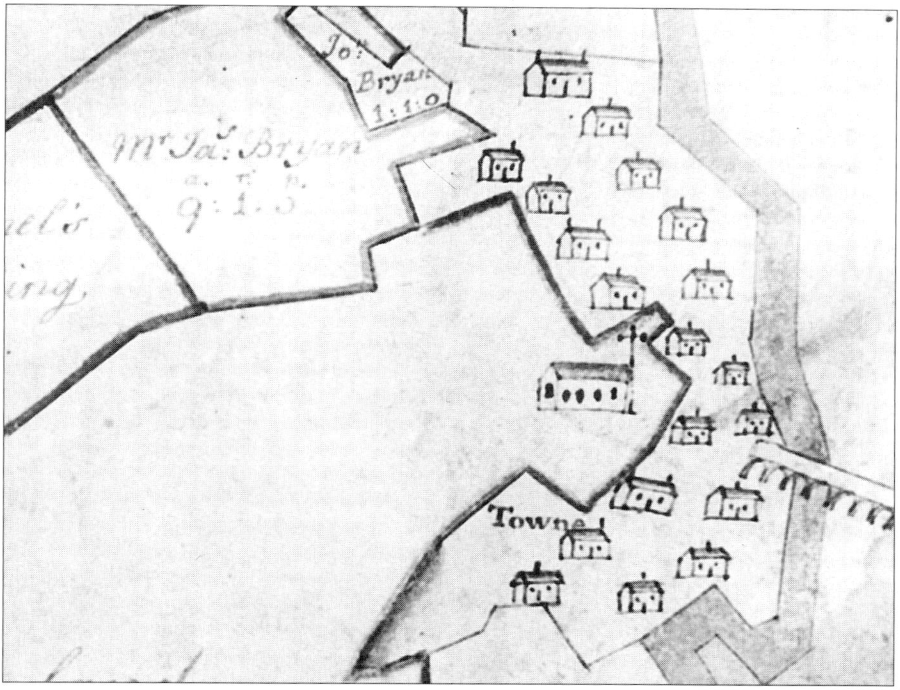

Figure 18.9 Copy of 1750 map of Proby estate showing Arklow town (NAI, M 6233).

William Chapman's 'Harbour and Canal report', dated 1791, contains a small plan of Arklow river estuary.[43] It is scaled two inches to a half mile and was engraved by George Gonne in Dublin. Nothing demonstrates more graphically than this little map the major topographical changes along Arklow's seaboard over the previous two hundred years. Urban detail is scant but the sinuous channels of the Avoca river, and its archipelago of sandy islands, stands out boldly. This emphasis on the river delta places Chapman's plan in the grey zone between marine chart and land map. But as the Avoca river mouth was to play such an important role in urban evolution, these transitional maps are a significant element in Arklow's cartography. Its inclusion in the original 1791 harbour survey was not the only publication of this map. In a report by the Royal Dublin Society in 1879, the same plan is reproduced under the name of 'Forster and Co., Dublin'. The only additional information is the scale of fathoms for the river's channels and the words 'Plan of harbour of Arklow previous to it being improved by the Hibernian Mining Company.'[44] The first purely local town map is derived from a description of the battle of Arklow fought on Saturday 9 June, 1798. It was drawn in 1800 to illustrate the relevant chapter in Sir William Musgrave's *Memoirs of the Different rebellions in Ireland.* There is no indication as to the actual surveyor, nor is the plan drawn to any definite scale.[45] Later editions of Musgrave's book contain key letters on the Arklow plan to indicate certain phases in the battle. The map encompasses all the urban area of the time along with features such as military camp earthworks, redoubts and the fortified militia barracks. Contemporary field patterns are shown as are some principal buildings such as the rectory and charter school. Shaded lines represent the built-up area. Roads and topographical features, though geographically distorted in some instances, represent a fairly accurate depiction of Arklow *c.*1798.

Roads and tracks giving access to Arklow from Wexford are shown on Valentine Gill's 'Wexford County Map' of 1811. There is little other detail on it relevant to the study area.[46] More informative is A.R. Nevill's 'County Survey' of 1798. On the portion covering Arklow barony are church sites, water mills, charter schools, mansions and demesne land. Wooded areas are indicated and the slow extension of the 'new line' mail coach road is charted to the county Wexford boundary.[47]

The period from 1812 to 1820 was a fruitful time for local surveying. As well as the Gill and Nevill surveys, a number of thematic maps were made such as that included in the informative *Statistical Account* by William Shaw Mason in 1816.[48] Again the theme is Arklow harbour and estuary. It is scaled at twenty perches to the inch and was drawn and surveyed by William Jackson of Oulart in 1812. As with Chapman's plans, the urban detail is scant except for the prominence given to the parish Church of Ireland, a deference perhaps to the Arklow rector, Henry L. Bayly, who actually wrote the excerpt for Mason's book. The map shows the start of the river embankments which, as the century progressed, radically transformed the town's development and layout.

The predilection for harbour improvements is also represented on a survey made in December 1821 by Captain Hardy R.N. on a scale of seventy-two perches to three inches.[49] New embankment works and a more detailed topography are shown along the Avoca river outfall. Hardy's plan also highlights the extension of the built-up area into the hitherto uninhabited land on the south shore of the river.

The great watershed of Irish map history is the Ordnance Survey. Born out of necessity for efficient local administration, the early surveys of the last century represent a standard for cartographic skill that has never been, nor is likely to be, equalled. Arklow barony was surveyed throughout 1838 along with the rest of county Wicklow. The first fruits of this painstaking work are two small unpublished 'fair plans' of the Arklow area on a five inch to one mile scale. One map encompasses urban Arklow south of the river and the other a portion of Kilbride parish. Both are signed by Col. Henry Tucker, Royal Engineers on 28

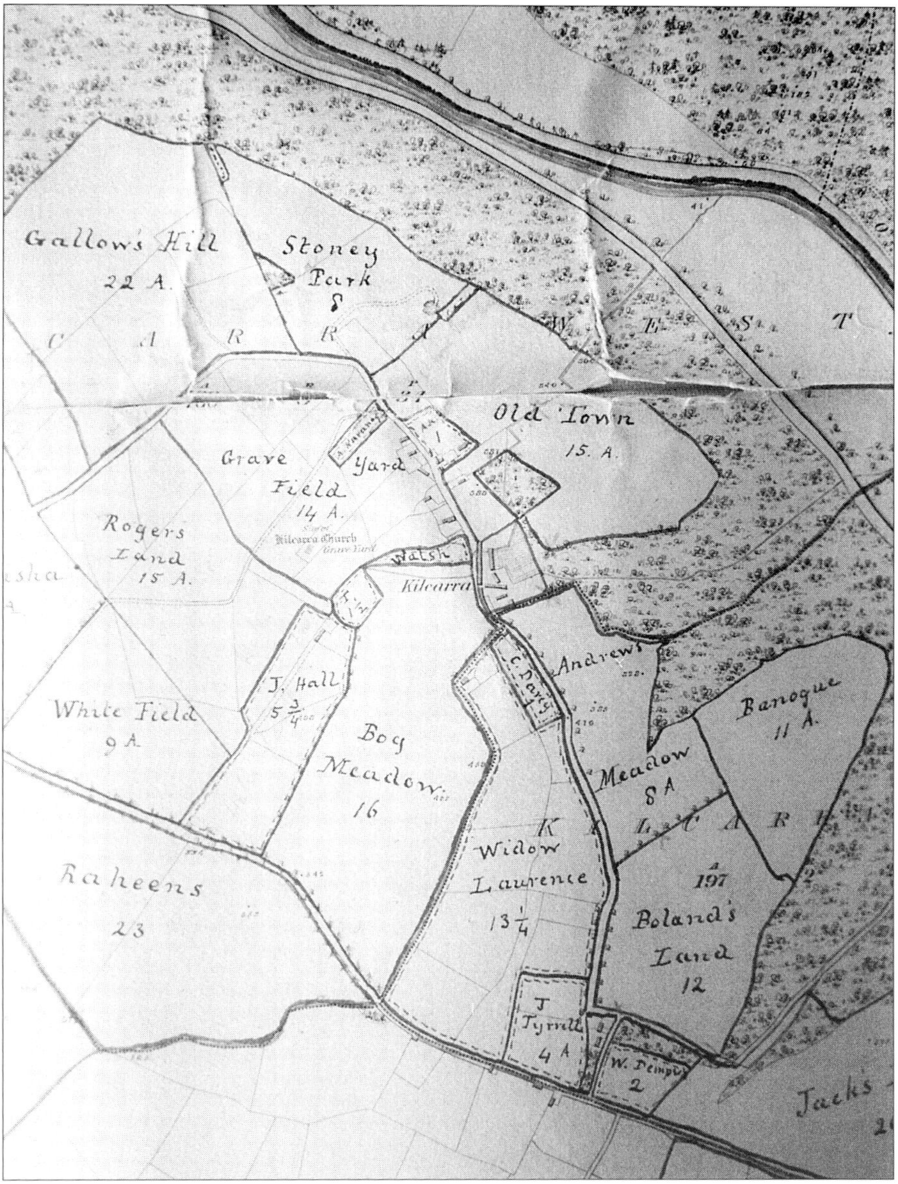

Figure 18.10 Part of Glenart demesne from Proby estate map 1845 (A.P.C.).

June, 1839. As well as depicting the built-up area, roads and landscape, details of some individual buildings with their specific use and location is included. Though much of this information was incorporated into the first official six inch map issue, other detail was unfortunately dropped form the finished work. For example, the Arklow town 'Fair Plan' shows an enlargement of its Fishery Quarter called 'The Chapel Ground' on which is indicated the location of an eighteenth-century chapel site. Likewise a margin drawing of part of Main Street locates the town market house. Neither feature was included in the published work.[50] Arklow barony is covered in the first edition Ordnance Survey by sheets numbered 23, 24, 29, 30, 31, 32, 34, 35, 36, 39, 41, 44, and 45, all issued in May 1840.

William Proby's personal atlas of six-inch O.S. maps of south county Wicklow has survived in a private collection. On eleven sheets, including those which encompass his Arklow estate, the earl plotted in his own hand the distance from Glenart Castle to various places such as Glendalough, Rathdrum and Greenane Bridge.[51] He also marked in the boundaries of the eight-hundred acre demesne of Glenart with its parklands, woods, plantation, farm and traditional field names along with their acreage.[52] Almost from the inception of the Ordnance Survey, the private estate cartographer passed across the bourne of obsolescence. Within the Carysfort estate, up to its subsequent break-up in 1944, there is only one example of a private map and that in itself is based on Ordnance Survey scales.[53] The six-inch Arklow maps of 1840 are primary source material into industry, mines, watermills, farms, raths, antiquities, and ancient occupation sites. The town of Arklow is engraved in minute detail and many features, long passed the threshold of human memory and tradition, are preserved.

Between 1840 and 1843, as part of the poor law valuation, instituted in 1838, Arklow was fully mapped, building by building, on a scale of five inches to one mile. The surveyor was a Robert MacMicken and tabulation of buildings was carried out by John McCready.[54] By 1843 the task was complete and the first fully scaled detailed town plan was drawn. The 'Primary Valuation Map' is of light pink colouring for housing and deep black lines for boundaries. Because it is a manuscript map and is still used for subsequent revisions of town valuation, the drawing text is heavily altered and much original detail has been obliterated. Despite the changes this map provides interesting geographical information. When used in conjunction with Griffiths' Primary Valuation lists, valuable geographical, and topographical detail of Arklow can be reconstructed. Though the original survey has been irrevocably changed, it appears that at some time in its early history, private draughtsmen working for the Carysfort estate were allowed access to the original unrevised map for copying purposes. Among the archives from the estate is an almost perfect copy of McMicken's and McCreedy's original work. Though bearing a date of 1873, it represents the text of the Arklow valuation map as it appeared in 1860. The copy was commissioned as part of an estate management scheme by William

Figure 18.11 Extract from Townsend-Trench valuation map of Arklow 1873 (A.P.C.).

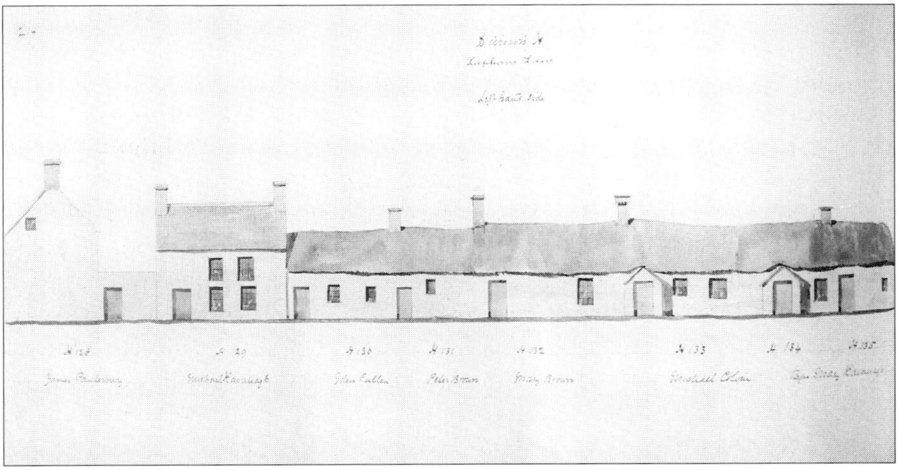

Figure 18.12 Extract from Townsend-Trench illustrated valuation of Arklow 1877 (A.P.C.).

Townsend Trench who adapted it to suit the needs of the landlord. Trench's plan provides an important town survey, filling as it does those gaps drawn over the primary valuation map.[55]

In 1886 the Ordnance Survey produced a set of twelve zincographed plans of Arklow scaled approximately 10 feet to one mile. In all, the series of large-scale plans covers five of the county's towns. Baltinglass, scaled at 1:500, unpublished *c.*1843; Bray, scaled 1:500, unpublished *c.*1843; Wicklow, 1:500, unpublished *c.*1843; Arklow 1:500, published 1886; Bray, 1:500, published 1878; Greystones, 1:1056, published 1883; and Wicklow, 1:1056, published 1896.[56] These rare and very beautiful works were never re-issued or revised and they stand, especially the coloured thirteen sheets for Bray (1878), as the high point of Victorian cartography. On such a scale there is an abundance of detail. The black and white Arklow plans illustrate individual premises and boundaries. Civic services such as water pumps, street lamps, gas lines, wells, and even communal privies are recorded. Other information includes place-names and laneways, long obsolete. As far as Arklow's cartographic record is concerned, it appears these plans fulfilled most requirements for professional and legal use. After their appearance in 1886, no subsequent private survey of Arklow appears to have been undertaken. For all their perfection few intact sets of all twelve plans have survived.[57] Arklow local authority has a few sheets which cover the then (1886) built-up area. Carysfort estate archives has not a full set, though it has multiple copies of some sheets. Some of these reveal interesting detail. On plan No. XL 1617, the area and piling layout for St Saviour's parish church of Ireland has been drawn in by the architect, Sir Arthur Bloomfield. Another plan, XL 1624, shows the terminus of the Avoca mineral railway and part of the South Quay railway embankment. On it is shown the final stop for the ore trucks from Avoca, which is a buffer made with typical Arklow fishery improvisation, from old ships' anchors.[58] Regretfully, there is not a full run of the county Wicklow town plans held in the county. Collections are on file in the National Library of Ireland, Trinity College New Map Library, and in the National Archives.

Estates 1690-1900

The era of the landed gentry lasted from 1690 to the late nineteenth-century Land Acts. The final phase of estate management has left us a rich legacy of county maps, more by accident than by design, and their appreciation cannot be better exemplified than by the introduction to E.R.R.Green's essay on the Downshire estate maps:

> The importance of these maps is clear, not merely for the local historian, but for all those whose work is based, or should be

> based, on the firm foundation of local studies – geographers, archaeologists, social and economic historians, students of placenames and genealogists.[59]

At this juncture it is worth considering the fortune of the bulk of county Wicklow's estate maps. They are the perennial poor relations of landlords' records and, for many reasons, their long-term survival was always in jeopardy. Maps are generally of perishable material and they were nearly always, except in exceptional circumstances, difficult to store. For these reasons, surveys, plans and maps, prone to soiling and general wear and tear were often confined to the pyre when estates were sold off, while more manageable records were preserved. Estates throughout county Wicklow, from 1690, displayed remarkable continuity in ownership over two hundred years. Based on surviving records, it is probable that all or most of them were surveyed and mapped at least twice in their history.[60] About seventy-five families in close alliance, socially and maritally, along with the established Church of Ireland, owned most of county Wicklow.[61] As proprietors of the land, they also regulated county affairs, civic and judicial. From the eighteenth century 'properties of inheritance' (the definition of an estate), two selections have been made which typify the types of property and their cartographic archive. Deference has been made to equitable geographic distribution. The first example is a middle-sized estate, at its greatest extent 7,000 acres.

Ballyarthur, home of the Mitchelbourne-Symes-Bayly family, is located near Woodenbridge in the south-east of the county. It was originally part of the vast Ormond-Butler holdings. In 1580, it passed on to the Brabazons and that family built a residence on the site of an old sporting lodge of the Ormonds.[62] In 1690, the lands were purchased by Colonel Richard Symes who commissioned a demesne survey of Ballyarthur in 1700. If the entire Ballyarthur estate was mapped in 1700, that plan has not survived. A descendant, Rev James Symes, repeated the commission in 1812 when a new demesne map was made. Comparison of both reveals much of the social and economic activity over a part of Wicklow at a century's interval. The Symes also produced descriptive maps to illustrate events and topics which were of personal interest to them, such as the Ballinvalley gold rush of 1796, and the line of a proposed coach road from Newbridge (Avoca) to Arklow.

The 1700 demesne map was surveyed on 10 March of that year by Edward Johnson.[63] It is laid down to a scale of twenty perches to one inch, a popular scale for estate maps. The map measures 26 x 21 inches. It is paper reinforced with a jute backing and linen edging. The text is written in brown and black inks. Housing plans are drawn in red. The draftwork has a plain utilitarian quality and this may reflect a lack of practice in the embellishment that was a later hallmark of estate cartography. There are two reference panels on the plan. The first, of thirty-five entries (in standard English numerals) outlines aspects of the land utilisation and economy of a great estate nearly three hundred years ago. Depicted on the survey are cherry orchards, deerparks, sawpits and limekilns, kitchen gardens and fishing pools on the Avoca river, as well as lawns and leisure walks. On the second reference panel are twenty-seven items in Roman numerals. These give a comprehensive account of the woodlands on the demesne. Timber acreage, location and types of trees, along with their dates of planting, all help to throw light on wood and coppice management on a typical estate in Williamite Ireland.

The later demesne map was plotted by John Jackson of Oulart (county Wexford) in 1812.[64] It is highly coloured in hues of green and, as expected on a well ordered estate 112 years on, carries much more detail than the 1700 map. It measures forty-nine inches by forty-three inches on a linen background. Jackson followed faithfully the 1700 survey, as his map is of the same orientation and is also scaled at 20 perches to the inch. There are ninety-eight reference numbers which document the demesne structure and economy. The Symes family was especially progressive in matters agricultural and in silviculture and were, in 1812, regarded as model farm innovators. A comparison of both maps sheds interesting light on development and pace in rural management over eleven decades, for on the later map the plantations laid down by Colonel Symes are shown in their maturity. On the 1812 survey, the Aughrim river's junction with the Avoca is located at the place where the former river is described as the Darragh river or River of Oaks.

Another plan originating at Ballyarthur is not an estate map at all, but does exhibit a growing awareness of the importance of cartography to illustrate a feature. This was a plan Rev Edward Lambert Bayly had drawn up to show Earl Fitzwilliam of Malton the precise location of the county Wicklow gold mine.[65] The two-colour paper map has no identifying surveyor but it might have been drafted by John Jackson. The area surveyed includes Croghan Kinsella mountain, the Gold Stream at Ballinvalley; secondary details include the route of the old post road to Aughrim and the location of several mills. The Rev E.L. Bayly also submitted a map to the county Wicklow grand jury of the proposed coach road from Avoca to Wicklow. While the map was catalogued by Ainsworth in 1964, its present whereabouts is unknown.[66] But it does appear that Bayly's argument, backed up by his survey, was instrumental in the decision to construct the 'New Line' or Vale Road, in 1816.

Blessington was dominated by the huge estate of the Hill family, Viscount Hillsborough in the Irish peerage. Though domiciled in county Down, the Wicklow estate came into its possession by way of a marriage settlement with William Hill and Elenor Boyle, daughter of the archbishop of Armagh. The Boyles owned Blessington estate since Elizabethan times.[67] It covered 16,000 acres and encompassed 31 townlands, including the town of Blessington.

The cartographic records of the estate of Lord Hillsborough are probably Ireland's best preserved and catalogued estate map collection. The county Wicklow section contains 86 maps dating from 1770 to 1858.[68] There are a number of undated maps probably made prior to 1770. Seven maps and plans cover the town of Blessington. An undated sketch plan within this group is probably of late seventeenth-century origin and may be the oldest in the Downshire collection. It shows the village layout, its buildings and corn mill. The remaining six plans, of which only one is dated (1770), illustrate the expansion of Blessington in the late eighteenth century. A similarity to his signed work would indicate that these plans were prepared by the professional surveyor John Brownrigg. One of the most revealing is an undated plot on paper of 'The Blessington New Inn'. Its inclusion reflects a trend by many responsible Irish landlords to provide, and improve, public and civic buildings.

Between 1785 and 1806 there were six surveys of Lord Hill's entire county Wicklow estate made by John Brownrigg and John Longfield. All scaled to the usual estate measurements of 20 perches to the inch.[69] Of special interest in these surveys is the portion of the estate now drowned by the Poulaphouca Reservoir. Another map by Brownrigg was surveyed in 1798, and shows road detail, housing and plantations in the region at the crucial time of the 1798 rebellion. Outlying townlands of the estate were surveyed by Daniel O'Brien but are uncatalogued in the county Wicklow portion of the Downshire archive. Among them is an interesting detailed survey of the lands of Harristown and Leigh dating from 1763.

One of the treasures of the collection is a portfolio of thirty maps by the estate surveyor Robert Manning made between 1856 and 1858 which cover the following districts: Ballydonnel North, Ballydonnel South (2 copies), Ballylow (3 copies), Ballynabrocky (4 copies), Ballynasculloge Upper, Ballynasculloge Lower, Ballysmuttan, Ballyward, Blackrock, Blessington, Butterhill, Blackhall, Crosscoolharbour (2 copies), Deer Park, Dillonsdown, Edmondstown, Haylands, Hempstown, Holyvalley, Newtown Great, Newtown Little, Newtown Park, Old Court, Seagraves Castle, Three Castles, Walshestown. Some of the above plans are paired.[70]

Bound in a red leather volume, these thirty maps are the culmination of the private surveyor's skill and are a suitable requiem to their art before the Ordnance Survey consigned private map-making to a secondary role. In this capacity the surveyors were generally employed preparing and drawing in overlay on O.S. sheets. Mineral maps and mining regional sheets prepared for the Avoca mines are good examples. Likewise, railway companies, cutting the routes through Wicklow, commissioned private work.

The early editions of the County Wicklow Ordnance Survey 1838-1888

A recurring motif of the Victorian era is an allegorical tableau, 'Art with Industry'. This theme was duplicated repeatedly, in sculpture, in heroic painting, on medallions and on numerous town hall windows throughout the British empire. There are few instances of this artistic pairing better expressed, on a practical level, than in the great cartographical undertaking that was the first Irish Ordnance Survey, and especially the series of six inch to one mile maps produced between 1829 and 1846.

The original of the Ordnance Survey had its roots in Britain in 1791. As part of the Military and War Department, its early function was to provide maps for use in the Napoleonic wars.[71] A primary consideration for the parliamentary committee which instituted the Irish Ordnance Survey in 1824 (the Spring Rice committee) was that of assessing the whole country for a systematic rate structure and, more locally, a county cess.[72] The mapping of Ireland was a huge undertaking and under its gifted director, Colonel Thomas Colby, the Ordnance Survey employed 2,139 men at its peak in the summer of 1840 at a cost of £800,000.

County Wicklow was surveyed throughout 1838. The provision of accurate maps was not the only brief of the survey. At the same time a programme was undertaken across the county recording its wealth of antiquities, especially ecclesiastical ruins and ancient religious sites. Townlands, baronies, parishes and other territorial divisions, such as the newly established poor law unions, were tabulated in special indexes and name books to act as official references for future planning. Accurate knowledge of the townlands of Wicklow occupied centre stage of the Ordnance Survey.[73] Great attention was focused on divising a definitive toponomy and fixing permanent townland boundaries. Until the setting up of the boundary commission, no single authority was charged with officially defining where one townland finished and another began.[74] As a result of the survey's work, county Wicklow was divided into 1,332 townlands, each painstakingly mapped. It was to the credit of the surveying staff that they succeeded in incorporating, onto various maps with a minimum of ambiguity, such potentially confusing aspects as the county's seven Ballinvalleys and Ballards or the eleven Kilmurrys.[75]

The retention of indigenous placenames together with a costly scholarly study into their origin was one of the enduring cultural legacies of this great survey. There were influential critics who saw the name study of Wicklow as a chance for massive anglicisation or normalisation as they interpreted it.[76] An inventory and description of ancient monuments scattered throughout the countryside was summarised by the antiquarians John O'Donovan (1809-61), his brother-in-law, Eugene O'Curry (1796-62) and Thomas O'Connor in a collection of informative letters to the survey director. Besides enquiry into monuments, comment was made on different placenames, legends and local lore relevant to the different parishes. In 1928, extracts from forty of the county Wicklow letters were published under the editorship of Rev Michael Flanagan. Collectively the thirty-two volumes of the Irish Ordnance Survey letters form one of the most important secondary roles of the survey.[77] Additional sources emanating from the project were the name books, surveyors' field note books and an immense correspondence of administration letters, instructions and reports generated by the size of the project. Concurrent to much of the actual survey transactions are the records of the Primary Valuation of Ireland overseen by Richard Griffith. Running parallel with the survey, if not always in harmony, Griffith's valuation was one of the main reasons why the survey was undertaken as accurate mapping was a prerequisite for uniform and fair valuation.

In 1842, there emerged from the Ordnance Survey printing presses at Mountjoy House, Phoenix Park, Dublin, 42 maps in black and white on a scale of six inches to one mile covering all of county Wicklow. On request the Ordnance Survey coloured the county map series. These special orders were usually bound atlases for statutory bodies and officialdom. With delicate colouring and minutely detailed engraving, an edition of these sheets in pristine state is a creation of great beauty. No comprehensive survey had ever been taken of the Wicklow mountain fastness or its immediate upland prior to 1838. All too often the map-makers of the day, public and private, dismissed over half the county as 'uninhabited bogge', 'mountainy land' or took the line of least resistance and left vast tracts as blanks.[78] The first comprehensive survey of this mountain tract was covered by about half the maps on the 6" scale, issued by the Ordnance Survey. No mountain top, lake, glen, glacial corrie, streamlet or featureless plateau was neglected nor were such antiquities as lay on them. All were plotted down. Some surveying had been done on the high land of the county forty years earlier, in pursuance of the military road project (to flush out the last Wicklow rebels).[79] The 1838 survey was the first undertaking in which the whole Wicklow massif came under the scrutiny of trained surveyors.

Historical emphasis on the importance of the maps cannot be overstressed especially in relation to mountain Wicklow. This was the county of pre-Famine, when its population was at its greatest extent in recorded history. Habitations and the trappings of these multitudes dot the early Victorian landscape, throwing light upon living patterns before the catastrophe of 1845-48 and its aftermath. Allied to the cartographic record of small tenant and labourer is the full flowering of the Anglo-Irish settlement pattern, the result of two and a half centuries of ascendancy social engineering frozen forever in the various maps as embellished 'Garden Ornament' to show demesne and plantation. Both these extremes of Irish life, from subsistence small holder to ermined earl, were to change dramatically by the next survey revision in 1888. A perusal of maps from north to south Wicklow along its mountain spine will reveal much of the economic state of the county without reference to any other research material.

Kippure mountain, on sheet 6, was crucial to the first survey as the triangulation for most of the county was made from observations from its summit. A true height for Kippure was ascertained in 1839 from an initial sea level calibration made from the flat sands of Brittas Bay.[80] Later, an adaption of a mean sea level of all Ireland was made from a tidal measurement at Dublin's Poolbeg lighthouse in 1883. On many nights throughout 1839 and later, the summit of Kippure was to glow in the incandescence of the lately invented 'Drummonds' limelight, a device for sighting accurately from mountain to mountain. Its nocturnal use struck the local peasantry with awe.[81] The presence of a police outpost at Kippure House was a reminder that agrarian disturbance was not far from the surface of Wicklow rural society and police stations in remote locations were a feature in every parish.

Overlooking the source of the Dargle river, the 2,107 feet high Tonduff mountain appears on sheet 7. As on all the first edition 6" maps, spot heights, instead of the now familiar contour line, used to show altitude. Extensive plantations and an enclosed deerpark, the property of Viscount Monck of Charleville, demonstrate a contrast to scattered hovels which cluster up to the four hundred incline level, that upland threshold where the cultivation of the potato crop peters out.[82]

Greystones, in 1838, consisted of ten houses with no discernible harbour or any formal structure of streets. These would not evolve until the coming of the railway. The no. 8 sheet, which includes the town, is dominated by Kilruddery House and demesne, the quintessential example of a great Irish peer's residence. Though the county Wicklow survey of 1838 is replete with seats of the landed gentry, a depiction of garden embellishment and formality did not necessarily convey a true account of the economic health of some of these estates. Many were run-down, victims of poor management, long standing neglect and encumbered with debt. But it was beneficial for the engraver and cartographer to depict the gentry residences in good light, for these sections of the public were most of the paying customers for the Ordnance Survey maps, paying in 1840 two shillings and sixpence each a sheet.[83]

Wicklow's military road from Aghavannagh barracks to Rathfarnham had been in existence forty years when its route was resurveyed as part of Sheet No. 11. Few features break the bleak Wicklow mountain bog other than the road. What does stand out is a line of spot heights descending from Gravale mountain to ascend neighbouring summits, demonstrating clearly the pattern of triangulation. Measuring and plotting in these lonely regions meant the surveyors or the 'sappers' had to live in tents. Inclement weather and lack of premises for lodgings was not the only discomfort. There were other, more portentous troubles. For many small-holders at loggerheads with landlord or agent, surveyors meant revalued estates and rent increases. More socially explosive were the enclaves of squatters living in remote mountain hollows who never paid rent now being finally sucked into some landlord's grasp as a result of improved surveys. For these reasons, some of the original field work was carried out under an armed police escort.

Lough Tay and the glacial valley of Luggalaw is depicted on Sheet No. 12. Luggalaw House, the isolated retreat of the La Touche family, is engraved in fine detail. This house was originally constructed to the order of Peter La Touche, the prominent eighteenth-century banker, but was gutted by fire in 1956 and rebuilt along its exact lines by Lord Iveagh.[84] Absence of tree cover and plantation allowed the surveyors to accurately plot the course of many small mountain streams and springs and from this detail draw up a comprehensive survey of county Wicklow's water catchments.[85] Information gleaned from this aspect of the project has stood the test of time and data originally gathered over a century and a half ago is only now superseded by remote sensing.

On Sheet No. 16 is a stark contrast to the field and settlement pattern of lowland Wicklow. A notable feature is the dense concentration of small holdings and cultivation plots typical of the pre-famine community structure, located near Corragh, in the barony of Lower Talbotstown, clustered to the 400-metre level. Comparison with the same area plotted on the 1911 map revision shows the upheaval that

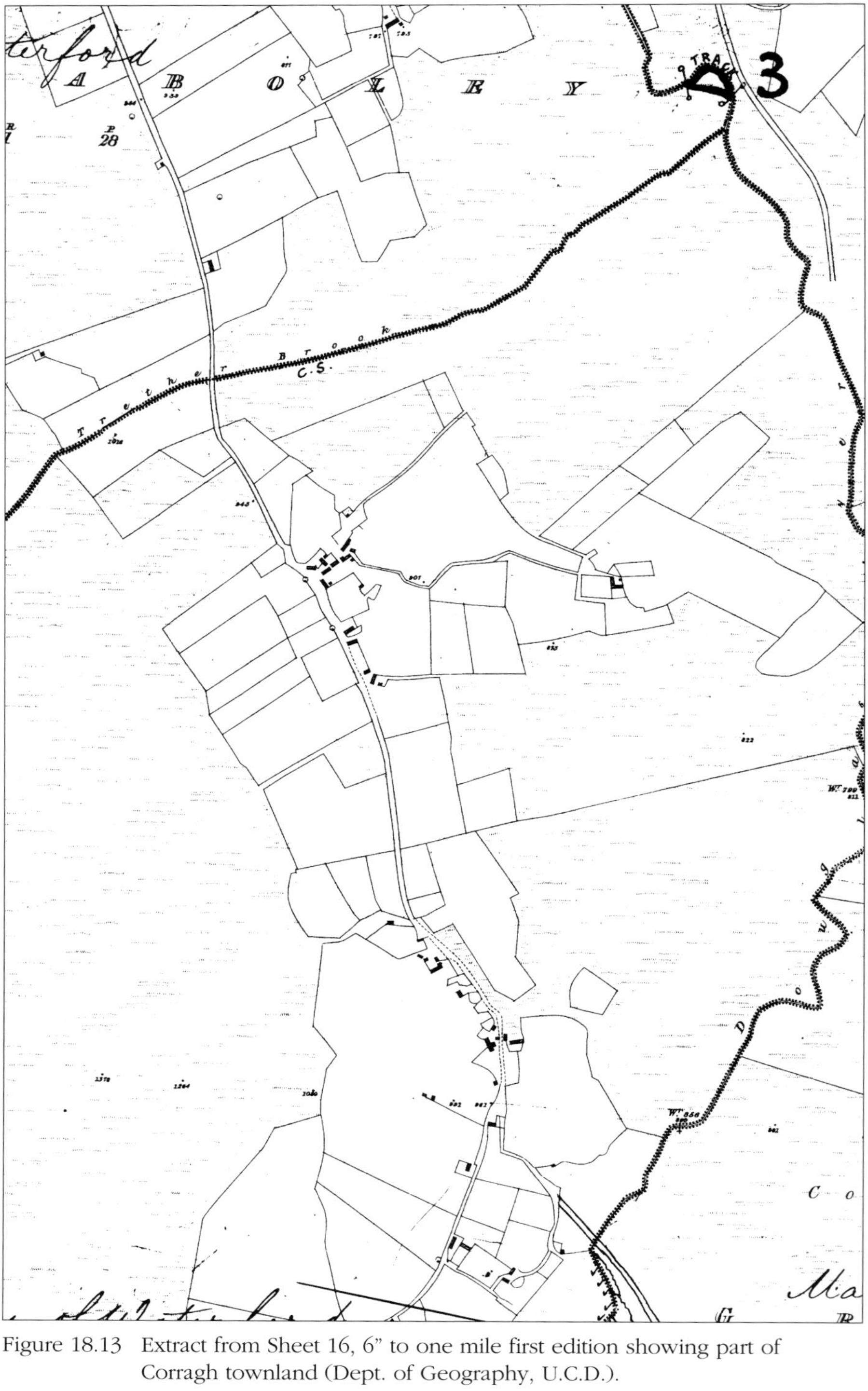

Figure 18.13 Extract from Sheet 16, 6" to one mile first edition showing part of Corragh townland (Dept. of Geography, U.C.D.).

followed the famine and its long aftermath of depopulation, for this portion of Corragh is now entirely uninhabited plantation with no vestige of cabin or track.

The Wicklow mining industry was mapped in part on Sheet No. 17, which shows the lead mining region known as Old Luganure. Prominent on the map is Lough Nahanagan, beautifully engraved and surrounded by carefully hatched and stippled outlines of cliff and corrie. The treeless outfall of the lake is broken only by the course of the Glendasan river and a tributary stream, both of which show sluice works installed by the mining engineers. Another portion of this map has plans of the mining process works, its watermills (Luganure had no steam engine), service installations and habitations, as all were recorded in 1838.[86] A distinctive feature was the 'big' water wheel, the sight of which, in this remote landscape, excited the eminent writer Thomas Carlyle on his visit to nearby Glendalough in 1844.[87] Prominent also on Sheet No. 17 is an ancient route from east to west, the St Kevin's pilgrim's track which then extended for some hundreds of yards. A contrast between the 1838 and current surveys reveals the loss of this antiquity whittled down to its present fragment, measuring little more than 25 feet.

Lugnaquillia mountain and Table mountain mark the summits of the Wicklow granite chain. One ancient earthwork prominently marked in the centre of an otherwise inhospitable terrain is 'Cavanagh's Camp', site of an entrenchment dating from *c.*1597.[88] Possibly O'Curry visited it while recording the ruins of Glendalough near where he lodged on the day and night of a hurricane which entered Irish folk memory as the 'Big Wind' of 1839.[89]

Part of the historic Glenmalure and its encompassing mountains are plotted on Sheet No. 23. Further information relevant to the lead mining industry of county Wicklow is recorded in some detail such as the stamp mills, (water operated wheels with displaced beam operated as hammer), smelting floor, and structures for separating lead ore called 'process retorts', as well as indicated trial working and productive tunnels. Sites associated with the Elizabethan wars are mapped as Phelim's Castle and Friary but the latter owes more to traditional lore than to solid archaeological evidences. Late eighteenth-century military history is recalled in the southern portion of the military road and the barracks at Drumgoff, closely associated with the Wicklow rebels Holt and Michael Dwyer. A wayside inn at Drumgoff recognises the burgeoning Wicklow tourist industry.[90] This 1840 map of Glenmalure also shows the site of the celebrated spa well of Drumkit. Wells of cuprum-iron waters abound in the area and were fashionable visiting places in the seventeenth century for those who wished to sample their

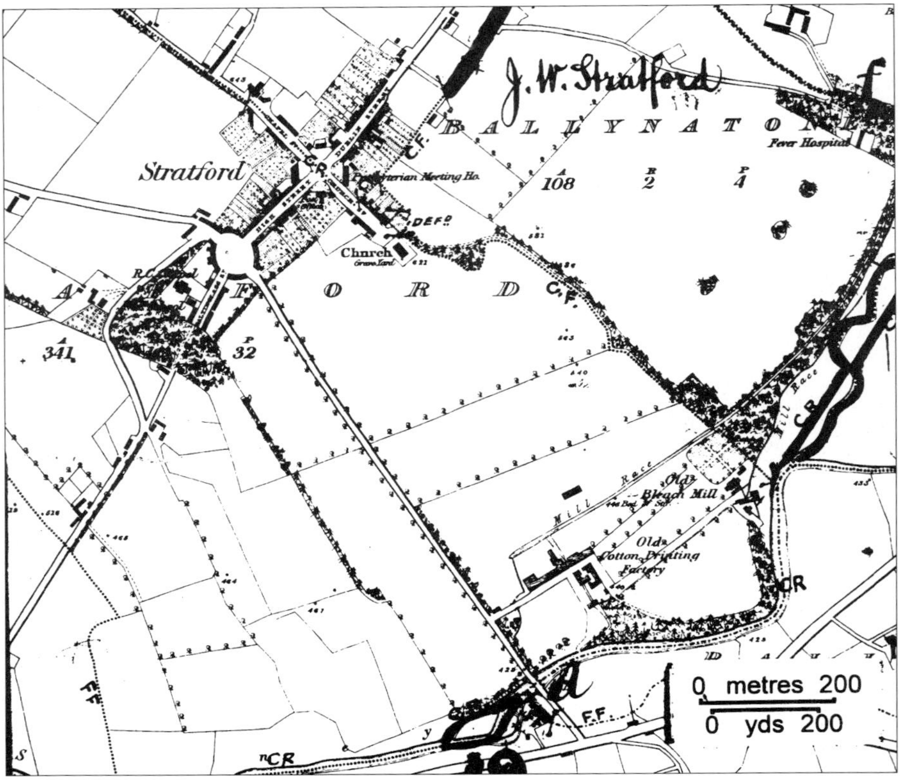

Figure 18.14 Extract from reworked Sheet 21, 6" to one mile showing Stratford-on-Slaney.

curative powers. Writing as early as 1666, the traveller Dineley observed persons of quality braving poor roads and the odd 'Tory' to savour the waters, notwithstanding its 'blew scum and noxious odour.'[91]

A culmination of the mountain tract can be seen with Sheet No. 28. A barren Aughavanagh plateau illustrates the open wind-swept nature of the high ground. Aughavanagh barracks is the only substantial feature. In service as a police post, part of it was leased as a sporting lodge to the proprietor of Avondale, William Hayes Parnell. The absence of population, considering the pressure for land in pre-Famine times might owe something to a succession of very severe winters which occurred in the middle decades of the nineteenth century.[92]

Other commercial activity besides mining and agriculture is documented on the maps. The survey sheds light on the county Wicklow linen industry and the 'model' village movement related to this trade. Of relevance to these are Sheets Nos. 21 and 27, published in April 1840. On the former, the town of Stratford-on-Slaney is beautifully drawn. The planned town is shown with its original layout unaltered.

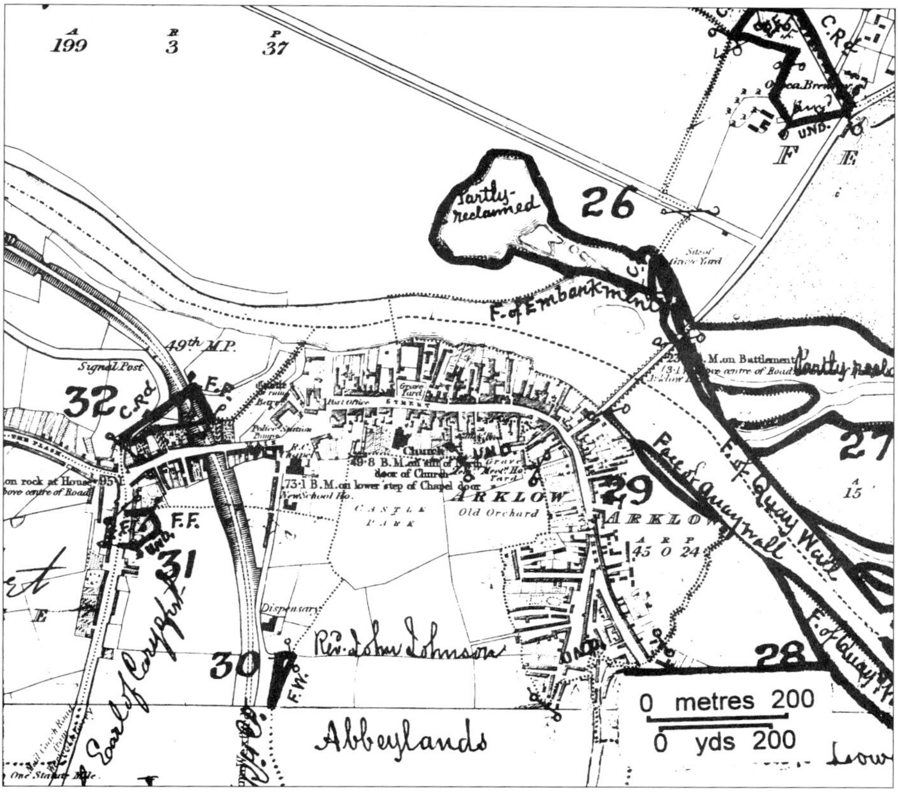

Figure 18.15 Extract from reworked 6" to one mile first edition showing Arklow (Dept. of Geography, U.C.D.).

Baltinglass, on Sheet No. 27, is an ancient town and its medieval core and long established streets and lanes deterred remodelling on a plan like Stratford-on-Slaney. Baltinglass linen industry, though in decline in 1838, shows on the town map as tuck mill, linen green and bleach mill. Here, perhaps, it should be well to recall that the ability of the cartographic medium to look into the past has its limitations and the reality of the 1838 town, like most contemporary villages, was prone to poor hygiene standards, poverty and investment shortages.

One of the most important aspects of the early maps is their record of topographical features now utterly lost. The construction of the railways in 1861-66 altered many miles of countryside. Along the railway route there were houses, fields, commons and urban structure cleared for line access. A small number of ancient monuments also suffered oblivion such as Killynee church near Arklow (Sheet No. 40).[93] Other destructions were permanently recorded. On Sheet No. 10

published in 1840 there is rendered in fine detail the drowned landscape beneath the lakes. The geography of the lost townlands can still be ascertained by reference to the 1838 survey and its 1888 revision. A fine stipple represents bog and river marsh. This technique was one of those rare applications where the engraver of the map could depart from his handwork and use a punch machine.[94] The names of the townlands and field names are indicative of the terrain, Redbog, Sallyhole Bog, and Killough Bog. A land-use feature is the Boystown Fox Cover, a deliberately encouraged scrub to provide sport for the great passion of Georgian gentlemen. Other lost man-made features were pre-famine dwellings, portions of road, the Blessington corn mill buildings, the mill race, and sluices.[95]

Part of the drowned valley is also prominent on Sheet No. 18, published in 1840. Roundwood reservoir, created in 1868, attracted wide interest at the time. Use of the 1840 map and Wicklow's geographical survey were crucial in helping to select a suitable site for the Dublin city water supply. Again a water mill and its ancillary works were destroyed as well as four houses, and on the immediate site of the filterbeds, a circular rath ninety feet in diameter was dug up.[96]

The issue of the 42 map sheets for Wicklow, perfect as they were, was but a beginning of the Ordnance Survey's work. All requirements were not satisfied by the 6 inch map. In their wake flowed a host of other cartographic works. Covering one inch to the mile, the geological survey maps were most important. These six sheets (nos 120, 121, 129, 130, 138, and 139) were issued in 1855 under the technical direction of Joseph Bette-Jukes. Each sheet was accompanied by a memoir, a written account of the geological history of the Wicklow landform with special references to its mineral wealth in lead, copper and sulphur ores. No. 138 gives a detailed description of the Avoca mines based on the best knowledge of the day and has some illustrations of that area. Valuation maps have already been alluded to. Originally devised for the accurate rating of the houses, county Wicklow towns were mapped by the survey for the valuation office. Of rare beauty are the thirteen sheets for Bray surveyed throughout 1870 and published in 1871. These hand-coloured town plans were tinted by children for sixpence a day and were originally sold to the public for five shillings.[97]

In 1870, the original Wicklow copper plates were irredeemably altered when the route of the Dublin, Wicklow and Wexford railway was engraved across them. A general revision was carried out on the six inch scale in 1888. It is by comparison with the first edition that the full impact of social change wrought by the famine and the subsequent depopulation becomes apparent. Other major social shifts included the growth of towns along the rail route, and a gradual change in field pattern where alterations in land tenure were beginning to show. Estates and 'big houses' were more realistically represented when 'garden ornament' was toned down.

Specialist maps were also printed on the survey's presses. Boundary maps, again under the aegis of the Valuation Office, settled a final size and boundary on what had hitherto been the cause of disputation at public inquisitions – the size and limitations of rateable areas. Another reference map was the townland index series. For the first time a diagrammatic outline for each townland and barony was depicted on a series of five 1" key maps. Later, in 1911, a single index map was added which was in essence a compilation of the original five sheets.[98]

The impact of the first Ordnance Survey was profound. All sections of the community who had needs cartographical were loud in their praise. Almost at once the private map-maker and surveyors were redundant. Estate agents, the judiciary, grand juries, rail companies, poor law unions, local government, and private individuals swiftly adopted the new maps for their many uses. One of the most beautiful and expensive sets was bought by the county Wicklow grand jury for its deliberations. Boxed in mahogany, each map, constructed from joined 6" coloured and varnished sheets, is linen-backed and encompasses each of county Wicklow's five baronies.[99]

As a historical source for Wicklow, several salient points emerge from the cartographical record. The most important ones were the scope and thoroughness of the landscape changes by the post sixteenth century landowners. Most of this development was accomplished in a 150-year period between 1600 and 1750. In many instances one overlay did not completely eradicate an earlier one and close study of the field network of the 1838 survey sheets can often reveal an early pattern. Proto-industrial activity was recorded in the mining operations in the valleys of Glenmacnass, Glendasan, Glenmalure, the Ballinvalley goldfield (Sheet No. 39) and on Sheet No. 35 a complex of workings in the vale of Avoca.

Since 1838, there have been numerous maps of town and county issued across a whole series of scales. Recent maps relate to just one subject such as river catchment, highways and roads, communications, contours or woodlands. In urban areas the modern need for maps extends underground to show services, water, waste disposal and ESB supplies.

Sophisticated as current cartography is, many maps are still based on conceptions and techniques first tried and tested back in 1838 by the 'Sappers'. Modern surveying methods have dispensed with the chain and the prismatic theodolite. Laser ranging and remote sensing by satellite is replacing the traditional cartographer in Wicklow as elsewhere. Perhaps technology will reach a stage in the not too distant future when imaging from space will finally replace the map altogether. But however sophisticated becomes a Landsat photograph from 600 km of, say, Wicklow town and its hinterland as is covered by sheet no. 25, it will never duplicate the beauty created when craftsmen and surveyors successfully merged art with life as they did in 1839.

Figure 18.16 Cartouche from A. R. Nevill's map (T.C.D.).

References

1. G. Hayes-McCoy, *Ulster and other Irish maps c.*1600 (Dublin, 1964), p. 15.
2. J. Harrington (ed.), *English travellers in Ireland* (Dublin, 1991), pp 61-2.
3. J.H. Andrews, *Irish maps* (Dublin, 1978), p. 4.
4. G.H. Orpen, 'Rathgall, county Wicklow, Dun Galion and the Dunum of Ptolemy', *R.I.A. Proc.*, xxxi (1913), C, p. 47. Also his 'Ptolemy's Map of Ireland,' *R.I.A. Proc.*, xxiv (1894).
5. N.L.I., *Ireland from maps* (Dublin, 1980), no. 1.
6. The river name 'Ovoca' or 'Avonmore' does not appear on any of the Ormond deeds relating to their Wicklow holdings. It is referred to as 'Great Water' or 'Black Water'. In sixteenth century State papers, Lords Deputies Grey and Russel on their Wicklow campaign always referred to the river as the 'Blackwater'. I am indebted to J.H. Andrews for his suggestion that I re-examine the validity of placing Ptolemy's placenames in a purely Wicklow context.
7. N.L.I., *Ireland from maps*, no. 2.
8. L. Price, '*O'Byrnes country in the sixteenth century*', *R.S.A.I. Jn.*, vi (1936), pp 63-6.
9. T. Westropp, 'Early Italian maps of Ireland from 1300 to 1600 – with notes of foreign settlers and trade', *R.I.A. Proc.*, xxx (1912-3), C, p. 317.
10. Ibid., p. 422 – for name list derived from portolan maps.
11. M. Andrews, 'The map of Ireland A.D. 1300-1700,' *Belfast Natural History Proceedings* (1922-3).
12. *Cal. Ormond deeds 1413-1509*, for Arklow references.
13. T.C.D., Ms F/3/17; M. Ronan, 'Archbishop Bulkeley's visitation of Dublin, 1630' in *Archiv. Hib*, viii (1941).
14. N.L.I., I*reland from maps*, no. 4.
15. J. Goghe, *Hibernia, Insula non procul ab Anglia 1567* (Reprint, Public Record Office, London). Original reference P.R.O., MPF 68.
16. J. Hardiman, A catalogue of maps, charts and plans relating to Ireland preserved amongst the manuscripts in the library of Trinity College Dublin with preliminary observations, *R.I.A. Trans*, xiv (1824), pp 63-8. Also Hayes-McCoy, *Ulster and other Irish maps c.1600,* for details of Elizabethan warfare.
17. Lord Deputy Russel's journal, 16 Oct. to 19 Nov., 1597, *Cal. Carew Mss*, ii, pp 250-2.
18. For Lythe's Survey see J.H. Andrews 'The Irish surveys of Robert Lythe,' *Imago Mundi*, xix, pp 22-31.
19. J.T. Gilbert, *Facsimiles of National Mss of Ireland* (London, 1874-84), ii, no. 25, Sir Henry Harrington's Defeate in the Berns Countrie near unto Wickloe anno 1599, original in T.C.D., Mss 1209-12.
20. W. Fitzgerald, 'Manor and castle of Powerscourt, county Wicklow in the sixteenth century, formerly a possession of the earls of Kildare,' *Kildare Arch. Soc. Jn.*, vi (1909), pp 129, 131-5.
21. Earl of Kildare, 'The Lansdowne maps of the Down Survey' in *R.I.A. Proc.*, xxxiii (1918-20), C, p. 387.
22. BL, Egerton Mss 1758; N.L.I., microfilm, n. 853, p. 576, barony survey of Rathdown.
23. Ibid., barony map of Newcastle. It is unclear why Petty highlighted this particular section of road. It is possible he wished to show the principal access in 1658 from the capital to the assizes town.
24. Ibid., barony map of Talbotstown.
25. Ibid., barony map of Ballinacor.
26. Price, *Placenames*, iv, p. 245.

27. J. Meagher, 'Notes on the parish boundary of Arklow', *Reportorium Novum*, iii (1962), pp 168-9.
28. P. Power, Ballydonnell and Coolanearl county Wicklow historical survey, unpublished typescript in Wicklow County Library, Greystones.
29. Egerton Mss, barony map of Arklow. For Dunganstown Castle, see P. Harbison (ed.) *Beranger's views of Ireland* (Dublin, 1990), Plate 6, p. 26.
30. T. Chubb, *The printed maps in the atlases of Great Britain and Ireland, a bibliography 1579-1870* (London, 1927), p. 409.
31. T.C.D., Gilbert Austin Coll., no. 56, *An actual survey of the county of Wicklow* by Jacob Nevill, 1760.
32. J.H. Andrews, 'Charles Vallancey and the map of Ireland', *Geographical Journal*, cxxxii (1966), pp 52-3.
33. For reproduction of large sections of Taylor and Skinner road maps see S. Watson, *The gentleman and citizen's almanack of Ireland 1794-1800*, pp 110-128. Original copy in the possession of Mr E. Bayly, Ballyarthur.
34. T.C.D., OLS Papyrus case 5, no. 31, T. 'This map of said county taken from actual surveys A.R. Nevill *c*.1810.' Although bearing a date of 1810, Nevill published his map in 1798.
35. The Nevill maps were widely adapted by guide book authors and published in various editions by M.H. and J.W. Allen, over two sheets 1" to 1 Mile from 1814 to 1834.
36. P.R.O., Kew, MPF 69. *Map of the newly made county of Wicklow or Fernes*, 1597.
37. Price, O'Byrne's country, pp 64-5.
38. Power collection, Arklow, 'Abbeylands of Arklow,' a coloured map by B. McKay (1988), reproduced from barony map of Arklow in Egerton Ms.
39. P. Power (forthcoming), 'Lost geography, the three shires of Arklow,' for *Arklow Hist. Soc. Jn.*, 1994/5.
40. P. Power, *The Arklow calendar, a chronicle of events from the earliest times to 1900 A.D.* (Limerick, 1981), pp 55-7; NAI, M 6233 (1) Proby map.
41. G. Taylor and A. Skinner, *Maps of the roads of Ireland*, 2nd edition (London, 1783), pp 141-2.
42. NAI, 999/452. A list of freeholders of county Wicklow entitled to vote at the election called for 1745. Endpaper to the above: A list of noblemen and gentlemen with estates of inheritance, edited by P. Power, 1991.
43. W. Chapman, *Report on the improvement of the harbour of Arklow and the practicability of a navigation from hence to Ovoca* (Dublin, 1792), frontispiece.
44. G. Kinahan, 'On Arklow beach and river,' *R.D.S. Scien. Proc.*, ii (1880), plate 17.
45. R. Musgrave, *Memoirs of the different rebellions of Ireland*, ii, plate 8 (Dublin, 1802). For a military appraisal of the Musgrave map see G. Hayes-McCoy, 'Topography of a battlefield, Arklow 1798', *Irish Sword*, i, p. 50.
46. V. Gill, *County Wexford 1808*, 1" to 1 mile. One sheet copy, 1798 Room, Wexford County Museum, The Castle, Enniscorthy. This survey was published on four sheets in 1811 and 1816 by W. Fadden.
47. A.R. Nevill, *Actual survey of county Wicklow*, 1798.
48. William Jackson of Oulart? (Surveyor), A plan of the River of Arklow with proposed improvements of its Harbour *c*.1812 from W. Shaw Mason, *A statistical account or parochial survey of Ireland*, ii (Dublin, 1816), p. 55.
49. W.L. Hardy, 'A Plan of the mouth of the Ovoca, December 1821', *R.D.S. Scient. Proc.*, iii (1822), pp 250-4, Plate 16.
50. J.H. Andrews, *A Paper landscape, the Ordnance Survey in nineteenth century*

Ireland (Oxford, 1975), p. 129. See also marginal sketch on fair plan for 29 1839 for Abbey Lane school.

51. *Ordnance Survey first edition*, Arklow Barony, bound volume of fourteen 6 inch maps formerly property of the earl of Carysfort comprising sheets nos. 23, 24, 29, 30, 31, 32, 34, 35, 36, 39, 41, 44, 45; Arklow Property Company, courtesy John Fogarty, Arklow, county Wicklow, hereafter A.P.C., O.S. volume.
52. A.P.C., O.S. volume, Sheet 40, 22 November, 1845.
53. W.T. Trench, *Arklow town rental map 1873*, colour, Hodge and Smith Printer. A.P.C., collection.
54. B. McKay, 'Robert McMicken and the Arklow connection 1840,' *Arklow Hist. Soc. Jn.* (1986), pp 10-12; P. Ferguson, Maps and records of the valuation office, unpublished B.A. dissertation presented to Dept. of Geography, UCD (1977).
55. W. Townsend-Trench, *Arklow town rental map 1873*, A.P.C. collection. Along with the Arklow plan of 1873, Townsend-Trench produced an illustrated valuation book of Arklow's streets and lanes, building by building. Comprising 215 watercoloured pages and index, it is a unique architectural portrait of Arklow as it was in 1877, the year Townsend-Trench completed it. The original volume, which was commissioned by Lord Carysfort, is now in the care of its owners Arklow Property Company. A full-size photostat copy is in N.L.I., Ms 2705, and a full-colour slide copy is in the possession of the author.
56. Andrews, *A paper landscape*, appendix G, p. 334.
57. P. Power, The 1885 1:500 town plans for Arklow, catalogue of plans and maps held by A.P.C., 1987, Wicklow County Library.
58. Arklow town plan 1:500, sheet XL-1617-1885 and sheet XL-1623-1885, A.P.C., Arklow, county Wicklow.
59. E.R.R. Green, 'A catalogue of the estate maps etc. in the Downshire office,' *U.J.A.*, xii (1949), p. 3.
60. Power, Index to some county Wicklow estate papers.
61. Ibid.
62. J. F. Ainsworth, Report on the Bayly papers (from 1657) the property of Major E. A. Bayly, Ballyarthur, Woodenbridge, relating to the families of Mitchelburne, Symes and Bayly and to lands in counties Wicklow and Wexford and letters on the 1798 rebellion, N.L.I., reports on private collections no. 95.
63. E. Johnson, Map of Ballyarthur demesne in the barony of Arklow and county of Wicklow 1700, Ms map in the possession of E. Bayly, Woodenbridge, county Wicklow.
64. William Jackson of Oulart, A survey of the demesne of Ballyarthur, seat of the Rev Symes 1812, Ms map in possession of E. Bayly, Woodenbridge, county Wicklow.
65. City of Sheffield archives, Fitzwilliam Wentworth Woodhouse Muniments, W.W.M. – 25-A, *The Wicklow gold field and Mount Croghan.*
66. Ainsworth, Report on the Bayly papers, item 359. This map is now missing.
67. E. Lodge, *The peerage and baronetage of the British Empire as at present existing* (London, 1887) (Downshire succession), pp 207-8.
68. P.R.O.N.I., D. 671.
69. Green, 'A catalogue of the estate maps in Downshire office,' p. 11.
70. P.R.O.N.I., D. 671.
71. C.F. Close, *The early years of the Ordnance Survey* (London, 1926), pp 2-8.
72. *House of Commons Papers 445*, Spring Rice Report, viii (1824), p. 5.
73. O.S. Name Books, county Wicklow.
74. *Third report of his majesty's commissioners of ecclesiastical revenue and patronage in Ireland* (1823), pp 97-101.

75. H.M.S.O., *General alphabetical index to the townlands and towns, parishes and baronies of Ireland* (Dublin, 1861, repr. Baltimore, 1992).
76. Andrews, *A paper landscape*, pp 121-2.
77. M. O'Flanagan (ed.), Letters containing information relative to the antiquities of the county of Wicklow, collected during the progress of the Ordnance Survey in 1838 (Bray, 1928).
78. J. Nevill (1760), op. cit.; A.R. Nevill (1810), op. cit.
79. B.L., Ms 32451, A. Taylor, Military survey of Sallygap 1801.
80. Andrews, *A paper landscape*, p. 111.
81. Ordnance Survey, *Ordnance Survey of Ireland, an illustrated history* (Dublin, 1911), p. 14. During the erection of the radio communication equipment on Kippure Mountain in the early 1960s, local folk memories revived of earlier engineering activity dating from the previous century. These stories invariably involved 'fairy lights,' limelights' and 'sappers' lights' and were specific to Kippure and surrounding summits. Liam Price surmised that this was a folk memory which owed its origin to the first generation of ordnance surveyors engaged in survey work on Kippure and he, too, had heard such local tales during his researches in the area. However, according to J.H. Andrews, author of the seminal history of the first Ordnance Survey *The paper landscape*, the Drummond Limelight was only used on one occasion at a Northern Ireland location in the early days of the survey. How fact may be distinguished from folklore at this point of time is difficult to tell. Perhaps Kippure's 'fairy lights' may have their origin in the use of the signal flares or some such devices as opposed to the original limelight. (Reminiscences of the late Andrew Kettle, Post office engineer related to the author).
82. R.N. Salaman, *The history and social influence of the potato* (Cambridge, 1949).
83. Ordnance Survey correspondence general order – 1 April 1834 – issued from Dublin.
84. M. Bence-Jones, *Burke's guide to Irish country houses*, 2nd edition (London, 1988), p. 195.
85. Ordnance Survey, *River catchment map of Ireland*, scaled 1 inch to 10 miles (Dublin, 1868).
86. C.H. Law (Publishers), *Geological map of the mining districts of Wicklow*, scaled ½ inch to 1 mile (1852).
87. T. Carlyle, *Reminiscences of my Irish journey in 1849* (London, 1852), p. 73.
88. Price, *Place-Names*, iii, p. 176.
89. O.S. letters.
90. Wright, *Guide to county Wicklow*, p. 93.
91. T. Dineley, 'Extract from Journal of Thomas Dineley giving some account of his visits to Ireland in the reign of Charles II,' *R.S.A.I. Jn.* (1858-9), p. 49.
92. F.E. Dixon, 'Weather in old Dublin' in *Dublin Historical Review*, 13 (1952), p. 96.
93. Meagher, 'Parish boundary of Arklow', p. 168.
94. Andrews, *A paper landscape*, p. 134.
95. S. Ó Súilleabhain, 'Beneath the Poulaphouca reservoir', *Folk and farm: essays in honour of A.T. Lucas* (Dublin, 1947), pp 201-3.
96. 'Roundwood Reservoir,' *Dublin Builder*, 6 (1864), p. 65.
97. *Ordnance Survey, an illustrated history*, p. 32.
98. J.H. Andrews, *History in the Ordnance map. An introduction for Irish readers* (Dublin, 1974).
99. It is the intention of Wicklow County Council to house the barony maps in the Old Wicklow Jail Heritage Centre.

Chapter 19

THE MINING COMMUNITY AT AVOCA 1780-1880

D. COWMAN

Avoca's mining history

Avoca's mineral deposits extend across the valley of the Avoca river: the mine names are derived from the townlands in which the workings were located. These were Upper Ballygahan, Ballymurtagh and Lower Ballygahan on the west of the river and Tigroney, Cronebane and Connary to the east. Exploitation of the mineral lodes apparently commenced in the early eighteenth century; records of mining in Ireland before that date make no reference to Avoca.[1]

The first located reference is to a mining lease at Tigroney granted to a partnership of eleven people in 1734. Their initial capital was £1,100.[2] Rev Wynne was cited as chief instigator of this operation but, according to his own account, Martin O'Connor was mainly responsible. He claimed to have commenced mining there sometime before 1745, but 'received a hurt', was laid up for seven weeks and when he returned the mine was closed. O'Connor planned to build a smelter and a new harbour at Arklow.[3]

A letter dated 1752 refers to the cessation of mining at Ballymurtagh but mentioned that 500 people were working at Cronebane on the east side of the Avoca river. There in the upper strata they also discovered quantities of valuable silver.[4] The extraction of copper from the waters running from the mine, through a process of precipitating the copper-sulphate onto scrap-iron, was worth approximately £1,000 yearly in the mid eighteenth century.[5] The total value of precipitate between 1758 and 1764 was estimated at £17,260.[6] Mining or the collection of precipitated ore continued up to 1778 with 840 tons of copper being exported from the area over the previous six years.[7] That significant mining did take place during the period 1750 to 1780 was confirmed when a systematic clearing out of the old workings took place some thirty-five years later.[8] Indeed, problems of pollution there are mentioned as early as 1752.[9]

The second phase of mining lasted about thirty years from 1780 and completed the pollution process. Rich salmon fisheries were completely destroyed by emissions from the mine and long after this phase of operations had ceased all fish life downstream to Arklow was destroyed.[10] The sulphurous nature of the ore-body was a major contributor to this. The sulphur was kilned and refined for a period during the Napoleonic Wars.[11] There was then a gap of about ten years followed by a resumption of mining from 1820 to 1880 which created the 'sheerest sterility' in the area in the early 1840s.[12]

Sixty years in the life of a non-renewable resource is a long time. The 1820s to *c.*1855 was a prosperous period for most Avoca mines particularly during the 1840s when sulphur was in demand. From 1855 there was a period of uncertainty in the sulphur trade and the beginnings of a decline in the price of copper. However, most mines survived the following decades by alternating their output of either sulphur, copper or iron to meet demand.

A great deal of primary sources have survived for the mines at Avoca.[13] There are also a number of good nineteenth century accounts of mining activity which are particularly strong on the geology of the area.[14] From these it would be possible to write a more technical history of the Avoca mines. However it is the purpose of this study to consider only the social implications of this industrial activity on the rural community of Avoca and its hinterland.

Employment at Avoca Mines, to *c*.1800

Sometime before 1780 John Howard Kyan had acquired ownership of Ballymurtagh, probably having discovered that the main mineralised area there was not on line with the east Avoca lode but displaced further south by a fault.[15] He also mined at Cronebane. Kyan successfully sought parliamentary grants in 1783 and 1785 to begin the difficult process of smelting the ore.[16] Both operations, according to later reports, were spectacularly unsuccessful. Around 1786 he came to a leasing arrangement with Roe and Company who had a smelter at Macclesfield and had just lost their lease in a similar orebody at Parys Mountain in Anglesea.[17] This company purchased outright the mineral rights of Tigroney and Cronebane on the east side of the river. It began work in Avoca in May 1787 and by July had about 100 men employed in all major mining sites there.[18]

Roe & Co. later changed their name to the Associated Irish Mining Company (AIMC). Exactly a year after commencing, AIMC discovered a vein of solid copper ore at Cronebane said to be between six and eighteen feet wide.[19] Over the following years they concentrated increasingly on this lucrative deposit. Having picked over Kyan's old waste tip at Ballymurtagh, and extracted ten tons of copper from it, they abandoned it, much to his chagrin.[20] Kyan then formed a partnership with the two Camac brothers, who probably provided the capital, to reopen Ballymurtagh under the patriotic name the Hibernian Mining Company – presumably to distinguish from the foreign competitors across the valley.

From 1789 the rival mining companies flooded the area with their half-penny tokens. In response to shortage of coinage the English company, Associated Irish Mining Company, (AIMC) issued a large number of copper tokens – forty-two variants of 1789 alone are recorded – bearing shovels, a windlass, hammers and even a bishop's head on the face. The Hibernian Company retaliated later in the year with their own coins bearing a harp playing Hibernia backed in many by the initials of chairman Turner Camac with the names Camac, Kyan and Camac around the edges. In some the edging had the motif 'Industry has its sure reward'.[21] Some 185 variants on this patriotic motif were coined in 1792: its English rivals managed a total of only sixty-four variations during their six years of issuing between 1789 and 1795. However, one of their later issues seems directed against the Hibernian Company as it shows a lady holding scales of justice and the message 'For change, not fraud'.

For details of the mining and smelting operations carried out by the Hibernian Company we have to rely on later comment, which is generally disparaging. Richard Griffith, for instance, commented:

> They expended an immense capital on a succession of expensive but useless surface works, consisting of a large smelting works on the sea shore in Arklow where coal could not be landed except in summer months; of building of five large conical kilns for calcining ore in only one of which a single fruitless trial was made and in a great variety of less prominent but very costly projects. Little attention was paid to the actual mine workings so that access routes to the ore were ill contrived and the expense and difficulty of raising the ore from the bottoms unusually great.[22]

Among the 'very costly projects' planned, but not constructed, was a canal between Arklow and Avoca with a link to Glenmalure and a branch to Kilkenny for the transportation of coals.[23] In the context of practical matters a later manager of Ballymurtagh described how the mine was pumped:

> They used a very primitive and inefficient means of draining the mine by a series of wooden pumps one above the other, each worked by a set of men – a most precarious and uncertain system and in itself sufficient to prevent all well-doing and retard their progress in bringing the minets to the productive beds of ore beneath.[24]

All in all, they left the mine 'in a ruinous state' for their successors.[25]

This operation, however, did create employment and distributed wealth – £60,000 before any ore was raised. A slightly later report estimates the expenditure at a massive £200,000.[26] Kyan died penniless while his more resourceful son had to work in a factory.[27] These efforts at mining terminated sometime after 1797, the date of the Hibernian Company's last recorded coinage. Meanwhile over that same decade (1787-1797) the English company was reported as having spent £48,914-16s. on wages and development at Avoca.[28]

The impact of this massive input of capital into a largely rural economy goes unrecorded. Only circumstantial and secondary evidence survives about the Ballymurtagh operation run first by Kyan and then in partnership with the Camac brothers as the Hibernian Mining Company. More social evidence is available about the impact of its rival's (AIMC's) mines east of the valley because of the survival of its records.

AIMC's Miners, 1787-*c*.1800

The surnames of the early Associated Irish Mining Company workers suggest that they had come from Anglesea – Fawcett, Leviston, Watson, Miller, Parker, Mason, Coffee. However, there was also a Burn (Byrne), a Doyle and a McKeogh, skilled miners who could possibly have transferred from the Hibernian Mining Company's operation.[29] A Joseph Byrne is noted as coming from Anglesea that November, suggesting that Wicklowmen had been involved in the mines there. Over the next two years the workforce continued to grow so that by October 1789 eighty people were employed on the surface and probably about the same number underground. Table 19.1 lists those regularly employed on surface operations at Cronebane, Tigroney and Ballygahan. Their rates of pay are somewhat better than those cited for agricultural labourers in the area at about the same time – 10d per day in summer and 8d in winter, less almost 1d (2 guineas p.a.) for rent of a cottage and acre.[30]

Some sixty of the eighty surface workers had surnames of Irish origin: the four smiths listed were apparently Welsh or Cornish – two Griffiths, a Daniel and a Penrose. The menial pump operators had local Wicklow names – five Kavanaghs, Toole, Kelly, Lawless and Madden. However, some of the better-paid jobs also seem to have gone to Irish people; the masons were named Garrety, Beaghan and Smith while the cooper was Doyle. On the other hand it is difficult to account for the names of the six cart-drivers: Robinson, Jennet, Gaffney, McGreagh and two Temperleys. The records indicate the merging of local and imported skills in the operation of the mines.

Table 19.1

Surface workers, 1789[31]

Number employed	*Type of work*	*Daily pay*
9	pump operators	10d
10	labourers	10-16d
10	masons	20-26d
4	smiths	20-26d
3	carpenters	20-24d
6	cart drivers	8-13d
8	labourers at launders & whims	10-20d
3	sawyers	12d
1	cooper	24d
30	(role not clear or unspecified)	10-20d

TOTAL 80 direct employees on surface activities, for Oct. 1789 paid £107-14/-

Apart from the benefits to the local economy of the spending power of mine employees, benefit through purchase or subcontract was more widely distributed as the sampling for 1787 to 1789 (table 19.2) shows.

As ore production increased, the greatest potential for secondary employment lay in transporting it the sixteen or so miles to Wicklow for shipment to Macclesfield. Production figures vary from a low of 70 tons in 1788 to 2,577 tons in 1808. In March 1789, for instance, the manager had 112 tons of ore ready at the mine and would 'employ every horse and cart that could be procured', but the local farmers' horses 'are employed getting corn and potatoes into the ground.' In

Table 19.2

Other beneficiaries[32]

10,000 bricks from Kilmacow for making kilns	
201 barrels of lime from Carlow	
26cwt of coal from Kilkenny	
William Judd for washing 8¾ tons ore @ 22/-	£9-12- 6d
John Manning for a handsaw and gimble	5-11d
B. Kavanagh for unloading the little kiln	10- 0d
J. Jenkinson for 4 lead lights and 2 windows	9-10d
M. Kavanagh for fencing boundary ditch	£4
John Manning for nails, etc.	11-10d
Mary Johnson's car, owed 49 days @ 19d per day	£3-19- 7d
Carriage of timber from Arklow, 4 cars @ 2/2d	8- 8d
Henry Butler for 14 barrells of lime	£1- 7- 1d
Mr. O'Brien: 2 suits of grove (grave?) cloaths	3- 9d
Hugh Byrne for one cargoe of iron from Clash	£1- 2- 9d
4 porters 2 days discharging ship & 1/- for drink	13- 0d
450 bricks	14- 6d

May he had five local farm carts working at nineteen and a half pence per day; by September he was in difficulty again with a hundred tons of ore to be transported; in December he had to halt operations in order to use the mine's own horses to transport ore to Wicklow.[33] This raises several questions. Could it be that the local farming community was unwilling to adapt to the market opportunities provided; 19d per day being nearly twice a labourer's wage? Why then did the company not make a rational decision between paying more or investing in its own haulage system? This it reluctantly did in 1791 with the purchase of three mules and carts. However, they sold these in January 1795 for £50 to William Mates who undertook to bring the ore to Wicklow for 6/6d per ton and coal or other commodities on the return journey at 4/- per ton.[34] If local farmers lost a useful income supplement, presumably the labourers Mates employed as carters profited.

The subcontracting system was the preferred option of most British mining companies, particularly for underground work. The ore faces were auctioned off to mining teams who contracted to raise a particular tonnage of a specified mineral content. The company would provide support services at fixed charges. Thus the account of William Markham's team for October 1789 reads –

Raised 160 tons ore @ 3/3d	£26
Deductions for blasting powder	£1-15-0
3 pickhilts	1/5d
19 candles	11/1d
Money advanced	£3-17/3d
NET PAID	£19-15-2

The money advanced was a loan given by the company to support the members of the mining team until completion of contract at the end of the month.[35] The numbers in Markham's team are not specified but eight would be a reasonable average. This would have given about two shillings per day if divided equally but the likelihood was that the labourers would have earned considerably less than the skilled men and the risk-taker, Richard Markham. However, no detail survives about the internal arrangements within each team.

A similar system applied to teams contracting to do development work. John Paul contracted to sink a shaft 138 feet (23 fathoms) deep to the old working for 15/2d per foot and to clear out the bottom. This work took about six months –

Cut 23 fathoms @ £4-11/-	£105-15/9d
Cleared the bottoms, 33 'shifts' (?) @ 20d	2-15/–
ditto, 34 'shifts' @ 10d	1- 8/4d
	£109-19-1d

Deductions	
For not cutting 1½ foot ground square	£6-16- 6d
273 candles	£6-16- 3d
gunpowder	£18-19- 9d
2 shovels, 5 hilts and sharpening	£3- 5- 2d
Raising 2824 buckets	£4- 4- 2d
Money advanced, May-Sept	£55-10-10
Deducted	£99-19- 4d
Net paid	£13-19- 9d

John Paul's team were fined according to a fixed rate for not sinking the shaft straight and had to pay a modest sum for the company to raise the waste from the shaft. Between advances and final settlement they earned nearly £70 over the six months.[36] Assuming a small team of six for this operation, three labourers could have averaged ten pence per working day and three skilled men, two shillings. This seems to be reasonably representative of monies earned by AIMC's employees.

That labourers could pick up mining skills and compete with the trained miners is suggested in an incident of August 1789:

> John Kircut, Nathaniel Holman, John Vivian and John Martin [all Cornish men] – have run away from their bargains and it is set again to six of the natives that were labourers in the works at the same price Kircut and company had it.[37]

This was a potential source of tension and two years later the skilled men were reported to have 'cheerfully acquiesced' to limiting the number of labourers allowed underground.[38] That difficulties continued is reflected in the company having to set fixed wages for the labourers on every team at 6/6d per week for the first year, 7/7d for the second year and 8/8d thereafter.[39] While this made mine labouring comparatively well paid, it came out of the pockets of the skilled men who took the financial risks. Some of them resorted to other means to raise their own income.

One basic ploy was to make the company dependent by drawing more advance money than they would actually earn. In June 1791 it seems this was attempted and the team leaders were accused of 'idleness' and refused any further advances. The leaders then stopped work and handed back their tools. However, 'in some little time' they ended their protest and returned. The company then sacked the ringleaders for 'combination'.[40] Two years later (September 1793) five Cornish team leaders got together and swore 'not to bid for each other's bargain'. Not alone were they immediately dismissed but their names were circulated to other mine owners 'to guard them against such men who have behaved so improperly here'.[41] A safer way was to bribe the agent in charge of the auctioning process. In November 1802 this agent was dismissed for 'gross peculation' having received 'several sums of money from the several bargain takers'.[42]

Table 19.3 sets out earnings for underground workers over a typical twelve-week period in 1802. The mining teams varied greatly in their composition ranging from John Byrne's team of four miners with three labourers to Archibald McInnin's mining on his own with four labourers in attendance. In all 121 were then employed underground, 79 of whom were labourers. Earnings per team varied. Fardy Doyle's team were lucky over those months with black copper ore up to two and a half feet wide, whereas Thomas Doyle ran out of ore and had to abandon his contract. What happened to Thomas Kavanagh is not stated. He and the others who had nothing for themselves by the time they paid their labourers, probably had to borrow 'subsistence' from the company to be paid back when times were better. The major expense for each of the miners was the candles, tools, timbering and the sharpening of their chisels which account for most of the 'deductions'.

Few social or personal details survive to illuminate the lives of the miners in the early 1800s. A rockfall in Cronebane in 1802 killed a boy. Some months later his father or brother was promoted and given 'a suit of underground clothes' costing 4/4d. Towards the end of that year 'very little work was done' throughout the mine due to 'ill success' at a number of ore faces which left the miners 'dispirited'. The following spring mining almost ceased due to an outbreak of influenza among the miners,[43] and three years later the same thing happened 'with great sickness and mortality prevailing in the country'.[44] The human suffering that lay behind these stark reports does not emerge. One miner from Derbyshire found his own solution: 'Contriving to make his co-partners drunk he absconded with about £20, their property and that of the labourers. Efforts to locate him have proved futile'.[45]

The socio-political element: 1798 and sequels

The rivalry between the Hibernian Mining Company and the English Associated Irish Mining Company (AIMC) as expressed in their coinage may have had deeper social and political dimensions. Kyan and Camac had apparently given employment in 1792 to a number of Defenders who had been driven out of county Louth.[46] As national and local tensions rose in 1796 the Hibernian Mining Company set up two corps of yeomanry – The Castlemacadam Infantry (commanded by Turner Camac) and the Castlemacadam Cavalry (commanded by his brother

Table 19.3

Earnings of Mining Teams 1802

Head of Team	*Total earned £ s d*	*Payment less deductions & subsistence*	M	L	*Comments on ore face*
Fardy Doyle	136-6-0	39-5-0	2	10	'promising black ore 1'-2½' wide'
Pat Cavanagh	85-11-5	52-6-4	3	4	'Scattered into strings (not retaken)'
Cornelius Hogan	48-12-7	30-1-4	3	3	
Thomas Doyle	19-0-1	2-17-8	2	2	'No immediate prospect of ore (abandoned)'
Andrew Cavanagh	61-2-0	16-5-11	3	3	
Edward King	39-5-3	10-19-1	3	3	'ore sparingly scattered'
Archibald McInnins	47-18-6	27-2-2	1	4	'ribs of coarse grained ore'
John Byrne	28-18-6	9-18-3	4	3	'discontinued'
Thomas Cavanagh	31-17-10	7-4-3	3	5	
Michael Byrne	32-11-7	owes	2	10	'ore much dispersed in rock'
Edward Doyle	46-1-6	15-11-8	2	6	'strong branches of ore'
John L. Cavanagh	108-7-8	62-8-9	3	12	'massive ribs and strings of good grained ore – rather scattered'
John Smogles	44-1-9	23-7-5	2	1	
John Brennan	73-6-2	48-5-8	2	9	
John T. Cavanagh	23-7-1	8-7-7	3	3	
Dan Byrne	32-0-6	16-5-8	2	1	
Nick Reed	31-19-1	23-18-6	2	0	

(M = miners, L = labourers)
Source: N.L.I., Ms 16307.

James).[47] The local gentry was highly suspicious about these, one comment being that they were potentially 'the most dangerous body of men to the peace of the country'.[48] There were grounds for such apprehensions: the Camacs were suspected of republican sympathies and their partner Kyan was a close kinsman of Esmond Kyan of

Wexford, a local leader of the United Irishmen. That a significant number of this yeomanry was actively involved in the United Irishmen was clearly established by early 1798.[49] It was, for instance, reported that the Hibernian Mining Company's workers had selected one James McQuillan, *alias* James Collins, to tour the area acting as an *agent provocateur*, stirring up local Orangemen in order to find out what their real plans were.[50] He was discovered and in March 1798 both the Camacs' infantry and cavalry corps, comprising Ballymurtagh miners, were formally disbanded.[51]

Meanwhile, the rival English mining company (AIMC) had organised their own yeomanry. In November 1796 they spent £150-2-2d, largely on cloth, hats and trimming for uniforms, plus £2-10-11d for a drum. Within a month this miners' militia had arms coming in through Wicklow.[52] Its establishment is probably related to the discovery of gold on the slopes of Croghan Kinsella to the south west of Avoca mines where the local peasantry had resorted in large numbers during 1795. Drinking booths had been set up so that 'a spirit of animosity' quickly established itself amongst those competing over panning locations. The squatters were driven off by the Kildare militia who took over the area on behalf of the state until legal entitlement to the gold was decided.[53] The AIMC was then contracted to identify the source of the gold on behalf of the state and it was in anticipation of the local hostility this would generate that the 'Volunteer corps' (as they called themselves) was set up.[54]

Apart from their activities in the gold mines the Cronebane 'Volunteers' appear to have done little during 1797 except post handbills in the locality that October headed 'Declarations of Cronebane'. This seems to have been a solemn oath to be taken by each of the yeomen swearing that they would never join the United Irishmen and would be ever loyal to King George III. Presumably the Cronebane officers were well aware of sedition among their rival's two corps. However, forty-four of AIMC's own employees, who had volunteered for service, could not take such a solemn oath and were dismissed to be replaced by loyal men. Nevertheless, as political tension rose locally the following spring (1798), it was decided that they all needed new uniforms![55]

When trouble did break out in May 1798 mining ceased, or as the report put it:

> – the works having continued suspended from 31st May to 30th September in consequence of the unhappy disturbances which broke out into open acts of violence in this country –[56]

Some ninety of the miners in their militia role were despatched to Rathdrum. A small payment in August may be indicative of their activities – tuition fee of £2-10-11 for 'Cronebane Drummers and Fifers'.[57] How much in total this cost the company in terms of lost production is not itemised but it must have been about £60,000 reckoned on the slump in their production in 1798-1799 in comparison with previous and successive years. The miners, moreover, were paid from 1/- to 1/4d per day while on service and the three months' operation cost the company a further £377-11-2d. A side effect of security precautions in December 1798 is recorded when the mines had to close for three weeks 'for want of (explosive) powder'.[58]

Whatever the Volunteers did in 1798 greatly pleased the English shareholders of AIMC and they awarded a ceremonial silver plate worth 50 guineas to their chief representative at Avoca:

> ... as a token of the highly grateful sense we entertain of the spirited and judicious conduct of our friend and partner, Capt. Mills of the Cronebane Corps during the momentous period of the rebellion in Ireland.

Plate was also awarded to First Lieutenant Weaver (worth 30 guineas) and Second Lieutenant Blood (20 guineas).[59] Surprisingly, this mining militia continued in existence over the next eight years or so; 102 new uniforms, for instance, being ordered in 1804. Mining must have suffered as many of the miners were doing over 100 days' service per year. But the early 1800s were peak years of profitability for the company and presumably they felt they could afford such indulgence. Part of their reasoning may have been the threat of continued violence and the potential which the gold workings seemed to offer. The following expenditure of January 1804 suggests both:

Subsistence for sundry men to guard this M	£16-16-4[60]
Turf for Rathdrum guard house	12-4
Turf and straw for Gold Mines guard house	£ 1-14-1
Payments to Volunteers for 1803	£130-12-9
Various	£30- 8-6
	£180- 4-7

The 1798 period may have proved difficult for the Hibernian Mining Company's extravagant enterprises west of the Avoca river – their last token issue was 1797. They were still reported to be treating ore in Arklow in 1800 though this operation must have ceased shortly afterwards.[61] On the eastern side of the river AIMC began to experience difficulty from about 1805. This was partly due to trouble marketing ore and partly due to the fact that the more readily accessible ore was nearly worked out and prices did not warrant further investment in pumping equipment. From 1808 AIMC's operation was wound down owing to 'the depressed state of the market and other untoward events' as a retrospect of 1811 puts it.[62] In the meantime its operation was reduced to harvesting the precipitate but they also had a team of miners driving a long deep level which would unwater Cronebane and leave them strongly placed for an upturn in prices. This, however, came far too late. The company may have also tried unsuccessful expedients such as selling the sulphur and in 1810 manager Mills wrote that 'everything is going steadily to ruin'.[63] While the social consequences of this can only be imagined, surviving evidence indicates that the Associated Irish Mining Company did its utmost to keep the eastern Avoca mines productive.[64]

A revived community, *c*.1825 to *c*.1855

An investigator in 1853 commented on how difficult it was to make sense of what was happening to the east Avoca mines in the early 1800s.[65] AIMC did not succeed in selling their mine and Cronebane-Tigroney was still in its hands in 1822 when they managed to lease it, first it would seem to a Mr Johnson. Then one, or both mines seem to have been acquired by the Dublin-based Imperial Mining Company from 1824 to the early 1830s. About 1832 the Cornish firm of Williams & Co. of Truro acquired them on a 31-year lease, though the AIMC continued as lessors.[66]

In the same year Connary began to produce copper, first mined by landlord Joseph Salkeld but later (post 1837) by a consortium under the title Connaree Mining Company.[67] Henry Hodgeson leased the Hibernian Mining Company's mines at Ballymurtagh and Ballyghahan by 1822 and may have been responsible for the seventeen tons exported from there in that year. Realising that he needed development capital he set up the Wicklow Copper Mining Company by 1830. This company operated Ballymurtagh for the next half century while Ballygahan remained the private mine of Hodgeson, with production beginning in 1828.[68]

The social consequences of increased mining activity are not commented on. A considerable number of outsiders came to work here in the 1820s as the almost 50 per cent increase in population (3,518 to 5,155) in Castlemacadam parish up to 1831 suggests. The increase over the next decade, when production levels soared, was only 10 per cent i.e. 5,633 in 1841.[69] Most likely, a number of miners from the previous phase of operations were still available to lend expertise though it was reported that at least one manager from Cornwall was brought in.[70]

It is difficult to account for the success of Avoca at this period,

Table 19.4

Copper production at Avoca 1822-1840 (Tons)

	1823-5	1826-8	1829-31	1832-34	1835-37	1838-40
Connery				2892	5183	1127
Ballygahan		57	167	411	957	1911
Tigroney	480	2829	4856	3675	4995	4726
Cronebane	3001	4129	5252	5710	8247	4104
Ballymurtagh	1340	1006		5359	15022	15111
'Wicklow'	400	2286	1012	132		

Source: *Memoirs of the geological survey of Great Britain*, ii, part 2 (London, 1848), p. 313.

particularly in view of the efforts which had been made by AIMC to keep the mines operating at a time of better, though less stable, copper prices. Peak copper production was reached sometime during the 1830s; the viable copper seams were worked out shortly after, as is suggested by falls in production.

Avoca's mines were on the point of closure in 1839[71] when a major difficulty arose in getting sulphur from Sicily which up to then had a near monopoly on the market. Suddenly the pyritic iron in which the copper was embedded became very valuable and the three Avoca operations were quick to avail of the market opportunities.[72] Copper mining was greatly reduced and waste heaps were 'mined' for their discarded sulphur content. Even roads where mine waste had been used as metalling were ripped up for recycling.[73] The reason for such haste would appear to have been the exorbitant price of 37 shillings per ton fetched by the first loads of this 'waste', shipped 28 December 1839. While the price had dropped to 30 shillings per ton within a year and to 20 shillings by 1850 it was nevertheless a most remunerative operation.[74] All the mines concentrated mainly on sulphur production over the next fifteen years or so.

Estimates of the employment given at this period vary. One source of the mid 1830s puts it at one thousand people employed at Ballymurtagh alone.[75] Two commentators in the early 1840s agree that 'about 2000 people, miners and their labourers' were employed over the entire area.[76] A third more formal source puts the number as high as 2,380.[77] The slight disparity may arise from the difference between those directly employed by the mining companies and those with occasional work or on sub-contract. Amongst these would have been carters and handlers.

Table 19.5 gives some idea of the tonnages which had to be transported to Arklow or Wicklow and the figure may be even higher

Table 19.5

Production of Copper and Sulphur 1840-1852

	1840	'41	'42	'43	'44	'45	'46	'47	'48	'49	'50	'51	1852
Copper	11	5	11	9	10	10	8	5	4	4	4	2	2
Value	25	12	25	20	24	22	18	10	8	8	8	4	5
Sulphur	40	77	40	39	35	39	30	41	41	46	74	102	98
Value	35	70	35	35	30	35	25	40	43	46	76	106	100

(weight x 1000 tonnes, value x £1000)

Source: W.W. Smyth, *Record of the school of mines* i, part 2 (London), p. 380.

as the statistics are incomplete. In 1845 for instance, over 18,000 tons of ore are recorded from Ballymurtagh alone and the other mines would have produced an equal amount between them. This had to be transported from Avoca the thirteen miles or so to either Wicklow or Arklow and in the late 1850s, up to 2,000 people locally were earning money from cartage.[78] Each load was half a ton in weight and required a full day's journey to either port at a cost of 2/6d.[79] One authoritative source in 1841 estimated, 'that the mines in this neighbourhood pay at least £20,000 a year for carting the ores to the port'. The overall consequences for the local economy were thus expressed:

> There are from 500 to 1000 car(t)s daily employed carting this ore to the ports of Arklow and Wicklow, and a vast number of coasting vessels employed conveying it from there to Dublin for shipment: for the ports of Wicklow and Arklow are so bad that large vessels cannot enter and the few that go to the roadstead are obliged to have their cargo taken to them in lighters, an expensive and tedious operation.

He adds: 'Nearly all the fisherman's boats during the winter are also employed conveying the ore to Dublin for shipment'.[80] Some of the spin-off benefits of haulage were presumably diminished in the late 1840s when Henry Hodgeson of Ballygahan opened a railway to Arklow[81] which was also used by the WCMC in which he was a major shareholder. The other mines continued to send ore by horse and cart.[82] While there are no statistics for income distribution from such activity, it can be assumed that the local economy benefited significantly whether from primary or secondary employment. Among the tertiary beneficiaries from mining at Avoca up to the late 1830s were the manufacturers and retailers of alcohol.

Advocates of temperance tended to exaggerate the problem of alcohol so one must put into perspective, for instance an assertion that on pay-day the miners immediately started drinking and then 'spent the night in fighting while their wives and children begged in vain for some of their wages'.[83] Somewhat more reliably, the mines doctor blamed ill health among the miners on insufficient diet partly due to 'their abundant use of whiskey'.[84] A dramatic improvement was brought about by the temperance movement from about 1840: 'the temperance society – has created a most wonderful change.' On pay-days the fighting had stopped and 'not even one gallon of whiskey is sold' according to one source and 'no whiskey whatsoever' according to another.[85] While this no doubt contributed greatly to the general sense of well-being amongst miners' families, there was still the problem of their living conditions.

Statistically at least, Avoca miners seemed to live in somewhat greater comfort than their compeers in a similar mining situation at Knockmahon, county Waterford. There, about half the workers lived in one roomed *bothāns*, with more than one family in occupation of 40 per cent of them.[86] In Avoca only one third of the houses were *bothāns* and a mere eleven per cent of these housed more than one family. Less than one in six of the better houses containing at least two rooms contained more than one family. There were also thirty solid, several-roomed 'second class' houses in the vicinity of the mines.[87] Furthermore, houses here were in great demand.[88] It was observed of industrially crowded Ballymurtagh in 1833 that 'The houses in this townland — are valuable being on the mining company's works. The smallest house lets at 12d per week', equivalent to a day's work for a labourer. Similar comments were made about the adjoining area.[89]

One well-placed individual in 1844 remarked that most of the ordinary labourers in Wicklow lived in 'cabins of the most wretched description'.[90] A French visitor to Avoca in 1836-'37 gave graphic details of housing:

> Along the Avoca valley I saw cottages so miserable they are impossible to describe. Most of them have neither the size nor the type of organisation that one would find in sheds to house animals. They are propped against the ditches which line the road and are, without doubt, the most misfortunate of structures, scarcely having a wall that merits the name, without chimneys or windows and none without a small heap of straw and farm dung — the traveller could never suppose that these were human habitations.[91]

Overcrowding too must have been a factor. Some 2,132 people living on the 1,722 acres which comprised mines, pump-houses, sorting sheds and stables for all four mines were sharing their sounds, smells and shadows. On steeply sided Tigroney-Connary hill, 274 houses were perched and across the valley, 410 people in 63 houses lived in. 'Wretched, dirty and filthy habitations' as one visitor observed.[92] A slightly later account refers to the environment as 'desecrated by the encroachment of the mines' and dominated by 'squalid ruins and gigantic mechanisms'.[93] Mine manager Barnes of Ballymurtagh commented on the 'Great want of comfort, order and cleanliness in the dwelling of the miners' and that the well paid lived in the same condition as the poorest, a condition he attributes to 'want of forethought and recklessness of character' of the miners.[94] A visitor to Avoca entered three such homes each being squalid, one roomed *bothâns*. The worst had no furniture; the best of the three was shared by a miner's wife and four children. Their total furniture was two beds, a stool, a small bench and a pot. The middle, mud-built *bothân* was described as follows:

> —-one apartment. It was neither air nor water-tight and the floor was extremely damp. The furniture consisted of a small bedstead with very scanty bedding, a wooden bench and one iron pot. The embers of some furze burned on the floor and there was neither chimney nor window.[95]

Edward Barnes and his uncle lived in Ballymurtagh close to the mines and the squalid housing of their employees. The paradox that was Avoca was even more strongly emphasised with the erection of a hotel close by to service the developing tourist industry.[96]

Mining gave no guaranteed security of income. The main Avoca mines, however, provided relatively continuous employment between 1825 and the late 1860s. Surviving account books[97] suggest that there was reasonable stability of income, averaging 12 shillings per week. Mines' inspector, Frederick Roper was there on a market day and saw 'all kinds of supplies, principally of food for sale' with 'upwards of 1,000 people' in attendance.[98] That regular supplies of food were available is apparent by the absence of reference to the Avoca area as a distressed district in the famine relief reports – as distinct from Baltinglass, 'a nucleus for misery', Wicklow 'an almost pauper population of 25,000 souls' and Arklow, 'stricken by cholera'.[99]

Table 19.6 indicates that the general population trend was downwards particularly amongst the poorest section. The numbers in first, second and third class houses actually increased whereas the occupants in the one roomed *bothâns* were dramatically reduced from 265 to 67 in the decade to 1851.[100] Perhaps these were the marginal

Table 19.6

Population in the Avoca mining area (parish of Castlemacadam)

	1821	*1831*	*1841*	*1851*	*1861*	*1871*	*1881*	*1891*
Connary			170	143	170	111	49	28
Cronebane			375	258	269	203	109	84
Tigroney			626	396	375	298	206	171
Ballygahan			173	144	119	61	35	30
Ballymurtagh			450	410	229	212	103	67

Source: *Censuses of Population* 1821-91, county Wicklow, Arklow barony, Castlemacadam parish.

people, the hangers on, those not so much looking for work as for the pickings of what working activity could bring 'Strollers' as they were known locally.[101] As late as 1860 such marginals caused difficulty for a mining company which had been set up to work the area south west of Avoca at Carysfort. The Carysford Mining Company rumoured to have discovered gold on its leasehold, found its workings besieged by 'idlers and persons of bad character together with the surrounding peasantry'.[102]

Both major mining companies in Avoca had contributory insurance schemes, and a pension scheme for widows, thereby affording some security against sickness and accidental injury.[103] While a doctor blamed ill-health partly on the 'unwholesomeness of the mines', it was pointed out that the absence of cholera from the area during the epidemic of 1832-33 was due to the cleansing power of sulphur.[104] There appears to have been reasonable safety procedures in place on both sides of the valley and even though there were some dramatic near-misses, few fatalities are reported. The manager at Ballymurtagh was specifically concerned about safety standards and Hodgeson at adjoining Ballygahan claimed that the only fatality he had in ten years was due to 'imprudence'.[105] Nevertheless Ballygahan had a lucky miss in 1835 when it was noticed that the rats 'which were living in great numbers underground' were seen to be deserting the mine possibly because of creaking sounds and the smell of sulphur from friction. The miners escaped before a section of roof some 80 yards long and 40 yards deep by about 10 feet wide broke off and collapsed, smashing its way through all levels beneath.[106] An even worse collapse happened seven years later when waste material from abandoned levels crashed down into the deeper active workings. The vibrations brought down an entire section of the mine, opening a surface chasm down to 420 feet which swallowed several sheds. Fortunately it was St. Patrick's Day and nobody was in or about the mine at the time. Another such collapse swallowed up a house with a child in it – the only casualty – occurred in 1850.[107] The east side of the valley was not as prone to such runs, the only documented one being towards the end of Tigroney's life in 1872 when the floor under six miners, who survived, collapsed.[108]

The majority of the miners according to an 1840 report were illiterate. Their children faced a better future: both WCMC and Hodgeson at Ballymurtagh provided their own schools and there were three other schools in the locality by 1841.[109] Their presence and the work of the temperance movement caused one analyst to observe in the context of Avoca:

> I do not hesitate to assert that the existing generation in this country is half a century in advance of that which is dying off — we were ignorant for learning was denied us; we were improvident for we had no future; we were drunken for we sought to forget our misery. That time has passed away for ever.[110]

Many of the miners themselves did not share this optimism. English Mines Inspector Roper reported of his arrival in Avoca in 1841:

> ... an absurd rumour having gone abroad that I had come over from France to hire men to work at the mines and fortifications there, and that I had a ship in Dublin all ready for them, I had at least a hundred applications from strong able men, miners and others, who expressed themselves ready to go.[111]

Some emigrated shortly afterwards: 'many went over to England but were disappointed and came back again'.[112] A local farmer – witness to the Devon Commission when asked whether miners were any better off than agricultural labourers replied 'Yes they are but the work is more laborious and it is very dirty. Saving your honours, they are covered over with it so that few might like to take it'.[113] A visitor in 1850 describes the miners trudging homewards with their clothes smelling of sulphur and the stumps of candles still stuck to their caps.[114]

Hope proferred and deferred, *c.*1855-*c.*1870

By the early 1860s the desire expressed by many of the workers to leave Avoca had been realised despite the huge quantities of sulphur being raised. The chairman of the newly reformed Connaree Mining Company reported in 1861 of 'the great difficulty in procuring a sufficient and permanent supply of miners and labourers.'[115] He concluded that the only way of attracting them was to build houses for the workmen, 'making it in their interest to attach themselves permanently to the mine'.[116] At Ballymurtagh from 1866 the long established Wicklow Copper Mining Company had to build houses and even provide gardens due to the 'scarcity of labourers'.[117] Apparently even this inducement did not succeed as two years later shareholders were told that labour shortage was due to ignorance on the part of the miners: the company intended to build no more cottages as the miners preferred to pay the same rent for a one roomed cottage as for the fine four roomed ones built by the company.[118]

Scarcity of labour is also referred to in Tigroney during the 1860s.[119] In 1872 Captain Oates, the mine manager, explained that he was setting rails into the mine, not because this was a cheaper way of removing the ore, 'but I find it more easy to obtain men to push a waggon than to wheel a barrow.' Shortly afterwards he reported that he had thirteen men simply breaking pyrite (sulphurous) rock, 'and could as easily put as many more to work if they could be obtained'. He does provide an explanation for that shortfall: 'demand for men in England has caused several able-bodied ones to leave in the last twelve months'. He was left with 'sluggish beings – the castaways from other mines'. However, he intended to 'knock them to their senses'.[120]

Oates had trouble either buying or hiring horses: 'sadly put out for horses' as he expresses it at the end of August 1872. He had given somebody £20 to buy one but no horses were available at two local fairs. Even an offer of 5/- per day to local carters had no takers.[121] The problem was also reported from a small mine east of Avoca where the agent there claims to have had to travel 'hundreds of miles' in search of horses.[122] Such difficulties caused Oates to break down the various handling costs per ton of 'wet ore' (21 cwts) at Tigroney in 1872.[123]

Ore-face extraction	1-6d
Handling within the mine	4d
Bringing ore to the surface	5d
Handling on surface	5d
Carting to rail head	9d
Loading onto railway carriages	2d
Freight, handling shipping etc.	3-9d approx
Total cost per ton, ore face to smelter	7-4d

At the same time, according to the company's own figures (March-Sept. 1872) the following were their sales receipts:[124]

Ore	*Tons*	*Price per ton*	*Total Value*
Sulphur	3000	17-6d	£2625
Iron	1500	13-6d	£1020-10/-
Copper Py.	300	45-0d	£ 675
'Riddlings'	200	9-0d	£ 90
Totals	5000		£4410-10/-

Total mining, handling and freight charges for 5,000 tons at 7-4d per ton should have amounted to approximately £1,835, leaving a profit of over £2,500. It would seem from this that the Wicklow Copper Mining Company, at least at this stage, had scope to pay more to attract new workers, to kept the loyalty of those they had and to hire sub-contractors for carriage.

A similar analysis cannot be made for the high-output 1860s as even contemporaries had difficulty getting either production statistics or costs.[125] However, some indication of the distribution of profits is possible. From the limited data available it is apparent that almost half sales income went on wages with 'stores', directors' fees, plus royalty and dividends, accounting for most of the other half.[126] Any balance went into a contingency fund. In 1857 the Wicklow Copper Mining Company could barely keep up with demand for pyrite (sulphur) and refers to the 'urgent and pressing demand for deliveries'. In that financial year they raised and shipped some 35,000 tons of ore, mainly pyrite – over a hundred tons per working day from Ballymurtagh alone.[127]

Cartage, however, was not a major factor as the WCMC had the use of the railway built by Hodgeson to transport his ore from adjoining Ballygahan to Arklow. Furthermore, the WCMC of Ballymurtagh made a brave attempt to diversify once the downturn started in 1865. It proposed a chemical plant for Arklow and a smelter nearby. This could have had enormous employment potential for the area and indeed it was envisaged that an entire new town would grow around the smelter.[128] No more was heard of this project but in 1868 a fertiliser factory was set up in Wicklow. Its fate goes unrecorded as does the origins of a similar factory which they acquired in Arklow in 1870.[129] These attempts, with all their employment potential, were, however, doomed to failure in the light of the huge tonnages of richer sulphur being cheaply quarried out of the Rio Tinto mines in Spain from 1865.[130] In 1873 the company's 'Chemical and Artificial Manure Works' in Arklow had to close and other attempts to give added value to Ballymurtagh production failed for the same reason.[131]

Hope proffered and deferred had long been offered to the work-force. Even during times of prosperity there had been set-backs, during the Crimean war between 1854 and 1856 and again during the American Civil War. As the company explained to their shareholders on the latter occasion: 'Mining operations of any description are liable to interruptions such as the present, and we cannot expect to form the exception'.[132] The workers may not have been quite so philosophical. As their number dropped they may have been aware of the promise that the proposed railway through Avoca to Dublin would have on ore sales from 1857 onwards. Its building over the next two years and the incorporation of Hodgeson's rail into the system by 1859 did not result in significant increase in either output or employment.[133]

Decline of a community from *c*.1870

The trend from 1870 was downwards. Footnotes in the published censuses for 1881 and 1891 specifically mention the failure of the mines as being the cause of the dramatic drops in population in many of the adjoining townlands. Cronebane seems to have first closed about 1863[134] even before the permanent downturn in prices was manifest. One can only assume that demoralisation of the workforce preceded the admission to the shareholders of such failures as management blamed the workers for the decline in the company's fortunes: 'The state of the labour market has interfered with the profitable results of the company's business', the Ballymurtagh shareholders were told in 1872. Apparently they did not believe this as the following meeting was marked by the use of 'strong and impolite language'.[135] Nevertheless while these shareholders were assured by the end of 1874 that everything was in place for the time 'when a revival of trade takes place', the evidence on the ground was of a mine being run down. A year later this was admitted to shareholders when they were told that underground pumping had ceased two months previously.[136]

How the two companies in east Avoca dealt with the same problem is not known, nor is the decline in their production. While there are quite extensive records concerning the Connary company, which was resuscitated in 1855, most of it relates to disputes among the directors and between shareholders and directors.[137] A coup by the shareholders in 1868 allows a glimpse into the consequences of such acrimony. The shareholders state:

> We found the affairs of the company in a sad and lamentable state as regards the books, there being no cash book — (and) open fraud in the cost sheets. (there was) extraordinary dereliction of duty and flagrant abuse of confidence'. [The mine itself was] in a deplorable state machinery neglected much useless material bought.

One can presume that the miners had their own sarcastic perspective on this, including a view on the only 'well ordered' arrangements being those 'for the comfort of the directors'. Over £5,000 was unaccounted for and cash was missing from the safe.[138] Further investigation indicated that the mine had been doing far better than reported from 1863 which enabled the directors to pilfer the profits that shareholders did not know had been made – up to £20,000 on some estimates with £16,861 being taken in 1865-66. Such profits for directors obviously were at the expense of the local economy both in the short and in the long term. By 1868 the miners were owed £250.[139] Nevertheless the mine continued to operate.[140]

A tendentious report of 1885 somewhat colourfully suggests that 'in more prosperous times' (of the early 1860s?) each head of mining family there

> was reckless and devoid of thrift, a result largely attributable, perhaps, to the hopelessness of his position and to his political serfdom. Again, almost every head of family was then the owner of a horse, or at least an ass, with which some younger members of the family drew the ore his father raised to seaboard. Each family could therefore exist without land, or, at least, with at least as much miserable mountainside to graze a goat or two.[141]

There is no direct evidence that Avoca mining families supplemented their incomes by farming and cartage.[142] Certainly for most of them the mines had ceased to be a source of employment by the late 1870s.

The last cargo sold by the Connary company had gone by mid-1875 after which the mine was formally abandoned.[143] When it was inspected later that year with a view to re-commencing operations, it was found to be flooded and deemed 'no good'.[144] Small tonnages of iron produced here over the next four years may have been the pickings of the waste heaps.[145] The other Avoca mines kept ticking over into the 1880s though on a vastly reduced scale with precipitated copper continuing to be collected. An attempt was made in the mid-1880s to find a market for ochre gathered from the upper levels of the eastern Avoca mines. Across the river in Ballymurtagh and Ballygahan, eight men were working at removing the ore-rich pillars which had once supported the mine roof. 'Such a scene of desolation it would be hard to conceive' was one perceptive comment on Avoca mines in August 1887.[146]

The consequences for the mining families of Avoca are not formally recorded though one rather polemic account states:

> The young men emigrated and many of the old people and children sought refuge in the much detested workhouse. Those

who escaped this institution have since engaged in a continuous and most pitiful struggle with starvation.

This source suggested that many went to the equally fraught English mining districts in hope of work where they were 'scarcely-welcome visitors'. Others emigrated to America.[147] Indeed when one inquirer went to Avoca in 1887 he could find nobody there who could tell him anything about mining traditions.[148]

A commentator in the 1920s implicitly blamed management for the failure of the Avoca enterprise:

> Owing to the mines being poorly equipped and also the fact that they had not kept up with modern mining developments the output gradually decreased and since 1880 the mines have only been worked in a small way.[149]

More recent analysis suggests that the absence of detailed knowledge of the Avoca ore-body and its configuration may have been a significant factor in the decline of mining.[150] Current research indicates that the geology of the district is extremely complex.[151] While the mines have since been worked intermittently and substantial tonnages produced, neither the scale of operations nor the numbers employed have remotely competed with the golden era of Avoca mining in the nineteenth century.

References

1. Hamner papers in addenda to *C.S.P. Ire.*, 1601-1603, pp 670-1 and provenance in preface lxxx-lxxxiii: this comprises a comprehensive list of mineral sites with attributed date of 1497 though it may date from 1600. John Powell, refiner at Silvermines also provides a list of known mines *c.*1650 in T.C.D., Ms 883, pp 9-13. Neither mention Avoca.
2. NAI, D. 7994h, Tigroney indenture, Hoey and Hume to Brownrigg and Co.
3. Idem., mentions Wynne as do most later sources. However, Anon., *The mines of Wicklow* (Law of London, 1856), p. 43 casts some doubt on whether Wynne played an active role. O'Connor's claims were published in pamphlets, 'State of the copper trade in Ireland for the consideration of the House of Commons' (*c.*1730) and 'The case of Martin O'Connor of Silvermines,' 1762 (N.L.I. mf. p. 4034).
4. Letter from W. Henry in *Philosophical Transactions*, xlvii (1753). The anonymous contributor to *The complete Irish traveller* (London, 1788), p. 65, blamed the closure of Ballymurtagh on 'dissension among the proprietors.'
5. *Petition to the house of commons to restrain harbour officers at Wicklow from charging higher duties on precipitate ore*, dated 19 Jan. 1760, House of Commons Journals, ix, 1753-56 (Dublin, 1763), p. 173.
6. J. Rutty, *An essay towards a natural history of the county of Dublin*, ii (Dublin, 1772), p. 22.

7. 'Dublin imports and exports' 1773-1778, N.L.I., Ms Customs' books, Wicklow customs' area.
8. N.L.I., Ms 16304, 16307, proceedings of the Associated Irish Mining Company from Aug. 1787, reporting monthly on clearing out the old workings.
9. G.T. Stokes (ed.), *Bishop Pococke's tour in Ireland in 1752* (Dublin and London, 1791), pp 159-160.
10. W. Shaw Mason, *A statistical account or parochial survey of Ireland*, ii (Dublin, 1816), pp 27-8.
11. T. Weaver, 'Geological relations of the east of Ireland', in *Transactions of the Geological Society*, v (London, 1819), p. 103.
12. J. Fraser, *Guide to the county of Wicklow* (Dublin, 1842), p. 50.
13. N.L.I., Ms 16304-16348 Avoca Mines Papers covering years 1787 to 1886. For a convenient summary of manuscript references to these see *An index to mineral and mining public records and manuscripts in Ireland* (Geological Survey of Ireland, 1988), pp 33-5.
14. The most comprehensive is *The mines of Wicklow* (1856).
15. An uncatalogued 'Rough Plan' in Geological Survey of Ireland collection dated August 1827 by A. Herviere shows deep and shallow adits facing Tigroney but more southerly workings labelled 'Old Hibernian Company'. A later uncatalogued map in G.S.I. by W.W. Smith (n.d. *c.*1850) calls the adits Whaley's.
16. *Statutes at Large from III Edward II to XXVIII George III*, viii; *Irish Statutes*, iii (Dublin, 1798), p. 412, 23-24th George III (grant 500); p. 841, 26th George III (amount not clear).
17. For background see J.R. Harris, *The copper king: a biography of Thomas Williams of Llanidan* (Liverpool, 1964).
18. N.L.I., Ms 16304, *passim* expenditure and proceedings from May 1788.
19. Wright, *Guide to county Wicklow*, p. 74.
20. N.L.I., Ms 16304, expenditure and proceedings from May 1788.
21. Dalton and Hamer, *The provincial token coinage of the 18th century, part xiii, Ireland* (London, 1917), introduction and p. 457.
22. R. Griffith, *The metallic mines of Leinster* (Dublin, 1828), p. 20.
23. *'Act for the better enabling certain persons to open and work mines ... and to open and improve the harbour of Arklow ...'* Irish statutes at large, iii, 32nd George II, pp 279-283.
24. E. Barnes, *A brief description of Ballymurtagh mine, the property of the Wicklow copper mining company* (Dublin, 1864), p. 6.
25. S. Haughton, 'Geological and statistical notes on Irish mines,' *Geological Society of Dublin Journal*, v (1853), p. 285.
26. De Lacotayne, *A Frenchman's walk through Ireland, 1796-1797*, translated by J. Stephenson (London, 1917); Wakefield, *Account of Ire.*, i, p. 137.
27. *D.N.B.*, ii, p. 347, 'Kyan, John Howard.' His son is reputed to have discovered that timber soaked in copper sulphate (such as issued from Ballymurtagh) was preserved and gave his name to this method of treating timber – 'Kyanization'.
28. *'Act for the enabling of certain persons to open and work mines,' Irish statutes at large*, iii, p. 943, 38th George III, ch. XL.
29. N.L.I., Ms 16304, June-Nov., 1789.
30. R. Musgrave, *Memoirs of the different rebellions in Ireland*, i(Dublin, 1801), p. 30.
31. N.L.I., Ms 16304, collated from reports under names of individual mines Oct. 1789 which is taken as a representative month in the early years of the operation.
32. Ibid., the first three being March, August and September 1787, the next 8 Oct. 1787 and the last 5 June to Aug. 1787.

33. Ibid., March, May, September, December 1789.
34. N.L.I., Ms 16305, Jan. 1795.
35. N.L.I., Ms 16304, Oct. 1789, Cronebane mine, Markham.
36. Idem for John Paul.
37. Ibid., August 1789.
38. N.L.I., Ms 16305, July 1791.
39. N.L.I., Ms 16307, July and Aug., 1801 proceedings; Ms 16309 Sept. 1801, minutes setting out rates of wages.
40. N.L.I., Ms 16305, June 1791.
41. Ibid., September 1793.
42. N.L.I., Ms 16309, Nov. 1802.
43. Ibid, proceedings Feb., June and Dec. 1802, March 1803.
44. N.L.I., Ms 16308, proceedings April 1806.
45. N.L.I., Ms 16309, minutes Dec. 1800.
46. Musgrave, *Memoirs*, p. 300.
47. W. Richardson, *History of the origin of the Irish yeomanry with the steps taken to bring forward the measure previous to its final adoption* (Dublin, 1801); *A list of the counties of Ireland and the yeomanry corps in each county* (Dublin, 1798), p. 91. I would like to thank Ruan O'Donnell for these and for the references immediately following from the National Archives.
48. NAI, 620/18A/6, J. Parnell to T. Coke, 3 Sept. 1796.
49. NAI, S.O.C. papers 1017/62; 620/17/30/64.
50. Musgrave, 1801, *Memoirs*, pp 301, 306.
51. N.L.I., mf. p. 5641, Hardy to Fitzwilliam, 15 Mar. 1798.
52. N.L.I., Ms 16306, expenditure Nov. and Dec. 1796.
53. J. Buckley, 'Note and transcript of letter from Lord Lieutenant Camden to the prime minister, 8 Oct. 1795' in *R.S.A.I. Jn.*, xliii, pt i, 1913, pp 183-5.
54. While there is no direct reference to this in Ms 16306, two of AIMC personnel published near contemporary accounts of it: A. Mills, 'A mineralogical account of the native gold lately discovered in Ireland' in *Philosophical Transactions of Royal Society*, pt. 1 (1796) and R. Kirwan, 'Report of the gold mines in the county of Wicklow with observations thereon,' *Dublin Society Transactions*, ii (1801).
55. N.L.I., Ms 16306, 1797, passim; April (new uniforms) and Oct. 1798 (payment of handbill, 1797) expenditures. Musgrave, *Memoirs*, p. 303, quotes oath and reaction to it.
56. October 1798 report from N.L.I., Ms 16306, removed from bound volume and hanging framed in the bar of the Avoca Vale Hotel.
57. Ibid., April-Aug. 1798.
58. Ibid., Jan-Dec. 1798 with copper standard taken from Hunt (op. cit.).
59. N.L.I., Ms 16307, resolution of 21 Jan. 1802.
60. Ibid., passim expenditures to volunteers being made either in Dec. or Jan. with table from Jan. 1804.
61. R. Fraser, *General view of agriculture and mineralogy, present state of the county of Wicklow* (Dublin, 1801), p. 17.
62. N.L.I., Ms 16307, passim and Ms 16308, March 1811.
63. Ibid., April, 1810. Wakefield, *Account Ire.*, i, p. 133. N.L.I., Ms 16309, April, 1810, Mills' comment and passim from 1808 almost monthly references to the deep level.
64. The concern is expressed in Ms 16309, passim. Its practical expression is shown in Thomas Weaver's plan entitled 'Plan and section of Cronebane and Tigroney mines in the county of Wicklow – from July 1794 to 1812,' in G.S.I. files, unreferenced, including detailed 1" = 200ft. and 1" = 360 ft. maps.

65. Haughton, 'Geological and statistical notes,' p. 283.
66. N.L.I., Ms 16309, passim, reports of meetings especially 16 July 1828, 28 Feb. 1834 and 28 Jan. 1834. Following a thirty-eight year gap records of AIMC resume in 1872.
67. J. Binns, *The miseries and beauties of Ireland*, ii (London, 1837), mentions Salkeld. While no detail has emerged about this operation, there were considerable surface workings by 1838 as shown on 6" O.S. map Wicklow, sheet 35. Extensive underground operations are indicated in sections of the mine by Roberts, G.S.I. WO11, 512, *c.*1838.
68. Anon, *The mines of Wicklow*, pp 47-8. The Hibernian Company also continued as a lessor for the next forty years before amalgamating with Wicklow Copper Mining Company in 1862.
69. Census of population (Ireland), 1821, 1831, 1841, Castlemacadam parish, Arklow barony, county Wicklow.
70. *Reports of commissioners – Children's employment in mines I*, H.C., 1841, xvi. Reports of Frederick Roper include statement from Henry Hodgeson, director of Ballymurtagh who says the majority of his workforce was Catholic; also J. Forbes *Memorandum made in Ireland in the autumn of 1852* (London, 1853), p. 30.
71. *Mining Journal* (hereafter *M.J.*) (1858), p. 134, informed anonymous article 'Mineral wealth in Ireland' suggesting their impending closure in 1839.
72. *M.J.* (1840), pp 324, 348, 412, editorial on Avoca sulphur potential. Most mid-nineteenth century sources (e.g. Barnes (1864) op. cit., p. 7) refer to how the king of Naples raised brimstone prices in 1839.
73. *Report select committee on industries (Ireland)*, H.C. 1888, app. no. 9, synopsis of evidence of A.G. Ryder, Manager, Ovoco Mineral Company Ltd., p. 744.
74. S. Haughton, 'Geological and statistical notes,' p. 283.
75. H.D. Inglis, *Ireland in 1834; a journey through Ireland during the spring, summer and autumn 1834* (London, 1834), i. p. 34.
76. R. Kane, *The industrial resources of Ireland* (Dublin, 1845, 2nd ed.), p. 407.
77. Second report of the railway commission, Ireland, HC, xxxv, 1837-8, app., no. 9, p. 69.
78. *M.J.* (1858), p. 134, Anon on Avoca.
79. S.C. & A.M. Hall, *Ireland, its scenery, character*, etc. (London, 1841), p. 337.
80. Roper, HC 1842, op. cit., p. 853 (quoting Hodgeson) and p. 855 for his own comments.
81. A. Webb, *Recollections of a three day tour in the county Wicklow in the summer of 1850* (Dublin, 1851), p. 29.
82. Anon, *The mines of Wicklow*, pp 55-6.
83. Kane, *The Industrial resources of Ireland*, p. 407.
84. Binns, *The miseries and beauties of Ireland*, ii, p. 209.
85. *Children's employment in mines*, H.C. 1841, xvi, evidence of Frederick Roper, p. 856; Kane, *The industrial resources of Ireland*, p. 407.
86. D. Cowman, 'Life and work in an Irish mining camp, *c.*1840: Knockmahon copper mines Waterford,' *Decies*, xiv (Old Waterford Society, May, 1980), p. 33.
87. *Census of population*, 1841, county of Wicklow, barony of Castlemacadam.
88. Six inch O.S. map, 1838, Wicklow sheet 35, shows clustering of houses particularly in Ballymurtagh, Tigroney, Crobenane and Connary with comparatively few houses in adjoining areas.
89. NAI, Valuation office house books, Wicklow county, barony Arklow, parish Castlemacadam, see townlands Ballymurtagh, Ballygahan, Castlemacadam and Kilqueeny.
90. *Devon commission*, iii, p. 708.

91. *Excursions pittoresque et artistique en Irlande pendant les annees 1836-7*, trans. Professeur Garrick (Paris, 1839), p. 99.
92. Inglis, *Ireland in 1834*, p. 29.
93. J. Forbes, *Memorandum made in Ireland in the autumn of 1852,* i (London, 1853), pp 29-30.
94. *M.J.* (1837), p. 30, 'Irish mining operations' by E.B. whom I assume to be Edward Barnes.
95. Inglis, *Ireland in 1834*, p. 30.
96. NAI, Valuation office house books, 1833, townlands Ballygahan and Ballymurtagh, Kilqueeny and Castlemacadam, Castlemacadam parish, Arklow barony, county Wicklow.
97. N.L.I., Ms 16329 *passim* to Sept. 1865.
98. *Children's employment in mines*, H.C. 1841, xvi, p. 856.
99. *Correspondence July 1846 to Jan. 1847 related to measures adopted for relief of distress in Ireland*, H.C. 1847, p. 402 (434). Boyle to Walker from Wicklow, 16 Dec. 1846.
100. *Census of population, Ireland, 1841 and 1851*, parish Castlemacadam, barony of Arklow, county of Wicklow 1841 and 1851.
101. *Poor Inquiry, 1835*, App. 4, p. 156, evidence of Rev Thomas Webber.
102. NAI, Q.R.O. 2B 46 31 (826), Carysford Mining Company correspondence, July 1860. It is possible that the company was exaggerating the problem in order to obtain a gold prospecting licence.
103. N.L.I., Ms 16329, accounts, payments into and out of medical and widows' pensions scheme.
104. Binns, *The miseries and beauties of Ireland*, ii, pp 208-9, quoting Nicholson; NAI, M 1A 46 11, cholera papers, county Wicklow (Arklow).
105. Barnes, *Ballymurtagh mine*, p. 12 and Hodgeson quoted by Roper in evidence to *Children's employment in mines*, H.C. 1841, xvi, p. 855.
106. W.W. Smyth, 'On the mines of Wicklow and Wexford', in *Records of the school of mines*, i (London, 1853).
107. Anon, *The mines of Wicklow*, pp 91-3, including sketch to show what happened in 1845.
108. N.L.I., Ms 16338, report of Capt. Oates to directors, 13 Dec. 1872.
109. N.L.I., Ms 16309, minutes, 30 Mar. 1834 'Resolved that £10 per annum be paid to Mrs Moorehead the schoolmistress for the purposes of affording instruction to the children of the miners.' Hodgeson told Roper that he was building a school for his miners' children and that there were two other schools in the area. See Roper's evidence to *Children's employment in mines*, H.C. 1841, xvi, p. 855.
110. Kane, *Industrial resources*, p. 407.
111. Roper, see n. 70.
112. *Devon commission*, iii, p. 695, evidence of Michael Hudson.
113. Ibid., p. 700, evidence of John Nolan.
114. A. Webb, *Tour in the county of Wicklow*, p. 26.
115. *M.J.* (1859), 'Advertisement and prospectus for shares,' p. 474.
116. *The Dublin Builder*, no. 21, 15 Feb. 1861, p. 438.
117. *M.J.* (1866), p. 641.
118. *M.J.* (1868), p. 767.
119. N.L.I., Ms 16339, letter to Capt. Oates from Cornwall 24 Dec. 1863 and Ms 16338 letter of 7 Apr. 1865.
120. N.L.I., Ms 16338, reports from Capt. Oates to the directors, 6 Dec. 1872, 1 Feb. 1873 and 28 Mar. 1873.

121. Ibid., 23, 27 and 30 Aug. 1872.
122. *M.J.* (1857), pp 189 and 277.
123. N.L.I., Ms 16638, report 23 Sept. 1872.
124. Ibid., 12 Mar. 1873.
125. *M.J.* (1846), p. 516, editorial claiming information was being withheld and indeed over the next ten years there is almost nothing reported on any of the Avoca mines in that paper.
126. N.L.I., pamphlets, p. 2411, half-yearly reports of Wicklow Copper Mining Company, 1857-'59.
127. N.L.I., pamphlets, p. 2411, Wicklow Copper Mining Company half-yearly reports, March and Sept. 1857, March 1858.
128. *M.J.* (1865), p. 684 and *M.J.* (1866), p. 248.
129. *M.J.* (1868), p. 767; *M.J.* (1870), pp 866 and 895 reports WCMC.
130. G.H. Kinahan, *Economic geology of Ireland* (Dublin, 1866) footnote, p. 111.
131. *M.J.* (1873), pp 362, 1153, 1184.
132. N.L.I., pamphlets 2441.
133. Ibid., Director's reports 1 Sept. 1857 and 1 Sept. 1861. For some context see W.E. Shepherd, *The Dublin and south eastern railway* (Newton Abbot, 1974), pp 32-3.
134. *M.J.* (1872), p. 206.
135. Ibid., pp 1060, 1088.
136. Ibid. (1874), p. 841; (1859), p. 724. There are many other reports on the company in *M.J.*, from 1856 to 1873.
137. *M.J.* (1855), *et seq.*
138. Ibid. (1868), pp 192-3.
139. Ibid. (1868), Irish mining shares market, pp 289-90, 361-392.
140. Ibid. (1875), 3 Jan., notice to creditors re closure of Connary.
141. Ryder evidence to *Select committee on industries*, H.C. (1888), p. 746.
142. Such does seem to have been the position in Allihies in the 1830s and 1840s to judge by evidence from there. See R.A. Williams, *The Berehaven copper mines* (Sheffield, 1991, British Mining no. 42).
143. G.S.I., W101254 Connarree 'Plan of abandoned mine 1876' with covering letter signed Joseph Dickenson, 20 Oct. 1875.
144. N.L.I., Ms 16338, letter 23 June 1875 and two letters dated 23 July 1875.
145. *Mineral Statistics* (published annually by H.M.S.O.), 1875-79.
146. R.J. Cruise, 'Ovoco mines' in *Memoirs of the Geological Survey of Ireland*, Sheets 138, 139 (H.M.S.O., 1888).
147. Ryder, evidence to Select committee on industries, H.C. 1888, p. 746.
148. Cruise, loc. cit., p. 30.
149. H.S. Mackey, *Report on the development of Avoca mines* (Wexford, 1920), p. 1.
150. J.S. Platt, typescript analysis, undated (*c.* 1980) in unsorted bundle of Avoca material in G.S.I. Mr Platt was the most recent manager in Avoca and had a keen interest in its history.
151. F.M. Williams, W.A. Sheppard and P. McArdle, 'Avoca mine, county Wicklow: a review of geological and isotopic studies' in C.J. Andrew, R.W. Crowe, S. Finlay, W.M. Pennell and J.F. Pyne (eds.), *Geology and genesis of mineral deposits in Ireland* (Dublin, 1986), pp 71-82.

Chapter 20

WICKLOW BEFORE AND AFTER THE FAMINE

K. HANNIGAN

This essay deals with the social and demographic structure of Wicklow in the pre-famine period, examines the extent and course of the famine in Wicklow and considers how the county changed in the post-famine period.[1]

Pre-famine Wicklow

Wicklow's population in 1841 was higher than it had ever been before or has ever been since. According to the census of that year there were 126,143 people living in the county. This had risen from 110,767 in 1821 and 121,557 in 1831 but may already have begun to decline in the years immediately preceding the famine. The population was overwhelmingly rural-based. In the towns the main concentrations were at Arklow, which had a population of 3,254, followed by Bray which had a population of 3,169 (a third of whom were in county Dublin), then Wicklow (2,794) and Baltinglass (1,928).

Overall the county had 21,182 families of whom 14,032 were chiefly employed in agriculture and 4,740 were in trade and manufacture. Out of a total of 50,861 individuals who were returned as having an occupation, by far the largest single category of employment was farm labour. Overall in the county there were 6,211 farmers with 9,466 holdings of various sizes.[2] Farm servants or labourers numbered 21,914 while a further 6,835 people, mostly female, were employed as domestic servants. The 1831 census which differentiated between occupiers of land and agricultural labourers showed that agricultural labourers tended to be proportionately more numerous in the eastern lowland baronies of Newcastle and Rathdown, where they outnumbered farmers by more than three to one, than in other parts of Wicklow (see table 20.1). In the upland baronies of Ballinacor and Talbotstown the numbers of farmers and labourers were about equal, while elsewhere in the county there was a slight preponderance of labourers.

The county's main sources of non-agricultural employment (apart from domestic service) derived from fishing and mining and the trades

Table 20.1

Agricultural labourers in co. Wicklow 1831

Barony	*Population*	*No. farmers*	*Farmers as % total pop.*	*No. agricultural labourers*	*Ratio of agricul. labs to farmers*	*Agricul. labs as % of total pop.*
Arklow	22796	1085	4.8	1792	1.7	7.9
Ballinacor	23839	1937	8.1	2114	1.1	8.9
Newcastle	15770	623	4	2035	3.2	12.9
Rathdown	11652	364	3.1	1230	3.4	10.6
Shillelagh	14204	911	6.4	1248	1.4	8.8
Talbotstown Lower	14784	1113	7.5	1478	1.3	10
Talbotstown Upper	18512	1556	8.4	1422	9	7.7

(Source: *Census of Ireland, 1831*)

of boot making, dressmaking and tailoring. There were 638 fishermen in the county, the majority of them based in Arklow, Wicklow and Bray.[3] Herring fishing, which was largely concentrated in Arklow, took place annually in two six-week periods beginning in May and November. The Arklow herring fishery was said to be the best in Ireland after Galway; the size of the catch in a normal season allowing the fishermen to survive for most of the year on the money earned from the intensive activity of these two six-week spells.[4] Between catches the dredging of the oyster beds seems to have bridged the gap.[5] It was a style of life that was to prove in its own way as precarious as that of the subsistence smallholders in the rural uplands. As can be seen in appendix I, the distribution of the herring catch through the county provided an important supplement to the diet of many of the poor.

According to the census there were 721 miners employed in the county in 1841, mostly at Avoca and Connary, but also at Glenmalure and Glendalough. The numbers employed by the mines, when extended to carters and craftsmen of various sorts, amounted to several thousands and was on the increase in the early 1840s, with the onset of a boom caused by the sudden demand for pyrite. It was reported at this time that there were a thousand carters sub-contracting to bring the ore from Avoca to Arklow and Wicklow.[6] The mining operations in the Avoca valley were on such a scale as to make the barony of Arklow quite unlike any other in the county. It contained more than one and a half times as many non-agricultural labourers as the rest of Wicklow combined and had almost three times as many non-agricultural labourers per head of its population as any other barony. It also had the greatest population density of any Wicklow barony (see table 20.4).[7] The mines had changed the agricultural economy of the area. Potatoes sold to the miners were grown on land which in other areas would have been set as conacre. When agricultural employment became scarce, the labourers drifted towards the alternative employment offered by the mines. However, for those used to agricultural labour, work in the mines was very much an alternative to be avoided. One witness to the Devon commission when asked if miners were in a better condition than the agricultural labourers answered:

> Yes, they are; but the work is more laborious, and it is very dirty. Saving your honours, they are covered over with it, so that few men would like to take to it.[8]

Although rural Wicklow (the county as a whole excluding towns of 2,000 and upwards) had the lowest population density of any county in Leinster, the picture was distorted by its mountainous centre which was largely uninhabited or sparsely inhabited. Only 56.1 per cent of Wicklow's land was arable compared with Meath's 94.3 per cent and Wexford's 88.5 per cent. On the arable land, where most of the county's population was concentrated, there was a much higher density. Taking arable land only into account, Wicklow was fourth highest of the twelve Leinster counties, ahead of the neighbouring counties of Wexford and Carlow.[9] Here as in other areas, therefore, Wicklow was a county of contrasts. Parts of its mountainous interior bore a closer resemblance to the wildest parts of the north and west than to the rest of Leinster. Charles Edward Trevelyan, assistant secretary to the treasury, was to comment on this during the winter of 1846-47 when famine made an unexpectedly early and devastating appearance in Wicklow:

> The barren mountains which make it so attractive to the tourist, have allowed the existence of a state of society, and a dependence upon the potato, approaching to what prevails in the wildest districts of the west, and it is only within the present century that this district has lost its former reputation for lawlessness.[10]

Most farming in the county was arable. As Ó Gráda has stated, in attempting to envisage the countryside at this time we must imagine a rural landscape very different from that of Ireland today. Most of the low-lying land was tilled, with comparatively little meadow or pasture.[11]

There were 9,467 holdings over one (Irish) acre in county Wicklow in 1841. Only 2,001 of these were over 30 acres, 5,572 were under 15 acres.[12] Compared with Leinster and Ireland as a whole, Wicklow had relatively fewer smallholders and relatively more medium to large farms as indicated in Table 20.2.

Holdings under 1 acre were not covered by the census, but as can be seen from the Devon commission returns (Table 20.3) the numbers were substantial, especially in the northerly poor law unions of Naas and Rathdown.

Most people in the county who were questioned by the Devon commission in 1844 stated that agriculture was improving, but the

Table 20.2

Farm sizes in Wicklow compared with Leinster and Ireland as a whole

Year 1841	*Farms under 15 acres (%)*	*Farms of 30 acres or more (%)*
Wicklow	58.9	21.4
Leinster	71.3	13.3
Ireland	81.5	7.03

(Source: *Census of Ireland, 1841*)

Table 20.3

Numbers of farms of varying sizes in Poor Law Unions of county Wicklow, 1845

Poor Law Union	*under 1 acre*	*Greater than 1 and less than 5 acres (and this as % of all holdings over 1 acre)*	*Greater than 5 and less than 20 acres (and this as % of all holdings over 1 acre)*	*Greater than 20 and less than 50 acres (and this as % of all holdings over 1 acre)*	*Greater than 50 acres (and this as % of all holdings over 1 acre)*	*Total holdings over 1 acre*
Baltinglass	143	710 (20.1%)	1089 (30.8%)	939 (26.5%)	799 (22.6%)	3537
Naas	3051	1544 (33.1%)	1463 (31.3%)	712 (15.3%)	949 (20.3%)	4668
Rathdown	2130	709 (37.1%)	644 (33.7%)	330 (17.3%)	229 (12%)	1912
Rathdrum	171	956 (21.5%)	1187 (26.7%)	1063 (23.9%)	1244 (28%)	4450
Shillelagh	208	611 (18.3%)	1251 (37.4%)	967 (28.9%)	516 (15.4%)	3345

(Source: Devon Commission)

condition of the small farmers and labourers was a cause of worry. Many of the small farmers had come to rely on the loan funds for payment of their rent and were becoming increasingly indebted to them. One witness told the Devon commission that even farmers holding from ten to thirty acres were dragging out a miserable existence, unable to afford meat even once a week and living mainly on potatoes and milk.[13] The condition of the labourers was considerably worse. In many places they received as payment only their potato ground and their cabin. Elsewhere their earnings were supplemented by the potato yield of their small plots of land. The situation by which the labourers were in effect paid less than the cost of their food allowed farmers in good times to have access to inexpensive labour but was dangerously unstable. When on the one hand the potato crop failed and on the other the cost of foodstuff increased, many of the smaller farmers could not afford to employ labour at subsistence rates. Unable to employ labour, they were unable to sow their crops. This set in motion a cycle that was difficult to break.

Some consolidation of smallholdings had taken place in the years preceding the famine and there had been sporadic clearances. The tenacity with which tenants clung to uneconomic holdings surprised some, but the bond between people and land transcended economic reasoning. One evicted tenant near Baltinglass was said to have died of grief over the loss of his holding.[14] Evicted tenants became labourers or simply drifted to the nearest town. When cabins were pulled down in Ashford in 1842, for instance, most of the occupants moved onto the Common at Rathnew where they joined a growing throng several hundred strong who lived there in rent-free squalor.[15]

Set against the rest of Ireland, Wicklow was undoubtedly one of the better-off counties, with a strong and comparatively wealthy gentry. The county's proximity to Dublin was one of the main factors influencing its development in the 1840s. It was largely because of its proximity to the capital, and its ease of access, that Wicklow had such numbers of resident gentry, while movement to the capital had significantly effected the county's social structure. In no other part of Ireland was there such a high rate of inter-county migration as there was between Wicklow and Dublin. The pull of the metropolis had resulted in one-seventh of Wicklow's native-born population living in the capital in the 1840s. Many of these were women working as domestic servants. The large number of females coming from Wicklow to Dublin was considered to be so great as to distort the balance of sexes then remaining. This was particularly so among those of marriageable and child bearing ages. Within the age band 26 to 35, 62 per cent of Wicklow's population was male and only 38 per cent female.[16]

In contrast to Wicklow's uniquely high rate of migration to Dublin, movement further afield was on a smaller scale. There was little seasonal migration of agricultural labourers. A total of only 251 harvest workers travelled to England and Scotland from county Wicklow in the summer of 1841 compared with 10,430 from county Mayo. Indeed it seems that agricultural labour may have migrated into parts of Wicklow at harvest time.[17]

Of all counties outside Ulster, nineteenth-century Wicklow had the highest proportion of Protestant inhabitants, a reflection of its intensive settlement in the seventeenth century followed by two centuries in which the mineral and timber resources of the county drew large numbers of entrepreneurs and artisans. Figures collected by the Commission on Public Instruction in 1834 show that Protestants of all denominations accounted for almost 22 per cent of Wicklow's population in 1831.[18] Figures collected in 1766 which survive for only some parts of the county suggest that the proportion of Protestants in the county was then higher with the relative decline in the intervening years being greatest in the west of the county around Baltinglass and Blessington.[19] In the county as a whole during the years up to the mid-nineteenth century the Roman Catholic population increased at a faster rate than the Protestant.

The baronies of Arklow, Rathdown and Shillelagh all had over 25 per cent Protestant populations in 1831 with Newcastle having just under 25 per cent. The highest concentrations were in the lowlands, in the valleys, and on the lower slopes of the mountains. Many of the larger estates supported strong Protestant communities, usually situated close to the demesne lands. This was apparent even as late as 1901 in the disposition tenants in Dunganstown where in 15 of the 87 townlands, Protestants amounted to 50 per cent or more of the population while 45 of the townlands were 100 per cent Roman Catholic. Here the greatest concentration of Protestants was around the Acton estate at Kilmacurragh where some townlands were 100 per cent Protestant.[20] The main concentrations of Protestants in the county were as follows; in the north east of the county from Bray to Delgany and inland to Powerscourt and Calary; in the south east in the area stretching from north of Wicklow town to Arklow and inland from Rathdrum to Woodenbridge; in the extreme south, especially in the parish of Carnew, but stretching north as far as Hacketstown and Moyne, and in the west of the county from Donard and Donaghmore to Stratford-on-Slaney. All these areas had parishes in which in 1831 the Protestant population exceeded 30 per cent (Figure 20.1).

The area with the lowest relative number of Protestants was in the barony of Talbotstown Lower. The barony was just under 12 per cent

Protestant. In 1831, however, the main concentrations here were within the parishes of Donard and Dunlavin and in the town of Blessington. Outside these areas, Protestants constituted only 5 per cent of the population.

Most of Wicklow's Protestants were Episcopalians. As one might expect, however, the development of the mines accounted for the existence of modestly, strong Methodist congregations for a time in Castlemacadam and Connary while Carnew and Tinahely, within the ambit of the Fitzwilliam estate, also contained Methodist congregations of some significance. Apart from these, Wicklow town had the only other significant congregation of Methodists in mid-century.[21] Orrs' cotton factory at Stratford-on-Slaney, which according to Atkinson in 1815 employed about 1,000 of the surrounding population, a figure that is probably exaggerated, drew much of its workforce from Scotland and the North of Ireland, accounted for the county's only sizeable Presbyterian community in 1831.[22]

George O'Malley Irwin in his *Handbook to the county of Wicklow*, published in 1844, made the rather optimistic statement that the misery which had continued to press the people of Ireland to the earth in other counties was comparatively unknown in Wicklow, where the land comfortably supported those by whose labour it was rendered productive.[23] Other bench-marks by which progress could be measured, however, also indicated improvement. The county had been remarkably peaceful in the decades before the famine. All those who gave evidence to the poor law commission of 1835-36 were agreed that, apart from some protests here and there against the payment of tithes, the county was perfectly peaceable. Likewise those giving evidence to the Devon commission in 1844 said that there had been little or no agrarian outrages. According to Irwin, inebriation among the peasantry had nowhere so completely subsided as in the county of Wicklow. The testimony of those who visited Avoca in the 1840s would suggest that this was true of the miners whose phenomenal consumption of whisky had been reduced to minuscule proportions by the activities of a temperance society and the expediency of miners' wives collecting their wages.[24]

But though Wicklow may have been better off than many other counties, poverty was still endemic among the labourers and cottiers. Twenty-eight per cent of families in county Wicklow lived in one-roomed mud cabins (see table 20.4). There were concentrations of these habitations around most towns and villages, particularly in the more densely populated eastern part of the county, where the greatest numbers of landless labourers were concentrated, and around Baltinglass in the west. In some parishes one-roomed mud cabins constituted 40

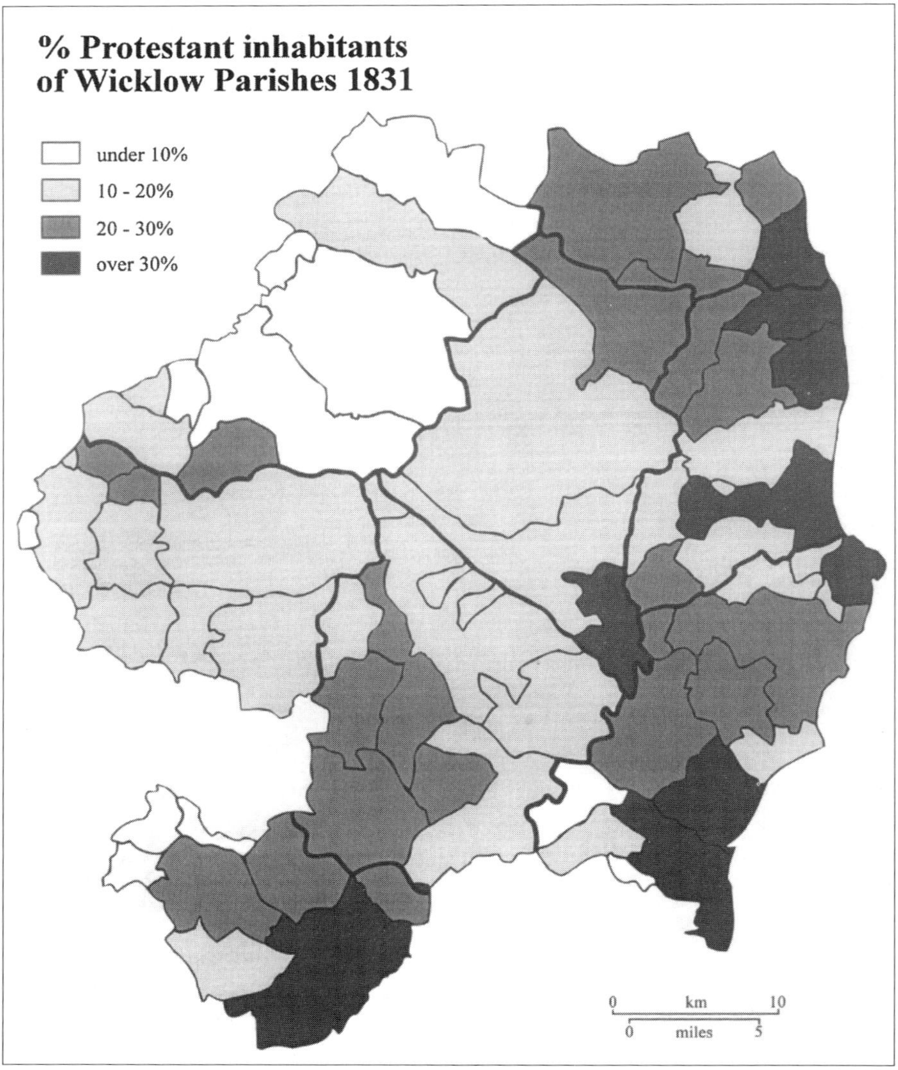

Figure 20.1 Percentage Protestant inhabitants of Wicklow parishes 1831 – shown as percentage of total inhabitants.

per cent or more of the inhabited houses. These were Ennereilly (48 per cent), Redcross (44 per cent), Kilmacanogue (44 per cent), Rathnew (42 per cent), and Arklow (40 per cent). In Ballinalea, beside Ashford, 37 of the 51 inhabited houses were one-roomed mud cabins.[25]

Poverty is difficult to measure or quantify in objective terms. Most contemporary opinion in the county suggested that things were improving in the years before the famine. The poor law commission of 1835-36 asked whether the general condition of the poor had

Table 20.4

Comparative statistics of extent of 4th class houses, population density, and numbers of agricultural and general labourers in Wicklow baronies 1831 and 1841

Barony	*Percentage 4th class houses to total no. of houses 1841*	*Density 1841*	*Percentage of ag. labs. to pop. 1831*	*Percentage of gen. labs to pop. 1831*
Arklow	30	.375	7.9	5
Ballinacor North	26	.138	9.8	.9
Ballinacor south	28	.198	7.8	.4
Newcastle	33	.314	12.9	.5
Rathdown	29	.33	10.6	1.7
Shillelagh	23	.317	8.8	1.4
Talbotstown Lower	27	.174	10	.2
Talbotstown Upper	26	.285	7.7	.4

(Source: *Census of Ireland 1831 and 1841*)

improved, deteriorated, or remained stationary since the end of the Napoleonic wars in 1815. Most respondents in county Wicklow stated that there had been a slight improvement. Mokyr's tentative analysis of these returns for the country as a whole indicates that Wicklow and Wexford were alone among Irish counties in registering more positive than negative responses.[26] However, the optimism was by no means unanimous, and it may be significant that in Wicklow the most strongly negative responses came from among the Roman Catholic clergy who were most familiar with conditions among the very poor.

There was general agreement among those who gave evidence to the poor law commission in Wicklow that a major barrier to improvement was the propensity of those with little or no means to marry young. The destitute were said to enter into marriage with the feeling that their condition could not be made worse. Parents, it was said, tried to get their daughters married off young as they would otherwise become beggars in middle age when, it was stated, most women considered themselves past field work. Another consideration inducing the poor to marry was the hope that they would thereby have children to assist them in old age. The small tenants and those who possessed anything themselves were said to be more cautious and 'seek for, and require, money, or some equivalent, with their wives'.[27] The increase in the county's population in the first half of the nineteenth century, therefore, was more pronounced among the poorer classes. As early as 1814 the rector of Arklow reported that the population of the parish, and more particularly of the town, had increased rapidly over the previous twenty years and attributed this to the improvement of the herring fishery which afforded subsistence to all who were engaged in it. Young men of eighteen or nineteen frequently married on obtaining a share in their fathers' herring boats. Their friends would unite in helping to build a thatched cabin in which they were enabled by their earnings to maintain a family that generally increased with each succeeding year.[28]

Among the labourers and cottiers, conditions were particularly hard in the summer months when the previous year's supply of potatoes began to run out. Although some of the new crop was ready for digging around the middle of August, this tended to be on the lands of the more comfortable farmers who had better land, used better seed, and had better means of fertilising the ground. The labourers' crop was usually not ready until September or even later. The period between the expiry of one crop and the digging out of the next amounted to what was described as an annual return of temporary half-famine. One witness from west Wicklow who gave evidence to the poor law commission of 1835-36 told how it was customary for the wives and children of the poorer labourers to take to the road or become beggars during these months every year. W. F. Grene, a justice of the peace at Kilranelagh, told the commission that in seasons when potatoes were scarce, the labourers were in a dreadful state of destitution, living on nettles, prassagh (wild mustard) and other weeds.[29] Daniel Kavanagh, the Catholic curate of the parish of Carnew told the Devon commission in October 1844 that the small tenantry were deteriorating in his area because of the activities of middlemen. He claimed that the poorer people were famishing and that a fund had to be raised to relieve unemployed labourers.[30]

Potatoes were universally the food of the poor. Replies to the poor law commission from 29 respondents in county Wicklow indicated that in most areas the labourers who were not boarded by the farmers ate little else for much of the year. Where the labourers were fed by their employers, their staple food was better and included butter and occasionally bacon. Eleven of the twenty-nine respondents in county Wicklow reported that herrings were also part of the diet of the poor. Oatmeal, mostly in the form of stirabout, and milk also featured. Although wheat was extensively grown on low lying lands along the coast, only among the mining communities of Castlemacadam was bread reported as being included in the diet of the poor.[31]

Famine and near-famine conditions had occurred before the 1840s. The poor law commission of 1835-36 was told of near-famine conditions in the barony of Talbotstown Upper in 1834 when but for the advance of government aid, hundreds would probably have died starvation. The situation was said to have been worse four years and seven years previously.[32] While the Irish Poor Law of 1838 savoured of a philosophy which regarded poverty as something to be discouraged rather than alleviated, and ensured that relief in the new workhouses would be the last resort of the destitute, it did at least mark the beginnings of government involvement, however inauspicious, in a co-ordinated plan of poor relief. Whatever else may have been expected of them, it can hardly have been envisaged that the workhouses in Baltinglass, Naas, Rathdown, Rathdrum and Shillelagh, which opened their doors to the destitute poor of Wicklow in 1841 and 1842 would serve to record such a rising tide of misery as that which broke upon them so soon after their establishment.[33]

The extent and course of the Famine in Wicklow

It is frequently assumed that Wicklow, along with the east of the country generally, was relatively untouched by the great famine of the 1840s. While it is true that the scale of distress did not approach that which obtained in parts of the south and west, it would be wrong to disregard the part that famine and near-famine had in shaping the county as it emerged in the second half of the nineteenth century. The accounts of contemporaries, including Elizabeth Smith of Baltiboys, James Boyle, the engineer in charge of the Board of Works' relief operations in Wicklow during 1846 and 1847, and numerous members of the clergy and gentry point to a subsistence crisis that was real and frightening. The extent of this is partly hidden from us by the massive migration to and through Dublin, which had already started before the famine, and by the efforts of those in the county who participated in schemes of relief, both official and private. They had no doubt that what Wicklow was experiencing in these years was a famine and that had they not taken action many would have died.

The first reports of the potato blight in Wicklow in 1845 were received by Dublin Castle in October and November. Bartholomew Warburton, the resident magistrate in Baltinglass, wrote on 29 October that he was not unduly concerned by the appearance of the disease, claiming that in the previous season there had been instances of disease being checked by admitting air into the pits.[34] Three days earlier Elizabeth Smith of Baltiboys noted in her diary that the blight had attacked some large conacre fields where the poor man's supply for the next nine months might, without active measures speedily taken, fail him entirely. Typically, however, she had no doubt that the situation could be overcome. Even in the worst cases of disease, the starch could be removed and mixed with wheaten flour to make bread.

Corn was abundant and, though it was rising in price because of the panic over the potato blight, she was confident it would fall. Her only cause for concern was the fear expressed by her husband that 'the want of energy of the lower orders, their idleness, and their ignorance, will prevent their setting to work to supply themselves with this change of food.'[35] The belief that even potatoes damaged by the blight could be used for food was widely held but wildly optimistic.

Initial impressions of the effects of blight varied greatly. From Kilbride near Arklow the vicar, Rev William Daly, reported on 10 November that he feared much of the potato crop was in a bad way. The earl of Wicklow, lieutenant of the county, writing from Shelton Abbey on 15 November, however, stated that a great quantity of the potatoes in the county were as yet undug, especially along the eastern shore where they were not usually dug until around Christmas. Those dug unripe had deteriorated in the pits, but those not yet dug had remained sound. On 29 November Warburton was still inclined to be dismissive of the general alarm. He estimated that potatoes were not more tainted than were generally used for feeding pigs and cattle. In fields examined he could not observe that there was cause for so general a panic. However, he said the most alarming accounts came from those who supported themselves by planting potatoes on conacre and from small farmers. Here too he was quite sceptical claiming that these people were quite careless whether or not they preserved the good potatoes, hoping they would get off paying their rent and would be supported by subscription.[36]

By January 1846 it was clear that the situation in the east of the county at least was giving rise to concern. Local relief committees had been, or were being, established in parishes throughout the county to co-ordinate relief efforts and to liaise with government. Initially the greatest distress in this first famine year seems to have been among the agricultural labourers in the east of the county and in the populous centres of Arklow and Baltinglass, where sharply rising food prices had an immediate effect. The vicar of Newtownmountkennedy reported that few parts of Ireland had suffered more from the failure of the potato crop as had his neighbourhood. In Newcastle it was estimated that one half of the potato crop had been lost, while in Killiskey the amount lost was two thirds. In the south of Wicklow around Carnew and Shillelagh the loss was less extensive, ranging from one third to one fifth. But even in areas like Hacketstown, where the loss of the potato crop had not been extensive, shortages were taking place because the available stock was being purchased for other areas and pushing prices up.[37] The main problem in this initial period, and indeed for most of the famine period in Wicklow, was not the absolute absence of food but the gap which opened up between the cost of basic foodstuffs and what the labourers could afford to pay.

In Arklow the crisis was compounded by the coincidental failure of the herring fishery, a factor which may also have contributed significantly to the distress along the whole coastal strip, affecting not only the fishermen themselves but also those who relied on herrings as a cheap supplement in their diet. By June 1846 the rector of Arklow, Henry Brownrigg, secretary of the town's relief committee, was reporting extreme distress in the town.[38]

Though the partial failure of the 1845 potato crop resulted in considerable distress, this was probably no worse in intensity than the famines which had been experienced in parts of the county several times already in the century. Indeed, the increasingly effective information gathering and relief measures which had been developing meant that something of a tried and tested formula for relief of distress came into operation and probably worked more effectively than ever before. The combined effects of local relief committees, the distribution of cheap food, public works and the new poor law, had seemed to cope adequately with the situation. The workhouses covering county Wicklow had never in this period exhausted their capacities. It has been stated that had the potato famine of 1845 lasted just one year, it would probably have merited no more than a few paragraphs in the history books.39 If the potato harvest of 1846 had been a success, the crisis of 1845-46 might simply have been remembered as one more in the series of periodic food shortages.

According to returns made by the constabulary, 14,861 acres in Wicklow were re-planted with potatoes in 1846. This was 88.1 per cent of the amount planted in the previous year. The amount re-planted varied considerably between baronies with the sharpest decline in the coastal baronies of Rathdown, Newcastle and Arklow and the least decline in Shillelagh and Ballinacor South (see table 20.5). Although the amount of conacre land in the county declined overall by one fifth the picture barony by barony was again very different. In the baronies of Arklow and Newcastle the amount of conacre land re-planted in 1846 was considerably less than it had been in 1845 while in Shillelagh and Ballinacor South it had actually increased.[40]

It is likely that these figures indicate the areas worst hit by the failure in 1845, both in terms of actual crop loss and in terms of fall-out among the cottiers and smallholders unable to re-plant. It is significant that the baronies which experienced the sharpest reduction in land re-planted after the first famine winter were those which had the highest proportions of agricultural labourers.

The renewed appearance of the blight, this time resulting in the

Table 20.5

Extent of land planted with potatoes and conacre land in Wicklow 1845-46

Barony	*No of acres planted with potatoes 1845*	*% of potato land let in conacre 1845*	*No. of acres planted with potatoes 1846*	*Amount planted in 1846 as % of that planted in 1845*	*% of potato land let in conacre 1846*
Arklow	2,469	12.2	2,054	83.2	6.7
Ballinacor North	1,714	_	1,583	92.4	_
Ballinacor South	2,759	3.2	2,606	94.5	4.8
Newcastle	2,268	8.3	1,790	79	6
Rathdown	804	3.1	585	72.7	3.2
Shillelagh	2,272	2.3	2,186	96.2	4.3
Talbotstown Lower	1,611	11	1,458	90.5	10.7
Talbotstown Upper	2,974	13.3	2,599	87.4	10.7
Total	16,871	7.3	14,861	88.1	6.6

(Source: NAI, Relief Commission Papers, RLF COM lV/2, constabulary returns for county Wicklow)

complete destruction of the potato crop, and the response of government to it, turned the crisis of 1845-46 into a disaster in 1846-47. In Wicklow, despite the fact that statistical evidence points to a prolonged period of excess death and distress over the entire period from 1846 to 1850, it was the winter of 1846-47 which was remembered by those who lived through it as the famine period. Many contemporaries referred to the famine as the famine of 1847.

The destruction of the potato crop in 1846 came suddenly. Many contemporaries vividly recalled the speed with which it happened. Fr John Gowan, the curate in Glendalough, dated the appearance of the blight in his area precisely to 19 July 1846:

> It was a very warm day. I was descending the mountains going towards the seaside about 3 o'clock on that day when I saw a thick white fog gradually creeping up the sides of the hills. When I entered it I was pained with the cold. I at once feared some great disaster. The next morning, when I travelled about in discharge of my duty, I found the whole potato crop everywhere blighted. The leaves were blackened and hanging loosely on their stems, and a disagreeable odour filled the air.[41]

By August the potato disease had appeared in every electoral division of every poor law union in the county.[42] From Ashford, Arthur Stanley

Bride, secretary of the local relief committee, wrote on 6 August that the people were digging up their potatoes and disposing of them as quickly as they could, fearing to keep them over. This, he thought, would result in the potato market being well supplied and cheap for the moment but the wholesomeness of this food worried him. He also reported that fever was prevalent in the Ashford region and was on the increase.[43]

August also marked the scaling down of the relief commission which had co-ordinated the government's relief policy in the previous year. The main relief effort for the coming winter was to be through a renewed and closely-monitored programme of public works. Because there had been widespread complaints that landlords had personally benefited from relief works organised in the previous year, a new system for controlling and financing such schemes was introduced by the government. The funds would be provided by government in the first instance but would have to be repaid from local taxes. Before public works could commence in any barony, extraordinary presentment sessions had to be held, authorised by the lord lieutenant. Works proposed at the sessions had to win the approval of Board of Works inspectors before they could be sanctioned by the treasury. The result was considerable delay in commencing such schemes in the areas most in need of them.[44]

Early in September 1846 questionnaires were distributed to ascertain how long the potato crop would supply the labouring population with food. Extant returns to this questionnaire from Carnew, Hacketstown, Rathdrum, Tullow and Tinahely indicate that the supply was expected to last only until the end of September or middle of October. Most replied that the labouring population would not be able to subsist until the harvest season of 1847 without some form of public relief works and that no public relief works had been set in train or planned in any of these districts.[45] By the end of the month people throughout the county were clamouring for the start of relief works.

It was becoming obvious that the almost complete destruction of the harvest in areas which had not been badly hit the previous year, and the fact that many of these areas were remote from the normal channels of supply, meant that the crisis had changed not only in scale but also in its nature. For the agricultural labourers on the more densely populated lowlands, the problem would continue to be the gap between what they could afford to purchase and the cost of food. For the cottiers and smallholders on the slopes of the mountains and in the isolated glens, who had subsisted almost totally on the produce of their land, the absence of any infrastructure to provide an alternative source of food brought them to the brink of starvation and even beyond in the winter of 1846-47.

By December alarming reports were coming in from all parts of Wicklow. James Boyle, superintendent engineer for the Board of Works Relief Department in county Wicklow, graphically charted the deepening crisis.[46] The towns of Baltinglass and Dunlavin had almost completely exhausted their supplies. In Wicklow town there were scarcely provisions for one week. Public works had been started there and 620 people were employed on them. A special presentment session was to be held in the town on 18 December but he estimated that it would require £3,400 to provide relief works for the people of the town alone for three months, whereas the annual taxes collected from the entire electoral division of Arklow was only £3,000-£4,000.

Boyle's report on conditions in the town and neighbourhood of Arklow was made on 17 December. Relief works were employing 650 in the town and its environs. Due to the absence of a suitable harbour or landing place, Arklow was dependent for its supply of food on the towns of Wicklow and Enniscorthy. Although Enniscorthy was the more remote, he thought it the more desirable place from which to supply Arklow as in Wicklow the supply was said to be in the hands of one or two individuals who owned the mills and who were in every sense monopolists. He estimated that there was not enough food in the town to feed its population for four days and warned of what would happen if there were a fall of snow heavy enough to disrupt or delay communications. In the rural district there was comparatively little food. Such stocks of grain as had been grown had either been consumed in place of potatoes or had been sold to pay rents. In travelling through the country he had been struck by the absence of corn stacks and still more by the absence of field labour. Seed was being sold off by the farmers, some from a feeling of insecurity, others from a desire to avoid having the appearance of the means of paying rent. Large landowners were being urged by their loyal servants to sell off their grain for fear of it being plundered. No preparations were being made for the following year's crop and not one third of the usual quantity of ground was being tilled or sown. Only towards the north and north-east of the county was there any indication that farmers were preparing for the future.

Other reports from James Boyle, which followed in quick succession, recorded the worsening conditions. Carts which had been sent from Arklow to Enniscorthy for meal returned empty because people there would not allow any further transport of food towards county Wicklow. On the evening of 17 December the Avoca mills which had supplied the mine workers ran out of meal. Destitution had spread from the cottiers to reach the small farmers of from one to six acres and was rapidly overtaking those who held even bigger farms. Wicklow had been slow to commence public works and by the middle of December, despite the obvious distress, only 1,225 people were employed on the public works in the county, fewer than in any other county in Ireland outside Ulster.[47]

The situation in the county continued to worsen in 1847. One measure of the level of distress is the extent to which the workhouses, the last resort of the destitute, were filling up. From the middle of November the workhouses covering the county which had not filled in the previous year, or indeed ever before, began to report that they had reached capacity. Baltinglass was reported full on 14 November, Rathdrum on 5 December, Rathdown on 12 December, Naas and Shillelagh on 18 January.[48] By the middle of January the numbers employed in the public works in the south and west of the county had risen above five thousand. James Boyle summarised a tour which he made during the second and third weeks of January when he travelled nearly 190 miles through the baronies of Upper and Lower Talbotstown, Ballinacor South, Shillelagh and Arklow. Many of the public works were over-crowded. On one 2½-mile stretch of road near Tinahely, 570 men were working. In the Barony of Ballinacor south one tenth of the population was employed on the public works. In Tinahely itself there were scarcely two days' provisions. The same was true for the other principal towns. Dunlavin and Carnew had only three days' provisions. Baltinglass and Arklow were equally destitute. To these towns thousands of labourers employed on the public works resorted on pay nights to purchase food for the ensuing week. With food prices continuing to climb relentlessly, the pay of one shilling per day for those on the public works was no longer sufficient to feed themselves and their families. Boyle was struck by the appearance of young men who when they joined the relief works a few weeks previously had a stout appearance but were now being seen to faint from hunger. Many of those whom he had known he could now scarcely recognise. Dysentery and dropsy were becoming very prevalent and dropsy, in particular, becoming more frequently fatal. Three days later Boyle again reported from Arklow, dwelling particularly on the scarcity of food at Tinahely. Tinahely the capital of a great barony, including some of the wildest and poorest glens and districts, was dependent for its food supply on Carlow and Enniscorthy. In turn what he termed the miserable district and town of Hacketstown relied in great measure on Tinahely. He again expressed fears for what might happen if a heavy fall of snow were to interrupt traffic between Wicklow and the supply centres of Carlow and Enniscorthy.

The snow storm which had been dreaded for so long came on the night of 6 February and the following morning, isolating large parts of the county. James Boyle reported on 10 February from Arklow that the district was covered with eight inches to five feet of snow and that there had been several deaths from hunger. In the mountainous region around Sheeanna, where one of Boyle's assistants, Lieut. Anderson, had been stranded while attempting to cross from Rathdrum to Tinahely, there were reports, reminiscent of those from the south and west of Ireland, that whole families had simply taken to their beds in resignation.[49]

Bowing to the inevitable, the government had issued instructions to relief committees in December for the establishment of soup kitchens, and in January a widespread scheme of relief, using soup kitchens, was put in train. In the towns and more populous areas of Wicklow soup kitchens had been established before the snowstorm. Seven hundred families were being relieved from the soup kitchen in Arklow. Had it not been for this, it was believed many people would by then have perished.[50] A soup kitchen had also been established in Wicklow town from where the secretary of the relief committee, James M. Barry, reported at the end of January that 471 families, numbering 2,277 persons, were receiving relief.[51]

From Ashford, Arthur Stanley Bride of Broomfield wrote on 12 February that many were starving and he claimed that if the bad weather continued they would have in this lovely part of the country a charnel house too frightful to contemplate ... Some think that such distress could not exist so close to Dublin. Let those that doubt come here.[52]

Boyle penned an alarming report from Arklow on 25 February stating that 30 men who had been on the public works had died, some actually on the work, some returning from it. He was perplexed by the fact that the labourers were refusing to leave the public works and accept agricultural work which by now was being offered by some of the farmers and stated that no labourer would, if he could avoid it, accept employment in preparing the food of another year. He was convinced that some sort of organisation was afoot among the labourers in the south of the county especially in the barony of Ballinacor south, close to the Wexford border, to prevent farmers taking men from the public works. He was equally puzzled by the fact that despite the presence of recruiting parties in Baltinglass and Arklow, which he termed the two great seats of misery in Wicklow, scarcely a man had enlisted. All looked forward to better times resulting from some great event which they did not seem to comprehend. He believed the situation in and around the town of Baltinglass to be especially critical. There were 500 men employed on the public works in this area but only 200 of them would receive employment in agriculture:

> They are generally speaking a most dangerous and inflammable community, chiefly consisting of the rejected from other districts and counties, bound by no ties of connexion or character, living on a property where there is neither a resident landlord nor agent.

In the baronies of Shillelagh and Ballinacor south, where there were 2,903 men employed on the relief works, he reported that the mortality was great and rapidly increasing.[53]

Boyle's fears were echoed on 12 March by Daniel McCoy, assistant engineer in the Board of Works Relief Department, who described conditions in the districts of Tinoran, Baltinglass, Kiltegan and Rathdangan. He said that many of the small farmers were positively starving and there was not one third of the land in the district planted. The labourers and the small farmers were in the most awful condition.[54]

By the beginning of March 1847 the numbers employed on public relief works in Wicklow had reached a peak of 6,678 or 5.29 per cent of the county's population.[55] In order to force labourers back into agricultural work for the spring and summer, a decision had been taken to close down the public works. This was to begin with an immediate reduction of 20 per cent from 20 March with the rest to follow by 1 May.[56] Such a blunt instrument caused widespread panic. Arthur Stanley Bride wrote from Ashford on 19 March to report that he had taken 20 per cent of the labourers off the public works as instructed. The following day he noted that those laid off were walking starving through the country. The workhouse in Rathdrum was full with a surplus of 242. The following week, 26 March, Bride observed that all the remaining men had been dismissed from the public works. As he wrote nearly 200 were at his door imploring relief and, he claimed, few know the destitution and misery prevailing there so close to the seat of government.[57]

By the middle of March, however, it seems that the nadir had been passed. Although destitution would continue to prevail among the labourers and small farmers, the establishment of food depots by the British Association at Arklow and Wicklow and in the west had ensured that food supplies, however meagre, were getting through. Arklow was certainly beginning to get through the worst. Fr James Redmond, the parish priest, gave a peculiarly exultant account of the situation in the area in three letters which he wrote in mid-March 1847. He stated that of ten thousand people only two had died in the previous week, one a farmer, the other a townsman whom, he claimed, had been too proud or too indolent to take the soup: 'Two persons in seven days in time of Famine die out of ten thousand! Blessed be the God of Heaven.'

In the previous six weeks he estimated that 30 members of his flock, young and old had died. As far as he was aware, none of these had been between 15 and 60 years of age. Although the soup kitchens had greatly alleviated the situation in Arklow, there were problems. Those in outlying area such as Ballycoog and Johnstown were having to travel long distances in a weakened state to obtain their food. In addition, there seems to have been considerable resentment at the fact that relief by means of public works was being substituted by soup kitchens, making the poor objects of charity. A boiler of soup had been spoiled at Coolgreaney. It is clear from Redmond's reaction that this was an act of sabotage directed against the new, and what was perceived to be demeaning, form of relief.[58]

Some indication of the extent of destitution in co. Wicklow at this time can be gauged from the figures compiled by the relief commissioners in respect of people who were supplied with food rations in the spring and summer of 1847 (table 20.6).

Table 20.6

Numbers supplied with food rations in each Poor Law Union Spring and Summer 1847

Union	*Maximum number of persons supplied with food on any one day*	*Proportion per cent. to the population of persons relieved*
Baltinglass	6,450	15.9
Naas	12,931	24.8
Rathdown	5,839	13.2
Rathdrum	12,365	21.8
Shillelagh	7,201	20.7

Within these unions individual electoral divisions had higher percentages of the population on relief. Rathdrum, with 48 per cent on relief, was the highest in Wicklow, followed closely by Delgany with 47 per cent. Other electoral divisions with over 30 per cent receiving relief were Arklow (35 per cent), Ballymore-Eustace (34 per cent) and Dunganstown (31 per cent).[59]

There are various indications that conditions had improved throughout the county by the summer of 1847. From Arklow, Captain Samuel Hore wrote on 3 August to the Central Relief Committee of the Society of Friends to report a remarkable improvement among the fishermen. Financial assistance provided by the Quakers in June had allowed 161 nets to be released from pawn. Many families which had been all but destitute were now in comparative comfort. By November a large proportion of those whose nets had been released had a surplus for the use of their families for the coming winter.[60] There were also many contrary indications of continuing destitution, however, with roads throughout the county thronged by destitute paupers, some of them dying of fever.[61]

Several sources point to 1847 as being the worst year of famine in Wicklow. The number of deaths recorded in the county for that year, at 2,776, was the highest for any year in the period. The crime statistics also showed a sharp increase in crimes against property. Lieut. Anderson, the commissariat's inspecting officer for county Wicklow reported in his journal for the week ending 16 January 1847 that sheep stealing was daily becoming more frequent and that several outrages of a more serious nature had occurred in his neighbourhood.[62] In Baltiboys, Elizabeth Smith recorded that her neighbour, John Hornidge, who had insisted in going around armed like a bandit because of the dangerous times, had shot himself accidentally, and, as it turned out, fatally.[63] The effect of the crisis in increasing crimes against property, clearly famine-related offences, is strikingly apparent in the official statistics. The vast majority of recorded crimes in the county during the years 1846 to 1850 involved cattle and sheep stealing and these reached a peak in 1847.[64] One of the resident magistrates, Bartholomew Warburton, observed from Tinahely on the quarter sessions in April 1847 that there had been nearly double the number of cases of any other sessions since he had been in the county.[65] In July 1847, following the summer quarter sessions for the county, he reported from Bray that the number of convictions had been unprecedented. He stated that the magistrates had felt obliged to meet the increase in crime by exemplary punishments. At the spring quarter sessions they had tried using more lenient punishments but this had not had the desired effect.[66] By 1849 a more concerned Warburton, reporting from the summer quarter sessions observed that he had never experienced so fearful a calendar since he came to the county, with nine crimes out of ten under the heading of larceny:

> The greater number of cases in the other divisions of the county principally arose from robberies committed in the several workhouses with a view of getting sent to gaol where they are better fed and also by persons not admitted to the workhouse that they might be sent to gaol.[67]

Despite the increase in crimes against property and the alarm of the resident magistrates, the often repeated fears about a more general breakdown in order did not materialise. There were no major disturbances and, despite reported cases of intimidation against farmers, who attempted to take men off the public works, the overwhelming demeanour of the county remained peaceful. Landlords who wrote to the relief commission expressed surprise at the docility of their labourers.

Deaths

According to the figures compiled for the 1851 census, deaths in the decade 1841-51 in Wicklow amounted to 16,930. The pattern over these years is shown in Table 20.7.

Clearly in order to make sense of these figures one must try to isolate the deaths which would normally have occurred in any year from those caused by famine and its attendant diseases. A glance at the statistics seems to show that the annual death rate in Wicklow more than doubled during the worst of the famine years. However, civil registration of deaths was not introduced in Ireland until 1864 and the figures compiled for the census were compiled retrospectively. It is likely that deaths in the pre-famine years are under-estimated. Mokyr has put the average annual excess death rate in Wicklow during the years 1846-51 at between 14.6 and 10.8 per thousand of the population. This was higher than in the neighbouring counties of Carlow, Wexford, Kildare and Dublin but only a fraction of the excess death rate in the south and west of Ireland. Mayo, which had the highest excess death rate of all, was more that five times greater then Wicklow.[69] Moreover, the extent to which the effects of famine can be deduced from these figures depends on whether deaths from contagious diseases are regarded as a direct consequence of famine. Of the 16,930 recorded

Table 20.7

Total of deaths county Wicklow in each year from 1841 to 1851[68]

Year	*Deaths (Ireland)*	*Deaths (Leinster)*	*Deaths (Wicklow)*
1841 (208 days)	16,907	5,919	287
1842	68,732	20,734	1,098
1843	70,499	21,557	1,168
1844	75,055	22,942	1,150
1845	86,900	25,387	1,275
1846	122,889	33,402	1,630
1847	249,335	59,208	2,776
1848	208,252	50,536	2,426
1849	240,797	60,360	2,264
1850	164,093	42,994	2,244
1851 (80 days)	46,261	12,271	612
Total 1841-51	1,349,720	355,310	16,930

deaths in county Wicklow only 29 were ascribed to actual starvation. However it is clear from the reports of contemporaries that there were many famine-related deaths, particularly in the winter of 1846-47, which, while not solely due to actual starvation, were hastened by hunger. The most common causes of death were consumption (2,796 deaths) infirmity, debility and old age (2,730), fever (2,172), and marasmus or wasting (1,175). The first three were common causes of death in normal years but took a higher toll in the years 1847-50 in a population weakened by malnutrition. Fever was more closely related to the spread of famine and was documented in Wicklow at an early stage in 1846. Returns from the dispensaries at Redcross, Dunganstown and Annamoe, and from the medical inspector of Wicklow Fever Hospital and Gaol published in March 1846 reported fever prevalent in all these areas and attributed it to the consumption of diseased potatoes and poor food. It was at its most severe in the year 1847.

Unlike many parts of Ireland, Wicklow escaped lightly from cholera. Overall in the ten year period there were 98 deaths from cholera in the county. Of these 68 occurred in Bray during the epidemic of 1849. Elizabeth Smith recorded two deaths in the mountains near Baltiboys, while at Naas there was a serious outbreak with several fatalities occurring in the workhouse. Neither Wicklow town nor Arklow had any recorded cases of cholera in the entire period 1846-50.[70]

Emigration

While Wicklow may have experienced a small number of famine and famine-related deaths, it seems for a time to have experienced a high rate of emigration. Already before the Famine, assisted emigration had been used to clear uneconomic holdings on the Fitzwilliam estate.[71] Pre-famine emigration tended to come not from among those who were reduced to destitution but from those who could afford the fare. The poor law commission of 1835-36 had been told that emigration had declined in the previous five years because of a want of means.[72] From 1847 many of the smallholders who could manage to scrape together the funds, began to emigrate, some leaving large arrears of rent in their wake. This process accelerated through 1848 and 1849 and seemed to contemporary observers to have become a torrent. Elizabeth Smith was among those who gave financial assistance to tenants wishing to emigrate and wrote of quantities going to America even in the unseasonable month of November 1848. In April 1850 she wrote that:

> ... there are very few boys left on our side of the country; there will be few men soon for they are pouring out in shoals to America. Crowds upon crowds swarm along the roads, along the

> bye roads, following carts with their trunks and other property. We have forty children as yet in the girls' school; but I don't really think there will be half that number by Autumn.

In October 1850 she described the numbers gone to America as countless.[73]

The level of emigration from Wicklow in these years is not apparent from official statistics, however. Comprehensive information on emigration from Irish counties began to be collected only in 1851 when rates had declined. According to the official statistics, 8,668 people emigrated from county Wicklow to places outside the United Kingdom in the period 1851-56.[74] This represented 8.75 per cent of the county's population in 1851 but was less than the rate of emigration for Leinster as a whole (which in any case would have been distorted by the peculiar circumstances of Dublin). It is almost certain, however, that emigration from Wicklow during the famine years was at a much higher rate. The largest scheme of privately-assisted emigration in the county was from the Fitzwilliam property and here records exist for the famine period. About 850 families on the Fitzwilliam estate were helped to emigrate in the years 1847-56 and the records show that the overwhelming majority of these emigrated in the period 1847-51, before they would have been recorded in official statistics.[75] Emigration from this estate was more intensive and better organised than from other parts of the county and therefore perhaps not typical, but some indication may be obtained from its relative disposition pre- and post-1851 as to trends generally in this period. Apart from the assisted emigration from the Fitzwilliam estate, most emigration from county Wicklow involved individuals or individual families rather than large organised groups. However, a large proportion of the 965 assisted emigrants from Irish workhouses in 1848-49 came from Wicklow[76] while Fr Thomas Hore led a mass exodus of parishioners from Whitechurch (Tinahely) and Killaveny aboard a chartered ship to found a colony in Arkansas in 1850.[77]

Migration to Dublin must also have played a significant role in helping to dilute the effect of famine in Wicklow. There were reports in 1847 of gangs from 'the mountainous districts of Dublin and Wicklow' wandering around the suburbs of the capital to the great alarm of the residents, and there is evidence that a large proportion of those involved in food riots in Dublin had drifted in from county Wicklow. Of eight people arrested following one bread riot in Dublin in January 1847, two were from county Wicklow.[78] The numbers of Wicklow-born people living in Dublin increased by over 58 per cent between 1841 and 1851. By 1851 more than a fifth of all Wicklow-born people lived in Dublin.[79]

Post-famine demographic and agricultural trends

Emigration obviously contributed to the overall decline in the population of the county between 1841 and 1851. Wicklow's population, which had been rising up to 1841, declined by 21.5 per cent over the next ten years. This was double the rate of decline in Wexford, about one-third greater than Kildare, and about equal to Carlow. It may be misleading to ascribe the decline entirely to the effects of the famine and emigration. Evidence from the Trinity College estates, which occupied 21 townlands in Wicklow and on which a special census was taken in 1843, shows that there had been an actual decline amounting to 13.75 per cent in its population between 1841 and 1843. There is also evidence in these records that fertility had begun to decline in the five years prior to 1843.[80] This would have been very much in line with what witnesses in Wicklow the poor law enquiry in 1835-36 and the Devon commission in 1844. There had been concerted efforts by landlords and clergymen of all denominations in these years to discourage people from marrying without means.

The decline in population was to continue well into the twentieth century. Between 1841 and 1951 the population of Wicklow more than halved. Between 1841 and 1861 the county's population declined by 31 per cent. Here, however, countywide statistics are deceptive. The rate of decline varied greatly within the county with the greatest decline in the south west. While the population of Shillelagh, Talbotstown Upper and Ballinacor south almost halved between 1841 and 1861, Arklow, Rathdown and Ballinacor North lost one-fifth or less (see table 20.8).[81] It is clear, however, that other factors must be taken into account in assessing these figures. The slight increase in the barony of Rathdown between 1851 and 1861, for instance, reflects the rapid expansion of Bray following the extension of the railway and disguises decline in other parts of the barony.

Table 20.8

Population decline in Wicklow baronies 1841-61

Barony	*Pop. 1841*	*Pop. 1851*	*% decline 1841-51*	*Pop. 1861*	*% decline 1841-61*
Arklow	25,263	21,919	13	20,444	19
Ballinacor North	10,196	9,469	7	8,192	20
Ballinacor south	15,491	11,046	29	8,806	43
Newcastle	16,444	12,794	22	11,760	28
Rathdown	11,423	9,500	17	9,614	16
Shillelagh	14,057	10,326	27	7,773	45
Talbotstown Lower	14,638	11,437	22	9,916	32
Talbotstown Upper	18,631	124,87	33	9,946	47

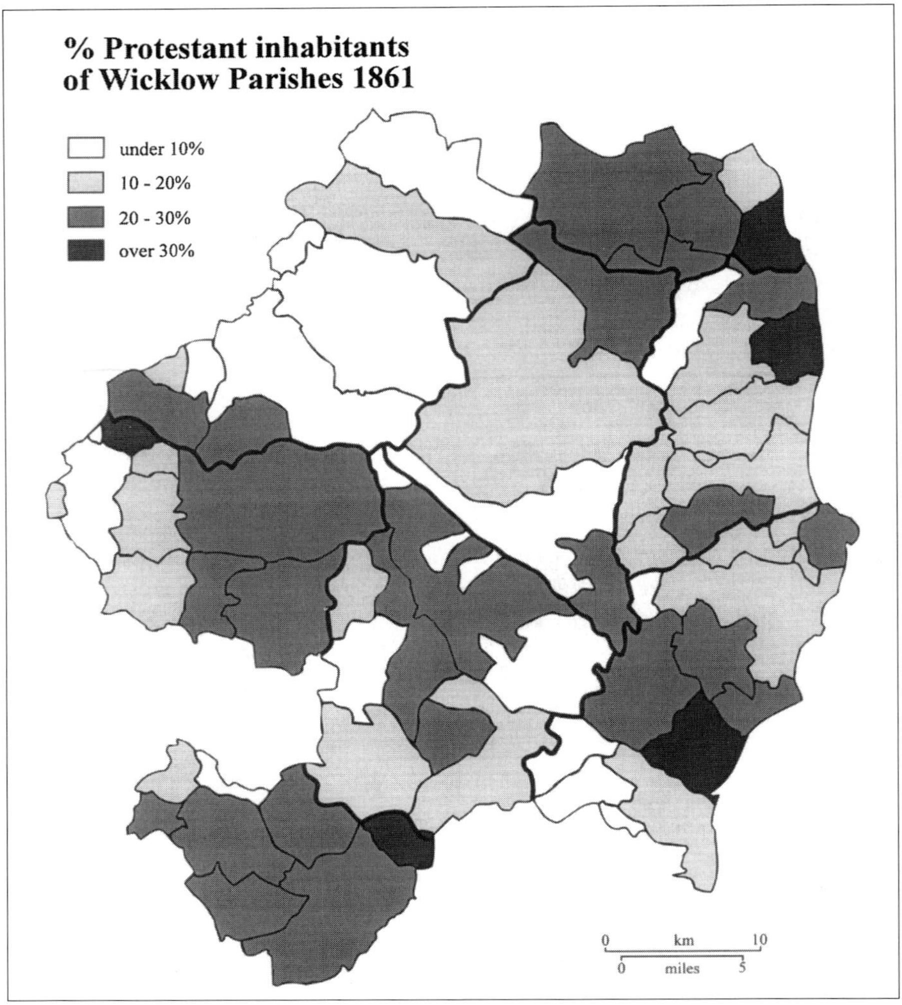

Figure 20.2 Percentage Protestant inhabitants of Wicklow parishes 1861 – shown as percentage of total inhabitants.

Population decline was also unevenly spread among social groups and religious denominations. The decline in population affected Catholics more than Protestants, though this varied from place to place. Although the overall proportions remained fairly constant throughout the century, there were great variations within the county (see figs 20.2-20.3). The main towns, with the exception of Bray, experienced a sharp decline in their Protestant populations between 1831 and 1901. A large proportion of the Protestant artisan class disappeared from areas of county Wicklow over the course of the century. The failure of woollen and cotton manufactories in Greenan, Glenmalure and Stratford-on-Slaney led to a drastic

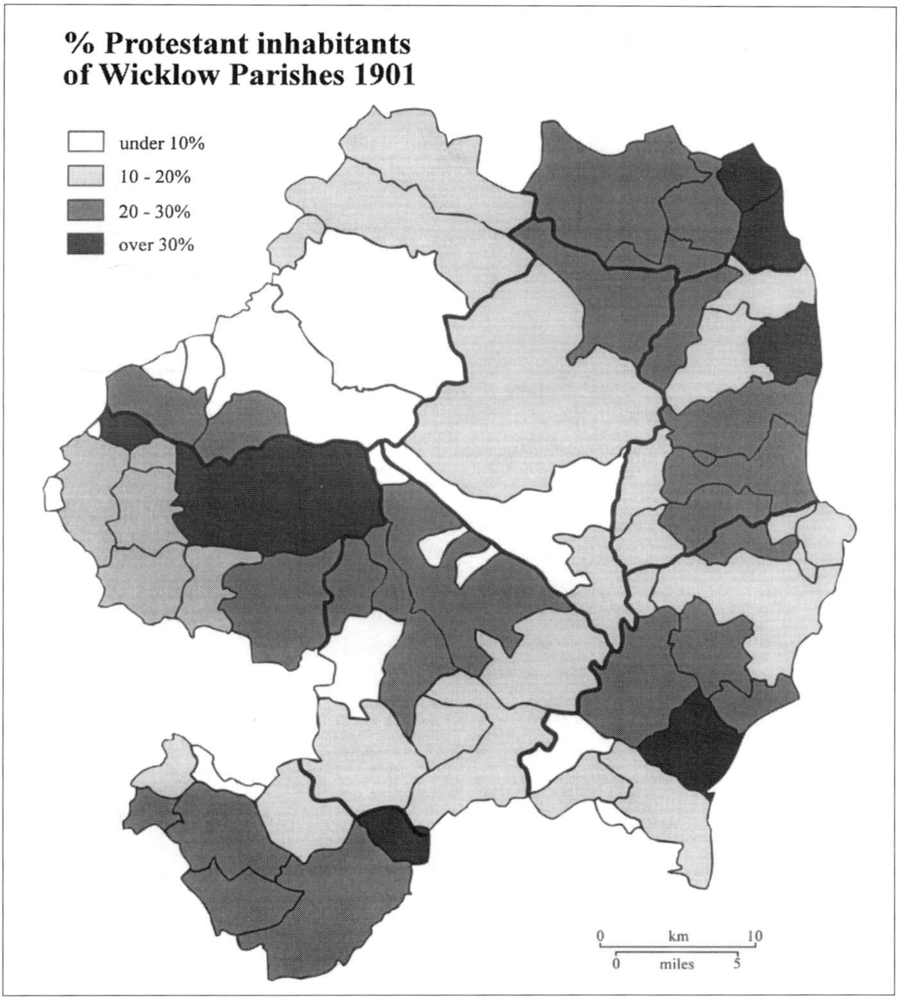

Figure 20.3 Percentage Protestant inhabitants of Wicklow parishes 1901 – shown as percentage of total inhabitants.

decline in the Protestant population of these villages and towns. Many of the mining communities of Glenmalure, Glendasan, Kilmacoo and Connary had come from Wales and south-west of England and such communities proved to be remarkably transitory. When the mines declined entire communities vanished leaving less trace on the social landscape than the mine works had on the physical. In rural areas, on the other hand, strong Protestant farming communities survived intact and, with the overall decline in population, strengthened in relative terms.[82]

This was very evident in the parish of Donaghmore where the population halved between 1831 and 1861, and halved again between

1861 and 1901. Here the rate of decrease was much greater among Catholics than among Protestants. In relative terms the Protestant population of Donaghmore increased from 19 per cent to 36 per cent between 1831 and 1901. In the civil parish of Ballinacor between 1831 and 1901 the Catholic population declined by over two thirds while the decline in the Protestant population was just under one half. In contrast, the neighbouring parish of Rathdrum, containing at the beginning of the century the strongly Protestant town of Rathdrum, had in 1901 less than a third of its Protestant population of seventy years before while the Catholic population remained almost stable. In Knockrath which in 1831 had contained the flourishing mines of Glenmalure, a mere one eighth of the Protestant population of seventy years before was represented in 1901 while the parish had managed to retain 37 per cent of its Catholic inhabitants.[83]

The survival of stable and long-established Protestant farming communities in some areas, whilst in neighbouring areas communities of artisans, miners and tradespeople disappeared, produced some striking contrasts in the demographic landscape of the county by the end of the century. In the Glen of Imaal, the electoral district of Imaal South which had a population of 351 in 1901, was more than 50 per cent Protestant while just to the North the electoral division of Luglass contained 280 Catholics but not a single Protestant. On the other side of the mountains the electoral division of Calary, comprising the two townlands of Ballinastoe and Glasnamullen and with a population of 254, was 58 per cent Protestant while the neighbouring electoral division of Togher, containing most of Roundwood village and the townlands north of it and with a population of 464, was 96 per cent Catholic.

In the north east of the county, the rapid growth of Bray and Greystones in the latter half of the century due to the development of the railway network saw the development of strong Protestant communities. Greystones, in particular, witnessed the extraordinary phenomenon of the growth of a new town which was overwhelmingly Protestant, uniquely so for a town outside Ulster. A mere hamlet in 1841, by 1861 it was over 70 per cent Protestant and by 1926 the town had the highest percentage of Protestants of any town in Saorstát Éireann with 57.9 per cent.

By 1861 the cotton works at Stratford had long since gone and of the 135-strong Presbyterian congregation of thirty years before, not a single person remained. Between the decline of Stratford and the growth of Bray and Greystones towards the end of the century, both of which also attracted strong Presbyterian congregations, the Kilpedder Witness, which flowered for a brief period on the Clarke estate in the 1850s was the only significant community of Presbyterians in the county.[84]

Direct comparison of pre- and post-Famine farm sizes is hampered by the use of Irish acres in the 1841 Census and statute acres in most subsequent surveys. However, the 1841 census provides some basis for comparison, while the Devon Commission, 1845, and the annual agricultural statistics from 1847 provide directly comparable data for Poor Law Unions. All show a steady decrease in the number of smallholdings (tables 20.9 and 20.10).

Many of these smallholders were among those who had emigrated. Others had become agricultural labourers. Notwithstanding the fact that many smallholders had joined their ranks, the numbers of labourers had also begun to shrink and would continue to do so for the rest of the century and beyond. As pasture replaced tillage the face of the countryside also changed, with the once familiar patchwork of corn, barley wheat and potatoes giving way to large expanses of pasture and meadow.

Table 20.9

Number of holdings of various sizes in Wicklow Poor Law Unions 1845 and 1847

Poor Law Union	*Total holdings 1845**	*Total holdings 1851**	*% decrease 1845-51*
Baltinglass	3,680	2,902	21.1
Naas	7,717	4,726	38.8
Rathdown	4,042	2,593	35.8
Rathdrum	4,621	3,466	25
Shillelagh	3,553	2,595	27
Total	23,613	16,282	31

* Including holdings less than 1 acre

Table 20.10

Number and size of holdings over 1 acre in Wicklow 1841-91

Year	*Total over 1 acre*	*More than 1 and less than 30 acres*	*Above 30 acres*	*Total acreage under crops*
1841*	9,467*	7,466*	2,001*	not available
1847	9,383	5,431	3,952	119,197
1851	8,189	4,443	3,746	127,727
1861	8,058	4,327	3,731	118,904?
1871	7,598	3,924	3,674	117,424
1881	7,282	3,631	3,651	107,433
1891	7,080	3,465	3,615	98,138
1891 as % of 1847	75.5	63.8	91.5	82.3

(Source: *Census of Ireland* 1841 and *Annual Agricultural Returns* 1847-99)

* Acreages given in the 1841 Census were Irish acres and the figures are therefore not directly comparable with those from 1847 to 1891 which were given in statute acres.

Appendix I

The food of the poor: Poor Law inquiry replies to question concerning diet

Parish and correspondent	Diet
Castlemacadam (including Redcross) Rev William Wingfield	Ordinary diet potatoes.
Castlemacadam Rev Thos Webber	Potatoes, buttermilk, oatmeal and occasionally salt herrings. The better sort of farmers give meat to their men. A good deal of meat is consumed by the miners; they might be more comfortable were the men not so fond of whiskey and the women of bread and tea.
Drumkay and Kilpoole Joseph Pim	Potatoes and milk and little else where labourers feed themselves; where farmers feed them stirabout, butter, salt herrings, perhaps a little bacon once a week.
Glenealy Joseph Dickson J.P.	Potatoes, milk or herrings if they diet themselves. Farmers give bacon and butter and potatoes.
Kilbride and Enereilly Rev M. John Mayers	Potatoes and oatmeal.
Annacurragh and Killaveney Rev Charles O'Brien	Potatoes, herrings and milk. (funds supplied by their wives or children begging).
Derrylossary Rev L.W. Hepenstal	Potatoes and stirabout and milk frequently with meat.
Derrylossary William Bookey J.P.	Potatoes, milk, butter and eggs occasionally.
Glendalough and Derrylossary Rev J. Johnson P.P.	Potatoes with poor milk.
Newcastle St George Knudson	Oatmeal and potatoes and occasionally milk.
Newcastle Rev William Archer	Potatoes, milk, salt and herrings.
Newcastle James L. Andonin J.P.	Potatoes, herrings, oatmeal and milk.
Delgany, Kilcoole and Kilmacanogue Arthur Jones J.P.	Oatmeal made into cake or stirabout and potatoes and milk.
Delgany, Kilcoole and Kilmacanogue John Dick	Potatoes, oatmeal, milk and herrings.

Parish and correspondent	Diet
Delgany, Kilcoole and Kilmacanogue Rev William Cleaver	Potatoes and meal; fish in some districts.
Kilquade and Kilmurray Rev Charles B. Kennett P.P.	Potatoes (seldom with milk), sometimes a salt herring. As to animal food, they never taste it.
Powerscourt Rev Robert Daly	Potatoes and milk with herrings and a little bacon.
Carnew Robert Chaloner	Potatoes.
Carnew Jos. Syms J.P.	Potatoes, sometimes alone, more generally with milk or herrings.
Carnew Thos de Renzy J.P.	Potatoes, sometimes with milk, sometimes with herrings, rarely without either and rare use of flesh meat.
Clonmore Rev P. Healy P.P.	When provided by themselves is of the lowest. Half of the year they live on dry potatoes and at best only procure a little buttermilk or a few herrings at certain seasons. When fed by the farmers and employed at hard work (they receive) butter each day at one of their meals and meat sometimes twice a week. If work is light generally potatoes and milk.
Ballynure Rev Thos. Taylor	Potatoes and milk.
Baltinglass Rev Henry Scott	Potatoes and milk – milk not always to be had.
Baltinglass, Ballynure, Rathbran and three parishes in Kildare Rev Daniel Lalor P.P.	Potatoes, sometimes with milk, sometimes dry.
Dunlavin and Tubber Rev M. Morgan	Potatoes! Potatoes! Potatoes! the ordinary diet, sometimes with stirabout or milk.
Granabeg and Kilbeg Rev Arthur Germaine	Labourers at their own tables potatoes and milk.
Kilranelagh and Kiltegan Rev William Scott	Potatoes, in summer with milk but not in winter, occasionally salted or fresh herrings.
Kilranelagh and Donaghmore Francis W. Greene J.P.	Three-quarters of the year potatoes with oaten meal.
Rathbran Rev Mark Lyster	Potatoes and milk.

(Source: Poor Law Commission 1836, Vol XXXI, Appendix D)

References

1. An earlier draft of parts of this article appeared in the *Wicklow Historical Society Jn.*, No. 5, 1992, under the title 'Wicklow in the Famine Years'. I am grateful to Dr. Cormac Ó Gráda of the Department of Economics, UCD, and to Dr. Mary E. Daly of the History Department, UCD, for their comments on that article.
2. *Census of Ireland, 1831*, *Census of Ireland, 1841.*
3. *Census of Ireland, 1841.*
4. The Rev. Henry Lambart Bayly, 'Statistical account of the parish of Arklow', in William Shaw Mason, *Statistical account or parochial survey of Ireland*, ii (Dublin, 1816), pp 39-40, 45, 55-57.
5. Forster to Trevelyan, 22 Feb. 1847, *Correspondence from January to March 1847 relating to the measures adopted for the relief of the distress in Ireland, commissariat series (hereafter correspondence from January to March 1897)*, pt. ii, H.C., [796], LII. 333, 1847, p. 176.
6. See Des Cowman's chapter in this volume also Des Cowman, 'Life and labour in three Irish mining communities circa 1840', *Saothar 9* (1983), pp 10-19.
7. *Census of Ireland 1831* and *Census of Ireland, 1841.*
8. *Devon Commission*, iii, p. 700.
9. *Census of Ireland, 1841.*
10. Trevelyan to Mr. S. Jones Lloyd, 26 January 1847 *Correspondence from January to March 1847*, p. 19.
11. C. Ó Gráda, *Ireland before and after the Famine. Explorations in economic history, 1800-1925* (Manchester, 1988), p. 51.
12. *Census of Ireland, 1841.*
13. *Devon Commission*, iii, p. 542.
14. *Poor inquiry* (1836), xxxiii, p. 105.
15. *Devon Commission*, iii, p. 705.
16. *Census of Ireland, 1841.* For comments on the abnormally high migration of females from Wicklow to Dublin and seasonal migration of agricultural labourers see the *Introduction to the general report*, pp xxiv-xxvii.
17. Ibid.; also T.W. Freeman, 'Land and People, *c.*1841' in *N.H.I.*, v, p. 251.
18. *First Report of the commissioners of public instruction, Ireland (hereafter First report of commissioners public instruction)*, H.C. 1835, [45] [46] xxxiii.
19. N.A.I., M 2476, Religious Census 1766, and G.O., Ms 537.
20. N.A.I., CEN 1901 Wicklow 43-45.
21. *First report of the commissioners of public instruction.*
22. Ibid. and A. Atkinson, *The Irish tourist* (Dublin, 1815), pp 226-30.
23. G. O'Malley Irwin, *The illustrated handbook to the county of Wicklow* (London, 1844).
24. Ibid.; also Des Cowman, 'Three Irish mining communities', p. 16, and R. Kane, *The industrial resources of Ireland* (Dublin, 1844, reprint Shannon, 1971), p. 407.
25. *Census of Ireland, 1841.*
26. J. Mokyr, *Why Ireland starved: a quantitative and analytical history of the Irish economy, 1800-1850* (London, 1983), p. 12, *Poor inquiry*, 1836, xxxi, supplement to app. F.
27. *Poor inquiry*, 1836, xxxiii, evidence of Rev. Daniel Lalor PP., Baltinglass.
28. Bayly, 'Parish of Arklow', pp 39-40.
29. *Poor inquiry*, 1836, xxxi, app. D, p. 48
30. *Devon Commission*, iii, pp 543-46.
31. *Poor inquiry*, 1836, xxxi, app. D, pp 146-54; *Devon Commission*, iii, p. 695.
32. *Poor inquiry*, 1836, xxxi, app. E, p. 23.

33. *Thirteenth report of the poor law commissioners* (1847). For an account or the role of the workhouses during the famine, see Eva Ó Cathaoir's chapter in this volume.
34. N.A.I., Relief commission papers, RLF COM, II/3, abstracts of incoming correspondence for county Wicklow.
35. Elizabeth Grant, *The highland lady in Ireland: journals 1840-50*, edited by P. Pelly and A. Tod (Edinburgh, 1991), pp 197-8. An earlier selection from the diaries of Elizabeth Smith (née Grant) was published under the title *The Irish journals of Elizabeth Smith, 1840-50*, edited by D. Thomson and M. McGusty (Oxford, 1980). While many of the extracts are common to both volumes, each contains material not contained in the other. Both have been used in the preparation of this essay.
36. N.A.I., RLF COM, II/3 (dates as cited in text).
37. Idem.
38. N.A.I., RLF COM, II/1/4014 (2903 attached).
39. Ó Gráda, *Ireland before and after the Famine*, p. 5.
40. N.A.I., RLF COM, IV/2, Constabulary returns of the potato crop, county Wicklow.
41. J. Gowan, 'The Irish Famine of 1847' in M. Assisi (ed.), *Sisters of the Holy Faith* (Dublin, 1967), pp 32-9
42. *Thirteenth report of the poor law commissioners* (1847).
43. N.A.I., RLF COM, ii/1/5127.
44. T.P. O'Neill, 'The organisation and administration of relief, 1845-1852' in R.D. Edwards and T.D. Williams (eds), *The Great Famine: studies in Irish history* (Dublin, 1956), p. 221; J.S. Donnelly, 'The administration of relief, 1846-7', in *N.H.I.*, v, pp 299-300.
45. N.A.I., RLF COM, II/2A (Wicklow)/5878.
46. Boyle's reports for 16 December 1846, 17 January 1847, 20 January 1847, and 25 February 1847 are contained in *Correspondence from January to March 1847*; Boyle's reports for 17 December 1846, 19 December 1846, and 10 February 1847 are contained in the Relief Commission Papers in the National Archives, RLF COM, 11/2a (Wicklow)/8462, 8633 and 10893.
47. Return showing daily average number of persons employed on public works in Ireland for week ending 19 December 1846 in *Correspondence from July 1846 to January 1847 relating to the measures adopted for the relief of distress in Ireland (Board of Works series)*, H.C., 1847, [761], p. 431.
48. *Thirteenth report of the poor law commissioners*, 1847.
49. N.A.I., RLF COM, II/2A/11008 (Wicklow).
50. Boyle report (see footnote 46).
51. N.A.I., RLF COM, II/2B/9454 (Newcastle).
52. N.A.I., RLF COM, II/2B/10782 (Newcastle).
53. Boyle reports (see footnote 46).
54. N.A.I., RLF COM, II/5/10/13868.
55. *Sixteenth report of the commissioners of public works (Ireland)*, 1847-48, Appendix R.
56. T.P. O'Neill 'Organisation and administration of relief', p. 234.
57. N.A.I. RLF COM, ii/2B/14736 and 15721½ (Newcastle).
58. Ibid., II/5/2/12.
59. *Seventh report of the relief commissioners*, 1847-48, supplementary appendix, part ii, pp 20-21.
60. Society of Friends, *Transactions during the Famine in Ireland in 1846 and 1847* (Dublin, 1852), pp 390-91.

61. See for instance letter of John Norris, Constable, Aughrim, 16 June 1847 in K. Hannigan (ed.) *The Famine: Ireland 1845-50 (facsimile documents)*, Dublin (1982).
62. *Correspondence from January to March 1847 relating to the measures adopted for the relief of distress in Ireland (Board of Works series)*, H.C., 1847, [797], p. 116.
63. Thomson and McGusty, *Journals of Elizabeth Smith*, pp 147-149.
64. See tabulated return of outrages in Wicklow 1846-50 reproduced in *Wicklow Historical Society Jn.*, i, No. 5 (1992), pp 52-53.
65. N.A.I., Outrage reports, OR, 1847/32/106.
66. N.A.I., OR 1847/32/179 and OR 1847/32/182.
67. N.A.I., OR 1849/32/103.
68. *Census of Ireland, 1851.* These statistics were recorded retrospectively on the census forms in 1851 by the relatives of those who had died. It is felt that figures for the country as a whole are an underestimate as they represent only those whose relatives survived and who remained in the country to provide the information in 1851. This factor would have been present to a greater degree in areas of greatest death and emigration. For Wicklow, given the lower rates of death and emigration in these years, the figures are probably correspondingly more reliable.
69. Mokyr, p. 267.
70. *Census of Ireland, 1851*; *Report of the commissioners of health concerning epidemics*, 1846-50 (1852).
71. *Devon Commission*, iii, p. 544.
72. *Poor inquiry*, 1836, xxxiii, p. 137.
73. Thomson and McGusty, *Journals of Elizabeth Smith*, pp 204 and 250.
74. *Commission on emigration and other population problems 1948-54*, Dublin, 1955; Kerby A. Miller, *Emigrants and Exiles: Ireland and the Irish Exodus to North America* (New York and Oxford, 1985), pp 569-79.
75. Paul Gorry, 'Index to the Coolattin Estate emigration records 1847-56' in *Journal of the West Wicklow Historical Society Jn.*, i-iii.
76. David Fitzpatrick, 'Emigration, 1801-70' in *N.H.I.*, v, p. 590. See also Eva Ó Cathaoir's chapter in this volume.
77. K. Hannigan, 'Eye-witness accounts of the Famine in County Wicklow in *Wicklow Historical Society Journal*, Vol. 1, No. 6 , 1993, pp 11-26. A full account of this enterprise in contained in Jim Rees *A Farewell to Famine* (Arklow, 1984). See also K.P. Schmitz, 'Father Thomas Hore and Wexford, Iowa' in *The Past* No. 11, 1977, and 'Passenger List of the *Ticonderoga*' in *The Past* No. 12, 1978. I am grateful to Conor O'Brien, Joan Kavanagh, and Jim Rees for bringing these articles to my attention.
78. O. Callaghan, 'A study of Dublin 1845-50: the impact of the Great Famine on the city', unpublished B.A.history dissertation, U.C.D. (1971). I am grateful to Dr. Fergus D'Arcy of the History Department, U.C.D, for bringing this dissertation to my attention.
79. *Census of Ireland, 1851.*
80. F.J. Carney, 'Pre-Famine Irish population: the evidence from the Trinity College estates' in *I.E.S.H.*, ii (1975), pp 35-45.
81. *Census of Ireland, 1861.*
82. *Census of Ireland, 1861, 1891, 1901 and 1926.* Also N.A.I. manuscript returns of 1901 census for county Wicklow.
83. Ibid.
84. Anon. *Greystones Presbyterian Church 1887-1987*, Greystones (1987).

Chapter 21

THE EVOLUTION OF FORESTRY IN COUNTY WICKLOW FROM PREHISTORY TO THE PRESENT

MARY KELLY QUINN

'This is no place for a tree' said the sour black soil,
'poor lost embryo, soon to perish
Famished, waterlogged, slowly poisoned,
Hypnum, sphagnum, heather and sedge,
These uncouth ones alone I cherish.'
But the rock said to the scarlet berry –
'Welcome, friend, here's ample for sharing;
Thrust your roots in my garnered humus,
Search my fissures, my crumbling crystals,
Food is there for your hardy rearing.'

(from *The mountain tree* by Hugh Connell)

Changes in woodland or tree cover impact greatly on the aesthetic and environmental quality of an area and on the economic and social life of its inhabitants. Wicklow is today one of Ireland's most heavily afforested counties with 18 per cent of its total area under forest, compared to the national average of 5 per cent. The forests of sitka spruce which now predominate in Wicklow are relatively young, most having been planted since the early 1920s, and are very different from the largely deciduous woodlands of earlier centuries.

The seeds of our woodlands were sown during the amelioration of climate which followed the last ice age nearly 20,000 years ago. When Mesolithic people arrived in Ireland between 9,000 and 8,000 years ago, they found a climate somewhat warmer than today, fewer peatlands and extensive deciduous woodlands. The density of the forests probably confined man to coastal regions and stretches along rivers. His hunting-gathering lifestyle would have had little impact on the landscape. Therefore, for the next two thousand years forest cover remained relatively unchanged and perhaps reached its maximum at this time.[1] In county Wicklow the remains of upland forests can still be seen in cutaway bogs such as the pine stumps which were found at Turlough Hill and south east of the television mast at Kippure, above Glencree. Some of the pine stumps, located below peat on a mineral soil, were estimated to be 4,200 years old.[2] Other pollen studies support the existence of pine and birch forest to an altitude of 460m (1,500ft) in upland Wicklow.[3] The valleys presumably had extensive cover of oak, elm, ash and hazel on fertile soils. On sandy and acidic soils there would have been a mixture of oak, pine and birch, while waterlogged soils carried sally and alder. These woodlands would have looked very different to those of today which are largely a product of eighteenth and nineteenth-century management. They were probably not dominated by oak but supported a variety of trees depending on soil conditions.[4]

Why did these forests disappear? Deteriorating climate and the arrival of Neolithic farmers (between 6,000-5,000 years ago) initiated forest decline which marked the start of a period of great change and activity in the Irish landscape.[5] In the 5,500 years since the beginning of the Neolithic period, native forest cover has declined to less than 1 per cent today (0.2 per cent represents ancient woodland). An increase in rainfall and lower temperatures led to the waterlogging of soils and the spread of blanket bog. The impact of man at this altitude appears to have been limited. Certainly there is little evidence of burning. Lowland forests were affected by farming and grazing by domestic animals. However, it is assumed that early farmers were unable to fell large areas of woodland. Instead they probably ringed the bark, killing the trees, and planted crops under the leafless canopy. The later introduction of the plough accelerated forest decline. Some authorities maintain that our treeless landscape may date back to the Bronze Age.[6] On the other hand others have suggested that, as a result of recurrent forest regeneration, the greater part of the country was still clothed in trees up the twelfth century.[7] Forest cover, however, was greatly reduced and there were also changes in its composition. Native Scots pine as well as the elm were extinct by the twelfth or thirteenth-century whereas hazel expanded, presumably into areas of cleared woodland abandoned by farmers.

Attitudes to forests and their importance to the people of ancient Ireland can be appreciated from the Brehon Laws. These essentially held that land (including woodland) was held in common by the people of the *tuath* (the people/territory ruled by a minor king). The Bretha Comaithchege (judgements of neighbourhood) arranges trees in four groups according to their economic importance.[8]

1. 'Chieftain' trees: oak (*dair*); hazel (*coll*); holly (*cuileann*); yew

(*ibur*); ash (*fuinnse, fuinnseann* or *fuinnseog*); pine (*ochtach* or *giúis*); apple (*aball*).

2. 'Common' trees: alder (*fernn*); willow (*sail*); hawthorn (*scieth*); rowan (*caerthann*); birch (*bithe*); elm (*leam*) and another (*idha*) which is not known from its Irish name.

3. 'Scrub' trees: blackthorn (*draidean* or *droigen*); elder (*trom*); white hazel (*fincoll*); aspen (*crithach*); arbutus (*caithne*); and two others not known from their Irish names, *feorus* and *crann-fir*.

4. 'Bramble' trees: fern (*raith*); bog-myrtle (*rait*); furze (*aiteand*); briar (*dris*); heath (*fraech*); ivy (*eideand*); broom (*gilcach*); gooseberry (*spin*).

The status of each tree was determined by its size and produce; the oak was deemed noble due to its size and appearance and its *meas* or mast of acorns. Substantial fines were specified for damage to trees. The fine (*dire*) for illegally cutting a branch was a yearling heifer (*dairt*). If a larger limb was cut the fine was a two year old heifer. The cost of cutting the tree at the base was a milch-cow (*bó*).[9] Woods at this time provided not just timber but a variety of food for man and his animals. Every person of the *tuath* had an equal right to the timber and produce of the wood, varying from 'the night's supply of kindling' and 'the nutgathering of every wood' to 'timber of a carriage for a corpse'.[10] *The Hermit's Song* was a poem written in seventh century Old Irish by a hermit living alone in a woodland. The wood provided shelter: 'A hiding turf, a green-barked yew is my roof,/While nearby a great oak keeps me tempest-proof'. It also provided a variety of food: 'I can pick my fruit from an apple like an inn,/Or can fill my fist where hazels shut me in.'

The written evidence for the distribution of woodland in county Wicklow is poor for the earlier period. However, it may be possible to get some appreciation of its extent from townland names, which were more or less fixed by the eighth century. McCracken cautions against the use of placenames for this purpose, stating that a townland name in itself cannot be taken as indicating that the wood survived until Tudor times.[11] At best placenames tell us of the existence of some type of tree cover at the indeterminate time when these names were fixed and no more. It is clear from the many tree-related placenames that, except for the mountain tops, large tracts of ancient woodland existed in Wicklow. Names such as *Kelshabeg, Kelshamore, Coillach, Ballynagran, Kilmore, Rosahane* and *Craobhach* describe large wooded districts. Oak apparently dominated these woodlands as confirmed by such names as *Lackandarragh, Derrybawn, Glendarragh, Knockaderry, Ballinderry* and *Tomdarragh.* The Derry river, Derry Water, Derreen river and Derrybawn river all take their names from *daireach* 'abounding in oaks'. The first two rivers flow through the famous wooded areas of Coolattin and Shillelagh. However, there were other trees in the Wicklow woods such as ash (*Coolafunshoge, Ballinafunshoge*), birch (*Bahana, Barnavay*), willow (*Corsillagh, Parknasilloge*), hazel (*Barnacoyle, Callowhill*), holly (*Cullenmore, Lugaculleen*), elder (*Troman, Trumonmore*) and yew (*Oghil, Newry* and *Newrath*). Some areas were apparently covered with woody scrub (*Knocknadrosse, Moneymeen, Rossana, Tomcoyle* and *Ruba Scolage*). Some written evidence for a wooded county in the eighth century can be extracted from St Kevin's Life which describes the valleys east and west of the mountains of the Wicklow Gap as being covered in dense deserted forest.[12] *The Irish Lives* of St Kevin narrate that when he left Glendalough, he was carried in a litter through the wood, which made way for him and that he blessed it. This is the probable origin of the name 'Hollywood'. Price suggests that the clearing of a way for the old pilgrims' road of the seventh and early eighth centuries was through the wooded areas of Slievecorragh and Scalp mountains, both close to Hollywood.[13] There is also a reference in early church records to the wooded district of Kiltagarren, which was near Lackan and Kilbeg.[14] The northern part of the ancient forest survived into the Middle Ages as the royal forest of Glencree.[15]

The Anglo-Norman invasion had important implications for woodlands in the vicinity of Dublin and Wicklow. They brought with them the idea of private ownership of the land and what stood upon it, a concept alien to Irish law.[16] Even though the Normans did not come to Ireland as conquerors, they nevertheless tried to introduce the forest laws of England.[17] During the reign of Henry II (1154-1189) the forest laws were still in full force and the passion of the Norman kings for 'the chase' reached its peak. As soon as a firm footing was obtained in Ireland, a royal forest was established. A royal forest was not necessarily a large expanse of woodland. The term forest was a loose one which was applied to an area of land, with or without trees, that was subject to forest law. The woods of Wicklow, because of their proximity to Dublin, were particularily attractive. A large proportion of land in the county came under the operation of forest laws as may be seen by the license granted by Henry II in 1229 to Luke, archbishop of Dublin, for 'the deafforestation of certain lands of that state'.[18] Land was set aside as a royal park in the valley of Glencree. At the time of the Norman invasion (1170 A.D.), the Glencree valley and its hinterland was an area of wild forest and moorland belonging to the Uí Briúin sept.[19] Pollen analysis indicates that the area was more densely wooded prior to the invasion.[20] Le Fanu, through analysis of its placenames, has described the probable boundaries of this park and its vegetation:

> a beautiful park stretching along Ballyross and the steep hill sides of Crone, up to the bald crest of Malin, and the black peaty moorland of Tonduff; diversified by the lighter green of the birches of Bahanagh and the hazels of Ballycoyle and broken here and there by the grey rocks of Ballyreagh, the green glade of Cloon, the foaming torrent of Aska Bawn, flashing down to the river forks of Ballylerane, or the white head of Knockbawn rising above the oaks of Lackandarragh.[21]

In 1244, eighty deer were sent from the royal forest at Chester to stock the king's park at Glencree. Later in 1269 the king sent a present to Eustace le Poer of twelve fallow deer from the Glencree forest. The park was apparently in close proximity to the Kilternan and Glencullen properties of the abbot and monks of St Mary's Abbey, Dublin and in 1291 the abbot was accused of hunting in the king's forest with nets, engines and greyhounds.[22] Le Fanu suggests that if *leporarii* is rightly translated 'greyhound' it would support the belief that open ground existed within the forest.[23] However, Glencree must have had good oak trees: in 1280 seven oaks were given to John de Wallop from the park at 'Glincry'. Three years later William le Devenais, keeper of the king's demesne lands, received twelve oaks and in 1285 the Dominican friars of Dublin received fifteen oaks from Glencree for their church. In 1289 the abbot and convent of St Thomas were granted twenty oaks fit for timber from the king's wood in 'Glincry' and William Burnell was given twelve oaks. Queen Eleanor, wife of Edward I, established large timber works in the valley for the purpose of providing wood for her castle, then in the process of erection at Haverford. This marked a more sweeping and systematic onslaught on the forest timber. William de Moenes (one of the family from which Rathmines derives its name) was keeper and manager of these works and a very considerable thinning of the forest must have been effected at this period. Between 1288 and 1292 pannage (the right to feed hogs on acorns) was practised at Glencree.[24]

The selling of the underwood was a profitable business. The judiciary rolls of Edward I in 1305 mark the last entry on Glencree forest and record a complaint by Thomas de Sandely, a carpenter, that he was kept for three weeks in irons in the castle of Dublin at the suit of John Mathew, the royal forester at Glencree, who charged him with stealing timber. It appears that the culprit was caught in the act but escaped and fled to Dublin where he was arrested. It seems probable that due to the withdrawal of large numbers of English from Ireland for the war in Scotland, and Edward I's expedition to Flanders, the forest had to be abandoned. The Irish advanced from their strongholds in the mountains and destroyed the park. By the sixteenth century the royal forest of Glencree had faded from memory. However, in 1597, Henry Wallop remarked that the area beside Enniskerry was full of woods and that many timbermen lived there, so some areas may have escaped destruction or were at least regenerated.[25] Pollen analysis indicates the complete disappearance of oak pollen in the early modern period: its existence in surface layers of peat coincides with the planting of oaks by the government authorities in 1853.[26]

Neeson suggests that the tradition of silviculture which is so marked a feature of modern Wicklow is derived from this period.[27] While forests were in Norman hands they were exploited for the English market. The Normans introduced resources and machinery to fell and export timber, but except for Wicklow there was no significant attempt at management.[28] At this time the Gaelic population of county Wicklow was almost exclusively confined to the wooded uplands above the 180m (600ft) contour, where pastoral activities formed the basis of their economy.[29] Uncharted dense forests were major assets for a lightly armed, highly mobile Irish army. Richard II realised that the greatest threat to the Anglo-Norman colony was the Leinster forest. In 1399 he employed five thousand people to cut a way through the forest for the royal army on its trek from the Barrow valley (stronghold of Art Mac Murrough) to the Wicklow coast.[30] From their woodland refuges Mac Murrough's men picked off stragglers at the rear of the royal army. The foolhardy expedition left Richard with a famished and very much reduced army by the time he reached the coast. Two centuries after Richard's invasion, the Wicklow forests, although less extensive, were still harbouring the Leinster clans. Some pollen evidence supports the conjecture that the violence and disruption of the Viking and Norman periods allowed some new woodland to appear on deserted farmland.[31]

Little reference is made to Irish woods during the later medieval period until the Tudor conquest in the sixteenth century reinforced the perception of forests as the strongholds of Irish 'woodkernes' as well as wolves.[32] The woods are described in the State Papers as 'a shelter for the ill-disposed' and 'the seat and nursery of rebellion'. Blackwood in county Kildare was apparently a half-way resting place for rustlers and their stolen cattle, as they roamed to and from the glens of Wicklow.[33] A piece written in the time of Elizabeth I noted that there were plenty of woods in Ireland except in Leinster, where they have been 'cut down because they harbour the Irish rebels' and now 'they are enforced in those parts, for want of fuel, to burn turves'.[34] Elizabeth ordered the destruction of woods both to deprive the Irish of shelter and to supply timber to England where there was already a shortage.[35] Glenmalure, at the time of Fiach Mac Hugh, was described as 'a valley, or combe, being in the middle of the wood, of great length between two hills ... the sides full of great and mighty trees, and full of bushments and underwoods'.[36] Later, Red Hugh O'Donnell was concealed 'in a solitary part of a dense wood' in Glenmalure after his second escape from Dublin Castle. Shillelagh was the principal abode of Feagh M'Hugh O'Byrne. It was a very large wooded area and probably the most famous on the east coast of Ireland. As early as 1444 it supplied timber for the construction of the chapel of King's College, Cambridge and Henry VIII's chapel in Westminster Abbey.[37] Later Shillelagh oak was used in the roofing of Westminster Hall in the 1660s[38] and in the building of Trinity College Dublin and St Patrick's Cathedral.[39] In the time of Charles II some of the finest timber from Shillelagh was also sent to Holland for 'the use of the Stadthouse and other buildings constructed on poles driven close together to the number of several thousand'.[40] By the beginning of the sixteenth century the Pale had been so thoroughly cleared of accessible timber that landowners were advised to compel tenants to plant trees, especially oak.[41] There is no reference to Wicklow although it is reasonable to assume that accessible timber was exploited whereas woods in the more remote areas of the county remained intact.

Intense exploitation of Irish woods by the New English occurred during the seventeenth century and this was particularly true for Wicklow. Large quantities of timber were needed for iron works, pipe-staves, ship building and bark for tanning. Very often conflict arose between the various interests. In 1609 and 1611 the council of lords directed, that 'in view of the great abundance of timber in Ireland, and the great waste thereof for pipe-staves and other minor uses as well as export, no timber in the king's woods may be used for such purposes but should be retained for navy requirements'.

It is difficult to estimate the extent of woodland in Wicklow at the beginning of the seventeenth century. The Down Survey maps of 1655 show some woodlands but only forfeited lands were surveyed and it is an incomplete record. Some woods are referred to as timber woods but many are classified as woody pastures. The density of tree cover in the latter category is unclear. Table 21.1 gives only the probable location of these woods as many of the placenames used in the Down Survey have changed or were misinterpreted by the surveyors. Price records an extract taken by W. Monck Mason from the Down Survey reference sheet of Bishop's Lordship which notes 'much wood about the two Boolies': the 'two boolies' being the townlands of Ballyknockan and Ballynastockan, which adjoin Kilbeg (*Coill beag*).[42] The Brabazon

Table 21.1

Wicklow woods referred to in The Down Survey

Name in Down Survey	*Present Name and Probable Location*	*Description*	*Size – Plantation Acres*
Fassaroe	Fassaroe	Wood	27
Oldcourt	Oldcourt	Wood	23
Killebeg	Killbeg (west Wicklow)	Arable & Woody Pasture	743
Bolenastokane	Ballynastockan	Mountain pasture & Wood	453
Bollenknockin	Ballyknockan	Mountain pasture & Wood	373
Kildalough	Glendalough area	Arable & Woody Pasture	1,680
Kellafeene	near Trooperstown	Arable & Woody Pasture	297
Castlekevin	Castlekevin	Arable & Woody Pasture	685
Tomrealan	Tomriland	Arable & Woody Pasture	790
Setrim	near Tomriland	Arable & Woody Pasture	626
Ballinecurbeg	Ballinacorbeg	Arable & Woody Pasture	137
Clonbreen/Clonbroon	near Moneystown	Wood	141
Balliheage	Ballyteige	Woody Pasture	145
Ballinatoan	Ballinatone	Arable & Woody Pasture	354
Clarogheightragh	near Clarabeg	Arable & Woody Pasture	218
Seekeene		Arable & Woody Pasture	641
Drumin	Near Delgany	Unprofitable Wood	53
Ballerogan	Ballyrogan	Wood	41
Ballimckaher	Ballymacahara	Arable & Woody Pasture	192
Kelloghter		Wood	16
Killaderry		Arable & Woody Pasture	58
Ballynamina	Baltinamina	Plantation	*c.*103

property had 200 plantation acres of wood and underwood in 1679.[43]

Rackham, using the Civil Survey of 1654-56 for three-quarters of the country, calculated a woodland cover of just 2.1 per cent. While no Civil Survey exists for Wicklow he extrapolated a figure of between 3 per cent and 4 per cent for the county.[44] Even then Wicklow appears to have had a forest cover greater than the national average. It is clear from references to woods during the seventeenth century, that there was sufficient woodland in Wicklow at the beginning of the century to support the expansion of timber-consuming industries. In 1654 there was an organised forestry department in the county with staff consisting of a wood reeve earning £100 a year, four assistants and a clerk with annual salaries of £26 and £20, respectively.[45] The names on the Hearth Money Rolls of 1669 may suggest that imported, skilled forest labour was used. Charcoal was exported from the county to south Wales in the early 1600s. A network of over fifty iron works was established in Wicklow around 1640 by an Englishman called Bacon. His daughter married a Chamney, who exploited Shillelagh timber and continued the business in the county into the next century, having managed over fifty iron works of various types.[46] Despite earlier exploitation, large areas of woodland remained at Shillelagh and it continued to be the most important timber producing region in the county. In 1608, Sir Arthur Chichester reported that the woods at Shillelagh were sufficient for the king's ships for twenty years.[47] In 1634 it was described as having an 'abundance of woods, more than many thousand acres'. Five years later Strafford estimated that if the wood were near London it would yield £50,000.[48]

The Shillelagh woods were heavily exploited for many purposes from the middle of the seventeenth century. Wentworth (or Strafford), during his term as lord lieutenant of Ireland, imposed export duties on pipe-staves but exempted himself from the regulations. In 1641, his agent was given permission to export timber from Shillelagh for 'the private advantage' of his employer.[49] In 1661, the earl of Strafford contracted with certain merchants for using the woods at Shillelagh for pipestaves.[50] A conflict arose between the individual exploitation of the woods and the demands of the crown for shipbuilding. Great quantities of timber were required for the building of navy and merchant ships which had a life span of only thirty years. Timber was consumed by the hundreds of tons. Oak, elm and beech were the main timbers used in the construction of the hull, while the masts and spars were of pine and spruce.[51] An order was made to halt the felling until the Shillelagh woods could be inspected for timber suitable for shipping and several surveys appear to have been undertaken to assess their potential value for shipbuilding. In 1670, Peter Brousdon reported that the Shillelagh woods on the Strafford estate were still extensive, being 'nine or ten miles in length'.[52] However, they were unsuitable for shipbuilding as the timber was full of defects and holes.[53] Yet, the previous year several hundred thousand staves had been sold by the earl of Strafford to a London merchant.[54] In 1671 the vast woods of the Shillelagh area were mapped by Andrew Yarranton who lamented that 'great quantities of timber lay rotting in the woods called Shelela'. He calculated that there was enough wood to make one hundred men of war and several hundred barges.[55] However, transport of the timber would be a problem: 'the mountains and the bogs have so locked them up, that they could not be brought to any sea port to be employed in the building of ships.' He proposed that the Slaney should be made navigable to enable timber to be transported to Wexford port, where he estimated that ships could be built at a fraction of their cost in England.[56] Another valuation of the Shillelagh woods was commissioned by the high court of chancery in Ireland in 1671. The total acreage returned was 3,905 with an estimated value of £10,000. The cost of exploiting this timber (felling, carriage) was estimated to be 'such as that ye profit per tunn will be so inconsiderable (if any sometimes) as not to answer the hopes of so great a sum as £10,000'.[57] Much of the biggest timber trees had been removed in 'many great falls of recent years or others stand rotten and much decayed' while there has been no 'improvement of the sapling for thirty years'. The difference of opinion probably explains why Yarranton's proposal for improved navigation of the Slaney river was never undertaken and why the trade in pipe-staves continued to be of greater importance. Strafford reputedly made huge profits from the sale of pipe staves.

Ireland in 1600 was substantially forested but by 1711 it was a net importer of timber.[58] Two centuries of merciless exploitation had ravaged the forests.[59] Timber became scarce in many parts of the country. It was decided in 1720 that timber allowances to tenants should not include even the lop or top of timber felled – a savage restriction when timber was such a vital ingredient in everyday life.[60] These harsh restrictions did little to encourage tree preservation or planting among tenants and is probably the root cause of the negative perception of trees which has persisted to recent times. Young noted:

> In conversation with gentlemen, I have found the very same gentlemen laid the destruction of timber to the common people, who they say have an aversion to a tree; at the earliest age they steal it for a walking stick, afterwards for a spade handle, later for a cart shaft and later still for a cabin rafter. That the poor do steal it I am certain, but I am clear the gentlemen of the country may thank themselves. Is it the destruction of sticks and handles that have has destroyed millions of acres? Absurdity. The worthless landlord cuts down their acres and leave them unfenced against cattle and then he has the impudence to charge the scarcity of trees to the sticks of the poor and have introduced a penalty of forty shillings on any poor man in possession of a twig.[61]

The beginning of the eighteenth century also marked the start of a period of great estate plantings for aesthetic, commercial and game management purposes. The impetus for this move may have been the political stability of the period in combination with a growing awareness of declining timber resources. As many as twenty-one parliamentary acts, aimed at preserving trees and encouraging planting were introduced between 1634 and 1785.[62] The parliamentary act of 1698 prescribed the number of trees to be planted in each county.[63] It is not clear how the figures were calculated but presumably they were based on the suitability of each county for planting. A relatively low figure of

3,250 was assigned to Wicklow (similar to the figures for Leitrim and Carlow).

Wicklow's timber resources were apparently adequate to supply a variety of industries in the eighteenth century and well into the first half of the nineteenth century. The planting and management of woodlands were undertaken in many parts of the county. The general availability of turf for fuel may have alleviated tenants' timber requirements. The best woodland in eighteenth-century Wicklow was to be found in the east, especially in the valleys of the Avonmore, Avonbeg and Avoca rivers; these provided revenue for the many large estates in the area. East Wicklow's deeply incised valleys, sculptured during the ice age, were incorporated into the landscaping of the demesnes. Soils in the east of the county tend to be more fertile than their counterparts in similar locations in the west[64] and this was an added bonus for settlers. The mountains were sometimes cultivated to altitudes as high as 350m (1,000 ft).[65] A survey of the mountain lands of Butterhill and Ballydonnel noted that the greater part had been cultivated at some time in the past.[66] The 1700s and 1800s were also marked by the creation of magnificent gardens. The ideal landscape at that time was one where 'art and nature in just union reign'.[67] This approach suited Ireland where a mild moist climate results in plant growth which quickly outstrips attempts to tame it. 'In the French garden nature is tamed by art but in the gardens of Ireland nature reigns supreme'.[68] The dramatic landscape of Wicklow provided a magnificent backdrop to its many gardens. Mountains frame them or form a focal point as in the case of the Sugarloaf mountain and Powerscourt gardens. Kilruddery, one of Ireland's oldest gardens, was laid out in a formal design at the end of the seventeenth century. The later gardens of Powerscourt, Bellevue, Rossana, Mount Usher and Luggala were more natural in style and involved extensive planting of trees and shrubs, many of them exotic. Many new tree species were introduced to the country at this time. Before the end of the seventeenth century Spanish chestnut, Scots pine, stone pine, lime, walnut, hornbeam, plane as well as English and Dutch elm had been introduced. The following century saw the introduction of various pines, silver fir, horse-chestnut, American red oak and Turkey oak. Hayes in 1794 commented on fine mature exotic trees, some of which must have been planted in the preceding century. There were very large sycamores in Shillelagh, Rathdrum and Kilmacurra. An avenue of Spanish chestnuts, 110 years old, was felled at Dunganstown in 1793. There were also large Spanish chestnuts at Rossana. Mount Usher had very fine evergreen oaks and a variety of specimen conifers were to be seen at Powerscourt and Kilruddery.[69]

However, the county's cartographic heritage, prior to the first ordnance survey, is not particularly revealing on woodland. A 1707 map by Nevill shows a three-acre coppice north-east of Ballyeustace. There was extensive woodland near Arklow. A Carysfort estate map of towlands near Arklow shows 500 plantation acres of woodland in 1726 or approximately 5 per cent of the area.[70] Kilcarney and Knocknegifty, part of the Piedmont estate, had just two clumps of fir trees and some ash in 1767 and a recommendation for the planting of 640 timber trees was made for Knocknegifty.[71] Old coppice woods could be found near Rathdrum at Ballinderry and just north of it was Clara coppice. South of the area was Ballygannon with approximately 33 per cent woodland cover. Small pockets of wood were also indicated at Corballis and Bahana.[72] The Taylor and Skinner maps of the roads between Wicklow and Arklow around 1777 show extensive woodlands in the valleys of the Avonmore, Avonbeg and Avoca rivers, along the lower reaches of the Vartry near Glenealy and the upper reaches of the Potter's river as well as the valley of the Dargle in the Charleville Estate.[73] A number of good maps for the Meath estate confirm the existence of woodland in the Rathdrum to Ballinaclash district. A map from 1787 by Arthur Nevill shows a wood and adjoining copse at Ballinacarrig, south of Rathdrum. A later (1805) beautifully detailed map by Nevill depicts the same wooded area with no change in overall size – two acres of wood and one of copse.

Other Meath estate maps show woodland in Ballinaclash. In 1805 the wooded area was twenty-two acres; by 1815 it had increased to twenty-three acres. Woodland in Cullentragh amounted to forty plantation acres in 1808, together with two woodrangers' pastures of sixty-four acres. The 1818 woodland estimate in this area was just six acres. The 1804 maps also show some copse wood in Ballinderry but no acreage is given. Woodland was also recorded at both Ballyhad and Ballinafunshoge in 1803. The same maps show an extensive Clara Wood but no acreage is given as the latter was not part of the Meath estate. The Rathdrum area appears to have retained extensive woodland into the nineteenth century. A detailed mapped survey of the woodlands of Clonerkin was compiled by Nevill in 1805. The two pockets of wood in upper Ballinatone were less than an acre in extent but they had some fine timber and great bark; the three-acre wood at Ballinatone was described as 'not being very close but having the potential for fine timber and bark'; Ballinanty's ten-acre wood was capable of producing thirty-five barrels of bark to the acre; and the remaining two parcels of the Clonerkin woods were Grace's Wood, near Ballyeustace/Ballyshane and at Ballymoney. Both were just over six acres in extent. Grace's Wood was described as being the worst of the woods while that at Ballymoney was the best, having the potential to produce more than forty barrels of bark to the acre. These Clonerkin woods are also marked on the 1827 survey of county Wicklow by Baldwin and Cradock. The Meath estate papers have many references to the sale of bark which appears to have been a profitable business. In 1814 the sale of bark from Ballymanus wood amounted to £1,255.4s.11d. West Wicklow appears to have had little wood cover at this time. Surveys of Ballynabarny, Rostyduff and Killaderrig, as early as 1723, indicate a scarcity of woodland in this area which was later confirmed by the 1839 O.S. maps.[74] Elizabeth Smith constantly reflected on the scarcity of timber in her countryside and noted that the tenants were grateful for even the hedge trimmings for their firewood.[75]

Reports, surveys and tourist guides supplement our knowledge of woodland nature, distribution and use in Wicklow during the eighteenth and early nineteenth century. The various surveys highlight extensive coppicing of woodland. The Malton estate had thriving coppices in the early 1700s at Shillelagh, Cosha or Cashaw, Rathdrum, Wicklow and Newcastle.[76] In 1731, a valuation of the coppices was undertaken by John Lee.[77] The total area was estimated to be 923 (plantation) acres or just over 1.3 per cent of the area of the estate. An earlier survey by Moland returned a figure of 897 acres with the largest coppices at Coolattin (120 acres), Tomnafinnoge (107 acres), Coolalug and Killaveny (182 acres), and Roddenagh (100 acres).[78] An estimate of the coppices was undertaken by Jones using archival material in Sheffield City Library.[79] By 1749, 2.5 per cent of the estate, some 1,450 plantation acres, was coppices and scrub wood. The scrub woods, although often managed as coppice, were generally unfenced and therefore distinguished from the other coppices. The surveys indicate a general increase in the size of the coppices composed of oak with some birch, hazel and ash.[80] Apart from the pure oak stands, there appear to have been three other stand mixtures. On the valley floors and lower slopes there were birch-hazel-oak woods. Hazel was absent at higher elevations. Thirdly, on the free-draining steep slopes, there were ash-hazel-oak woods such as the Avonmore valley, south of Rathdrum. Alder and sally were locally important on wet ground. The estate provided both underwood, bark and timber from large trees, whose by-products were used in ship building, tanning, charcoal production and building projects. Timber was provided for buildings in Dublin, courthouses at Athy, Carlow and Wicklow, repairs to market houses at Blessington and Newtownmountkennedy, new churches at Coolkenna, Donard, Inch and Kilcullen, church repairs at Ballymore, Baltinglass, Carnew, Clonegal, Donaghmore, Hacketstown, Hollywood, Kilcommon, Limerick and Tullow, and for a new gaol at Carlow.[81]

Cordwood for charcoal accounted for only a small percentage of the income generated from timber in the Malton estate, and may have been a by-product of bark and timber production.[82] Income from the estate coppices was considerable, being over six times the average annual outgoings.[83] However, in later years many coppices were damaged by cattle grazing. Large parcels of mature trees and coppice were put on the market until well into the 1770s. Jonathan Chamney, who operated the Shillelagh iron works, bought over half of the wood sold between 1730 and 1760.[84] Chamney also appears to have ignored the legal requirement to plant trees. It was reported of Chamney that 'from Rashenmore to Ballybegg are two miles long, not one tree planted all the way'.[85] This undoubtedly accelerated the loss of Shillelagh woodland. Efforts were made to encourage care of the coppices and planting of trees. After 1730, head tenants were obliged to plant both fruit and timber trees. The estate in every lease reserved the right to plant one or two acres on each farm and trees were also given out to smaller tenants to plant around their cabins.[86] Hayes lamented the demise of the oakwood in the Deerpark near Coolattin and noted that the last remaining concentration of wood was around Malton demesne.[87] In 1728 there were 2,150 mature oak in the Deerpark, described as 'the glory and ornament of the Kingdom of Ireland'. The previous year nearly 900 oaks were sold to Chamney or were felled for the use of tenants.[88] Young, in his tour of Ireland in 1778, reported that there are 'no great oak woods since the Shillelegh woods were cut down about twelve years ago' (*c.*1766).[89] The iron works had ceased operation in 1756.[90] By 1830 the wood was gone and all that remained was an old trunk known locally as the Sprig of Shillelagh.[91] However, the practice of planting in the parks and gardens, encouraged by the estate, continued after the estate coppices had gone, and this is still a feature of the Shillelagh area today.[92]

There were other coppices in Mount Kennedy demesne. Young wrote that the Mt. Kennedy country is enclosed within various mountains and high lands. There are many copses on the sides of the mountains of birch, oak, ash and holly which are generally cut at twenty-five year's growth for poles for building cabins, the bark for tanning and the smaller branches for charcoal. They are worth £12 to £25 an acre. Many are on very steep sides and to a great height.[93]

Tourist guides and other accounts of travel in the eighteenth and early nineteenth centuries give a good visual picture of woodland in the county. Even then Wicklow attracted large numbers of tourists and a well-worn itinerary from Dublin to the county's many beauty spots was established. Arthur Young described the Dargle Glen as containing 'one of the finest ranges of woods I have seen anywhere'[94] and Wakefield wrote of the Vale of Arklow that 'the extent of the woods induced me to imagine I was in the midst of one of those immense forests seen only on the continent'.[95] Such comment on woodland was apparently rare at the beginning of the nineteenth century.

In 1794 Hayes wrote that there were considerable Scots pine at Ballybeg and at the property of Symes of Hillbrook.[96] Shelton, the seat of Lord Viscount Wicklow, was also finely wooded. It was to Shelton that the first beech was taken into Ireland. Trees were propagated from their mast and distributed to other parts of the country. At Rossana there were also several species of fine timber, 'among these the Milltown oak is most considerable.' He notes that there were considerable numbers of healthy oak of good growth for their age in the adjoining woods of Coolattin. But the best trees in the district of Shillelagh were in the demesne of the Rev Symes at Ballybeg and in the neighbourhood of Fairwood Park, the hunting lodge built by Strafford. Of this period Hayes wrote that:

> such has been the waste of timber in Ireland during the last century from the unsettled state of the Kingdom and other causes such as the introduction of iron forges and furnaces that there scarcely exists in many districts a sufficiency to favour the supposition that we ever possessed a valuable growth.[97]

However, he believed that a more attentive survey might reveal a greater number of large trees still standing. Hayes undertook a survey of the maritime districts of Wicklow and Dublin.[98] In Shillelagh there were few specimens then remaining of the celebrated oak. The woods belonging to Colonel Symes at Ballyarthur near Arklow were 140 acres in extent, the oldest trees there being not much more than 100 years. Part of this area was coppice wood. By 1822 the woods at Ballyarthur were 260 acres and said to be one of the finest in Ireland.[99] Wright also commented on Shelton Woods which now 'consist chiefly of oak trees which from their too great closeness have all run to a height of about 40ft bearing no foliage but scanty toppings at the top'.[100] Hayes noted that the act which gave to the tenant the profit of such woodlands on his farm, as he may fence up for coppice at his own expence, subject to certain restrictions, had been very effective.[101] An example quoted refers to the considerable thriving tract of woods in Glendalough which was fenced from cattle by James Chritchly, a tenant of the see of Dublin. This contrasted with the apparently wholesale destruction of woodland in other parts of Glendalough:

> I am sorry to say that I have been eye witness to the fall of nearly

> 200 acres of beautiful and well grown oak in a romantic valley; on the see lands of Glendalough, three times within the space of 24 years. The produce of each sale, to the several archbishops never exceeded 100; as I am informed, it amounted once only to £50 or 5s/acre, for a coppice, which had it been preserved for the same number of years, though not containing a single reserve of a former growth, would have produced £30/acre or £6,000 in the place of £50.[102]

A pamplet written in 1794 observed that:

> The banks of the Avonmore are either covered with close coppice wood or with scattered oak and ash of lofty growth ... on the front and side (of Avondale house) spreads a smooth lawn ... rising to a hill crowned with large beech and uncommonly thriving fir. On the back of the house the ground ... covered with ancient oaks, the roofs of many of which are a hundred feet perpendicular over the topmost summit of others.[103]

In 1801 Archer in his *Statistical Survey of county Dublin* observed that 'timber rises in value every year, on account of its scarcity, and is likely to continue rising as the small quantity remaining is, on an average, being cut down in the proportion of 4-1 of that planted'. In the same year *Frazer's Statistical Survey of county Wicklow* recorded that the woods in the county were principally coppices which are usually cut at thirty years growth.[104] However, most of the woods belonged to absentee landlords and as a result were generally neglected until they reached felling age. Frazer estimated that the actual loss suffered by the mismanagement of the woods of non-residents in the county for the previous ninety years – assuming the woods to amount to only 2,500 acres (a very low estimate) – was £1,063,750. He further noted that before the 'late unfortunate disturbances' (1798), planting was going on rapidly in the county and a number of candidates had applied for the tree premiums of the Dublin Society. However, despite damage to fences, the trees planted were doing well and specific reference is made to planting near the marquis of Waterford's lodge in the uplands.

A report on the agriculture and livestock of the county of Wicklow prepared under the direction of the Royal Dublin Society by Thomas Radcliff in 1812 highlighted an example of the skilful management of woods in the county, again at Ballyarthur:[105] 'The society's gold medal was awarded to Rev. James Symes of Ballyarthur whose objective was to protect rather than to cut down, to improve instead of to destroy –

the fences have been kept secure; and a regular system of thinning has taken place.' Radcliff outlines the season's work and price of produce – birch bark in 1809 – £10 a ton and oak bark – £29 a ton. The map included in this report shows woodland above Arklow, at Avondale, Powerscourt, Shillelagh, to the east of Baltinglass and north-east of Stratford.

We move into the first half of the nineteenth century with the impression of good woodland in many eastern parts of the county. Extensive planting was being undertaken and except for a number of cases, woods were generally well managed. The first edition O.S. map gives the most accurate estimate of woodland distribution at the beginning of that century.

The largest expanse of woodland was in the Arklow area especially around Glenart Castle and Shelton Abbey. There had been little change in forest cover in this area since the 1726 survey. Extensive woodland was located in the valley of the Avonmore (Cronybyrne, Glenwood, Derrybawn), at Glenealy, the Devil's Glen and the Enniskerry area (Dargle Glen). Coolattin, Humewood, the Coronation Plantation and Mount Kennedy estate also has good tree cover. The Coronation Plantation, a rectangular block of some 500 acres of woodland near Kippure House, was planted by the marquis of Downshire to honour the coronation of King William IV. It was planted to supply timber for the estate and for 'the improvement of the county and the benefit of the working classes'.[106] The west of the county had only small pockets of woodland. Pure conifer plantations were concentrated here, because there was probably a need to establish forests due to the relative scarcity of substantial tree cover.

A significant change occurred in the species composition of the woods at this time. The majority was no longer pure deciduous wood because of the practice of using conifers as a nurse crop for the hardwoods. Indeed on the later O.S. map many of these mixed woods were marked as deciduous wood, presumably because the conifers had been felled. A rough estimate of the tree cover in 1839 was 2.5 per cent. The second edition O.S. map at the end of the nineteenth century shows little change in woodland cover (2.6 per cent), apart from conifer expansion into the uplands of west Wicklow at Glenbride Lodge. This is presumably the same plantation which Frazer referred to as 'growing well'.[107]

Tree planting commenced again in the last century and continued well into the latter half of the nineteenth century. Landowners were now sufficiently secure to begin tree planting, as an economic crop rather than an anemity, on their estates. Edward Cooke wrote ... 'I do not know what value to put on an acorn and yet I am fully convinced that sowed

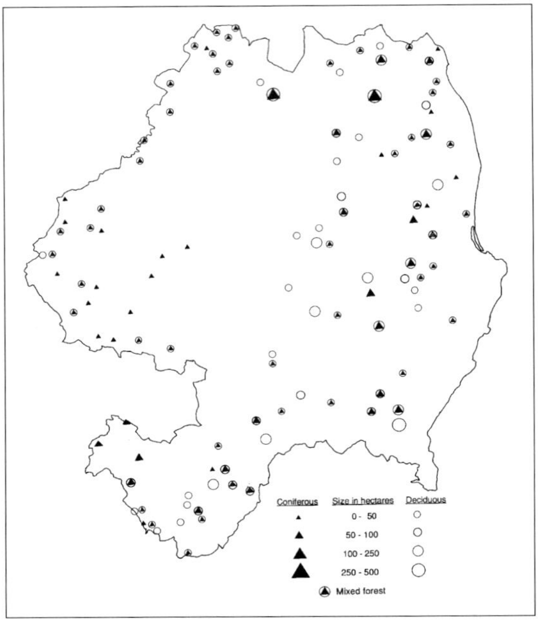

Figure 21.1 Tree cover in county Wicklow, 1837. Source: Ordnance Survey 6" to one mile, first edition, 1837.

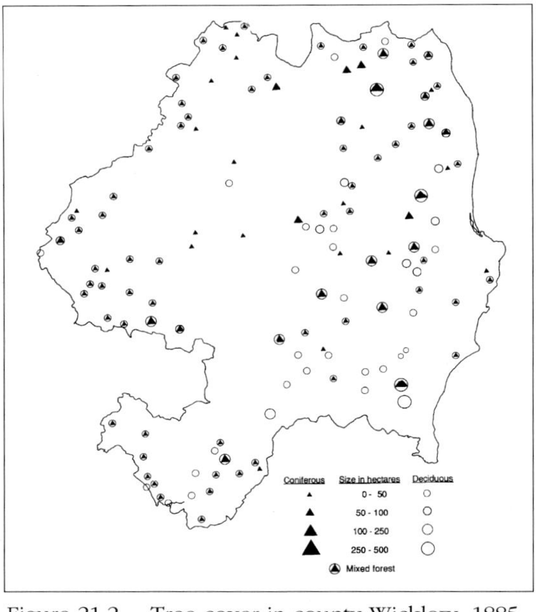

Figure 21.2 Tree cover in county Wicklow, 1885. Source: Ordnance Survey 6" to one mile, first revision, 1885.

in proper soils and preserved would produce in forty years (£10) and I fancy so especially if planted in the county of Wicklow'.[108] Thomas Acton of Kilmacurra was one of the pioneer planters in the county. As early as 1730 he had an item for 'dibbing' trees. He received a premium from the Dublin Society (now the Royal Dublin Society) around 1750, for the planting of foreign trees.[109] The greatest number of these plantings was a general mixture of the common hardwood trees with a nurse crop of conifers or alder and birch as evident from the ordnance survey maps. Wakefield wrote of the Devil's Glen at the beginning of the nineteenth century that 'the principle timber in the rocky glen is oak and in all modern plantations the beautiful larch occupies a most conspicuous place'.[110] The Dublin Society was founded in 1731 to promote and encourage industrial and agricultural development.

Table 21.2 lists the premiums which were awarded for tree planting in county Wicklow, a relatively small number compared with other parts of the country. Frazer, in his *Statistical Survey*, reiterated the complaints of the small farmer about the society's premiums, namely that they did not extend to plantations, less than ten acres, as they could not always spare ten acres in one area without encroaching on meadow or pastureland.[111] He further commented that 'if premiums had been granted to small tenants or even cottiers for planting a rood or two round their cabins, as is doing by Lord Fitzwilliam, it might have the effect of giving the lower classes a love of trees, and be a greater means of preventing their wanton depredations on them than any penalties.' There was also an obligation to register trees planted. Most of the records for the greater part of the eighteenth century were destroyed in the Four Courts fire in 1922. Those remaining for the period 1891 to 1906 have been extracted for Wicklow (table 21.3). The greatest number of registrations, four, was in 1897. Rev Edward Bayly, as a tenant of Carysfort in the parish of Arklow, planted and registered 4,926 trees as well as a large number of fruit trees and ornamental shrubs.[112] Almost 30 per cent of these were softwoods.

The most popular hardwood was beech while only sixty-six oak trees were planted. An 1850 Ordnance Survey valuation of the woods in the Ballinacarrig area noted approximately twenty-seven acres of woodland, an increase on the 1805 figure. Later in 1879 John Morris, a tenant on the farm of Ballinacarrig, gave notice to the earl of Meath of his intention to plant and register 400 trees.

Obtaining a reliable source of tree seedlings was a problem for those who wished to plant large numbers of trees. The act of 1710 laid down that compulsory planting had to be done from trees out of nurseries and not from existing wood. The Dublin Society offered premiums for new nurseries or extensions of existing ones. Between 1766 and 1806,

Table 21.2

Details of tree planting which qualified for premiums paid by the Royal Dublin Society 1741-1804

Year	*Value of Premium*	*Details*	*Area/Numbers planted*
1741/42	–	Timber trees planted by Joseph Leeson, Russellstown.	21,897
1759	–	Richard Symes, Ballyarthur was entitled to premium for most oaks grown from seed sown on not less than 2acres and not less than 2 barrels of sound acorns to an acre.	not given
1767/68	–	Samuel Hayes planted beech under 5 years in age and not nearer to each other than 15ft.	2550
GOLD MEDAL			
1784	£8	Trees planted by Edward Hodgins	2 acres
1790/91	£18	Oak planted by Col. Symes	6 acres
	£34	Coppiced wood fenced by Francis Synge	17 acres
	£4	New nursery ground prepared and planted by Edward Hodgins	1
1791	£23.10s.7d	Charles Frizell enclosed and planted forest trees	10 acres
1796	£40	Henry Allen enclosed and planted forest trees	10 acres
1797/98	–	Planting of forest trees by Ann Symes & Marquis of Waterford	not given
1799/1800	£40	Forest trees planted by 1800 Francis Grene	10 acres
1800/01	£40	Forest trees planted by Morley Saunders	10 acres
1803	£3/acre	Oak planted by Viscount Powerscourt and Rev. James Symes.	not given
	£40	Timber trees planted by Francis Greene (also entitled to medal)	10 acres
1804		Timber trees planted by	
	£47	Francis Greene	12 acres
	£96	Morley Saunders	25 acres
	£9	Rev James Symes	3 acres (oak)

684 went to Wicklow for tree planting while 40 went to nurserymen.[113] These were relatively small figures when compared with the 1,887 (nurserymen) and 1,794 (planters) awarded to Galway. The following is a list of nurserymen operating in Wicklow in the eighteenth and nineteenth centuries.[114] Included are the premiums received from the Dublin Society.

A great variety of trees was raised, from the common oak to rarer specimens such as *Ilex altaclarensis 'Hodginsi'*. This cultivar was raised in a nursery around 1810 and is now growing in the grounds of a house formerly owned by John Jameson at Glencormac south of Bray.

Table 21.3

Registration of Trees 1891-1901

Year	*Trees planted by*	*Species*	*Numbers*
1890/91	John D. Valentine	Larch	200
	Davidstown	Beech	400
	Parish of Donaghmore	Scotch Fir	50
1893/4	Edward Cullen	Silver Fir	12
	Barnacoyle	Larch	200
	Parish of Killiskey	Spruce/fir	250
		Scotch Fir	200
	John Joseph Burne	Ash	80
	Templerainy	Scotch Fir	100
	Parish of Kilbride	Larch deal	100
1895/96	Abraham Hobson	Larch	200
	Killmagig	Spruce	150
	Parish of Castlemacadam	Fir Deal	50
	Daniel Somers	Larch Fir	200
	Thomastown	Spruce	250
	Parish of Arklow	Scotch Fir	250
	James G. McPhail	Cupressus	24
	Glege or Church Hill	Abies	76
	Parish of Wicklow	Pinus	59
		Thuja	40
		Retinispora	12
		Miscellaneous	50
1896/97	John Morris	Larch Deal	350
	Ballinacarrig	Birch	100
	Parish of Rathdrum		
	John Coates	Larch, Spruce	
	Tomcoyle	and Fir	800
	Parish of Preban		
	James Byrne	Larch	1,750
	Tinakelly Lower	Scotch Fir	750
	Aughrim	Spruce	500
	Parish of Ballykine		
	William J. Shephard	Scotch Fir	1,000
	Ballydowling and Cullen Upper	Larch	1,000
	Parish of Dunganstown		
1897/98	Francis J. Minchin	Larch	300
	Mooretown	Spruce	200
	Donaghmore	Laurels	150
1900/1	John Maane Robinson	Larch	7,750
	Coolgarrow		
	Parish of Ballintemple		
1905/6	John Jackson	Fir and Spruce	2,000
	Lisheen	Larch	100
	Parish of Kilbride		

Table 21.4

List of nurserymen

Buller, William. Died 1757. Tinnahinch.
Coles, Philip. £3 premium on 17,000 oak in 1790.
Faulkner, Samuel. Premium on 1 acre in 1790.
Hidgins, Edward. Dunganstown. Premium on 3 acres in 1786. Gave gift of plants to Botanic Gardens in 1797 and supplied plants in 1808. The nursery, under an Edward Hodkins, was still supplying plants to the Botanic Gardens in 1846.
Kirwan, Martin. Premium on 1 acre in 1786.
Long, William. 48/- premium on 14,000 trees between 1785 and 1790.
Reilly, James. £14 premium on 2 acres and 33,000 trees, 1790.
Reilly, John. 28/- premium on 14,000 oak in 1790.

Glencormac (Avoca Handweavers) has many other interesting trees planted in the 1800s as well as a line of yew trees thought to be part of the old avenue leading to Hollybrook and to be aged between 700 and 800 years.[115]

Woodlands reached their maximum area in the second half of the nineteenth century. Some of the later tourist guides describe a well-wooded county. The Halls in 1853 noted that the valley of the Dargle had 'hills on either side clothed by gigantic trees'.[116] Another nineteenth-century traveller described the Devil's Glen:

> the west is covered to its summit with indigenous oak forest of this county. As we enter (the overhanging foliage has hitherto concealed its character) the scene that at once bursts upon the sight is inconceivably grand and beautiful. We are between two huge mountains, the precipitous sides of one being covered with the finest forest trees, of innumerable forms and hues, the greater number having been planted by the hand of nature. The other is half naked and rugged.

He commented that the Glen of the Downs was 'clothed with the most luxuriant foliage from the base to summit of each side'.[117] The valley of the Avonmore continued to draw attention: 'The Copse Wood of fully three miles and a half, being the largest in Wicklow. The vale of Avoca and the hills around Castle Howard are also well planted'.[119] Prince Puckler Muskau on his visit to the Avondale area remarked: 'In this paradise every possible charm is united. A wood which appears measureless in extent, two noble rivers, the most varied and luxuriant shrubberies and thickets. In short changing scenery at every step, yet never diminishing in beauty'.[119]

The availability of substantial local supplies of timber, from such areas as Shillelagh and Coolattin as well as Ballyarthur (renowned for the quality of its larch), probably prompted the establishment of the John Tyrrell Ltd shipyards in Arklow in 1864. Bayly of Ballyarthur had well-managed woods so that supplies could be maintained.[120] Timber also came from the Carysfort estate and from Avondale. Shipbuilding had continued to make hugh demands on timber resources. In the nineteenth century it was estimated that the British navy would require the timber of 1,000 acres to maintain the navy for one year.[121] A variety of imported timber, including teak, was used for ship-building together with local supplies of oak, beech and larch. Arklow was one centre where ship building has been carried on on a small scale for hundreds of years. The export of ore from copper mines had also significantly contributed to the development of its shipping business.

Glendalough did not maintain its woodland. The landscape painting by Walford, dated to 1818, depicts it as relatively treeless. A tourist in 1853 wrote that 'except along the borders of the lower lake and the heights that divide the mountains of Lugduff and Derrybawn, not a tree is to be seen and scarcely a scrub large enough to shelter a lamb'.[122] It is hard to fancy that a few centuries ago the now barren district was a huge forest – a den for wolves and a nest for outlaws or that almost in our own time the lesser hills were covered with foliage'.[123] Another traveller wrote of this area: 'The vale is dark and cheerless even in summer and being almost without a single tree, has a gloomy aspect. At the head of the valley a mining company has planted the hill behind their cottages – a great improvement to the landscape'.[124] In 1857 the mining company planted in the region of 0.25 million trees. These were to be used as mining props but because of the closure of the mines many of these trees, Scots pine, survived on the northern slopes of the valley. Much of the area was apparently stripped of timber in the early nineteenth century for fuel and charcoal.[125] Paddy Healy has surveyed over eighty oval platforms in Glendalough, located along the north and south sides of the Upper Lake, west and south-west of Reefert Church and also above the cliffs on Derrybawn and Camaderry mountains.[126] Most of these platforms are believed to have been used for burning charcoal for smelting iron ore in the 1600s and 1700s. Charcoal production and iron smelting in Glendalough stretches back at least into medieval times. In 1979, excavations in the east of the valley uncovered evidence for extensive medieval iron workings.[127] The adjoining Derrybawn, in contrast, was well wooded and managed.

Some of the present oaks in this area show signs of having been coppiced in the past.

The passing of the land acts in 1881 resulted in little further planting and large areas were cleared from then onwards. By the beginning of the twentieth century remaining pure broadleaved woodlands in the country as a whole accounted for only 16 per cent (oak 9 per cent) of the total tree cover. This consisted mainly of old demense woods, ornamental plantations and former coppices. Wicklow was estimated to have 17,644 acres of woodland in 1902.[128] Coppicing was now a lost art. The fall in the value of the underwood probably meant that coppicing was unlikely to be revived.[129] Roddenagh wood near Aughrim was considered to be one of the finest coppice woods of 179 acres of oak. It was cut during the First World War and later bought by the government in 1922. It was then coppice oak scrub which was cleared and planted with a variety of conifers. The war took its toll on many woods. Shillelagh wood was sold to the Arklow potteries during the war shortages. Many woods had been interplanted with larch, probably as a nurse crop for the oak but also for its commercial value. Other commercial plantations of conifers accounted for one-fifth to a quarter of the woodland area but their management was poor. Some of the areas in county Wicklow which were planted with conifers prior to 1900 included, Ballyreagh Wood near Enniskerry – 1,100 statute acres of pine and larch, some spruce, silver, and douglas fir planted in 1870; Garryduff wood Rathdrum – 473 acres of larch, Scots pine and a little spruce planted 1845-1849; Whaley Abbey, a douglas fir plantation in 1885. These marked the rather tentative beginnings of our present coniferous forests.

The collapse of the landlord system forced the state to assume responsibility for the production of timber. However, before 1922 only 1,200 acres were planted. A forestry school was established at Avondale, the former home of Samuel Hayes and, later, Charles Parnell. Many of the first forests in the country were planted in Wicklow. The afforestation of valleys with conifers began after 1920 with the planting of Crone and Ballyreagh in Glencree, Lugduff in Glendalough, Ballyboy and Clohernagh in Glenmalure and the Aughrim-Aghavannagh valley.[130] Some planting (43 ha) had been carried out in Glendalough prior to 1922, most of it by the mining company operating in the valley. Conifers from western North America were the chief tree species planted. Douglas fir was planted on well-drained slopes below 1,000ft while sitka spruce was used on wet ground and exposed grassy areas extending right up to 1,800ft. The sitka spruce, indigenous to western North America, dominates the Wicklow forests today. It was not used in plantations before 1909. When first used it was planted with other conifers and not as pure stands. A variety of other species were tried on suitable soils in various parts of the county. The first state plantation of contorta pine was at Ballintombay near Rathdrum.[131] In 1908, Forbes, the director of forestry, procured from Tasmania packets of eucalyptus seed which were first raised at Avondale.[132]

The Second World War and post-war years took a heavy toll on our trees. In 1938, Ireland had one per cent forest cover. Hardwoods comprised only 26 per cent of this, while mixed forests accounted for just over 48 per cent. The remainder was softwood plantations. More than half of this cover was felled in the ten years between 1938 and 1947.[133] Table 21.5 shows that the afforestation of county Wicklow with conifers accelerated from the 1950s to give us the present tree cover of just under 18 per cent. The most significant feature of this tree planting was its expansion into upland moorland areas. In 1958 mountain areas (1200 ft-1500 ft) which were previously unplantable because of the poverty of the soil, were ploughed with a Cuthbertson plough. These areas were then planted with sitka spruce (75 per cent) and Pinus contorta.[134] Table 21.5 shows the amount of new planting in each decade.

The river valleys retained pockets of native deciduous woodland, much of which had been effected to some degree by eighteenth and nineteenth-century management. The most significant remaining woodlands are to be found in Clara Vale, the Glen of the Downs and Glendalough.

It is fitting to conclude this historical account with the great oaks of Wicklow. The Fitzwilliam estate at one time comprised 90,000 acres, stretching from Coolattin to Rathdrum, much of which was tree covered. In 1977, the Fitzwilliams sold the remaining 3,000 acres of their estate. Since then most of Coolattin has been felled. In 1978 a tree

Table 21.5

State planting in county Wicklow

	hectares
Pre 1920	563
1920-29	1,053
1930-39	1,717
1940-49	2,654
1950-59	6,532
1960-69	6,141
1970-79	5,360
1980-89	5,251
1990-93	1,200

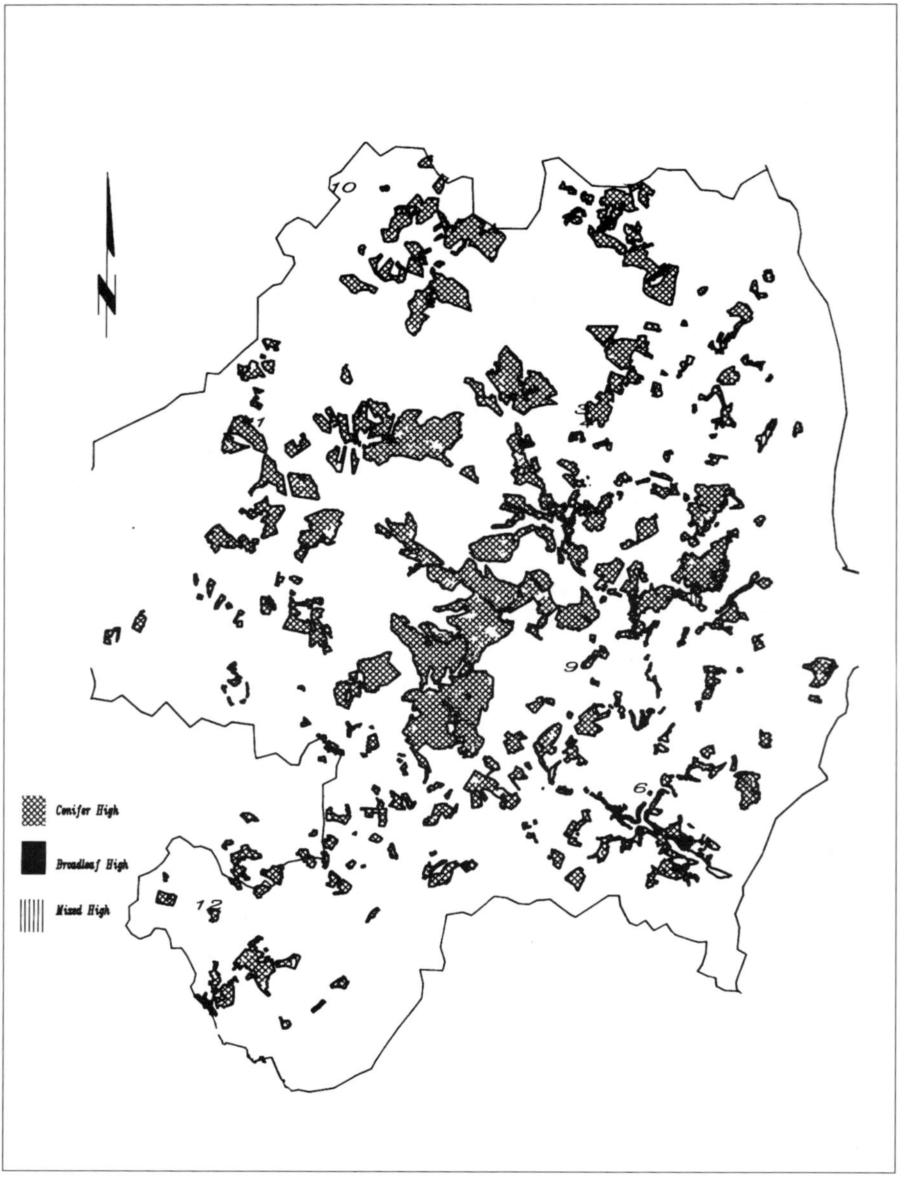

Figure 21.3 County Wicklow forests, 1994.
Source: Coillte teoranta.

preservation order was placed on some of the 750 acres of predominantly oak woods at Coolattin. However, when faced with the possibility of a massive compensation bill from the owners, felling was permitted on condition that only 25 per cent to 30 per cent of the total number of trees in Brow Wood would be cut. Some replanting did take place but history repeats itself in the reported absence of adequate care of the young trees. In 1987 a prohibition order was placed on further felling. Later a licence was given to fell 323 mature oak trees in Tomnafinnoge. This was apparently only the first phase of an agreed programme which would have resulted in the felling of 90 per cent of the trees in Tomnafinnoge over a six to ten year period. A long campaign to save these trees ended with the purchase of the wood for conservation by Wicklow County Council in March 1994.

What has been the environmental impact of the changes in trees cover which have occurred over the centuries? We can only theorise on the effects of reduced tree cover on our small windswept island. Today, the re-afforestation of the country, largely monocultures of conifers, may also be contributing to environmental damage. Research in Europe and northern USA has shown that plantations of evergreen trees, on poor base soils, can cause acidification of streams draining these forests. This has been linked to the ability of the trees to intercept acidic pollutants from the atmosphere or precipitation. In many rivers and streams such a process has had undesirable effects on fish and other aquatic life. There are other ways in which plantation forestry may have a negative impact on freshwater life, such as by shading or by altering the hydrology of the rivers and streams which drain these forests. A major national project was initiated in Ireland in 1990 to assess the possible impacts of afforestation on salmon and trout waters. The impetus for this project was the rapidly expanding afforestation programme and potential loss in revenue resulting from damage to game fisheries. A large percentage of our important salmonoid waters receive some drainage from coniferous forests. Of particular concern were the headwaters of these streams where salmon and trout spawn and spend up to three years of their life. The juvenile stages are extremely sensitive to acidification. Therefore, effects at this stage could have enormous implications for the game fisheries in the lower courses of the rivers. Interdisciplinary teams from three universities undertook biological, chemical and hydrological monitoring of rivers and streams in three regions, Wicklow (University College Dublin), Galway/Mayo (Trinity College Dublin) and Cork (University College Cork). The Wicklow project has surveyed thirty three streams in the catchments of the Liffey, King's and Avonmore rivers and the Vartry reservoir. Results suggest that streams within large areas of closed canopy evergreen forest tend to be more acidic than non-afforested systems. Associated with the increase in acidity is an undesirable increase in toxic aluminium concentrations. Effects on the ecology of these streams whose catchment areas consist of more than thirty per cent closed canopy forest cover ranged from the loss of some aquatic insects such as the mayfly to elimination of trout populations in

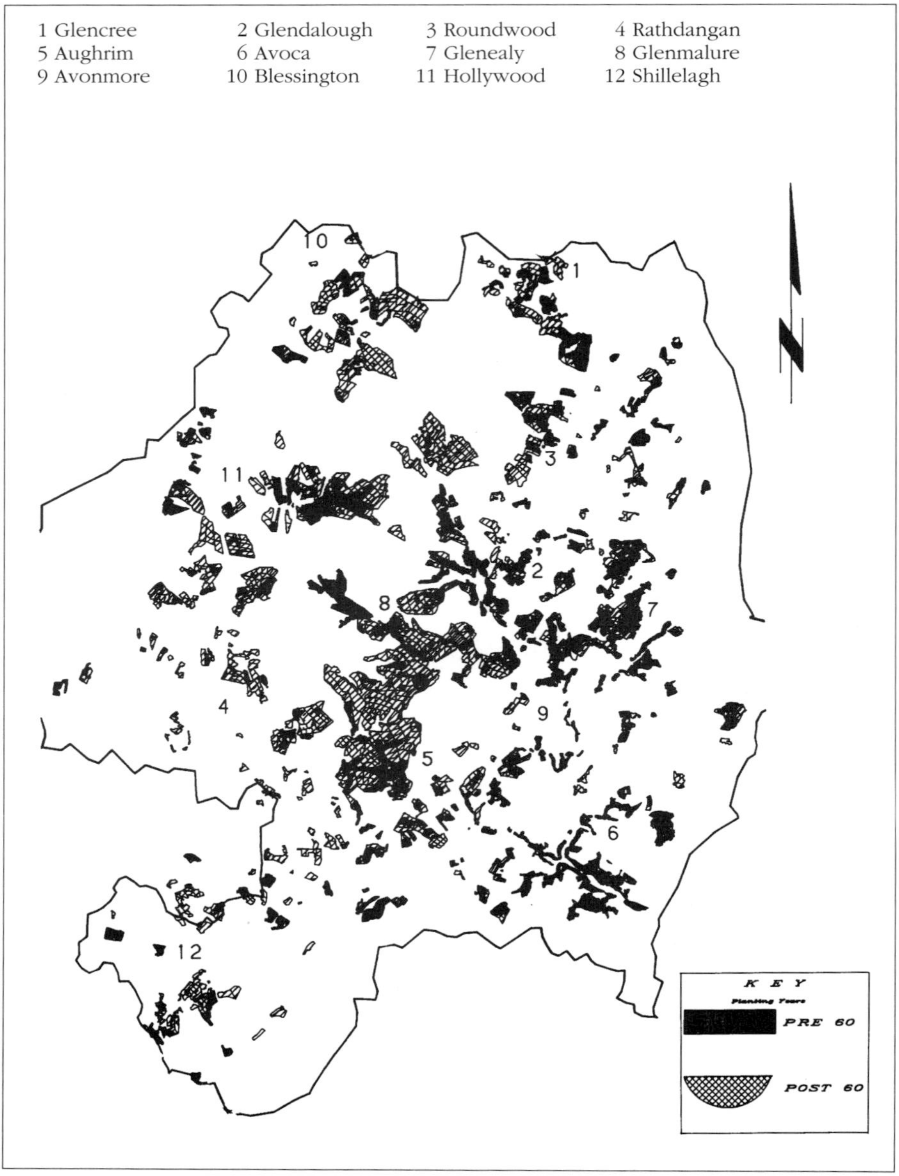

Figure 21.4 County Wicklow forests planted before and after 1960.
Source: Coillte teoranta.

a number of streams in the county. These potential deleterious impacts of forestry on water quality must be taken into consideration in future planning of afforestation programmes in county Wicklow.

The demand for timber continues to rise despite the variety of other materials at our disposal today. With diminishing sources of foreign hardwood timbers the wisdom of a home timber industry is obvious. However, history and modern research must surely highlight the need to plan a sustainable industry which contributes to the quality of our environment.

References

1. J. Cross, 'Status and value of native broadleaved woodland' in *Irish Forestry*, xliv (1987), p. 82.
2. S. Hakansson, in *Radiocarbon*, xvi (1974), pp 307-30.
3. K. Jessen, 'Studies in late Quarternary deposits and floral history of Ireland' in *R.I.A. Proc.*, lii (1952), B, pp 85-290.
4. Cross, 'Native broadleaved woodland,' p. 82.
5. E. Neeson, *A history of Irish forestry* (Dublin, 1991), p. 13.
6. K.J. Edwards, 'The anthropogenic factor in vegetational history' in K.G. Edwards and W.P. Warren (eds.) *The quarternary history of Ireland* (London, 1985), pp 187-220.
7. Neeson, *Irish forestry*, p. 27.
8. F. Kelly, *A guide to early Irish law* (Dublin, 1988), p. 144.
9. Idem.
10. Neeson, *Irish forestry*, p. 28.
11. E. McCracken, *The Irish woods since Tudor times* (Newton Abbot, 1971), p. 22.
12. A.P. Smyth, *Celtic Leinster – towards an historical geography of early Irish civilization AD 500-1600* (Dublin, 1982), p. 25.
13. Price, *Place-Names*, iv, p. 216.
14. Ibid., p. 240.
15. Smyth, *Celtic Leinster*, p. 26.
16. Neeson, *Irish forestry*, pp 33-6.
17. Ibid., pp 36-8.
18. Ibid., pp 42, 295-6.
19. C. Scott, *The stones of Bray* (1913), p. 18.
20. C. Gorman, 'The pollen analysis of a monolith taken above Glencree, county Wicklow and correlation with the history of the area.' unpublished Master of Applied Science thesis, UCD (1987), p. 33.
21. T.T. Le Fanu, 'The royal forest of Glencree' in *R.S.A.I. Jn.*, xii (1883), p. 269.
22. Ibid., pp 270-77.
23. Ibid., p. 270.
24. Gorman, 'Pollen analysis,' p. 33.
25. Le Fanu, 'Glencree,' p. 276.
26. Gorman, 'Pollen analysis,' p. 39.
27. Neeson, *Irish forestry*, p. 42.
28. Ibid., p. 47.
29. Smyth, *Celtic Leinster*, p. 108.
30. Ibid., p. 109.
31. O. Rackham, *The history of the countryside* (London, 1988), p. 112.
32. Neeson, *Irish forestry*, p. 48.
33. H.E. Hore, 'Woods and fastnesses, and their denizens in ancient Leinster' in *U.J.A.*, vi (1960), p. 233.
34. Ibid., p. 233.
35. Le Fanu, 'Glencree,' pp 50-51.
36. Hore, 'Woods and fastnesses,' p. 234.

37. S. Hayes, *A practical treatise on planting and the management of woods and coppices* (Dublin, 1794), p. 110.
38. McCracken, *Irish woods*, p. 50.
39. P. Lennon, Eighteenth-century landscape change from estate records – Coolattin estate, Shillelagh, county Wicklow,' unpublished B.A. geography dissertation, T.C.D. (1979), p. 60.
40. Hayes, *Practical treatise*, p. 111.
41. Hore, 'Woods and fastnesses,' p. 233.
42. Price, *Place-Names*, iv, p. 239.
43. A.C. Forbes, 'Tree planting in Ireland during four centuries,' in *R.I.A. Proc.*, xli (1941), B, p. 188.
44. Rackham, *History of the countryside*, p. 113.
45. E. McCracken, 'The woodlands of Ireland circa 1600' in *I.H.S.*, xi (1959), p. 285.
46. R. Loeber, 'Settlers' utilisation of the natural resources,' see this volume.
47. *Cal. S.P. Ire.*, 1608-1610, p. 88.
48. Hore, 'Woods and fastnesses,' p. 235.
49. McCracken, *Irish woods*, p. 100.
50. *Cal. S.P. Ire.*, 1660-62, p. 429.
51. Neeson, *Irish forestry*, pp 79-90.
52. Lennon, Coolattin estate, pp 61-2.
53. McCracken, *Irish woods*, p. 50.
54. Hayes, *Practical treatise*, p. 111.
55. Lennon, Coolattin estate, p. 62.
56. Ibid., p. 62.
57. Huntington Library, San Marino, Ms HA 14,245, A survey of the Strafford estate, county Wicklow, 1671.
58. Neeson, *Irish forestry*, pp 63, 67.
59. Ibid., p. 91.
60. Ibid., pp 72-6.
61. Young, *Tour*, ii, p. 62.
62. Neeson, *Irish forestry*, pp 301-8; M.L. Anderson, 'Items of forestry interest from the Irish statutes prior to 1800 A.D.' in *Irish Forestry* (1944/45), pp 6-35.
63. Anderson, op. cit., pp 7-8.
64. M. Bulfin, 'Upland soils of Wicklow have good potential' in *Farm and food research*, x (1979).
65. T.W. Freeman, *Pre-famine Ireland* (Manchester, 1957), p. 187.
66. Letter from Thomas Murray to Lord Downshire, 28 July 1840, concerning the improvement of mountain land on the Blessington estate cited in W.A. Maguire (ed.), *Letters of a great Irish landlord – a selection from the estate correspondence of the third marquess of Downshire 1809-45* (Belfast, 1974).
67. E. Malins and The Knight of Glin, *Lost demesnes* (London, 1976), p. xv.
68. P. Bowe, *The gardens of Ireland* (London, 1986), p. 9.
69. Hayes, *Practical treatise*, pp 119-57.
70. N.L.I., Ms 6,232 (1).
71. N.L.I., Ms 9,999.
72. N.L.I., Ms 22,017. 'A survey of several parcels of land lying in an about the town of Rathdrum in the manor of Fairwood.' Accompanying notes are given in Ms 4944.
73. G. Taylor and A. Skinner, *Maps of the roads of Ireland, surveyed 1777* (London and Dublin, 1778).
74. N.L.I., Ms 5255.

75. D. Thomson with M. McGusty (ed.), *The Irish journals of Elizabeth Smith* (Oxford, 1980).
76. M. Jones, 'Coppice wood management in the eighteenth-century: an example from county Wicklow' in *Irish Forestry*, xliii (1984), p. 17.
77. N.L.I., Ms 3982, 'Valuation of the coppices and woods belonging to Lord Malton' by J. Lee, 1731.
78. Lennon, Coolattin estate, p. 65.
79. Jones, 'Coppice wood management,' pp 21-2.
80. Ibid., p. 22.
81. Ibid., p. 27.
82. Ibid., p. 29.
83. Ibid., p. 30.
84. Ibid., p. 67.
85. Lennon, Coolattin estate, p. 64.
86. Ibid., p. 67.
87. Hayes, *Practical treatise*, p. 110.
88. Jones, 'Coppice wood management,' p. 22; Hayes, *Practical treatise*, pp 111-12.
89. Young, *Tour*, ii, p. 122.
90. McCracken, *Irish woods*, p. 69.
91. Ibid., p. 50.
92. Lennon, Coolattin estate, p. 69.
93. Young, *Tour*, ii, p. 125.
94. Ibid., p. 134.
95. Wakefield, *Account of Ire.*, ii, p. 53.
96. Hayes, *Practical treatise*, p. 118.
97. Ibid., p. 116.
98. Ibid., pp 119-57.
99. Wright, *Guide to county Wicklow*, p. 80.
100. Ibid., p. 84.
101. Hayes, *Practical treatise*.
102. Idem.
103. E. McCracken, 'Samuel Hayes of Avondale' in *Irish Forestry*, xxv (1968), p. 40. Samuel Hayes of Avondale, represented Wicklow in the house of commons from 1783 to 1790. In 1788 he introduced a bill to explain and amend the Act of 5 and 6 George III entitled 'An act for encouraging the cultivation and better preservation of trees.'
104. R. Frazer, *General view of agriculture and mineralogy, present state and circumstances of county Wicklow* (Dublin, 1801), pp 266-71.
105. T. Radcliffe, *A report on the agriculture and livestock of the county of Wicklow prepared under the direction of the farming society of Ireland* (Dublin, 1812), pp 305-9.
106. W. St John Joyce, *The neighbourhood of Dublin* (Dublin, 1921), p. 380.
107. Frazer, *General view*, p. 266.
108. E. McCracken, 'Notes on eighteenth-century Irish nurserymen' in *Irish Forestry*, xxiv (1967), p. 40.
109. Forbes, 'Tree planting in Ireland,' p. 182.
110. Wakefield, *Account of Ire.*, ii, p. 55.
111. Frazer, *General view*, p. 266.
112. J. Ainsworth, Report on the Bayly papers, p. 115.
113. McCracken, 'Notes on nurserymen,' p. 43.
114. Ibid., pp 57-8.

115. *The trees of Glencormac*, n.d., a pamphlet produced by Avoca Handweavers.
116. S.C. Hall, *Hand-books for Ireland-Dublin and Wicklow* (London and Dublin, 1853), p. 113.
117. Ibid., pp 155, 165.
118. C. Black, *Black's guide to Dublin and the Wicklow mountains with plans of Dublin* (Edinburgh, 1868), p. 92.
119. Ibid., p. 94.
120. Neeson, *Irish forestry*, pp 86-9.
121. Ibid., p. 82.
122. Hall, *Hand-books*, pp 123-4.
123. Wright, *Guide to county Wicklow*, p. 117.
124. Black, *Dublin and the Wicklow mountains*, p. 89.
125. G.F. Mitchell, *The Irish landscape* (Glasgow, 1976), Plate 30.
126. P. Healy, Supplementary survey of the ancient monuments at Glendalough, county Wicklow, O.P.W. Parks and Monuments (unpublished).
127. C. Manning, Excavations at Glendalough, Office of Public Works, unpublished, pp 344-46.
128. Petrie, S.M., 'Observations on Irish forestry in year 1904' in *Irish Forestry*, vi (1949), p. 12.
129. Ibid., p. 13.
130. H.M. Fitzpatrick, *The forests of Ireland* (Dublin, 1966), p. 64.
131. Ibid., p. 65.
132. M. O'Beirne, 'Notes on eucalyptus species at Avondale, county Wicklow' in *Irish Forestry*, vi (1949), p. 24.
133. Statistics prepared for the fifth British Empire Forestry Conference, Great Britain, June 1947, in *Irish Forestry*, v (1948), p. 33.
134. Fitzpatrick, *Forests of Ireland*, p. 87.

Chapter 22

FROM GRAND JURY TO COUNTY COUNCIL: AN OVERVIEW OF LOCAL ADMINISTRATION IN WICKLOW 1605-1898

B. DONNELLY

The modern administrative county of Wicklow has its origins in the early sixteenth century. In an indenture made at Dublin on 4 July 1542 Thady O'Birne, described as captain of his nation, and other nobles inhabiting 'a certain country between the Wynde Gates and the town of Arclowe in the county of Dublin' petitioned the King that their country might be erected by authority of parliament into a county, with the name of the county of Wicklow, so that henceforth they might hold their lands from the crown and a sheriff and other officers might be constituted there. The lord deputy and council ratified their submission, provided that the King should accept it within a year, but nothing was to come of this proposal.[1] In the late 1540s instead, three administrative zones were created in what is now the county, corresponding to the areas inhabited by the three septs of the O'Byrnes, O'Tooles, and Kavanaghs, each ruled by an English captain from a convenient fort.[2]

In 1578 a royal commission issued for the areas south and east of Dublin to be bounded out into a shire, to be named and called the county of Wicklow. Sir William Drury, the lord Justice, defined the boundaries of the county but 'findinge that there were not sufficient, and [fewer] gent. to be shriffes, nor freeholders to make a jury for her Maiestie' the matter was let drop.[3]

It was thus not until 1605 that Sir Arthur Chichester as lord deputy completed the work of a generation earlier by having the country of the Birnes and Tooles surveyed and distinguished into a county. The shiring of Wicklow was finally completed only in the following year and, as Litton Falkiner points out, the county nearest the metropolis was of all the last to be brought effectively within the scope of the English government.[4]

As a result of the shiring of Wicklow a framework of local administration was introduced at county, borough, and parish level around which developed a panoply of functions, juridical, charitable and medical, which was to to survive until the establishment of the county council by the Local Government Act of 1898. The development of these and other administrative bodies is considered in this essay.

The origins of local administration; grand jury, parishes and municipalities

At the top of the county's administrative structure came the grand jury. Under the grand jury system a King's officer known as the sheriff was appointed and twice a year, in spring and summer, he called together twenty three of the largest landowners in the county and made up a grand jury to meet the judges who came on circuit.

As well as having certain legal and semi-judicial functions, the grand jury gradually developed as an instrument of administration for such matters as the repair of roads and bridges, the erection of courthouses and gaols, and the raising of the necessary finances, by means of a local tax known as county cess levied on the occupiers of the land. The obligations placed on freeholders of serving on juries, together with the expenses of attending at assizes and sessions made such duties onerous and unpopular.[5] Rolls of Fines, which survived mainly for the year 1619, showed how unpopular these duties were. Petty constables and jurors were fined for not attending sessions; tradesmen, chiefly millers and victuallers, for not bringing in their weights and measures on time, or for excessive tolls and inhabitants of baronies and parishes for not mending bridges, making highways and other works passed as presentments.[6] Nevertheless, a further act in 1634 made inhabitants of shires, baronies and towns liable to repair or build bridges and roads. The justices of assize in their circuits and the justices of the peace at quarter sessions could, with the assent of the grand jury, tax every inhabitant reasonably to pay for such works. The names of persons to be taxed were to be set out in a roll and two collectors were to be appointed for each barony to levy the sums by distress and sale. Two surveyors were to be appointed to whom the collectors paid the sums collected. Both surveyors and collectors were to be allowed reasonable charges.

Grand jurors, representative of the new plantations, meanwhile played a major role in indicting those involved in the confederate rebellion in the 1640s as outlaws and removing their title to land. In many instances persons were indicted without evidence and solely upon knowledge of the grand jury.[7] By 1647 one hundred and forty six Byrnes, twenty four O'Tooles, fourteen members of the old English family Archbold and five Wolverstons had been outlawed in county Wicklow. The results of such indictments are evident from the fact that whereas almost half the land in Wicklow in 1641 was owned by catholics, by 1688 this had fallen to between ten and fourteen per cent.[8]

Grand jury functions were extended in the eighteenth century. As early as 1712 the grand jury had some responsibility for creating work for the poor. In that year Sir W. Fownes, [Victor] Harris and Thomas Acton were appointed to be overseers of a workhouse to be built at Wicklow pursuant to a late Act of Parliament for the encouragement of the Hempen and Flaxen Manufacture.[9]

This workhouse appears to have been built within limits of the Borough of Wicklow and was completed in 1715.[10]

Along with the grand jury, the parish also became an integral part of the administration of local government in the county in the seventeenth and eighteenth centuries. An act of 1613 required parishioners to meet during Easter Week, choose surveyors of roadworks and arrange for householders, cottiers and labourers to work six days repairing and cleaning the roads. An insight into the operation of this system in Wicklow in the late seventeenth century is given in surviving vestry minute books. In Delgany, for example, we find in the minutes the names of those persons appointed churchwardens, sidesmen and surveyors of the highways for particular years. The parish was also responsible for its own poor and for foundling children. Under a 1715 Act a minister and churchwardens were empowered with the consent of a justice of the peace to board out any child found begging in their parish, or any other poor child with the consent of the parents, to any honest or substantial protestant housekeeper or tradesman who undertook to maintain the child until the age of 21, if a menial servant, or the age of 24, if an apprentice to a trade.[11] Under the terms of a 1774 Act it was directed that in every parish in the kingdom a annual vestry was to appoint three overseers to provide for the maintenance and education of deserted children.

Many foundlings were transported from rural Ireland to the foundling hospital in Dublin from where they were put out to nurse in the country. County Wicklow was long associated with the practice of taking in nurse children from Dublin. The Delgany parish burial registers contain many references to the burials of nursed children from Dublin from the early 1740s. In the 1780s a notorious abuse was highlighted in which children, given at nurse to persons by the foundling hospital in Dublin,[12] were then hired out to beggars or carried about the country by their nurses in order to excite the feelings of the humane and the charitable.[13] In 1791 at the Wicklow Assizes several persons were convicted for counterfeiting the brand used on children by the foundling hospital. Pretended nurses had claimed wages for the nursing of upwards of 150 children in this manner.[14] When, in 1792, the grand jury and freeholders of county Wicklow recorded their appreciation of William Wilberforce for bringing forward a bill for the abolition of the slave trade, the *Freeman's Journal* commented acidly that the issue of foundling children was one that would better attract their attention.[15]

Payments to the poor were made in some parishes in the county from the early eighteenth century. The recipients were usually members of the established church. A poor list which appears in the Delgany vestry minute book for 1716 contains eight names including that of Martha Salt – 'widow of William Salt who was killed in the rebellion [of 1688] by the rapparees at Cloghoge ...'.[16] Parish cess was also levied to provide coffins for the poor, salaries for parish officers, repairs to churchyards and clocks, collectors' and apploters' fees etc. The parish vestries also appointed poundkeepers.

Policing of areas fell to both the grand jury and the parishes and local watches throughout the county are noted in the records of both. The grand jury ordered on the 16 July 1712 that £31 be raised on the Half Barony of Rathdown for a watchhouse to be built in the town of Fasseroe and appointed Captain Richard Lambert overseer for it.[17] At a meeting of the Delgany vestry on 2 April 1711 two overseers were each appointed to the Delgany and Kilcoole constablewicks. On 6 April 1713 Thomas Hodgeon of Kindlestown was appointed petty constable of Delgany and John Cullen of the Downe, petty constable of Kilcoole. These offices were distinct from the overseers of the highways. An Act of 1715 barred 'papists' from serving as high or petty constables and made all appointments subject to appraisal by the county grand juries.[18] Constables were obliged to repair to fires and assist in extinguishing them. Under an Act of 1719 watchmen were to be selected from the inhabitants of parishes by one or more justices of the peace, within corporations by chief magistrates, and within manors and liberties by seneschals. Catholics might serve, though they were specially debarred from service in times of tumult and danger.[19] The watchmen were to be provided with watch-bills, staves and halberts and could stop and examine all suspected persons and if necessary arrest and detain such persons until the next day when they were to be carried before a justice of the peace to be dealt with according to law.[20]

Planned colonisation in the seventeenth century dramatically increased the incorporation of towns in Wicklow. Wicklow was incorporated in 1613, Carysfort in 1628, Baltinglass in 1663 and Blessington in 1669. Wicklow Corporation's charter placed the power of returning two members of parliament in the portreeve and free burgesses, a privilege which they exercised up until the Act of Union, when the borough was disenfranchised. The charter provides a good example of the legal framework of urban government. The corporation consisted of a portreeve, free burgesses, and a number of freemen. The portreeve was chosen annually on 24 June by the free burgesses, three of whom formed a quorum for the purpose. There were twelve free burgesses, elected by the portreeve and free burgesses, from among the freemen elected for life. All freemen were eligible to be free burgesses. By 1833 only four free burgesses were resident in Wicklow and no catholic had been elected a burgess. Catholics had enjoyed only a short-lived participation in municipal affairs in Wicklow borough when some were admitted freemen to the corporation in 1687 under an order of James II allowing them to take an oath of fidelity instead of the oath of supremacy and to be elected to the magistracy or bear any office in the town of Wicklow. One Catholic admitted on 28th of March 1687 was William Wolverston. The borough sent two catholic representatives, Francis Toole and Thomas Byrne, to the Jacobite parliament of 1689.[21] Catholics were later debarred from holding municipal office by one of the penal laws and were efffectively denied the freedom of the corporation by the oath of supremacy and other oaths.[22] The freemen of the corporation of Wicklow were admitted by the portreeve and free burgesses. The right to freedom was acquired by birth, apprenticeship, or marriage and freemen were also admitted by 'grace especial'.

The minute books of the borough chronicle many aspects of the town's development. A bridge was built there around 1687 and appears to have been subsidised to the amount of £19.9s being 'Lynin Cloath Money given by the county'. By 1707 part of the streets had been paved and other parts gravelled. Military victories were celebrated. Seventeen shillings and three pence was spent for the battle of Ramilles. Poor orphans were maintained from rents due to the corporation. In 1713 sums were paid for putting up the town clock and for gasing the market house, perhaps an early form of fumigation. The buying of 'a greate for the town shoar' in 1716 indicates the existence of a drainage system. By 1720 a schoolmaster was being paid by the borough on an annual basis. The freemen attended the meetings of the corporation, shared in the appointment of the inferior officers, in the making of bye-laws and in the disposition of the landed property of the corporation. Each freeman was entitled to send a horse or cow to the common known as the Murrough and was exempted from the toll collected on the importation of coals and the harbour dues.

The limits of the corporation included the entire town of Wicklow, with the exception of the Castle of Wicklow, and towards the land, according to ancient usage, they extended for a mile in every direction. In 1833 the landed property of the corporation contained between 200 and 300 acres. The portreeve's court – the equivalent of a petty sessions court – was in 1833 being held in Rathnew which was considered more central and convenient. While the collection of market tolls had ceased by 1833 the portreeve exacted a toll of a barrel of coal from each cargo of coal imported by persons who were not freemen.

Harbour dues on every vessel above 20 tons burden were also taken by the portreeve and later let by him to the town serjeant. Pilotage charges were imposed in January 1833 and the revenue was paid to the pilots as remuneration for their labour. The revenue of the corporation was expended on several payments to the portreeve and the town serjeants, repairing the streets and quays, and paying interest on a debt of £200 borrowed for building a market house.

Of the other seventeenth century boroughs, Baltinglass, incorporated by a Charter of Charles II in 1663, was defined as the built town and 300 acres contiguous. Although empowered to have all the officials consistent with proper local administration, there is little evidence that Baltinglass functioned according to the letter of its charter. By 1832 the corporation was virtually extinct, there being only two burgesses and no freemen.

Blessington, incorporated by charter granted to Michael Boyle, Archbishop of Dublin and Chancellor of Ireland in 1669 had similar privileges and provisions for a local administration. The only reason or the maintenance of town status was to retain the entitlement to return two members to parliament. Blessington lost its corporation and entitlement to parliamentary representation in 1800, for which Arthur, marquis of Devonshire, received compensation of £15,000.

The Borough of Carysfort was incorporated by a charter in 1628 but there is no evidence that the charter was acted on for any corporate purpose, except that of returning members to parliament. At the time of the Union a sum of £15,000 was awarded to John, earl of Carysfort, as compensation for the loss of representative franchise of the borough. Lands granted for the use of the school of Carysfort were afterwards vested in the commissioners of Education in Ireland.

Catholics were excluded from local government – from corporations, from the magistracy, from grand juries and vestries. When the Wicklow grand jury met on the 7 April 1715 there were about 50 bills of indictment before them, mainly relating to the stealing of animals, timber, hides and wool.[23] Some related to transgressions under the penal laws. William Cavanagh, a catholic priest, was indicted for saying mass, not having taken the oath of abjuration. Charles Byrne, another priest, was also indicted for saying mass.[24] When they met on the 22 April 1715 the grand jury proclaimed several persons 'out on their keeping' in armes as raparees or tories and there were several cases of robbery in Shillelagh for which compensation was levied on the popish population.[25] The grand jury stated that they knew of '... no person sent abroad to be [educated as monks] or popish priests nor of any inlisted for the Pretender ...'.[26] The Popery Act of 1704 prohibited pilgrimages or religious processions and on St. Kevin's Day, 1714, Thomas Ryves, High Sheriff, and a posse[27] of magistrates and Protestant gentlemen disrupted the annual pilgrimage to Glendalough and 'pulled down their tents, threw down and demolished their superstitious crosses, filled up and destroyed their wells, and apprehended and committed one Toole, a popish school master'.[28]

The areas on which presentments were levied varied according to circumstance. In 1735 it was decided that the manor pound at Ballymanus should be repaired for £4 which was to be raised on the manor inhabitants. When in 1733 a person named Hennessy was robbed in Shillelagh half barony by four tories, two of them catholics and two protestants, it was ordered that the money was to be levied equally on the catholics and protestants of the half barony. Under a 1727 Act the grand Juries were empowered to take action to appoint overseers if parish authorities failed to do so and regulations with regard to six days labour were tightened up. Provision was made for emergency action in the case of sudden damage – two neighbouring justices could spend 40 shillings for urgent repairs and claim reimbursement from the grand jury. The practice of providing a stock of tools in a central storehouse in each parish was approved. From 1733 the grand juries appointed the baronial High Constables who served a one year non-renewable term and whose principal duty was the collection of the county cess. Among those appointed at the Assizes in 1739 were Francis Revill of Ballyduff for Arklow, Edward Hatton of Drombaun for Newcastle and John Booth of [Killough] for Rathdown. A mention of the six days labour at the vestry in Delgany on 15 April 1734 indicates the existence of a well developed network of roads in the locality:

> It was at the same presented and agreed to by the Parishioners that the six days labour for mending the High Roads should be applied to the mending of the following roads viz
> to Killincarrick,
> From the church to the Downs Bridge, to the North end of the Glynne of the Downs, to the old Watch House, to the Wicklow Road by Kindlestown
> From Templecarrick to Ballydonagh to Redford
> From Mr Thomas Fox's to the North end of the Glyn of the Downs

Compulsory labour on the roads, as Maxwell points out, was almost always grudgingly given and the work done was often of a very indifferent nature.[29] Around 1760 it was finally decided to allow a system of payment for labourers on roadworks and the system of setting a road to contract for a number of years was developed and was to continue in the county until the early twentieth century.[30]

The Assizes were social as well as judicial events. William Fairbrother of Glenealy had first served as a member of the Wicklow grand jury at the Spring Assizes of 1757.[31] In the Spring of 1765 he served again and his diary account provides an interesting insight into that occasion:

> 8 April, Monday. Up before 6, drest, sett off for Wicklow, Geo and I went over the hill. Took lodgings at Billy Williams. Went into Court, grand jury sworn, went up to room, there all the morn. Burke the Highwayman tried and found guilty. We did not go to dinner till past 6. Satt drinking all the night and until 6 in the morning almost. Then I went to Williams. Geo in bed from 12. Slept well, very wet morn, but cleared up about 12. Windy. 9 April, Tuesday. Up about 10. Drest. Break [fast]. Up to grand jury Room. Satt there most of the morn. The 6 Megans were tried and found guilty. 5 to be hanged and 1 transported.[32] Went to dinner about 5. Satt til past 7. Went to Court about 8. Sorting notices for presentments. Did not go down to the judge til nigh 11. I left the court soon after and went to lodging. Slept well. A showery windy day ...[33]

The law operated, on occasion, with some degree of sensitivity. Lane-Poole noted from the Presentments Book of 1734 that on several occasions a man in custody for his fees was discharged as 'a very poor man'.[34] The *Freeman's Journal* reported in April 1784 on the acquittal of two men, Daniel Finn and Patrick Dowd, for highway robbery at the Wicklow Assizes as the only evidence against them was their own confession, which it was alleged was improperly obtained, as they were for twelve hours imprisoned in an outhouse.[35] When two lads of 15 or 16 were detected in the act of plundering an orchard in September 1788, a local magistrate reasoned with their prosecutor that the usual punishment, a gaol sentence, would only harden their minds and prevent their reformation. A compromise was reached whereby the boys were warned and were alternately tied for a night to the gibbet on Black-a-moor Hill from which hung the body of an executed criminal named Walter Read.[36] Read had been hung and gibbetted on the 19th of July 1788 for his part in the murder of a Dr. Vincentio Pandolphi in October 1785. Justice could be administered in a more medieval fashion. Among the irons and other implements in the custody of the Wicklow gaoler, Thomas Manning, in 1737 was a branding iron.[37] James Wilson was branded on the hand for stealing three lambs in 1734.[38] At the Wicklow Assizes in the autumn of 1772 John Honige was found guilty of stealing cloth for which he was burnt on the hand.[39] Terence Doyle and Michael Sheil, found guilty of manslaughter at the Lent Assizes in 1798, were burned in the hand and imprisoned for two months.[40] Executions were sometimes enlivened by the oratorical flourishes of the departing criminal. George Manly, convicted of murder at Wicklow in 1738, told the assembled crowd:

> My friends, you come to see a man leap into the abyss of death. You will say I have killed a man. Marlborough, Caesar, and Alexander killed millions, and they are heroes. I am the murderer of one, and must be hanged.[41]

In 1787 the lord Lieutenant was empowered to appoint chief constables in baronies. The grand Juries were empowered to appoint 16 sub-constables within the same districts. Some of the constables appointed in county Wicklow under this act proved inefficient and at a meeting of magistrates held at Kilcoole on 3 August 1791 a list of nine suggested replacements was recommended to the incoming grand jury.[42] A further Act in 1792 allowed grand Juries to appoint additional constables, who were known as baronial constables, to each district. One of the most famous sub-constables in the early 1790s was Joseph Holt, later to become a rebel in 1798. The unsettled state of the country during the 1790s led to the introduction of greater controls particularly with regard to the registration of arms.[43] Certificates of licences were issued by magistrates to persons considered suitable to keep arms. Blacksmiths had to obtain certificates from magistrates that they were fit and proper persons to keep forges and had to enter into recognizances not to make pikes.

Health in local government

The beginnings of a modern health service at county level began in 1765 when an Act was passed making provision for the erection and support of an infirmary for each county in Ireland. The county infirmary in Wicklow opened in 1766 and was thereafter supported by grand jury presentments, parliamentary grants and local subscriptions. Only those surgeons who had been duly examined and certified competent by a board consisting of the governor general and surgeons attached to Steevens, and Mercers, Hospitals could be appointed to a county infirmary. The prison reformer, John Howard, visited the county infirmary at Wicklow on 3 June 1787 and later reported to a committee of the Irish House of Commons as follows:

> This hospital is situated in the main street, and is much out of repair. The yard is very uneven and foul, without a Privy. There is a garden, but it is occupied by the apothecary. The house which contains eight apartments might be rendered much more commodious than it is at present. There are ten beds in bad order, and nine patients. There is a deputy treasurer at 10l. per annum; the apothecary has 25l. for making up the medicines, as they are laid in by the governors; and there are two maid servants and a porter attending there.[44]

By the late 1820s the county infirmary was treating 613 persons each year. A dispensary attached to it treated 1000 extern patients each year. In the early 1840s it was described as a very well-managed institution which was considered sufficient to meet the wants of the eastern portion of the county. It was also noted that fit cases were sometimes refused for want of room, but they were put into lodgings in the town, and attended until there were vacant beds. In 1817 another county infirmary opened in Baltinglass and continued in operation there until 1868. By the late 1820s, 1,500 people were being treated there annually. The effective radius of these infirmaries was limited and in the early 1840s it was pointed out that an area like Shillelagh was so remote from the two Wicklow infirmaries that few but the more serious cases were sent to either.[45]

In 1805 the grand Juries were authorised to give grants to dispensaries in rural areas and in 1814 and 1818 they were allowed to assist in the erection and maintenance of fever hospitals. By the early 1820s dispensaries, administered by committees of management and supported partly by subscriptions and partly by a grand jury grant of equal amount, were in operation in Arklow, Bray, Coolattin, Dunlavin, Enniskerry, Newtownmountkennedy, and Rathdrum. By 1850, the network of dispensaries had extended to Annamoe, Ashford, Aughrim, Avoca, Ballinastoe or Calary, Blessington, Carnew, Delgany, Redcross and Dunganstown, Kiltegan, Newcastle, Rathvilly, Shillelagh and Tinahely. MacDonagh has pointed out that Ireland had one of the most advanced health services in Europe in the early nineteenth century, if policy and structure were to be taken as criteria.[46] In 1851 dispensaries were placed under the control of the poor law unions.

Fever hospitals, supported, like the county infirmary, by grand jury presentments, parliamentary grants and local subscriptions, opened in Newtownmountkennedy and Enniskerry in 1814, in Stratford-on-Slaney and Bray in 1817 and in Arklow in 1818.[47] Crises rather than any deliberate policy caused the setting up of these hospitals and the building rate was hastened considerably by each fever epidemic.[48] Bad weather which did much to cause food shortages also resulted in turf famines which deprived the poor of usable fuel. The absence of fires and hot water created the optimum conditions for the breeding of the typhus-carrying louse. Huddled together for mutual warmth in conditions of squalor, the poor inevitably became infested with vermin. Traditional practices like waking the dead also played a part in spreading typhus.[49] Between 1815 and 1817 the failure of the harvest was followed by a fever epidemic of unprecedented magnitude. It is likely that at least 65,000 people died of typhus over the entire country.[50] A Select Committee on the State of Disease in Ireland reported that in county Wicklow the disease had been most prevalent among the wretched peasantry in the mountains, in a tract commencing above Newtownmountkennedy and extending to Tullow in county Carlow...' Wandering beggars were blamed for the spread of the disease.[51] There were further epidemics in 1826 and a great wave of typhus spread over the country between 1845 and 1846.[52]

From 1817 cholera spread slowly across Europe from India, where it was endemic, and reached Ireland in March 1832. The symptoms were particularly unpleasant – the Irish for cholera was *tonn taosgach agus crampaidhe* – purging, vomiting and cramps. Almost half of those who contracted the disease in Ireland died as a result. According to the census of 1841 a total of 119 people died of cholera in county Wicklow between 1831 and 1832, 45 in rural districts and 74 in civic districts. This was undoubtedly a conservative estimate – at least 46,000 people died in the country at large, the incidence of the disease in Ireland being about double that of England and Wales.[53] The fear engendered by cholera was undoubtedly due in part to the indiscriminate nature with which it afflicted all classes, whereas typhus was to a much greater extent, the disease of the poor.[54]

Fever hospitals opened in Wicklow in 1836 and in Tinahely in 1845, the latter for paying patients only. During the famine many temporary fever hospitals were opened – at Tinahely between April and September 1847, in Baltinglass between March 1847 and July 1849, in Newcastle or Killadreenan between June and September 1847, and at Blessington between December 1847 and August 1850. Carnew Dispensary was also used occasionally as a fever hospital up to 1852.

Health – mental

While under the Vagrancy Acts of 1714 and 1744, two or more justices of the peace were allowed to commit 'furiously mad' or 'dangerous' persons to a secure place, generally the local gaol,[55] it was not until the early nineteenth century that moves were made to provide for the treatment of mental illness on a broad scale. The Richmond Lunatic

Asylum was opened in Dublin in 1817 and a network of asylums was established around the country over the following decades. The Richmond took in patients from several outlying counties including Wicklow. In the early 1830s this asylum usually held about 10 Wicklow patients supported by the grand jury. By the 1840s the county was entitled to send 27 patients to the Richmond. The Wicklow grand jury considered the establishment of a separate asylum in the county in the 1860s and the cost to the county of maintaining lunatics in the Richmond was a source of continued irritation.[56] In 1895, when additional buildings were to be erected at the Richmond, the Wicklow grand jury sought an exemption from the lord lieutenant with regard to the county Wicklow proportion of the proposed outlay because the number of patients going to the asylum from county Wicklow did not, as a rule in their average number, fill the number of beds for which the county was assessed and paid. The number of Wicklow lunatics maintained there, however, rose dramatically in the 1890s, from 108 in 1890 to 166 in 1898.[57] The average cost per patient in the Richmond, excluding casual receipts and amounts from paying patients, was £28.4s.5d for the year 1896. At the spring assizes in 1898 the grand jury suggested that the state should provide for the care and maintenance of dangerous lunatics and that the incoming county councils should be responsible only for harmless lunatics.

Synge provides an insight into public perceptions in county Wicklow of the asylum. Among the peasants of the Wicklow hills, of Ireland in general the madhouse, he suggested, was less dreaded than the union workhouse. The union, a home of refuge for 'tramps and tinkers', was looked on with supreme horror by the peasants; the asylum they knew better.[58]

Law and order

In the early nineteenth century the grand jury continued to exercise important functions with regard to the appointment and support of the police. At the summer assizes, 1819, presentments were made for 9 sub-constables in the Barony of Arklow, 14 in the Barony of Ballinacor, 11 in the Barony of Newcastle, 10 for the Half Barony of Rathdown, 7 for the Half Barony of Shillelagh, 14 in the Upper Half of the Barony of Talbotstown and 10 for the Lower Half of the Barony of Talbotstown.[59] Under an 1822 Constabulary Act, implemented in Wicklow in 1823, a county constabulary was established. Sixteen constables or sub-constables were to be appointed for each barony, half barony or other division of a barony within each county and force strength remained determined by the standard of the barony until 1828. The senior constabulary officers and chief constables were thereafter to be appointed by the lord Lieutenant. The percentage of Catholics in the police in Wicklow remained very low in the 1820s. In 1824 only 12 per cent of the police in the county were catholics compared with 26 per cent for Leinster. Palmer suggests that the reason was the greater availability of protestant recruits in the county, but sectarian tensions in the aftermath of the 1798 rebellion may also have contributed to the exclusion of catholics from the force.[60] In 1824 the jurisdiction of the Dublin police was extended, enabling them to act in cases of treason and felony in Kildare, Wicklow and Meath. On the 1st of January 1836 there were in the county 4 first class chief constables, including sub-inspectors, 23 constables, 116 sub-constables and 5 horses. The cost of this force in 1835 had been £5,417-12-03 of which £2877-08-02 was chargeable against the county. There was also a force of Peace Preservation Police in the county consisting of 1 magistrate, 1 chief constable, 7 constables, 36 sub-constables and 2 horses.[61]

By the mid nineteenth century wide powers were given under the grand jury laws with regard to the regulation of traffic on the roads, the curtailment of nuisances etc. Persons turning horses and cattle loose on public roads, negligently driving cattle, flying kites, setting off fireworks or making slides on ice and snow, leaving ploughs and harrows on the road, slaughtering beasts on the road etc. could all be prosecuted under the grand jury laws. Dogs were not allowed within 50 yards of any public road unless they were muzzled or had a block of wood of sufficient weight fastened to their necks to prevent them from being dangerous. Justices of the peace could order the seizing or killing of dangerous dogs. Persons carrying timber crosswise on carts and carriages on any public road were liable to prosecution.[62] All cart, car or dray owners were required to have their names and residences painted upon some conspicuous part of the right or off-side of such carriages in legible letters not less than one inch high. Carts had to be under proper control and drivers who refused to divulge the names and addresses of the owners of carts were liable to prosecution. There were specific rules of the road in operation with which traffic had to comply. Drivers of carriages, riders of horses etc., on meeting any other traffic, had to keep to the left, and on passing other traffic, to pass to the right.

The meetings of the grand jury in the mid nineteenth century appear to have been non-contentious affairs. At the Wicklow summer assizes in 1858 the chief justice congratulated the grand jury on the condition of the county of Wicklow and attributed this happy state of the county to the fact of the uniform residence of the landlords within it.[63] There were, however, inherent weaknesses in the structure of grand jury system. The grand juries had no corporate existence and had no direct authority, except in a limited way through their officers, to maintain actions against those who had failed in their duties or obligations.

COUNTY OFFICERS

The county officers in Wicklow in the nineteenth century included the following:

The lord lieutenant of the county

The office of lord lieutenant for a county was initiated in Ireland in 1831. The holders were the chief military authorities in their counties and had a large control over the militia and appointments to it. Their military jurisdiction was abolished by the Army Regulation Act, 1871. The lord Lieutenants of counties were appointed by the crown (or subject to the direction of the Sovereign, by the Viceroy). The earl of Wicklow was lord Lieutenant until the late 1860s when he was succeeded by the earl of Meath The earl of Milltown served as Lieutenant in the 1880s and the earl of Carysfort in the 1890s.

Custos rotulorum

The custos rotulorum was the chief civil authority in the county, had custody of the county records and administered the oath of office to under-sheriffs. He was appointed by the viceroy, by letters patent under the Great Seal of Ireland. From the 1830s to the early 1850s the earl of Meath served in this office. From then on the person holding office as lord Lieutenant invariably also held the post of custos rotulorum. The custos rotulorum was charged with the custody of the county records and up until the the passage of the County Courts Act in 1877, was responsible for the appointment of the clerk of the peace.

Deputy lieutenants

These were offices which conferred social rank. The appointment rested with the lord lieutenant of the county, subject to the sanction of the viceroy. The average number of deputy lieutenants in county Wicklow in the nineteenth century usually ranged between 13 and 19.

The high sheriff

The high sheriff was appointed by the lord lieutenant from a list of three names, submitted to him by a judge going on assize.[64]

The duties of sheriff included the conduct of elections for parliamentary representatives, the election of coroner, the service of writs for both the superior and the county courts and the selection of the grand jury. The sheriff needed a substantial income and on his appointment had to enter into recognizance to the crown of £1,000 before the barons of exchequer. While the office was one which enhanced the personal and political influence of the holder, the financial implications of the position were potentially ruinous. Creditors could sue the sheriff if debtors escaped the sheriff's bailiffs.[65] The sheriff had the power of appointing a sub-sheriff who could perform the duties of the office, but was answerable for the act of such a deputy. A list of the high sheriffs of Wicklow to 1898 appears in Appendix I.

The clerk of the crown

The clerk of the crown acted as the clerk of the court of assize, as well as the secretary of the grand jury for criminal business.

He acted as public prosecutor, prepared and sent bills of indictments, kept the crown book and entered rules and judgements. It was the duty of the clerk of the crown to file and keep all affidavits, maps, plans and estimates for grounding any presentments or affidavits accounting for public money, to deliver copies of all presentments to the grand jurors, to deliver copies of all discharged queries to the treasurer of the county, to make out queries on all presentments to the grand jury, to record the fiat of the judge, to receive traverses etc. In May 1818 John Pollack, the clerk of the crown for Wicklow, appointed William Curtis as his deputy. Curtis acted as deputy clerk of the crown in Wicklow for the following 30 years, being reappointed after John Pollack's death by his son, A.H.C. Pollack. Curtis resided at 3 Harcourt Street in Dublin and informed a government commission in 1842 that he always attended in county Wicklow before and after assizes, 'whilst my presence was necessary', and always discharged his duties in person with assistants. He also acted as deputy clerk of the crown for Kilkenny county and city and for county Wexford. In 1846 John McMahon became clerk of the crown for county Wicklow and acted thereafter without a deputy. Paul Dane, who became clerk of the crown in 1868 became the first clerk of the crown and peace around 1878. William G. Toomey, who had served as solicitor to the grand jury, became clerk of the crown and peace in the late 1880s.

The clerk of the peace

The clerk of the peace performed the same duties at quarter sessions as the clerk of the crown at assizes, acted as Assistant Barrister at civil bill proceedings and registered electors for counties and boroughs. In March 1834 John Mills, clerk of the peace for Wicklow, appointed Samuel Fenton as his deputy. Mills died in March 1838 and his successor, Charles Hamilton, reappointed Fenton as deputy clerk of the peace. Hamilton received a salary of £277 as clerk and Samuel Fenton received as his deputy £77 in addition to the fees of the office. Fenton was based in Gloucester Street in Dublin City but had offices in the Courthouse in Wicklow and in Baltinglass which he attended between two and three months of the year and where there were persons throughout the year to receive notices and attend to communications. He also acted as solicitor and a land agent for a private gentleman in county Wicklow. Fenton succeeded Hamilton as clerk of the peace around 1858 and served as such until the 1870s when the office was amalgamated with that of clerk of the crown.

Treasurer of the grand jury

The duties of the treasurer included the issuing of warrants to collectors of the cess, keeping an office open in the assize town into which collectors paid their collections, and laying his accounts before the grand jury at each assizes.

John Revell jun served as treasurer for county Wicklow from his election by the magistrates of the county in February 1830 to the 1860s when the post was amalgamated with that of secretary. In 1842 he told a government commission that he received a salary of £185 together with a sum of £212-10-0 as interest on exchequer bills. He stated that he did not receive any fees, had been elected for life and resided altogether within the county of Wicklow and within three miles of the county town. He had an office attached to the county courthouse where he attended for three days previous to, during and six days subsequent to each assizes and frequently at other periods. He also had an office open daily at his own residence for attending to the business of his office.[66] Sir George Hodson, the foreman of the Wicklow grand jury, told the government commission in 1842 that he regarded the post of county treasurer as being almost a sinecure and thought that the duties might well be united with those of county secretary.

Secretary of the grand jury

The duties of the secretary of the grand jury included keeping an office open for the purpose of receiving applications for presentments which were then open to public inspection and making schedules of approved applications printed copies of which were distributed to the county Surveyor, the foreman of the grand jury and the judge of assize. The secretary was appointed by the grand jury. At the spring assizes of 1834 B.S. de Renzie was appointed secretary. The *Wicklow Newsletter* was later to recollect that de Renzie was at this point '... an elderly gentleman, a retired Militia Captain:- his sight was much impaired, he lived at a great distance from the town of Wicklow ...' The paper ascribed his appointment to 'that veneration for antiquity and military attainments which characterised the past generation ...'.[67] in 1842 he told a government commission that he received from the presentments the sum of £120 from which he had to provide stationery etc., the sum of £10 at each assizes for the distribution of schedules, posting notices etc. and about £60 per annum in fees for printed forms of applications.[68] He had a permanent office at the courthouse at Wicklow and one at Baltinglass '... for more than two months previous to each road sessions, for the accommodation of the public in that part of the county ...'. He attended some days previous to and during each assizes in Wicklow. He commented that '... the county being intersected by a chain of mountains and most of the sessional towns being on the outskirts of it, makes the travelling on the sessional tours very arduous and expensive, occupying 40 days in each year ...'.

De Renzie also acted as clerk to the Dublin and Carlow Turnpike Trust and as an agent for a small property 'for a gentleman residing in England', functions which he had performed previous to his employment by the grand jury in 1834.

In 1842, following the death of de Renzie, Marcus Maingay became secretary and acted until his own death in September 1858.[69] Samuel Fenton acted as secretary briefly in the late 1850s. In March 1859 George Wynne was appointed secretary. Wynne had been for some years in the army, had subsequently been for a short time secretary to lord Massereene, had been abroad for some years, and had a relative secretary in an adjoining county.[70]

Among his opponents in the election for secretary were J Maingay, son of the late secretary and Robert Courtenay junior, son of the Sub-Sheriff of the county. The *Wicklow Newsletter* made no secret of its sympathy with the 'young blood of the county, the sons of our old friends and well tried county officers ...' who were disappointed at the election.[71] During his tenure the offices of secretary and treasurer were amalgamated. George Wynne resigned at the end of at the summer assizes, 1882. At the spring assizes in 1883, his son, Edward N. Wynne, was elected secretary and treasurer of Wicklow grand jury. Wynne was a marksman of note[72] and served for a time as Honorary secretary and treasurer of the county Infirmary in Wicklow.[73] He became a justice of the peace in May 1887. In 1899 he became the first secretary and acting treasurer of the Wicklow county council.

County Surveyor

The duties of the county surveyor included attending at presentment sessions and affording professional advice, making applications for the repair of roads when necessary and causing roads to be repaired in cases of neglect by contractors etc.

In April 1834 William Hampton became the first county surveyor to be appointed for county Wicklow. He told a government commission in 1842[74] that he resided and had an office in the county '... and am always attending at it when not travelling or inspecting the works of the county; I cannot exactly state the number of days, but suppose they might be 45 or 50 in each year; drawing plans, writing letters, instructing my assistants in the discharge of their several duties ...'. He commented that he had '... only 3 assistants (costing £150 per year) allowed me for 8 baronies ...'. The foreman of the grand jury stated to the commission that there was a lack of control over the operations of the several road contractors by the county surveyor who could not possibly be present at all times when inspection was required. The county surveyor recommended persons for the post of surveyor's assistant. Hampton seems to have appointed his son, Robert, assistant county surveyor in 1837.[75]

James Boyd succeeded Hampton as county surveyor around 1846. Boyd had served as county surveyor in Clare from the 1830s and had his son Campbell Boyd made assistant county surveyor in Clare in 1836. Campbell Boyd seems to have been appointed assistant county surveyor in Wicklow during the tenure of his father and served in that capacity until the early years of the twentieth century.

James Boyd was replaced by Henry Brett in 1853. Brett seems to have served as county surveyor in Mayo in the 1830s and 1840s and in Waterford in the early 1850s.[76] In the early 1880s Carter Draper replaced Brett as county surveyor. Draper was later to become the first surveyor for Wicklow County Council.

Under the grand jury system all public works of any description, such as the making of new roads, building of bridges etc. and the maintenance and repair of existing works had to be carried out by contract. When there was no tender for a particular contract the county surveyor, under an 1857 Act, could execute the works himself. Unfortunately under the grand jury Acts it was difficult to purchase machinery which restricted the range of work which a county surveyor could carry out.

Coroners

The duties of coroners in respect of which they obtained grand jury presentments was that of holding inquests when persons were slain or died suddenly or in prison. In some of the Boroughs such as Baltinglass, the Sovereign acted as coroner. Originally coroners were obliged to have an estate or inheritance of the value of £50 or a freehold estate of £100 a year. They were later elected in Ireland by popular suffrage and had to be medical doctors, barristers, solicitors or justices of the peace of five years standing.[77] At the spring assizes 1824 five coroners received payment for carrying out inquests – Alexander

Moore, John L. James, William P. Higginbotham and Mathew Hudson. By 1834 a fifth coroner, J.B. McClathchy had been appointed for county Wicklow but from 1840 there were generally two. The Hudson family were prominent as coroners in the county for most of the nineteenth century – Mathew Hudson, was replaced as coroner by Robert Hudson around 1840. He resigned in 1859 and was replaced by Mathew Hudson Jones who was elected unopposed in March of that year.[78] Jones was a guardian in Rathdrum union.

Two members of the Newton family also served as coroners – Hibert Newton from around 1850 and Philips Newton from the early 1860s.

The coroner was authorised to direct that dead bodies be brought into the nearest convenient tavern, public house, or house licensed for the sale of spirits and the owners or occupiers of such premises were obliged to permit this.

Other county employees

Other employees of the grand jury in the 1820s included the surgeon of the Infirmary and gaol at Wicklow, the surgeon of the second infirmary at Baltinglass, Protestant and Catholic chaplains of the gaol, the gaoler at Wicklow, the assistant gaoler at Wicklow, the courtkeeper at Wicklow, the bridewell keeper at Baltinglass, the courtkeeper at Baltinglass, the crier at assizes and crier at sessions. In 1819 the Court-House keeper at Baltinglass was a woman named Mary Doran. The length of tenure of certain office holders was considerable. The Rev. Robert Porter retired as chaplain of Wicklow gaol in March 1858 after 48 years service.[79]

Grand Juries – limitations

Hoppen points out that in such counties as Wicklow in the early nineteenth century Tory landlords and their agents established quasi-permanent election organisations to supervise the registries, pay the travel expenses of sympathetic voters, and manipulate the granting of leases according to the changing demands of local politics.[80] The registration of voters was a matter of vital importance both before and after the Franchise Act of 1850. This Act simplified procedure and gave the county vote to £12 rated occupiers. In 1859 regular registration work constituted the most common form of Tory organisation in such counties as Wicklow,[81] and while, until 1874, the Whig Fitzwilliam interest regularly held one of the county seats, a mass of well organised Tory proprietors invariably held the other.[82]

While Catholics were permitted to serve on grand Juries from 1793 their composition remained overwhelmingly protestant due to the concentration of property in protestant hands and religious and political discrimination. The magistracy remained overwhelmingly Protestant to the end of the nineteenth century. In the early 1890s, for example, there were 116 justices of the peace in county Wicklow, of whom 101 were Protestant Episcopalians and only 13 Roman Catholics.[83] In Kildare, where the number of justices of the peace was the same, 34 of them were Roman Catholics. The majority of both Protestant Episcopalian and Roman Catholic justices were landed proprietors and it is significant that merchants, as a class, were all but excluded from the magistracy, only three justices in this period coming from their ranks. One of these was Episcopalian, one Methodist and one Catholic.[84] In Wicklow, as in other parts of the country, the majority of grand Jurors came from a small, interconnected group of landed families. grand jury resolutions frequently reflected their political outlook. The Wicklow grand jury regularly presented addresses of loyalty to the reigning monarch.[85] In the last two decades of the century these were anti Home Rule in character, much to the chagrin of local nationalists. At the spring assizes in 1886, for example, the grand jury expressed their unabated devotion and loyalty to the person and throne of Her Most Gracious Majesty Queen Victoria, and their unswerving attachment to the legislative union existing between Ireland and Great Britain and expressed their conviction that any change tending to weaken or impair such union would be fatal to the prosperity and progress of Ireland and fraught with the gravest danger to the British Empire. At the spring assizes of 1887 and 1893 similar resolutions were passed. Other preoccupations sometimes manifested themselves as when, at the spring assizes in 1895, the grand jury applied to the secretary of state to prohibit the taking or destroying of the eggs of pheasant, partridge, quail, heathgame, grouse, wild dick, widgeon, golden plover, pochard, sheldrake, goldfinch, snipe, teal and woodcock, within the limits of the county of Wicklow at large.

The main objections raised against the grand jury system were based on the manner in which they were constituted which was unrepresentative of the body of the ratepayers, their temporary character and the fluctuating nature of their membership which had no continuity from one Assizes to another.

The grand jury and the poor law system

After 1840 the grand jury system ceased to expand to any great extent. In contrast, the structure of the poor law system, being modern and efficient and more easily subject to central control, was adapted on nearly all occasions where a new local function was created or an old one modified. In 1844 the poor law unions were taken as the marriage registration districts, in November 1851 the boards of guardians took over the new system of medical relief under the Medical Charities Act, in 1861 the machinery of the poor law was used for defraying the expenses of the Cattle Disease Act for Ireland and in 1874 the guardians became rural sanitary authorities and in certain cases urban sanitary authorities.

The Medical Charities Act of 1851 led to the modernisation and extension of the old grand jury dispensary network under the boards of guardians and made a domiciliary medical service available to thousands of people in county Wicklow for the first time. The dispensary system played a vital role in the fight against smallpox and by the end of the nineteenth century midwives had been authorised in virtually every dispensary district in the Wicklow unions.[86] The poor law hospital system soon complemented that of the grand jury. The 1862 Poor Law Amendment Act opened the workhouse hospitals to the non-destitute sick. The Act also gave the power to boards of guardians to place orphans and deserted children with foster parents. Boards were also empowered to recover from a putative father the cost of maintaining his illegitimate child on the poor rate, after the mother had made a sworn statement, supported by corroborative evidence, before petty sessions. At a meeting of Rathdrum guardians on the 9th of April 1864, the Chairman stated that proceedings were being taken against 5 putative fathers of illegitimate children in the workhouse. Such cases were, however, difficult to pursue successfully.[87] Grand jury presentments continued to be made into the latter half of the nineteenth century to persons, sometimes clergymen, for the support of deserted children in each barony or half barony. The children ranged in age from infancy to about 10 years and were nursed by women[88] who were named in the presentment books. At the summer assizes of 1857 presentments were made for the support of 12 deserted children in the Barony of Shillelagh, 1 in Upper Talbotstown, 1 in Rathdown, 2 in Newcastle and 3 in South Ballinacor.

The poor law system settled into a supporting role for the grand jury in respect of mental health. In general, dangerous lunatics from the county appear to have been transferred to the Richmond asylum while harmless lunatics and the mentally retarded were maintained in workhouses.

While an infrastructure for the treatment of disease was in place in the county by the mid nineteenth century, the Nuisance Removal and Diseases Prevention Acts of 1848 and 1849 had utilised the poor law system to assist in the prevention and spread of fever and cholera, there was considerable local concern with regard to the absence of adequate legislation to deal with the question of sanitation. Early nineteenth century pioneers of sanitation such as Edwin Chadwick had highlighted the medical benefits of sanitary reform. It was believed that contagion arose from miasms emitted from filth. While such thinking was based on a concept of disease that was notably incomplete by modern standards these theories had enough truth in them to work. The miasmatic theory was the first generalization of epidemiology to be actually justified by its fruits.[89] Many local medical men in Wicklow had no doubt as to the the dangers which a lack of sanitation posed. William Nolan of Wicklow Fever Hospital in a letter to the *Wicklow Newsletter* on the 24th of June 1865 complained that his representations to the cabin-holders of Rathnew concerning the '... very great danger arising from the cess pools which are to be found opposite each cabin reeking with filth and abominations of every sort ...' were to no avail.[90] An editorial in the *Newsletter* in September 1865 strongly supported the necessity of a good sanitary law. The Sewage Utilization Act of 1865 constituted the board of guardians as the 'sewer authority' in any town or village in the union not under the control of a municipal authority. The following year a Sanitary Act was passed which consolidated and tidyied up the earlier public health legislation and which was primarily concerned with the prevention and treatment of cholera. The cholera epidemic of 1866 primarily affected the towns of Arklow, Wicklow and Bray and the *Freemans Journal* noted on 21st of September 1866 that nearly all those who had died in Arklow at that point had been from a district where the sewerage was bad. The 1866 Act introduced the sanitary inspector or inspector of nuisances to the local scene.

The whole issue of sanitation transformed the structure of local government in Ireland. In Britain the Royal Sanitary Commission of 1866-69 resulted in the formation of the Local Government Board in 1871 and a similar body was set up in Ireland in the following year which absorbed the poor law commissioners and took in other public health functions too. In 1874 a new Public Health Act was passed which established urban and rural sanitary authorities. The boards of guardians became the rural sanitary authorities for those areas which did not come under the jurisdiction of urban authorities.

The boards of guardians who administered the poor law unions were, to a much greater extent than the grand juries, microcosms of the surrounding community being made up of representatives of the land-owning class, the ex-officios, and representatives elected by the rate-paying public, mainly tenant farmers. The posts of honour and power on these boards, chairman, vice-chairman and deputy vice-chairman were for most of the nineteenth century in the hands of the land-owning element. In Baltinglass union the Saunders, Westby and Dennis families held the officers posts for much of the nineteenth century. In Shillelagh Earl Fitzwilliam held the post of chairman from the 1840s to the 1890s and the other positions were generally in the hands of magistrates. In Rathdrum union members of the Acton, Parnell, Tottenham, Drought and Gilbert families generally occupied these posts. As Feingold points out, the Poor Relief Act of 1838 which established the poor law introduced the Irish countryman to representative local government for the first time and established the conditions whereby he could become involved in politics either as a poor law guardian or as a voter.[91] The boards of guardians enabled farmers to express themselves politically within the established governmental framework. Membership of these boards was however, closed to those at the bottom of the economic ladder. Elected guardians were required to meet property qualifications higher than that required for the franchise. The average qualification in the 1870s and 1880s was about £20. Subsistence farmers, cottiers, labourers and most artisans were excluded by the £4 qualification from the franchise as well. Nevertheless, between 1872 and 1882 about half the boards of guardians in the three southern provinces gradually removed all the landowners occupying offices and replaced them with tenant occupiers. At a Tenant Right meeting in Rathdrum on the 3rd of January 1880 poor law guardians and town commissioners were present.[92] At a meeting of the Ladies Irish National Land League, Rathdrum, on the 7th of March 1881, it was proposed and seconded 'that the ladies of this branch of the Land League, who are entitled to a poor law vote, pledge themselves to support no candidate at the coming election, except a member of the Land League'.[93] At the subsequent poor law elections in Rathdrum union two land leaguers, Thomas Delahunt and John Doyle, topped the poll for the Wicklow division after an active canvass. In the Arklow Division, the candidates nominated by the Land League were elected after a contest.[94]

The following year there were elections in two divisions, Wicklow and Killiskey. The latter seat was vacant due to the resignation of Lieut. Colonel Tottenham and a conservative candidate, Mr G. Crofton, won the seat after a contest with a home ruler, Mr J. Gaskin. In Wicklow Electoral Division Thomas Delahunt and John Doyle again topped the poll with nearly a hundred votes more each than the previous year. The *Wicklow Newsletter* commented that the home rulers worked very hard while the conservative party did very little and not even a canvass was organised.[95]

Feingold divides counties into (a) 'radical' counties whose union offices were in 1886 filled by more than 60 per cent tenants or (b) 'conservative' counties whose union offices were in 1886 filled by more than 60 per cent landowners. He classes county Wicklow as 'conservative'. Feingold found no relationship between poverty and radicalism and, while counties with the highest prevalence of large farms showed the strongest tendency towards radicalism, Wicklow was the exception. This was due, he thought, to the fact that the Catholic population was relatively small. Feingold noted that where the population had a higher proportion of Protestants the tendency towards radicalism decreased. In Wicklow Unionist and anti-Land League organisation in the county seems to have been particularly well developed as typified by such bodies as the West Wicklow Loyal Association and the County Wicklow Property Defence Association.[96]

Municipal development – nineteenth century

Following the abolition of its corporation, the town of Wicklow adopted the Lighting, Cleansing and Watching Rate Act on the 13th of September 1841. No rates were levied for some years as the corporate property was found adequate to cover the expenses. The town was lighted with gas in 1858. Even in the 1880s the cleaning, watering and gas lighting of the streets was defrayed out of corporate property.[97] In 1881 the town commissioners constructed waterworks at Ashtown, one and a half miles from the town, which provided an abundant and pure water supply.[98] Perhaps the most remarkable example of municipal development was that of Bray. Its transformation from 'no more than a rude fishing village and posting town'[99] to a large town took place with an extraordinary rapidity in the early 1850s owing to the advent of the Dublin, Wicklow, and Wexford railway in 1854 and the energy and enterprise of William Dargan. On the 9th of October, 1857, sanction was obtained by 'the chief influential inhabitants' to constitute themselves into an incorporate governing body for the management of the township affairs utilising the Towns Improvement (Ireland) Act of 1854. In 1866, under the terms of the Bray Township Act, the commissioners, as reconstituted under the Act, took over those powers formally vested in the grand jury with regard to roads, bridges and township works.

The town commissions enabled the catholic inhabitants of Wicklow's towns, particularly businessmen who were virtually excluded from the grand jury system, to participate in municipal government for the first time, and provide a pool of knowledge and expertise which facilitated the transition to local democracy on a county basis after 1898. Many nineteenth century town commissioners and their families played a prominent role in local administration into the twentieth century. Nathaniel Haskins, a native of Tinahely, established a business in Wicklow town around 1868 and became a town commissioner in the 1870s. His sons Jack, David and Nathaniel later served on Wicklow Urban District Council.[100] Members of the McPhail family were closely associated with administration in Wicklow town in the late nineteenth and early twentieth centuries. One of the most prominent local nationalists on the Wicklow town commission was Joseph McCarroll, a Tyrone man and ex-teacher who came to Wicklow around 1870 and established himself in the town as a shipping broker and agent of the Dublin and Wicklow Manure Company. He had served as a Town commissioner from the 1870s and quickly became the acknowledged leader of nationalists in the district.[101] Other Wicklowmen such as Denis Cogan were to utilise, for the benefit of the county, an expertise gathered through service on other municipal authorities. Cogan had been a member of Dublin Corporation in 1885 and the Irish Times was later to report that 'due to his financial genius the debts of that body were successfully consolidated and its first loan floated'.[102] He later served for many years on Wicklow County Council and was M.P. for East Wicklow between 1900 and 1907.

The 1898 Local Government Act

The two decades following the passing of the Public Health (Ireland) Act of 1878 saw no major changes in the structure of local government. While nationalist opinion looked askance on the unrepresentative nature of the grand jury system the struggle for Home Rule rather than democratic local administration remained the priority. The Local Government (Ireland) Act was an attempt to reduce the jumble of authorities and place county government on a representative basis.

Up until 1899 the right to vote in local elections was confined to those who were ratepaying occupiers or owners. The Local Government Act made the parliamentary electorate (plus peers and qualified women) the local government electorate. Thus householders and persons occupying part of a house could vote in local elections. Multiple votes proportionate to the amount of rateable property were abolished. While women could become guardians and district councillors they were debarred from county and borough councils until 1911, when they were admitted by the Local Authorities (Ireland) (Qualification of Women) Act of that year.[103]

While the new Local Government Act was initially greeted with mixed feelings by nationalists they quickly adjusted to the new situation and used it to full advantage, particularly in political terms.[104] The new councils were to provide valuable experience in the art of administration and a fresh channel for local political enthusiasms. The 1898 Local Government Act saw the demise of the grand jury as an organ of local government and all fiscal functions were transferred to the county and rural district councils. The functions of the grand jury were thereafter confined to adjudication on Bills of Indictment sent up to them at the assizes.

The elections of councillors for the new urban district councils highlighted the sophistication of the nationalist political machine. In Wicklow town, for example, the nationalist '98 ticket' secured an overwhelming victory. 73 of the 487 voters on the register were women to whom the franchise had been extended by the Local Government Act. The total poll was 396. The *Wicklow Newsletter* paid sardonic tribute to nationalist organisation, commenting that of the 76 voters who could not mark their own papers, 66 were illiterates, '... and the marvellous accuracy with which the large majority of these illiterates voted for the '98 ticket' spoke volumes for the excellent tutoring they had previously received..'.[105] The *Newsletter* did, however, express its approval of the choice of Chairman by the three new urban district councils in the county. In Bray, Mr James E. McCormick, 'a well known, clever, business man' was elected, in Arklow Mr Daniel Condren 'another astute and far seeing gentleman possessing considerable business capacity', and in Wicklow Mr James P. Byrne, 'a clever and popular member of the medical profession'.[106]

As a result of the 1898 Local Government Act five rural district councils were established in county Wicklow, with control of sanitation, housing, roads and public works within their respective districts. The rural district councillors also acted as poor law guardians. Under the 1898 Act women could become guardians and rural district councillors.

The elections of county councillors for the new Wicklow County Council were held in April 1899. The county had been divided into nineteen county electoral divisions each returning one county councillor (with the exception of Bray, which returned two).[107] Contests took place in 14 of the 19 electoral divisions in the county. Three unionists and 17 nationalists were returned (see appendix II).[108] The unionists were all returned after contests. Viscount Powerscourt was elected for Powerscourt county electoral division, Viscount Milton for Rathdrum county electoral division and Dr Norman Thompson for Delgany county electoral division. Thompson had been one of the Honorary Secretaries of the Rathdown Branch of the County Wicklow Property Defence Association during the Land War.[109] Sir Henry Cochrane, while an unsuccessful unionist candidate in Bray, topped the poll for the poor law election for the east ward in that town. The *Wicklow Newsletter*, while regretting the fact that none of the old grand jury had been elected, confessed that '... with a few exceptions we believe the county councillors selected will prove equal to the proper discharge of the fiscal business of the county...'. The paper particularly praised the election of the nationalists Mr T.J. Troy, Mr M. Langton, Mr E.P. O'Kelly, and Mr James Byrne who '... are sound, practical businessmen and are not likely to encourage jobbery or corruption of any kind ...'. The new county council also included such veteran nationalists as Denis J. Cogan and Joseph McCarroll.

The first general meeting of Wicklow County Council took place on 22 April 1899. Under the terms of the 1898 Act three grand jury nominees could be nominated to the first county council – the Wicklow nominees were Richard Drought, William Morris and David Mahoney. The council also included 5 ex-officio representatives from the rural district councils within the county and two members co-opted at the first meeting – William Murphy and William Harrington. The former had been defeated by Viscount Powerscourt in the Powerscourt division at the county council elections. Mr Edward P. O'Kelly J.P., a nationalist merchant from Baltinglass and Chairman of Baltinglass poor law union was elected the first Chairman of Wicklow county council. Mr Michael Byrne J.P., a nationalist farmer from Tinahely and Chairman of Shillelagh union, was elected Vice Chairman. For the first time resolutions carried by the main county authority reflected the political aspirations of the majority of the inhabitants of the county. Resolutions asserting the right to a full measure of home rule and the restoration of a native parliament, endorsing the finding of the financial relations commission (that Ireland was overtaxed to the extent of at least two and a half millions a year), affirming the right of Catholics to university education and directing the attention of the government to the painful condition of the evicted tenants, were put and declared carried, the grand jury nominees and Dr Thompson (unionist) dissenting.[110]

Appendix I

High Sheriffs of county Wicklow 1800-1899

1556/7	Robert Pyfoll, Gent. for one year Sheriff of the county, Territory or Country called O'Byrnes Country in the Marches of Dublin. – (3 & 4 Phil & Mary s.3.)
1558	Bryan McTeig Oge O Byrne, Gent, of Ballynvalley – (4 & 5 Phil. & Mary, s.9.)
1559	Patrick Barnewall, Gent, of Kilmahoole, for one year of this country and county Dublin (1 Eliz. s. 23)
1563	George Wolverston of Stilorgan
1566	Francis Agarde
1569	Robert Pyfore
1570	Francis Agarde

Sheriffs Proper (appointed after the establishment of the county)

1609	John Wolferston
1612	Gerald Byrne
1613	James Eustace
1614	Sir Henry Belyng
1618	Calcot Chambre
1617	Philip Pilsworth (Kildare)
1618/19	Sir Richard Graham [or Grehan]
1620	Sir Richard Graham [or Grehan]
1621	Robert Walker
1622	John Potts
1623	Edward Leigh
1624	Thomas Daniel
1625	Bryan Cavanagh
1628	Pierse Sexton
1633	Samuel Loftus
1640	Bernard Talbot
1643	Robert Kennedy
1645	Edw. Loftus
1655	John Ponsonby
1656	William Coddington
1657	Daniel Hutchinson
1658	Chidley Coote
1661	Robert Hassells
1662	William Matthews
1663	John Hackett
1664	Cromwell Wingfield
1665	Humphrey Abdey
1666	Richard Buckley
1667	William Reeves
1668	Richard Edwards
1669	John Loftus
1670/71	John Boswell
1672	Thomas Graham

1673	James Moore
1674	John King
1675	John Byrne
1676	Alexander Heydon or Heyden
1677	Robert Stratford
1678	Christopher Usher
1679/80	John Warren
1681	Laurence Hudson
1682	Alexander Heydon or Heyden
1683	Philip Cradock
1684	William Hoey
1685	John Stockton
1686	Sir Robert Kennedy
1687	Francis Meara
1688/89	Thady Byrne
1690	Ambrose Wall [26 Nov 89]
1691	John Price (10 July from the camp of K. William III at Crumlin)
1692	Robert Stratford [19 Nov. 91}
1693	William Mathews [22 Sep. 92]
1694	William Hoey
1695	John Whitehead or Whitshead
1696	Thomas Burows or Burrows
1697	Evan[s] Price
1698	Hugh Eccles
1699	Anthony Archer
1700	Owen Jones
1701	John Hoey
1702	Richard Edwards
1703	Robert Graydon
1704	John Lovett
1705	Tichbourne West
1706	Edward Stratford, Belan, county Kildare.
1707	Sir William Fownes
1708	Henry Percy, Snugboro.
1709	Joshua Allen
1710	Robert Stewart
1711	Thomas Acton, West Aston.
1712	Abraham Nixon
1713	Kendrick Fownes
1714	Thomas Ryves
1715	John Boswell, Ballycurry, alias Boswell's Court.
1716	John Hayes
1717	Richard Mitchelburne
1718	John Stephens
1719	Laurence or Lorenzo Hudson
1720	Simon Goodwin
1721	Richard Wingfield
1722	Robert Saunders
1723	John White, Ballyellis.
1724	Richard Reade, Temple Lyon.
1725	Arthur Baldwin

1726	Robert Percy, Snugborough.
1727	Richard Chapel Whaley
1728	William Hume, Butterswood.
1729	John Heighington, Donard.
1730	Thos. Hawkduel or Hawkshead, Ballintruer.
1731	Thos. Eaton
1732	Richard Archer
1733	William Westby
1734	William Ryves
1735	Geo. Pendrill or Pendred
1736	John Stratford, Baltinglass
1737	John Hayes
1738	Joseph Chamney
1739	James Griffith Carroll
1740	Abraham Nixon, Money.
1741	John Smith, Baltiboys.
-	William Goodwin, Talbotstown. (J. Smith decd.)
1742	William Goodwin, Talbotstown.
1743	Edward Chamney, Knockloe.
1744	Robert Baldwin, Redcross.
1745	Henry Acton, West Aston.
1746	Henry Monck, Charleville.
1747	Laurence Steele, Aghavannagh.
1748	Samuel Onge, Ballynaclash.
1749	Ralph Howard, Shelton.
1750	Forster Adair, [Grove Hill,] The Crosses.
1751	Henry Bond, Shankill.
1752	Richard Symes, Ballyarthur.
1753	Thomas Smith
1754	Hugh Eccles, Cronroe.
1755	[Janat] Eaton, Wicklow.
1756	Richard Baldwin
1757	Robert Hoey, Dunganstown.
1758	Morley Pendred Saunders, Tankardstown, Saundersgrove.
1759	James Edwards, Oldcourt.
1760	James Carroll Jnr., Ballynure.
1761	Dennison Hume, Humeswood.
1762	Hon. Richard Wingfield, Dublin.
1763	Henry Brownrigg, Rathdown.
1764	John Usher, Mount Usher.
1765	Isaac Ambrose Eccles, Cronroe.
1766	Charles Powell Leslie, Tubber.
1767	Mitchelburne Symes, Coolboy.
1768	John Smith, Baltyboys.
1769	William Hume, Humeswood.
1770	William Fairbrother, Foxhall.
1771	William Tighe, Rossana.
1772	George Carroll, Ashford.
1773	Samuel Hayes, Hayesville.
1774	Patrick Boyd
1775	Thomas Ryves, Rathsallagh.

1776	George Putland, Hawksview.
1777	Nicholas Westby, High Park.
1778	William Parsons Hoey, Hoeysville.
1779	Morley Saunders, Saundersgrove.
1780	Andrew Murray Prior, Claremount.
1781	Thomas Acton
1782	Hopton Scott, Ballygannon.
1783	Sir Francis Hutchinson Bart., Ballycullen.
1784	Hon. Richard Wingfield, Powerscourt.
1785	Sir James Stratford Tynte Bart., Dunlavin.
1786	Robert Hodson, Hollybrook.
1787	Archibald Hamilton Foulks
1788	Samuel Falkener, Castletown.
1789	Richard Hornidge, Tulfarris.
1790	William Patrickson, Blessington.
1791	Arthur Knox, Woodstock.
1792	William King, Baltinglass.
1793	Thomas King, Kingston.
1794	Charles Stanley Monck, Charleville.
1795	Robert Gore, Sandymount.
1796	Thomas Hugo, Drummin.
1797	Peter La Touche, Bellevue.
1798	Walter Carroll, Ballynure.
1799	Thomas Archer, Mt. John.
1800	Thomas Archer, Mt. John.
1801	Wm. Eccles
1802	James Critchley
1803	Wm. Heighington
1804	William Francis Grene
1805	John Middleton Scott
1806	Edward Westby
1807	James Wall
1808	John Blachford, Altidore.
1809	John Knox, Woodstock.
1810	George Mears John Drought, Ballyfree.
1811	Isaac Ambrose Eccles, Clonroe.
1812	Charles Tottenham, Ballycurry.
1813	Robert Howard, Castlehoward.
1814	John Hornidge, Russelstown.
1815	Major General John Stratford Saunders, Golden Fort.
1816	Daniel Mills King, Kingston.
1817	Francis Hoey, Dunganstown.
1818	George Gun, Mount-Kennedy.
1819	John Synge, Roundwood.
1820	William Acton, West Aston.
1821	Alexander Carroll, Ashford.
1822	Robert Saunders, Saunders Grove.
1823	Thos Hugo, Drummin.
1824	Robert Holt Truell, Clonmannon Hill.
1825	Sir Robert Hodson, Hollywood.
1826	Henry Carroll, Ballynure.

1827	William Jones Westby jun., High Park.
1828	Daniel Tighe, Rossana.
1829	William Truelock Bookey, Annamoe.
1830	Francis Synge Hutchinson, Palermo, Bray.
1831	Hon. Grenville Levison Proby, Glenart.
1832	William Parsons Hoey, Hoeyfield.
1833	Wm. Kemmis jnr., Ballinacor.
1834	Sir George Fredrick Hodson, Hollybrook House.
1835	William Beresford, Templecarrig.
1836	John Parnell, Avondale.
1837	Edward Symes Bayley, Ballyarthur.
1838	David La Touche, Luggelaw.
1839	John Michael Henry Baron de Robeck, Rathcoole.
1840	Thomas Johnson Barton, Merrion Square, Dublin.
1841	John Synge, Glenmore Castle.
1842	Joseph Pratt Tynte, Tynte Park.
1843	Richard Hudson, Spring Farm.
1844	Francis Synge, Glenmore Castle.
1845	William Wentworth Fitzwilliam Hume, Humewood.
1846	Charles Tottenham, Ballycurry.
1847	Robert Craven Wade, Dunganstown.
1848	Lord Brabazon, Kilruddery.
1849	Robert A. Gun Cunningham, Mount Kennedy.
1850	Richard Howard Brooke, Castle Howard.
1851	George Hudson, Templecarrig.
1852	Rt. Hon. James Gratton, Tinnehinch.
1853	Sir Ralph Howard, Bushy Park.
1854	John Brennan, Kingston Lodge.
1855	George Putland, Bray Head.
1856	Andrew W. Byrne, Croneybyrne.
1857	Thomas Acton, West Aston.
1858	Joseph Salkeld, Ovoca, Rathdrum.
1859	Lt. Col. Charles J. Tottenham, Woodstock.
1860	William Robert La Touche, Bellevue.
1861	Christopher O'Connell Fitzsimon, Glencullen.
1862	Coote Alexander Carroll, Ashford.
1863	William Henry Ford Cogan, Tinode.
1864	Charles Putland, Bray Head.
1865	Joseph Scott Moore, The Manor, Kilbride.
1866	Hon. William Proby, Glenart Castle, Arklow.
1867	St. Vincent B. Hawkins Whitshed, Killincarrig.
1868	Robert Francis Ellis, Sea Park.
1869	Daniel Mahony, Grangecon.
1870	O'Neill Segrave, Kiltimon.
1871	Henry Pomeroy Truell, Ballyhenry.
1872	William Richard O'Byrne, Glenealy.
1873	Meade Caulfield Dennis, Fortgranite, Baltinglass.
1874	Charles Stewart Parnell, Avondale.
1875	Sir John Esmonde, Ballynastragh, Gorey.
1876	James Stuart Tighe, Rossana, Ashford.
1877	Julius Casement, Cronroe, Ashford.

1878	Robert J.P. Saunders, Saunders' Grove, Baltinglass.
1879	Gordon E. Tombe, Bromley, Newtownmountkennedy.
1880	R. Howard Brooke, Castle Howard, Ovoca.
1881	Charles George Tottenham, Ballycurry, Ashford.
1882	Charles William Barton, Glendalough House, Annamoe.
1883	Lord Brabazon, Kilruddery, Bray.
1884	Baron de Robeck, Gowran Grange, Naas.
1885	George Booth, Lara, Greystones.
1886	Capt. Cornwallis Robert D. Gun Cunningham, Mount Kennedy, Newtownmountkennedy.
1887	Hon. Henry Power Charles S. Monck, Charleville, Bray.
1888	Major Charles Robert Worsley Tottenham, Woodstock.
1889	Colonel D'Oyly Battley, Belvedere Hall, Bray.
1890	Captain Charles E. Pennefather, Rathsallagh, Grangecon.
1891	Sir Robert Adair Hodson, Hollybrooke, Bray.
1892	Lieut. Col. Fortescue Joseph Tynte, St. Austin's Abbey, Tullow.
1893	Captain Henry Segrave, Kiltimon, Newtownmountkennedy.
1894	Fletcher Moore, The Manor, Kilbride.
1895	Edward Henry Charles Wellesley, Bromley, Greystones.
1896	William Hume Hume, Humewood, Kiltegan.
1897	Sir Henry Cochrane, Woodbrook, Bray.
1898	Captain Quintin Dick, Grosvenor Crescent, London.

Appendix II

Members of the First Wicklow County Council

Elected Members

C.E.D.	*Name, Address and Occupation of Member*
Arklow	Edmond C. Walsh, 1 Vale Road, Arklow (returned unopposed) nationalist.
Ballyarthur	Thomas J. Troy, Ferrybank, Arklow, shipowner (returned after contest) nationalist.
Baltinglass	Edward P. O'Kelly J.P., Baltinglass, merchant (returned unopposed) nationalist.
Bray	William Burke, Castle Street, Little Bray, (returned after contest) nationalist.
	Martin Langton, 1 Fitzwilliam Terrace, Bray, (returned after contest) nationalist.
Blessington	William Osborne, Ballyknockan House, Blessington, contractor (returned after contest) nationalist.
Carnew	Michael Byrne J.P., Coolalug House, Tinahely, farmer (returned unopposed) nationalist.
Delgany	Dr. Norman Thompson, Kindlestown, Delgany, physician (returned after contest) unionist.
Dunlavin	Joseph Dunne, Merginstown Glen, Dunlavin, farmer (returned after contest) nationalist.
Glendalough	Dennis J. Cogan, 115 Thomas Street, Dublin, also Brockagh, merchant (returned after contest) nationalist.

Glenealy	William Costelloe, Ardanairy, Tonelegee, Wicklow, farmer (returned after contest) nationalist.
Hollywood	Anthony Metcalfe J.P., Lemonstown, Ballymore Eustace, farmer (returned unopposed) nationalist.
Newcastle	Simon T. Doyle, Delgany, farmer (returned after contest) nationalist.
Ovoca	James Byrne, Tinnakilly Lower, Aughrim, auctioneer and farmer, (returned after election – James Byrne received the same number of votes as a nationalist opponent and the result was decided by drawing lots) nationalist.
Powerscourt	Viscount Powerscourt K.P., P.C., Powerscourt, Enniskerry, peer (returned after contest) unionist.
Rathdangan	Michael Kelly, Englishtown, Kiltegan, (returned unopposed) nationalist.
Shillelagh	Thomas Sheppard, Boley, Shillelagh, farmer, (returned after contest), nationalist.
Rathdrum	Viscount Milton M.P., Carnew Castle, Carnew, (returned after contest) unionist.
Tinahely	Edward Byrne, St. Mullins, Tinahely (returned after contest) nationalist.
Wicklow	Joseph McCarroll, Church Street, Wicklow, merchant (returned after contest) nationalist.

Nominees of the grand jury
(as a temporary provision grand juries were allowed to nominate at the first county councils)
Richard R. Drought J.P., Ballinacooley, Glenealy.
William G. Morris J.P., Windgates House, Bray.
David Mahoney D.L., 34 Fitzwilliam Place, Dublin and Grangecon, Athy.

Ex-Officio members of the council council
James H. Coleman, Griffinstown, Baltinglass (chairman of Baltinglass no. 1 rural district council)
Alfred Zeller, Lackan, Blessington (chairman of Naas no. 2 rural district council)
Thomas Lawless, The Hotel, Delgany (chairman of Rathdown no. 2 rural district council)
Patrick J. Carey, Tomanierin, Aughrim (chairman of Rathdrum rural district council)
Joseph Gahan, Boley, Shillelagh (vice-chairman of Shillelagh rural district council)

Co-opted members of the county council
William G. Murphy, Mullinaveigue, Roundwood (William Murphy, a nationalist, had been defeated by Viscount Powerscourt in the county council elections for Powerscourt Division)
William Harrington, Cherryfield, Templeogue, county Dublin.

References

1. *Cal. Carew Mss 1515-1574*, p. 193.
2. R. Loeber, *The geography and practice of English colonisation in Ireland from 1534-1609* (Dublin, 1991), p. 18.
3. John Dymmok, 'A Treatise of Ireland' in *Tracts relating to Ireland*, ii, (Irish Archaeological Society, 1843), p. 13.
4. C. Litton Falkiner, 'The counties of Ireland, an historical sketch of their origin, constitution and general delineation', *R.I.A. Proc.*, xxiv (1903) C, pp 169-94.
5. *Cal. S. P., Ire., 1611-14*, p. xxxiv.
6. *P.R.I. rep. D.K. 33*, pp 43-4.
7. A writ of exigent required the appearance of a party to answer the law under pain of outlawry.
8. *N.H.I.*, ix, p. 52.
9. N.L.I., Ms 7227, Lane-Poole Notebook, p. 44. Around 1893 over 75 different types of records, including the presentment and query Books of the Wicklow Grand Jury were accessioned by the Public Record Office of Ireland from the local crown and peace offices in the county. Edward Stanley Lane-Poole, (1854-1931) orientalist and historian, worked on the presentment books subsequently in the Public Record Office. While the original volumes were destroyed during the siege of the Four Courts in 1922, a notebook containing information obtained by Lane-Poole from them is preserved in the National Library of Ireland.
10. Ibid., p. 51.
11. 2 Geo. I, c.17.
12. The declared object of the Foundling Hospital was the preservation of the lives of deserted or exposed infants by their indiscriminate admission from all parts of Ireland, putting them out to nurse in the country until they were of a proper age to be drafted into the hospital and educating them in such a manner as to qualify them for being apprenticed to trades or as servants. The foundlings were to be brought up as Protestants. The mortality rate among infants in the hospital was notoriously high.
13. *F.J.*, 11-13 October 1787.
14. Ibid., 9-11 August 1791.
15. Ibid., 19-22 May 1792. The Foundling Hospital was closed to further admissions in January 1830. The poor law commissioners and subsequently the local government board took over responsibility for the remaining foundlings who included many invalid adults boarded out mainly in remote parts of Leinster, See Joseph Robins, *Custom House people* (Dublin, 1993), p. 80.
16. Martha Salt last appears on the list of parish poor in 1730.
17. N.L.I. Ms 7227, p. 44.
18. 2 Geo. I, c.10.
19. 6 Geo. I c.10.
20. Ibid.
21. J.G. Simms, *The Jacobite Parliament of 1689* (Dublin Historical Association, 1974). The English parliament of William and Mary declared the Jacobite Parliament to be 'an unlawful and rebellious assembly' and all its acts and proceedings 'absolutely null and void'.
22. Kenneth Milne, 'The Corporation of Waterford in the eighteenth century', in William Nolan and Thomas P. Power (eds.), *Waterford: history and society* (Dublin, 1992), p. 334.
23. N.L.I., Ms 7227, p. 54.
24. Ibid., p. 60. Under the act for registering the popish clergy, only registered priests

were allowed to celebrate mass under pain of imprisonment or banishment. As the conditions attached to registration were so onerous, most Irish priests preferred not to register.

25. Ibid., p. 51.
26. Ibid., p. 50.
27. Eighteenth century magistrates had authority under ancient statutes to raise the 'power of the county' (*posse comitatus*) in the event of sudden outbreaks of disorder.
28. *The last county: the emergence of Wicklow as a county, 1606-1845* (Wicklow, 1993), pp 23-24.
29. Constantia Maxwell, *Country and town in Ireland under the Georges* (rev. ed., Dundalk, 1949), p. 200.
30. The last reference to statute labour appears in the Delgany vestry minute book on 2 October 1758. The last reference to overseers of the highways and roads appears on 2 October 1764.
31. N.L.I., Ms 7227, p. 70.
32. Two headstones side by side at St Saviour's Priory (The Monastery), Glendalough, commemorate Michael and Joseph Meagan, who were hanged on 26 April 1765, aged 30 and 28 respectively.
33. A book of historical notes on Killiskey Parish compiled by the rector includes an extract from the diary of William Fairbrother of Gleneasly for the period 1-7 April 1765. Mr Richard Drought, who inherited Mr Fairbrother's estate, sent the original to the rector.
34. N.L.I., Ms 7227, p. 60.
35. *F.J.*, 27/29 April, 1784.
36. Ibid., 23/25 September, 1788.
37. N.L.I., Ms 7227, p. 65.
38. Ibid., p. 60.
39. *F.J.*, 5/8 September, 1772.
40. *Commons Jn. Ire.*, xviii, p. cccxlv
41. *Our Boys*, 14 August, 1940, p. 816.
42. N.L.I., Ms 5024 (meeting of 3 August 1791).
43. Ibid., contains names of persons registering arms in the Kilcoole area in 1796.
44. *Commons Jn. Ire.*, xii pt. 2, p. dccccxliii.
45. Supplementary appendix to report on medical charities pursuant to the 46th section of the Act 1 & 2 Victoria, c. 56, p. 235.
46. O. MacDonagh, *Ireland* (Englewood Cliffs, New Jersey, 1968), p. 27.
47. Mr Phelan and Dr. Corr noted in the early 1840s that two of these fever hospitals received no subscriptions but they each received part of the county grant.
48. Timothy P. O'Neill, 'Fever and public health in pre-Famine Ireland', *R.S.A.I. Jn.*, ciii (1973), p. 7.
49. Ibid., pp 2-3.
50. Ibid., p. 10.
51. Ibid., p. 9.
52. 1,287 persons died of fever in the county between 1831 and 1841 and 2,171 in the following decade.
53. O'Neill, 'Fever and public health', p. 21.
54. Ibid., p. 25.
55. The 1744 Act also allowed local authorities to board out detained lunatics in private 'madhouses', but these were rare.
56. *Wicklow Newsletter*, 14 July, 1865.

57. Wicklow County Council archives, minutes of Wicklow County Council, 27 February, 1911.
58. Mark Finnane, *Insanity and the insane in post-famine Ireland* (1981), p. 129.
59. Wicklow County Council archives, printed grand jury presentment book, Summer Assizes 1819. The Sub-Constables presented for at the Summer Assizes in 1819 were as follows;
Barony of Arklow:- James Winterbotham, Thos. Norton, Wm. Hill, jun., John Grafton, Edw. Gregory, J. Kelly, Wm. Evans, John Long and T. Long.
Barony of Ballincor:- Wm. Paslow, Thomas Harrison, T. Doolan, John Coleman, P. Robinson, John Graham, John Hawkins, Alex. Halfpenny, T. Rice, John Mills, John Halfpenny, R. Allen, Joseph Wright and Forbes Flaherty.
Barony of Newcastle:- Thos. Smith, Jas. Orr, R. Jones, Robert Fox, John Thompson, Chas. Quinn, P. Hughes, Alex Warnock, Walter Storey, Jno. Fitzpatrick, and A. Dunbar.
Half Barony of Rathdown:- Thomas Hamilton, Joseph Cooper, Wm. Walker, Wm. Booth, of Ballinteskin, W. Booth jun., Wm. Fox, Robert Cuthbert, T. Basset, Thomas Walker and Mich. Barry.
Half Barony of Shillelagh:- James Codd, Geo. Thompson, David Price, Rich. Bedlow, Wm. Williams, Thomas Lennon and David Page.
Upper Half, Barony of Talbotstown:- Geo. Pearson, L. Smith, W. Cooper, Robert McBride, Wm. Thornton, T. Roe, John Steward, Jno. Robinson, Mich. Doran, Thomas Rubotham, Simon Lawrenson, T. Cope, Marks Weeks and M. Hawkins.
Lower Half, Barony of Talbotstown:- Henry Giltrap, Henry Norton, Wm. Scarf, John Forster, Henry Cordell, James Redden, Wm. Redden, Mat. Valentine, Mich. Valentine and J. Keegan.
60. Palmer, *Police and protest*, p. 249.
61. Minutes of evidence taken before the select committee on county cess (Ireland), appendix No. 1.
62. In cases where the timber projected more than two feet beyond the wheels and sides of the cart or carriage.
63. *Wicklow Newsletter*, 10 July, 1858.
64. At the beginning of the nineteenth century it was usual for the serving sheriff to name three suitable successors. He passed their names to the judge of assize on the summer circuit, who passed them to the lord chancellor who presented them to the lord lieutenant, the latter normally appointing the first name on the list.
65. Virginia Crossman, *Local government in nineteenth century Ireland* (Belfast, 1994), p. 8.
66. Appendix to report of the commissioners to revise the grand jury laws, Ireland, 1842, appendix A, see p. 9, [386] xxiv, sess. 1842
67. *Wicklow Newsletter*, 5 March, 1859.
68. Grand jury commission [386] xxiv, sess 1842, appendix c, p. 31.
69. *Wicklow Newsletter*, 11 September 1858. The correspondent noted that '... he had won, by his business-like habits and courteous demeanour, the respect of all who had official intercourse with him; and equally, in his private capacity, as a country gentleman, did he succeed in obtaining, by the kindness of his disposition, and the amiability of his character, the regard of a most numerous circle of friends...'.
70. Presumably Henry E. Wynne who had been appointed secretary to the Wexford Grand Jury in 1856.
71. *Wicklow Newsletter*, 5 March, 1859.
72. Minutes of meeting of Wicklow County Council, 8 August, 1904.

73. *Thom's Directory*, 1891, p. 1193.
74. Grand jury commission [386] xxiv sess. 1842, appendix B, see p. 19.
75. NAI, OPW 1/1/9, letter book relating to the appointment of county surveyors and assistants, 1836-1847, p. 21.
76. Ibid., pp 4, 11, 40-1, 44, 66, 128.
77. R. Barry O'Brien, *Dublin Castle and the Irish people* (2nd ed., 1912), p. 158.
78. *Wicklow Newsletter*, 19 March, 1859.
79. Ibid., 27 March 1858.
80. K. Theodore Hoppen, *Elections, politics and society in Ireland, 1832-1885* (Oxford, 1984), p. 282.
81. Ibid., p. 291.
82. Ibid., p. 305.
83. Of the Roman Catholic justices of the peace, 5 were landed proprietors, 3 were farmers, 1 was a solicitor, 2 were in the constabulary service, 1 was a member of the medical profession and 1 was a merchant or manufacturer.
84. The Catholic merchant justice of the peace was probably Peter P. Morrin, a miller and merchant from Baltinglass.
85. Wicklow County Council archives, grand jury presentments, spring assizes 1820, county at large sessions, presentment no. 131.
86. *Report of the Local Government Board, 1899*, p. 970.
87. *Wicklow Advertiser*, 9 April, 1864.
88. Wicklow County Council archives, spring assizes 1844, Half Barony of Shillelagh, presentments.
89. Charles-Edward A. Winslow, *The conquest of epidemic disease* (Madison, Wisconsin, 1980), pp 242-249.
90. *Wicklow Newsletter*, 24 June, 1865.
91. William L. Feingold, *The Revolt of the tenantry: the transformation of local government in Ireland, 1872-1886* (Boston, Mass., 1984), p. 233.
92. *Wicklow Newsletter*, 3 January, 1880.
93. Ibid., 12 April, 1881.
94. Ibid., 26 March 1881.
95. Ibid., 25 March 1882.
96. Ibid., 12 February 1882.
97. *Thom's Directory*, 1890.
98. *Slater's Directory*, 1894.
99. Arthur L. Doran, *Bray and environs* (Bray, 1903), p. 19.
100. *Wicklow People*, 24 October, 1942.
101. Obituary of Joseph McCarroll, *Wicklow People*, 13 March, 1920.
102. *The Irish Times*, 5 August 1940 includes an article on personal details of surviving members of the Old Irish Parliamentary Party. Denis J. Cogan was born in 1859 in county Wicklow. He built up a large business as a wholesale provision merchant in Dublin. He was one of the founders of the Hibernian and General Fire Insurance Company and was an extensive agriculturist. He was the Irish Parliamentary Party M.P. for East Wicklow between 1900 and 1907. He was a member of Dublin Corporation in the 1880s and was one of five leading businessmen nominated jointly by the Dublin Chamber of Commerce and the Dublin Mercantile Association to represent voters on the commercial register of the Dublin Corporation when it was taken over from the control of commissioners around 1930.
103. The extension of universal suffrage to local government did not take effect until 1935. The 30 year age minimum for women voters enacted in the Representation

of the People Act, 1918, was retained for women local electors until that date.

104. The Local Government Act of 1898 was severely criticised by Michael Davitt and John Dillon but was warmly welcomed by John Redmond and Tim Healy.

105. *Wicklow Newsletter*, 21 January, 1899.

106. Ibid., 28 January, 1899.

107. The nineteen county electoral divisions (each comprising a number of district electoral divisions) were Arklow, Ballyarthur, Baltinglass, Blessington, Bray, Carnew, Delgany, Dunlavin, Glendalough, Glenealy, Hollywood, Newcastle, Ovoca, Powerscourt, Rathdangan, Rathdrum, Shillelagh, Tinahely and Wicklow.

108. In neighbouring Wexford two unionists and seventeen nationalists were returned, in Dublin six unionists and fourteen nationalists, and in the province of Leinster, twenty unionists and two hundred and twenty two nationalists.

109. *Wicklow Newsletter*, 7 January, 1884.

110. Viscount Powerscourt (unionist) abstained from voting and Viscount Milton (unionist) was not present at that stage of proceedings.

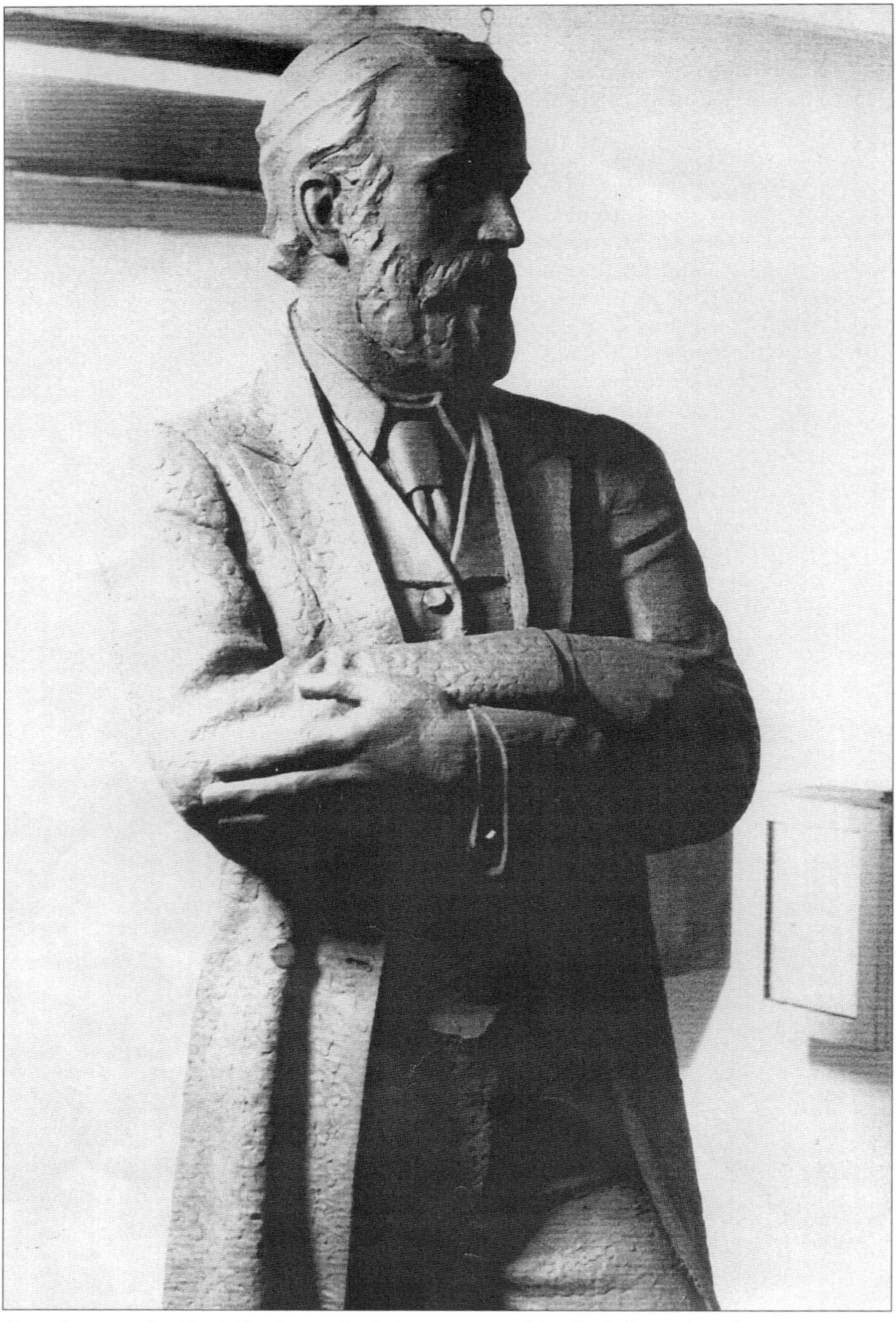

Parnell statue by Fred Conlon at Rathdrum, erected by Rathdrum Development Association with the financial support of Avondale Chemical Company (Kathleen Conlon).

Chapter 23

PARNELL AND HIS NEIGHBOURS

R. F. FOSTER

Parnell's connections with Wicklow have been the subject of continuing interest – most recently evidenced in the development of a lively and stimulating annual symposium at Avondale, which was inaugurated in 1991 as a fully-fledged summer school. Significantly, it has been inspired and nurtured by the dedication and commitment of a group of local people; academic input, while welcomed, is kept correctly in its place.[1] This seems apposite, in an involvement that commemorates the most hard-headed (and possibly worst educated) of Irish national leaders; it is also appropriate as a testimony to Parnell's continuing interest in, and identification with, the people of his native place and county. This in turn is a pointer to a vital theme in Irish history: the importance of place. On one level, the analysis of large subjects and issues – like the 1798 Rising or the Famine or the War of Independence – more and more emphasises local aspects and local variations; on another, historical initiatives are increasingly taken from the localities too. This is not a recent development; the anniversary year of Parnell's death was also the centenary of the foundation of the

Plate 23.1 Avondale House, county Wicklow.

Cork Archaeological and Historical Society, while other local historical societies originated over fifty years before that. And in 1912 AE wrote, with characteristic generosity and prescience: 'Citizenship in the true sense is created much more by the non-political than by the political movements in our time. The highest developments of humanity, of civic and patriotic life the world has known, have been in the small states, in communities no larger than Sligo.'[2]

Or, indeed, Wicklow. And Parnell's connections with his native county are symbolised in Avondale, his family's house, perched in an idyllic setting in one of the loveliest parts of the county. The situation of the house, too, is emblematic: close to Rathdrum, but not dominating it; one of a number of fine houses in that part of Wicklow, built between the mid-eighteenth and mid-nineteenth centuries; not aggressively large, nor cordoned off by miles of avenues and barriers of gate-lodges. Its great glory is not its architecture but its planting: those unique stands of trees planned by Samuel Hayes, and continued by the Forestry Commission.[3] In this Avondale is fairly representative of those houses scattered through east Wicklow (such as Westaston, Clonbraney, Clonmannon, Inchinappa, Glendalough) which, unlike the great Italianate *palazzi* of Kildare, have a certain integral relationship to their surroundings. This might be taken to symbolise the existence of a middling gentry – families like the Humes, Actons, Tottenhams, Howards, Synges, Tighes, Westbys, Grattans, Truells, Brookes, Bayleys, Probys and Parnells.[4] Several of these families had prominent eighteenth-century ancestors who had been active in politics and were retrospectively claimed for the 'Patriot' tradition: notably the Grattans, the Tighes and – again – the Parnells. These families, and the world they inherited, formed the background to Parnell's early life; and it was a background with which he kept up connections, though those connections naturally altered as his extraordinary political career distanced him from them.

The fact that his career was so extraordinary means that Parnell tends to be seen very much as a figure who stands alone: 'glamorously unique, as well as uniquely glamorous'.[5] But there were tissues, threads and connections which bound him to Rathdrum and continued to do so. Some were personal, and disappeared into obscurity: like the closest friend of Parnell's youth, Major Bookey of Derrybawn. The two young men, served in the Wicklow Rifles together, experimented on their sawmills together, played cricket together, socialised together; when the youthful Parnell and his drunken brother-in-law Arthur Dickinson were prosecuted for rowdy behaviour in the hotel at Glendalough in 1869,[6] Bookey was, fortunately, the magistrate in the case. With Bookey's death by drowning off Algiers in 1875, a link to

Parnell's Wicklow life is lost.[7] It is possible, even likely, that had he lived, their friendship would have been threatened by politics: as happened with Parnell's other great friend among his neighbours, his exact contemporary John Barton.

The Parnells were, however, closely linked into the cousinage of the local county. Many of their local relationships stemmed from the Howard family connection, created when Parnell's grandfather William Parnell-Hayes married Frances Howard. This brought relationships to the Powerscourts and Carysforts, since Frances's two sisters married into these families. Sir Ralph Howard of Castle Howard, MP for the county in Parnell's youth and a great local magnate, was a powerful figure in the Parnell children's lives, especially after their father's premature death; he became guardian for many of their financial interests, and was involved in litigation against Mrs Parnell over them.[8] The huge Fitzwilliam estate at Coolattin near Shillelagh, whose agent Robert Chaloner was a key figure in local life, was also important in Parnell's world; Chaloner was a friend of his father's, and had co-operated with him in famine relief measures in 1846-7. Years afterwards, at the height of the Land War in 1881, Parnell would uncharacteristically defend the administration of Coolattin: 'As to the Fitzwilliam estate in Wicklow, I know a great deal about it; it is so well managed that the tenants up to the present refused to join the Land League.'[9] In fact, a great deal of material relating to the Fitzwilliam estate has survived, and does show a complex and ambitious scheme of management: free schools, widows' pensions, a carefully structured approach to aided emigration, a Poor Shop, and well-meaning but probably infuriating attempts to regulate hostile relationships between tenants ('Edward Kelly is not to beat his wife Johanna any more and his wife is not again either to keep company with the Kirwans of Ballyconnell or to go into their house.')[10] The estate also paid a half of all improvement expenses, and limited rent increases to 5 per cent. This may seem whistling against the wind, and the attempts at social control equally hopeless and misplaced: the tone of landlord benevolence is grating at best nowadays, and often seems objectively self-interested. What is interesting, however, is that the evidence for nineteenth-century estate management in Wicklow does present a picture of involvement and amelioration on the landlords' part which was hardly typical, and more closely resembles the English norm. The Fitzwilliams may have been unusual; they were certainly unusually rich. And a squirearchical approach might be expected on their estate, since the owners were English Whig grandees rather than local Anglo-Irish (or Irish) Tories.

This could also explain their committed resistance to sectarian education. The estate paid grants to schoolmasters who founded hedge schools, for instance,[11] and opposed the attempts made by a bigoted local protestant clergyman to institute separate schooling. Lord Fitzwilliam had already alienated protestant foundations like the Erasmus Smith Board by opening his school to catholics alongside protestants, and appointing roman catholic priests to his Schools Committee.[12] Schools on the Grattan estate were similarly 'open to all'.[13] An exceptionally good relationship with local catholics was also evident on the Powerscourt estate (and not only because of Lord Powerscourt's friendship with the famous Father Healy of Little Bray[14]).

Wicklow had its bad landlords too (there were terrible evictions at Crony Byrne during the Famine); and before the Parnellite revolution it was not overwhelmingly Liberal in political terms either, generally returning Conservative members. The family interest of Lord Wicklow, notorious for political dictation to tenants, was Tory.[15] However, the impressive figure of James Grattan represented the Radical Whig interest between 1827 and 1841; Lord Monck was a prominent Liberal MP in the 1850s; and Sir Ralph Howard was described by Chaloner in 1848 as representing 'the Liberal cause'.[16] But where Orangeism appeared in the county, it was not among the gentry, and local JPs were opposed to its manifestations.

If there was a tradition of good local relationships in nineteenth-century Wicklow, it may have been because of the prevalence of secondary residences there; many houses like Avondale were owned by people who drew their major income from larger estates elsewhere in Ireland but preferred to live in Wicklow and could therefore – in a sense – afford a more liberal and relaxed attitude to their holdings there.[17] For instance, the Tighe family came to Rossana because an ancestor was ordered by his doctor to live in the country; his estates were in Kilkenny, but he so disliked that county that he bought the Wicklow holding as well.[18] Parnell's father, in fact, not only possessed another estate in Armagh, but also bought a far larger holding in Carlow just before he died.

At the same time, the liberal attitudes of local gentry went deeper than this, and were represented in the attitudes and writings of Parnell's grandfather: campaigner against English exploitation of Ireland, enemy of bad landlords, and early advocate of Catholic Emancipation. In his *Enquiry into the causes of popular discontents in Ireland* (1805), William Parnell violently attacked the Union:

> You tell us to interest ourselves in the glory of the English government; we tell you we cannot. Why? Because we cannot love our stepmother as our mother ... Give us, then, back our independence; hunt our trade from your ports; that national spirit

which lightened our shackles can assert its freedom; leave us to our rebellions, the courage that repressed them once can repress them again; take back the lenitives you would apply to our religious distinctions: we shall not always be bigots but shall one day acknowledge the maxim that by removing religious distinctions we remove religious animosities. These are evils that time and experience will remedy and we might yet be a happy and wealthy people; but if you destroy the principle of national honour you destroy the very principle of wealth and happiness and our misery will be such as our baseness deserves, our poverty as complete as your narrow jealousy could desire.'[19]

The language derives from late eighteenth-century 'patriotism'; but it also anticipates the rhetoric of early Home Rule. In a sense both William Parnell and his neighbour James Grattan, another liberal pro-catholic, were attempting the impossible: the situation of an Irish landlord in the early nineteenth century made liberal initiatives effectively unviable. History, and the prejudices of their neighbours, were too strong for them. Nonetheless, they tried; and William Parnell found his own niche in history, since it has recently been established that it was he who first hit on the subscription idea which funded Daniel O'Connell's Catholic Association.[20]

William Parnell's ideas were in many other ways ahead of his time, if less immediately influential. He propagandised for educational reform and agricultural innovation; he worked long and hard for a reversal of landlord attitudes towards 'those unfortunate beings who are placed at the extremity of the scale of degradation, the Irish peasantry',[21] and constantly reverted to this preoccupation in his writings; the surrounding miseries of the tenantry, he said, made a landlord's existence almost unbearable.

What is striking here is the sense of an interdependent connection between a reforming landlord and his dependants; and, even more remarkable for the time, the fact that religious differentiation did not enter into this. It is the kind of scenario conjured up by the didactic novelists of the early nineteenth century (amongst whom William Parnell must himself be numbered) but which bore little resemblance to normal reality. Himself a liberal Protestant, William Parnell was close to catholic activists, and dedicated his one novel to 'the Priests of Ireland'. His son John Henry Parnell during his short life achieved a similar reputation for good relationships with his catholic neighbours, and the record of his activity on the Rathdrum Poor Law Union Board of Guardians bears this out; he also campaigned for building a catholic church at Rathdrum and warmly praised the good work done by orders of nuns.[22] And this also bears upon an aspect of Charles Stewart Parnell which is not often paid attention, but which has direct relevance to his Wicklow background.

Parnell was a Protestant; a member of the Synod of the Church of Ireland; and dutifully took some part in local parish organisations like the Select Vestry when he was living at Rathdrum. His private religious feelings appear to have been agnostic, with an inclination (like others of his family) towards the Plymouth Brethren. But from the first stirrings of his political career, it is notable that he sustained extremely good relationships with local Catholic clerics. The parish priest at Rathdrum in 1875, Father Galvin, gave him influential backing in his first political contest; Father Galvin's brother, also a priest, befriended Parnell and his brother John on their American tour in 1872. The Reverend James Redmond of Arklow was another local priest who brought heavy pressure to bear on Parnell's behalf in the 1875 Meath election. A later parish priest at Rathdrum, Father Dunphy, was an even closer friend and associate; when he moved to Arklow he worked closely with Parnell not only in political organisation, but also in his development of quarries at Big Rock, and in campaigns to develop Arklow harbour. More surprisingly, these local clerical friends remained friends, even during the terrible days of the Split (there were more Parnellite priests than one might think).[23] After the Kilkenny election of December 1890, when Parnell allegedly had quicklime thrown in his eyes, he spent Christmas Day with Father Dunphy, now based in Waterford. Father Dunphy told him he would always have something to eat and drink from him and asked him, reasonably enough, 'Where was your brain? Why did you not get three sensible men to advise you?' Parnell said that he was getting old, like Father Dunphy, and would accordingly get sense.[24] Not many people could talk to Parnell like that, especially at that stage of his life. Like Major Bookey at Derrybawn or John Barton at Glendalough or the Gaffney family at Avondale, Father Dunphy knew Parnell as a Wicklow neighbour: and his testimony, were it available to us, might accordingly clarify several aspects of the enigma.

Parnell, of course, was a Wicklow gentleman and conscious of it; his brother's memoir emphasises this, and stresses his irritation at foreigners (American as well as English) who did not recognise 'an Irish gentleman' when they saw one.[25] This identification as 'an Irish gentleman' was not as inimical to support for Home Rule as might be supposed, at least in the 1870s. It is interesting to note that Wicklow's first Home Rule MP, Andrew O'Byrne, who was returned in 1874, was a landlord, owner of Cabinteely House, a JP, and High Sheriff for the county; he had been a close ally of Parnell's father on the Rathdrum

Poor Law Guardians' Board. Many of Isaac Butt's early Home Rule party were from a similar background.[26] As a general rule, this ceases to be true from 1880. But significantly, one of Parnell's closest friends in the party was another obscure and forgotten figure, the Wicklow MP and Parnell's neighbour at home, W. J. Corbet. Corbet, a regular guest at Aghavannagh shooting-parties and a frequent visitor to Avondale, remained a firm supporter of Parnell's to the end – as a Wicklow neighbour as well as a political ally.

Indeed, the support in Wicklow for Parnell could sometimes come from unexpected quarters: here again, neighbourliness may have counted for more than political affiliation. When the practice of 'ploughing matches' at Avondale was instituted (originally to work Parnell's land when he was imprisoned in Kilmainham), several of those who contributed help were not Home Rulers. And the local newspaper, the *Wicklow Newsletter,* owned and edited by the firmly Unionist William McPhail (who had bought the press to set it up from the Tighes at Rossana) sustained an odd relationship with Parnell – at once antagonistic and affectionate. Parnell's politics were consistently attacked by the paper; but his Wicklow identification was seen as a cause for pride, and the paper warmly endorsed his campaigns for improving the harbour facilities at Wicklow and Arklow, and his creation of local employment in mines and quarries. In the terrible last year of his life, the *Newsletter* took a Parnellite rather than anti-Parnellite line, while every now and then reminding itself and its readers that its line was officially Unionist. Its leader on Parnell's death was genuinely grief-stricken and memorialised him as a great son of Wicklow as well as a magnanimous employer and good landlord:

> In one connection particularly do we desire to speak of his sad demise, and that is as it regards Wicklow itself. In the death of Mr Parnell we have lost a benefactor in the true sense of the word. What he has done for the people of the county, and what he intended to do, will never be adequately realised. How much his heart was centred here, and how deep an interest he displayed in the home of his childhood, was little thought of. It was absorbed in the whirl of political excitement, but we are now beginning to faintly see the inmost recesses of his heart. The walls of his study at Brighton were hung with engravings of Avondale, for which he ever retained an abiding love ... Mr Parnell's life was sacrificed for Ireland. No matter how we may condemn his policy, he lived to aid her progress. When the archbishop of Dublin taunted him with the money he received from the Irish people, he replied that the inhabitants of Arklow could explain how he employed it. And

> well they might. It was in the recent speech he delivered in Wicklow he made use of those words; and to the minds of those who were aware of his interest in the county, they carried emphatic conviction.[27]

These identities meant more to Parnell himself than is often realised. He was a conspicuously good landlord: building cottages for his tenantry (one of whom went to great lengths to conceal from him the fact that the chimney smoked, for fear of disappointing him);[28] letting rents run for long periods, and keeping them below recommended valuation levels; remaining deeply preoccupied with his experimental sawmills on the estate, which at their height employed twenty-five people (the buildings are still there, on the left of the avenue as one approaches the house); engaging in turf production for various purposes at Aghavannagh. (Ahead of his time in this as in much else, he also started a peat-litter industry in Kildare.) The estate overall employed more than a hundred and fifty people. The efforts of many hostile journalists to prove the Land League president a bad landlord in private life all failed. They very often confused him with his brother Henry, who was an absentee, managing his Carlow estates purely as land speculations and quite prepared to evict non-paying tenants. Parnell, however, was uniformly praised by his tenants, and never made money from his rent-rolls, already declining when he took over the estate.

In fact, there is a strong case for arguing that it was the issues of tenant right and the general agricultural position that brought him into politics, rather than the inspiration of the Fenian ideal – whatever that came to mean later.[29] (His sister Anna certainly denied that this played any part in their youthful conditioning.[30]) Avondale must have demonstrated to him the logic of land reform, for all concerned. He was, in fact, the archetypal encumbered landlord; the estate was burdened with mortgages, inherited and acquired.[31] Parnell was, unlike many of his colleagues, a genuine farmer; T. P. O'Connor merrily recalled that most of the agrarian leaders could not tell a cow from a horse, nor a field of oats from a field of potatoes, and Parnell had to explain these mysteries to his followers.[32] His early and consistent embrace of the land purchase ideal – peasant proprietary – was probably encouraged by the realisation that the traditional system had not worked at Avondale.

And this also helped to inspire the non-political activities for which his neighbours knew him best, and which brought him back into contact with them: stone-quarrying and mineral explorations. In 1882 he had been excited to discover granite stone-quarries 'on my own land', at Ballyknockan.[33] From producing beechwood paving-setts in his sawmills, he progressed to turning out granite setts from his stone quarries – the major ones at Big Rock, Arklow, and minor efforts elsewhere. (We think of Parnell's monument as the Gauden's statue at the top of O'Connell street in Dublin; he might prefer it to be the paving stones at the other end, on O'Connell Bridge, which were supplied to Dublin Corporation, against Welsh competition, from Parnell's quarries at Arklow.) Parnell's preoccupation with his quarries, and his developments at Arklow, brought him back into the mainstream of local politics. His relationship with his relative, Lord Carysfort, had turned sour over politics, and bitter mutual criticism had been exchanged over their respective espousals of the Wicklow and Arklow harbour schemes. However, the development of Big Rock, and Parnell's subsequent support of the Arklow harbour scheme which was intimately linked with it, meant that they began to co-operate again.[34] His political biographers tend to express surprise at Parnell's obsession with these matters – at the fact, for instance, that his first enquiry of a visitor to him in Kilmainham Jail in 1881 was about the progress of the Wicklow harbour works.[35] Similarly, during his highly controversial interview with Lord Carnarvon in 1885, on which so many speculations about a Tory Home Rule initiative were based, Parnell devoted much valuable time to expounding the success of his quarries, and the significance of the Dublin Corporation contract, as an earnest of the industrial resources of Ireland.[36] His preoccupation with his mines and quarries during 1891 struck some people as evidence of delusion.[37] But considered in the context of Parnell's local identity, such obsessiveness comes as no surprise. Even when he was strategically lying low, during the high political fever of 1885, he emerged to give an eagerly-awaited address on St Patrick's Day in London. Most of it was devoted to the Arklow and Wicklow harbour schemes. Political analysts might interpret this as a Machiavellian red herring dragged across the tracks, or as a deliberate exhibition of impassiveness. But it is more easily explained simply as a genuine expression of what meant most to him at the time.[38]

It is of a piece with his economic ideas, which increasingly tended towards protectionism for Irish industry; and significantly, he first endorsed the principle openly in a speech at Arklow. In the world of political calculation, this was read as a deliberate snub to Joseph Chamberlain, at the time pressing his own schemes for Ireland. In historical terms, it might be noted as another of those steps which alienated Ulster yet further from any association with Home Rule. (The same was true of Parnell's endorsement of denominational education, which he embraced and adhered to from an early stage – another indication that his attitude towards catholicism and its social agenda was far warmer than that of many Protestant politicians, Irish or English.) But the point of the speech is surely that an encouragement was being expressed to local Wicklow industry and that this was Parnell's priority. Sharply focussed as always, he seems not to have been juggling the larger implications.

In the very first political speech ever reported from Parnell (during the 1874 Dublin election campaign), he gave his reasons for wanting Home Rule. It would encourage manufactures, develop fisheries, and stimulate a resident gentry, who would be socially and politically responsible.[39] These were sentiments spoken from platforms where he was accompanied by warmly supportive catholic priests, and where a significant amount of Fenian influence had been brought into play on his behalf behind the scenes. In a sense, all the elements of his future career are there; and it is possible that their order of priorities, and relative weighting, did not alter as dramatically as might be assumed.

And these priorities should, I think, be related not only to his family background (they closely echo William Parnell) but also to the ethos of nineteenth-century Wicklow. Even in the Land War, local Land League priests like Parnell's friend Father Dunphy found themselves rather grudgingly praising the record of local landlords for reducing rents below Griffith's Valuation and keeping up the 'kind and considerate traditions of their families'.[40] The *Wicklow Newsletter*, though Tory, Unionist and pro-landlord, called on local landlords to grant rent abatements, and approvingly published lists of those that did. Corbet, one of the new Home Rule MPs for the county, was himself a landowner and a popular one; he also denounced advocates of violent methods. Even a lashing from Michael Davitt failed to rouse the supine tenantry of Blessington in December 1880.[41] Unpopular landlords like Lord Brabazon rapidly reduced their rents by 50 per cent; the general level of agitation in the county was very low, a phenomenon remarked with varying degrees of disapproval by visiting politicians.[42] The focus of most of the local criticism was the Fitzwilliam estate, but this tended to concentrate on the interventionist practices of re-cropping, reallocation, drainage and so forth, rather than evictions; in the words of one tenant, 'introducing English ideas, contrary to the feelings and views of the Irish people'.[43] Relationships with landlords were more fraught in the less prosperous west of the county, as local opinion admitted; this was a tradition of long standing, at least to judge by the diary of Mrs Smith of Baltiboys, who lacerated her landlord neighbours with a fine Scots impartiality in the 1840s.[44] Even she, however, had felt that 'the Irish gentleman is at last waking from his dream of idle pleasure, which never satisfied, which deteriorated his character, impoverished his resources, spread distress round him, and left him to drown religion in the bottle.' Neighbours of hers in west Wicklow like Lord Downshire, Lord Milltown and Hugh Henry, may have approximated to the type; the interesting thing is that there seem to have been much fewer of them on Parnell's side of the county. Reading between the lines of Mrs Smith's diary, which ends in the early 1870s, it is clear that she felt the whole structure of landlordism was doomed. And by the 1880s it was increasingly clear to farsighted people that the Irish land system had run its exploitative course, and a new world was looming.

Some of Parnell's neighbours saw this development as apocalyptic; we need only look at the publications of the local Irish Loyal and Patriotic Union (a pro-landlord rump, dominated by Lord Meath and his cronies). Yet Parnell's neighbours, like himself, came from a tradition where landlords maintained good relations with tenants, even if the system's *raison d'etre* was increasingly doomed; where opposition to the Union had been a deeply felt commitment among families like the Tighes, Ponsonbys, Grattans, and Parnells; where

Plate 23.2 Gladstone at Kilruddery House. Included are Mr. Pratt Saunders, Lord Brabazon, W. E. Gladstone, Mrs. Gladstone, Miss M . Gladstone, Earl of Meath, Countess of Meath, Lady A. Brabazon, Spencer Lyttelton (Irish Architectural Archive).

estates had been given more attention than was the norm (though this may have been at the expense of a larger holding elsewhere, which met the bills), and where modern initiatives and productivity plans featured surprisingly. Here, too, relationships between catholics and protestants were easier than in many other areas; and, possibly, relationships across social divides too (Anna Parnell's evolution towards radical politics and feminism was probably aided by her friendship with the Comerford family, millers at Rathdrum). And, despite the conventional Unionism of run-of-the-mill gentry politics, it is worth remembering that at the end of her life Mrs Smith of Baltiboys supported Isaac Butt's Home Government Association, since she gave up all hope of Britain running Ireland effectively after the Famine; and that not only James Grattan and William Parnell, but later local gentry like Andrew Byrne and Viscount Monck, embraced liberal politics. Ged Martin, indeed, has pointed out that Monck by the 1860s was overseeing in Canada the kind of extension of devolved government which Parnell would press for in Ireland a decade later.[45]

The dramatic convulsions of politics in the 1880s, and the revolutions of the subsequent period, jolted these complacent continuities out of existence. And where they did exist, the reformist ideas of the Wicklow gentry probably depended on oldstyle deference politics, one of the first casualties of the new order. But they have great relevance to the conditions of the early 1870s, when Parnell entered politics; and the influence of his background and conditioning in Wicklow stayed with him all his life. As with his father and grandfather, the idea of appropriate behaviour on the landed gentry's part was central to his thinking. No-one who has read the memoirs of those who knew him, or the accounts of newspaper reporters who tracked him round Avondale, can doubt that he was himself most at ease in that role. Paul Bew, indeed, has put at the very centre of Parnell's motivation his belief in the necessity of regenerating the landlord class and constructing a political and social order where they could play a viable national role; at key points in his career he certainly returned to this.[46]

Considering Parnell's Wicklow life also restores to the centre of the picture his preoccupation with developing and protecting the mineral and industrial resources of the country: to him Wicklow, with its uniquely varied geology and topography, was a potential microcosm of what an industrially developed Ireland might be under Home Rule. And another aspect of Parnell's Wicklow life reminds us of something rarely enough stressed about Parnell himself, perhaps because we view his career backwards, through the clericalised politics of the Split: that is, his easy friendships with catholics and his lack of bigotry. He himself represented a belief in the possibilities of a future pluralist Irish

Plate 23.3 Lying-in-state of Erskine Childers at Glendalough House (Irish Architectural Archive).

identity – unrealistic as that may have been in contemporary terms. But it probably reflected the variety, tolerance and depth of relationships to be found around his part of Wicklow: a syndrome which might well apply to any rural Irish community when explored in detail. It is certainly borne witness to in any number of individual memoirs, though often lost sight of in the cut-and-dried overall picture of confrontational monoliths.

In conclusion one might return to the question of place, locality and identity, and the ethos of neighbourhood. Over at Glendalough House lived John Barton, an exact contemporary of Parnell's and like him a fanatical cricketer; he also had a sawmill, the largest in the area, and possibly inspired Parnell to emulate him. They were close friends as young men, but politics sundered the friendship completely; Barton was a strict Unionist. However, in 1888, during a storm, a great tree came down in front of Glendalough House, and Parnell asked permission to test his sawmill on it. This was granted, and Parnell rode over to inspect the tree. Barton's seven-year-old son was lifted up to the window by his nurse, to see the great man arriving by permission at the house where he had once been a frequent and casual guest. That son, Robert, like Parnell, went on to follow a predictable course early in life: rugby, Oxford, the army. But like his Childers relations, after 1916 he took another path – resigning his commission, joining Sinn Féin, commencing a career as a nationalist which took him into Portland prison, the first Dáil cabinet, and the Treaty negotiating chamber. Shortly before the end of his life, well over ninety, he talked to me about Parnell: the inspiration of that glimpse from the window remained. It is in its way a Carlylean moment: a sudden conjunction of the personal and the 'world-historical'. But it also puts back in focus the world of Parnell and his neighbours, the symbiotic way in which his life reacted upon theirs, and theirs upon his.

References

1. Papers delivered at the symposium over recent years have been collected in Donal McCartney (ed.), *Parnell: the politics of power* (Dublin, 1991). This essay, in fact, derives from the address given in August 1991 at Avondale, to inaugurate the summer school.
2. AE [George Russell], *Co-operation and nationality* (Dublin, 1912), pp 59-60.
3. See E. Neeson, *A history of Irish forestry* (Dublin, 1991), pp 122-3, for the most recent commentary.
4. For a commentary on the 'middling gentry' of nineteenth-century Cork see I. d'Alton, *Protestant society and politics in Cork 1812-1844* (Cork, 1980), p. 26.
5. See my 'Parnell, Wicklow and Nationalism', in McCartney, op. cit., p. 32, which expands some of the ideas in this essay.
6. See my *Charles Stewart Parnell: the man and his family* (Brighton, 1969), pp 120-21.

7. There is a memorial pulpit dedicated to him in St John's Church, Laragh.
8. See Foster, *Parnell: the man and his family,* pp 82-85.
9. Parliamentary speech reported in *Pall Mall Gazette,* 17 June 1881.
10. See N.L.I. MS 4955, 4962, 3983, 3984, 4965.
11 N.L.I., MS 3988, p. 41, records a payment to 'Mr Healy, who has now established a classical school in Carnew'.
12. See N.L.I., MS 8816 for details of this lengthy saga.
13. See James Grattan's notebook for 1823, N.L.I. MS 5777.
14. See Anon [W. J. Fitzpatrick], *Memories of Father Healy of Little Bray* (Dublin, 1896).
15. James Grattan's notebooks (see N.L.I., MS 3853) refer to Lord Wicklow's political dictation to his tenants in the 1830s; Chaloner's letter-books indicate that the practice continued in the following period. Wicklow tenant voters, however, had a name for recalcitrance and independence on other estates; see Tottenham papers, N.L.I., mic. n. 4905 p. 4937. And Grattan saw his return in 1832 as accomplished 'in spite of them all', 'them' being the neighbouring grandees (Foster, *Parnell: the man and his family,* xix).
16. N.L.I., MS 3987, Robert Chaloner's letter-book. MS 3987, pp 211-18, a draft standard letter of April 1848, asking for local support for Howard's candidature.
17. For detailed consideration of this point see Foster, *Parnell: the man and his family,* xii-xiv.
18 N.L.I., MS 4814, Mrs Caroline Hamilton's family reminiscences.
19. Pp 59 *et seq.*
20. In a letter to Denys Scully, 3 Dec. 1811. 'Why not ... call every nerve & sinew of the Catholic body into action by quarterly meetings of all the *Parishes* throughout Ireland ... I perceive a great many more contingent advantages from this plan but I think that you will perceive these too. I shall only mention one; which is affording you a regular fund of money without being burthensome to anyone ... I think nothing would give more union to the Catholic body than to raise generally & annually a very small voluntary contribution, if only a penny from each labourer, a shilling from each farmer & five from each gentleman. Your parish collectors & your Treasury would be the connecting medium between you & the people – so small a donation could scarcely become an object of great obloquy. It might be raised for the ostensible purpose of paying the law expenses where poor Catholics were oppressed; & for the necessary expenses of your petitions; but your executive in Dublin might be allowed a sum for secret service money accountable to a select committee, for contesting the elections of members inimical to your cause, and for remunerating the newspapers & employing the press ... In one word, instead of a Parliament, I would propose an executive & the people.'

    This long letter of strategic advice, of which the above is only an extract, lays down the tactics and organisation adopted by O'Connell and Scully a decade later. See B. Macdermot (ed.), *The Catholic question in Ireland and England 1798-1822: the papers of Denys Scully* (Dublin, 1988), pp 301-4.
21. Foster, *Parnell: the man and his family,* p. 17.
22. See N.L.I., MS n. 6-8, pp 201-3 for Poor Law Union records. It remained true that his doctrinal disagreements with catholicism ran deep, at least in his youth; see Foster, *Parnell: the man and his family,* pp 40-41.
23. Roscommon was one place where this phenomenon was noted. See also F. S. L. Lyons, *Charles Stewart Parnell* (London, 1977), p. 584.
24. *Waterford Star,* 27 April 1895; quoted in Paul Bew, *C. S. Parnell* (Dublin, 1980).

25. See Foster, *Parnell: the man and his family,* pp 121-2; also J. H. Parnell, *C. S. Parnell: a memoir* (London, 1914).
26. See Foster, 'Parnell, Wicklow and nationalism', in McCartney, op. cit., pp 20-21.
27. *Wicklow Newsletter,* 10 Oct. 1891.
28. Foster, *Parnell: the man and his family,* p. 168.
29. For a discussion of this see my 'Interpretations of Parnell' in *Studies,* Winter 1991.
30. See her long letter taking issue with Barry O'Brien's biography in the *Gaelic American,* 16 Jan. 1907.
31. For details see *Parnell: the man and his family,* pp 113, 128-30, 151, 191, 193-6, 290.
32. T. P. O'Connor, *C. S. Parnell: a memory* (London, 1891), p. 22.
33. For Parnell's discovery, see his letter to Katharine O'Shea in K. O'Shea, *Charles Stewart Parnell: his love story and political life* (London, 1914), ii, 53.
34. See Foster, *Parnell: the man and his family,* pp 200 ff.
35. 'Parnell as a Prisoner in Kilmainham', *Irish Weekly Independent,* 7 Oct. 1883.
36. Rather to Carnarvon's bewilderment; see his account in Carnarvon MS 60829, British Library.
37. See for instance Standish O'Grady, *The story of Ireland* (London, 1904), p. 203.
38. Lyons, op cit., p. 278 for the circumstances. An interesting illustration of Parnell's preoccupation, not often noted, occurs on pp 190-200 of Lord Ribblesdale's *Impressions and memories* (London, 1927), and describes 'A Railway Journey with Mr Parnell' in the summer of 1887. Parnell talked vehemently about the possibilities of local industrial development under Home Rule, as well as afforestation, fisheries and tillage improvement.
39. See *Parnell: the man and his family,* p. 138.
40. Ibid., p. 170.
41. *Pall Mall Gazette,* 14 Dec. 1880.
42. For Redmond's remarks see *Wicklow Newsletter,* 7 Dec. 1881.
43. Evidence to the Land Commission as reported in *Pall Mall Gazette,* 17 June 1881. See however *Hansard* clxii, 1597, for unfavourable remarks from Corbet, who said that Lord Fitzwilliam was 'kind and indulgent' only to 'sycophants and parasites' and claimed that leases and administrative practice on the estate left much to be desired.
44. Published extracts are in D. Thomson and M. McGusty (eds.), *The Irish journals of Elizabeth Smith* (Oxford, 1980); the diaries are the subject of an important Ph.D. thesis by Andrew Tod (Edinburgh, 1979).
45. Dr Martin made this point in a lecture, 'Parnell and the problem of biography', which was part of the inauguration ceremony for the Parnell Memorial Fellowship at Magdalene College, Cambridge, in October 1991.
46. Bew, op. cit., passim. See *Hansard* cccii, 151 *et seq.*, for a particularly interesting speech of 21 Jan. 1886 by Parnell on Home Rule, the Empire, landlords, and his own protestantism.

Chapter 24

A RIGHTFUL PLACE IN THE SUN — THE STRUGGLE OF THE FARM AND RURAL LABOURERS OF COUNTY WICKLOW

ROSS M. CONNOLLY

'The federation's one aim is to lift the most downtrodden of our nation to their rightful place in the sun.'
Seán Dunne, organising secretary, addressing the first delegate conference of the Federation of Rural Workers, October 1946.

The first indications of industrial organisation amongst farm and rural labourers can be traced to the Land and Labour Leagues which sprang up around the time of the Land League campaign in the latter half of the nineteenth century.

Except for the coastal strip on the eastern seaboard, county Wicklow is mainly mountainous and during the nineteenth century was made up of small farms and landholdings. Just over 50 per cent of the land was arable, the rest being given over to sheep grazing and turbary. A few large estates were held by prominent landlords such as Lords Fitzwilliam, Meath, Powerscourt and Waterford and five others, each of whom held over 10,000 acres. In some cases, such as Powerscourt, a substantial portion was mountain land, yielding mainly grazing and turbary. Contemporary accounts say little about land agitation in the county during the latter half of the nineteenth century. Branches of the Land League were active but there appear to have been only isolated incidents, in spite of (or perhaps because of) the county being the home of the leader of the Irish Parliamentary Party and the Land League – Charles Stewart Parnell, who himself owned some 4,000 acres at Avondale.

The most notorious land conflict occurred just across the south Wicklow border in Coolgreaney in 1887 when 100 tenants of the Brooke estate were evicted because they had adopted the Plan of Campaign of the National League (the successor of the Land League). The Plan of Campaign in essence was that the tenants would seek a reduction in rents, refuse to pay any increase, and if opposed by the landlords, lodge their rents in a trust fund until a settlement was reached. Michael Davitt was a witness of the harrowing scenes, as was a young boy named William Forde whose family was one of the first victims. It was an experience Bill Forde carried with him for the rest of his life and powerfully influenced his subsequent involvement in the republican and trade union movements in county Wicklow.[1]

While there had been booming industrial activity in the urban areas of Bray, Wicklow town, Arklow, and mining in Avoca, it had not been matched in the rest of the county. There was widespread discontent amongst agricultural labourers. This had been recognised by the Land League, which had sought to harness that discontent in order to push forward its programme of land reform for the tenant farmers. The League initiated the Irish Labour and Industrial Union in August 1882, in which Parnell and Davitt were both involved. Its purpose was 'to promote and harmonise the interests of agricultural labourers and urban workers.' The labourers had played a vital part in the agitation of the previous few years from which tenant farmers had gained so much. Parnell, however, urged the agricultural labourers to moderate their claims and avoid conflict with the farmers. The Avondale Treaty between Parnell and Davitt followed in September 1882. This established the Irish National League and included in its objects the development and encouragement of the labour and industrial interests of Ireland, with an emphasis on improving the conditions of agricultural labourers. Michael Davitt, however, had to compromise on several fundamental issues such as land nationalisation.[2]

In this way it was hoped that any discontent felt by agricultural labourers would be diverted into the larger struggle against the landlords for the land. Eventually the land question – insofar as the farmers were concerned – was largely resolved. This was small comfort to the farm labourers. According to Clarke and Delaney, 'Unlike the tenant farmers, they (the labourers) did not win the land, if we except the 50,000 who ultimately received one acre each. There were not sufficient rural industries to retain them and a class that had numbered at least 350,000 at the start of the Land War shrank within fifty years to 160,000, and was halved again during the following quarter century.'[3] This created a sense of betrayal amongst farm and rural labourers, and led to the founding of local organisations of farm labourers and smallholders. These organisations adopted various titles such as 'Land and Labour League' and 'the Irish Trade and Labour League.' Their sense of betrayal is illustrated by, for example, the Killiskey Labour League in county Wicklow when in March and April 1899 it adopted a Mr Giffney as a Labour candidate for the local elections, which were being held for the first time. He informed the league that the 'farmers' candidates would oppose the erection of labourers' cottages and any other candidates likely to better the conditions of workingmen.'[4] The farm and rural labourers were learning fast that their salvation no longer lay with the National League and the tenant farmers. Their efforts to redress their grievances, although accompanied in some cases by strike action, were not successful, and ultimately the Land and Labour Leagues were absorbed into the more powerful trade union movement as it gathered strength in the early 1900s.

The second decade of the 1900s was marked by increasing militancy amongst farm labourers. Disillusioned with the effectiveness of the National League and local land and labour leagues they turned to strike action and trade union organisation. The growing recognition by rural workers of an identity of interest with their unionised colleagues in the towns was shown in the action of the Oulart Irish Trade and Labour League and the Leinster council of the GAA in voting funds for the locked-out workers of Pierce's of Wexford in 1911.[5] A farm strike broke out at Crumlin in county Dublin in 1915 and another in Rathnew in county Wicklow, the latter organised by the Trades and Labour Benefit League in March 1916.[6] There was also a dispute at Hacketstown in the south of the county over farm wages in 1917.[7] One of the first of the land and labour leagues to join up with the Irish Transport and General Workers' Union was at Blanchardstown in county Dublin in March 1917.[8] This branch, although located in county Dublin, actually affiliated to the Bray and Dun Laoghaire Trades and Labour Council.[9] The level of agricultural wages had been recognised as very low and the British government set up an Agricultural Wages Board, with union representation in September 1917, to fix legal rates of pay. Its first order fixed a rate of twenty-five shillings a week in county Dublin and twenty shillings in the rest of the country.

The ITGWU not only continued its policy of militant action on the ground, but also resorted to the courts on several occasions to enforce orders of the Wages Board. Unrest in the countryside was spreading. There were strikes of farm labourers in Dungarvan and Callan, and again in 1919 in Carlow, Kerry, Offaly, north Cork and county Dublin.[10] Against this national scenario, however, activity by the ITGWU was almost non-existent in the rural areas of county Wicklow. It was active only in the town of Bray from 1910 and in Arklow in Kynoch's munition factory during the 1914-18 Great War. The level of inactivity may be explained by the arrival on the scene in 1917 of another trade union, the County Wicklow Labourers' Association, organised under the energetic and skilful guidance of its secretary, James Everett and chairman, J. de Courcy. The new organisation in county Wicklow probably also owed its inspiration to an earlier trade union formed in Wicklow town in June 1899 when a large meeting of dock labourers and other workers was held. After a long debate about conditions, a decision was taken to 'establish a labour league in Wicklow in the interests of the workingmen of the town.'[11] The league went on to do battle with local employers, particularly over employment of non-union labour and rates of pay. It also paid strike pay to its members. It is likely that James Everett, who was a native of Wicklow town, would have been influenced by the struggles of the earlier organisation.

Although no original documents appear to be extant, the County Wicklow Labourers' Association seems to have started about July or August of 1917, since it was holding its first half-yearly executive meeting in Wicklow town on 26 January 1918. Terms such as 'union' and 'association' were freely interchangeable in contemporary reports, so while titles are different they appear in fact to refer to the same organisation. In January 1918 an advertisement was published by the 'County Wicklow General Labourers' Association,' in the local papers. James Everett was named as secretary of the new union, and J. de Courcy as chairman. At this time the union was involved in a strike of farm labourers at Col. Leslie-Ellis's property at Magheramore, a strike which was called because of the employment of non-union labour and which lasted for eleven weeks.[12]

J. de Courcy addressed a recruiting meeting that month in Shillelagh, beside the Coolattin estate of Earl Fitzwilliam, who was also an extensive coalmine owner in Britain. de Courcy claimed that since the start of the association over 2,000 labourers had received increased wages of twenty-three shillings per week (this would have been an advance on the Wages Board rate). Membership in the branch rose rapidly to seventy. Meetings were held in Bray, Roundwood, Rathdrum, Tinahely, Delgany, Greystones and Arklow. Meetings were also reported from many other areas, referring to the 'Labourers' Association,' and in Baltinglass even a Blacksmiths' Society was formed. The union extended its organisation to Carnew and Barndarrig, Aughrim and Tinahely in south Wicklow, as well as to Redcross and Avoca. At one stage the union listed twenty-nine branches in the county, stretching from Bray in the north to Shillelagh in the south, and west to Baltinglass. The village of Tinahely recorded a membership of 136, and over 300 men joined at Enniscorthy.[13]

By February 1918 the union was so impressed with its progress that it mandated its chairman to arrange a conference with a view to forming a Leinster or even an all-Ireland organisation of labourers. Its optimism was a reflection of its rapid expansion in counties Wexford and Wicklow.[14]

So confident was the union of its strength that it decided to organise a Labour parade and demonstration in Wicklow town in April 1918.

One of the biggest meetings and processions by workers ever witnessed took place in the town, when resolutions dealing with labour matters and opposition to conscription were adopted. Even some of the villages were not to be left out and Tinahely and Ashford Labour organisations also staged demonstrations against conscription. Obviously the union's members felt strongly about British attempts to conscript Irish workers into the Great War, and this influenced its decision to affiliate in 1918 to the Irish Trade Union and Labour Congress because of the latter's national stand on the issue.[15]

The most serious strike dealt with by the union in 1918 was at Ballyteskin. Arbitration or any discussions had been refused by the Farmers' Union and they had decided to lock out their workers. Lord Wicklow had refused to come to terms on wages and conditions and the employees took strike action, most of them getting work elsewhere. There was also a dispute over increased wages with the Dublin and Wicklow Manure Company (forerunner of today's Irish Fertiliser Industries, Arklow) which obtained its noisome raw material of animal bones from the Rathdrum Workhouse – the work of unfortunate orphans confined there. The company made an offer in January 1919, but further talks were requested by the union. Some violence occurred during the dispute, from which the union was at pains to dissociate itself. There was a further strike there in 1920. Even workers at the Wicklow convent went on strike in March 1919, an action which drew clerical disapproval. Twenty-five timber workers at Clarke's of Rathnew also went on strike when their demand for an increase in pay of seven shillings and sixpence was refused.[16]

In January 1919 the half-yearly meeting of the union's executive was attended by delegates from Ashford, Aughrim, Avoca, Barndarrig, Ballyteskin, Ballynattin, Rathnew, Newcastle, Kilcoole, Glenealy, Rathdrum, Laragh, Templerainey and Wicklow. Issues which were discussed included affiliations, the new unemployment benefit which had been introduced by Lloyd George's government and the new scales of pay announced by the Agricultural Wages Board. A demand was made for twenty-six shillings a week for every man working more than ten hours a day, while those 'boarded and lodged' were to get thirteen shillings a week. The forthcoming county and rural district elections were also considered and each branch was urged to form an election committee. Clearly the union was determined to get into the political arena quickly.

The issue of amalgamation with other unions was also on the agenda, and it seems that this was a preparation for eventual amalgamation with the Agricultural and General Workers' Union of county Wexford, which had also been making strides in organisational terms under the leadership of Seán Etchingham.[17] An IRB man who had been active in Wexford during the 1916 Rising, Etchingham was responsible for getting the GAA to support the ITGWU men locked out by Pierce's of Wexford in 1911.[18] Subsequently Everett's organisation was described as 'The County Wicklow Branch of the AGWU.' Amalgamation with the ITGWU, however, did not take place for more than another year.

Meanwhile in January 1919 the ITGWU was holding a meeting of its 'Gardeners and Garden Workers' Section' (a nice distinction in employment status!) in the Trades Hall in Bray for the purpose of organising those workers in the town. There would appear to have been rivalry between the unions in this area, as the Agricultural and General Workers' Union, holding its half-yearly meeting at that time, recorded delegates from Kingstown and Blackrock branches of the 'Gardeners and Garden Workers' Union.' One of the disputes dealt with at that meeting was a lock-out of men by Killiney (county Dublin) Rural District Council.[19]

In the previous year the AGWU had affiliated to the Irish Trade Union and Labour Congress and its delegates attended the Annual Meeting of Congress in Drogheda in August 1919, one of its delegates being James Everett. Congress had on its agenda consideration of a major restructuring and re-organisation of the trade union movement, and the delegates from the AGWU would have met the leaders of the ITGWU there.[20] Possibly as a result of the debate and contacts made at Congress along with the ongoing policy of the union to seek amalgamations, William O'Brien and Tom Kennedy of the ITGWU travelled to the executive meeting of the Agricultural and General Workers' Union in Enniscorthy on 13 June 1920. It was agreed to wind up the AGWU and join with the ITGWU. James Everett, who had been general secretary of the 'Wicklow General Workers' Union' since 1917, became the Transport Union's organising secretary for county Wicklow.[21]

Making good use of the excellent organisation he had built up in the years since 1917, James Everett stood and was elected in 1922 as the first Labour Dáil deputy for county Wicklow, a seat he held until his death. He was twice a minister in inter-party governments in the years after the Second World War. One of his most active workers was John Conroy of Wicklow town, who subsequently became the ITGWU organiser and eventually general secretary of the ITGWU. With young Jim Larkin, Conroy helped to heal the split in the national trade union movement some fifty years later.

This era of active trade union campaigning was drawing to a close as the ITGWU found itself forced to wind down its activities in rural areas. There had been a massive increase in organisation among farm workers between 1918 and 1920 when the farm membership of the

ITGWU had risen from 10,000 to 40,000. After 1920, however, the collapse of farm prices brought an aggressive reaction from farmers who demanded cuts in wage rates. These were fiercely resisted and the ITGWU found itself supporting a growing number of strikes throughout the countryside. The costs of strike pay and heavy organisational expenses which are a feature of rural organisation, forced a policy change on the union. In 1923 it had spent over £128,000 on farm strikes. Costs of that magnitude could not be sustained and the union gradually disengaged itself from the organisation of farm workers.[22] In county Wicklow it withdrew into the towns of Bray, Wicklow and Arklow, with some organisation among the county council workers. James Everett devoted his political talents to looking after his rural constituents.

There was a long hiatus in the organisation of farm workers until the Second World War. Their plight during the years of the war had worsened: even the Minister for Industry and Commerce admitted that their real income in 1944 was only 90 per cent of their income in 1939. A Labour Party motion in Seanad Éireann in 1944, to reconstitute the Agricultural Wages Board to admit representatives of agricultural workers (a right they had enjoyed under the British) and ensure them a living wage, was defeated.[23]

Responding to many demands James Larkin Senior and his union, the Workers' Union of Ireland (formed by a break-away in 1924 from the ITGWU), decided in 1943 to set up a branch of rural workers, mainly in county Dublin and adjoining areas. In 1944 he appointed Seán Dunne, a native of Bray, as secretary of the farm workers' branch of the union.[24] Seán Dunne had been a republican activist interned in the Curragh and had also figured prominently in the butcher's strike which gripped Dublin and Bray in 1946. He had been arrested for 'anti-scab' activity then, and along with Luke Connor (subsequently a Labour mayor of Camden Town in London) had led a hunger march from Bray to Rathdrum in 1935.[25]

Insistent demands for organisation were coming into the Workers' Union of Ireland from areas outside county Dublin and Larkin recognised that a new approach was needed. In fact he was goaded by the attitude of the then Minister of Agriculture, Dr James Ryan, in the Dáil when Larkin Senior attempted to get the Agricultural Wages Board reformed. He swore he would make the Minister swallow his words.[26] Although the genesis of a new union came directly from Larkin and the Workers' Union of Ireland, the actual impetus for a national union for farm and rural workers originated with the Irish Women Workers' Union, which tabled the following motion for the 1944 Annual Meeting of the Irish Trade Union Congress in Drogheda:

> That as soon as circumstances permit, the national executive will summon a special conference in a rural area to discuss plans for the organisation of agricultural and rural workers, men and women, with a view to raising their standard of wages, hours and working conditions.[27]

The union was motivated by the conditions of its own female members working on farms, who were in an even more desperate situation than their male colleagues. Addressing Congress, Louie Bennett of the Irish Women Workers' Union said that women working on the farms had been the 'down and out' people of the movement. She had been horrified at what she heard of their conditions when groups of women workers on fruit farms had joined the union. Mrs M. Buckley, also of the IWWU, said that Congress had no conception of the slavery of these women in the fields, doing harvesting work in all sorts of weather. The women had been working for less than sixpence per hour.[28] The motion was adopted but the actual conference was not convened by Congress until 17 March 1946, when rules for the new union were drawn up and arrangements made to start organising. The Workers' Union of Ireland arranged to transfer all its farm and rural members to the new organisation, as did the Irish Women Workers' Union. The new union was called the Federation of Rural Workers, and its first provisional executive included James Larkin Junior as president and Seán Dunne as organising secretary. It was the first example of a new union being launched by a national trade union congress. Larkin Senior, however, did not like the title of the new union: he would prefer it to have been called a union of land workers, not rural workers, but did not elaborate on the distinction.

The original concept was for a federation of semi-autonomous county unions, controlled by a national executive. The practical operational demands of the new union, however, dictated a more orthodox centralised control by the national executive council over the organisation, the appointment of full-time officials and financial returns to head office. The counties, however, were allowed to hold their own conventions and elect their own county executives.[29]

The conference was hardly over before a widespread strike took place in county Dublin which resulted in victory for the new union, with pay rises of nine shillings per week (on rates of thirty-two shillings and sixpence and thirty-seven shillings), a 48-hour week (the norm was fifty-four), paid holidays and a weekly half day (these were previously almost non-existent).[30]

The success of the new union fired other areas around the country, including county Wicklow. In Bray, organisation, particularly amongst the men on Lord Meath's estate, was undertaken by Bill Forde, whose family had moved to Bray after the Coolgreaney evictions.[31] A policy of campaigning along political lines by holding after-Mass meetings outside rural churches was adopted, followed up by local contacts and establishment of branches. Organising the new union was not easy, however, and considerable reliance had to be placed on the services of other unions' officials and political activists. In county Wicklow, for example, the federation's representative to its national conference in October 1946 was James Morgan, who was also elected to the national executive. James Morgan came from near the village of Kilcoole, but was in fact employed as a shop assistant in Findlater's of Bray. He was an ardent socialist, a member of the Labour Party and a close colleague of Seán Dunne. Along with other Workers' Union of Ireland activists who had been involved in the Bray butchers' strike of 1946, they did most of the foot slogging, or bike pedalling, organising work in the county in its early months. Significantly when nominations were taken for the Agricultural Wages Board area committees, the county Wicklow branch of the federation could not supply one. James Morgan, because of his occupation, would not have qualified.[32]

By 1948 matters had improved: county Wicklow representatives to the annual conference were Patrick Doyle of Delgany (also a Labour activist) Edward Kearney of Rathnew, Denis Moore of Shillelagh and Joseph O'Hara of Baltinglass. Three of these were rural workers. Denis Moore, who came from the Coolattin estate in south Wicklow went on to become county organiser. The 1949 conference also included representatives from Enniskerry and Ballymoney and Denis Moore replaced James Morgan on the national executive.[33]

Farm workers' wages were again being regulated by an Agricultural Wages Board appointed by the government, with local advisory committees. Because of government policy laid down in 1946 the wages of county council labourers, forestry workers and employees of small rural businesses were effectively controlled by the Agricultural Wages Board. This policy decreed that such rates of pay must be strictly related to the wages paid by local farmers. Labourers' rates of pay throughout rural Ireland were therefore effectively controlled by the Agricultural Wages Board.[34]

This policy had a double effect: county council and forestry workers turned to the new union and the federation pushed to secure representation on the Agricultural Wages Board (in spite of opposition by the then minister in 1944 to worker representation). With the defeat of the Fianna Fáil government in 1948 and the introduction of a more relaxed policy by the inter-party Minister for Agriculture, James Dillon, the federation succeeded in its aim and got its representatives, among them Paddy Murphy, appointed to the Agricultural Wages Board. The influence of the board over road and forestry workers was gradually eliminated and their wages were determined in their own right as industrial workers. Finally the federation saw the board abolished and replaced by the Industrial Relations Act 1976.[35]

I joined the federation in 1947 as a clerical assistant, but it was not long before Seán Dunne discovered I had experience of speaking at political meetings. Immediately I was taken out on an apprenticeship course for organising rural workers at rallies and after-Mass meetings. The late Paddy Murphy (who went on to become president of the federation) was then county Dublin secretary, but of course was not let rest on his laurels. Soon the two of us were travelling the country in a battered Ford Prefect, addressing meetings wherever possible. As we were both twenty at the time, we reckoned we were probably the youngest trade union organisers in the country.

Most meetings were held in time-honoured fashion outside church gates after Sunday Mass. We had no public address system then, and a strong voice and lungs were essential. Frequently we had no stand or platform and made use of the bonnet of the long suffering car. It wasn't long before we found we were facing strong opposition – from the farmers, which was natural enough, but also from the clergy. The general election of 1948 saw the defeat of the Fianna Fáil government after sixteen years in power and the installation of the inter-party government, which included the Labour Party. During the campaign for the election there had been a determined effort to whip up anti-communist hysteria against the Labour Party and Clann na Poblachta (a newly-formed radical republican party led by Seán MacBride). This had been mainly orchestrated by Seán MacEntee, a Minister of the Fianna Fáil government. Many of the Labour candidates in the election had been active in organising the new federation and there was a perception, not entirely unfounded, in Fianna Fáil that the Labour Party hoped to use the organisational strength of the federation to extend the party throughout rural Ireland.[36] Consequently the smear campaign was bound to rub off on the new union. This gave welcome ammunition to many of the clergy who had a vested interest in opposing the spread of the union, since many of them came from farming families and the small-town middle class. Paddy Murphy and I discovered that, at the Masses held before our church gate rallies, they were using the pulpits and their captive audience to abuse the union and all connected with it.

We adopted a simple stratagem. We made a point of arriving early for each Mass and would take our seats directly below the pulpit where the priest could not fail to see the two strangers. When he saw the two 'communist agitators' staring him in the face as he rose to deliver his anti-union sermon, it is remarkable how often he decided to deliver a different gospel of the Lord. One of the first places we tested this policy, with great success, was in a small village church in west Wicklow. In fairness to the rural workers of the time, there is little evidence that any of them was intimidated by the anti-union rantings from the pulpits.

Organisation in county Wicklow spread gradually and soon nearly every village in the county had its own small branch. Where farm workers were thin on the ground, county council labourers and gangers, and forestry men joined. The level of organisation never reached that achieved by the Agricultural and General Workers' Union of James Everett, but then economic circumstances had changed drastically in the countryside in the intervening years. The main focus of farm worker organisation in south Wicklow was around the Coolattin estate where there were twenty-five workers. In north Wicklow, organisation stretched from Lord Meath's estate at Bray, also with about twenty-five men, down to Newcastle, where there were prosperous farmers, giving a membership in the north county of about 300. The heavy afforestation programme undertaken by the new inter-party government under the influence of Seán MacBride, gave much needed employment in the mountainous areas of the county and brought more men into the federation's ranks. It even extended its activities into mining, hitherto a preserve of the ITGWU, and organised the men in the Avoca mines for a period.

The federation affiliated to the Bray Trades and Labour Council in 1952 in respect of its north Wicklow membership, thus adding a considerable boost to that body, and also supplied the council with a new secretary, myself, for the next fifteen years.

Active work by the federation's representatives on the Agricultural Wages Board had succeeded in upgrading county Wicklow land, which had been classed as a low pay area. The board had classed county Wicklow into two areas, B and C, the latter covering the rich lands of south Wicklow. In 1954 workers in these two areas qualified for a minimum wage of four pounds ten shillings and four pounds seven shillings respectively, for a 54-hour week. By 1956 the federation's representatives on the board (Paddy Murphy being the principal one) had succeeded in pushing all of county Wicklow into area B, with a minimum wage of four pounds fourteen shillings and the Bray district (i.e. Lord Meath's estate) into area A with a rate of five pounds per week.[37]

These were marginal victories, however, as the government had the final say through its appointed chairman of the board. Disillusionment with the Wages Board system grew and the federation agitated for the establishment of an agricultural Labour Court on the lines of the industrial Labour Court. This was promised by the government in early 1955, and at its annual convention that year, the county Wicklow branch called for an assurance from the government that it would continue the policy of a legal minimum wage under the proposed new court. The convention also made a claim for a farm wage of five pounds per week, half-holidays and annual holidays and improvements in the working conditions of forestry workers.

By 1957, however, the county Wicklow federation was condemning the failure of the government to honour its promise about the agricultural Labour Court and increasingly the union resorted to industrial pressure. Improvements in wages had been won in 1952 through a threatened strike in north county Wicklow, and by 1957 farm wages had risen to four pounds fifteen shillings in the county, marginally above the Wages Board minimum. However, by contrast, the county convention noted that farm workers in Northern Ireland were receiving six pounds seven shillings for a 48-hour week at this time, and the union's efforts on behalf of county council and forestry workers had brought their wages ahead of the farm workers. It was clear that a crisis was looming on the farm front.[38]

The farming scene in the 1950s was totally different to what it is today. Tractors were few and far between; the combine harvester was almost unheard of, and nearly all milking was done by hand. Farming was labour intensive where it was not devoted entirely to ranching, and most farming on the east coast was mixed. By the mid-fifties I had become engaged almost full-time in county Wicklow. Most of the organising was done on a bike in all weathers, a heavy raincoat and good rubber boots being essential equipment. A hired car was a luxury provided only when it was necessary to bring the members of the county executive together or attend a special meeting too far away to be reached by bicycle. I saw much of the working conditions on the land at first hand, and there was very little of the idyllic pastoral scene about it.

On one occasion I had to visit members on a farm in Delgany, owned by Dr James Ryan, who had been Minister for Finance in the Fianna Fáil government, and who also, as a young medical student, had ministered to my wounded grandfather in the GPO in 1916. By the standards of the time he was a reasonably good employer, so the conditions I found were not exceptional. The four members were in a field thinning turnips. This required them to spend their working day on their hands and knees, working down seemingly endless muddy rows of plants. Their only protection was old sacking tied over their trousers, and their heavy overcoats. That scene, and others such as the tyranny of hand-milking cows seven days a week, was duplicated on many farms.

Discontent with the Wages Board grew among the farm workers and the federation became convinced that further progress would now be dependent on resorting to strike action. The union's plan was to take selected areas with high concentrations of farm workers, attempt to force up wages by private bargaining, and thus bring pressure on the Wages Board to raise the minimum rates.

Because the number employed on individual farms was generally small (and thus organisationally weak), the ordinary process of dealing with each employer separately could not be pursued. One of the areas selected for union action was north county Wicklow and demands were served on about twenty farmers in an area stretching from Bray to the villages of Newcastle and Newtownmountkennedy.

The farmers did not take the threat seriously and apparently believed the union was trading on past bluffs. They were obdurate and negotiations broke down. I then found myself in the unusual position for a union organiser of having to persuade the workers of the absolute necessity of taking strike action. Strike action was familiar to farm workers in county Dublin and county Kildare, but it was nearly forty years since strikes had taken place in county Wicklow. Nevertheless, with the help of local leaders, a vote for strike was agreed.

The uneasiness of the union members was evident in the long discussions which took place on the question of picketing. The problem of milking cows and caring for livestock had to be resolved. It is not in the nature of men who work on the land to deny care to their stock, or neglect the crops, a virtue which many farmers shamelessly exploited.

It was agreed that cows should be milked, but no milk delivered, and only essential feeding carried out. There was even reluctance to milk the cows onto the ground, and I know some men continued to take their daily perk of a quart of milk home throughout the strike. On the appointed day, however, pickets arrived outside all the farm gates, causing consternation amongst the farmers and something of a sensation in the local community.

Within a week several of the bigger farmers had re-opened negotiations and soon an acceptable settlement was reached. Now we were faced with a dilemma: if the men on the bigger farms returned to work, a lot of men on the smaller farms where only one or two were employed, and whose employers had made no move to negotiate, would be left isolated and in a very weak position. Faced with this a new tactic was tried, after a great deal of persuasion of the strike members. No worker would return to work in the area until all farmers had agreed to the same settlement terms. The reaction of the farmers who had already settled may be imagined, but the men stuck to their guns.

As was anticipated, the large farmers – who had most to lose – brought considerable pressure on their reluctant neighbours, pressure which the union could not have exercised. In a matter of days, offers of settlement flooded in and the strike was settled. All the members in north Wicklow returned to work on the same day.

This was the last major strike of farm workers in county Wicklow. Within a decade increased mechanisation had changed the face of agriculture. The Meath estate, which once supported over twenty families, is now managed by machines and a couple of men; the Coolattin estate in south Wicklow was sold off by the Fitzwilliam family and fell into the hands of speculators, who stripped it of its fine oak woods. The recession of the late fifties brought increasing unemployment and reductions in staff on the county councils and in the state forests with the inevitable result of drastically reducing membership of the federation, particularly in county Wicklow. Eventually the federation amalgamated with its sister organisation, the Workers' Union of Ireland, from which it could be said to have spawned originally, and became the Federated Workers' Union of Ireland in 1980. Gradually organisation among local authority workers in the county and in the Avoca mines, which had enjoyed a resurgence from Canadian investment, drifted back to the ITGWU. The ITGWU also monopolised the majority of workers in Arklow and Wicklow Town. In Bray the two unions divided the industrial workers between them, until ten years later they in turn came together to form the Services, Industrial, Professional and Technical Union (SIPTU), the One Big Union first visualised by Connolly and Larkin.

The flight from the land and the scourge of unemployment decimated organisation among farm and rural labourers in the county thereafter. However, for a brief period after the Second World War they had re-asserted themselves and had regained their 'rightful place in the sun.'

References

1. P. Doyle, 'The Coolgreaney Evictions 1887', *Enniscorthy Echo* and Aug/Sept 1966 issue of *The Delegate,* Newsletter of the Bray and District Trades Union Council.
2. T.W. Moody, *Davitt and the Irish revolution 1846-82,* p. 542.
3. Clarke, Delaney, *Irish peasants – violence & political unrest 1780-1914,* p. 334.
4. *The Wicklow Star,* April 1899.
5. D. Greaves, *The formative years – history of ITGWU,* Dublin, 1982, p. 68.

6. *Wicklow People,* 24 March 1916.
7. Ibid., 31 March 1917.
8. Greaves, *The formative years,* p. 180.
9. Annual Accounts 1923, Bray & Dun Laoghaire Trades and Labour Council.
10. Greaves, *The formative years,* p. 246.
11. *The Wicklow Star,* June 1899.
12. *Bray and South Dublin Herald,* January 1918.
13. Ibid., January/February 1918.
14. Ibid., 16 February 1918.
15. *Wicklow People,* 18 January 1919.
16. *Bray and South Dublin Herald,* 27 April 1918.
17. *Wicklow People,* 18 January 1919.
18. Greaves, *The formative years,* p. 68.
19. *Wicklow People,* 25 January 1919.
20. Greaves, *The formative years,* p. 247.
21. Ibid., p. 276.
22. *Saothar* 14, 1989, p. 78, review by Paddy Bergin of Daniel G. Bradley's *Farm labourers – Irish struggle 1900-76,* Belfast, 1988.
23. Report of Administrative Council of the Labour Party, 1944, p. 14.
24. P. Murphy, *The federation of rural workers,* Dublin, 1988, p. 6.
25. *Unity,* Journal of FWUI, vol. 2. no. 1, 1985.
26. ITUC, *Report of proceedings,* 10 July 1946.
27. Ibid., 7 July 1944.
28. Ibid., 10 July 1946.
29. *Report of NEC to Irish Trade Union Congress, xxiii* – organisation of rural workers.
30. Murphy, *Rural workers,* pp 29-30.
31. *The Delegate,* no. 10 1966, Newsletter of Bray and District Trades Union Council, article by C. Brien.
32. Murphy, *Rural workers,* pp 25-7.
33. Murphy, *Rural workers,* pp 43, 53.
34. Dáil debates 15 February 1946, Col. 348 31/146, Col. 1102/3-15.
35. Murphy, *Rural workers,* p. 61.
36. See *The Irish People,* no. 195, 14 February 1948 for an insight into this 'anti-communist' campaign. Of the 14 Labour deputies in the new Dáil, B. Corish (Wexford), D. Desmond (Cork), Seán Dunne (county Dublin) and J. Larkin (Dublin) had all been associated with the formation of the FRW.
37. *The Labour Party, Annual Report 1955-6,* p. 19.
38. *Irish Independent,* 24 January 1955.

Poulaphouca reservoir from Ballyknockan.

Chapter 25

'THE WATER WAS THE SHERIFF': THE LAND BENEATH THE POULAPHOUCA RESERVOIR

FIACHRA Mac GABHANN

This chapter reconstructs the farms, fields and the social dimensions of the rural society which formed the 6,500 acres of north-west Wicklow drowned in 1939 to provide water for the rapidly expanding Dublin metropolitan area.

The realisation that the proposed Poulaphouca reservoir would bury beneath waters captured from the Liffey and King's rivers the material fabric of a rural community inspired a team of Dublin scholars to undertake a hasty survey of the doomed valley.[1] This survey and accompanying photographic evidence is used extensively in the chapter. State bodies were involved in directing the evacuation: details of the transactions are found in repositories such as the Valuation Office, the offices of the Electricity Supply Board and the National Archives.[2] These official sources have been complemented by the testimony of those who were forced to relinquish homeplace and the land of their ancestors.[3]

The mountain lands south of Dublin city with their large, relatively unpopulated river catchment districts constitute an ideal water source for the city (fig. 25.1). Reservoirs impounding the Vartry and Dodder Rivers had been constructed using natural valleys as storage places in 1867 and 1884 respectively.[4] Fast-flowing rivers fed by run-off from mountain streams and cleansed through natural filtration on granite sands were ideally located to sate the voracious thirst of the rapidly growing Dublin metropolitan district. As early as 1902 the suitability of the narrow gorge of Poulaphouca where the Liffey drops from hill to lowland was identified as a natural dam site both for impounding water for the generation of electricity and for the provision of water for Dublin.[5] In the 1920s various sites were investigated and the Commission of Enquiry into the Resources and Industries of Ireland proposed the immediate construction of a series of dams on the river Liffey because of its proximity to Dublin.[6] There were some misgivings concerning the impermeability of the Liffey's northern slopes but

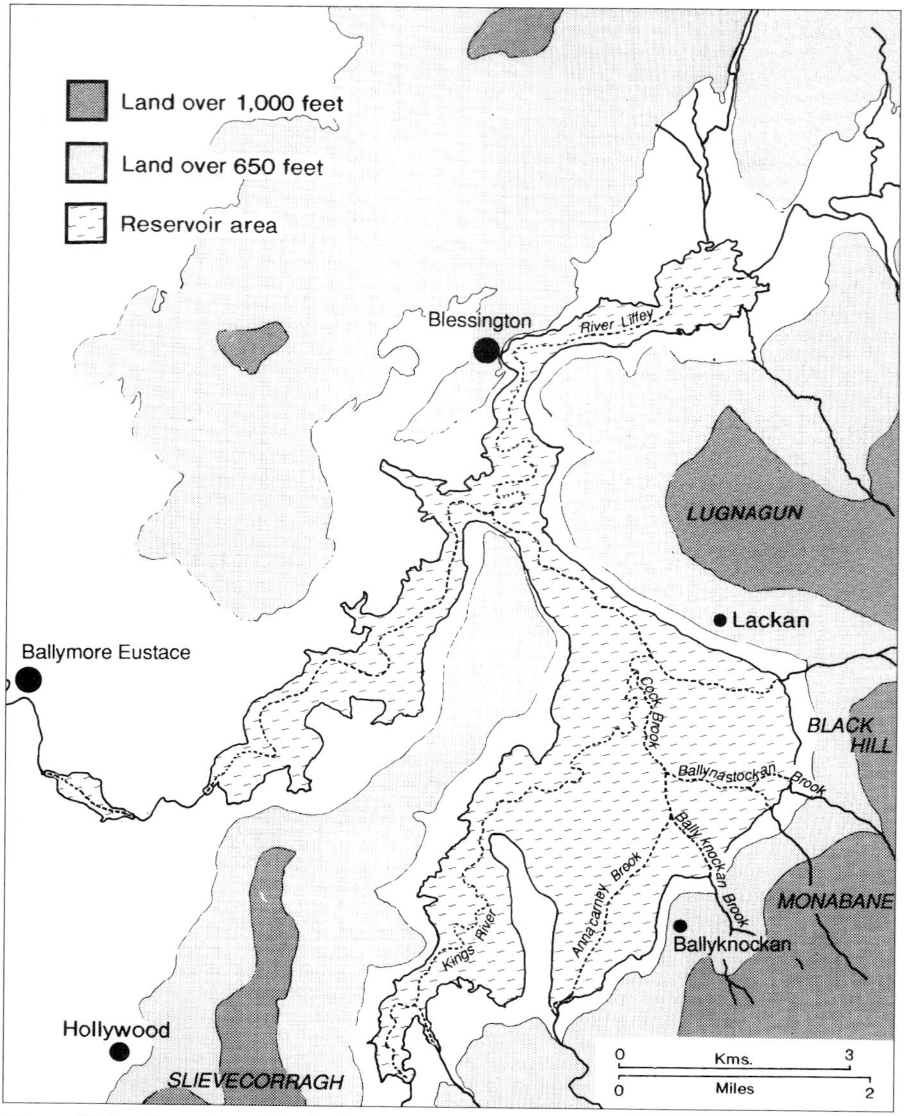

Figure 25.1 Location of Poulaphouca reservoir.

nonetheless the scheme was put out to tender. One tender submitted by the Anna Liffey Power Development Co. Ltd estimated that the project would cost some £1.2 million to finalise in contrast to the annual coal import bill of £3 million.[7] However, the government decided not to proceed with the Liffey project but moved instead to construct the massive hydro-electric plant at Ardnacrusha on the Shannon near Limerick city.[8]

Proposals for the Liffey project were rejected because of questions on management, constitutional authority (of the scheme developers), and whether or not it was relevant to the country as a whole.[9] Perhaps the anticipation of the founding of the semi-state Electricity Supply Board prompted such caution. With the advent of Fianna Fáil to government in 1932, public policy emphasised self-sufficiency in the Irish economy. The provision of power from natural resources to fuel the national drive towards industrialisation was one of the prerogatives of the Electricity Supply Board established in 1926. In November 1936 the young, dynamic Minister for Industry and Commerce, Seán Lemass, introduced the Liffey Reservoir Bill to the Dáil[10] citing increasing national demand for electricity, the strategic location of the proposed site in relation to Dublin and the additional advantage of having a reservoir to meet the ever growing demands for water in the Dublin urban district as the primary reasons for the scheme. Dublin Corporation, in return for its right to draw up to twenty million gallons a day from the reservoir, would pay £1.2 million to the ESB. The labour intensive demands of such a major engineering project – some 1,200 men would have well-paid employment for a three-year period – ensured the quick passage of the Liffey Reservoir Bill. Apart from the work at Poulaphouca a dam was to be constructed downstream at Golden Falls in county Kildare. Rivers were dammed and an intake tunnel a mile long led the water to the very high surge tank from where it was propelled to giant turbines producing 30 million units of electricity.[11] The original level used for land acquisition behind these dams was the crest level of the dams viz, 622ft (189.6m) OD for Poulaphouca Reservoir. Thus, 622ft is the maximum flood level of the reservoir which would generate a lake of 5,600 surface acres; the normal high water level of 612ft (186.6m) generates a reservoir with a surface area of 4,960 acres. The shore length of the Poulaphouca Reservoir is about thirty-five miles.

Although there was some local dissent, it would appear that the very scale and urgency of the project led to its passive, if unwilling, acceptance. Local politicians and the parish priest of Valleymount, whose parish would be physically sundered and whose parishioners would be reduced in number, were critical of the scheme. There was little, however, that a group of smallholders could do to stem the tide and the national interest was invoked to silence opposition. By late 1938 the evacuation of the proposed reservoir site had begun: thatch was burned, buildings were razed and their sites disinfected. Road bridges at Blessington, Burgage More and Baltyboys Upper were blown up.[12] Trees and bushes were cut, collected into lots and left for floating to suitable sites when the reservoir had filled. By early 1940 the valley was silent. Over the following two years the slowly drowning land attracted the transients: farmers from the high ground grazed stock freely in the receding grass; the army used the depopulated swathes for artillery practice and last in the grim procession were the hunters 'snaring rabbits easily caught because of the rising water'.[13] James Cullen of Lackan paid his final visit to the old home in August 1940 to rescue pigs and was met by household things floating out the kitchen door on the rising surge.[14]

Elizabeth Smith's country lost most. Ballinahown was obliterated from the map and Baltyboys Upper and Lower, Burgage More and Burgage Moyle, Haylands, Horsepasstown, Lackan, Russelltown, Tulfarris and Valleymount all lost more than 40 per cent of their Ordnance Survey acreage (table 25.1 and fig. 25.2). Baltyboys House, home of the redoubtable nineteenth century diarist, was left perched on the shoreline of the inland lake. There is a subtle irony underlying the choice of the reservoir site. Geologists such as Farrington, have noted that a glacial lake, formed by the damming of melt water by the slowly retreating midlandian ice sheet, had covered this valley floor for thousands of years.[15] The midlandian glaciation explains the variable land quality of the valley floor. Limestone drift, deposited north and south of Baltyboys, provided the texture which drew gentry graziers such as Smith of Baltyboys, Hornidge of Tulfarris, Finnamore of Ballyward and Milltown of Russborough. This arc of grassland faced the foothills of high Wicklow across the valley where the poor were gathered in their untidy cluster assemblage. Between the Liffey and the King's river and beyond to Slieve Corragh and the hills around Hollywood, absentee landlord indifference created a densely populated district based on thin soils, granite, and the commonage of bog valley and high mountain. None of the hill clusters, safe in their high retreats, was touched by the reservoir; some such as Ballynastockan, Ballyknockan and Johnstown lost bottom land. Holdings in the better endowed limestone drift, such as at Baltyboys, ran with the gradient towards the Liffey and King's rivers in plots of some sixty acres. In Carrig, Sroughan and Lackan townlands, plots ran parallel from the river against the gradient up Lugnagun in divisions of approximately thirty acres. Further south along the thin foothills, minuscule holdings serving quarryman as much as farmer were huddled together. Farm fragmentation, a residual element of rundale, characterised the clusters as far south as Johnstown. Not even the Land Commission could impose state geometry here.[16]

In much of the reservoir area and contiguous hill lands the final transfer of ownership from landlord to tenant under the land purchase acts had not been fully realised. The marquis of Waterford at

Table 25.1

Land, Holdings and Houses lost to the Reservoir

Townland	*Percentage of Townland*	*Holdings which lost Land*	*Houses Submerged*
Annacarney	18.0	8	—
Ballinahown	100.0	10	8
Ballynastockan	12.0	18	—
Ballintober	11.0	2	—
Ballyknockan	20.0	24	7
Ballymore Eustace East	5.0	2	—
Ballyward	6.0	1	—
Baltyboys Lower	52.0	22	3
Baltyboys Upper	49.0	9	8
Bishopsland	18.0	3	—
Bishopslane*	0.3	1	—
Blackditches Lower	1.0	1	—
Blessington	23.0	8	2
Britonstown	29.0	1	2
Broadleas Commons	3.0	6	—
Burgage More	56.0	14	2
Burgage Moyle	52.0	5	3
Butterhill	31.0	7	5
Carrig	18.0	8	—
Carrigacurra	7.0	12	2
Crosscoolharbour	23.0	8	4
Fallarees Commons	85.0	2	—
Glashina	3.0	3	1
Glebe East	85.0	2	—
Harristown	9.0	2	—
Haylands	40.0	4	—
Horsepasstown	48.0	1	—
Holyvalley*	0.4	9	—
Humphreystown	26.0	9	3
Johnstown	14.0	8	—
Kilmalum	4.0	1	—
Knockieran Lower	22.0	3	—
Lackan	48.0	36	15
Lockstown Lower	22.0	3	—
Monamuck	84.0	18	4
Oldcourt	16.0	7	—
Rathballylong	15.0	1	—
Russborough	16.0	2	—
Russellstown	64.0	1	—
Silverhill Lower	9.0	3	—
Sroughan	19.0	7	—
Threecastles	23.0	8	3
Tulfarris	72.0	1	1
Valleymount	59.0	10	3
Walterstown	2.0	1	—
Total		**309**	**76**

Sources: Valuation Office archives.

* Land in these townlands, although under the 622ft contour, was considered unviable to keep and was restored to the previous owners by the ESB.

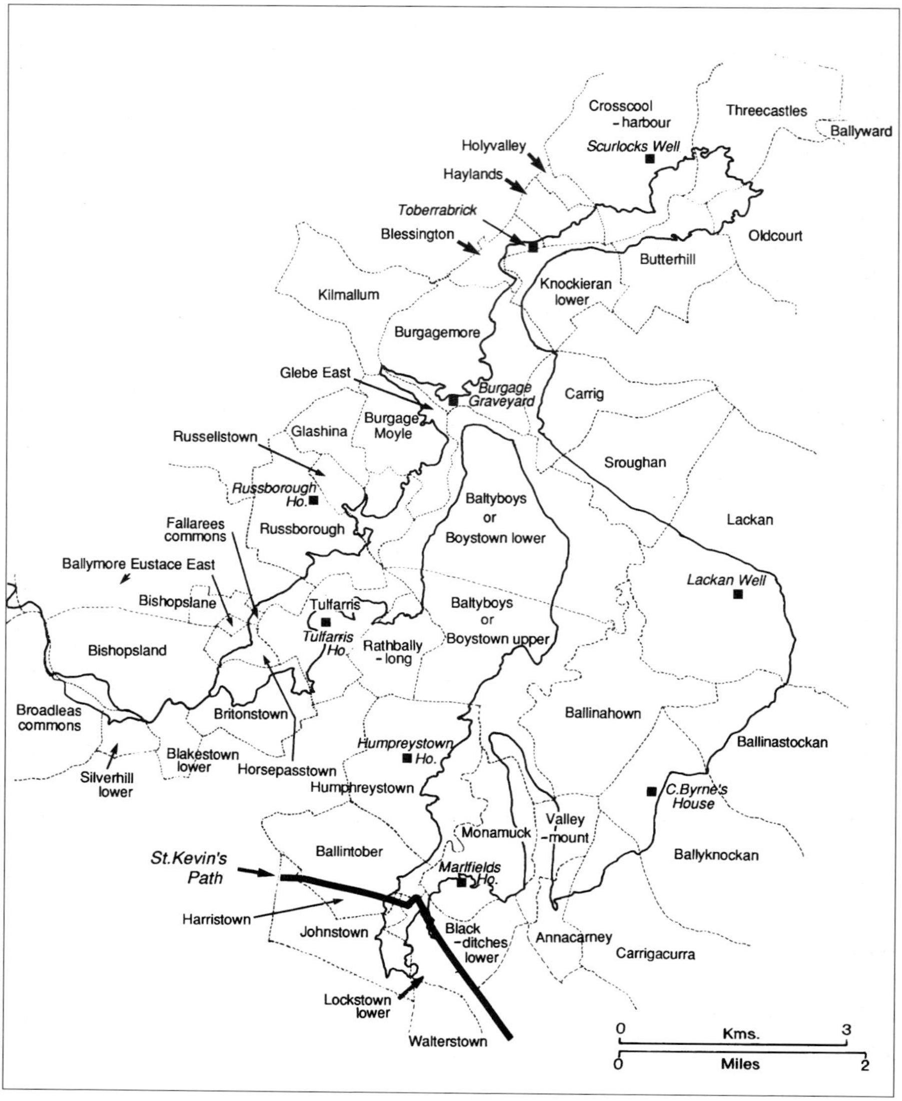

Figure 25.2 Townlands in reservoir area and sites referred to in text.

Curraghmore owned eight of the more peripheral mountain townlands (derived initially from episcopal ancestors) between the Liffey and the King's rivers: Elizabeth Graydon Stannus was returned owner of the residual part of the Smith property now shorn of its Big House: Captain Edward Hornidge of Tulfarris House was lessor of Tulfarris, Britonstown, Horsepasstown and part of Russborough.[17] The nature of tenancy was directly related to the chronology of land purchase acts in the district. In the areas untouched by landlord or Land Commission, survivals of older land systems were evident. An insight into cluster origins and associated land use regimes is provided in Ballinahown townland. Here, in the comparatively recent early years of the century 185 acres had been divided among two members of the Quinn family who decided to hold it in common. By 1939 a cluster of three houses, housing three related Quinn families, had evolved: John (senior), John (junior) his son, and Joseph a brother of John (senior). The land was allocated in three unequal shares. These shares known locally as 'stints' gave each a share in the fields thereby equalising land quality but not land area. John (senior) had a half share in each division whereas the other two, his son John and brother Joseph, held a quarter share each. Pasture land was grazed according to a similar quota system and an inventory of stock was carried out annually on May Day to ensure compliance with the regulatory system.[18] The arable was in a large open field of six acres. Such an inheritance and land use system would progressively reduce field size and encourage fragmentation.

It is a tradition locally that land in the bottoms in Lackan townland was not divided into individual farms until 1939.[19] Prior to this cows grazed on undivided, unfenced, common land. Ninety acres of this townland remained undivided until 1940 and was described in the valuation records as leased to the 'tenants of the townland' by the owners of the Smith property.[20] The rough summer grazing on the high mountain of Moanbane (*Móin Bhán* – the white bog) was allocated in collops. Farmers of Ballyknockan townland were allowed graze cows and sheep free in proportion to the rental paid for land downslope to the marquis of Waterford. It was also permissible for those with grazing rights to sell them on an annual basis. One farmer stated that his father had a 'stint' for sixty sheep on this 'preserve' and he claimed that two cows or four young cattle or six sheep were equivalent to a collop. Others gave different ratios of stock to the collop which indicates the absence of rigorous management practices in the mountain.[21]

Fieldnames and economy

The several hundred fieldnames collected by Ó Súilleabháin and his rescue team afford insights into the hidden geography of what was a diverse area in terms of land quality, land ownership and land use. Echoes of the long fugitive Irish language were found in some ninety fieldnames, although the majority of names may be of relatively recent origin suggesting that the bottom lands were settled in the modern historical period. Fieldnames, though primarily concerned with intimate scale details of location, when aggregated convey a general impression of topography and land quality (table 25.2). Many of the names along

Table 25.2

Irish Fieldnames

Townland	*Recorded Name**	*Possible Original Form*
Ballyknockan	the fussock	an fásach (the pasture)
	glass the silluk	glas na saíleach (meadow of the willows)
	the rillig	an reilig (the graveyard)
	the mullawn	an mullán (the hillock)
	farnathray	fearann an trá? (ploughland of the (river) beach)
	the ling	an linn? (the pond)
	carrawllugh	ceathrú an locha (quarterland of the lake)
	farnafowlach	fearann? (ploughland of the plundering)
	the kunop	an cnap? (the heap)
	the rath	an ráth (the fort)
	the rideogs	na raideoga (the bog myrtles)
	carnasilloge	carn na saileog (the heap of the sally trees)
Baltyboys Lower	the cosheer	an chois thiar? (the western foot of a valley or water channel)
Burgage More	inch-a-clare	inse an chláir (holm of the level land)
	lástrum	lios? droma (the fort of the ridge or hill)
Carrig	riligeen bank	an reiligín (the small graveyard)
Humphreystown	the cloovaun	an chluain bhán? (the dry or fallow meadow)
Johnstown	the riasg field	an riasc (the wet or rough land)
	inse na circe	ínse na gcoirce/na circe (the holm of the oats/of the hen)
Lackan	the mooneens	na móinîní (the little marshes)
	locharavó – er	loch an rátha mhóir? (lake of the big fort)
	kishanagonna	cois áth na gcúnach? (the foot of the fort of the mosses)
	baunagash	bán na gaise (lea ground of the stream)
	the cruckawns	na cnocáin (the small hills)
Monamuck	the keeb	an chíb (the sedge/mountain grass)
Russborough	the buaile bhán	bhuaile bhán/buaile an bháin (the fallow booley/the booley of the pasture)
	the tóchar lane	tóchar (causeway)
Valleymount	the fassock	an fásach (the pasture)

* Most of these fields were numbered by the surveyors and may be located by correlating the source material with Liam Price's map currently held by the Geography Department, UCD.

the rivers included the element 'inch' which is derived from *inse* – 'holm, water meadow'. Sometimes these incorporated scale such as *inse beag* – the small inch, *inse mór* – the big inch; ownership as in 'Murphy's Inch' or land use as in *inse na coirce* – the inch of the oats. Names denoting poor drainage and indifferent land such as *the riasg* –

marsh, the coarse field, the furry field, the pond field, or the 'fussock' from *fásach* – 'waste, uncultivated, uninhabited' – were common. Land use was reflected in names such as 'the bull field', 'the cabbage garden', 'the pasture', 'Thady Browne's Boolye' and 'the *buaile bhán*'. The latter two names contain the element *buaile*, 'milking place in summer pasturage'. Neither in townland nor in fieldnames is there much evidence of non-agricultural, economic activity but the memory of a long defunct flax mill in Ballinahown was held in the names of two bleaching fields known as the upper and lower tinters. Four fields, appropriately in the northernmost lime-starved townlands, had the name 'limekiln field' and the survival of a number of 'brick fields' suggests the local exploitation of the clay deposits.[22]

Many fieldnames indicate location in relation to the farm dwelling such as 'the middle field', 'the back lodge' and 'the field fornith the door'. Traditionally, individual surnames, often recording former owners, were given to fields incorporated into new farms. These are invaluable indices of settlement density and the continuous rationalisation of farm size. Examples abound in the reservoir area such as 'John Lennon's bog', 'Murphy's Inch', 'Butler's Field', 'Brady's Field' and 'Thady Browne's Boolye'. Fieldnames in Irish were generally densest in the south-east of the reservoir coincident with the poorest land and the smallest holdings. The names recorded for William Twyford's large farm in Ballinahown townland could be replicated in the English midlands (table 25.3).

Farm settlement in the valley was dispersed, each within its own fields and generally recessed down boreens away from the main roads. Local authority housing was road orientated and devoid of the outbuildings found on farms. It is certain that this landscape had been shaped by improving landlords in the nineteenth century but in many respects the valley was a microcosm of the robust, self-sufficient Ireland preached by Éamon de Valera. Turf, potatoes, vegetables, milk, butter and eggs were all produced locally; there was a traditional pig trade with Dublin and pigs were also killed and salted for home consumption. Ballinahown village which specialised in pig rearing earned the local sobriquet 'pigtown'.[23] James Cullen's farm in Lackan townland typified the area. A dairy herd of eight cows, a flock of forty breeding ewes and two mares for farmwork and breeding were the bedrock livestock. In recessionary times when stock and feeding were comparatively cheap these numbers could be augmented. Cows and horses never left the home farm but the sheep were moved to the common grazing above Lackan in summer before returning in late autumn to warmer, kinder climes. Blessington Fair, religiously held on the thirteenth of each month, except when it happened to be a Sunday,

Table 25.3

Fieldnames in Ballinahown and Baltyboys Upper

Townland	*Landholder*	*Fieldname*
Ballinahown	John Clarke	the inches
		sally park
		the back lodge
		the little field
		the big field
		the field over the pond
		the big bog
		the little bog
		the high field
Ballinahown	William Twyford	the lower inch
		sally park
		the lower tinter
		the haggard
		the upper tinter
		the paddock
		the bank
		the high field
		the field fornith the door
		the whites field
		the flat inch
		the daisy field
		the wood field
		the burrow field
		The bog field
		The red scar
		The big height
		fitz's inch
Baltyboys Upper	Michael Fitzpatrick	the little meadow
		the black field
		connors acre
		the bank
		the inches
		the fussock
		the knock
		the lodge
Baltyboys Upper	Butler	butler's field
		the upper brick bank
		the lower brick bank
		the inches
		the big meadow
		the little lodge
		the little field
Baltyboys Upper	Joe Farrell	the stone wall meadow
		brady's field
		the Inch
		the wall field
		the brick fields
		butler's field

provided an outlet for young surplus stock and butter.[24] The Browns of Butterhill in addition to ten cows, kept a shorthorn bull; three shillings were charged for the servicing of a cow. Joe Brown, a nephew, remembered the machinery used on the 125-acre farm: a double boarded plough (for potatoes and turnips), and another, a 'jib' for straight ploughing; a three part harrow, a spring harrow and a roller; an eleven-piked and later a fourteen-piked corndrill; and a 'wheel driven mowing machine' – one for the meadows, another for the corn, operated by foot stirrups which would overturn the corn gathered on the blades. Oats was the dominant cereal grown in the entire reservoir area and fertilisers included farmyard manure and lime, the latter collected by horse and cart from a kiln in Naas. In addition a yellow clay which apparently served as a good fertiliser was taken from a 'marl' pit at Woodenbridge, Butterhill and spread by shovel. A maddock was used to clear furze on more hilly ground.[25]

A common type of rick stand was made of granite quarried nearby in Ballyknockan. One found in the haggard at Butler's house in Baltyboys Upper was described as a platform consisting of seven legs and caps and twelve stretchers; each cap, circular in shape and 1 foot 9 inches in diameter stood on a leg about 2 feet 6 inches from the ground, with six legs arranged in a circle and one in the middle supporting stretchers roughly 8 feet long; on this surface a platform of 11 feet diameter was placed. A set of legs, caps and stretchers would have cost £2 in 1940. This so-called 'oat stack' prevented vermin reaching the platform as the caps protruded 6 inches or so out from the leg; the stand was dismantled when not in use. A less sophisticated platform constructed with soil lined by stones and rectangular in shape, was found on the smaller farms.[26] Haycocks were held down with home spun ropes called twisters, woven from straw, and weighted with stones.[27]

Prevalent in the byres of the valley was an animal tying device consisting of wire bent into a ring, attached to a rope which divided in two to go around the animal's neck or horns. It could be used for either goats or cows and was called 'ringadan' or 'lingadan'. In some cow houses, sliding wooden rails called 'bales' tied cattle during winter.[28] Valley residents in Carrigacurra, Ballyknockan, Valleymount and Ballinahown townlands cut turf on the Killough bog in Ballinahown. This bog of *c.*180 acres was owned by John Mahon who resided at the 'Tan House' or Bog Lodge in this townland. The £2,700 which Mahon received in compensation was hardly any consolation to the scores of others who cut turf here. Starting in April, the cutting was done with both breast and wing slanes, 'using ponies and asses and carts and creating large clumps on the old bog road', between Valleymount and Ballyknockan. All the turf would be drawn out by the end of August – in the exceptional year of 1939, the cutting ran late into September. The Red Bog in Ballyknockan, leased to several townlanders, provided brick clay for brickworks in Kilbride, just north of the reservoir, which closed in 1936, two years after opening, when the bog had been fully exploited.[29]

Hardware goods which could not be home made were supplied by local carpenters, the Kelly brothers of Blessington and Tom Jones of Knockieran, and blacksmiths Jack Tyrrell and Tom Shannon of Blessington. Carpenters were responsible for maintenance and at times the manufacture of the contemporary modes of transport, from the block-wheel solid dray and trapcar to the less common jaunting car that carried five people. The communal business of threshing one's oats in October led to the sharing of farm machinery otherwise unaffordable: a drum thresher, owned by Jim Valentine of Donard and pulled by horses, was used by the Browns of Butterhill.[30]

The symbolic landscape

'It is impossible,' wrote a correspondent in the *Leinster Leader*, 'to realise the wealth of loving feeling for their old homesteads that ages of habitation amongst the glorious mountains and valleys of the district generated in the young and old.'[31] The national papers were initially more concerned with lauding the triumph of technology over impoverished nature. The *Irish Independent* pictured the nemesis: 'where now lie thousands of acres of bog and poor pastureland will then lie an immense shimmering sheet of oriental water. Boats with coloured sails and dipping oars will be skimming over its calm surface.'[32]

Attachment to homeplace and empathy with the landscape of childhood and ancestors is one of the more enduring traits of the Irish countryman. Scattered throughout the doomed district were the ancestral shrines, the symbolic sites and holy places, invested with generations of prayer and pilgrimage. The loss of such a personal heritage was deeply felt by a spiritual and traditional people. One of the holy sites with such a sacred aura was the holy well located in a field below Lackan village. This well was known as St Boden's Well, Fr Germaine's Well or simply Lackan Well. The origins of the well were variously ascribed. Some attributed its supernatural status to Fr Germaine, parish priest of Baltyboys, much revered by his parishioners and much distrusted by local landlords such as Elizabeth Smith of Baltyboys House. Others associated the well with the legendary Bishop Boden whose footprint was reputedly imprinted on a stone beside it. Yet another origin story linked both the mythical figure of Boden and the nineteenth-century pastor Germaine, claiming that the well was known locally as Thighnavilla, possibly *tigh na meala* (house of the honey), until Fr Germaine blessed the site and placed two fish in the water. The water would hold its curative powers as long as the fish remained within the well. Whatever its origins the well was a focal point in the calendar of local religious festivities. On 1 May, perhaps inferring association with the festival of Bealtaine, the community, after benediction service in Lackan chapel, proceeded to the well in the wake of Ballyknockan band. Drowning of the well, it was believed, would release the fish and deprive the waters of their healing power. The community was not mollified by the erection of a new well by the Electricity Supply Board higher up the hill and when the old site was once more revealed during the severe drought of the summer of 1978, thousands flocked in pilgrimage to the shrine of their ancestors.[33] Two other holy wells at Tobernabrick (*Tobar na mBreac* – the well of the trout) east of Blessington and Scurlock's well beside the old graveyard in Coolcrossharbour townland were both lost beneath the water. A lone tree, accorded sanctity because of its proximity to Scurlock's well and bedecked with medallions and rags of former supplicants, was, according to local residents, cut down and burned in the preparatory work of clearing the site.[34]

The forced abandonment of Burgage More graveyard caused great resentment in the community. Graveyards bonding living and dead were, next to the home hearth, sites which linked families across the centuries and rarely have they been disturbed in rural Ireland. A Burial Rights Committee was established to ensure re-internment in the new Burgage graveyard on the high ground. The rough unsculptured granite cross sited outside the old graveyard and bearing the date 1400 testified to its antiquity. When removed, this cross of St Mark reputedly shed blood which ceased after it was prayed over by the local parish priest and then re-erected at the new site.[35] A 'clournaun' (*ceallúrnán*) or burial ground for unbaptised children in Lackan townland escaped drowning but a field known locally as the 'relig field' in Ballyknockan was lost to the reservoir.[36]

The valley was within the sphere of influence of St Kevin's monastic settlement of Glendalough and local tradition had it that St Kevin's Walk followed the townland boundary between Humphreystown and Ballintoher and crossed the King's river into Monamuck at a ford of stepping stones. Local informants told the surveyors that they had often ploughed through the paving stones in the townlands of Blackditches, Togher and Bawnoge en route to the Sally Gap some eight miles to the north. This route of great antiquity was still used by the people of Blackditches but it was to be sundered by the water.[37]

Because Wicklow's gentry claimed the middle ground for their house sites there were few material associations with landlordism across the valley floor. One 'gentry' house, Marlsfield's house, though above the projected water level, had to be abandoned because of its proximity to the reservoir. Built by the La Touche banking family, whose influence and money permeated all of north Wicklow, the house had been garrisoned by a troop of yeomanry in 1798 and tradition claimed that 'many a man was flogged and scourged' there.[38]

Remembered history was everywhere evident. On the gable wall of Dr Byrne's house in Ballyknockan was the legend:

'The Emergency Land Grabber
Defeated here 1888
God Save Ireland.'

These words inscribed on a piece of local granite by master craftsmen commemorated the eviction of a blind woman and her sister from this house by a local middleman in 1888. A defiant community built a new house in one day for the evicted couple and when the middleman's men tossed it during Sunday Mass it was quickly repaired. This house escaped inundation in 1939.[39]

Vernacular architecture

The vernacular architecture of the valley dwelling closely resembles the housetypes discussed by F. H. Aalen in this volume.[40] Houses of the direct entry type,[41] usually with a single door into the kitchen unit and usually with upright gables[42] were numerically superior to the so-called hearth-lobby houses[43] which commonly have hipped roofs and a screen or jamb wall, separating the main kitchen entrance from the adjacent hearth, forming a lobby immediately inside the door. The direct entry houses surveyed ranged from one structural unit to three structural units in length. Some had outhouses attached at one end, such as Miley's three unit house in Monamuck townland. Likewise Peter McDonald's house in Valleymount townland, which also had three outhouses attached, forming an extended farmyard layout with the farm buildings built along the continuation of the long axis of the dwelling.[44] Two further farmyard types associated with the direct entry house in the reservoir area were also recorded. One of these, the 'half courtyard' type[45] in which two sides of the farmyard were utilised by the dwelling house and a range of outhouses at right angles to it, was found at Flemings in Monamuck townland and at Twyfords in Baltyboys Upper townland. The other farmyard type recorded was the scattered farmstead as in Ballinahown village where there was no formal farmyard layout, the buildings seemingly having been erected as the need for them arose wherever suitable terrain permitted. The Wicklow Mountains area was one of only a handful of places in the southeast of Ireland where this type of farmyard layout was found at this time.[46]

Four of the houses recorded were clearly of the hearth-lobby type,[47] three had upright gables and one had a byre attached, features redolent of the direct-entry houses found in these valleys. A characteristic feature of this house type, the 'jamb wall', was recorded in Butlers of Baltyboys Upper townland as being 18 inches thick with an opening (*c.* 1 foot x 7 inches) facing the kitchen door. When this door was open, as was the normal practice in country houses, a person sitting at the hearth or window opposite had a view of the yard outside. Butler's house had the additional feature of a 'blind window', etched 8 inches deep in the wall opposite the jamb wall window, and it was used to store socks and old pipes.[48] In another house, Fox's of Woodenbridge, Butterhill townland, the jamb wall with a window in it called a 'spy hole', supported a cross beam forming a mantlepiece, to the right of which a loft called the targ (*tailleog*) was created.[49] The hearth in these hearth-lobby houses was located towards the centre of the building apart from the one-unit house in which the fire was located at the gable wall. This was also the hearth position in direct-entry houses recorded. The internal organisation of space, with a bedroom behind the fire in many instances, corresponded in both house types. A further common feature in both house types was a loft over the bedroom opposite the fire.[50]

Four examples of two-storey slated farmhouses belonging to large farms were also recorded.[51] At least one was of hearth-lobby type[52] but it is unclear from the material to hand whether the other three houses belonged to the vernacular building tradition, or if they were of formal design. One of the latter, called 'The Bog Lodge' and owned by Paddy Twomey in Ballinahown townland, had six rooms with modern doors, fireplaces and chimneys and was said to have been built no less than one hundred years earlier on a farm of about 200 acres.[53] Another, Matt Brown's house in Butterhill townland, was situated on almost 125 acres. It had a kitchen, 'back kitchen', a parlour downstairs and two bedrooms upstairs. Outhouses surrounding an enclosed yard at the back of the house included stables, a few cattle houses, a coach house, and a loft over the stables to store corn.

In Ballyknockan townland, just at the south-east of the reservoir, a granite quarry, employing several cutters, provided the entire area with suitable materials for floors and walls of houses and outhouses, for barn stands, gate posts and even pig troughs. Special features such as cutstones forming nooks beside the fire for storing and drying turf were also made of granite. It was not used exclusively, however, although flags seem to have been the common floor covering. Cairn's house in

Plate 25.1 Direct-entry thatched house, Ballinahown. The upper walls were of sod (Dept. of Irish Folklore, U.C.D.).

Plate 25.2 Lobby-entry gabled wall house, with granite outhouses roofed with slate (Dept. of Irish Folklore, U.C.D.).

Plate 25.3 Ballinahown cluster
(Dept. of Irish Folklore, U.C.D.).

Plate 25.4 Quinn houses in Ballinahown
(Dept. of Irish Folklore, U.C.D.).

Ballyknockan, for example, had a concrete floor, though the walls were of granite.[54] Sod was much more rarely used in construction. Matthew Lennon's house in Ballinahown townland could not support a stone chimney as the upper gable walls were of sod.[55] Another house known locally as the 'Black House' situated at the Priest's Bridge in Lackan townland, and owned by Mr Kavanagh, was described by a neighbour as a 'booley house'.[56] It had layered sods of walls up to 60cm thick with the grass side placed downwards. The house measured 7m in length and 4m in width. The walls reached only to kitchen door height.[57] Internally, a three-sided wattle canopy – a common hearth feature in the area – was placed over the fire, resting on an oak breast-beam which formed a mantlepiece over the wide fireplace. The entire canopy structure was plastered with mud and whitewashed on the outside.

The prevalent roof structure consisted of a series of A-shaped couples tied by collar braces. Lying across the couples, and attached to them by wooden pegs, were runners.[58] On this wooden framework, often of bog oak retrieved from local bogs,[59] rested the first layers of vegetable roofing materials. In the south-east of the study area, this was generally straw which was presumably sewn to the couples by straw rope or yarn. Only one house, P. McDonald's in Valleymount townland, was recorded as having an underthatch of sod.[60] Thatching was done in the technique typical of the south-east of Ireland at the time – thrust thatching.[61] In the late 1930s there were four thatchers in the immediate townlands: John Brennan and Peter Geoghegan of Lackan; James Butler of Baltyboys and James Twomey of Carrigacurra, the latter being one of the many displaced by the construction of the reservoir.[62] Oaten straw was the preferred material, lasting up to ten years, but it is clear that some houses used rushes which needed replacing every two years.[63] A thatcher's pay was about three shillings per day (fifteen new pence) and a three-bay house would take twelve or thirteen days to thatch.[64] Slate, found on roughly one-fifth of the dwelling houses was confined mainly to dwelling-house roofs, and outbuildings, even those associated with the two-storey houses, were usually thatched, though some had corrugated iron roofs. Corrugated iron was also being used as roofing material for dwelling houses; it had replaced the thatched roof of Pat Lawlor's house in Lackan, for example.[65]

Other features recorded were the internal wooden window shutters found in many houses,[66] the use of heather for floor brushes,[67] the prevalence of sprigs of blessed palms in the houses and outhouses,[68] and the house-leek (Sempervivum), grown from cracks in the walls and used to cure cattle flux.[69] Precautionary measures against another common cattle disease, blackleg, were also recorded. In one instance the hind leg of a cow which had died from blackleg had been hung in the chimney by a cord for sixty years, 'probably as a preventative against the other cattle being affected'.[70]

The local blacksmith's craft was to be seen, from iron flower-shaped railing decorations for windows in Ballinahown village, to the metal 'rack' suspended from a bog-oak beam set transversely into the chimney to hold a strong wire called the catch from which a pot or kettle was suspended over the fire.[71] This hanging crane was the usual type found in the district, although a fire crane standing beside the fire was also in evidence in some houses; one was said to have been made seventy years previously by a smith called Farrell of Valleymount townland.[72]

Evacuation

The 6,500 acres of lost land stretched across thirty-eight townlands in the barony of Talbotstown Lower in county Wicklow and seven townlands in the barony of Naas Upper in the contiguous area of east Kildare. Table 24.1 shows the land claimed by the reservoir on a townland basis and the number of houses submerged (fig. 25.3). Because of the relative recency of the evacuation and the division of responsibilities between the Electricity Supply Board, who were generally concerned with the engineering aspects, and the Irish Land Commission, whose primary function related to the re-settlement of migrants from the valley, it is difficult to track down documentation. The unavailability of Land Commission documents relating to the migration process means that there is no official list of people evacuated and migrant numbers have to be inferred from the number of houses submerged.

The Electricity Supply Board paid an average of £9 per statute acre to each landholder together with £100 disturbance money.[73] These figures conceal the variable nature of awards which were based, like the nineteenth-century valuation, primarily on land quality and market access. Not all farmers, however, lost complete farms and the ESB had to assess the extent to which the land lost affected the future viability of the farm. Some of the landowners refused the compensation offered and brought claims to arbitration courts specially convened in Blessington courthouse. The amount sought by claimants and the figure finally paid by the ESB varied widely. Table 25.4 shows, for example, that seventy-four acres without a house in Crosscoolharbour on the north of the reservoir was valued at £2,150, whereas seventy acres with a house across the reservoir in Lackan townland was valued at £1,250. From the final public land valuation of the reservoir in 1940 it is possible to calculate the compensation figures. The lowest valued land was in Ballynastockan at three shillings an acre – whereas the highest was in Russellstown at eighteen shillings and six pence.

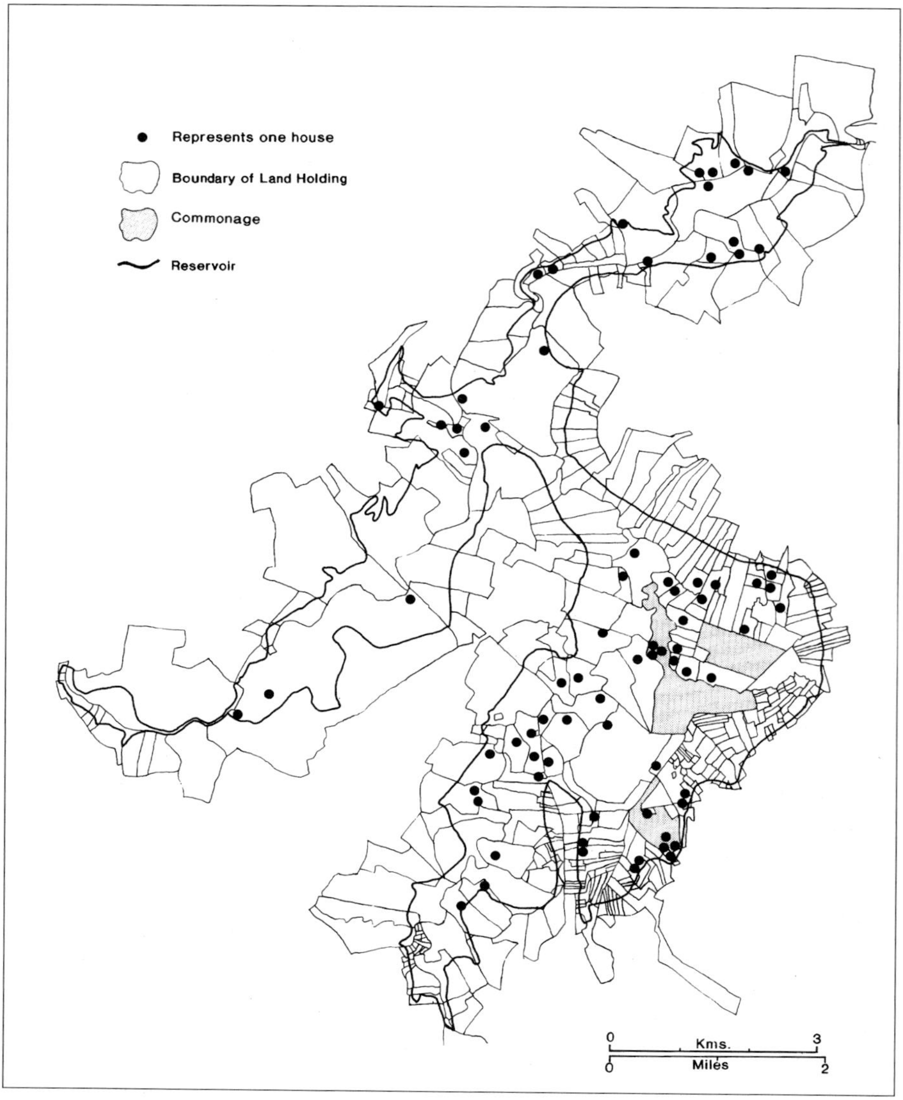

Figure 25.3 Houses in reservoir area.

There was little time for grieving. The first notice (of proposed relocation) came in the Christmas post of 1937.[74] James Cullen had not settled with the ESB by the time of the building of the dam in 1940.[75] Having travelled to see several prospective farms in Kildare he was eventually forced to evacuate his old home in Lackan and move to that county. Matt Brown, according to his nephew, was given twelve months to move. The Burial Rights Committee formed to oppose the

Table 25.4

Some Compensation Cases Brought to Arbitration

Townland	*Landowner*	*Claimed*	*Acres*	*Settlement*
Ballinahown	John Quinn (Sen)	£2,540	73 + house	£1,400
	John Quinn (Jnr)	£1,355	38 + house	£800
	Joseph Quinn	£2,477.10s	72 + house	£1,350
	Patrick Clark	£2,507	73 + house	£1,460
	John Mahon	£5,685	266 + house	2,700
Carrig	Mrs Margaret Murphy	£721	11	£194
Crosscoolharbour	William Hamilton	£3,865	74	£2,150
Humphreystown	Miss Esther Shannon	£1,000	8 + house	£407
Lackan	James Cullen (Sen)	£1,346	41 + house	£975
	Michael Parker	£1,944	70 + house	£1,250
	Edward Miley	£2,460	52 + house	£1,200
	Patrick Browe	£735	15 + house	£475
	Martin White	£900	14	£300
	Patrick J Lawlor	£2,050	60 + house	£1,025
	Mrs Julia Lawlor	£1,300	34 + house	£600
Kilmalum	John Rowel	£1,750	22	£550

Source: Local and National Newspapers

drowning of the Burgage graveyard and the Disturbed Owners Association representing anxious landowners give some idea of the depth of opposition to the reservoir, compulsory purchase and inadequacy of compensation.

The element of compulsion and the rapidity with which the ESB moved to secure possession awakened dormant images of Cromwell's soldiery and rapacious landlords. Landowners were dismayed by the valuation placed on their farms and the general opinion was that the semi-state body was measuring value in purely monetary terms. Bill Twyford aptly evoked local sentiment: 'The Arbitrator was the devil and the court was in hell ... The feeling of the local people was that it was back to the days of Cromwell, that they were evicted whether they were willing or not; there was no sheriff needed. The dam was built and the water was the sheriff.'[76] Many argued that they were about to lose a family home which rooted them in this Wicklow valley for generations past. The Shannons were said to have lived in Baltyboys Upper for over 600 years.[77] Money could never compensate for the loss of such primal associations. 'They couldn't have been more sorrowful,' Rosie O'Reilly remembered in later years, 'leaving ancestors before them.'[78] Some clung defiantly to house and home until the water crept in around the kitchen hearth and quenched the fire. The Twyfords of Ballinahown were one such family and Jack Callaghan from the same

Table 25.5

Destination of Migrants (where located)

Name	*From – Townland*	*Moved To*
Patrick Clarke	Ballinahown	Broadleas Commons, county Kildare
John Quinn (Sen)	Ballinahown	Ballymore Eustace
John Quinn (Jnr)	Ballinahown	Donadea, county Kildare
Matthew Reid	Ballinahown	Clondalkin, county Dublin
Matthew Lennon	Ballinahown	Lackan
Patrick Shortt	Ballyknockan	Annacarney
The Cahills	Ballyknockan	Carrigacurra
The Kehoes	Ballyknockan	Carrigacurra
The Conlons	Ballyknockan	Carrigacurra
The Mulvey Sisters	Ballyknockan	Ballyknockan
John Dargle	Ballyknockan	Ballyknockan
James Byrne	Baltyboys Lower	Baltyboys Lower
Jock Byrne	Baltyboys Lower	Burgage More
Essie Shannon	Baltyboys Lower	Broadleas Commons, county Kildare
Joseph Tyrrell	Baltyboys Lower	Baltyboys Lower
James Butler	Baltyboys Upper	Donadea, county Kildare
The Cahills	Baltyboys Upper	Harold's Cross, Dublin
Patrick Fitzpatrick	Baltyboys Upper	Baltyboys Upper
Patrick Shannon	Baltyboys Upper	Dublin
John Mahon	Baltyboys Upper	Eadestown, county Kildare
Michael Twyford	Baltyboys Upper	Kilmurry, Baltinglass
The Browns	Butterhill	Baltyboys Upper
The Floods	Humphreystown	Humphreystown
The Bolgers	Humphreystown	Humphreystown
Christy Miley & Sister & Mother	Monamuck	Crosscoolharbour
James & Miles Fleming	Monamuck	Geoghanstown, Brannockstown
Joseph Quinn	Monamuck	Valleymount
The Mileys	Lackan	Tober, Dunlavin
Edward Miley	Lackan	Gormanstown, Dunlavin
The Lawlors	Lackan	Mullycagh, Hollywood
The McLoughlins	Lackan	Threecastles
The Mackeys	Lackan	Donadea, county Kildare (one to Kylebeg, Lackan)
The Browes	Lackan	Ballinastockan
The Cullens	Lackan	Donadea, county Kildare
Jack Carroll	Lackan	county Meath, later Glashina
Patrick McDonald	Valleymount	Fryanstown, Dunlavin
Peter McDonald	Valleymount	Valleymount
Ed & John McDonald	Valleymount	Mullycagh, Hollywood
The Callaghans	Valleymount	Ballinastockan

place simply raised the turf fire up into the hob stone as the water breached the door. He was eventually taken out by neighbours who feared he would drown but the sight of his settle bed floating around the lake for months after conveyed the haunted image of the dismemberment of the home sanctuary.[79]

Dammed water dramatically changed the geography of the valley. Ballinahown townland was lost and with it the bog road linking Valleymount and Ballyknockan villages. The Catholic parish of Valleymount was sundered and the priest now had an extra journey of six miles in serving the spiritual needs of his parishioners in Lackan and Valleymount churches. He also lost the contributions of over forty families. Many believed that those who had lost everything and who had received compensation, however inadequate, were better off than those whose farms had been substantially reduced but who had not lost their homes. The former group could start anew whereas the latter had to conform to a reduced farm with little hope of acquiring additional land. The afforestation of Ballyward begun in 1928 and the revival of Ballyknockan granite quarries together with the work of dam construction were not sufficient to prevent the migration of all displaced by the reservoir. Table 25.5 suggests that the majority were re-located within five miles of their old homesteads. All except three families migrated to rural areas, usually to farms made available by the Land Commission who had by then embarked on their most extensive scheme of migration from western Ireland to grazier farms and landlord demesnes in the east; Poulaphouca migrants moved to Mullycagh, Hollywood and Donadea, county Kildare. Valley residents in local authority housing were generally re-housed close to their old locations. Migration did not necessarily improve the economic prospects of those displaced. Julia Quinn of Ballinahown, re-located to a farm in Kildare, knew that her new more fertile land would be rated more that seven times higher than her Wicklow farm.[80]

References

1. Immediately prior to the flooding, scholars including Seán Ó Súilleabháin and Liam Price surveyed the valley. Ó Súilleabháin's material is primarily in Vol. 654 of the Irish Folklore Manuscripts, Department of Irish Folklore, UCD, while Liam Price's collection is currently held by Dr F. H. Aalen of TCD. For further information on the survey see P. Lysaght, and F. Mac Gabhann, 'Rural Houses in the Poulaphouca Reservoir Area', *Sinsear* vii (1993), p. 1, and S. Ó Súilleabháin, 'Under Poulaphouca Reservoir', Lucas, *Folk and Farm* (1977), pp 200-7.
2. Valuation Office, 6 Ely Place, Dublin 2; Private archives (inspected with special permission), ESB, Lower Fitzwilliam Street, Dublin 2; National Archives, Bishop Street, Dublin 1.
3. Interviews with the following were conducted by F. Mac Gabhann: Terry Mahon, Valleymount, 12/10/91; Mrs Mackey, Dunlavin, 12/10/91; Jessie Clarke,

Blessington, 08/11/91; Fr Cantwell, PP, Valleymount, 15/11/91. Liffey Valley Heritage Study Group kindly furnished typescripts of interviews with the following: Rosie Reilly, Blessington, 13/12/91; Joe Brown, Baltyboys Upper, 03/10/91; Stanley Miller, Blessington, 26/09/91; Dicky Gyves, Blessington, 07/10/91; Kathy Tyrrell, Baltyboys Upper, 16/10/91; Nano Miley, Donard, 24/09/91.

4. Vartry and Dodder Schemes.
5. NAI, D/T S 3939, William Tatlow's address to the 'Irish Section of Electrical Engineers'.
6. Held in the Department of Agriculture Library, Kildare Street, Dublin 2.
7. NAI, D/T S 8302, Dept. of Industry and Commerce files.
8. Ibid.
9. Ibid.
10. Dáil Debates, November 1936.
11. Information provided by J. H. Godden, Deputy Station Manager, Turlough Hill.
12. M. Kelly, 'Tales of a Drowned Land' in *West Wicklow Hist. Soc. Jn.* (1983-84), pp 39-42.
13. Ibid.
14. Ibid.
15. A. Farrington, 'Glacial Deposits in West Wicklow', *Irish Geography*, 1957.
16. Valuation Office archives.
17. Ibid.
18. Ibid 12.
19. Ibid 12.
20. Ibid 16.
21. I.F.C. 654: 160.
22. Several thousand fieldnames recorded by the survey (see note 1) are contained in the aforementioned collections et passim.
23. Stanley Miller, Blessington (see note 3).
24. Ibid 12.
25. Joe Brown, Baltyboys Upper (see note 3).
26. I.F.C. 654 et passim.
27. Ibid 25.
28. Ibid 26.
29. Rosie O'Reilly of Blessington interviewed by Dr Séamus Ó Catháin, broadcast on 'Folklands', RTE Radio 1, 29/07/1987; RTE sound archive and Department of Irish Folklore, UCD.
30. Ibid 25.
31. *Leinster Leader* 24/05/1938.
32. *Irish Independent* 27/06/1936.
33. G. McClafferty, 'On The Well That Appeared to Many', *Sinsear* 1 (1979), pp 28-33.
34. Liam Price Collection (see note 1).
35. Ibid 29.
36. I.F.C. 654 et passim.
37. Ibid.
38. Ibid.
39. Ibid.
40. Sources on contemporary local vernacular architecture are primarily: the Poulaphouca Reservoir Survey, 1939; IFC 654: 45-170; The Dept. of Irish Folklore, UCD; and the Department's photograph archive (see note 1).

41. C. Ó Danachair, 'The Traditional Forms of the Dwelling House in Ireland', *R.S.A.I. Jn.* (1972), cii, pp 79-81, 84-88.
42. A. Gailey, *Rural houses of the north of Ireland*, Edinburgh (1984), pp 140-164.
43. A. Gailey, op cit., pp 140-141, 164.
44. C. Ó Danachair, 'Farmyard forms and their distribution in Ireland,' *Ulster Folklife* 27 (1981), Fig. 1, 65-66; A. Gailey, op. cit., pp 233, 241.
45. C. Ó Danachair, 'The Combined Byre-and-Dwelling in Ireland', *Folklife* 2, (1964), 62; F. H. Aalen, in this volume.
46. Ó Danachair, Farmyard forms', (1981), pp 70-72; Gailey, *Rural houses*, pp 233(d), 241.
47. A further two-storey house photographed by D. Ó Cearbhaill in 1939 was also a hearth-lobby house. Department of Irish Folklore, UCD, archive photograph.
48. I.F.C. 654: 59.
49. Information from Liam Price collection, held by Dr F. H. Aalen; similar lofts are mentioned on I.F.C. 654: 121, 137.
50. I.F.C. 654: 61, 137; also mentioned in Liam Price's material.
51. I.F.C. 654: 111; and Liam Price material.
52. Ibid 47.
53. Liam Price material.
54. I.F.C. 654: 91.
55. I.F.C. 654: 99, 101.
56. Liam Price material.
57. Ibid; see F. H. Aalen, in this volume.
58. I.F.C. 654: 63, 129.
59. I.F.C. 654: 129, 179.
60. I.F.C. 654: 129-131.
61. C. Ó Danachair, 'The Questionnaire System' (Roofs and Thatching of Traditional Houses), *Béaloideas* 15 (1945), p. 209.
62. I.F.C. 654: 63, 147.
63. I.F.C. 654: 47.
64. I.F.C. 654: 63-64.
65. Liam Price material.
66. I.F.C. 654: 137.
67. I.F.C. 654: 149-151 (locally known as 'Green Brooms').
68. I.F.C. 654: 65.
69. I.F.C. 654: 145.
70. I.F.C. 654: 89.
71. I.F.C. 654: 51, 103.
72. I.F.C. 654: 103.
73. From research conducted by Mr M. Lennon of Lackan, Blessington.
74. Kathy Tyrrell, Baltyboys Upper (see note 3).
75. Ibid 12.
76. Bill Twyford of Blessington on 'Folklands' (see note 29).
77. *Irish Independent* 06/10/1937.
78. Ibid 29.
79. Terry Mahon, Valleymount (see note 3).
80. *Irish Independent* 06/10/1937.

Phoul A Phuca (Bartlett).

Chapter 26

A SELECT BIBLIOGRAPHY OF COUNTY WICKLOW

JOAN KAVANAGH

This is a select list of books, pamphlets and articles relating to county Wicklow. Articles in journals are not included but most recent articles on the history of the county have appeared in the journals listed in section 2 below. For a comprehensive listing of articles in journals readers are directed to the 'Bibliography of the local history collection in Bray public library' published as appendix iv to O'Sullivan, J., Dunne, T., and Cannon, S., *The book of Bray* listed in section 6 below, and to the excellent card index of sources for Wicklow local history which is available in Wicklow County Library. The County Wicklow Heritage Project has compiled an extensive database index of sources for the history of Wicklow and its people and is glad to offer advice to researchers.

Entries in this bibliography are grouped within the following categories:

1. Guides and directories
2. Journals
3. Archaeology, geology, physical geography and topography
4. Biography, memoirs and letters
5. Folklore, music and sport
6. Places
7. General

1. GUIDES AND DIRECTORIES (see also under PLACES below)

Anon. *A three days' tour in the county Wicklow* (London, 1849)

Dublin & Wicklow mountains; access routes for the hill walker (Dublin, 1984)

Carson's illustrated guide: guide to county Wicklow (Dublin, 1882)

Anon. *A guide to the county of Wicklow* (Dublin, 1835)

Anon. *West Wicklow: a comprehensive guide to the area, with illustrations and map* (Dublin, 1971)

Black, A. and C. *Black's guide to the Dublin & Wicklow mountains* (Edinburgh, 1865)

Boyle, K. and Bourke, O. *et al, The Wicklow way: a natural history field guide* (Dublin, 1990)

Bradbury, J. *Dublin and the county of Wicklow: how to see them for 4½ guineas* (1886)

Brunker, J.P. *Flora of the county Wicklow* (Dundalk, 1950)

Cantwell, B.J. *Memorials of the dead in county Wicklow* (4 vols. 1974-78 and supplementary index, 1986)

Costello, C. *Guide to county Kildare and West Wicklow* (Naas, 1991)

de Lion, C. *The Croghan valley: a guide to Aughrim and Glenmalure* (Dublin, 1968)

Ferrar, J. *A view of ancient and modern Dublin, with it's improvements to the year 1796, to which is added a tour to Bellevue, in the county of Wicklow, the seat of Peter La Touche, Esq.* (Dublin, 1796)

Fewer, M. *The Wicklow way from Marley to Glenmalure: a walking guide* (Dublin, 1988)

Flynn, A.and Brophy, J. *The book of Wicklow: towns & villages in the garden of Ireland* (Blackrock, 1992)

Fraser, J. *Guide to the county of Wicklow* (Dublin, 1842)

Fraser, R. *General view of agriculture and mineralogy, present state and circumstances of the county Wicklow* (Dublin, 1801)

Heffernan, D.E. *Handbook of the county of Wicklow* (1860)

Herman, D. *Hill strollers' Wicklow* (Dublin, 1990)

Herman, D. *Hill strolls around Dublin: a guide to 24 short walks in the Dublin and Wicklow mountains* (1984)

Herman, D. and others. *Irish walk guides: the East., Dublin / Wicklow* (Dublin, 1979)

Irwin, G. O'Malley. *The illustrated hand-book to the county of Wicklow* (Dublin, 1844)

Irwin, G. *Irwin's Dublin guide and the county of Wicklow* (Dublin, 1857)

Mc Cormick, J. *The higher lakes of Wicklow (Wicklow, 1994)*

Malone, J.B. *Walking in Wicklow: a guide for travellers (afoot or awheel) through the Wicklow mountains* (Dublin, 1964).

Malone, J.B. *The complete Wicklow way – a step by step guide.* Revised edition updated by Jimmy Murphy with an introduction by James Plunkett (Dublin, 1993).

Moriarty, C. *Irish wheel guides: 1 Dublin and North Wicklow* (Dublin, 1980)

Moriarty, C. *On foot in Dublin & Wicklow exploring the wilderness* (1989)

Owens, J. *Ar dtir féin. Excursions in and about Dublin and Wicklow to places of historic interest where ruins of cromlechs, castle, ancient churches, holy wells, etc. still exist* (Dublin, 1900)

Porter, F. *Porter's post office guide and directory of the county of Wicklow* (Dublin, 1910)

Powell, G.R. *The official railway handbook to Bray, Kingstown, the coast and the county of Wicklow* (Dublin, 1860)

Powell, G.R. *Pleasure tours in the environs of Dublin and the county of Wicklow* (1853)

Powell, G.R. *The tourist's picturesque guide to Wicklow and Dublin* (London, n.d)

Power, P.J. *The pocket guide to South East Wicklow* (Arklow, 1989)

Price, L. *The place-names of county Wicklow: the Irish form and meaning of parish, townland and local names* (Wexford, 1935)

Price, L. *The place-names of county Wicklow* (7 vols., Dublin, 1945-67)

Radcliff, T. *A report of the agriculture and livestock of the county of Wicklow prepared under the directions of the Farming Society of Ireland* (Dublin, 1812)

Redmond, P. *Wicklow rock-climbs: Glendalough and Luggala* (Dublin, 1973)

Tierney, M. *Cahill's Arklow and Wicklow county guide and directory* (Dublin, 1979)

Vesey, J.B. *Dublin and Wicklow in colour* (Norwich, n.d.)

Webb, *Recollections of a three day tour in the county Wicklow in the Summer of 1850* (Dublin, 1851)

Wicklow calling: Wicklow's history, industries, people, games (Dublin, 1968)

Wicklow County Council, official guide book to county Wicklow (Castleblaney, 1985)

Wicklow County Council, six years of real progress 1985-1991 (Wicklow, 1991)

Wright, G.N. *A guide to the county of Wicklow* (London, 1822)

2. JOURNALS

Arklow Historical Society Journal (1982–)

Ashford and District Historical Journal (1991–)

Journal of the Greystones Archaeological/ History Society (1992–)

Imaal; Journal of St. Kevin's Local Studies Group (1985)

Bray Historical Record (1986–)

Bray Journal (1985– continued as the *Journal of the Cualann Historical Society* 1990–)

Glendalough; the enchanted valley of St Kevin, Journal of the Glendalough Historical and Folklore Society (1991–))

Roundwood and District History and Folklore Journal (1988–)

Journal of the West Wicklow Historical Society (1984–)

Wicklow Journal (1987–)

Wicklow Historical Society Journal (1988–)

3. ARCHAEOLOGY, GEOLOGY, TOPOGRAPHY and PHYSICAL GEOGRAPHY

Anon. *A pictorial and descriptive guide through the beautiful Wicklow district* (London, 1905)

Anon, *The mines of Wicklow* (London, 1856)

Argall, P.H. *Avoca Mines Limited: a case history of mining in Ireland* (Arklow, 1975)

Barnes, E. *A brief description of Ballymurtagh mine, the property of the Wicklow Copper Mining Company* (Dublin, 1864)

Coad, J. *The angling excursions of Gregory Greendrake, Esq., in the counties of Wicklow etc.* (1832)

Collins, J.F., Farrell, E.P., O'Toole, P. *Soils of Avondale Forest Park, Rathdrum* (Dublin, 1980)

County Wicklow Heritage Project. *The lost county: the emergence of Wicklow as a county 1606-1845* (Wicklow, 1993)

Curtis, T. and Young, R. *Areas of scientific interest in county Wicklow* (Dublin, 1976)

Grogan, E. and Hillery, T. *A guide to the archaeology of county Wicklow* (Wicklow, 1993)

Inamdar, D.D. *A total magnetic survey of county Wicklow* (Dublin, 1973)

Mackey, *H.S. Report on the development of Avoca mines* (Wexford, 1920)

Moriarty, C. *The book of the Liffey* (Dublin, 1989)

O'Cléirigh, N. *Archaeological heritage of the barony of Arklow* (Arklow, 1982)

Office of Public Works. Sites and Monuments Record, Archaeological Survey of County Wicklow, 1986.

O'Neill, H. and Nicholl, A. *Fourteen views in the county of Wicklow from original drawings* (1835)

Simoens, G. *The gold and the tin in the South East of Ireland* (Dublin, 1921)

Turner, K. *If you seek monuments: a guide to antiquities of the barony of Rathdown* (Rathmichael, 1983)

Warren, W.P. *Wicklow in the Ice Age. An introduction and guide to the glacial geology of the Wicklow district* (Dublin, 1993)

4. BIOGRAPHY, MEMOIRS, LETTERS

ACTON FAMILY

Ball-Acton, C.B. An appreciation. Compiled chiefly from his letters and journals (Privately printed, 1906)

BYRNE, MYLES

Byrne, M. *Memoirs of Miles Byrne.* 2 vols., (Paris, 1863)

Gwynn, S. (ed.) *Memoirs of Miles Byrne* (Dublin, 1906)

BYRNE, WILLIAM

The trial of William Byrne of Ballymanus (Dublin, 1799)

BYRNE, WILLIAM MICHAEL

Ridgeway, W. *A report of the trial of Michael William Byrne* (Dublin, 1798)

BYRNE FAMILY

Edge, J. *The O'Byrnes and their descendants* (Dublin, 1879)

MacAirt, S. (ed.) *Leabhar Branach: the book of the O'Byrnes* (Dublin, 1944)

Rees, D. *The green bough of liberty* (London, 1979)

CHILDERS, ERSKINE HAMILTON

Young, J.N. *Erskine H. Childers. President of Ireland* (Gerrard's Cross, 1985)

CHILDERS, ROBERT ERSKINE

Burke, W. *The zeal of the convert, the life of Erskine Childers* (New York, 1985)

McInerney, M. *The riddle of Erskine Childers* (Dublin, 1971)

DEVLIN, ANNE

Cullen, L. *The Ann Devlin jail journal,* (ed.) J.J. Finnegan (Cork, 1968)

McKown, R. *The ordeal of Ann Devlin* (London, n.d.)

DWYER, MICHAEL

Campion, J.T. *Michael Dwyer or the insurgent captain of the Wicklow mountains, a tale of '98* (Dublin, n.d.)

Cargeeg, G. *The rebel of Glenmalure: a history of Michael Dwyer* (Perth, 1988)

Dickson, C. *The life of Michael Dwyer with some account of his companions* (Dublin, 1944)

O'Donnell, R. 'Michael Dwyer' in Bob Reece (ed.) *Irish convict lives* (Sydney, 1993)

Sheedy, K. *Upon the mercy of government, the story of the surrender, imprisonment and transportation to New South Wales of Michael Dwyer and his Wicklow comrades* (Dublin, 1988)

GRANT, ELIZABETH

Grant, E. *The highland lady in Ireland: journals 1840-50* (ed.) Patricia Pelly and Andrew Tood) (Edinburgh, 1991)

McGusty, M. & Thomson, D. (eds.) *The Irish journals of Elizabeth Smith* (Oxford, 1980)

GRATTAN, HENRY

Grattan, H. *Memoirs of the life and times of the Rt. Hon. Henry*

Grattan, (ed.) by his son, 5 vols. (London, 1839-42)

HALPIN, ROBERT

Rees, J. *The life of Captain Robert Halpin* (Arklow, 1992)

HANBIDGE, WILLIAM

Hanbidge, M. *The memories of William Hanbidge* (St. Alban's, 1939)

HEALY, FR. J

Anon (W.J. Fitzpatrick) *Memories of Father Healy of Little Bray* (Dublin, 1896)

Healy, Fr. J. *Memoirs of Father Healy of Little Bray* (London, 1904)

HOLT, JOSEPH

Holt, J. *A rum story, the adventures of Joseph Holt, thirteen years in New South Wales (1800-12)*, (ed.) P.O'Shaughnessy (Perth, 1988)

Holt, J. *The memoirs of Joseph Holt*, (ed.) T.C. Croker, (2 vols. London, 1838)

O'Donnell, R. 'General Joseph Holt and the historians' in Bob Reece (ed.) *Irish convicts: the origins of convicts transported to Australia'* (Dublin, 1989)

MEATH FAMILY

Meath, M. *The diaries of Mary countess of Meath: edited by her husband* (London, n.d.)

MONCK FAMILY

Batt, E. *The Moncks and Charleville House* (Dublin, 1979)

MURRAY, DANIEL (ARCHBISHOP)

Meagher, M. *Notices of the life and character of his Grace Most Rev. Daniel Murray late archbishop of Dublin, as contained in the commemorative oration pronounced in the Church of the Immmaculate Conception, Dublin on occasion of his grace's month's mind. With historical and biographical notes* (Dublin, 1853)

O'CONNOR, FRANK

O'Connor, F. *My father's son* (Dublin, 1968)

O'TOOLE FAMILY

O'Toole, J. *The O'Tooles, anciently Lords of Perscourt (Feracualan), Fertir Imale; with some notices on Feagh MacHugh O'Byrne, chief of Clan-Ranelagh* (Dublin, 1869)

O'Toole, P.L. *History of the Clan O'Toole and other Leinster septs* (Dublin,1890)

PARNELL, C.S.

Anon.. *The uncrowned king: The life and public services of the Hon. Stewart Parnell* (Philadelphia, 1891)

Bew, P. *C.S. Parnell* (Dublin, 1980)

Callanan, F. *The Parnell split* (1992)

Ervine, St. J. *Parnell* (London, 1936)

Foster, R.F. *Charles Stewart Parnell: The man and his family* (1976)

McCartney, D. (ed.) *Parnell, the politics of power* (Dublin, 1991)
Heaslip, J. *Parnell: a biography* (London, 1936)
Hurst, M. *Parnell and Irish nationalism* (London, 1968)
Lyons, F.S.L. *The fall of Parnell, 1890-1891* (London, 1960)
Lyons, F.S.L. *C.S. Parnell* (London, 1977)
Kissane, N. *Parnell: a documentary history* (Dublin, 1991)
McCartney, D. *Parnell: the politics of power* (Dublin, 1991)
McDonald, J. *The island storm awakens the Phoenix* (1986)
O'Brien, C.C. *Parnell and his party 1881-90* (Oxford, 1964)
O'Brien, R.B. *Life of Charles Stewart. Parnell* (2 vols. London, 1898)
O'Shea, K. *Charles Stewart Parnell: his love story and political life* (London, 1914)
Parnell, J.H. *C.S. Parnell: a memoir* (London, 1916)
Power, J.W. *Words of the dead chief* (Dublin, 1894)
Robbins, Sir A. *Parnell, the last five years* (London, 1926)

PARNELL FAMILY

Cote, McL. J. *Fanny & Anna Parnell. Ireland's patriot sisters* (1991)
Dickinson, E. *A patriot's mistake: reminiscences of the Parnell family, by a daughter of the house* (London, 1905)

POWERSCOURT FAMILY

Daly, R. (ed.) *Letters and papers by the late Theodosia A. Vicountess Powerscourt* (London, 1838)

SMITH, ELIZABETH

See Grant, Elizabeth

SYNGE, J.M.

The Synge manuscripts in the library of Trinity College, Dublin (Dublin, 1970)
Green, D.H. and Stephens, E.M. *J.M. Synge, 1871-1909* (New York, 1959)
Grene, N. *Synge: a critical study of the plays* (London, 1975)
Mickhail, E.H. *J.M. Synge: interviews and recollections* (London, 1972)
Saddlemyer, A. (ed.) *The collected letters of John Millington Synge* (Oxford, 1983)
Stephens, E. *My Uncle John* (London, 1974)
Skelton, R. (ed.) *J.M. Synge: collected works* (Oxford, 1962-8)
Synge, S. *Letters to my daughter: memories of John Millington Synge* (Dublin, 1931)

WHALEY, THOMAS ("BUCK")

Sullivan, Sir E. (ed.) *Buck Whaley's memoirs* (London, 1906)

WICKLOW FAMILY

Earl of Wicklow *Fireside fusilier* (Dublin, 1958)

5. FOLKLORE, MUSIC AND SPORT

Donard G.A.A. – A history, 1884-1984 (Donard, 1984)

Sons of Saint Nicholas. A history of Dunlavin G.A.A. Club (Dunlavin, 1984)

Brophy, J. *The leathers echo: a story of hurling, handball and camogie in county Wicklow from 1884 to 1984* (Naas, 1984)

Brophy, J. *By the banks of the Dargle: a history of Bray Emmets G.A.A. Club 1885-1985* (Bray, 1985)

Flannery, M. (ed.) *Greystones R.F.C.: record of a half century* (Dublin, 1987)

Liffey Valley Heritage Study *Memories of the Liffey valley* (Blessington, 1992)

O'Toole, M. *In the shadow of Sliabh Cualann* (Bray, 1988)

Shorter, D.S. *A legend of Glendalough and other ballads* (Dublin, 1919)

Tobin, J. *Bray Wanderers: old and new* (Wicklow, 1987)

6. PLACES

ANNACURRA

Pattison, J.A. I.T.A. topographical and general survey. Barony of Ballinacor (South) Parish of Annacurra and Killaveny. Surveyed in 1943

ARDOYNE

Eustace, E.A.R. *Short history of Ardoyne parish, diocese of Leighlin* (Carlow, 1967)

ARKLOW

Lambart Bayly, H. 'Statistical account of the parish of Arklow'. in William Shaw Mason, *Statistical account or parochial survey of Ireland , Vol II* (Dublin, 1816)

D'Arcy, P.J. I.T.A. topographical and general survey. Baronies of Arklow and Gorey Parish of Arklow. Surveyed in 1942.

Forde, F. *Maritime Arklow* (Arklow, 1988)

Morris, J. *The story of the Arklow lifeboats* (Coventry, 1987)

Murphy, H. *The Kynoch era in Arklow 1895*-1918 (Arklow, 1977)

Power, P.J. *The Arklow calendar, a chronicle of events from earliest times to 1900 A.D.* (Arklow, 1981)

Rees, J. and Charlton, L. *Arklow – last stronghold of sail: Arklow ships, 1850-1985* (Arklow, 1985)

ASHFORD

D'Arcy, P.J. I.T.A. topographical and general survey. Barony of Newcastle. Parish of Ashford. Surveyed in 1942.

AVOCA

D'Arcy, P.J. I.T.A. topographical and general survey. Barony of Arklow. Parish of Avoca. Surveyed in 1942.

de Lion, C. *The vale of Avoca* (Dublin, 1967, revised 1986, reprinted 1991)

Dempsey, P. *Avoca: A history of the vale* (Dublin, 1912)

BALLYNAGRAN

MacEiteagain, D. and O'Byrne, E. *Ballynagran: an historical perspective* (Wicklow, 1994)

BALTINGLASS

Chavasse, C. *Baltinglass and its Abbey* (Baltinglass, 1962)

Earl, L. *The battle of Baltinglass* (London, 1952)

Pattison, J.A. I.T.A. topographical and general survey. Barony of Talbotstown Upper. Parish of Baltinglass. Surveyed in 1943. Includes photographs

BARNDARRIG

D'Arcy, P.J. I.T.A. topographical and general survey. Barony of Arklow. Parish of Kilbride and Barndarrig. Surveyed in 1942.

BLESSINGTON

Pattison, J.A. I.T.A. topographical and general survey. Barony of Talbotstown Lower. Parish of Blessington. Surveyed in 1943.

Taylor, R.M. *St. Mary's Church, Blessington 1683-1970* (Greystones, 1970)

BOYSTOWN

Pattison, J.A. I.T.A. topographical and general survey. Barony of Talbotstown Lower. Parish of Boystown. Surveyed in 1943.

BRAY

Bland, F.E. *The story of Crinken, 1840-1940* (Bray, 1940)

Bray Cualann Historical Society, *A short history of Bray* (Bray, 1992)

Brien, C. *In the lands of Brien: a short history of the Catholic Church and other institutions in Bray and district from earliest times* (Bray, 1984)

Connolly, R. M. *'By common council and common action' : an outline history of Bray and District Council of Trade Unions 1917-1992* (Bray, 1992)

Craig, T. *A guide to Bray and the picturesque scenery in its vicinity* (Dublin, 1884)

D'Arcy, P.J. I.T.A. topographical and general survey. Barony of Half Rathdown. Parish of Bray. Surveyed in 1943

Doran, A.L. *Bray and environs* (Bray, 1903, reprinted 1985)

Flynn, A. *Famous links with Bray* (Bray, 1985)

Flynn, A. *History of Bray* (Bray, 1986)

Garner, W., *Bray: architectural heritage* (Dublin 1980)

Lynam, J. and Convery, L. *Bray Head and minor crags around Dublin* (Dublin, 1978)

Mansfield, C. *The Aravon story* (Dublin, 1975)

Martin, C. *A drink from Broderick's well* (Dublin, 1980)

Martin, C. *The bridge below the town 1940-1980* (Bray, 1984)

Martin, C. *The woodcarvers of Bray 1887-1914* (Bray, 1985)

O'Sullivan, J., Dunne, T. and Cannon, S. *The book of Bray* (Dublin, 1989)

O'Cathaoir, B. (ed.) *Holy Redeemer Church 1792-1992: a Bray parish* (Bray, 1991)

Pakenham-Walsh, W. (ed.) *Aravon school register, 1862-1928* (York, 1929)

Scott, G.D. *The stones of Bray* (Dublin, 1913)

Seymour,F.J. *A hundred years of Bray and it's neighbourhood from 1770-1870 by an old inhabitant* (Bray, 1978)

CALARY

Jennings, R. *Calary Church and parish, diocese of Glendalough :150th anniversary, 1834-1984* (1984)

DELGANY

Flannery, J. *Between the mountains and the sea: the story of Delgany* (Delgany, 1990)

DUNGANSTOWN

Heavener, R. Credo: *Dunganstown, an age-old Irish parish with a living message for everyman today* (Jordanstown, 1994)

DUNLAVIN

McGee, S.R. *Dunlavin, co. Wicklow: a retrospect* (1935)

Pattison, J.A. I.T.A. topographical and general survey. Barony of Talbotstown Lower. Parish of Dunlavin. Surveyed in 1943. Includes photographs

Warke, R.A. *St. Nicholas's Church and parish, Dunlavin 1817-1967* (1967)

ENNISKERRY

Brien, C. *Church of the Immaculate Heart of Mary, Enniskerry, co. Wicklow, 1859-1959* (n.d.)

D'Arcy, P.J. I.T.A. topographical and general survey. Barony of Half Rathdown. Parish of Enniskerry. Surveyed in 1943

Kennedy, D.J. *History around you: Enniskerry sources* (Foxrock, 1986)

GLENCREE

Evans, H. *From revolution to reconciliation, the story of Glencree* (Bray, 1978)

GLENDALOUGH

Barrow, L. *Glendalough and Saint Kevin* (Dundalk, 1972 reprinted Dundalk, 1984)

Doyle, D. *The story of Glendalough* (Dublin, n.d.)

Fanning, Bill *Tales and yarns of Glendalough and the Wicklow Hills told to John D. Vose by Bill Fanning, shepherd of Glendalough*

(Blackpool, 1988)
Hogan, M. *Glendalough* (1903)
Leask, H.G. *Glendalough: official historical and descriptive guide* (Dublin, n.d.)
MacGowan, K. *Glendalough* (Dublin, 1982, 1983, 1988)
McAllister, R. *A guide to Glendalough* (Dublin, n.d.)
Moloney, D.J. *History of Glendalough* (Wicklow, 1925)
Nolan, J. *The history and antiquities of Glendalough* (Dublin, 1871)
Noonan, P.J. *Glendalough and the Seven Churches of St. Kevin* (Wicklow, 1950)
O'Connell, Sir J. *Glendalough, its story and its ruins* (Dublin, 1950)
O'Nuanain, P. *Glendalough* (Wexford, 1934)
Price, L. 'Glendalough; St. Kevin's Road' in J. Ryan (ed.) *Feil-sgribhinn Eoin Mhic Neill: essays and studies presented to Professor Eoin MacNeill* (Dublin, 1940)

GLENEALY

Corbett, R.J.H. *A short history of Glenealy and its Church of Ireland Parish* (Glenealy, 1992)

GREYSTONES

Anon. *Greystones Presbyterian Church 1887-1987 and the Kilpedder Witness from 1851* (Greystones, 1987)
D'Arcy, P.J. I.T.A. topographical and general survey. Barony of Half Rathdown. Parish of Greystones. Surveyed in 1943.
French, S. *Greystones 1864-1964* (1964)
Paine, D. *A pictorial history of Greystones, 1855-1955: a collection of old photographs compiled by Derek Paine* (n.d.)
Smal, C. (ed.) *Ancient Rathdown and St. Crispin's Cell: a uniquely historic landscape* (Greystones, 1993)
Webb, R. *Tree survey in Greystones* (Dublin, 1977)

HOLLYWOOD

Hollywood I.C.A. Local History Group *Hollywood: a Wicklow village* (Hollywood, 1990)
Hollywood I.C.A. Local History Group *Hollywood: a pictorial record* (Hollywood, 1992)

KILCOOLE

Martin, F.X. *The Howth gun-running and the Kilcoole gun-running, 1914* (Dublin, 1964)

KILLISKEY

Vandeleur, W.E. *Notes on the history of Killiskey Parish* (Dundalk, n.d.)

KILQUADE

D'Arcy, P.J. I.T.A. topographical and general survey. Barony of Newcastle and Half-Rathdown. Parish of Kilquade. Surveyed in 1942.

Masterson, J.P.P. *A garden and a grave: Kilquade* (Wicklow, 1952)
MOUNT USHER
Jay, M. *Mount Usher Gardens, Ashford, Co. Wicklow* (Dublin, 1983).
Walpole, E.H. *Mount Usher 1868-1928. A short history.*
NEWCASTLE
Jennings, R. *Glimpses of an ancient parish. Newcastle, co. Wicklow. 1189-1989* (Wicklow, 1989)
POWERSCOURT
Powerscourt, M. W. *A description and history of Powerscourt* (1903)
Stokes, Rev. A.E. *The parish of Powerscourt* (1963)
The Seventh Viscount Powerscourt *A description and history of Powerscourt* (London, 1903)
RATHDRUM
Pattison, J.A. I.T.A. topographical and general survey. Barony of Ballinacor. Parish of Rathdrum. Surveyed in 1943. Includes photographs
ROUNDWOOD
D'Arcy, P.J. I.T.A. topographical and general survey. Barony of Ballinacor. Parish of Roundwood and Glendalough. Surveyed in 1942
Nevin, M.G. *Roundwood and Moneystown. An essay in parish history* (Wicklow, 1985)
Robinson, N. *The Vartry, A cruise up the Vartry with an Alderman: or how to see the Dublin Waterworks* (1866)
RUSSBOROUGH
Beit, Sir A. *Russborough* (Dublin, 1978)
WICKLOW
Clarke, M. *Wicklow Parish. A history of the development of the present catholic parish with an account of various religious foundations of medieval times* (Wexford, 1944)
D'Arcy, P.J. I.T.A. topographical and general survey. Barony of Arklow. Parish of Wicklow. Surveyed in 1942
Kavanagh, J (ed.). *De La Salle, Cill Mhantáin 1912-1987* (Wicklow, 1987)
Lynch, G. *Cill Mhantáin: A historical guide to the Catholic Parish of Wicklow* (Wicklow, 1983)
Noonan, P.J. *Wicklow: A guide to the town* (Wicklow, 1947)
Wicklow. A charming health and holiday resort. The official handbook issued under the auspices of the Wicklow Urban District Council (Cheltenham, n.d.)

7. GENERAL

Aalen, F.H.A., Gillmore, D.A. and Williams, P.W. *West Wicklow: background for development* (Dublin, 1966)

Aalen, F.H.A. *Rural Surveys and the role of local development associations: a case-study in West Wicklow* (Dublin, 1967)

Armstrong, G.F. *Stories of Wicklow* (London, 1886)

Barlow, J. *Wicklow, the garden of Ireland: gleanings from its past, with a preface by Tomás Ó Cléirigh* (1934)

Campion, Dr. *The last struggles of the Irish sea smugglers: a historical romance of the Wicklow coast* (Glasgow, 1869)

Cantwell, Brian J. *A Cantwell miscellany* (1960)

Convery, F.J., Flanagan, S., Parker, A.J. *Tourism in co. Wicklow: maximising its potential* (Dublin, 1989).

Connolly, R.M. *The labour movement in county Wicklow* (Bray 1992)

Cullen, L. *Personal recollections, of Wexford and Wicklow insurgents of 1798* (Enniscorthy, 1959)

Cullen, L. *'98 in Wicklow: the story as written by Rev. Bro. Luke Cullen O.D.C., 1793-1859* (ed.) M. Ronan (Wexford, 1938)

Doyle, C. *From Dauntless to Annie: a history of Wicklow lifeboat station* (Wicklow, 1990)

Evans, E.B. *An outline of the history of the county of Wicklow regiment of militia together with a succession list of the officers of the regiment from the formation in 1793 to the present time* (1885)

Fayle, H. and Newham, A.T. *The Dublin and Blessington steam tramway* (Surrey, 1963)

Hayes, S. *A practical treatise on planting and the management of woods and coppices* (Dublin, 1794)

Hutchinson, C.D. (ed.) *The birds of Dublin and Wicklow* (Dublin, 1975)

Maguire, W.A. *The Downshire Estates in Ireland 1801-1845: the management of Irish landed estates in the early nineteenth century* (Oxford, 1972)

McClaren, A. *A minute description of the battles of Gorey, Arklow and Vinegar Hill: together with the movements of the army through the Wicklow mountains* (1798)

Redmond, B. *The story of Wicklow, Wexford and Carlow: our land in story, a series of Irish local histories.*(Dublin, n.d.)

Rees, J. *A farewell to famine* (Arklow, 1994)

Ronan, M. V. (ed.) *Insurgent Wicklow: the story as written by Bro. Luke Cullen O.D.C.* (Dublin, 1948)

Shepherd, W.E. *Dublin and South- Eastern Railway* (London, 1974)

Smyth, A.P. *Celtic Leinster: towards an historical geography of early Irish civilization A.D. 500-1500* (Dublin 1982)

Whitty, S.J. *The flaming wheel. Nature studies in the counties of Dublin and Wicklow* (Dublin, 1924)

Index of Places

Index of Persons